ISBN 978-1-333-42324-7
PIBN 10502531

1 MONTH OF
FREE
READING

at

www.ForgottenBooks.com

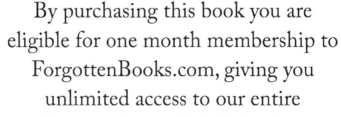

By purchasing this book you are
eligible for one month membership to
ForgottenBooks.com, giving you
unlimited access to our entire
collection of over 700,000 titles via
our web site and mobile apps.

To claim your free month visit:

www.forgottenbooks.com/free502531

NOTICE TO PURCHASERS

It is respectfully requested that purchasers of THE HISTORY OF THE BRIGHAM FAMILY discovering errors or omissions therein send the correct information immediately to Miss Emma E. Brigham, care of The Grafton Press, 6 Beacon Street, Boston, Mass. By special arrangement with the publishers, all purchasers of this book will be notified of corrections received within one year, that proper entry of them may be made in each volume.

June 1, 1907.

ADDITIONS AND CORRECTIONS

ADDITIONS AND CORRECTIONS

ADDITIONS AND CORRECTIONS

IN CRUCE SALUS

Brigham

AMILY

EVERAL THOUSAND
F THOMAS BRIGHAM
... 653

By

ER BRIGHAM

ngland ...ical Society,
... Record ...ociety of
... Thomas Bradley ...ion,
...an Revolution, ...

and edited by
E. BRIGHAM

...GHAM, Associate Editor

...TON PRESS

A...

MCMVII

THE HISTORY OF THE
BRIGHAM FAMILY

A RECORD OF SEVERAL THOUSAND DESCENDANTS OF THOMAS BRIGHAM THE EMIGRANT, 1603-1653

By

W. I. TYLER BRIGHAM

Late Member of the New England Historic Genealogical Society,
Southern History Association, British Record Society, Society of
Colonial Wars, Governor Thomas Dudley Association,
Sons of the American Revolution, etc.

Collated and edited by

EMMA E. BRIGHAM

WILLIAM E. BRIGHAM, Associate Editor

THE GRAFTON PRESS

GENEALOGICAL PUBLISHERS

NEW YORK   MCMVII

Copyright, 1907,
By THE GRAFTON PRESS

CONTRIBUTORS TO THE BOOK FUND

The following named Special Contributors, by their generous provision, made possible the preparation and publication of *The History of the Brigham Family:*

Arthur L. Allen of Pittsburg.
Alfred Brigham of Boston.
A. Ward Brigham of New York.
Charles O. Brigham of Toledo.
Edmund D. Brigham of Chicago.
Edmund S. Brigham of Boston.
Elizabeth F. Brigham of Brookline.
Emma E. Brigham of Boston.
George E. Brigham of Boston.
George French Brigham of Sharon, Wis.
Helen F. Brigham of Cambridge.
Helen S. Brigham of Fitchburg.
Henry H. Brigham of Chicago.
Joel Brigham of Wauseon, Ohio.
Johnson Brigham of Des Moines, Iowa.
Mary E. Brigham of Medfield, Mass.
Mary M. Brigham of Cambridge.
William E. Brigham of Somerville, Mass.
Dwight R. Burrell of Canandaigua, N. Y.
Rose Brigham Coxford of New York.
Sarah L. Hill of Newton, Mass.
Elmer P. Howe of Boston.
George A. Lowe of Salt Lake City.
Henry Brigham Rice of Boston.
L. Frederick Rice of Boston.

CONTENTS

ILLUSTRATIONS

PREFACE

After almost incredible obstacles *The History of the Brigham Family* is herewith submitted to the living descendants of Thomas Brigham, the Puritan. Until this volume, the only record of this great American family was to be found in the conscientious volume, *Brigham,* issued by Rev. Abner Morse, A. M., in 1859. The idea of taking up and developing the work so well begun by Mr. Morse had its inception with Dr. B. A. R. Brigham of Chicago, through whose instrumentality the Brigham Family Association was organized 18 Oct., 1893 (see Appendix). It was and always has been the main purpose of the Association to publish a family history, but Dr. Brigham personally assumed the task and responsibility of preparing the work, although drawing heavily upon members of the family throughout the country for support. In 1896, by reason of ill health, he had become so incapacitated for work that he was compelled to relinquish the task he had laid out for himself.

Since its organization, Willard Irving Tyler Brigham of Chicago had served the Association modestly, but with marked ability as historian, and in 1901, the task of bringing genealogical order out of existing chaos was placed in his competent hands. He already had attracted some notice in the genealogical field and had made good progress with the Tyler Genealogy. No family ever was blessed with a more painstaking and conscientious, yet brilliant historian. He had abandoned a promising career at the bar to take up work of this class, and for years had been studying and traveling in pursuit of genealogical knowledge, particularly with reference to the Tyler and Brigham families. His historical sketches of the Brigham Family, including a most exhaustive attempt to trace its origin in Great Britain, were collated and published in an official report in 1901. Revised by Mr. Brigham, these constitute an important feature of the present work. The pictures of scenes in Great Britain which appear herein are from original photographs taken by Mr. Brigham on this trip.

Acting under a definite arrangement with the officials of the B. F. A., Mr. Brigham entered bravely upon his work in the summer of 1901. He had practically to start anew, but after the decease of Dr. Brigham, he negotiated, on behalf of the B. F. A., the return of the records gathered by the Doctor, which had been retained by his estate. These were of material assistance, although the papers had been much injured by lack of care and were often difficult to decipher. These papers were destroyed by our genealogist after he had carefully copied them all, hence we have been unable to consult them for purposes of verification.

President Charles O. Brigham of Toledo devised the plan under which an arrangement was made with Willard I. T. Brigham to complete and publish 350 copies of the Family History within three and one-half years, the original term of five years having been shortened by the receipt of the Doctor's papers. Ill health soon drove Willard to Arizona, where he continued his work for two years, practically from a dying bed. His one prayer was that he might live long enough to complete the work he had undertaken. This, however, was not to be, for he died in Auburn, California, 26 Sept., 1904. None except those intimately associated with him and his work can appreciate the sacrifices made by him and his devoted wife, the hardships and discouragements under which he labored and the debt of gratitude which all of the name and blood of Brigham owe to his memory.

Mr. Brigham's death was a stunning blow to the enterprise. So thoroughly, however, had his work been done that the Publication Committee found it practicable to place the data, all in the hand-writing of the genealogist, in the hands of an editor.

A competent person was found in Miss Emma E. Brigham of Boston. She had been actively identified with the B. F. A. since its inception (librarian-curator 1893-1896, secretary 1896-1900, treasurer 1900-1906-7), and by means of intimate associations had acquired a more accurate and thorough knowledge of the Brigham lines than anyone else. She had also the advantages of large executive training and a good literary equipment. At great self-sacrifice, Miss Brigham collated and edited the MS. left by the deceased genealogist, meantime adding names and data representing about one thousand persons.

A third tragic event in the career of *The History of the Brigham Family* was the death, 2 May, 1906, of Charles O. Brigham of Toledo, President of the B. F. A., and Chairman of the Publication Committee, but for whose personal influence and financial aid it would have been well-nigh impossible to continue the work. Notwithstanding the great loss of President Brigham's able and enthusiastic co-operation in everything appertaining to the family publication, the work was continued to completion, and is herewith respectfully submitted. It doubtless has been impossible, owing to the circumstances under which this volume was compiled, to avoid

errors, omissions and misunderstandings. We believe, however, that
The History of the Brigham Family is substantially accurate. No
pains to make it so have been spared. Our readers will bear in
mind, of course, that the names, dates and other facts contained in
the book are not the personal compositions of the author or editors,
but, in a great majority of cases, have been contributed by others.

In the preparation of this book for the press, the work of our
genealogist has been revised and verified to the extent of our ability,
and much new matter has been added. The chapter on " Thomas
Brigham, the Emigrant," was wholly rewritten by Mr. Henry A.
Phillips of Boston. All except letters C and D of the Appendix,
are by the editors. The name of Rev. Abner Morse cannot be too
highly honored by the Brigham Family for his service in collecting
and publishing its earlier records; but Mr. Morse worked under
great disadvantages and discouragements—practically without assistance of any kind, in fact—and it is not surprising, therefore,
that we frequently have been compelled to omit reference to many
statements which in his book stand forth as interesting and apparently important. In other cases, Mr. Morse's was the only authority
available and we have accepted it with this fact in mind.

In addition to the invaluable pages of Mr. Morse, we are especially indebted to the late Rev. Lucius R. Paige and Hon. Charles
Hudson, whose histories of Cambridge and Marlboro respectively
have supplied us with much useful information; and to Mrs. Harriette M. Forbes, formerly of Westboro, from whose *Diary of Rev.
Ebenezer Parkman of Westboro* (editor) and *The Hundredth
Town,* we have drawn freely for facts and color unobtainable
elsewhere. Our warmest thanks are due Mrs. Edwin E. Nelson of
Fort Worth, Texas (Mrs. Willard I. T. Brigham), for her cordial
assistance to the editors in the early period of our labors. Mrs.
Nelson has fulfilled to the letter every agreement made by her late
husband, as far as lay in her power, and placed at our disposal
everything in her possession that could aid us to complete the task
our genealogist was compelled to relinquish.

We would record our obligations also to Messrs. S. Ingersoll
Briant, president of the Westboro Historical Society, E. M. Goddard, assistant state librarian of Vermont, and Ernest D. Bugbee
of Springfield, Mass., for the loan of valuable portrait and locality
plates; to Mr. Thomas M. Hutchinson of Winchester, Mass., for
unique data establishing beyond question the location of Thomas[1]
Brigham's " Farme on Ye Rocks "; to Mr. Charles D. Elliot of
Somerville, Mass., for the use of his excellent " Map of Cambridge
in 1635," whereby we are enabled to show the site of the original
13-acre grant to Thomas[1] Brigham in Watertown and of the homestead where he died; to Mr. Weston F. Hutchins of Boston for

great assistance in the collation of war records and preparation of the general index; and to Mr. L. Frederick Rice of Boston for special aid of a financial nature at a recent most critical period.

It is with pleasure, also, that we acknowledge our wholly satisfactory relations with Messrs. Frederic H. and Thomas B. Hitchcock of the Grafton Press, whose interested co-operation, helpful suggestions and practical skill in book-making have been of great service to this undertaking.

Owing to sharp limitations as to time and money, the references in the Index have been confined to the genealogical section, and to persons of or directly connected with the Brigham Family; notwithstanding that we would have preferred a broader and slightly different arrangement.

The first and most natural question to be asked of the genealogist relates to the over-sea origin of our common ancestor. What and where was the origin of Thomas Brigham, the Puritan? It was one of the primary purposes of these researches to answer this question; and it implies no discredit to the ability of the genealogist, no reflection upon the Brigham line that the answer is still in doubt. More or less exhaustive descriptions of British Brigham names and places will be found in succeeding pages, but we have thought it well to embody here the latest conclusions respecting the English ancestry of Thomas Brigham the Puritan, reached by Mr. Willard I. T. Brigham. How indefatigably he worked to discover the facts his chapters devoted to research in Great Britain attest. Had he lived to make his purposed second visit to Great Britain, the conclusions might have been decisive. We quote Willard I. Tyler Brigham, as follows:

It was formerly my impression that perhaps all the Brighams sprang from a common Brigham ancestor, whose origin I was inclined to attribute to Yorkshire. Later researches, however, led me to the changed belief that there were no less than *four distinct Brigham lines*, founded by individuals, who assumed this surname in the early days, when it became the proper thing to have a surname; and that they assumed this particular name because they lived at one or another of the four Brigham places.

From which branch descended our " Thomas the Puritan," I regret my present inability to say, though I incline to the opinion that it was Yorkshire. I made thorough search among wills in the Perogative and Exchequer Court of York, and the Durham Probate Court, in hopes of gleaning some clue which would lead to an intelligent solution of the vexatious problem, but in vain. In the Canterbury Probate from 1598 to 1660 occur but eleven Brigham wills, the residence of four being in London, three in Yorkshire, and one each in Oxford, Surrey, Sussex and Kent counties. At Durham Probate I was disappointed in not finding a single Brigham will. As its jurisdiction extended (until recently) over Northumberland, as well as Durham County (both of which lie just above Yorkshire), I was prepared to find many Brigham estates.

York Probate, however, makes a better showing; in fact, the largest, I fancy, of any court in the Kingdom. From 1437 to 1602, I found thirty-two Brigham wills. This latter year was the one at which I began to make careful search, which I found to embrace the period between 1602 to 1660; during which time I found eighteen Brigham estates. . . . My regret was poignant that not a clue was found tending to point out the origin of our " Thomas the Puritan "

Let us not forget that Mr. Morse never made any personal research in England and that Mr. Brigham's work there was the first attempted on a scientific basis. It is profoundly to be hoped that the invaluable records of Mr. Brigham's painstaking industry in this field, herewith preserved, will inspire some ambitious family historian of the future to a quest which will be rewarded with complete success.

Boston, May, 1, 1907.

HISTORY

HISTORY

I

ETYMOLOGY OF BRIG-HAM

Our family tree must be considered under two heads, *Brig* and *ham*. Ferguson (*Popular County Histories, Cumberland*) contains this statement: " The Saxon equivalent of ton or tun (which mean, we need hardly remind, a *town*) is heim and ham." *Ham-let* is still used to designate a small *village*.

Again, Teller (*An Anglo-Saxon Dictionary*) states: " The Latin word which appears most nearly to translate it (i. e., ham) is *vicus*. . . . In this sense, it is the *general assemblage of the dwellings in each particular district,* to which the arable land and pasture of the community were appurtenant: the *home* of all the settlers in a separate and well-defined locality: the collection of the houses of the freemen." In another paragraph, the same author observes: " Ham, a dwelling, fold, or enclosed possession. It is so frequently coupled with words implying presence of water as to render it probable that (like the Friesic ' hemmen ') it denotes a piece of land surrounded by paling, wickerwork, etc., and so defended against the stream, which would otherwise wash it away." (Citing *Codex Diplomaticus Aevi Saxonici*) " Ham-steall=homestead."

Grimm's *Deutsches Worterbuch* contains, " *Hame, hamen,* used in Netherlands and middle Germany, meaning a net (collective sense, like home). Hamm, found in Bremen Dictionary in the sense of any enclosure; especially, meadow; but also, forest, house, or farm."

Roemer's *Origins of the English People and the English Language,* pp. 190 *et seq.,* has this interesting summary: " By far the most important elements which enter into Anglo-Saxon names are the suffixes *ham* and *ing*. Like many other Saxon forms, *ham* signifies primarily an *enclosure;* something that *hems in;* a meaning not very different from that of *ton* and *worth,* or even the Norse *by*." Again (p. 474), the same author states: " The Saxons preferred country to city life; generally dwelt near forests in *clusters* of *houses, called ham*."

" Ham " is our English *home,* and has a very ancient history. *Ham* is of Aryan parentage; and exhaustive research would discover some form of the word in all the languages of such origin. The word is found in all parts of Europe whose people contributed to the Anglo-Saxon conquest of England.

Passing to the "Brig" of our Brig-ham, there is not the same certainty of meaning. There are three roots—with the distinct meanings, *bridge, hill, strife*—all of which in the lapse of time have assumed the form "brig." As Brigham is a *place* name, we must consult the environment, and let probabilities determine.

Speaking of the several localities:—"Brigham," Yorkshire and Cumberland, as well as the modern hamlet by the same name (near Keswick), "Bridgeham" (formerly *Brig*ham), Norfolk (all in England), as well as "*Birg*ham (the *historical Brig*ham), Berwick, Scotland,—the writer concludes that the "brig" was derived, in each instance, from the root signifying *bridge,* because all five places are upon *bridgeable* streams: most, in fact, possessing bridges to this day, while to the Scotch Brigham attaches tradition of an ancient bridge.

II

ORTHOGRAPHY OF BRIGHAM

Early English spelling was phonetic. Words were spelled in a variety of ways. This variance was increased by the composite complexion of the nation. Composed of members of the Brigantes, Celts, Scandinavians, Danes, Saxons, Angles, Frisians, and Normans (with their digressive vowel and consonant tones, not to mention individual vagaries), conventional orthography was for ages an impossibility.

From records covering more than a thousand years, the writer found the following forms of Brigham: "Bringeham, Briccham, Bricgham, Brygcham, Brycgham, Brygham, Brycham, Brigholm, Briggeholm, Briggham, Briggeham, Briggam, Briglam, Briglame, Brighame, Brigh'm, Brigeham, Birgeame, Birgham, Bridgeham, and Brigham: twenty-one ways all told. More might be found; especially if the Latin ("declined") forms were included. Of the foregoing, only two (Bridgeham and Brigham) are known by the writer to have crystallized into patronymics.

Seeming discrepancies disappear by bearing in mind:—

1. The Saxons had several forms for their word bridge, *i. e.,* bryeg, brygc, bricg, brigg, and brye; all equivalent to the "brig" in our surname.

2. The Teutonic word *hame* was taken by colonizers to England; and lingers in the "North countrie."

3. *Holm* was (formerly) interchangeable with *ham.* Brigham (Scotland) was sometimes styled (in early days) Brigholm.

4. The letter h is an aspirate; and so, inserted or dropped, does not influence the pronunciation. We now spell our name "Brigham" but pronounce it "Brig'am," is if the h were omitted.

5. The insertion of e, elision of a, and doubling of g are readily accounted for; by individual idiosyncracy, as well as by divergence of racial phonetics. In Hotten's work (*List of Emigrants*) we find "Thomas Brig(g)ham," the second g in parentheses, to indicate the conventional spelling.

6. But the changing of historic "Brigham" (Scotland) to modern "Birgham" (pronounced Bur-jam) is to us inexplicable; although "North countrie" dialecticians may see a logical transition.

III

ENGLISH BRIGHAM PLACES

There appear to have been several early Brigham localities whose names have been changed in succeeding centuries, as we learn from the *Domesday Book* (p. 83, b).

Whatever may be the modern appellations of the places there mentioned the author has not learned.

BRIGHAM, NORFOLK

Bricgham, Norfolk Co., is mentioned (among other places) in Calendar Close Rolls (Ed. 2, 1313-1318, p. 373). This is the "Royal Manor of Bridgeham," mentioned in the Records of the Historical MS. Com. (London), Vol. 10, prt. 3, pp. 81, 199 (Gowdy MSS.). It was called *Brigham* in the Middle Ages until after 1500 (see *Particulars for Grants, Index Locorum—Henry VIII.*, Pub. Rec. off., London).

Stacy (*Hist. Norfolk Co.*, 1829) says it was named from the bridge which was the passage to Rowtham Cross, a way much frequented by pilgrims traveling from Suffolk and other parts to our "Lady of Walsingham."

Bridgham is situated two miles from the Harling Road Station and six from Thetford Station on the Great Eastern Ry. No Brigham is there. In fact, the only one in *Norfolk Co. Directory* lives in Norwich (an old Brigham habitat), twenty miles distant.

Bridgham parish contains the Manor of Hackford and the village of Rondham (whose church was burned many years ago). Its ancient church has an old Norman north porch, and, as there is no tower, its two bells hang in a yard-house.

BRIGHAM, YORKSHIRE

The most persistent Brigham line (so far as records show) were dwellers in this town, from the time of the Norman Conqueror (1606) to the present generation; a pedigree of heirship can be found in Poulson's *Holderness*.

From *Monasticon Eboracense* (Burton, York, 1758) we ascertain (p. 218) that the Priory of Bridlington (founded in the reign of K. Hen. I.) had lands at " Brigham " from various donors.

Chronica Monasterii de Melsa (1242-'69) has an account from William of Driffield, 9th Abbot, of an "inquisition" held at the "Hermitage of Brygham."

From Dugdale's *Visitation* (from Heralds' College, 1655-73) we learn, that from the time of Glover's *Visitation* (1585), the families of gentlemen in Holderness had decreased in number from 39 to 17: of which latter number appears " William Brigham of Brigham & Wyton, Esq., aged 52."

Sheahan & Whellen's *History and Topography of the City of York and the East Riding of Yorkshire* (1856, p. 473) recites:—

" Brigham Township extends over an area of 1,470 acres, and contains 139 inhabitants. The ratable value is £1,553. The family of Brigham possessed the whole of the Brigham Estate, . . . and their pedigree is fully recorded in Heralds' College from 1100 to 1853. . . . The Hamlet of Brigham is situated on the River Hull, near Frodingham Bridge, about five miles southeast from Driffield and one mile southwest of Foston."

BRIGHAM, CUMBERLAND *

This is a very ancient settlement, and has been the theater, in earlier ages, of stirring and important events.

Inquisitio Eliensis (p. 515, a) records the early " Church in Brigham, with 12 acres of free land, rated at 2 shillings."

The parish of Brigham (which includes ten townships) lies on the south side of the River Derwent, spanned by a fine bridge, whose opposite shore was the site of a Roman fortress. The locality is a few miles west of Cockermouth, and a few east of Workington (its seaport), being in Allerdale ward, and the archdeaconry of Richmond. It is about five and one-half miles in extent, north and south, and four miles east and west.

Soon after " The Conquest," this locality passed from William de Meschines to Waldeof, who, it is believed, built here a great castle, which became the baronial seat of his successors, the lords of Allerdale. Situated upon " The Marches," between two hostile nations (Scotland and England), these lords were courted by both great powers, and almost continually at war in behalf of that kingdom to which might temporarily be owed a changeful allegiance.

---

* Published authorities: Nicholson & Burns Hist. Westmoreland & Cumberland, Vol. II, p. 59; Hutchinson's Hist. Cumberland, Vol. II, p. 104; Carlisle's Topographical Dict. of England; Lewis' Top. & Hist. Dict. of England., p. 232; Magna Britania; Annals of the Caledonians, Picts & Scots, (Ribson, Edby., 1828), Vol. II, p. 228; *Cronicon Cumbriae.*

St. Bridget's Cathedral Brigham Cumberland, England

The castle, built of material brought from the old Roman fortress over Durwent, was in 1648 garrisoned for the royal cause; but after a month's siege dismantled. The gate house and adjoining rooms (including double dungeon capable of guarding 100 prisoners) were the last relics of the ruins to pass into oblivion. The castle and manor descended from Waldeof to Fitz Duncan (nephew of the Scottish King Malcolm); and his coheiresses—who married into the families of Albemarle and Lucy—shared in moieties. On the death of William de Fortibus, Earl of Albemarle, without issue, this moiety lapsed to the crown, was bestowed upon Piers Gavestone, and in 1323 granted by K. Ed. II. to Anthony, Lord Lucy, who possessed, by inheritance, the other moiety. His sister and heiress, Maud, in 1369, settled the property upon her second husband, Percy, Earl of Northumberland. The next Lord was Seymour, Duke of Somerset, by marriage with the only daughter of the last Earl Northumberland; thence unto the Earls of Egremont, to whom belong the court-leets and dismissions for the copyhold tenants of Brigham.

Brigham Church (dedicated to St. Bridget and formerly rectorial) is a discharged vicarage, valued in the King's Books (in 1808) at £ 20, 16, 0 1-2, situated in the diocese of Chester, archdeaconry of Richmond and deanery of Copeland. The modern East End of the village is called " Eller Beck " Brigham.

The published inscriptions of the graveyard from 1666 to 1876 (H. T. Wake, Cockermouth, 1878) do not show a single decedant of the name Brigham. The present vicar does not think the family has ever been prominent in the community; though he cites one who died in Cromwell's day, fighting in defense of Cockermouth castle. But in 1216-'72 there was a noble family of the name there whose male line, that of Waldeve de Brigham, was early extinct.

BRIGHAM, BERWICKSHIRE

Brigham (modern Birgham—pronounced Bur-jam), Berwickshire, Scotland,* is a very ancient settlement situated at the head of Tweed navigable waters (in salmon fishing second only to the Tay); and, as its name implies, once spanning its flood by a bridge, now only a tradition. Lying on " The Marches," it was for ages rent by wars between the ever-contending England and Scotland; and is but three miles from famous " Wark " castle, nor far from Norham

* Some published authorities: Lewis' Topographical Dict. of Scotland (1846), p. 128; Carlisle's Topo. Dict. of Scot. (1813); Statistical Acc. of Scot. by Haddington (1845), p. 50; Ordnance Gazetteer of Scot., Groome, (London), p. 157; Ridpath's Border Hist., pp. 104, 166; Exchequer Rolls of Scotland; Chronicle of Roger de Hovenden; Acts of the Parliaments of Scotland, pp. 66, 441, 442, Vol. II, pp. 124, 125; Haile's Annals of Scotland; Calendar Patent Rolls.

similarly famed, in the midst of a district immortalized by the poet-novelist, Scott. That Brigham was anciently an important center we may infer from meetings of parliament held, and " Brigham Treaty " confirmed here.

This village is situated in the parish of Eccles (so called from its number of ancient churches). Ecclesiastically, it is a chapelry, appendant to the rectory of Eccles, the ancient seat of Cistercian nuns (antedating preserved history), whose nunnery (according to Hovenden and the *Melrose Chronicle*), refounded by Gospatrick, Earl of March, is now only a fragment of ruins. The town is on the main highway from London to Edinburgh, and noted for several several ancient events, among them being the following:—

In 1188, William the Lion, King of Scots, with his bishops, earls, barons, and vassals met (at Brigham) Hugh, Bishop of Durham, who was sent by English King Henry II. to collect a " Saladin tenth " tax to carry on the Holy Land crusades. The tax was not granted.

March 17, 1290, Queen Margaret held here a parliament, at which letters were drafted by the magnates of Scotland regarding the marriage of their Queen with Prince Edward (son of K. Ed. I. of England). This assembly also communicated its consent to the Norway King, whom it requested to send his daughter speedily to England.

July 18, 1290, the " Treaty of Brigham " was here consummated (Patent 18 Ed. I., m. 9); but renounced by the Scottish King Baliol two years after. By this marriage contract between Q. Margaret and Prince Edward, the independence of Scotland was recognized. (The death soon after of the young queen, in one of the Orkneys, defeated the intended marriage.)

According to de Hovenden, " Bricgham " was in 883 the property of St. Cuthbert. In the *National MSS. of Scotland* (Craig, 1867), prt. 1, facsim. 7, one may see a facsimile of a charter of English King William II. to Durham church, 1097-1100, including the " Messuage of Brycgham," with adjacent lands, woods, and waters, and all wrecks of ships and other customs, to God and St. Cuthbert forever.

In the Exchequer Rolls of Scotland are found various spellings of the locality and references to some of its subdivisions.

In the MSS. Dept. of the British Museum, we examined an interesting small parchment with red seal, being the Appointment of a Deputy to hold " Jours de Marches " at Brigehamhalgh, A. D. 1394.

1. Earl Grey Monument, Newcastle-on-Tyne. 2. Brigham Forge. 3. Site of
Ancient Chapel "Birgham." 4. Field of Parliament where
Treaty of Brigham was ratified.

IV

AUTHOR'S JOURNEY TO BRIGHAM PLACES

Four places in Great Britain bear the name of Brigham: one in Yorkshire, and two in Cumberland, England; the fourth is just over the border, in Berwickshire, Scotland.

Starting from London, four hours finds one at York, the ancient Roman capital. Here change cars for Driffield, situated in the East Riding of Yorkshire. About half way you change at Market Weighton, thence a short run across the "Wolds" reaches Driffield, early capital of the "Saxon Kingdom."

In a dogcart we make our five-mile drive to Old Brigham, Yorkshire, through a landscape of level, fertile farms, studded with substantial buildings, surrounded by abundant ripening crops. Much of the distance we are alongside a canal, which runs from Driffield toward Hull. We saw only one boat, and that *drawn by a man* whose mother was tending rudder. As the craft sat low, it carried cargo. The man, with broad strap across his arms and chest, slowly drew it through the water.

At four cross-roads, we found a signboard, one of whose arms pointed toward "Brigham" hard by. Soon we climbed a slight rise, called "Brigham Hill," which commands a pleasant view in all directions.

As we proceed up "Brigham Lane," we pass the post-office and an old sand pit on the right, while on the left are a few low buildings occupied by a blacksmith and harnessmaker. In the rear is a farm called "Little Brigham." Just over the brow of the hill we reach the "Manor House," whose extensive buildings betoken that the proprietor, Mr. Stork, is a prominent breeder of hackney horses. At the foot of the hill, by the canal, stands the public house, known for generations as "The Brigham Arms." In truth the family coat-of-arms used to grace the sign; but forty years ago, when the place was sold by the Brighams, it was taken down, never again to be seen there.

A drawbridge spans the canal, and below the "Arms" is "Brigham Landing;" years ago a thriving hamlet, now simply a rural district, with no distinction to individualize it. In an adjoining field ("Sledmere Farm"), a stone slab chronicles in Latin * the passing

---

* Translation: "William Brigham, surgeon, firm and zealous in the faith of his ancestors, lived 56 years. He died at Manchester on the 10th before the Kalends of August, in the year 1815. In memoriam of a most kind and indulgent father, William, his eldest son, caused this stone to be erected here within the relics of his ancestral territory, handed down to this time from the Norman Conquest, through a continuity of ancestors."

of the Brigham race, after continuous possession from the Norman Conqueror's time. The generous erector neglected to enclose or even raise it above surrounding meadows. We fear another half century will have witnessed its overthrow.

Witness the extent of this ancient estate: An extract from *Coram Rege Rolls* (40 Ed. iii.), being taken from an Inquisition *Post Mortem* at York Castle: George Brigham, Lord of the Manor of Brigham Yorkshire, died without issue in 1576, leaving real property, which by marriage settlement had been entailed upon his nephew, Francis Brigham, as follows: " 15 messuages, 20 cottages, 5 tofts, 16 crofts; 1200 acres of arable land, 800 acres pasture, 1200 acres meadow, 500 acres moor and marsh, 500 acres turf, in Brigham." Surely this 4200-acre estate is no inconsiderable property; and as it was in the family 750 years, have we not cause for pride because of the tenacity with which succeeding generations clung to one of our clan cradles?

On our way to Scotland, we stopped at Newcastle-upon-Tyne, the magnificent " second city " of the United Kingdom. Our family have been prominently identified with this city. Though veiled in obscurity, it is certain that for at least three generations, from 1486 to 1550, they were in the lead of Newcastle families. During that period, Robert, Christopher, and Robert Brigham, each in turn, became sheriff and afterward mayor of this city.

Christopher B., a merchant of means, founded " Brigham Hospital," near the north walls, contiguous to Pilgrim Gate. This institution has disappeared. The city walls have been demolished; while along the western boundary of the Brigham Hospital site runs Grey street, one of the grandest avenues in all England; and opposite towers the monument dedicated to Earl Grey, the distinguished reformer.

In proof of the dignity of said Christopher, we might add, King Henry VIII. (Pat. 4 Hen. VIII., p. 2, m. 8) granted him a patent, whereby he was excused from serving on juries, etc., and had the privilege of *sitting with his hat on in the presence of the King and his heirs.*

To reach Brigham, Scotland, *via* the east coast, you change at Berwick and go to Coldstream; whence a four-mile drive is made over fine roads, through a beautiful rolling country of first-class farms. Brigham is a single street a mile long, made up chiefly of one-story scattered cottages, including ale-houses and a post-office. A few cots are ruinous, and others have been pulled down. The two principal farms are " Long Birgham " and " Birghamhaugh." When the spelling became changed I know not, but Birgham (Bur-jam) it is now altogether called. In history it is known as Brigham.

BRIGHAM, YORKSHIRE
1. Brigham Monument: Estate held by Brigham Family from 1100 to 1853.
2. Manor House. 3. Brigham Arms and Landing. 4. Brigham Hill.

The town lies a half mile from the Tweed, to which it runs parallel. The river offers excellent trout and salmon fishing, especially at the bend to "Dub," a deep, still pool between rapids. From Birghamhaugh bend to its mouth, the Tweed is the boundary between England and Scotland; and it is tradition that a bridge (as the name of the village suggests) once spanned the flood at this place; but no trace remains. The same lamentable truth holds of the ancient chapel, whose site is pointed out. Birgham's (Brigham) recorded history dates back more than 1,000 years.

Its early annals were glorious. In 1188 Henry II. sent ambassadors thither, who met with the Scotch King, to consider contribution to one of the crusades; in 1290 the Scots met here to ratify the proposed union of Prince Edward of England with Margaret of Scotland; in 1290, the "Treaty of Brigham" was solemnized here, providing for the freedom of Scotland; in 1291, the twelve competitors for the Scotch throne met here, to present their claims. They still point out a field as the place where Parliament convened.

In the old burying ground (some of whose stones reach back into the 1600's) not a Brigham name is found. The present lord paramount is Earl Home, whose chief residence is a few miles distant toward Coldstream. He now fishes in "Brigham Dub," and shoots game in the preserve "Birgham Wood."

Carlisle (*Topographical Dict. of Scotland*), speaking of Birgham, says: "During 1830-'31, no less than ninety-four persons emigrated to America." Perhaps many years before a Brigham performed a similar act. We doubt much, however, that there was any by the name still living there at the time when "Thomas the Puritan" began to figure in our pedigree. Let me not forget to mention, the vulgar phrase, "Go to Birgham," is frequently used in the neighborhood, in the sense of our phrase, "Go to Halifax."

Brigham, Cumberland, lies southwest of its Tweed namesake: like which, in the days of inveterate border strife, it belonged now to Scotland, now to England, as each might become the victorious aggressor. Borne many a mile through purple heather, we change cars at Carlisle, from which a short run brings one to Brigham, Cumberland. Nearing the town, we see the long stone bridge (whose prototype ages ago gave name to the place) spanning the Derwent.

Hard by the station stands the time-honored church dedicated to St. Bridget, whose masonry has been largely modernized. On the vestry wall hangs a small brass tablet dated 1633, in memory of one Swinburne, Knight. Some interesting fragments of carved stone (formerly parts of the edifice) are placed about the altar. The environing churchyard contains a choice collection of unique slabs, very large and massive. They reach back into the 1600's, but no

Brigham name is found. Near the old vicarage, but graded quite over when the railway was built, is the historic location, " Nun's Well," to whose merits the poet Wordsworth composed a sonnet. A more commonplace spot, in its present aspect, would be hard to find.

To reach the village, walk a mile up a good hill, passing through " Brigham Low Houses," consisting of two country inns, the " Lime Kiln " and the " White Sheaf." At the latter, they recalled the visit of our kinsman, the late Dexter H. Brigham of Springfield, Mass., who at our first Marlboro meeting, kindly gave us all as a souvenir, an excellent cut of Brigham church.

In going up " Brigham Hill " you pass along a causeway, from which you look down on either side fifty feet or more into vast pits, the beds of worked-out lime kilns, and try to realize what a great industry this must have been from time immemorial. Three kilns are in present use.

Reaching the height of land, and the one winding street of the older village, you see at a glance what a diary of history lies about, could it but play the oracle and speak. Old farm-houses and barns are interspersed with newer town residences. We turn westward, and descending gradually some half mile come to the modern Brigham schoolhouse, built in solid masonry in excellent taste, surrounded by a substantial high stone wall. The children come trooping to dinner, their wooden-bottomed shoes, as they romp along, resounding like a squadron of horse guards. Retracing our steps, we turn off at a private gateway leading to the Fletcher mansion, late home of the chief citizen of the community.

The east end of the village, on the height of ground, consists of modest but substantial and well-designed modern residences, whose front yards bloom with a profusion of beautiful flowers. From proximity to a small stream, it is frequently called " Eller Beck " Brigham. Beyond was " Brigham Commons "; but about a score of years ago it was divided among property owners, and is hedged off into many a sightly field.

From Brigham to Keswick is a delightful ride through the famous Lake District of England, bounded by oval hills, covered with purple heather. Up the Greta River from Keswick a short mile we reach the *hamlet* of *Brigham.** The lower portion, called " Brigham Nook," consists of a neighborhood of well-kept cot-

---

* A courteous letter from the Vicar, Rev. H. D. Rawnsby, contains the following: " Brigham by Keswick is in the ecclesiastical district of St. John's, carved out of the ancient parish of Crosthwaite in 1866. It has, so far as known, no founder, but took its name from the fact, at some time, probably in the XII or XIII century, a bridge would be put up across the river, the builders of said brig being, in all likelihood, the members of the monkish Brotherhood of St. Anthony, who were gathered here to h l   en le across fords and   ide them over the hills and to

BRIGHAM, CUMBERLAND
1. Main Street.   2. Schoolhouse.   3. Approach to St. Bridget's Church.
4. Bridge over Derwent.

tages, one ale-house, and an excellent school erected in 1851, attended by about one hundred pupils of both sexes from the agricultural and manufacturing population, a part of the instruction being garden-work. At this place, "Brigham toll-bar" (or bridge) of masoury crosses the Greta, leading toward Skiddaw, most famous of the mountains, only one and one-half miles distant.

Passing through the village, a short walk upon the left-hand road brings the visitor to "Brigham Forge," a picturesque sheltered spot, where the Greta is spanned by another stone bridge, and the power from the fall drives electric and laundry plants.*

V

HERALDRY AND BRIGHAM "ARMIGERS"

The science of heraldry was devised to distinguish persons and property and record descent and alliances. It dates from the twelfth century. The earliest document, compiled about 1240, is a roll of arms of the King and nobility in the reign of Henry III.; by which time armorial ensigns had become hereditary.

There is a great abuse of arms in the United States of America, where their use is proscribed by the Constitution, and they are displayed merely for sentiment, often without knowledge of rules appertaining to the science. Hence the erroneous assumption of arms, because borne by a family of the same name, though proof of descent be inadequate or even entirely lacking. Another abuse is the common adoption by ladies of crests upon their note paper, notwithstanding that crests belong exclusively to gentlemen.

The subject is here treated, not that the American Brighams are known with certainty to be of "armigerous" descent, but because many bearing this surname are recorded among the gentry of Great Britain, and are thought worthy of some attention in this work.

The Herald's College of Scotland does not contain any Brigham information; † but the English College of Arms in London has

ferry pilgrims across to the shrine of St. Herebert of Derwenwater. There really is no history attaching to this little Brig, or Bridge, Hamlet or Brighamlet."

See also "Keswick and Its Neighborhood," pp. 56, 57. (Windermere, 1852).

* In the ancient register of the Diocese of Carlisle is recorded the will of Thomas "Brigholme," A. D. 1361. (Hist. MSS. Com.—London, Eng.—Vol. IX, p. 196, b.)

"Lyon Office, Edinburgh, 14 Dec., 1900.

† "Sir:—There is no doubt, as you say, the name Brigham is more English than Scottish. No arms have ever been recorded here for any one of the name.

. . . . . .

"J. Balfore Paul,
"Lyon King of Arms."

considerable. We had a " search " made through the Records only, and secured numerous items (mainly corroborative of published pedigrees).

Burke's *General Armoury* has the following items:

1. Brigham (Cannon End, Co. Oxford), Argent, a fleur-de-lis within an orle of marlets sable.

2. Brigham (Cumberland), same arms.

3. Brigham or Briggam (Yorkshire), same arms. Crest, a boar's head bendways couped sable.

4. Brigham (Yorkshire), Argent a fesse sable between three Arefoils slipped gules (another of the second). Crest, on a cloud a crescent between two branches of palm in orle.

5. Brigham (Yorkshire), Argent, a fesse between three trefoils slipped gules.

6. Brigham (Yorkshire), Argent, a saltire engrailed vert. (Another sable.)

7. Brigham (Foxley House, Co. Chester, formerly of Brigham, Yorkshire), Argent, a saltire engrailed vert. Crest, out of a ducal coronet a plume of feathers. Motto, *In cruce salus.*

8. Brigham (   ), azure, a chevron between three lions rampant or.*

To these, we add the arms of the " New Castle " branch:

9. Argent, a saltire engrailed vert; in chief, a crescent sable.

We meet with numerous items, scattered through the records, concerning Brighams; which (considering that it is a " place " surname) shows a rather surprisingly early distribution of the family name; for in the earlier ages the British were, as a rule, very tenacious of accustomed localities, and families remained identified with certain places for centuries.

SOME BRITISH BRIGHAM PEDIGREES †

From *Inquisitions and Assessments Relating to Feudal Aids* (1284-1431, Vol. I., pp. 424, 487), the " Bryghams " appear to have been early domiciled (or interested in lands, at least) in " Faleton, Harrygg Hundred, Devon " Co.; " Thomas de Brygham " owned three-fourths of a knight's fee there in 1346; and " John de Brygham " the same amount in 1428. But the family either removed or died out.

" Robert de Brigham " in 1332 was proctor for the Prior of Ely. (*Hist. MSS. Commis.*, Vol. VI., p. 296, MSS. Lord Leconfield, Petworth House, Sussex.)

* We have not learned where these arms were used.

† We include here pedigrees from such sources as to render it clear that the families possessed coat armor, though no record of it is preserved.

About 1300 we find a record of three generations in Lincolnshire —Richard, Thomas, and Richard de Brigham.   (*Calendarium Genealogicum*, Vol. I., p. 259; Vol. II., p. 693.)

Marshall's *Visitation of Northumberland* has this pedigree:

Knight.

ARMS: *Three bendlets; on a canton, a spur.*

Wm. Knight, Co. Dechy= ·   Hobson of Cambr. town.
Rector Gransden Parva
Co. Cambr., o.   about
1645 *æ.* abt. 63.

Wm. Knight, eldest son, == Anne dau. John Hacker Flintham,
Gransden Parva, o. about | Nott. Co.
24 Feb. 1659 *æ.* 69.

Jane (eldest of 7 daus.)= Thomas Brigham, Swavesey, Cambrsh.

From a *Catalogue of Ancient Deeds* (Vol. I., p. 523, c. 1372), under date "Thursday in the Octave of the Purification, 17 K. Ed. I." (A. D. 1289), Warwickshire, we note, "Grant by Sarah, late the wife of Thomas Sorel of Birmingham, to Robert de Brigham, of her bondmen and villeins, Richard, son of Peter le Bule; Arice, daughter of Humphrey Frideau, and Agnes, daughter of Galfrida, daughter of Margaret, of the same place, with all their belongings."

Coming now to the neighborhoods of the *Brigham places,* we find, as anticipated, the *Brigham surname* in evidence, though the records are, as a rule, fragmentary.

In Norfolk County (seat of the "royal manor of Brigham"— modern Bridgham), we find one "Alande Brigham" as early as 1297 (*Coram Rege Rolls,* K. Ed. I., p. 289).

In Parkin's *Topographical History of the County of Norfolk* (Vol. VI., p. 144) the heirs of one William de Brigham are named, as being part owners in a knight's fee of land in Bradenham Manor in 1347.

Over the remains of Adam Brigham, who died at Norwich, England, in 1685, aged 54:

> "In youth, I poor and much neglected went,
> My gray and wealthy age in mirth I spent,
> To honors then, I courted was by many,
> Altho' I did in nowise seek for any;
> But what is now that wealth, that mirth, that glory?
> Alas! 'Tis grave, 'tis dust, 'tis mournful story:
> Ne'erless, my soul through Christ a place enjoys
> Where blessed Saints with him in God rejoice."
>
> ("*Chronicles of the Tombs,*" by Thos. Jos. Pettigrew, p. 448).

There are Brighams in Norfolk to-day who appear to have descended in unbroken local lines for centuries.

Of Brigham, Cumberland, we find families:—" John de Brigge-haim" appears as witness to a grant about 1210 (*Calendar of Docs. Relating to Scotland,* Vol. I., p. 97). This may be the " John " found in the following pedigree, whose male line early died out:

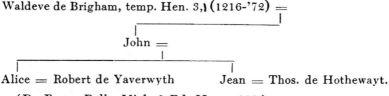

Waldeve de Brigham, temp. Hen. 3,) (1216-'72) =

John =

Alice = Robert de Yaverwyth   Jean = Thos. de Hothewayt.

(*De Banco Rolls, Mich,* 2 Ed. II., m. 220.)

From the *De Banco Rolls* (MSS. Series, Vol. XXVIII., p. 863) one finds that in 1274 John and Thomas Brigham, sons of Adam de Brigham, had lands in Galenter. From *Coram Rege Rolls* (p. 583, 23 Ed. III., 23 Ric. II.), Thomas Brigham was in Cumberland in 1381. *Ibid.,* 14 Hen. IV. has this pedigree:—

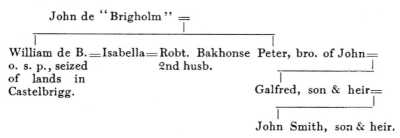

John de "Brigholm" =

William de B. = Isabella = Robt. Bakhonse   Peter, bro. of John =
o. s. p., seized   2nd husb.
of lands in
Castelbrigg.   Galfred, son & heir =

John Smith, son & heir.

But the Brighams of Cumberland early either died out or removed; for there is no evidence of them in the preserved parish records of Brigham (Cumb.), which run back about 300 years; we get no light from Brigham graveyard, whose epitaphs run back to 1660; nor do the wills for the Deanery of Copeland disclose any Brigham estates.

Concerning Brigham, Berwickshire, Scotland: notwithstanding there are no Brigham wills of this county of record between 1562 and 1670 (the period of our search); notwithstanding, moreover, that " Lyon King of Arms " writes me, " I do not think any one of the name [Brigham] ever possessed land in Scotland, or that the family was conspicuous in any way "—there are brief scattered notes which are more hopefully eloquent. Indeed, it would be strange had not someone assumed for his surname the name of that town shown by records to have been of the early importance of Brigham, Berwick. But, being upon " The Borders," the devastations of innumerable conflicts have destroyed local records.

From Whellen's *History of Cumberland* (based on Nicholson and Burn & Hutchinson) we learn:—

"Sir Ranulph Bonekill had issue Alexander, whose son Adam gave Aiverthwaite, parcel of his Manor of Uldale, to the priory of Carlisle. Said Adam had issue a son Alexander, whose daughter and heiress was married first to John Stuart, Kinsman of the King of Scotland, and afterwards to *David Brigham,* a Scottish Knight renowned for his prowess and bravery; and by this marriage the Manor of Uldale passed to the Brigham family. This David Brigham was a companion of William Wallace, who was executed at London (temp. Ed. I.), for resisting that King, having joined with Robert Bruce. Wallace was of extraordinary strength, and Brigham an exceedingly good horseman; whence came the Scots' rhyme:

> "The man was ne'er so wight nor gend,
> But worthy Wallace durst him bide;
> Nor ever horse so wild or wend,
> But David Brigham durst him ride."

Palgrave (*Docs. and Recs. Illustrtg. Hist. Scotland,* Vol. I., pp. 193, 291, 315 and 355) shows that this "David de Breghyn" resided at Brigham, Scotland, and was upon the scene at about the "Treaty of Brigham" epoch.

William Brigham, 1525, is seized of lands in the "Lordship of Brigham" (*Exchequer Rolls of Scotland,* Vol. XV., p. 638). In 1559 "Adam Birgem" is seized of lands in the same (*Ibid.,* p. 445).

In 1590, "Elizabeth Birgen, haeres Adami Birgen, patris" has "2 terris husbandiis cum 12 acris terrarum, in dominio de Birgen." (*Retornak Rolls, Scotland,* Vol. II., Berwick, No. 489.) From *Reg. of the Privy Council* of *Scotland* (Vol. IV., p. 675) it appears that the wife of the above Adam Brigham was "Issobell Edzeare"; also that their daughter Elizabeth married "Alex. Diksonn* of Newton in Brigham."

It thus plainly appears that the male Brigham line of Brigham, Scotland, died out in the latter part of the sixteenth century.

We add one other stray note of this Kingdom (*Calend. of Docs. Relating to Scotland,* Vol. IV., p. 233). "John Brigholme," a Scotch merchant, has warrant for safe conduct for one year, with his vessel, "Gyles, 60 tone," to trade in England with 12 mariners.

It is, however, in connection with Brigham, Yorkshire, that we find the most persistent and satisfactory pedigree, so far as records show. It runs back to Norman times; a period so remote that very few English families presume to trace their (certain) origin from any anterior source.

* Dickson is a common surname thereabouts. I found stones bearing it in the old Brigham churchyard.

Poulson's *History of Holderness** (East Riding of Yorkshire), Vol. II., pp. 268, 269, 270, contains a magnificent pedigree,† credited to *Harleian MS.*, 1487, p. 300 (from Glover's and St. George's *Visitations*, 1484-1485, 1612, edited by Foster), and a MS. vol. of *East Riding Pedigrees* in Burton Constable Library.

BRIGHAM OF WYTON AND BRIGHAM

WYTON.   The family of Brigham is first mentioned as holding this manor 35 Hen. VIII.; but at what time it came into their possession is not ascertained.   In that year Thomas Brigham, Esq., held the manor of Wyton, " 3 mess. 3 cott. 4 crofts, 6 bovates of arable, and 40 acres of land here, of the heirs of Thomas Constable, Kt., as of his manor of Constable, be the service of Knt.'s fee; Geo., son and heir."

ARMS: ‡ *Argent, a saltire engrailed vert.*

Poulson says " this family is now become extinct."   This is error; see Sheahan & Whellen's *History and Topography of the City of York and the East Riding of Yorkshire* (1856).   The said Dr. Wm. Brigham removed from Brigham to the city of Manchester, whereby the family became " extinct " upon the estate of Brigham, which probably accounts for Poulson's statement; for it is certain that it was Dr. Wm. Brigham, Esq.,§ whose residence was Foxley House,‖ Lymm, Cheshire, who sold the very last Brigham property in Brigham, Yorkshire, removed the " Brigham Arms " from the Inn, and erected a monument herein elsewhere referred to at length.   Said

---

* We had the good fortune to procure, at reasonable price, a new (uncut) copy of this, now rare and valuable, treatise, the full title of which is: " The History and Antiquities of the Seigniory of Holderness, in the East Riding of York, Including the Abbies of Meaux and Swine, with the Priories of Nunkeeling and Burstall; Compiled from Authentic Charters, Records and the Unpublished Manuscripts of the Rev. William Dade, Remaining in the Library of Burton Constable; with numerous embellishments; by George Poulson, Esquire, * * * Hull, MDCCCXL." It is composed of two quarto volumes, aggregating more than 1,000 pages, and by far the most valuable book which has been written of this part of York, wherein is situated Brigham.

† Parcels of this pedigree also recorded:—Harl. MS. 1415, fol. 87, b.; 1420, fol. 84, b.; Dugdale's Visit. 1665/6, (Lon. Her. Coll. " Recs. C. 40, 109 "); Add. MS. 18,011, fol. 103, b.; Her. Coll. Recs. (London) " C. 13, 173 " and " Norfolk IX, 211 "; Harl. MS. 1394, pp. 113-115, 349; (this MS. has many biographic, land and marriage notes); 805, fol. 75.

‡ Glover and St. George give the arms: " argent a fesse sable bet. 3 trefoils slipped gules."   (Probably used by one branch of the family). Also, the motto: " Promisit se nussurum arma Londinum."

§ This family of " Foxley House " is recorded in Burke's " Seats & Arms," Vol. IV, and Walford's " County Families, etc."

‖ I had a letter from the present owner of Foxley House, L. Clark, Esq., who kindly promised me a picture of the house and chapel.

"Squire" Brigham had an only daughter, who had the misfortune to marry an unscrupulous Frenchman, to whose criminal actions her death was doubtless due. She had a child, whose whereabouts and descendants (if any) are to the writer unknown.*

We include here the following pedigree, because it is believed to be of Yorkshire origin.

(Brigham of Cannon End.)†

ARMS: *Argent a fleur-de-lis within an orle of martlets sable.*

Anthony Brigham, Cofferer of the household to (Q. Eliz.) ‡ = ——

Thomas, Patentee for the Stanneries in Cornwall under Q. Eliz.; ob. s. p.	Xtofer, of Cannon Inde in Com.	=daughter of ——Weldon, Cofferer to King Henry VIII.
Thomas, eldest son = Dorothy, daughter living Ao. 1634. of John Lyne of Norwich.		Wm. 2d son. Hedon, 3d son.

Thomas, son and heir. Anthony, 2d son. Elizabeth. Rachell. Dorothy.

Newcastle-upon-Tyne § appears to have been the metropolis with which the Brighams were most historically connected. For at least a century, this family seems to have been in the lead: Robert Brigham was Sheriff of the city in 1486, and Mayor in 1499; Christopher Brigham was Sheriff in 1495, and Mayor in 1504, 1505; Robert Brigham was Sheriff in 1540, and Mayor in 1550, in which latter year he was also "Governor of the Merchants' Company."

The arms ‖ of this branch are: "Argent, a saltire engrailed vert;

---

* I have had some very pleasant correspondence with Rev. I. Kennedy, Vicar of Foston-on-the-Wolds (only a mile from Brigham). He kindly cited to me the records of the Leet Courts, which used to be regularly held at Brigham, up to about forty years ago.

† See Harl. MS. 1480, fol. 44; Her. Coll. "Records, C. 29, 126; D. 25, 5."

‡ It appears that said "Anthony" was not "Cofferer," but Bailiff of the King's Manor of Caversham (Pat. 35, Hen. VIII, p. 14, m. 6).

§ Authorities: Tanner's Notitia Monastica; Leland's Itinerary, Vol. V, p. 114; Wallis' Northumberland, Vol. II, p. 218; Hist. Antiquities of Newcastle, Brand (London, 1789), Vol. I, p. 342, Vol. II, p. 240; Welford's Hist. of Newcastle, Vol. II, p. 322; Vestiges of Old Newcastle, Knowles & Boyles.

‖ London Her. Coll. ("Recs. C. 41, 7. C.") erroneously attributes to this family the arms of the "Horsleyie" family: "An annulet, bet. 3 horses' heads, couped and caparisoned."

in chief, a crescent sable." The crescent is (in the writer's opinion) used for " difference " (as heralds say), to indicate that this New-castle branch sprang from (not the eldest, but) the " second son '' of the parent stock. The remainder of the coat stamps them as (undoubtedly) of Yorkshire Brigham origin. Going yet farther, the writer concludes that the Newcastle branch is descended from " *Robert* " Brigham (the " *second* son " of John and Elizabeth Brigham) in the seventh generation from Walter Brigham, of Brigham, according to the said Poulson pedigree.

From Flower's *Visitation* (1563, 1564) is learned: (1) that Wm. Lewen, son and heir of William, " Marchant " (and armiger) mar. Jane, dau. of Christopher " Brygam," both families of Newcastle. (A second wife, by whom 5 ch.—" Crystofer, Edward, Robert, William, and " Mighill.") (2) Christopher Mitford, 4th son and heir of Robert, of Segell, Northumberland (armiger), mar. Agnes, dau. of Christopher Brygham.

Marshall's *Visitation* (1615) has this pedigree:

John Jackson (armiger), of New = Jane, dau. and sole heir of Wm.
Castle.   Brigham, of New Castle.

Wm. Jackson, Town Clerk of = Isabell, dau. Gilbert Read, New
New Castle.   Castle.

Henry Jackson, of Cotam = Dorothy, dau. of   John Jackson, of
Mandaville,   Bishoprick   Mansfield.   Grayes Inn.
of Duresne.

We close our Newcastle remarks with a curious church item:

" Robert Darell, Archdeacon of Northumberland, made a covenant Oct. 9, 1537, with F. Roland Harding, Prior of the Blake Friers, Newcastle-on-Tyne, between 6 and 9 A. M. daily, devoutly to say for the souls of William Darell and *John Brigham,* late of Newcastle, Merchant, their wives and children the *De profundis,* etc., ending *Absolve quaesumus Domine,* and *Sede ad dextram.*"

LONDON BRIGHAMS

The Brigham family has been identified with the British metropolis for several hundreds of years, as is proved by items scattered through the records, although we find no pedigree preserved.

" Rob. Briggeham, A. M.," 31 Jan., 1427, became Rector of the parish church of St. Andrew-Hubbard (sometimes called St. A. juxta Eastcheap), which stood in old Rope Lane, (London), and had a history antedating 1389. It was burned by the " Great Fire,'' and the parish united with St. Mary-Hill. (*An Eccles. Paroch. Hist. of the Dios. of London*, Newcourt, 1708.)

One Richard Brigham was "Coach-maker to Kings James I. and Charles I.," as appears by a "Grant, Sept. 13, 1619, to John Banks and Richard Brigham, of the office of Maker of the King's Coaches and other Carriages." (*Calendar of State Papers*—Dom. Ser., Vol. CLI., p. 77.) "1620-1622. Third accompt. Bill of John Banckes and Richards Brigham, Coachmaker to the King. For chariots and other vehicles. A rich chariot for the King cost, in all, £15." Again, "1624-1625. Two long bills (respectively 13 and 9 pp.) of Richard Brigham, for reparations of the King's caroches and chariots. He made the total £368, but took £280 in satisfaction. There were two new coaches: one is said to be of the German fashion, with the roof to fall asunder at his majesty's pleasure [*i. e.*, a sort of landau]. The other was of the Spanish fashion. The like of them were never made before in England." (*Histor. MSS. Commis.*, Lon., Vol VI., p. 326b, MSS. of Sir F. U. Graham, Bart., Netherby, Cumb.; and Vol. VII., prt. 1, p. 250a, MSS. of Lord Sackville, at Knole, Kent.)

George Brigham was also a "royal coachmaker"; the same authority (Vol. II., p. 583), some readable facts follow: Aug. 13, 1645.

"George Brigham, coachmaker to the late King,

Thomas Brigham, his brother and administrator, *et al.*,

all of London."

Then come two pages of legal proceedings, disclosing that one Thomas Brigham resided in Duke's Place, London; George Brigham, deceased, was in arms and died at Oxford; proceedings over a £200 debt owed the George Brigham estate, wherein said Thomas Brigham will not release one Pilchard of his imprisonment, and says that the committee shall make dirt of his bones before he will give up the mortgage; there is an order for Thomas Brigham to be brought before the committee for contempt. Later, John Brigham, of Cottenham, County Cambridge, as executor of Thomas Brigham, deceased, was apprehended to answer contempt for not delivering up certain writings; he was discharged from restraint, upon performing order of the committee.

Concerning Thomas Brigham, "Patentee for the Stanneries" (*i. e.*, tin mines) in Cornwall, we find some interesting facts. In the first place, this was a very valuable grant. The mines were very old; in fact, the same sought out by the Phoenicians and other inhabitants of the Mediterranean Sea, before the dawn of the Christian era. In the *Calendar of State Papers* (Domestic Series), preserved in the Public Record Office, London (Vol. CLI., p. 13, sec. 4) we find:

"June 7, 1603.   Allegations against the patent granted to Thomas Brigham and Humphrey Wemmes by the late Queen, for pre-emption of tin." (P. 152, sec. 45) Sept. 25, 1604.   Warrant to Sir Richard Smith, Receiver General of Cornwall, to deliver tin at a certain rate to such persons as now lend money in repayment thereof, and to redeliver to Thomas Brigham and Humphrey Wemmes the tin sold by them to the Company of Pewterers. (Docquet.) (P. 157, sec. 75) Oct. 14, 1604.   Reply of Thomas Brigham and Humphrey Wemmes to an annexed petition to the King by the Master, etc., of the Pewterers' Company against the monopoly granted to them of the pre-emption of tin.   (P. 335, sec. 57) Nov. 14, 1606. Decree of the Court of Star Chamber against Richard Glover, et. al., Pewterers of London, for endeavoring to frustrate a patent granted to Thomas Brigham and Humphrey Wemmes, for pre-emption of tin in Cornwall and Devon." There was a "Warrant to advance £20,000 on loan to Thomas Brigham and Humphrey Wemmes, patentees for the pre-emption of tin, on their delivery of tin worth more than that, they having already disbursed £60,000, and being unable to disburse more.   They will add £1,000 to their former rent of £2,000, and lend the tinners £10,000 yearly."

"London, Feb. 23, 1618.   Assignment by John Langley to Richard Brigham, both being of Lambeth, of the Keepership of the Archbishop of Canterbury's Mansion House, grounds and pasture land, called Lambeth Park." (*Calend. State Papers,* Domestic Ser., Vol. CLI., p. 523, sec. 29.)   This Richard Brigham, Esq., of Lambeth, London (Comptroller of the house of the Archbishop Abbot), married Emelyn, daughter of Sir Robert Hudson, Bart. Their only daughter, Anne, married Thomas, Lord Leigh; they having but one child, Anne, who died young." (*Magna Britannia.*)

John Brigham of the City of Westminster, London, in 1637, was married in the local abbey of St. Peter, to Anne, daughter of Sir Thomas Aylesbury.   Her eldest sister, Frances, was the first Countess of Clarendon, and thus grandmother of Queen Mary II., and Queen Anne. (*London Marriage Licenses,* 1521-1869, by Jos. Foster.)

Nicholas Brigham, poet, jurist, and historian (for a biographical sketch see elsewhere herein) was buried in "Poet's Corner," Westminster Abbey, beside his daughter Rachel, whom he lost at the age of four.

The *London Directory* for 1900 does not contain any Brigham "liverymen."   But therein appear: Henry George Brigham, Surgeon, Buckingham Palace Road, Dr. John K. Brigham, Finsbury Pavement, John (the proprietor of "coffee rooms"), and George E. ("boatmaker").

VI

As far as preserved records establish, Nicholas Brigham * was the greatest scholar, the most versatile and honored genius of all who have borne the Brigham name. By tradition his birth was from the prominent family of Caversham, Oxford, the founder of which, Anthony Brigham, was Bailiff of the King's Manor there under Henry VIII.; but his name does not appear in the pedigree of Brigham. Nicholas is reported to have finished his education at Hart Hall (now Hertford College). He appears to have removed thence to one of the Inns of Court, where he made a thorough study of law and history. His love for poetry, however, was a lifelong passion, as manifested in many flights of his Pegasus.

Biographers say he died in December, 1559, but from the probate of his estate, into which I examined, it is determined that he passed away on the " 20 Feb. 1558." He was buried in " Poet's Corner," Westminster Abbey, beside his daughter Rachel, whom he lost at the age of four. Camden, in his work (published in 1606) upon those entombed at Westminster, gives the full inscription upon the grave of the daughter, but he does not mention anything of the sort concerning the father.

The epitaph follows: " *Rachael Brigham, filia Nicolai Brigham quadrimula obiit, sita est juxta Galfridum Chaucerum. Obiit* 1557, *21 Junii.*"

Dean Stanley (*Westminster Abbey*, p. 15) says: " There was nothing to mark the grave [of Chaucer] except a plain slab, which was sawn up when Dryden's monument was erected. It was not till the reign of Edward VI. that the present tomb, to which apparently the poet's ashes were removed, was raised, near the grave, by Nicholas Brigham, himself a poet, who was buried close beside, with his daughter Rachel."

From the foregoing we might infer possibly that Nicholas never

* Do not confound this Nicholas with the one spoken of elsewhere as " Teller of the Exchequer " to Queen Mary. The fact that they both bear the same name, are prominent and in London at the same period makes it a question of easily mistaken identification. In fact, the best modern English biographer of Nicholas, the poet, falls into this error, of making these two persons one. It is clear, however, that Nicholas, the " poet," died in 1558, and that his estate was administered upon in the Commissary Court of the Dean & Chapter of Westminster; while concerning Nicholas, the " Teller," I find him living as late as "1563," at which time he " entered into hall, gardens and premises of her Majesty's (Q. Elizabeth) Almshouses of Westminster." Very likely the two were nearly related; but in what degree I am unable to say, save that I do not believe the relationship could have been that of father and son.

had any epitaph, although historians agree that he was herein buried near the tomb of Chaucer, father of English poets, to whom Brigham had caused a monument to be erected.

Chaucer's ruinous tomb yet remains, black with antiquity and slowly crumbling to dust; but the exact spot of Brigham's grave cannot be determined. Even his epitaph, like that of his little daughter, has disappeared.

A modern movement to repair the tomb evoked the following restatement: "An examination of the tomb by competent authorities has proved . . . there can exist no doubt, from the difference of workmanship, material, etc., that the altar tomb is the *original* tomb of Geoffrey Chaucer; and that instead of Nicholas Brigham having erected an entirely new monument, he only added to that which then existed the overhanging canopy," etc. (*Notes and Queries,* London, 1st Ser., Vol. II., p. 141; quoting from *Athenæum.*)

He left no will, and it is impossible to decide whether he left issue. He did, however, leave children of his brain, in several notable works, namely: (1) *Rerum Quotidianarum Venationes* (or a Diary of Memoirs, in 12 Bks.). (2) *Venationibus Rerum Memorabilum,* in 1 vol., being biographic in character, from which Bale, in his *Scriptores,* published in 1559, makes extract touching two (now obscure) English writers. (3) *Diversorum Poematum,* in 1 vol., being a collection of poems from his own pen. But the only production now known is his epitaph on Chaucer.

Pitts, his biographer, thus summarizes the record of his achievements, which I render into English: "Nicholas Brigham . . . In poetry, above the common crowd; eloquent as an orator; an experienced jurisconsult; a signally successful historian; as an antiquarian researcher into the lore of ancient Albion, very diligent."

VII

EARLY AMERICAN BRIGHAMS *

Aside from Thomas, " The Puritan," of Watertown, Mass., 1635, we find some other Brighams of early date who should be mentioned

* Briggs' " Shipbuilding on North River," etc., 1640-1872, p. 366, states: " There was built in Scituate in 1698 the ship ' Providence,' 100 tons, Capt. Thos. Lillie=owners, Capt. Juo. Thomas, Saml. Lillie, John Borland and Joseph Brigham of Boston."

This is an error, for Joseph Bridgham of Boston, whom we find (Recs. Mass., Vol. V, p. 538), " 1st Ch. Boston, made free in May Court 1678." He died 1708/9, and was buried in King's Chapel ground. But, as witness of how persistent the error was, we find on the tombstone of a descendant (in King's Chapel), " Sarah, Dau., to Mr. Jos. and Mrs. Abigail Brigham, aged 1 month decd. Oct. 7, 1728."

in this work, that they may not be confused with the line of Thomas Brigham the Puritan, our common ancestor.

But first, let us introduce a name merely suggestive. From Hotten's *List of Emigrants,* etc., 1600-1700, p. xix., a register of all such persons as embarked themselves in the good ship called the " Hercules " of Sandwich (Eng.), and taken to the " plantation called New England in America," etc.: " Tho. Bridgen of Faversham, husbandman and his wife," 5 March, 1634. From Boys' *Hist. Sandwich, Eng.,* 1692, pp. 750-1. (See also *N. E. Hist. Gen. Reg.,* Vol. XV., p. 29.)

Savage (*Gen. N. E.*) informs us that this Thomas " Bridgen or Brigden " settled in Charlestown, Mass., 1634; had two sons, Thomas and Zachariah (grad. Har. Col. 1657 and prchd. Stonington, Mass.), and daus. Mary and Sarah.

Equally suggestive is an entry in Bond's excellent *Hist. Watertown, Mass.,* wherein the land of one " John Brigan " in 1642 was a boundary line of a lot of E. Child.

JOHN BRIGHAM OF NEW PROVIDENCE, 1633

His name is known from a letter in the Bouverie MSS., preserved at Brymore, near Bridgewater, Eng. (*Hist. MSS. Com.,* Vol. X., prt. 6, p. 85). In this letter, which is dated Oct. 28, 1633, Wm. Rudyerd, Wm. Rous, Roger Floyde, and John Brigham write from the Island of Providence (one of the Bahamas) to —— (probably John Pym, the great English leader) concerning the hardships of life and agriculture on the Island. In the *Calendar of State Papers* (Domestic Ser., Vol. CLI., A. D. 1581-'90, Q. Eliz., p. 146, sec. 35), we learn that Mr. Secretary (probably Walsingham) has been informed by Mr. Anthony Brigham that he approves of the Western discoveries in America; recommends the formation of a company, and advises them to hearken to the offers of Sir Philip Sidney and Sir George Peckham. This " Anthony " Brigham may be the very one who was " Bailiff " to Queen Elizabeth; and the " Western discoveries in America," to which reference is made, are undoubtedly those in the West Indies. So we are justified in believing that the " company " recommended was formed, that they did " hearken " to " Sir Philip Sidney " (or someone), and that this letter of " John Brigham " and others is information returned by them, as settlers of the " Company " in the New World. It is entirely natural that we should inquire *what became of this John Brigham,* who was settled and writing back to England some year and a half before our Thomas the Puritan was sailing out of London.

Paige's *Hist. Cambridge* (Mass.) records: " Brigham, Sebastian, about 1638, bought house and garden at the northwest corner of Holyoke and Winthrop Sts , which he sold to John Bridge in 1639. He probably removed to Rowley."

Morse's Brigham book (p. 3) finds " no further trace " than shown by Cambridge records.

There are preserved several entries in the *Records* of *Massachusetts.* Vol. II., p. 87, states that Sebastian Brigham (then of Rowley), by action of the General Court, Nov. 13, 1644, " hath liberty to sell wine and to keepe an ordinary."

Ibid., p. 187, May 26, 1647, The Rowley Co., having chosen Sebastian B. their Captain, he is confirmed by Gen. Crt. *Ibid.,* Vol. III., pp. 62, 105, 183: Capt. S. B. of Rowley is " Deputy " in 1646, 1647, and 1650. *Ibid.,* p. 186: He was appointed by the Gen. Crt., May 23, 1650, one of a Commission to lay out the boundaries of Haverhill, Mass. From the published *Records of Rowley, Mass.*, we learn that Sebastian Brigham was a large landholder.

From the *Records* of *Rowley; Mass.* (printed), Proem, p. vi.: " Sebastian Briggam was the Captain of the first military company. Had wife, Mary. Returned to England about 1657.† Four children were born here." ‡

VIII

MARLBORO AND ITS BRIGHAMS

As Marlboro, Mass., whose original boundaries included the pres-ent Northboro, Southboro, Westboro, and Hudson, is the Mecca of the American Brigham, it is well here to give a brief summary of the place and its Brigham inhabitants. In 1656, thirteen of the leading settlers of Sudbury (the first town to the east) received from the General Court favorable answer to their petition for a new township grant: Marlboro being the result.

Heading the list of petitioners, and one of the first to move to Marlboro, was Edmund Rice, who took with him his second wife, the widow of Thomas Brigham the Puritan, with her young Brigham family, whose names, however, do not appear upon the records for

* See also Essex Instit. Coll., Vol. XX, p. 137.

† Blodgett's " Early Settlers of Rowley, Mass." says returned with family about 1656 or earlier.

‡ Farmer's " Geneal. Reg. makes Sebastian's son ' John ' Brigham, a graduate of Harvard Coll.; 1669." The " Bridgham " family is entitled to this honor. The earliest " Brigham " graduate was " Benjamin, 1764."

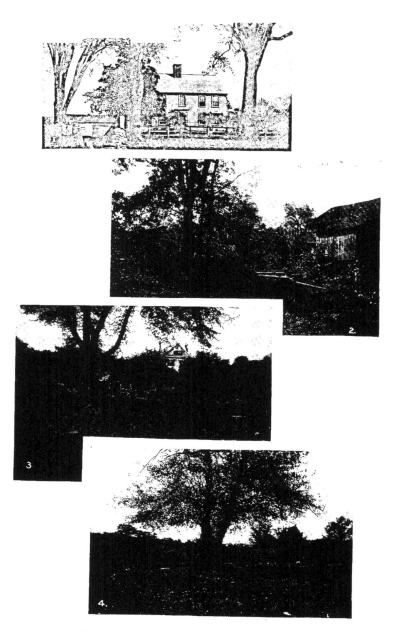

1. Priest Whitney Place, Northboro. 2. John[2] Brigham's Mill Dam,
Northboro. 3. Samuel[2] Brigham's Tanyard, Marlboro.
4. Burial Plot, Last of the Indians, on Thomas[2]
Brigham Farm, Marlboro.

some time. They settled upon the north side of "The Pond," not far from Williams' Tavern; and for the succeeding two and a half centuries, the Brighams have continued to people the scene.

At the time of Philip's War, they fled to Watertown. On their return, such was the feeling against Indian perfidy, a petition was made to the General Court to divide the 6000-acre "Indian Plantation," a part of and contiguous to Marlboro. Although this was denied, the people, under the leadership of John Brigham, took a deed from the Indians to these lands, 15 July, 1684; and though this was declared "null and void" by the General Court, the white proprietors proceeded to divide and settle these lands, under the supervision of their agent, the said John Brigham, who was their surveyor. In the 1686 list of proprietors we find the names of all the young Brighams, and their alliances, for the first time set out, viz.: Mercy Hunt (former widow of the Puritan Brigham, who before this time had married her third husband, William Hunt, also then dead), Thomas Brigham, John Brigham, Samuel Brigham, John Fay, (husband of Mary Brigham), and William Ward (husband of Hannah Brigham). Feeling uneasy over the adverse action of the Court, in 1683; the proprietors agreed that their grants "shall stand good to all intents and purposes, if they be attested by John Brigham, their Clerk." And so it stood, until, after a generation, having acquired title by possession, the General Court confirmed it.

The first mill in town was built by John Brigham (before Philip's War) on Assabet River (now in Northboro), and the site was only recently abandoned.

The first tannery in town was built by Samuel Brigham, and continued in the family for generations. The shoe industry is now the most important by far in town; and Francis Brigham, one of Samuel's descendants, more than fifty years ago started in Hudson a shoe factory, which is the leading business of that town.

In 1689, John Brigham was one of a committee of two chosen by the town, when the tyrant Andros was superseded by the Colonial Government.

At this period new settlements to the westward were being made (e. g., Shrewsbury, Brookfield, Rutland, Worcester, and Grafton), and the Brigham family, with others, sent its colonizers.

In Queen Anne's War, Samuel Brigham was one of the committee to assign the inhabitants to the twenty-six log forts erected. Among these, we see: "4. Capt. [Samuel] Brigham's Garrison." "10. Thomas Brigham's Garrison," which included his son Jonathan. "14. Nathan Brigham's Garrison," and David Brigham of Edmund Rice's Garrison. In this war Samuel Brigham was the lieutenant of Capt. Howe, and thereafter received a bounty for destroying an Indian.

In 1717, in reply to petition of Thomas Brigham and others, about half the town land, with other added (including the Rice and Fay farms to the westward) became the new town, "Westboro"; and among its first inhabitants are David and Jotham Brigham, with the Rice, Ward, and Fay families (related by intermarriage) represented. Subsequently, Northboro, Southboro, and Hudson were carved out of the parent town; in all of which the Brighams were interested.

Some Marlboro records covering a period of many years were lacking (and entirely lost in the Town Hall fire of 1903; showing the town's wise foresight in having had published a history, by Charles Hudson, 1862; to which the present writer owes so much), but in 1756, we find Thomas and Capt. Ephraim Brigham on a committee of five to repair the meeting-house "on the foreside and two ends," including glazing "with sash glass, set in wood."

In the military history of Marlboro, the Brighams have held conspicuous places. Numbers took a hand in the French and Indian Wars, as exhibited by meager records; (Lieut. Ephraim, Sergt. Benj., Corps. Asa and Ithamar, privts. Paul, Noah, etc.); and when we come to the Revolution, we have full evidence of their bravery. In the preliminary stages, George Brigham was one of the committee of five to draw up a "Covenant of non-consumption of British goods"; and was one of three to represent the town in the "Provisional Government."

We now come to the immortal day of Concord and Lexington, 19 April, 1775; upon which day marched out from old Marlboro Captain William Brigham and Company, including 2d Lieut. Ithamar B., Sergts. Henry and Joseph B., Corp. Lewis B., and privates Lovewell, George, Gershom, and Alexander Brigham; in Barnes' Company marched 2d Lieut. Paul Brigham, Corp. Antipas B., and private Jonathan; in Gates' Company, privates Henry, George, and Uriah; in Howe's Company, private Joel. In the same year, enrolled with the "eight months" men, we find Capt. Paul, and privates Jonathan, Abraham, Artemas, William, Uriah, Henry, and George Brigham. Among others who fought during this war are Lovewell, John Gott, David, Phineas, David, Paul, Daniel, Samuel, Stephen, and Aaron Brigham. (For fuller detail, turn to the Appendix, and individual records.)

Illustrating school activity: Thomas and Jotham Brigham were on the school committee of five, in 1745; Samuel Brigham received £57.10 for teaching "two school quarters," in 1747; in 1771, Capt. Ephraim Brigham left £111, a permanent fund, the interest to be annually expended for a school for "writing and cyphering." "Brigham School," thus created, gave to older pupils in the spring

BRIGHAM CEMETERY   MARLBORO

(after "common school" closing) this additional instruction; until the fund was merged in the general appropriations.

We are likely to forget that slavery once existed in New England. In 1771, the Assessors return " 1 slave owned by Hannah Brigham." In 1770, the Brigham "polls" in town, with the number in each family, appear as follows: Samuel 1, Uriah 1, George 2, Ithamar 1, Paul 1, Ephraim 3, Joseph 2, Benjamin 3, Asa 1, Solomon 1, Caleb 2, and Winslow 1. Ephraim was one of the largest taxpayers. At the beginning of the next century, the Brighams number 25 polls; making, with the Howes and the Rices, 73 of the 277 taxpayers.

" Brigham Cemetery " is situated on West Main Street; an enclosure of some acre and a half, reached through a little lane and commanding a pleasing landscape to the southwest. It was named after Capt. William Brigham and Lydia his wife, who died in 1793, of smallpox (one of the most dreaded foes of the early settlers); and, as forbidden to be buried in a public cemetery, were here entombed. In 1808 this land was deeded by Capt. William's son, Col. Ephraim Brigham, Esq., to the Unitarian Society; and over Ephraim's remains, in 1887, Lucius L. Brigham of Worcester erected a fine gray granite monument. About thirty Brighams are here buried, in a ground which, since 1882, has been kept in excellent condition by the income of the " Gibbon Fund."

Of Marlboro civil officers, we find:

Selectmen: Samuel Brigham, 1707, '10; Samuel, 1741, '42, '44, '46, '48, '49, '54; Jedediah, 1741, '43, '47, '52; Ephraim, 1749, '50, '54, '56-'59, '61, '62, '65, '67, '69; Joseph, 1749, '62, '64; Samuel, 1755; Joel, 1763, '72; Uriah, 1765, '68, '69; Winslow, 1770-'80, '82, '84, '86, '88, '89, '91; Joseph, 1771; George, 1774-'76; Ithamar, 1775, '76, '78, '79, '82; Paul, 1777; Solomon, 1777; William, 1778, '82, '85; Daniel, 1792-'94, '97-1813; Aaron, 1795, '96, 1802-'05; Joseph, Jr., 1799, 1801; Paul, 1801; Ithamar, 1801, '06, '09, '11, '13; Ephraim, 1808; Jedediah, 1810, '14-'16; Ashbel S., 1816; Ephraim, 1824, '25; Francis, 1846, '47; George, 1856.

Town Clerk: Samuel Brigham, 1754, '55; Uriah, 1769; Winslow, 1770-'80, '82; Daniel, 1807-'13; Jedediah, 1814.

Town Treasurer: George Brigham, 1741; Ephraim, 1742, '43, '50, '52-'64; Daniel, 1801-'13; Jedediah, 1814-'18; George, 1855.

Assessors: Samuel Brigham, 1739, '40; Ephraim, 1747, '59-'63, '65, '68; Winslow, 1769, '73, '77, '81, '82, '84-'86, '88; Asa, 1773, '74; Paul, 1775, '76; Uriah, 1788; Daniel, 1794-'99; Aaron, 1800-'06, '10; Jedediah, 1804, '08; Charles, 1849; Aaron, 1852.

Representatives to General Court: John Brigham, 1689, '92; Samuel, 1697-'99, 1705; Nathan, 1726, '30; Samuel, 1741; George,

1776, '77, '81; Paul, 1777; Winslow, 1783, '84; Daniel, 1803, '10, '12-'19; Francis, 1850, '52.

Delegate to Constitutional Convention, 1779, Winslow Brigham; Committee of Correspondence, 1776, Paul Brigham; 1780, Joel Brigham.   Justice Peace, Joseph Brigham, appointed 1804.

Of the three original Brigham settlers, two historically identified their names with two homesteads: Thomas, west of town (on present Glen St.), and Samuel, east of town (on present E. Main St.). John Brigham seems to have been too busy to " keep home " here; but he is identified by his mill (on the " Priest Whitney place ") in Northboro, as well as his later homestead in Sudbury.

THOMAS BRIGHAM THE EMIGRANT

THOMAS BRIGHAM, THE EMIGRANT·
1603-1653

1 THOMAS[1] BRIGHAM, born probably in England in 1603;
died in Cambridge, Mass., 8 Dec., 1653; married, probably in
1637, Mercy Hurd, born probably in England; died in Marlboro,
Mass., 23 Dec., 1693.

Governor Winthrop has left a graphic narrative of sixty-four
days on shipboard coming hither from old England in 1630.*
The Rev. Richard Mather also kept a journal of his passage, in
1635, which occupied twelve weeks and two days from taking
ship at Bristol to the landing at Boston.† These stories present
a vivid picture of the perils and privations attending the long
voyage Thomas Brigham encountered a little earlier in the latter
season, from the somewhat more remote port of London. He must
have first set foot on the New England shore early in June, for in
one of the few passenger lists ‡ of that time which have escaped
loss or destruction we read:

" VIII April 1635. Theis under written are to be transported
to New England imbarqued in the *Suzan* and *Ellen,* Edward
Payne Mr (Master). The p'ties have brought certificates from
yᵉ Ministers and Justices of the peace yᵗ they are no subsidy
men; and are conformable to yᵉ orders and discipline of the
Church of England.   *   *   *

" THOMAS BRIGHAM   32 "

*   *   *

Aboard the same ship were Symon Crosby and his wife and infant, future neighbors in Cambridge; Ralph Hudson and Percival Green, who were to be fellow-townsmen there, and also two
boys, Benjamin and Daniel, with their father, the learned and
reverend Peter Bulkley, who the same year was to found the
town of Concord and long was its pastor and benefactor.

The record quoted, which is the earliest we have of Thomas
Brigham, shows that he was born in 1603, wherein occurred the

* Winthrop's *History of New England.*   † *Richard Mather's Journal.*
‡ Hotten's *Original Lists.*

death of Queen Elizabeth and the beginning of the reign of the House of Stuart, which brought so much misfortune to the Puritans of England.

We may yet learn from what English town or hamlet he came, for the great mass of unprinted and inaccessible parish and probate records is slowly yielding each year to patient antiquarians more particulars of those who passed to New England.

Landed in "the Massachusetts," perhaps he first went to live in Watertown; but of that we have no intimation further than the fact that his largest piece of planting ground was situated within Watertown territory. This, however, was adjacent to the bounds of Cambridge and only fourteen minutes' walk from the centre of the latter settlement, while on the other hand Watertown village was nearly three miles distant. In fact it was in a district long ago taken from Watertown and made part of Cambridge.

Dr. Bond, who made an exhaustive study of the early settlers in Watertown, says: "Probably he (Thomas Brigham) did not reside in Watertown" (*Genealogy and History of Watertown*, p. 1006).

A visitor in 1633 thus described the village, which in 1638 was to be renamed Cambridge:

"By this side of this river is built Newtown which is three miles by land from Charlestown & a league & a half by water. This place was first intended for a city but upon more serious consideration, it was not thought so fit, being too far from the sea, being the greatest inconvenience it hath. This is one of the neatest & best compacted towns in New England, having many structures & many handsome contrived streets. The inhabitants are most of them very rich & well stored with cattle of all sorts, having many hundred acres of ground paled in with one general fence, which is about a mile & a halfe long, which secures all their weake cattle from the wild beasts. On the other side of the river lieth all their meadow & much ground for hay." *

An examination of the map of Cambridge as it was in 1635, drawn by Mr. Charles D. Elliot, shows that the original settlement, called "the town," lay between the present college yard and the marsh at the river's edge. To the eastward stretched the first "planting field," "the small lots" and "the large lotts" forming "the Neck." To the westward of "the Town" lay the "West End" and beyond that the "West End Field." In "the West End" just within the encircling fort or stockade lived Thomas Brigham.

The General Court in 1634, and again in 1635 and 1639, ordered that records of every man's houses and lands should be taken,

---

* *New En. land's Pros ect Jossel n 1634.*

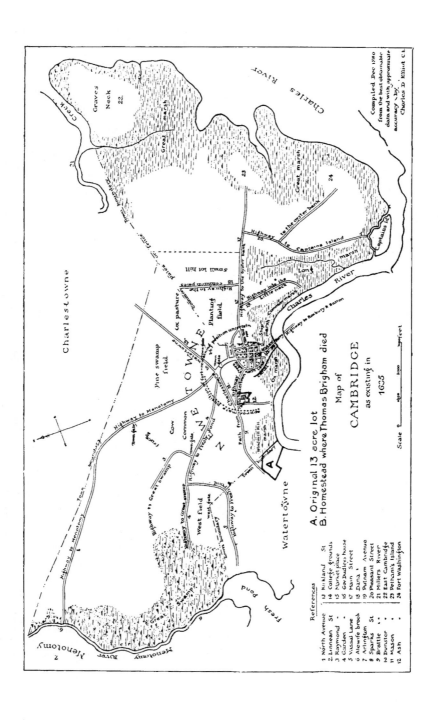

Map of
CAMBRIDGE
as existing in
1635

A. Original 13 acre lot
B. Homestead where Thomas Brigham died

Scale 0   400   2000   3000 feet

Compiled Dec 1880
from the best obtainable
data and with approximate
accuracy by
Charles D. Elliot C.E.

References

1 North Avenue
2 Linnean   St
3 Raymond   "
4 Garden   "
5 Vassall Lane
6 Alewife brook
7 Arlington   St
8 Sparks   St
9 Brattle   "
10 Pleasant Street
11 Mason   "
12 Ash   "
13 Kirkland   St
14 College grounds
15 Market place
16 Gov Dudley's house
17 Main Street
18 Dana   "
19 Putnam Avenue
20 Pleasant Street
21 Millers River
22 East Cambridge
23 Pelham's Island
24 Fort Washington

entered in the town book and a transcript thereof handed into court, and that such record should be a sufficient assurance of title.

The towns were slow in responding. The larger part of such an inventory for Cambridge, and that which enumerates about seventy proprietors, follows the date of September, 1639.

Thomas Brigham's property is described as follows:

" In the West end one house with three acres of Land and a halfe the highway ,to watertowne North Joseph Isack Southeast Symon Crosb (y) Southwest, the high waye to the Windemill Hill West." (*P. R.*, p. 64.)*

Situated thus at a corner, the lot can be identified with exceptional certainty; the " highway to watertowne," now Brattle Street, and the " high waye to the Windemill Hill," now Ash Street, being two very early thoroughfares, which have maintained their identity from 1630 to the present day. If the curious reader cares to follow Ash Street to the river, he will notice that the " Winde mill hill " was a low one, being rather a projection of the higher land into the marshes; and looking up the Charles River, as it comes down through the broad meadows, it is still evident why, in 1632, the mill was removed to Boston, because only when the wind came from across these meadows to the west had it force to propel the sails.

Forty-one pages further on, in the *Proprietors' Book*, this description is repeated, except that we now have " *one Dwelling house with out houses.*" *Elizabeth* Isaacke is now on the Southeast and " John Benjamin and An Crosby on the South west." Their father Symon died in 1639. When this property was deeded in 1654, it is described as " conteyning the late mansion house of the s^d Thomas Brigham with the Edifices, Barn, Cow houses and about three acres and a halfe to the same adjoyning a part whereof is a garden & orchards."

Radcliffe College has lately acquired a portion of this estate, known as the Greenleaf estate, as it lies directly across Brattle Street from its grounds which contain " Faye House," " Agassiz Hall " and the Gymnasium building, and eventually will form its principal quadrangle.

The *Watertown Book of Possessions* describes Thomas Brigham's property in that town as follows (A. D. 1639):

" Thomas Brigam.

" 1. Thirteen Acres of upland more or less and one Acre of Meddow bounded the East with John Marrett & Cambridge line the West with Thomas Andrews & Robert Keies the North with Cambridge Street the South with River & Samuel Saltonstall."

* *P. R.* refers to the *Proprietors' Record* of Cambridge, and to the pages as numbered in the printed publication.

Here again the bounds are of exceptional clearness: the river, Cambridge Street (now Brattle Street) and the "Cambridge line" (now Sparks Street).

If the curious reader has followed Ash Street to the "Winde mill hill," he has noticed along the foot of its short western slope a group of ancient willows, the willows that Lowell loved and sang:

> ". . . an ancient willow spreads
> Eight balanced limbs, springing at once all round,
> His deep ridged trunk with upward slant diverse,
>   In outline like enormous beaker. . . .
>   "This tree
> Is one of six, a willow Pleiades,
> The seventh fallen, that lean along the brink
> Where the steep upland dips into the marsh,
> Their roots like molten metal cooled in flowing,
> Stiffened in coils and runnels down the bank.
> The friend of all the winds, wide armed he towers
> And glints his steely aglets in the sun.
>   —*Under the Willows*, *James Russell Lowell.*

This group of willows bounds at one end a portion of the Metropolitan Park which lies between the Charles River and Mt. Auburn Street. At its other end Thomas Brigham's "Watertown Field" came down to the stream. Inland from "the willows" the narrow Longfellow Park extends up to the front of Craigie House and as a memorial preserves the vista of which that poet was so fond, looking across the "meadows on yᵉ south side the river," as the old records call them, where is now "Soldiers Field," and its huge white stadium, which gathers within it of an afternoon, a crowd in numbers double the whole population of Massachusetts in the days of Thomas Brigham.

If we go up Sparks Street from the river as far as Brattle Street, observing that what is now Hubbard Park (or two and one-half acres of it) substantially represents the lot that John Marrett owned at the northeast corner of Thomas Brigham's land, then follow Brattle Street to Lowell Street, and thence by that street to the park, then to the river front, and then along the water to where Sparks Street would enter it, we shall have compassed the Watertown property of Thomas Brigham. We have also included about three acres at the corner of Mt. Auburn Street and Lowell Street that belonged to Samuel, the son of Sir Richard Saltonstall, the exact boundary line of which is uncertain.

At the back of the *Cambridge Proprietors' Book,* without date but by the context perhaps as early as 1636, is recorded: "Lootts Given out By the towne one the South side of Charles River: in two Sever (al) Divissions: to severall men as followeth." In these as " 53 " Thomas " Bridgham " received in " The Lower Division " 4 acres and in " the Upper division " 4 acres 7 (poles).

Thomas was made by the General Court a Freeman of the Massachusetts Bay Company, April 18, 1637,* and thus became a member of the body politic and acquired the right to vote. Preliminary to this he must have been a member of Cambridge church, but its records for the early years are lost. The oath required of a Freeman by the law of 1634 was as follows:

I, A. B., being by God's providence, an inhabitant and ffreeman within the jurisdiction of this Commonweale, doe freely acknowledge myselfe to be subject to the governm^t thereof doe heere sweare, by the great and dreadful name of the everlasting God, that I wil be true and faithful to the same, and will accordingly yeilde assistance and support thereunto, with my pson and estate, as in equity I am bound, and will also truely indeav^r to maintaine and preserve all the libertyes and privilidges thereof, submitting my selfe to the wholesome laws and orders made and established by the same: and furth^r, that I will not plott nor practise any evil against it, nor consent to any that shall so doe, but will timely discover and reveale the same to lawfull authority now here established, for the speedy preventing thereof. Moreover, I doe solumnely bynde myselfe, in the sight of God, that when I shall be called to give my voice touching such matter of this state, wherein freemen are to deale, I will give my vote and suffrage, as I shall judge in myne owne conscience may best conduce and tend to the publique weale of the body, without respect of psons, or favor of any man.

Soe helpe mee God, in the Lord Jesus Christ.

" Oc'tob^r the firste 1639 " he was chosen constable and " joined with the Townsmen " or selectmen (*T. R.*, p. 36).†

" Att a Towne meeting the first Monday in Mar 1639 It is ordered that all that is not outsyde fence in the west ffeilde but common ffence betweene that and the other twoe new ffeildes shall be Removed by the owners of the same and sett upp uppon the lyne betweene Cambridge and Watertow and to lessen their charges they shall be abated in ev^{r}ie five Rod one Rodd and w^t shall remaine: to be done att a generall charge as the other Rayles and this to be done before the first of August next ensuing uppon the penalttie of 5^s a rod for ev^{r}ie defaulte. The wch order Thomas Parrishe and Thomas Briggam shall see to be fulfilled uppon the forfit of XX^s a man " &c.—(*T. R.*, p. 39).

---

* *Records of the Mass. Bay Colony*, i. p. 373.

† *T. R.* refers to the *Town Records* of Cambridge, and to the pages of the printed publication.

At " a Court of Assistants, or Quarter Court, held at Boston, the 3rd of the 10th mo. 1639," Thomas Brigham was one of the twelve jurymen on the trial of " Marmaduke Peirce, being indited upon suspition of murther, was found not guilty, but was bound to the good behavio^r, and to appear at the next Court, and to pay the witnesses and Nico. Davis was bound in 20$^£$ for his appearance.—" (*Colonial Records.*)

In the fall of 1640 land was granted: to Joseph Cook 400 acres, to Mr. Samuell Shepard 400 acres, to Captaine Cooke and Edward Goffe each 600 acres and to John Bridge 350 acres. When:

There were then p'sent six of the seven Townsmen that subscribed * unto theis Grauntes n ly	John More Thomas Briggam Thomas Marret Edw^{r}d Goff John Bridge Joseph Cooke (*T. R.*, p. 41.)

Xth Novemb^r 1640 Att a Towne meeting generally of all the Inhabit   There were chosen for Townsmen as followeth:

Tho: Marret
Thoms Parrish
Thomas Briggam
Joh Stedman
Abrahm Shawe
(*T. R.*, p 43)

8 9th month called Novem: 1642.
Att a towne meeting . . . there were chosen . . . ffor Constables for this p^{r}sent yeare   Tho Briggam
Edwa: Oakes
(*T. R.*, pp. 46-47.)

Anno 1645 were graunted by the Towne these forty seaven Lotts, on the west side of Monotamye river, to the sev^{r}all inhabitants of the Towne as followeth
Thomas Brigham one acr more or lesse William Manninge east, John Bruer west Charlestown lyne north Comon south.

These 47 lots, of from one to 3½ acres each, were all adjacent to the Charlestown line with the common land to the south of them. Thomas Brigham's is the sixteenth from the east end.

In the yeare 1645 . . .

Alsoe granted the land on this side the water † lying beyond (5) miles, unto the seaventh mile for small farmes. The names of the prsons & quantities followeth, onely they that fall by lott between the 5th & 6th mile, there quantity is to be multiplied by 8: and they that between the sixth & seaventh mile there quantity to be multiplied by nine. & what the land on this side the water Cometh short to make up the prties prpor-

* In the original record these names are all entered by the clerk.
† Menotime.

tions here after mentioned of the land on yᵉ other side the water, to begin at the nerest, & soe on.

ac
Itm to Herbert Pelham, Esq. late Mʳ Bucklies house   - 13 - 00
1 lott Tho: Brigham   - 10 - 00
(*T. R.*, p. 67.)

There are 25 lots in all.

We do also agree and give the land at Menotime for their full prpor- tions of all the lands in ye Towne except Rich: Jacson John Betts: and Tho: Brigham (*T. R.*, p. 69).

The Church book of Disbursements contains this entry:

1645. Payd our brother Briggam for something for clothinge for his sone   0 : 7 : 6
(Paige's *Hist. of Cambridge*, p. 258.)

This may refer to Sebastian Brigham or to John Brigham. As we read it, this does not seem consistent with the estate which Thomas Brigham possessed before and after this date.

At a towne meting: 8ᵈ: (4) mo 1646:

Thomas Brigham delinquent in yᵉ Breach of the about hogs, viz: for his wives rescuing of two Hogs from yᵉ Impounder when He should a driven them to pound, for ten at one time and two at another being unringed, and thre being impounded allsoe for two oxen of his: Breaking yᵉ order.   (*T. R.*, p. 53.)

Thomas Brigham for ye Breach of yᵉ Hog order to pay for yᵉ two rescued away by his wife Vˢ and for ye other   00 - 07 - 06

4 (9)mo 1646
Severall men fined ( ) Breach of the orders concerning oxen and hogs . . .

Bro. Brigham (for 10 hogs at one time and
              (4 at another and 3 at another   4ˢ - 00
              (without a keeper and some unringed
(*T. R.*, p. 54)

The list of the offenders, of which this is one, includes over forty names, or a large part of the inhabitants of the hamlet.

11ᵗʰ 8. 1647
It is ordered that Bro. Goffe and Bro: Ed: Oakes shall gather up the fines due to Bro. Cane for his fines of the oxen.

s   d
of Robert Parker   - 0 - 8 - 2
of Tho: Brigham   - 0 - 7 - 8 etc

The list of 18 names ends with

of Elder Champnis   - - 0 - 8

According to this account every man is Bated one third prt of what he ough(t) to a payde By the towne order wch is 3ᵈ pr heade. & we have Concluded that every man shal pay according to this.   & soe he pay but 2d. pr heade for every default. & theese men are to be sattisfied out of the fines for there gathering them up (*T. R.*, pp. 62, 63).

Severall Officers Chosen to order the prudentiall affaires of this Towne for this present yeare Ensueing the date hereof.
8ᵗʰ 9ᵗʰ 1647
for Townsmen   (John Bridge
                (Tho: Marret
                (John Stedman
                (Tho: Brigham
                (Tho: Beale   (*T. R.*, p. 69.)

13ᵗʰ (1) 1647/1648   .
Whereas It hath bine formerly ordered and published that all out fences be sufficiently made by the owners thereof before the last of this prsent month and the penalty of 6ᵈ pr rod, for every rod that is found failing: It is now ordered that there shalbe 12ᵈ a month penalty for every rod that shalbe found delinquent after the last of this prsent month is expired: to be demanded of the owners of such fence from time to time the saide monthly fine untill such time as the fence be made sufficient . . .
   John Bridge, Tho: Marrett, Tho: Brigham and Tho: Beale are appoynted to see this ordered uppon the owners of the fence belonging to the West feilde (*T. R.*, p. 73).

17ᵗʰ 3ᵗʰ mo. 1648.
Thomas Brigham Bought of Williams Hamlett, ten acʳ of land in fresh Pond med. abutt. William Holman, Nathaneell Sparahauke, John Doget, Richard Champnis, Susan Bloget, and William Man, North West, the greate swamps South East, Widow ffisher Souwest (*P. R.*, p. 134).

7ᵗʰ of the 6ᵗʰ mo: 1648
thease presents witnes that thomas Brigham of Cambrigd having A percell of land about three akers more or les adioning to the west field in Cambrigd bounds being bounded Watertowne highway to the fresh pond Southwest great swamp north Robert parker East: hee doth freely Resigne up all his right & Intrest in the same into the hands of the towns- men from him and his for ever. Condition that they dispose of It as that Care be made to maintain the fence that is layd upon that land to beare and secure the said thomas brigham from all future damages theareby

In presence of   his T marke
     Roger bancroft   thomas brigham
     Jonathan bower
     thomas danforth
this land the towns men doe asigne to thomas Marrit upon Condition hee make the fence.

11th 10th mo 1648
thomas Marrit Resigned up this land againe into the towns hand. the note of thease acts put upon file (*P. R.*, p. 154).

12 of (10) 1648 . . .
Lands layd out, on the Rocks, on the North side the River Impr. To Thomas Brigham:
Seventy two acr's Charlestowne line on the north. Cow Comon East (*P. R.*, p. 138).

The interesting story of the recent discovery of the location of this " small farme " is told in the Appendix to this book.

8th of the 11th 1648: . . .
Liberty granted to Thomas Brigham to fell some timber on the Comon for the Repaireing of his house and out fences, prvided it be before the first of June next Ensueing: (*T. R.*, p 79).

23th 12th mo. 1648
Uppon an apoytment, of a generall meeting of the proprietors of the Lands within the west feild, we then found according to a division made of the fence appurtayneing to the same, formerly: everymans pportion as here followeth in order, begining at the first foure Railes next the greate Swamp adjoyning to the ox pasture and ending at water Towne Line next Wm Hamletts The fence is divided in the generall for one acre of land, 3 pole of fence. . . .

	foot	
Tho: Brigam	12	(*P. R.*, pp. 335-7.)

Thomas Brigham's is the 72d lot in 89 items.

At a generall meeting of the pprietors of the necke of land by the consent of the major pt of the pprietors there was an adition of fence added to eache pprietor for the preserving of it from stroy·
The fence was thus devided in order following

	rod	foot	inch
Impr To mr Cooke half that which lay agst his land and his ption for his land in the neck	5	12	
To Mr Herbert Pelham	16	5½	
To Tho: Danforth	04	14	
Robt: Broadish	02	07	
Wm Homan	00	01	
Tho: Bridgham	00	12	

Then follow 28 others (*P. R.*, pp. 338-9).

The only reference to Thomas Brigham preserved in the Watertown records, other than the description of his property already quoted, is as follows:

It is Ordered, yt acording to the complaynt of those two men apoynted by the towne, for the seeing unto the sufficiency of fences, wee have awarded, Thomas Brigham to pay unto the sd men, yt is Garrett Church & John Trayne, the some of five shillings, for that he did not sett up his pt of fence wth his neighbors according to order (First September, 1651, *Watertown Records,* vol. i. p. 23).

January 12 1651 . . . Goodman Brigham is Cost by the Townsmen the Sum of 10ˢ: to Garrett Church & John Trayne the Town offeceres for ye not regulating his hogs according to the Towne orders (*Ibid.*, p. 28).

The Devission of Shaw Shine: *

4 (4) 52
The Number of evrie mans lott, and Quantity of acres is as followeth

89/ Tho: Briggam   180 acres.

(*T. R.*, pp. 97, 98.)

14 (12) 1652
Robert Parker hath liberty to Sell some timber, for his use, as also John ffessington, for enlarging his barne, and Tho: Brigham for railes (*T. R.*, p. 101).

14 : 12 : 1652
It is agreed between Ri: Jacson, Tho: Brigham on the one prty and Mʳ Joseph Cooke, Edward Goffe, and Tho: Danforth on yᵉ other prty, yᵗ all differences about the fence in the necke of land, appertyning to Cambridge; shall be referred to the hearing and determination of Deacon Monsell and Tho: Perce of Charles Towne, to determine the matter in difference between the marsh and upland, each prty to procure one of the said arbitrators at or before the 10ᵗʰ of March next ensueing.

Joseph Cooke	Richard Jackson
Edward Goffe	Thomas Brigham
Thomas Danforth	(*T. R.*, p. 157.)

the 28ᵗʰ 10ᵗʰ mo. 1653
The proprietors of the wood Lotts meeting together agreed to devide the remainder of the wood Lotts apperteyning to these Lotts formerly Devided in to foure Squadrants, wch was accordingly done by lott being in evrie Squadrant thirty acres. . . . In yᵉ 4ᵗʰ Squadrant next Spy pond

Tho: Oakes	02
Edw: Winship	02½
Mʳ Michell	06
Abra: Errington	01¼
ffranc: Whitmore	00¾
Ri: Champney	03½
Tho: Chisholme	04
The towne Lott	01½
Tho: Brigham	02
Jno: ffessington	- 01¾
Andrew Belshar	- 01½

26¾

(*T. R.*, pp. 64, 65.)

* Shawshine was set off from Cambridge in 1655 and incorporated as the town of Billerica, previous to which the Cambridge men who had received grants in that territory, with a few exceptions, united in what is called the "Great Deed," conveying all their rights to the inhabitants of Billerica. Thomas Brigham's lot, No. 89, was included in that conveyance.

The following entry, which must belong before 1654, is found at the end of the Town Book, printed upside down, the date on the preceding page being for 1703:

		s	
Robert Parker	49 - 08		2
Thomas Bredgham	44 - 07		8
Rich Wyeth	26 - 04		4
Will man	16 - 02		8
Holman	10 - 01		8
Elder ffrost	15 - 02		6
Grene	18 - 03		0
Dansfurth	6 - 01		0
Crackbone	13 - 02		2
ffrench	05 - 00	-	10
Holms	28 - 04	-	8
Shaw	12 - 02	-	0
Gibsonn	11 - 01		10
hildreth	8 - 01		4
Coopr	6 - 01	-	0
Oak	2 - 00	-	4
Brandish	10 - 01	-	8
Eldr Chpns	4 - 00		0

47

(*T. R.*, p. 350.)

Thomas Brigham died the 8th day of the 10th month, 1653 (Old Style), or December 19th, 1653 (New Style).

He was buried, there is convincing reason to believe (Mr. Morse notwithstanding), in the old Burial Ground on the south side of the Cambridge Common, a few minutes' walk from his mansion; but no stone remains to mark the spot. Only one of the existing stones * records a death as early as 1653, that of Ann Erinton, who died two days after Thomas Brigham. The stone next in age is ten years later, and commemorates Elizabeth Cutter, sister-in-law of Mercy Brigham's sister, if Mr. Morse's supposition is correct.

WILL OF THOMAS BRIGHAM, THE PURITAN †

In the name of God Amen, I Thomas Brigham of Cambridge being at this pnt writing weake in body, and not knowing how the Lord will dispose of me, whether for life or death, and haveing yet through the mercy of God, a good memory and sound understanding, do hereby ordeine and make this my last Will & Testiment, my poare Soule wch I do beleive is imortall and shall live when my body is dissolved to dust, I do desire by faith humbly to comitt and leave it in yᵉ Armes of the everlasting mercies of God

* *Cambridge Epitaphs*, Harris, 1845.

† Both the will and the inventory are copied from the original documents.

the father in his deare and Eternal Sonne Jesus Xt, who when I
was altogether full of Enmity agst him, and a miserable undone
child of wrath, did then send his holy word accompanied with the
irresistable power of his ow^n blessed spirit to make knowne and
apply the exceding and abundant riches of his grace to my Soule,
by wch faith I have desired to live, and do now desire to dy, and
go to that Lord Jesus who hath Loved me to the Death that I a
poare sinner might live, my body I comitt it to the earth to be
decently buried at the discretion of my Executrix, and as for my
children, and outward blessings wch the Lord hath bin pleased of
his goodnes to blesse me wth all and for a time to make me Steward
of my will is that they be thus disposed of as followeth, vizt. my
just debts being first sattisfyed, my will is that my loveing wife
shall have to her owne vse one third pt of my estate, according
to the Law of the Country: and to my Eldest sonne Thomas I
give one third pt of the remainder of my estate, and the rest of
my estate to be equally divided between my other 4: children Jno
and Mary and Hannah and Samuell my will is that my wife shall
have the vse of my whole estate dureing her widow hood, for the
bringing up and education of my children and in case the Lord
shall provide for my wife by mariage, it shall then be at the will
and discretion of the overseers of this my last will and testament,
whether my children with their portions shall continue with her
or not, and as they see meet to dispose of them and their portions
for their education and bringing up. I do appoint my wife to be
sole Executrix of this my last will and Testament and do also
desire my Loveing Brethren Thomas Danforth, Jno. Cooper, Thomas
Fox, Jno. Hastings, and William Towne to be overseers of this
my last will and testament: and in witness hereof I do hereunto
put my hand and seale this 7th of the 10th mo. 1653,

Read & signed in the   his T marke
presence of John Cooper   Thomas Brigham (Seal)
    John Hastings
    Tho: Danforth   Proved 3^d 8m 1654,

At a County Court held at Cambridge the 3: (8mo) 1654

Thomas Danforth, John Cooper, Thomas Fox and Jno. Hastings
appearing before the Court, Attested upon oath that the within
named Thomas Brigham deceased: being of a sound mind and
good memory made this his last will & testament
                                    Thomas Danforth Recorder.
    Entered & Recorded 25-11-1654, Mid. Prob., L. V., p. 41 and
43-7.
By Tho: Danforth
        No. 1733
        Recorder

INVENTORY OF THE ESTATE OF THOMAS[1] BRIGHAM

The 10: of the 12 mo: 1653
And Inventery of the Goode and Chattells of Thomas Bridgham
Latly deceased followeth

'

	£	s	d
Imprs one Cloake and a cloth suite	02 - 00	00	
It one stufe Coate and a water stufe ould suit & shett band } & other linen		02	00
It one large cloth Coat	0 - 13	04	
It one cloth stragt Coat & a new paire of breches one hatt 6s 8d	1 - 16	08	
It a paire of boots shoes and stockens	0 - 10	00	
It In silver	0 - 11	02	
It 3 silver spones	0	12	00
In the paler			
It: one great bedstadle	1	00	00
It one feather bed and boulter larg	4	10	00
It one feather bed fine teken 3 pellows	3	15	00
It one litle feather bed "	1	10	00
It one grene ruge and a paire blankets	3	10	00
It Cartenes and vallance	1	00	00
It one paire of hollon shets	1	06	08
It 4 paire of flaxen shets	1	08	00
It 2 paire of corse shets	0	13	04
It 9 pellows 3s 4d p pece	1	10	00
It one dammeske cobbert cloth	0	02	06
It one Calecoe cobbert cloth	0	02	06
It one fine table cloth	0	04	00
It 3 short table clothes	0	06	08
It one duessen of napkins	0	06	00
It 3 cors napkines	0	01	00
It 3 towells	0	01	04
It 2 small trunkes wherein the lenen is	0	10	00
It one levery table & cloth	0	10	00
It one cubbert table and cloth	1	06	08
It 2 Joyne cheyers a buffet stolle	0	10	00
It 2 cobbert clothes	0	03	04
It 2 peces of branch stufe 4 Chusenes	0	03	04
It 4 chusens	0	02	08
It 4 £ Carret sed	0	08	00
It ¼ Carraway sede	0	05	00
It a parcell of ould [ ] with one bible and a greater bible	1	00	00
It one warmin pane	0	02	00
It a table basket	0	02	00
It 11 £ of wollen & Cotten yarne 2s 6d	1	07	06
In the hall			
It a table a forme & Carpet cloth	0	15	00
It a small table & cloth	0	03	00
It 2 chests	0	13	04
It 4 Joyne cheyers	0	10	00

[1] Thomas Brigham, 1654-1753.

	£	s	d
It 3 Joyne stoles	0 -	02 -	00
It one Coselet & pikes	1 -	10 -	00
It a paire of horsman pestoll and a cutlash and belte	1 -	10 -	00
It a Corliver and sword & belt	0 -	13 -	04
It a lanthorne	0 -	01 -	00
It one paire of Cobbornes		- 15 -	00
It 2 stone Jauges other small things	0 -	01	06

In the checken [kitchen]

It one halfe headed bedstadle blockbed boulster a ruge Coverlet a paire of blankets curtenes & vallance and a bed suttell [settle]	3 -	00 -	00
It a tranell bed 2 ould Coverlets with a chaffe bed & boulster	1 -	00 -	00

47 - 16 - 06

	£	s	d
In the Chambers			
It one flocke bed and boulster one Covelut a shet and a paire of blankets	1	00	00
It a table		03	04
It a wennowing cloth		10	00
It a small spining whelle		01	00
It a sadle and bridle a brest gurt and a ould sadle	0	00	00
It 6 sickle and hockes [hooks]	0	03	00
It a hand sawe shave and 2 seives	0	03	00
It 3 paire of woll cards	0	02	00
It 3 corne seives	0	02	00
It a childs Cradle	0	04	00
It 7 bush wheate	1	15	00
It 19 bush Indian	2	17	00
It 3 bush ½ rye	0	14	00
It 6 bush pease	1	04	00
It sieve and stafe	0	02	8
It 3 barrell & 3 halfe barrell	0	08	00
It 2 dressed skines	0	03	00
It 43 £ peuter	2	03	00
It 2 bell Candlesticks	0	03	00
It 3 peuter porrengers	0	02	06
It one double salt and one single	0	02	00
It one peuter quart pot	0	02	06
It one small flaggon	0	04	00
It a bere cup and a small beaker	0	02	00
It bere pot of peuter	0	01 -	4
It a chamber vessell	0	01 -	8
It a scummer and brasse Candlestic	0	03 -	00
It a brasen baken pan	0	02	6
It 2 Iron pots and pothockes	0	13	00
It 2 peuter basine a wine cup and a peuter botle	0	03	6
It one duessene ockeme spons	0	06	00
It more 8 ockeme spones	0	02	0
It one ould brase pot	0	10	0
It: 2 trammells 5s a spett & foot	0	07	6
It one Cobbourne firepan & tongs	0	08	0
It a duessene of trenchers	0 -	01	0

	£	s	d
It one salt boxe with other small thg	0	01	6
It 4 wembems a gouges 3 chesseles	0	06	0
It 3 paire hinges	0	03	0
It a mattocke 3s 6d a pease meax 1s	0	04	6
It a hummer pinsonne 2 paire hocks	0	03	0
It a parrcel of ould Irom	0	10	0
It 2 bettell rings 3 wedges	0	05	0
It 2 brasse Cetles	1	10	0
It a brasse morter and a Iron pestell	0	05	0
It a some beffe and porke & butter & suit	3	10	0
It 2 bere barrell	0	05	0
It one payle and a Iron bayle	0	01	0
It one chuerne and stafe	0	03	6
It 4 chese Fats 2s 5 trayes 20d	0	04	0
It 3 remnant of narrow cloth	3	17	9
It 5 yds sarge 7s 6d p yd	1	17	6
It one ould hodghead	0	02	0
It 14 ewe shepe 40s a pece	20	00	0
It 2 oxen 15£	15	00	0
It 2 steres come 3 yere ould one heifer come 3 yere ould one heifer with calf	15	10	0
ıt 2 stere come 2 yere	05	00	00
It one Cow with Calfe 5£ 5s	05	05	00
It one black ould Cowe 4£	04	00	00
It one pyd Cowe	4	10	00

67 : 04 : 03

It 3 Calfes of the last yeare	4	10	00
It 4 Cowes	18	00	00
It the dwelling house & barne with 4 Akors of land adiojg	70	00	00
It the lot bought of Goodman Doggett in watertowne	40	0	00
It the upland and medowe in the hether end of watertowne	60	00	00
It 10 Akors in rocke medow	15	00	00
It 9 Akors salt marsh	13	10	00
It a small farme on Charlestown line	10	00	00
It one ould gray mare	15	00	00
It one young Mare	15	00	00
It one pyboll mare with foll	15	00	00
It one mare 4 yere ould	16	00	00
It one yearing mare Colt	07	00	00
It Daneel Mykene a Scot	15	00	00
It Anne Keche 6 years to serve	08	00	00
It a Cart and whelles	1	10	00
It one plow chane and yoake	0	06	00
It one swine	1	10	00
It 5 yds Canvis 2s p yd	0	10	00
It one harrow	0 - 08 - 00		
It about 8 Akors rye on the ground	8 - 00 - 00		

334 : 04 : 00
47 : 16 : 06
67 : 04 : 03

449 : 04 : 09

Edward Goffe
John Bridge
Edward mitcheasonn

At a County Court held at Cambridge 3 (8 m°) 1654 Mercy Brigham Executrix of the last will and Testament of the within named Thomas Brigham deceased, Attested upon oath that this above & w'hin written is to her best knowledge a true Inventory of the whole estate of her husband Thomas Brigham deceased, and if any more shall hereafter appeare shee will truly discover and certifie the Same.

Entered & Recorded the
26 (12) 5:4—   Tho: Danforth: Recorder.
    Tho: Danforth Recorder.

Certain terms in the inventory are thus explained:

Livery table, a *delivery* or serving table.

Joine chair or *joine stool,* such furniture framed with joinery work.

Buffet stool, a cushion for the feet, or small ottoman.

Cob-irons, andirons.

Ockumy spoons, Ockimy or *Ockamy,* a " mixed metal."

Pease meake, Peas hook.

Cheese fatt, a vat or round box.

Piggin, a wooden dipper.

October 20, 1651, by act of Parliament, certain Scotch prisoners were made free. A large number of them seem to have come to Charlestown in December, 1652. In the list was one Daniel Mackajne (*Suffolk Deeds,* vol. i. p. 6). It seems possible it was he who appears in the inventory as Daneel Mykene. Thomas Brigham may have paid his passage money, to be repaid subsequently in labor as was then a custom, so that at the death of Thomas Brigham the value of labor then due was £15.

A better understanding of Thomas[1] Brigham's property is gained by a consideration of the disposition made of the real estate after his death.

In March, 1654, " whereas the Lord hath in his wise providence so disposed that the s^d Mercy Brigham the relict widdow of the s^d Thomas Brigham is now married to Edmund Rice of Sudbury," etc. the overseers of the will sold to Thomas Fox, one of their number, for £40, the " Watertown field " estimated to contain 20 acres more or less (see Note 1 at the close of this generation), and at the same time deeded to John Hastings, another of their number, for £60, the mansion house with garden and orchard, also a lot in the Neck and also a wood lot and the town rights appertaining to these (see Note 2).

Neither of these deeds was recorded until 31 years later, and by some mischance the authority to make these sales which the overseers had obtained from the General Court was not properly entered until 30 years after making the deeds, when a second application was made and received approval from the General Court. Meanwhile in 1681 the children of Thomas Brigham, now about 30 and 40 years of age, sold in two pieces the 10 acres their father had owned in Rockie meadow (see Note 3), and also another 10 acres of his meadow and swamp land (see Note 4).

Still later, and 42 years after their father's death and when their mother had been dead two years, they appear to have been ignorant of these deeds that have been quoted as made by the overseers, or else they felt the overseers had not fulfilled the requirement of the General Court that they (the overseers) should give proper surety for the rights of the heirs. They therefore formally made claim for their rights to the property, Samuel Hastings having, meanwhile, acquired the properties deeded both to his father and to Thomas Fox. The quaint ceremony is recorded as follows:

" THO: BRIGHAMS CLAIME

" These may certifie all p^{r}sons whome it may concerne that we ye subscribers p^{r}sent at ye house of Samuel Hastings in Cambridge in the County of Middlesex in New England in ye 27th of September 1695, and there being desired by Thomas Brigham, Samuel Brigham & Hannah Ward to bear Witness to what demands of Land or Claimes made by them of Lands in ye possession of ye above s^d Samuel Hastings & then & there we heard John Brigham aforesaid which is of Marlburrough Demand in the behalfe of ye Rest, the Possession of ye Lands as followeth, viz: the Homestall which is four acres with the Dwelling house Barn & all that was upon ye Land, wth all ye Towne Rights & priviledges Divisions or allotments whatsoever belonging to ye same also nine acres of marsh neer Mr Hough's farme at the Great Creek on ye Neck in Cambridge. Also a Feild Called by ye name of Watertowne Feild, with two little Lotts adjoining called by ye name of Keys ffeild and Wilcocks Lott in one Intire parcell Containing by Estimation 20 acres or thereabouts, bounded Northerly by a highway partly & partly by land in the Possession of Goodman Wise (Withe ?) & Goodman Hicks, Southerly by Land which was Mr Sam^{ll} Saltinstalls Easterly by ye Land now in the Possession of John Marrett, upon the day above written we heard John Brigham afores^d upon the Land afore mentioned, make Demand of Samuell Hastings aforenamed all ye Lands above mentioned as it was theire portions left by theire ffather Thomas Brigham Deceased and Samuel Hastings owned he was in Possession of s^d Lands Demanded & in p^{r}ticular the land here mentioned being in the bounds of Watertowne.

"Also we see John Brigham at the same time cut off a Twigg of an apple tree with an apple upon it & carry it away off ye Homestall as a Testimony of his Challenge made to ye Land here mentioned. Also we see Thomas Brigham John Brigham & Samuel Brigham cutt Twiggs off trees & Ears of Corn upon ye Lands herein mentioned lying in Watertowne & carry them away as a Testimony of theire Challenge of the Said Land being theires by theire ffathers Will And in Testimony hereof, In Witness hereunto We have set our hands this Twenty Seventh of Septemb^r one thousand Six hundred ninety and Five.

"David Downing.
"Israel Cheever

"Camb^r. 27. Septemb^r. 1695

"Charlestowne Septemb^r 28 1695   Rec'd in ye office Record & Entered by Sam^{ll} Phipps Record^r."

On the same day the heirs also went through the ancient form of challenge, at the "small Farm on the Charlestown line," which had passed in some way into the hands of Thomas Danforth, one of the overseers of the estate, but the deed for which he had never recorded. What they did is thus told in the ancient record:

"We that have subscribed our Names Do Testifie and say that we were desired on ye 27th of Septemb^r 1695. By Tho. Brigham, John Brigham, Samuel Brigham & Hannah Ward the Children of Thomas Brigham Deceased all of Marlburrough in the County of Mid^x in the Massachusetts Bay in New England to go along with them to a ffarme upon the Rocks within the bounds of Cambridge, within the aforesaid County, which ffarme is asserted by them to be Eighty Acres, with the meadow belonging to it according to Town Grant, & then & there upon ye aforesaid Land, & on the day above mentioned We See Thomas Brigham, John Brigham & Samuel Brigham mark severall Trees wch was the bounds of said Land & cut out the marks upon the Trees which marked wth T. D. & set theire own names on them Set up a New Corner Stake, Cut off a Tree & Carried it off the said Land, and a Twigg or young growth they cut and carried off, and there they did declare that they did it as Challenging all the said ffarme, as theire own proper right, being part of their portions left by their ffather Brigham Dece'd, with all the rights priviledges and appurtenances belonging to the same.

" In Witness hereof as a Testimony to all that above written
We Thomas Phille brown and Andrew Wilson set unto our hands
this 27th Day of Septemb[r] 1695
" Cambridge Septemb[r]. 27th. 1695.

> " Thomas ffillebrowne
> " Andrew X Wilson his mark.

" Charlestown Septemb[r]. 28. 1695
" Received ffor Record and Entered By

> " Sam[ll] Phipps Record[r]."

Mid. Prob., vol. vii. pp. 7, 8 and 9 (at the back of the book).

Samuel Hastings was the son of John Hastings.

Suit was brought against Samuel Hastings (see Note 5).
Eight years passed, and in 1703 the heirs united in a deed for
this property to the Danforth estate (see Note 6).

Thomas Brigham married probably in 1637 his wife Mercy,
but of this date there is no record. We know she must have been
a woman of unusual strength, force and determination. The Rev.
Abner Morse says, on the authority of tradition, that her maiden
name was Mercy Hurd, that she was 10 or 15 years younger
than her husband, and that, persecuted in England for noncon-
formity, she came to New England with her sister, who married
William (?) Cutter. Tradition should be taken as a clue to the
truth rather than truth itself, for investigation where practicable
is likely to find the basis of truth small in tradition a century old.
The *Cutter Genealogy* states that when William Cutter returned to
England, probably he was a bachelor.
She married for her second husband, 1 March, 1655, Edmund[1]
Rice, then of Sudbury, but who removed in 1660 to Marlboro, where
he died 3 May, 1663. He was born 1594, and came from Bark-
hamstead, Hertfordshire, England; settled in Sudbury in 1638-9;
resided on east side of Sudbury River in the southerly part of what
is now Wayland, near the great meadows. .   . He was selectman in 1644, and deacon of the church in 1648. His first wife
was Tamazine, who came with him from England; also eight
children. His residence in Marlboro was in the westerly part of
the town, on an old county road leading from Marlboro to Northboro, and in the bend, as it passes around the northerly side of
Williams Pond, a short distance north of the ancient Williams
Tavern. He was intrusted by the General Court (1640 and 1643)
with various duties. He was buried in Sudbury and his estate
settled by his widow.

On her second marriage she took with her to Sudbury and Marlboro all her children (*History of Cambridge*, p. 501).

Children of Edmund Rice and Mercy (Hurd) (Brigham) Rice:
   i Ruth, b in Sudbury, Mass., 29 Sept., 1659; died 30 March, 1742, æ. 83; married 20 June, 1683, Samuel, son of Capt. Samuel and grandson of Gov. Thomas Welles of Conn. (Gov. Welles settled at Hartford, 1636; Capt. Samuel settled at Weathersfield; Samuel resided at Glastonbury, Conn.); her husband was b. 13 April, 1660; d. 28 Aug., 1731. On the first day of June, 1684, a deed was made by Samuel and Ruth (Rice) Welles to Eleazer Howe of Marlboro, of her land inherited from her father, 12½ acres, bounded by Samuel Brigham. She made her " mark." Their first child, who d. in infancy, was named " Mercy."
   ii Ann, b. in Marlboro, 19 Nov., 1661; probably married Nathaniel Gary (Gerry) of Roxbury, Mass., 12 Nov., 1685; he was b. 4 July, 1663, son of Nathaniel Gery and Ann Dugglas, who were married in Roxbury, 14 Oct., 1658.

A petition for a division of Edmund Rice's estate was signed 16 (4) 1663 by his widow Mercy with eight elder and two younger children. His inventory made a total of £556 0s. 7d (*Mid. Files*).
His inventory made a total of £556 0s. 7d (*Mid. Files*).
Mercy married, 1664, as her third husband, William Hunt, then of Marlboro, but formerly an early settler in Concord. He was made Freeman 2 June, 1641, and was a large land holder. His first wife Elizabeth, the mother of his children (Nehemiah, Samuel, Elizabeth and Isaac), died 27 Dec., 1661. His will probated 17 Dec., 1667, made the following provision for his widow:

" I doe give and bequeath to Mercy Hunt my well beloved Wife all my cart and plow Irons here at Marlboro, one spade, also one bedstead and Cord, one pair of Curtains & Valionts, one Chest, one cupboard, two Cushion stools, two Joyn-stools, three Cushions, two frying pans, one peuter flaggon, one peuter bowle, one peior of Tongs, three small peuter plates, one winnowing sheete, one forke, one little keeller, two hand pigine pails, one booke, one fine sheet " (*Hunt Family Gen.*).

She died in Marlboro, 23 Dec., 1693, after a third widowhood of 26 years. During this period she saw two bloody Indian wars. The 26th of March 1676, the Marlboro people were assembled in their meeting house for worship when the alarm was sounded and they barely reached the garrison house in time to find safety from the attacking Indians, who burned houses and barns and destroyed orchards and cattle. The people shortly retreated to the towns to the eastward, where they remained for some months until peace was assured.

GRAVE OF SAMUEL[2] BRIGHAM, MARLBORO CEMETERY

MERCY HURD'S CAP BOX "

The *Jeffrey Papers* preserve tax lists for New England towns the year of Andros' rule (1688). The "Invoice" for Marlboro contains the following:

Widow Hunt for person and estat	00	05	06	0
Thomas Brigham for persons and estate	00	12	01	0
John Brigham " " " "	00	12	01	0
Samuel Brigham " " " "	00	04	10	4
William Ward " " " "	00	05	07	0
John Faye " " " "	00 : 04 : 04 : 0			

The sum total of the whole is	19	03	03	4

The whol Number of the Males
is one hundred & five-   Heads
                                        105

(Endorsed)
   Marlboro Rate   5 Sept. 1688
   £19 3 3
   Wm. Ward   )
   John Fay   ) Constables   (*Hist. Gen. Reg.*, 1882, 191.)

It will be noted that the constables are the husbands of the widow Hunt's two elder daughters.

The little oak chest, of which a picture is given, presents the visible link that spans the years from Mercy Brigham to her children of so many generations later who read these pages. Mr. Thomas Brigham Rice of Barre,* who now owns it, and who received it from his mother, Mrs. Nancy (Brigham) Rice, daughter of Henry Brigham, as a child knew it, then in his grandmother's possession, as "Mercie Hunt's cap box," but he had no conception who Mercy Hunt was until he learned in the *Brigham Genealogy* at its publication in 1859 that she and Mrs. Thomas[1] Brigham were one and the same person.

The box measures inside in length $22\frac{1}{2}$ inches, in height $9\frac{1}{2}$ inches, in width $7\frac{3}{4}$ inches, and is of English oak one inch thick. The larger part of the furniture which was brought over in the Puritan migration is distinctly Jacobean in style, that is, dating from the first half of the seventeenth century, very different from the carving on Mercy Brigham's box. Nor is the latter of the preceding Tudor style, which prevailed in the 16th century. The picture of the box was submitted to an accomplished architect of Boston, one of English birth and training, especially versed in English Gothic art. He pronounces the box to be work in the

* Thomas Brigham Rice[7], b. 1817, Nancy Brigham Rice[6], Henry Brigham[5], Uriah[4], Samuel[3], Samuel[2], Thomas[1].

Gothic style of the 15th century, or even, probably, as old as the 14th century.

Children of Thomas[1] and Mercie Brigham:
2   i   Mary[2], b. probably in Cambridge about 1638.
3   ii Thomas, b. probably in Cambridge about 1640.
4   iii John, b. in Cambridge, 9 March 1644-5.
5   iv Hannah, b. in Cambridge, 9 March, 1649-50.
6   v   Samuel, b. in Cambridge, 12 Jan., 1652.

NOTE 1.—DEED TO THOMAS FOX BY THE OVERSEERS OF THE ESTATE OF THOMAS[1] BRIGHAM, DECEASED, 1656-7

To All People to whome this prsent writing shall come greeting Whereas Thomas Brigham late of Camb in the County of Middlesex in New England deceased was in his lifetime seazed of an estate of inherytance in fee simple of and in   of land lying wthin the limits of Watertowne in the forenamed County and is by estimation about twenty acres more or less being bounded with the common cuntry highway and widdow Daniell on the North Wm Dixson on the North West Mr. Samll Saltonstall on the South West Charles river South and Thomas Marrit on the east also whereas the sd Thomas Brigham by his last will and testament bareing date the 7th of the tenth month Ann. domini 1653 (read and proved at a county court held in the same place October the eight Anno Domini 1654 as may more fully appear in the records of that county in the first book of wils and inventories page forty) nominated and appointed his loveing wife Mercy Brigham sole executrix of that his last will and testament And his loving friends Thomas Danforth Jno Cooper Jno Hastings Thomas Fox and William Towne overseers thereof and further ordered in that his last will and testament that in case of the marriage of his relict widdow that then his overseers of that his last will according to their best discretion should dispose of his Children and their portions for their education and bringing up. Also whereas the Lord hath in his wise providence so disposed that the sd Mercy Brigham the relict widdow of the sd Thomas Brigham is now married to Edmund Rice of Sudbury Senr. who hath received the full portion or legacy due to the sd Mercy his wife, and hath a cleare release of the Remainder of the Estate to be disposed of by the above said overseers for the Benefitt and behoofe of the children of the sd Thomas & Mercy: as may more fully appear by an Instrument signed by the sd Edmund and Mercy his wife, bearing date Anno Dom   Also whereas the above sd overseers preferring a Petition to the Generall Court of that Colony held at Boston Anno: Dom. 1656— obtained Liberty and full power to make sale as well of the above sd parcell of Land, as of other the state of Inheritance whereof the sd Thomas Brigham died seized, as may more fully appear by the Records of that Court. Now know ye that the above named Thomas Danforth John Cooper, John Hastings and William Towne (for and in Consideration of fowety pounds sterl. secured to be paid to them or their assignes for the use and behoofe of the children of the sd Thomas Brigham by the above named Thomas Fox with due dammages Annually for the forbearance thereof untill the sd fourty pounds be demanded and fully paid by the sd Thomas Fox, as may more fully appeare by his bil given for security thereof baring the same date wth these presents Have given granted bargained and sold asiened infeeffed and confirmed and by these presents do fully clearly and absolutely give grant bargaine and sell assieu infeeffe and confirm unto the sd Thomas Fox his heirs and

assignes for ever the above named pᵣcell of land be the same twenty acres
more or less according to the bounds and limmits above named with all
and singular the priviledges and appurtenances thereof to the same ap-
purtaineing or in any wise belonging To Have And to Hold the sᵈ
bargained premises and every part and parcell thereof to him the sᵈ
Thomas Fox his heirs & assigns forever to his and their only proper use
and behoofe In Witness whereof the above named Thomas Danforth
Jnᵒ Cooper Jnᵒ Hastings and William Towne have hereunto put their
hands and seals the twenty and first day of the first month in the Year
of our Lord God one thousand six hundred fifty and four——

Thomas Danforth and seale
Jnᵒ Cooper and seal
Jnᵒ Hastings and seal
William Towne his mark & seal

signed sealed
and delivered
in the pᵣsents of
Edward Goffe
David Fish

This deed was acknowledged freely and legally by Thomas Danforth
Jnᵒ Cooper John Hastings William Towne the 9 of March 1656/7 before me

Daniel Gookin

Entered 6. 1. 8½
By Tho: Danforth R   (*Mid. Deeds*, vii. 447.)

NOTE 2.—DEED TO JOHN HASTINGS BY THE OVERSEERS
OF THE ESTATE OF THOMAS¹ BRIGHAM,
DECEASED, 1656-7

. . . Whereas Thomas Brigham late of Cambridge in the County
of Middlesex in New England dece'd. was in his life time seized of an
estate of inheritance in fee simple of and in one messuage or tenement
scittuate lying and being within the limmits of sᵈ Towne, conteyning the
late mansion house of the sᵈ Thomas Brigham with the Edifices, Barn,
Cow houses and about three acres and a halfe of land to the same
adjoyning, being bounded on the South East by Abraham Errington, on
the South west Simon Crosby alias now Thomas Longhorne, the Highway
North and West a part whereof is a garden and orchards. Also within
the Neck of land in the great marsh commonly so called about seven
aċres and a halfe of marsh more or less and is bounded with Oyster bank
Bay east, Thomas Danforth west, Richard Jackson north, Thomas Fox
south, Also the woodlott appertaining to the sᵈ house, lying a part thereof
in the ox pasture commonly so called and another part or addition there
unto belonging beyond Mills ware, commonly so called as may appeare
in the Towne Book, with all other Town rights and priviledges, in Common
to the sᵈ House apperteyning Also whereas the sᵈ Thomas Brigham by
his last Will and Testament bearing date the seventh of the tenth month
Anno Domini 1653: read at a County Court held in the same place.
octob. 6. 1654: as may more fully appeare by the Records of that County
in the first Book of Wills and Inventories pag. 407 . . . [*here follows*
as in deed to Thomas Fox] . . . Now know yee that the above named
Thomas Danforth John Cooper Thomas Fox and William Towne for and
in consideration of Sixty pounds sterl. Secured to be paid to them and
their Assigns for the use and behoofe of the children of the sᵈ Thomas
Brigham by the above named John Hastings as more fully appears by

his bill given for security thereof having the same date with the p^rsents . . . and confirmed unto the said John Hastings . . .

In Witness whereof . . . the twenty fifth of the first month called March in the year of our Lord God One thousand six hundred fifty and four.

Thomas Danforth & seal
John Cooper & seal
Thomas Fox his mark & seale
William Towne his mark & seale

Signed sealed & delivered
in the p^rsence of
Edward Goffe
David Fiske

This deed of sale was fully and legally acknowledged by Thomas Danforth, John Cooper, Thomas Fox and William Towne to be their Act and Deed the 9th 1mo 1656/7

Before me
        Daniel Gookin Magistrate
Recorded 24. 12. 1685
    by Tho: Danforth R.   (*Mid. Deeds,* x. 656.)

Confirmation of acts of Overseers by the General Court:

At a Gen^ll Court held at Boston: 28: January 1684 In answer to the petition of the overseers of the Children and estate of Thomas Brigham for confirmation of the Sale of certain houses and lands left by him to his wife and children The Court on perusall of the will of the s^d Brigham thinks meet to grant petition Provided that the overseers do give security to the County Court to the use of ye children for the principall and Effects as is exprest in ye petition It appearing to this Court that the above order was passed by the Gen^ll Court in the year 1656 and altho the engrossing thereof was omitted by the Secretary yet do find it was entered in the Register of the Courts Acts of the Deputies This Court the Secretary to enter s^d order in this Courts Records.

As attest   Edward Rawson Secret.
Recorded 24. 12. 1685
    by Tho: Danforth R.   (*Mid. Deeds,* x. 654.)

NOTE 3.—SALE BY HEIRS OF THOMAS¹ BRIGHAM, 1681

Grantors: Thomas Brigham and Samuel Brigham of Marlbury £24. (Consideration.)
Grantee: George Lawrence of Watertown.
In Cambridge, part of Rocky meadows
5 acres:
Bounded:

Southerly, Watertown line.
Westerly, Cambridge Common.
Easterly, John Gemery.
Northerly, George Lawrence.
2nd May 1681.
Signed, Thomas Brigham & (seale)
        Jno Brigham   & (Seale)
        Samuel Brigham   & (Seale)
In presence of
Nicholas ffessendin
Wm. Ward Jr.   (*Mid. Reg.,* iv. 159.)

SALE BY HEIRS OF THOMAS[1] BRIGHAM

Grantors: Thomas Brigham, Samuel Brigham, John Brigham of Marlbury,
      Yeomen.
£24. (Consideration.)
Enoch Sawtle of Watertown: Grantee.
In Cambridge, parcel of meadow land.
Part of Rockie meadow.
5 acres.
Bounded.——
N. & E. Philip Jones. *S. & W.* George Lawrence.
2nd May 1681.
In presence of,
  Nicholas ffessinden
  Wm. Ward Jr.   (*Mid. Reg.*, viii. 55.)

NOTE 4.—SALE BY HEIRS OF THOMAS[1] BRIGHAM, 1681

We Thomas Brigham, John Brigham, Samuel Brigham & William Ward,
all of Marlbury in the County of Middlesex, Husbandmen, for & in
consideration of fifteen pounds of currant money of New England, by us
already received of Nicholas Fessenden of Cambridge in the same county,
Glover . . . sold . . . unto said Nicholas Fessenden a platt of
meadow & swamp lying in Cambridge bounds, conteyning about ten
acres, as it is stated in the town book, be it more or less bounded, the
above Nicholas Fessenden Southerly, Monotoma River westerly, the great
swamp easterly, formerly in the possession of Edward   Sen[r] . . .

In witness whereof we the above[sd] Thomas Brigham, Jn[o] Brigham,
Samuell Brigham, & William Ward and o[r] wives Mary & Sarah Brigham
with Hannah Ward in acknowledgement of our free consent to this act
& deed of our husbands & y[e] utter relinquishing of o[r] Dower right in
the above granted .   y[e] 27th day of y[e] 10th m the year of o[r] Lord
God   1681.

                (seale) Thomas Brigham.
                    John Brigham   (seale)
                    Samuel Brigham
        (seale)
                    William Ward (seale)
                    (*Mid. Reg.*, viii. 134.)

NOTE 5.—SUIT AGAINST SAMUEL HASTINGS

William the third by y[e] grace of God of England Scotland France
& Ireland King Defender of the ffaith &c To y[e] Sheriff of our s[d] County
under Sheriff or Deputy Greeting   We Command you to attach y[e] goods
or Estate of Samuel Hastings Sen[r] of Cambridge in s[d] County Gunsmith
to y[e] value of three hundred pounds & for warrant there of to take y[e]
body of him Samuel Hastings if he may be found in yo[r] precinct, and
him safely keep.   So that you have him before our Justices at our next
Inferio[r] Court of Common Pleas to be holden for s[d] County at Charlestown on y[e] Second Tuesday of Decemb[r] next, Then & there to answer to
Thomas Brigham John Brigham, Samuel Brigham & Hannah Ward &

John Fay & Samᶫᶫ Fay children of Mary Faye all of Marlburrough in yᵉ County of Middˣ being the Children & heires of theire ffather Thomas Brigham late of sᵈ Cambridge Yeoman dece'd In an action upon the Case For that yᵉ said Samuell Hastings hath entered into & with holdeth from yᵉ plts the possession of a homestall Containing three acres & a halfe more or less as bounded in the Town Records of Cambridge with all yᵉ buildings and Ediffices thereupon and being and appurtenances & Town Rights thereunto belonging and Also of a certain parcell of Saltmarsh Containing Seven acres & a halfe as it stands

Recorded in the Records in Cambridge Town Book wᵗʰ yᵉ prvriledges & appurtenances thereof & being at a place in sᵈ Cambridge called Long Marsh or Great Creek   The said Homestall & appurtenances & seven acres & a halfe of marsh being Scittuate in said Cambridge   As also a Certain parcell of Land Scittuate & being in Watertowne in said County Containing Twenty Acres or thereabouts called by the name of Watertowne ffeild, Keys ffeild & Wilcoxs Lott, all in one Intire parcell and bounded Northerly partly by a highway, partly by land in the Possession of Goodman Withe and Goodman Hicks Southerly by Land that was Samᶫᶫ Saltonstalls, Easterly by Land in the possession of John Marritt wᵗʰ the priviledges & appurtenances thereof, all wᶜʰ homestall of three acres and halfe and the Seven acres and halfe of Salt Marsh, and Twenty acres of Land more or less Sued for, formerly belonged to yᵉ aforesaid Thomas Brigham Dece'd the ffather of yᵉ pltˢ & by him to them bequeathed in his Last Will & Testament as part of theire portions, & therefore of right belongs to yᵉ plts.   The with holding the possession whereof from yᵉ plts. is to theire Dammage one hundred and Twenty pounds, as shall then & there appear with Dammages, and have you there this writt.

Witness John Phillips Esq. at Charlestowne

Septembʳ 28ᵗʰ: 1695 In yᵉ Seventh year of our Reign

Samll: Phipps Cler——

Decembʳ 7ᵗʰ: 95 Rece'd to be recorded with)
        yᵉ Return on yᵉ Contrary side)
        & Entered
        By Samᶫᶫ Phipps Recordʳ

Middˣ Ss Septemb yᵉ 28ᵗʰ: 1695:

I have attended yᵉ Body of Samᶫᶫ Hastings within mentioned, & taken bond of him to the value of three hundred pounds . . .

    By me Jnᵒ Waite
    Under Sheriff for yᵉ County aforesaid—

Know all men by these prsents that We Samuel Hastings Senʳ of Cambridge Gunsmith as principall & Reuben Luxford of sᵈ Cambridge as Surety doth bind our Selves our beires Jointly & Severally unto John Waite of Charlestown under sheriff for the County aforesaid in the summ of three hundred pounds, on Condition that the within mentioned Samuel Hastings Shall prsonally appear before his Majestie's Justices at theire next Inferior Court of Common Please to be holden for sᵈ County at Charlestown on yᵉ Second Tuesday in December next then & there to answer to Thomas Brigham, John Brigham, Samuel Brigham & Hannah Ward & John Fay & Samᶫᶫ Fay Children of Mary Fay all of Marlburrough in sᵈ County of Middˣ being the Children & heirs of their Father Thomas Brigham late of said Cambridge in sᵈ County Yeoman Dece'd in an action upon the Case according to the Tenour of the within written Writt & that I or he said Samuel Hastings shall abide yᵉ order of yᵉ Court, &

not Depart without Licence, as Witness our hands this 28th Day of Septembr. 1695

> Samuel Hastings
> Ruben Luxford
> (*Mid. Prob.,* vol. vii. pp. 16, 17, 18; *back of book.*)

NOTE 6.—ABSTRACT OF DEED FOR THE 72-ACRE FARM, A. D. 1703

Grantors: Thomas Brigham and Samuel Brigham of Marlburrough and John Brigham of Sudbury.

. . . especially ffor and in consideration of the Sum of Sixteen Pounds pd to ye Children of Thomas Brigham late of Cambridge Dece'd by Thomas Danforth Esq. and Thomas Fox called Overseers of ye Estate of sd Thomas Brigham Dece'd: and Thirty pounds in money to us in hand at and before the Sealing and Delivery of these presents of Francis Foxcroft of Cambridge Esq. one of the Executors of the last will and Testament of ye Honble Thomas Danforth aforesaid well and truly paid   the receipt whereof Wee the said Thomas Brigham, Samll Brigham and John Brigham Do hereby . . . grant . . . the said Francis Foxcroft Esq. Samuel Sparhawk and Daniel Champney Joint Executrs of the last will and testament of the Hon. Thomas Danforth . . . all right the said Thomas Brigham Samuel Brigham and John Brigham may . . . have in   . . that tract or prcell of land comonly called or known by ye name of Brighams farme: Scituate, lying and being on ye Rocks neer Oburn Line within the Township of Cambridge .   containing by Estimation Seventy Two acres be the same more or less and is butted and bounded as it should be recorded in Cambridge Towne Booke of Records . . . In witness whereof . . . have set their hands and seals the Twenty Sixth Day of February Anno Domi: one thousand Seven hundred and three . . .

> Thomas Brigham & seale
> John Brigham   & seale
> Samuel Brigham & seale

Ack before John Leverett J: Pais—

> Feb. 26 1703.   (*Mid. Deeds,* xiii. 527.)

SECOND   GENERATION

SECOND GENERATION

2 MARY[2], daughter of Thomas and Mercy (Hurd) Brigham; born probably in Cambridge, Mass., about 1638; died in Watertown, in 1676; married John Fay, the emigrant, who settled in Marlboro, Mass., and died 5 May, 1690, æ. 50.

Mary was *the first Brigham born in America,* and as such deserves especial mention. Paige, in his *History of Cambridge* (pp. 501-2), a most thorough and painstaking work, chronicles that " Mary went to Sudbury and Marlboro with her mother, brothers and sister, when her father died, where she married John Fay of Marlboro." And he cites evidence, as already indicated by a legal document (*Mid. Prob. Recs.,* vii. 9), wherein, joining with other complainants, John Fay and Samuel Fay, *children of Mary Fay* of Marlboro, and heirs of Thomas Brigham, late of Cambridge, began suit September 28, 1695, to recover certain lands in the possession of Samuel Hastings, who possessed also the Puritan Brigham homestead. John Fay Sr.'s wife was Mary, and there was no other Fay in Marlboro at that time of suitable age to be the father of said John, Jr., and Samuel Fay, parties to said suit. Paige was undoubtedly correct, and we must include in our genealogy of the Brighams the children of John and Samuel Fay, sons of Mary (Brigham) Fay. Both of them had large families, among them being sons who became the heads of numerous branches (see *Fay Family*). There was also a daughter, Mary Fay, who married Jonathan[3] Brigham, her cousin, and a son of Thomas[2] Brigham; they had 10 children, thus starting several male lines of Brighams. Hudson, in his *Hist. of Marlboro,* does not conflict with Paige's position; and he adds that John Fay retired (with most other Marlboroites), during King Philip's War, to Watertown, where he buried his wife Mary and a young son David, just coming five years.

John Fay, the husband of Mary Brigham, came to America when he was eight years of age. No mention is made of his parents. He is found in Marlboro as early as 1669. He married (2) Susanna, daughter of William Shattuck of Watertown and widow of Joseph Morse. As will be seen, she married for her third husband, Thomas[2] Brigham.

Children (Fay), born in Marlboro:
    i John[s], b. 30 Nov., 1669; d. in Westboro, 5 Jan., 1747; m. (1) Elizabeth, dau. Benjamin and Elizabeth (Sweetman) Wellington, b. 29 Dec., 1673; d. 8 March, 1729; m. (2) Levinah[4], dau. of

Elnathan[8] Brigham; res. Westboro. Ch. (by first wife):

  1 *Bathshebah*[4], b. 1 Jan., 1693; m. John Pratt of Westboro.
  2 *Eunice*, b. 2 June, 1696; m. Isaac Pratt of Westboro.
  3 *Mary*, b. 29 Sept., 1698; d. 20 Nov., 1704.
  4 *John*, b. 5 Dec., 1700; m. 17 April, 1721, Hannah Child.
  5 *Lydia*, b. 24 Nov., 1702.
  6 *Dinah*, b. 5 Sept., 1705; m. David Goodnow, in 1722.
  7 *James*, b. 27 Dec., 1707; m. 1727, Lydia Child of Watertown.
  8 *Mehitabel*, b. 18 June, 1710; m. ———— Fletcher.
  9 *Benjamin*, b. 15 Aug., 1712; m. (1) Martha Mills; (2) Elizabeth Stow.
  10 *Stephen*, b. 5 May, 1715; m. Ruth Child.

 ii David, b. 15 Oct., 1671; d. 28 Sept., 1676.

iii Samuel, b. 11 Oct., 1673; d. in Westboro, 10 Nov., 1732; m. 16 May, 1699, Tabitha, dau. of Increase and Record Ward, b. 16 May, 1675. He res. in Westboro. Ch.:

  1 *Rebecca*[4], b. 19 Feb., 1700; m. William Nurse of Shrewsbury, Mass.; had 9 ch.
  2 *Tabitha*, b. 14 Aug., 1702; m. William Maury of Brookfield.
  3 *Samuel*, bap. 6 May, 1705; m. (1) Deliverance Shattuck of Watertown; m. (2) Elizabeth (Hastings) Cutler; had 24 ch., 14 by first wife and 10 by second wife.
  4 *Jeduthun*, b. 7 June, 1707; m. 1739, Sarah Shattuck of Watertown.
  5 *Abigail*, b. 19 Jan., 1709; m. Thomas Converse of Killingly, Conn.
  6 *Ebenezer*, b. 12 April, 1713; m. (1) Abigail ————; m. (2) Thankful Hyde; m. (3) Mary Mason; had 18 ch.
  7 *Mary*, b. 28 March, 1720; d. unm. prior to 1746.

 iv Mary, b. 10 Feb., 1675; m. Jonathan[8] Brigham, 8.

3   THOMAS[2], son of Thomas[1] and Mercy (Hurd) Brigham; born probably in Cambridge, Mass., about 1640; died in Marlboro, Mass., 25 Nov., 1716; married (1), 27 Dec., 1665, Mary, daughter of Henry and Elizabeth (Moore) Rice, (daughter of John and Elizabeth Moore of Sudbury), and granddaughter of Edmund Rice, the emigrant, and his wife, Tamazine; married (2), 30 July, 1695, Susanna, daughter of William Shattuck of Watertown and widow (1) of Joseph Morse and (2) of John Fay, whose first wife was Mary, the sister of Thomas. It will be noted that every descendant of Thomas[2] is also a descendant of Edmund Rice, who is an ancestor of many colonial families in eastern Massachusetts. He had a large number of children, some of whom were of mature age at the time of the emigration.

Thomas went to Sudbury and Marlboro with his mother when she married Edmund Rice. On attaining his majority he bought of his stepfather, for £30, a town right in Marlboro of " 24 acres, with the frame of a dwelling house thereon, with all the privileges of the town commons and further additions of allotments to be made thereto." August 28, 1665, having completed payment for the same, he received a deed from the Executors of Edmund Rice.* This land, situated near Williams Pond in the southwest part of the town, was the beginning of his large farm, which included many acres stretching away toward Chauncey Pond in Westboro. Thomas Brigham also was one of the purchasers of the old plantation "Ockoocangansett," which had been reserved for the Indians out of the ancient boundaries of Marlboro, and which many contended they forfeited by their perfidy during Philip's War. Certain leading men of Marlboro, including the Brighams of the day, obtained, without the consent of the General Court, title to this plantation of 5800 acres and formed a company. The amount paid never can be known, because of the subsequent disappearance of the deed, but the sum doubtless was nominal.

Miss Martha L. Ames, a descendant of Thomas[2], residing on the old Joseph Brigham place in Marlboro, owns a very early Brigham deed, dated "May 10, 1706," being a conveyance of $13\frac{3}{4}$ acres of meadow land, as explained by a map, going to Thomas[2] Brigham, out of "Cow common" land, and certified to by his brother "Dr. John," who had been chosen "surveyor and clerk" by the proprietors. On the old Thomas Brigham homestead, on the south side of present Forest Street, beyond the confluence of Glen Street, something like a score of rods from the highway and at the foot of Crane Hill, is a slightly raised rectangular plot, about 30 x 75 feet, from whose center springs a mature apple tree. Here rest the last of the Marlboro Indians, whose earlier generations listened to the great Indian Apostle Eliot. Their last chief expired in his wigwam, near Williams Pond, and was buried at this place on the Brigham farm, where thirty other individual graves could be made out by the last generation of Marlboro citizens. This spot has always been sacredly preserved by the owners of the Brigham farm. The successive owners of the "old home place" since the Rices are as follows:

* The parchment deed of this purchase is owned by Charles F. Brigham, of Allston, Mass., who relates that when a boy he boasted at school that he had a deed on parchment at home, and being dared to produce it, he tore a small piece off one corner of it and carried it to school to vindicate his statement. The interview afterward with his father was not pleasant. This deed runs from Benjamin Rice to Thomas Brigham, and upon it Mercy Rice made her "Mark" in place of a signature.

Thomas and John Brigham (with others) oppose petition of some fellow-citizens that the Gen. Court appoint a Committee to inquire into and settle certain municipal difficulties. The Committee was, however, appointed, and its adjustment recorded in the "New Town Book." A later Committee seems to have supported this adjustment (Hudson's *Marlboro*, p. 46).

Thos. and Sam'l Brigham supported the Rev. Emerson in the controversy of 1701 (*Ibid.*, p. 102.)

Thos. Brigham's "Garrison" about 1710 in Queen Anne's War, near Warren Brigham place (*Ibid.*, p. 109).

Thos. Brigham and 22 others of Marlboro in 1702 petitioned the Gen. Court that Chauncey (Western Marlboro) might be enlarged westward. Resulted in 1717 in setting off of Westboro. David, son of Thos., already settled there (*Ibid.*, p. 113).

Thos. and Jno. Brigham in Marlboro before 1665; two of the first 44 proprietors (*Ibid.*, p. 247).

(1) Thomas[2] Brigham; (2) Gershom[3] Brigham; (3) Benjamin[4] Brigham; (4) Warren[5] Brigham; (5) Benjamin Thomas[6] Brigham, son of Barnabas; (6) Elisha Bond, who bought it of Benj. T. Brigham; (7) Bradford Latham, son-in-law to Bond; (8) George F. Nichols, who bought it in 1893 from Latham; Mr. Nichols' wife is Abbie A.[8], daughter of Addington M.[7] Brigham of Marlboro. The last male Brigham owner of the place is said to have strikingly resembled his paternal ancestry, having "thick, wavy black hair, black eyes and red cheeks; a fine looking man."

The Thomas[2] Brigham homestead has long been known as the "Warren Brigham place," from its fourth owner, who died at the age of 87, more than half a century ago. Up to his time there had been no Warren Brighams. This fact inspired some research, which resulted in discovering that Gershom[3] Brigham, the second owner, had married Mehetabel Warren, daughter of Joseph Warren of Medfield.

Like the sites of the homes of so many of the first settlers, that of Thomas[2] Brigham's house seems almost to have been chosen for the landscape effect. The brook which gives the outlet to Williams Pond flows through the home lot. A few rods above the brook stood the house. From it the higher hills appear to encompass the valley of the brook, except where they break to the northwest and a narrow opening discloses the peak of Mt. Wachusett looming up twenty miles away. The first dwelling, a log hut built by Thomas[2], was burned during his absence by flax catching fire. In 1706 he built a frame house, which was left for an "ell" by his son Gershom, who built a two-story house about 1724. The old house was used as a garrison in Queen Anne's War. This "ell" was finally taken down in 1791, by Warren Brigham. Mrs. Lucy B. Brown of Marlboro was the last occupant of the Gershom Brigham house, from which she moved in 1859; the house was uninhabited for some time and was finally razed. The Gershom Brigham house "was clapboarded but never painted outside; only two rooms were finished; the sitting-room and the principal bedroom were plastered and painted." About 1825 the present house was built on the opposite side of the road from the old house, by Barnabas[6] Brigham. The old well, from which many Brigham pilgrims drink, still exists.

Thomas[2] unquestionably was one of the principal citizens of the town and must have held offices of responsibility, but an important volume of the town records was lost many years ago, hence there is no connected record of town officers or of town proceedings from 1665 to 1739. The church records are also fragmentary or nonexistent for the early period. His lands, however, were

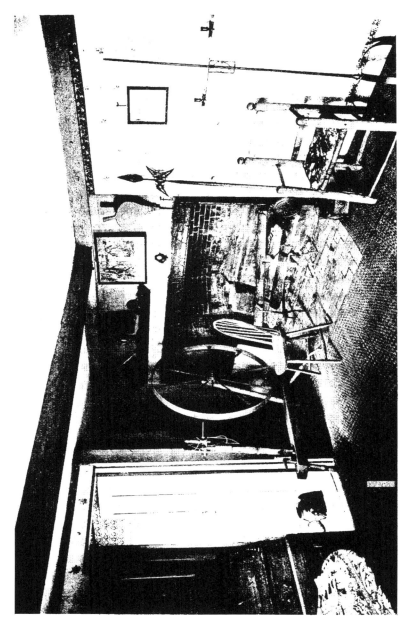

Room in Joseph[4] Brigham House, Marlboro

Showing the chair in which Thomas[2] Brigham died

extensive, lying in what now are four townships.* They divided
into comfortable farms for his descendants and made many of
them well-to-do. He executed his will 21 April, 1716, and died
25 Nov. of the same year in his chair, which is now in the possession of Miss Martha L. Ames. His will, which was approved 2
Jan., 1717, is as follows:

WILL OF THOMAS² BRIGHAM

In the Name of God Amen: This Twenty first Day of April Anno
Domini one Thousand seven hundred and sixteen & in the second
year of the Raigne of our Soveraigne Lord Georg of Great Brittian
&c King   I Thomas Brigham of the town of Marlborough in
the County of middlesex in the Province of the massachusetts
Bay in New-England yeoman being vere weak of Body but of
perfect mind & memory Praised be God for it Knowing that it
apoynded for men once to Dy Do make and ordain this my Last
will & Testament first I bequeth my soul into the hands of Almighty
God my maker hoping that through the merratorious Death of
Jesus Christ my only Savour to know the free pardon of all my
sins: And my Body to be Buried in Christian Like Decent &
Cortly maner at the Discrestion of my hereafter Named Executors:
And as for such Worldly Estate as it hath pleased God to bless
me with hear in this world I Give and Dispose of the same in the
maner and forms following *Item* I will and Give to my Son
Elnathan Brigham and to his heirs Three acres of land in Etton
farm next adjoining to the seven acres I have given him by Deed
Lying side by sid with it And also Twelve acres of Land in s^d
farm some where towards the uper End of the s^d farm. *Item* I
will and Give unto my two sons Nathan Brigham and Jonathan
Brigham and to theirs all that part of my Etton farme that lies
on the easterly side of Assabeth River except what I have Given
to my son Elnathan Brigham. *Item* I will and Give unto my
Two sons Nathan Brigham & Jonathan Brigham and to their heirs
Twenty two acres of the thirty acres that is laid out to me in
Etton farme to have it on the Southerly end of the s^d Thirty acres
And also the pece of Land that Joyns to it on the westerly side.
Item I will and Give unto my two sons David Brigham and Ger-
shom Brigham and to their heirs eight acres of the thirty acres

* Thomas and John Brigham (inter alias) in 1671 asked for grant of General
Court 40 or 50 miles south or southwest of Marlboro. Refused as outside jurisdiction of Province of Mass. Bay (DeForest's *Hist. of Westboro*, p. 19).
    In 1672 grant to Thomas B. (and Sam. Goodenow) in easterly Northboro of
to-day (*Ibid*).
    Thos., Jno., Sam'l and Nathan Brigham (inter alias) in 1702 petitioned for west-
erly extension of Marlboro (refused). Called " Kerly pet'n " from first signer, p. 33.

that is Laid out to me in Etton farme to have it on the northerly end of the s^d Thirty acres And also all the Rest of my Etton farme that lies on the westerly side of Assabeth River I Give to the s^d David Brigham & Gershom Brigham & to their heirs Except what is Given to others of my Children: *Item* I give unto my son David Brigham & to his heirs all my meadow in Hokamok meadow and Brook meadow. *Item* my will is that all my Books be Equally Divided amongst all my Children. *Item* I will and Give unto my Daughter mary Houghton the wife of Jonas Houghton junr of Lancaster the feather bed I ly upon with all the furnituer to it also I Give unto my Daughter mary Houghton above s^d one Cow and my Great Brass Kittle that is at my son Jonathans and all my movable Goods with in Dors viz Brass Iron pewter with all my utensils in the house Except my part in the Barrels And Except Likewise some particular things that I have or shall Dispose of to som particular persns. *Item* I Give unto my Daughter mary Houghton above mentioned & to her heirs Thirty six pounds in money to be paid by my sons as followeth: Twenty pounds to be paid to her or her heirs by my son Gershom Brigham within three years after my Deccas at three several payments viz six pounds thirteen shillings & four pence a year. And ten pounds to be paid her or her heirs by my son David Brigham within two years after my Decease And fourty shillings to be paid to her by my son Nathan Brigham And fourty shillings to be paid to her by my son Jonathan Brigham And fourty shillings to be paid to her by my son Elnathan Brigham these three last to be paid to her or to her heirs within one year after my Deceas: *Item:* I will and Give unto my two sons David Brigham and Elnathan Brigham my Lot of Cedar Swamp that is in Chancy swamp: *Item* I will and Give unto my son Gershom Brigham all my utensils for Husbandtre And one halfe my Lot of Sedar swamp in Cran Swamp And also my part in the barrels   Item I will and Give unto my Daughter mary Brigham the wife of Jonathan Brigham the Twenty shillings which John Emes oweth me   *Item* my will is that all my Cattle and horses be Equaly Divided amongst all my Children except what I shall Dispose of in my Life time   *Item* I Give unto my son Jonathan Brigham my bigest Brass Kittle here in the house: *Item* I do hereby Constitute ordain and apoynt my Three sons Nathan Brigham, Jonathan Brigham & Gershom Brigham to be my executors of this my Last will and Testament Revoking & Disalowing of all other wills & Testaments what soever, Rattefying and Confirming this to be my Last will and Testament in wittness whereof I the s^d Thomas Brigham have hereunto put my Hand &nd fixed my seal the Day and year above written   *Item* my will further is that if there be any part of my estate ether Real or personal be Left undisposed & which at present I have

not thought of that it be Equaly Divided amongst all my Children
These lines were writen before signing and sealing there is three
words bloted out in the thirteenth Line & there is three words
bloted out in the twentieth Line & three words Likewise bloted out
in the twenty third line which was done before signing & sealing

Thomas Brigham   (Seal)

Signed sealed and Delivered
in presence of witnesses
Gershom How
Ephraim How
Jno Banister
Eleasar How

(On the reverse is written the following.)

The Lines may sertifie whom it may Concern that where as in
the within writan will I Thomas Brigham have Given unto my
two sons Nathan Brigham Jonathan Brigham Twenty two acres
of a pece of Land in Etton farme wch I Did then Call thirty
acres And it apears that there is in the s^d peace Thirty three acres
& one quarter of an acre wch three acres and one quarter not mentioned in the within wretten will I Give to my to sons Nathan
Brigham & Jonathan Brigham to be Equaly Divided between them
and Likewise what I have Given to my two sons Nathan Brigham
and Jonathan Brigham in the within wreten will in Land it is to
be Equally Divided between them And also what Land I have
Given to my two sons David Brigham & Gershom Brigham is
Likewise to be Equaly Divided between them And where I have
made Assabeth River the Dividing Line between any of my sons
my meaning is the main Body of the s^d River in witness where of
I the s^d Thomas Brigham have here unto put my hand and seal
this May 19th 1716

There is four words bloted out in the second line & six bloted
out the sixth Line and all the seventh Line & one word in the eigth
line which was Sow before signing & sealing

Thomas Brigham   (Seal)

Signed sealed & Delivered
in presence of witnesses
Eleazar How
Gershom How
Jno Banister

Midelsx   Eleazer How and Gershom How apeared before me
and mad oath that they saw this instrument sined and sealed and
at the same time saw John Banister sine as a witness the above said
Thomas Brigham being in perfect memory at that time

January 1: 1717/18

Tho How   Justice of peace

Cambridge Jan 2, 1717   (*Mid. Prob. Rec.*, 1733.)

Children, by first wife, born in Marlboro:

    i Thomas³, b. 24 Feb., 1666-7, and no further reported; probably died before his father.

7   ii Nathan, b. 17 June, 1671.

    iii David, b. 11 Aug., 1673; died young.

8   iv Jonathan, b. 22 Feb., 1675.

9   v David, b. 12 April, 1678.

10 vi Gershom, b. 23 Feb., 1680.

11 vii Elnathan, b. 7 March, 1683.

    viii Mary, b. 26 Oct., 1687; m. Capt. Jonas Houghton of Lancaster, Mass., 30 July, 1710; he d. 15 Aug., 1739, æ. 56.* Ch. (Houghton), b. in Lancaster:

      1 *Silas⁴,* b. 26 Oct., 1713.

      2 *Betty,* b. 20 March, 1715-16.

      3 *Mary,* b. 8 March, 1720-21.

      4 *Prudence,* b. 21 Oct., 1723.

      5 *Persis,* b. 31 July, 1726.

      6 *Jonas,* b. 21 April, 1728.

      7 *John,* b. 13 Feb., 1731-2.

4 JOHN², son of Thomas¹ and Mercy (Hurd) Brigham; born in Cambridge, Mass., 9 March, 1644-45; died in Sudbury, Mass., 16 Sept., 1728; † married (1) Sarah ‡ ————, who died between 1691 and 1698; she was the mother of his children; married (2) Deborah ————, who died 7 Feb., 1716-17; married (3), 22 May, 1717, Sarah Bowker, who survived him.

John, known as "Dr." Brigham, founder of the "lost tribe" of our family, undoubtedly was the most brilliant of the children of Thomas¹. Drake (*History of Middlesex County,* vol. ii. p. 141 *et seq.*) describes him as "one of the most popular and remarkable men of his day, having considerable capacity for public affairs, unusual ability as a surveyor and some ambition as a land speculator." Lewis (*History of Worcester County,* vol. ii. p. 1332) refers to him as "John Brigham, the doctor, surveyor, Commissioner of the General Court, land speculator and the most enterprising man in town." It is the very exuberance of his activity, his ubiquitous absorption here and there, into this and that problem of the place and hour, that make the fragmentary gleanings of him so fascinating yet unsatisfactory. Drake states that "he was returned as representative from Marlboro in 1688 and from Sudbury in 1706." The first date we cannot verify, as the records are lacking, but we learn from the State Archives (*Recs. Gen. Crt. of Mass.,* vol. vi. pp. 16, 220) that John Brigham represented Marlboro in 1689 and 1692; and he was returned from Sudbury for the term of "May 30, 1705—Apr. 12, 1706." (*Acts and Resolves of the Province of Mass. Bay,* vol. viii. p. 115). He also was a Marlboro delegate to the convention called against the "Tyrant Andros."

* See Lancaster Records.   * Sudbury Records.

‡ *Hist. of Westboro* says he m. a dau. of Josiah Haynes.

He began business for himself by erecting a sawmill, with rude flutter wheel, the first turned on Assabet River, it may be, near the site of one existing in Morse's day owned by Hayes and Bush in Northboro on Howard's Brook; he having received, in 1672, a grant of land on Licor Meadow Plain. Hudson says (p. 231): "It is difficult to tell when or where the first mill was erected. It is probable, however, that the first was a sawmill and was erected in that part of the town now included in Northboro, by John Brigham. It was near the center of the present town of Northboro, on a stream which constitutes one of the principal tributaries of the Assabet River. This mill was erected before Philip's War." Whitney's *History of Worcester* (1793) points out that "a little north of the meeting-house runs a small but lasting stream from the hills in the westerly part of the town, on which is a sawmill which performs considerable work in spring and fall." Rev. Joseph Allen says he was the first white settler of Northboro.

He surveyed the Marlboro Indian Plantation of about 6000 acres in 1672; was granted the extensive "Coram farm"* for his services as surveyor; surveyed and mapped out Sudbury Township in 1708.

John Brigham appears to have been the leader in the attempt of some of the principal citizens of Marlboro to possess themselves of the Indian Plantation, Ockoocangansett, which, they alleged, had been forfeited by the Indians through their participation in King Philip's War. The General Court, in 1684, refused the prayer of the petitioners for permission to purchase the Plantation of the Indians; whereupon, says Hudson, it appears that the principal inhabitants of Marlboro, headed by John Brigham, resolved to possess the Indian lands. To cut the knot which they could not untie, on the 15th of July, 1684, they obtained, without the consent of the General Court, a deed of the Plantation from the Indians. This deed the General Court promptly declared null and void; notwithstanding which, the purchasers proceeded at once to take possession of the Plantation and to lay out and divide the lands.

"The 29th of October, 1686: At a meeting of the proprietors of Ockoocangansett Plantation, it was ordered that every proprietor should have laid out to him in some of the best of the land lying as conveniently as may be to the town of Marlboro, thirty

---

* "The 'Coram Farm' was granted John Brigham in 1672, as compensation for services as surveyor. The principal part of 'Coram Farm' lay on the northern side of the old Marlboro line, now (1826) farms of Nahum, Asa and Lewis Fay, John Green and Stephen Williams......The Indians burnt John's house a few days after his removal" (*Top. and Hist. Sketches, etc.,* Rev. Jos. Allen; Pamphlet, 1826; p. 25, note).

acres for a first division of upland, and Mr. John Brigham is agreed, withall, to lay out the abovesaid lands, and to have five shillings a day, the one half in money, the other half in corn, rye at four shilling per bushel, and Indian at three shillings per bushel, and to have his diet all the while he is about the work. Also at the same meeting it was agreed that John Maynard Sen., and Richard Barnes, should join with John Brigham, to order the laying out of the land, and order highways according to their best discretion, and they to have two shillings a day for their pains, in corn at country prices. Also, at the same meeting, it was agreed that when the lots were laid out, every proprietor should draw his lot."

At a meeting of the proprietors, in December of the same year, continues Hudson, it was voted that Major Hincksman and others " should have the thousand acres of land which was surveyed by John Brigham, and signified by the plats under his hand, should be recorded in the Company's Book of Records, so that it make a final settlement of all differences about the said land, as to any further claimes." Among the fifty-two proprietors were included John, Samuel and Thomas, sons of Thomas[1] Brigham, Mercy Hunt, their mother, and John Fay and William Ward, who had married their sisters. Dr. John appears to have received, besides his share, other lots for his services. " Sept. 24, 1691, he, for £16, conveyed to Daniel Rice his 30 acre right in the Indian Plantation   " In 1693 the proprietors agreed that their grants of land " shall stand good to all intents and purposes, if they be attested by John Brigham their Clerk." In March, 1708, says Morse, they chose Dr. Brigham on a committee "to act about their title." The General Court, still keeping faith with the Indians, steadfastly refused to confirm the purchase, but in 1719 finally ended all controversy by annexing the territory to Marlboro. Hudson does not excuse this mild fraud upon the Indians, but, he says, " The people of Marlboro have at least this apology: they acted in accordance with the spirit of the age."

Morse concisely gives details of his later life as follows: " Dr. Brigham   Nov. 9, 1697, he then of Sudbury, for £70 received of Joseph Freeman of Preston, Conn., a deed of 130 acres in Sudbury, bounded on the south by the Lancaster Road and on the E. by the five miles of land *first* granted to Sudbury. This tract is presumed to be the farm now owned and occupied by Captain William Rice. Oct. 7, 1698, he sold for £10, to Nathaniel Oke, 12 acres E. of his sawmill in what is now Northboro."

Dr. Brigham lived in Marlboro near and northwest from the

present French church. He evidently drew many lots of the town's commons. His old homestead in Northboro was situated on what is now Berlin Street, just on the edge of Northboro Center village, across Howard's Brook, where the site of his mill is still used for that purpose. A good part of the dam is of native rock, attesting John's shrewd selection of an advantageous spot. This farm has long been known as the " Priest Whitney Place," from the occupancy of the Rev. Peter Whitney, an honored historian of Worcester Co., who, having been ordained in 1767 and dying in 1816, built a fine mansion house in 1780, still standing in half-neglected picturesqueness. In 1839 Silas Haynes came into possession; succeeded in 1852 by Mr. S. McClure, with whom, in September, 1894, the writer had an interview. North of the residence at the orchard end, opposite some fence bars, two rods distant, is a level piece of meadow plowed over many times by Mr. McClure, who remembers well the spot where the plow touches " the white sand," which was filled into the cellar of the original John Brigham house. This spot is about 18 x 20 feet. In the rear it slopes down quickly to lower marshy ground, where was a spring, probably first used by John, four or five rods east, but now filled, although recognized in an identation of the rounded slope.

In 1684 John was one of the grantees from the Indians of land from which was formed the " Plantation of Sudbury," * whither he removed from Northboro, and he long lived on the old Sudbury and Marlboro Road near Sudbury town line. The old homestead building (where Abijah Brigham once lived) stood about ten rods west of the present Lucius Brigham house, and was a large old-fashioned red building with long sloping roof.† He served six years as selectman in Sudbury and was placed on important committees.‡

It is worthy of note that the given names of his seven children recall those of his family dear to his heart: Sarah, his wife; Mercy, his mother; Mary and Hannah, his sisters; Thomas, his father, Thomas his eldest brother, Samuel his other brother, and lastly himself. Singularly enough, he had just enough children in all and just enough of each sex to go around the beloved circle.

Judge Forbes of Worcester stated in a letter to the writer that

---

* Vide Hudson's *Sudbury, Wayland and Maynard*, pp. 4, 5.
† See *History of Westboro* (Deforest & Page), for description of " Brigham Farm " and account of John Brigham's grant, pp. 459 and 19.
‡ Same, p. 31. " Town Rate in 1680 for John Brigham *et al.* to kill rattle-snakes " (q. v.).
Same, p. 42. " Petition of John Brigham & 30 others in 1716, Nov. 23, for lots west of Marlboro for a town; it was first movement towards incorporation of Shrewsbury."

he did not think any one knew the grave of John Brigham. The late James S. Draper of Wayland (E. Sudbury) stated that as far as he was aware, no gravestones of Brighams existed in that town. With reference to the present condition of the old burying-grounds in Worcester Co., see Jewett's *History*, also Hudson's *History of Sudbury*.

WILL OF JOHN[2] BRIGHAM

In The Name of God Amen. The Fourteenth Day of September Anno Domini One Thousand Seven Hundred and twenty-eight and in ye Second Year of ye Reign of our Sovereign Lord George the Second by ye Grace of god of Great Brittan France & Ireland King Defender of ye faith I John Brigham Senr. of Sudbury in ye County of Middlesex In his Majesties Province of ye Massachusetts Bay in New England Yeoman: Being very aged but of perfect mind & memory Thanks be Given to God: therefore Calling unto mind the mortality of my Body and Knowing that it is appointed for all men once to Die Do make and ordain this my last will and testament that is to Say principally and first of all: I give and Recommend my soul into ye hands of god that gave it me and my Body I recommend to ye Earth to be Buried in Decent Christian Burial att ye Discrestion of my Executor hereafter named Nothing Doubting but at ye General Resurrection I shall Receive the same again by the mighty Power of god, and as touching such worldly Estate wherewith it hath Pleased God to Bless me in this Life, I Give Demise & Dispose of ye same in ye following manner & forme. Imprimis My Will Is That my Executor First of all Should Pay all my just Debts and Funerall Charges out of my Personal Estate.

Item: My Will is that my well beloved wife Sarah Brigham Enjoy one Third Part of all my Houseings, Orchards, Lands & meadows whatsoever Dureing natural Life & One Third part of my moveable Estate Forever, viz:————After my Just Debts & Funeral Charges Being paid as above Said.

Item: My Will Further Is That my Son John Brigham his heirs and assigns Shall have my homestead That is all my Lands Orchards & Meadows Which I Bought of Robbart man In Said Sudbury with all my Other Lands and Meadows adjoining or Belonging thereunto with all ye Buildings that Thereon is Allso I give & Bequeath unto him his heirs and assigns my Gulfe Meadow in Said Sudbury Allso Five acres of Land Laid out to ye Right of Mr. Robbart Fordom in Said Sudbury joyning to and bounded Easterly by land in ye Possession of Peter Plimpton All which is

Upon Condition that my said son John Brigham shall within Two
Months Next after my Decease Give or Tender to Give Sufficent
Security for ye payment of Two Hundred & Forty Pounds unto my
Four Daughters as namely Sarah Mary Hannah & Mercy: that is to
Each of them ye sum of Sixty Pounds apiece to be paid to Them
Their Heirs or assigns In Four Payments ye First Payment not
to be made until one year after my Decease and then Sixty Pounds
a year untill One Year after my Decease and Then Sixty Pounds
a year untill ye Two Hundred & Fourty Pound be Payd: Further-
more my will is that all my lands In Sudbury Marlborough and
Westborough not Desposed of as above Said Shall be Equally
Divided to & Amongst my Children Namely John Brigham Junr
Sarah Goodenow, Mary Fay Hannah Ward & Mercy Perry to
them Their Heirs and Assigns forever: Furthermore it is my will
and order That my Four Daughters Above mentioned their Heirs
or assigns shall take ye above said John Brighams part in ye above
mentioned outlands In part of pay to them or their Heirs of ye
Legacy of Two Hundred & Fourty Pounds above mentioned:
By a Just Apprizement In Case They Do Not agree Other ways
uppon his offering & Secureing of it to them & their Heirs forever
& The Rest to be payed in Cattle or Bills of Credit or money as
it passes from man to man. Furthermore it is my will that all
my Rights in Common in Sudbury; Marlborough; & Westborough
Shall be Equally Divided amongst all my Children. Furthermore my will is That all my Personal or Moveable Estate not
Disposed of As Above Said Shall Be Equally Divided amongst
all my Children namely John Brigham Thomas Brigham Sarah
Goodenow, Mary Fay Hannah Ward & Mercy Perry. And Furthermore as a Reason why I have not Given to my son Thomas
Brigham no more in this my Last will & Testament is because I
have Given him by Deed of Gift in Land and Housings & Other
ways about Four Hundred pounds. Further the Reason why I
have given To my Son Thomas Brigham so much in Time Past by
Deed of Gift and Other ways was Partly in Consideration of his
Living so much Longer with me Then The Rest of my Children:
Furthermore it is my will that my Executor Pay ye Sum of five
pounds apeice out of my above mentioned outlands To Japhet
and Lydia Perry when they come of age in Money or Bills of
credit: Memorandum I Give to my Wife Sarah Brigham as a
Token of my Love to her ye Curtains that Shee made her selfe &
ye Lesser of ye Two Brass Kettles Free & Clear to come into no
apprizement with ye Rest of ye Estate. Furthermore it Is My
Will That all ye Deeds of Gifts Given To Any of my Children
I Ratify & Confirm to be to them & their Heirs forever and

that if any of ye above mentioned Children Molest Each Other by Vertue of my Lands Given Them by Deeds of gift Shall by These Presents forever be Bared and Excluded from haveing any Right Title or Interest of or unto any of my Estate both Real & personal above named. And furthermore my will is That my Children Shall give Deeds of Quit Claim Each to Other if it Be Requested or Demanded by them before ye Division of my Estate amongst my said Children Above named in this my Last will & Testament. Furthermore I constitute make & ordain my well beloved son John Brigham my Sole Executor to this my Last will and Testament In Witness whereof I: ye Said John Brigham Senr. have hereunto set my Hand & Seal the Day and Year above mentioned.

John Brigham Senr
+   (Seal)
his mark

Signed Sealed Published
pronounced & Declared by
ye Said John Brigham
as his last will and testament
in presence of us ye subscribers
John Eveleth
Daniel Haynes
Jotham Brown
Uriah Moore

    Furthermore it is my will & order that if ye above named Mary Fay does proceed in marring against my will with one Tounsend School master late of Westbury that I do alow her but five shillings out of my Estate & her legacy above mentioned but it is my will and order that ye legacy made to her shall Return to ye Children to be divided amongst them and not to be paid untill two years after my decease and to be at ye disposal of my Executor and Gershom Fay. This was writ before signing & sealing.

(The inventory of his personal estate amounted to £186, 11s. 9d.)

Children (by first wife), the two youngest born in Sudbury; the others born in Marlboro:
    i John³, b. 19 Aug., 1667; d. 2 Dec., 1667.
12 ii Sarah, b. 27 March, 1674.
13 iii Mary, b. 6 May, 1678.
14 iv John, b. Nov., 1680.
    v Hannah, b. 27 March, 1683; m. 2 Feb., 1708-9, Oliver, son of Increase Ward; b. Marlboro, 1686; res. Marlboro. Ch. (Ward):
      1 *Dinah⁴*, b. 26 Dec., 1709.
      2 *Experience*, b. 25 Sept., 1711; m. 26 April, 1733, Jesse Smith of Lexington, Mass.

3 *Thankful*, b. 9 May, 1713.
4 *Deborah*, b. 15 Jan., 1714-15.
5 *Hannah*, b. 15 Jan., 1714-15.
6 *Sarah*, b. 15 Jan., 1714-15.
   4, 5 and 6, triplets, d. in infancy.
15 vi Thomas, b. 6 May, 1687.
   vii Mercy, m. 23 March, 1715, Ebenezer Perry from Dedham to Sudbury. They res. in Sudbury; he d. intestate about 1732-3, and she m. (2) Samuel Streeter of Framingham, Mass. Ch. (Perry), b. Sudbury:
      1 *Obadiah⁴*, b. 19 Nov., 1716.
      2 *Sarah*, b. 24 Aug., 1718.
      3 *Ebenezer*, b. 28 Feb., 1721; not mentioned in settlement of his father's estate, 1732-1738.
      4 *Mary*, b. 7 Jan., 1723.
      5 *Esther*, b. 24 June, 1724.
      6 *Mercy*, b. 2 Sept., 1727.
      7 *Elizabeth*, b. 11 Oct., 1728.
   viii Samuel, m. 23 Aug., 1716, Abigail Monroe (or Moore); res. Sudbury, but had no children recorded.

5 HANNAH², daughter of Thomas¹ and Mercy (Hurd) Brigham; born in Cambridge, Mass., 9 March, 1649-50; died in Marlboro, Mass., Dec., 1719; married (1) Gershom Eames * of Marlboro, who went to Watertown, Mass., on the breaking out of King Philip's War, where he died 25 Nov., 1676; married (2) William, son of William - Ward (who was in Sudbury as early as 1639, and owned land there); born in Sudbury, 22 Jan., 1640; died in Marlboro, 25 Nov., 1697.

The historians have had a good deal of trouble over Hannah with respect to her marriage, Morse having married her to Samuel Wells of Glastonbury, Conn., and Hudson (p. 357) concurring with the historian of Shrewsbury that Gershom Eames married Hannah Johnson, daughter of Solomon and Hannah Johnson. The Sudbury records show the birth of a Hannah, daughter of Solomon Johnson (who was Solomon, Jr.), but she would have been only 14 years old when Gershom Eames married Hannah Brigham. Paige corrects these errors (pp. 501-2), and we can support him with overwhelming evidence. Paige first quotes two Massachusetts public records; one wherein her name is given as Hannah Ward and another where William Ward, her husband, joins with Thomas², John², and Samuel² Brigham, in 1681, in conveying to Nicholas Fessenden certain of the Thomas¹ Brigham land in Cambridge. Paige continues:

" I do not find any Hannah Ward in that town who could represent herself as a daughter of Thomas Brigham, except the wife of William Ward, who united with the Brighams in the sale of

* The name in the early records is spelled with an E, but most of the families have dropped the E and spell it *Ames* (Hudson's *History of Marlboro*, p. 358).

the Cambridge land. This Hannah had been the wife of Gershom
Eames; and is supposed by her descendant, Andrew H. Ward, in
his *History of Shrewsbury* (p. 457) to have been a daughter of
Samuel Johnson of Sudbury. But I think it more probable that
Thomas Brigham was her father, and that John Brigham, who
witnessed the execution of her will, Oct. 30, 1714, was her brother."

Hannah Eames had two children: Hannah (named for herself)
and a posthumous daughter, Mary. She lived in Marlboro both
before and after her marriage to Mr. Ward, although she probably
accompanied her first husband to Watertown at the time of King
Philip's War. In her will, executed 30 Oct., 1714, she makes
pathetic reference to the boy Elisha, who was killed or stolen
by the Indians. After the usual introductory formula, she devises
as follows:

WILL OF HANNAH BRIGHAM-EAMES-WARD

FIRST: I will that all those debts and duties as I do owe in
Right or conscience to any person or persons whatsoever shall
well and truly be paid in convenient time after my decease by my
Executor hereafter named.

Item: I give to my well beloved son Gershom Ward whom I
likewise constitute make and ordain my onely and sole executor
of this my last will and testament and all my lands and other
Estate which I shall dye seazed by him freely to be possessed, he
fulfilling those things hereafter specified: First I will that he the
aforesaid Gershom doe take the sole care of my daughter Hannah
Eames and provid for her both in sickness and in health with the
help of what Estate she hath and what of right belongs to her
during her Natural Life. And further it is my plesuer that the
Bed and Bedding which she uses and a white cow and all the
puter that I shall leve that is marked with Eames leters with all
her other things be called hers: it is my will also that his heirs
or administrators stand obliged to the performance hereof and
her funeral to be at his charge.

Item: I will that there be paid unto my four other children
by my Executor above named to wit: to William and Nahum Ward
and to Mary Keyes and Bethiah Brigham twenty shillings apiece
within one year after my Decease and if Elisha shall ever come
again that my executor pay him twenty shillings also and if any
of my children should dy before the time of payment then to their
heirs also. I apoint my well beloved kinsmen Samuel Goodenow
and Joseph Straten to be the over seer of this my will, Ratifying
and confirming this to be my last will and testament in witness

hereof I have set my hand and seal the Day and yeare above written.

her

Signed Sealed Published   Hannah H Ward   (Seal)
pronounced and Declared   mark
by the said Hannah Ward
as her last will and testament
in the presents of us the
subscribers viz:
John Brigham (original signature.)
Joshua Rice
Joseph Straten

Will filed Dec. 1719.
Record of Probate 27 June 1720
Inventory 2 Feb. 1721.

The inventory of her personal estate showed £85 15s. 9d. Her real estate was valued at £160, and consisted of 11 acres of pasture in Marlboro, 54 acres "wast" land and 5 acres of swamp and meadow in Marlboro.

Children (*Eames* or *Ames*), born probably in Marlboro:
i Hannah³, b. 3 Feb., 1675.
ii Mary (posthumous), b. 1677; d. 1772, æ. 95 yrs. and 1 mo.; m. 11 March, 1696, John, son of Elias and Sarah (Blanford) Keyes of Marlboro; moved to Shrewsbury about 1723; built a new house and part of the family slept in the new one and part in the old one, just before the building was completed. In Aug., 1723, both houses were burned and two of his sons sleeping in the new house perished. He was a Major and d. 1768, in his 94th year. Ch. (Keyes).
   Gershom⁴, b. 1 March, 1698; m. about 1718, Sarah ———— moved to Boston and became wealthy; 5 ch.
   2 Mary, b. 24 Oct., 1700; m. 1720, Daniel Rand.
   3 Solomon, b. 30 Aug., 1703; m. Sarah ————. 2 ch.
   4 Hannah, b. 9 July, 1706; m. 1725, Gershom Flagg.
   5 Thankful, b. 24 May, 1709; m. 1728, Jonas Keyes.
   6 John, b. 30 April, 1712; burned to death, Aug., 1723.
   7 Sarah, b. 5 March, 1715; m. 21 Dec., 1721, Joshua Wilder.
   8 Stephen, b. 2 April, 1718; also burned to death, Aug., 1723.
Children (*Ward*) born in Marlboro (as per Hudson's History of Marlboro):
iii William, b. 27 March, 1680; m. Jane Cleveland, and res. in the part of Marlboro which is now Southboro. He rose to the rank of colonel and was a J. P. Ch:
   1 Hezekiah; 2 Elisha; 3 William; 4 Charles; et al.
iv Bethiah, m. Elnathan³ Brigham, 11.
v (Col.) Nahum, b. 18 Dec., 1684; m. 16 July, 1714, Martha, dau. of Capt. Daniel and Elizabeth (Kerley) Howe; b. 30 July, 1687;

followed the sea in early life, and then moved to Shrewsbury, where he was a Colonel, J. P., Rep. and Judge. Their sixth child was (Gen.) *Artemas*[4], b. 1727; grad. Harvard Coll., 1748, was Major in the French War; at the opening of the Revolution was appointed General and Commander-in-chief of all the forces raised by the Colony; he had command of the troops besieging Boston until the appointment of Washington as Commander-in-chief. He then commanded the right wing of the besieging army until the capitulation, after which he had command of the department of the East. He served several terms in Congress, was president of the governor's council, and until his death judge of the Court of Common Pleas for Worcester County.

vi Elisha, b. 12 Jan., 1686; was killed or taken captive by the Indians in Worcester, 1709, while riding post from Marlboro to Hadley.

vii Bathshebah, b. 16 May, 1689; d. 6 Oct., 1693.

viii Gershom, b. 3 Jan., 1693; rep. Marlboro, 1738; d. unm., 1739.

6 CAPT. SAMUEL[2], son of Thomas[1] and Mercy (Hurd) Brigham; born in Cambridge, Mass., 12 Jan., 1652; died in Marlboro, Mass., intestate, 24 July, 1713, æ. 61; married Elizabeth, daughter of Abraham and Hannah (Ward) Howe (who was a settler in Marlboro by 1660, and probably came from Roxbury, Mass.); born in Marlboro, 5 April, 1665; died there, 26 July, 1739, æ. 74.

Samuel, at the time of his mother's marriage to Edmund Rice, was 3 years old, and went with her to Sudbury and Marlboro. The glimpses we have of his early manhood are meagre. We first note that he had a " 25 acre grant in the first laying out of Worcester, in 1673; it lying in the Eastern Squadron next to the County Road to Boston." He was a lieutenant of Capt. Thomas Howe and was rewarded by government for military services in Queen Anne's War. A garrison was established at his house in this war. Feb. 25, 1694, he sold 2 lots of meadow in Marlboro to Thomas Beman. In 1707 he drew a lot of 21 acres and a lot of 103 acres south of Tobacco Meadow, bounded by the path to his Stony Brook Meadow, where, in his right, his heirs drew other lots. April 23, 1708, he purchased of Obadiah Ward, Jr., a 10½-acre right in the lands of Marlboro; and in that year he became bound for Joseph Parre to Francis Holmes of Boston in the penal sum of £100. In the years 1699 and 1703, it has been stated, he was town treasurer, although Hudson says that the town records for that period are missing. He was selectman in 1707 and 1710, and representative to the General Court in 1697-99 and in 1705. According to Hudson, he resided three-fourths of a mile east of the East Village, near the old tanyard of the late Capt. Daniel Brigham.

To Samuel Brigham is due the honor of founding in old Marlboro the tanning and shoe trades. Many of Samuel's descendants are in the shoe business in Marlboro, in one capacity or another, as are also the descendants of Thomas². The first tannery in the town was erected by Samuel² about 1700, near his dwelling house on present East Main Street, one-quarter of a mile east of the old Village Academy. This tannery, which is said to have been the first west of Charlestown, descended in regular succession (Jedediah³, Winslow⁴, Daniel⁵) to Capt. Daniel⁶, who retired from active business in the early 1850's, when the tannery ceased to be used. In 1859 Capt. Daniel's son Dennison owned the site. For many years the tannery was being taken down piecemeal, and it was wholly demolished by 1876. The place is now owned by Francis C. Curtis, who married a Brigham, and through the kindness of Timothy Brigham Patch, we were permitted to see the outlines of the tanyard as it looked some fifty or a hundred years ago when the plant was at its highest development. An eye witness in 1894 might have seen a rectangular field by the roadside (Main Street), of about an acre in extent, enclosed by stone walls, wherein towered a magnificent old elm; hard by an ancient well spring, covered by one of the stones formerly used for grinding bark (the other stones serving as a backdoor step at the house of Mr. Curtis, a few rods distant). To the north of the spring were remains of the old Samuel " flats," of small size, whose chestnut timbers are well preserved. Near by used to stand a curry shop, bark shed, bark mill, and a second curry shop which served sometimes for a dwelling. This last has been converted into a house known as " Glen Cottage." The main part of the old Jedediah³ house is about 20 x 40 feet, falling off to a leanto on the side, which was built in 1718 or thereabouts. It has been removed to No. 36 School Street. An ell had been removed to an adjoining lot a short time before we saw the house.

Samuel Brigham lies buried in the Old Cemetery in the rear of the Academy in Marlboro, the only one of the second generation of Brighams whose grave is marked. The headstone is rather ornate. Undoubtedly Thomas² and his mother also lie in this cemetery, but the places are unknown. Samuel² died intestate. The widow and eldest son, Samuel³, were appointed administrators of the estate, and John² Brigham appears on their bond. She was made guardian of the younger children. The inventory made soon after his death amounted to £1263 8s. At this time the land was estimated at £800. On 12 March, 1719-20 a Commission, appointed by the Judge of Probate, rendered their statement. These gentlemen were, John Maynard, a son-in-law, Caleb Rice, Nathan Brigham and William and Nahum Ward, the last three being nephews of the deceased Capt. Brigham. They valued the estate at £2191, 4s. They set off to the widow in right of dower half the dwelling house and about 237 acres of land. The whole valued at £730 8s. Samuel, the eldest son, received the other half of the dwelling house and 136 acres of land besides " Rock Island, the Cedar Swamp and the Rights," the whole consisting of " Land, Improvements and Buildings," valued at £603 19s. He was to pay Jotham, his brother, £132 16s.; the same to Lydia, the third daughter; to Hepsibah, £36 4s., and to Persis, the fourth daughter, £36 11s. Jedediah, the second son, received 258 acres of land, valued at £230, he paying to Hepsibah £37, 3s, and to Persis, £60 1s. Timothy, the fourth son, received 65 acres of land and some meadow and other lots valued at £173 17s., he paying to Hepsibah, £41 1s. Charles, the fifth son, had 87¾ acres of the first division of the land and some meadow and swamp valued at £142 6s. 8d., he to pay Hepsibah, £9 10s. 8d. Antipas received 104 acres, and certain Rights, he paying Hepsibah, £8 17s. 4d. Elizabeth, the eldest daughter, received a little more than 59 acres of land valued at £169, she to pay Persis, £36 4s. As will be seen by the foregoing, Samuel² was a large landowner and it is evident that he was a character of great weight in the community.

Children, born in Marlboro:
   i Elizabeth³, b. 24 March, 1685; m. 16 Oct., 1711, Samuel Robinson.
   ii Hepsibah, b. 25 Jan., 1686; m. 1719, John, son of John, Jr., and Lydia (Ward) Maynard.
16   iii Samuel, b. 25 Jan., 1689.
17   iv Lydia, b. 6 March, 1691.
18   v Jedediah, b. 8 June, 1693.
19   vi Jotham, b. 23 Dec., 1695.
20 vii Timothy, b. 10 Oct., 1698.
21 viii Charles, b. 30 Dec., 1700.
      ix Persis, b. 10 July, 1703; m. 22 Nov., 1721, Edward Baker, Jr., b. Lynn, Mass., 16 July, 1696, a first settler of Westboro, Mass.; had 10 children, of whom we have a record of one. Ch. (Baker):
        1 *Samuel⁴*, b. Westboro, 27 Aug., 1722; he moved to Berlin, Mass., where he had a family; was Judge of the Court of Common Pleas, 1775-1795; Councillor and Senator; built a stone house in Berlin, which is still standing; the most prominent man in the town history; was at the battle of Lexington. A cut of his house is in the Hist. of Berlin, p. 269.
       x Antipas, b. 16 Oct., 1706; d. Grafton, Mass., 23 April, 1746. Less distinguished than his brothers; left a house and a farm of 260 acres in Grafton. Lieut. Nathan Brigham of Southboro was one of the appraisers of his estate, on which his brother Samuel of Marlboro administered, 7 June, 1747.

THIRD GENERATION

THIRD GENERATION

7 CAPT. NATHAN[3], son of Thomas[2] and Mary (Rice) Brigham; born in Marlboro, Mass., 17 June, 1671; died there 16 Feb., 1746-7; married (1) Elizabeth, daughter of Isaac and Frances (Woods) Howe (not, probably, the daughter of Abraham and Hannah [Ward] Howe, as stated in *Marlboro History*) of Marlboro; born 17 Jan., 1673; found dead, kneeling by a chair in her home, 29 March, 1733; married (2) Mehitable (Gould) widow of Jonas Eaton of Charlestown, Mass. (See Wyman's *Charlestown Genealogies and Estates,* pp. 130, 317).

Morse states that he settled on a part of the Thomas[2] homestead, his house being a garrison house in Queen Anne's War. He was a weaver. He inherited the town-right of his father and drew shares of the public land in this right. He held town offices and was 7 years a selectman and for the last time in 1738; was representative in 1726 and '30· April 5, 1733, he made his will, giving his son Thomas 100 acres where he then resided, a house, 6 acres of meadow in Marlboro and 70 acres in Sutton; also a 16 acre town-right, originally John Rediet Jr.'s. His wife, Mehitable, received £20 for a mourning suit, and Ephraim, who had the homestead, was to support her and pay her funeral expenses. March 26, 1746-7, the heirs signed an agreement dividing his estate.

Children, born in Marlboro:
22   i Nathan[4], b. 28 Nov., 1693.
23   ii Thomas, b. 22 Feb., 1695.
      iii Tabitha, b. 20 Aug., 1698; d. unm. 6 Feb., 1730-1.
24   iv Elizabeth, b. 4 Jan., 1699-1700.
25   v Sarah, b. 14 Dec., 1701.
26   vi Zipporah, b. 14 Sept., 1704.
27   vii Hannah, b. 9 March, 1706.
28   viii Ephraim, b. 20 Jan., 1707-8.

8 JONATHAN[3], "ENSIGN," son of Thomas[2] and Mary (Rice) Brigham; born 22 Feb., 1675, in Marlboro, Mass.; died there, 4 Jan., 1768, æ. 93; married 26 March, 1696, his cousin, Mary, daughter of John and Mary Fay (2); born in 1675; died 9 Nov., 1781.

He settled on a part of the Thomas[2] homestead in Marlboro, where he was tythingman, 1704; constable, 1714; moderator, 1715, and selectman in 1719, '22 and '32· He was commonly called the " Indian Warrior." One day while chopping in the woods he saw a savage preparing to take aim at him; he seized his own musket, stepped forward in full view, exclaiming as he did so, " Shoot straight, you dog." Both fired at the same moment, when the Indian dropped his gun, and giving a tremendous whoop, bounded high into the air and fell dead. His bullet passed close to the ear of Jonathan, who escaped unhurt.

Children, born in Marlboro:
29   i Keziah⁴, b. 1697.
30   ii Zerviah, b. 9 Oct., 1698.
     iii Mary, b. 27 Oct., 1701; and no further reported.
31   iv Ruth, b. 30 April, 1704.
     v Thankful, b. 4 Feb., 1705-6; d. 23 Sept., 1706.
32   vi Jonathan, b. 14 March, 1707.
     vii Thankful, b. 21 April, 1709; d. at Southboro, 9 March, 1796; unm.
33   viii Jesse, b. 10 July, 1710.
34   ix Joel, b. 2 Oct., 1714.
35   x James, b. 2 Oct., 1717.

9   DAVID³, son of Thomas² and Mary (Rice) Brigham; born in Marlboro, Mass., 12 April, 1678; died in Westboro, Mass., 26 June, 1750; married (1) Deborah ————, who died 11 Oct., 1708; married (2) 21 Aug., 1709, widow Mary (Leonard) Newton, who died 1 Dec., 1741 (see *Rice Family*); married (3) ————, who survived him.

Morse says that he was surveyor in Marlboro, 1711, but on the division of the town in 1717, was thrown into Westboro, where he held town offices, 7 years as sealer of leather, and 6 years as selectman. As one of the privileged class, he was, by the vote of the town, allowed a pew in the meetinghouse. He settled on a wild tract of about 500 acres, including the present Hospital Grounds and several adjacent farms in Westboro and Northboro, and built his house about 60 rods east of the present Insane Asylum. His house was burnt,* during his old age, with much of its contents. June 14, 1748, he made his will, ratifying deeds of farms and land which he had previously given to his children, and giving his wife room in his house and the use of all in-door movables which, after her decease, were to be equally divided among his children and his son-in-law, Edward Newton; but such as Jonas had supplied since the burning of the house were, on the strength of his word, to be first surrendered to him. To Jonas, who had already given security to provide for his step-

* " Oct. 16, 1737..........N.B. The Congregation disturbed P.M. by ye burning of Mr. David Brigham's House, but when the people gathered in again, and were composed, I went on with ye rest of my sermon. A very sorrowful Providence! a great Loss! but I trust ym and all of us to profit by it, yt our hearts may be taken off from temporal transitory Enjoyments."
" 18 Oct., 1737..........Proceeded to Mr. Brigham's to see their Desolations. A Sorrowful Sight! I desire heartily to sympathise."
" 19 Oct., 1737. Mr. Brigham's son David fetched away divers things which we lent ym in yeir necessity."
" 11 Nov. 1737. My oxen were at work for Mr. David Brigham's to cart stones "

mother, he gave a 14 acre town-right, a part of the right purchased by his father of Rice; also all his stock and tools for carpentry and husbandry, making some reservations for his daughter Deborah. He gave his apparel to be equally divided among his 5 sons. Jonas was to pay the funeral charges of his parents, and be the executor of the will. This trust he so far performed as to obtain the receipts of the heirs, 29 June, 1750, 3 days after the death of their father, but his will was not proved until 22 Aug., ensuing.

Children (by first wife), born in Marlboro:
36   i John[4], b. 22 April, 1704.
      ii David, b. 30 Sept., 1708; d. s. p., 29 Nov., 1741, 2 days before his stepmother.
Children by second wife:
37   iii Silas, b. 9 Aug., 1710.
      iv Jemima, b. 24 Aug., 1712; m. Edward Newton; perhaps his second wife.
      v Deborah, b. 17 Sept., 1714; m. 14 Nov., 1752, Francis Harrington of Worcester, Mass. Ch. (Harrington), b. W.:
            1 *Mary[6]*, b. 16 Dec., 1753; m. 13 Feb., 1777, Jonathan Stone, Jr., of Worcester; no ch. recorded at Worcester.
            2 *Prudence*, b. 20 April, 1755; m. 6 July, 1780, Josiah Perry of Worcester; ch. (Perry):
                  i Josiah[6]; ii Mindwell; iii Nathan; iv Sophia; v William.
            3 *William*, b. 18 Nov., 1756; m. 29 May, 1781, Mary Perry; no ch. recorded at Worcester.
38   vi Levi, b. 21 Aug., 1716.
39 vii Jonas, b. 25 Feb., 1718.
40 viii Asa, b. 2 Dec., 1721.

10   GERSHOM[3], son of Thomas[2] and Mary (Rice) Brigham; born in Marlboro, Mass., 23 Feb., 1680; died there, 3 Jan., 1748-9; married 18 May, 1703, Mehitabel, daughter of Joseph and Experience (Wheelock) Warren, born in 1684. (This Joseph Warren was an early settler of Medfield and his wife's father, Ralph Wheelock, was the founder of the town. The latter held the degree of A. M. from Clare College, Cambridge, Eng. His house was burned in King Philip's War.)

Gershom settled on the homestead of his father in Marlboro, and was surveyor for the west end of the town, 1710; tythingman, 1716; constable, 1721; one of a committee to " seat the meeting," 1727; selectman, 1733. It is probably a mistake that Morse calls him " Doctor."

Children, born in Marlboro:
41   i Martha[4], b. 6 Oct., 1704.
42   ii Joseph, b. 21 Apr., 1706.
      iii Abigail, b. 25 Nov., 1708; m. 25 March, 1729, John Snow of Marlboro; they probably moved away. Ch. (Snow), b. Marlboro:
            1 *John[5]*, b. 25 Nov., 1729.
43   iv Gershom, b. 4 Nov., 1712.
44   v Benjamin, b. 19 Feb., 1714-15.

11   ELNATHAN[3], son of Thomas[2] and Mary (Rice) Brigham; born in Marlboro, Mass., 7 March, 1683; died in Mansfield or Coventry, Conn., 10 April, 1758; married in 1705, Bethiah, daughter of William and Hannah (Brigham) Ward. Bethiah died in Coventry, Conn., 15 April, 1765, æ. 82. He drew 17 acres in his father's right; was surveyor in 1715; removed to Mansfield, Conn., 1717.

Children, the six elder born in Marlboro, the two younger in Mansfield.
  i Uriah[4], b. 30 April, 1706; d. 9 July, 1710, in Marlboro.
  ii Jerusha, m. 1729, Benjamin Robinson of Windham, Conn.; had 2 sons and 3 daus.
  iii Priscilla, b. 3 April, 1709; m. 2 Jan., 1726, Matthias Marsh of Coventry, Conn. Ch. (Marsh), b. Coventry:
    1 *Elizabeth[5],* b. 1 Oct., 1727.
    2 *Matthias,* b. 28 Dec., 1729.
    3 *William,* b. 10 Jan., 1738.
    4 *Bethiah,* b. 2 Nov., 1743.
  iv Levinah (Morse says " Dinah "), b. 31 Aug., 1711; d. s. p., 8 March, 1749; m. 16 Dec., 1729, John Fay, son of 2; b. in Marlboro, 30 Nov., 1669; d. 5 Jan., 1747; he m. (1) Elizabeth Wellington, by whom a large family.
  v Prudence, b. 28 Jan., 1715; d. 3 Feb., 1715, in Marlboro.
45 vi Elnathan, b. 7 April, 1716.
46 vii Paul.
47 viii Uriah, b. about 1723.

12   SARAH[3], daughter of Dr. John[2] and Sarah Brigham; born in Marlboro, Mass., 27 March, 1674; married Samuel, son of Samuel Goodenow (who was the son of Samuel, who was son of Thomas, a petitioner from Marlboro); born in Marlboro, 30 Nov., 1675; died 12 May, 1716. The elder Samuel had a garrison house in 1711, in the present town of Northboro; it was his daughter who met with the tragic death by the Indians.

Children (Goodenow), born in Marlboro:
  i David[4], b. 26 Feb., 1704; m. 29 Dec., 1746, Martha Bannister. Ch.:
    1 *Sybil[5];* 2 *Lovina;* 3 *John;* 4 *Stephen;* 5 *Adina;* 6 *Mary;* 7 *Martha;* 8 *Calvin;* 9 *Ebenezer.*
  ii Jonathan, b. 16 July, 1706; d. 25 Dec., 1803, in Westboro; m. 20 Feb., 1727, Lydia Rice, who d. 4 Dec., 1747. Ch.:
    1 *Lydia[5];* 2 *Mary;* 3 *Jonathan;* 4 *Levi;* 5 *Ebenezer;* 6 *Surviah;* 7 *Tabitha;* 8 *Submit.*
  iii Thomas, b. 18 May, 1709; m. 7 Apr., 1734, Persis, dau. of **Edward** Rice of Marlboro and sister of Lydia *supra.*
  iv Mary, b. 5 April, 1712; m. 6 Jan., 1731, Beriah Rice, a loyalist, who moved to Nova Scotia.

13   MARY[3], daughter of Dr. John[2] and Sarah Brigham; born in Marlboro, Mass., 6 May, 1678; married Gershom, son of John and Mary (Brigham) Fay; born in Marlboro, 19 Oct., 1681; died 24 Nov., 1720. He was a first settler of Northboro.

On the 18th of August, 1707, as Mrs. Fay and Miss Mary, daughter of Samuel Goodenow, Sr., were gathering herbs near the Goodenow Garrison House (situated near the stream known as Stirrup Brook, on the " great " road), a party of 20 or more Indians issued from the woods and came towards the two women, who immediately ran for the fort. Miss Goodenow was lame and was soon captured, dragged across the brook to a wood on the hillside, killed and scalped and there her mangled remains were afterward buried. Mrs. Fay reached the fort and succeeded in closing the gate before the Indians could capture her. There was one man in the garrison, the rest being at work in the fields. The savages tried to break through the inclosure, but the man in the fort fired all the muskets in the place as fast as Mrs. Fay could load and hand them to him, and was thus able to repel the Indians until the men outside, hearing the report of the muskets, came to their relief. Mrs. Fay's heroism saved her two children's lives.

Children (Fay), born in Marlboro:
  i Gershom⁴, b. 17 Sept., 1703; m. Hannah ————.
  ii Mary, b. 10 July, 1705; m. George Smith.
  iii Susanna, b. 18 Nov., 1707; subject to constant nervous trembling, believed to have been caused from her mother's fright over the Indians before her birth.
  iv Sarah, b. 2 Oct., 1710; m. Timothy Billings.
  v Silas, b. 12 Aug., 1713; m. Hannah ————.
  vi Timothy, b. 26 June, 1716; m. 1738, Lydia Tomblin; res. Northboro.
  vii Paul, b. Aug., 1719; d. 28 March, 1790; m. 1752, Rebecca Rice, who d. 26 Jan., 1807, æ. 75. Ch.:
    1 *Nahum⁵*, b. 27 July, 1757; m. Lucy Warren.
    2 *Asa*, b. 19 Sept., 1761; m. widow Grace Mahan.
    3 *Persis*, b. 11 Dec., 1768; m. Col. William Eager.

14 JOHN³, son of Dr. John² and Sarah Brigham; born in Marlboro, Mass., Nov., 1680; died, probably in Sudbury, 16 Sept., 1729; married Martha ————, who died 13 Nov., 1734.

Morse tells us that John probably inherited the homestead of his father in Sudbury, and as his executor, 30 Dec., 1728, exhibited to the Registry of Probate for Middlesex County an inventory of his estate amounting to £203.16.9, but died before proceeding further, leaving his wife Martha to complete the settlement, and also to administer upon his own estate. This she undertook, but, in her turn, died before completing either and was succeeded by her daughter Hannah, æ. 21, who accomplished the undertaking, paying out of her grandfather, Dr. John's estate, £74.18.1 to each of her aunts, Goodenow, Fay, and Ward, and to her aunt Perry £57.1.4, and a bequest to Jeptha Perry;

and to her uncle Samuel, his father's oxen. His real estate is presumed to have been conveyed mostly to his sons during his lifetime. The inventory of John Jr.'s estate, presented by his widow, 8 March, 1730, amounted to £487.5.3. At his death he was one of the selectmen of Sudbury.

Children, born in Sudbury:
    i Hannah⁴, b. 4 Feb., 1712-13; not reported after 1734; probably d. unm.
48 ii Samuel, b. 27 April, 1716.
49 iii Sarah, b. 29 March, 1718.
    iv *John, b. 1 April, 1720; m. 12 March, 1750, Abigail Johnson; probably went to Willington, Conn., " 6 Nov., 1763," according to " dismissal " from Sudbury church; no ch. recorded at Willington. Ch., b. Sudbury:
       1 *Abigail⁵*, b. 5 Dec., 1751.
    v Phebe, b. 5 Oct., 1721; m. ———— Hubbard.
    vi Abigail, b. 31 Dec., 1723; m. ———— Prescott.

Morse states that these children, except the eldest, having been left in their minority, Samuel chose David Haynes for his guardian, but Sarah, Phebe and Abigail, 10 Feb., 1734, were placed under the guardianship of John Green until 3 April, 1738, when Sarah, having married Samuel Brown, her sisters chose him for their guardian, and probably removed with them to Rutland. Brown received his discharge in Middlesex County, 24 June, 1745, with the receipts of Phebe Hubbard and Abigail Prescott.

15 THOMAS³, son of Dr. John² and Sarah Brigham; born in Marlboro, Mass., 6 May, 1687; married 24 Dec., 1724, Elizabeth Bowker. He settled in Sudbury, Mass., but probably removed to Rutland, Mass.

Children, born in Sudbury:
50 i John⁴, b. 14 Sept., 1726.
    ii Sarah, b. 10 March, 1735; m. 13 March, 1765, Reuben Willis of Sudbury. Ch. (Willis), b. Sudbury:
       1 *Asa⁵*, b. 2 Sept., 1765.
       2 *Sarah*, b. 24 April, 1768.
       3 *Mary*, b. 11 Oct., 1770.
       4 *Asa*, b. 17 Feb., 1773.
       5 *Eunice*, b. 28 July, 1775.
       6 *Reuben*, b. 5 Jan., 1779.
       7 *Joel*, b. 17 Aug., 1781.
51 iii Abijah, b. 26 Aug., 1737.

16 CAPT. SAMUEL³, son of Capt. Samuel² and Elizabeth (Howe) Brigham; born in Marlboro, Mass., 25 Jan., 1689; died in Grafton, Mass., 1 Sept., 1771; married 23 Aug., 1716, Abigail Moore, who died 20 Nov., 1731, æ. 35. Curiously, both Morse and Hudson, in their respective histories, say that Samuel, son of Dr.

* *Colonial War Record:* On alarm list, 2d Sudbury Co., Capt. Josiah Richardson, 1757.

John Brigham, also married Abigail Moore on the foregoing date, besides giving the marriage as here entered.

Morse says in part: In Dec., 1727, leave was granted by the General Court to him and 39 others (among them Charles and Nathan Sr. of Marlboro) to purchase Grafton of the Indians, under restrictions and conditions which seem to have been strictly observed. Samuel settled in the south part of Marlboro and served her in all the offices in her gift, particularly as moderator of meetings, assessor, 1739, '40, town treasurer (not named by Hudson), town clerk, 1754, 1755, selectman, 1741, '42, '44, '46, '48, '49, '54; in 1716, one of a committee " to seat the meeting." 1747-49 he administered upon the estate of his brother Antipas. Samuel left a large estate; settled without an administrator.

Children, born in Marlboro.
    i Samuel⁴, b. 13 June, 1717; d. 14 June, 1717.
    ii Sybillah, b. 15 Oct., 1718; d. 27 Sept., 1807; m. 1736, **Eleazer** Goddard, a farmer of Framingham and Athol, Mass., who d. 18 Nov., 1762.*
    iii Mary, b. 13 April, 1720.
    iv Abigail, b. 10 Dec., 1721; d. 27 Sept., 1755.
52   v Samuel, b. 3 March, 1723.
    vi Phineas, b. 18 Dec., 1725; d. 23 Aug., 1736.
53   vii Uriah, b. 10 Sept., 1727.
54 viii George, b. 17 March, 1730.

17   LYDIA³, daughter of Capt. Samuel² and Elizabeth (Howe) Brigham; born in Marlboro, Mass., 6 March, 1691; married, 5 April, 1711,* Jonathan, son of Thomas and Sarah (Hosmer) Howe; (his grandfather John Howe was one of the petitioners from Marlboro of 1657); he died in Marlboro, 22 June, 1738, æ. 51.

Children (Howe), born in Marlboro:
    i Timothy⁴, b. 24 May, 1712; d. 15 Oct., 1740.
    ii Prudence, b. 3 Nov., 1714; m. Isaac Howe of Leicester, Mass.
    iii Bezaleel, b. 19 June, 1717; m. Anna ————, who d. 28 June, 1773. Ch.:
       1 *Susanna⁵; 2 Timothy; 3 Edith; 4 Darius; 5 Bezaleel.*
    iv Charles, b. 30 April, 1720; m. Lydia ————. Ch.:
       1 *Theodore⁵; 2 Calvin.*
    v Eliakim, b. 17 Jan., 1723; m. 15 Dec., 1747, Rebecca **Howe**; moved to Henniker, N. H. Ch.:
       1 *Otis⁵; 2 Tilly; 3 Rhene; 4 Anna; 5 Molly; 6 Jonathan.*
    vi Lucy, b. 20 March, 1726.
   vii Lydia, b. 12 April, 1729; d. y.
  viii Mary, b. 12 Aug., 1730; d. y.
    ix Lydia, b. 29 June, 1732; m. 21 Sept., 1752, Timothy Goodenow.

* *Genealogies of Watertown*, p. 256.
* There is a mistake in the *History of Marlboro* in regard to the month of this marriage; three different dates are there given, and Morse gives another. The marriage was in either May or April.

18   LIEUT. JEDEDIAH³, son of Capt. Samuel² and Elizabeth (Howe) Brigham; born in Marlboro, Mass., 8 June, 1693; died 21 May, 1763; married 18 May, 1720, Bethiah, daughter of Joseph and Dorothy (Martin) Howe, born 7 March, 1695; died 23 June, 1756.

Morse tells us that Jedediah inherited the tannery and seems to have settled at the homestead.   He served in many minor town-offices and particularly in those of selectman (1741, '43, '47 and '52), sealer of leather, etc.   In 1746 he was chosen to a seat at the Concord Court as petit juryman.   He owned lands at Prince-ton, Bolton, Lancaster and Marlboro.   Dec. 21, 1762. " being in-firm in body and mind," he made his will, bestowing his estate upon his children.   To Winslow he left the homestead and tannery, half a mile east of Spring Hill, on the road from Marlboro to Boston, and made him his sole executor.   The will was proved 13 June, 1763.

Children, born in Marlboro:
55   i   Dorothy⁴, b. 2 March, 1721.
56   ii Solomon, b. 25 May, 1723.
57   iii Francis, b. 13 Aug., 1725.
58   iv Lucy, b. 15 May, 1727.
       v   Bethiah, b. 31 March, 1729; d. 7 Oct., 1745.
59   vi Stephen, b. 2 Nov. or 11 Feb., 1731 or 1732.
       vii Abner, b. 1734; d. Princeton, Mass.; unm., 1821, æ. 87.
60   viii Winslow, b. 30 Aug., 1736.

19   JOTHAM³, son of Capt. Samuel² and Elizabeth (Howe) Brigham; born in Marlboro, Mass., 23 Dec., 1695; died 23 Nov 1759; married Abigail ————, who died as his widow, 24 March, 1768.   He settled in Marlboro and served often as surveyor; 1734 was constable; 1738 petit juryman; 1745 on the school-committee.

Children, born in Marlboro:
61   i   Betty⁴, b. 15 Nov., 1719.
62   ii Abraham, b. 25 Feb., 1720-1.
       iii Edmund, b. 15 Nov., 1724; he was in the Colonial Wars under Capt. Timothy Brigham.
       iv Oliver, b. 4 Sept., 1727; m. 9 Aug., 1757, Sherah, dau. of Jonathan Johnson of Marlboro; b. 5 March, 1736; he moved to Petersham, Mass., where selectman 1769.
63   v   Asa, b. 1 Nov., 1729.
       vi Persis, b. 2 Jan., 1734.
       vii Abigail, b. 9 July, 1737; d. 11 Sept., 1740.
64   viii Antipas, b. 25 May, 1740.
65   ix Abigail, b. 22 April, 1745.

20   COL. TIMOTHY³, son of Capt. Samuel² and Elizabeth (Howe) Brigham; born in Marlboro, Mass., 10 Oct., 1698; died in Southboro, Mass., 1 Oct., 1775; married (1) Martha, daughter of Jonathan and Mary (Kerley) Johnson; born in Marlboro, 26

Jan., 1701; died 23 Sept., 1757; married (2) 12 April, 1759,
Mrs. Sarah, daughter of Rev. Mr. Prentice of Lancaster, Mass.,
and widow of Dr. Joshua Smith, who died in Shrewsbury, Mass.,
1756. (She had 5 sons and 1 daughter by first m.)

Col. Timothy was a soldier, a patriot and a very distinguished
citizen, and was in the Colonial Wars. A leader in the movement
to set off Southboro from Marlboro, the first town-meeting of
Southboro was held at his house, 14 Aug., 1727. He was often
moderator of town-meetings; 24 years town treasurer of Southboro; selectman for the same number of years; conspicuous in
all municipal affairs; Representative, 1753, 1756 and 1769, and
among the first to take a stand with the colonies in the Revolutionary struggle; he was first on a committee of rights who reported
a series of spirited resolutions in 1773; he died during the siege
of Boston. He often acted as guardian to minors, and on 13
June, 1746, Jonathan Fay, son of John, receipted for such service.
His will made 4 May, 1774, gave his wife Sarah half of his
personal property and the improvement of one third of his real
estate; to her son, Joshua Smith, he gave the other half of his
personal property and the improvement, for seven years, of two
thirds of his real estate. After the death of his widow, and seven
years after his own decease, he gave all his real estate to his
nephew, George Brigham, son of his brother Samuel. To his
brother Charles he gave his best hat and wig and whatever might
be due from him to his estate; also Flavel's works, the *Exposition
of Genesis and Exodus,* and Dr. Coleman's work on the *Parable
of the Ten Virgins.* George Brigham was to pay his brother
Uriah £40, in instalments, and £40 to Timothy Smith, son of
Joshua, when he was twenty-one years old. To Baxter How,
whom he brought up, he bequeathed a cow and a debt which he
would owe the estate. He made his wife Sarah, and Joshua Smith,
his brother Charles, and nephew George Brigham his executors.
The will was proved 7 Nov., 1775. Col. Timothy had no children.
He was Capt. and Col. in 1757, from Southboro. See *Mass.
Archives.*

21 *CHARLES³, son of Capt. Samuel² and Elizabeth (Howe)
Brigham; born in Marlboro, Mass., 30 Dec., 1700; died in Graf-
ton, Mass., 17 March, 1781; married Mary Peters of Newport,
R. I., who was born 1716, and died 19 Feb., 1797.

Charles settled in Grafton after having disposed of his lands
in Marlboro, and he became, in 1727, one of the 40 proprietors
under the sanction of the General Court. Was one of the ablest

* *Colonial War Record:* (Probably in 1725) " Centinel " 3 weeks and 1 day in
Capt. Nathan Brigham's Troop of Horse. 25 March, 1757, with Capt. Sam. Warren.

and most distinguished of the citizens of Grafton, held the most
important town offices and was her Representative to the General
Court.   He was appointed by the Royal Governor, a magistrate,
an office of very great dignity, in his day, and one that was
sparingly bestowed.   He settled upon Brigham Hill, on a rich
tract of land, which was afterward the country residence of his
descendant, the late William Brigham of Boston.

Children, born in Grafton:
  i Charles⁴, b. 29 Oct., 1732; d. 21 Jan., 1755, unm.
  ii Daniel, b. 28 April, 1735; d. about 1759; * was a soldier at Crown
     Point at time of decease. Daniel was drafted into the army for
     the war of 1758. Just before leaving home, as he was passing
     up the road late one afternoon for the cattle, he was startled to
     see before him a man wrapped in an Indian blanket. He recognized
     the face and figure of the man as his own. It disappeared. His
     brother also saw the figure. He went to the war with the convic-
     tion that he would not return. He fell ill at Crown Point and when
     near the point of death an Englishman found him attended by a
     friendly Indian wrapped in an Indian blanket, and brought back
     the account to Grafton. The place where the apparition was seen
     is not far beyond the Brigham homestead in Grafton on the old
     road just after passing the long bridge.—*The Hundredth Town.*
  iii William, b. 26 March, 1739.
  iv Mary, b. 12 Dec., 1740; m. Moses Parks, and res. in New Marl-
     boro.
  v Sarah, b. 19 April, 1743; m. Moses Leland, Jr., a farmer; b. in
     Sutton, Mass., 1745; d. S., 1769. Ch. (Leland), b. in Sutton:
     1 *Charles⁵*, b. 1766; d. 1777.
     2 *Prudence,* b. 1769; m. Ephraim Harrington of Grafton. Ch.
       (Harrington): i Sally⁶; ii Mary; iii Martha; iv Prudence; v
       Harriet; vi Ephraim.
67   vi Anna, b. 18 March, 1745.
     vii Timothy, b. 23 Nov., 1747; d. 9 Feb., 1747-8.
68 viii Persis, b. 4 Jan., 1755.
     ix Elizabeth, m. Nahum Warren of Grafton, and probably d. s. p.

* *Colonial War Record:* 25 March, 1757, with Capt. Sam. Warren. 1759, Private,
Whipple's Co., Ward's Regt., 18 2-3 days at Pontosook (Pittsfield) to recruit forces.

FOURTH GENERATION

FOURTH GENERATION

22 *LIEUT. NATHAN[4], son of Nathan[3] and Elizabeth (Howe) Brigham, born in Marlboro, Mass., 28 Nov., 1693; died in Southboro, Mass., 15 Sept., 1784, æ. 91; married (1) 24 Dec., 1717, Dina, daughter of Edmund and Ruth (Parker) Rice of Westboro, Mass.; married (2) about 1729, Elizabeth (Ward) Snow.

Morse gathered the following facts: Prior to the second division of the original township of Marlboro, in 1727, Nathan held several minor town offices, but in the new town of Southboro, to which he was set off, he appears at once among her principal citizens, serving the first year as a selectman and soon after as treasurer. He was repeatedly placed on committees for hiring schoolmasters and chosen for the 29th time as a selectman at the age of 77 years, at which he remonstrated and was, with public thanks, excused. He lived near the houses of Samuel and Dana Brigham in the north part of Southboro, and is presumed to have inherited the lands southeast of Crane meadow, drawn in his grandfather Thomas' right. He did inherit the Bible, law-book, cane and sword of his father Nathan. He retained his vigor to a great age and when in his 90th year used to mount his horse without assistance.

Children (by first wife), born in Marlboro:
    i Dina[5], b. 5 Sept., 1719; m. 9 Nov., 1743, Jonathan Witt, Jr.
    ii Eunice, b. 4 Oct., 1721; m. 8 Sept., 1742, Hezekiah Newton (see Addenda).
69   iii Moses, b. 2 Jan., 1722.
    iv Persis, b. 3 April, 1724; d. 12 July, 1740.
70   v Elizabeth, b. 18 Dec., 1725.
Children (by second wife), born in Southboro:
71   vi Nathan, b. 13 March, 1730.
72   vii Hepsibah, b. 1 June, 1732.
73   viii Edmund, b. 12 Aug., 1733.
74   ix William, b. 8 April, 1735.
    x Phineas, b. 11 Oct., 1737; d. 16 July, 1740.
    xi Tabitha, b. 27 Aug., 1739; d. 5 July, 1740.
75   xii Ebenezer, b. 24 June, 1741.
76   xiii Elijah, b. 5 Sept., 1743.

23 †THOMAS[4], son of Capt. Nathan[3] and Elizabeth (Howe) Brigham; born in Marlboro, Mass., 22 Feb., 1695; died there, 25 Nov., 1765; married, 25 Jan., 1719-20, Sarah, daughter of Jo-

---

* *Colonial War Record:* Centinel (probably 1725), Capt. N. Brigham.
† *Colonial War Record:* First Marlboro Co., 1757.

seph and Sarah (Howe) Stratton, born in Marlboro, 30 Nov., 1700,* died there, his widow, 15 Sept., 1775. Her father was assigned to the garrison of Capt. Nathan Brigham, when she was 11 years old, and Thomas was 16.

Morse says that he settled in the south-west part of Marlboro, where he was constable and tythingman, and in 1740 and 1743, selectman, and sealer of leather 6 years; 1738 a petit jury-man, and 1731 member of a committee to procure a school-master; 1757 he administered on the estate of David Burnham of Southboro. 13 Aug., 1765, he made his will, giving to his wife Sarah the use of half his house; his pew in the meeting-house; all his household stuff, and his horse and chaise, while she remained his widow; $7\frac{1}{2}$ bushels of corn, $7\frac{1}{2}$ bushels of rye, $1\frac{1}{2}$ of wheat, all ground; 6 score weight of pork, 5 do. of beef; the apples, cider and sauces of all kinds that she might need; 2 cows and 5 sheep, kept summer and winter; 26s. 6d. in cash, and a supply of fire-wood, all to be supplied her annually by his sons Ithamar and Paul. To his sons Aaron, Ezekiel, and Elisha he gave one right in the great Crane swamp, to be equally divided between them, and each was to receive from his executors £20, within 3 years after his decease.

To his grand-daughter, Lydia Bigelow, he gave £133, to be paid her within 5 years after his death; also his desk and all his household stuff after the death of his wife, and all that belonged to her aunt, Sarah Brigham, provided she should marry and leave heirs of her body; but otherwise, all after her death should go to his children or their heirs; to Ithamar and Paul he gave his wearing apparel, his husbandry tools, and steelyard; and after the death of their mother, his clock, chaise and pew; and to Paul the half of his house reserved for her; his money and stock he ordered to be equally divided among his children and grand-children; to his sons Ithamar and Paul, he gave his homestead, and all his lands in Marlboro, Westboro and Southboro, and a right in little Crane swamp, and made them his executors. His will was proved 6 March, 1766. In 1858 his house, north of the then Alden Brigham place, was still standing.

Children:

77   i Aaron⁵, b. 17 March, 1720.
78   ii Lydia, b. 14 March, 1721-2.
79   iii Ezekiel, b. 14 Feb., 1723-24.
80   iv Elisha, b. 25 Nov., 1726.
81   v Ithamar, b. 6 Oct., 1729.
        vi Sarah, b. 12 March, 1731-32; d. unm., 21 July, 1765.
        vii Thomas, b. 23 April, 1734; d. 3 June, 1740.
82   viii Paul, b. 26 March, 1737.
        ix Ephraim, b. 6 April, 1739; d. 22 June, 1740.
        x Abner, b. 13 Jan., 1741-2; d. 28 Sept., 1746.

* *Histor   Marlboro; Morse sa s " ι οι "*

24   ELIZABETH[4], daughter of Capt. Nathan[3] and Elizabeth (Howe) Brigham; born in Marlboro, Mass., 4 Jan., 1699-1700; d. there, 11 Oct., 1757; married 25 April, 1722, John, son of Samuel Stow (who was in Marlboro by 1684, descended from John of Roxbury, emigrant of 1634; a member of the Ancient & Hon. Artillery Co.; in King Philip's War); born in Marlboro, 30 March, 1696; died there, 2 July, 1761.

Children (Stow), born in Marlboro:
  i *Elizabeth[5], b. 17 July, 1723; m. 20 May, 1752, John Eager of Marlboro; he d. 9 April, 1777. Ch. (Eager):
       1 *Joseph[6];* 2 *Luke;* and 2 d. y.
 ii Manasseh, b. 8 Nov., 1724; d. in Southboro, 1776; m. 17 Nov., 1747, Dinah Morse, b. in Marlboro, 8 Oct., 1729; she was descended from Joseph of Watertown.
 m Hannah, b. 14 July, 1726.
 iv Miriam, b. 7 Jan., 1729; d. 7 July, 1741.
  v Mary, b. 2 Sept., 1730; d. 11 Jan., 1814; m. 9 June, 1752, Asa Howe of Petersham; des. from John of Marlboro; b. there, 31 Jan., 1728. Ch. (Howe): *John[6]*, b. Marlboro.
 vi Keziah, b. 8 Sept., 1732; d. 17 Jan., 1823; m. 27 Nov., 1755, Abner, son of Joseph Morse, des. from Joseph of Watertown; b. Marlboro, 5 Nov., 1727; d. 3 June, 1810; moved to Paxton. Ch. (Morse):
       1 *Aaron[6];* 2 *Elijah;* 3 *Stephen;* 4 *Kezia.*
vii Abigail, b. 7 Aug., 1734; d. 25 Sept., 1823; m. 26 Dec., 1753, Ebenezer, son of Eben. Hagar; b. 16 March, 1728; d. in M., 19 Dec., 1798. Ch. (Hagar):
       1 *Joel[6];* 2 *Elizabeth;* 3 *Nancy;* 4 *Lovice;* 5 *Abigail;* 6 *Cate.*
viii Ephraim, b. 30 March, 1736;˙ d. 19 Oct., 1752.
 ix Sarah, b. 4 April, 1738; d. 17 Dec., 1804; m. 12 Feb., 1761, William, son of Eben Hagar, des. from William of Watertown; b. 21 April, 1733; d. 9 Jan., 1811. Ch. (Hagar):
       1 *Ephraim[6];* 2 *Lydia;* 3 *Eben;* 4 *William;* 5 *Martin.*
  x John, b. 17 Nov., 1740; d. 18 Feb., 1828; m. 4 June, 1766, Grace, dau. of Micah Newton; b. 12 June, 1746; d. 26 May, 1824. Ch.:
       1 *Elizabeth[6];* 2 *William;* 3 *Mary;* 4 *Sarah.*

25   SARAH[4], daughter of Capt. Nathan[3] and Elizabeth (Howe) Brigham; born in Marlboro, Mass., 14 Dec., 1701; died there, 5 Nov., 1744; married 14 Mch., 1727, Capt. Uriah, son of Zeruhbabel and grandson of William Eager (Morse has it "Hager,") of Marlboro; born there, 4 Apr., 1700; died there, 30 Dec., 1780; marched on the Lexington Alarm.   He married (2) Rebecca Rice, who d. s. p. 1790.

Children (Eager), by first wife, born in Marlboro:
  i Nathan[5], b. 9 Feb., 1731; m. 1755, Sarah Goodnow.
 ii Mary (or Sarah), b. 27 May, 1733.
iii Fortunatus, b. 6 July, 1735; m. 13 June, 1758, Mehitable Bigelow.
 iv Elizabeth, b. 21 Jan., 1737; d. 24 July, 1740.

* In one place the *History of Marlboro* says she died 25 May, 1750; again that
she was married 20 Ma   ₁   ain that she died in 180₁

    v Uriah, b. 5 Feb., 1740; m. 29 March, 1764, Tryphosa, dau. of
Joseph Bush; b. in Marlboro, 13 July, 1736; d. 8 Feb., 1802;
he d. 30 Sept., 1813; was in the Revolution. Ch.:
     1 *Rebecca*; 2 *Mary;* 3 *Triphena;* 4 *Moses;* 5 *Lydia; 6 Hep-
zibah.*

   vi Hannah, b. 29 Dec., 1741; m. 10 Feb., 1761, Uriah Newton, Jr.,
b. in M., 17 May, 1736; des. from Richard of Marlboro. Ch.
(Newton):
     1 *Jonathan*.

26 ZIPPORAH⁴, daughter of Capt. Nathan³ and Elizabeth
(Howe) Brigham; born in Marlboro, Mass., 14 Sept., 1704; died
there, 2 May, 1790; married John Warren Jr., born in Marlboro,
3 Apr., 1701; died 27 Dec., 1783; descended from John of Watertown, the emigrant of 1630. He was an important Marlboro
citizen.

  Children (Warren), born in Marlboro:
    i Elizabeth⁵, b. 31 March, 1734; m. 13 June, 1754, Asa Brigham, 63.
   ii John, b. 16 Oct., 1735; d. 25 Apr., 1737.
  iii Anne, b. 27 Aug., 1737; m. 26 Oct., 1757, Larkin, son of Col.
Abraham Williams, and grandson of Abraham, a proprietor of
Marlboro, in 1663; b. 29 Dec., 1728; moved to Chester about 1774,
where probably d. Ch. (Williams), b. Marlboro, except youngest:
     1 *Anna*; 2 *Ephraim;* 3 *John;* 4 *Larkin;* 5 *Louisa;* 6 *George;*
     7 *Anna;* 8 *William,* b. in Chester; settled in New Fane, Vt.,
and gave name of " Williamsville " to the place of his residence.
   iv Lieut. John, b. 19 June, 1739; m. 27 Jan., 1763, Rachel, dau. of
Jonathan Barnes; b. 13 July, 1740; a prominent citizen. Ch.:
     1 *Anna*; 2 *William.*
    v Persis, b. 9 Apr., 1741; m. ———— Arnold.
   vi Hastings, b. 20 Feb., 1743; d. 17 Nov., 1760, in Albany in the
French War.
  vii Catherine, b. 3 Nov., 1745; d. in M., 1 Feb., 1826; m. 21 Feb.,
1763, Bailey, son of Aaron Eager; b. in Marlboro, 7 Feb., 1741;
d. 26 Feb., 1790. Ch. (Eager):
     1 *Lucretia*; 2 *Abraham;* 3 *Stephen;* 4 *Jonathan.*
 viii Thaddeus, b. 20 March, 1747; d. 18 June, 1821; m. 27 Dec., 1770,
Lucy, dau. of Samuel Stevens; b. in M. 21 Jan., 1752; d. 17
June, 1821. Ch.:
     1 *Lydia*; 2 *John;* 3 *Samuel,* m. Betsey W. Brigham; 4 *Hastings;*
     5 *Lucy;* 6 *Sarah;* 7 *Edward,* a missionary to Ceylon; 8 *Eliza-
beth;* 9 *Sophia;* 10 *Millicent.*

27 HANNAH⁴, daughter of Capt. Nathan³ and Elizabeth
(Howe) Brigham; born in Marlboro, Mass., 9 March, 1706; was
living as late as 1783; married 7 June, 1732, Jabez, son of Caleb
Rice, and gr.-grandson of Edmund Rice the emigrant; born in
Marlboro, 2 Feb., 1702; died 1783.

  Children (Rice), born in Marlboro:
    i Hannah⁵, b. 9 March, 1737; d. 30 March, 1751.
   ii Caleb, b. 7 May, 1740; d. 28 Dec., 1776; grad. Harvard Coll.,

1764; m. Mary, dau. of Rev. Nathan Stone, first minister in
Southboro. Ch.:
    1 *Caleb*⁶*;* 2 *Nathan;* 3 *Ephraim;* 4 *Solomon.*
  iii Jabez, b. 17 July, 1746; d. 3 Nov., 1809; m. 27 June, 1776, Alice
Howe, who m. (2) Simon Goddard. Ch.:
    1 *Hannah*⁶*;* 2 *Sally;* 3 *Jabez;* 4 *Abel.*
  iv Noah, b. 10 Sept., 1751; d. 1 Oct., 1820; grad. Harvard Coll.,
1777; m. (1) 1778, Sarah Cazeneau of Boston, who d. 15 May,
1781; m. (2) Mrs. Hannah (Palfrey) Cole of Boston, who d. 17
Sept., 1826. Ch.:
    1 *Henry*⁶*;* 2 *Sarah;* 3 *Sophia;* 4 *William;* 5 *Rufus;* 6 *Hannah,*
and others who d. y.

28   CAPT. EPHRAIM[4], son of Capt. Nathan[3] and Elizabeth
(Howe) Brigham, born in Marlboro, Mass., 20 Jan., 1707-8; died
there, 7 Feb., 1771; married, 15 April, 1730, Hannah Willard of
Grafton. She married (2) Joseph Wilder, 6 Apr., 1774.

Was lieutenant in the engagement at Charlestown, N. H., 3
Aug., 1746. Settled in Marlboro in the School District No. 3, of
Morse's day and was one of the largest taxpayers in the town,
and a prominent citizen; was treasurer 1742, '43, '50, '52-64;
assessor 1747, '59-63, '65, '68; selectman 1749, '50, '54, '56-59,
'61, '62, '65, '67, '69; jury-man, moderator, etc. There were 32
heirs to his estate, none of whom were his descendants. One hundred
and thirty-three pounds were left to Marlboro under the care of the
selectmen and the minister for the time being. The proceeds of £22
were to be paid to the minister for preaching, in person or by proxy,
an annual sermon to promote the present and future reformation and
happiness of the young; and the income of the remainder was
to support a school in the middle of the town, distinct from the
district schools, for "Writing and cyphering." The "Brigham
School" was to be kept open about a month in the spring for
older pupils. Fund now merged in the general appropriation.

The line is extinct.

Children, born in Marlboro:
  i Hannah[5], b. 26 March, 1732; d. 21 Sept., 1736.
  ii Ephraim, b. 10 Aug., 1748; d. 25 Sept., 1748.

29   KEZIAH[4], daughter of Jonathan[3] and Mary (Fay) Brigham; (dates of birth and death unknown); married 13 Dec.,
1718, Elias, son of James Keyes; born in Marlboro, Mass., 1694;
died in New Marlboro, Mass., 27 Feb., 1756; he was one of the
16 founders of the church in Shrewsbury, Mass., where he moved;
in 1744 moved to New Marlboro.

Children (Keyes), born in Shrewsbury:
  i Elias[5], b. 22 July, 1719; went to New Marlboro. Ch.:
    1 *Zenas*⁶*.*
  ii Mary, b. 13 April, 1721; d. 1724.

iii David, b. 20 Sept., 1722.
iv Robert, b. 18 April, 1725.
v Mary, b. 12 Dec., 1726.
vi Charles, b. 29 April, 1728.
vii Keziah, b. 13 Feb., 1730.
viii Paul, b. 16 Sept., 1731.
ix Zenas, b. 9 March, 1733; d. 1740.
x Martha, b. 27 June, 1736.
xi Thaddeus, b. 17 June, 1738.
xii Deliverance, b. 14 March, 1740.

30 ZERVIAH[4], daughter of Jonathan[3] and Mary (Fay) Brigham; born in Marlboro, Mass., 9 Oct., 1698; died in Shrewsbury, Mass., 1 July, 1736; married, 16 Mch., 1724, Ebenezer Bragg, a carpenter from Ipswich to Marlboro and thence to Shrewsbury, Mass.; he died there, 4 Sept., 1766, æ. 67; he m. (2) Sarah ————, by whom 11 children.

Children (Bragg), by first wife, born in Shrewsbury:
i Ebenezer[5], b. 7 March, 1725; m. 5 Oct., 1751, Sibilla Bouker. Ch.:
1 Nathaniel[6]; 2 Timothy; 3 (Dea). John.
ii Zerviah, b. 29 June, 1727; d. y.
iii Lydia, b. 27 Jan., 1729.
iv Abiel, b. 25 June, 1730; m. Abigail Wilson. Ch.:
1 Lovisa[6]; 2 Elizabeth.
v Elizabeth, b. 10 Jan., 1732.
vi Moses, b. 19 Aug., 1733.
vii Mary, b. 4 Jan., 1735.
viii Zerviah, b. 22 June, 1736; d. y.
ix Thankful, b. 22 June, 1736; d. 7 April, 1756.

31 RUTH[4], daughter of Jonathan[3] and Mary (Fay) Brigham; born in Marlboro, Mass., 30 April, 1704; died there, 14 Oct., 1791; married (second wife), 12 July, 1727, Joseph Howe Jr., of Marlboro; born 19 Feb., 1697; died 18 Feb., 1775; (by his first wife, Zerviah, he had a child Zerviah); he was a large owner of land in New Marlboro, Mass.

Children (Howe), by second wife, born in Marlboro:
i Joseph[5], b. 1 Feb., 1728; d. 26 Sept., 1800; m. 21 May, 1751, Grace, dau. of Simon Rice, who d. 23 Jan., 1816, æ. 87. Ch.:
1 Lovina[6]; 2 Reuben; 3 Simon; 4 Samuel; 5 Lucy; 6 Eli; 7 Daniel; 8 Miriam; 9 Hepsibah; 10 Joseph, and others who d. y.
ii Dorothy, b. 4 May, 1730; d. 30 May, 1764; m. 20 Nov., 1750, Col. Cyprian Howe, b. in Marlboro, 29 March, 1729; was in the Revolution; m. (2) Mary Williams. Ch. (by first wife) (Howe):
1 Martha[6]; 2 Jabez; 3 Phebe; 4 Catee, m. Joel Brigham, 88.
iii Dinah, b. 11 Oct., 1731; m. Josiah Willard.
iv Thaddeus, b. 30 May, 1733; m. 12 April, 1757, Levinah[5] Brigham, 117.
v Elizabeth, b. 12 Dec., 1734; m. Dr. Rice of Barre, Mass.
vi Samuel, b. 22 May, 1737; d. 1756, in the French War.

vii Phineas, b. 25 Jan., 1739; d. 14 March, 1832; m. (1) 11 Dec., 1764, Dorothy Burnet, who d. 9 Dec., 1781; m. (2) 1783, Sarah Brooks, who d. 22 July, 1784; m. (3) 4 Jan., 1798, Lydia Ruggles, who d. 1837 æ. 84. Ch. (by first wife):
1 *Sylvanus[6]; 2 Elizabeth; 3 Jedediah; 4 Gilbert; 5 Lovice.*
Ch. (by second wife):
6 *Phinehas.*
viii Artemas, b. 15 Jan., 1743; d. 17 Nov., 1813; m. 28 March, 1767, Mary, dau. of Gershom Bigelow; who d. 15 Aug., 1810, æ. 65. Ch.:
1 *Elisha[6]; 2 Catherine; 3 Mary; 4 Jonas; 5 Lydia; 6 Sally; 7 Stephen,* m. Susanna Brigham, dau. of 169; 8 *David; 9 Samuel;* 10 *Levi;* 11 *Jabez;* 12 *Moses.*
ix Miriam, b. 5 Dec., 1744; d. 14 Nov., 1825; m. April, 1763, Timothy, son of Gershom Bigelow; b. in Marlboro, 1 Nov., 1738; d. 6 Nov., 1817. Ch. (Bigelow).
1 *David[6]; 2 Lydia; 3 Ephraim.*

32 *JONATHAN[4], son of Jonathan[3] and Mary (Fay) Brigham; born in Marlboro, Mass., 14 March, 1707; died there, 4 Jan., 1768; married, 3 April, 1733, Damaris, daughter of Benjamin and Mary (Graves) Rice, born in Marlboro, 20 July, 1711; died 9 Nov., 1751. He lived in Marlboro and was survevor there in 1743 and constable in 1749.

Children, born in Marlboro:
83   i Noah[5], b. 24 Nov., 1734.
ii Mary, b. 25 April, 17—; d. s. p. in Northboro, Oct., 1807; m. Thaddeus, son of Gershom and Hannah (Oaks) Fay of Northboro, whose first wife was Thankful Rice. He d. in Northboro, 22 July, 1822, æ. 91., s. p.
iii Matthias, b. 24 Aug., 1742; d. 18 Aug., 1752.
iv Damaris, b. 15 April, 1746; d. 12 July, 1752.

33 †CAPT. JESSE[4], son of Jonathan[3] and Mary (Fay) Brigham; born in Marlboro, 10 July, 1710; died in Northboro, 8 Dec., 1796; married, 4 June, 1734, Bethiah, daughter of Jacob Rice; born 13 Aug., 1712; died 19 Dec., 1794.

Morse says he settled in Westboro, in that part which, in 1766, became the east part of Northboro; was a large land-owner. Was one of a committee to build the Northboro Precinct meeting-house, in 1744, etc.; in 1766 he was selectman and held other town offices. He made his will 8 Sept., 1767, giving to his wife her thirds and all his in-door movables, to be disposed of at her pleasure to his 3 daughters. To son Timothy, to whom he had previously given lands and buildings, he bequeathed half of his right to the undivided lands of Marlboro. To son Artemas he gave his buildings and lands in Northboro, his lands in Leicester and Paxton, all his live-stock and tools, his firearms, sword and cane, requiring him to provide a horse for his mother to ride at

* *Colonial War Record:* First Marlboro Co., 1757.
† *Colonial War Record:* "Ensign" Train Band, 1757; Capt. 2d Westboro Co., 1762.

times when she should have occasion; to pay £52 to his sister
Rice; to his sisters Vashti and Mary, each £66, and to provide
them with room in his house so long as they should live single.
Artemas was sole executor.

Children, born in Westboro:
84   i Timothy[5], b. 16 Feb., 1735-6.
85   ii Artemas, b. 29 Sept., 1739.
       iii Persis, b. 7 March, 1741-2; d. 17 Sept., 1745.
86   iv Sarah, b. 21 Feb., 1745-6.
       v Vashti, b. 27 Feb., 1748; m. ——— Gage.
       vi Mary, b. 6 Sept., 1750; m. ——— Gassett.

34 *JOEL[4], son of Jonathan[3] and Mary (Fay) Brigham; born
in Marlboro, 2 Oct., 1714; died at son Jonathan's in N. Y., April,
1797; married 17 March, 1740-1, Mary Church.

Morse says that he kept a public house in Marlboro for more
than 50 years; was selectman in 1763 and 1772; had extensive
land and business connections, and sustained a considerable loss
in Continental money; was a noted Whig. About 1783, after the
death of his wife, he removed with his sons to Madison, N. Y.

Children, born in Marlboro:
87   i William[5], b. 20 March, 1741-2.
       ii Zerviah, b. 10 June, 1745; d. 31 Aug., 1746.
       iii Zerviah, b. 5 July, 1747; m. ——— Maynard of Worcester,
       Mass. She d. and he m. a second time.
88   iv Joel, b. 5 April, 1751.
89   v Jonathan, b. 29 Oct., 1754.
90   vi John, b. 16 April, 1758.
91   vii Samuel, b. 3 Dec., 1760.

35 †JAMES[4], son of Jonathan[3] and Mary (Fay) Brigham;
born in Marlboro, Mass., 2 Oct., 1717; died in Brookfield, Mass.,
15 March, 1794; married Anna, daughter of Elisha Rice of Brookfield, Mass.; born, 5 July, 1726; died in Brookfield, 9 May,
1799.

Morse says that he settled on a tract of one thousand acres
on the south side of the Quabog River in Brookfield, which his
father had purchased, 7 Nov., 1722, for about $250, more or less.
He built his house one and a half miles south-west of the Brookfield Depot (formerly South Brookfield). He is on a list of men
who served to the credit of the 3d precinct of Brookfield, dated
30 June, 1778, credited with 8 months' service.

Children, probably born in Brookfield:
92   i Tilly[5], b. 6 June, 1748.
93   ii Elisha, b. 6 Jan., 1750.
94   iii Jonathan, b. 22 Oct., 175—.

* On Committee of Correspondence, 1780.
† *Colonial War Record:* " Corporal." Relief of Fort William Henry, 1757.

36 *JOHN[4], son of David[3] and Deborah Brigham; born in Marlboro, Mass., 22 April, 1704; died in Shrewsbury, Mass. to which town he moved and where he made his will, 20 July, 1767; he married Susanna ———; born in 1708; died 12 Feb., 1761.

By will, his two sons divided his farm, Samuel being executor. His two daughters were each to have a cow and one half of the indoor movables. They were to be furnished room in the house and firewood, and to have their cows kept at halves.

Children, born in Shrewsbury:

    i Deborah[5], b. 11 Dec., 1737; d. unm., at Shrewsbury, 22 Oct., 1816, æ. 79.

95 ii John, b. 25 July, 1739.

96 iii Samuel, b. 1 July, 1741.

    iv Susannah, b. 5 July, 1745; d. s. p. 12 March, 1830, æ. 85; m. 24 Nov., 1785, David, son of Deacon Jonathan Nelson of Upton, Mass.; he d. in Shrewsbury, 12 May, 1827, æ. 90; (m. for his first wife Susannah Bacheller, who d. in 1785, and had seven sons and two daughters (see *Hist. of Shrewsbury*).

37 †SILAS[4], son of David[3] and Mary (Newton) Brigham; born in Marlboro, Mass., 9 Aug., 1710; died, 11 March, 1791; married (1) Mindwell Grout, who died 8 June, 1741; married (2) (published 30 Jan., 1743) widow Tabitha (Prescott) Sawyer of Lancaster, Mass.

Morse says he became associated with her as administrator on her former husband's estate. See *Hist. of Lancaster*

Children (by first wife), born in Westboro:

    i ‡ Jemima[5], b. 23 March, 1736-37; m. 25 Jan., 1763, Constantine Hardy of Westboro.

  ii Mary, b. 19 April, 1739; d. 14 Jan., 1740.

* *Colonial War Record:* On Alarm List Shrewsbury Co., 1757. In 1759, " invalid."

† *Colonial War Record:* Private in Train Band, 1757, Shrewsbury, 1st Co., Capt. Ward.

‡ "27 March, 1737......N. B. Mr. Silas Brigham and Mr. Eleazer Pratt of Shrewsbury had desired me to baptize yeir Children. Accordingly, in my usual manner I desired ye Children might be brought forth to Baptism. But only one appeared. I looked about till I conceived yt something had befallen ye other or those concerned with it. I proceeded and baptised Mr. Pratt's (wh was ye Child yt was brought) wn the prayers were over we proceeded to ye last Singing; in ye Time of the ye last Singing Mr. Brigham and his Child came in—After ye Blessing and wn I was down in ye Alley going out, Mr. Brigham asked me whether his child could not be baptized. I ans'd. it could not now. My Reasons are these. Besides that, when I am spent with the foregoing Services, it is too much to expect me to repeat ym over again. Besides that, such a custom indulged would involve us in great irregularity and Difficulty, but this administration for my known Friends would have forced me to make it a custom, and besides the impatience of many of the Congregation to get away home, being they live 4, 5, or 6 miles off. Besides those Reasons, I would urge yt was so very sudden upon me yt I could not judge wh way I could vindicate it if I should proceed. Again by ye suddenness I was too much confused to have my Power at command to perform the Devotions; nor was I furnished therfor (Eccl. 5; 1, 2). So it would have been nothing short of horrible Presumption for me to have done it."—*Parkman Diary.*

The Editor of the Diary adds: " Poor Silas and poor Mindwell! How they must have worried and how flushed his young face must have been when he marched

Children (by second wife), born in Lancaster:
97 iii David, b. 4 April, 1745.
    iv Mindwell, b. 7 Feb., 1746-47.
    v Mary, b. 1 March, 1748-49.

38 COL. LEVI[4], 6th child and 4th son of David[3] and his 2d wife, Mrs. Mary (Leonard) Newton Brigham (widow of Edward Newton); born 21 Aug., 1716, in Marlboro, Mass., upon his father's farm, in that portion of the town which was set off as Westboro, in 1717; died in Northboro, Mass., 1 Feb., 1787; married, 6 June, 1745, Susanna, daughter of *Joseph[3] (Joseph[1], John[2]) and Mrs. Mary (Harrington) Rogers Grout; born in Watertown, Mass, 2 March, 1720; died in Northboro, 17 March, 1816.

When his father divided his farm among his children, Levi[4] received and settled upon the northerly portion of it, most of which, at the division of Westboro, in 1766, was set off into Northboro, of which town it formed the south-east corner. He was born, lived and died upon the same farm, and yet was, at different periods of his lifetime, a citizen of 3 different towns.

In 1763 he was one of the selectmen of Westboro, and subsequently held the same office in Northboro for 7 years. He was also sealer of leather. In 1757, when 41 years old, he was Cornet of the Shrewsbury Troop of Horse, commanded by Captain Benja-

down the aisle, after all the hurry, to have his pride in his first-born so humbled by the Minister's censure! "
    The Church Records say under date of April 3, 1737: "Jemima of Silas and Mindwell Brigham baptized by Rev. Mr. Prentice of Grafton."
    * Joseph[3] Grout was the 2d child and only son of Joseph[2] Grout (John[1]) of Watertown and his wife Susanna Hagar. He was born in Watertown 6 Feb., 1683, and resided there until March, 1733, when he removed, with his family, to Westboro, where he died in 1759. 3 Jan., 1717, he married Mrs. Mary (Harrington) Rogers, widow of Daniel Rogers and dau. of Edward and Mary (Ockington) Harrington of Watertown; she was b. 2 Jan., 1693.
    Joseph[2] Grout, was a son of Capt. John[1] Grout and his 2d wife, Sarah Busby. He was b. in Sudbury 24 July, 1649, and removed to Watertown, where in 1675 he was a Trooper in Capt. Thomas Prentice's Middlesex Troop of Horse and served during the campaign against the Narragansetts in the early part of King Philip's War. About 1680 he m. Susanna, dau. of William and Mary (Bemis) Hagar of Watertown, by whom he had 3 ch. He d. in 1720, his wife outliving him.
    Capt. John[1] Grout, was b. about 1616, probably in England, emigrated to New England about 1634, and was in Watertown in 1640 with wife Mary......by whom he had a son John, b. 1641, but who must have d. soon afterward, for he m. (2) Sarah, dau. of Nicholas & Bridget (......) Busby, by whom Capt. John had a dau. Sarah, b. in Watertown, 11 Dec., 1643.
    During 1643 he removed to Sudbury where he acquired land and was made a Sergeant of the Military Company. Oct. 7, 1662, sundry inhabitants of Sudbury petitioned the Gen. Court that John Grout "be allowed to practice the mistery of chirurgery." In 1685 he was made a Freeman and in 1667 the town records refer to him as Ensigne Grout, which rank he held during King Philip's War and as late as 1685, during which year the Gen. Court granted the claim of Ensigne Grout for compensation for losses sustained during the Indian attack on Sudbury, April 21, 1676. In 1688 Lieut. John Grout was appointed one of the custodians of the public stock of ammunition, and the Vital Records of Sudbury show that Capt. John Grout d. 25 July, 1697. John Grout also served the town of Sudbury 30 years as selectman and 7 years as town clerk.

SIGNATURES TO AGREEMENT OF THE HEIRS OF COLONEL LEVI BRIGHAM

min Eager, attached to the 3d regiment of Militia of the counties of Middlesex and Worcester. He served as delegate from Northboro in the Provincial Congress during its 3 sessions, 7 Oct., 1774, to 10 Dec., 1774, 1 Feb., 1775, to 29 May, 1775, and 31 May, 1775, to 19 July, 1775.

March 23, 1776, he was commissioned Lieut. Colonel in Col. John Goulding's 6th Worcester County regiment of militia of which *Job Cushing of Shrewsbury was Major and subsequently Colonel. In 1778 Col. Brigham received £27 from the town of Northboro for his services in the war since 19 Apr., 1775.

Children, all born on the home farm in Westboro:
98   i Levi⁵, b. 26 Aug., 1746.
     ii Joseph, b. 21 Nov., 1747; d. 13 Feb., 1760, killed by a fall.
     iii Elijah, b. 14 Jan., 1750; d. 12 Sept., 1750.
99   iv Elijah, b. 7 July, 1751.
100 v Susanna, b. 21 Jan., 1754.
101 vi Winslow, b. 18 June, 1756.
     vii Josiah, b. 12 Aug., 1758; d. unm., 9 Jan., 1788, in Westboro. He was a doctor, and is mentioned in the Diary of Rev. Ebenezer Parkman, as living with his brother-in-law, Breck Parkman, at different times. He was often at the parsonage, with Elijah, Moses and Samuel Brigham, to dine and to sing.
     viii Mindwell, b. 18 Aug., 1760; d. 1 Feb., 1784.
     ix Anna, b. 28 May, 1763; d. unm., 30 May, 1790.

39 †CAPT. JONAS⁴, son of David³ and Mary (Leonard) Newton Brigham; born in Westboro, Mass., 25 Feb., 1718; died there, 25 Sept., 1789; married 16 Jan., 1745-6, Persis Baker, who died 3 Nov., 1784.

He settled on land in Westboro inherited from his father, and built about 20 rods south of the present Insane Asylum. He was one of the most distinguished citizens of Westboro, and through life stood high in the public esteem and confidence; was elected to town offices soon after attaining his majority, a thing of very rare occurrence in his time; was repeatedly selected to look after the interests of schools and was once placed on a committee to prepare instructions for the school committee of the town; he seems to have been a man of considerable education. He often served as surveyor and constable, and was 7 years selectman, between 1764-77. As moderator of town meetings, member of

* Five years later, in 1781, Col. Brigham's son Winslow married Col. Cushing's daughter Alice.
    † *Colonial War Record:* Lieut. Westboro Train Band, 1757· " Acting Capt." Relief of Fort William Henry, 1758.
    ‡ " 6 Jan., 1779. Capt. Jonas Brigham and his wife were so benevolent as to present me with a Cheese. I take ye more notice of this because he has been so long aloof, but I rejoice in his friendly Disposition."
    " 9 Oct., 1780. Hear much of *Bears*—One is killed by Capt. Jonas Brigham and Others—weighed 300. I dined at Capt. Brigham's, I visit at Col. Brigham's   "
—*Parkman Diary.*

vigilance committees and delegate to the County Congress at the beginning of the Revolutionary struggle, and during its continuance, he appears to have been an efficient and enlightened patriot.

Children:

102   i Martha⁵, b. 1 Nov., 1746.

❬103   ii Jonas, b. 29 Oct., 1748.

    iii Hannah, b. ————; d. in Westboro; m. Rev. Halloway, son of Elisha Fish of Upton, Mass., b. there, 2 Aug., 1762; grad. Dartmouth Coll., 1790; res. in Marlboro, N. H., where d. 1 Sept., 1824; in 1840 she returned from Marlboro, N. H., to Westboro to reside with her nephew, Halloway Brigham, where she died; had no children, but adopted Hannah Halloway Brigham.

    iv Antipas, b. 23 July, 1750; d. 12 Nov., 1756.

    v Eli, b. 17 May, 1752; after grad. from Dartmouth College, A. B., 1778, he became a merchant in Lancaster, Mass., and in about 8 years failed in business; subsequently called on his brother in Bakersfield, Vt., with a team and load of goods, enroute for Canada. He was known to have taken the ice-road to Lake Champlain, but was never heard of afterward; his friends believed he was lost in the lake; no family.

104   vi Edward, b. 21 May, 1754.

105 vii Barnabas, b. 29 March, 1756.

106 viii Antipas, b. 15 March, 1758.

107   ix Daniel, b. 12 June, 1760.

108   x David, b. 31 March, 1762.

    xi Persis, b. 23 April, 1764; d. 3 Feb., 1775.

109 xii Joseph, b. 20 April, 1766.

    xiii William, b. 12 May, 1768; d. 7 Dec., 1779.*

40 †MAJOR ASA⁴, son of David³ and Mary (Newton) Brigham; born, 2 Dec., 1721, in Westboro, Mass; died in Fitzwilliam, N. H., 6 Nov., 1777; married 23 Jan., 1745, Mary Newton, who died 17 Dec., 1795, æ. 70. See *Westboro Vital Records.*

He resided in Shrewsbury, Mass., until 1775, where, in 1747, he was admitted to the church. His house was still standing in 1894 in an excellent state of preservation, when the author visited it.

"In September, 1894, I visited the old Shrewsbury homestead of Capt. Asa Brigham, my direct ancestor and the 4th generation from Thomas the Puritan. The house is situated, approximately, a half mile east of Brigham Hill and 2½ miles south-east of the

---

* "Dec. 6, 1779. Was called away to see a young son of Capt. Jonas Brigham viz; his son William in his 12th year, who was throught to be under extremely dangerous Symptoms. I went prayed, breakfasted there."......

"Dec. 7, 1779. Mr. Edward Brigham came to acquaint me that his Brother dyed this morning and to desire me to attend ye Funeral on Thursday; at nine A. M. I remonstrated, but it was settled, I suppose."

"Dec. 9, 1779....I did not go to Capt. Brigham's as I was at first desired. Mr. Edward had come yesterday and told me his Father would conform to ye proposal to bring ye Corps to ye Meeting-House. They did so and I prayed there. After this they proceeded to ye Interment, and I went to ye Grave with ym. We re-entered ye Meeting-House and having prayed already began with singing. Preached on ps. 68, 26-28."....—*Parkman Diary.*

† *Colonial War Record:* Corporal, 1757.

present site of the Shrewsbury post-office on the road described as "the back road from the old pike road to Westboro." It faces north and stands on a slight elevation at a point where the road makes quite a bend toward the east. To the north-west, a newer and more modern house has been built and just across the road a barn, the original one having been torn down long since. The premises are at present occupied by Mr. George Freeman. The old house has a gable roof, is 2 stories high below the eaves, and at the time of its erection must have been quite a pretentious structure. It has 22 windows and 2 outside doors— 1 in the front and 1 in the back. In the center of the house, dividing it into 2 equal parts, is an immense fire-place, oven and chimney, constructed of stone and brick. At the south side of the house is a hall connecting the 2 rooms of the ground floor; in this hall are 2 doors, 1 leads to the cellar, and the other is an outside door; a stairway leads to the next floor. The 2d floor has another stairway which leads to the attic. Two rods south of the house is the old well which originally supplied the barn as well as the house, and the pipes which carried the water to the barn are still in position 8 feet below the surface, and serve to carry off the excess of water; it is said that at no time since the well was dug has the water been below this pipe. The stumps of 2 huge Elms may be seen, one of which I measured and found to be $17\frac{1}{2}$ ft. in circumference. In 1893, during a heavy storm, one of the large divisions of the tree was split off and falling on the roof of the house made quite a hole in it; the tree was so badly disfigured it was cut down. Mr. Freeman presented me with a cane turned from this tree."

He was the first captain of So. Militia Co. of Shrewsbury, and moved to Fitzwilliam, 1775, where he was moderator 1775 and '77; selectman, 1776; on Committee of Safety and Treasurer, 1777. See *Hist. of Fitzwilliam.*

Children, all born in Shrewsbury:

110   i Alpheus[5], b. 30 April, 1746.
111   ii Molly, b. 10 March, 1748.
112   iii Leonard, b. 7 May, 1750.
       iv Levinah, b. 21 Feb., 1752; m. 14 July, 1774, Antipas, son of Isaac Harrington of Troy, N. H.; b. in Grafton, Mass., 30 Sept., 1753. Morse says "had ch." *Troy Hist.* does not mention him.
113   v Stephen, b. 13 May, 1754.
114   vi Elizabeth, b. 26 Sept., 1756.
       vii Asa, b. 10 Sept., 1758; d. Barnard, Vt., 1839; m. Sally Newton; was in the Revolutionary War; served in R. I., in 1778, in Col. Josiah Whitney's Regt.; res. Barnard. Ch., b. there:
       1 *Sophia*[6], b. 24 Feb., 1786.
       2 *Cloe,* b. 16 July, 1789; m. ————; res. Barnard.
       3 *Sally,* b. 2 May, 1792.

    4 *Asa*, b. 16 June, 1794; went west in 1830.
    5 *Alden*, b. 28 Oct., 1796; m. 1822, Lydia Lathrop Smith; res. Barnard, where d. 1872; ch.: Dennis S.[7] of Albany, N. Y.
    6 *Polly*, b. 8 Sept., 1798.
  viii Thankful, b. 13 June, 1760; d. 28 July, 1849; m. 6 Dec., 1786, Dr. Isaac Moore Farwell, b. in Townsend, Mass., 12 April, 1757; d. in Paris, N. Y., 11 Aug., 1840; grad. Dartmouth Coll.; went to Utica, N. Y.; was selectman and town clerk of Fitzwilliam, N. H.   Ch. (Farwell):
    1 *Lyman*[6], b. 5 Oct., 1798.
    2 *Eli*, res. Watertown, N. Y.
    3 *More*.
    4 *Samuel*, res. Utica.
  ix Lyman, b. 19 Nov., 1762; in Revolutionary War, July 1780; received £9 bounty (*Fitzwilliam Town Records*); res. Augusta, N. Y. 3 daus.
115 x Josiah Newton, b. 30 March, 1765.

41 MARTHA[4], daughter of Gershom[3] and Mehetabel (Warren) Brigham; born in Marlboro, Mass., 6 Oct., 1704; died, 15 Oct., 1782; married 22 Feb., 1725, Capt. Joseph, son of John and Jerusha (Garfield) Bigelow; born in Marlboro, 1 Jan., 1703; died, 24 Jan., 1783.   Resided in Shrewsbury in 1729, and was selectman in 1748.

Children (Bigelow), born in Shrewsbury:
  i Capt. Joseph[6], b. 9 Nov., 1726; m. Olive Beaman. Ch.:
    1 *Stephen*[6], and several daus.
  ii Martha, b. 3 May, 1728; d. y.
  iii Charles, b. 22 April, 1729; m. Lucy Bennett. Ch.:
    1 *Andrew*[6]; 2 *Joseph*; 3 *Charles*; 4 *Solomon*; 5 *John*; and daus.
  iv Martha, b. 10 March, 1733; d. 13 July, 1742.
  v Stephen, b. 10 Jan., 1735; d. unm., 1756.
  vi Anna, b. 14 Jan., 1737; m. 26 Oct., 1757, Samuel Hastings.
  vii Mehitable, b. 14 Sept., 1739; d. 1746.
  viii Solomon, b. 13 Oct., 1746; m. 6 April, 1769, Mary Demmon, who m. (2) William Small of Fitchburg. Solomon d. s. p.
  ix Mary, b. 18 Sept., 1748; m. 2 June, 1768, Isaac Moor of Bolton, Mass.   Ch. (Moor):
    1 *Isaac*[6]; 2 *Solomon*; and 5 daus.

42 * JOSEPH[4] son of Gershom[3] and Mehetabel (Warren) Brigham; born in Marlboro, 21 April, 1706; died 29 July, 1786; married (1) 26 Aug., 1728, †Comfort, daughter of John Bigelow who, previous to her birth, had been a captive among the Indians, ⸝taken 15 Oct., 1705; (after his liberation he named his first-born Comfort and his second Freedom; Miss Ames of Marlboro corrects the Morse record); she d. 24 Sept., 1755, æ. 48; married

* *Colonial War Record:* Centinel (probably 1725), Capt. N. Brigham. Marlboro Alarm List, 1757.
† *History of Marlboro.*

Joseph[4] Brigham House, Marlboro

(2) 3 May, 1757, Ruth, daughter of Joseph Rice of Marlboro, and widow of Elisha Ward; born in Marlboro, 1 Sept., 1721; died 1 Feb., 1786.

He resided in Marlboro and built the Joseph Brigham-Ames house. He was surveyor in 1734; petit jury-man, 1738; constable, 1740; selectman, 1749-50, '62, '64, '71; warden, 1766, and tythingman, 1775.

Children (by first wife), born in Marlboro:

   i Mehetabel⁵, b. 14 July, 1729; d. in Berlin, Mass., 1762; m. 1748, Capt. Samuel Jones Jr., b. in B., 1726; d. 23 Jan., 1797; he bought, in 1748, 137 acres, which included the land now a large part of the central village of Berlin, where he built "Jones Inn," in 1749; was a man of energy and good judgment; assistant sheriff. He m. (2) Dorothy Whitcomb, dau. of John, who had children. Ch., (Jones), b. in Berlin:

     1 *Mehetabel⁶*, d. y., probably in Marlboro.
     2 *Samuel*, b. 22 March, 1751; d. y.
     3 *Solomon*, b. 5 March, 1753; d. y.
     4 *Samuel*, b. 14 Feb., 1757; m. Martha Fay, and had a family; moved to Marlboro, N. H.
     5 *Sally*, b. 19 Aug., 1758.
     6 *Solomon*, twin to Sally.
     7 *Levina*, b. 1761; m. Stephen Coolidge.

116 ii Sarah, b. 13 May, 1731.
117 iii Lavinah, b. 10 July, 1733.
   iv Joseph, b. 14 June, 1735; d. 17 July, 1742.
   v Comfort, b. 29 July, 1737; d. 17 July, 1742.
   vi Martha, b. 9 Sept., 1739; m. 20 Jan., 1763, Daniel Barnes, Jr.; b. 19 July, 1736. Ch. (Barnes), b. in Marlboro:

     1 *John⁶*, b. 6 Nov., 1763; m. 8 March, 1785, Sarah, dau. of Abram Howe.
     2 *Martha*, b. 9 May, 1766; m. 28 Aug., 1783, Fortunatus Brigham, 168.

118 vii Stephen, b. 15 Oct., 1741.
119 viii Joseph, b. 27 Sept., 1743.
   ix Comfort, b. 26 Aug., 1745; d. 19 May, 1771; m. 14 March, 1770, Daniel, son of Samuel Stevens; b. 7 May, 1746; d. 7 Nov., 1810; he m. (2) 2 June, 1772, Lydia Brigham, dau. of 44; m. (3) Lavinia Barnard, and had ch.; was in the Revolution; res. in Marlboro. Ch. (Stevens), by first wife, b. Marlboro:

     1 *Samuel⁶*, b. 21 Feb., 1771; d. 29 Aug., 1775.

   x Jonah, b. 19 Nov., 1747; d. 1 Dec., 1827, s. p.; m. 1771, Sarah Walker.
   xi Lucy, b. 19 Aug., 1752; m. Samuel Stratton, son of 61.

43 *†GERSHOM⁴, son of Gershom³ and Mehetabel (Warren) Brigham; born in Marlboro, Mass., 4 Nov., 1712; died, ————— ————; married, 26 Mch., 1741, Mary, daughter of Henry and

* *Colonial War Record:* Capt. Fay's Train Band, 1757.
† "December 27, 1779....Called at Mr. Gershom Brigham's and begin to take *Thomas's Spy* of him" (*The Worcester Spy*).
"Jan. 22, 1780. Elias goes on Racketts to Mr. Gershom Brigham's. A newspaper of Dec. 30, is ye last."

Rebecca (Heywood) Lee, who died in Westboro, 5 Sept., 1780.*
He resided in Westboro where he held town offices 1748-65.

Children, born in Westboro:
    i Hepsibah⁵, b. 20 Jan., 1741-2, and no further reported.
120 ii Gershom, b. 15 Oct., 1747.
    iii Seth, b. 22 June, 1750; res. and d. in Westboro; no family reported (Vide *Hist. of Gardner*).
    iv Silas, b. 27 March, 1753; res. and d. in Westboro; no family recorded.
    v Timothy, twin to Silas, res. in Westboro, and was selectman in 1764.
    vi Joseph, b. 23 Aug., 1757; d. y.
    vii Mary, twin to Joseph, probably m. 12 Dec., 1776, Jonathan Prescott, Jr., of Lancaster, Mass.

44 †SERGT. BENJAMIN⁴, son of Gershom³ and Mehetabel (Warren) Brigham; born in Marlboro, Mass., 19 Feb., 1714-15; died ——————————————; married Hannah Merrill.
He is supposed to have inherited the ancient homestead of his grandfather, Thomas, through his father Gershom, and to have left it to his youngest son Warren, who left it to Benjamin Thomas⁸ Brigham, son of 488. Warren weighed about 200 pounds and was of medium height.

Children, born in Marlboro:
121 i Benjamin⁵, b. 11 March, 1741-2.
122 ii Caleb, b. 20 Nov., 1743.
123 iii Benajah, b. 15 March, 1745-6.
124 iv Hannah, b. 1 May, 1748.
125 v Gershom, b. 27 June, 1750.
    vi Warren, b. 16 Nov., 1753; d. 10 Jan., 1840, s. p.; m. Lucy Marble, who d. 19 Nov., 1858, æ. 90. He was well educated, but eccentric, and desired to keep everything " as it always was."
    vii Lydia, b. 28 Feb., 1758; d. 28 Dec., 1782; m. 2 June, 1772, Daniel, son of Samuel Stevens, whose first wife was Comfort Brigham, dau. of 42. Ch. (Stevens):
      1 *Samuel⁶*, b. 29 Oct., 1776; d. 16 Jan., 1791.
      2 *Lydia*, b. 18 May, 1778; d. 11 April, 1842; m. 1795, Seth, son of Edmund and Hannah (Gassett) Rice of Westboro. Ch. (Rice): i Lydia⁷, b. 12 April, 1796; ii Sophia, b. 6 Feb., 1798;

---

* " Aug. 3, 1780....Visit Mr. Gershom Brigham's wife who languishes.
" Aug., 1780. On Deac. Wood's Horse I rode to Mr. Gershom Brigham's to see his Wife who is dangerously ill. The State of her Soul is deplorable as well as her Body. She was very sorry yt she had neglected ye Lord's Supper. She was in much Confusion. I prayed with her and ye Family. I dind there."
" Aug. 31, 1780. Mr. Gershom Brigham brings his Wife's Earnest Desire yt I would visit her again & preach a Sermon there to-day. I complyed—delivered a short Discourse (as I could) from several passages in Isa. 55. ' Hear and your Soul shall live.' May God bless what was delivered. Mrs. B. is brot very low."
" Sept. 5, 1780. Mr. Gleason came and informed yt Mr. Gershom Brigham's Wife dyed this morning; and ye Survivors desire me to attend ye Funeral next Thursday."
" Sept. 7, 1780. I rode one of Alexander's Horses to ye Funeral of Mrs. Brigham (Wife of Mr. Gershom) & prayed there......"—*Parkman Diary.*
† *Colonial War Record:* Sergeant, 1757.

iii Samuel, b. 11 Nov., 1799; iv Lucy, b. 20 Aug., 1801; v
Hollis, b. 26 June, 1803; vi Emeline, b. 26 April, 1805.
3 *Edward,* b. 10 March, 1781; d. 1 Aug., 1782.
viii Levinah, b. 2 Sept., 1760; m. 16 Dec., 1779, John Fay, Jr.; res.
Marlboro. Ch. (Fay), b. Marlboro:
1 *Windsor*, b. 15 July, 1780.

45 ELNATHAN[4], son of Elnathan[3] and Bethiah (Ward)
Brigham; born in Marlboro, Mass., 7 April, 1716; died 2 Sept.,
'1802, in Mansfield, Conn. He settled on the homestead in Mansfield, Conn.

Children, born in Mansfield:
126 i Stephen[5], b. 1744.
    ii Elnathan, b. 1757; d. s. p., 1835; m. Mary ————; res. Tolland,
    Conn. Was a pensioner in 1832, and probably was the one re-
    corded as being in Capt. Rudd's Co., Tyler's Brigade, when
    attempting to dislodge the British from Newport, from Aug.
    2-Sept. 12, 1778, and was at the battle of Long Island. Also in
    Capt. Waterman's Co., 6 Sept. to 8 Sept., 1781, and on duty
    in New London.

46 PAUL[4], son of Elnathan[3] and Bethiah (Ward) Brigham;
born in Mansfield, Conn.; died in Coventry, Conn., 3 May, 1746;
married, 1 July, 1741, Catherine Turner, who married (2), 18
Oct., 1750, in Coventry, Benjamin Carpenter Jr., and had children, Alvin and Mabel. Resided in Coventry.

Children:
127 i Thomas[5], b. 7 March, 1742.
    ii Dinah, b. 14 Nov., 1743; d. 16 March, 1836; m. (1) Medad Curtis,
    who d. in Conn.; they had son *John*[5], who moved to Ohio; she m.
    (2) 9 April, 1776, Elisha Tracy.
128 iii Paul, b. 6 Jan., 1746.

47 URIAH[4], son of Elnathan[3] and Bethiah (Ward) Brigham;
born in Mansfield, Conn., about 1723; died in Coventry, Conn.,
25 Jan., 1777, æ. 54. He settled in Coventry and married (1)
Lydia Ward, who died 14 Dec., 1750; and married (2) Ann,
daughter of Amos Richardson of Coventry, 28 May, 1754. He
was a patriot, and his anxiety for his country is believed to have
hastened his death. He was very plain in all his tastes.

Children (by first wife), born in Coventry:
129 i Hannah[5], b. 9 April, 1746.
    ii ("Capt.") Gershom, b. 1750; d. s. p. in C. about 1834, æ. 84;
    m. 13 Jan., 1774, Anne Parker of C., who died 18 Aug., 1815,
    æ. 66; was an inn-keeper. In vol. ii. of *Recs. Conn.,* he is granted
    leave, May, 1778, to "keep a house of publick entertainment where
    he dwells til next Mch. 1, provided he executes proper bond to
    Treasurer of Windham Co." He lived on the "great road"
    from Hartford to Boston.

Children (by second wife):
  iii Roger, b. 28 Oct., 1755; d. Nov., 1760.
130 iv Bethiah, b. 14 July, 1757.
131 v Anna, b. 14 Oct., 1759.
  vi Norman, b. 2 Dec., 1761; d. Aug., 1782, after release from British Prison Ship in N. Y. Harbor.
132 vii Don Carlos, b. 21 Feb., 1764.
133 viii Cephas, b. 7 Dec., 1765.
  ix Martha (or Marcia), b. 28 Jan., 1770; bapt. in Coventry, 1778; m. ———— Edgarton.
  x Lucy (or Lucia), b. 6 Nov., 1771; bapt. in Coventry, 1778; m. 31 Aug., 1800, Dr. Rice of Glastonbury, Conn.

48   SAMUEL⁴, son of John Jr.³, and Martha Brigham; born in Sudbury, Mass., 27 April, 1716; was drowned; married Mary ————. He lived in Sudbury.

Children, born in Sudbury:
  i Martha⁵, b. 1 Aug., 1739; m. 27 April, 1775, John Goodnow. Ch. (Goodnow), b. Sudbury:
    1 *Elizabeth⁶*, b. 10 Feb., 1770.
    2 *Jonas*, b. 4 Dec., 1775.
    3 *Nahum*, b. 14 Dec., 1777.
    4 *Martha*, b. 19 May, 1780.
  ii Mary, b. 25 Sept., 1741; m. 14 Jan., 1761, Samuel Balcom of Sudbury; no ch. recorded.
  iii Sarah, b. 2 Jan., 1744; m. Reuben Willis.
  iv John, b. 31 Jan., 1746.
  v Samuel, b. 31 Jan., 1746; m. 6 June, 1776, Hannah Brintall; he was on the Sudbury muster-roll of 1775; no ch. recorded in Sudbury.
  vi Phebe, b. 17 June, 1748; d. y.
134 vii Hosea, b. 6 Sept., 1750.
  viii Phebe, b. 13 Jan., 1751.
  ix Hannah, b. 1 Feb., 1754; m. 2 Feb., 1775, Samuel Gleason. Ch. (Gleason), b. Sudbury:
    1 *Joel⁶*, b. 15 July, 1775.
    2 *Ruth*, b. 5 Sept., 1777.
    3 *Molly*, b. 21 March, 1781.
135 x Joel, b. 5 March, 1756.
136 xi Jonas, b. 26 May, 1758.

49 SARAH⁴, daughter of John Jr.³ and Martha Brigham; born in Sudbury, Mass., 29 Mch., 1718; married, 18 Mch., 1736, Capt. Samuel Brown; born in Chelmsford, or Rutland, Mass., 8 Dec., 1700.

He was in the French and Indian Wars. He went from Concord to Rutland (now Paxton), Mass., where he resided south-east of Turkey Hill Pond; held town offices and was in the military service; he malted barley and made brick; was moderator (1765) of the first Paxton town meeting; subscribed to the first church covenant when organized in 1767; will dated 1 June, 1776;

son Abel became executor 23 April, 1794. See *Hists. of Rutland* and *Paxton*.

Children (Brown), born in Rutland:

    i *Abel*⁵, b. probably 1739.

    ii Martha, b. probably 1743; m. ———— Williams.

    iii Abigail, b. probably 1746; m. ———— Davis.

    iv Samuel, b. 1749.

    v Alpheus, b. 1752; had a descendant, Charles Brigham Brown, who was local historian of Rutland.

    vi Abijah, b. Paxton, 9 Oct., 1755; d. 1834-6; m. 1775, Phebe, dau. of Dr. Solomon Parsons of Leicester, Mass.; b. 1755; a " Minute Man," and marched to Lexington with Capt. Phineas Moore; afterward in the Continental Army 3 years; moved to Swanzey, N. H. Ch.:

        1 *Elizabeth*⁶, b. 9 Oct., 1779; d. 13 July, 1865; m. Stephen Green of Leicester, Mass., b. 24 Dec., 1772; d. 6 March, 1842; had 6 ch. the 3d one, Samuel, was living in Spencer, Mass., in 1905; has a son, Charles A. Green of Malden, Mass.

        2 *Phebe*, b. 14 July, 1781.

        3 *Sarah*, b. 17 Nov., 1783; m. Philemon Whitcomb of Swanzey, N. H., and Fayston, Vt., who had Zelinda, who m. Merrill Tyler, who had Laura E., who m. Dr. Gershom N. Brigham, 598, father of the author of this volume.

        4 *Solomon*, b. 23 July, 1785.

        5 *David*, b. 1787.

        6 *Abijah*, b. 1789.

        7 *Brigham*, b. 1790.

        8 *Jerusha*, b. 19 March, 1792.

        9 *Harriet*, b. 21 June, 1794.

        10 *Orrin*, b. 3 Aug., 1796.

        11 *Jonathan Hubbard*, b. 8 June, 1798.

50 *JOHN⁴, son of Thomas³ and Elizabeth (Bowker) Brigham; born in Sudbury, Mass., 14 Sept., 1726; married " Cate " (Catherine) Willis.

Children, born in Sudbury:

    i Elijah⁵, b. 9 Oct., 1773; d. 7 Sept., 1775.

137 ii Samuel, b. 3 March, 1775.

138 iii Elijah, b. 13 Oct., 1776.

139 iv Eber, b. 28 June, 1778.

    v Catherine, b. 2 April, 1780; probably d. unm.

    vi John, b. 20 Feb., 1783.

140 vii William, b. 20 Dec., 1784.

    viii Elizabeth, b. 15 June, 1786; d. unm., 16 April, 1875.

    ix Sally, b. 4 Aug., 1788; d. Sudbury, 1 Sept., 1870; m. 1809, Elisha Maynard.

    x Abigail, b. 5 Jan., 1790.

    xi Mary, b. 2 Dec., 1793; d. unm., 1 March, 1846.

    xii Chloe, b. 3 March, 1795; d. 1 April, 1836; m. 1815, Cyrus Willis.

* There may be an intermediate generation (" Capt. Isaac ").

51 *LIEUT. ABIJAH[4], son of Thomas[3] and Elizabeth (Bow-ker) Brigham; born in Sudbury, Mass., 26 Aug., 1737; died there, 2 April, 1814, æ. 76; married 5 June, 1759, Eunice Willis, b. 16 Jan., 1741; died 9 March, 1826, æ. 85.

Was a Lieut. in the Revolution and on the Sudbury muster roll of 1775; he marched on the Lexington alarm from Sudbury to Cambridge. Was in Capt. A. Wheeler's Co., Col. E. Howe's regi-ment, as 2d Lieut., commissioned 5 July, 1776; also, enlisted 20 Oct., 1779, as 2d Lieut. in Capt. A. Cranston's Co., Col. Denny's regiment. Was a blacksmith, and resided on the ancient Dr. John Brigham homestead in Sudbury, where he was selectman in 1778, '81' and '87· The dates of his children and some of his later descendants are taken from his old Bible in possession of Newell Willcomb, who lives on the John Jr. homestead and who married Emma, youngest daughter of Lewis Brigham of Maynard, Mass.

Children, born in Sudbury:
    i Abel[5], b. 25 March, 1760; he was a soldier in the Revolution from Sudbury in 1775; he settled in Paris, N. Y. Ch.: *Abel, Jr.*[6], and 2 daus.
141   ii John, b. 19 May, 1762.
142 iii Joseph, b. 26 Sept., 1764.
    iv Eunice, b. 7 Feb., 1767; d. 1773.
    v Reuben, b. 21 Sept., 1769; settled in Paris, N. Y. Ch.:
       1 *Reuben, Jr.*[6]
       2 *George*, and daughters.
    vi Elizabeth (Betsey), b. 14 April, 1772; d. 1781.
   vii Abner, b. 31 Oct., 1774; d. 16 Aug., 1807; m. Persis Bowker, 20 April, 1797. Ch.:
       1 *Sophia*[6], bapt. Sudbury, 6 Jan., 1799.
       2 *Louisa.*
  viii Eunice, b. 5 July, 1779; m. 11 Dec., 1798, Loring Wheeler.

52 †DR. SAMUEL[4], son of Capt. Samuel[3] and Abigail (Moore) Brigham; born in Marlboro, Mass., 3 March, 1723; died, West Indies, 1756; married (1), 24 Nov., 1747, Elizabeth Wood, who died s. p.; married (2), 9 Jan., 1752, Anna, daughter of Dr. Benjamin Gott of Marlboro; born there, 8 Jan., 1731; ‡she mar-ried (2) §Capt. Maynard of Westboro, Mass., and died 6 July,

---

* *Colonial War Record:* In 1755, private on Crown Point expedition. Also 13 weeks with Capt. Samuel Dakin.
   In 1758, with Capt. Henry Spring, Col. William Williams.
† *Colonial War Record:* Surgeon, 14 weeks on Crown Point expedition, Col. Joshua Browne.
‡ She is the " Cousin Maynard " of Rev. E. Parkman's Diary; she was a niece of Madam Parkman. " Mrs. Maynard dined here " is a frequent note in the *Diary*, particularly on Sunday.
§ " Capt. Maynard has the reputation of being the wealthiest man of his day in Westboro, and his house, burned a few years ago, was solid and handsome......
The work on his farm for many years was performed by slaves, and he was loth to give them up, so loth, that the heavy stone walls by the side of the avenue leading to his house are said to be among the very last labor performed by slaves in Massa-chusetts " (Foot-note, *Parkman Diary*, p. 62).

1799, and was interred in the ancient burying-ground in Westboro, near the south wall.

Dr. Samuel settled in Marlboro and was chosen selectman in 1755; he represented Marlboro in the General Court in 1741. History states that he received £59 10s. for teaching " 2 quarters " in 1747. He went to the West Indies as an army surgeon, was taken with yellow fever and died there.

Children (by second wife), born in Marlboro:

  i Elizabeth[5], b. 11 Aug., 1752; d. 20 June, 1798; m. 17 Dec., 1778, Dea. David Goodell of Marlboro, b. 1716; they probably had no children.*

143 ii Anna, b. 29 Oct., 1753.

  iii Susannah, b. 12 April, 1755; m. 4 Oct., 1770 (?), Elisha, son of John Hudson (who with 8 sons was in the Revolution); b. in M., 174—; was in the French War, 1756-58-60); was in the Revolution from Northboro; moved to Canada, where died. Ch. (Hudson), b. Marlboro:

  1 *William[5]*, b. 29 March, 1770.

  2 *Samuel*, b. 25 Dec., 1771.

  Others, names unknown.

144 iv Samuel, b. posthumous, 21 Aug., 1756.

53 †LIEUT. URIAH[4], son of Capt. Samuel[3] and Abigail (Moore) Brigham; born in Marlboro, Mass., 10 Sept., 1727; died there, 22 Oct., 1782; married, 12 July, 1750, Sarah Breck, daughter of Dr. Benjamin and Sarah (Breck) Gott (Mrs. Gott was the daughter of Rev. Robert Breck of Marlboro and sister of Madam Parkman); born in Marlboro, 21 March, 1729; died 31 Jan., 1815.

Morse says of Uriah that he was brought up a gentleman's son and never performed a day's labor in his life; that he lived in the style of the English gentry, receiving the visits of the *elite* from far and near, keeping an open house, in which there was no limit to his hospitality. His estate bore the strain of such a lavish style of living better than might have been expected, lasting through his time, but was so involved, at his death, that the administrators had employment for 30 years. He resided in the

---

* " 17 Dec., 1778....At eve there were two marriages, viz: Mr. David Godell to Miss Elizabeth Brigham (Cousin Maynard's Dauter) 8 Dollars.   . . .

" 20 Dec., 1778. ......Mr. David Goodell the Bridegroom and his Bride together with her mother Maynard dined here, as did Mr. Elijah Brigham. P. M. The Bridegroom preached on I Cor. 6. 19-20, and I hope to ye Glory of God. He went from ye Meeting House, with his new Spouse, to Capt. Maynard's."

" 9 June, 1779. Sophy, with Mr. Brigham, in Mr. Newton's Chaise goes to Marlboro. Mr. Goodell here and shows me ye Certificate of his Ordination at large, or as a Missionary, to go to the State of Vermont."

" 5 Feb., 1788o. ......Hear that Mr. David Goodall and his Wife were come from Athol & passed by to Capt. Maynard's yesterday........He is going to Marlboro, his Father being dyed lately."—*Parkman Diary.*

† *Colonial War Record:* Lieut. 1762, 3d Marlboro Co., Capt. Thomas How, Jr., Col. Ward.

south part of Marlboro on a part of the estate which had belonged to his father.* Was chosen warden in 1764 and selectman in 1765, '68 and '69' and town clerk in 1769.

Children, born in Marlboro:
145   i John Gott⁵, b. 8 Feb., 1750-1.
146   ii Henry, b. 26 Oct., 1752 (N. S.).
     iii Sarah, b. 22 Jan., 1755; m. in Sudbury, 14 March, 1782, Dr. Nathaniel Gott of Wenham, Mass.; settled in Guildhall, Vt., and rem. to Cooperstown, N. Y.; 1 son.
147   iv Uriah, b. 11 July, 1757.
     v Abigail, b. 31 Dec., 1759; m. David Wait; res. Sterling, Mass.; 2 sons and 3 daus.
     vi Persis, b. 7 April, 1762; m. Alexander Watson; res. Frankfort, N. Y.
148   vii Edward, b. 13 June, 1764.
     viii Nathaniel, b. 17 Aug., 1766; d. y.
     ix Robert, b. 14 Dec., 1769; d. y.
     x Anne, b. 16 Aug., 1773; m. Charles Safford; res. Lancaster, Mass., and d. s. p.
     xi Robert Breck, b. 2 Jan., 1776; d. about 1815, in Worcester, Mass., unm.

54 †GEORGE⁴, son of Capt. Samuel³ and Abigail (Moore) Brigham; born in Marlboro, Mass., 17 March, 1730; died in Southboro, Mass., 27 March, 1808; married Mary, daughter of Ebenezer Bragg of Shrewsbury, Mass.; born 4 Jan., 1735; died 4 Feb., 1822.

George settled first on a farm in the south part of Marlboro, which his father left him. His uncle, Col. Timothy, made him his heir, and he came into possession of another fine farm in Southboro, where he removed and resided until his decease. In 1774 was on a Committee of Safety to draw up a covenant of non-consumption of British goods; selectman in 1774, '75 and '76; in 1775 on a committee of 3, representing Marlboro, in the Provisional Government; representative to the General Court in 1776, '77' and '81' from Marlboro, and chosen representative from Southboro 9 May, 1785. In one year, 1771, he lost six children by death, and 2 the year of the dreadful epidemic, 1775. *Hist.* ₒf *Marlboro,* p. 186.

Children, born in Marlboro:
     i Phineas⁵, b. 25 May, 1755; d. 3 July, 1755.
     ii George, b. 22 July, 1756; d. 26 Aug., 1782.
149   iii Phineas, b. 7 Oct., 1757.

* " 18 Apr., 1780. ......Mr. Stone and I rode together to Marlboro. I visited our Kinsman, Lt. Uriah Brigham, where I lodged."
" 19 Apr., 1780. A Storm of Rain and Snow—but I ventured to try for Home. Sat out in ye Morning under another Disadvantage, viz., the Horse lame—got to Captain Edmund Brigham's and dined there. Arrived safe at home about 3 P. M."
Parkman Diary.
† *Colonial War Record:* 26 April, 1757, with Col. Abe Williams from Marlboro.

iv Timothy, b. 11 Feb., 1759; d. 6 Jan., 1804, unm., in Southboro.
v Louisa, b. 27 Sept., 1760; d. 18 Sept., 1771.
vi Ashbel, b. 3 March, 1762; d. 27 Sept., 1771.
vii Mary, b. 18 Dec., 1763; d. 27 Aug., 1771.
viii Thankful, b. 7 May, 1765; m. Capt. Daniel Brigham, 162.
ix Zerviah, b. 6 Apr., 1767; d. 11 Sept., 1771.
x Samuel, b. 27 Jan., 1769; d. 1 Sept., 1771.
xi Stephen, b. 7 Jan., 1771; d. 3 March, 1771.
150 xii Ashbel Samuel, b. 2 March, 1772.
xiii Mary Louisa, b. 6 May, 1773; d. 2 Sept., 1775.
xiv Stephen, b. 8 Aug., 1774; d. 11 Sept., 1775.
xv Frances, b. 24 Dec., 1776; m. Nathan Brigham, son of 71.
xvi William, b. 2 April, 1779; m. Mary Graves; was mortally wounded in the battle of Tippecanoe, and d. 8 Dec., 1811, in Vincennes, Ind., s. p.
xvii Infant, d. unnamed.

55 DOROTHY[4] (Morse calls her "Dorotha"), daughter of Lieut. Jedediah[3] and Bethiah (Howe) Brigham; born in Marlboro, Mass, 2 March, 1721; died 4 Sept., 1796; married, 25 Jan., 1738-9, Thomas, son of Thomas and Rebekah (Perkins) Howe; born in Marlboro, 20 June, 1716.

Children (Howe), born in Marlboro:
i Sibyl[5], b. 29 May, 1740; d. 23 July, 1822; m. Peter Wood from Concord to Marlboro; J. P. and prominent man, who d. 5 March, 1820. Ch. (Wood):
1 *Dorothy[6];* 2 *Thomas;* 3 *Martha;* 4 *Anna;* 5 *Moses;* 6 *Jedediah.*
ii Fiske, b. 23 June, 1741; m. Lydia Bigelow of Shrewsbury, Mass., dau. of 78.
iii Antipas, b. 16 April, 1745; m. Catherine Tainter; moved to Princeton, Mass. Ch.:
1 *Catherine[6].*
iv Artemas, b. 11 March, 1747; moved to Templeton.
v Francis, b. 26 June, 1750; d. 28 Feb., 1833; m. Mary Hapgood; res. Marlboro. Ch.:
1 *Joseph[6];* 2 *Francis;* 3 *Lewis;* 4 *Ezekiel;* 5 *Thomas;* 6 *Polly;* 7 *Lucy;* 8 *Lydia;* 9 *Lambert;* 10 *Abigail.*

56 SOLOMON[4], son of Lieut. Jedediah[3] and Bethiah (Howe) Brigham; born in Marlboro, Mass, 25 May, 1723; died there, 1 Feb., 1807; married (1), 1 Aug., 1754, Martha Boyd; married (2), Sally ———, who died 16 Jan., 1797. He settled near Feltonville in Marlboro where his grand-son, Charles[6] Brigham, long resided; was selectman, 1777; overseer of the poor, 1779 and '80; grand jury-man, 1782.

Children, born in Marlboro:
151 i Lovewell[5], b. 1 Dec., 1754
ii Bethiah, b. 31 July, 1756; d. 24 Aug., 1848, unm., æ. 92.
iii Charles, b. 20 Aug., 1758; d. y.

iv Timothy, b. 22 Nov., 1760; d. 15 Nov., 1811, unm.
v Artemas, b. 24 Jan., 1763; d. y.
152 vi Ivory, b. 30 April, 1765.

57 FRANCIS[4], son of Lieut. Jedediah[3] and Bethiah (Howe) Brigham; born in Marlboro, Mass., 13 Aug., 1725; died about 1810 (see *N. E. Hist. Gen. Reg.*, vol. 29, p. 69); married Phebe, daughter of Jabez and Phebe (Eager) Ward; born in Marlboro, 22 Nov., 1730; died in New Marlboro, Mass., about 1800. He was a first settler in New Marlboro, and kept a public house during the Revolution.

Children, born in New Marlboro:
   i Lucretia[5], m. Jonathan Harmar of N. M. Ch. (Harmar) (Morse says " Harman "), b. N. M.:
      1 *Jonathan[6]; 2 William; 3 Lovisa; 4 Origen; 5 Belinda.*
153   ii Artemas.
   iii Origen, M. D., d. about 1812, s. p.; m. Eleanor Soule; he was a physician and surgeon in the Revolution; was the leading physician in Schoharie, N. Y., where he died; original member of the Society of the Cincinnati; was Surgeon's mate with Warner in Bailey's 2d Regt., in 1781.
   iv Clarissa, m. ———— Hathaway, and res. in Vermont.
   v Candace, m. Seth Norton; res., s. p., New Marlboro.
   vi Jedediah, d. Vernon, N. Y., 1835; m. Olive Clark. Ch., b. Vernon:
      1 *Candace[6]; 2 Emma; 3 George; 4 Henry Augustus,* a lawyer in Western N. Y.
   vii Catherine, m. Maj. Jonathan Chapman; res. Chatham, N. Y.; o. s. p.
154 viii John, b. 1767.
   ix Francis, d. unm., Syracuse, N. Y.; res. Vernon, N. Y.
   x Sophia, d. unm., at Westfield, N. Y., about 1841.

58 LUCY[4], daughter of Lieut. Jedediah[3] and Bethiah (Howe) Brigham; born in Marlboro, Mass., 15 May, 1727; died in Berlin, Mass., 14 May, 1778; married Col. Silas Bailey of Berlin, where he died, 30 Oct., 1793, æ. 70. He was a plucky patriot,* and interested in Shay's Rebellion; married (2) Mrs. Elizabeth (Rice) Brigham, widow of Capt. Paul Brigham, 82, of Marlboro, and married (3) Catherine, daughter of Eleazer Howe of Marlboro.

Children (Bailey), by first marriage, born in Berlin:
   i Lieut. Timothy[5], b. 9 Feb., 1749; killed in the Revolution, 1780; m. Martha Rice, and left small family.
   ii Bertha, b. 4 Oct., 1752.
   iii Major Silas, b. 22 July, 1756; res. Northboro, where d. 3 Oct., 1840; m. Lavinia Bartlett. Ch.:
      1 *Timothy[6]; 2 Silas; 3 Holloway; 4 Calvin; 5 Levina; 6 Lewis;* 7 *Lucy;* 3 d. y.

* " 11 Nov., 1780........At eve Col. Silas Bailey here, returning from Rhode Island, his son Timothy dyed there & is buryd."—*Parkman Diary.*

iv Lucy, b. 6 Jan., 1759; m. Jabez Fairbanks, who was grandfather of Col. Silas Fairbanks of Hudson, Mass.

v Amherst, b. 27 July, 1761; d. in Berlin, 9 Nov., 1830; m. Lydia Barnes of Bolton, Mass.; he had the homestead. Ch.:

1 *Lucy*[6]; 2 *William*; 3 *Persis*; 4 *Sarah*; 5 *Calvin*; 6 *Hannah*; 7 *Zilpah*; 8 *Lucinda*; 9 d. y.

vi Calvin, b. 2 Jan., 1763.

59 *STEPHEN[4], son of Lieut. Jedediah[3] and Bethiah (Howe) Brigham; born in Marlboro, Mass., " 2 Nov., or 11 Feb.," 1732 (*Marlb. Hist.*); died in Princeton, Mass., 17 April, 1821; married, 4 Jan., 1757, Betsey, daughter of Col. John and Dinah (Keyes) Weeks, born in Marlboro, 26 Jan., 1736; died 6 Sept., 1787. Moved to Princeton, where was one of the earliest planters.

Children, born in Princeton:

155   i John[5], b. 8 Aug., 1758.

    ii Betsey, b. 5 Feb., 1760; d. 1840; m. 22 March., 1789, Jonathan Newton; res. Alstead, N. H. Ch. (Newton):

1 *Asa*[6]; 2 *Silas*, who had the homestead; 3 *Joel*; 4 *Betsey*.

156 iii Stephen, b. 9 Aug., 1762.

157 iv Abner, b. 31 May, 1764.

158 v Asa, b. 2 June, 1767.

159 vi David, b. 8 April, 1771.

   vii Lucy, b. 9 Jan., 1774; d. 28 Aug., 1843; m. 2 Nov., 1806, Samuel Russell; res. E. Sudbury, Mass. Ch. (Russell):

1 *Reuben*[6], b. 23 April, 1808; d. s. p. in St. Louis, 20 Aug., 1849; moved West; m. Jane Patterson of Circleville, O.

2 *Abby*, b. 21 April, 1810; m. 28 March, 1857, Dea. Waldo Winter; res. Clinton, Mass.

3 *Sarah*, b. 8 Nov., 1811; unm.

Other ch. names unknown.

160 viii Silas, b. 12 Aug., 1776.

   ix Lydia, m. Nov., 1796, Elijah Wild.

   x Persis, m. 15 May, 1796, John Whitcomb, b. in Lancaster, Mass., 6 May, 1770; drowned, W. Boylston, Mass., 11 Sept., 1820; she d. in Ware, Mass., 1830; res. Princeton. Ch. (Whitcomb):

1 *Sally*[6], b. 21 March, 1797; m. (1) Oliver Nash; m. (2) Elijah Kennon; had a family by each m.; res. Medford, Mass.

2 *Persis*, b. 17 May, 1799; d. in Barre, Vt., 1872; m. Henry Keyes; 4 sons and 1 dau.

3 *Betsey*, b. 1801; d. 1883.

4 *John A.*, b. 14 Sept., 1803; d. in Boston, 1851; m. Caroline Pierce; 6 sons and 1 dau.

5 *Lydia*, b. 2 Jan., 1806; d. in Boston, 1863; m. Thomas Ayer of Boston; 2 daus. and 1 son.

161 xi Aaron, b. 13 March, 1781.

60 †WINSLOW[4], son of Lieut. Jedediah[3] and Bethiah (Howe) Brigham; born in Marlboro, Mass., 30 Aug., 1736; died there 29

---

* *Colonial War Record:* 1757, 2d Marlboro Co., Capt. J. Weeks' Train Band.
† *Colonial War Record:* Private 1756, Capt. Howe, 15 weeks, 1 day. In Col. Willard's Regt., Crown Point. 1757, Private 2d Marlboro Co., Capt. J. Weeks' Train Band.

‡ *History of Marlboro*, p. 377.

Aug., 1791; married 29 July, 1760, Elizabeth, daughter of Daniel Harrington of Marlboro (whose great-grandfather was a proprietor of Watertown); born in Marlboro, 20 March, 1737; died 25 Oct., 1815.

Morse says: "Winslow was an uncommon man and a distinguished citizen. Up to the time he came upon the stage, the municipal affairs of Marlboro from the first, had been, in a great degree, managed by the Brighams, although they had constituted only a fraction of her numerical population; but during the eventful period of our Revolutionary struggle, he and his namesakes seem to have had almost the entire control." Apparently no vigilance committees were organized "until the last year of the war, when, with a new settler, arrived a spirit of jealousy or rivalry, and every Brigham, save one, was displaced from office; and he who had held the highest in the town was insulted with the lowest and a committee of vigilance and correspondence chosen. But this overturn lasted but one year. The Brighams were re-elected, and Winslow again chosen town clerk and selectman, in which offices he had served the preceding ten years and he was continued for years afterwards as selectman." He was town clerk, 1770-'80-'82; assessor; 1769-'73-'77-'81-'82-'84-'86-'88; Rep. to General Court, 1783-'84; delegate Constitutional Convention, 1779; selectman, 1770-'80-'82-'84-'86-'88-'89-'91.

He resided on the homestead of his great-grandfather, and carried on the tannery. Aug. 4, 1791, he made his will. He provided with great care for his wife, Elizabeth, "so long as she remains my widow." His daughters, Lucy Brigham and Elizabeth Barnes, were each to receive money to be paid by their brothers, Daniel and Jedediah. His sons, Aaron, Artemas, Amariah, and John Winslow, were each to have money to be paid by the same, and he expressed a desire that John Winslow should have a liberal education. "To Daniel and Jedediah he bequeathed all his real and most of his personal property. Daniel was to have the Indian pasture of 34 acres, the tan-yard of one acre; and Jedediah the remainder of his lands and buildings, and to be sole executor."

Children, born in Marlboro:
162   i Daniel⁵, b. 25 Dec., 1760.
163   ii Aaron, b. 22 Nov., 1762.
      iii Jedediah, b. 5 Jan., 1765; d. 3 Sept., 1766.
164   iv Jedediah, b. 15 Sept., 1766.
165   v Elizabeth, b. 5 March, 1769.
      vi Amariah, b. 30 May, 1771; d. Feb., 1798, unm., in Conn.
      vii John Winslow, b. 10 Jan., 1774; d. Norfolk, Va., Aug., 1826; m. 1793, Hannah Lewis, b. in Wellfleet, Mass., 17 June, 1774; d. 7 May, 1801, in Boston; he was a sea-captain. Ch.:

      1 *Mary Ann*⁶, b. May, 1794; d. Nov., 1821, unm.
      2 *Hannah,* d. before 1801.
      3 *John Winslow,* d. before 1801.
      4 *Helen,* d. before 1801.
166 viii Artemas, b. 13 May, 1776.
167   ix Lucy, b. 28 June, 1779.
      x Lydia, b. 7 Jan., 1782; d. 7 Aug., 1784.

    61 BETTY⁴, daughter of Jotham³ and Abigail Brigham; born in Marlboro, Mass., 15 Nov., 1719; married, 23 Feb., 1741-42, Jonathan, son of Joseph and Sarah (Howe) Stratton; born in Marlboro, 28 Dec., 1714; died 10 Aug , 1758.

    Children (Stratton), born in Marlboro:
      i Jonathan⁶, b. 29 Sept., 1742; m. 10 Sept., 1765, Abigail, dau. of
          Jonathan Barnes, who d. 30 Dec., 1794. Ch.:
          1 *Abigail*⁶; 2 *Jonathan;* 3 *Aaron;* 4 *Moses;* 5 *Sally;* 6 *Samuel;*
          7 *Lydia;* 8 *Anna;* 9 *Phebe.*
      ii Betty, b. 11 April, 1744; m. 4 Sept., 1764, William Brigham, 87.
      iii Sarah, b. 20 March, 1746; m. Daniel Barnes.
      iv Samuel, b. 30 Dec., 1748; m. Lucy Brigham, dau. of 42.
      v Lucy, b. 4 Dec., 1750; d. 1 April, 1771.
      vi Aaron, b. 6 Sept., and d. 19 Oct., 1753.

    62 ABRAHAM⁴, son of Jotham³ and Abigail Brigham; born in Marlboro, Mass., 25 Feb., 1720-1; died 10 Nov., 1788; married, 26 Feb., 1752, Phebe Martin, who died 17 Jan., 1806, æ. 77 years, 8 mo., 23 days. He resided in Marlboro and was in the Revolution. Marched on the Lexington alarm, Capt. Wm. Brigham's Co., Col. Jonathan Ward's Regt., service 14 days.

    Children, born in Marlboro:
      i Lucy⁵, b. 30 Oct., 1753; d. in M., 8 June, 1835; m. 7 Nov., 1771,
          David, son of Nathaniel Wyman of Hopkinton, Mass.; b. about
          1746; went to Marlboro, 1754; removed to Marblehead; d. in
          Marlboro, 3 Feb., 1838. Ch. (Wyman), one of whom (supposed
          to be eldest child):
          1 *Asenath*⁶, burned to death in Marlboro, 21 Nov., 1857, æ. 85
          (*Hist. of Marlboro,* p. 480).
168   ii Fortunatus, b. 29 Sept., 1759.
      iii Anna, b. 1 March, 1763; m. Samuel Barnes; res. Warwick.
      iv Gardner, b. 30 April, 1766; d. 29 Dec., 1779.

    63 *ASA⁴, son of Jotham³ and Abigail Brigham; born in Marlboro, Mass., 1 Nov., 1729; died 18 Nov., 1806; married, 13 June, 1754, Elizabeth, daughter of John and Zipporah (Brigham) Warren; born 31 March, 1734; died 15 Aug., 1807.

    He settled in Marlboro and was assessor in 1773-4.

    * *Colonial War Record:* Corporal from Marlboro, 26 April, 1757, Capt. (Col.) Abraham Williams' Co.

Children, born in Marlboro:

    i Elizabeth⁵, b. 18 Dec., 1754; d. 3 June, 1827; m. 20 Feb., 1776, Francis (Morse says: "Aaron," see *Hist. Marlboro,* p. 448), son of Samuel and Lucy (Barnes) Stevens; b. in Marlb., 8 Feb., 1749; d. 1829. Ch. (Stevens), b. in Marlb.:

        1 *Capt. John⁶*, b. 12 Jan., 1777; m. Mary Brigham, dau. of 162.
        2 *Capt. Aaron,* b. 26 Jan., 1779; m. 19 May, 1806, Mary, dau. of Capt. William Gates; was a prominent citizen of Marlb., living in 1861. Ch.:

           i William F.⁷; ii Lyman G., iii Loriman G.
169 ii Lewis, b. 24 March, 1756.
170 iii Jotham, b. 18 Nov., 1761.
    iv Hastings, b. 9 March, 1764; d. 28 Aug., 1805, unm. in Marlboro.

64　*ANTIPAS⁴, son of Jotham³ and Abigail Brigham; born in Marlboro, Mass., 25 May, 1740; married Catherine, daughter of Benjamin and Elizabeth (Morse) Woods; born 4 April, 1733.

Moved to St. Albans, Vt., where charter member of Congregational Church in 1803. Was in the Revolution.

Children:

    i Catherine⁵, b. 10 Feb., 1767; d. 23 Feb., 1831; m. 14 May, 1786, William, son of Ivory and Sophia (Banister) Bigelow; b. in Marlboro, 8 Jan., 1764; d. there, 30 Dec., 1807. Ch. (Bigelow), b. in Marlboro:

        1 *John⁶*, b. 25 Oct., 1786; d. 1824; m. 3 Sept., 1809, Hepsibah Barnes; res. Hudson, Mass. Ch.: i John⁷; ii Sidney, and daus.
        2 *Edward,* b. 18 Nov., 1788; m. Thirza Bartlett; res. Bethlehem, N. Y. Ch.: i William⁷; ii Ivory; iii Stephen; iv Elijah, and others.
        3 *Asa,* b. 19 Jan., 1791; d. 1829; m. 4 Oct., 1809, Lucy Hapgood; res. Concord, Mass. Ch.: i Clarence⁷; ii Ernest, et al.
        4 *Abigail,* b. 11 April, 1793; m. 31 Dec., 1808, Levi, son of Artemas Howe; b. 30 April, 1787. Ch. (Howe): Elisha⁷, William, and daus.
        5 *Jotham,* b. 14 March, 1795; m. Lois Drury; went to St. Louis, Mo. Ch.: Jotham⁷, Windsor, and 2 daus.
        6 *Artemas,* b. 14 Jan., 1798; d. unm., 1823.
        7 *Levi,* b. 14 Dec., 1799; m. 13 Feb., 1823, Martha B. Howe; res. W. Boylston. Ch.: i Francis⁷; ii George; iii William, and daus.
        8 *Adeline,* b. 1 Feb., 1802; m. 26 Sept., 1822, Ebenezer Witt.
        9 *Luther,* b. 1 Nov., 1805; m. Hannah Tucker; res. W. Boylston. Ch.: Elmer⁷, and 2 daus.
       10 *William,* b. 16 Dec., 1807; went to sea, U. S. N., and was never heard from.

    ii Abigail, b. 22 May, 1768.
    iii Sabrina, b. 23 Dec., 1770; m. Daniel Rice.
    iv Lucretia, b. 12 Oct., 1773.

65　ABIGAIL⁴, daughter of Jotham³ and Abigail Brigham; born in Marlboro, Mass., 22 April, 1745; died 27 April, 1805; married,

  * *Colonial War Record:* Marlboro, 26 April, 1757, Capt. (Col.) Abraham Williams' Co.

25 Feb., 1767, Peter Bender; he died in Bolton, Mass., æ. 87. He married a second time.

Children (Bender), born in Marlboro:
    i Samuel⁵, b. 1 March, 1768; m. a Barnard of Northboro.
   ii John, b. 4 Nov., 1769; a Boston merchant; d. on voyage to South Carolina.
  iii Jotham, b. 19 Dec., 1771; grad. Harvard College, 1796; studied law; d. 1800.
   iv Louisa, b. 15 April, 1774; m. 1801, Isaiah L. Greene, a Member of Congress.
    v Betsey, b. 10 Sept., 1776; m. 21 Oct., 1799, David Greenough of Boston. Ch. (Greenough):
       1 *Horatio⁶,* b. 6 Sept., 1805; d. in Somerville, Mass., 18 Dec., 1852; the noted sculptor; the colossal statue of Washington, in front of the Capitol in Washington, D. C., his greatest work; res. Italy.
       2 *Dau.,* m. Thos. B. Curtis of Boston.
       3 *Dau.,* m. Chas. Huntington of Boston.
       4 *Richard Saltonstall,* also a sculptor, b. 1819; dau. m. ——— Blight of N. Y.
   vi Stephen, b. 9 July, 1779; went to sea; d. abroad.
  vii Jacob, b. 23 Sept., 1781; grad. Yale Coll.; studied law; changed name to " Hastings "; d. in N. Y. State.
 viii Henry, b. 31 May, 1784; d. about 1856; a Lieut. in War of 1812.
   ix Abigail, b. 18 May, 1787; m. Joseph Sawyer of Bolton.

66 *WILLIAM⁴, son of Charles³ and Mary (Peters) Brigham; born in Grafton, Mass., 26 March, 1739; died there, 1 Aug., 1833; married, July, 1768, Sarah, daughter of Rev. Solomon Prentice of Grafton; born there, 1 July, 1744; died 2 Feb., 1834. Her father was the first minister of Grafton.

Morse says that William inherited the Charles Brigham homestead in Grafton, which originally embraced nearly or quite the whole tract known as " Brigham Hill." A well-educated man for his time, and a " great reader," he yet had no taste for public office or employment. He was offered a justice's commission, then a great honor, which he declined. He was straight, tall, and muscular, and this is probably the original type of the race. He ·was wont " to jump over fences 5 and even 6 feet in height, without touching hand or foot; and when 90 years old would rather walk than ride 1 or 2 miles, and would accomplish the distance nearly as soon as a boy." He never took medicine, and died of old age.

Children, born in Grafton:
171   i Charles⁵, b. 27 July, 1769.
172   ii Susanna, b. 27 Nov., 1770.
       iii Solomon, b. 26 Nov., 1772; d. s. p., 7 June, 1817; m. Lucy, dau. of Andrew Adams, Jr., of Grafton, b. 14 March, 1778; a farmer of Grafton.
    * *Colonial War Record:* Grafton, 1757, Train Band, Capt. Sam. Warren.

173   iv Sally, b. 12 Sept., 1780.
174   v Persis, b. 4 Aug., 1786.

67   ANNA[4], daughter of Charles[3] and Mary (Peters) Brigham; born in Grafton, Mass., 18 March, 1745; died 11 Sept., 1831; married (1) Samuel Harrington; born in Grafton, 10 June, 1743; died 3 Oct., 1773; married (2) Henry, son of the Rev. Solomon Prentice; had a family by his first wife, Sarah Rice; he died in Grafton, 1781; was hotel-keeper at the " Center " (see *Hist. of Grafton*).

Children (Harrington), born in Grafton:
    i Mary[5], b. 11 Sept., 1765; m. Martin Smith.
   ii Anna, b. 29 Aug., 1767; m. Fortunatus Harrington.
  iii Samuel, b. 31 Aug., 1769; d. 3 Oct., 1802; m. Abigail Putnam.
   iv Joshua, b. 13 March, 1771; m. Polly Adams.
    v Lucy, b. 13 July, 1773; m. Perley Goddard.
Child (Prentice), born in Grafton:
   vi Charles, b. 21 Aug., 1781; d. s. p.; m. Widow Elizabeth (Case) Merriam, who d. 1851; was town clerk of Grafton, 1836-53; selectman and assessor, 1852-53.

68   PERSIS[4], daughter of Charles[3] and Mary (Peters) Brigham; born in Grafton, Mass., 4 Jan., 1755; died about 1780; married, 1775, Lieut. Noah B., son of Capt. Aaron Kimball; born in Grafton, 19 May, 1756; died 21 Aug., 1806; was at the " Lexington Alarm " in company commanded by his father; was selectman and on the school-committee in Grafton; (he married [2], 12 Dec., 1782, Mary Chase, by whom probably Betsey, Anna, and Persis).

Children (Kimball), born in Grafton:
    i Capt. Oliver[5], b. 9 May, 1776; d. 31 March, 1819; m. (1) Hannah ————, b. 1787; d. 29 April, 1809; m. (2) Catherine ————, b. 1786; d. 13 Sept., 1819; a prominent merchant of Grafton and Westboro; representative, etc. Ch.:
      1 *Mary[6];* 2 *Hannah;* 3 *Noah;* 4 *Hannah;* 5 *Charles;* 6 *Catherine;* 7 *Oliver.*
   ii Polly, b. 7 Aug., 1779; d. 11 Dec., 1850; m. Daniel Cook of Worcester, Mass. Ch. (Cook):
      1 *Persis[6];* 2 *Mary;* 3 *Elizabeth;* 4 *Nancy;* 5 *Laura;* 6 *Oliver.*

FIFTH GENERATION

FIFTH GENERATION

69 MOSES[5], son of Lieut. Nathan[4] and Dina (Rice) Brigham; born in Marlboro, Mass., 2 Jan., 1722; died in Westboro, Mass., 3 Dec., 1769; married 2 May, 1749, Mehetabel, daughter of Joseph Grout of Westboro, Mass.; who died 30 Aug. 1795.

" The house which he occupied is the one now standing on East Main street, owned by George A. Ferguson. This, more than a hundred and twenty-five years ago, had received the usual addition for the married son's accommodation. The immense chimney with three flues is of brick, which was manufactured very early in the young town's history, from the ' clay lands ' in Marlboro, Southboro, and Northboro. This house was built by Moses Brigham, and here he brought his bride, Mehetabel. She was a member of the Grout family, and her wooing by young Brigham caused many heart-burnings and wild frenzies of jealousy to the daughter of his stepmother. One evening, when she knew that he planned to ride over to see Mehetabel, she slipped out to the stable and hamstrung Selim, his favorite horse. Moses Brigham lived here until his death; then his son-in-law, Jonathan Forbes, took possession of the north end, and the widowed Mehetabel lived in the south end. It remained in the possession of the Forbes family until 1870. It has the usual curiosities of the carpentry of those days, one of the doors—that from the sitting-room to the kitchen—having dim heart-shaped panes of glass set in the upper half."—*The Hundredth Town.*

He was surveyor in 1757; tythingman in 1760; and constable in 1762.

Children, born in Westboro:
175   i Sarah[6], b. 18 April, 1751.
176   ii Moses, b. 31 May, 1753.
177   iii Phineas, b. 23 July, 1755.
178   iv Mehetabel, b. 31 Jan., 1758.
179   v Ebenezer, b. 3 March, 1761.
      vi Mary, b. 27 July, 1764; m. Amasa Braman, M. D.; res. Sutton.
180   vii Joseph, b. 23 Sept., 1766.

70 ELIZABETH[5], daughter of Lieut. Nathan[4] and Dina (Rice) Brigham; born in Marlboro, Mass., 18 Dec., 1725; married Capt. Jedediah Fay, born in Westboro, Mass., 30 Jan., 1727 (?). They resided in Ashford, Conn.; he was Capt. in the French Wars and also Deputy to the General Assembly.

Children (Fay), born in Ashford:
    i Jedediah⁶, b. 21 April, 1760.
    ii Elizabeth, b. 29 April, 1762.
    iii Ephraim Brigham, b. 7 June, 1764.
    iv Nathan, b. 2 March, 1768.

71 *CAPT. NATHAN⁵, son of Lieut. Nathan⁴ and Elizabeth (Ward) Brigham; born in Southboro, Mass., 13 March, 1730-1; died there, 9 Feb., 1806; married (1), 6 Feb., 1751, Martha Gleason; and married (2), 15 June, 1769, Mary Hudson, who died his widow, 16 Dec., 1825, æ. 82.

Morse's account of this noted Indian fighter is as follows: " He was a Lieut. in the first French War and a distinguished officer. In the service he became warmly attached to Capt. Thomas Gage, afterwards Gen. Gage. To avenge the massacre at Fort William Henry, he and a party volunteered, under the command of Capt. Rogers, to penetrate into Canada, attack and burn the town of St. Francis, and retreat. Having accomplished the task, they were pursued and overtaken by the Indians, who killed and scalped 30 of their number. The remainder fled into the wilderness, and for the most part perished. Of the few who lived to return was Lieut. Brigham, whose deeds of valor were eulogized in ballads. He settled in Southboro, one-half a mile east of the meeting-house. Among other town offices he was chosen one of a committee to ' seat the meeting' in 1778; and one to revise the constitution reported to the towns, in 1786, for their consideration."

The male line is extinct.

Children, born in Southboro.
    i Nathan⁶, b. 30 July, 1772; d. 21 Feb., 1839; m. Frances, dau. of 54. He resided in Southboro. Ch., b. there:
        1 *Mary Mills⁷*, b. 22 July, 1805; d. 15 Aug., 1811.
        2 *Susanna Maria*, b. 5 April, 1807; m. Lincoln Brigham, 432.
    ii Thomas Gage, b. 20 March, 1774; d. 6 Oct., 1775.
    iii Mary, b. 21 Dec., 1775; d. s. p., 2 March, 1853; m. (third wife) Ebenezer Brigham, 195.
    iv Sarah, b. 25 Sept., 1778; d. unm., 17 March, 1840.
    v Martha, b. 19 June, 1781; d. unm., 11 July, 1805.
    vi Ephraim, b. 9 Aug., 1784; d. unm., 1 Feb., 1848.

72 HEPSIBAH⁵, daughter of Lieut. Nathan⁴ and Elizabeth (Ward) Brigham; born in Southboro, Mass., 1 June, 1732; died in Corinth, Vt., 27 Dec., 1815; married, 21 March, 1748, Col. John Taplin (whose father's name was Mansfield " Tapley," but all his children save one changed the name to " Taplin "), born in Charlestown, Mass., 1726; died in Corinth, 9 Nov., 1803.

* *Colonial War Record:* Lieut. Capt. Taplin, 1759; Lieut. " to westwards," 1760; Capt., 1761; Capt., 1763; presents bill, £7 12s 6d.

JUDGE ELIJAH BRIGHAM (99)

FORBES (MOSES^5 BRIGHAM) HOMESTEAD
In Westboro, Mass.; built before 1764

He raised a Southboro Co. and served in the Revolution from March, 1775, to March, 1776, in Col. Bagley's Regt. Was also out in 1758, '59, 1760, '61 at Fort Cumberland, N. S., as "Col." He was Judge of the Court of Common Pleas of Gloucester Co., N. Y. (comprising half of the present State of Vt.), in March, 1770. Was an original proprietor of the town of Corinth and Representative in 1780 (Vide Well's *Hist. of Newbury, Vt.,* and O'Callahan's *Doc. Hist of N. Y.*).

Children (Taplin), born in Corinth:
    i John⁶, b. 14 July, 1749; d. in Montpelier, Vt., 20 Nov., 1835; had 21 children (see Thompson's *Hist. of Montpelier, Vt.*).
    ii Brigham.
    iii Hepsibah.
    iv Elisha.
    v Mansfield, b. 1754.
    vi William, b. 1755; d. 17 Feb., 1806.
    vii Nathan, d. 7 July, 1824, æ. 73.
   viii Gouldsburn, b. 1758; d. 16 Nov., 1862.
    ix Polly, m. Robert Lovewell.
    x Hepsibah, m. Zaccheus Lovewell.
    xi Johnson, b. 1 July, 1766; d. about 1848.

73   CAPT. EDMUND⁵, son of Lieut. Nathan⁴ and Elizabeth (Ward) Brigham, born in Southboro, Mass., 12 Aug., 1733; died in Westboro, Mass., 29 June, 1806; married (1), 2 Nov., 1757, Sarah, probably daughter of Samuel Lyscom, born 27 Dec., 1734; died 27 May, 1769; married (2), Elizabeth Bevel, of Marlboro, born 1740; died in Westboro, 11 May, 1825; she was brought up by Mrs. Ruth Ward, who became the second wife of Joseph Brigham of Marlboro, and lived in the old house, still standing, and occupied by Miss Martha L. Ames; it was in this house that Elizabeth Bevel was married.

Capt. Edmund was also deacon; he settled near Chauncey Pond in the northeast part of Westboro, and was an important citizen. He was warden in 1774; member of a committee of vigilance and correspondence, '77 and '78; selectman, '79, '87, '88, '91, 93. Was also Captain of the Company of Minute Men who marched on the Lexington Alarm. He took 18 men to the Northern Army, (who each had a bounty of £9), and at the surrender of Burgoyne he had command of a company of volunteers. Was kicked by a horse, which incapacitated him for further service in the army. British prisoners, destined for Boston, under charge of officers, accompanied him on his journey home, and were encamped on his grounds for a night, as they passed through Westboro. During the halt, a Hessian prisoner drew a map of Capt. Brigham's fine farm as the one he intended to draw for his service in conquering the country. This map was discovered, about 1800, by a citizen from the vicinity of Westboro, hanging upon the wall of an inn in Germany, and recognized. Up to this time, his descendants have failed to find the grave of this Revolutionary hero.* He is mentioned several times in the Parkman *Diary*.

His will, allowed 2 Sept., 1806, is as follows:

In the name of God, Amen. I, Edmund Brigham of Westboro in the county of Worcester and Commonwealth of Massachusetts, Gentleman, considering the uncertainty of this mortal life, and being weak in body, yet am of sound and disposing mind & memory, (blessed be God therefor), do this ninth day of November in the year of our Lord one thousand eight hundred & four, make & ordain this my last will & Testament in manner and form following, that is to say,

First & above all, I commit my soul to God, in hope of acceptance through the righteousness of an all-sufficient Saviour, and my body to the earth to be decently buried in a christian-like manner, at the discretion of my executors, nothing doubting, that at the general resurrection my soul and body will be united: And touching such worldly estate as God in his Providence has been pleased to bestow upon me, I would and do dispose of it as follows viz, Imprimis, I give unto my dearly beloved wife, Betsey Brigham, the use & improvement of the easterly room in my now dwelling house in Westboro aforesaid, & the chamber over said room, (reserving a priviledge for my daughter Betsey Brigham to make it her home in said part of said house untill her marriage) and the priviledge of doing her work in the kitchen, cheese room and cellar of said house as shall be convenient for her, with liberty of using the aqueduct water in said house, and to pass and repass to & from the well to use that water at any and all times and liberty to pass and repass to & from all parts of said house as shall be necessary in order to perform her washing, baking & all other necessary work, so long as she shall remain my widow. I also give & order my executors to deliver unto my said wife, four bushels of rye meal, six bushels of Indian meal, Seventy-five pounds of pork, Seventy-five pounds of beef, one bushel of salt, twelve pounds of tallow, ten pounds of flax, & five pounds of sheeps wool, all the aforesaid articles to be of good quality and to be delivered at my said house yearly and every year so long as she shall remain my widow, and I also give unto her seven dollars in money, to be paid her by my executors yearly and every year, so long as she shall remain my widow, also a sufficient quantity of firewood for her use, to be brought to said house and cut fit for her fire; also cyder, beer, apples and all sorts of sauce which she may need, & to be carried to meeting & else-

* Early in the 'seventies Mr. Hosea W. Brigham of Winchester, N. H., a great-grandson, saw Capt. Brigham's gravestone in the old cemetery in Westboro. It should be found and restored.

where in a carriage as she may require, by my two sons Pierpont
& Dexter Brigham so long as she remains my widow;

And I also give and bequeath unto my said wife & to her Heirs
& assigns forever, all my household furniture & two good cows, &
the said two cows, or other two instead thereof, to be kept for her
during the time she remains my widow, at the expence of my two
sons aforesaid, and in case my said wife should be sick & infirm
while she remains my widow, my two said sons, Pierpont & Dexter,
are to provide for her a nurse & Doctor at their expence, and in
case of her decease while she is my widow, my two said sons are
to give her a decent christian burial; furthermore, in case my said
wife should intermarry after my decease, & providentially, again
be left a widow, my will is, that she may return to my said house
if she shall choose so to do, and in that case, it is my desire & will
that my two said sons Pierpont & Dexter shall provide & do for
her in all respects as they are above directed & ordered to provide &
do for her while she remains my widow.

Item, I give unto my sons Edmund Brigham, Roger Brigham,
Samuel Brigham and Lyscomb Brigham, all my wearing apparel
to be equally divided amongst them, and they to make the division
if possible, otherwise, my desire is, that they choose a man, or men
to divide it for them, whose determination shall be final.

Item, I give unto my grandchildren born of my daughter Hepzibah Brigham, deceased, & late wife of Capt. Antipas Brigham,
unto each and everyone of them that shall be living at my decease,
one dollar, to be paid when the youngest shall arrive at the age
of twenty-one years, this together with what I have heretofore
given my said daughter, I consider as their portion of my estate.

Item, I give unto my daughter, Sally Read, (wife of Daniel
Read), fifty dollars, to be paid in four years after my decease.

Item, I give unto my daughter Betsey Brigham, one good cow,
& one hundred dollars, to be paid in one year after my decease, I
also give her a priviledge of living in that part my said house,
the improvement of which is given to my said wife, and this priviledge reserved in that article as aforesaid, and this priviledge to
be enjoyed by said Betsey, untill her marriage, & if my S'd. wife
shall die or marry, Sd. Betsey shall improve the priviledges in and
about said house, as given to my Sd. wife, till Sd. Betsey shall
marry.

Item, I give unto my son Eli Brigham Four hundred dollars, one
moiety thereof to be paid in two years after my decease, and
the other moiety thereof in three years after my decease, and I
give him the privilege of making my said house his home for the
purpose of depositing his clothes &c untill his marriage, but not
in that part to be improved by my said wife & daughter.

Item, I give unto my two said sons Pierpont Brigham & Dexter Brigham, and to their heirs and assigns forever, all my right which I have in the cedar swamp which lays in common & undivided with my brother Nathan Brigham and the heirs of my brother Elijah Brigham deceased, & myself, and also an eight acre right in the common lands, (which right was given me by my father in & by his last will & testament) together with all the remainder of my estate, both real and personal (which is not herein otherwise disposed of) to be equally divided between them, excepting my four wheel carriage and harness, which I give to my said son Pierpont, they paying all my just debts, funeral charges & legacies aforesaid, and providing for my said wife (their mother) everything as is given and secured to her in the former part of this will equally between them: but my desire and will is, that the real estate aforesaid, shall not be subjected to a division between them untill my said son Dexter shall arrive at the age of twenty-one years, and if at any time there should, (unhappily and contrary to expectation) any dispute arise between said Pierpont & Dexter, respecting a division of the real or personal estate, or both, herein given to them, and they cannot agree to divide the same, my will and direction expressly is, that such disputes shall be decided by three impartial inteligent men, known for their probity and good understanding, two to be chosen by my two said sons, each having the choice of one, & the third by those two, which three men, thus chosen, shall make such division, and when made, shall be, to all intents & purposes as binding on the parties as if it had been made by any legal process whatsoever.

Finally, I constitute and appoint my two said sons Pierpont Brigham and Dexter Brigham, the executors of this my last Will & Testament hereby revoking & disannulling all former wills & bequests by me made.

In witness whereof I have hereunto set my hand & seal, the day and year first above written.

EDMUND BRIGHAM.   (Seal.)

Signed, sealed, published & declared by the said Edmund Brigham to be his last will & testament, In the presence of

NAHUM GALE
SAMUEL BELLOWS
ANDREW PETERS.

Children (by first wife), born in Westboro:
181   i Edmund⁶, b. 19 Oct., 1758.
    ii Hepsibah, b. 29 July, 1760; m. Antipas Brigham, 106.
182 iii Roger, b. 28 Feb., 1762.
183 iv Samuel, b. 6 Dec., 1763.
184   v Sarah, b. 15 March, 1765.
    vi Elizabeth, b. 2 Dec., 1766; d. 20 Oct., 1785, unm.

185 vii Lyscom, b. 19 May, 1769.
Children, by second wife:
186 viii Pierpont, b. 16 Sept., 1780.
187 ix Betsey, b. 7 May, 1782.
188 x Eli, b. 31 July, 1784.
189 xi Dexter, b. 25 May, 1786.

74 *CAPT. WILLIAM[5], son of Lieut. Nathan[4] and Elizabeth (Ward) Brigham, born in Southboro, Mass., 8 April, 1735; died in Marlboro, Mass., 20 April, 1793, of the small-pox; married (1), 4 Sept., 1759, Rebecca Ball, who died 14 Dec., 1768; married (2), Lydia Chamberlain of Westboro, Mass., who died 8 Feb., 1793; æ. 49 of the small-pox.

He resided near Gates Pond in Marlboro, and was tythingman 1762; warden '73; field-driver '74, and selectman '78, '82, and '85. Was Commander of a Company of Minute-men in Col. Jonathan Ward's regt., and marched with them on the Lexington Alarm, 19 April, 1775. His old house still stands. He was the founder of Brigham cemetery in Marlboro.

Children (by first wife), born in Marlboro:
190 i William[6], b. 27 Feb., 1761.
191 ii Rebecca, b. 1 Feb., 1763.
iii Peter, b. 27 Dec., 1764; m. ———— Bent; res. Westboro.
iv Abigail, b. 4 March, 1766; m. 18 Jan., 1787, Paul, son of Silas Barnes; b. 10 Oct., 1761, in Marlboro (Vide *Hist. of Marlboro* and *Bigelow Family.*
v Hollis, b. 4 Dec., 1768; d. *ibid.*
Children (by second wife), born in Marlboro:
192 vi Ephraim, b. 9 Oct., 1771.
vii Hollis, b. 14 March, 1773; d. unm., 8 June, 1837.
193 viii Willard, b. 18 June, 1775
ix Lydia, b. 29 Dec., 1776; m. Artemas Brigham, 166.
x Polly, b. 30 Jan., 1779; m. 16 Aug., 1797, Willard Howe of Marlboro.
xi Patty (Martha), b. 22 March, 1782; m. Caleb Brigham, 293.
194 xii Sophia, b. 12 June, 1784.
xiii Dana, b. 8 June, 1787; d. unm., with lockjaw, in Cambridgeport, Mass.

75 †EBENEZER[5], son of Lieut. Nathan[4] and Elizabeth (Ward) Brigham; born in Southboro, Mass., 24 June, 1741; died ————; married Martha ————. Morse records that he made his will 20 Feb., 1765, giving all of his estate to his wife Martha and his little daughter Patty, and the offer of his mare and saddle, at £13, 6s.8d. to his brother Elijah. He resided in Westboro, Mass.

Child, born in Westboro:
i Patty[6], b. ————; d. ————.

* *Colonial Wars:* Southboro Train Band, Col. Tim. Brigham, 1757.
† *Colonial War Record:* Priv. Capt. Maynard, 1759; also with Col. Williams.

76 ELIJAH[5], son of Lieut. Nathan[4] and Elizabeth (Ward) Brigham; born in Southboro, Mass., 5 Sept., 1743; died there, 8 Jan., 1804; married, 7 Jan., 1768, Ruth, daughter of Ezra and Abigail (Trowbridge) Taylor of Southboro; born 9 March, 1747; died 10 April, 1831.

Morse gives the story of his life substantially as follows: He resided on the homestead of Lieut Nathan in the west part of Southboro, and was a very distinguished citizen. Was chosen a member of the Provincial Congress that met at Watertown, 31 May, 1775; was one of a committee in 1778 to report on a proposed constitution for Massachusetts, and again, in 1780, to revise the constitution which had been offered and rejected by the town, and instructed to report objections proper to be adopted and returned to the convention. The reports of this committee, of which he was the principal member, are able, and if they were the product of his mind, he was a reasoner and draughtsman of rare ability. He was probably the one who was in Capt. Josiah Fay's company of Minute-men, as Lieut., and marched on the Lexington Alarm. From 1776 to 1812, his name was more intimately connected than any other man's with all the important civic transactions of Southboro. He served about 30 years as selectman, represented the town in the General Court 6 years during 1789-1800, as often as they voted to send.

Children, born in Southboro:
195   i Ebenezer[6], b. 5 April, 1768.
        ii Fanny, b. 12 Sept., 1769; m. Paul[6] Brigham, 211, and res. St. Albans, Vt.
196   iii Sylvester, b. 16 Jan., 1771.
197   iv Dinah, b. 5 Nov., 1772.
         v Persis, b. 7 Aug., 1774; d. 8 June, 1829; m. Ashbel Samuel Brigham, 150.
198   vi Elijah, b. 19 July, 1776.
199   vii Trowbridge, b. 17 Sept., 1778.
200   viii Lincoln, b. 17 June, 1780.
201   ix Hepsibah, b. 7 May, 1782.
         x Lavina, b. 26 Dec., 1784; d. 23 July, 1786.
        xi Nancy, b. 11 Dec., 1786; m. (1) Levi Ward, who d. s. p., in Westboro, 1836; m. (2) Jotham, son of Josiah Bartlett of Southboro; b. 7 April, 1783.
202   xii Martha, b. 6 June, 1790.
203   xiii Taylor, b. 29 April, 1793.

77 *AARON[5], son of Thomas[4] and Sarah (Stratton) Brigham; born in Marlboro, Mass., 17 March, 1720; made his will 8 Sept., 1768; married (1), Dec., 1740, Elizabeth, daughter of Js. Brown; she died at Rutland Dis. probably early in 1761, æ. about 49; married (2), in 1761, Sarah Winchester.

* *Colonial War Record:* Sergt. Train Band, 1757.

Morse's account says that he settled in Grafton. The inventory of his estate was presented 31 Oct., 1768. He made ample provision for his wife Sarah, " except paying a physician." He gave all his lands in Grafton to his two sons Thomas and Ephraim, and the avails of his lands in Shrewsbury, to his sons Amariah and Moses, and authorized their guardian to sell the property. He gave to his daughters Dorothy, Lydia, Lucy, and Rebecca, their own mother's apparel; and he made Thomas and Elisha (or either one of them) his executors (see Pierce's *Hist. of Grafton*).

Children (by first wife), born in Grafton:
   i Aaron⁶, b. 30 Aug., 1741; d. unm.
   ii Sarah, b. 2 Sept., 1742; d. unm.
   iii Elizabeth, b. 30 Oct., 1743; d. 4 Aug., 1760.
   iv Dorothy, b. 24 Dec., 1744; d. unm.; a division of her estate was ordered 13 July, 1769.
   v Thomas, b. 7 Feb., 1745-6; d. unm.; no further reported by Grafton records.
204 vi Ephraim, b. 2 March, 1746-47.
   vii James, b. 23 Aug., 1748; d. unm.
   viii Amariah, b. 3 Jan., 1749-50; d. 28 Jan., 1752.
   ix Lydia, b. 6 Sept., 1753; d. unm.
   x Lucy, b. 6 Dec., 1754; d. unm.
   xi Rebecca, b. 22 Feb., 1756; d. 15 April, 1759.
   xii Amariah, b. 18 Sept., 1757; m. twice, and d. in Millbury or Sutton; was in the Revolution in 1775, 1777, 1778, and 1779, short services.
   xiii Rebecca, b. 26 April, 1759; m. ———— Smith, and res. Montpelier, Vt.
   xiv Joseph, b. 28 April, 1761.
Children (by second wife), born in Grafton:
   xv Elizabeth, b. 19 April, 1763; d. 13 March, 1764.
   xvi Moses, b. 8 April, 1765.

78 LYDIA⁵, daughter of Thomas⁴ and Sarah (Stratton) Brigham; born in Marlboro, Mass., 14 March, 1721-22; died in Stow, Mass., 17 March, 1748; married, 14 April, 1747, Dea. Amariah, son of Samuel Bigelow of Marlboro; born 14 Sept., 1722; died in Stow, 8 March, 1780; (he married [2], Sarah Eveleth of Stow, and had sons Francis, Abel, Amariah, Levi, Elnathan, and daughter Sarah). He was selectman, assessor, etc.
Child (Bigelow), born in Stow:
   i Lydia⁶, b. 1 March, 1748; m. 31 March, 1767, Fiske Howe, son of 55; b. 23 June, 1741; she inherited £133 by her Grandfather Brigham's will, and other things if she had " heirs of her body "; moved to Templeton, Mass., where he was town treasurer, etc. Ch. (Howe):
     1 *Thomas⁷;* 2 *Ephraim;* 3 *Lambert,* who moved to Cleveland, O.

79 EZEKIEL⁵, son of Thomas⁴ and Sarah (Stratton) Brigham; born in Marlboro, Mass., 14 Feb., 1723-4; died in Grafton,

Mass., 4 April, 1788; married (1), Martha, daughter of Samuel
Bigelow of Marlboro, born 21 Oct., 1724; died 1 Aug., 1764; married (2), Millicent Sherman, who died æ. 70. Resided in Grafton.

Children (by first wife), born in Grafton:
- i Sergt. Abner[6], b. 19 Feb., 1750-1; m. Molly Emerson; moved
  to Hartland, Vt.; was in the Revolution, as a corporal in Capt.
  Luke Drury's Co., in 1775; may have gone to Quebec under Col.
  Arnold, Sept., 1775; sergeant, in 1779, under Col. J. Chase.
- ii Martha, b. 23 April, 1753; m. Benjamin, son of Benjamin and
  Rebecca (Parler) Leland, b. in Grafton, 1747; d. there 1828;
  he was a farmer. Ch. (Leland), b. in Grafton:
    - 1 *Huldah[7]*, b. 1774; m. Asahel Warren; res. Springfield and
      Weathersfield, Vt.
    - 2 *Daniel,* b. 1776; m. (1) Mary Forbush; m. (2) Sally Mor-
      gan; had 12 ch.; res. Weathersfield, Vt., and Barre, Mass.
    - 3 *Capt. Benjamin,* b. 1779; m. Lucy Barnes; res. Boston till
      1816, a mfr., then in New York and Philadelphia, where d.
      1842; ch.: Benj.[8], and 6 others.
- 205   iii Ezekiel, b. 30 March, 1755.
- 206   iv Isaac, b. 30 May, 1757.
- v John, b. 3 July, 1759; d. unm., 25 Nov., 1839, in Oxford; interred in Grafton.
- vi Miriam, b. 10 March, 1761; m. Joseph Gallop.
- vii Huldah, b. 1 Dec., 1762; m. Moses Rockwood.

Children (by second wife), born in Grafton.
- viii Sarah, b. 23 Aug., 1766; m. 8 Aug., 1790, Aaron Hall of Grafton;
  moved to Weathersfield. Ch. (Hall), b. in Grafton:
    - 1 *Sally[7]*, b. 20 Nov., 1790.
    - 2 *Aaron,* b. 4 June, 1793.
- ix Jacob, b. 6 Dec., 1769; m. Polly Dudley; moved to Reading, Vt.
- x Millicent, b. 26 Dec., 1771; d. in Weathersfield, 1814.
- xi Lydia, b. 29 Sept., 1774; m. 20 May, 1811, Isaac Stone of Ward
  (Auburn).
- xii Anna, b. 27 Aug., 1776; d. 18 April, 1847, in Oxford, unm.

80 *ELISHA[5], son of Thomas[4] and Sarah (Stratton) Brigham;
born in Marlboro, Mass., 25 Nov., 1726; died in Grafton, Mass.,
very aged; married Sarah ————. He resided in Grafton. The
male line is extinct.

Children, born in Grafton:
- i Elisha[6], b. 12 April, 1758; d. 28 Feb., 1776.
- ii Charles, b. 9 Oct., 1761; d. 6 Aug., 1776.
- 207   iii Sarah, b. 29 April, 1767.
- iv Molly, b. 18 March, 1769; d. 29 Aug., 1823, unm.

81 †CAPT. ITHAMAR[5], son of Thomas[4] and Sarah (Stratton)
Brigham; born in Marlboro, Mass., 6 Oct., 1729; died there, 3 May,
1784; married (1), 13 Sept., 1753, Ruth, daughter of Daniel and

* *Colonial War Record:* In Train Band, Capt. Warren.
† *Colonial War Record:* "Ensign" with Capt. Rice; Corporal First Marlboro
Co., 1757.

Mary (Bigelow) Ward, born 20 Feb., 1732; died 29 May, 1766; married (2), 29 March, 1768, Mary, daughter of Abraham and Mary (Rice) Beaman, of Marlboro; born 1 Dec., 1734; died, his widow, 13 May, 1813. He lived in Marlboro, where Alden Brigham afterward resided, and was selectman in 1775, '76, '78, '79 and '82· Probably was Lieut. in Capt. Wm. Brigham's Co., and marched on the Lexington Alarm.

Children (by first wife), born in Marlboro:
    i Ruth⁶, b. 17 Sept., 1756; d. unm., 20 Sept., 1797.
208 ii Ithamar, b. 7 Nov., 1758.
209 iii Daniel, b. 15 Nov., 1760.
    iv Silas, b. 21 Oct., 1763; d. 27 Sept., 1838; m. Persis Stow, who d. 31 March, 1835; he res. in Southboro and Northboro; this line is extinct. Ch.:
        1 *Otis⁷*, b. 4 June, 1793; d. 3 Oct., 1813.
    v Abner, b. 29 May, 1766; d. 5 July, 1766.
Children (by second wife):
210 vi Abner, b. 21 Dec., 1768.
    vii Abraham, b. 14 Nov., 1771; d. unm.

82 *CAPT. PAUL⁵, son of Thomas⁴ and Sarah (Stratton) Brigham; born in Marlboro, Mass., 26 March, 1737; died there, 4 June, 1777; married, 9 Aug., 1757, Eliza, daughter of Abraham and Persis (Robinson) Rice (she married [2], Col. Silas Bailey of Berlin); she was born 12 Oct., 1736; died 30 March, 1793. He settled in Marlboro, where was assessor, 1775-76; selectman, '77; on Committee of Correspondence, 1776, '77, and Representative, 1777. He marched on the Lexington Alarm in Capt. Daniel Barnes' Co., as 2d Lieut. He is in a list of officers commissioned 25 May, 1775, and saw considerable service in that year. He was Capt. of the 5th Co. of Col. Ezekiel Howe's Regt., commissioned 5 July, 1776.

Childen, born in Marlboro:
    i Persis⁶, b. 17 March, 1760; d. 17 June, 1760.
211 ii Paul, b. 17 June, 1761.
212 iii Samuel, b. 14 Sept., 1762.
    iv Miriam, b. 9 Jan., 1764; d. 10 Jan., 1776.
213 v Thomas, b. 25 Dec., 1765.
    vi Aaron, b. 7 Feb., 1768; d. 10 Oct., 1771.
    vii Sarah, b. 16 Oct., 1769; d. 10 Oct., 1771.
    viii Pierpont, b. 22 Nov., 1772; d. 31 Aug., 1775.
    ix Eli, b. 16 Oct., 1773; d. 29 Aug., 1775.

83 †NOAH⁵, son of Jonathan⁴ and Damaris (Rice) Brigham; born in Marlboro, Mass., 24 Nov., 1734; died there, 3 Feb., 1805; married, 5 July, 1758, Miriam Allen; married (2), 19 May, 1771,

---

* *Colonial War Record:* First Marlboro Co., 1757.
† *Colonial War:* First Marlboro Co., 1757; Relief Fort William Henry, 1759.

Martha Tomblin, who died 27 May, 1813.   He was in office in Marlboro in 1798.

Children (by first wife), born in Marlboro:
   i Damaris[6], b. 24 April, 1759.
   ii Anne, b. 25 June, 1761.
   iii Matthias Rice, b. 4 Jan., 1765; m. 15 Sept., 1791, Anna Gleason.
   iv Lydia, b. 28 Oct., 1767; m. 12 Oct., 1797, James Wright.

Children (by second wife), b. in Marlboro:
   v Miriam, b. 30 Oct., 1772; m. 17 April, 1792, Simeon Cunningham.
   Ch. (Cunningham), b. in Marlboro:
      1 *Miriam[7],* who had three children.
      2 *Simeon,* who had ch.: Miriam[8]; Anna; Emma L., who m. ———— Rice, and had 2 ch.; Charles.
      3 *Nancy,* had 1 dau.
      4 *William L.,* d. unm.
      5 *Levy,* had several ch.
      6 *Martha,* had Harriet; Frederick; Anna; Fannie; Ellen.
      7 *Jonathan Brigham,* m. 1836, Sarah Proctor of Gloucester, Mass.; about 1839 he changed his name by dropping the " Cunningham," and was known thenceforth as " Jonathan Brigham," and under the name of " Brigham " his children grew up and were married. Ch., b. in Marlboro: Lydia[8], b. 1837; m. 1870, James Bliss, a merchant of Boston; she res. there, a widow; Sarah, d.; Martha Washington, probably m. Charles L. Brigham, son of 354; Mary, d.; Frank, d.; William, d.

84 *COL. TIMOTHY[5], son of Capt. Jesse[4] and Bethiah (Rice) Brigham; born in Westboro, Mass., 16 Feb., 1735-6; died in Northboro, 5 Oct., 1828, in his 93d year; married Lydia Wood, born 8 Nov., 1740.

Morse says that he inherited from his father an extensive farm in the east part of Northboro, the value of which he lost through the depreciation of Continental money after its sale.   In extreme old age he was supported by the town, the first instance of the kind to be found in the history of the race.   Although poor, he was received with profound respect, and entertained with free hospitality, wherever he called during life.   In 1764 he was selectman of Westboro; in 1777, after the division of the town, selectman of Northboro.   In 1775 he entered the Revolutionary army as Captain; was second in command under Capt. Samuel Wood of Marlboro of the company of Minute Men, which marched down to Cambridge on 19th of April, 1775, and which was in the battle of Bunker Hill, on the 17th of June following.   He received £18 from the town for the first term of service; is supposed to have removed his family from Northboro, soon after, and to have further served in the field.

   * *Colonial War Record:*   Westboro Train Band, 1757; served also 1758.

Children, probably born in Westboro, except the 3 youngest, born in Northboro:

    i Eber[6], b. 25 Nov., 1761.

    ii Persis, b. 16 Jan., 1764.

    iii Samuel, b. 14 Dec., 1765.

    iv Kitte, b. 11 Dec., 1767.

    v Lydia, b. 26 Dec., 1769; perhaps d. y.

    vi Sally, b. 13 Jan., 1772.

    vii Lewis, b. 4 Jan., 1774.

    viii Nabby, b. 29 Dec., 1775.

    ix Luther, b. 3 April, 1778; m. Rosomond Jones, and moved to Waterford, Me., from Stowe, Mass. Ch.:

        1 *Lydia*[7], m. Rufus Priest.

        2 *Mehitable.*

        3 *Sophie,* m. Abel, son of Stephen Moore from Stow.

        4 *Mary,* m. Joseph Flint.

        5 *Lewis,* m. ———— Swallow.

        6 *Calvin,* m. ———— Ball.

        7 *Maria,* m. Nathan Hilton.

214   x Polly, b. 15 April, 1781.

    xi Betsey, b. 22 Oct., 1783.

85 *LIEUT. ARTEMAS[5], son of Jesse[4] and Bethiah (Rice) Brigham; born Westboro, Mass., 29 Sept., 1739; died, in a fit at home, 25 Nov., 1802; married, Keziah, daughter of Josiah and Thankful Rice, born Northboro, Mass., 31 Jan., 1741; died, his widow, 27 Sept., 1806.

He inherited the homestead of his father and resided where his grandson, Fred William Brigham resided, in the east part of Northboro. He served in the Revolutionary War in 1775, marching on the Lexington Alarm, and as a sergeant in 1777; the town voted him £18 for volunteer service. He was assessor in 1778; selectman in 1788 and '89·

Children, the 2 eldest born in Westboro; others in Northboro:

    i Jesse[6], b. 10 Dec., 1762; m. 18 Dec., 1782, Elizabeth Henderson.

215   ii Gardner, b. 20 Feb., 1764.

216   iii John, b. 24 May, 1766.

217   iv Henry, b. 4 Dec., 1768.

    v Azuba, b. 16 July, 1771; d. 2 Aug., 1778.

    vi Lucinda, b. 8 Feb., 1774; m. 9 June, 1793, Amos, son of Amos and Sarah (Graves) Rice; b. in N., 7 March, 1767; d. in Belfast, Me., Nov., 1806; moved to E. Andover, Me. Ch. (Rice), the 2 elder b. in Northboro:

        1 *Serrel*[7], b. 17 Aug., 1794; d. y.

        2 *Betsey Curtis,* b. 1 Sept., 1795.

        3 *Lanson,* b. E. A., 7 Feb., 1801.

    vii Betsey, b. 26 June, 1776; d. 1 Aug., 1778.

    viii Joel, b. 16 Nov.; 1778; d. 28 Aug., 1779.

    ix Lucy, b. 21 July, 1780; m. 1800, David Knowlton, b. 1779; d. 6 Sept., 1823; moved to N. Y. State. Ch. (Knowlton), 6 b. in Shrewsbury; the 3 youngest in N. Y.:

* *Colonial War Record:* Private in Train Band, 1757.

   1 *Julia Ann[7]*, b. 4 Dec., 1800.
   2 *Eli*, b. 28 Oct., 1802.
   3 *Artemas Brigham*, b. 15 Sept., 1804.
   4 *Elbridge Gerry*, b. 4 Oct., 1806.
   5 *Abraham*, b. 8 Dec., 1808.
   6 *Lucy Caroline*, b. 3 Sept., 1811.
   7 *David Bacheller*.
   8 *Marietta*.
   9 *Harriet*.
218   x Lovell, b. 22 Oct., 1782.
219   xi Moses, b. 21 April, 1786.

   86 SARAH[5], daughter of Capt. Jesse[4] and Bethiah (Rice)
Brigham, born in Westboro, Mass., 21 Feb., 1745-6; died in North-
boro, Mass., 23 Dec., 1798; married (second wife), 15 Jan., 1767,
Dea. Seth, son of Seth and Dorothy (Robinson) Rice, born in West-
boro, 9 Nov., 1737; (married [1] Rachel Coolidge and had chil-
dren). He was deacon of the Northboro church and died there, 2
Jan., 1815.
   Children (Rice), born in Northboro:
      i Sarah[6], b. 16 June, 1768; d. 28 March, 1844; m. Jonathan Pat-
      terson of Northboro, who res. in Maidstone, Vt., and Eaton, Que.
      Ch. (Patterson):
         1 *Sarah[7]*, b. 16 July, 1793; m. Joel Bartlett of Northboro.
         2 *Sabra*, b. 6 Dec., 1794; d. 10 March, 1801.
         3 *Isaac C.*, b. 15 May, 1796; d. unm., 9 Nov., 1821.
         4 *William*, b. 3 April, 1798; m. Eliza Norcross.
         5 *Anson*, b. 5 March, 1801; m. Maria Gilbert; res. Trumbull,
         Conn.
         6 *Benjamin F.*, b. 3 May, 1803; m. Levinah Platt; res. Trum-
         bull.
         7 *Lawson B.*, b. 8 Aug., 1805; m. Savilla Dunkley.
         8 *David*, b. 29 Jan., 1807; m. Louisa Alexander of Winchester,
         N. H.; res. Boston.
         9 *Mary*, b. 15 July, 1810; m. Harwood Proctor.
         10 *Sophia*, b. 3 Aug., 1812; d. 3 Nov., 1841; m. Edward Proctor;
         res, Franklin, Mich.
      ii Rachel, b. 8 Oct., 1770; d. 22 July, 1837; m. Jotham Bartlett of
      Northboro. Ch. (Bartlett):
         1 *Clarissa[7]*, b. 11 Feb., 1793.
         2 *William L.*, b. 21 Jan., 1796.
         3 *Sarah*, b. 3 March, 1797; m. Nahum Eager.
         4 *Jotham*, b. 1 Nov., 1798; d. y.
         5 *Holloway*, b. 15 Jan., 1800.
         6 *John*, b. 8 March, 1801; m. Sally Munroe.
         7 *Lawson*, b. 15 May, 1802.
         8 *Jonathan*, b. 26 April, 1804; m. Louisa Warren.
         9 *Sophia*, b. 29 Dec., 1805; d. 23 March, 1835; m. Stephen
         W. Jeffrey.
         10 *Salina*, b. 22 Jan., 1808; d. y.
         11 *Mary E.*, b. 26 Dec., 1812; d. 2 May, 1848; m. Abraham M.
         Bigelow.
         12 *Franklin D.*, b. 24 July, 1814; m. Mary E. Munroe.

m Baxter, b. 4 May, 1772; d. 28 March, 1854; m. Mary Chandler.
Ch.:
  1 *Harriet*[7], b. 6 Feb., 1795.
  2 *Ermina*, b. 29 Aug., 1798; m. Rev. Bennett Roberts.
  3 *Anthony C.*, b. 4 Oct., 1800; d. 7 April, 1832.
  4 *Louisa F.*, b. 1 Dec., 1802; d. 18 Aug., 1826.
  5 *Baxter*, b. 30 July, 1807.
  6 *John*, b. 1 Dec., 1811; m. (1) Susan K. Knowlton; m. (2)
    Elizabeth Morse.
iv William, b. 18 Sept., 1774; d. 14 Dec., 1826; m. Lois Munroe. Ch.:
  1 *Israel C.*[7], b. 3 Nov., 1799; d. 1 Dec., 1853; m. (1) Mary E.
    Munroe; m. (2) Mrs. Almira L. Davis.
  2 *Sarah Brigham*, b. 7 Dec., 1800; d. y.
  3 *Sarah Brigham*, b. 21 Dec., 1801; d. 18 Sept., 1841; m. John
    Andrews.
  4 *Polly*, b. 9 Jan., 1804; m. Sumner Chapin.
  5 *Susannah*, b. 1805; d. 1826.
  6 *William*, b. 6 June, 1807; m. Lydia Wilson.
  7 *Lewis*, b. 23 Nov., 1809; m. Susan A. Brigham, 522.
  8 *Reuben*, b. 23 Sept., 1811; m. Harriet F. Kettell.
  9 *Lydia F.*, b. 16 Nov., 1813; m. Dana M. Clapp.
  10 *Abraham M.*, b. 30 July, 1815.
  11 *Lois C.*, twin to Abraham; m. Jerome Wells.
  12 *Charles*, b. 30 Dec., 1817; d. y.
  13 *Charles L.*, b. 10 Oct., 1823; d. unm., 22 Feb., 1850.
 v Polly, b. 9 Feb., 1782; d. 14 March, 1852; m. Isaac Davis. Ch.
(Davis):
  1 *Polly*[7], b. and d. 1803.
  2 *Adaline P.*, b. 4 Nov., 1804; m. John Patrick.
  3 *Isaac Brigham*, b. and d. 1806.
  4 *Henry G.*, b. 4 Nov., 1807.
  5 *Isaac Brigham*, b. 24 Dec., 1809; d. 1832.
  6 *Ann Eliza*, b. 3 Oct., 1811.
  7 *John*, b. 25 Oct., 1813; d. 1844.
  8 *Sarah R.*, b. 25 March, 1816.
  9 *Hannah G.*, b. and d. 1818.
  10 *Hannah G.*, b. 9 Nov., 1819; d. 6 March, 1850; m. Franklin
    Whipple.
  11 *Cyrus*, b. 18 June, 1822; m. Elizabeth W. Bruce.
  12 *Caroline G.*, b. 27 Sept., 1825; d. 1839.
vi Sapphira, b. 13 Dec., 1784; d. 1 Sept., 1841; m. Maj. Oliver Sawyer of Berlin, Mass. Ch. (Sawyer):
  1 *Lewis*[7], b. 2 Feb., 1812.
  2 *Oliver B.*, b. 5 June, 1816; m. Angeline A. Baldwin.
  3 *Lucy F.*, b. 9 Sept., 1819; d. 30 Dec., 1847; m. Stephen Sawyer.
  4 *Sophia R.*, twin to Lucy.
vii Seth, b. 25 March, 1788; m. Alice Brigham, 250.

87 WILLIAM[5], son of Joel[4] and Mary (Church) Brigham;
born in Marlboro, Mass., 20 March, 1741-2; died, æ. 80; married,
4 Sept., 1764, Betty, daughter of Jonathan and Betty (Brigham)
Stratton (61); born in Marlboro, 11 April, 1744. He lived in
Northboro, Mass., and moved to Tunbridge, Vt., also lived in
Lowell, Vt.

Children:

    i *Lydia⁶*, b. Northboro, 27 May or March, 1765; m. 3 or 8 Nov., 1785, Dea. Moses, son of Robert Eames; b. in Marlboro, 4 June, 1763; d. 24 June, 1825. The early records spell this name with an " E," but most of the families have dropped the " E," and spell it " Ames." Ch. (Eames), b. in Marlboro:

        1 *Lewis⁷*, b. 31 Aug., 1786; d. 11 June, 1856; m. (1) 24 May, 1812, Nancy Childs, who d. 1819; m. (2) 1821, Mehitable Forbush.

        2 *Lucinda*, b. 11 Jan., 1789; d. unm., 20 June, 1833.

        3 *Nancy*, b. 1 March, 1792; m. 23 July, 1809, Levi Bigelow, b. 28 Oct., 1790; d. 3 April, 1859; they had 14 ch. He was a district school teacher, town officer, rep. to the Gen. Court, and J. P.

    ii Betty, b. 19 Feb., 1767; d: y.

    iii William, b. 27 Dec., 1769; d. 6 March, 1771.

    iv William, b. 12 Jan., 1772.

220   v Silvanus, b. 17 Jan., 1774.

    vi Betty, b. 21 Feb., 1775; although Morse says " 1776," which is probably an error, although Betty may have been b. in 1776, and Samuel in 1777.

    vii Samuel, b. 7 April, 1776; d. 12 Feb., 1859, in Ogden, N. Y.; m. ————. Ch.:

        1 *Henry O.⁷*, who res. Ohio.

221 viii Lucy, b. 24 March, 1778.

    88   JOEL⁵, son of Joel⁴ and Mary (Church) Brigham, born in Marlboro, Mass., 5 April, 1751; died in New Marlboro, Mass., about 1840; married (1), 2 Jan, 1776, Katee, daughter of Col. Cyprian and Dorothy (Howe) Howe, born in Marlboro, 28 Dec., 1757; married (2) Polly Butler. About 1783 he moved to Madison, N. Y., but came back to New Marlboro before his decease. He was a Commissary in the Revolution.

Children, four probably born in Marlboro:

    i Mary⁶, b. 1776; d. y.

    ii Mary, b. 1778; d. y.

    iii Charles, b. 1779; d. y.

    iv Susan, b. 1780; d. y.

    v Thankful.

    vi William, b. 24 Sept., 1812; d. New Marlboro, 21 Dec., 1863; m. 24 April, 1844, Elizabeth, dau. of John, Jr., and Lucy (Langdon) Dodge; b. in N. M., 24 April, 1817; d. 4 June, 1856; he was a farmer and res. N. M. Child, b. in N. M.:

        1 *Ellen E.⁷*, b. 19 March, 1848; m. 27 Feb., 1878, Louis M., son of Samuel and Ursula (Day) Williams, b. in Canaan, N. H., 17 Sept., 1851; res. Stafford, Kan., where moved from Putnam, Conn. Ch. (Williams), b. in Putnam: i Robert Longfellow⁸; ii Elizabeth Langdon, twins, b. 8 Feb., 1879; iii Henry Trumbull, b. 8 Sept., 1880; iv Ursula Louise, b. 30 Dec., 1886.

    vii Son, probably Henry G.

    89   JONATHAN⁵, son of Joel⁴ and Mary (Church) Brigham; born in Marlboro, Mass., 29 Oct., 1754; died in Mayville, N. Y.,

26 July, 1848; married (1), 5 Jan., 1774, Lydia Stevens, born 8 May, 1758; died in Mayville, 4 Feb., 1828; married (2), Sarah (Olds) Brigham, widow of his cousin Jonathan, 94. He resided first in Marlboro; moved to Madison, N. Y., 1796; thence to Sheridan, N. Y., 1810; last to Mayville, in 1813.

Children (by first wife), all born in Marlboro, except the youngest born in Madison:

222   i Stephen⁶, b. 24 Aug., 1780.

   ii Susanna, b. 12 Feb., 1783; m. 1805, Henry Titus of Augusta, N. Y., and moved to Penfield, Ontario, in 1812, where she d. 3 Aug., 1813. Ch. (Titus):
   1 *Franklin⁷;* 2 *Lysander;* 3 *Mary;* 4 *Samuel;* 5 *Haven;* 6 *William.*

   iii *Haven, b. 23 May, 1785; d. ————; m. 19 Feb., 1809, Eunice, dau. of Ephraim Herrick of Augusta, N. Y., who was a soldier of the Revolution; removed with his father in 1796 to Madison, N. Y.; a tanner by trade; built the first tannery in Sheridan, N. Y. (in company with his brother Windsor), where settled in 1810. In 1815 built a 40-ton schooner, " Kingbird," which ran between Dunkirk and Buffalo, taking out his lumber and bringing back merchandise, etc. In his later years he resided s. p. in Fredonia, N. Y., in retirement.

   iv*Windsor, b. 1 Oct., 1787; d. 25 July, 1835, of the cholera; he had taken passage on a boat from Detroit to Dunkirk, N. Y., but bad weather intervened and they were carried by the port and he died on the passage; was interred in Buffalo in an unknown spot; m. about 1812, Marinda Cone of Mayville, N. Y. In 1796 he removed to Madison with his father and in 1810 he settled in Sheridan; when he went there he took a pack of 50-pound weight of tools, provisions, etc.; in company with his brother Haven he built the first sawmill in the place, but soon sold out to Haven; being a carpenter he took a contract to build the first building at Mayville, and he built the second sawmill in Sheridan. Ch.:
   1 *Eliza;* 2 *Melissa,* who m. Harrison Barker; 3 *Angeline;* 4 *Marcia;* 5 *Sarah;* 6 *Squire;* 7 *Leroy,* who d. y.; 8 *Samuel,* who d. y.

   v Lydia, b. 30 Dec., 1789; d. of apoplexy in Sheridan, 18 April, 1853; moved from Madison to Chautauqua Co. in 1810; m. Barnabas Cook in Augusta. Ch. (Cook):
   1 *Nelson⁷;* 2 *Emogene;* 3 *Salinda;* 4 *Angeline;* 5 " *Wartus* " or *Lyanda;* 6 *Haven;* 7 *Edward;* 8 *Cynthia.*

   vi Jonathan, b. 13 Oct., 1791; d. unm., in Mayville, æ. 23.

   vii William, b. 23 Sept., 1793; d. in Sheridan, 28 June, 1829; m. Philatheta Farnsworth. Ch.:
   1 *Lydia Ann⁷;* 2 *Eunice;* 3 *Jonathan;* 4 *Edward.*

   viii Edmund, b. 15 July, 1796; m. (1) Lucinda Pratt, who d.; m. (2) ————· res. in Mayville, s. p.

   90   JOHN⁵, son of Joel⁴ and Mary (Church) Brigham; born in Marlboro, Mass., 16 April, 1758; died in Chadwick Bay, N. Y.,

* Vide *History of Chautauqua Co.,* p. 537.

20 Aug., 1828; married, in 1779-80, Abigail, daughter of James and Abigail (Ward)* Williams of Marlboro and Rutland, Vt., born 26 Feb., 1764; died, in Chadwick Bay the next day after her husband, and they were interred in one grave at Fredonia, N. Y.

He was a soldier in the wars of 1775 and 1812. In 1790 he moved to Fitzwilliam, N. H., and in 1795 to Madison, N. Y., and in 1808 to Chadwick Bay, where he took up a tract of wild land, built a log house and opened a farm. A principal street, leading out of Dunkirk village, and first opened by him, bears his name.† He was a highly respected and honored citizen.

Children, the 2 eldest born in Marlboro:
223   i John⁶, b. 7 Oct., 1780.
224   ii James, b. 6 Nov., 1782.
225   iii Walter.
226   iv Nabby, bapt. in Fitzwilliam, 13 March, 1791.

91   SAMUEL⁵, son of Joel⁴ and Mary (Church) Brigham, born in Marlboro, Mass., 3 Dec., 1760; died 2 March., 1813; in Augusta, N. Y.; married Phebe Davis, (dau. of Daniel, a kinsman of Gov. John Davis), of Worcester, who married (2) Israel Rice, of Madison, N. Y.; she died 9 Feb., 1843, æ. 82. He was a farmer, and moved, about 1796, to Madison, N. Y.

Children, born in Paxton, Mass.:
227   i Joel⁶, b. 12 Sept., 1785.
   ii Samuel, b. ———; d. æ. about 17.
   iii Phebe, b. 16 Oct., 1790; d. in Springhill, O., 27 Nov., 1855; m. 11 Feb., 1811, in Augusta, N. Y., Russell Munn; b. 17 Feb., 1786; d. Wauseon, O., 25 Nov., 1889. Moved to Springhill, O., in 1854. Ch. (Munn), b. in New York:
     1 *Asa C.⁷,* b. 26 June, 1813; d. 23 Jan., 1871; m. Florence Guthrie. Ch.: i Dr. Allison⁸, res. Crystal Lake, Mich.; ii Celia, m. George Stores.
     2 *Marshall Davis,* b. 22 May, 1816; d. 8 Dec., 1896; m. Elvira Guthrie. Ch.: Coralia.
     3 *Phebe L.,* b. 15 May, 1818; d. in Toledo, O., 10 Dec., 1899; m. 1852, H. B. Williams, who d. in Toledo, 31 Dec., 1892. Ch. (Williams): Phebe⁸, b. 29 March, 1855; m. 28 Dec., 1877, S. J. Clark, proprietor of a job printing house in Toledo.

92   CAPT. TILLY⁵, son of James⁴ and Anna (Rice) Brigham, born in Brookfield, Mass., 6 June, 1748; died there, 17 Aug., 1808; married Rachel, daughter of Joseph Walker of Brookfield.

He inherited a third of his father's one thousand acres in Brookfield and also the house built by James in 1722, which was next owned by Joel⁶. The old house was burned down a few years ago

* She was the daughter of Daniel and Mary (Bigelow) Ward.
† *History of Chautauqua Co.*

GERSHOM[4] BRIGHAM HOUSE, WESTBORO, MASS.

CAPTAIN TILLY[5] BRIGHAM HOUSE, BROOKFIELD, MASS.

and the place is owned by Joseph[7] Brigham. His service in the Revolution was a little over 13 mos., beginning June 30, 1778.

Children, born in Brookfield:
    i Bathsheba[6], b. 4 Jan., 1782; m. Joseph W. Hamilton; res. in Brookfield. Ch. (Hamilton):
      1 Cheney[7], who lived in Barre, Mass.
228 ii Barna, b. 11 Nov., 1784.
   iii Ruth, b. 27 May, 1787; d. about 1813; m. Capt. Benjamin Barrett; res. Brookfield. Ch. (Barrett), b. there:
      1 Sophia A.[7], m. Luther Stowell; res. Brookfield.
      2 Henry P., m. Selura Tuttle; res. W. Brookfield.
229 iv Joel, b. 2 June, 1790.
    v Lydia, b. 5 March, 1793; m. Proctor Sanford; res. W. Brookfield. Ch. (Sanford):
      1 Charles B.[7], res. Brookfield.
      2 Harriet A., m. Washington Tufts, who was station agent at B.
   vi Mary, b. 3 Aug., 1796; m. Washington Hamilton; res. Jamesville, N. Y. Ch. (Hamilton):
      1 James T.[7]
      2 George W.
      3 Mary A.
      4 Nancy M.
  vii Fanny, b. 27 Nov., 1798; m. Daniel Holt from Western, now Warren, Mass.; res. a retired merchant in New York. Ch. (Holt):
      1 Sarah F.[7], m. William A. Cromwell, merchant; res. N. Y. Ch. (Cromwell): i William A.[8], Jr. d.; ii William A., 3d., d.; iii Mary F.; iv Maria A.
      2 Maria A., d. ———; m. William P. Bridgman; res., a merchant, in N. Y. Ch. (Bridgman): i Daniel H.[8], d.; ii Emily F.
 viii Asenath, b. 19 March, 1801; m. John Hobbs of Brookfield, both d.
   ix Salem, b. 7 Sept., 1803; d. æ. 4.

93 ELISHA[5], son of James[4] and Anna (Rice) Brigham, born in Brookfield, Mass., 6 Jan., 1750; died there, 8 Sept., 1808; married Patience Walker. He inherited one third of the one thousand acres which belonged to his father, in Brookfield. He went to war from Brookfield, in 1777, and was at the battle of Saratoga; was a private in Capt. Asa Danforth's Co. of Vols.

Children, born in Brookfield:
230 i James[6], b. 22 Feb., 1783.
231 ii Silvanus, b. 30 July, 1785.
   iii Hannah, b. 16 Dec., 1788; m. Joshua Knights. Ch. (Knights):
      1 Rebecca[7], d.

94 JONATHAN[5], son of James[4] and Anna (Rice) Brigham; born in Brookfield, Mass., 22 Oct., 175—; died there, Feb., 1841; married Sarah Olds, who became the second wife of his cousin

Jonathan, 89. He inherited one-third of the homestead in Brookfield. Was in the Revolution in 1778.

Children, born in Brookfield:
  i Silas⁶, b. 3 Nov., 1774; d. 21 Jan., 1795; killed by an accident.
  ii Lot, b. 13 April, 1778; m. Sally Worcester, and settled in Vermont.
  iii Elisha, b. 8 Nov., 1780; d. unm., probably in Richmond, N. H.
  He was very fond of attending auctions and created much amuse-
  ment by his purchases.
  iv Sally, b. 22 Oct., 1783; m. Edward Parker; res. Brookfield.
  v Catherine, b. 11 July, 1787; m. (2) Josiah Burrows.
  vi Betsey, b. 30 Sept., 1790; m. ———— Wyman; probably res. a
  while with Elisha in Richmond.
  vii William, b. 7 Oct., 1793; d. in Pelham, Mass., æ. 80; m. Harriet
  Hoar; res. in Pelham. Ch.:
    1 *George*, b. 1 March, 1842; d. 5 Oct., 1887.
    2 *Meriva Jane*, b. 1844; m. ———— Crosby; res. 1903. Cooley-
    ville, Mass.

95 *JOHN⁵, son of John⁴ and Susanna Brigham; born in Shrewsbury, Mass., 25 July, 1739; died in Phillipston, Mass., 5 Feb.,
1818; married, 12 March, 1760, Zerviah, daughter of Eleazer and
Persis (Newton) Rice of Westboro, Mass., born 11 Sept., 1741;
died in Phillipston, 10 Feb., 1818. According to Morse his father
gave him half of the Shrewsbury farm.

Children, the 3 eldest born in Shrewsbury, the others in Phillipston:
  i Miriam⁶, b. — Dec., 1762.
  ii Eunice, b. 20 March, 1766; d. in Fitzwilliam, N. H., 21 June,
  1853, æ. 87; m. 12 Dec., 1787, John Cobleigh, b. 18 Dec., 1762;
  res. in Fitzwilliam. Ch. (Cobleigh), b. there:
    1 *John⁷*, b. 21 March, 1789; d. in Fitzwilliam 6 February, 1870.
    2 *Amos*, b. 18 April, 1790; d. in Fitzwilliam, 19 Feb., 1824.
    3 *David*, b. 26 July, 1791; d. in Marengo, Mich., 26 May, 1858.
    4 *Eunice Brigham*, b. 15 Nov., 1792; d. in Bakersfield, Vt., 13
    Sept., 1835.
    5 *Chloe*, b. 6 Feb., 1801; d. in Bakersfield, 27 April, 1831.
    6 *Bathshebah*, b. 14 April, 1803; d. in Fitzwilliam, 8 Sept., 1854.
  iii John, b. 26 Dec., 1767; d. ————————; m. (1) ————————; m.
  (2) Widow Susan Washburn; he moved to New York State,
  probably to Malone, but no record is there. Ch. (by first wife):
  1 *Eleazer⁷;* 2 *John;* 3 *William.* Ch. (by second wife): 4 *Rox-
  anah*, d. æ. 4; 5 *Julia.*
  iv Chloe, b. in Phillipston, Mass., 6 Feb., 1772; d. in Georgia, Vt.,
  29 June, 1848; m. 22 Sept., 1793, Israel, son of Benjamin Joslin;
  b. in Killingly, Conn., 22 Feb., 1770; d. in Georgia, 31 Dec., 1855;
  they res. in Georgia. Ch. (Joslin), b. there:

* *Colonial War Record:* Shrewsbury, 1757, Capt. Ward, Train Band. Shrews-
bury, 1759 æ. 19) in Col. Abe Williams' Regt. for invasion of Canada. Shrewsbury,
Private, 1760, Capt. Maynard's Co. to westward, 8 mos. 21 days. Centinel, Capt.
Josiah Brown's Troop of Horse, 5 days.

1 *Serviah*[7], b. 13 Sept., 1794; d. in Georgia, 1867.
2 *Israel*, b. Aug., 1796; d. 1797.
3 *Abigail*, b. 15 Nov., 1797; d. in Georgia, 1847.
4 *Levi*, b. 10 Dec., 1799; d. in Oneida, N. Y., 1876; a lawyer.
5 *Israel*, b. 8 March, 1802; d. 14 April, 1871; m. Hannah
    Colton. Ch.: i Edward B.[8]; ii Dana I. (M. D. in St. Louis);
    iii Hannah L.; iv Dwight C.; v. Mary P.; vi Ellen L.; vii
    John C.; viii Chas. W., Cairo, Ill.; ix Walter C., Cairo, Ill.
6 *Polly*, b. 8 May, 1804; d. 11 July, 1823.
7 *Infant*, b. 23 March, 1808; d. 1808.
8 *Benjamin Barrett*, b. 27 April, 1809; d. 1851; a farmer.
9 *Chloe Priscilla*, b. 26 June, 1811; d. 1874.
10 *Charlotte Nelson*, b. 18 June, 1817.
    v Susannah, b. 5 Dec., 1776.
   vi Timothy, b. 17 June, 1779; perhaps went to Canada.
   vii Nahum, b. 5 April, 1781; perhaps d. y.
232 viii Samuel, b. 16 Jan., 1782.
    ix Abigail, m. ———— Josslyn.

96 SAMUEL[5], son of John[4] and Susanna Brigham; born in
Shrewsbury, Mass., 1 July, 1741; died there, 28 Feb., 1836; æ. 94;
married, 1774, Rachel, daughter of Phineas Underwood of Westford, Mass., born, 1746; died 21 Dec., 1810, æ. 64.

    Probably was a private in Capt. Job Cushing's Co. of Minute-men
which marched on the Lexington Alarm. He was admitted to the
church in Shrewsbury in 1780. According to Morse he received
half of his father's farm in Shrewsbury, and was sole executor of
his father's will.

Child, born in Shrewsbury:
233   i John[6], b. 22 March, 1788.

97 DAVID[5], son of Silas[4] and Tabitha (Prescott) Brigham;
born in Lancaster, Mass., 4 April, 1745; died in Shrewsbury, 27
Sept., 1824, æ. 80; married (1), 21 March, 1766, Mercy, daughter
of Dea. Benjamin Maynard, who died, with her infant, 10 Nov.,
1766, æ. 22; married (2), 13 Oct., 1768, Martha Chamberlain, of
Westboro, who died 9 Aug., 1807, æ. 59; married (3), in 1809,
Hannah Marcy, of Brooklyn, Conn. He settled in Shrewsbury.
He was in Capt. Ross Wyman's (Artillery) Co., Col. Jonathan
Ward's Regt., which marched on the Lexington Alarm; in 1777,
marched on an alarm at Bennington in Capt. John Maynard's Co.,
Col. Job Cushing's Regt.

Children, born in Shrewsbury:
234   i Nathaniel[6], b. 27 July, 1769.
235   ii Edmund Trowbridge, b. 9 March, 1771.
      iii Mercy, b. 10 June, 1773; d. 28 Aug., 1776.
      iv Prescott, b. 24 June, 1775; d. 22 Sept., 1776.
       v David, b. 6 Aug., 1777; d. 26 Aug., 1880.

236   vi Prescott, bap. 16 April, 1780.
    vii Martha, b. 16 March, 1782; m. 20 Nov., 1800, Balch Dean, b.
           in Dedham, Mass., 7 March, 1775; removed to Shrewsbury and d.
           there, 1857.   Ch. (Dean):
           1 *Elizabeth*[7], b. 31 Dec., 1801; d. s. p. in Worcester, ————;
             m. 6 June, 1827, James Harvey Gerald, probably of Wrentham;
             her mother res. with her.
237 viii Mercy, b. 21 March, 1784.
238   ix David, b. 15 Aug., 1786.
    x Ebenezer, b. 28 April, 1789; d. 14 Sept., 1861.   Morse tells us
           that in 1814 he emigrated to the west, and in 1828 settled in
           Blue Mounds, Territory of Michigan, now in Dane Co., Wisconsin,
           where he lived until his death; was unm.; had large profits
           from the rise in real estate, and was proprietor of a large tract
           of land; one of the original proprietors of the city of Madison;
           was well known and highly regarded where he lived and labored.
            The Dane County Bar adopted the following resolutions at
           the time of his death:
           " That we regard it as a privilege to bear our testimony in this
           public manner to the unblemished morals, the ardent patriotism,
           the benevolent character and generous heart of our esteemed and
           lamented friend."
    xi Luther, bapt. 10 June, 1791; d. 29 Aug., 1793.

    98   LIEUT. LEVI[5], son of Col. Levi[4] and Susanna (Grout)
Brigham; born in Westboro, Mass., 26 Aug., 1746; died in Fitzwilliam, N. H., 26 April, 1821; married 9 July, 1771, Tabitha,
daughter of Phineas and Prudence Hardy; born in Westboro, 10
May, 1745; died 26 April, 1818.

He moved to Fitzwilliam about 1772, in the infancy of the
country, travelling on foot, packing his provisions, and submitting
to hardships now unknown to pioneers.   He kept a tavern on
" Brigham Hill," in the east part of Fitzwilliam, and was collector in 1774 and '86; selectman in 1774, '75, '76, '78 and '81;
Lieut. of Militia, '75; on the Committee of Safety, '78·   He held
nearly every office in the gift of the people from time to time (see
History of Fitzwilliam).

Children, born in Fitzwilliam:
239   i Lydia[6], b. 24 Aug., 1772.
240   ii Joseph, b. 2 June, 1774.
    iii Anna, b. 14 March, 1776; d. 16 March, 1776.
241   iv Hannah, b. 12 March, 1777.
242   v Levi, b. 19 Dec., 1778.
243   vi Tabitha, b. 30 Sept., 1780.
244   vii Anna, b. 26 April, 1782.
    viii Rufus, b. 22 Nov., 1783; d. 27 May, 1802.
245   ix Mindwell, b. 11 April, 1785.
246   x Susannah, b. 3 April, 1790.

99 *HON. ELIJAH[5], son of Col. Levi[4] and Susanna (Grout) Brigham; born in Westboro, Mass., 7 July, 1751; died in Washington, D. C., 22 Feb., 1816; married (1), 21 Sept., 1780, Anna Sophia,† daughter of the Rev. Ebenezer and Hannah (Breck) Parkman, of Westboro; born there, 18 Oct., 1755; died there, 26 Nov., 1783; married (2) 20 April, 1786, Mrs. Sarah (Lambert) Hammock, of Marlboro, widow of Charles; born 26 Feb., 1750; died 22 March, 1787; married (3), 16 Dec., 1792, Sarah, daughter of Gen. Artemas Ward of Shrewsbury, Mass., (grandson of 5); born 28 July, 1756; died, his widow, 5 Feb., 1838.

He graduated from Dartmouth College, A.B., 1778; A.M., Dartmouth and Harvard (ad eum.), and Yale, 1792; began the study of law, but for some reason unknown abandoned it before he was admitted to the bar. When he went to college, his father gave him a horse, which was all the start he had toward his higher education. He settled in Westboro as a merchant with Breck Parkman. Elijah, after Mr. Parkman's death, continued to live in the parsonage, which is generally called the "Judge Brigham house"; "built in 1748. . It has been much altered and modernized. . . . Mr. Parkman bought the land which constituted his farm of Nathan Brigham of Southboro." He was selectman in 1785, '89, and '96. He represented Westboro in the General Court, 1791 and '93; served 12 years as a member of the Senate; 2 years as executive counsellor, and 16 years as a judge of the Court of Common Pleas

* " 25 June, 1780. Mr. Elijah Brigham . . . propounded."
   " 9 July, 1780. Mr. Brigham . . . admitted into ye Church."
   16 July, 1780 . . . Mr. Brigham and Sophy were published for the last time.
   " 15 Aug., 1780 . . . I returned at eve. Mr. Elijah here de die in diem."
   " Sept., 1780 . . . Mr. Elijah Brigham privately spoke to me of his joining in Trade with Breck.
   " 7 Sept., 1780 . . . He (Mr. Wm. Spring of Brimfield) dined with us as did Mr. Elijah Brigham (who keeps shop for Breck).
   " 20 Sept., 1780 . . . N. B. Mr. Brigham asked me whether it would suit me to have the Marriage of my Dauter to him to be to-morrow? . . . Sent my Complements to his Father and Mother, & Request they would come—likewise his Brothers and Sisters. He acquainted me with his desire to wait on Squire Baker and his Lady with his Invitations to ye wedding; also ye two eldest Dauters. To which I consented. My Dauter Cushing rode to Capt. Maynard's to invite him and his wife. The Return was that Mrs. Maynard was confined with illness " (she was the widow of Dr. Samuel Brigham, before her second marriage).
   " 21 Sept., 1780. Mrs. Parkman I hope is better. Sophy has unhappily a good deal of a cough. I had a most agreeable sight of my children & their Consorts at Dinner, viz.: Wm. & Lydia, Mr. Cushing and Sarah, Breck & Susé (born Brigham), Sam'l. & Sally & Mr. Brigham with Sophy. To God be Praise and Glory! Towards evening according to Invitation, Joseph Baker, Esq. and Lady, Mr. Winslow Brigham and Miss Alice Cushing of Shrewsbury, Mr. Hazeltine and Miss Mindwell Brigham, Master Fisk and Miss Anna Brigham, and Mr. Josiah Brigham came to wait on ye Solemnity of the Marriage of Mr. Elijah Brigham to my Dauter Anna Sophia, which was performed; and after ye Covenant, Mr. Cushing prayed. . . . Mrs. P. was not able to attend."
   " 22 Sept., 1780. . . . Sam and Breck with their wives wait on ye Bridegroom and Bride, to Coll. Brigham."—Parkman Diary.
   † " She also kept a journal in which is frequent mention of Mr. Elijah Brigham, but it ends in July, 1778 "—The Hundredth Town.

for Worcester County; was a member of Congress from 1810 until death.

Morse paid the following tribute to his character:

" Of this man I cannot speak in justice to convictions, and escape the suspicion of extravagance among strangers, while among his acquaintance who survive, nothing would fail of a hearty response which I might say commendatory of his social and domestic virtues, his commercial integrity and honor, his great common sense and refinement, his patriotism and political integrity; his wisdom and benevolence, his fidelity to every official and important trust, and his services in the advancement of the moral, civil, and educational interests of the community in which he lived. ' Stranger, tread lightly at the grave of one such as thou oughtest to be, true to his conscience and country ! ' "

Children (by first wife), born in Westboro:
    i Anna Sophia[6], b. 26 July, 1781; d. 17 Oct., 1864; m. 9 March, 1813, Joseph F. Boardman of Boston, Mass., b. 1781; d. 21 June, 1858. Ch. (Boardman), b. in Boston:
        1 *Maria Ann[7]*, b. Sept., 1814; d. 31 March, 1870.
        2 *Anna Sophia Brigham*, b. 27 Jan., 1817; d. 5 Feb., 1863.
247 ii Elijah, b. 21 April, 1783.
Child (by second wife):
    iii Sally, b. 27 Jan., 1787; d. 26 Feb., 1867; m. 31 Oct., 1821, John, son of Dea. Isaac and Mercy (Lawrence) Gregory; b. in Ashby, Mass., 20 Jan., 1779; (he m. [1] Sarah Call and had 2 ch.); res. Charlestown, where d. 14 April, 1853. Ch. (Gregory), b. in Charlestown:
        1 *Sarah Brigham[7]*, b. 18 Sept., 1822; res. in Cambridge, Mass.
Children (by third wife):
248 iv Ann Maria, b. 14 July, 1794.
    v Sally Sophronia, b. 22 Dec., 1795; d. 3 Dec., 1810.
    vi Dana Ward, b. 9 March, 1797; d. unm., 23 Nov., 1830.
    vii Susanna Walter, b. 4 May, 1798; d. 24 Dec., 1825.
    viii Catherine Martha, b. 21 Jan., 1801; d. in DeWitt, Ia., 24 July, 1881; m. 18 Feb., 1830, George Henry, son of Dr. Abraham and Charlotte (Hale) Lowe of Lunenburg, Mass.; b. in Ashburnham, Mass., 12 May, 1803; d. in DeW., 21 Dec., 1866; was a merchant in No. Brookfield, Mass., 1841-56, and served as selectman for several years; moved to DeWitt in 1857. Ch. (Lowe), the eldest b. in Fitchburg, the others in Ashburnham:
        1 *Emma Catherine[7]*, b. 4 June, 1834; m. 20 Dec., 1865, Maj. Chas. Merrill Nye of DeWitt. Ch. (Nye): i Martha W.[8], b. 15 Dec., 1866; ii George L., b. 3 Aug., 1869; m. Ethelyn Webber of Salt Lake City; iii James Brigham, d. y.; iv Susanne K., b. 30 July, 1879.
        2 *George A.*, b. 16 May, 1836; d. 4 Jan., 1903; m. 9 Oct., 1866, Anna M. Dewing of No. Brookfield, b. 23 March, 1840; a merchant in Salt Lake City, U. Ch.: i Catherine A.[8], b. 23 Oct., 1873; ii Alice, d. y.
        3 *Susan Brigham*, b. 21 March, 1840; res. unm., in DeWitt.

100 SUSANNA[5], daughter of Col. Levi[4] and Susanna (Grout) Brigham; born in Northboro, Mass., 21 Jan., 1754; died in Westboro, Mass., 10 Nov., 1834; married, 9 Jan., 1777, Breck, son of the Rev. Ebenezer and Hannah (Breck) Parkman; born 27 Jan., 1748-49, in Westboro; died in W., 3 Feb., 1825.

She is described in *The Hundredth Town* as a rather stately, but most gracious lady, always performing kindly deeds, and much beloved in the community.* Some years before his marriage, Breck opened a store in one end of the little house still standing on South Street in Westboro, using the other end for a dwelling place. At this time it stood between the parsonage and the church.† He was the ancestor of all the Parkmans who remained in Westboro. Elijah Brigham, who married Sophy Parkman, went into business with him in 1780. There are descendants of Susanna in the 9th and 10th generations whom the limits of this work will not permit us to enter.

Children (Parkman), born in Westboro:
  i Hannah Breck[6], b. 22 Oct., 1778; d. 6 Sept., 1834; m. 25 June, 1801, Dr. John Eugene Tyler, b. 10 April, 1766; d. 25 Jan., 1820; a physician in Westboro, and later a merchant in Boston. Ch. (Tyler):
    1 *Hannah Parkman[7]*, b. 25 Sept., 1803; d. 1857; m. Onslow Peters. 6 ch.
    2 *Susan Brigham,* b. July, 1806; d. 9 Nov., 1821.
    3 *Anna Sophia,* b. 28 Jan., 1809; d. 20 Jan., 1889; m. Dea. Christopher Colombus Denny (who m. [1] Susan B. Rockwood[7]); he was a merchant of Keene, N. H., and a manfr. in Leicester. Ch. (Denny): 2 d. y.; iii Parkman Tyler[8], b. 20 Dec., 1851; m. 3 times; grad. Worcester Polytech. Inst.; cashier Leicester Nat. Bank to 1904, and treas. Leicester Savings Bank, 1890 to present time; 1 son.
    4 *Sarah A.,* b. 11 June, 1811; d. 1875; m. John A. Fayerweather of Westboro.

* Aug., 1772. Susie Brigham undertakes to make a DuCape for Mrs. Parkman; later she made sundry gowns, stayed after meeting, lodged, worked for Sophy and Hannah in making new crape gowns. Another time, Breck, nigh evening goes home with Susie Brigham.
    In December: " Miss Susie Brigham here still." A month later, " Susie Brigham here with Miss Abbie White, stayed over night."
    In Apr., 1773: " Susie Brigham came last night which makes the ninth person beside my own family. So to-day we are thirteen."
    Breck bought a clock at vendue and 3 Sept., 1777, he set it up, and it measured the hours for forty-eight years in the " best room "; it now belongs to Robert Breck Denny of Boston.
    † 13 Dec., 1778. " Breck is out of wood. Susé herself and the child, her sister Mindwell and Billy Spring came up here to be with us over ye Sabbath. Breck, his family & Br. Josiah dind here." 14th, " Breck had wood brot. him. Susé &c. returned home."
    24th. " Breck and his dine here on a roast Turkey of his providing."
    13 Jan., 1779. " Susé rode to Capt. Maynard's in ye Sleigh and safely, but in returning ye Mare took a start, and tore away with Speed from Susé, who had got out of the Sleigh, and came home o' foot; but ye mare first, broke ye Sleigh and threw out a case of Gin—however broke but one Bottle (which might at this time stand at..........Dollars), but no Mischief done to Life or Limb. The praise to God."
    22 June, 1780. " My wife and Susé ride to her Father's and to Capt. Jones'. They bring home little Hannah who has been Weaning."—*Parkman Diary.*

     5 *John B.;* 6 *Charlotte C.;* 7 *Maria T.,* all d. young.

     8 (*Dr.*) *John Eugene,* b. 9 Dec., 1819; d. 9 March, 1878; m. (1) Caroline A. Denny; m. (2) Augusta M. Denny[7]; at the head of McLean Insane Asylum, Somerville, Mass.; later a physician in Boston.

  ii Susanna Brigham, b. 13 April, 1781; d. 4 June, 1836; m. 5 Oct., 1809, Rev. Elisha Rockwood, b. 9 May, 1778; d. June, 1858; of Westboro and Swanzey, N. H. Ch. (Rockwood):

     1 *Elisha P.*[7], b. 19 June, 1811; d. 22 Jan., 1828.

     2 *William O.,* b. 12 Feb., 1814; d. 1879; m. ,1842, Helen M. Moore; res. Indianapolis.

     3 *Susan Brigham,* b. 1 Oct., 1815; d. 1843; m. (as first wife), Christopher C. Denny (who m. [2] Anna S. Tyler).

     4 *Hannah A.,* b. 1 Feb., 1817; m. Dexter Brigham, Jr., 439.

     5 *Robert B.,* b. and d. 1822.

 iii Charles, b. 26 May, 1785; d. 13 Sept., 1834; m. 26 Jan., 1811, Joanna P., dau. of Jonathan Fay of Concord, Mass.; b. 27 Oct., 1784; d. 3 Dec., 1826. Ch.:

     1 *Joanna F.*[7], b. 21 Feb., 1812; m. Dr. Henry H. Rising.

     2 *Charles B.,* b. 13 June, 1813; d. unm., 26 June, 1885.

     3 *Mary A.,* b. 23 Sept., 1814; d. 1836.

     4 *Lucy P.,* b. 16 Aug., 1817; m. Nahum Fisher of W.

     5 *Susan B.,* b. 19 April, 1820; d. 28 June, 1871.

     6 *Hannah S.,* b. 12 Nov., 1822; m. Henry Taft of Lowell.

     7 *Samuel,* b. 29 Aug., 1824; d. 1845 or '47·

     8 *Maria D.,* b. 17 May, 1826; m. 1 March, 1854, George T. Leach, who d.; she res. Dorchester, Mass.

  iv Robert Breck, b. 29 Sept., 1787; d. unm.

   v Anna, b. 31 Dec., 1792; d. 1 Jan., 1807.

  vi Mary Augusta, b. 12 May, 1796; d. 23 Dec., 1812.

 vii Charlotte Sophia, b. 5 Feb., 1800; d. 24 Nov., 1884; m. 13 May, 1824, George Denny, a merchant of Boston, b. 1 April, 1801; d. 14 Jan., 1852; Prest. Granite Bank of Boston, and treasurer of Sullivan R. R. Ch. (Denny):

     1 *Augusta M.*[7], b. 28 Feb., 1825; d. 1899; m. 1852, Dr. John Eugene Tyler.

     2 *George P.,* b. 10 May, 1826; d. 1885; m. Nancy A. Briggs.

     3 *Charles A.,* b. 13 March, 1828; m. 1860, Jane S. Bigelow.

     4 *Charlotte E.,* b. 7 Feb., 1830; d. unm., 7 Aug., 1854.

     5 *Robert Breck,* b. 8 Dec., 1832; m. 1856, Valeria K. Titcomb; a wool dealer in Boston; owner of the old family clock.

     6 *Edward W.,* b. 12 Nov., 1836; m. Kate Brown.

     7 *Dr. James H.,* b. 2 Nov., 1838; of New York and Boston.

     8 *Mary H.,* b. 20 Sept., 1840.

     9 *John A.,* b. 14 Jan., 1843; d. 3 Feb., 1845.

  101 WINSLOW[5], son of Col. Levi[4] and Susanna (Grout) Brigham; born in Westboro, 18 June, 1756; died in Northboro, 4 Sept., 1837; married, 16 May, 1781, Alice, daughter of *Col. Job and

    * Col. Job[5] Cushing, son of Rev. Job[4] and Mary (Prentice) Cushing of Shrewsbury; born 1728; d. 1808; m. 1752; Rev. Job[4] Cushing, was b. 1694; H. C., 1714; m. 1727, d. 1760. He was a son of Matthew[3] and Jael (Jacobs) Cushing of Hingham. Mathew[3] Cushing, son of Daniel[2] and Lydia (Gilman) Cushing of Hingham, was b. 1660; m. 1683; d. 1715. Daniel[2] Cushing, son of Mathew[1] and Nazareth (Pitcher) Cushing, was b. 1619, in Hingham, Eng.; came to New England in 1638 with his father and mother; m. 1645; d. 1699. Mathew[1] Cushing, b. 1588, m. Nazareth Pitcher in 1619; came to America in Ship *Diligent,* with wife and 5 children; settled

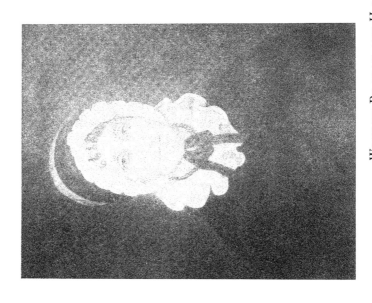

WINSLOW BRIGHAM AND HIS WIFE ALICE CUSHING (101)

Lucy (Stone) Cushing of Shrewsbury, and grand-daughter of the Rev. Job Cushing, of Shrewsbury; she was born in Shrewsbury, 23 Feb., 1757; died in Northboro, 7 Feb., 1847.

He was a farmer and resided in the south-east corner of Northboro. He served six years as selectman. He was a private in Capt. Silas Gates' Co., Col. Ward's Regt.; enlisted 4 Dec., 1775; on muster list of Captain Timothy Brigham's Co., Col. Cushing's Regt., 30 Jan., 1776; also Capt. Ebenezer Belknap's Co. and Capt. Nathan Fisher's Co., Col. Wade's Regt. Service in No. Kingston, R. I., from 23 June, 1778-1 Jan., 1779; also on muster roll, Jan.-Nov., 1778.

Children, born in Northboro:
 i Emery Cushing⁶, b. 22 Sept., 1782; d. 13 March, 1783.
 ii Emery, b. 5 Jan., 1784; d. 21 Feb., 1785.
249 iii Nathaniel, b. 7 Oct., 1785.
250 iv Alice, b. 11 March, 1787.
251 v Josiah, b. 1 Sept., 1788.
252 vi Lucy Cushing, b. 27 Sept., 1789.
 vii Nancy, b. 1 Oct., 1791; d. 11 May, 1792.
 viii Nancy, b. 2 Dec., 1792; m. 1 Feb., 1839, Maj. Eli Prouty of Spencer; d. s. p. 2 Oct., 1877.
 ix Emery, b. 15 April, 1794; d. 26 Jan., 1820; m. Lucy Claflin Corbett, 6 Oct., 1818; no issue.
 x Mindwell, b. 5 May, 1796; m. Abr. M. Brigham, 1812; d. 1 Jan. 1870.
 xi Winslow, b. 11 Dec., 1797; d. unm. 5 Dec., 1818, in Quincy, Mass.
 xii Lydia Cushing, b. 11 Aug., 1799; d. 17 March, 1837, in Worcester, Mass.; m. Thos. T. Farnsworth, 1820; res. Worcester; no issue.

102 MARTHA⁵, daughter of Capt. Jonas⁴ and Persis (Baker) Brigham; born in Westboro, Mass., 1 Nov., 1746; married, 19 Jan., 1768, Capt. John, son of Capt. Stephen Maynard (whose second wife was Widow Anna [Gott] Brigham), born in Westboro, 1743. He moved to Shrewsbury, Mass., 1771; Representative, 1781.

Children (Maynard), the eldest born in Westboro, others in Shrewsbury:
 i Martha⁶, b. 23 Nov., 1769; m. 1785, Fred K. Crosby.
 ii Josiah, b. 18 Sept., 1771; d. Barnard, Vt., 1796.
 iii John, b. 5 Oct., 1773; d. in Bakersfield, Vt., 1816.
 iv Edward, b. 25 April, 1775; moved to Bakersfield.
 v Antipas, b. 6 April, 1777; res. Waltham, Mass.
 vi Hepsibah, b. 12 March, 1779; m. Elijah Hardy of Westboro.
 vii William, b. 20 Sept., 1781.

103 CAPT. JONAS⁵, son of Capt. Jonas⁴ and Persis (Baker) Brigham; born in Westboro, Mass., 29 Oct., 1748; died in Bakersfield, Vt., in 1826; married (1), published 26 Jan., 1771, Anna Draper of Watertown; who died in 1802; married (2), 10 Nov., 1810, Polly Wyman.

He settled first in North Brookfield, Mass. In 1774 he was a Minute Man, and marched at the time of the Lexington Alarm as a Sergeant. He was Lieut. from Brookfield in 1777, and was in the battle of Saratoga. His commission as Capt. of the Mass. militia was signed by John Hancock, 1 July, 1781.

He moved to Bakersfield and was very prominent in all the affairs of the town, and was the first elected Representative to the General Assembly. The second year there was no election but he was elected for 17 consecutive years thereafter. On the division of the town he fell within the limits of Enosburg, where he was moderator in 1797.

Children, born in North Brookfield, except the youngest born in Bakersfield:
253   i Michael⁶, b. 2 March, 1772.
254   ii Eli, b. 14 Dec., 1774.
     iii Hannah, b. 7 July 1776; m. Col. Holley Taylor; res. St. Albans, Vt.; d. s. p., over 70.
     iv Sally, b. 7 Dec., 1778; d. unm.
     v Patty, b. 27 April, 1780.
255   vi Jonas, b. 14 March, 1782.
ꞌ256 vii Luther, b. 15 May, 1785.
257 viii Asa, b. 1786.
     ix Betsey, b. 1788; d. y.
258   x Cheney, b. 22 April, 1793.

104   EDWARD⁵, son of Capt. Jonas⁴ and Persis (Baker) Brigham; born 21 May, 1754, in Westboro; died 5 May, 1838; married, 30 Sept., 1779, Sally Miller.* He was in the Revolutionary War. He was a private in Capt. Edmund Brigham's Co. of Minute Men which marched on the Lexington Alarm; also was sergeant in 1775-1776, and in service at Dorchester and New York. He may have been out in 1780-'81 also. Moved to Milton, Vt., and was a member of the First Church in that place.

Children:
     i William⁶, b. about 1780.
259   ii Edward, b. 1782.
     iii Baker, b. 1786.
     iv Lorin, b. 1788; father of Elon⁷, b. 1822.
     v Miller, b. 1793.

105   BARNABAS⁵, son of Capt. Jonas⁴ and Persis (Baker) Brigham; born in Westboro, Mass., 29 March, 1756; died in North Brookfield, Mass., 30 Jan., 1817; married, 28 Feb., 1790, Eunice Mandell, of Barre, Mass.

He was a private in Capt. Edmund Brigham's Co. of Minute-men,

---

* " 30 Sept., 1779. Returned at eve. I married Mr. Edward Brigham to Miss Sally Miller, heretofore of   The Fee given was $20 . . . "—*Parkman Diary.*

Maj. Gen. Ward's regt., which marched on the alarm of April 19, 1775. He was in Capt. Todd's Company, Col. Craft's Regiment of Artillery, from North Brookfield, from February 1 to May 8, 1776. He settled in North Brookfield (see Hist. of that town).

Children, born in North Brookfield:

    i Henry[6], was a good scholar and entered college, but did not grad.
260 ii Otis, b. 2 July, 1795.
    iii Nancy, b. ————.

106 ANTIPAS[5], son of Capt. Jonas[4] and Persis (Baker) Brigham; born in Westboro, 15 March, 1758; died in Schoharie, N. Y., about 1840; married (1), 24 Jan., 1780*, Hepsibah[6], daughter of Capt. Edmund[5] and Sarah (Lyscom) Brigham (181); born 29 July, 1760; died 11 March, 1789; (2), Lydia, daughter of Joseph and Mary (Reed) Cutler, born in Warren, Mass., 2 Dec., 1769; died 16 Jan., 1798; (3), 7 April, 1799, Julia Whitney, of Northboro; (4), Mary Hall. He moved to St. Albans, Vt. He was probably a private in Capt. Edmund Brigham's company, which marched Aug. 21, 1777, to re-inforce the Northern Army; proceeded to Hadley and there counter-ordered.

Children (by first wife):

    i Nahum[6], b. 8 April, 1781, and no further reported.
    ii William, b. 24 Dec., 1782.
    iii Nelly, b. 2 July, 1784.
    iv Antipas, b. 4 March, 1786.
    v Hepsibah, b. 11 Jan., 1788.
    vi Persis, b. 9 March, 1789.

Children (by second wife):

    vii Rensselaer, b. 2 Aug., 1791; was deaf and dumb.
    viii Lydia, b. ————; m. Aaron Bliss of Warren.
    ix Mary, b. 7 July, 1796; l. unm., at Hardwick, N. Y.

* The winter of 1779-80 was very cold and much snow fell. On the 29th of Dec., 1779, Mr. Parkman records:
"A very dismal morning. Storm continues till about nonn. Snowbanks very high, one nigh my saddle-house 6 feet high. Roads blocked up . . . My son Breck had also designed to go in a double sleigh to Ashburnham, but no Team nor Sleigh can stir. How wonderful are the Works of ye Great God! "
    On the 30th he records:
"I keep close to my Study, tho Mr. Antipas Brigham had requested me to go to Capt. Edmund's to marry him. But nobody disturbs me. . . . Enough to do to keep warm."
    24 Jan., 1780. "An urgent message from Mr. Antipas Brigham to go to Capt. Edmund Brigham's with request to marry him. I went, but with great Difficulty, by reason of ye deep snow. My sons Breck and Elias drew me on a light sled as far as Mr. Haskill's, nigh which a number of young men, Brighams, accompanied me on foot to ye House, where I performed ye Solemnity. After ye Supper they brot me to Mr. Gale's, who kindly obliged me to locate there."—*Parkman Diary.*
    "The tradition of Mr. Parkman's ride to the wedding is still preserved in the Brigham family, with some of the incidents of the trip—that the old minister lost his wig, and the racketmen were at no small trouble to recover it; but all finally ended well."—*The Hundredth Town.*

107   DR. DANIEL⁵, son of Capt. Jonas⁴ and Persis (Baker) Brigham; born in Westboro, Mass., on the old David Brigham homestead, 12 June, 1760; died in Marlboro, Mass., 12 June, 1837; married Anna, daughter of Abram Munroe of Northboro, Mass., born there, 22 July, 1766; died 9 April, 1850.

He studied medicine in Harvard College. Entered the Revolutionary Army as surgeon's mate and was at West Point when Maj. André was captured; after the war he was surgeon in the Fifth Regt. of Mass. Militia. He practiced medicine in Northboro, then in Berlin, about 1800, and about 1826 in Marlboro, where he resided on the farm on Brigham St., occupied now by Addington M. Brigham. His high rank in his profession is indicated by the distance he was often called to go in cases of consultation. Many of his surgical instruments are now in the possession of his grandson, Addington.

Children, born in Northboro:
    i Persis Baker⁶, b. 26 April, 1784; d. 1808.
261   ii Barnabas, b. 14 April, 1786.
262 iii Daniel, b. 27 Jan., 1788.
    iv Anna, b. 8 Aug., 1790; m. Capt. Prentice Keyes; res. Northboro.
263   v Lois, b. 14 April, 1793.
264 vi Abraham Munroe, b. 25 March, 1796.

108   DAVID⁵, son of Capt. Jonas⁴ and Persis (Baker) Brigham; born in Westboro, 31 March, 1762; died ————, 1851; married, 21 Feb., 1787, Lucy Harrington of Westboro, sister of Lawyer Nahum Harrington; born 17 Sept., 1765; died 13 Aug., 1846. She was a very superior woman. He settled on a part of the extensive homestead of his grandfather, David, and resided near the present Insane Asylum. At his home were held many friendly meetings of his descendants and others of the Brigham race, precursors of the Brigham Family Association.

Children, born in Westboro:
265   i Otis⁶, b. ————, 1788.
    ii Elmer, b. ————, 1790; d. 1796.
   iii Arethusa, b. 2 Oct., 1792; m. 29 Jan., 1821, Rev. John Milton, son of Dea. Reuben Putnam; b. in Sutton, Mass., 26 Feb., 1794, and d. at Yarmouth, Me., 19 Sept., 1861; educated at Brown Univ.; settled in Dunbarton, N. H. Ch. (Putnam), b. in Dunbarton:
       1 *Jane Brigham⁷*, b. 19 Nov., 1821; d. 11 Sept., 1824.
       2 *Carleton Elliott*, b. 21 July, 1823; d. 29 Aug., 1824.
       3 *Milton A.*, b. 13 June, 1825; d. 25 Aug., 1826.
       4 *Antoinette M.*, b. 12 Oct., 1827; d. 7 Aug., 1828.
       5 *Antoinette B.*, b. 17 May, 1829.
       6 *Henry M.*, b. 10 June, 1831.
       7 *George A.*, b. 7 Aug., 1833; d. 1 March, 1834.
       8 *George A.*, b. 8 May, 1835.

266 iv David, b. 2 Sept., 1794.
    v Hannah, b. 2 Oct., 1796; d. 20 May, 1889; m. 11 Dec., 1829,
       Silas Paine of Randolph, Mass. Ch. (Paine):
       1 *Silas B.⁷*, d.
       2 *Nancy*, m. Wm. Johnson of St. Louis, Mo.
       3 *Silas H.*
267 vi Elmer, b. 8 Sept., 1798.
268 vii Holloway, b. 2 Sept., 1801.
    viii Lucy Harrington, b. 1805; d. 11 Oct., 1887; m. 5 March, 1835,
       Benj. Pond, M. D., who d. 7 June, 1857; res. Westboro. Ch.
       (Pond):
       1 *Alfred⁷*, b. 1 March, 1836; d. 3 Nov., 1856.
       2 *Lucy Gale*, b. 16 April, 1839; res. 1903, Westboro; was long
          a teacher.
    ix Martha, b. 1808; d. 6 May, 1886; m. 26 Dec., 1832, Harrison O.,
       son of Otis Fay; b. 20 Jan., 1807; res. Westboro. Ch. (Fay):
       1 *Albert E.⁷*, b. 11 Aug., 1835; d. 23 June, 1890; m. Amelia A.
       ————. Ch.: i Mattie⁸; ii Lucy, both d. y.

109 JOSEPH⁵, son of Capt. Jonas⁴ and Persis (Baker) Brigham; born in Westboro, Mass., 20 April, 1766; died 29 Dec., 1837;
married Lucy Warren, born 23 Aug., 1769; died 15 June, 1856.

Children, born in Westboro:
    i Lowell⁶, b. 19 Dec., 1790; d. unm., 20 Nov., 1849.
    ii Harriet, b. 19 Sept., 1795; d. 11 July, 1868; m. 26 Oct., 1826,
       William F. Stone, b. in Saxonville, Mass., 10 April, 1784; d. in
       Cambridge, Mass., 26 March, 1857; he was Register of Deeds
       for Middlesex Co., 1821-1845. Ch. (Stone):
       1 *William L.⁷*, b. 1829; d. unm., 1857.
       2 *Mary W.*, b. 1833; d. 1899; m. 1880, Calvin Dimick of Cam-
          bridge.
       3 *Harriet B.*, b. 1835; d. unm., 1858.
       4 *Olynthus B.*, b. 3 April, 1838; res. Westboro, unm.

110 ALPHEUS⁵, son of Major Asa⁴ and Mary (Newton)
Brigham; born in Shrewsbury, Mass., 30 April, 1746; died in
Jaffrey, N. H., about 1826; married, 1764, Lydia Green, of
Westboro, who was killed about 1830, "frozen to death" in in-
human quarters "provided" by her son-in-law, Foster, who had
been deeded the farm by her husband, Alpheus, in consideration
of the care to be bestowed upon them in their old age.

He was settled in Jaffrey, N. H., by 1775, "Lot 4, Range 10."
Was in the Revolutionary War, in Capt. Abijah Smith's Co., for
New York, mustered 21 Sept., 1776; was a prominent man and held
many town offices and was on many important committees; was
"deer-reeve" there in 1775.

Children, born in Shrewsbury, except the 2 youngest, born in Jaffrey:
    i Asaph⁶, b. 2 June, 1765.
    ii Wright, b. 23 June, 1768.
269 iii Sylvanus, b. 10 Feb., 1771.

270   iv Abel, b. 31 July, 1773.
 v Joseph, b. 2 May, 1777; d. ——————; m. 30 May, 1796,
  Polly, dau. of Thos. and Sarah (Bigelow) Dutton of Jaffrey;
  b. 18 Aug., 1779; she m. (2) David Wilkins, and d. in Greenfield,
  2 Feb., 1830. Joseph moved West.
 vi Lydia, b. 12 April, 1782; d. 21 May, 1859; m. 7 June, 1807,
  Jedediah Foster of Jaffrey, who lived on her father's farm until
  1836, when he left town. Ch.: *Alpheus[7]*, d. 1819, æ. 10.

111   MOLLY[5], daughter of Major Asa[4] and Mary (Newton)
Brigham; born in Shrewsbury, Mass., 10 March, 1748; died in
Fitzwilliam, N. H., 23 Nov., 1822; married, 5 June, 1778, Benjamin
Davison, who was at Fitzwilliam by 1767; died there, 25 April,
1820, æ. 76.

Children (Davison), born in Fitzwilliam:
 i Mindwell[6], b. 1 March, 1778; d. 18 Oct., 1849; m. Richard
  Gleason, who d. s. p., in F., 1843, æ. 70.
 ii Molly, b. 2 June, 1780; m. 8 May, 1806, Nathan Winch, b. 1781;
  d. 1851, in Troy, N. H. Ch. (Winch):
  1' *Nathan[7]*; 2 *Mary*; 3 *Arethusa*; 4 *Calvin.*
 iii Sylvene, b. 23 Dec., 1781; d. 8 March, 1851; m. 21 Feb., 1811,
  Aaron Townsend, b. 1779; d. 1854. Ch. (Townsend):
  1 (*Rev.*) *Luther[7]*; 2 *Aaron.*
 iv Asenath, b. 4 April, 1785; d. s. p., 11 Feb., 1858; m. Nathan
  Winch of Troy (husband of Molly).
 v Arethusa, b. 26 Feb., 1787; d. unm., 12 April, 1811.
 vi Benjamin, b. 5 March, 1789; d. 20 Sept., 1860; m. (1) Abigail
  Marshall of Jaffrey, N. H.; m. (2) Nancy Colburn of Rindge,
  N. H. Ch., by first wife:
  1 *Abigail[7]*, m. (1) Daniel Prescott; m. (2) Dea. Oren Brooks.
  2 *Benjamin Brigham*, b. 22 Sept., 1818; d. 16 Nov., 1861; m.
  Almira Pierce of Jaffrey. Ch., by second wife: *Five*, all of
  whom d. y.

112   LEONARD[5], son of Major Asa[4] and Mary (Newton)
Brigham; born in Shrewsbury, Mass., 7 May, 1750; died in Milton,
Vt., 1 Jan., 1821; married (1), Mary, daughter of Capt. Silas
Wetherby; who died in Walpole, N. H., Jan., 1777; married (2),
in 1780, Abigail Forbush, of Walpole, who died in 1832.

He resided in Walpole, N. H., and moved to Milton, Vt. Him-
self and wife were original members of the First Church of Milton.
Was in the Revolutionary War, from Fitzwilliam, N. H., in the
"Ti" army; Corporal, in 1775.

Children (by first wife), born in Walpole, N. H.:
 i Luther[6], b. Oct., 1775; d. about 1840, s. p., in Canada.
 ii Infant, d. y.
*Children (by second wife), born in Walpole, except the last 3 born in
Milton:*   :,
271   iii Asa, b. 18 June, 1781.
 iv Calvin, b. ——————, 1782; d. in Milton, 1803.
 v Leonard, b. 1784; d. æ. 11.

272 vi Rufus, b. 9 Feb., 1786.
273 vii Jonathan, b. 23 Oct., 1788.
    viii Nabby, b. Oct., 1789; d. ——————; m. (1) 1812, Moses
         Stratton of Milton, Vt., who d. in Malone, N. Y., in 1836; m.
         (2) in 1838, Judson Tyler of Hartford, O., who d. in Filmore,
         Minn., in 1855. Ch. (Stratton):
         1 *Amanda*⁷; 2 *Selona*; 3 *Arvin*; 4 *Harriet*; 5 *Hiram*.
274   ix Silas, b. Oct., 1791.
       x Lois, b. Aug., 1793; m. 1816, Eben Saxton of Croton, O.; had
         9 ch.: 2 daus. were *Calista*⁷ and *Charlana*.
      xi Polly, b. April, 1796; m. in 1829, Henry Bliss of Croton, O.,
         who d. in 1853. Ch. (Bliss): *Hiram*⁷ of Croton.
     xii Leonard, b. 1798; d. probably s. p., 1827; m. 1825, Roxy Taylor.
275 xiii Hiram, b. Nov., 1800.

113   CAPT. STEPHEN⁵, son of Major Asa⁴ and Mary (Newton) Brigham; born in Shrewsbury, Mass., 13 May, 1754; died in
Vernon, N. Y., 11 Oct., 1849; married, 1 Feb., 1781, Sarah,
daughter of Joshua and Betty (Bent) Harrington; born in Fitzwilliam, N. H., 14 Jan., 1754; died 15 November, 1841.

He early moved to Fitzwilliam, and thence in 1790 to Whitestown, N. Y., and thence, about 1812, to Vernon, N. Y. Was in the
Revolutionary War, at Bunker Hill under Capt. Whitcomb. Was
selectman in 1789. Was a very pious church member.

Children, the first 6 born in Fitzwilliam, the 2 last in Whitestown:
276   i Sullivan⁶, b. 29 Dec., 1781.
277 ii Stephen, b. 11 April, 1783.
    iii Arethusa, b. 19 March, 1785; d. 28 Aug., 1794.
     iv Polly, b. 18 Aug., 1786; m. at Westmoreland, N. Y., 25 Jan.,
        1810, Barney Spalding (son of Uriah), b. Rutland, N. Y., 21
        March, 1782; d. there, 7 Dec., 1866; a farmer. Ch. (Spaulding),
        b. in Pinckney, N. Y.
        1 *Darwin*⁷, b. 18 March, 1812; d. 1 April, 1844; m. Cynthia Ann
          Wheeler of Henderson, N. Y. Ch.: Delia⁸, m. Newell Mathews
          of Watertown, N. Y.
      v Sally, b. 24 April, 1788; d. 20 July, 1818, in Denmark, N. Y.;
        m. 31 March, 1814, Ebenezer Cheever.
278 vi John, b. 24 March, 1790.
    vii Lucinda, b. 8 May, 1792; d. 26 Aug., 1794.
   viii Electa, b. 3 March, 1794; d. in Utica, N. Y., 1883; m. 13 Jan.,
        1814, Leonard Moore of Union, Ct., who moved to Utica. Ch.
        (Moore), b. in Utica:
        1 *Alexander Hanson*⁷, d. in U., 9 April, 1852; of firm of Dibble,
          Work & Moore, N. Y. City. Ch.: Horatio⁸, of Utica.
        2 *Lansing C.*, d. 1873; m. S. M. Dempsey; res. N. Y. City.
          Ch.: William⁸ (d); Frederick L., unm., a broker in N. Y.
          City.
        3 *Electa Brigham*, b. 25 Aug., 1825; res. unm., in Utica.

114   ELIZABETH⁵, daughter of Maj. Asa⁴ and Mary (Newton) Brigham; born in Shrewsbury, Mass., 26 Sept., 1756; died
15 Feb., 1823; married, 21 Nov., 1780, Joshua Harrington, Jr.,

born in Framingham, Mass., 13 Sept., 1755; died in Fitzwilliam, N. H., 20 Sept., 1834. She moved to Fitzwilliam with her father; her husband inherited a mill from his father, which, in turn, he left to his sons, Joshua and Elijah. For further details of this family, see *Hist. of Troy. N. H.*

Children *(Harrington), born in Fitzwilliam:*
- i Anna⁶, b. 29 June, 1781; d. 16 Feb., 1857; m. William Marshall of Troy, N. H.
- ii Daniel, b. 15 Dec., 1782; moved to Vt., where he d.; m. 24 Jan., 1809, Mary, dau. of Jesse Forristall of F.; b. 11 April, 1786; d. in Fitz., 23 June, 1819.
- iii Betsey, b. 18 April, 1784; m. 10 Jan., 1805, Asa, son of Abijah Stowell; moved West.
- iv Joshua, b. 29 Sept., 1785; m. (1) Nelly Gates of Dublin, N. H.; m. (2) Ruth Hall; in 1820 moved to Alstead, N. H., and then to Pittsford, N. Y. Ch.:
    - 1 *Sally⁷;* 2 *Lyman;* 3 *Eleanor;* 4 *Joshua;* 5 *Leonard Brigham,* b. 1818; m. Eunice Grant of Lyme, N. H.; 6 *Charles;* 7 *Lucy A.;* 8 *George F.;* 9 *Mary J.*
- v Elijah, b. 23 April, 1787; d. 15 May, 1870; m. (1) 1 Feb., 1810, Prudence Newell, who d. 3 June, 1827; m. (2) Mrs. Tabitha Tolman. Ch.:
    - 1 *Nelson⁷;* 2 *John;* 3 *Alonzo Brigham;* 4 *Daniel;* 5 *Patty;* 6 *Elizabeth;* 7 *Jacob Newell;* 8 *Arbee Reed;* 9 *Frances E.;* the last two d. y.
- vi Sally, b. 17 June, 1789; d. 1 Feb., 1800.
- vii Polly, b. 12 June, 1791; d. 1833.
- viii Lyman, b. 2 March., 1794; d. 1800.

115 JOSIAH NEWTON⁵, son of Major Asa⁴ and Mary (Newton) Brigham; born in Shrewsbury, Mass., 30 March, 1765; died ————; married (1), in Fitzwilliam, N. H., 14 Feb., 1793, Sarah, daughter of David and Sarah (Fisher) Perry; born 16 May, 1774; died 3 May, 1803; married (2), Mary Alsworth, from Ellington, Conn., who died in 1827. He moved to Hartwick, N. Y.

Children *(by first wife), born in Hartwick:*
- 279 i Elijah⁶, b. 1790.
- ii Josiah, ⎫ twins, d. unm.
- iii Sally, ⎭
- iv Mary, d. unm., in Dryden, N. Y., 186—.
- 280 v David, b. 27 Oct., 1799.
- 281 vi Perry, b. 17 April, 1801.
- vii Phebe, m. (1) ———— Carpenter; m. (2) ———— Harding; res. s. p., in Cortland, N. Y.

Children *(by second wife), born in Hartwick:*
- viii Rebecca, d. unm., 1861, in Whitestown, N. Y.
- ix Lucinda, m. ———— Butler. Ch.:
    - 1 *Lucinda E.*
- x Electa, d. unm, 1863, in Whitestown, N. Y.

116 SARAH⁵, daughter of Joseph⁴ and Comfort (Bigelow) Brigham; born in Marlboro, Mass., 13 May, 1731; died before 1791; married, 4 June, 1755, Dea. Benjamin, son of Joseph and Thank-

ful (Barrett) Tayntor; born in Marlboro, 3 Jan., 1733; died in Worcester, N. Y., 1798. They lived in Woodstock, Conn., Shrewsbury, and Princeton, Mass. He was in the Revolution.

Children (Tayntor), the two elder born in Woodstock, the third in Shrewsbury, and the rest in Princeton:

  i Sarah⁶, b. 12 March, 1756; m. Ebenezer, son of Elijah and Huldah (Keyes) Rice of Holden, Mass.; (his second wife was Ruth Eveleth of Stow); settled in Hubbardston. Ch. (Rice):
    1 *Rollin⁷;* 2 *Ebenezer;* 3 *Sarah,* who moved to Illinois.

  ii Miriam, b. 28 April, 1758; m. 1787, Stephen Potter of Marlboro.

  iii Anna Sophia, b. 19 June, 1760; m. 1786, Cyrus Kingsbury of Worcester, Mass. Ch. (Kingsbury):
    1 *Cyrus⁷.*

  iv Lucy, b. 30 Oct., 1761; m. Abel Hubbard of Holden; moved to Putney, Vt.; had 9 ch.

  v Lucretia, b. 30 Oct., 1763; d. y.

  vi Joseph, b. 2 Nov., 1765; d. y.

  vii Electa, b. 28 July, 1767; d. y.

  viii Patty, m. John Perry of Holden.

  ix Benjamin, b. 1768; d. in Russia, N. Y., 1835; m. Dinah Houghton of Worcester, N. Y. Ch.:
    1 *Benjamin⁷;* 2 *Sarah;* 3 *Olive;* 4 *Cyrus;* 5 *Lavina;* 6 *Mary;* 7 *Jonah;* 8 *Phileta.*

  x Joseph, b. 6 July, 1775; d. in Lebanon, N. Y., 1847; m. Abigail Fuller. Ch.:
    1 *Abigail⁷;* 2 (Dea.) *Joseph;* 3 *Patty;* 4 (Rev.) *Orasmus;* 5 *Lucy;* 6 *Ira;* 7 *Erasmus;* 8 *Cyrus;* 9 *Rufus.*

117 LAVINAH⁵, daughter of Joseph⁴ and Comfort (Bigelow) Brigham; born in Marlboro, Mass., 10 July, 1733; died Aug., 1784; married, 12 April, 1757, Thaddeus, son of Joseph and Ruth (Brigham) Howe (31); born in Marlboro, 30 May, 1733; (he married [2] Mrs. Prudence Holman, who died, s. p., 1831); he died 18 March, 1799.

Children (Howe), born in Marlboro:

  i Susanna⁶, b. 22 June, 1758; d. April, 1837; m. 2 Nov., 1778, Gershom Rice, Jr., b. in Marlboro, 3 July, 1755; d. April, 1837. Ch. (Rice):
    1 *Stephen⁷;* 2 *Anna;* 3 *Susanna;* 4 *Mary;* 5 *Henry.*

  ii Nanne, b. 15 Feb., 1760; d. 3 Nov., 1814; m. 11 July, 1781, Jonas Morse, b. in Marlboro, 29 Nov., 1759; d. 1799; she was his 2d wife. Ch. (Morse):
    1 *John W.⁷;* 2 *Nancy;* 3 *Henry;* 4 *Willard.*

  iii Jonah, b. 22 Feb., 1762; d. 8 Dec., 1834; m. (1) 8 March., 1792, Betty Cranston, who d. 1806; m. (2) 15 June, 1806, Mrs. Catherine (Howe) Wheeler, who d. 4 Jan., 1851, æ. 81. Ch.:
    1 *Lovina⁷;* 2 *Betsey;* 3 *Lydia;* 4 *Martha;* 5 *Thaddeus,* m. Charlotte Brigham, 390; 6 *Lyman;* 7 *Rufus;* 8 *Diana;* 9 *Cranston;* 10 *Dexter;* 11 *Freeman.*

  iv William, b. 4 Dec., 1764; d. 21 July, 1820; m. 27 Sept., 1785, Elizabeth, dau. of John Stowe; b. in Marlboro, 12 Sept., 1767; d. 3 June, 1835. Ch.:
    1 *Joel⁷;* 2 *William;* 3 *Elizabeth;* 4 *Sarah.*

> v Lovina, b. 23 March, 1767; d. 17 July, 1851; m. 11 June, 1787,
> Moses, son of Samuel Sherman; b. in Marlboro, 28 June, 1761;
> d. 28 June, 1833.
> vi Aaron, b. 15 May, 1770; m. Sarah Dana of Oxford, Mass.;
> moved to Lunenburg, Vt.
> vii Martha, b. 5 Feb., 1773; d. 22 July, 1848; m. 9 March, 1796,
> Francis Barnard (son of Joel; des. from Robert of Andover);
> b. in Marlboro, 18 Dec., 1768; d. 28 Dec., 1858. Ch. (Barnard):
> 1 *Elizabeth⁷;* 2 *Loring;* 3 *George;* 4 *Daniel;* 5 *Mary;* 6 *William;* 7 *Edward.*
> viii Stephen, b. 10 Aug., 1776; d. y.

118 STEPHEN⁵, son of Joseph⁴ and Comfort (Bigelow) Brigham; born in Marlboro, Mass., 15 Oct., 1741; died about 1811; married (1), 1764, Jemima Snow; married (2), ——— Wilder. He moved to Shrewsbury, thence to West Boylston, Mass. Probably was a private in Capt. Maynard's Co., Col. Cushing's Regt., which marched on alarm at Bennington, in 1777; discharged after 3 days' service.

Children (by first wife), born in Shrewsbury:
>   i Martha⁶, b. 9 Sept., 1766; d. 23 May, 1784.
> 282 ii Edmund, b. 29 Sept., 1769.
>   iii Sarah, b. 21 Feb., 1772; m. Gershom Flagg of Boylston.
> 283 iv Jabez, b. 28 Aug., 1775.
>   v Dolly, b. 10 July, 1777; d. 1782.
> 284 vi Stephen, b. 21 Sept., 1779.
>   vii Dolly, b. 20 Dec., 1783; d. s. p., 10 Jan., 1858; m. (1) Rev.
>   Reuben Ball; m. (2) Jas. Libby of Bridgton, Me.
Children (probably by second wife):
> 285 viii Levi, b. 8 June, 1787.
>   ix Lucinda, b. ———; m. Simon Plympton of W. Boylston; d.
>   s. p.

119 LIEUT. JOSEPH⁵, son of Joseph⁴ and Comfort (Bigelow) Brigham; born in Marlboro, Mass., 27 Sept., 1743; died 25 Aug., 1810; married Lydia, daughter of Daniel and Zeruiah (Eager) Barnes, who died 23 May, 1784, æ. 41 yrs., 38 days.

He resided in Northboro, Mass., and was selectman in 1799 and 1801; Justice of the Peace, 1804. Marched on the Lexington Alarm in Capt. William Brigham's Co.; was 2d Lieut. in Capt. Paul Brigham's Co., commissioned 5 Sept., 1776, and performed other service. Commission is preserved by Miss Martha L. Ames, his descendant.

Children, born in Marlboro:
> 286 i Lydia⁶, b. 16 Aug., 1766.
>   ii Lucy, b. in Marlboro, 31 Dec., 1771; d. June, 1855; m. 1791,
>   Samuel R. Rice. Ch. (Rice):
>   1 *Lucy⁷;* 2 *Patty;* 3 *Lydia;* 4 *Edmund;* 5 *Ashley;* 6 *Elvira;*
>   7 *Serena;* 8 *Wheeler.*
>   iii }
>   iv } Twin boys, d. y.

120 DR. GERSHOM⁵, son of Gershom⁴ and Mary (Lee) Brigham; born in Westboro, Mass., 15 Oct., 1747; married in 1772 (intentions, June 6), Esther Belknap, who died Oct., 1801. He practiced medicine in Westboro and also several years in Fitzwilliam, N. H., where he was the first doctor and held town offices. He was in Westboro in 1780.*

Children, the 4 elder born in Fitzwilliam; the twins and probably Nathaniel and Josiah in Westboro:
    i Sally⁶, bapt. 16 June, 1776; m. 3 June, 1793, Silas, son of John Witherby; b. in Westboro, 20 Feb., 1769. Ch. (Witherby), b. in Westboro:
        1 *Mary⁷*, b. 1796; 2 *Jeremiah*, b. 1798; res. in Boston; 3 *Joel*, b. 1800; res. N. Y.; 4 *Jesse Brigham*, b. 1807; res. N. Y.; 5 *Esther Louisa*, b. 1810.
    ii Joseph Warren, bapt. 5 May, 1776; d. y.
    iii Patty, m. Ebenezer Belknap, and res. Boston. Ch. (Belknap):
        1 *George⁷*, d. y.; 2 *Martha*, m. Benj. H. Goodell, res. Worcester; 3 *Eunice*, m. Ammon Cate of Boston; 4 *Louisa*, m. Capt. James Paxton; res. Baltimore.
    iv Jesse, bapt. 31 May, 1778; d. unm., in Worcester.
287   v Joseph, b. 28 May, 1780.
288   vi Benjamin, twin to Joseph.
    vii Nathaniel, m. Nancy Brown; res. Westboro. Ch.:
        1 *Harriet⁷;* 2 *Maria;* 3 *Julia*, who probably res. Providence, R. I.
289 viii Josiah, b. 19 Dec., 1791.

121 REV. BENJAMIN⁵, son of Benjamin⁴ and Hannah (Merrill) Brigham; born in Marlboro, Mass., 11 March, 1741-2; died in Fitzwilliam, N. H., 13 June, 1799; married (1), 6 June, 1771, Lucy, daughter of Jonas and Lucy (Eager) Morse of Shrewsbury, Mass.; born 25 April, 1840; died 22 April, 1793; married (2), 11 Feb., 1795, Puah Mellen, widow of John (she had nine children by her first marriage), who died 4 Feb., 1821, æ. about 76.

He graduated from Harvard College, A. B., 1764. In 1770 he received an urgent call from the church in Fitzwilliam to become its pastor. He was to receive two lots of land of 100 acres each, and two other lots were to be reserved for the use of the minister. He was to receive eighty pounds in money and an annual salary of £53 6s.8d., from time of acceptance for three years, then an additional sum yearly until it had reached £66 13s. 4d. He accepted, and spent the rest of his life in charge of this church. He was a man of fine character and a minister who preserved harmony in his parish. Several of his manuscript sermons are extant. He was Representative to Exeter Provincial Congress, 1775. He was interred in the

* "2 June, 1780. Dr. Gershom Brigham makes me a visit respecting the baptism of his new-born Twins."—*Parkman Diary.*

central part of the old graveyard in Fitzwilliam, and in 1809 the town appropriated $20 to buy gravestones for him.

Children (by first wife), baptized in Fitzwilliam:
290   i Lucinda⁶, bapt. 22 March, 1772.
    ii Lucy, bapt. 13 June, 1773; m. 27 Nov., 1793, Gen. James Humphrey; res. Athol, Mass.
    iii Benjamin Franklin, bapt. 3 Sept., 1775; d. 13 Oct., 1801; m. 8 Nov., 1796, Sally, dau. of Abner and Martha (Ward) Haskell; she was dismissed, 12 March, 1804, to a church in Penn.; he moved from Fitzwilliam to Colchester, Vt., in 1799. Ch., b. in Fitzwilliam:
        1 *Fanny*⁷, b. 22 Dec., 1796.
        2 *Benjamin Franklin,* b. 24 Jan., 1799.
        3 *Adolphus,* b. 5 Sept., 1801.
291   iv Elisha⁶, bapt. 1 Aug., 1779.

122   CALEB⁵, son of Benjamin⁴ and Hannah (Merrill) Brigham; born in Marlboro, Mass., 20 Nov., 1743; died 13 Sept., 1829; married 3 Sept., 1766, Hannah, daughter of Daniel and Zeriah (Eager) Barnes; born 4 April, 1743. He was born at the original homestead of Thomas² in Marlboro, and held town offices there as late as 1776.

Children, born in Marlboro:
    i Hannah⁶, b. 17 April, 1767; m. Mr. Gates of New Marlboro, Mass.
    ii Dorothy, b. 27 Aug., 1770; d. unm.
292   iii Willard, b. 1 Oct., 1772.
    iv Francis, b. 25 Aug., 1776; d. 24 Nov., 1796, while attending Harvard Univ.
293   v Caleb, b. 26 Dec., 1778.
    vi David, b. 8 March, 1781; m. Betsey Trowbridge; moved to New York; a son was a printer or editor in Albany, N. Y.

123   BENAJAH⁵, son of Benjamin⁴ and Hannah (Merrill) Brigham; born in Marlboro, Mass., 15 March, 1745-6; died 7 Dec., 1822; married, 12 Sept., 1771, Abigail, daughter of Peter Bent of Marlboro, a descendant of the distinguished Peter Bent; born 29 Jan., 1754; died in Boston, 1837. He first resided in Westboro, where he was chosen on a school committee in 1778; afterwards he resided in Marlboro, where he was constable in 1785.

Children, probably the 5 elder born in Westboro, the others in Marlboro:
    i Annas⁶, b. 15 March, 1772; m. Jonathan Barnard of Lancaster, Mass., who d. 5 March, 1824, æ. 60. Ch. (Barnard), b. in Lancaster:
        1 *Jonathan*⁷, b. 23 Dec., 1795; d. 12 Feb., 1799.
        2 *Benajah,* b. 13 Sept., 1798; d. 4 Oct., 1805.
        3 *Julia,* b. 28 Dec., 1803; d. 5 Sept., 1805.
294   ii Benajah, b. 7 June, 1774.

295 iii Ephraim, b. 2 July, 1776.
296 iv Peter W., b. 10 May, 1779.
297 v Jabez, b. 12 March, 1781.
    vi Mary, b. 4 July, 1784; m. (1) William Lancaster; m. (2) Rev. ————; res. New Salem.
    vii Zenas, b. 20 March, 1786; d. in West Medway, Mass., where he res. 28 May, 1878; m. 1816, Nancy, dau. of Ralph Mann, of West Medway; she d. 1826. Ch., b. in Westboro:
      1 *Marian A.*[7], b. 16 Jan., 1817; d. 6 July, 1896; m. 28 April, 1836, Eleazer T. Bullard of West Medway, who d. 1888. Ch. (Bullard): i Nancy Brigham[8], b. 15 Feb., 1838; ii Marian Adelaide, b. 20 June, 1839; d. 3 Sept., 1875; m. Warren H. Howe of Marlboro; (had Mabel, who m. Herbert J. Mann of Boston and Nashua); iii Julia Estelle, b. 16 Feb., 1851; d. July, 1852; iv William Brigham, b. 3 Sept., 1853; v Helen Florence, b. 23 June, 1855.
    viii John, b. 16 Sept., 1790; m. and removed West.
    ix William, b. 28 Dec., 1792; d. in Westboro, 9 Oct., 1818.

124 HANNAH[5], daughter of Benjamin[4] and Hannah (Merrill) Brigham, born in Marlboro, Mass., 1 May, 1748; died 14 Jan., 1815; married, 21 June, 1769, Hezekiah Maynard, Jr., of Marlboro; born 20 Jan., 1742; died 14 March, 1824.

    Children (Maynard), born in Marlboro:
    i Bethiah[6], b. 9 April, 1770.
    ii Zadock, b. 4 Sept., 1771; d. 1776.
    iii (Capt.) Abel, b. 3 June, 1773; d. 31 Oct., 1811; m. Nancy ————. Ch.:
      1 *William*[7].
    iv John, b. 9 Aug., 1775; m. 7 Sept., 1794, Dorothy Hayden. Ch.:
      1 *Thomas*[7]; 2 *Martin*; 3 *Susanna*.
    v Silas, b. 12 Sept., 1777; d. 4 Aug., 1806.
    vi Calvin, b. 3 Aug., 1779.
    vii Hannah, b. 28 Feb., 1782.
    viii Hezekiah, b. 29 Feb., 1784.
    ix Luther, b. 9 Aug., 1785; d. 6 Feb., 1815.
    x Joel, b. 26 May, 1788.
    xi Charles, b. 9 June, 1790.
    xii Willard, b. 7 Sept., 1792; d. 6 Jan., 1815.

125 GERSHOM[5], son of Benjamin[4] and Hannah (Merrill) Brigham; born in Marlboro, Mass., 27 June, 1750; died in Fayston, Vt., 22 Oct., 1817; married, 23 May, 1783, Sarah, daughter of Samuel and Mary (Loring) Allen; born in Northboro, Mass., 9 Dec., 1756; died in Fayston, 30 Aug., 1829.

He had land of his father Benjamin, just west of the old Warren Brigham place on Glen St., where he built a house and barn near the intersection with Forest St.; it was sold by Gershom when he moved to New Hampshire. He marched with Capt. William Brigham's Co. of "Minute Men" in 1775. In 1795 Gershom moved from Marlboro to Winchester, N. H. (*vide* deed which exists of property owned there), and 12 years later, 1807, to Fayston, Washington Co., Vt., where he settled upon the homestead which descended to his son, Elisha, then to Elisha's son-in-law, George O. Boyce, who married Elisha's daughter, Laura. He came to a wooded wilderness which had to be cleared, and as his health was not strong for many years (he was a paralytic), Elisha took charge of affairs, before his father died at the age of 68. He was a man about 5 ft. 7 inches in height, rather spare, black hair and eyes. Sarah Allen was tall with light brown hair and very light blue eyes standing out prominently; her forehead was very high, broad, and rather retreating. They lie buried in the hill cemetery overlooking the home of their closing years.*

Children, the 5 eldest born in Marlboro, the others in Winchester, N. H ·
298   i Leonard Warren⁶, b. 16 July, 1785.
299   ii Polly, b. 17 Oct., 1786.
       iii Sarah, b. 16 May, 1789; d. s. p., April, 1830; m. George Grimes.
300   iv Elisha, b. 22 Oct., 1792.
301   v Benjamin Baxter, b. 28 May, 1795.
302   vi Alvin L., 21 Oct., 1798.
303   vii Rebecca M., b. 27 Feb., 1802.

126   STEPHEN⁵, son of Elnathan⁴ and ———— Brigham; born in Mansfield, Conn., 1744; died 7 May, 1816; married (1) ————; married (2), Hannah, daughter of Bennet and Eliza beth (Spofford) Field, born 26 May, 1747. He resided in Mansfield.

In Sept., 1777, he was permitted to transport to Boston, by land, 1600 lbs. of rye and wheat flour, 400 lbs. cheese and 200 lbs. butter, to be exchanged for iron and steel; also to exchange for salt, 2 tons of rye and wheat flour, 1400 lbs. cheese, 600 lbs. butter; also to drive to Boston, 40 fat cattle and 250 fat sheep. He was appointed Ensign of the 8th Co., 5th State Regt., May, 1779 (*Recs. of Conn.,* Vol. 1).

Children (by first wife), born in Mansfield:
       i Eunice⁶, b. 15 Feb., 1776; d. 9 June, 1841; m. 23 Feb., 179 , Elijah Royce; res. Woodstock.
       ii Asenath, m. ———— Wright.
       iii Anna, m. ———— Parker.
       iv Lucretia, m. Isaac Morey. Ch. (Morey), b. in Coventry:
          1 Elisha⁷.
Children (by second wife), born in Mansfield:
304   v Elizabeth.
305   vi Stephen, b. 5 Feb., 1774.
       vii Hannah, d. unm., in Mansfield.

* Two slate stones are in the old " Waite Cemetery "—each with urn and drooping willows at top. " Gershom Brigham died Oct. 22, 1817, aged 68 years. Clay to clay and dust to dust." " Sarah (Allen) wife of Gershom Brigham died Aug. 30, 1829, aged 73 years. Dust to dust and clay to clay." On each is a quartrain (almost illegible) at the bottom.

Eng'd by E.P.Hall & Sons 18 Barclay St N Y

Paul Brigham

viii Clarissa, m. (1) Gerry Russ; m. (2) Raphael Storrs, who d.;
    res. Mansfield.
  ix Elisha, d.; m. ————; res. New York. Ch.:
    1 *Elisha⁷*, and 2 daus.
   x Spofford, m. ———— Myrick; res. s. p., Rockville, Ct.
  xi Polly, b. about 1785; d. 27 April, 1807, æ. 22; m. Cephas Dun-
    ham; res. Willington, Conn. Ch. (Dunham):
    1 *Lewis Brigham⁷*, res. Marquette, Ia.
  xii Sally, d. 27 June, 1808, æ. 20.

127   CAPT. THOMAS⁵, son of Paul⁴ and Catherine (Turner)
Brigham; born in Coventry, Conn., 7 March, 1742; died there, 10
May, 1800; married, 5 Feb., 1769, Susanna Eels, who died 21 June,
1813. He resided in Coventry, Conn.

Children, born in Coventry:
306   i Alexander⁶, b. 26 Jan., 1770.
      ii Salinda, b. 26 April, 1772; d. 29 Dec., 1775.
307   iii Orleans, b. 10 Dec., 1773.
      iv Thomas, b. 13 July, 1775; d. 27 Nov., 1775.
308   v Don Ferdinand, b. ————.
309   vi Royal, b. 27 Sept., 1779.
     vii Eunice, b. 17 Dec., 1782; d. of consumption, 1 Nov., 1805, in
       Coventry.

128   LIEUT.-GOV. PAUL⁵, son of Paul⁴ and Catherine
(Turner) Brigham; born in Coventry, Conn., 6 Jan., 1746; died in
Norwich, Vt., of a long and distressing illness, 15 June, 1824; mar-
ried, 6 Oct., 1768, Lydia Sawyer of Hebron, Conn., who died 19
Sept., 1838, æ. 93.

He had served in the Connecticut militia in every grade from corporal to captain, long enough, at the time of the Revolutionary War,
to be exempt from service. Nevertheless, he entered the Continental
Army as captain, 1 Jan., 1777, and served 4 years in Col. Chandler's
regiment, afterwards commanded by Col. Isaac Sherman; received
his discharge 22 April, 1781; was in the battles of Germantown,
Fort Mifflin and Monmouth, and wintered in Valley Forge, 1777-'78.
In 1782 he removed from Coventry, Conn., to Norwich, Vt., where
he was town clerk, 1784-'96; high sheriff of Windsor Co. 5 years;
appointed Judge of County Court for Windsor County, June, 1785,
serving 5 years; in 1788, elected Brig.-General of 3d Brigade;
1787, elected chairman of committee to apprehend, in Vermont, the
supporters of Shay's Rebellion, who had fled there; in 1788, member
of State Land Commissioners; was member of the Legislature; in
1791, elected to Vermont Council, and was on committee to nominate
men for the first Board of Trustees of Univ. of Vermont; also elected
Maj.-General of 4th Div. of Militia. He received 27 elections
from the people at large, 1 as Presidential Elector, 5 as Councillor,
21 as Lieut.-Governor, when he declined further election. He was
the first elected Lieut.-Governor and served 20 years. He received

the degree of Hon. A. M. from Dartmouth College in 1806. He had a military funeral.*

Children, born in Coventry:
310   i Thomas⁶, b. 23 March, 1769.
       ii Mary, b. 12 Oct., 1770; d. March, 1773.
311 iii Don J., b. 24 March, 1774.
312   iv Paul W., b. 26 Oct., 1776.
        v Lydia, b. 5 Oct., 1778; d. 1872; m. Joseph Lathrop, a farmer of
          Middlesex and Worcester, Vt., who d. 1837. Ch. (Lathrop):
          1 Benjamin⁷, had a family in Worcester, Vt.
          2 Dwight, had 2 daus.; res. Berlin, Vt.
          3 Brigham, had a family in western part of N. Y. State.
          4 Lucia, m. Stephen Willey of Middlesex, Vt.; 3 ch.
          5 Albert, d. early in New Orleans, La.

129   HANNAH⁵, daughter of Uriah⁴ and Lydia (Ward) Brigham; born in Coventry, Conn., 9 April, 1746; died 6 April, 1813; married, 19 May, 1766, Jacob Baker, son of Dea. Jonathan and Hannah (Baker) Gurley; born in Mansfield, Conn., 28 July, 1742; died 20 Feb., 1804. Was a farmer, prominent man, holding town offices, and a leading member of the North Parish church in Mansfield. Was in the Revolution.

Children (Gurley), born in Mansfield:
    i Lydia⁶, b. 6 June, 1767; d. 12 Aug., 1787; m. 24 Dec., 1786,
      Benjamin Pierce of Brooklyn, Conn.
   ii Artemas, b. 9 April, 1769; d. 18 May, 1822; m. (1) Sarah Steele;
      m. (2) Mrs. Martha (Shepard) Hovey; was a farmer, representative, etc. Ch.:
      1 Lovinia⁷; 2 Sarah; 3 Abigail; 4 George; 5 Charles; 6 Infant; 7 Infant; 8 Uriah Brigham of Deansville, N. Y.
  iii Jacob Baker, b. 2 Aug., 1771; d. at res. in New London, Conn.,
      24 Sept., 1856; one of the ablest lawyers in the city; m. Elizabeth Griswold of Lyme, Conn.; was grad. Dartmouth Coll., 1793.
      Ch.:
      1 Sarah⁷; 2 Mary; 3 Charles, who d. soon after grad. from
        Yale Coll., 1827; 4 Elizabeth; 5 Ursula; 6 Hannah; 7 Hannah Brigham; 8 John; 9 Ellen; 19 Lydia; 11 Ann.
   iv Uriah, b. 30 May, 1774; d. 4 Oct., 1775.
    v Ebenezer, b. 25 July, 1776; d. 3 July, 1864; m. Sally Balcom;
      a farmer. Ch.:
      1 Jacob⁷; 2 Emily; 3 Ebenezer; 4 Joseph, d. y.; 5 Sarah.
   vi Abigail, b. 7 Feb., 1778; d. 29 Jan., 1855; m. Elijah Hinckley
      of Cambridge, Vt. Ch.:
      1 Chauncey⁷.
  vii Uriah Brigham, b. 19 Nov., 1780; d. Oct., 1783.
 viii Mercia, b. 24 March, 1782; d. Dec., 1783.
   ix Lucia, b. 14 Nov., 1784; d. unm., 20 March, 1864.
    x Hannah, b. 5 May, 1791; d. 18 March, 1884; m. Anson Turner,
      a farmer of Mansfield. Ch. (Turner):
      1 Ursula⁷; 2 Mary, both d. y.; 3 Phineas; 4 Henry; 5 Hannah
        Brigham, d. unm.; 6 Jacob.

* Compiled from Gov. & Council of Vt., Vols. iii and iv.

130 BETHIAH[5], daughter of Uriah[4] and Ann (Richardson) Brigham; born in Coventry, Conn., 14 July, 1757; died in New Lisbon, N. Y., 20 July, 1838; married, 30 Jan., 1782, Zaccheus, son of Andrew Downer; born in Norwich, Conn., 13 Nov., 1755; moved to Utica, N. Y., where he died 17 July, 1851. He was in the Revolution from Vermont and pensioned; a Justice of the Peace and contributor to the press.

Children (Downer), all but the youngest born in Sharon, Vt..
   i Norman[6], b. 25 Oct., 1782; died in Utica, N. Y., 25 Jan., 1854;
     m. (1) Phebe Davis; m. (2) Laura Gregory. Ch.:
       1 *Don S.[7]; 2 Lovina; 3 Norman; 4 John; 5 Charles; 6 Mary;*
       7 Phebe; 8 Diana; 9 Almira.
   ii Don, b. 25 Feb., 1784; d. 25 March, 1850.
   iii Jeannette, b. 30 March, 1786; d. 5 March, 1854; m. (1) ————
     Blood; m. (2) ———— Reed.
   iv Dana, b. 4 July, 1788; d. in Utica, 22 Sept., 1863; m. Cynthia
     Munger. Ch.:
       1 *Edward[7].*
   v Mary, b. 17 May, 1791; m. Uriah Kimball; they moved to Wis-
     consin, and she d. 9 April, 1830.
   vi Andrew Otis, b. 25 July, 1796; d. in Detroit, Mich., 3 June,
     1876; m. Esther Emerson. Ch.:
       1 *Mary J.[7]; 2 Sarah M.; 3 Emily E.; 4 William A.; 5 Henry E.*
   vii Zaccheus, b. in Springfield, N. Y., 8 March, 1799; d. Sullivan,
     Ind., Sept., 1876; m. Harriet Thatcher. Ch.:
       1 *Albert F.[7]; 2 Sanford B.; 3 Augustus; 4 Ava C.; 5 Julia A.*

131 ANNA[5], daughter of Uriah[4] and Ann (Richardson) Brig-ham; born in Coventry, Conn., 14 Oct., 1759; died 11 Feb., 1845; married, 17 May, 1781, Lemuel, son of Samuel White; born in Coven try, 30 Dec., 1758; moved to Batavia, N. Y., where died, 7 Aug., 1850.

Children (White).
   i Percy[6], b. 14 Jan., 1782; d. 20 Sept., 1798.
   ii Brigham, b. 1 July, 1783; d. 27 June, 1839.
   iii Grace, b. 15 Dec., 1786; res. Middlebury, Vt.
   iv Laura, b. 16 April, 1788; m. Reuben Ross of Middlebury.
   v Chester, b. 1 Feb., 1790; d. 10 Feb., 1790.
   vi Chester, b. 14 Feb., 1793; m. Lucy Topliff; he was a farmer in
     Batavia, N. Y. Ch.:
       1 *Harrison[7]; 2 Mary; 3 Emily; 4 Lemuel; 5 Maria; 6 Laura;*
       7 Ann; 8 Eliza; 9 Kirke.
   vii Lemuel, b. 9 April, 1796; d. 5 May, 1840; m. Eliza Mathews;
     he was a harness maker in Buffalo, N. Y. Ch.:
       1 *William C.[7]; 2 Ann M.; 3 Eliza; 4 John B.; 5 Walton O.*
   viii Lucy, b. 9 June, 1802; d. 15 Nov., 1820.

132 DON CARLOS[5], son of Uriah[4] and Ann (Richardson) Brigham; born in Coventry, Conn., 21 Feb., 1763; died 27 March, 1843; married, 7 June, 1789, Mary (or Polly) Greenleaf; born in

Coventry, 7 Jan., 1764; died 30 Oct., 1845. He resided in Mansfield, Conn. (some records say Hartford). Was in the Revolution, as he is noted in records as being a pensioner in 1832.

Children, born in Mansfield:

    i (Dr.) Norman⁶, b. 7 March, 1790; d. s. p., 15 Oct., 1871, in Mansfield, where res.; m. Pamelia Dunham, who d. 11 Jan., 1872; was a physician of professional eminence and extensive practice; served in many town offices, and was representative a number of times.

    ii Gurdon, b. 23 April, 1792; d. 11 June, 1804.

    iii Mary, b. 12 Feb., 1794; m. 1 Sept., 1825, John Kingsbury of Tolland, Conn. Ch. (Kingsbury), b. in Tolland:

        1 *John B.⁷*, m. (1) Mary Ann Kellogg; m. (2) Carrie Rogers; res. Rockville, Conn.

        2 *George*, m. Mary Crone. Ch.: i Adelaide⁸, res. W. Hartford; ii Jennie, m. Halsey L. Allen, res. Rockville; iii Elizabeth, m. Elmer Adams, res. s. p., Rockville; iv Mary, m. Frank Holton, res. Ellington, Conn.; v George, d. y.

313   iv Charles, b. 29 Jan., 1797.

    v David, b. 10 March, 1802; d. 19 Jan., 1804.

    vi Eliza Ripley, b. 3 April, 1805; d. 5 April, 1891; m. 9 Dec., 1834, Richmond C. Lovet of Tolland, Conn. Ch. (Lovet), b. in Tolland:

        1 *Eliza T.⁷*, b. 10 June, 1836; m. 1860, Daniel S. Hunter of Brooklyn, N. Y. Ch. (Hunter): i Mary E.⁸, m. Frank U. Smith of Minneapolis, Minn.; ii James F., m. Cornelia Adams, New Haven, Conn.; iii Bernie, unm., res. Brooklyn; iv Harry R., m. res. Brooklyn.

        2 *Eugene*, b. 7 April, 1838; m. Emma Weis; res. Merced Falls, Cal. Ch.: Merton⁸, m. and res. Palo Alto, Cal.

    vii Susan Ann, b. 31 Dec., 1807; d. Tolland, 1 Feb., 1863; m. 29 Nov., 1831, John Webb Gager of Tolland. Ch. (Gager), b. in Tolland:

        1 *Mary B.⁷*, b. 25 Aug., 1833.

        2 *Andrew*, b. 19 Oct., 1835; d. 3 Sept., 1901.

        3 *Ann Eliza*, b. 5 Nov., 1839; d. 1 Aug., 1870.

        4 *Lois*, b. 11 Jan., 1847; d. 26 April, 1899.

        5 *Charles A.*, b. 6 March, 1851.

133 CEPHAS⁵, son of Uriah⁴ and Ann (Richardson) Brigham; born in Coventry, Conn., Dec., 1765; died (probably) in South Coventry, Conn., 17 May, 1841; married, 14 May, 1786, Amelia Robertson, born about 1764; died in 1845, æ. 81. Her family were of Newbury, Mass. He resided in So. Coventry, where he held many town offices, and was a member of the General Assembly of Conn.

Children, born in South Coventry:

    i Anna⁶, m. 9 Oct., 1806, Roderick Dimock of Mansfield, Conn.; res. Coventry.

    ii Lucia, m. Horace Russ; res. Coventry.

    iii Sally, m. 29 Nov., 1810, Artemas Russ of Mansfield; res. Coventry.

    iv Uriah, m. (1) 26 April, 1825, Emily Wright; m. (2) Harriet Nye: res. s. p., Coventry.

314   v Daniel R., b. 6 Aug., 1895.
     vi Eveline L., m. Gurdon Fuller; res. Vernon.
    vii Maria, m. 4 July, 1821, Levi Allen; res. Mansfield.
   viii Emily, m. Roderick Dimock; res. Coventry.
    ix Julia, m. Abner Mason; res. Coventry.
315   x Edwin G.

134 HOSEA⁵, son of Samuel⁴ and Mary Brigham; born in
Sudbury, Mass., 6 Sept., 1750; he was living in Hubbardstown,
Mass., in 1782, where he died, 17 Dec., 1817; married Catherine
Davis of Holden, Mass., who died in Hubbardstown, 19 Oct., 1823,
æ. 74 (Vide *Hist. of Hubbardston*).

Children, born in Hubbardston:
316   i Peter⁶, b. 2 Oct., 1781.
317   ii Joseph, b. 9 Aug., 1785.
   iii Samuel, b. 12 May, 1787; moved to New York State.
   iv Betsey, b. 12 Aug., 1792; d. 15 March, 1851.

135 JOEL⁵, son of Samuel⁴ and Mary Brigham; born in Sudbury, Mass., 5 March, 1756; died there, 25 June, 1813; married, 25
April, 1784, Elizabeth, daughter of John and Esther Maynard;
born in Sudbury, 25 March, 1759; died there, 6 Sept., 1846. He
was a soldier from Sudbury, 1775-1782; had a fine Revolutionary
record. The full story is too long to print here. He was 5 ft. 10
in. in height; had a " ruddy " complexion and dark hair.* He resided in Sudbury and Leominster, Mass.

Children, born in Sudbury:
318   i Asa⁶, b. 16 Feb., 1785.
    ii Betsey, b. 8 July, 1786; d. in Sudbury, 27 Oct., 1830; m. ———
      Carlton.
319 iii Joel, b. 16 March, 1788.
    iv Esther, b. 28 Sept., 1789; m. 9 June, 1811, William Hunt, Jr.
      Ch. (Hunt):
        1 *Abel⁷;* 2 *Mary;* 3 *Andrew;* 4 *Lizzie;* 5 *Asahel;* 6 *Thomas;*
        7 *George;* 8 *Abbie.*
    v Lucinda, b. 14 March, 1791; m. Reuben Moore, 23 Dec., 1821.
      Ch. (Moore):
        1 *Eunice E.⁷,* m. Edwin Harrington of Sudbury, 27 Nov., 1845.
        Ch. (Harrington): George E.⁸, b. 27 Oct., 1846; m. (1) Alice
        E. Brown, 13 June, 1878; she d. 19 Nov., 1879; m. (2) M.
        Edna Newton; 3 ch.
320   vi Polly, b. 29 Dec., 1792.
   vii Sally, b. 1 April, 1794; d. 9 Oct., 1796.
   viii Otis, b. 15 May, 1796; d. in Sudbury, 12 June, 1842; m ———.
      Ch.:
        1 *Elizabeth⁷.*
    ix Sally, b. 20 Dec., 1797; m. Joel Dakin; no further reported.
    x John, b. 29 Nov., 1799; no further reported.
    xi Rebecca, b. 5 March, 1801; no further reported.
321 xii Nancy, b. 16 Aug., 1803.

* See *Mass. Records of Sailors and Soldiers*, p. 530.

136   JONAS⁵, son of Samuel⁴ and Mary Brigham; born in Sudbury, Mass., 26 May, 1758; resided for a time at " Nelson "; thence to Dublin, N. H., where died, 11 Feb., 1850; married (1), in Sudbury, 10 Nov., 1780, Polly Wyman; married (2), 1807, Dorcas, widow of Oliver Pratt. Was probably in service with the Northern Army in the Revolution, in 1777.

Children (by first wife), born in Sudbury:
    i Levi⁶, b. 29 Feb., 1781.
    ii Jonas, b. 22 Sept., 1783.
Children (by second wife):
    iii Ruel, b. 30 May, 1808; m. (1) 2 June, 1835, Prudence, dau. of James Burns, b. 17 Dec., 1811; d. 11 Oct., 1848; m. (2) 28 Jan., 1850, Maria J., dau. of Moses Cragin, b. in N. Y., 2 Jan., 1832; he probably res. for a while in Dublin. Ch. (by first wife).
        1 *Jane*⁷, b. 19 Jan., 1838.
        2 *George*, b. 15 Sept., 1843; d. 7 March, 1845.
    iv Mary H., b. 1 April, 1818.

137   CAPT. SAMUEL⁵, son of John⁴ and Cate (Willis) Brigham; born in Sudbury, Mass., 3 March, 1775; died 28 Nov., 1843; married, 3 Jan., 1799, Lucy Osborn, who died 9 Sept., 1825. Resided in Waltham, Mass.

Children, born in Sudbury:
    i George⁶, b. 25 Feb., 1800; d. in Newton, Mass., 6 Sept., 1873.
    ii Henry, b. 5 April, 1802; d. in Newton, Mass., 27 Nov., 1874.
    iii Cynthia, b. 9 June, 1804; d. 20 Sept., 1886; m. 24 Nov., 1841, Dea. Adin Cummings of Rindge and Jaffrey, N. H.; b. 4 Dec., 1797; d. 28 July, 1870. Ch. (Cummings):
        1 *John C.*⁷, b. 1843; d. 1863, on the way home from the Civil War.
    iv Warren, b. 12 June, 1806; d. in E. Jaffrey, N. H., 31 May, 1882.
    v John, b. 10 Aug., 1808; d. unm., 18 Feb., 1869, in Abington, Mass.
    vi Eliza, b. 9 June, 1810; d. in Concord, Mass., 10 July, 1845; m. Jefferson Reed, who d. 18 Sept., 1878. Ch. (Reed) ·
        1 *Lucy*⁷; 2 *Charles;* 3 *George.*
    vii Samuel, b. 22 Oct., 1812; d. 22 Oct., 1813.
    viii Lucy Ann, b. 27 June, 1815; m. Henry H. Hart, who d. 23 April, 1882.
    ix Sarah, b. 27 May, 1817; d. unm., in Rindge, N. H., 6 March, 1847.

138   ELIJAH⁵, son of John⁴ and Cate (Willis) Brigham; born in Sudbury, Mass., 13 Oct., 1776; died in Waltham, Mass., 26 Oct., 1848; married (1), 20 March, 1803, Mary, daughter of Capt. Isaac Gleason, Jr.; born 2 Feb., 1779; died 18 May, 1815; married (2), Leonora ————, who died 17 July, 1840, æ. 54.

Children (by first wife), born in Sudbury:
322   i Danforth Phipps⁶, b. 30 Dec., 1803.

323 ii William, b. 27 March, 1805.
    iii Mary, b. 4 July, 1806; d. 30 Aug., 1825.
    iv Elijah, b. 29 June, 1808; d. unm., 14 Aug., 1837, in Sudbury.
    v Charles, b. 17 April, 1810; d. 13 Oct., 1810.
    vi Charles, b. 6 June, 1811; d. 26 Nov., 1811.
    vii Catherine, b. 23 March, 1813; d. 5 July, 1876, in Lowell, Mass;
       m. 31 Aug., 1832, Otis Bullard of Lowell; res. Boston. Ch.
       (Bullard):
       1 *Mary Jane*[7], b. 25 Nov., 1833; d. 15 Sept., 1834.
       2 *George Jefferson,* b. 26 Aug., 1836; d. 16 Jan., 1837.
       3 *Lucy Frances,* b. 12 Jan., 1840; d. 22 April, 1841.
       4 *George Francis,* b. 22 March, 1841; m. 10 March, 1864, Elvira
        Caroline Rowe of Thornton, N. H.; res. Lowell.
    viii Isaac, b. 27 July, 1814; d. 3 Dec., 1814.
Children (by second wife), born in Sudbury:
    ix Martha Ann, b. 7 Jan., 1823.
    x Leonora Wellington, b. 22 April, 1824.
    xi Mary Elizabeth, b. 21 Jan., 1829.

139 EBER[5], son of John[4] and Cate (Willis) Brigham; born in
Sudbury, Mass., 28 June, 1778; married, 3 Dec., 1809, Lucy Arnold
of Lancaster, Mass., who died 24 Aug., 1863.

Children, born in Sudbury:
324 i Samuel[6].
    ii James, d. before 1861; m. 27 Jan., 1833, Lucy Balcom, who d.
       13 Sept., 1861. Ch.:
       1 *Infant*[7], d. 1841, æ. 1 year.
       2 *Miranda,* m. ————————; has a son res. Lowell, Mass.

140 CAPT. WILLIAM[5], son of John[4] and Cate (Willis) Brigham; born in Sudbury, Mass., 20 Dec., 1784; died there, 3 July,
1879; married (1), 1812, Sarah Osborn, who died 24 May, 1859;
married (2), 12 June, 1860, Mrs. Mary B. Christie.

He was Capt. of a Militia Co. in 1812, and offered himself for the
war, but was never called out; he was selectman from 1817-1824;
filled many other town offices, but declined many; chairman of the
Congregational Church Building Committee, and chairman for four
years of the Committee for building the Town House; a member
of the Committee on the " Wadsworth monument," representative to
the General Court from 1832-37, and thus one of the leading citizens
of Sudbury, and a very benevolent man, withal.

Children, born in Sudbury:
325 i Rufus[6], b. 11 Jan., 1818.
    ii Sarah, d. ————————; m. Robert Scott of Newport, Vt., who d.
       Ch. (Scott):
       1 *Lillian*[7]; 2 *Bert A.;* 3 *Arthur F.*

141 JOHN[5], son of Lieut. Abijah[4] and Eunice (Willis) Brigham; born in Sudbury, Mass., 19 May, 1762; died in Rutland,

Mass., 10 Jan. (or June), 1833; married, 20 May, 1786, Ann Eunice Moore of Sudbury; born 10 April., 1768; died in Watertown, Mass., 20 May, 1862, æ. 94. Resided in Sudbury and Rutland, and was a member of the militia of Sudbury; was in the Revolutionary War in 1776, and in 1779.

Children, the first 5 born in Sudbury, the last 4 in Rutland:

326   i   Roxey[6], b. 7 Jan., 1788.

      ii   Oreb, b. 25 July, 1789; d. unm., in Watertown, Mass., 12 Dec., 1869, æ. 80.

327   iii   Abijah, b. 17 March, 1791.

      iv   Susannah Woodward, b. 15 May, 1793; d. unm., in Watertown, Mass., 5 Oct., 1879.

328   v   John, b. 22 March, 1795.

      vi   Sewell, b. 2 March, 1797; d. unm., in Watertown, 11 April, 1870.

    vii   Horatio, b. 16 Sept., 1800; d. unm., in Burke Co., Ga., 20 Sept., 1835.

   viii   James Moore, b. 4 Jan., 1807; d. unm., in Watertown, 8 Jan., 1855.

329   ix   William, b. 11 Aug., 1810.

142   JOSEPH[5], son of Lieut, Abijah[4] and Eunice (Willis) Brigham; born in Sudbury, Mass., 26 Sept., 1764; died there, 12 Jan., 1842; married, 5 April, 1795, Rebecca, daughter of Charles Haynes (who was in the Revolution); born in Sudbury, 29 Jan., 1770; died there, 12 Jan., 1853. Was a farmer and resided in Sudbury.

Children, born in Sudbury:

      i   Nancy[6], b. 11 March, 1796; d. 14 June, 1878; m. (1) 28 Oct., 1819, Daniel Crocker of Albany, N. Y., who d. 9 May, 1825; m. (2) 14 July, 1833, Benjamin Harris of Russellville, Ala. Ch. (Crocker):

         1   *Alphonso[7]*, d. unm., 6 July, 1851.

         Ch. (Harris):

         2   (*Dr.*) *John C.*, b. in Russellville; d. s. p., 8 Aug., 1899.

         3   *Rebecca B.*, m. Harvey Sargeant of Russellville. Ch. (Sargeant): i Lucy[8], m. ———— Williams; ii B. Harris; iii H. Owen; iv Bessie; v Rebecca.

330   ii   Lewis, b. 27 Oct., 1797.

331   iii   Eunice, b. 19 Dec., 1798.

      iv   (Rev.) Alanson, b. 11 Oct., 1802; d. unm., in Meadville, Pa., 24 Aug., 1833; grad. A. B., Harvard College, 1826; A. M., Div. School, 1831; was a Unitarian clergyman.

      v   Esther H., b. 30 March, 1805; m. 25 Dec., 1833, Josiah H. Adams. Ch. (Adams):

         1   *Caroline[7]*, b. 21 July, 1825; d. ——————; m. ———— Toyier; had dau. Carrie[8], who m. ———— Johnson.

         2   *John*, b. 21 May, 1827; d. ————; was Supt. Fitchburg Ry.; had a son John F.[8]

         3   *Joseph B.*, b. 24 Feb., 1830; d. ——————; m. ————. Ch.: Josephine[8], who m. ———— Lord, and d. Oct., 1904.

         4   *Rebecca*, b. 24 March, 1832; d. ————.

         5   *Eunice*, b. 1 March., 1835; d. ————.

332 vi Rebeccah, b. 28 Aug., 1807.
333 vii Charles, b. 16 July, 1811.
　　viii Abijah, twin to Charles; d. unm., on home farm, 9 April, 1897.

143 ANNA[5], daughter of Dr. Samuel[4] and Anna (Gott) Brigham; born in Marlboro, Mass., 29 Oct., 1753; died, 1803; married, 21 May, 1772, Isaac Davis; born 27 Feb., 1749; died 27 April, 1826. She was brought up at the home of Capt. Maynard in Westboro, whom her mother married as her second husband. She lived in Westboro after her marriage.* Some of her descendants live there still.

Children (Davis), born in Westboro:
　　i Phineas[6].
　　ii Isaac, b. 1779; † m. Polly Rice, dau. of 86.
　　iii Joseph. *no ltoin ball - liveo northcofo*
　　iv John, (Gov.), b. 1787; d. 1854; was called " Honest John Davis." He represented his town in the Legislature and was sent to Congress as senator; he was thrice governor of Massachusetts, serving in 1834-35, and 1841-43.

144 DR. SAMUEL[5], son of Dr. Samuel[4] and Anna (Gott) Brigham; born in Marlboro, Mass., 21 Aug., 1756, a posthumous child; died in Boylston, Mass, 24 June, 1830; married, in Northboro, 17 Feb., 1789, Mary, daughter of Stephen and sister of Dr. Stephen Ball of that place; born in Northboro, 10 May, 1766; died in Boylston, 10 Aug., 1852.

He was one of 4 young men from Westboro, of the name of Brigham, who joined the same class at Dartmouth College on the eve of the Revolution, the others being the future Hon. Elijah[5] Brigham, and Moses[6] and Eli[5] Brigham. Samuel joined the army under Washington in 1777, as paymaster, and was present at the execution of Maj. André. He returned to college and was graduated in 1779. He then read medicine with Dr. Stephen Ball of Northboro, and began to practice in that part of Boylston which was once Shrewsbury. The old homestead is in the northeast part of Boylston, about half a mile from the town line of Berlin, and about 4 miles from Clinton, where some of his descendants live. Great things were expected of him, but before he could take the rank among practitioners which he might have attained, he met with a serious accident to the calf of his leg, was incapacitated from walking without crutches, and thus seriously handicapped in his profession as a country doctor.

---

* " Isaac Davis, a young tanner, who came to town to teach his trade to Capt. Maynard's son, had married Anne Brigham, step-daughter of Capt. Maynard, in 1772. They had four sons. . . . They were living at this time in the house recently occupied by Hiram Broaders. In 1781 they bought the Dea. Tonlin place which has been known since as the Davis homestead. Isaac and his sons became wealthy men, and they and their descendants, who take pride in the name of Davis, have held many positions of honor and trust."—*Parkman Diary.*
† " 31 Oct., 1779, I baptized Mr. Davis' son Isaac."—*Parkman Diary.*

He became a magistrate and a writer of essays and verse. Morse states that he read some of Dr. Brigham's writings which showed him to have been a man of letters and of original thought as well as a patriot. Morse also says that he composed music as a recreation. This may very well have been the case, as he was brought up in the home of Capt. Maynard in Westboro, who was the richest man of his day there, and undoubtedly young Brigham had opportunities for self-culture and training beyond the curriculum of the college. He was related to the Parkmans and often mentioned in the *Parkman Diary.*

Children, born in Boylston:

    i Rowena, b. in 1789; d. 17 July, 1839; m. 7 Jan., 1808, Timothy Whitney, Jr., of Boyleston. Ch. (Whitney):

        1 *Theresa*[7], b. 14 Aug., 1808; d. 13 Aug., 1810.

        2 *Mary*, b. 30 Nov., 1809; m. 24 Feb., 1829, Timothy Hastings.

        3 *Theresa*, b. 19 Feb., 1811; m. 21 May, 1816, Lyman Maynard.

        4 *Rowena*, b. 7 March, 1813.

        5 *Amos*, b. 28 Feb., 1815; d. in Worcester.

        6 *Emily*, b. 10 Jan., 1817; m. ———— Lawrence.

        7 *Dorothy*, b. 19 Sept., 1818.

        8 *Lucy*, b. 8 Dec., 1820.

        9 *William*, b. 5 April, 1823; m. Ruth Crossman.

      10 *Daniel*, b. 22 June, 1825; d. unm., in Worcester.

      11 *Sarah*, b. 22 Oct., 1827; m. Samuel Elliott.

      12 *Catherine E.*, b. 29 Oct., 1829.

      13 *Harriet N.*, b. 22 June, 1834.

      14 *Samuel M.*, b. and d. 1836.

   ii Sally, b. 17 April, 1791; d. in No. Bangor, N. Y., 31 May, 1832; m. in Boylston, 2 Sept., 1805, Benjamin Eager. They removed to No. Bangor. Ch. (Eager):

        1 *Mary*[7], (or *Polly*), b. 16 March, 1806; m. Luther Howe; 11 ch.

        2 *Nahum Brigham*, b. 11 Feb., 1808; m. and had 6 ch.

        3 *John W.*, b. and d. 1809.

        4 *Elizabeth G.*, b. 23 Oct., 1810; d. 9 Oct., 1892; m. 7 June, 1832, Sanford Cornish, who d. in 1891; they removed to Oshkosh, Wis.; 15 ch.

        5 *Benjamin*, b. 10 March, 1813; d. 19 Aug., 1877; m. and had 5 ch.; res. Allegan, Mich.

        6 *John W.*, b. 13 June, 1815; d. at sea, unm.

        7 *Lewis*, b. 8 Dec., 1816; m., had 6 ch.; res. Mattawan, Mich.

        8 *Sarah A.*, b. 2 June, 1819; m. Warren French; res. Mattawan, Mich.; had 6 ch.

        9 *Martha A.*, b. 2 Dec., 1821; m. Herman Sanborn; res. Lawrence, Mich.

      10 *Harriet*, b. 23 Oct., 1823; d. 2 April, 1844.

      11 *Joseph T.*, b. 22 Aug., 1825; d. unm., in California, 6 Jan., 1853.

      12 *Almira L.*, b. 11 Jan., 1828; m. William Moody; res. Pentwater, Mich.

      13 *George E.*, b. 8 Nov., 1829; d. y.

      14 *Adaline*, b. 18 Feb., 1832; m. James Lytle; 2 ch.

  iii Stephen B., b. 16 Nov., 1793; m. Jemima Flagg. In his **mother's** will he was left a wooden clock and one sheep. Ch., b. in Boylston:

    1 *Nahum Ball*, b. 26 Sept., 1817; d. in Worcester, 4 Sept., 1860; m. 20 Feb., 1840, Harriet S. Hapgood, who d. 11 Aug., 1848, æ. 29; m. (2) Mary E. ————, who survived him. He owned land in Boylston on road to Berlin, which was sold in 1860, by order of the court. No ch. reported.

    2 *Maria*, m. Augustus Wright.

334 iv Samuel, b. 19 Feb., 1795.

335 v Mary, b. 13 April, 1797.

    vi Ann Gott, b. 30 Aug., 1799; d. in Berlin, 29 Sept., 1874; m. (1) 2 Oct., 1827, Leonard, son of Daniel Carter, b. in Berlin, 19 March, 1792; d. there 18 Sept., 1849; [he m. (1) Persis Bailey, and had a family]; m. (2) 6 Jan., 1852, Amos, son of Levi Wheeler of Berlin, d. there, 6 Oct., 1867; (he had a family by a first m. but s. p., by second m.). Ch. (Carter), b. Berlin:

    1 *Leonard*, b. 2 March, 1830; 2 *Lydia Ann*, b. 16 June, 1834; d. in Berlin; m. Oliver Sawyer; 3 *Mary E.*, b. 4 Nov., 1838; m. David B. Whitcomb; res. Cal.

    vii Infant, b. 23 Aug., 1801; d. y.

    viii Sophia, b. 22 Nov., 1803; m. (1) ———— Martyn; m. (2) Shadrach Whitney, a bro. of Timothy, who m. her sister Rowena. Ch. (Whitney):

    1 *Sophia*, m. Chas. Bridge of Lowell, Mass., and Marlboro.

    2 *Betsey*, m. James Anderson of Sutton, Mass.

    3 *Sally*, m. Luther F. Woodbury of Oxford, Mass., and Worcester.

    ix Theresa, b. 14 Oct., 1804; m. Otis Flagg of Boylston. Ch. (Flagg), b. in Boylston:

    1 *Martha*, m. John M. Sargent.

    2 *Sarah*, m. Francis A. Davidson.

336 x Jonas Ball, b. 28 April, 1807.

    xi Lydia, b. 2 Nov., 1809; m. Edward Whitney of Cambridge, Mass. Ch. (Whitney), b. in Cambridge:

    1 *Edward*, a sea-captain; d. in Cambridge.

    2 *Frances*, m. Frank Crane of Chicago. Ch. (Crane):

      i Lizzie, m. ———— Harrison; res. Philalelphia.

      ii Charles; iii Minnie; iv John; v James.

145 JOHN GOTT[5], son of Uriah[4] and Sarah Breck (Gott) Brigham; born in Marlboro, Mass., 8 Feb., 1750-1; died 30 April, 1816, according to Hudson's *Hist. of Marlboro;* Morse says "10 Jan., 1833"; married Mary Collins. He resided in Marlboro. He was in the Revolution, in Capt. Morse's Co., Col. Howe's Regt. He was 5 ft. 9 in. in height, of a dark complexion.

Children, born in Marlboro:

    i Hepsibah[6], b. 30 Oct., 1794.

337 ii John Gott, b. 2 Aug., 1796.

146 HENRY[5], son of Uriah[4] and Sarah Breck (Gott) Brigham; born in Marlboro, Mass., 26 Oct., 1752; N. S.; died in Barre, Mass., 16 Jan., 1829; married, 25 March, 1781, Anna, daughter of Nathaniel Phillips; born Charlestown, Mass., 7 June, 1758; died

in Barre, 16 Oct., 1848.   Her father's house, Bow St., Charlestown, was burned at the Battle of Bunker Hill.   Henry was an
officer in the Revolution.   He went to Barre about 1782, where he
was a farmer and selectman and a very prominent citizen.   He was
of a serious nature.

Children, all but the eldest born in Barre:
> i Betsey⁶, b. in Marlboro, 7 Jan., 1782; m. July, 1810, Warren
> Sibley of Barre, who d. Feb., 1816. Ch. (Sibley):
>> 1 *Orlando*⁷, d. y.
>> 2 *Henry Brigham*, b. 8 Nov., 1812; d. 5 March, 1883; m.
>> Caroline, dau. of Luke Stone, 12 Feb., 1832; he was Deputy
>> Sheriff of Barre. Ch. (Sibley): i Charles W.⁸; ii Caroline;
>> iii Ellen and 5 d. y.
>> 3 *Warren Hicks*, m. Roxana Adams; res. New London, Wis.;
>> had a family.
> ii John, b. 24 Nov., 1783; d. 6 Dec., 1787.

338   iii Nathaniel, b. 1 Dec., 1785.
339   iv Nancy, b. 4 March, 1789.
340   v Henry, b. 14 Nov., 1791.
> vi Sarah, b. 19 Aug., 1794; d. in Barre, unm., æ. over 80.
341   vii Maria Theresa, b. 20 Sept., 1800.

147   URIAH⁵, JR., son of Uriah⁴ and Sarah Breck (Gott) Brigham; born in Marlboro, Mass., 11 July, 1757; died in Bakersfield,
Vt., 16 Sept., 1820; married, 25 Dec., 1790, Elizabeth, daughter
of Col. Josiah Fay * of Southboro, Mass.; born there, 28 April,
1767; died in Boston, 9 Nov. 1837.

Uriah was assessor in Marlboro in 1788; about 1796 he moved
to Bakersfield, with his wife and two children, in an ox-team.   The
estate of Uriah, Sr., was a long time in being settled, and there were
eleven children to share it; therefore we find his sons pushing out
into the wilderness and among the settlers of new towns.   Uriah,
Jr., was appreciative of intellectual attainments, and was instru-
mental in establishing a small but valuable library for the use of
the pioneer settlement, from which his own children benefited.   It is
said that he never allowed anything to interrupt his children when
they wished to read.   He was one of the leading citizens of Bakersfield.   Appears to have been a private in the Revolution from
Marlboro, in Capt. Gates' Co., Col. Ward's Regt., in 1776; and in
1777, in Capt. Wm. Morse's Co., Col. J. Read's Regt.

Children, the 2 elder born in Marlboro, the others in Bakersfield:
> i Mary⁶, b. 31 July, 1792; d. 14 July, 1858; m. Hubbel Mitchel,
> who d.; they res. Fairfield, Vt.; she was widely celebrated for
> her knowledge of the use of medicine, and was a superior nurse.
> Ch. (Mitchel):
>> 1 *Melissa*⁷; 2 *Deborah*; 3 *John*; 4 *Temple*; 5 *Fanny Fay.*

* Col. Fay died while in service on Long Island, in the Revolution, and his
remains were buried in Trinity Church cemetery, N. Y. City. His wife, Mary Fay,
was fined $300 (?) by the authorities of Southboro for breaking the Sabbath by going
a mile on horse-back to see her sick daughter.

ii Elizabeth, b. 8 Jan., 1794; m. Cheney Brigham, 258.

iii Uriah, b. 3 Sept., 1795; d. 14 Nov., 1814; he was in the battle
of Plattsburg.

iv Robert, m. (1) Polly Lucas, who d. at the birth of her child; m.
(2) Mary ————, who survived him; he d. s. p., in Burke,
N. Y., 7 Dec., 1867.

v Breck, b. about 1798; was drowned in 1816.

342 vi Josiah Fay, b. 11 Oct., 1801.

343 vii Peter Bent, b. 4 Feb., 1807. ⅃ ⅠᎥᏅ⅂⅂

344 viii Benjamin Gott, b. 10 June, 1808.

ix Sarah, b. 5 March, 1809; m. James B. Jacobs, who d.; she res.,
a widow, for many years in Boston; she d. 24 Nov., 1891. Almost her entire estate was left to the town of Bakersfield, Vt.,
her native place. Ch. (Jacobs):

1 *James B.⁷,* d. 20 Dec., 1854, æ. 19; was interred in Mt. Auburn
Cemetery.

148   EDWARD⁵, son of Uriah⁴ and Sarah Breck (Gott) Brigham; born in Marlboro, Mass., 13 June, 1764; died 29 May, 1826;
married Beulah Hawes, born 14 Feb., 1770; died 15 Jan., 1834.
He was a tanner and lived in Petersham, Mass.

Children, born in Petersham:

i Harriet⁶, b. 11 Dec., 1792; d. in Barre, Mass., 30 Dec., 1864; m.
9 March, 1814, Paul Rice of Barre, who d. Ch. (Rice), b. in
Barre:

1 *James B.⁷,* b. 7 May, 1829; d. in B., 14 July, 1886; m. 17
Sept., 1868, Mary M. Wilson of Barre. Ch.; i Mary L.⁸; ii
Martin P.

2 *Harriet S.,* b. 28 Dec., 1830; d. in Weathersfield, Vt., 14
July, 1876; m. 10 Sept., 1854, Elias W. Ellis, who d. in Weathersfield, 30 May, 1879. Ch. (Ellis):

i James E.⁸, b. 13 Oct., 1863; m. 1887, Nellie C. Boynton; res.
Claremont, N. H.; 1 ch.

ii Roxana, b. 22 June, 1794; d. in St. Almand, C. E., 16 April,
1881; m. 3 April, 1830, John P. Deal of St. Almand. Ch.
(Deal), b. there:

1 *Edward F.⁷,* d. in Boston, 20 April, 1901; m. ———— Emerson,
who d. 1903. Ch.: i (Dr.) George F.⁸; ii (Dr.) Edward E.,
both of Malden, Mass.

2 *Elvin M.,* res. unm., Highgate, Vt.

3 *Hiram B.,* res. unm., St. Almand, Can.

4 *Daughter.*

345 iii Nancy, b. 10 May, 1796.

346 iv Artemas, b. 22 Oct., 1799.

v Mary Ann, b. 26 Sept., 1801; d. 27 June, 1828, unm.

vi Elvira, b. 14 June, 1803; d. 8 Jan., 1890; m. 16 April, 1828,
James, son of James H. Holland; b. in Barre, 14 March, 1799;
d. there, 22 Sept., 1880. Ch. (Holland), b. in Barre:

1 *Maria Louisa⁷,* b. 2 May, 1830; d. 25 March, 1899; m. 16
Nov., 1852, Joseph G. Balcom, b. in Hague, N. Y., 1 June, 1820;
d. in Gardner, Mass., 10 Sept., 1891. Ch. (Balcom): James
L.⁸, m. Mrs. Ida Gale Hemmenway of Gardner.

2 *Mary B.,* b. 26 Nov., 1832; d. 2 Feb., 1899; m. 22 May, 1855,

J. Henry May; res. No. Brookfield, Mass. Ch. (May): Henry
L.⁸, m. Mabel W. Tenney; res. Medford, Mass; 3 ch.

    3 *Harriet E.,* b. 20 April, 1841; d. s. p., in No. Brookfield, Mass.,
31 March, 1880; m. (1) 22 Oct., 1862, David R. Woods of
Barre, who d. 1873; m. (2) Isaac M. Boyd, who d. 1891.

  vii Catherine, b. 18 Jan., 1805; d. in Boston, 4 July, 1874; m. 2
April, 1833, Charles Sibley, b. 14 Jan., 1808; a coal dealer in
Chelsea, Mass., where he res. and d. Ch. (Sibley), b. in Chelsea:
    1 *Charles Edward*⁷, b. 1 March, 1835; d. y.
    2 *Nelson Hawes,* b. 28 Sept., 1838; d. 1900; in Civil War; a
bank clerk and Chelsea City Marshal.
    3 *Catherine A.,* b. 9 April, 1841; d. y.
    4 *James B.,* b. 2 Dec., 1842; d. y.
    5 *Mary Louisa,* b. 5 Feb., 1845; d. y.
    6 *Charles Alonzo,* b. 12 July, 1848; m. Harriet Merrill; res.
Highgate Springs, Vt. Ch.: i Charles⁸; ii Floyd.
 viii Robert Morris, b. 23 Aug., 1806; d. unm., 8 Feb., 1889, in
Petersham.
347 ix Sarah Breck, b. 20 May, 1808.
   x James Sumner, b. 5 Feb., 1811; m. Clarie Henley; d. s. p., in
Boston, 22 Aug., 1862.
348 xi Edward, b. 1 Jan., 1814.

149 PHINEAS⁵, son of George⁴ and Mary (Bragg) Brigham;
born in Marlboro, Mass., 7 Oct., 1757; removed to Eaton, N. Y.,
1810, from Southboro; died there, 17 March, 1813; married, 1785,
Susanna, daughter of Phineas Howe of Hopkinton, Mass., born 19
Feb., 1767.

Children, born in Southboro, except the 2 elder born in Marlboro:
349   i Timothy⁶, b. 8 Feb., 1786.
350   ii Phineas, b. 31 Dec., 1787.
    iii Susanna, b. 16 Dec., 1789; d. 1809, æ. 19 yrs., 11 mos.; m. Ebenezer
Damon. Ch. (Damon):
    1 *Susan Brigham*⁷, b. 31 Oct., 1809; d. 17 Oct., 1885; m. Rev.
Chancellor Hartshorn. Ch. (Hartshorn): i Emma M.⁸, b. 3
Dec., 1829; d. 24 Dec., 1872; m. Alonzo M. Poe; 2 ch.; ii John D.
b. 22 May., 1832; res. Mexico, N. Y.; 3 ch.; iii Frances Mary,
b. 24 Nov., 1835; m. Prof. DeV. Wood, Stevens Inst., Hoboken,
N. J.; 4 ch.
351   iv Sophia, b. 5 May, 1792.
    v Louisa, b. 19 May, 1794; d. 11 Nov., 1796.
   vi George, b. 30 May, 1796; d. æ. 16 days.
  vii Louisa, b. 6 June, 1797; d. 14 Feb., 1860; m. 27 Nov., 1817,
Harry Knickerbocker. Ch. (Knickerbocker):
    1 *Amelia*⁷, b. 22 Aug., 1819; m: Rev. William Holroyd; res.
Cincinnatus and Wyanette, N. Y. Ch. (Holroyd): i Amelia⁸;
ii Cordelia; iii Mary; iv William; v Daniel; vi Zira.
    2 *Louisa,* b. 25 April, 1822; d. 6 Jan., 1854; m. Zira Parce, of
No. Pitcher, N. Y. Ch. (Parce); i Judson⁸, d.; ii Frank.
    3 *Franklin,* b. 25 March, 1826; m. Huldah Eldredge; res. Holley,
N. Y. Ch.: i Adelbert⁸; ii Frank.
    4 *Henry,* b. 29 Nov., 1833; m. 24 Dec., 1861, Helen M. Bourne;
res. Cincinnatus. Ch.: i Irving B.⁸; ii Elbert.

352 viii George Howe, b. 14 Dec., 1799.
ix Fitch, b. 11 Jan., 1803; d. unm., Madison, N. Y., æ. 41.
353 x Salmon, b. 15 July, 1805.

150 ASHBEL SAMUEL[5], son of George[4] and Mary (Bragg) Brigham; born in Marlboro, Mass., 2 March, 1772; died there, 13 July, 1839; married, 24 Aug., 1794, Persis[6], daughter of Elijah and Ruth (Taylor) Brigham (76) of Southboro; born there, 7 Oct., or Aug., 1774; died 7 June, 1829. He inherited his father's farm in the south part of Marlboro, where Barnabas Brigham resided in Morse's day, and which is described under 541. Was selectman, 1816.

Children, born in Marlboro:
354 i Ashbel[6], b. 1 July, 1800.
355 ii Varnum, b. 8 July, 1802.
iii Nahum, b. 24 June, 1804; d. 3 Dec., 1808.
356 iv Charles, b. 26 Sept., 1806.
v George, b. 10 April, 1811; d. 23 May, 1870; m. Abby Mallard; was town treasurer of Marlboro in 1855, and selectman in 1856. Ch.:
1 *Lizzie M.[7]*, b. 5 April, 1848.
357 vi Mary, b. 21 March, 1815.

151 LOVEWELL[5], son of Solomon[4] and Martha (Boyd) Brigham; born in Marlboro, Mass., 1 Dec., 1754; died April, 1824; married Betty Rice, who resided in Saxonville, a widow, in Morse's day. Was on the Committee to erect " Spring Hill " Meeting-house, in 1805, the location of which caused a division in the church, and the erection of two meeting-houses instead of one (see *Hist. of Marlboro*). He appears to have marched on the Lexington Alarm and to have been in the army in 1777 and in 1780.

Children:
i Sally[6], b. 22 Feb., 1791, in Saxonville; d. 28 Feb., 1873; m. 1 July, 1814, John, son of Calvin Pierce; b. in Bolton, Mass., 23 March, 1786; d. there, 28 April, 1853. Ch. (Pierce), b. in B.:
1 *Susan M.[7]*, b. 30 Nov., 1815; m. Levi Johnson.
2 *Harriet E.*, b. 19 Nov., 1817; d. 2 June, 1821.
3 *John E.*, b. 22 Aug., 1819; m. (1) Elizabeth Lovejoy; m. (2) Emeline Trufant; m. (3) Elizabeth Woodbury; res. s. p., in Charlestown, Mass.
4 *Albert*, b. 17 May, 1821; m. Abigail Moody; res. Boston. Ch.: i John[8]; ii Judson.
5 *Addison B.*, b. 16 May, 1826; m. Mary W. Sanderson. Ch.: i Susan[8]; ii Harriet; iii Grace.
ii Nabby, b. 27 Dec., 1792; m. Nathan Fuller; res. Saxonville.
iii Miriam, b. 17 June, 1794; m. Nathan Polly; res. Waltham.
358 iv Artemas, b. 27 April, 1796.
v Sophia, b. 3 Nov., 1797; d. 7 May, 1802.
vi Patty, b. 29 Oct., 1799; m. (1) Stillman Corey; m. (2) ——— Safford; res. Fitchburg.

vii Lydia, b. 28 Aug., 1801, in Marlboro; m. 5 Jan., 1824, Dexter, son of Nathaniel Bigelow; b. in Framingham, 16 Jan., 1795; d. 19 May, 1875; a paper manufacturer. Ch. (Bigelow), b. in Framingham:

    1 *George William*[7], b. 31 Oct., 1824; m. Grace Hoyt; res. Framingham. Ch.: i George[8]; ii Dr. Enos, and 2 daus.

    2 *Elizabeth Ann*, b. 21 Dec., 1829.

viii Stephen, b. 13 March, 1804; d. 28 May, 1806, from a scald.

ix Eliza, b. 13 May, 1807; m. John Works; res. Ashland.

x William, m. at Hopkinton, where is said to have res., but there is no record.

152   IVORY[5], son of Solomon[4] and Martha (Boyd) Brigham; born in Marlboro, Mass., 30 April, 1765; died 4 June, 1853; married, 19 Feb., 1800, Sally, daughter of Edward and Sally (Dunn) Wilkins of Marlboro; born 15 April, 1779; died 24 Aug., 1849.

Children, born in Marlboro:

i Betsey[6], b. 26 Aug., 1800; d 17 Sept., 1883; m. Phineas Haskell, who d.; res. Marlboro. Ch. (Haskell):

    1 *Caleb*[7], b. 11 Dec., 1819; d. 23 May, 1900; m Betsey Clark; res. Marlboro. Ch.: Nelly F.[8]

    2 *Sarah E.*, b. 4 March, 1822; d. unm., 24 Dec., 1844.

    3 *William B.*, b. 7 Nov., 1825; d. 27 Oct., 1851; m. Catherine M. Bruce. Ch.: Mary E.[8], b. 19 July, 1850.

    4 *Susan M.*, b. 14 June, 1827; d. 13 April, 1851.

    5 *Seth G.*, b. 24 Oct., 1829; m. Mary Magennis; res. Marlboro.

    6 *Lucy*, b. 22 Dec., 1831; d. 26 March, 1905; m. Jan., 1852, Geo. L. Manson, b. 6 Nov., 1827; a merchant and postmaster in Feltonville (now Hudson). Ch. (Manson): Sarah R.[8], b. 19 Dec., 1852.

    7 *Roena*, b. 17 Oct., 1836; d. 1 Jan., 1853.

    8 *Arethusa*, b. 23 Feb., 1839; m. 12 Nov., 1884, Joseph Durst; res. Hudson, Mass.

    9 *Nathan L.*, b. 25 June, 184—; d. 28 March, 1844.

ii Edward, b. 1802; d. 1803.

iii (Col.) William, b. 20 May, 1804; d. 22 Jan., 1839; m. Harriet Randall, who m. (2) David Coolidge, and d. 12 Sept., 1877, æ. 67; Col. William was a trader. Ch.:

    1 *William*[7], d. 24 May, 1855, æ. 19.

iv Solomon, b. 9 Nov., 1806; d. 6 Jan., 1843, s. p.; m. Lucy Ball, and res. Marlboro, where was a farmer.

v Francis, b. 3 April, 1811; d. æ. 2.

359 vi Francis, b. 12 April, 1813.

360 vii Charles, b. 11 Dec., 1815.

viii Infant.

153   DEA. ARTEMAS[5], son of Francis[4] and Phebe (Ward) Brigham; born in New Marlboro, Mass.; died there, about 1802, where he also resided; married Mary Cornish. He was in the Revolutionary War, a private in Capt. Caleb Wright's company of Minute Men, Col. John Fellows' Regt., which marched on the Lexington Alarm. He was also a corporal in Lieut Hermon's Co., of

Col. John Brown's Berkshire Co. Regt. He was in several other companies and regiments, and was discharged 16 Oct., 1780.

Children, born in New Marlboro:
361   i Artemas Ward[6], b. 25 Dec., 1781.
     ii Harvey, m. Lois Bidwell; res. Painsville, O. Ch.:
       1 *Nelson B.*[7], m. Maria Milliken. Ch.: i Jenny A.[8]; ii **Emma.**
       2 *Ann P.*, m. Rev. B. Y. Messenger; res. and d. in Illinois. Ch.:
       (Messenger): i Mary Ann V.[8]; ii William.
       3 *Eliza L.*, m. Halbert E. Paine; res. Milwaukee, Wis.
     iii Pliny, twin to Harvey, m. Polina Kasson; res. and d. Canaan, Conn·
       (or Mass.; nothing in Canaan records). Was in the War of
       1812, as a corporal at New London, under Capt. Moses **Hayden,**
       3 Aug., to 16 Sept., 1813.
     iv Joseph C., lived and d. unm., Rochester, N. Y.
     v Polly, m. Jabez Ward; res. and d. in Illinois or Vernon, N. Y.
     vi Clarissa, m. (1) Asher Robinson; res. Westmoreland, N. Y.; m.
       (2) ――――― Shepherd; d. in Clinton, N. Y.
     vii Parley, m. Matthew Smith; res. and d. Vernon, N. Y.
     viii Cynthia, m. Thomas Wilcox; res. Westmoreland, N. Y., and moved
       to Michigan.
362   ix Betsey.

154   JOHN[5], son of Francis[4] and Phebe (Ward) Brigham; born in New Marlboro, Mass., 1767; died in Chatham, N. Y., 9 Nov., 1806, to which place he had removed the same year; married Phebe Clark.

Children, born in New Marlboro:
363   i John Clark[6], b. 10 Feb., 1794.
364   ii Harry, b. 19 June, 1796.
365   iii Amariah, b. 26 Dec., 1798.
366   iv Eliza, b. 27 Aug., 1801.
     v Lewis, b. 1805; d. in Hudson, N. Y., 1829, æ. 24.
     vi Phebe Ann, b. 1808; d. in Whitestown, N. Y., 1828.

155   JOHN[5], son of Stephen[4] and Betsey (Weeks) Brigham; born in Princeton, Mass., 8 Aug., 1758; died in Ackworth, N. H., 2 April, 1841; married, 24 Jan., 1788, Lydia Howe from Princeton, who died 28 Nov., 1859. He was in the Revolution. There was John, a corporal, and John, a private, from Princeton, and probably it was the service of one man. As a corporal he served only 27 days in Oct., 1777; marching to reinforce Gen. Gates at Saratoga; as a private he served a little over 3 mos. in Col. Rand's Worcester Co. Regt. in 1780. Resided first at Alstead, N. H., and went to Ackworth in 1805.

Children, born in Alstead:
     i Joel[6], b. 10 Jan., 1790; d. 2 Sept., 1795.
367   ii Rufus, b. 29 June, 1791.
     iii John, b. 21 April, 1793; m. 22 July, 1835, Mrs. Eunice H. Clark;
       res. Worcester, Vt. Ch., b. there:

    1 *Lydia*[7], b. 7 June, 1836; m. ———— Ide. Ch. (Ide): i Eunice[8]; ii Mary, d. y.

    2 *Susan,* b. 25 Aug., 1838.

    3 *George W.,* b. 25 Dec., 1840.

    4 *Silas H.,* b. 17 May, 1843.

    5 *Marshall R.,* b. 1 June, 1846; res. Worcester.

iv Lucy, b. 6 Aug., 1795; m. 12 Dec., 1821, Jared Beckwith of Alstead and Pana, Ill.; b. 12 March, 1794. Ch. (Beckwith):

    1 *William*[7], b. in Alstead, 14 Oct., 1822; m. and res. in Oregon.

    2 *Joel,* b. 17 June, 1824; d. 29 April, 1850; m. Lottie Cowgill; res. Pana. Ch.: John[8].

    3 *Silas H.,* b. 7 March, 1829; d. 7 Jan., 1853.

    4 *Milan Sumner,* b. 6 June, 1830; 22 Oct., 1857, m. Flora M. Putnam; res. Lebanon, Mo. Ch.: i Herbert H.[8]; ii Flora H.; iii Walter E.; iv Lucy M.; v Arthur M.; vi Vera V.; vii Forest P.; viii Fanny O.; ix Gertrude.

    5 *Lydia A.,* b. 26 Nov., 1831; 3 Jan., 1854, m. Parker Grimes of Springfield, Vt. Ch. (Grimes): i Flora[8]; ii Lillie; iii Allie.

368 v Polly, b. 16 Sept., 1797.

vi Matilda, b. 12 June, 1800; m. 10 Dec., 1819, Martin Mason; res. s. p., Moretown, Vt.

vii Silas, b. 22 July, 1802; m. 4 Jan., 1834, Sarah Manchester of Little Compton, R. I. Ch.:

    1 *Sarah E.*[7], b. 1 Sept., 1839; d. 14 Jan., 1845.

    2 *Charles W.,* b. 6 Apr., 1841; d. unm.

    3 *Beriah W.,* b. 2 June, 1843; d. unm.

    4 *Henry W. R.,* b. 14 June, 1846; d. unm.

viii Lydia, b. 21 Aug., 1804; d. s. p., 13 April, 1828; m. 12 June, 1826, Henry McClure; res. Moretown, Vt.; he m. twice after her death, and had a family.

ix Betsey, b. 30 Oct., 1808; m. 30 Dec., 1833, Almond Wetherbee of Northfield, Vt. Ch. (Wetherbee):

    1 *Mary M.*[7], b. 20 June, 1836; m. John Nichols of Montgomery, Ala.

    2 *Angeline A.,* b. 8 July, 1839; m. Albert S. Brownell of Elmhurst, Ill. Ch. (Brownell): i Harry G.[8]; ii Helen A.

    3 *Lydia M.,* b. 14 Sept., 1844; m. Charlton Badger of Northfield, Vt. Ch.: (Badger): i Angeline E.[8]; ii George K.

156 STEPHEN[5], son of Stephen[4] and Betsey (Weeks) Brigham; born in Princeton, Mass., 9 Aug., 1762; died in Alstead, N. H., 16 July, 1839; married 13 Feb., 1791, Louisa M. Howe, born 24 May, 1768; died 9 July, 1830. In 1790 he went to Alstead, being one of the early settlers of the town; was a farmer.

Children, born in Alstead:

i William[6], b. 15 Dec., 1791; d. 13 Jan., 1792.

ii Louisa, b. 9 April, 1793; m. 28 March, 1821, John B., son of Philip Proctor; b. in Groton, Mass., 6 March, 1792; a farmer, res. Sullivan, N. H., and Rutland, Vt. Ch. (Proctor):

    1 *John B.*[7], b. 28 Nov., 1823; m. 22 Feb., 1853, Charlotte Reynolds at Rutland Center. Ch.: i William[8], d. y.; ii John; iii Mary, who m. A. H. McNeil.

    2 *David N.,* b. 27 May, 1826; d. 18 Nov., 1826.

3 *Maria L.*, b. 24 Oct., 1827; d. 24 March, 1902; m. 18 Oct., 1852, George A. King, who d. 21 June, 1891; res. W. Rutland. Ch. (King): i Frank E.[8]; ii Alice L.; iii William H.
4 *Elbridge W.*, b. 17 Jan., 1832; d. 15 May, 1832.
5 *Stephen W.*, b. 13 Nov., 1835; d. 23 Jan., 1903; res. W. Rutland, Vt. Ch.: i Ella[8]; ii Lucy; iii Iola; iv Nina.
iii Persis, b. 28 June, 1795; d. 6 Sept., 1834, in Dalton, N. H.; m. 16 Jan., 1817, Alvin Brooks of Alstead, b. 24 Aug., 1793; d. in Dalton, 31 May, 1856. Ch. (Brooks):
1 *Louisa M.*[7], b. 26 Jan., 1818; d. 9 Sept., 1837.
2 *Rachel P.*, b. 3 Jan., 1820; d. 7 Dec., 1846.
3 *Austin*, b. 22 Dec., 1821; d. 15 Sept., 1850.
4 *Elvira C.*, b. 27 Jan., 1824; m. 12 Nov., 1850, James McQuesten at Manchester, N. H.
5 *James N.* b. 16 April, 1827.
6 *Benjamin B.*, b. 4 Nov., 1829.
369 iv Aaron, b. 20 Oct., 1797.
370 v Lydia, b. 26 Feb., 1800.
371 vi David, b. 25 March, 1802.
372 vii Abram, b. 1 April, 1807.

157 ABNER[5], son of Stephen[4] and Betsey (Weeks) Brigham; born in Princeton, Mass., 31 May, 1764; died, probably in Princeton, 12 Jan., 1823; married Elizabeth, daughter of Ebenezer and Charity (Bugbee) Childs; born in Woodstock, Conn., 29 Dec., 1767; died in Marietta, O., 31 May, 1841.

Abner went to Vermont, but subsequently returned to Princeton, where he resided on the old Brigham home farm, half a mile west of Wachusett Mountain. This farm was in the family for over seventy years, occupied by three generations of Brighams, Stephen[4], Abner[5], and Lucius[6].

Children, born in Princeton:
373 i William[6], b. 23 Nov., 1789.
ii Betsey, b. 28 Feb., 1792; d. 12 Aug., 1825; m. Luther Whitaker of Princeton. Ch. (Whitaker), b. in Princeton:
1 *Harriet*[7], m. Warren Williams; res. Worcester, where d. æ. about 85. Ch. (Williams): i Mary[8], b. 1842; d. unm.; ii Charles, res. Worcester.
2 *Charles*, has a dau., Mrs. Moses Goodnow[8] of Princeton.
3 *William*, d. in N. Y.
4 *Aaron*, res. Westboro, Mass. (5 and 6 names unknown.)
iii Nancy, b. 8 July, 1794-6; m. 23 Jan., 1823, Joseph Hardy, Jr.; res. Worcester; had four or five children; one dau. is Mrs. Edwin Spear[7], 513 63d Street, Englewood, Ill.
374 iv Lucius, b. 2 Dec., 1797.
v Sophia, b. 27 Feb., 1800; d. in Waterford, O., 8 Nov., 1834; m. Leicester Converse. Ch. (Converse):
1 *Benjamin G.*[7], res. 1903, Gypsum, Kan. Ch.: Frank G.[8], of Kalma, Wash.
vi Lucy, b. 12 June, 1802; res. and d. unm., in Marietta, 26 Sept., 1887.

   vii Louisa, b. 17 Aug., 1804; res. and d. unm., in Marietta, 24 Aug.,
      1879.
  viii Asa, b. 24 March, 1807; res. and d. unm., in Marietta, 31 July,
      1866.
    ix Sarah M., b. 15 Aug., 1809; d. unm., in Marietta, 10 Aug., 1839.
     x Charles C., b. 19 Nov., 1811; d. in Beverly, O., 30 July, 1865;
      m. 30 Aug., 1842, Relief B., dau. of Michael Story of Beverly;
      b. 1 Jan., 1821; d. in Marietta, 8 Feb., 1901. He went west at the
      age of 16 and attended Marion Coll. in Missouri; became a
      farmer and res. in Beverly, where a deacon in Presbyterian church.
      Ch., b. in Beverly:
       1 *Lucy E.*[7], b. 15 June, 1843; res. unm., in Marietta.
       2 *Asa M.*, b. 23 Sept., 1849; m. 26 July, 1876, Mary Richards;
        res. Zanesville, O. Ch.: Arthur[8], b. 1 Sept., 1877.

158 LIEUT. ASA[5], son of Stephen[4] and Betsey (Weeks) Brigham; born in Princeton, Mass., 2 June, 1767; died there, 29 Oct., 1794; married, 1791, Elizabeth, daughter of William* and Sibyl (Parker) Marean; born 26 Aug., 1770, in Hubbardston, Mass.; died 22 March, 1843; she married (2) Ezra Holden and had two sons, Joseph and Justinian, who died. Mr. Holden died 18 May, 1806. Asa settled on the homestead in Princeton, with his father, but dying at the early age of 27, left a small family of very young children. The male line is extinct.

Children, born in Princeton:
375   i John[6], b. 24 Nov., 1791.
376   ii Betsey, b. 18 May, 1793.
     iii Sally, b. 4 April, 1795, posthumous; d. 21 July, 1814.
     iv Asa, twin to Sally, d. 20 Jan., 1817.

159 DAVID[5], son of Stephen[4] and Betsey (Weeks) Brigham; born in Princeton, Mass., 8 April, 1771; died in Lowville, Lewis Co., N. Y., 27 March, 1853; married, 13 Feb., 1802, Sarah, daughter of Judge Veeder of N. Y. State; born 20 June, 1775; died 24 June, 1823. He removed to Mohawk Flats, N. Y., about 1795, and raised tobacco; then settled on a tract of 100 acres of wild land in Lowville, which contained only 5 families.

Children, the 4 elder born in Denmark, N. Y., the others in Lowville:
     i Betsey[6], b. 3 Nov., 1802; d. 25 Jan., 1831.
    ii Nancy, b. 9 Sept., 1804; m. 27 March, 1834, Jacob Swart, b. 16
      Nov., 1809, at Charlton, N. Y.; res. Hadley, Mich. Ch. (Swart),
      the 5 younger b. in Hadley:
       1 *William*[7], b. in Glennville, N. Y., 8 June, 1835.
       2 *Maria*, b. in G., 24 May, 1837; m. 25 Feb., 1859, John T. Hart-
        well, b. in Denmark, June, 1839.
       3 *Sarah Ann*, b. 15 Sept., 1839; d. 16 Oct., 1841.
       4 *Emeline*, b. 20 Sept., 1841.

  * From Newton and Barre, Mass. He was Capt. and Major from Cambridge, in the Revolution; see *Mass. Pay Rolls*, Vol. 46, p. 19.

     5 *Stephen*, b. 16 Oct., 1845.
     6 *Ira*, b. 29 Sept., 1848.
     7 *George*, b. 22 Nov., 1850; d. 7 Oct., 1855.
  iii John, b. 21 Nov., 1806; m. Nov., 21, 1838, Eliza S. ————, b.
    12 Sept., 1809, at Sempronius, N. Y.; res. Hadley, Mich. Ch.,
    b. in Hadley:
     1 *Aaron G.*[7], b. 12 May, 1840.
     2 *John*, b. 29 Aug., 1842.
     3 *Eliza Jane*, b. 4 Sept., 1845; d. 21 Oct., 1847.
     4 *Samuel*, b. 2 Dec., 1850. .
     5 *Charles*, b. 29 Sept., 1853; d. 29 Aug., 1854.
377 iv Aaron, b. 21 Aug., 1809.
    v Maria, b. 2 Sept., 1811; m. in Lowville, ———— Townsend; res.
    Rochester, Minn.
    vi Stephen, b. 8 April, 1813.
   vii Jane, b. 3 Sept., 1815; m. ———— Vroman; res. Verona, Dane
    Co., Wis.

160 CAPT. SILAS[5], son of Stephen[4] and Betsey (Weeks) Brigham, born in Princeton, Mass., 12 Aug., 1776; died in Brownington,
Vt., 15 Jan., 1853; married, 23 Oct., 1807, Rhoda, daughter of John
and Demis (Gillett) Morey, of Orford, N. H.; born there 30 Jan.,
1787; died in Brownington, 7 Feb., 1862. He was apprenticed to
a tanner in Alstead, N. H., and finally settled in Brownington, Vt.

Children, born in Brownington:
378   i Edmund Sanford[6], b. 11 July, 1808.
379   ii Emily, b. 17 Dec., 1809.
380 iii John Morey, b. 30 April, 1812.
381   iv Charles, b. 26 Oct., 1814.
382   v Albert Smith, b. 19 Aug., 1816.
     vi Demis Morey, b. 18 Sept., 1818; she d. unm., in Newport, Vt.,
     14 Oct., 1891.
   vii Samuel Granger, b. 15 Sept., 1820; d. unm., 23 March, 1888.
  viii Mary Ann, b. 5 Aug., 1822; d. 11 May, 1887; m. Hiram Killam.
    ix Elizabeth Caroline, b. 7 Nov., 1826; d. s. p., 31 May, 1893; m.
    11 Dec., 1847, John L. Edwards; res. Derby, Vt.

161 AARON[5], son of Stephen[4] and Betsey (Weeks) Brigham;
born in Princeton, Mass., 13 March, 1781; died in Nashua, N. H.,
3 July, 1840; married, 3 Jan., 1808, Charlotte Read; born 14 Aug.,
1785; died in Marshall, Mich., 7 April, 1850. He resided in several
places and finally settled in Nashua (see *Hist. of Gilsum, N. H.*).

Children:
     i Cordelia P.[6], b. 10 April, 1809; d. unm.
383   ii Elbridge G., b. 29 April, 1809.
   iii Hannah R., b. 28 Dec., 1811; m. 10 April, 1834, Addison A. Ald-
    rich, b. 20 June, 1809; res. Monroe, Mich. Ch. (Aldrich):
     1 *Addison L.*[7], b. 14 March, 1836.
     2 *Hannah Maria*, b. 6 Feb., 1838; m. James Brown; res. Monroe.
     3 *Anna Eliza*, b. 8 July, 1846; d. y.

    iv Wealthy M., b. 22 Dec., 1813; m. Claudius B. Webster, Sept., 1845; res. Marshall, Mich.· Ch. (Webster):
       1 *Infant*[7], d. y.; 2 *Arabella*, b. 22 Feb., 1849.
    v William H., b. 1 April, 1816; d. unm., either in Nashua or Vt.
384 vi Micajah R., b. 3 April, 1818.
    vii Mary Ann, b. 1 June, 1821; d. s. p.; m. George Gould of Nashua.
    viii Edward R., res. Illinois.
    ix Eliza Ann, b. 2 Sept., 1823; d. unm.

162   CAPT. DANIEL[5], son of Winslow[4] and Elizabeth (Harrington) Brigham; born in Marlboro, Mass., 25 Dec., 1760; died there, 11 Oct., 1818; married Thankful, daughter of George and Mary (Bragg) Brigham (54); born 7 May, 1765; died 14 Dec., 1824. Inherited the tannery of his father, filled every office in the gift of the town, and was the most prominent citizen of his day; selectman in 1792-'94-'97-1813; assessor, 1799; town treasurer, 1801-1813; town clerk, 1807-1813; representative to the General Court, 1803, '10, '12,-'19.

Children, born in Marlboro:
    i Mary[6], b. 12 Jan., 1783; m. 10 April, 1803, Capt. John, son of Francis and Elizabeth (Brigham) Stevens (63); b. in Marlboro, 12 Jan., 1777; d. 3 Feb., 1822; a prominent citizen. Ch. (Stevens), b. in M.:
       1 *Eliza B.*[7], b. 10 Sept., 1803; m. 1825, Sidney[7] Brigham, 451.
       2 *Mary Ann*, b. 24 Oct., 1805; m. 1829, Curtis[7] Brigham, 462.
       3 *Adeline*, b. 12 Jan., 1808; d. unm., 1836.
       4 *Harriet*, b. 25 Dec., 1809.
       5 *John W.*, b. 5 Feb., 1812.
       6 Charlotte, b. 19 April, 1814; m. Dennis F. Witherbee, son of 201.
       7 *Almira*, b. 26 May, 1818.
385 ii George, b. 19 Oct., 1784.
386 iii Daniel, b. 7 Aug., 1786.
    iv Dexter, twin to Daniel; d. unm., Oct., 1838, in Seneca Falls, N. Y.
    v Elizabeth, b. 1 Oct., 1788; d. s. p., 17 April, 1863; m. (1) 10 June, 1812, Abraham, son of Silás Gates; b. in Marlboro, 1 March, 1775; d. s. p., 22 July, 1829; m. (2) 13 Sept., 1831, Dea. Stephen R. Phelps, whose 1st wife was Martha[6] Brigham, 202. Mr. Gates kept the famous " Williams Tavern " in Marlboro, and gave $1000 to endow Marlb. Academy. Ch. (Gates):
       1 *William Bradford*[7], who d. y.
    vi Thankful, b. 15 Feb., 1791; m. 9 Dec., 1813, Rufus, son of Abraham Stow; b. in Marlboro, 30 July, 1789. Ch. (Stow), b. in Marlboro:
       1 *William Bradford*[7], b. 14 March, 1828; 2 *Almira*, m. Dea. Levi Baker; res. Marlboro; 3 *Phebe*, m. ——— Eager; res. Marlboro; 4 *Catherine*, m. John H. Maynard, res. Marlboro; and 6 other children.
387 vii William, b. 3 Aug., 1793.
388 viii Winslow, b. 29 May, 1795.
    ix Amariah, b. 23 July, 1797; d. unm. 30 July, 1826, in Bermuda.

389   x Freeman, b. 4 May, 1800.
390   xi Charlotte, b. 1 June, 1802.
391   xii Harriet, b. 4 Dec., 1804.
392   xiii Laura Ann, b. 17 March, 1807.

163   CAPT. AARON[5], son of Winslow[4] and Elizabeth (Harrington) Brigham; born in Marlboro, Mass., 22 Nov., 1762; died in Marlboro, 23 March, 1831; married, 28 Sept., 1785, Betty (or Betsey), daughter of Edward and Submit (Forbush) Barnes; born 2 April, 1766; died 4 May, 1858. Resided near Williams Pond; was assessor in 1800-'06, '10, and selectman in 1795, '96, 1802-'05. Was in the Revolution as a private in Capt. Amasa Cranston's Co., Col. Saml. Dennis' Regt., for a month in 1779; in 1780 was in the Continental Army and discharged Jan. 13, 1781. He was 5 ft. 8 in. in height and of a light complexion.

Children, born in Marlboro:
    i Lydia[6], b. 5 Feb., 1786; m. 12 Oct., 1808, Windsor, son of Benjamin Howe; b. in Marlboro, 12 Oct., 1785; d. 1857; res. Lowell, Mass.
    ii Sarah, b. 9 Dec., 1787; d. 4 July, 1791.
    iii Betty, b. 12 Aug., 1789; m. 25 March, 1809, Jonathan, son of Thomas and Abigail (Hapgood) Rice; b. in Marlboro, 30 Nov., 1786; d. 1860. Ch. (Rice), b. in Marlboro:
        1 *Abigail*, b. 21 July, 1810; m. 15 Nov., 1832, John F., son of Stephen Rice; b. in Marlboro, 7 Jan., 1809.
        2 *Eli*, b. 24 April, 1812.
        3 *Thomas*, b. 12 June, 1814.
        4 *Lucy*, b. 20 Aug., 1816.
        5 *Aaron Brigham*, b. 14 Feb., 1819.
        6 *Caroline E.*, b. 8 Feb., 1821.
        7 *Sarah Ann*, b. 11 July, 1823.
        8 *Joseph A.*, b. 16 Jan., 1826.
        9 *William*, b. 6 Aug., 1828.
        10 *Charlotte Brigham*, b. 6 March, 1834.
    iv Sally, b. 25 March, 1792; m. 1 Sept., 1811, Capt. Abraham, son of Archelaus and Lucy (Howe) Howe; b. 18 July, 1789; res. Lowell, where he d. (See *Hist. of Marlboro*.)
393   v Aaron, b. 20 March, 1798.

, 164   MAJOR JEDEDIAH[5], son of Winslow[4] and Elizabeth (Harrington) Brigham; born in Marlboro, Mass., 15 Sept., 1776; died there, 22 April, 1846; married, 17 Aug., 1791, Lydia, daughter of William and Lydia (Morse) Boyd; born in Marlboro, 18 June, 1770; died 28 April, 1824.

He inherited the homestead of his great-grandfather Samuel, near the tannery in the southeast part of Marlboro, and was active in town affairs; assessor in 1804 and '08; selectman in 1810, '14-'16; town clerk in 1814, and town treasurer from 1814-18. He also represented Marlboro in the General Court; was interested in military affairs and rose to the rank of Major.

Children, born in Marlboro:

   i Betsey Winslow[6], b. 28 Nov., 1791; d. 5 Oct., 1819; m. 1 June, 1813, Samuel, son of Thaddeus Warren; b. in Marlboro, 1 June, 1777; d. 3 Feb., 1852; he m. (2) Rebecca Morse. Ch. (Warren), b. in Marlboro:

     1 *Elizabeth Brigham[7]*, b. 22 April, 1814; m. (1) 1836, Dana Clark; m. (2) 1845, William Stetson, who d. 1890, æ. 91; she res. Marlboro in 1903; had 6 ch. by 2d marriage.

     2 *Samuel Edward*, b. 1 May, 1816; d. 12 Oct., 1888; m. 1839, Elizabeth Wilson, who d. 1890; 2 ch.

     3 *Lucy Stevens*, b. 25 Oct., 1817; d. 16 Sept., 1887; m. 1841, Edward Goodale; had 3 daus.

     4 *John Winslow*, b. 25 Sept., and d. 23 Oct., 1819.

  ii Lydia, b. 28 Oct., 1793; d. 23 Oct., 1875; m. 8 May, 1815, Lyman, son of Stephen Morse; b. 10 Nov., 1792; d. 17 Aug., 1849; res. Southboro, Mass. Ch. (Morse), exact order of birth not known; b. in Southboro:

     1 *Porter[7]*, b. 1816; d. Aug., 1858.

     2 *Ocean A.*, m. 26 Sept., 1842, Addison G. Fay.

     3 *Lyman B.*, b. 1820; d. 18 Sept., 1864; m. 4 Oct., 1847, Louisa C. Blodgett.

     4 *Burleigh*, b. 1822; m. (1) 1848, Ann Janette Brigham, dau. of 293; m. (2) 1857, Mary A. Wise.

     5 *Lydia B.*, m. 29 Oct., 1845, Moses B. Garfield.

     6 *Charles F.*, m. 26 Oct., 1855, Angie H. Bigelow.

     7 *Martha O.*, m. 1856, Lewis F. Ball.

     8 *Frederic H.*, m. 1858, Emily F. Hayden.

     9 *Jedediah*, m. 30 Sept., 1860, Margaret T. Sawyer.

  iii Lucy, b. 2 May, 1796; d. 5 Sept., 1830; m. 28 Dec., 1819, Timothy Patch of Stow, Mass., b. 12 Nov., 1793; d. in Nashua, N. H., 13 March, 1827. Ch. (Patch), b. in Stow:

     1 *Lucy Ann[7]*, b. 27 March, 1821; d. in Boxboro, Mass., 16 Aug., 1844; m. Levi H. Stevens. Ch. (Stevens): Mary L.[8], m. Alfred Brown of W. Acton, Mass.

     2 *John Winslow*, b. 23 Dec., 1822; d. in Neenah, Wis., 27 April, 1856; m. Mary A. Haskell. Ch.; i John W., Jr.[8]; ii Alfred B.

     3 *Timothy Brigham*, b. 14 Sept., 1824; d.; res., 1904, s. p., in Marlboro; m. Lucy A. Bennett.

394 iv Jane, b. 23 April, 1798.

   v Hannah L., b. 3 Oct., 1802; d. 31 March, 1832; m. George Peters, Jr.; res. Marlboro. Ch. (Peters): 1 *George L.*, b. 3 March, 1825; m. Ann M. Stevens. Ch.: 1 *Effie M.*; 2 *Lydia B.*

395 vi Ashley, b. 9 Oct., 1804.

  vii Jedediah, b. 11 Aug., 1806; d. unm., 1 Dec., 1829.

396 viii Joel, b. 16 Dec., 1808.

397 ix William Pitt, b. 30 Aug., 1811.

   x Augusta, b. 10 March, 1814; m. John W. Stevens of Marlboro. Ch. (Stevens), b. in Marlboro:

     1 *Ocean Augusta[7]*, b. 1 Dec., 1840; d. 16 Sept., 1861; m. Benjamin H. Witherbee.

     2 *Eliza Brigham*, b. 31 Oct., 1845; m. Frederick A. Lewis.

MAJOR JEDEDIAH BRIGHAM, OF MARLBORO (164)

165 ELIZABETH⁵, daughter of Winslow⁴ and Elizabeth (Harrington) Brigham; born in Marlboro, Mass., 5 March, 1769; died 29 Nov., 1831; married, 16 Sept., 1788, William, son of Solomon and Judith (Hapgood) Barnes; born in Marlboro, 3 Sept., 1766; died 7 March, 1823.

Children (Barnes), born in Marlboro:
   i Elizabeth⁶, b. 17 Dec., 1788; d. 23 Aug., 1845; m. 22 Oct., 1841, Elisha Crosby.
   ii Samuel, b. 20 April, 1790; d. 2 June, 1816.
   iii Winslow, b. 12 April, 1792; d. 1861; m. 1817, Nancy Newton.
   iv Solomon, b. 16 April, 1794; m. 17 April, 1822, Sarah Howe.
   v John, b. 17 June, 1796; d. 10 Sept., 1855; m. 1836, Sarah Bush.
   vi Judith, b. 16 Dec., 1797; m. 24 March, 1819, Eli Cunningham.
   vii Lucy, b. 15 July, 1800; d. 17 Oct., 1851; m. 4 Nov., 1819, James son of Sylvanus Howe; b. in Marlboro, 22 Feb., 1792.
   viii Lydia, b. 2 Nov., 1802.
   ix Catherine, b. 7 Feb., 1805; m. May, 1835, Amasa Bishop.
   x William, b. 17 May, 1807; d. 1 April, 1822.
   xi Emilia, b. 26 Feb., 1810; m. Sept., 1856, James Howe.
   xii Charlotte, b. 4 Jan., 1813; d. 1856; m. Nov., 1843, Joseph Johnson.

166 ARTEMAS⁵, son of Winslow⁴ and Elizabeth (Harrington), Brigham; born in Marlboro, Mass., 13 May, 1776; died 3 July, 1862; married, 1798, Lydia, daughter of Capt. William and Lydia (Chamberlain) Brigham (74); born 29 Dec., 1776. He settled in Bridgton, Me.

Children, born in Bridgton:
   i Lydia⁶, b. 5 July, 1799; d. 21 Jan., 1885; m. 26 May, 1825, William P. Holden of Bridgton, b. 1 Nov., 1799; d. 11 Nov., 1889. Ch. (Holden), the 2 elder b. in Raymond, Me., the 2 younger in Waterville, Me.:
      1 *Lydia Augusta⁷*, b. 26 Oct., 1827; d. 2 Dec., 1883; res. Portland, Me.
      2 *Esther Damon*, b. 21 Sept., 1829; a teacher, res. Hudson, Mass.
      3 *Laura Ann*, b. in Portland, 7 Aug., 1834; d. 6 Dec., 1859; res. Hudson.
      4 *Charles William*, b. 7 Aug., 1837; m. 18 Sept., 1864, Martha S. Willard of Harvard, Mass., b. Sept., 1849; res. Hudson. Ch.: i William O.⁸, b. 15 June, 1867; a teacher, res. Hudson; ii (Prof.) Charles A., b. 14 July, 1872; at Dartmouth Coll; m. Gertrude Robinson of Allston, Mass.; iii Martha Martina, b. 5 May, 1876; res. Hudson.
      5 *Ellen Maria*, b. 25 Feb., 1840; d. 29 April, 1865.
   ii Laura, b. 26 March, 1801; d.; m. Larkin Woodbury, who d.; res. Lynn, Mass.
   iii Jefferson, b. 25 Jan., 1803; d. 12 April, 1850; unm.; a manfr. of woolen goods; res. Bridgton.
398 iv James Madison, b. 14 March, 1805.
   v Sophia, b. 9 Jan, 1808; d. in Bridgton; m. Alpheus Gibbs of Bridgton and Boston. Ch. (Gibbs), b in Bridgton:

1 *Sophia*[7], b. 1828; d. y.

2 *Aaron*, b. 20 July, 1830; m. 1858, Eliza Walker of Bridgton; he was a farmer. Ch.: i Benjamin W.[8], m. Leola Dodge; res. s. p., Bridgton.

3 *Charles B.*, b. 22 Jan., 1835; m. 1858, Sarah Billings; res. Bridgton. Ch.: i Harry C.[8], d. s. p., 1902; ii Fred C., res. Bridgton.

4 *Lydia A.*, b. 28 Aug., 1837; m. 16 Aug., 1867, Col. Elias Briggs, son of Jacob Baldwin; he was Lieut. Col. of 8th Mo. Cavalry Vols., U. S. A., in Civil War.; res. Edna, Kan. Ch. (Baldwin): i Edwin Miles[8], b. 22 July, 1868; d. unm., 14 May, 1890; ii Julia Anna, b. 15 Aug., 1870; m. 17 Sept., 1890, Ollie W. Ball; 2 ch.

5 *Mary E.*, b. 9 April, 1840; m. Micajah Gleason; res. Bridgton. Ch. (Gleason): i Charles E.[8], of Bridgton; ii George, res. Camden, Me.; iii William, d. unm.

vi Dana, b. 16 Jan., 1811; d. 20 Feb., 1867; m. Mary Ann Larrabee; res. Westbrook, Me. Ch.:

1 *Mary A.*[7], m. J. H. Fogg of Portland, Me.; d. s. p., soon after.

2 *Joseph D.*, m. Etta Hazleton; res. a merchant, Westbrook, Me., s. p.

vii Mary, b. 14 May, 1813; d. 25 May, 1875; res. unm., in Boston.

viii Dexter, b. 28 Feb., 1816; d. 24 Oct., 1822.

ix Ann, b. 30 March, 1819; d. 27 Sept., 1854; m. 29 March, 1840, Elijah H. Bagnall, b. 1816; they res. Chelsea, Mass. Ch. (Bagnall), b. in Chelsea:

1 *Wilbur Fisk*[7], b. 14 Jan., 1841; d. 28 Dec., 1859.

2 *Emma Brigham*, b. 16 July, 1843; d. 28 Nov., 1862.

3 *Edwin Elijah*, b. 6 Nov., 1845; d. 14 June, 1864.

4 *Anna Theresa*, b. 9 July, 1848; d. 4 Feb., 1865.

5 *Charles Dana*, b. 5 June, 1851; m. 9 Jan., 1879, Mary L. Belcher, b. 15 Dec., 1859; res. Dorchester. Ch.: Florence May[8], b. 5 Dec., 1879.

6 *Henry Ward*, b. 4 Jan., 1854; d. 1 July, 1875.

167 LUCY[5], daughter of Winslow[4] and Elizabeth (Harrington) Brigham; born in Marlboro, Mass., 28 June, 1779; died 23 Nov., 1850; married, 29 Oct., 1799, Capt. Eli (known as " Dea."), son of Peter Rice; born in Marlboro, 8 Oct., 1777; died 4 May, 1851. He was a deacon, Justice of the Peace, and Representative to the General Court.

Children (Rice), born in Marlboro:
i Levina[6], b. 19 Oct., 1800; m. 21 April, 1817, Otis Russell, b. in Marlboro, 24 April, 1793; they had 17 ch.; she d. 28 Aug., 1883.

ii Matthias, b. 10 July, 1802; d. 8 June, 1841; m. Martha Brigham, 587; res. Fitchburg, Mass.

iii Lucy Brigham, b. 2 April, 1804; d. 10 Jan., 1805.

iv Emily, b. 10 Nov., 1806; d. 4 Feb., 1836; m. 18 April, 1826, Edward Phelps, b. 28 March, 1805; he m. (2) Sophronia Rice.

v Betsey, b. 7 Oct., 1808; d. 27 Aug., 1819.

vi Lucy, b. 16 Jan., 1811; d. 11 Feb., 1812.

vii Sophronia, b. 1 Feb., 1813; d. 3 Sept., 1877; m. Edward Phelps, widower of her sister Emily.

viii Peter, b. 10 March, 1815; d. unm., 25 Feb., 1841.

ix Laura A., b. 27 April, 1817; d. 16 Dec., 1875; m. William Hersey.

x Sophia, b. 5 March, 1819; m. 1851, Dennis Witherbee; res. Marlboro; living in 1905.

xi Winslow Brigham, b. 24 May, 1821; d. 3 July, 1876; m. 23 Nov., 1842, Emeline L. Stow; moved to Ohio.

xii Abraham W., b. 7 May, 1823; d. 12 Sept., 1885; m. 1844, Abby W. Albee.

168 FORTUNATUS[5], son of Abraham[4] and Phebe (Martin) Brigham; born in Marlboro, Mass., 29 Sept., 1759; died 4 Nov., 1834; married, 28 Aug., 1783, Martha, daughter of Daniel and Martha (Brigham) Barnes; born 9 May, 1766, in Marlboro; died 10 Oct., 1860. Resided in Northboro.

Children, born in Northboro:

i Polly[6] (Mary), b. 3 Nov., 1783; m. Moses[6] Brigham, 219.

ii Phebe, b. 4 July, 1785; d. 22 Oct., 1813; m. George Chase; res. Northboro. Ch. (Chase):
1 *Mary Ann[7]*, b. 20 Jan., 1811.
2 *George B.*, b. 28 Aug., 1813; d. 12 April, 1857.

iii Abraham, b. 11 July, 1788; d. Nov., 1813; m. Betsey Wright; res. Northboro. Ch.:
1 *Lyman[7];* 2 *Lucy,* m. ———— Miller.

iv Nancy, b. 29 June, 1791; d. 10 June, 1850; m. Joel Brigham, 490.

v Samuel, b. 24 April, 1794; d. 13 Dec., 1795.

399 vi Samuel, b. 20 Sept., 1796.

400 vii Martin, b. 25 Aug., 1799.

401 viii Lincoln, b. 13 May, 1803.

402 ix Edward Leonard, b. 8 Oct., 1806.

x Martha Barnes, b. 22 Aug., 1809; m. Moses William Maynard, b. 29 Sept., 1805; res. Worcester, Mass. Ch. (Maynard):
1 *Martha Adelaide[7]*, b. 8 Oct., 1833; d. 31 July, 1865.
2 *Malcolm Williams,* b. 22 Dec., 1836.
3 *Myron,* b. 8 July, 1839; d. 27 Dec., 1843.
4 *Mander Alvan,* b. 15 Sept., 1841.

169 LEWIS[5], son of Asa[4] and Elizabeth (Warren) Brigham; born in Marlboro, Mass., 24 March, 1756; died 22 Feb., 1803; married, 18 Sept., 1786, Mary, daughter of Benjamin and Susanna (Weeks) Rice; born in Marlboro, 8 April, 1767; died 15 June, 1797. He settled in Marlboro. He probably marched on the Lexington Alarm in Capt. Wm. Brigham's Company.

Children, born in Marlboro:

403 i Asa[6], b. 31 Aug., 1788.

ii Sukey (or Susanna), b. 12 April, 1790; m. 29 Jan., 1809, Stephen, son of Artemas and Mary (Bigelow) Howe; b. in Marlboro, 21 March, 1780; his grandmother was Ruth[4] Brigham, 31. Ch. (Howe), b. in Marlboro:

        1 *Nahum B.*[7], b. 5 June, 1809; 2 *Mary L.*, b. 7 May, 1812; 3
        Elbridge, b. 15 Nov., 1816; res. Marlboro; 4 *Benjamin S.*,
        b. 12 Dec., 1823; 5 *Alfred G.*, b. 8 July, 1825, and 2 other
        daus.
  iii Sally, b. 5 June, 1792; m. 18 July, 1811, Rufus Bruce of Sudbury.
      Ch. (Bruce):
        1 *Rufus L.*[7], res. New Orleans.
   iv Mary, b. 16 Aug., 1794; m. Amory, son of Abraham and Eliza-
      beth (Wetherbee) Howe of Marlboro; b. 3 Sept., 1795; they res.
      N. Y., and had 12 ch., several of whom are in the learned pro-
      fessions.
    v Abigail, b. 2 Aug., 1796; m. Benjamin Weeks Allen; res. Am-
      herst. Ch. (Allen):
        1 *Benjamin W.*[7]; 2 *Susan*; 3 *Mary*; 4 *Lewis*; 5 *James*.

170   **JOTHAM**[5], son of Asa[4] and Elizabeth (Warren) Brigham; born in Marlboro, Mass., 18 Nov., 1761; died 26 March.,
1810; married Lucy Thompson of Sudbury, who died in Lancaster, Mass., 20 Dec., 1830, æ. 71.   Resided in Marlboro and was
a farmer and tailor.

Children, born in Marlboro:
    i Betsey[6], b. 30 July, 1785; m. Int., 28 Feb., 1806, James Mallard
      of Lancaster; she joined the church in Lancaster, in 1807. Ch.
      (Mallard), born in Lancaster:
        1 *Eliza Brigham*[7], bapt. 2 Feb., 1807; d. 11 Jan., 1810.
        2 *James*, bapt. 19 Jan., 1809; d. 11 Jan., 1810.
        3 *James*, bapt. 15 Feb., 1811; d. 10 Aug., 1813.
        4 *Ann Sophia*, bapt. 24 April, 1814.
        5 *Abigail*, bapt. 29 Sept., 1816.
   ii Lucy, b. 15 Jan., 1787; m. 30 May, 1808, Edward, son of Edward
      and Submit (Forbush) Barnes; b. 30 April, 1778; d. 24 Jan.,
      1851; she was living in the early sixties. Ch. (Barnes):
        1 (*Dr.*) *Edward F.*[7], b. in Marlboro, 1809; m. Maria E. Brig-
        ham, dau. of 354.
        2 (*Dr.*) *Henry*, b. 1811; res. Northboro.
        3 (*Dr.*) *Charles W.*, res. Wayland.
        And 5 others.
404 iii Otis, b. 8 Oct., 1788.
405 iv Henry, b. 3 May, 1790.
406   v John, b. 1 Aug., 1792.
407 vi Hastings, b. 4 Aug., 1794.
408 vii Sophia, b. 11 July, 1796.
  viii Charles Lee, b. 14 Oct., 1800; m. Roama V. Atkins; res. Dor-
      chester, Mass.

171   **CAPT. CHARLES**[5], son of William[4] and Sarah (Prentice)
Brigham; born in Grafton, Mass., 27 July, 1769; died there, 2
Dec., 1847; married, 20 Oct., 1797, Susanna, daughter of Dea.
Nicholas Baylis, who was brother of Dr. William Baylis of Digh-
ton and father of Nicholas Baylis, a justice of the Supreme Court
of Vermont; she was born 10 Aug., 1778; died 10 June, 1837.

Capt. Charles was, 18 Sept., 1792, sergeant in Wheeler's Co., 2d
Regt., 2d Brigade, 7th Div. of the Militia; resigned as captain 20
Jan., 1809. Inherited the homestead on "Brigham Hill" in Grafton, and lived there until his death, which, owing to his excellent
health and constitution, was the result of almost his first sickness.

Children, born in Grafton:

409   i Charles⁶, b. 22 May, 1799.
      ii Susanna Baylis, b. 13 Feb., 1802; d. 5 March, 1804.
      iii Susanna Baylis, b. 24 May, 1804; m. 1844, Dr. Josiah Kittridge;
         res. Nashua, N. H.; d. s. p.
410   iv William, b. 26 Sept., 1806.
411   v Nicholas, b. 2 Oct., 1808.
      vi Solomon, b. 12 Nov., 1810; d. unm., a merchant in Grafton, 8
         Oct., 1841.
412   vii Hannah, b. 11 March, 1813.
413   viii Sarah, b. 7 May, 1815.
      ix Lucy Abigail, b. 25 July, 1817; was grad. Mt. Holyoke Sem.,
         1839; m. 1861, Francis Merrifield; s. p.
414   x Maria Caroline, b. 26 June, 1820.
      xi Cornelia Antoinette, b. 17 Nov., 1823; was at Mt. Holyoke Sem-
         inary in 1843; m. 5 July, 1860, Calvin Taft of Worcester, Mass.,
         where she resides, s. p.

172   SUSANNA⁵, daughter of William⁴ and Sarah (Prentice)
Brigham; born in Grafton, Mass., 27 Nov., 1770; died 9 Sept.,
1850; married, 6 March, 1792, Capt. Ephraim, son of Col. John
Goulding of Grafton; born there, 4 Sept., 1765; died 14 Jan., 1838.
Was a tanner and owned much land; was a prominent citizen and
frequently served as selectman.

Children (Goulding), born in Grafton:

      i Susanna⁶, b. 25 March, 1793; m. Ezekiel Brigham⁷, son of 205; s. p.
      ii Sally, b. 24 Jan., 1795; d. unm.
      iii John, b. 19 Jan., 1797; was grad. Yale Coll., A. B., 1821; M. D.,
         Yale, 1824; settled in Stratford, Conn., where d. 10 Jan., 1860.
      iv Ephraim, b. 25 Feb., 1799; d. 25 June, 1800.
      v Ephraim, b. 11 July, 1801; m. (1) Eunice Dunsmore; m. (2)
         Emily Carter; res. Millbury, Mass.
      vi William, b. 22 Dec., 1804; d. in N. Y. City; m. Ada Jewett.
      vii Solomon E., b. 28 Nov., 1807; m. (1) Lucy A. Nichols; m. (2)
         Nancy P. Robinson.
      viii Lucy E., twin to Solomon, m. Harvey J. Pratt.
      ix Palmer, b. 11 Oct., 1809; m. (1) Fanny W. Maynard; m. (2)
         Ann Cutting.
      x Charles, b. 15 Nov., 1812; m. Emily A. Miles; res. Mobile, Ala.

173   SALLY⁵, daughter of William⁴ and Sarah (Prentice)
Brigham; born in Grafton, Mass., 12 Sept., 1780; died 26 Aug.,
1870; married (1) 1798, Benjamin, son of Nathaniel Kingsbury;
born in Dedham, Mass., 1776; died in Grafton, Aug., 1799; he

owned a store there; married (2) Jeremiah Flagg of Grafton (who married [1] Lydia Drury); born 26 Dec., 1779; died 27 Aug., 1847.

Child (Kingsbury), born in Grafton:
  i Benjamin⁶, b. 24 March, 1799; brought up by his grandfather Brigham; m. 16 Nov., 1825, Hannah Stone of Grafton; b. 23 May, 1804; d. 27 May, 1872; he owned mills in Centreville; held many town offices; State Representative, etc. Ch.:
    1 Sarah⁷; 2 Julia, both d. y.
    3 Albert, of Kingsbury Bros., Quincy, Ill.
    4 Henry, oil operator in Penn.
    5 William; 6 Hannah, both d. y.
    6 Lyman, res. Quincy, Ill.
    7 Charles, Gen. Mgr. Chester & Iron Mt. Ry., Chester, Ill.
    8 Horace, res. Titusville, Pa.
    9 Edward, was grad. Harvard Coll., 1875, and Law School, 1876; practices in Worcester.
Children (Flagg), born in Grafton:
  ii Lydia D., b. 27 Nov., 1802; m. George W. Hale.
  iii Charles A., b. 25 Nov., 1804; res. Boston.
  iv Sarah A., b. 11 Jan., 1807; d. 16 Jan., 1832.
  v Jeremiah, b. 30 Nov., 1810; m. Eliza W. Turner; cordwainer; had sons:
    1 George⁷; 2 Charles; 3 William, all of Boston.
  vi Samuel C., b. 19 Oct., 1819; d. 25 May, 1841.

174 PERSIS⁵, daughter of William⁴ and Sarah (Prentice) Brigham; born in Grafton, Mass., 4 Aug., 1786; died 5 March, 1871; married, 1804, Leonard, son of Paul Wheelock of Grafton; born 4 Sept., 1785; died 13 July, 1858.

Children (Wheelock), born in Grafton:
  i Daniel Brigham⁶, b. 7 March, 1805; m. Sophia Brigham⁷, dau. of 297.
  ii Sophronia, b. 7 Aug., 1807; m. Willard S. Wood.
  iii Gardner L., b. 27 July, 1810; d. 25 March, 1870; m. 1832, Caroline A. Wood, b. 7 Oct., 1813. Ch.:
    1 Henry⁷; 2 Clarendon; 3 Susan; others d. y.
  iv Mary Brigham, b. 28 Aug., 1813; d. 1 Sept., 1874.
  v Leonard S., b. 15 July, 1815; m. (1) 1835, Adaline A. Doane; m. (2) 1838, Abby Pollard; m. (3) 1845, Lucy Pollard. Ch.:
    1 Charles⁷; 2 Candace; 3 Francis; 4 Ida; others d. y.
  vi Solomon Brigham, b. 7 Sept., 1817; m. Ruth Hall.
  vii William R., b. 17 Aug., 1822; m. Caroline E. Brewer.
  viii Francis A., b. 21 Oct., 1828; m. Esther C. Briggs.

SIXTH   GENERATION

SIXTH GENERATION

175 SARAH[6], daughter of Moses[5] and Mehitabel (Grout) Brigham, born in Westboro, Mass., 18 April, 1751, at the homestead; died there, 20 Aug., 1827; married, 2 July, 1772, Jonathan, son of Dea. Jonathan Forbes of Westboro; born there, 1 March, 1746; died there, 5 June, 1805.

Through this marriage, the old Moses Brigham house on West Main Street passed into the Forbes family. Sarah's husband was a deacon in the church, and one of the leading men of the day. She willed each of her grand-children a Bible.

Children (Forbes), born in Westboro:
  i Moses[7], b. 18 April, 1773; d. s. p.; m. 22 May, 1797, Abigail Baker, b. 1 Sept., 1776.
  ii (Dea.) Jonathan, b. 6 Dec., 1775; d. 6 Jan., 1861; m. 17 Jan., 1802, Esther, dau. of Ebenezer and Esther (Fay) Chamberlain; b. 28 April, 1780; d. 2 Feb., 1867; res. in Westboro, in the "Forbes house"; held most of the town offices, and was a leader in the church. Ch., b. in W.:
    1 *Susanna Brigham[8]*, b. 16 April, 1803; d. s. p., 22 Aug., 1851; m. Rev. Charles Forbush, 6 Nov., 1833.
    2 *Julia Miranda*, b. 25 June, 1804; d. in Alexandria, Va., Feb., 1868; m. 29 Nov., 1832, Rev. John Wilde; 1 dau.
    3 *Jonathan*, b. 20 Nov., 1806; d. 24 Jan., 1820.
    4 *Daniel H.*, b. 13 Sept., 1809; d. 18 May, 1854; m. (1) Jane Baker; m. (2) Mary A. White; 3 ch. by 2d wife.
    5 *Esther Louise*, b. 22 June, 1810; d. Oct., 1812.
    6 *Moses*, b. 26 Sept., 1812; d. 25 April, 1851; m. Eliza L. Southwick of Grafton; 2 ch.
    7 *Ephraim Trowbridge*, b. 25 March, 1815; d. 2 Aug., 1863; m. 13 Sept., 1842, Catherine, dau. of William and Nancy (Avery) White; b. 25 July, 1815. Ch.: i Catherine S.; ii Esther L.; iii William T., m. dau. of 414; iv Frank W.
    8 *Eliza Sophia*, b. 7 Jan., 1821; d. unm.
  m (Maj.) Holland, b. 7 July, 1777; d. 4 Nov., 1842; m. 7 Nov., 1803, Polly Wheelock, b. 5 Sept., 1783; d. 25 Feb., 1858. Ch.:
    1 *Mary W.[8]*, b. 14 March, 1805; d. 14 April, 1882; m. ———— Bowman, d.
    2 *Holland*, b. 22 July, 1806; d. 17 June, 1870; m. Lydia A. Brigham, dau. of 296.
    3 *Joseph W.*, b. 26 Aug., 1810; d. s. p., 4 Sept., 1876; m. Lucretia ————.
    4 *Charles B.*, b. 20 Oct., 1813; m. Marion Rider, dau. of 237.
    5 *Julia S.*, b. 30 June, 1816.
    6 *John S.*, b. 30 June, 1817; m. Persis G. Bowman.
    7 *Ephraim*, b. 27 April, 1818; m. Harriet Childs.
    8 *George B.*, b. 4 March, 1823; m. Nancy Temple.

9 *Sarah A.,* b. 22 Oct., 1826; m. Solomon J. Taft.
10 *Henry B.,* b. 26 Aug., 1829; m. Anna Harrington.
iv Ephraim, b. 11 Sept., 1779; d. s. p., 8 Nov., 1817; m. Mary Goddard.
v Sarah, b. 13 Oct., 1782; d. s. p., 12 Oct., 1851; m. John Sanborn.
vi Hannah, b. 18 April, 1785; d. s. p.; m. Silas Maynard.
vii Elias, b. 10 Aug., 1787; m. 5 Nov., 1811, Mary Wadsworth, b. 9 Jan., 1791; d. 15 Oct., 1861. Ch.:
    1 *Ebenezer W.*[8], b. 14 Jan., 1813; m. Lutheria Longley.
    2 *Elias E.,* b. 9 Oct., 1814; m. (1) Harriet T. Harrington; m. (2) Hepsibah G. Clapp.
    3 *Lewis,* b. 25 Oct., 1816; m. Clarissa Farnham.
    4 *Mary G.,* b. 24 Dec., 1818; m. Thomas H. Wetherby.
    5 *Hannah E.,* b. 19 Nov., 1820; m. 23 Jan., 1848, Thomas B. E. Pope.
    6 *Lucy B.,* b. 12 Nov., 1824; m. William H. Harrington.
    7 *Sarah Brigham,* b. 3 May, 1827; d. 29 Aug., 1845.
viii Nancy, b. 24 May, 1790; d. 30 June, 1832; m. Samuel Chamberlain.
ix Achsah, b. 22 June, 1794; d. 16 Sept., 1880; m. 30 Nov., 1815, Eli Chamberlain. Ch. (Chamberlain):
    1 *Sarah*[8]; 2 *Harriet;* 3 *Lyman H.;* 4 *Joshua M.;* 5 *Achsah;* 6 *Daniel H.;* 7 *L——— T.*

176 MOSES[6], son of Moses[5] and Mehitabel (Grout) Brigham; born in Westboro, Mass., 31 May, 1785; died in Delaware, near London, Province of Ontario, Canada, 13 Aug., 1814; married (1), 9 Sept., 1781, Wealthy Johnson of Lebanon, N. H., who died 9 Jan., 1790, æ. 30; married (2) Lucinda, daughter of Dr. Gideon Tiffany of Hanover, N. H., originally from Attleboro, Mass.

He was graduated from Dartmouth College in 1778 in the same class with his distinguished kinsman, the Hon. Elijah Brigham of Westboro. Moses taught school in Westboro,* and is often mentioned in the *Diary of the Rev. Ebenezer Parkman,* being one of the frequent visitors to the parsonage. He was one of the original grantees of Concord, Vt., and settled as a merchant in Hanover, N. H., where, about 1800, he became embarrassed and closed business. In 1801 he removed with his brother-in-law, Tiffany, and most of his family, to the vicinity of London, Ontario, and with him embarked in land speculation on an extended scale, having purchased the " Delaware Property " on the river Thames.

Children (by first wife), born in Hanover:
i Wealthy Clarinda[7], b. 29 June, 1782; d. 7 June, 1841; m. 1808, John Ham, A. M., of Gilmanton, N. H.; they had 6 ch.

* " 24 Jan., 1779. Master Moses Brigham who keeps school at ye East Quarter of ye Town dind here."
" 26 Mch., 1779. P. M. came Mr. Alexander accompanied by his uncle Miller. Stays not long. Mr. Caleb Harrington invites and waits upon him to his House and thence he intends to go to Master Moses.
" Moses Brigham who is to be found at his school or at his Lodging, Mr. Andrews."—*Parkman Diary.*

415　ii Bela Brewster, b. 4 Feb., 1784.
　　iii Susan Laurinda, b. 2 March, 1786; d. in Northampton, Mass.,
　　　　17 Feb., 1862; m. 27 Aug., 1806, John F. Munroe from Marl-
　　　　boro to Northampton, where he d. 1 Nov., 1856. Ch. (Munroe):
　　　　1 *Susan Lorinda Brigham*⁸, b. 31 Dec., 1821; d. 11 Jan., 1897;
　　　　m. Henry Shepherd of N., b. 19 June, 1811; d. 20 Nov., 1900.
　　　　Ch. (Shepherd): Thomas M⁹., res. unm., in Northampton;
　　　　the founder and donor of the Henry Shepherd Surgery build-
　　　　ing at Northampton.
　　iv John Hartman, b. 6 June, 1788; d. 13 Aug., 1790.
　　Children (by second wife), born (probably) in Hanover, N. H.:
　　　v Fanny Lucinda, m. Seneca Allen; res. Monroe, Mich.; 11 ch.
　　　vi Lucy Malinda, m. Abraham Truax, and d. ——————; res.
　　　　Trenton, Mich.; 5 ch.
　　vii George Dean, d. 1831; killed by an explosion; m. Fanny Huston;
　　　　res. Truago, Mich.
　　viii Maria, d. in Truago, Mich., unm., in 1837.
　　ix Sophia, m. Carlos Colton; res. Toledo, O.; 4 ch.

177　PHINEAS⁶, son of Moses⁵ and Mehitabel (Grout) Brigham; born in Westboro, Mass., 23 July, 1755; married Lydia,
daughter of David and Lydia (Maynard) Batherick.

He resided in Westboro. Was a private in Capt. Edmund Brigham's Co. of Minute Men, and marched on the Lexington Alarm.
He enlisted in the army, and in 1777 marched with Capt. Brigham
to reinforce the Northern Army, but went only as far as Hadley
and returned. He saw further service in 1778.

　　Children, born in Westboro:
　　　i Eli⁷, b. 23 May, 1780; m. Dulcena ——————. Ch., b. in Grafton:
　　　　1 *Lydia*⁸, b. 3 Oct., 1804.
416　ii Phineas, b. 28 March, 1782.
417　iii Willard, b. 20 Sept., 1784.
　　iv Lydia, b. 23 Sept., 1787; d. y.
　　　v Nahum, b. 10 Feb., 1790; d. y.
　　vi Stephen, b. 3 June, 1792; d. in Westboro, unm., æ. 23 or 24.
418　vii Lambert, b. 7 June, 1794.

178　MEHITABEL⁶, daughter of Moses⁵ and Mehitabel
(Grout) Brigham; born in Westboro, Mass., 31 Jan., 1758; died
there, 11 Dec., 1844; married, 11 Jan., 1776, John, son of Capt.
Benjamin Fay;* born in Westboro, 25 Aug., 1748; died there, 7
June, 1837.

* " 5 Aug., 1780. Mrs. Fay (John Fay's wife) came to be examined, but I
could spend but little Time with her.
" 11 Aug., 1780. Mrs. Mehitable Fay (wife of John) here with her Relation,
which I corrected and copy'd. *Josiah Brigham came to Breck* again to live with him.
They clear ye lower Well.
" 12 Aug., 1780. Mr. John Fay was examined—left a Relation to be corrected
and transcribed. He dines here.
" 25 Aug., 1780. Mr. John Fay, with his Relation here, and signs it."—*Parkman
Diary.*

Children (Fay), born in Westboro:
    i Polly[7], b. 22 Dec., 1778; m. 1821, Elias Miller. Ch. (Miller):
        1 *Elias[8];* 2 *John;* 3 *Harriet.*
    ii Mehitabel, b. 20 Feb., 1781; d. 25 March, 1781.
    iii Mehitabel, b. 19 March, 1782; d. unm.
    iv John, b. 19 April, 1784; m. 1806, Betsey, dau. of Daniel Noyes
      of Shrewsbury. Ch.:
        1 *Betsey[8]*, d. y.; 2 *(Dr.) Henry,* a physician of N. Y. City.
    v Joseph, b. 27 Sept., 1786; d. 1 March, 1864; m. Eunice Fay.
      Ch.:
        1 *Joseph Brigham[8];* 2 *Maria;* 3 *John.*
    vi Lucy, b. 26 Jan., 1789; d. 18 Jan., 1848; m. Willard Gates of
      Worcester, Mass. Ch. (Gates):
        1 *Henry[8].*
    vii Edward, b. 19 July, 1791; d. in Albany, N. Y., 1832; m. Priscilla
      Price. Ch.:
        1 *Mary[8];* 2 *Lucy;* 3 *Marcia;* 4 *Sarah.*
    viii Susan, b. 20 Sept., 1794; d. 3 July, 1873; m. Jonas Stone of
      Winchendon and Westboro. Ch. (Stone):
        1 *Jonas[8].*
    ix Josiah, b. 29 Dec., 1797; m. Mary W. Warren; res. Westboro.
      Ch.:
        1 *Hercules[8];* 2 *Martha.*
    x Charles Miles, b. 24 Sept., 1800; m. (1) Frances Spurr; m. (2)
      Mrs. Althea Waters; m. (3) ———— Fitz. Ch.:
        1 *Ellen[8]*, m. ———— Daniels.
    xi Nancy Maria, b. 15 April, 1803; d. unm., 28 March, 1839.

179 **EBENEZER[6]**, son of Moses[5] and Mehitabel (Grout) Brigham; born in Westboro, Mass., 3 March, 1761; died in Townshend,
Vt.., 15 Dec., 1839; married, 28 Sept., 1782, Judith Hazeltine; born
in Westboro, 18 Jan., 1762; died in Townshend in 1854. He moved
to Townshend, Vt., by 1790, where he was an important citizen,
and a Captain of Infantry, in 1812.

*Children, the elder probably born in Westboro, the younger probably
in Townshend:*
419   i John Hazeltine[7], b. 14 Aug., 1783.
    ii Ebenezer B., b. 1785; d. 1786.
    iii Eben, b. 1787; d. 1790.
420   iv Moses, b. 1789.
    v Nathan, b. and d. 1791.
    vi Eli Whitney, b. 1792; d. unm., 1815.
    vii Alonzo, b. and d. 1794.
    viii Lyman H., b. 1795; d. 1887.
    ix Judith, b. 1797; d. 1880.
    x Wealthy Clarinda, b. 22 March, 1800; d. 28 June, 1844; m.
      Elijah, son of Jacob and Sarah (Boutelle) Allen of Millbury,
      Mass. Ch. (Allen):
        1 *Elvira W.[8]*, b. 15 Feb., 1825; m. Artemas E. Fairbank; 3 ch.
        2 *Brigham Elijah,* b. 17 Jan., 1827; killed 16 July, 1861, in first
          battle of Bull Run.
        3 *Julia P.,* b. 20 Sept., 1829; d. 27 June, 1891; m. 2 June,
          1852, Leonard Wood of Leominster, Mass.; 2 ch.

4 *Boutelle E.*, b. 27 June, 1833; m. (1) Lizzie S. Whitney; m. (2) Mary Pierce; m. (3) Anna Jaquith.; 2 ch.
5 *Ellen D.*, b. 1 Sept., 1842; m. 16 Nov., 1864, Frederic S. Coolidge; 3 ch.

180 JOSEPH[6], (A. B. and A. M., Harvard, 1788; *ibid.* Dartmouth), son of Moses[5] and Mehitabel (Grout) Brigham; born in Westboro, Mass., 23 Sept., 1766; died in Canada, 14 Sept., 1821, and interred by the grave of his brother Moses, in Delaware, near London, Ontario; married, 1 Jan., 1794, Sally Woods, born 7 June, 1776; died 21 Feb., 1806.

He studied law with Hon. Levi Lincoln, Sr., of Worcester, and opened an office in Marlboro; practiced there and in adjacent towns until after the death of his wife. Moved to Albany, N. Y., and thence, after the War of 1812, to Canada.

Children, born in Marlboro:
    i Eliza Chandler[7], b. 27 Jan., 1795; d. 25 April, 1823; m. Martin L. Stow, A. M., of Concord, Mass.; res. Northboro.
   ii Lydia Vose, b. 19 April, 1796; d. unm., 11 May, 1821.
  iii Sally Clarinda, b. 29 Jan., 1798; d. 14 Feb., 1885; m. 17 Oct., 1820, John Cotting of Marlboro; res. Ch. (Cotting):
        1 *John Francis*[8], b. 4 May, 1822.
        2 *Joseph Clarendon*, b. 14 April, 1825.
        3 *Sarah B.*, b. 23 Feb., 1828.
        4 *Charles William*, b. 21 Aug., 1833.
        5 *Mary Caroline*, b. 9 Feb., 1836.
        6 *Henry E.*, b. 13 May, 1840.
421 iv Joseph Clarenden, b. 20 Dec., 1800.
    v Moses Woods, b. 18 Dec., 1802; murdered in a P. O. in Texas.
   vi Francis Lincoln, b. 21 July, 1803; d. unm., a dentist, in New Bedford.
  vii Caroline Maria, b. 20 Feb., 1805; d. 1868, in Framingham, Mass., m. Richard Farwell, A. M., who d.; res. Marlboro. Ch. (Farwell):
        1 *John M.*[8], b. 2 Dec., 1825; res. Marlboro.
        2 *Lucy W.*, b. 6 May, 1827; (d.); m. S. E. Morton.
        3 *Willard Brigham*, b. 26 Jan., 1829; res. an editor in San Francisco, Cal.

181 EDMUND[6], son of Capt. Edmund[5] and Sarah (Lyscom) Brigham, born in Westboro, Mass., 19 Oct., 1758; died in Templeton, Mass., 22 Apr., 1840; married Mary, daughter of Lieut. John and granddaughter of the Rev. John Martyn (who was the first settled minister of the church in Northboro, Mass., a graduate of Harvard College in 1724, who married Mary Marrett of Cambridge, Mass.). She was born in Northboro, 24 Nov., 1762; died in Templeton, 2 May, 1835.

Edmund learned the saddler's trade and resided with his father on the old home place in Westboro until July, 1782, when he moved to Gerry, now Phillipston, Mass., and thence to Templeton, about

1790. On a division of the Martyn estate in Northboro, his wife received a five-dollar gold piece, a chaise, and a stony farm in Templeton. · In the midst of the struggle to raise crops from between the rocks, and all the difficult labor required in a new country, 12 children were born, 10 of whom were raised to maturity and 6 of whom have left descendants. He is noted as being in a train band, year not given. He marched on the Lexington Alarm from Westboro in his father's company, and was on duty in Cambridge for some time afterward. He is named in his father's will among the 4 sons who are to share in the distribution of the Captain's wardrobe.

Children, the 2 elder born in Westboro, the next 3 in Gerry, and the others in Templeton:
422   i Polly⁷, b. 6 Feb., 1780.
423 ii John, b. 7 June, 1782.
     iii Edmund, b. 28 March, 1784; d. 15 April, 1784.
     iv Betsey, b. 8 Nov., 1787; d. 16 Aug., 1849; m. Nixon Ball of Southboro.
     v Abigail, b. 25 Sept., 1789; d. unm., 18 March, 1860.
424 vi Lyscom, b. 28 March, 1792.
425 vii Edward, b. 26 May, 1795.
     viii Susan, b. 10 July, 1798; d. 15 May, 1879; m. James Arnold of Boston, who d.; she lived in Marlboro on the site of the present Baptist church; a woman of graceful manners, she was a successful milliner, and was associated with her sister Roxana, a very capable woman, in this business in Marlboro for a number of years.
     ix Dexter, b. 20 Aug., 1800; d. unm., 4 Nov., 1832, at Whitingham, Vt.; he was a very smart business man, but a cripple.
     x Roxana, b. 30 July, 1803; d. unm., in Southboro, 3 Jan., 1880.
     xi Infant, b. 24 Dec., 1804; d. next day.
426 xii Lewis, b. 4 June, 1806.

182 ROGER⁶, son of Capt. Edmund⁵ and Sarah (Lyscom) Brigham; born in Westboro, Mass., 28 Feb., 1762; died in Jaffrey, N. H., 18 Nov., 1837; married Elizabeth Rich of Truro, N. H., who died in Jaffrey, 3 Sept., 1850, æ. 88. He was at Jaffrey in 1793. He is mentioned in his father's will as one of the 4 sons to share in the Captain's wardrobe. He belonged to the train band in Westboro, and was in the Revolution in 1778 and 1779, in which latter year he was a corporal.

Children, the 2 elder born in Phillipston, Mass., the others in Jaffrey:
     i Sally⁷, b. 9 Sept., 1790; d. in Jaffrey, 3 March, 1879; m. 11 Dec., 1817, Joel Oaks Patrick of Jaffrey, b. in Fitzwilliam, N. H., 8 Nov., 1793; d. in Jaffrey, 31 March, 1870; a merchant, hotel keeper and carpenter. Ch. (Patrick), b. in Jaffrey:
        1 *Dexter⁸*, b. 9 Dec., 1818; m. (1) Mary Ann Nutting; m. (2) Eliza J. Wentworth; res. Waltham, Mass. Ch., by 2d wife: i Mary⁹, m. Leroy Brown of Waltham; ii Dexter, m. Rosella Bigelow; res. Waltham.

2 *Joel*, b. 30 Oct., 1820.
3 *Sarah*, b. 26 Jan., 1825; m. 8 May, 1859, David A. Cutler; res.
E. Jaffrey.
ii Eli, b. 19 Oct., 1792; m. Abigail Russell of Dublin, N. H.; res.
McDonough, N. Y.
iii Lora, b. 27 June, 1795; m. ————; res. Dunbarton, N. H.
iv Dexter, b. 30 April, 1798; d. 1800.
v Betsey, b. 6 July, 1806; m. 17 Sept., 1835, Charles Lincoln, who
d. 7 Oct., 1859, æ. 60. Ch. (Lincoln), b. Jaffrey:
1 *Rohanna*[8], b. 1836; d. 13 Feb., 1865.
2 *Sarah A.*, b. 1842.

183 SAMUEL[6], son of Capt. Edmund[5] and Sarah (Lyscom)
Brigham; born in Westboro, Mass., 6 Dec., 1763; died in Westboro,
11 June, 1823; married, 5 May, 1785, Lydia Ball of Westboro,
who died 16 March, 1827.

He was a farmer and moved to West Waterford, Me., but returned to his native place in the latter part of his life. He is
mentioned in his father's will as one of the 4 sons among whom
the Captain's wardrobe was to be divided. An old tradition is
that when a child he was very large of his age, and, to save him
from conscription at a time when boys were being called upon to
enter the army, his mother, mindful of his tender years, put him
in one of the big ovens to hide him from the soldiers. On one
occasion, either he or one of his brothers got into earnest political
discussion with a neighbor, on a summer's evening, while putting
the cows out to pasture for the night; they stood at the bars as they
talked, and when the dawn came it found them there, the debate
still going on.

Children, born in West Waterford:
i Lucy[7], b. in 1786; m. Amos Smith of Waterford. Ch. (Smith),
b. in Waterford:
1 *Hazen*[8], moved West.
2 *Betsey*, m. ———— Barker of Quincy, Mass. Ch. (Barker):
i Hendrick[9] of Holden, Mass.; ii Henry of New York.
3 *Verona*, m. ———— Black of Holden, Mass.
4 *Hendrick*, m., had two sons; went West.
5 *Sarah*, m. ———— Rand of Roxbury, Mass.; 1 dau.
6 *Henry*, book dealer in New York City.
7 *Calvin*, d. y.
8 *Charles*, res. in Boston; had 2 sons and daus.
9 *Cyrus*, res. Hopkinton, Mass.
427 ii Samuel, b. in 1788.
iii Polly, b. 1789; m. Amos Smith of Holden, Mass. Ch. (Smith):
1 *Julia A.*[8], b. in Holden, 13 May, 1816; m. (1) Ephraim Smith;
m. (2) John Hammond of Sanbornton, N. H. Ch.:
i Julia A.[9], m. Albert E. Lyon of Leominster, Mass.
ii Lizzie B., b. and d. 1856.
428 iv Lyscom, b. 1791.
429 v George Ball, b. 23 Jan., 1793.

430   vi Bryant, b. 10 Feb., 1794.
431   vii Levi, b. 27 May, 1796.
      viii Nahum, b. Jan., 1798; d. in Boston, —————; m. Lucy
        Blood of Groton, Mass.; he res. in Boston, a coal dealer. Ch.:
          1 *Thomas J.*⁸, b. 29 July, 1824; d. unm.
          2 *Lucy Ann,* b. 8 June, 1824; m. 15 Aug., 1854, Horace Phil-
           brook, b. 20 Nov., 1820; bank clerk, Boston; s. p.
          3 *Sarah E.,* b. 2 Dec., 1833; m. Franklin Smith; one child.
      ix Antipas, b. Jan., 1800; d. in Plymouth, Mass.; m. Mercy S.,
        dau. of Seth Morton of Plymouth; he is interred in the famous
        old burying-ground there. Ch., born in Plymouth:
          1 *Antipas*⁸, b. in 1828.
          2 *Mary Ann,* b. in 1830.
432   x Lincoln, b. 22 Nov., 1801.
      xi Sophia, b. Sept., 1804; d. unm., in Boston, 29 Oct., 1830.
      xii Thomas J., b. 14 Aug., 1806 (Morse also says " 1805 "); d. ——
      ——; m. 21 April, 1831, Eliza A. Cowden of Boston; res.
      Boston. Ch.:
          1 *James Henry*⁸, b. 21 Feb., 1832.
          2 *Thomas Dexter,* b. 24 March, 1834.
          3 *Eliza Ann,* b. 23 June, 1836; m. Hosea Tarbell; res. Boston.
           Ch. (Tarbell): Ann B.⁹, b. 4 May, 1859.
          4 *Nahum G.,* b. 30 July, 1837; d. in Boston, 7 May, 1840.
          5 *Levi L.,* b. 13 Feb., 1841.
          6 *Mary F.,* b. 28 Aug., 1845.
          7 *Andrew B.,* b. 29 April, 1847; d. 26 Dec., 1847.
433 xiii Dexter, b. 24 Sept., 1808.

184   SARAH⁶, daughter of Capt. Edmund⁵ and Sarah (Lyscom) Brigham; born in Westboro, Mass., 15 March, 1765; married
in 1784, Gen. Daniel, son of John Reed; born 1761; died in Wardsboro, Vt., 31 Aug., 1845. He resided in Wardsboro and was in
the Revolutionary War and was a General in the Militia of Vt.

Children (Reed), born in Wardsboro:
    i Joseph⁷, b. 14 May, 1784; d. 2 Nov., 1849.
    ii Davis, b. 17 April, 1786; res. Wardsboro, and had 3 ch.
    iii Alexander H., b. 16 June, 1804; m. (1) Serena Gray; m. (2)
      Eunice Melvin. Ch. (by 1st wife):
        1 *Cordelia*⁸; 2 *Alexander;* 3 *Charles;* 4 *Andrew;* 5 *Henry.*
    iv Elijah.

185   DEA. LYSCOM⁶, son of Capt. Edmund⁵ and Sarah (Lys-
com) Brigham; born in Westboro, Mass., 19 May, 1769; died in
Shutesbury, Mass., 24 Aug., 1845; married (1), 29 Nov., 1792,
Martha, daughter of Benjamin Fay of Westboro; born there, 5
April, 1775; died in Shutesbury, 9 Feb., 1818; married (2) Betsey
(Hammond) Hoar, a widow.

He resided for a time in Pelham, Mass., thence to Shutesbury,
Was a deacon of the Baptist church and a very religious man; engaged in farming. He was named in his father's will as one of the
4 sons to share in the Captain's wardrobe.

Children (by first wife), the 2 elder born in Westboro, the next 3 in Pelham:
434   i Curtis[7], b. 21 May, 1793.
      ii Martha.
      iii Ebenezer, d. æ. 17.
435   iv Benjamin Fay, b. 25 Aug., 1800.
      v Stillman, d. y., unm.
Children (by second wife), born in Shutesbury:
436   vi Hubbard Hammond, b. 31 Oct., 1819.

186   CAPT. PIERPONT[6], son of Capt. Edmund[5] and Elizabeth (Bevel) Brigham; born in Westboro, Mass., 16 Sept., 1780; died in Westboro, 6 Oct., 1836; married Anna, daughter of John Warren of Westboro.

He was a captain in the War of 1812. He settled on a farm in the northeast part of Westboro, the homestead of Capt. Edmund. He was joint executor of his father's will with his brother Dexter, and they divided the larger part of the estate between them.

Children, born in Westboro:
      i Anna E.[7], d. 15 June, 1895; m. 17 April, 1826, Charles Brigham of Grafton, Mass., 409.
      ii Martha W., b. 3 April, 1813; m. Dexter Brigham, 433.

187   BETSEY[6], daughter of Capt. Edmund[5] and Elizabeth (Bevel) Brigham; born in Westboro, Mass., 7 May, 1782; died in Whitingham, Vt., 20 Apr., 1880; married (1) Capt. Asa Godfrey; born in Westboro, 30 May, 1786; died 15 Dec., 1842; married (2) Hezekiah Murdock, who died 7 Aug., 1864, æ. 88.

She resided in Whitingham, Vt., after her marriage. She is the "Betsey" mentioned in her father's will, and was of a very lively disposition and considered "good company." She said once, "You can't throw a stone in Westboro, Northboro, or Southboro, but you'll hit a Fay or a Brigham." Her nephew, H. W. Brigham, was afflicted at one time with a compound fracture of the arm. The doctor, after an examination, stated that there was proud flesh in the arm. Aunt Godfrey remarked: "You never saw a Brigham who didn't have 'proud flesh.'"

Children (Godfrey), probably born in Whitingham:
      i Elizabeth B.[7], b. 21 March, 1811; d. 13 Feb., 1831, unm.
      ii Asa Augustus, b. 2 Feb., 1813; d. 30 May, 1840; m. 6 Jan., 1833, Anna D. Foster.
      iii Mary Augusta, b. 2 Feb., 1813; m. 27 Nov., 1838, David Barker, b. 8 Sept., 1807; d. 8 June, 1854; res. Whitingham. Ch. (Barker):
            1 *Olive E.*[8], b. 6 Oct., 1839.
            2 *Asa A.,* b. 24 Sept., 1841.
            3 *Charles A.,* b. 30 Oct., 1842.

188   ELI[6], son of Capt. Edmund[5] and Elizabeth (Bevel) Brigham, born in Westboro, Mass., 31 July, 1784; died in Sterling, Mass., 30 Oct., 1865; married in 1810, Polly, daughter of Peter Fay; born in Southboro, Mass., 15 Oct., 1791; died 29 Dec., 1876.

He was a farmer. He resided first in Bolton, Mass., and then moved to Sterling. In his father's will he was left $400 in money and the privilege of keeping his clothes in the house until his marriage.

Children:
    i Edmund Fay[7], b. 6 April, 1812; d. 24 Dec., 1812.
437 ii Edmund Fay, b. 28 Oct., 1813.
    iii Parkman, b. 23 Feb., 1816; d. unm., 5 May, 1868.
    iv Mary E., b. 16 Dec., 1818; d. unm., 18 Sept., 1873.
    v Peter Fay, b. 14 June, 1821; d. unm., 28 Nov., 1900; was an honorable citizen of Sterling.
    vi Eli, b. 28 April, 1823; d. 16 Sept., 1824.
    vii Laura A., b. 15 Jan., 1826; d. 24 June, 1826.
    viii Eli, b. 14 July, 1828; d. 8 March, 1832.
    ix Jane M., b. 16 April, 1832; d. unm., 1 Feb., 1903.
    x Harriet A., b. 6 June, 1834; d. 1 March, 1837.

189   DEXTER[6], son of Capt. Edmund[5] and Elizabeth (Bevel) Brigham; born in Westboro, Mass., 25 May, 1786; died there, 22 Dec., 1870; married (1), 28 March, 1816, Catherine, daughter of John Warren of Westboro; born 7 Sept., 1792; died 13 Nov., 1825; married (2), 1 Jan., 1827, Mary Ann, daughter of Willard Gould of Westboro; born 24 Jan., 1804; died 22 Aug., 1889.

He was in Capt. Pierpont Brigham's company in the War of 1812. Was a trader and inn-holder, in the old stage-coach days, in Westboro. Was joint executor of his father's will with his brother Pierpont, and the larger part of the estate was inherited by them. He retired from business a number of years before his death; was a man of capacity for affairs, with a wide reputation for skill as an inn-keeper.

Children (by first wife), born in Westboro:
438 i Catherine Warren[7], b. 11 Dec., 1816.
439 ii Dexter, b. 23 Jan., 1819.
    iii Angeline, b. 31 July, 1821; d. 18 July, 1822.
440 iv Angeline, b. 27 Jan., 1824.
Children (by second wife), born in Westboro:
441 v Mary Ann, b. 6 Dec., 1829.
442 vi Achsah Elizabeth, b. 10 April, 1832.
443 vii Charles Edmund, b. 3 July, 1834.
    viii Henry Pierpont, b. 13 Oct., 1838; d. unm., 18 April, 1896; was in business in N. Y. and Boston.
    ix Francis Augustus, b. 23 May, 1841; d. 28 Dec., 1841.
444 x Sarah Louisa, b. 13 Jan., 1845.
    xi Emma Augusta, b. 24 June, 1849; d. unm., 20 Aug., 1875.

190 LIEUT. WILLIAM[6], son of Capt. William[5] and Rebecca (Ball) Brigham; born in Marlboro, Mass., 27 Feb., 1761; died in Southboro, Mass., 20 March, 1834; married Sara Baker, who died his widow, at Southboro, 14 March, 1850, æ. 82.

Children, born in Southboro:
   i Sally[7], b. 1 Oct., 1787; d. 11 Sept., 1823; m. Lieut. Larkin Newton; res. Southboro.
445 ii Baker, b. 9 Jan., 1792.

191 REBECCA[6], daughter of Capt. William[5] and Rebecca (Ball) Brigham; born in Marlboro, Mass., 1 Feb., 1763; married, 27 Feb., 1781, Ephraim, son of Silas Jewell of Stow, Mass.; born 19 Aug., 1760; died in Kirtland, O., 13 July, 1845.

Children (Jewell):
   i Hollis[7], b. ————————, 1781; d. in Georgia, Vt.
   ii Ephraim, b. 23 May, 1783; res. Oberlin, O.
   iii Willard, b. 15 July, 1785; res. St. Albans, Vt.
   iv Samuel, b. 26 Aug., 1792; res. St. Albans Bay, Vt.
   v Lydia, b. 2 April, 1795; m. Elbridge Brigham, son of 211.
   vi Martha, b. ————————, 1796; d. unm., 22 Oct., 1836.
   vii William, b. ————————, 1798; d. 12 Feb., 1809.
   viii Ira M., b. 5 July, 1803; res. Kirtland, O.
   ix Eurata, b. ————————, 1807; d. 5 Feb., 1852; m. Reuben Fuller.
   Ch. (Fuller):
     1 *Esther*[8]; 2 *Lydia;* 3 *Sidney;* 4 *Marietta;* 5 *Martha;* 6 *Francis;* 7 *Franklin;* 8 *Anna;* 9 *Amelia;* 10 *Sophia;* 11 *Eurata.*

192 COL. EPHRAIM[6], son of Capt. William[5] and Lydia (Chamberlain) Brigham; born in Marlboro, Mass., 9 Oct., 1771; died in Saxonville, Mass., 13 Sept., 1847; married (1), 3 Nov., 1794, Lucy, daughter of Peter and Levina (Howe) Rice; born 21 Dec., 1774; died 20 Feb., 1814; married (2), 15 March, 1815, Mary, daughter of Daniel Hubbard of Leicester, Mass., born 8 Feb., 1789; died his widow, in Saxonville, Aug., 1870.

He was a resident of Marlboro, Sudbury and Saxonville, Mass., at different times during his life. In Marlboro he was for some time town treasurer and in 1808, '24 and '25 he served as selectman. Elected general, but declined to qualify. Was one of the leading men of his day. He deeded Brigham Cemetery to the town of Marlboro, in 1808.

Children (by first wife), who appear all to have been born in Marlboro:
446 i William C.[7], b. 7 Aug., 1795.
447 ii Matthias, b. 29 Nov., 1796.
448 iii Lucy, b. 11 March, 1798.
449 iv Ephraim, b. 21 Oct., 1799.
450 v Harriet, b. 14 March, 1801.
451 vi Sidney, b. 28 Dec., 1802.

452 vii Elijah, b. 17 Nov., 1804.
453 viii Peter, b. 18 Sept., 1806.
454   ix Lydia, b. 2 Jan., 1809.
       x Sophia, b. 5 Dec., 1811; d. in Saxonville, 17 June, 1883; m.
          26 March, 1830, Josiah Stone of Saxonville; a farmer, b. 28
          Oct., 1801; d. 6 Sept., 1881. Ch. (Stone), b. in Saxonville:
          1 *Elizabeth*, b. 25 Dec., 1830; m. John A. D. Gross; res.
          Newton Centre, Mass.
          2 *Martha E.*, b. 17 March, 1838; unm.; res. Newton Centre.
          3 *Caroline B.*, b. 3 March, 1839; d. 3 June, 1846.
          4 *Eugene.*
          5 *Josiah Eugene*, b. 8 May, 1847; d. at Nogales, Mexico (where
          he was U. S. Consul), 11 July, 1893.
      Children (by second wife), born in Marlboro:
       xi Mary H., b. 27 April, 1816; d. unm., 30 March, 1837.
455 xii Jane E., b. 20 Dec., 1818.
     xiii Caroline C., b. 22 Dec., 1821; d. Oct., 1897; m. 17 Jan., 1843,
          William, son of Paul A. Ingraham of Peacham, Vt.; was a
          retired merchant in Watertown, Mass.; 25 years town clerk,
          selectman, and 2 years representative. Ch. (Ingraham):
          1 *Ralph Waldo*, b. 19 Oct., 1845.
          2 *Isabel Frances,* b. 10 Sept., 1849; m. 26 Sept., 1875, Edward
          C. Graves of Boston. Ch. (Graves): Chester C.*, b. 18 July,
          1878.
          3 *Alice Choate*, b. 25 May, 1856; m. Edwin F. Fearing of New-
          ton, Mass. Ch. (Fearing): William I.*, b. 23 June, 1888.
      xiv Charles C., b. 9 April, 1824; d. 3 Oct., 1826.
456   xv Charles F., b. 5 June, 1829.
457 xvi Lucius L., b. 1 Sept., 1832.

193   WILLARD*, son of Capt. William[5] and Lydia (Chamberlain) Brigham; born in Marlboro, Mass., 18 June, 1775; died in
Rindge, N. H., 7 Feb., 1843; married in 1806, Abigail, daughter
of David and Elizabeth (Foye) Munroe; born in Lexington, Mass.,
10 July, 1771; died in Rindge, 10 Feb., 1843. He settled in
Rindge, in 1821, in the south part of the town. Was an upright
man and highly respected.

Children, born in Marlboro:
458   i Abigail', b. 22 May, 1807.
459   ii Sarah Foye, b. 5 May, 1809.
460 iii Willard Chamberlain, b. 10 April, 1811.

194   SOPHIA*, daughter of Capt. William[5] and Lydia (Chamberlain) Brigham; born in Marlboro, Mass., 12 June, 1784; died
in Montpelier, Vt., 1855; married (third wife), 8 Oct., 1822, Hon.
Jeduthun Loomis, born in Tolland, Conn., 5 Jan., 1779; died in
Montpelier, Vt., 12 Nov., 1843.

He studied law and settled in Montpelier, 1805, where was selectman, 1813 and 1814; Judge of Probate. He was continually
in office from 1807 until death. Was twice married before his

Monument to Colonel Ephraim Brigham
In Brigham Cemetery, Marlboro; erected by Lucius L. Brigham of Worcester

Brigham marriage, and had two sons by his second wife, (Charity Scott of Peacham, Vt.), Dr. Gustavus H. and Chauncey.*

Children (Loomis), born in Montpelier:
   i Charity[7], m. Charles Dana of Woodstock, Vt. Ch. (Dana):
     1 (Dr.) Charles[8], of 53 W. 53d St., N. Y. City, a leading nerve specialist of international reputation.
     2 John C., Public Librarian, Newark, N. J.
     Also three other sons, names unknown.
   ii Rebecca, m. Joseph Prentiss, moved to Winona, Minn.
   iii Charles, res. Cincinnati, O.

195 EBENEZER[6], son of Elijah[5] and Ruth (Taylor) Brigham; born in Southboro, Mass., 5 April, 1768; died in Southboro, 26 Feb., 1852; married (1) Betsey Champney, who died 22 June, 1799; married (2) Elizabeth (Rice) Wilder; who died 22 Feb., 1827, æ. 65; married (3) Molly Brigham, (dau. of 71), his cousin, who survived him. He resided in Southboro.

Children (by first wife), b. in Southboro:
461   i Samuel[7], b. 23 Oct., 1789.
    ii Betsey, b. 28 Feb., 1792; d. unm., æ. 28.
Children (by second wife), born in Southboro:
462 iii Curtis, b. 17 March, 1801.
463 iv Dana, b. — Oct., 1802.
    v Elijah, d. unm., æ. about 40.

196 SYLVESTER[6], son of Elijah[5] and Ruth (Taylor) Brigham; born in Southboro, Mass., 16 Jan., 1771; died in Southboro, 24 Nov., 1858; married ———— Patty Nichols, who died 22 May, 1836, æ. 62. He resided in Southboro.

Children, born in Southboro:
464   i Dennis[7], b. 10 Dec., 1795.
    ii Emily, b. 29 Jan., 1797; m. Newell Bellows; res. Westboro.
465 iii William Ashbel, b. 24 Oct., 1798.
466 iv Lowell, b. 6 Dec., 1800.
467   v Trowbridge, b. 27 Sept., 1802.
    vi Sophia, b. 17 Sept., 1804; m. (1) Edmund Whipple; m. (2) Dea. Tuttle; res. Littleton.
    vii Lyman, b. 29 March, 1806; d. 3 Nov., 1808.
   viii Ruth, b. 26 Feb., 1809; d. 31 Oct., 1827, æ. 18.
    ix Harriet, b. 11 April, 1811; m. James Williams; res. Southboro.
    x Otis, b. 13 July, 1813; d. 28 Nov., 1836, æ. 23.

197 DINAH[6], daughter of Elijah[5] and Ruth (Taylor) Brigham; born in Southboro, Mass., 5 Nov., 1772; died there or in Wendell, Mass., Sept., 1857; married Joseph Williams of Southboro and Wendell.

* Vide Thompson's *Hist. Montpelier*, pp. 208 et seq.

Children (Williams):
  i Lincoln⁷, b. in Southboro.
  ii Martha.
  iii Avis.
  iv Joseph.
  v Elijah Brigham.
  vi Hollis.
  vii Louvinia.
  viii James, b. 24 Aug., 1812; d. 21 Dec., 1869; m. 1847, Maria, dau.
    Eben Cutler of Shrewsbury, Mass.; res. Worcester, where a
    real estate dealer. Ch.:
      1 *Ella M.⁸,* 24 July, 1849; m. David L. Fiske of Grafton, Mass.;
        she grad. Boston School of Oratory. Ch. (Fiske): i Mavida⁹;
        ii Rebecca C.; iii Georgiana K.
  ix William.
  x Moses.
  xi Nancy.

198   CAPT. ELIJAH⁶, son of Elijah⁵ and Ruth (Taylor)
Brigham; born in Southboro, Mass., 19 July, 1776; died there,
8 May, 1861; married (1) (pub. Charlestown, Mass., 27 May,
1803), Sophia, daughter of Elijah and Mary (Allen) Houghton;
born in Lancaster, Mass., 15 June, 1775; died 25 Jan., 1816;
married (2) Jane Fisk, who died March, 1852.

From 1803 to 1813, he kept a store and tavern in Southboro;
he afterward kept the "Black Horse" tavern in Union Street,
Boston, and was engaged for some time in the "forwarding"
business. He was in the war of 1812.

Children (by first wife), born in Southboro:
  i Seleucus⁷, b. 21 Aug., 1805; d. 31 March, 1806.
  ii Mary Sophia, b. 27 Jan., 1809; was a teacher in Boston; d. unm.,
    30 Dec., 1888.
  iii Adaliza, b. 16 Oct., 1811; d. unm., 21 Nov., 1835.
468   iv Elijah Sparhawk, b. 20 April, 1813
  v Angeline A., b. Nov., 1819.
  vi Rosalinda M., twin to Angeline. These ladies were for many
    years prominent educators in Boston, retiring some years ago
    to their home in the country, Chichester, N. H., where they reside
    in 1906.

199   TROWBRIDGE⁶, son of Elijah⁵ and Ruth (Taylor)
Brigham; born in Southboro, Mass., 17 Sept., 1778; died, probably
in St. Albans, Vt., 21 July, 1836; married (1) in Southboro, 12
Jan., 1803, Asenath Eaton, born 8 Oct., 1775; died 21 May, 1821;
married (2) in St. Albans, 6 Dec., 1822, Mary Caldwell, born
10 Oct., 1782, in New Hampshire; died 22 Nov., 1836. Resided
in St. Albans.

Children (by first wife), probably born in St. Albans:
  i Hartwell⁷, b. 30 Aug., 1803; d. in Waddington, N. Y., 21 Jan.,
    1831; res. there; m. (1) Oct., 1825, in Fairfield, Vt., Delia

Wright, who d. there, 8 Sept., 1828; m. (2) 4 Jan., 1832, in Waddington, Sarah McDowell, who d. there, 13 July, 1839. Ch.:

1 *Mary Elizabeth*[8], b. 21 Jan., 1827, in Canada; m. in Wisconsin, Oct., 1854, David Bailey; she d. Oct., 1855, in Davenport, Ia.

2 *Louisa Dorinda*, d.

3 *Jane Maria*, b. 26 Feb., 1828; d. in Waddington, 1850.

469   ii Emily, b. 1 Jan., 1805.

  iii Dorinda, b. 17 April, 1808; no further reported.

470   iv Stowell, b. 1 Aug., 1809.

  v Fanny, b. 4 May, 1812; res. in Niles, Mich., unm., about 1857; aided Morse in rescuing the records of her family.

Children (by second wife), born in St. Albans:

  vi Almira A., b. 14 Aug., 1825; d. 12 Sept., 1825.

  vii Miranda A., b. 8 Jan., 1827; d. 19 April, 1827.

200   LINCOLN[6], son of Elijah[5] and Ruth (Taylor) Brigham; born in Southboro, Mass., 17 Jun, 1780; died in Troy, N. Y., 18 Nov., 1831; married 13 June, 1802, Lucy, daughter of Elisha and Hannah (Flagg) Forbes of Westboro, Mass.; born 3 June, 1779, died in Worcester, Mass., 21 Oct., 1837. She was admitted to the church in Arlington, Mass., in 1810; dismissed to the church in Cambridgeport, in 1827. He resided in Cambridge, Mass., where was selectman in 1823.

Children, born in Cambridge:

  i Lucy Maria[7], b. 28 April, 1803; d. s. p., in Newton, Mass., 19 Sept., 1882; m. (1) 11 Sept., 1834, Rev. David Peabody of Lynn, afterwards Professor of Rhetoric and Belles-Lettres at Dartmouth College, where he d. 17 Oct., 1839; m. (2) Rev. Daniel L. Furber of Newton Centre, Mass.

471   ii Joseph Lincoln, b. 15 Nov., 1804.

472   iii Erastus Forbes, b. 26 Aug., 1807.

  iv Elijah Dana, b. 17 Aug., 1813; d. s. p., 6 April, 1868; was a merchant in Boston for a number of years. President of the Metropolitan Ry.; Commissioner General of Mass., during the Civil War, with rank of Capt., and Government Purchasing Commissioner in Boston as Brevet Major (see *N. E. Hist. Geneal. Reg.*, vol. xxii. p. 468).

473   v Lucy Forbes, b. 9 Sept., 1818.

474   vi Lincoln Flagg, b. 4 Oct., 1819.

201   HEPSIBAH[6], daughter of Elijah[5] and Ruth (Taylor) Brigham; born in Southboro, Mass., 7 May, 1782; married 6 Sept., 1801, Caleb son of Zaccheus Witherbee; born in Southboro, 3 April, 1779; moved to Marlboro in 1806, where he died 3 Jan., 1853.

Children (Witherbee), born in Marlboro, except the 2 eldest born in Southboro:

  i Jabez S.[7], b. 12 Sept., 1802; m. Harriet Brigham[8], 391.

  ii Elijah Brigham, b. 19 July, 1804; m. Louisa Brigham, dau. of 210.

  iii Nancy M., b. 3 Dec., 1806; d. 11 Nov., 1807.

  iv Nancy M., b. 19 Oct., 1808; d. unm., 21 Nov., 1829.

v Nahum, b. 12 April, 1811; m. 30 April, 1835, ——————.
vi Dennis F., b. 25 July, 1813; d. 1857; m. 20 May, 1835, Charlotte, dau. of Capt. John and Mary (Brigham) Stevens, and granddau. of 162.
vii John Brigham, b. 10 June, 1816.
viii Sarah, b. 26 Oct., 1818; d. 27 Sept., 1840.
ix William Wallace, b. 21 Feb., 1821; m. Elizabeth G. Brigham, dau. of 388.

202   MARTHA⁶, daughter of Elijah⁵ and Ruth (Taylor) Brigham; born in Southboro, Mass., 6 June, 1790; died 17 Aug., 1829; married 1807, Dea. Stephen R., son of Roger and Elizabeth (Rice) Phelps; born 3 Dec., 1788; he married (2), Elizabeth Brigham, (dau. of 162), and widow of Abraham Gates. He resided in Marlboro and was deacon in the West Parish church.

Children (Phelps):
i Nancy⁷, b. 19 Feb., 1807; m. John Cathell; res. Cincinnati, O.
ii Charles, b. 27 June, 1808; m. 1834, Mary R. Wilson; res. Marlboro.
iii Henry Roger, b. 25 Jan. (*Hist. Marl.* says " June "), 1810; m. Harriet Davis; res. Syracuse, N. Y.
iv Winslow, b. 20 Oct., 1811; d. 12 Feb., 1826.
v Martha, b. 17 Sept., 1813; m. William Wilson; res. Marlboro.
vi John, b. 28 May, 1817; m. 9 Oct., 1838, Sarah Charlotte Wilson; res. Marlboro, where was manufacturer, several years town clerk, and representative.

203   TAYLOR⁶, son of Elijah⁵ and Ruth (Taylor) Brigham; born in Southboro, Mass., 29 April, 1793; died there, 4 Feb., 1870; married (1) Arethusa Fay; married (2) 11 March, 1827, Ann Jacobs of Cambridge, Mass. He resided in Southboro.

Child (by first wife), born in Southboro:
i Edward A.⁷, b. 9 Jan., 1817; d. 27 Dec., 1876, s. p.; m. 9 Nov., 1843, Drusilla D. Whitney; res. Northboro. They adopted *Clarissa Augusta⁹*, dau. of Jonathan L. and Arethusa⁸ (Brigham) Patch, and granddau. of 483.
Children (by second wife):
ii Arethusa Ann, m. Dexter Newton of Southboro, who d. in 1890. Ch. (Newton), b. in Southboro:
  1 *Francis D.⁸*, m. (1) Ella A. Strickland, who d. s. p.; m. (2) Ellen J. Miller. Ch.: Roland S.⁹
  2 *Ida L.*, d. y.
  3 *Ada M.*, living, unm.
  4 *Cora A.*, living, unm.
iii Georgiana Baxter, m. Lyman Newton of Southboro, who d. in 1902. Ch. (Newton), b. in Southboro:
  1 *Edward E.⁸*, m. (1) Mary Chandler; m. (2) —————— res. Kansas City, Mo.; 3 children.
  2 *Charles R.* (d.). Ch.: Charles L.⁹ (d); Chester.
  3 *Lillian*, res. in Southboro, unm.
iv Lucretia L., res. unm., in Southboro, in 1903.
v Charles W., d. at Charlestown, Mass., Nov., 1853, æ. 18.

vi " Halloway " Baxter, b. 2 March, 1840 (changed name to *Henry*);
m. ————. Ch.:
    1 *Ella*[8].
vii George Taylor, b. 25 Feb., 1844; m. Emma Hayes; res. in Union,
N. H. Ch ·
    1 *Chesley*[8].
viii Martha, d. 27 July, 1853, æ. 6.

204   EPHRAIM[6], son of ,Aaron[5] and Elizabeth (Brown) Brigham; born in Grafton, Mass., 2 March, 1746; died in Colebrook, N. H., 26 Feb., 1802; married Sarah ————; born 22 Dec., 1747; she married (2) 21 June, 1803, David Tyler, from the vicinity of Piermont, N. H. He moved to Colebrook, N. H.

Children, the 2 elder born in Grafton, the others in Colebrook:
475   i Aaron[7], b. 29 March, 1771-2.
      ii Betty, b. 26 Feb., 1773-4.
      iii Sarah, b. 23 June, 1776; d. unm., in Lempster, N. H.
      iv Elisha, b. 3 July, 1778; d. Jan., 1779.
      v Louisa,, b. 21 Dec., 1779.
      vi Ephraim, b. 13 March, 1781-2; d. Jan., 1782-3.
      vii Dorothy, b. 10 Dec., 1783.
      viii Susannah, b. 10 May, 1785; d. May, 1785.
476   ix Thomas, b. 7 July, 1786.
      x Rebekah, b. 26 Aug., 1788; d. 28 April, 1804.
      xi Ethelinda, b. 19 July, 1794; m. Jesse Tyler, b. in Piermont, N. H.,
      5 March, 1785. Ch. (Tyler):
          1 *Simon*[8]*;* 2 *Hazel;* 3 *Hosea B.*, b. 1816, living in Alderbrook,
          N. H., in 1896; had a son James[9]; 4 *James;* 5 *Martin* (perhaps of Lunenburg, Vt.); 6 *Milo;* 7 *Pierpont;* 8 *Alvira;* 9
          Annie.

205   LIEUT. EZEKIEL[6], son of Ezekiel[5] and Martha (Bigelow) Brigham; born in Grafton, Mass., 30 March, 1755; died there, 14 Dec., 1828; married 5 Feb., 1783-4, Patience Gowing, who died, his widow, 5 Nov., 1834. He settled in Grafton, probably on land drawn in the right of his grandfather Nathan, who was one of the 40 proprietors of that town by consent of the General Court, in 1727. The male line is extinct.

Children, born in Grafton:
      i Martin Greenleaf[7], b. 22 Feb., 1784; d. 14 April, 1790.
      ii Betsey, b. 6 July, 1785; d. unm., 10 April, 1838.
      iii Polly, b. 23 April, 1787; d. in Oxford, Mass., 11 Oct., 1866; m.
      26 March, 1825, (second wife), Capt. John, son of Joseph Hurd;
      b. in Oxford, 20 May, 1779; d. 30 April, 1866; was Capt. of
      Militia and deacon in the Cong'l church; m. for his first wife,
      Mary Stone, by whom a family. Ch., by second wife (Hurd),
      born in Oxford:
          1 *Caroline P.*[8], b. 10 Sept., 1827; d. in Oxford, 2 March, 1860; m.
          1 Sept., 1849, A. Bradford, son of Bradford Hudson, b. in
          Oxford, 4 June, 1826; he m. (2) Mrs. Cordelia (Davis) Sumner; was in the Civil War. Ch. (Hudson). i Oliver B.[9]; ii
          William W. of Grafton.

iv Ezekiel, b. 18 Feb., 1789; d. ——————; probably s. p.; m. Susan, dau. of Capt. Ephraim and Susanna (Brigham) Goulding; born 25 March, 1793.
v Oliver M., b. 24 Dec., 1793; d. unm., 28 Feb., 1861.
vi Abijah, b. 20 Aug., 1795; d. 10 March, 1813, æ. 18.
vii Diadema, b. 27 July, 1801; d. unm.

206   DR. ISAAC[6], son of Ezekiel[5] and Martha (Bigelow) Brigham; born in Grafton, Mass., 30 May, 1757; died in Milford, Mass., 12 June, 1825; married 6 April, 1786, Elizabeth, daughter of Rev. Amariah Frost, of Milford; born 6 Sept., 1754; died there 3 Jan., 1829.

He probably went to Milford after his father-in-law's death, in 1792, and lived in the parsonage; was graduated from Brown University, in 1804, A. M., and M. D. in 1824; practiced many years in Plainfield, N. H. Probably was the one who marched on the Lexington alarm in Capt. Luke Drury's Co. He seems to have remained in the army and was a sergeant in 1779. Line is now extinct.

Children, uncertain where they were born:
 i Horace[7], b. 1787; d. 1810; was very promising; in the employ of Maj. John Claflin, who esteemed him so highly that he named his son, who became the merchant prince in New York, Horace Brigham Claflin.
 ii Isaac, b. 1794; d. 13 March, 1858; m. 3 Oct., 1830, Wealthy Donovan, who d. 9 Feb., 1860, æ. 54; was for many years the town sexton in Milford, and lived in the old parsonage at West and Congress streets. Ch., b. in Milford:
  1 *Elizabeth Frost*[8], b. 9 Sept., 1831; d. 17 Dec., 1849.
  2 *Horace*, b. 16 April, 1834; d. 4 March, 1855.
  3 *Emily Alice*, b. 19 May, 1838; d. 19 Aug., 1850.

207   SARAH[6], daughter of Elisha[5] and Sarah Brigham; born in Grafton, Mass., 29 April, 1767; died there, 6 June, 1826; married 18 April, 1782, Zebulon Daniels, born in Medway, Mass., 1758; died in Grafton, 14 Feb., 1825.

Children (Daniels), born in Grafton:
 i Lusiny[7], b. 1 May, 1783; m. P. Parker, and d. 1825.
 ii Otis, b. 28 Sept., 1786; d. 1869.
 iii Philena, b. 20 Sept., 1788; d. 1878.
 iv Emory, b. 10 March, 1792; d. in Ohio, 1851; m. Mary Hastings.
 v Sarah, b. 27 March, 1796; d. 6 Sept., 1870; m. A. Crosby.
 vi Charles, b. 16 Aug., 1798; d. 11 Sept., 1874; m. Eliza Hastings. Ch.:
  1 (Gen.) *Horace*[8] of R. I.; 2 *Lewis*; 3 *Henry* of Troy, N. Y.; 4 *Joseph*; 5 *Louisa*, m. Charles Taft; 6 *Elisha*; 7 *Mary*, m. Sumner Fifield; 8 *Martha*; 9 *Aaron*; 10 *Lucy*; 11 *Marcus*.
 vii Nancy, b. 26 Feb., 1801; d. 10 Oct., 1834.
 viii John, b. 22 Nov., 1806; m. Nancy Chase.

208 ITHAMAR[6], son of Capt. Ithamar[5] and Ruth (Ward) Brigham; born in Marlboro, Mass., 7 Nov., 1758; died there, 12 March, 1836; married Catherine Barnes, born 27 Jan., 1765; died 13 April, 1804. He resided in Marlboro, and was selectman in 1801, 1806, 1809 and 1811-1813. Probably ,was private in Capt. Wm. Morse's Co. of, Volunteers, and marched to reinforce army under Gen. Gates, Oct. 1777.

Children, born in Marlboro:

  i (Dr.) Levi[7], b. May 1, 1784; d. 8 Dec., 1818; res. Raymond, Me.; m. ———————. Ch.:
   1' *Catherine*[8], m. Orin H. Newton, who d.; res. Clinton.
   2 *Joseph B.*, res., a merchant, in Boston.
477 ii Aaron, b. 29 Dec., 1785.
  iii Moses, b. 22 July, 1788; d. 2 May, 1875; m. Susan, dau. of. Joel Fosgate of Berlin, Mass.; she d. 19 Sept., 1885, æ. 90; res. on a part of the homestead of Thomas, the son of Nathan, in Marlboro. Ch., b. in Marlboro:
   1 *Susan F.*[8], b. 1 Jan., 1816; d. 28 Oct., 1853; m. 20 Sept., 1838, John Holyoke, and res. Marlboro. Ch. (Holyoke): i Arvilla M.[9], b. 25 April, 1840; d. 12 Oct., 1840; ii Helen M., b. 18 Oct., 1841; iii Martha E., b. 20 Feb., 1850.
   2 *Lucy M.*, b. 31 Oct., 1820; m. H. S. Bowman; res. Marlboro.
  iv Jonas, b. 29 Aug., 1790; became an officer in the U. S. Army in the War of 1812, and d. 9 Feb., 1822, in New York.
478 v Eli, b. 18 July, 1794.
479 vi Abel, b. 13 Feb., 1797.
  vii Judith, b. 5 Oct., 1799; d. 21 Oct., 1864; m. Joel, son of Nathan Bullard of Medway, b. June, 1794; d. in Berlin, 8 Nov., 1850; a blacksmith in Berlin. Ch. (Bullard):
   1 *Martha S.*[8], b. 15 Aug., 1825; d. 27 Oct., 1898.
   2 *Henry M.*, b. 22 Aug., 1826; d. 9 May, 1860.
   3 *Harriet H.*, b. 26 Sept., 1831; d. 21 Nov., 1875.
   4 *Mary C. J.*, b. 8 July, 1834; d. 10 Nov., 1882; m. Wm. R. Patch of Fitchburg. Ch. (Patch):
    i Carrie L.[9], m. Charles Woodward of Berlin.
   5 *Jane M.*, b. 23 Aug., 1836; res. unm., in Berlin; P. O. address, Northboro.
   6 *James M.*, b. 23 Aug., 1836; d. 29 April, 1893; m. Arvilla Hadley. Ch.: i Wm. S.[9]; ii Frank H.; iii Charles M., all of Greendale, Mass.

209 DANIEL[6], son of Capt. Ithamar[5] and Ruth (Ward) Brigham; born in Marlboro, Mass., 15 Nov., 1760; died 7 March, 1807; in Bridgton, Me.; married Anna Beaman of Marlboro, born 1 March, 1761, died 8 April, 1855, æ. 94. They removed to Bridgton about 1789. He had a good Revolutionary record. Was in the army in 1777, 1779, 1780, and was discharged 13 Jan., 1781. He was 5 ft. 11 in. tall, of a dark complexion.

Children, born in Bridgton:

  i Ithamar[7], b. 20 Jan., 1790; d. 2 Nov., 1858, unm.
  ii Rutha, b. 24 Sept., 1792; d. 22 July, 1822; m. Jan., 1817, Richard

Davis from New Hampshire, b. 22 July, 1791; d. 19 April, 1860; res. in Bridgton. Ch. (Davis):

    1 *Alvina⁸*, b. 14 Jan., 1818; d. 23 Aug., 1828.

    2 *Alvin*, b. 6 Aug., 1821; m. 12 Aug., 1858, Caroline, dau. of Hon. N. S. Littlefield of Bridgton; res. there.

480 iii Daniel, b. 4 June, 1794.

481 iv Aaron, b. 11 March, 1796.

     v Nancy, b. 24 Sept., 1798; d. 22 April, 1853; m. Richard Davis, widower of her sister Rutha. Ch. (Davis):

    1 *Rutha⁸*, b. 22 June, 1825; d. 29 Sept., 1827.

    2 *Richard H.*, b. 28 Jan., 1828; res. in Bridgton, unm.

    3 *Eliza J.*, b. 22 Jan., 1830; res. in Bridgton.

482 vi Henry, twin to Nancy.

210   ABNER⁶, son of Capt. Ithamar⁵ and Mary (Beaman) Brigham; born in Marlboro, Mass., 21 Dec., 1768; died in Marlboro, 4 Nov., 1828; married, 21 June, 1794, Dorothy, daughter of Peter and Sybil (Howe) Wood; born in Marlboro, 30 Nov., 1767; died there, 6 July, 1854, æ. 87. He was a farmer and resided in Marlboro.

Children, born in Marlboro:

483 i Loring⁷, b. 19 March, 1795.

   ii Alden, b. 4 May, 1797; d. 7 Sept., 1797.

484 iii Abner, b. 21 June, 1798.

   iv Nancy, b. 15 July, 1800; d. in Barre, Mass., 19 April, 1896; m. (1) 1827, John O. Sullivan, who d. s. p., 1829; m. (2) 1832, Walter Felch, who d. s. p., 1872; she res. in East Boston, Mass.

485 v Adolphus, b. 4 Dec., 1802.

   vi Louisa, b. 31 March, 1805; d. 11 Aug., 1890; m. 12 April, 1829, Hon. Elijah Brigham Witherbee, son of 201; who removed to Flint, Mich., and d. 26 Feb., 1847. Ch. (Witherbee):

    1 *Austin B.⁸*, b. 22 May, 1832; d. 2 Feb., 1871; m. 1856, Molly A. Thompson; had a family.

  vii Alden, b. 12 March, 1807; d. s. p., in Colebrook Springs, Mass., 25 Nov., 1877; m. 6 Dec., 1835, Laura Ann Brigham, dau. of 293, who d. 8 July, 1897, æ. 84; she was bed-ridden for years; he was a successful schoolteacher in the District Schools for many years; res. on a part of his gr.-grandfather's homestead, and became an authority on the cultivation of choice fruit in his neighborhood. He was an ardent spiritualist and wrote on the subject in verse and prose.

 viii Austin, twin to Alden; d. unm., 16 Jan., 1829.

211   DEA. PAUL⁶, son of Capt. Paul⁵ and Eliza (Rice) Brigham; born in Marlboro, Mass., 17 June, 1761; died in St. Albans, Vt., of apoplexy, 17 Nov., 1838; married Fanny, daughter of Elijah and Ruth (Taylor) Brigham (76), born 12 Sept., 1769, in Southboro, Mass.; died in St. Albans, 31 May, 1865.

He was a soldier of the Revolution in 1780. A selectman of Marlboro in 1801; removed to St. Albans, March, 1803, having disposed of his father's homestead which he inherited. He with his wife and Antipas Brigham, (64), were 3 of the 9 charter members of the Congregational church in St. Albans in 1803. He was 5 ft. 8 in. in height, of a dark complexion.

Children, the 4 four younger born in St. Albans, others in Marlboro:

486   i Pierpont[7], b. 2 Aug., 1785.

   ii Josiah, b. 5 Aug., 1787; d. unm., 3 March, 1810.

   iii Lovina, b. 11 April, 1789; d. unm., in St. Albans, 10 Nov., 1878.

   iv Sumner, b. 13 Dec., 1791; d. unm., 20 Dec., 1813.

   v Elbridge, b. 10 March, 1794; d. 13 Feb., 1845; m. 3 Nov., 1817, Lydia Ball Jewell, b. 2 April, 1795; d. 20 March, 1862; res. St. Albans. Ch.:

     1 *Josiah Sanford*[8], b. 15 Aug., 1818; d. unm., in Phillipsburg, Can., 10 June, 1892; a physician, grad. McGill Med. Coll.

     2 *Lincoln Sumner*, b. 14 Nov., 1821; d. unm., 3 April, 1853, in Phillipsburg.

   vi Jonah, b. 25 Jan., 1797; d. 21 July, 1799.

   vii Paul, b. 7 July, 1799; d. 25 Nov., 1803.

   viii Elijah, b. 31 July, 1801; d. 16 Nov., 1813.

   ix Elisha, b. 31 Oct., 1803; m. (1) 15 March, 1832, Nancy Jenison, who d. 23 March, 1845, in Monroe, Mich., where they removed; m. (2) 20 Jan., 1848, Mrs. E. A. Comstock, who d. 3 May, 1850; m. (3) 12 Nov., 1854, Orphia S. Curtis. Res. Ravenna, O. Ch.:

     1 *Adelia*[8], b. 14 Dec., 1833; m. June, 1854, J. W. Turner; res. Coldwater, Mich.

     2 *Edgar*, b. 10 July, 1836; d. 5 Sept., 1837

     3 *Sophia*, b. 12 April, 1837; d. 13 April, 1839.

     4 *Mary*, b. 16 Dec., 1838.

     5 *Elenora P.*, b. 30 June, 1840; d. 6 Aug., 1850.

     6 *Fanny H.*, b. 27 Jan., 1843; m. ——— Ward; res. Washington, D. C.

487   x William D., b. 14 Jan., 1806.

   xi Moses W., b. 29 Feb., 1808; d. 2 Jan., 1839, with lockjaw, in Charleston, S. C.

   xii Lummus, b. 24 July, 1810; m. Catherine Creps, who d. 24 June, 1858; res. Toledo, O. Ch.:

     1 *William B.*[8], b. Sept., 1834.

     2 *Frances L.*, m. John Worts; res. Toledo.

     3 *Frederica;* 4 *Catherine;* 5 *Sarah;* 6 *Florence;* 7 *Emma*, who d.; 8 *Julia*.

212 SAMUEL[6], son of Capt. Paul[5] and Eliza (Rice) Brigham; born in Marlboro, Mass., 14 Sept., 1762; married in 1787, Asenath, daughter of Barnabas Bailey. He resided in Berlin, Mass. He was a farmer and weaver, and invented a new shuttle.

Children, born in Berlin:

   i Elizabeth[7], b. 5 Nov., 1787; d. unm., 27 Sept., 1841.

   ii Seraphine, b. 5 June, 1789; d. in Nashua, N. H., 1870; m. Josiah Crosby, from Scotland to Berlin, where res. on Dr. Daniel Brigham's place, and d. 15 Sept., 1866, æ. 84. Ch. (Crosby), b. in Berlin:

     1 *Nancy*[8], d. y.

      2 *Josiah Quincy,* b. 28 Feb., 1830; lost an arm in the Civil
        War; afterward in Treasury Dept., Washington, D. C.; had
        res. in Stoneham, Mass.
      3 *William H.,* b. 26 Dec., 1833; proprietor of National Hotel,
        Washington, D. C.
488 iii Barnabas, b. 13 March, 1791.
    iv Sophia, b. 25 Aug., 1796; d. unm., æ. 28.
     v Eli, b. 7 Aug., 1799; d. 1832, probably in Washington, D. C.;
       m. Lucy Crosby; res. for a time in Pittsburgh, N. H. Ch.:
       1 *Lucy S.*[8], m. Andrew Madison, Washington, D. C.
       2 *Lucinda;* 3 *Romanzo;* 4 *Elizabeth,* m. ————, in Wash-
       ington, D. C.

    213   THOMAS[6], son of Capt. Paul[5] and Eliza (Rice) Brig-
ham; born in Marlboro, Mass., 25 Dec., 1765; died in Berlin,
Mass., 9 March, 1821; married 6 May, 1795, Azubah, daughter
of William Babcock; born 15 Oct., 1764; died in Berlin, 11 Oct.,
1847. He was a farmer and resided in Berlin. The male line is
extinct.

   Children, born in Berlin:
     i Paul[7], Capt. and farmer, b. 12 April, 1796; d. in Berlin, s, p.,
       24 June, 1869; m. 31 Oct., 1844, Harriet[7] (Brigham) Phelps,
       450; res. on the homestead of his father in Marlboro, and
       served in various town offices and was, for years, selectman.
489 ii Thomas, b. 17 Oct., 1797.
   iii Sybil, b. 10 May, 1799; d. unm., 4 July, 1879.
    iv Elizabeth, b. 14 Feb., 1805; d. s. p., in Northboro, 16 Sept.,
       1873; m. John F. Newton, who d. in Northboro, 7 June, 1888.
     v Azubah, b. 4 Oct., 1809; d. 1 March, 1835, unm.

    214   POLLY (MARY)[6], daughter of Col. Timothy[5] and Lydia
(Wood) Brigham; born in Northboro, Mass., 15 April, 1781; died
in Richmond, Wis., 21 Sept., 1862; married 18 April, 1802, Seth
Hill, born in Cornwall, 9 Dec., 1783; died in Richmond, 24 Nov.,
1859. He was a deacon in the Presbyterian church. She moved to
New York State and thence to Richmond, Wis.

   Children (Hill), the 3 younger born in Danby, N. Y ·
     i Sarah[7], b. 5 Feb., 1805; d. 18 Aug., 1884; m. 8 Sept., 1825,
       Stephen Bettis of Buffalo, N. Y. Ch. (Bettis):
       1 *Henry*[8], architect in Buffalo.
       2 *Addie,* m. Rev. Mr. Taylor.
     ii Mary, b. in Hamilton, N. Y., 25 April, 1807; d. 14 Oct., 1882;
       m. 28 Sept., 1828, Lyman Bradley of Spencer, N. Y. Ch.
       (Bradley):
       1 *Edwin*[8].
       2 *Augustus L.,* dentist in Spencer.
       3 *Chas. E.,* Lieut. in the Civil War.
       4 *Mary A.,* m. Dr. T. F. Bliss of Springfield, O.
   iii Esther, b. 22 Oct., 1810; m. 20 March, 1828, William Patterson
       of Richmond, Wis. Ch. (Patterson):

1 *Seth*[8], of Howard, Kan.
2 *Martin,* who was in the Civil War.
3, 4 and 5, killed in the Civil War.
iv Nancy, b. 5 Aug., 1815; d. 16 April, 1890; m. John M. Evans
of Whitewater, Wis.
v Elizabeth, b. 22 Dec., 1825; d. about 1880; m. 22 Dec., 1844,
Joseph Prentice. Ch. (Prentice):
1 *Elmina*[8], m. ———— Terry of Los Angeles, Cal.
2 *Fred F.,* res. Magnolia, Wis.

215 GARDNER[6], son of Lieut. Artemas[5] and Keziah (Rice)
Brigham; born in Northboro, Mass., 20 Feb., 1764; married Sarah
Rice, 10 April, 1785; resided in Northboro. He was probably a
private in the Revolution, in 1781.

Children, born in Northboro:
  i Betsey[7], b. 29 Jan., 1786.
490 ii Joel, b. 13 Dec., 1788.

216 JOHN[6], son of Lieut. Artemas[5] and Keziah (Rice) Brig-
ham; born in Northboro, Mass., 24 May, 1766; died in Rochester,
N. Y., æ. 63; married 21 March, 1790, Lois Fisk; resided Paxton,
Worcester County, and later, moved to New York State and west.

*Children, born in Massachusetts, except the fourth and fifth born in
Rochester:*
  ı Benjamin[7], m. Sallie Coolidge; no ch. recorded.
491 ◦ ii John Swarrow, b. 24 May, 1803.
  iii Charles.
  iv Sobeiski.
  v Pulaski.
  vi Clarissa, m. Aaron Davis. Ch. (Davis):
    1 *Edward*[8], who d. æ. 20.
    2 *Gideon,* who went to Texas before 1861.
  vii Maria, m. Jacob Forbes. Ch. (Forbes):
    1 *Mary*[8]; 2 *Horace;* 3 *Clarissa;* 4 *Levi;* 5 *Thomas.*
  viii Arethusa, m. Levi Wright. Ch. (Wright):
    1 *Charles*[8]; 2 *Stephen.*
  ix Lois, m. Samuel Waite. Ch. (Waite):
    1 *Harriet*[8]; 2 *Mary;* 3 *Oliver.*
  x Eucla, b. 1806; d. in Somnauk, Ill., Nov., 1900; m. 1831, Alvarius
    Gage. Ch. (Gage):
    1 *Sallie*[8]; 2 *Lois;* 4 *Sobeiski;* 5 *Ellen.*

217 HENRY[6], son of Lieut. Artemas[5] and Keziah (Rice)
Brigham; born in Northboro, Mass., 4 Dec., 1768; died there 20
Oct., 1853; married (1) 1793, Susanna Harrington, born 14 Feb.,
1769; died 28 Aug., 1805; married (2) 1806, Hannah Bride, born
in 1772; died 19 Oct., 1807, æ. 34 yrs. 10 mos. 24 days; married
(3) 1816, Betsey Newton, born in 1781; died in 1871, æ. 90. The
last wife resided at the old homestead in Northboro until her death.

Child (by first wife), born in Northboro:
492   i Henry[7], b. 30 Oct., 1798.
Child (by second wife), born in Northboro:
    ii Artemas, b. 29 June, 1806; d. unm., in Northboro, in 1837.
Children (by third wife), born in Northboro:
    iii Charles Edward, b. 11 March, 1817; died in Northboro, in 1891.
    iv Elizabeth Newton, b. 8 May, 1818; unm.; res. at the homestead.
    v Hannah Bride, b. 9 Sept., 1819; m. George Ball; had 5 children; res. Southboro.
    vi Susanna Harrington, b. 29 Dec. (Morse says " Sept."), 1820; m. 19 June, 1844, Stephen Hunt, Jr., b. in Northboro; perhaps they moved to Southboro. Ch. (Hunt), b. in Northboro:
      1 *Henry A.[8]*, b. 1845.
      2 *Ellen F.*, b. 1848.
      3 *Frederick S.*, b. 1849.
      4 *Arthur Brigham*, b. 19 Jan., 1858.
    vii Frederick William, b. 15 Dec., 1821; d. unm., in N., in 1885.
    viii Sarah Ann, b. 1 Dec., 1824; m. Jan., 1851, George Emerson Rice, b. in Marlboro, 29 May, 1818; she d. and he m. (2) Nov., 1863, Mary A. Allen. Ch. (Rice), b. in Marlboro:
      1 *Mary S.[8]*, b. 5 Feb., 1852.
      2 *Charles E.*, b. 16 Jan., 1854; d. 19 July, 1877.
      3 *Sarah E.*, b. 2 Sept., 1857; m. Oct., 1881, Charles H. Sloan.
      4 *Son*, b. Aug., 1862; d. 12 Oct., 1862.

218   LOVELL[6], son of Lieut. Artemas[5] and Keziah (Rice) Brigham; born in Northboro, Mass., 22 Oct., 1782; died in Worcester, Mass., 19 Feb., 1849; married, 1806, Lucy, daughter of Stephen Phelps of Marlboro, Mass., born 20 April, 1788; who died. He probably married a second time, although no record appears of such marriage. He was a farmer in Northboro and is said to have moved to West Boylston, Mass.

Children, probably born in Northboro:
    i Lucinda[7], b. 13 Sept., 1809; d. 22 March, 1810.
493   ii Stephen P., b. 11 Oct., 1810.
494   iii William Russell, b. 27 Dec., 1812.
    iv Joseph, b. 14 Oct, 1824; m. twice in W. Boylston, but names of wives not learned.

219   MOSES[6], son of Lieut. Artemas[5] and Keziah (Rice) Brigham; born in Northboro, Mass., 21 April, 1786; died 25 Nov., 1874, æ. 88; married Mary[6], daughter of Fortunatus Brigham, (168), born in Marlboro, 3 Nov., 1783; died 13 June, 1869. He resided in Binghamton, N. Y.

Children, born in Binghamton:
    i Eliza[7], b. 7 Aug., 1807.
    ii Elmer W., b. 29 May, 1809; d. in Binghamton, 18 March, 1895; m. in 1833, Ruth Ann Robie, b. in N. Hampshire, 1813; d. in Binghamton, 12 March, 1899. He was the first brick manfr. in Binghamton, and was a contractor and builder, also. He and his wife each lived to be eighty-five years old. Of their eleven chil-

Colonel Ephraim Brigham Homestead, Marlboro

dren eight d. and we have no records of their names. The children who lived were the 2d, 5th and 8th, b. in Binghamton:

2 *John R.*[8], res. Portland, Oregon.

5 *Edward C.,* res. Portland, Oregon.

8 *Porter Elmer,* b. 1849; m. 1877, Mary Parker Cramhall of San Francisco, Cal., b. 1855; he is a merchant in Portland, Oregon. Ch., b. there:

    i George Chase[6], b. 1882; ii Helen Katherine, b. 1885.

iii Edward, b. 14 April, 1811; d. 2 Oct., 1872; m. (1) Sarah Ann Tissot; m. (2) Clarissa Swain. Ch., of whom there were probably nine, the names of five only being known:

1 *Sarah Ann*[8], m. Elmer L. Andrews of Lestershire, N. Y.; she res. Binghamton.

2 *Charles E.,* res. Binghamton.

3 *Eubulus H.,* res. Horn Brook, Pa.

4 *Benjamin F.,* res. Horn Brook, Pa.

5 *Clara E.,* m. ———— Bennett; res. Topeka, Kan.

iv Fanny E., b. 26 Oct., 1812; d. 21 Aug., 1888; m. ———— Delemater.

v Mary, b. 16 Feb., 1816.

vi Elijah W., b. 21 Sept., 1826; in 1893 he res. in Binghamton; m. ————. Ch.:

1 *Julia F.*[8], b. 19 Sept., 1851; d. 13 Nov., 1859.

2 *Frederick S.,* b. 15 Aug., 1858; d. 10 June, 1902.

3 *John L.,* b. 11 Dec., 1861; d. 14 Sept., 1901; m. ————. Ch.: Ethel L.[9], b. 18 Nov., 1888.

4 *Harry E.,* b. 7 March, 1872; m. ————. Ch.: i Bessie L.[9], and ii Grace L., twins, b. 27 June, 1892.

220   SILVANUS[6], son of William[5] and Betsey (Stratton) Brigham; born in Northboro, Mass., 17 Jan., 1774; died in Lowell, Vt., 7 March, 1843; married ————

Children:

    i Perle[7].

    ii Charles, b. in Lowell, Vt., 15 Sept., 1803; d. 15 Aug., 1853; m. Jerusha Dewey (dau. of Asa), b. in Hanover, N. H., 7 Nov., 1805; d. 25 April, 1850; a farmer in Lowell. Ch., b. there:

1 *Ann D.*[8], b. 16 May, 1827; m. 29 April, 1847, George S. Noyes, Architect, Chelsea, Vt., who d. 26 Nov., 1867; 5 children, one, Mrs. Pliny C. Bliss of No. Lexington, Mass.

2 *Asa Dewey,* b. 29 Aug., 1828; m. in the West; a butcher and res. Abington, Pa.; 5 children.

3 *Harvey S.,* b. 16 Dec., 1829; a butcher in Abington; 1 dau.

4 *Frank A. H.,* b. 1 Dec 1831; m. Angeline Northrup; a farmer in Abington.

5 *Amanda S.,* b. 16 Jan., 1834; d. 8 June, 1856.

6 *Charles P.,* b. 15 May, 1837; d. 25 Aug., 1842.

7 *Emily A.,* b. 24 Feb., 1840; drowned 15 Aug., 1863, with 4 cousins.

m Levi, who res. in Lowell, Vt.

221   LUCY[6], daughter of William[5] and Betsey (Stratton) Brigham; born in Northboro, Mass., 24 March, 1778; died

————; married, 13 Oct. 1796, Solomon Willard Cushman, born in Norwich, Vt., 10 June, 1773; resided in Tunbridge, Vt., and died 22 Dec., 1822.*

Children (Cushman), born in Tunbridge:
   i Marietta[7], b. 30 March, 1797; d. 21 March, 1800.
   ii Solomon, b. 16 April, 1799; d. 5 Nov., 1821.
   iii Porter, b. 3 Nov., 1801; m. (1) Eunice Osgood; m. (2) Asenath West; 7 ch.
   iv Marilla, b. 15 March, 1804; unm.
   v Ira, b. 26 July, 1806; d. at Chelsea, Vt., 17 May, 1850; m. Emily Adams of Ripton, Vt.
   vi Malvina, b. 10 Dec., 1808; m. (1) Benjamin H. Adams of Tunbridge, in 1838; he d. 13 Oct., 1849; m. (2) Nathaniel Stockwell of Waitsfield, Vt., in April, 1852; res. Tunbridge; 4 ch.
   vii Minerva, b. 24 Aug., 1811; m. Alvin Ordway of Tunbridge, in 1833; 8 ch.
   viii Dennis, b. 24 Aug., 1811; unm.
   ix Frances, b. 28 April, 1814; m. Jude Moulton of Tunbridge, 25 Oct., 1846. 2 ch.
   x Ziba Chapman, b. 3 July, 1819; m. Laura Quaid of Randolph, Vt., in Nov., 1848; 2 ch.

222 STEPHEN[6], son of Jonathan[5] and Lydia (Stevens) Brigham; born in Marlboro, Mass., 24 Aug., 1780; died in Sheridan, N. Y., 13 Nov., 1856; married in 1800, Mary Wilcox, in Madison, N. Y.; he removed with his father, in 1796, to Madison, N. Y.; in 1817 he moved to Chautauqua County.

Children:
   i Willard W.[7], b. in Augusta, N. Y., 16 July, 1802; m. (1) 6 Oct., 1825, Electa Robinson, who d. in Dunkirk, 16 Feb., 1853; m. (2) 25 Aug., 1853, Louisa C., dau. of E. R. Thompson of Dunkirk. Mr. Brigham was a commission merchant, well known upon the Lakes; res. in Dunkirk, s. p.
   ii Edward; iii Charlotte; iv Lucetta; v Paulina; vi Mary; vii Harriet.
   viii William H., m. 26 Dec., 1839, Nancy B., dau. of Cyrus Shattuck, originally from N. H.; res. in Dunkirk; assessor, collector, mail agent and prominent man. Ch.:
      1 Catherine Maria[8], b. 25 June, 1845.

223 JOHN[6], son of John[5] and Abigail (Williams) Brigham; born in Marlboro, Mass., 7 Oct., 1780; died in Pomfret, N. Y., 8 Jan., 1850; married, 20 Feb., 1807, Sarah Eaton of Paris, N. Y. He resided for a time in Paris, now Clinton, N. Y. In 1808 he went from Madison County to Chadwick Bay, now Dunkirk, N. Y.

Children, all but the eldest probably born in Dunkirk; they are all deceased, but dates of death not known in each case:
495   i Lodasca[7], b. in Madison Co., N. Y., 13 Dec., 1807.
      ii Phebe, b. 1809; d. in Laporte, Ind., 29 Jan., 1837; m. Curtis Travis; moved to Indiana about 1832; he m. again. Ch. (Travis):

* Vide *Cushman Genealogy.*

1 *Eliza Madeline*[8]; 2 *Nelson Albert;* 3 *John B.;* 4 *Wesley.*

iii Walter E., b. 1811; m. (1) 28 April, 1844, Sophia Bussing; m. (2) 13 Feb., 1853, Ann A. Saunders. Ch.:
1 *Laurens Orlando*[8], b. 29 Jan., 1845; d. unm., in U. S. N., Civil War.
2 *Minerva A.*, b. 11 April, 1849; m. ———— Shepard; res. Silver Creek, N. Y.
3 *Frank W.*, b. 23 Jan., 1854; d. before 1904.

496 iv Orlando, b. 5 Feb., 1813.

v Polly, b. 1815; m. 11 Feb., 1835, Moses Luce of Pomfret. Ch. (Luce):
1 *John*[8], who d.
2 *William*, m. Clarissa Rood; res. Cassadaga, N. Y.
3 *Curtis*, res. 1904, Arkwright, N. Y.
4 *Sarah*, m. Charles Spencer of Fowlerville, Mich.
5 *Moses.*
6 *Lodasca*, m. Allen Erwin of Sinclairville, N. Y.
7 *Martha*, m. ———— Dexter, Cardot, Mich.

vi Henry, b. 1816; m. 21 May, 1839, Selinda Chase; res. Cropsey, Ill. Ch.:
1 *Julia*[8], b. 14 Feb., 1844; m. ———— McCullough; had 2 ch.

497 vii Nabby, b. 1818.

viii John Williams, b. 1820; m. Delacia Perry of Warren Co., Pa.; res. Dunkirk, where he was a member of the firm of Brigham & Brigham, seed merchants. Ch., b. in Dunkirk:
1 *George Raymond*[8], b. 22 Oct., 1853; res. Nebraska.
2 *Daughter*, d. y.

498 ix Nelson, b. 11 June, 1822.

x Jackson, b. 1824; m. in Pomfret, 6 Feb., 1849, Maria Balcom; moved to York, Neb. Ch.:
1 *Alice M.*[8], b. 28 Feb., 1851; m. ———— Pratt; res. York.
2 *Charles W.*, b. 14 Dec., 1855; res. York.
3 *Ida*, res. York; m. ————.
4 *George.*

xi Sarah, b. 1826; d. abt. 1854; m. Nicholas Wilson; moved to Matamora, Ill. Ch. (Wilson):
1 *Corwin*[8], b. 7 Sept., 1850.
2 *Marvin*, b. 22 Feb., 1852.
3 *John B.*, b. 22 Dec., 1853.

xii Almary, b. 1830; m. (1) Elijah Plank; m. (2) ———— Chilson of Topeka, Kan.

xiii Harriet, b. 1832; m. Nicholas Bussing of Pomfret. Ch. (Bussing):
1 *Emma*[8]; 2 *Almara;* 3 *Sarah;* all of whom died; 4 *Jerome*, d. 19 Jan., 1904, Chautauqua Co., N. Y., and had 5 ch.

xiv Fanny, b. 1833; m. 19 Sept., 1854, at Pomfret, Ezra Merrill; res. Fairburg, Ill. Ch. (Merrill):
1 *Alice*[8], b. 20 Feb., 1855; 2 *Jay*, b. 14 Nov., 1858; 3 *Delia;* 4 *Roland;* 5 *Vinie;* 6 *Forest;* 7 *Lee;* 8 *Sanford.*

224 JAMES[6], son of John[5] and Abigail (Williams) Brigham; born in Marlboro, Mass., 6 Nov., 1782; died in Fredonia, N. Y., 31 Jan., 1861; married there, 4 March, 1811, Fanny Risley, who died at the home of her daughter Philena, in Dunkirk, N. Y., 26 Jan., 1869.

He moved to Madison, N. Y., with his father in 1795, and settled in Fredonia. He assisted in the erection of the first mill and in the establishment of the first school and church in Fredonia, and was to the end of his days a respected and influential citizen. They are remembered with deep affection by their few surviving children and will ever be held in honor by their posterity.

Children, born in Fredonia:
499   i Fidelio Williams[7], b. 5 Dec., 1812.
      ii Philena Warren, b. 13 April, 1816; d. in Dunkirk, N. Y., 24 Feb., 1886; m. 26 Jan., 1840, John Freese, who survived her only a few years. Ch. (Freese):
         1 *Helen Sophia*[8], b. 22 Nov., 1840; m. about 1870; res., a widow, Jersey City, N. J.
         2 *Fanny Brigham*, b. 7 July, 1843; d. 29 Dec., 1846.
         3 *James Brigham*, b. 15 Dec., 184—; d. 29 Sept., 1846.
         4 *George Brigham*, b. 7 July, 1848; d. 13 April, 1853.
         5 *Ada Belle*, b. 26 Feb., 1850; res., with sister, Jersey City.
500 iii Wesley Hervey, b. 13 May, 1819.
      iv James Risley, b. 31 Jan., 1821; d. in Pittsburg, 26 July, 1843.
501   v Levi, b. 6 Jan., 1824.
502   vi George French, b. 18 Nov., 1827.
      vii Sophia French, b. 29 Sept., 1830; d. 3 Jan., 1840.
     viii Henry Hanson, b. 30 July, 1833; unm., res. in White River, Wisconsin; a local agent at that station for Wis. Cen. Ry. Co.
      ix Helen Harriet, b. 30 July, 1833; d. 12 March, 1836.

225 WALTER[6], son of John[5] and Abigail (Williams) Brigham; born in Marlboro, Mass., 1787; died in Dunkirk, N. Y., 5 Sept., 1827; married in 1812, Mary Child, daughter of William Dix of Holden, Mass.; born in Holden, in 1790, and died at the home of her son Robert, in Amboy, Ill., 1 Nov., 1857. She married (2) Mr. Taylor of Ripley, N. Y.

Walter visited England in 1818, and was at the manor of Brigham and the borough of Cockermouth but his MSS. were lost. After his return from travel abroad, he became a merchant in Westfield and Dunkirk, N. Y.

Children, the second and third born in Pomfret, N. Y ·
503   i Mary Ann[7], b. 18 Dec., 1814.
      ii Lydia Maria, b. 27 Oct., 1819; d. unm., in Spirit Lake, Ia., 28 March, 1901.
     iii Robert McMann, b. 18 June, 1824; m. 6 June, 1850, Mary Ann Kenyon of Westfield, N. Y.; res. Amboy, Ill.; d. s. p. 30 Jan., 1892.
      iv Walter Dix, b. 21 April, 1828; d. unm., in Dunkirk, 23 Sept., 1863.

226   ABIGAIL[6], (or NABBY), daughter of John[5] and Abigail
(Williams) Brigham; born in Fitzwilliam, N. H.; baptized 13
March, 1791; died ———; married, 25 Oct., 1810, Hon. (Gen.)
Elijah, son of Elijah and Phoebe (Bills) Risley; born 17 May,
1787; died ———, 1869.

He was a merchant and very prominent man of Chautauqua
County, N. Y.; a member of Congress in 1850-'52. He and his wife
occupied a high place in the esteem and affections of the people
of Fredonia, N. Y., where they resided, and where they celebrated
their 54th marriage anniversary in 1864.

Children (Risley), born in Fredonia:
 i Florilla C.[7], b. 1 Oct., 1811; d. in La Salle, N. Y., 24 June, 1874;
  m. Chauncey Tucker, b. 10 Jan., 1805; d. in L. S., 25 April, 1874.
  Ch. (Tucker), b. in Fredonia:
   1 *Florella[8]*, d. y.
   2 *Henry C.*, b. 24 Oct., 1835; d. 7 June, 1887; an attorney,
    Niagara Falls, N. Y.; m. Clara Warren; 6 ch.
   3 *Risley*, b. 10 Oct., 1848; a manufacturer; President Buffalo
    Envelope Co.; res. s. p., Buffalo; m. Matilda C., dau. of
    Jonathan Jewett.
 ii Hanson Alexander, b. 16 June, 1814; d. in W. Newton, Mass., 23
  Aug., 1893; m. 3 Dec., 1835, Harriet H. Crosby, b. Sept., 1816;
  d. 28 Sept., 1868. Ch.:
   1 *George F.[8]*, b. 18 Oct., 1836; d. 17 March, 1841.
   2 *Mary C.*, b. 10 March, 1838; d. 15 March, 1841.
   3 *Walter R.*, b. 25 May, 1842; d. 7 July, 1847.
   4 *Olive F.*, b. 15 July, 1844; adopted by Hon. William H. Sew-
    ard, and assumed name of Risley-Seward in 1868; res. Wash-
    ington, D. C.
   5 *Harriet D.*, b. 5 March, 1850; m. Alfred Rodman of Dedham,
    Mass.; 1 son.
 m Sophronia, b. 15 Sept., 1816; d. 5 Sept., 1875; m. 7 Feb., 1841,
  Charles F. Matteson of Fredonia, who d. April, 1882; res.
  Fredonia. Ch. (Matteson), the 3 younger b. in Fredonia:
   1 *Katherine[8]*, b. 16 Jan., 1844.
   2 *Isabelle*, b. 22 Sept., 1851; d. Oct., 1852.
   3 *Charles R.*, b. 29 Jan., 1855; d. 7 Feb., 1855.
   4 *Abby J.*, b. 29 Jan., 1855; d. 29 Oct., 1858.
 iv Laurens Green, b. 27 March, 1819; d. Jan., 1893; m. 7 June,
  1842, Henrietta E. Houghton, b. 8 July, 1821; d. 6 Feb., 1897.
  Ch.:
   1 *Evelyn[8]*, b. 26 Feb., 1843; d. 15 July, 1890; m. 22 Nov., 1871,
    George H. Stetson of Bangor, Me
   2 *George H.*, b. 13 April, 1847; m. 24 June, 1868, Emilie B.
    Schutt.
 v Delia, b. 13 Oct., 1824; d. Aug., 1881; m. 28 Dec., 1843, Hon.
  T. P. Grosvenor of Buffalo, who d. 1880. Ch. (Grosvenor):
   1 *Ellen D.[8]*, b. 13 May, 1845, in Buffalo; d. 1 June, 1898; m.
    28 Dec., 1868, Milton B. Cushing, Paymaster U. S. A., who d.
    about 1886.
   2 *Charles P.*, b. Nov., 1858, in Dunkirk; d. 7 Jan., 1899.
 vii Minerva, ·b. Aug., 1825 (Morse says " 1828 "); d. in Dunkirk, 10
  Feb., 1897; m. Frank C. Cushing, a lawyer, who d. Oct., 1858.

227   LIEUT. JOEL[6], son of Samuel[5] and Phebe (Davis) Brigham; born in Paxton, Mass., 12 Sept., 1785; died in Lodi, Ohio, 3 Oct., 1837; he was shot through the abdomen by Indian "Longfinger," from an ambush; married 8 Oct., 1809, Polly Ann, daughter of Benjamin and Susan Durkee, of Augusta, N. Y.; born in Washington, Conn., 7 Oct., 1786; died in Lodi, 13 Sept., 1840. He was a Lieutenant in the War of 1812. He removed from Augusta, N. Y., to Dunkirk, N. Y., about 1816 and thence to Lodi in 1834.

Children, the first 3 born in Augusta, the last 4 in Dunkirk:
504   i Elmina[7], b. 2 July, 1810.
505   ii Dexter, b. 28 Oct., 1812.
506   iii Winfield Scott, b. 30 Dec., 1814.
507   iv Joel, b. 10 Jan., 1818.
    v Haven, b. 2 June, 1820; d. 19 Feb., 1837.
    vi Theodore, b. 2 Jan., 1823; d. 19 Aug., 1835.
    vii Julius, b. 25 Aug., 1826; d. 26 Jan., 1840.

228   BARNA[6], son of Capt. Tilly[5] and Rachel (Walker) Brigham; born in Brookfield, Mass., 11 Nov., 1784; died 4 March, 1834; married Anna Hinds of Prescott, Mass.; born 11 May, 1785; died 24 Aug., 1861.

Children, born in Prescott:
    i Bathsheba[7], or "Basha," b. 18 Sept., 1805; d. in Prescott, 26 Sept., 1806.
    ii Charles F., b. 19 Jan., 1807; d. 19 Aug., 1866; a book dealer; res. Cincinnati.
    iii Nehemiah H., b. 13 March, 1809; d. 18 Sept., 1861; res. Prescott.
    iv Tilly, b. 4 Nov., 1810; d. 26 Sept., 1811.
    v Barna Lovering, b. 2 Feb., 1813; d. 21 Sept., 1876; a farmer in Richland, Mich.
    vi Henry, b. 25 March, 1815; d. 24 Sept., 1837; a trader in Verona.
    vii Marcia A., b. 14 Oct., 1817; res. Acme, Mich.
    viii Vesta C., b. April, 1819; d. 15 March, 1872; res. Northampton, Mass.
    ix Frances E., b. 17 July, 1821; res. Florence, Mass.
    x Mary J., b. 25 July, 1823; d. 22 Aug., 1855, in Fort Wayne, Ind.
    xi Lorenzo, b. 27 March, 1825; d. 10 Aug., 1825.
    xii Horatio G., b. 19 July, 1827; d. 30 July, 1830.
    xiii Samuel T., b. 4 Feb., 1829; retired; res. Florence, Mass.
    xiv Emory C., b. 24 Nov., 1832; d. 24 Aug., 1895; a jeweler; res. Florence, Mass.

229   JOEL[6], son of Capt. Tilly[5] and Rachel (Walker) Brigham; born in Brookfield, Mass., 2 June, 1790; died there about 1866; married 27 Feb., 1812, Basmath Hamilton. He resided on the original homestead in Brookfield, and engaged in farming.

Children, born in Brookfield:
    i Martha A.[7], b. 27 Dec., 1813; d. unm., in So. Framingham, Mass., 20 April, 1893.
    ii Persis A., b. 24 Oct., 1815; d. 24 April, 1893; m. 1837, Timothy M. Walker; moved to Springfield, in 1842, where he was a merchant. Ch.   1k   :

1 *Edward M.*[8]
2 *William B.,* both res. in Springfield.
iii Julia F., b. 2 Aug., 1817; m. Henry S. Waterman, who engaged in mining. Ch. (Waterman):
  1 *Charles H.*[8], b. 11 May, 1848; 2 *Mary A.;* 3 *Henry B.*
508 iv Jane Elizabeth, b. 11 July, 1819.
v Seraph A., b. 9 Feb., 1821; res. unm., So. Framingham, Mass.
vi Tilly, b. 1 March, 1823; d. unm., 1865, in N. Y. City, where he was with Wade Letter Press Co.
509 vii Salem Tilly, b. 17 Oct., 1824.
viii Lucius A., b. 10 June, 1827; res. unm., a hardware dealer in St. Louis.
ix Abbie H., b. 11 Sept., 1829; d. in So. Framingham, 2 April, 1884; m. Augustus Richardson, a straw-goods manufacturer; b. in Sterling, Mass., 28 Dec., 1823; d. 5 Feb., 1892; res. So. Framingham. Ch. b. there:
  1 *Addie C.*[8], m. Frederick P. Stearns of Dorchester, Mass., who d. 1905. Ch.: i Herbert[9]; ii Ralph.
  2 *Ella M.,* m. Frank H. Fales; res. s. p., So. Framingham.
  3 *Herbert A.,* m. Albina C. Jacobs; res. s. p., So. Framingham.
  4 *Kate E.*
  5 *Fred W.*
x Mary A., b. 20 May, 1831; d. 7 Dec., 1848.
xi Joseph W., b. 11 Dec., 1834; m. Juliana Hyde; res. on the old homestead in Brookfield. Ch.:
  1 *Alfred*[8]; 2 *Lucius.*

230 JAMES[6], son of Elisha[5] and Patience (Walker) Brigham; born in Brookfield, Mass., 22 Feb., 1783; died in Richford, Vt., 31 Oct., 1866; married 24 March, 1814, Marcia Hastings of West Richford; born 3 Nov., 1792; died in Richford, 5 June, 1879. He resided in West Richford.

Children:
i Infants[7], twin girls; d. at birth.
ii Lucie E., b. 14 Feb., 1816; d. 17 July, 1902; m. 9 Dec., 1840, Henry Branch, who d. 26 Feb., 1869; res. Berkshire, Vt. Ch. (Branch):
  1 *Viola E.*[8], b. 11 Aug., 1842; m. Peter Rockwell of Berkshire.
  2 *Mary E.,* b. 24 May, 1844; m. Charles Brainard of Berkshire.
iii Laura H., b. 26 Oct., 1817; d. unm., 17 Sept., 1900, æ. 82.
iv Nancy M., b. 11 Sept., 1819; d. 27 Dec., 1853; m. 2 March, 1853, Ambrose Sikes; res. Payson, Ill.
510 v Bostwick, b. Brookfield, Mass., 6 Aug., 1821.
vi Alfred (Rev.), b. in Brookfield, 27 Nov., 1823; d. in Newark Valley, N. Y., 21 Sept., 1896; m. 15 June, 1853, Fanny P. Tinker of Concord, N. H., who d. 27 Oct., 1901. Ch.:
  1 *William F.*[8], b. 2 April, 1854; d. 18 June, 1876.
  2 *Mattie,* b. 29 Oct., 1858; d. s. p., 21 Oct., 1891; m. 17 June, 1884, Melville D. Cameron.
  3 *Lottie,* b. July, 1861; d. 21 Sept., 1869.
  4 *Minnie,* b. April, 1863; d. 24 Aug., 1872.
vii Elizabeth, b. 6 Sept., 1825; m. in W. Brookfield, in 1869, Calvin E. Gilbert, who d. s. p., 30 Oct., 1901.
511 viii James E., b. in Caroline, N. Y., 17 July, 1827.

ix Marcia A., b. 4 Nov., 1829; d. 24 Feb., 1850.
x Rebecca K., b. 13 Nov., 1832; d. 26 Oct., 1846.

231 SILVANUS[6], son of Elisha[5] and Patience (Walker) Brigham; born in Brookfield, Mass., 30 July, 1785; married 1 Dec., 1808, Sarah, daughter of Elisha Rice of Brookfield; born 17 Sept., 1790. He was in the War of 1812, and went from Brookfield to Boston. He resided on part of the old homestead in Brookfield.

Children, born in Brookfield:
   i Lucy Rice[7], b. 26 April, 1809; m. (1) George Old; m. (2) Columbus Rice; d. in B., s. p., 9 Oct., 1882.
   ii Emeline, b. 22 Feb., 1811; m. Dexter Nichols of Sturbridge, Mass. Ch. (Nichols), b. in Sturbridge:
      1 *Henry W.[8]*, m. ———— Maynard. Ch.: i Maynard D.[9], res. California; has 1 boy; ii Homer; iii Walter; iv John; all res. Sturbridge and have families.
      2 *Sarah E.*, m. Farnum Southwick. Ch. (Southwick): Myron[9], who res. Warren, Mass., and has 5 ch.
   iii Amanda, b. 11 Jan., 1813; m. Calvin A. Davis, who d. in Brookfield. Ch. (Davis):
      1 *Frederick[8]*, d.
      2 *Ellen*, d.
   iv James Sullivan, b. 3 Aug., 1814; d. 7 Feb., 1815.
512 v Alexander, b. 10 Nov., 1815.
   vi Charles Lewis, b. 14 Nov., 1817; d. in Brookfield, 17 July, 1864; m. Betsey S. Harwood, and res. there. Ch.:
      1 *John H.[8]*, b. 20 Feb., 1857; d. 28 Aug., 1864.
      2 *Frank T.*, b. 21 Jan., 1860; d. 1 Aug., 1864.
   vii Frederick, b. 28 Oct., 1819; d.; m. Eliza J. Hobbs; res. Warren, Mass. Ch.:
      1 *Lucy J.[8]*, who m. J. M. Drake; s. p.
   viii Sarah, b. 16 Feb., 1822; d. *ibid.*
   ix John G., b. 18 Aug., 1823; d. 22 Jan., 1849, unm.
   x Seth, b. 8 April, 1828; d. unm., 4 Oct., 1876; he was a cripple, and assisted Rev. Abner Morse in his work.

232 DR. SAMUEL[6], son of John[5] and Zerviah (Rice) Brigham; born in Phillipston, Mass., 16 Jan., 1782; died in Bainbridge, O., 29 July, 1848; married (1) Lucy Churchill; married (2) Polly Wood; born 17 Jan., 1792; died in 1838; her father was a captain in the Revolutionary War.

Samuel resided at Bangor, N. Y., and then went west. He was a physician and surgeon, and musical, being considered a fine violinist. Several of his descendants inherited his musical gifts.

Children (all by second wife), 10 were born, but only 5 lived; the 3 younger b. in Bangor, N. Y.:
513 i Samuel[7], b. in Malone, N. Y., 8 May, 1817.
   ii Lucy Churchill, b. in N. Y. State, 31 July, 1822; d. 1 Nov., 1892; m. 31 Dec., 1845, Benjamin Sweet of Ohio. Ch. (Sweet):
      1 *Alcesta[8]*, b. in Bainbridge, O., 3 Aug., 1848; m. (1) 24 Oct., 1867, Nathan Phinney, who d. 5 July, 1876; m. (2) 28 Nov., 1881, Franklin S. Morris of Munroe, O.

2 *Leora*, b. 29 June, 1852; m. 12 Jan., 1905, Frank Russell, whose first wife was Emily A. Brigham, dau. of 513.

iii Polly Wood, b. in 1824; d. 11 Dec., 1893; m. in 1844, William R. Hatch of Berlin Heights, O.; a sailor. Ch. (Hatch):

1 *William E.*[8], b. 15 Sept., 1845.

2 *Arabella Z.*, b. 25 Sept., 1849; m. 15 Oct., 1871, Marion Sprowl, who d. 13 April, 1894. Ch. (Sprowl): i Hallie J.[9], b. 10 July, 1874; m. May, 1897, Ada Karcher; ii Francis L., b. 10 April, 1881; m. Oct., 1901, Ada Willinger; iii Rena B., b. 19 July, 1887; m. March, 1902, Alonzo Goodsite.

3 *Alice E.*, b. 6 Jan., 1854; m. 22 March, 1874, Alfred L. Dickinson. Ch. (Dickinson): Marian A.[9], b. 15 Sept., 1880.

iv Benjamin Franklin, b. 7 Aug., 1827; d. in Pleasantville, Ia., where he res. 19 Aug., 1905; m. Clara J. Elliot, 23 April, 1863; 5 children were born, all dying young. He was a farmer. His death leaves Mrs. Price, his sister, the last of her family.

v Abigail Rudd, b. in 1833; m. 22 Oct., 1855, Thomas Price of Huron, O., who d. s. p., 27 May, 1870; he was a great sportsman; res. in Chagrin Falls, O., where she now lives (1905). She has taken a great interest in the Brigham Family History, and has furnished a large number of records of the line.

233   JOHN[6], son of Samuel[5] and Rachel (Underwood) Brigham, born in Shrewsbury, Mass., 22 March, 1788; died 1 May, 1853; married 14 Aug., 1808, Sarah, daughter of Abraham Fay of Northboro, Mass., who died 25 March, 1869, æ. 82.

Children, born in Shrewsbury:

i Samuel Augustus[7], b. 18 Feb., 1809; d. Oct., 1846; m. Daphne Leggett, who m. (2) Nathaniel Green. Ch.:

1 *Susan A.*[8], b. 1845; d. 1846.

ii Abraham Fay, b. 3 March, 1810; d. at home of his dau., Mrs. Coburn, in Shrewsbury, 21 Aug., 1889; m. 13 June, 1850, Sarah Wingate, who d. 26 Sept., 1865, æ. 44. Ch., b. in Shrewsbury:

1 *Eliza Jane*[8], b. 8 July, 1851; m. 2 Oct., 1871, Henry L. Coburn, who d.; she res., a widow, in Shrewsbury. Ch. (Coburn): i Walter[9]; ii Frank; both d. y.

2 *May Fay*, b. 30 Jan., 1854; m. 31 Aug., 1870, Lozano C. Knowlton; res. Shrewsbury. Ch. (Knowlton): Helen B.[9], b. 1 May, 1886.

3 *George Edward*, b. 4 June, 1856; m. 19 May, 1880, Helen A. Hicks; res. Shrewsbury. Ch.: i Flora A.[9], b. 1 July, 1881; ii Walter E., b. 2 Oct., 1882.

4 *Dexter E.*, b. 9 May, 1859.

iii Abigail Martyn, b. 4 Feb., 1812; d. 24 Jan., 1885; m. (1) James L. Green of Millbury, Mass., who d. 1844, æ. 37; m. (2) Capt. Leander Sawyer, who d. 1882, æ. 74. Ch. (Green):

1 *James*[8]; 2 *Sarah*; 3 *Marion*; all d. y.

4 *Henry A.*, b. 7 Sept., 1841; m. Fannie M. Gates. Ch.: i Alice[9]; ii Albert; iii Marion; iv Florence; v Cora. Ch. (Sawyer):

5 *Abigail*, b. 28 April, 1852; she m. and d.

iv John, b. 29 June, 1818; d. probably unm., Nov., 1838.

v Charles Taylor, b. 14 Oct., 1826; d. unm., 4 March, 1861.

234 LIEUT. NATHANIEL[6], son of David[5] and Martha (Chamberlain) Brigham; born in Shrewsbury, Mass., 27 July, 1769; died 20 May, 1846; married 21 Nov., 1799, Sarah, daughter of John Mason, who moved from Medfield to Shrewsbury; she died 14 April, 1843. He moved from Shrewsbury to West Boylston, Mass.

Children, the 2 elder born in Shrewsbury, the others in W. Boylston:
514   i Luther[7], b. 10 Oct., 1800.
515   ii Calvin, b. 23 May, 1802.
516   iii John Mason, b. 26 March, 1808.
517   iv Henry Harding, b. 21 June, 1814.

235 EDMUND TROWBRIDGE[6], son of David[5] and Martha (Chamberlain) Brigham; born in Shrewsbury, Mass., 9 March, 1771; died in Shrewsbury, 28 Feb., 1858; married Elizabeth or Lucy Davis, of Ware, Mass.; she died at Shrewsbury, 4 May, 1853. He resided in Shrewsbury.

Children, the eldest born in Westboro, the second in Shrewsbury:
   i Elijah Augustus[7], b. 20 June, 1804; moved to Philadelphia, where d. 27 Jan., 1889; m. 17 May, 1825, Elizabeth, dau. of Thos. Witherby, Jr.; who d. 9 July, 1869. Ch.:
      1 *Susan Elizabeth*[8], b. 26 July, 1826; d. 15 Nov., 1870; m. Dr. Levi Curtis of Philadelphia.
   ii David Trowbridge, b. 6 Aug., 1806; a lawyer in Worcester; m. 24 Nov., 1831, Ann M. Peck; he d. s. p., in Keokuk, Ia., 9 July, 1865; was grad. Union Coll., A. B., 1829, P. B. K.; res. for a time at Alton, Ill.; was a member of the Iowa Senate.

236 PRESCOTT[6], son of David[5] and Martha (Chamberlain) Brigham; born in Shrewsbury, Mass., 8 March, 1780; died 28 May, 1862; married 6 April, 1814, Hannah, daughter of Gideon Rider of Shrewsbury; born in Shrewsbury, 24 July, 1788; died 16 Oct., 1846. He resided in Shrewsbury, and removed to Blue Mounds, Wisconsin, in 1838.

Children:
   i Ebenezer Prescott[7], b. 8 Sept., 1818; m. in 1838, Lucy Gibbs; res. in California. Ch.: 1 *Clarissa Damon*, b. 17 March, 1839; m. H. A. Goodell, and d. s. p. soon after.
   ii Martha Chamberlain, b. 16 Dec., 1823; m. 28 May, 1842, Thomas B. Cowles of Sauk Co., Wisconsin.

237 MERCY[6], daughter of David[5] and Martha (Chamberlain) Brigham; born in Shrewsbury, Mass., 21 March, 1784; died 12 Oct., 1867; married John, son of Gideon Rider, of Shrewsbury; descended from George Barbour, the emigrant; he was born in Hopkinton, Mass., 27 Jan., 1786; died in Phillipston, Mass., 17 Jan., 1862. They moved to Phillipston about 1820.

Children (Rider), the 6 eldest born in Shrewsbury, the 3 youngest in Phillipston:

 i Ann[7], b. 4 July, 1806; d. 19 Sept., 1829; m. 21 July, 1825, Rev.
  (Hon.) Charles Hudson, b. in Marlboro, 14 Nov., 1795; d. 4 May,
  1881; a soldier of the War of 1812; was a well-known historian of
  towns of Massachusetts, notably that of Marlboro; was in both
  branches of the Mass. Legislature many years, and also in Congress. Ch. (Hudson), b. in Westminster:
   1 *Harriet W.[8]*, b. 18 Aug., 1827; d. 26 July, 1828.
   2 *Harriet A.*, b. 13 Sept., 1829; d. 26 Sept., 1875; m. Henry M.,
    son of Rev. Stephen I. Smith; res. in Chicago for more than
    20 years; was one of the editors of the *Chicago Tribune;* also
    editor in Washington and Brooklyn, N. Y.; 4 ch.
 ii Martha Brigham, b. 15 June, 1808; d. 11 Jan., 1888; m. (second
  wife), 14 May, 1830, Rev. (Hon.) Charles Hudson, whose first
  wife was her sister Ann. Ch. (Hudson), b. in Westminster:
   1 *Martha Brigham[8]*, b. 10 April, 1832; d. 25 April, 1832.
   2 *Charles H.*, b. 10 July, 1833; m. Frances H., dau. of John
    Miller Nichols; was grad. from Harvard Univ., 1855; has been
    Supt., Chief Engineer and Gen. Manager on several southern
    R. R.'s; 5 ch.
   3 *(Col.) John W.*, b. 10 July, 1836; d. s. p., 1 June, 1872; m.
    Sophia W., dau. of Edward Mellen of Wayland, Mass.; was
    grad. from Harvard Univ., 1856; a lawyer in Boston; served 3
    years with 35th Regt., Mass. Vol., Army of the Potomac, and
    was Lieut. Col. Resided in Lexington.
   4 *Mary E.*, b. 31 March, 1839; res. Lexington, Mass., unm.
 iii Marion, b. 27 Sept., 1810; m. 4 April, 1839, Charles, son of Maj.
  Holland Forbes of Westboro and Royalston, Mass.; had 7 ch.,
  6 d. y.
 iv John, b. 28 Feb., 1813; d. 9 Sept., 1893; m. 1 Jan., 1839, Lydia,
  dau. of John Johnson; moved from Petersham, Mass., to Blue
  Mounds, Wis., 1847; served as assessor continually and as member
  of the school board; 6 ch.
 v Otis, b. 12 Aug., 1815; (spelled his name with a " y "); d. 6 June,
  1897; m. 5 April, 1838, Susan, dau. of John Mann; res. Lawton,
  Mich.; 7 ch.
 vi Jonas, b. 26 Aug., 1818; d. 10 March, 1868, in Barre, Mass.;
  m. Nancy, dau. of Charles and Lucy (Howe) Rice of Barre.
  Ch. (Rider):
   1 *Caroline Augusta[8]*, b. 3 Aug., 1843; d. unm., in No. Grafton,
    Mass., 20 July, 1904.
   2 *Ella Jane*, b. 4 July, 1850; res. unm., in Worcester.
   3 *Emma Josephine*, b. 4 Oct., 1852; m. Charles A. Hancock;
    res. Barre; 6 ch.
 vii Theodore S., b. 27 Jan., 1821; d. 21 May, 1873; m. (1) 2 April,
  1844, Rhoda, dau. of Capt. Jesse Forristall of Fitzwilliam, N. H.;
  m. (2) 2 April, 1846, Mrs. Lucy (Crittenden) Carr; 3 ch., by
  1st wife.
 viii Susan Dennis, b. 5 April, 1825; m. 3 Jan., 1849, Jonathan Bartlett Ackermann of Rye, N. H.; res. Derry, N. H.; 2 ch.
 ix Charles (spells his name with a " y "), b. 4 Aug., 1829; m. 27
  March, 1851, Martha A., dau. of Daniel Matthews; 6 ch.

238 DAVID[6], son of David[5] and Martha (Chamberlain) Brigham; born in Shrewsbury, Mass., 15 Aug., 1786; died in Madison, Wis., 16 Aug., 1843; married in Greenfield, Mass., 6 July, 1819, Elizabeth, daughter of Jerome Ripley of Greenfield; she died in Madison, 3 Nov., 1879, æ. 86. He received the degree of A. B. at Harvard College, 1810; became a tutor in Bowdoin College, where in 1815 he received the degree of Hon. A. M. He read law and in 1818 was established in Greenfield. Earlier he resided in Shrewsbury, Mass., and also in Fitchburg. He moved to Madison in 1839.

Children:

518 i Jerome Ripley[7], b. 1 July, 1825.

ii Marianne Elizabeth, b. 10 July, 1828; m. 10 April, 1849, Horace G. Bliss; they res. Madison and then moved to St. Paul, Minn. Ch. (Bliss):

1 *Brigham*[8], who was with the First Nat. Bank of St. Paul for 20 years; m. Carrie Kellogg. Ch.: Julia[9]

2 *Mary F.*, d. y.

239 LYDIA[6], daughter of Lieut. Levi[5] and Tabitha (Hardy) Brigham; born in Fitzwilliam, N. H., 24 Aug., 1772; died in F., 23 Nov., 1833; married 8 Sept., 1795, Elijah, son of Samuel Phillips of Athol, Mass.; born in Athol, 23 Jan., 1764; moved to Fitzwilliam about 1790, where he died 4 May, 1841.

Children (Phillips), born in Fitzwilliam:

i Belinda[7], b. 20 May, 1796; d. 13 Aug., 1798.

ii Lucy, b. 14 Jan., 1798; d. 4 Oct., 1805.

iii Elijah, b. 6 April, 1800; d. 26 Sept., 1805.

iv (Dea.) Rufus Brigham, b. 7 June, 1802; d. 5 Feb., 1882; m. 6 April, 1826, Mary, dau. of Dea. John Woodward; b. 8 March, 1799; d. 29 May, 1870. Ch.:

1 *Susan M.*[8], m. Charles Taft.

2 *Edward P.*

3 *Mary,* m. Chester Marsh of Windsor, Vt.

v Maria, b. 20 July, 1804; d. unm., 30 Oct., 1821.

vi Gardner, b. 27 Nov., 1806; d. 23 Dec., 1869; m. (1) Fanny Whitman, who d. s. p.; m. (2) Pamelia Carpenter of Westminster, Vt. Ch.:

1 *Julia A.*[8], b. in Keene, N. H., 13 Nov., 1840; m. Albert Cooper of Allston, Mass; 4 ch.

2 *Hattie S.*, b. in Keene, 27 Oct., 1842; m. Alfred P. Ranney of Westminster; s. p.

3 *Fannie M.*, b. 12 Feb., 1845.

4 *Eliza J.*, b. in Walpole, N. H., 15 June, 1847; d. 16 Sept., 1865.

5 *John G.*, b. 24 Dec., 1850; m., s. p.

6 *Lydia D.*, b. in Westminster, 9 Dec., 1856; d. 9 May, 1858.

7 *Herbert,* m. ——————; 4 ch.

vii Elijah, b. 11 April, 1809; killed by Indians in Bureau Co., Ill., 18 June, 1832.

viii Almond, b. 9 Oct., 1811; d. 3 Sept., 1879; m. 6 Oct., 1839, Kezia A., dau. of John J. Allen; b. 21 Jan., 1815; d. 10 Sept., 1877; moved to Marlboro, Mass. Ch. b. in Fitzwilliam:
    1 *Ella F.*[8], b. 28 Dec., 1840; m. Frederick J. Potter of Quincy, Ill.; res. Allston, Mass.; 1 ch.
    2 *Henry S.*, b. 20 March, 1844; d. 17 Feb., 1847.
    3 *(Dr.) Leslie A.*, b. 19 Aug., 1847; d. 3 April, 1896; res. Boston.
    4 *Anna M.*, b. 31 May, 1850; m. George R. Leland of Worcester, Mass.; 2 ch.
ix Levi, b. 30 Jan., 1814; d. 18 March, 1865; m. (1) 26 Oct., 1835, Submit, dau. of Emory Taft; b. 1812; d. Dec., 1860; m. (2) Mary, dau. of Henry Shirley. Ch.:
    1 *Helen*[8]; 2 *George H.*; 3 *Elmer E.*, Principal Park Col. School, N. Y. City; 4 *Lewis*; 5 *Herbert*; 6 *Harriet*.
x Winslow, b. 19 Jan., 1817; m. 21 April, 1847, Susan, dau. of Hyman Bent; b. 30 Dec., 1825. Ch.:
    1 *Herbert W.*[8]
    2 *Arthur L.*, b. 7 Sept., 1854; m. 7 Oct., 1878, Hattie Marie Keith, b. 9 July, 1858; res. Winchendon, Mass.; 2 ch.
    3 *Chester H.*, b. 27 May, 1868; m. 20 April, 1892, Anna May Merrill of Plymouth, N. H., b. 12 Jan., 1868; res. Fitzwilliam; 1 ch.
    4 *Wilbur H.*

240 CAPT. JOSEPH[6], son of Lieut. Levi[5] and Tabitha (Hardy) Brigham; born in Fitzwilliam, N. H., 2 June, 1774; died in F., 19 July, 1846; married 28 April, 1803, Polly, daughter of Francis and Sarah (Fisher) Perry Fullam; born 7 Jan., 1779; died 29 Sept., 1861.

He was selectman in Fitzwilliam 1805-'07, 1811-'19, 1826-'30; Representative, 1831 and 1832; Captain of the Artillery Co. He was a farmer and removed to Dover, Ill., 1832.

Children, born in Fitzwilliam:
    i Belinda[7], b. 28 Feb., 1804; d. 11 July, 1812.
    ii Rufus, b. 2 May, 1805; d. 28 June, 1812.
519 iii Silvester, b. 17 June, 1807.
    iv Mary, b. 23 March, 1809; d. 8 July, 1812.
    v Lucy, b. 16 June, 1811; living in 1893; m. 25 May, 1834, David Chase, b. in Royalston, Mass., 30 April, 1811; d. 1 July, 1882; was a farmer in Dover, Ill. Ch. (Chase), b. in Dover:
    1 *Lucy A.*[8], b. 10 April, 1840; d. 1880; m. Oscar Mead of Dover.
    2 *David Warren*, b. 11 Jan., 1844; m. Mary A. Codington; a farmer in Dover.
    3 *Mary E.*, b. 30 Oct., 1849; m. Arthur Trueitt in Dover.
    vi Polly, b. 2 Nov., 1813; res. Princeton, Ill.
    vii Nancy, b. 6 June, 1816; d. Oct., 1851.
    viii Eliza, b. 31 Aug., 1818; d. 23 Sept., 1863.
520 ix Joseph H., b. 31 Jan., 1823.

241 HANNAH[6], daughter of Lieut. Levi[5] and Tabitha (Hardy) Brigham; born in Fitzwilliam, N. H., 12 March, 1777; died 27 Oct., 1845; married in Fitzwilliam, 1 July, 1802, Capt.

William Fisher, son of David and Sarah (Fisher) Perry; born in Fitzwilliam, 9 Feb., 1776; died 18 March, 1871, æ. 95. He was prominent in obtaining the charter for the Fitzwilliam Artillery Co., in 1807, when the contest was close between Fitzwilliam and Dublin.

Children (Perry), born in Fitzwilliam:
i Infant[7], d. 19 Sept., 1803.
ii David, b. 14 Oct., 1804; d. 1 Oct., 1812.
iii Infant, b. 27 Nov., 1806; d. 4 Dec., 1806.
iv Sally, b. 30 Oct., 1807; d. 23 Oct., 1812.
v Tabitha, b. 6 Dec., 1809; d. 12 Oct., 1812.
vi William, b. 9 Jan., 1812; d. in Boston, 25 May, 1863; m. 30 May, 1841, Harriet, dau. of William and Elizabeth (Lennett) Springer of Gardner, Me., b. 16 July, 1816; d. 8 Jan., 1903; he res. Boston. Ch.:
    1 *Edgar W.[8],* b. 30 March, 1842; d. 27 April, 1842.
    2 *Hannah E.,* b. 20 June, 1843; m. George A. Smith of Boston; res. Boston; 2 ch.
    3 *Maria M.,* b. 5 April, 1845; d. 11 April, 1845.
    4 *William H.,* b. 11 Oct., 1847; served in the Civil War, 42d Reg. Mass. Vols.; d. in Boston, of disease contracted in the army, 11 Nov., 1864.
    5 *Sarah E.,* b. 11 Nov., 1853 (another record says " 4 Dec., 1854 "); m. in Boston, 8 Oct., 1885, Warren S. Locke of Lancaster, Mass., b. 10 June, 1853; res. Providence, R. I.; 4 ch.
    6 *Frederick G.,* b. 13 Jan., 1858; d. Oct., 1890; m. 10 Dec., 1884, Annie E. Mosely; was grad. Harvard Univ., 1879; 2 ch.
vii David, b. 4 May, 1814; d. 8 Feb., 1895; m. 4 May, 1847, Sophia, dau. of Nathaniel Keniston of Gardner, Me.; b. 11 July, 1821; d. 16 March, 1872; he kept a hotel in Fitzwilliam, and moved to Weston, Mass., 1866, where engaged in farming. Ch.:
    1 *Infant,* b. 28 Feb., 1848; d. 29 Feb., 1848.
    2 *Frank D.,* b. 24 April, 1849; m. 28 April, 1890, Sarah E. Cox of Gardner, Me., b. 30 May, 1848; res. s. p., Gardner.
    3 *Hattie S.,* b. 23 Jan., 1852; res. unm., Weston.
    4 *George S.,* b. 14 Nov., 1855; d. s. p., 10 July, 1904; m. 9 Oct., 1883, Charlotte Johnson.
    5 *Henry W.,* b. 15 July, 1857; m. 5 June, 1890, Mary Eloise, dau. of John H. Drew of Farmingdale, Me.; b. 7 Oct., 1861; res. Sharon, Mass.; 4 ch.
viii Sarah, b. 16 July, 1816; d. unm., 23 March, 1903.
ix Charles, b. 22 Nov., 1818; d. 23 Feb., 1901; m. 31 March, 1847, Maria, dau. of Calvin and Deborah (Brewer) Bemis of Swanzey, N. H.; b. 24 Jan., 1826; d. 2 Sept., 1903; res., a farmer, in Fitzwilliam. Ch.:
    1 *Calvin Brigham[8],* b. 27 Jan., 1848; m. in Fitzwilliam, 10 Nov., 1870, Julia E., dau. of Abner and Elizabeth (Bailey) Gage of Fitzwilliam; b. 27 Nov., 1846; he res. Keene, N. H., where in the granite, R. E. and Ins. business. Ch.: i William Fisher[9]; ii Walter Gage.
    2 *Charles William,* b. 3 March, 1855; killed instantly 22 Oct., 1879, by the kick of a horse.

242   LEVI[6], son of Lieut. Levi[5] and Tabitha (Hardy) Brigham; born in Fitzwilliam, N. H., 29 Dec., 1779; died in Boston, Mass., 20 Oct., 1826; married 6 Feb., 1821, Nancy H. Ayer, of Concord, N. H.; born 22 Sept., 1793; died 9 June, 1835.

He was an architect, and assisted in building the New Hampshire State House and also the Quincy Market, in Boston. He is interred under Saint Paul's Church, Tremont Street, Boston.

Children, born in Concord, N. H.:
    i Levi[7], b. 2 May, 1822; d. 1 Oct., 1843; grad. from Dartmouth College in 1843; was a private tutor at Port Tobacco, Md., where he d.
    ii Susan Ann, b. 25 June, 1825; d. in Concord, 10 May, 1863; m. 27 Sept., 1849, Col. John H. George of Concord, b. 20 Nov., 1824; d. 6 Feb., 1888; a lawyer of Concord. Ch. (George):
        1 *Mary H.[8]*, b. 23 July, 1850; d. 2 June, 1858.
        2 *Jennie P.*, b. 22 Feb., 1852; m. 1 Oct., 1873, Henry E. Bacon of Portland, Me. Ch. (Bacon): i George U.[9], b. 21 June, 1874; ii John H., b. 6 Nov., 1875; iii Elbridge, b. 28 Oct., 1878; iv Mary R., b. 25 Sept., 1888; v Henry E., b. 4 Oct., 1891.
        3 *Sidney W.*, b. 15 Oct., 1853; d. 17 March, 1857.
        4 *John P.*, b. 21 Jan., 1856; a lawyer.
        5 *Ann Brigham*, b. 10 March, 1858; res. unm., in Concord.
        6 *Charles P.*, b. 8 March, 1860; m. 1883 in Washington, D. C., Jennie P. Grayham; Capt. in the 16th U. S. Infantry, stationed in Atlanta, Ga. Ch.: i John W.[9]; ii Charles P.; iii John H.; iv Charlotte; v Elizabeth; vi Virginia.
        7 *Benjamin P.*, b. 6 March, 1862; m. 13 June, 1895, in Chicago, Ill., Lydia C. Harland. Ch.: Katherine[9], b. 13 Nov., 1899.

243   TABITHA[6], daughter of Lieut. Levi[5] and Tabitha (Hardy) Brigham; born in Fitzwilliam, N. H., 30 Sept., 1780; died in Fitzwilliam, 11 Oct., 1805; married, (second wife) 15 Jan., 1801, Capt. Aaron, son of Nathaniel Wright, of Sterling, Mass., born 9 Dec., 1766; died in Winchester, N. H., 26 Nov., 1866; he married (1) Lucy Bigelow, of Princeton, Mass., who died 1799; they had children; he married (3) Polly Blanding, widow of Seth Kendall of Athol. He was a farmer.

Children (Wright), born in Fitzwilliam:
    i Mary Ann[7], b. 18 Oct., 1801; d. 28 Sept., 1805.
    ii Tabitha Sophronia, b. 22 Oct., 1803; d. 2 Oct., 1805.
    iii Tabitha, b. 30 Oct., 1805; d. in F., 14 June, 1891; m. 6 June, 1827, Henry H., son of Asa Wheeler; a farmer, and town treasurer; b. in Sudbury, Mass., 18 Oct., 1805. Ch. (Wheeler), b. in Fitzwilliam:
        1 *Lyman K.[8]*, b. 1 May, 1828; d. 17 Oct., 1904, unm.; 3 years in the Civil War.
        2 *William H.*, b. 13 Sept., 1830; res. a druggist in Springfield, Vt.; m. 16 Sept., 1856, Harriet R., dau. of Asa Brewer of Fitzwilliam; b. 3 June, 1835; 5 ch.

    3 *Mary W.,* b. 17 Aug., 1832; d. unm.; res. Troy, N. H.
    4 *Edmund,* b. 30 July, 1835; m. 15 Jan., 1853, Carrie A. Allen
      of New Fane, Vt.; architect in Springfield, Mass.; s. p.
    5 *Maria,* b. 1 March, 1840; d. unm.
    6 *Charles W.,* b. 25 Dec., 1845; d. unm.; res. Troy, N. H.
    7 *Clarence H.,* b. 24 Aug., 1847; d. 7 Sept., 1881, unm.

244   ANNA[6], daughter of Lieut. Levi[5] and Tabitha (Hardy)
Brigham; born in Fitzwilliam, N. H., 26 April, 1782; died 1 April,
1860; married 26 Sept., 1804, Capt. Timothy, son of Samuel and
Betsey (Wetherbee) Kendall; born in Fitzwilliam, 25 Aug., 1782;
died there 14 Feb., 1851; his grandfather was one of the first
settlers of the town.   They resided for a time in Troy, N. H.

Children (Kendall), the 4 elder b. in Fitz., the others in Troy:
    i Lyman[7], b. 9 July, 1805; d. 5 May, 1828.
    ii Caroline, b. 22 June, 1807; d. 11 Nov., 1812.
    iii Clarissa, b. 29 Sept., 1809; d. 15 March, 1812.
    iv Timothy B., b. 14 Dec., 1811; d. 24 Oct., 1812.
    v Timothy, b. 9 Oct., 1813; d. 16 Dec., 1855; m. 10 May, 1839,
      Catherine, dau. of Stephen Wheeler of Troy, N. H.; b. 21 June,
      1819; d. 7 March, 1896. Ch.:
      1 *Charles W.*[8], b. 14 Aug., 1842.
      2 *Lucy A.,* b. 17 Jan., 1844; d. 8 or 11 Jan., 1899; m. 2 Nov.,
        1869, Jefferson Cary of Caribou, Me., b. 4 Sept., 1841; 1 ch.
    vi Caroline, b. 30 Jan., 1816; d. 24 Aug., 1836.
    vii Parkman, b. 13 Sept., 1818; d. 24 March, 1850, unm.
    viii Charles, b. 10 Jan., 1821; d. 9 Feb., 1837.
    ix George, b. 24 Oct., 1824; d. 14 Sept., 1854.

245   MINDWELL[6], daughter of Lieut. Levi[5] and Tabitha
(Hardy) Brigham; born in Fitzwilliam, N. H., 11 April, 1785;
died in Craftsbury, Vt., 17 May, 1863; married in 1805, Elijah,
son of Barakiah Scott; born 21 April, 1781; died in C., 11 Oct.,
1840.   They removed to Craftsbury in 1810.

Children (Scott), the first 3 born in Fitzwilliam, the others in Craftsbury:
    i Levi[7], b. 23 Oct., 1805.
    ii Sabin, b. 16 Sept., 1807; d. 31 May, 1902; m. in Craftsbury, 29
      April, 1830, Sarah Towle of C., b. 28 Oct., 1812; d. 28 March,
      1895. Ch., all but the youngest b. in C.:
      1 *Thaddeus*[8], b. 28 Aug., 1831; d. 11 Oct., 1871; was a R. R.
        man and lived in O.
      2 *Francis,* b. 6 Sept., 1833; a R. R. man, res. Alabama.
      3 *Orell,* b. 10 Nov., 1836; d. 13 Oct., 1872; a merchant in
        Alabama.
      4 *Sarah,* b. 4 Oct., 1842; res. Eden Mills, Vt.; a farmer.
      5 *Elizabeth,* b. in Lowell, Mass., 14 Sept., 1847; res. Eden Mills,
        a farmer.
    iii Amasa, b. 19 Sept., 1809.
    iv Mary Ann, b. 19 Aug., 1811.
    v Susan, b. 15 July, 1813; d. 29 April, 1819.
    vi Caroline, b. 15 Aug., 1815.

vii William, b. 19 Aug., 1817.

viii Catherine, b. 28 Aug., 1819; m. ———— Brown. Ch.:
  1 *J. C.*[8], res. Boston.

ix Laura, b. 2 Aug., 1821.

x Benjamin, b. 2 Aug., 1824.

246 SUSANNA[6], daughter of Lieut. Levi[5] and Tabitha (Hardy) Brigham; born in Fitzwilliam, N. H., 30 April, 1790; died 10 Feb., 1870, (or 1871); married 12 Aug., 1813, Ebenezer Potter, Jr., born 18 May., 1793, (or 1792); died 1 May, 1875.

Children (Potter), born in Fitzwilliam:
  i Sarah Harris[7], b. 30 Dec., 1814, or 1812; d. 30 Jan., 1843, or 1841; m. 8 Feb., 1837, Joseph A., son of John Warren of Grafton, Mass., b. 17 June, 1815; d. 24 June, 1903. Ch. (Warren):
    1 *Maria S.*[8], b. 7 March, 1838; m. Henry Rogers Hayden of Seneca Falls, N. Y., b. Nov., 1836; d. March, 1899; 10 ch.
    2 *John E.,* b. 6 Oct., 1840; m. ————————.
    3 *Sarah H.,* b. 10 Jan., 1843; d. 9 April, 1864.
  ii Levi Brigham, b. 15 Dec., 1815, or 1814; d. 24 Feb., 1883; m. 1 Sept., 1841, Hitty, dau. of John Wenzel of Framingham, Mass.; b. 1820; d. 1864; he was a farmer and moved to Wisconsin in 1839, and settled 7 miles from Milwaukee, on a farm now occupied by his son Milton, the place now called Wauwatosa. Ch., b. in Wanwatosa, except the 3d.:
    1 *Lucilla T.*[8], b. 28 July, 1842; d. 20 Aug., 1842.
    2 *Milton B.,* b. 6 July, 1845; m. 2 Aug., 1876, Sarah J. Church of Whitewater, Wis.; ch.: Charles M.; John C.; Alice H.; Marion E.
    3 *Henry B.,* b. in Fitz., 12 Jan., 1847; res. unm., Cooke, Montana.
    4 *Susan H.,* b. 18 Nov., 1849; m. 20 Feb., 1873, Maltby J. De Graff of Wanwatosa; 5 ch.
    5 *Eliza G.,* b. 27 Jan., 1853; d. 31 Dec., 1867.
    6 *Levi F.,* b. 27 March, 1855; m. Nov., 1882, Martha J. Wood; a banker, res. s. p., Harlan, Ia.
    7 *Mary H.,* b. 16 Nov., 1858; d. 1 April, 1902; m. 15 June, 1881, Chas. L. Church of Whitewater; 1 ch.
    8 *Charles W.,* b. 17 Jan., 1861; d. 5 April, 1861.
  iii Lydia Relief, b. March, 1818; d. 17 May, 1818.
  iv Rufus Baxter, b. 18 or 21 May, 1819; m. Mary, dau. of Moses Eames of Upton, Mass.; res. Fitchburg, Mass. Ch.:
    1 *Julia A.*[8], b. 5 June, 1842; m. 14 May, 1861, Leander Richardson of Royalston, Mass., who d. 1890; res. Fitchburg; 4 ch.
    2 *Sarah.*
    3 *Delia M.,* b. 13 Aug., 1850; m. 8 Nov., 1871, E. S. Fairbanks of Jaffrey, N. H.; 5 ch.
    4 *Mary E.,* b. 24 July, 1853; m. 21 March, 1872, Peter Russell of Randolph, Vt.; 4 ch.
    5 *Susie N.,* b. 30 April, 1858; m. 25 Oct., 1876, William Pulsifer of Rockingham, Vt., b. 2 April, 1855; 2 ch.
  v Tabitha Hardy, b. 13 Dec., 1821; m. 19 Jan., 1848, Edwin Burnham Carpenter of Brattleboro, Vt., b. 13 June, 1819; d. 3 Sept., 1891; she res. in Mendota, Ill. Ch. (Carpenter), the 4 elder b. in Brattleboro, the others in La Moille, Ill.:

    1 *Charles E.*[8], b. 16 May, 1849; d. 23 March, 1850.
    2 *Edwin P.*, b. 28 Jan., 1851; mfr. in London, Eng.
    3 *Hattie G.*, b. 18 Aug., 1852; m. 30 Sept., 1873, George S., son of Rev. Nathan Denison of Mendota; 5 ch.
    4 *Lena M.*, b. and d. 1855.
    5 *Minnie M.*, b. 4 July, 1859; d. 10 March, 1860.
    6 *Alice E.*, b. 20 Jan., 1861; d. 23 Aug., 1864.
    7 *Arthur E.*, b. 20 Jan., 1861; m. (1) 26 June, 1884, Kezia R. Inglis of Mendota, b. 25 May, 1852; d. 7 June, 1901; m. (2) Helen Hendry, b. 27 Oct., 1869; 3 ch.
  vi Hervey Gilbert, b. 18 July, 1823, or 1824; m. Mrs. Mary Wilder Aldrich; killed, s. p., in Mendota, 1866; res. Grafton, Mass.
  vii Lucy Ann, b. 4 Nov., 1826; d. 28 April, 1904; m. 4 Oct., 1843, Lewis, son of Lawson Moore of Framingham, Mass.; b. 1814; killed in the battle of the Wilderness, 6 May, 1864. Ch. (Moore):
    1 *Sarah E.*[8], b. 20 Jan., 1845; m. Charles A. Gleason of Worcester, 9 Nov., 1871; res. Boston; 1 ch.
    2 *Etta A.*, b. 16 Sept., 1849; m. 3 March, 1886; Lucius H. Wells of Belchertown, Mass., who d. 30 March, 1905; proprietor of Wells Chem. Bronze Wks.
    3 *Charles E.*, b. 25 Sept., 1852; went West in 1875; probably died.
    4 *John*, b. 27 March, 1855; d. 13 Aug., 1855.
  viii John Q. Adams, b. 4 April, 1830; m. Nancy Bradish; d. 1 July, 1850, s. p.

247 MAJOR ELIJAH[6], son of Hon. Elijah[5] and Anna Sophia (Parkman) Brigham; born in Westboro, Mass., 21 April, 1783; died 22 Jan., 1847; married (1) March, 1806, Nancy, daughter of Col. Nathan Fisher; she died 13 Jan., 1807, æ. 25; married (2) 13 April, 1808, Mary Bush of Boylston, Mass., who died in Westboro, 23 Sept., 1867, æ. 85.

Children (by first wife), born in Westboro:
521   i Elijah Parkman[7], b. 13 Jan., 1807.
Children (by second wife), born in Westboro:
   ii Mary Sophia, b. 25 Nov., 1809; d. unm., 2 Dec., 1886.
  iii Theodore Henry, b. 15 Nov., 1814; d. *ibid.*
   iv Theodore Frederick, b. Dec., 1815; d. probably s. p., 18 July, 1878; m. Sept., 1841, Caroline M. Fay of Westboro, b. 1816; d. 5 Jan., 1889.

248 ANN MARIA[6], daughter of Hon. Elijah[5] and Sarah (Ward) Brigham; born in Westboro, Mass., 14 July, 1794; died there, 14 Dec., 1880; married, 12 Oct., 1818, Ebenezer Morgan, son of Dr. Ebenezer Humphrey Phillips, born in Charlton, Mass., 19 Feb., 1792. He was, for 30 years, agent of the Boston and Worcester R. R. at Westboro, where he resided, and there died, 1 May, 1880.

Children (Phillips), born in Westboro:
   i Elijah Brigham[7], b. 20 Aug., 1819; d. in Brookline, Mass., 12 Sept., 1905; m. 2 Feb., 1845, Maria R., dau. of Henry Ayling of Roxbury, Mass. He was Master of Transportation for Boston

E. B. Phillips

& Worcester Ry.; first Supt. of Cleveland & Toledo Ry., 1852-58; Supt. Boston & Worcester Ry., 1858-65; Prest. Mich. So. & No. Indiana Ry., 1865-70; first Prest. Lake Shore & Mich. So. Ry., 1870-71; Prest. Phillips & Colby Construction Co., which built Wis. Cen. Ry.; he managed the latter 1871-78; Receiver of Grayville & Mattoon Ry. (Ill), 1878; Prest. Eastern Ry. (Mass.), 1879-83; Prest. Fitchburg Ry., 1884-89. Ch., the eldest and youngest born in Boston:

1 *Henry A.*[8], b. 19 Aug., 1852; m. 4 Oct., 1888, Florence Elizabeth, dau. of Col. Asa H. Waters of Millbury, Mass.; S. B., M. I. T., 1873; an architect in Boston.

2 *Anna M.*, b. in Cleveland, O., 21 Dec., 1856; m. 2 Feb., 1885, Cyrus A. Page, editor of the *Beacon,* Boston, b. 9 June, 1845; d. 10 May, 1898. Ch. (Page): i Phillips Ward[9]; ii Dorothy.

3 *Walter B.*, b. 2 April, 1864; m. 2 Oct., 1890, Gertrude Eleanor, dau. of Jacob E. Spring of Danvers, Mass.; A. B., Harvard Univ., 1886; a stockbroker in Boston. Ch.: Eleanor[9], Maud Brigham, Roger Spring.

ii Harriet Maria, b. 8 Aug., 1824; m. 2 April, 1850, Rev. Edward Clark of Reading, Mass.; was grad. Dartmouth Coll., 1844; Andover Theol. Sem., 1847; Chaplain Mass. Senate, 1862-64; Overseer Harvard Univ., 1862-64; Chaplain 47th Mass. Regt., 1863. They adopted a son who became the Rev. Francis Edward Clark, the founder of the " Christian Endeavor " societies; was grad. Dartmouth Coll., 1873; Andover Sem., 1876.

249 NATHANIEL[6], son of Winslow[5] and Alice (Cushing) Brigham, born in Northboro, Mass., 7 Oct., 1785; died there, 17 Sept., 1870; married, 22 April, 1812, Dolly, daughter of Silas* and Catherine (Newton) Ball of Southboro, Mass.; born, 11 April, 1786; died, 28 March, 1882. Nathaniel was a soldier of the War of 1812, and was Corp. in Capt. Pierpont Brigham's Co. of Mass. Militia. Served 10 Sept., 1814 to 1 Nov., 1814. He was drafted from Westboro and served in South Boston. His wife received a pension from 1 July, 1878, until her death.

Children, born in Northboro:
522 i Susan Augusta[7], b. 5 Jan., 1813.
523 ii Dolly Ann, b. 28 Feb., 1814.
524 iii Elijah Winslow, b. 18 July, 1816.
525 iv Catherine Ball, b. 8 Sept., 1818.
v Harriet Cushing, b. 25 March, 1820; d. unm., in Northboro, 5 Dec., 1873.
vi Nancy Maria, b. 16 Sept., 1821; d. unm., in Boston, 16 April, 1874.
vii Mary Prentice, b. 19 Feb., 1823; res. unm., in Northboro.

* Silas[7] Ball, son of Jonas[6] and ——— Ball of Marlboro; b. 1752; m. 1781; d. 1786. Jonas[6] Ball, son of Peter and Abigail (Dix) Ball of Watertown and Sudbury; b. 1736; d. 1807. Peter[5] Ball, son of Joseph[4] and Elizabeth (Parkhurst) Ball of Watertown; b. 1707; m. 1732. Joseph[4] Ball, son of John[3] and Sarah (Bullard) Ball of Watertown; b. 1674. John[3] Ball, son of John[2] and Elizabeth ——— Ball of Concord; b. 1644; m. 1665; d. 1722. John[2] Ball, son of John[1] Ball of Watertown and Concord; m. 1665; killed by Indians in Lancaster, 1675. John[1] Ball came from Wiltshire, Eng. Was made a Freeman in 1650; lived in Watertown and Concord and d. 1655.

    viii Nathaniel Walley, b. 12 Oct., 1824; d. 21 Sept., 1825.
    ix Josiah Quincy, b, 18 June, 1826; d. unm., 18 Aug., 1868; he res.
      at the American House, in Boston.
    x Nathaniel Sumner, b. 28 Feb., 1829; m. (1) March, 1852, Sarah
      Louisa Thompson, b. 20 Dec., 1832, in Leominster, Mass.; d.
      s. p., in Northboro, 29 June, 1879; m. (2) 1 Nov., 1881, Annis
      T., widow of Willard Jones of Worcester; res. Worcester, s. p.

250 ALICE[6], daughter of Winslow[5] and Alice (Cushing) Brigham; born in Northboro, Mass., 11 March, 1787; died in Milford, N. H., 19 Aug., 1862; married 22 April, 1812, Seth, son of Dea. Seth and Sarah (Brigham) Rice (86); born in Northboro, 25 March, 1788. Soon after his marriage, Mr. Rice made a journey to Canada and was never heard from again.

   Child (Rice), born in Northboro:
    i Lucy Brigham[7], b. 21 April, 1813; d. in Milford, N. H., 8 July,
      1900; m. 24 Sept., 1837, Thomas Treadwell Farnsworth of Groton.
      Ch. (Farnsworth), b. in Groton:
      1 *Lydia A.[8]*, m. Charles P. Whitney; s. p.
      2 *Lucy J.*, m. Lauren J. Blanpied; s. p.
      3 *Thomas H.*, d. unm., æ. 50.
      4 *George E.*, d. unm., æ. 22.
      5 *Georgianna M.*, d. y.
      6 *Alice M.*, d. unm., æ. 44.
      7 *Fred W.*, b. 8 Nov., 1854; m. Emlie M. Herschler of Red
        Wing, Minn.; res. Milford, N. H. Ch.: i Hazel A.[9]; ii Emlie
        B.; iii Harold T.; iv Kenneth A.; v Winston H.

251 JOSIAH[6], son of Winslow[5] and Alice (Cushing) Brigham, born in Northboro, Mass., 1 Sept., 1788; died in Quincy, Mass., 24 July, 1867; married 23 Nov., 1814, Elizabeth, only daughter of John Fisk of Northboro, born there, 18 Oct., 1791; died 10 Feb., 1866. Her mother was the daughter of the Rev. Abner Ballou, a Baptist clergyman.

    In April, 1811, Josiah went to Quincy to teach school and remained there until his death. In 1814 he went into business there, and continued in it for over 40 years. He was connected with several organizations and institutions as trustee, director and treasurer, and was president of the Quincy Savings Bank and the Quincy Stone Bank; was chairman of the school committee, town clerk, assessor and a Justice of the Peace. His military career began in 1814 and he was with the Quincy Light Infantry under command of Capt. Thomas Tirrell in its service in Boston in the War of 1812. After filling every subordinate place in the company he was elected in 1823, its commander. In 1826 he was chosen a Lieut. Col. in the Militia, but declined.

   Children, born in Quincy:
    i Abigail Fisk[7], b. 30 Dec., 1816; d. 1 July, 1885; m. 10 Nov.,
      1842, James A. Stetson, M. D., of Quincy. Ch. (Stetson):

1 *Josiah Brigham*[8], b. 23 July, 1843; d. 1895; m. Katie I. Lane.
2 *Elizabeth Fisk,* b. 20 Dec., 1845; d. 17 July, 1849.
3 *James H.,* b. 23 March, 1851; m. 1883, Clara M. Bayles of Camden, Me.; res. s. p., Quincy.
4 *Abigail.*

ii Elizabeth Ann, b. 2 April, 1820; m. 4 Nov., 1840, Charles F. Baxter, who was of the old firm of W. & S. Phipps & Co., Boston. Ch. (Baxter):
1 *Elizabeth F.*[8], b. 27 Oct., 1841.
2 *Charles Fuller,* b. 20 July, 1843; res. Dorchester.
3 *Langdon,* b. 29 July, 1849.

252 LUCY CUSHING[6], daughter of Winslow[5] and Alice (Cushing) Brigham; born in Northboro, Mass., 27 Sept., 1789; died in Blackstone, R. I., 21 Dec., 1861; married (1) 24 Nov., 1813, Jesse Wood Morse of Marlboro, Mass., 1785; died 7 May, 1832; married (2) 1838, Nathan White of Spencer, Mass.

Children (Morse), born in Marlboro:
i Jesse[7], d. y.
ii Stephen H., b. 10 Oct., 1821; d. 1902; m. in 1838, Lucinda Davis. Ch
1 *Burrill W.*[8], b. 1843.
2 *Winslow B.,* b. 1845.
3 *James B.,* b. 1847.
4 *Jessie C.,* b. 1856.
iii Winslow Brigham, b. 15 Nov., 1823; d. 18 Aug., 1893; m. (1) 31 March, 1847, in Northboro, Susan C. Carter, who d. 1855; m. (2) 1! May, 1856, Eugenia S. Carter, b. 23 June, 1838. Ch., b. in Berlin, Mass.:
1 *Susie Caroline*[8], b. 31 Aug., 1859; m. 1 May, 1883, Daniel H. Bassett, who d. 19 Jan., 1886; res. Berlin. Ch. (Bassett): i Eugenia L.[9]; ii Fred E.
2 *Lucy Sarah,* b. 21 Dec., 1862; d. Aug., 1866.
3 *Fred Winslow,* b. 6 Dec., 1866; a professor of chemistry in Durham, N. H.
4 *Jennie Eugenia,* b. 9 June, 1869; m. Philip G. Hilliard of Northboro.
5 *Sybil Eliza,* b. 6 Sept., 1872; d. May, 1874.
iv Emery* C., b. 25 April, 1826; d. 14 Feb., 1885; m. 7 July, 184~ Mary S. Spofford. Ch.:
1 *Mary A.*[8], b. 1859.
2 d. y.
3 d. y.

253 MICHAEL[6], son of Jonas[5] and Hann'
ham; born in North Brookfield, Mass., 2 Mar
Aug. 1802; married 21 Sept., 1796, Po¹¹
Rachel (Crosby) Tyler of Brookfiel'ʼ
she married (2) 17 April, 1805, W
and she died there, 19 July, 1ʳ
resided in North Brookfield.

Children, born in N. Brookfield:
   i John Tyler⁷, b. 1795; d. unm., 1849; a merchant in New York.
526   ii Anna Allen, b. 9 Dec., 1797.
527   iii Loring W., b. 30 Oct., 1799.
   iv Crosby, b. 1802; d. 25 Sept., 1803.

254   ELI⁶, son of Jonas⁵ and Hannah (Draper) Brigham; born
in North Brookfield, Mass., 14 Dec., 1774; died in Bakersfield,
Vt., 7 April, 1848; married (1) 3 Feb., 1803, Mary Harrington,
who died 22 Feb., 1822, æ. 46; married (2) Mercy Taylor, who
died 13 Aug., 1872. He resided in Bakersfield.

Children (by first wife), born in Bakersfield:
528   i Samuel Sumner⁷, b. 30 Oct., 1803.
   ii Jonas Draper, b. Jan., 1805; d. 29 March, 1822.
529   iii Sophia, b. 29 Sept., 1806.
530   iv Eli Whitney, b. Jan., 1809.
   v Mary, b. 26 Feb., 1812; d. in Chesterfield, N. Y., 25 March, 1873;
      m. 5 Oct., 1845, Nathan Hurd Winter of Chesterfield, where they
      res. Ch., b. there:
      1 *Fannie M.*⁸, b. 2 Oct., 1847; d. 11 Oct., 1893; m. 1867, Abram
         R. Bragg of Chesterfield. Ch. (Bragg): i Sumner A.⁹, m.,
         1 ch.; ii and iii d. y.; iv Hollis R.
      2 *Whitney Brigham*, b. 17 March, 1853; m. 1878, Addie A.
         Moore; res. Keesville. Ch.: i George H.⁹; ii Mary E.
531   vi Hubbard, b. 28 June, 1815.
   vii Lucy, b. June, 1821; d. 31 March, 1822.
Child (by second wife):
   viii Hollis, b. 2 June, 1825; d. s. p., in Bakersfield, 21 Aug., 1898;
      m. 12 May, 1870, Marion A. Brown of Bakersfield.

255   JONAS⁶, son of Capt. Jonas⁵ and Hannah (Draper)
Brigham; born in No. Brookfield, Mass., 14 March, 1782; died in
Bakersfield, Vt., 1 Jan., 1841; married Eunice Billings, who was
born 13 Aug., 1780; died 2 Sept., 1841. He was a farmer and resided
in Bakersfield. The *History of Vermont* contains interesting tales
of the hardships of the settlers of this town, of whom Jonas was one.
ᵀt took an entire week to go to mill and back again with their grain.

      ⁻ ⁻n, *born in Bakersfield:*
         ⁻da⁷, b. 15 April, 1806; d. 6 Aug., 1891; m. Metcalf Ayres,
         ⁻r; res. Bakersfield. Ch. (Ayres):
         ˢ who d. in the West.
            m. Horace Farwell. Ch. (Farwell): i Emma A.⁹,
            ⁻ʔ78, Eli Jones; 2 ch.; ii Harriet A.; m. 7 Jan., 1880,
            ʼvder; 4 ch.
            4 Nov., 1807.
            ⁻ov., 1809.
               ⁻l. 28 Feb., 1871; m. Ephraim Perkins;
               rkins):
                  d. 5 Dec., 1897; m. Elvira Ander-
                  June, 1858; d. 19 Aug., 1904; ii

Waldo B., b. 10 April, 1868; d. 22 Sept., 1868; iii George
E., b. 24 Jan., 1871; d. 30 March, 1872; iv Homer B., b. 13
Nov., 1879; d. 22 Oct., 1901; his widow is living in 1907.

  v Annah D., b. 18 April, 1814; d. unm., 17 April, 1894, in Bakers-
    field.

 vi Lovina, b. 7 June, 1816; d. s. p., 27 July, 1870; m. Horace
    Felcher.

vii Emily, b. 4 Oct., 1818; d. in Bakersfield, 16 Dec., 1883; m. 1844,
    Dea. James A. Perkins, a farmer of Bakersfield, who d. in 1889,
    æ. 82; he was deacon for 26 years. Ch. (Perkins):
    1 *Manlius R.*[8], b. 8 March, 1850; d. 31 May, 1893; m. 1 Jan.,
      1877, Laura G. Bradford. Ch.: i Harry B.[9], b. 17 March,
      1879; was grad. M. D., Univ. of Vt., 1903; on staff of Fletcher
      Hospital, Burlington, Vt.; ii Harley M., b. 28 April, 1883;
      a magazine correspondent and illustrator.
    2 *Emma Cornelia,* b. 1861; m. John W. Giddings; res. Cam-
      bridge Junc., Vt.

viii Jonas Michael, b. 23 Feb., 1821; d. ————————; m. Martha E.
     Church, who d. 1 March, 1871, æ. 35 yrs., 9 mos. Ch.:
     1 *Oscar Erastus*[8], b. 1 Sept., 1855; m. 15 May, 1892, Sarah J.,
       dau. of Wm. E. and Sarah (Reed) Neptune. Ch.: Helen
       Church[9], b. 16 Aug., 1894.
     2 *Fred,* b. 1 March, 1865; d. æ. 4 mos.
     3 *Clara E.,* b. 5 March, 1868; d. 12 Aug., 1870.

534 ix Moses B., b. 18 Sept., 1823.
535   x Jewett B., b. 25 Aug., 1826.

*256 DR. LUTHER[6], son of Jonas[5] and Hannah (Draper)
Brigham; born in North Brookfield, Mass., 15 May, 1785; died
in Ware, Mass., 28 Aug., 1856; married (1) Eunice Hawley of
Arlington, Vt., born 11 Jan., 1794; died in North Brookfield, 8
April, 1824; married (2) Betsey Ayers, born in North Brookfield,
7 Oct., 1800; died in Chicopee, Mass., 23 Oct., 1841; married (3)
Olivia L. Hadley, who died in Nashua, N. H., 5 Nov., 1850.

    Dr. Brigham was a graduate of the Philadelphia Medical Col-
lege and was a practicing physician in good standing, residing at
different times in Ware, Lowell and Chicopee, Mass. He was a
man of liberal culture, a fine speaker and often delivered lectures
and other public addresses. He was a Whig in politics, and attended the Congregational church. ·

    Children (by first wife):
      i Lucretia M.[7], b. 26 Oct., 1811; res. and d. in St. Albans, Vt.;
        m. Jason Lobdell. Ch. (Lobdell):
        1 *May*[8], who m. George Blanchard, and d.
     ii Jonas C., b. 27 July, 1813; d. in Detroit, Mich., 25 Jan., 1842.
536 iii Lemuel Hawley, b. 17 Aug., 1816.
     iv Martha Eliza, b. 27 July, 1818; m. John Warren Brigham, son
        of 327.
      v Hannah M., b. 21 Feb., 1821; m. Geo. Holt; res. Watertown,
        Minn. Ch. (Holt):
        1 *Emma*[8], m. Dr. Hiram Carson, and d.
        2 *Fred,* res. unm., in Chicago.

vi Eunice Jane, b. 9 April, 1823; d. 24 Jan., 1857, in Dickenson, N. Y.; m. Jason Lobdell, who also m. her sister Lucretia. Ch. (Lobdell):
  1 *Cassius*[8]; 2 *Henry*; 3 *Millie*, m. and res. Minneapolis.
Children (by second wife), the 8th and 9th born in Ware, Mass.:
vii George Homer, b. in Nashua, N. H., 18 Aug., 1830; d. unm., in Worcester, Mass., 22 May, 1857.
viii Elizabeth Ann, b. 16 Sept., 1831; m. 11 Jan., 1859, Hiram, son of Alvan Fowler of Westfield, Mass., b. there, 6 Jan., 1831; d. there, 3 Feb., 1891; he was a Civil Engineer. Ch. (Fowler), b. in Westfield:
  1 *Alvan Luther*[8], b. 7 Oct., 1859; m. Annie T. Simonds; res. New York City. Ch.; Alvan L.[9], b. 8 Dec., 1886.
  2 *Herbert Hiram*, b. 12 July, 1862; d. 25 July, 1862.
  3 *Esther Brigham*, b. 28 Jan., 1864; a missionary in India; she was educated at Smith College.
  4 *Lewis Henry*, b. 14 Oct., 1869; d. 9 Feb., 1876.
537 ix Luther Ayers, b. 7 Oct., 1832.
x Charlotte Rice, b. 27 Feb., 1834; d. in Ware, 8 June, 1835.
xi William Henry, b. 17 Oct., 1838; d. in Springfield, 3 Aug., 1839.
Child (by third wife), born in Nashua, N. H.:
xii Emma Frances, b. 28 April, 1847; m. 9 July, 1867, William Stoddard, b. in Fitchburg, Mass., 18 March, 1847. Ch. (Stoddard):
  1 *Anna Louisa*[8], b. 8 April, 1870.
  2 *Luther J. B.*, b. 15 June, 1874.
  3 *Curtis Duncan*, b. 22 Sept., 1881.

257 ASA[6], son of Capt. Jonas[5] and Hannah (Draper) Brigham, born in No. Brookfield, Mass., 1784; died in Bakersfield, Vt., 11 April, 1854; married, Sallie Hardy, born 1788; died 13 Aug., 1854. He resided in Bakersfield.

Children, born in Bakersfield:
i Amanda[7], b. 1809; d. soon after m., s. p., 1834; m. Dr. Truman Houghton of Bakersfield, b. 1807; d. 1879.
ii Lydia, b. 18 Dec., 1811; d. 4 Nov., 1889; m. Warren Houghton, a bro. of Dr. H.; b. 26 June, 1810; d. 18 July, 1886. Ch. (Houghton):
  1 *Marshall*[8]; 2 *Amanda*; 3 *Lodoiska*; 4 *Jay*; all probably deceased.
iii Bradley, b. 1814; d. s. p., 16 Feb., 1892; m. Dolly Potter, b. 1823; d. 21 Feb., 1892; a merchant in Bakersfield.
iv Baxter, b. 1 Feb., 1816; 'd. 27 Sept., 1856, in Bakersfield; m. 17 Sept., 1846, Laura Maria, dau. of Truman Chase of Westford, Vt., b. 24 Nov., 1822. She res. in Burlington, Vt. Ch
  1 *Dorr Baxter*[8], b. 27 Nov., 1847; d. 26 Sept., 1856.
  2 *Elva Maria*, b. 9 May, 1850; m. 12 Oct., 1875, Chauncey W. Brownell of Burlington, where res. Ch. (Brownell): i Carl Brigham[9], b. 27 April, 1877; ii Elva Mabel, b. 11 Feb., 1879; iii Chauncey Sherman, b. 23 Dec., 1880; iv Henry Chase, b. 1 Sept., 1887.
v Abigail, b. 1818; d. unm., in Hyde Park, Vt., 1894; res. Bakersfield, where interred.
vi Sarah, b. 20 March, 1820; d. s. p., in Charlotte, Vt., 8 June, 1896; m. John H. Sherman of Charlotte, b. 14 Dec., 1818; d. 15 April, 1888.

vii Rebecca, b. 1822; d. s. p., 1886; m. Henderson Gallup of Franklin, Vt., who d. before his wife.
viii Noah, b. 1825; d. 9 Aug., 1833.
ix Nahum, b. 9 May, 1827; d. unm., 1893, in Bakersfield.
538 x Waldo, b. 10 June, 1829.

258 CHENEY[6], son of Capt. Jonas[5] and Hannah (Draper) Brigham; born in Bakersfield, Vt., 22 April, 1793; died there, 28 Jan., 1865; married 20 May, 1821, Elizabeth, daughter of Uriah and Elizabeth (Fay) Brigham of Bakersfield, (147), born in Marlboro, Mass., 8 Jan., 1794; died in Bakersfield, 12 April, 1853. He was the first-born male in Bakersfield; was a farmer and always lived there.

Children, born in Bakersfield:
i Augustus Kendall[7], b. 31 Oct., 1821; d. in Bakersfield, 25 Nov., 1870; m. 16 March, 1854, Maria Shaw Lathrop, b. 3 Aug., 1833; d. 2 March, 1885; he was a farmer and res. in his native town. Ch
  1 *Susie Augusta[8]*, b. 5 June, 1871; m. 5 June, 1902, Bernard Joseph Cogan, b. in Liverpool, Eng., 1 Nov., 1873; res. Chicago. Ch. (Cogan): i Bernard Brigham[9], b. 10 April, 1903; ii Elizabeth Genevieve, b. 2 Oct., 1904.
ii Elizabeth Fay, b. 20 Jan., 1824; res. unm., in Brookline, Mass., in 1906.
539 iii Robert Breck, b. 1 Nov., 1826.

259 EDWARD[6], son of Edward[5] and Sally (Miller) Brigham; born in Westboro, Mass., 1782; died in St. Albans, Vt., where he resided. Name of wife unknown.

Children, born in Vermont:
i Edward[7], b. 1813.
ii Daniel P., b. in Milton, 1814; name of wife unknown; res, a painter, in Brookfield, Vt. Ch.:
  1 *Lucian[8];* 2 *Emma;* 3 *Charles,* (d.); 4 *Alice,* (d.).
iii Lucian V., b. 1817.
iv Phineas P., b. 1818.
540 v Leander D., b. in Milton, 16 Oct., 1820.
vi Lucian N., b. 1827.
vii Charles A., b. 1829.

260 OTIS[6], son of Barnabas[5] and Eunice (Mandell) Brigham; born in North Brookfield, Mass., 2 July, 1795; died in Needham, Mass., 6 Dec., 1862; married 11 April, 1830, Lucinda, daughter of Samuel and Hannah (Stowell) Pond; born in Dedham, Mass., 31 Oct., 1806; died 20 Oct., 1890. He resided in Dedham and Needham.

Children, the first 5 born in Dedham, the last 3 in Needham:
i Joseph Henry[7], b. 18 April, 1831; d. 14 Nov., 1899; m. 20 Nov., 1862, Mary E. Hamilton; res. 1872, in Medfield, Mass.
ii Francis Otis, b. 8 Nov., 1832; res. Stoneham, Mass.; d. 1904.

iii Horace Wait, b. 8 Oct., 1834; d. 8 March, 1835.
iv Hannah Lucinda, b. 24 April, 1836; m. 28 Feb., 1871, Eliakim
Holman Ross, b. 16 May, 1836. Ch. (Ross):
1 *Henry A.*[8], b. 9 Jan., 1872.
2 *Jenny E.*, b. 5 Nov., 1874; d. 26 June, 1881.
v Horace Wait, b. 8 Oct., 1838; d. 17 May, 1862.
vi George Frederick, b. 11 Sept., 1840; d. in Stoneham, 20 Jan.,
1869; m. 24 Nov., 1863, Sarah Ellis Gerry.
vii Charles, b. 23 Oct., 1843; d. 25 April, 1881.
viii Nancy Jane, b. 22 Nov., 1845; d. 21 April, 1878; m. 30 June,
1870, Frank D. Blake.

261 BARNABAS[6], son of Dr. Daniel[5] and Anna (Munroe)
Brigham; born in Northboro, Mass., 14 April, 1786; died in Marlboro, Mass., 4 June, 1865; married (1) 20 April, 1824, Mary,
daughter of William Fife of Bolton, Mass., born 9 Nov., 1796;
died 4 Aug., 1839; married (2) Mary, daughter of Eber and
Sarah (Barnes) Rice, born in St. Albans, Vt., 6 Jan., 1802; died
in Marlboro, 5 Sept., 1882.

He resided with his father in Berlin and Marlboro, and held
town offices in Berlin and was constable there many years. In
Marlboro they resided on the farm on Brigham Street, described
under 541. He and his wives were members of the Unitarian
church.

Children (by first wife), born in Marlboro:
i Abigail[7], b. 5 April, 1825; d. 4 June, 1883; m. 5 April, 1865,
William H. Howe, who d. 24 Feb., 1891. Ch. (Howe):
1 *Edgar Brigham*[8], b. 23 April, 1866; d. 13 Aug., 1869.
2 *Mary Eva,* b. 16 Dec., 1868; res. unm., in Marlboro.
ii Mary Ann, b. 17 Oct., 1826; d. in Santa Barbara, Cal., ————;
m. 1 May, 1849, Stephen G. Livermore, who d. in Cedar Rapids,
Ia. Ch. (Livermore):
1 *Ella M.*[8], b. 10 May, 1850; d. 17 Dec., 1855.
2 *Harry E.*, b. and d. 1855.
3 *Ida E.*, b. 27 Dec., 1862; m. and res. in Los Angeles, Cal.
4 *Emma M.*, b. 10 July, 1864; res. Santa Barbara.
iii William Fife, b. 21 Sept., 1829; d. s. p., 18 July, 1863, of southern
fever; m. 21 June, 1853, Frances Davidson, who d. Oct., 1904.
He enlisted in the 45th Regt., Mass. Vols.
iv Mindwell, b. 2 June, 1832; d. 15 July, 1880; m. 21 May, 1861,
Lawson M. Gassett, who m. again and res. in Pa., and d. Ch.
(Gassett):
1 *Arthur L.*[8], b. 12 Jan., 1867, res. in the West.
2 *Ella,* b. July, 1869; d. 1869.
3 *George,* b. in Grafton, Mass., ————————; res. in the West.
541   v Addington Munroe, b. 27 March, 1837.
Child (by second wife), born in Marlboro:
vi Joseph Edward, b. 12 May, 1844; d. 19 June, 1905; m. 25 Jan.,
1875, Mary Whitney, dau. of John Loring, b. in Marlboro, 18
Aug., 1842. He dealt in timber and at one time kept a hotel.
Was in the Civil War, during the last year of the conflict, in Co.
H, 17th Regt., Mass. Vols. Ch.:

1 *Alice May*[8], b. in Marlboro, 24 Nov., 1876; a well known musician; played with great effect for the 7th Reunion of the B. F. A.

262 DANIEL[6], son of Dr. Daniel[5] and Anna (Munroe) Brigham; born in Northboro, Mass., 27 Jan., 1788; died in Marlboro, Mass., 29 Nov., 1841; married Sarah M. Barnard, in 1813; born 13 March, 1789; died June, 1870.

Children, born in Northboro:
542   i Charles Amory[7], b. 26 Sept., 1814.
    ii Persis Baker, b. 7 Jan., 1816; d. unm., in 1898.
    iii Elizabeth B., b. 21 Oct., 1817; d. 23 Dec., 1835.
    iv Edward F., b. 22 July, 1819; d. March, 1869; m. 22 May, 1855, Martha A., dau. of Elisha Johnson; b. in Southboro, Mass., 28 Feb., 1832; res. No. Brookfield, Mass. Ch ·
      1 *Lizzie M.*[8], b. 5 May, 1858; d. 9 Jan., 1877.
      2 *Hattie S.*, b. in No. B., 22 July, 1865; res. unm., in Watertown, Mass.
    v Sarah Ann, b. 2 April, 1821.
    vi Hannah B., b. 13 June, 1823; d. 29 Oct., 1825.
    vii Daniel L., b. 18 Oct., 1825; d. 6 Sept., 1827.
    viii ————, perhaps one who d. in Framingham, 15 Sept., 1884, æ. 59.

263 LOIS[6], daughter of Dr. Daniel[5] and Anna (Munroe) Brigham; born in Northboro, Mass., 14 April, 1793; died in Westboro, Mass., 31 March, 1890; married 3 May, 1815, Capt. Theophilus, son of Dr. Benjamin Nourse; born in Berlin, Mass., 9 April, 1787; removed to Westboro, where he died, 24 April, 1824.

Children (Nourse), born in Berlin:
    i *Benjamin Bailey*[7], b. 31 March, 1816; d. 24 Sept., 1900; m. 19 Oct., 1843, Mary E. Langley. He was a manufacturer of plant trellises, etc.; an accurate surveyor and the best posted man on town matters; held many offices; in 1875 appointed Spec. Justice of First Dist. Court, E. Mass.; res. in Westboro. Ch.:
      1 *Frank*[8]; 2 *Henry*, both d. y; 3 *Emma*; 4 *Walter B.*, architect of Worcester; 3 ch.
    ii Jane, b. 10 Aug., 1817; m. 15 Oct., 1838, Charles P. Rice of Westboro. Ch. (Rice), b. in Westboro:
      1 *Charles Amory*[8], b. 26 April, 1840; m. (1) 6 April, 1866, Lizzie B., dau. of O. P. Wakefield of Lyndon, Vt.; b. 15 Jan., 1837; d. 6 July, 1873; m. (2) 18 Sept., 1876, Ella J., dau. of C. R. Cleveland of Guilford, Vt.; b. Athol, Mass., 19 Dec., 1851; 2 ch.
      2 *Jennie M.*, b. 28 June, 1847; d. 6 May, 1904.
      3 *Louise S.*, b. 28 June, 1847; m. 28 Nov., 1878, James Alexander Kelley, b. in Northboro, 9 June, 1835; res. Westboro, s. p.
    iii Catherine, b. 18 Jan., 1820; m. 8 May, 1844, Lyman G. Stephens of Westboro and Marlboro. Ch. (Stephens):
      1 *Frederick W.*[8], of Newton; 2 *George L.*
    iv Lois Brigham, b. 2 Sept., 1824; d. 22 June, 1851; m. 14 June, 1849, Henry W. Baldwin of Shrewsbury, Mass.; 1 ch., d. y.

264 ABRAHAM MUNROE[6], son of Dr. Daniel[5] and Anna (Munroe) Brigham; born in Marlboro, Mass., 25 March, 1796; died in Westboro, Mass., 26 Oct., 1882, æ. 86; married, in 1822, Mindwell, daughter of Winslow and Alice (Cushing) Brigham; born in Northboro, 5 May, 1796; died 1 Jan., 1870. He was the landlord of the American House, Boston, for many years.

Children, born in Boston:
  i Caroline Matilda[7], b. 1 Feb., 1823; d. 23 Feb., 1823.
543 ii Lydia Maria, b. 23 Nov., 1824.
  iii Henry Lyman, b. 7 June, 1828; d. 24 Aug., 1847.

265 OTIS[6], son of David[5] and Lucy (Harrington) Brigham; born in Westboro, Mass., 1788; died there 15 April, 1872; married (1) 16 June, 1819, Abigail, daughter of Zealous Bates of Cohasset, Mass., and sister of Rev. Joshua Bates, D. D., President of Middlebury, Vt., College; born 22 Jan., 1792; died 2 May, 1831; married (2) Adeline, sister of his first wife, born 10 May, 1801; died 2 Oct., 1866.

He was Captain in the war of 1812 and helped to raise troops for the Civil War. A prosperous farmer, he yet found time to devote to church and town affairs with great energy and success. For 40 years he was superintendent of the first Sunday-school started in Westboro. Was selectman 1827-'28, 1830-'33, 1836-'43; overseer of the poor and moderator of town meetings for many years. Was Representative from Westboro in 1839 and 1840. In 1834 he began to collect the genealogy of the Brighams, and his experience, like that of others who have followed him, was full of hardship. After 14 years he had found most of the records collected later by Morse. No encouragement to publish was given him and he drew a chart of the branch to which he belonged and sent the rest of the MSS. to various places where he hoped it might be of use, but it was beyond recovery when Morse needed it. He gathered annually at the old firesides in Westboro large companies of Brighams.

Children (by first wife), born in Westboro:
  i Henrietta A.[7], b. 5 April, 1820; d in Westboro, 25 Jan., 1896; m. 16 Feb., 1848, Samuel M., son of Dr. Samuel Griggs, b. in Grafton, Vt., 10 Sept., 1822; d. in Westboro, 7 Nov., 1886; was in business in Westboro; town clerk 31 years; representative and state senator, and a leader in the church. Ch. (Griggs), b. in Westboro:
    1 *Sarah Bancroft[8]*, b. 1 May, 1854; m. 17 May, 1883, Dr. Henry S., son of Franklin H. and Sarah (Hood) Knight of Worcester, Mass., b. there in 1853. Ch. (Knight): Roscoe Griggs[9], b. 16 Nov., 1886, in Amherst Coll, 1906.
544 ii George Otis, b. 9 Nov., 1821.
  iii Sereno Leroy, b. 9 April, 1824; d. unm., in the West, 8 Oct., 1860; was injured by a fall.

iv Ivers Jewett, b. 31 Oct., 1826; d. 11 Aug., 1847, unm.
545   v Joshua Bates, b. 28 Sept., 1828.
Children (by second wife), born in Westboro:
  vi Abigail Adeline, b. 21 March, 1833; d. 18 Nov., 1899; m. 26
     June, 1861, Orville K. Hutchinson; res. s. p., N. Y. City.
  vii Lucy Harrington, b. 1 June, 1834; res. unm., in Westboro.
  viii Ann Frances, b. 13 Dec., 1835; d. 9 Feb., 1843, of scarlet fever.
  ix Mary Jane, b. 21 Nov., 1837; d. 9 Feb., 1843, of the same disease.
  x Daniel Edward, b. 22 Dec., 1840; d. 30 Dec., 1840.

266   REV. DAVID[6], son of David[5] and Lucy (Harrington)
Brigham; born in Westboro, Mass., 2 Sept., 1794; died Bridge-
water, Mass., 18 April, 1888; married 1 March, 1819, Elizabeth
H. Durfee of Fall River, Mass.

Mr. Brigham studied two years at Brown University and finished
at Union Collēge, where he was graduated, A. B., 1818. Studied
theology under the direction of Drs. Emmons and Ide of Medway,
Mass. He was pastor in East Randolph, Mass., (now Holbrook),
1819-'36; in Framingham, Mass., 1837-'45; Bridgewater, Central
Square Church, 1845-'59. He retired from the ministry with im-
paired health and resided several years in Fall River. Was pastor
of a small church in Waquoit, a section of Falmouth, 1863-'69. In
1876 he attempted to fill the pulpit of the Second Church in Plymouth, Mass., but a serious illness interrupted his labors. He
served 62 years in the ministry. He was a man of great energy
of purpose.

Children, the eldest, fourth, fifth and sixth, born in Fall River:
  i Elizabeth Durfee[7], b. 1 May, 1821; m. 6 Nov., 1851, Valentine,
     son of Christopher D. Copeland; res. Bridgewater, Mass. Ch.
     (Copeland), b. in B.:
       1 *Lucy H. B.[8]*, m. F. Chapin Davis of Longmeadow, Mass.
       2 *Alice G.*, m. Herbert Pratt of Quincy, Mass.
       3 *Annie Gilbert*, a physician, res. Bridgewater.
546   ii David Sewall, b. E. Randolph, Mass., 17 March, 1823.
  iii Lucy Harrington, b. E. Randolph, 28 July, 1827; d. 17 Aug.,
     1853.
547   iv Charles Durfee, b. 21 July, 1831.
  v Thomas Russell, b. 7 Jan., 1834; m. in St. Louis, Mo., 7 Oct.,
     1869, Delia H. Larrimore; res. in St. Louis. Ch.:
       1 *Samuel Edward[8]*, b. 22 Aug., 1870; res. St. Louis.
       2 *Lucy Harrington*, b. 8 Aug., 1872.
       3 *David William*, b. 26 April, 1875; res. St. Louis.
       4 *Charles Sewall*, b. 11 July, 1881; d. *ibid.*
       5 *Chester Russell*, b. 26 Dec., 1892.
       6 *Thomas,* an adopted son.
  vi Martha Ann, b. 28 April, 1837; m. George August, son of Dea.
     Daniel King. Ch. (King):
       1 *Mary B.[8]*, m. Eugene H. Babbitt of New York City.
       2 *Alice W.,* m. Edgar G. Murphy of San Antonio, Texas.
       3 *Louise B.;* 4 *George G.*
  vii Mary Agnes, b. 21 Aug., 1839; d. 11 Aug., 1858.

267   HON. (DEA.) ELMER[6], son of David[5] and Lucy (Harrington) Brigham; born in Westboro, Mass., 8 Sept., 1798; died in Westboro, 3 March, 1871; married 14 May, 1823, Betsey Curwen, daughter of Joel and Hannah (Bond) Parker; born in Westboro, 20 Jan., 1799; died 29 Nov., 1875.

Dea. Brigham was a distinguished citizen of Westboro, serving the town in many ways, most ably. He engaged in farming. He represented the town three terms in the General Court and was a member of the State Senate and Governor's Council; held many town offices and was on several important committees; was treasurer of Westboro Reform School, and held the church office of Deacon from 1848-'69.

Children, born in Westboro:
  i   Ellen Elizabeth[7], b. 3 March, 1824; d. s. p., 13 Sept., 1848; m. 12 May, 1847, David W. Hill of Westminster, Mass.
548   ii   Janette Hannah, b. 9 Jan., 1827.
549   iii Merrick Putnam, b. 9 March, 1829.
  iv   Anna Parker, b. 18 Sept., 1832; d. 26 Feb., 1870, s. p.; m. 3 Feb., 1853, Charles A. Harrington, of Westboro.
  v   Sophia Augusta, b. 10 July, 1837; d. 17 April, 1842.
  vi Susan Parker, b. 4 Jan., 1840; d. 14 Oct., 1863.
  vii Charles Elmer, b. 14 March, 1842; d. 28 July, 1877, s. p.; m. 2 March, 1866, Ellen Davis.
  viii Calvin Lloyd, b. 30 July, 1844; d. 11 June, 1902; m. (1) 11 Oct., 1866, Mary Millicent, dau. of Josiah Brown; who d. 6 April, 1875; m. (2) 29 June, 1876, Ethie J., dau. of James Burpee of Sterling, Mass. Ch., by 1st wife:
    1 *Alice A.,* b. 10 May, 1868; res. in Marlboro, unm.

268   CAPT. HOLLOWAY[6], son of David[5] and Lucy (Harrington) Brigham; born in Westboro, Mass., 2 Sept., 1801; died 28 March, 1869; married, at Royalston, Mass., 31 Aug., 1823, Frances, daughter of Jonathan Read (Preceptor of Academy at Portland, Me.); born in Portland, 27 April, 1805; died, his widow, in Boston, 1 Sept., 1882.

Capt. Brigham was named after his uncle, Rev. Holloway Fish, who adopted him. He resided in Marlboro, N. H., until 1830, when he moved to Northboro, Mass., (some records say " Westboro ").

Children, the 3 eldest born in Marlboro, N. H., the younger in Northboro (or Westboro):
  i   Jane Putnam[7], b. 29 Aug., 1824; d. in Falmouth, Mass., 30 Sept., 1887; m. 15 April, 1846, Hon. Austin Belknap of Westboro, Mass.; res. in Somerville, Mass., where Mr. Belknap was mayor in 1875; he d. in 1902. Ch. (Belknap):
    1 *Jennie M.[8],* b. 1851; m. Roswell C. Downer. Ch. (Downer):
      i Cutler[9]; ii Helen.

2 *Frances R.,* b. 1857; d. 1871.
3 *Robert William,* b. ————; m. Dora Parkinson. Ch.
(Belknap): i Howard P.⁹ ; ii Stearns E., who d. 1893.
ii Hannah Farrar, b. 20 March, 1827; d. 10 June, 1906; m. 15
April, 1847, Calvin, son of Calvin and Anna (Holbrook) French
of Holbrook, Mass.; b. 11 Oct., 1811; d. 20 Dec., 1884. Ch.
(French):
1 *George Bradford⁸,* b. 28 July, 1853; m. 30 April, 1889, Abbie
F. Hollis, b. 5 July, 1860; she is in 8th gen., direct line from
Gov. Bradford. He is in business in Barristers Hall, Boston,
and res. s. p., Holbrook, Mass.
iii Maria E., b. 22 Sept., 1829; d. unm., 19 Jan., 1879.
iv Lyman M., b. 8 Feb., 1836; d. probably s. p., Aug., 1885; m.
22 Nov., 1864, Jennie Moody of Waterbury, Vt.; was a trader in
Essex Junc., Vt.
550 v Cyrus, b. 27 Dec., 1838.
vi Harriet Frances, b. 1 Jan., 1842; m. 1 Jan., 1870, William E.
Bryant; res. s. p., in Boston, Mass.

269 SYLVANUS⁶, son of Alpheus⁵ and Lydia (Green) Brigham; born in Shrewsbury, Mass., 10 Feb., 1771; died in Boylston,
N. Y.; married Amy, daughter of William Cox, who died in Galilee, Pa. He resided in Florida and Springfield, N. Y.
Children, the eldest and fourth born in Florida, N. Y.:
551 i Hiram Wright⁷, b. 29 Dec., 1799.
ii Samantha.
552 iii Cynthia M., b. 26 April, 1807.
553 iv William C., b. 12 July, 1802.
554 v Philip P., b. in Springfield, N. Y., 5 Sept., 1810.
vi Orville, b. 7 May, 1813; m. Sept., 1847, Mrs. Sophia Houghton,
widow of Hiram R.; he d. s. p.
vii Emeline B., b. 7 May, 1813; d. 11 Jan., 1889, s. p.; m. 2 Jan.,
1859, Calvin S. Marks.
555 viii Orrin A., b. in Boylston, N. Y., 4 May, 1820.
ix Jonathan.
x Amy d. y.
xi Alonzo, d. y.

270 ABEL⁶, son of Alpheus⁵ and Lydia (Green) Brigham;
born in Shrewsbury, Mass., 31 July, 1773; died in Rodman, N.
Y., 18 Oct., 1850; married, 1795, Phebe, daughter of Joseph
Wheeler, born in New Hampshire, 6 June, 1777; died in Rodman,
14 Nov., 1858. Was a teacher and merchant and resided in Westmoreland, Whitesboro, Watertown, and Rodman, N. Y.
Children, 3 eldest born in New Hampshire, others as indicated:
i Achsah⁷, a teacher, and d. unm., in Rodman, 14 Oct., 1849.
ii Lavantia, b. 1803; d. 18 Sept., 1870; m. Jan., 1830, Capt. John,
son of Tilly Richardson; b. in Mass., 1795; d. 30 March, 1870;
was a teacher; res. in Rodman. Ch. (Richardson):
1 *Mary Eliza⁸,* b. 5 Sept., 1834; m. 1867, Nathan Graham; res.
Lakeport, Cal.
2 *John Jay,* b. 24 Oct., 1836; res. Worthville, N. Y.

    iii Rebecca, m. 1835, William C. Johnson, b. in Walton, N. Y., 1804; d. 6 March, 1880; res. Aurora, N. Y. Ch. (Johnson):
      1 *Chrisfield*[8], author of *Hist.* of *Erie Co., N. Y.;* res. Ithaca, N. Y.

    iv Eliza, b. 1808, in N. Y. State; d. s. p., 2 March, 1823; m. March, 1822, Augustus R. Moin of N. Y. City.

    v Charlotte, b. in Watertown, N. Y., 24 July, 1816; d. 4 Aug., 1881; m. Dec., 1849, Elias Parkhurst, b. in England, and d. in Rodman, 1894; res. Rodman. Ch. (Parkhurst):
      1 *Adelbert*[8], who d. æ. 2.
      2 *Medora*, m. Frank Brown and was divorced.
      3 *Frank.*
      4 *Herbert.*

    vi Tracy Abel, b. Dec., 1818, in Watertown; left home, æ. 17; lived in Aurora, N. Y., then went to Ohio.

    vii Cornelia Jane, b. in Watertown, 12 Oct., 1820; m. 18 Nov., 1847, Caleb Eton, son of Joseph Hitchcock, b. in Vermont, 3 Sept., 1824; d. 28 Sept., 1852; she was a cheesemaker; res. in Watertown, Worth, Rodman and Richland, N. Y. Ch. (Hitchcock):
      1 *Julia C.*[8], b. 28 Feb., 1849; m. 1875, (1) Horace Draper m. (2) John Cole. Ch. (Draper): i Lillian E.[9] Ch. (Cole): ii Lena M.; iii Cornelia.
      2 *Eugenia Ella*, b. 3 Nov., 1850; m. 1871, Eugene Shoecraft of Mannsville, N. Y. Ch. (Shoecraft): i Jacob E.[9], grad. of Albany Med. College; ii Martha M.

    viii Lucy Ann, b. 10 June, 1822; d. unm., 12 Oct., 1848.

271 ASA[6], son of Leonard[5] and Abigail (Forbush) Brigham; born in Walpole, N. H., 18 June, 1781; died in Essex, Vt., about 1840; married in 1802, Lavina Bellows of Essex. He settled in Essex about 1812, and resided on " Brigham Hill," grown now to be a summer resort.

Children, born in Essex, except Calvin, who was b. in Milton, Vt.:
    i Warren[7], res. Essex.
556 ii Calvin, b. 1805.
    iii Sarah.
    iv Asa, who d.; m. Polly ————; res. Essex Junc.; has two grandchildren.
    v Rebecca, m. A. A. Slater, Essex Centre. Ch. (Slater):
      1 *John*[8].
    vi Lavina, m. E. B. Collins, Burlington, Vt.; 1 dau.[8], m. ———— Thayer; has dau., Etta[9].
    vii Rufus, m. ————. Ch.:
      1 *Martha*[8], who m. ———— Kimball. Ch. (Kimball): i Jennie[9]; ii Edwin B.
    · viii Lyman, res. Essex; m. ————————. Ch.: 1 dau., *Mrs. Harold Stevens*[8] of Burlington, Vt. Ch. (Stevens): i Edson C.[9], of Winooski, Vt.; ii Harrison A. of Burlington.

272 RUFUS[6], son of Leonard[5] and Abigail (Forbush) Brigham; born in Walpole, N. H., 9 Feb., 1786; died in Hampden, O., (whither he removed in 1835), 12 Dec., 1838; married (1) Dec.,

1815, Sophia Wheelock of Essex, Vt., born 1791; died 29 Aug., 1826; married (2) 14 April, 1830, Lydia Morgan of Essex, born 1791; died 27 May, 1857. He was a farmer.

Children (by first wife), born in Essex:
i David B.[7], b. 29 July, 1817; d. in Thompson, O., 4 April, 1845; m. Jane Clark; he was a farmer.
ii Sarah S., b. 20 June, 1819; d. 5 July, 1872; m. (1) 14 Feb., 1838, Douglas Hurlburt, a manufacturer of cloth; m. (2) 25 May, 1843, Chillion Strong, a farmer of Thompson, O. Ch. (Hurlburt):
1 *Diana*[8]. Ch. (Strong): 2 *Newton*.
Child (by second wife), born in Essex:
557 iii Daniel Morgan, b. 25 Sept., 1832.

273 JONATHAN[6], son of Leonard[5] and Abigail (Forbush) Brigham; born in Walpole, N. H., 23 Oct., 1788; died in Chardon, O., 1856; married, in 1812, Melinda Davenport of St. Lawrence Co., N. Y. He moved in 1817 to Madison, O., and in 1821 to Hampden, O., thence to Chardon, O.

Children, the 3 elder born in N. Y., the last 5 in Hampden:
i Laura[7], d. y.
ii Eliza, b. 13 April, 1815; m. in 1839, Milton Tilden of Unionville, O. Ch. (Tilden):
1 *Stella*[8].
iii Laura, b. 11 April, 1817; d. in 1852; m. in 1835, S. N. Burroughs of Montville, O.; 7 ch.
iv Leonard R. (Dr.), b. in Madison, 11 July, 1819; m. in 1844, Eliza S. Fancher of Auburn, N. Y.; res. Painesville, O.; Ed. Farmington Inst., O.; a popular lecturer on Medicine, Hygiene, etc.
v Eunice, b. in Madison, 10 May, 1821; a teacher in Lena, Ill.; m. in 1850, Alfred A. Ovary.
vi Daniel J., b. 10 May, 1823; m. 1851, Nancy Roberts of Lena, Ill.; res. Iowa.
vii Polly A., b. 18 Nov., 1824; m. A. A. Crary of Freeport, Ill.; res. Lena, Ill.
ix Orman H., b. 12 May, 1827; drowned in Akron, O., 1849.
x Melinda L., b. 19 June, 1833; teacher in Ill.; m. W. T. House, and moved to Wells Mill, Mo.
xi Lewis D., b. June, 1838; res. Lena, Ill.

274 SILAS[6], son of Leonard[5] and Abigail (Forbush) Brigham; born in Walpole, N. H., 16 Oct., 1791; died in Harpersfield, O., 26 March, 1850; married, 27 May, 1818, Polly, daughter of Archibald Harding of Locke, N. Y.; born 16 July, 1796; died in Ohio, 10 May, 1854. He was a farmer; was town trustee, and in the war of 1812.

Children, born in Harpersfield:
i Samantha[7], b. 11 April, 1820; d. 11 March, 1821.
558 ii Nelson, b. 21 Oct., 1821.
559 iii Hiram, b. 14 Feb., 1823.
iv Almond, b. 27 Nov., 1826; d. in 1827.

560   v Albert Crawford, b. 13 Nov., 1828.
   vi Paulina Lois, b. 4 Dec., 1831; d. 1878; m. 8 Dec., 1857, Jerome
      B. Vankirk; she was a teacher; res. Rush Lake, Wis. Ch.
      (Vankirk):
      1 *Frederick Euclid*[8], b. 12 Dec., 1858.
      2 *Flora May*, b. 25 March, 1860.
      3 *Weldon Brigham*, b. 18 May, 1862.
      4 *Orley Jerome*, b. 15 July, 1864.
      5 *Jennilla*, b. 31 Jan., 1867.
      6 *Alice Euphane*, b. 11 Sept., 1869.
   vii Mary Louise, b. 7 Jan., 1835; m. (1) 4 Jan., 1860, William Van-
      kirk, who d. in Rush Lake, 25 Dec., 1878; m. (2) 25 Dec., 1879,
      Jerome B. Vankirk, widower of her sister Paulina; she was a
      teacher; res. Rush Lake. Ch. (Vankirk), by first husband:
      1 *Luella Orsino*[8], b. 9 Nov., 1861; d. 4 Nov., 1862.
      2 *Genevra Estelle*, b. 3 May, 1864; d. 17 Oct., 1865.
      3 *Anna Louise*, b. 4 April, 1868.
      4 *Lyndon Jay*, b. 10 June, 1872.
561 viii George Washington, b. 22 Sept., 1836.
   ix Henry Harrison, b. 1 Sept., 1840; d. s. p., 12 Oct., 1867; m. 1865,
      Louisa Morrison; he was in the Civil War, 2d O. Cavalry; was
      twice wounded, one wound proving fatal; he was a farmer.

275   HIRAM[6], son of Leonard[5] and Abigail (Forbush) Brigham; born in Milton, Vt., Nov., 1800; died in Croton, Ohio, 1838,
where he moved in 1834; married, 1829, Hannah Carpenter of
Milton.

Children:
   i Silas Hermon[7], b. in Milton, 8 Nov., 1833; d. 13 June, 1879; m.
      6 Nov., 1860, Lucy A. Root of Granville, O., b. 6 Dec., 1839;
      she res. Hutsonville, Ill. Ch.:
      1 *Clara Belle*[8], b. in Pickerington, O., 2 Sept., 1861; d. at
         res. in Robinson, Ill., 21 May, 1885; m. Joseph Ferrel. Ch.
         (Ferrel): i Charles H.[9], b. 24 Sept., 1884; d. 19 July, 1887.
      2 *Luther Harvey*, res. Robinson, Ill; 4 ch.
      3 *Emma Cornelia*, b. Hardinsville, Ill., 15 Nov., 1865; m. Austin
         Price; res. Eaton, Ill.; ch. 1 dau.
      4 *Mary Luella*, b. Hardinsville, 20 July, 1870; m. William Aker-
         man; res. Eaton; 5 ch.
      5 *Omer Allen*, b. Robinson, 13 Jan., 1874; m. Bertha J. Stark;
         res. Hutsonville. Ch.: i Jennie Madge[9], b. 29 July, 1901; ii
         John Herman, b. 9 May, 1903.
      6 *Nina Cleone*, b. in Robinson, 4 Feb., 1877; d. 5 June, 1879.
   ii Harvey Carpenter, b. in Hartford, O.; m. 30 March (or Nov.),
      1861, at H., Mary H. Morrow of Johnstown, O.; res. E. St.
      Louis, Ill. Ch., b. in Robinson, Ill.:
      1 *Frank Clifford*[8], b. 11 Dec., 1864; d. 13 Oct., 1865.
      2 *George Morrow*, b. 16 April, 1867; a livestock dealer, E. St.
         Louis.
      3 *Willametta*, b. 9 Dec., 1869; m. E. E. Gordon; res. Robin-
         son, Ill.
      4 *Bertha Emeline*, b. 24 Jan., 1873; d. 27 July, 1874.

276   DEA. SULLIVAN[6], son of Capt. Stephen[5] and Sarah (Harrington) Brigham; born in Fitzwilliam, N. H., 29 Dec., 1781; died in Vienna, N. Y., 2 Oct., 1867; married (1), 5 Jan., 1804, Amanda, daughter of Uriah Spalding; born 9 Feb., 1778; died in Vienna, 3 Feb., 1849; married (2) Mrs. Nancy Bryan. He resided in Westmoreland, and in Vienna, Oneida Co., N. Y.

Children (by first wife), the elder ones born in Westmoreland:
    i Lucinda[7], b. 5 Dec., 1804; d. 27 Oct., 1841; m. 29 Sept., 18—, William E. Thorn of Washington, O., b. 3 Jan., 1803; d. 2 July, 1870. Ch. (Thorn):
        1 *Daniel W.[8]*, b. 5 Dec., 1837; m. 1868, Anna Whitmill; res. Samaria, Mich. Ch.: i Charles F.[9]; ii Adelaide F.; iii William J.; iv Pearl E., d. y.; v Euphemia E.; vi Gilbert A.
        2 *Theodore*, b. 30 Jan., 1839; m. 1871, Mary A. Pierce; res. Bedford, Mich. Ch.: i Maurice T.[9], d. y.; ii Mavor B.; iii George L.
562 ii Mavor, b. 16 May, 1806.
    iii Eliza, b. 29 Aug., 1808; d. 30 March, 1856; m. 1 April, 1840, Edward Doty; res. Rome, N. Y.
    iv Rollin, b. 12 Oct., 1810; d. 2 Jan., 1855; m. 4 March, 1849, Louisa Risley, who d.; res. Vienna.
    v Arethusa, b. 30 Oct., 1812; d. 25 Jan., 1858; m. 3 Oct., 1835, Ansel L. Johnson; res. Vienna.
    vi Faber, b. 21 Feb., 1815; d. 24 Nov., 1844, unm.
    vii Newell, b. 1 Jan., 1820; d. 25 March, 1841, unm.
    viii Sarah, b. in Vienna, b. May, 1823; m. 5 Oct., 1854, James D. Marks, b. in Vergennes, Vt., 22 June, 1812; d. in Vienna, 27 Aug., 1890; res. Vienna. Ch. (Marks), b. in Vienna:
        1 *Ira Brigham[8]*, b. 3 May, 1857; d. 30 March, 1861.
        2 *Charles F.*, b. 22 July, 1861; m. 27 July, 1881; res. Vienna.
        3 *Nellie Eliza*, b. 23 Oct., 1864; d. 27 Aug., 1872.

277   CAPT. STEPHEN[6], son of Capt. Stephen[5] and Sarah (Harrington) Brigham; born in Fitzwilliam, N. H., 11 Apr., 1783; died in Vernon, N. Y., 24 July, 1850; married (1), in 1824, Widow Ruby Wetmore, born 27 Jan., 1793; died 16 June, 1828; married (2), 1832, Elizabeth Stevens, born 20 Sept., 1802; died 7 Aug., 1870. He moved to Vernon with his parents; held town offices.

Children (by first wife), born in Vernon:
    i Harriet T.[7], b. 9 April, 1825; m. 29 May, 1849, Isaac Adams, Jr., b. 19 April, 1825; d. 28 Sept., 1879; in 1893 she res., a widow, Hill City, S. Dakota. Ch. (Adams):
        1 *Carolyn E.[8]*, b. 20 Oct., 1850; d. 10 Nov., 1877; grad. Wisconsin St. Univ. in 1871; Prof. Wis. St. Normal; m. 4 Oct., 1876, Rev. Cephas F. Clapp, Supt. of Missions, in Oregon.
        2 *Frederick Brigham*, b. 7 March, 1857; m. 16 March, 1882, Electa Barker. Ch. Cephas B.[9], b. 1885.
    ii Caroline, b. 1827; d. 1828.
Children (by second wife), born in Vernon:
    iii Eleanor E., b. 16 Dec., 1832; m. 14 Jan., 1869, Samuel Bragg; res. 2116 Norris St., Philadelphia.

  iv Richard Henry Lee, b. 7 Feb., 1835; d. 31 July, 1878; m. in
    1872; a farmer in Rutland, Wis.; he was in the 49th N. Y. Vols.,
    discharged disabled after hard service.
  v George Washington, b. 6 Nov., 1836; was Capt. in the 117th
    N. Y. Vols., and killed in the battle of Drury Bluff, Va., in 1864.
  vi Miriam C., b. 7 Aug., 1839; m. 11 Nov., 1868, Edwin Jackson of
    Stoughton, Wis.
  vii Sara M., b. 13 May, 1842; res. Madison, Wis.
  viii Emma O., b. 1845; d. 1852.
  ix J. Quincy Adams, b. 7 March, 1848; m. 15 Jan., 1875, Mary
    Carpenter; a farmer, res. Madison, Wis.

  278 DEA. JOHN[6], son of Capt. Stephen[5] and Sarah (Harrington) Brigham; born in Vernon, N. Y., 24 March, 1790; died in
Ogden, Monroe Co., N. Y., 16 July, 1868; married, 25 Jan., 1816,
Susan, daughter of David Moore, born 3 Jan., 1797; died 9 Feb.,
1848. He was a farmer and had a good property. Was captain
in the Militia and was in the War of 1812.

  Children, born in Ogden:
  i Caroline E.[7], b. 8 July, 1817; d. 4 April, 1894; m. 23 Feb., 1837,
    George W. Hiscock of Spencerport, N. Y. Ch. (Hiscock), b.
    there:
    1 *Franklin*[8], b. 20 Jan., 1840; d. 8 April, 1841.
    2 *Emily F.*, b. 25 Aug., 1845; m. 17 Oct., 1866, James F. Heakok
     of Spencerport.
    3 *Alice Susan*, b. 2 Oct., 1852; d. 12 Oct., 1877; m. 25 Jan.,
     1877, Myron H. Davis.
    4 *George L.*, b. 8 Nov., 1860; m. 16 Nov., 1881, Nettie M. Wilmot.
     Ch.: i Florence[9]; ii Herbert.
563 ii Orvill P., b. 10 Sept., 1818.
564 iii John D., b. 4 Dec., 1820.
565 iv Alonzo, b. 16 Nov., 1822.
566 v Milton, b. 18 June, 1825.
567 vi Charles, b. 17 March, 1827.
  vii Sarah, b. 3 Sept., 1832; d. 21 Jan., 1881; m. 9 April, 1857, Har-
    vey Pratt of Spencerport. Ch. (Pratt):
    1 *Charles B.*[8], b. 1 Feb., 1858; d. 1 Aug., 1885, in California;
     m. 30 Jan., 1884, Alice Porter. Ch.: Harry[9], d. y.
    2 *Helen E.*, b. 16 April, 1859; d. 13 March, 1884.
  viii Harriet, b. 22 June, 1837; m. 29 Oct., 1857, William W. Hart,
    of Spencerport, who d. 1901. Ch. (Hart), b. in Spencerport:
    1 *Edward Clarence*[8], b. 16 April, 1868; m. Julia L. Henderson
     in 1895. Ch. i Mildred[9]; ii Alice; iii Ethel.

  279 ELIJAH[6], son of Josiah Newton[5] and Sarah (Perry) Brig-
ham; born in Hartwick, N. Y., 1790; died in Clinton, N. Y., 18
May, 1858; married, 1818, Lydia Richards, of Jefferson Co., N.
Y., born 1797; died, March, 1868.

  Children, born in Vernon Center, N. Y.:
568 i Lewis E.[7], b. 4 Dec., 1820.
  ii Lyman, b. 1823; d. 1874; a butcher in New York City.

iii Phebe, b. 12 Jan., 1827; d. 28 Oct., 1896, in Utica, N. Y.; **m.** 1848, Willard, son of Wellington Camp, b. 1826. Ch. **(Camp),** b. in Clinton, N. Y.:
  1 *Jennie*[8], b. 18 June, 1853; m. 20 Aug., 1878, Wilford, son of William L. Burnham of Newport, N. Y.; b. 20 Jan., **1854.** Ch. (Burnham), b. in Utica: i Bessie I.[9], b. 26 Oct., 1879; **m.** 28 May, 1902, R. Clinton Jones; res. Utica; 2 ch.; ii **Marjorie** L., b. 8 Nov., 1884; res. Utica.
  2 *Mary,* b. 1855; m. —————---
  3 *Lena,* b. 1858; m. —————.
iv Mary, b. 9 Nov., 1828; res. Utica, in Old Ladies' Home; was **a** dressmaker.

280 **DEA. DAVID**[6], son of Josiah Newton[5] and Sarah (Perry) Brigham; born in Hartwick, N. Y., 27 Oct., 1799; died in Dryden, N. Y., 12 Jan., 1864; married, in Poughkeepsie, N. Y., 30 Aug., 1827, Catherine, daughter of Isaac Romaine; born in New York City, 2 Nov., 1802; died in Dryden, 18 April., 1858. He was a mechanic and resided in Dryden.

Children, born in Hartwick:
569 i Lyman Farwell[7], b. 26 Sept., 1828.
    ii Harriet Amanda, b. 20 July, 1830; d. 26 Jan., 1885; m. 6 **Feb.,** 1850, Simeon Squires, son of Squires Stiles; b. 19 June, **1824;** res. Dryden. Ch. (Stiles), b. in Whitney Point, N. Y.:
      1 *Laura Maria*[8], b. 5 Dec., 1851; a nurse, unm.
      2 *Ella Jane,* b. 12 Sept., 1853.
      3 *Mary Elizabeth,* b. 28 Dec., 1854.
      4 *Melvin Arthur,* b. 6 April, 1856; m. 1 Oct., 1885, Hattie, dau. of Frank Updegrove; res. Binghamton, N. Y. Ch.: i **Har-** riet[9]; ii Franklin.
      5 *Eva Frances,* b. 8 Sept., 1859; d. 11 July, 1873.
      6 *Hiland Thayer,* b. 26 July, 1861; res. Whitney's Point.
      7 *Willie,* b. 14 Dec., 1863; d. 11 July, 1873.
      8 *Fred D.,* b. 28 Feb., 1871; d. 1 Sept., 1871.
    iii Sarah Mariah, b. 8 Oct., 1831; m. 1 June, 1858, Elson P., son **of** Enos Wheeler; b. in Dryden, 25 Dec., 1828; a farmer, **res.** Dryden. Ch. (Wheeler), b. in Dryden:
      1 *Sara Jane*[8], b. 25 July, 1862; d. unm., 12 Sept., 1898.
      2 *Fred Romaine,* b. 1 Jan., 1866; res. unm., a farmer in **Dryden.**
570 iv Newton Josiah, b. 17 Sept., 1834.
    v Cornelia Melvina, b. 16 Feb., 1838; d. in Cortland, N. Y., 17 **Oct.,** 1885; m. March, 1861, John, son of Adam Simmons; b. in **Dryden,** 4 March, 1838; d. in D., 27 Oct., 1868. Ch. (Simmons), b. **in** Dryden:
      1 *Adam S.*[8], b. Dec., 1861.
      2 *Willison D.,* b. April, 1866; m. 4 April, 1894, Olive Ingerman; res. Sioux City, Da.

281 **DEA. PERRY**[6], son of Josiah Newton[5] and Sarah (Perry) Brigham; born in Hartwick, N. Y., 17 April, 1801; died ————; married, 2 Oct., 1827, Hannah, daughter of Capt. Amos Mason of Biddeford, Me. He was a trader in Boston.

Children:
    i Albert[7], b. 26 March, 1829; d. 29 March, 1829.
    ii Helen Augusta, b. 26 Jan., 1830; res. West Newton, Mass.
    iii Garaphelia M., b. 17 Nov., 1832; m. 13 July, 1853, Henry W. Jenkins.
    iv Charles Perry, b. 21 Sept., 1834; d. 1 April, 1836.
    v Aleathia Maria, b. 1 March, 1837; d. 19 May, 1851.
    vi Charles Perry, b. 22 July, 1839; d. (a son, *Percy*[8], is an actor).
    vii Sarah Anna, b. 18 June, 1842.
    viii Emma Josephine, b. 20 Aug., 1844.

282 EDMOND[6], son of Stephen[5] and Jemima (Snow) Brigham; born in Shrewsbury, Mass., 29 Sept., 1769; died in W. Boylston, Mass.; married (1), 7 Jan., 1795, Mary Brooks of Worcester, born 25 Oct., 1776; died 15 May, 1817; married (2), 26 May 1818, Eunice Plympton, born 5 Oct., 1788; died 1857. Was a farmer in W. Boylston.

Children (by first wife):
    i Mary[7], b. 6 Oct., 1797.
    ii Patty, b. 13 Nov., 1799.
    iii Hester L., b. 1 Nov., 1800.
    iv Fidelia, b. 17 Jan., 1804.
    v Almira, b. 9 April, 1806.
    vi Lucy, b. 2 Nov., 1808.
571   vii Stephen Nathaniel Brooks, b. 18 July, 1811.
    viii Nancy, b. 29 July, 1813.
Children (by second wife):
    ix Sarah, b. 12 July, 1819.
    x Frederick L., b. 24 May, 1821; res. Worcester; had 2 daus., one, *Mrs. Wm. C. Wheeler*[8], 9 Myrtle St., Cliftondale, Mass.
    xi Eunice E., b. 1 Feb., 1823.

283 JABEZ[6], son of Stephen[5] and Jemima (Snow) Brigham; born in Marlboro, Mass., in 1776; died, probably in Worcester, Mass., 14 June, 1834; married, in 1794, Nancy, daughter of Joseph Kingsbury of Worcester; she died in 1848. He resided in Worcester and was on the School Committee; he was also surveyor of high ways and hog reeve.

Children, born in Worcester:
    i Polly[7], b. 1 Nov., 1796; d. 14 Jan., 1855; m. 1812, Ephraim, son of Abel Bigelow of W. Boylston, Mass.; b. 20 Feb., 1791; d. 13 July, 1837; he was selectman, town clerk, and owned a cotton mill. Ch. (Bigelow), b. in W. B.:
        1 *Horatio Nelson*[8], b. 13 Sept., 1812; he was the " father " of Clinton, Mass.; a mill owner, and manufacturer. Ch.: i Henry[9]; ii Charles; both of Clinton.
        2 *Erastus Brigham*, b. 2 April, 1814; an inventor of weaving machines; a prominent citizen. Ch.: Ellen[9], who m. Rev. Daniel Merriman of Worcester.
572   ii Moses, b. 10 May, 1798.

iii Betsey, b. 3 Nov., 1800; m. 10 March, 1819, Simon Plympton; res. Millbury, Mass.
573 iv Hosea, b. 6 Dec., 1802.
v Nancy, b. 1806; d. 17 March, 1846; m. Rev. D. S. King of Boston; res. B.
574 vi Margaret, b. 1808.

284 STEPHEN[6], son of Stephen[5] and Jemima (Snow) Brigham; born in West Boylston, Mass., 21 Sept., 1779; died about 1819 in Roxbury, Mass., married Lucy, daughter of Aaron White of Roxbury; born 27 March, 1777; died about 1820. He was a merchant in Boston.

Children, born in Boston:
i William[7], who d. y.
ii Mary W., b. 2 Sept., 1806; d. in Roxbury, 4 Jan., 1892.
iii Stephen A., b. 28 June, 1808; d. unm., in Roxbury, 21 Nov., 1866.
iv Elizabeth D., b. 27 Feb., 1810; d. in Roxbury, 30 March, 1898.
575 v Lucy A., b. 8 Dec., 1811.
vi Louisa, b. 27 July, 1813; m. 18 Nov., 1844, Sanford Kendall; res., a widow, in Worcester. Ch. (Kendall):
1 *Sanford M.*[8], b. 21 March, 1847; d. 2 Sept., 1849.
vii Caroline, b. 15 Feb., 1815; d. unm., æ. about 17.
viii Henry Bigelow, b. 15 July, 1818; d. 24 Jan., 1887, in Lexington, Mass.; m. 26 March, 1860, Mary E., dau. of Samuel Dudley of Roxbury; he was a farmer; she res., a widow, in Lexington. Ch.:
1 *Mary L.*[8], b. in Roxbury, 3 March, 1862; res. Lexington.

285 LEVI[6], son of Stephen[5] and ———— (Wilder) Brigham; born in West Boylston, Mass., 8 June, 1787 (a family record says " b. Boston," but his parents res. W. Boylston); died in Boston, 17 July, 1864; married (1) Eunice, daughter of Isaac Monroe, of Keene, N. H.; born 23 Aug., 1788; died in 1813 or 1814; married (2), in 1814, Frances, also daughter of Isaac Monroe; born 12 Dec., 1793; died 18 June, 1858; married (3) Mrs. Taft, born Taylor, daughter of " Father " Taylor of Boston, the " Sailor preacher." Mr. Brigham was a wine merchant in Boston.

Children (by first wife), born in Boston:
576 i Levi Henry[7], b. 27 Nov., 1811.
ii Eunice Harriet, b. 26 Dec., 1813; d. 4 Dec., 1850; m. 1 Nov., 1836, Samuel S. Ball, b. 25 Dec., 1807; d. 1 Nov., 1838. Ch. (Ball):
1' *Harriet F.*[8], b. 1 May, 1838; d. 30 Dec., 1904; m. 9 Oct., 1860, Edward F. Thayer. Ch. (Thayer): Elsie[9], b. 17 June, 1872.
Children (by second wife):
iii Caroline Frances, b. 13 Dec., 1815; d. 2 June, 1854; m. 18 July, 1843, Erasmus Jones Andrews, a silk merchant in Boston; b. 19 Aug., 1811. Ch. (Andrews):
1 *Caroline Frances*[8], b. 19 June, 1845; m. 14 June, 1900, Edwin L. Sanborn; res. Commonwealth Ave., Boston, s. p.

2 *Harriet Ball,* b. 6 May, 1849; d. 18 Feb., 1881; m. 10 June, 1879, Edward W. Howe; s. p.
iv Frederick Augustus, b. 14 Feb., 1817; d. 5 April, 1848; m. 15 Oct., 1845, Harriet A. Norton of Worcester, Mass. Ch.:
    1 *E. Harriet*[8], b. 14 June, 1847; d. 9 Dec., 1849 (another record says 11 June, 1851).

286 LYDIA[6], daughter of Joseph[5] and Lydia (Barnes) Brigham; born in Northboro, Mass., 16 Aug., 1766; died in Marlboro, 4 April, 1850; married, 7 Nov., 1785, Dea. Moses Ames of Marlboro; born 4 June, 1763; died 24 June, 1825. He was a farmer and miller and was in the Revolutionary War.

Children (Ames), born in Marlboro:
i Lewis[7], b. 31 Aug., 1786; d. 10 June, 1856; m. (1) 24 May, 1812, Nancy Childs; ·m. (2) 2 May, 1821, Mehitabel Forbush; was a farmer and miller, and res. on the old Joseph Brigham place in Marlboro. Ch. (Ames), by first wife, b. in Marlboro:
    1 *Lucy*[8]; 2 *Moses;* 3 *Lydia;* 4 *Robert.*
    Ch. (Ames), by second wife, b. in Marlboro:
    5 *Robert;* 6 *Nancy;* 7 *Martha.*
    8 *Dr. Joseph,* who d. in Holden, Mass., 1 April, 1903, æ. 74 yrs., 3 mos.; a highly successful physician there for over 44 yrs.
    9 *Stephen.*
    10 *Martha L.,* who, with her brother Stephen, res. on the old Ames place in Marlboro (the Joseph Brigham place), is a well known genealogist. She carefully treasures many old deeds, wills and other documents relating to the Ames and Brigham families, as well as antique furniture and utensils, among them the chair in which Thomas[2] Brigham, died.
ii Lucinda, b. 11 Jan., 1789; d. unm., 20 Jan., 1833.
iii Nancy, b. 1 March, 1792; m. 23 July, 1809, Levi Bigelow; he taught school 20 years; J. P. 30 years; assessor 17 years; Rep. 4 years. Ch. (Bigelow):
    1 *Lydia*[8]; 2 *Leander;* 3 *Mary;* 4 *Cordelia;* 5 *Electa;* 6 *Levi;* 7 *Lambert;* 8 *Edwin;* 9 *Horace;* 10 *Julian;* 11 *William;* 12 *Ann;* 13 *Arthur;* 14 *Ada.*

287 JOSEPH[6], son of Dr. Gershom[5] and Esther (Belknap) Brigham; born in Westboro, Mass., 12 May, 1780; died in Shrewsbury, Mass., 29 Feb., 1836; married, in 1807 (intentions, Jan. 2), Hannah, daughter of Joseph and Lucy (Parker) Hardy, (Joseph Hardy's mother was Prudence Warren, whose paternal ancestor, Richard Warren, came over in the *Mayflower*). He resided in Westboro and Shrewsbury.

Children:
577 i Joseph D.[7], b. 19 July, 1807.
578 ii William Belknap, b. 26 April, 1809.
    iii Hannah, b. about 1810; d. unm., 21 Sept., 1842.
579 iv Charles Corriden, b. 1 Dec., 1813.
    v Roxana, m. 3 Nov., 1834, Silas Dinsmore of Worcester, Mass. Ch. (Dinsmore), b. in Worcester:

1 *Silas Everett*[8], b. 18 June, 1836.
2 *Henry C.*, b. 1839; d. 24 Aug., 1840.
3 *Emma*, b. 29 Dec., 1843.
4 *Anna*, d. y.

288   BENJAMIN[6], son of Dr. Gershom[5] and Esther (Belknap) Brigham; born in Westboro, Mass., 28 May, 1780; died in Shrewsbury, Mass., 30 Jan., 1831; married, 22 May, 1803, Lucy, daughter of Joseph Hardy; born in Westboro, 28 June, 1780; died in Shrewsbury, 27 June, 1861. He resided in Westboro and Shrewsbury.

> *Children, all born in Westboro:*
> i Loring[7], b. 21 Dec., 1804; d. 19 May, 1810.
> ii Susan Lee, b. 1 Nov., 1806; d. in Shrewsbury, 25 Sept., 1877; m. 31 March, 1828, William Hastings Knowlton (son of Dea. Joseph H.) of Shrewsbury; b. there, 8 March, 1807; d. there, 5 Aug., 1872. Ch. (Knowlton).
>   1 *Susan Ellen*[8], b. 26 Dec., 1828; d. 9 Oct., 1854; m. 1 Jan., 1849, Elhahan C., son of Ebenezer Wheeler; b. in Grafton, Mass., 1826; res. Shrewsbury. Ch. (Wheeler): i Inez[9]; ii Infant, d. y.
>   2 *Mary Adelaide*, b. 19 May, 1831; m. 17 April, 1855, Joseph Albert Nourse, a merchant of Shrewsbury. Ch. (Nourse): i Anna M.[9]; ii William K.; iii Albert; 2 d. y.
>   3 *William Everett*, b. 26 Sept., 1832; m. 7 Jan., 1856, Mary E., dau. of Lyman S. Brown; b. in Shrewsbury, 1837; a merchant there. Ch.: i Wm. E.[9]; ii Addie M.; iii Mabel E.; iv Edward L.; v Harry L.; 3 d. y.
>   4 *Lucy Maria*, b. 21 May, 1835; d. 30 Sept., 1850.
>   5 *Eliza Greenwood*, b. 18 Oct., 1837; d. 26 Nov., 1855.
>   6 *Martha Brigham*, b. 6 Oct., 1839; d. 13 Aug., 1840.
>   7 *Caroline E. A.*, b. 3 April, 1843; d. 9 Jan., 1868.
>   8 *Walter Brigham*, b. 2 Dec., 1845; d. 7 July, 1866.
> iii Mary Parker, b. 24 Jan., 1810; m. 6 April, 1830, Henry Benjamin Pratt, son of Shepherd; b. in Shrewsbury, 16 Sept., 1807; res. Shrewsbury. Ch. (Pratt), b. in S.:
>   1 *Susan Augusta*[8], b. 18 March, 1839; m. George J. Morey of Worcester, Mass. Ch. (Morey): Mary B.[9]
>   2 *Franklin Brigham*, b. 11 Aug., 1842; res. Shrewsbury; m. Emma A. Knowlton. Ch.: i Willis[9]; ii Mary; iii Frederick; iv Harry; v Florence; vi Bertram; vii Clifford.
>   3 *Marion Elizabeth*, b. 9 Nov., 1846; d. 10 June, 1851.
> 580 iv Owen Benjamin, b. 27 May, 1812.

289   COL. JOSIAH[6], son of Dr. Gershom[5] and Esther (Belknap) Brigham; born in Westboro, Mass., 19 Dec., 1791; died Westboro, 23 July, 1870; married Azubah Beeton of Westboro; born 15 May, 1795; died 6 Dec., 1883. A portrait of Col. Brigham, his wife and son, hangs in the rooms of the Westboro Historical Society.

Children, born in Westboro:

i Augusta Olivia[7], m. Henry Whitman of Providence, R. I.; he was a merchant, lawyer and notary public; res. Cranston. Ch. Ch. (Whitman), b. in Westboro:

1 *Henry Brigham*[8], b. 30 June, 1841; d. in Providence, 9 March, 1894; m. 6 Nov., 1872, Lucia Keyser Haskell of New York City; he grad. in 1864, Brown Univ.; was admitted to the Albany (N. Y.) bar, 1866; took an active part in politics. Afterward practiced law in Providence until his decease; his knowledge of statute and common law was marked, and he was a man of talent and rare cultivation. Ch.: Ralph Myers[9].

ii Josiah, m. ———— Maynard, and res. Westboro.

290 LUCINDA[6], daughter of Rev. Benjamin[5] and Lucy (Morse) Brigham; born in Fitzwilliam, N. H.; baptized 22 March, 1772; died ————; married (1), 5 May, 1793, Dr. Peter Clark Grosvenor, who died 14 Dec., 1794; he was town clerk of Fitzwilliam at time of death, which occurred when young; married (2), 10 Dec., 1795, Daniel Morse of Sturbridge, Mass., who died in Fitzwilliam, 1 Oct., 1812.

Child (Grosvenor), born in Fitzwilliam:

i Ebenezer Clark[7], b. 21 Sept., 1793; was grad. Univ. of Vt., 1813, and M. D. from Boston; moved to Darien, Ga., of which mayor; studied in Europe; was drowned in Darien, at an early age.

Children (Morse), born in Fitzwilliam:

ii Eliza, b. 13 Sept., 1796; m. Ziba Baldwin of Greenfield, Mass.

iii Harding, b. 1 Oct., 1798; d. 18 March., 1802.

iv Loring, b. 22 April, 1800; settled in Ackworth, N. H., where had a large family.

v Lemuel, b. 4 Sept., 1801; res. Hillsboro Bridge, N. H.

vi Curtis, b. Oct., 1803; d. in Geneseo, Ill., 1855.

291 ELISHA[6], son of Rev. Benjamin[5] and Lucy (Morse) Brigham; baptized in Fitzwilliam, 1 Aug., 1779; died ————; married, 1 Jan., 1810, Susannah (Sukey), daughter of Capt. Samuel and Rachel (Cary) Thayer; baptized in Boston, 12 Dec., 1787; died ————. Some records say he married Miss Williams, sister of his employer in Boston, but the family deny this.

He kept store awhile in Fitzwilliam, and went to Boston, where he became a clerk for Mr. Williams. He then moved to Cincinnati, O., where he went into business, and died.

Children:

i Cornelia S. Thayer[7], b. 3 Nov., 1810; m. James (?) Southgate.

ii Marcus Marcellus, b. 3 Aug., 1812; d. unm.

iii Julia Roxalina, b. 14 Feb., 1814; d. in Boston, ————; m. in Oxford, O., 1 Nov., 1833, Charles, son of Jabin and Mary (Tucker) Fisher; b. in Canton, Mass., 9 Dec., 1799; spent his youth in Washington, N. H.; went to Ohio; was a wholesale grocer in Cincinnati; d. in Yellow Springs, O., 28 March, 1869. Ch. (Fisher):

1 *Charles L.*[8], b. 2 March, 1835; m. 2 April, 1874, Laura Feder-
spiel of Fort Lee, N. Y.; grad. Union Theol. Sem.; res.
Corydon, Ind. Ch. (Fisher): i Samuel[9]; ii David; iii Garfield.

2 *Theodore B.*, b. 6 Oct., 1837; unm.

3 *Cornelia M.*, b. 4 July, 1840; d. in Worcester, Mass., 15 May,
1890; m. G. Stanley Hall, afterward Prest. of Clark University,
Worcester. Ch. (Hall): i Robert G.[9], b. Feb., 1881; ii Julia
Fisher, b. 1883.

4 *Sidney A.*, b. 18 March, 1842; m. 11 Feb., 1866, Angeline E.
Adsitt; res. San Francisco, Cal. Ch.: i Luman[9]; ii Philip A.
(Rev.), pastor of the First Presbyterian Church, Mill City,
Oregon.

5 *Horace*, b. 18 March, 1844; m. Kate Matson; res. Cincinnati.
Ch.: i William[9]; ii Clifford.

6 *Emma*, b. 31 May, 1855; a teacher in Boston.

7 *Susan Florence*, b. 1857; d. 1859.

iv Lucius Algernon, b. 16 Aug., 1816; m. Cornelia Taylor. Ch.:

1 *Edwin*[8], d. y.

2 *Stanley*, d. y.

3 *Edith*, m. ———— Hanna; res. Chicago.

4 *Eva*, m. ———— Longinotti; res. Chicago.

292 WILLARD[6], son of Caleb[5] and Hannah (Barnes) Brig-
ham; born in Marlboro, Mass., 7 Oct., 1772; died in Marlboro, 28
Aug., 1835; married, 5 Oct., 1797, Betsey, daughter of Oliver and
Betty (Howe) Russell of Marlboro; born 16 Oct., 1780; died 11
Dec., 1820. He inherited the homestead in Marlboro, one mile
S.W. of Feltonville; was a farmer and resided for a time in Berlin
Mass. Two of his sons became Congregational clergymen.

Children, born in Marlboro:
    i Harriet[7], b. 3 Oct., 1802; d. unm., in Hudson, Mass., 19 Sept.,
      1890.
581 ii Mary M., b. 1 Oct., 1804.
582 iii Levi, b. 14 Oct., 1806.
583 iv George, b. 12 Oct., 1808.
    v Hannah, b. 18 Jan., 1811; d. unm., in 1836.
584 vi Willard, b. 4 May, 1813.
585 vii Aaron, b. 7 April, 1817.
586 viii Elizabeth, b. 1 Dec., 1821.

293 CALEB, JR.[6], son of Caleb[5] and Hannah (Barnes) Brigham; born in Marlboro, Mass., 26 Dec., 1778; died 17 Aug., 1842;
married, Martha, daughter of William and Lydia (Chamberlain)
Brigham (74); born in Marlboro, 22 March, 1782; died 20 April,
1860. He was a farmer and music and dancing teacher, and an
unusually skilful performer on the violin. He resided in Marlboro.

Children, born in Marlboro:
587 i Martha Chamberlain[7], b. 2 Oct., 1803.
    ii Laura Ann, b. 1 July, 1805; d. 7 March, 1808.
    iii Francis Dana, b. 19 April, 1808; d. 7 March, 1883; m. 12 May,

1831, Sarah, dau. of Stephen Pope of Feltonville, b. 11 Jan., 1811; d. in 1892; was a merchant in Hudson many years. Ch., b. in Hudson:

    1 *George Austin*[8], b. 28 Sept., 1832; d. 24 July, 1834.
    2 *Charles Dana,* b. 16 June, 1835; d. 14 Oct., 1836.
    3 *Charles Austin,* b. 22 Aug., 1837; d. 5 Dec., 1860.
    4 *George Dana,* twin to Charles A.; d. 10 April, 1838.
    5 *Ella Frances,* b. 11 Nov., 1851; d. 10 July, 1853.

  iv Charles, b. 3 May, 1811; d. 8 April, 1886; m. 12 Oct., 1836, Rebecca Burr, dau. of Daniel and Rebecca (Burr) Tuttle of Fitchburg; b. 31 July, 1817; d. 7 Dec., 1875; res. Fitchburg, and was Purchasing Agt. for R. R. Co. Ch.:

    1 *Charles Lewis*[8], b. Fitchburg, 10 July, 1843; d. s. p., 11 March, 1894; m. at Hudson, 1 Jan., 1868, Mary L., dau. Henry and Louisa (Nourse) Whitcomb of Hudson; b. 22 April, 1847. (She m. [2] Wm. S. Pierce.)

  v Laura Ann, b. 20 April, 1813; m. Alden, son of Abner Brigham, 210.

  vi Austin P., b. 4 April, 1815; d. 4 Sept., 1818.

  vii Sophia, b. 1 July, 1817; d. 5 Sept., 1818.

  viii Sophia Austin, b. 24 June, 1820; d. 25 March, 1833.

588 ix Tileston, b. 25 Aug., 1822.

  x Ann Janette, b. 13 Dec., 1824; d. 1852 (another record says she d. 24 April 1854); m. in Marlboro, 5 Dec., 1848, Burleigh, son of Lyman and Lydia (Brigham) Morse; b. in Marlboro, 3 Sept., 1822; d. 25 Feb., 1896. Ch. (Morse), b. in Marlboro:

    1 *Ellen Augusta*[8], b. 28 June, 1849; res. Marlboro.

294   BENAJAH[6], son of Benajah[5] and Abigail (Bent) Brigham; born in Westboro, Mass., 7 June, 1774; died 23 Oct., 1852; married (1), in 1801, Sarah Lancaster, born in Salem, N. H., 15 Nov., 1783; died in Boston, Jan., 1828; married (2), in Boston, 4 Jan., 1830, Betsey, daughter of Job Turner; born in Pembroke, Mass., 15 Dec., 1793; died 1 March, 1871.

He was a grocer in Boston and a deacon of the First Universalist church. He is interred in the Old Granary Burying-ground, Tomb No. 65, which is on the right-hand side of the gate, near the fence.

Children (by first wife), born in Boston:

  i Sarah[7], b. 3 Dec., 1802; d. in Boston, 28 Oct., 1829; m. 1 May, 1822, Anson Dexter of Boston. Ch. (Dexter):

    1 *Anson Brigham*[8], b. 16 July, 1823; d. 26 Sept., 1844.
    2 *Sarah Lancaster,* b. 26 June, 1825; m. 10 May, 1847, William Ellery James. Ch. (James): i Annie Fay[9], b. 15 April, 1851; ii Brigham Dexter, b. 25 March, 1855.
    3 *Mary Ann Ruth,* b. 3 Oct., 1827; d. 27 May, 1829.

  ii Benjamin, (Rev.), b. 30 Oct., 1804; d. unm., in Boston, 21 Sept., 1831; A. M. at Harvard Univ., 1825; studied theology and was Chaplain U. S. N.; was with Prest. Bolivar 4 years; was a Unitarian clergyman, and a superior scholar and musician; he preached his last sermon in Brattle Street Church.

  iii Mary, b. 2 Dec., 1806; d. 7 Sept., 1807.

589 iv Mary Lancaster, b. 28 Dec., 1808.
　　v *Lucy*, b. 23 April, 1811; d. 7 May, 1829.
　　vi Charlotte, b. 20 Aug., 1813; d. in Brookline, Mass., 13 Feb., **1867**;
　　　m. 23 Feb., 1832, Isaac Bell of New Orleans. Ch. (Bell):
　　　　1 *Eliza James*[8], b. 16 Jan., 1833; d. 16 May, 1906; **m. 9 Oct.,**
　　　　1860, Charles Herbert Draper, b. 22 March, 1838; Prest. **Brook-**
　　　　line Nat. Bank; res. Brookline.
590 vii George, b. 20 Sept., 1815.

295　EPHRAIM[6], son of Benajah[5] and Abigail (Bent) Brigham; born in Westboro, Mass., 2 July, 1776; died —————; married Hannah, daughter of Thomas Twitchell. He inherited the
Benajah homestead in Westboro.

Children, born in Westboro:
　　i Hannah M.[7], d. —————; m. Benj. F. Green, who also d.;
　　　res. Shrewsbury, Mass. Ch. (Green):
　　　　1 *Charles*[8], who res. with his Grandfather Brigham, in West-
　　　　boro.
591 ii John W., b. 6 May, 1821.
　　iii Lucy H., d. —————; m. Charles C. Andrews; res. West-
　　　boro. Ch. (Andrews):
　　　　1 *Charles*[8].

296　PETER W.[6], son of Benajah[5] and Abigail .(Bent) Brigham; born in Westboro, Mass., 10 May, 1779; died 24 July, 1831;
married, 8 June, 1807, Lydia, daughter of William H. Valentine
of Hopkinton, Mass.; born 9 Aug., 1786; died in Worcester, Mass.,
6 Sept., 1871; she married (2) Thomas Beeton. Mr. Brigham settled in Boston as a mason and was the first American who put on
stucco work.

Children, born in Boston:
592　i William Augustus[7], b. 29 Aug., 1808.
　　ii Lydia Ann, b. 5 Feb., 1810; m. 5 Feb., 1829, Holland, son of
　　　Maj. Holland Forbes of Westboro, and grandson of 175; they
　　　res. in Salem, N. H., where he d. 17 June, 1870; she res., a
　　　widow, in Boston. Ch. (Forbes):
　　　　1 *John W.*[8], b. 9 Nov., 1829; d. in Carlisle, Pa,. 27 Nov., 1863;
　　　　m. Diantha Houghton of Swanzey, N. H. Ch.: i Julius W.[9],
　　　　b. 14 Oct., and d. 14 Nov., 1852; ii George H., b. 3 Feb., 1856;
　　　　iii Charles O., b. 4 March, 1862.
　　　　2 *Martha A. B.*, b. 4 July, 1834, in Brighton Mass.; m. A. H.
　　　　Merrill of Salem, N. H.
　　iii John Wells, b. and d. Sept., 1818.

297　JABEZ[6], son of Benajah[5] and Abigail (Bent) Brigham;
born in Westboro, Mass., 12 March, 1781; died 10 Jan., 1862;
married (1), 9 Feb., 1800, Sophia, daughter of John Hunt of Lancaster, Mass., who died in Grafton, 6 Feb., 1837, æ. 55; married
(2), in 1849, Phebe (or Phila) Wheeler. He was a mason by

trade, and built the first brick building in Bangor, Me. Resided in Grafton and Boston.

Children, the first, second and fourth born in Lancaster:

   i Francis[7], b. 22 Feb., 1800; d. in Grafton, 13 Sept., 1819.

   ii Mary Ann, b. 29 Dec., 1801; d. in Springfield, Mass., 27 Feb., 1870; m. in 1818, Dea. Robert, son of Daniel Prentice; b. in Townsend, Mass., 16 March, 1792; d. in Springfield (or Worcester), 17 April, 1864; res. a while at Grafton. Ch. (Prentice):

      1 *Mary Ann*[8], b. 6 Feb., 1819; d. 29 Sept., 1821.

      2 *Emily*, b. 16 Feb., 1821; m. Sanford J. Hall of Grafton, Mass. Ch. (Hall): i Mary S.[9]; ii Nellie F.

      3 *Benjamin Brigham*, b. 18 April, 1833; d. 18 Jan., 1858.

   iii Jabez, b. in Boston, 29 Aug., 1804; d. 26 Aug., 1805.

593 iv Franklin, b. 19 July, 1805.

   v Sophia, b. in Grafton, 7 June, 1806; m. 20 Nov. 1828, Daniel, son of Leonard and Persis (Brigham) Wheelock, 174; b. in Grafton, 7 March, 1805. Ch. (Wheelock), b. in Grafton:

      1 *Sophronia*[8], b. 20 Sept., 1829.

      2 *Lucian B.*, b. 20 Aug., 1831.

      3 *Persis B.*, b. 18 July, 1833.

      4 *Adaline A.*, b. 11 March, 1837.

      5 *Mary B.*, b. 13 April, 1840; d. 7 July, 1872.

      6 *Francis F.*, b. 23 Oct., 1847; d. 4 Nov., 1864.

594 vi Abigail D., b. in Grafton, 24 Oct., 1807.

595 vii Phebe, b. in Boston, 2 Aug., 1810.

   viii Jabez, b. 7 March, 1813; d. in Detroit, Mich., March, 1839, s. p.

   ix Warren, b. 24 March, 1815, in Grafton; living in 1904; m. (1) 9 Sept., 1842, Persis Carlton, who d. 8 Jan., 1868; m. (2) in 1870, Susan M. Carroll. Ch. (by first wife): *Levi*[8], b. 1853; d. 1855.

   x Emeline F., b. in Grafton, 7 Nov., 1821; d. in Millbury, Mass., 13 Feb., 1844; m. Aug., 1837, Andrew Holden of Millbury. Ch. (Holden), b. in M.:

      1 *Lizzie*[8], m. William Fenner. Ch.: Emma[9], m. Alfred H. Carr.

      2 *Emeline*, d. æ. 3.

596 xi Sarah E., b. in Grafton, 9 Sept., 1822.

298 LEONARD WARREN[6], son of Gershom[5] and Sarah (Allen) Brigham; born in Marlboro, Mass., 16 July, 1785; died in Brookfield, Vt., 15 Nov., 1834; married, in Roxbury, Vt., 17 Nov., 1811, Polly Wilcox, born in Woodstock, Conn., 25 Oct., 1783.

Children, the second and third born in Roxbury:

   i Son[7], d. y.

   ii Alzina, b. in 1812; m. Stephen Collis of Elmore, Vt.

597 iii Elisha Warren, b. 15 Nov., 1814.

   iv Eunice, b. ————; m. (1) 1848, Solon Simons; m. (2) Joseph Richards of Northfield, Vt., and had 2 children.

299 POLLY[6], daughter of Gershom[5] and Sarah (Allen) Brigham; born in Marlboro, Mass., 17 Oct., 1786; died in Waitsfield, Vt., 12 Aug., 1862; married Benjamin Carroll, a farmer of Fayston, Moretown, and Richmond, Vt.; born March., 1780; died 20 Jan., 1842.

Children (Carroll), the 3 elder born in Moretown, the 5 younger in Richmond:

    i Esther Wright[7], b. 2 Dec., 1813; d. .in Transit, Minn., 6 Dec., 1892; m. 1842, Almon Hall. Ch. (Hall):
       1 *Frank*[8]; 2 *Flora;* 3 *Ervin;* 4 *Ellen;* 5 *Robert;* 6 *Eva.*

    ii George B., b. 11 Oct., 1814; d. in Waitsfield, 13 April, 1886; m. Susan Johnson; a farmer. Ch.:
       1 *Eden*[8], res. Sioux City, Ia.; 2 *Burt.*

    iii Sarah Alsina, b. 27 Feb., 1816; d. 30 Aug., 1816.

    iv Alzina Sarah, b. Fayston, 2 Aug., 1817; d. in Kansas; m. Leander Marshall. Ch. (Marshall):
       1 *Henry*[8]; 2 *Willard,* of Nora, Ill.; 3 *Alphonso;* 4 *Ellen;* 5 *Bert.*

    v Alma Luana, b. 6 May, 1820; d. s. p., 18 Dec., 1893; m. William Wait of Waitsfield.

    vi Lawson, b. 6 Oct., 1822; d. in Fayston, 4 Jan., 1889; m. 1848, Maria Boyce; a farmer. Ch.:
       1 *Fred C.*[8]; 2 *George H.*

    vii Lovina D., b. 17 April, 1825; d. in Richmond, 30 June, 1847; m. Benjamin Hall. Ch. (Hall):
       1 *George B.*[8]

    viii Charles L., b. 3 Dec., 1827; m. Lucy Scribner; res. Robinson, Kan. Ch.:
       1 *L. Charles*[8]; 2 *Alice.*

    ix Pliny F., b. 7 Nov., 1831; m. Susan Poland; a farmer, res. Warren, Vt. Ch.:
       1 *Lovina*[8]; 2 *Lewis.*

300 ELISHA[6], son of Gershom[5] and Sarah (Allen) Brigham; born in Marlboro, Mass., 22 Oct., 1792; died in Fayston, Vt., 11 March, 1863; married, in Fayston, Sophronia, daughter of Samuel B. Ryder; she was born in Randolph, Vt., 20 June, 1799; died in Fayston, 24 Oct., 1876. Her father came from Plymouth, Mass., to Braintree, Vt.; came in by " blaised " trees, and planted the first fruit nursery in that town. Her mother was Lucy, dau. of Seth Chase, the 4th from Aquila Chase, who settled at Newburyport, 1646. Through the Ryders, Sophronia was descended from Mary, dau. of Richard Warren, one of the *Mayflower* (1620) passengers. Thus all of Elisha and Sophronia's descendants are of *Mayflower* stock. The Ryders are well represented in the graveyard on the Hill, at Plymouth. Samuel Ryder (or Rider) was one of the first settlers of Yarmouth on Cape Cod, from Plymouth, 1639.

When Elisha was 4 years old his father removed to Winchester, N. H., and when he was 16 they removed to Fayston in the Mad River Valley, where were only half a dozen recent settlers with small clearings and no roads. His father being infirm, Elisha took the lead in clearing up a wooded wilderness into the homestead which he inherited at his father's death. He was a quiet, devout, most peaceable man; scrupulously honest, suffering a wrong rather than committing one. The " pioneer of Methodism " in his town, he was class-leader, chorister, and financial and social supporter of the church. " Puritanism never thrived better this side of old Plymouth, in all its sterling simplicity and straight-forwardness, than here." His name is found in the earliest business transactions of the town, without interruption to the time of his death; he was collector, selectman, lister, district clerk, highway surveyor, committee man and juror. A consistent Whig, while the town was almost to a man Democratic, he never was elected to the Legislature. Elisha and his wife rest in that Waitsfield, Vt., cemetery, situated in Irasville.

Children, born in Fayston:
    i Harriet Jane[7], b. 22 Sept., 1818; d. in Cascade, Mich., Sept., 1881; m. 27 Oct., 1844, Bernard, son of Hon. Eber H. Baxter; b. in Moretown, N. Y., 6 July, 1824; moved to Cascade, Mich., and d. 20 Aug., 1881. Ch. (Baxter), b. Moretown:
      1 *William A. C.*[8], b. 15 Oct., 1845; d. y.
      2 *Aurilla S. D.*, b. 12 March, 1847; m. 12 Jan., 1866, Thomas J. Hurlburt. Ch. (Hurlburt): i Carrie[9]; ii Morris; iii Helen; iv William; v Ray, d. y.
      3 *Lucy Irene*, b. 15 Jan., 1852; m. 1873, William Hall of Grand Rapids, Mich. Ch. (Hall): i Ida[9]; ii Willie.
      4 *Bernard Nelson*, b. 11 June, 1855; d. about 1873.
598 ii Gershom Nelson, b. 3 March, 1820.
599 iii Elisha Aldis, b. 22 Dec., 1821.
    iv Lucy, b. 20 March, 1823; d. 21 July, 1865; m. (1) 15 Jan., 1843, Jacob Pierce; m. (2) 6 Oct., 1852, Charles Thompson. Ch. (Pierce), name was changed to Brigham:
      1 *Anson Orlando*[8], b. 11 Oct., 1843; m. Nov., 1865, Mary Mansfield of Fayston, Vt. Ch. (bearing name of Brigham): i Josephine[9], m. George Bliss; res. Springfield, Mass.; has 1 son; ii Minnie L., m. 17 Dec., 1890, James Burt of W. Randolph, Vt.; has 1 son.; iii Fred.
      Ch. (Thompson):
      2 *Charles Brigham*, b. 30 Aug., 1853.
    v Sophronia Delight, b. 17 May, 1825; d. in Flint, Mich., 10 May, 1901; m. 25 Sept., 1844, William H. Chaffee, d. in Fargo, N. D., Nov., 1882. Ch. (Chaffee):
      1 *Helen Adelaide*[8], m. 1865, Henry G. Perry of Toymonth, Mich. Ch. (Perry): i Charles[9]; ii Fred; iii Nellie; iv William.
      2 *Willis L.*, b. Jan., 1847; d. July, 1847.
      3 *William Henry*, b. 1848; m. 1869, Alice A. Moses; res. Cal. Ch.: i Ida[9]; ii Lois; iii Herbert.
      4 *Clarence*, b. and d. Aug., 1856.
600 vi Eusebia Miranda, b. 23 Aug., 1826.
601 vii Leander Howe, b. 17 April, 1828.
    viii Samuel Allen, b. 8 Nov., 1829; d. unm., 1893; rem. Portland, Oregon.
602 ix Albert, b. 3 May, 1832.
    x Anson Orlando, b. 27 March, 1835; d. April, 1835.
603 xi Sarah, b. 17 Oct., 1836.
604 xii Laura Artemesia, b. 27 Feb., 1840.

301 REV. BENJAMIN BAXTER[6], son of Gershom[5] and Sarah (Allen) Brigham; born in Marlboro, Mass., 28 May, 1795; died in North Plains, Mich., 2 Jan., 1855; married in Mexico, N. Y., 3 Sept., 1827, Sophia Cowing, born in Chesterfield, Mass., 18 Sept., 1802; died in North Plains, 18 Aug., 1881. He was a Baptist minister and farmer.

Children, the 3 youngest probably born in Shiawassee, Mich., the others in Penn.:

   i George Allen[7], b. 30 Dec., 1829; d. in Blair, Neb., 8 Jan., 1886; m. (1) Margaret Hawley; m. (2) ————; was a farmer, contractor and teacher. Ch

     1 *Martha[8]*, m.; res. Oklahoma.

     2 *Clarence S.*, b. in Blair, 1868; m. 1894; farmer and contractor; res. Cushing Oklahoma.

     3 *Carroll*, d.

     4 *Ollie*, m.; res. Oklahoma.

  ii Benjamin Keene, b. April, 1833; m. 14 Nov., 1858, Mary J. Dalzell; farmer, res. Muir, Mich. Ch.:

     1 *Elmer William[8]*, b. 22 Oct., 1861.

     2 *Mary E.*, b. 27 Aug., 1865; m. 1896, Moses Merithew; res. Muir.

     3 *George B.*, b. 25 Sept., 1879; m. 1900, Lottie Ely. Ch.: Lilia M.[9], b. 30 Jan., 1901.

  iii Martin A., b. 15 May, 1836; d. 20 Jan., 1885, s. p.; m. (1) Parmelia Conklin; m. (2) Mary Zimmerman, who d. 1890; res. North Plains.

  iv Noble S., b. 23 June, 1838; m. 10 Aug., 1862, Elsie Howe, b. 25 Dec., 1841; res. Battle Creek, Mich. Ch.:

     1 *Rhoda S.[8]*, b. 13 Feb., 1866; m. 10 Aug., 1885, Harley M. Dunlap, M. D.

   v Addie M. S., b. 24 June, 1840; m. William Frost of Fenwick, Mich., who d. Ch. (Frost):

     1 *Carrie J.[8]*, b. 11 Sept., 1874.

     2 *Major E.*, b. 28 Dec., 1876.

302 ALVIN LUCAS[6], son of Gershom[5] and Sarah (Allen) Brigham; born in Winchester, N. H., 21 Oct., 1798; died in Roxbury, Vt., 8 May, 1870; married, in 1820, Flora H., daughter of Timothy Baxter; born in Berlin, Vt., 21 July, 1804; died in Lowell, Mass., 29 April, 1871. He was a farmer.

Children:

   i Flora Ann[7], b. in Berlin, 13 Sept., 1822; d. 14 Aug., 1844.

  ii Alvin Ozro, b. 11 Feb., 1824; d. s. p., 25 March, 1865; was in the Civil War, and shot on picket duty, before Petersburg, Va.; m. 11 May, 1854, Lomelia, dau. of James Cady of Alstead, N. H.; b. 25 May, 1829; she m. (2) ———— Bickford, and res. a widow in Hyde Park, Mass.

605 iii William Baxter, b. 17 Nov., 1826.

  iv Alphonso Rice, b. 22 Jan., 1829; d. 7 Feb., 1841.

   v Maria Sarah, b. 23 Sept., 1830; m. 1 June, 1867, Newton C. Dodge; res. s. p., Lowell, Mass.

vi Alonzo Gleason, b. 5 Oct., 1835; d. unm., 3 Jan., 1883.
vii Son, d. y.
viii Aurora Cordelia, b. in Roxbury, 11 Sept., 1840; d. s. p., in
Lowell, Mass., in 1892; m. 8 Aug., 1862, George Cooper, who
was killed in the Civil War, in Kingston, N. C.
ix Don Alphonso, b. 7 Nov., 1845; d. unm., 18 March, 1866. He
was in the Civil War.
x Lomelia Ann, b. 24 Oct., 1848; d. 23 March, 1901; m. 2 July,
1871, George E. Maker; res. Lowell, where he was a merchant.
He was b. in Maine. Ch. (Maker), b. in Lowell:
1 *Elizabeth Florence*[8], b. 17 May, 1872; d. unm.
2 *Don Eugene*, b. 18 Feb., 1874; d. 12 July, 1898.
3 *George Alfred Brigham*, b. 23 March, 1889.

303   REBECCA M.[6], daughter of Gershom[5] and Sarah (Allen)
Brigham; born in Winchester, N. H., 27 Feb., 1802; died 1872;
married, 30 March, 1820, John Kneeland.   They resided in Strikely,
Canada, and moved to Rochester, Ind.

Children (Kneeland), born in Strikely:
    i John Allen[7], b. 5 Jan., 1821; res. unm., a farmer, Arcata, Cal.
    ii Benjamin Merrill, b. 28 Aug., 1822.
    iii Albert Cheney, b. 27 June, 1824; d. 12 March, 1845.
    iv Hannah Maria, b. 27 April, 1826; m. (1[1]) Abel Greenwood; m.
    (2) James C. Feeley. Ch. (Greenwood):
      1 *Laura*[8]; 2 *Abel*, res. Columbus, O.
      Ch. (Feeley):
      3 *James*, res. Mason City, Ia.
    v Sylva, b. 15 Nov., 1828; m. Royal Kennedy. Ch. (Kennedy):
      1 *Mandana*[8], m. A. M. Brinkerhoff of Garwin, Ia.
      2 *Cynthia*, m. James E. Blanchard of Oakland, Cal.
      3 *Cyrus M.*, of Humphrey, Neb. Has ch.: i Roy[9]; ii Edna; iii
      William; iv Asa.
      4 *Edwin A.*, res. Jewell, Kan.
      5 *Laura R.*, res. Stockton, Cal. Ch.: i Erol[9]; ii Inez.
      6 *Eva S.*
      7 *Clara B.*, d. y.
    vi Sarah Rebecca, b. 20 Jan., 1831; m. Mr. Abrams of Winterset, Ia.
    vii Asa K., b. 14 Feb., 1833; d. 7 March, 1845.
    viii Gilbert B., b. 9 Jan., 1835; res. Arcata, Cal. Has ch.:
      1 *Cynthia I.*[8]; 2 *Lydia L.*; 3 *Oscar E.*; 4 *Herman M.*; 5
      Viola R.
    ix Mandana P., b. 9 Sept., 1837; m. John Smith of Arcata, Cal.
    Ch. (Smith):
      1 *Udella*[8]; 2 *Rebecca E.*, m. Aaron F. Nelson of Sciota, Cal.;
      3 *Lasa K.*; 4 *Ellis S.*; 5 *Byron M.*
    x Lydia L., b. 15 Nov., 1839; m. Thomas Kennedy of Ingallston,
    Neb. Ch. (Kennedy):
      1 *Gilbert*[8]; 2 *William*; 3 *Mary E.*; 4 *Eudora E.*; 5 *Robert L.*;
      6 *Alta E.*; 7 *Udellus E.*
    xi Laura A., b. 6 Dec., 1841; d. 26 Jan., 1843.

304   ELIZABETH[6], daughter of Stephen[5] and Hannah (Field)
Brigham; born in Mansfield, Conn.; died there, 1845; married.
1798, Samuel Augustus Spalding of M., who died 1824.

Mr. Spalding kept a hotel for many years in Mansfield.

Children (Spalding), born in Mansfield:
  i Samuel Augustus[7], b. 1800; d. 1880.
  ii Brigham, b. 3 June, 1805; d. 6 Nov., 1887; m. (1) Lucretia
    Loveridge; m. (2) Dulcena Adams. Ch.:
      1 *Henry[6]*, m. (1) 23 Sept., 1863, L. M. Thomas; m. (2) 22
        Nov., 1875, Rebecca Wyeth of Montclair, N. J.; he d. s. p.,
        25 Nov., 1875, while on his wedding tour; was a New York
        importer.
      2 *Augusta*, b. in Woonsocket, R. I., 22 Oct., 1845; m. 8 April,
        1868, Allen Adams; res. s. p., Spencer, Mass.
  iii Franklin, b. 1807; d. 1870.
  iv Ursula, b. 15 Aug., 1809; d. unm., 14 Dec., 1861.

305 STEPHEN[6], son of Stephen[5] and Hannah (Field) Brigham; born in Mansfield, Conn., 5 Feb., 1774; died ————; married (1) Huldah Freeman; married (2) Elizabeth Huntington; at
the time Morse published the Brigham genealogy, he resided, in
his 86th year, in Mansfield, Conn.

Children:
  i Mary Ann[7], m. Chester Royce; res. Weathersfield, Vt.
  ii Betsey, m. April, 1827, Horace Nye of Tolland, Conn.; res., his
    widow, Mansfield, Conn.
  iii Julia, m. 26 March, 1833, Otis Sweet of No. Coventry, Conn.,
    who d.; she res. Mansfield.
  iv John, b. 26 April, 1810; was a merchant in Boston; unm. in
    the late fifties.
  v William Pitt, b. 16 March, 1813; m. Anna Fuller; was a mer-
    chant in Boston; his widow res. on Newbury Street, Boston. Ch.:
      1 *Anna F.[8]*
      2 *Mary T.*

306 ALEXANDER[6], son of Thomas[5] and Susanna (Eels)
Brigham; born in Coventry, Conn., 26 Jan., 1770; died in German,
N. Y., 30 July, 1839; married, in Bernardston, Mass., in 1795,
Sarah Whitten, born in Wareham, Conn., 11 July, 1770; died in
Brownsville, N. Y., 29 Aug., 1828. Moved to Brownsville, N. Y.,
in 1819. For a time, he kept a hotel in Perch River, N. Y.

*Children, the 2 elder born in Buckland, Mass., the others in Richfield,
N. Y.:*
606 i Sarah[7], b. 11 Sept., 1796.
    ii Anne, b. 25 Dec., 1798; m. John W. Edwards of Limerick, N. Y.
      Ch. (Edwards), b. in Limerick:
        1 *William G.[8]*, b. 17 March, 1830; m. Harriet McComber; res.
          Niles, Mich.
        2 *Sarah C.*, b. 11 May, 1832; m. O. C. Rounds; res. Niles,
          Mich.
        3 *Mary M.*, b. 12 March, 1834; m. Henry Barber; res. Hounds-
          ville, N. Y.
        4 *Hiram A.*, b. 30 May, 1836; m. Angelina Dickey; res. Niles,
          Mich.
        5 *Eliza Ann*, b. 30 July, 1838; d. y.

      6 *Helen A.,* b. 22 Nov., 1840.
    iii William, b. 11 Nov., 1801; d. 1809.
    iv Fanny, b. 23 Feb., 1805; m. Martin Watson; resided in German,
       N. Y.; she later went to Michigan, and lived there during her
       widowhood; date of death unknown; had 6 sons.
607   v George, b. 6 March, 1808.
    vi Eunice, b. 18 Dec., 1810; d. in California; m. Lucius Lummerce
       of Syracuse; had 2 sons who res. in California.

    307   ORLEANS[6], son of Thomas[5] and Susanna (Eels) Brig-
ham; born in Coventry, Conn., 10 Dec., 1773; died in Willet, N.
Y., 6 June, 1864; married Mercy Stafford, who died in Willet, 2
Aug., 1862, æ. 80.   He was an engineer and farmer, and was in
the War of 1812.

Children, born in Willett:
    i Orleans[7], b. 1792; d. s. p., in Willet, 10 Jan., 1864; m. Mercy E.
      Burt, a farmer.
    ii Eunice, b. 1815; d. in Upper Lisle, N. Y., 10 Aug., 1887, æ. 72;
      m. Hiram Snow. Ch. (Snow):
       1 *Fanny L.[8];* 2 *Hannah M.;* 3 *Mary J.;* 4 *Eunice M.*
   iii John, b. 1817; d. unm., in Willet, 12 April, 1861; a carpenter.
    iv Catherine, b. 1820; d. in McDonough, N. Y., 28 Jan., 1901, æ. 80;
      m. Fenner Darling. Ch. (Darling):
       1 *Thomas[8];* 2 *Milton;* 3 *Mary;* 4 *Joel;* 5 *Ellen;* 6 *Addie;*
       7 *Emery;* 8 *Elsie.*
    v Henry, b. 1823; d. in Preston, N. Y., 8 April, 1902, æ. 79; a
      farmer; m. Elizabeth McNeil. Ch.:
       1 *Henry[8]*, m. ———— Van Horn; res. unknown. Ch.: i Perley[9],
       m. ————; res. Whitney Point, N. Y.; ii Mary.
    vi Archibald, b. 1825; d. in Willet, 7 April, 1865; a farmer; m.
      Esther Rooks. Ch.:
       1 *Hiram[8];* a carpenter, unm., res. Cincinnatus. N. Y.
       2 *Ida A.*
       3 *Harriet L.*
   vii Thomas, d. unm., æ. 21.
  viii Hiram, d. in Ulysses, Pa.; a blacksmith; m. Larissa Lewis. Ch.:
      1 *John[8];* res. Addison, Pa.; 2 *Perry;* res. Ulysses.
      3 *Collins.*
    ix Royal, left home when a young man, and was never heard from.
    x Diantha, m. ———— Hill; had a family.
    xi Ruth, d. s. p, Oxford, N. Y., Feb., 1862; m. Russell Willoughby.

    308   DON FERDINAND[6], son of Thomas[5] and Susanna
(Eels) Brigham, born in Coventry, Conn., about 1776; died in
Tolland, Conn., 29 Sept., 1867; married, 7 Nov., 1802, Lois, daugh-
ter of Elias Palmer of Coventry.   He was a farmer and shoemaker.

Children, born in Coventry:
    i Sarepta[7], m. Elmer Barrows of Willington, Conn. Ch. (Barrows):
      1 *Brigham[8]*, res. Coventry; 2 *Sarepta,* m. ———— Bugbee; 3
      Henrietta, m. (1) Harrison Grant; m. (2) ————; res. Phila-
      delphia; 2 ch., Emily[9] and Minnie; 4 *Walter,* lawyer, Vineland,
      N. J.

ii John Palmer, b. 6 Dec., 1806; d. in Willington, 10 May, 1891; m. (1) 1833, Lurancy Johnson, who d. 1838; m. (2) 1839, Emily Waldo, who d. 1889. He was a farmer. Ch. (by first wife):
1 *Daughter*[8], d. y.; 2 *Daughter*, d. y. Ch. (by second wife) probably b. in Willington.
3 *Frances Ann*, b. 12 July, 1840; d. 1 June, 1858.
4 *John Palmer*, b. 4 Jan., 1843; d. 12 Sept., 1844.
5 *Ferdinand Palmer*, b. 25 Sept., 1844; d. 8 May, 1845.
6 *Henrietta Eliza*, b. 8 May, 1846; m. Albert Field, M. D., Easthampton, Ct.
7 *Mary Isabella*, b. 2 June, 1848; m. Adolph Korper, So. Willington.
8 *Charlotte Romelia*, b. 27 Oct., 1850; unm.
608 iii Lewis, b. 22 March, 1809.
iv Eunice Susan, m. Albert Newcomb; moved to Missouri; had 3 sons and 2 daus.; 2 sons killed in Civil War.
v Austin, b. 24 Jan., 1816; d. in Hartford, Conn., 4 Jan., 1890; m. 3 Jan., 1842, Rhoda Champion, b. in Lebanon, Conn., 15 Sept., 1812; d. in Hartford, 29 March, 1890; res. a farmer in Coventry. Ch., born there:
1 *Addie Champion*[8], b. 27 March, 1843; m. 15 Jan., 1868, William H., son of John J. White, b. in Hartford, 8 Jan., 1822; d. 7 April, 1884. Ch. (White): i William H.[9], d. y.; ii Herbert Brigham, b. 30 May, 1874; iii Addie Viola, b. 3 April, 1878.
vi Eliza Stowe, b. 21 Sept., 1818; d. unm., 31 May, 1889.
vii Wealthy Jane, b. 12 Sept., 1821; m. Rufus W. Tilden of Mansfield, Conn. Ch. (Tilden):
1 *Augusta R*[8]., unm.; 2 *Mary Jane*, unm.; 3 *Kate*, m. Edward Dimock; res. s. p., Mansfield Depot, Conn.; 4 *Rufus Webster*, res. Norwich, Conn.
viii Henrietta, d. young.

309 ROYAL[6], son of Thomas[5] and Susanna (Eels) Brigham; born in Coventry, Conn., 27 Sept., 1779; died 27 March, 1858; married, Aug., 1804, Hannah Tracy of Lisbon; born in 1777; died 1861. He went from Connecticut to Norwich, Vt., where he spent the rest of his life.

Children, the second and third born in Norwich:
609 i Royal[7], b. 17 July, 1805.
ii Jedediah Thomas, b. 24 Sept., 1811; d. in Norwich, unm., 13 Jan., 1875.
iii Lucy Ann, b. 1 Sept., 1816; d. in Norwich, unm., 9 May, 1900.

310 THOMAS S.[6], M. D., son of Lt.-Gov. Paul[5] and Lydia (Sawyer) Brigham; born in Coventry, Conn., 23 March, 1769; died in Wayne, Kennebec Co., Me., 6 May, 1844; married (1) Polly, daughter of Gen. James Dana of Mansfield (or Lebanon), Conn., and afterward of Cobleskill, N. Y. (who commanded a company at the battle of Bunker Hill and served seven years in the Revolutionary Army, which he left with the rank of Major); married (2) Mary French of So. Hampton, N. H.

Dr. Brigham removed to Norwich when thirteen years of age and was graduated from the Medical College in Hanover, N. H., and became celebrated in his profession. About 1809 he removed to Wayne, Me.

Children (by first wife), probably all born in Norwich:
610   i Polly[7], b. 21 July, 1794.
611   ii Lucia, b. 8 March, 1796.
      iii Laura, b. 13 Oct., 1800; m. 8 July, 1825, Luman McClintock, b. 2 May, 1803; res. Manchester, N. H. Ch. (McClintock):
         1 *Charlotte Jane[8]*, b. 23 June, 1826; m. 18 June, 1848, Henry H, Summers; res. Manchester, N. H. Ch. (Summers): i Luman H.[9], b. 11 May, 1849; ii Caroline H., b. 8 Oct., 1851; iii Clarence H., twin to Caroline, d. 3 June, 1858; iv Fred E., b. 7 Feb., 1854; v Charlotte A., b. 29 Aug., 1857.
         2 *Elizabeth*, b. 2 April, 1829.
         3 *Caroline*, b. 11 May, 1833.
         4 *William G.*, b. 27 Jan., 1838; m. 4 Dec., 1858, Elizabeth M. Davis; res. Manchester.
         5 *Luman B.*, b. 29 July, 1844; was a printer in Manchester.
      iv Charles, b. in 1806; d. at home of son in Iowa, about 1875; m. ————. Ch.:
         1 *Sidney[8]*, d. young in Lowell, Mass.
         2 *George*, res. Nevada, Ia.
612   v James Dana, b. ————.
      vi Thomas Jefferson, d. young.
Children (by second wife):
      vii Hannah, b. 1814; d. 17 Oct., 1849; m. Dr. Joseph Snelling Bishop (a des. of Edward Bishop of Salem, Mass., 1645) of Newport, Me. Ch. (Bishop):
         1 *Julia[8]*, b. in Newport; m. Alfred Tuck, who d. 24 Dec., 1897. Ch. (Tuck): Alfred[9] of Kennebunkport, Me.
         2 *Thomas Brigham*, b. 29 June, 1835; m. 1866, Sarah Ann Shivers, b. 4 Nov., 1847; was a broker in New York and Boston; a member of the Apollo Club. Ch.: Clarence Brigham[9], b. 11 July, 1869.
      viii Thomas Chandler, d. s. p.
      ix Mary Jane.
      x Sarah.
      xi Joseph, b. in Weld, Me.; m. ———— Ch., the 2 elder, names unknown; perhaps others, also:
         3 *Thomas Sawyer[8]*, b. in Weld, Me., 3 Oct., 1845; d. in W. Foxboro, Mass., 10 Dec., 1898; m. 16 Nov., 1873, Lois Ann, dau. of Amos Kimball, b. in Newton, N. H., 3 June, 1851; res. W. Foxboro. Ch.: i Nettie Gertrude[9], b. 2 Nov., 1874; ii Thomas Sawyer, b. 12 Nov., 1875; iii Amos Leslie, b. 31 Jan., 1877; iv Joseph Howard, b. 5 March, 1878; v Chester Goodell, b. 14 Jan., 1881; vi Olive L., b. 14 Feb., 1889; vii Lewis W., b. 22 May, 1890; viii Mary Elsie, b. 15 July, 1891; d. 4 Oct., 1891; ix Fanny M., b. 6 June, 1893; d. 15 Sept., 1895.

311   DON JOSEPHUS[6], son of Lt.-Gov. Paul[5] and Lydia (Sawyer) Brigham; born in Coventry, Conn., 24 March, 1774; died in Norwich, Vt., 28 Dec., 1856, æ. 82; married Anna Wright,

born in 1776; died 9 May, 1854. He resided in Norwich, Vt. The male line, is extinct.

Children, born in Norwich, Vt.:

i Sophia[7], b. 20 Oct., 1797; died in Norwich, s. p., 21 Aug., 1883; m. Samuel Wright; res. Norwich.

ii Cynthia, b. 24 July, 1799; d. ——————; m. Thomas Emerson o*f* Ridgway, N. Y. Ch. (Emerson):

1 *George*[8]*; 2 Ann; 3 Thomas; 4 Sophia; 5 Mary L.*, b. 14 Feb., 1833; m. —————— Oderkirk; res. Oak Orchard, N. Y.; 6 *Edward; 7 Charles; 8 Isabella,* d. 7 June, 1864.

iii Nancy, b. 3 July, 1801; d. unm., 9 Nov., 1887.

iv Phebe C., b. 20 July, 1803; d. 16 May, 1823.

v Lydia S., b. 19 April, 1805; d. unm., in Norwich, 27 ,Nov., 1891.

vi Olive, b. 26 March, 1807; d. in N., 9 March, 1885; m. 12 April, 1827, Stephen, son of Michael Blaisdell of Norwich; b. in Plainfield, N. H., 6 June, 1801; d. 4 Feb., 1854. Ch. (Blaisdell), b. in Norwich:

1 *Egbert*[8], b. 20 Dec., 1827; m. (1) Mary C. Hilton; m. (2) Melissa Russ. Ch. (by 1st wife): i Bell[9], m. Chas. W. Worman of Centerville, Ia. Ch. (by 2d wife): ii Carrie; iii Dennis; iv and v d. y.; vi Egbert, res. Norwich.

2 *George*, b. 7 Sept., 1829; m. Mary D. Houghton. Ch.: i Lizzie[9]; ii Nettie; iii Abel; iv Bessie, d. y. He res. Lowell, Mass.

3 *Ellen*, b. 9 March, 1831; d. 183—.

4 *Mary E.*, b. 20 Jan., 1833; m. George Burton; res. s. p., Norwich.

5 *Elizabeth*, b. 2 Nov., 1834; m. Frank Norton; 1 ch., d. y.; res. Norwich.

6 *Franklin*, b. 24 July, 1836; m. Lucy M. Frink.

7 *Edward*, b. 22 Sept., 1838; m. Ellen Mattoon; 2 ch., d. y.; res. Fitchburg, Mass.

8 *Henry*, b. 28 Sept., 1841; d. 1860.

9 *Amanda*, b. 20 May, 1844; m. (1) Charles C. Davis; m. (2) George Bemis. Ch. (Bemis): Harland[9], res. Providence, R. I.

vii Don A., b. 24 May, 1809; d. 23 Jan., 1894; m. in 1834, Susan R. Amsden, b. in 1814; d. 1879; res. Norwich. Ch.:

1 *Helen R.*[8], b. 27 April, 1838; d. 21 Aug., 1845.

2 *Eva,* b. and d. 1840.

3 *Susan J.,* b. 25 Jan., 1842; d. 30 Sept., 1845.

4 *Joseph A.,* b. 16 Jan., 1844; d. 6 Jan., 1845.

5 *Anna T.,* b. 14 Jan., 1846; m. Nahum Turner of Norwich; s. p.

6 *Walter L.,* b. 23 March, 1848; d. 1864.

7 *Mary E.,* b. 17 Nov., 1850; d. 1864.

8 *Grace F.,* b. 29 Oct., 1852; d. 10 Sept., 1853.

9 *Edgar,* b. 3 Aug., 1854; d. March, 1863.

10 *Nina A.,* b. 25 Nov., 1856; d. March, 1863.

viii Elvira, b. 17 July, 1811; d. in Lebanon, N. H., 12 April, 1893; m. 8 Nov., 1832, James Bly, Jr., b. in Norwich, 1 Aug., 1805; res. Lebanon, N. H., where he d. 29 Jan., 1888. Ch. (Bly), the 3 eldest b. in Norwich, the others in Lebanon:

1 *James Brigham*[8], b. 4 Jan., 1834; d. 13 Oct., 1863; m. in 1856, Marion Lester of Montreal, P. Q.

2 *Henry Osgood*, b. 20 Oct., 1838; m. 21 Dec., 1878, in Hanover, N. H., Helen A. Boutwell; res. there, s. p., in 1903.

3 *Harriet Osgood*, twin to Henry; d. 28 Oct., 1839.

4 *Ella Katherine*, b. 29 Aug., 1845; m. 21 Nov., 1867, James E. Warner of Lebanon. Ch. (Warner): Harriet E.*, b. 26 Oct., 1870; res. Ashburnham, Mass.

5 *Infant*, b. 29 Nov., 1847; d. *ibid.*

312   PAUL WOOSTER[6], son of Lt.-Gov. Paul[5] and Lydia (Sawyer) Brigham; born in Coventry, Conn., 26 Oct., 1776; died in Norwich, Vt., 3 Jan., 1865, æ. 89; married, 22 Feb., 1801, Mary Ayers of Haverhill, Mass.; born 16 March, 1782; died 28 Sept., 1869.

When his father moved from Coventry to Norwich, Vt., he rode on horseback behind his mother, at the age of 6 years. Resided for a time in Sharon, Vt., whence he went as representative to the General Court in 1804. Was a merchant. Inherited the homestead of his father, in Norwich, and in Morse's time was living there, æ. 83, and gave considerable assistance to that genealogist in his work.

Children, the 3 eldest born in Sharon, the others in Norwich, Vt.:

613   i Paul Wooster[7], b. 2 Nov., 1802.

    ii George, b. 17 June, 1804; res. Norwich, Vt., where d. 26 Jan., 1833; m. Elizabeth Trull of Roxbury, Mass. Ch.:

      1 *George C.*[8], b. in Norwich, 28 Jan., 1833; m. Abbie Willie of Roxbury, Mass.; res. Worcester and Holden, Mass. Ch.: i George W.[9], b. 16 Sept., 1856; d. in Boston, 1901; m. 25 Aug., 1883, Lottie E. Spurr; ii Lizzie E., b. Aug., 1860; m. H. C. Chapel.

    iii Mary, b. 25 May, 1806; died in Norwich, 14 Nov., 1828; m. Oct., 1826, Oliver S. Buell of Norwich. Ch. (Buell):

      1 *Loren*[8], res. Westville, N. Y.

614   iv William, b. 20 March, 1808.

    v Catherine, b. 23 July, 1810; d. 12 Oct., 1883; m. 26 Dec., 1832, Edwin Hebard, b. in Lebanon, N. H., 27 Aug., 1806; d. in Norwich, 8 April, 1878. Ch. (Hebard), b. in Norwich:

      1 *Lucius C.*[8], b. 2 Feb., 1835; m. Susan Eastman; res. Norwich. Ch.: i Mary[9]; ii Emma.

      2 *Susan E.*, b. 22 Aug., 1838; res. s. p., Norwich; m. 1 Jan., 1857, Curtis C. Sawyer, b. 1825.

      3 *George B.*, b. 2 Aug., 1840; d. unm., July, 1867.

    vi Louisa, b. May, 1813; d. 17 April, 1875; m. Oliver S. Buell (as his second wife) of Westville, N. Y. Ch. (Buell).

      1 *William B.*[8], b. Nov., 1832; res. E. Constable, N. Y.

615   vii James A., b. 24 June, 1816.

    viii Adaline E., b. 14 May, 1819; d. 28 April, 1885; m. 1 April, 1850, Alvin Pratt of Manchester, N. H. Ch. (Pratt), b. in Manchester:

      1 *Ella A.*[8], b. 30 Jan., 1852; m. R. S. Wallace of Manchester; s. p.

      2 *Mary P.*, b. Feb., 1855; d. æ. 2.

ix Albert, b. 21 April, 1823; m. in 1845, Harriet Harriden, who
d. 11 Oct., 1900; res. in 1903 in Manchester. Ch ·
1 *Albert*[8], b. and d. in 1855.
2 *Josephine E.*, b. in 1857; m. in 1886, D. J. Adams of Manchester. Ch. (Adams): Albert[9], d. y.

313 CHARLES[6], son of Don Carlos[5] and Mary (or Polly)
(Greenleaf) Brigham; born in Mansfield, Conn., 29 Jan., 1797;
died in Woodstock, Vt., where resided, 10 Jan., 1836; married, 7
Nov., 1824, Betsey Royce, born in Woodstock, 3 June, 1796; she
married (2), 21 Feb., 1821, Elisha Morey, and died in Coventry,
Conn., 15 April, 1862.

Children, born as indicated:
616 i Charles Frederick[7], b. in Woodstock, 13 Nov., 1825.
ii Laura Kendall, b. 2 Nov., 1828, in Coventry, Conn.; m. 1 Jan.,
1852, Edwin Cyrus Hoadley, b. in Mansfield, Vt., 7 March, 1828; d.
in So. Woodstock, Vt., 6 April, 1880. Ch. (Hoadley), b. in So.
Woodstock:
1 *Mary Elizabeth*[8], b. 5 Oct., 1852; d. 19 Jan., 1865.
2 *Jason Kendall*, b. 23 Dec., 1857; m. 13 Jan., 1881, Julia Arabella Lincoln, b. 8 Jan., 1859; ch.: i Walter E.[9], d. y.; ii Edith
L., b. 28 Dec., 1887; iii Forrest H., b. 15 March, 1895.
3 *Albert Edwin*, b. 7 Oct., 1871; unm.
iii Norman Carlos, b. in Mansfield, Conn., 8 Sept., 1835; m. 16
April, 1860, Mary Chase. Ch.:
1 *Don Carlos*[8], b. 30 March, 1861; m. 10 July, 1881, Ella Corbett.
Ch.: i Ruth[9], b. 13 Nov., 1882; d. in infancy; ii Maud Ella,
b. 3 April, 1884; iii Cora L., b. 9 Dec., 1885; d. 9 Dec., 1900.

314 DANIEL R.[6], son of Cephas[5] and Amelia (Robertson)
Brigham; born in South Coventry, Conn., 6 Aug., 1795; died about
1865; married Eliza, daughter of George Needham; born in Stafford, Conn., 6 Jan., 1796; resided in South Coventry, where he
died, 3 Dec., 1854.

Children, born in South Coventry:
i Daniel Watson[7], b. 6 April, 1821; d. in Williamsburg, N. Y.; m.
Elizabeth Brownell. Ch.:
1 *Mary A.*[8]; 2 *Marshall W.*; 3 *Anna E.*; 4 *James B.*
ii Henry Gray, b. 13 April, 1823; d. in Rockville, Conn., ————;
m. Mary A. Dimock; s. p.
iii Emily Wright, b. 1 Nov., 1826; m. (1) Lorin Edgarton; m. (2)
A. H. Brown; d. his widow, in Hartford, Conn., 20 Jan., 1901.
iv Frederick Benton, b. 13 April, 1829; died in New York; m.
Jane Smith. Ch.:
1 *Frederick E.*[8]; 2 *Charles.*
617 v George N., b. 2 May, 1831.
vi Edwin G., b. also 2 May, 1831; m. Sophronia Nye. Ch.:
1 *Henry*[8].

315 EDWIN G.[6], son of Cephas[5] and Amelia (Robertson)
Brigham; born in Coventry, Conn.; died in Hartford, Conn., Feb.,

1896; married Mariette Perrin, who died in Worcester, Mass. July, 1895. He resided in Vernon, Conn.

Children, born in Vernon:
    i Arthur Lee[7], m. 17 April, 1873, Louise Hecker; res. New York. Ch.:
        1 *Katherine*[8], b. 14 Aug., 1874.
        2 *Edna M.*, b. 22 Aug., 1885.
    ii Elbert, d. in Worcester, May, 1895.
    iii Mary, d. 1858, æ. 2½.

316 PETER[6], son of Hosea[5] and Catherine (Davis) Brigham; born Hubbardston, Mass., 2 Oct., 1781; married, 27 Oct., 1808, Mary Shirley. He died in Roxbury, Mass.

Children:
    i William E.[7], b. —————; d. Jan., 1889; m. Catherine Gay, who d. 29 Oct., 1900. Ch.:
        1 *William*[8], d. —————.
        2 *Augustus*, d. —————.
        3 *Justin*, m. —————; res. Worcester, Mass., and was living, 1905; dau. Myra J.[9]
        4 *Sarah J.*, b. 24 Nov., 1832; d. s. p., 25 Feb., 1902; m. 4 Jan., 1854, Capt. Augustus Ford, and res. Dorchester, Mass.; she was interested in the B. F. A., and a member at the time of death.
        5 *Louisa*, d.
        6 *Juliette*, d.
    ii, iii, iv and v have not been reported.

317 JOSEPH[6], son of Hosea[5] and Catherine (Davis) Brigham; born in Hubbardston, Mass., 9 Aug., 1785; died there, 18 Oct., 1864; married, 26 Feb., 1823, Rebecca (Brown) Lamb, who died 23 March, 1863. Resided in Hubbardston. The male line is extinct.

Children, born in Hubbardston:
    i Mary R.[7], b. 13 Jan., 1824; m. 30 Sept., 1845, Asa Bennett of Hubbardston. Ch. (Bennett), b. in Hubbardston:
        1 *Frederick*[8], b. 30 Nov., 1846; d. 12 Aug., 1848.
        2 *Mary Lizzie*, b. 16 Dec., 1849; m. 20 Aug., 1872, Howard McAllister of Chicago, Ill.
    ii Elizabeth, b. 27 April, 1828; m. 10 Nov., 1864, Alden Pollard of Hubbardston; he m. (1) Elizabeth Green, who had James A. Pollard, b. 1854, res. Leominster, Mass. Ch. (Pollard), b. in Hubbardston:
        1 *Mabel Alden*[8], b. 25 Dec., 1866.
        2 *Frederick Eugene*, b. 21 March, 1871.

318 ASA[6], son of Joel[5] and Elizabeth (Maynard) Brigham; born in Sudbury, Mass., 16 Feb., 1785; died there, 20 March, 1856; married Olive Gardner, who died 23 Feb., 1863.

Children:
    i Sherman[7], b. 4 Jan., 1812; d. 7 July, 1876.
    ii Sylvanus, b. 25 Aug., 1813; d. 10 Jan., 1860.

iii Rufus, b. 16 April, 1815; d. 26 Feb., 1881.

iv Henry, b. 27 Sept., 1816; d. 27 March, 1854.

v Charles, b. 16 April, 1818; d. 15 Feb., 1863.

vi Maria, b. 5 May, 1819; d. 23 Jan., 1884; m. Thomas Cousens. Ch.: (Cousens)·
  1 *George*[6].

vii Dennis, b. 23 Nov., 1820.

viii Christopher, b. 24 Feb., 1822; m. Eliza Tupper, and had 3 ch.

ix Lucy A., b. 1 April, 1824; m. Lorenzo F. Wood. Ch. (Wood):
  1 *Henry*[8]; 2 *Charles*; 3 *Ann Maria*, who m. John Bevins of London, Eng.

x Olive A., b. 24 Feb., 1826; d. y.

xi Olive A., b. 24 May, 1827; m. (1) Francis W. Ayers; m. (2) D. W. Carville. Ch. (Ayers):
  1 *Adelaide A.*[8], m. C. X. Dalton.
  2 *Henry W.*, m. Fanny Trefethen; has ch.: Henry W.[9]

xii Candice, b. 25 Dec., 1830; m. Thomas Sweet; has 2 ch.

xiii Andrew J., b. 25 Dec., 1832; m. —————.

xiv Sarah J., b. 9 June, 1834; d. 21 Aug., 1863; m. Rufus Harvey. Ch. (Harvey):
  1 *Thurber*[8]; 2 *Lizzie*.

319   JOEL[6], son of Joel[5] and Elizabeth (Maynard) Brigham; born in Sudbury, Mass., 16 March, 1788; died in Deerfield, Mass. where he resided, 16 Nov., 1829; married Elizabeth Brown, born 14 Oct., 1789 in Sudbury.   He was a farmer.

Children, the 2 eldest born in Sudbury, the 7 youngest in Deerfield:

i Emily[7], b. 17 Nov., 1812; d. 27 Feb., 1896; m. 24 April, 1845, William Smith of Conway, Mass. Ch. (Smith):
  1 *Maria Antoinette*, b. 13 March, 1846; d. 18 Feb., 1849.
  2 *Oscar Allen*, b. 23 Dec., 1847; d. 4 March, 1872.
  3 *George Elliot*, b. 30 June, 1850; d. 23 Nov., 1881; m. Annie Underwood. Ch.: Nettie A.[9], m. Frank Gordon of Peekskill, N. Y.

618 ii Abel, b. 11 Jan., 1814.

iii Charles, b. 23 April, 1815; d. s. p., date uncertain.

iv Dana, b. 23 Nov., 1816; d. 5 July, 1888; res. Deerfield, a farmer.

v Elbridge G., b. 27 Aug., 1818; d. in Deerfield, 30 Nov., 1875; m. (1) 8 May, 1849, Martha L. Smith, who d. 24 Jan., 1861, æ. 32; m. (2) Rebecca, dau. of Erastus Barret, and wid. of Frank Goodnough; a farmer, res. Deerfield. Ch. (by first wife), b. in Deerfield:
  1 *Frank S.*[8], b. 8 Feb., 1858; m. 31 March, 1888, Clara A. Smith; res. E. Deerfield, a farmer. Ch.: i Dwight[9], b. 12 March, 1889; ii Daisy, b. 3 March, 1890.

vi Joel, b. 23 April, 1820; d. unm., 26 July, 1889; a farmer, res. Deerfield.

viii Cephas, b. 26 Dec., 1821; d. in Newton, Mass., 31 Oct., 1890; m. 1846, Lucy E. Graves, who d. 11 July, 1887; res. Montague, Dedham and Boston, Mass.; a teacher, lawyer, trial justice and 1st lieutenant.

ix Leander, b. 23 March, 1823; d. in Montague, Mass., 19 June, 1888; m. Eliza —————.   He enlisted in Co. G, 56th Mass. Infantry, Civil War; a farmer. Ch.:

1 *Mary E.*[8], m. Felix McCue; res. Millers Falls, Mass.
2 *Julia*, m. W. E. Morrison; res. Greenfield, Mass.
3 *Hattie M.*, res. Montague.
4 *Edgar C.*, res. Montague.

x Lorenzo, b. 26 Sept., 1824; d. in Deerfield, where res. 28 Dec., 1893; m. ————; a farmer. Ch.:
    1 *Herbert S.*[8], res. Deerfield; 2 *Lillie;* 3 *Minnie;* 4 *Leslie;* 5 *Nettie.*

xi Horace, b. 31 March, 1828; d. in Deerfield, where res. 12 Aug., 1896; m. Sophronia Kent. Ch.:
    1 *George*[8]; 2 *Dorr;* 3 *William;* 4 *Dwight.*

320 POLLY[6], daughter of Joel[5] and Elizabeth (Maynard) Brigham; born in Sunbury, Mass., 9 Dc., 1792; maridtd, 2 Nov., 1820,. Capt. Thomas Stearns, born in Leominster, Mass., 1 April, 1794; (he married [1], June, 1817, Thirza ,Burrage, dau. of Dea. Williams, who died s. p., 1819). Was a tanner and currier and resided in Leominster.

Children (Stearns), born in Leominster:
    i William Alonzo[7], b. 14 Aug., 1821; d. 27 Dec., 1901; m. Mary Schutte; res. Boston.
    ii Oliver, b. 1 March, 1823; d. 1 Oct., 1898; m. 27 Oct., 1847, Charlotte A. Whitcomb; 1 ch., d. y.
    iii George, b. 16 March, 1826; d. 19 April, 1826.
    iv Thirza, b. 28 Sept., 1827; d. 20 Sept., 1846.
    v Henry, b. 19 Aug., 1829; d. in L., 14 Jan., 1882; m. 7 Sept., 1852, Mary A. Phipps of Holliston, Mass.; a man of solid worth; in the coal, ice and teaming business in Leominster. Ch.:
        1 *Clara Viola*[8], b. 25 June, 1853; m. Wilbur F., son of T. Dwight Wood; b. in Westminster, Mass., 5 Nov., 1851; manager of the Rodney Wallace farm in W. Fitchburg; 1 ch.
        2 *Emma Luella*, b. 21 June, 1856; d. 11 Dec., 1877.
        3 *Lizzie Anna*, b. 1859; d. 1863.
        4 *Etta Maria*, b. 2 June, 1865; m. (1) H. H. Hunt; m. (2) J. F. Gallagher; 4 ch.
    vi Caroline Matilda, b. 27 June, 1831; res. Leominster.
    vii Mary Ann, b. 22 Feb., 1833; d. 14 April, 1883; m. Josiah Pierce. Ch. (Pierce).
        1 *Edward W.*[8], m. Anna Tisdale. Ch. Ralph[9].
        2 *Gertrude A.*, m. Jos. Munro. Ch. (Munro): Marjorie[9].
        3 *Grace B.*, m. E. A. Onthank. Ch., 1 son.

321 NANCY[6], daughter of Joel[5] and Elizabeth (Maynard) Brigham; born in Sudbury, Mass., 16 Aug., 1803; died 12 May, 1891; married 6 May, 1829, Seth Brown.

Children (Brown):
    i George Henry[7], b. 17 Sept., 1831; m. (1) 29 Nov., 1860, Augusta P. Britton, who d. 30 May, 1874; m. (2) Frances E. Powers. Ch. (by first wife):
        1 *Georgietta Isabel*[8], b. 22 Oct., 1873; m. 2 Jan., 1896, Fred Z. Brown; 1 ch.

ii Chester Franklin, b. 12 Jan., 1835; d. 22 May, 1898; m. 2 Dec., 1858, Sarah J. Streeter. Ch.:
    1 *Eva Leila*[8], b. 19 June, 1872; m. Elton Ward Lacy, 1 Feb., 1898.
iii Alonzo A., b. 29 Jan., 1837; m. in New Zealand, in 1865, Janet Kennedy. Ch.:
    1 *Lizzie*, b. in Pabraka, N. Z., 7 Oct., 1866; m. (1) L. E. Bathrick; m. (2) 1900, S. M. Schatzkin; 2 ch.
    2 *John S.*, b. 20 Aug., 1868; m. 1900, Julia Kennel; 2 ch.
    3 *George F.*, b. 29 April, 1870; m. 1893, Alice I. Knowland; 3 ch.
    4 *Flora J.*, b. 15 Sept., 1872; d. 30 Oct., 1878.

322 DANFORTH PHIPPS[6], son of Elijah[5] and Mary (Gleason) Brigham; born in Sudbury, Mass., 30 Dec., 1803; died in Lowell, Mass., 18. Sept., 1875; married, 12 Apr., 1827, Hannah Walcott; born in Stow, Mass., 25 May, 1801; died 6 April, 1874. He was a city official in Lowell and representative to the Legislature in 1850; also resided in Wilmington, Mass.

Children, born in Lowell:
    i Eliza Jane[7], b. 16 March, 1828; d. 13 June, 1851, unm.
    ii Hannah Elizabeth, b. 10 Aug., 1829; d. in Lowell, 26 April, 1880; m. 15 Nov., 1860, John Higgins Nichols, who was in the Civil War, 2d N. H. Vols.; wounded at second battle Bull Run; honorably discharged; b. in Wilmington, Mass., 7 April, 1828. Ch. (Nichols), b. in Lowell:
        1 *Charles William*[8], b. 30 Oct., 1861; d. 18 Sept., 1864.
        2 *Fred*, b. 3 Dec., 1863; d. 3 Sept., 1864.
        3 *Carrie*, b. 26 Aug., 1866; d. 22 Aug., 1873.
        4 *Fred*, b. 29 Sept., 1867; m. 13 Sept., 1893.
        5 *Ulysses*, b. 3 March, and d. 20 March, 1869.
        6 *Theodore*, b. 28 April, and d. 17 May, 1872.
    iii Mary Ann, b. 1 Jan., 1831.
    iv Ellen Maria, b. 25 July, 1832.
619   v Charles William, b. 12 Aug., 1834.
    vi Caroline Louisa, b. 1 June, 1836; d. unm., 27 March., 1863.
    vii Henry Harrison, b. 19 Feb., 1841; d. unm., 2 Sept., 1873; 3 years in U. S. service during Civil War; Ark. and Fortress Munroe.
    viii Sarah Phipps, b. 22 June, 1843.
    ix Emeline Frances, b. 5 June, 1845.

323 DEA. WILLIAM[6], son of Elijah[5] and Mary (Gleason) Brigham; born in Sudbury, Mass., 27 March, 1805; died in Mass. Gen. Hospital, 20 May, 1879; married, 4 Aug., 1835, Abby Ann, daughter of Rev. William Muzzey (who graduated from Harvard College in 1793); born in Lexington, 15 June, 1806. Moved to Lexington about 1830, where he was deacon in the Unitarian church.

Child, born in Lexington:
    i Laura Muzzey[7], b. 20 July, 1836; res. unm., in Lexington.

324 SAMUEL[6], son of Eber[5] and Lucy (Arnold) Brigham; born in Sudbury, Mass.; died there, 10 April, 1853; married Hannah Sanderson.

Children, born in Sudbury:
  i Alfred[7], b. 10 Feb., 1846; m. 1 Oct., 1874, Mary Frances, dau. of Oliver Smith and Mary (Denton) Wells; b. 16 Feb., 1848; d. in Cambridge, Mass., 28 Jan., 1906; interred in Mt. Auburn. He is a grocer in Boston and res. Cambridge. Ch.:
    1 *Arthur Wells*[8], b. 23 Sept., 1875; m. 7 June, 1905, Ina F. Sears; is in business with father. Ch., b. in Dorchester: Sears[9], b. 12 March, 1906; d. 1 April, 1906.
    2 *Harry Austin,* b. 11 June, 1877; is a journalist, res. Cambridge.
    3 *Walter Sanderson,* b. 11 July, 1882.
  ii Georgiana.

325 RUFUS[6], son of Capt. William[5] and Sarah (Osborn) Brigham; born in Sudbury, Mass., 11 Jan., 1818; died there, 17 Nov., 1896; married, 3 Feb., 1842, Lucretia Moore, who died in Sudbury, 9 March, 1887.

Children, born in Sudbury:
  i Emily Elizabeth[7], b. 9 July, 1843; m. 20 Dec., 1888, Levi S. Jones; s. p., 1903.
  ii Lucretia Jane, b. 5 Aug., 1845; m. 29 Nov., 1877, George Washington Griggs of Scituate, Mass. Ch. (Griggs), b. in Scituate:
    1 *Bertha Helen*[8], b. 1 Oct., 1878.
    2 *Alice,* b. 20 Sept., 1881.
  iii William Rufus, b. 25 Dec., 1847; d. 26 Feb., 1861.
  iv Charles Nixon, b. 15 April, 1850; m. in 1878, Jennie Smith; res. in Dundas, Minn. Ch.:
    1 *Edith Lucretia*[8], b. 18 Feb., 1880; m. 28 Oct., 1897, Fred H. Hassin. Ch. (Hassin): i Russell R.[9], b. 28 July, 1899; ii Bernice, b. 19 Nov., 1901.
    2 *Gertrude C.,* b. 15 Aug., 1882; m. 15 Aug., 1897, Lewis A. Hall of Wells, Minn. Ch. (Hall): i Edgar C.[9], b. 26 Nov., 1899; ii Cecil D.
    3 *Ruby Inez,* b. 12 March, 1885.
    4 *Isabel Wanetta,* b. 18 Oct., 1887.
    5 *Herbert Clarence,* b. 14 April, 1890.
    6 *Jesse C.,* b. 28 March, 1899.
  x Herbert Storrs, b. 26 Nov., 1857; m. 27 March, 1881, Helen Lord of Kennebunk, Me., where he res. Ch., b. there:
    1 *Ernest Lord*[8], b. 17 Jan., 1882; grad. A. B., Bowdoin Coll., 1904.
    2 *Herbert Storrs,* b. 2 Dec., 1885.
    3 *Dean Nason,* b. 18 April, 1895.

326 ROXEY[6], daughter of John[5] and Ann Eunice (Moore) Brigham; born in Sudbury, Mass., 7 Jan., 1788; married Luke Robinson of Rutland, Mass.; moved to Watertown, Mass., where he was for many years proprietor of " Spring Hotel " and highly respected, and where he died, 7 Sept., 1870, æ. 89.

Children (Robinson):
  i Elizabeth[7], b. 6 July, 1806; m. Andrew Cole of Watertown. Ch.
    (Cole):
      1 *Harriet[8];* 2 *Susan;* 3 *Adaline;* 4 *Francis;* 5 *Henry P.;* 6
      Mary E.; 7 *Caroline;* the last three are living in Newton, Mass.
  ii Edwin, b. 2 Aug., 1808; m. Bathsheba Bates. Ch ·
      1 *Edwin[8];* 2 *Frank;* 3 *Ellen,* m. Charles Lowe of Newton.
  iii Rufus, b. 3 Sept., 1810; d. Sept., 1813.
  iv William, b. 12 Oct., 1812; d. July, 1817.
  v Mary, b. 8 July, 1815; d. July, 1817.
  vi Francis, b. 16 Oct., 1818; d. 1883; m. Martha Cutter of Weston,
     Mass. Ch.:
      1 *Mabel[8],* a teacher in Washington.
  vii George, b. 8 Dec., 1821; m. Helen Young; res. Lexington,
      Mass. Ch.:
      1 *George[8],* who d.; 2 *Jennie,* res. Waltham.
  viii William, b. 1 July, 1827; m. (1) Abbie W. Robbins; m. (2)
       Ione Streeter of Woburn, Mass. Ch. (by first wife):
       1 *William[8];* 2 *Mary;* 3 *George Frederick;* 4 *Ruth W.;* 5 *Theo-
       dore B.*
       Ch. (by second wife):
       6 *Wallace;* 7 *Wilhelmine* (d.); 8 *Philip.*
  ix Ellen, b. 6 Dec., 1832; d. April, 1838.

327 ABIJAH[6], son of John[5] and Ann Eunice (Moore) Brigham; born in Sudbury, Mass., 17 March, 1791; died 7 Feb., 1892;
married Melissa Stratton of Rutland, Mass.; resided in Rutland.

Children, born in Rutland:
  i Clarissa[7], m. Daniel Hitchings, and res. Chelsea, Mass. Ch.
    (Hitchings):
      1 *Henry[8];* 2 *Lucy;* 3 *Charles B.,* m. ———— Jones; 4 *Frank;*
      5 *George;* 6 *Martha.*
  ii Lucy.
  iii Lavinia Moore, b. 1 Dec., 1821; m. Robert Lewis Goddard of
      Petersham, Mass., b. 21 May, 1822; d. in Palmer, Mass., 15 Jan.,
      1887; res. Palmer. Ch. (Goddard):
      1 *William Lewis[8],* b. 1 Aug., 1846; d. 1 Aug., 1873.
      2 *Frank Ballard,* b. 6 Oct., 1851; d. 9 Nov., 1858.
      3 *Lisette Martha,* b. 15 Nov., 1861; d. 12 Jan., 1877.
  iv John Warren, m. Martha Eliza Brigham, dau. of 256. Ch.:
      1 *Warren[8],* m. ———— Adams, and d. Ch.: i Ethel, m. W. B.
      C. Fox, res. Dorchester; ii Enid; iii Edith.
      2 *Ella,* m. George Marchant of Minneapolis, Minn.
      3 *Frank.*
      4 *Lura,* d.

328 JOHN[6], son of John[5] and Ann Eunice (Moore) Brigham;
born in Sudbury, Mass., 22 March, 1795; died in Watertown, Mass.,
24 May, 1874; married (1) Mary Leveritt of Burke Co., Ga.; married (2), 8 July, 1844, Mary (Crafts) Brigham, widow of his
brother William.

At the age of eighteen he went to Georgia where he secured a large plantation and also engaged in mercantile business; resided on the Savannah River, 70 miles above the city of Savannah, in place known as "Brigham's Landing"; returned to Watertown in 1840, and engaged in the lumber trade, purchased the historic "Coolidge Tavern," where tradition says Washington stayed the night previous to taking command of the Continental troops in Cambridge. He seemed to possess energy and business ability like his distinguished ancestor, Dr. John, and was highly respected in the communities where he resided.

Children (by first wife), born in Georgia:
620   i William[7], b. 19 July, 1819.
621   ii Elizabeth Ann Eunice, b. 15 Jan., 1824.
622   iii John, b. 13 Feb., 1827.
Child (by second wife), born in Watertown:
      iv Maria, b. 25 Feb., 1847; res. unm., Watertown.

329   WILLIAM[6], son of John[5] and Ann Eunice (Moore) Brigham; born in Sudbury, Mass., 11 Aug., 1810; died in Watertown, Mass., 23 April, 1843; married (1), 17 April, 1834, Adeline, daughter of Thaddeus Cole of Watertown; born 1813; died 1836; married (2), 15 March, 1837, Mary Crafts (who married [2] her first husband's brother, John); born in Cambridge, Mass., 7 June, 1813; died in Watertown, 15 Nov., 1902. He resided in Watertown; first entered the dry goods business, and later associated himself with his brother John in the lumber business, in which line he continued until his death.

Child (by first wife), born in Watertown:
623   i William Theodore[7], b. 12 Sept., 1835.
Children (by second wife), born in Watertown:
      ii George, b. 16 March, 1838; d. y.
624   iii Charles, b. 21 June, 1841.

330   LEWIS[6], son of Joseph[5] and Rebecca (Haynes) Brigham; born in Sudbury, Mass., 27 Oct., 1797; died there, 8 Sept., 1875; married, 27 May, 1838, Almira Bowker, born 12 Aug., 1810. The old red house on the homestead of Dr. John, where Lewis lived, was taken down about 1830 to help build the new house; it stood west of the present residence, at the angle of the Marlboro and Fitchburg roads in northwestern Sudbury; in 1897 there was still to be seen the cellar hole of the old house, 10 rods west of present residence; also a ruined cider-mill, over 100 years old, on right of Fitchburg road, west of present house. He was a farmer.

Children, born in Sudbury:
      i Martha Ann[7], b. 9 March, 1839; m. 1 June, 1859, Hiram Greene, a merchant; res. Mass. Ave., Boston. Ch. (Greene):
         1 *Julia H.*[8]
      ii Rebecca Haynes, b. 1 July, 1840; m. 20 June, 1859, Thomas Albert Bent; res. Somerville, Mass. Ch. (Bent):

1 *Carrie* F.[8]
iii Nancy Elizabeth, b. 25 April, 1843; res. unm., Boston.
iv Esther Louisa, b. 16 Dec., 1846; d. unm., 8 May, 1902; res.
   Boston.
v Lewis Alanson, b. 25 Feb., 1850; d. æ. 9 days.
vi Emma Almira, b. 9 Aug., 1851; m. 20 March, 1872, Newell Wilcomb, a farmer; res. on the old Dr. John place in Sudbury. Ch.
   (Wilcomb):
   1 *Fanny* A.[8], b. 11 Dec., 1874; m. James Haire of Maynard,
     Mass. Ch. (Haire): Claude Brigham[9].
   2 *Lewis*, b. 26 Nov., 1877; d. 1879.
   3 *Alice Emma*, b. 19 Sept., 1880; d. æ. 15 years.
   4 *Ida Louise*, b. 21 Nov., 1885; d.

331   EUNICE[6], daughter of Joseph[5] and Rebecca (Haynes)
Brigham; born in Sudbury, Mass., 19 Dec., 1798; died in Springfield, Mass., 13 March, 1856; married, 16 Oct., 1834 (as his second
wife), Rev. Addison Parker.

Children (Parker):
   i Sarah Frances[7], b. in Methuen, Mass., 26 July, 1837; m. 17 Aug.,
     1865, Elias C. Atkins, b. in Bristol, Conn., 28 June, 1833; d.
     in Indianapolis, Ind., 18 April, 1901; he was the founder of the
     firm of E. C. Atkins & Co., saw manufacturers; was a man of
     marked influence in his State. Ch. (Atkins):
     1 *Mary* D.[8], b. 1867; m. Nelson A. Gladding of I.; 2 ch.
     2 *Henry* C., b. 1868; m. Sue Winter of I.; 3 ch.
     3 *Sarah Frances*, b. 1870; m. Thomas Reed Hackley of I.; 4 ch.
     4 *Emma L.*, b. 1872; m. Edward B. Davis; 1 ch.
     5 *Carra*, b. 1874; m. Arthur D. Gates; 1 ch.
  ii Rev. Addison, b. in Danbury, Conn., 12 Nov., 1839; is a Baptist
     clergyman in Richmond, Ind.; was grad. from Brown Univ. and
     Newton Theolog. School; was a sergeant in the Civil War;
     filled many Baptist pulpits in the East and West; m. 18 Sept.,
     1866, Mary L. Boyden of Dedham, Mass. Ch.:
     1 *Wilson* B.[8], b. in Natick; res., an architect, in Indianapolis.
     2 *Edith M.*, b. in Charlestown, Mass.; m. Dr. Woodbridge O.
       Johnson, a missionary to Taiku, Korea, Asia; 4 ch.

332   REBECCA[6], daughter of Joseph[5] and Rebecca (Haynes)
Brigham; born in Sudbury, Mass., 28 Aug., 1807; died 1856; mar-
ried, 9 Jan., 1834, Lawrence Thompson, a wealthy planter of
Prides Station, Ala.

Children (Thompson), born in Alabama:
   i Sarah[7], d. y.
  ii Lawrence, d. y.
 iii Rebecca, m. Dec., 1866, William W. Baylis of Florence, Ala.
     Ch. (Baylis):
     1 *Annie* T.[8], d. y.
     2 *William B.*, unm., res. Louisville, Ky.
     3 *Mary*, m. (1) Morgan; (2) Ashcroft.
  iv Annie S., d. unm., Nov., 1866.
   v Joseph N., m. 1869, Lucie B. Malone; res. Tuscombia, Ala. Ch.:
     1 *Humphrey* B.[8]; 2 *Lawrence K.*; 3 *Joseph N.*; 4 *Lucien B.*

vi Mary Nancy, m. Dr. Joseph P. Pride.   Ch. (Pride):
1 *Empson T.*[8], d. unm.
2 L. *Thompson*, m. May Mahoon, res. Prides Sta., Ala.; 5 ch.

333   CHARLES[6], son of Joseph[5] and Rebecca (Haynes) Brigham; born in Sudbury, Mass., 16 July, 1811; died —————; married Eunice Hagar, daughter of Francis Garfield.   Resided in Greenfield, Mass., and was very much interested in the project of a family history.

Children, born in Greenfield:
   i Maria[7], b. 16 July, 1852; d. 7 Oct., 1862.
   ii Dorcas, b. 17 April, 1855; d. 9 April, 1856.
   iii Alanson, b. 5 July, 1859; m. Stella, daughter of Jason Moore; b. 7 Oct., 1863; res. Greenfield.   Ch.:
      1 *Lewis*[8], b. 14 Aug., 1889.
   iv Jane, b. 3 Oct., 1862; m. ————— Damon; a widow, res. with bro. Joseph, in Greenfield.
   v Lucy, b. 25 Sept., 1865; d. 10 Feb., 1866.
   vi Joseph, b. 9 April, 1868; res. in Greenfield, unm.
   vii Eunice, d. unm., 1892.

334   SAMUEL[6], son of Dr. Samuel[5] and Mary (Ball) Brigham; born in Boylston, Mass., 19 Feb., 1795; died in Clinton, Mass., 15 July, 1877; married Alethina Howe, who died in 1880. He probably resided in Boylston and Lancaster, Mass., and Machias, Me.

Children, born as indicated:
625   i Abel[7], b. in Boylston, Mass., 26 Oct., 1815.
626   ii Dolly, b. 30 Oct., 1817.
627   iii Samuel Davis, b. 22 March, 1821.
628   iv Levi Edwin, b. in Lancaster, 17 Jan., 1825.
      v James Lawson, b. 18 Feb., 1831; d. y.
629   vi John D., b. in Machias, Me., 5 Aug., 1834.

335   MARY[6], daughter of Dr. Samuel[5] and Mary (Ball) Brigham; born in Boylston, Mass., 13 April, 1797; died in Shrewsbury, Mass., 30 Oct., 1867; married, 9 April, 1822, Solomon, son of David Mahan of Northboro, Mass.; born there, 16 July, 1792; died in Shrewsbury, 28 Dec., 1873.   He was a farmer and moved to Shrewsbury.

Children (Mahan), born in Shrewsbury:
   i Mary Ann[7], b. and d. 1823.
   ii George Henry, b. 19 Dec., 1824; d. in Shrewsbury, 14 March, 1903, unm.
   iii Mary Ann, b. 22 July, 1826; m. William H. Perry, a farmer in Shrewsbury; 25 years assessor; 15 years on school committee. Ch. (Perry).
      1 *Marian*[8], m. Joseph E. Warren of Marlboro.
      2 *Zella*, m. Samuel H. Johnson of Shrewsbury.
      3 *Abbie*, m. Alvin S. Dearth of Worcester.

iv Harriet Elizabeth, b. 1 May, 1830; m. Jonas Cummings, a farmer in Shrewsbury; d. 1873. Ch. (Cummings):
1 *John*[8]; 2 *Mary*; 3 *Ida*.
v John Davis, b. 8 Feb., 1835; m. Elizabeth J. Orne; res. Charlestown, Mass.
vi Sarah Jane, b. 10 Sept., 1836; m. George A. Newton, a farmer of Shrewsbury. Ch. (Newton):
1 *George*[8], d. æ. 13.
vii Caroline S., b. 18 July, 1844; m. Abel O. Perry, who d. in Worcester, 1898.

336 JONAS BALL[6], son of Dr. Samuel[5] and Mary (Ball) Brigham; born in Boylston, Mass., 28 April, 1807; died 1 March, 1872; married, 9 April, 1835, Lucinda, daughter of Capt. John Howe of Boylston; born 19 May, 1809; died 16 May, 1861. Resided in Westboro, Mass., and probably in Grafton.

Children:
i Joshua Leland[7], b. 16 March, 1836; d. 2 Feb., 1837.
ii Harrison M., b. 4 Feb., 1838; res. Westboro.
iii Abbie L., b. 25 Feb., 1840; res. Westboro.
iv George E., b. 1 March, 1842; d. 7 July, 1849.
v Silas H., b. in Grafton, Mass., 5 June, 1844, or 1846; m. 1866, Abbie Flanders. He is Supt. of Construction, and res. 320 Madison St., Waukegan, Ill. Ch.:
1 *Lena*[8], m. Ralph Draper Smith. Ch. (Smith): i Florence Marie; ii Kathryn Brigham; they res. Keene, N. H.
vi Mary E., b. 25 Dec., 1845 (?).
vii Edmund L., b. 7 Dec., 1848.
viii Henry A., b. 22 Sept., 1850; d. 28 May, 1854.

337 JOHN GOTT[6], son of John Gott[5] and Mary (Collins) Brigham; born in Marlboro, Mass., 2 Aug., 1796; died 27 Nov., 1871; married, 9 Jan., 1820, Lucy, daughter of Benjamin and Abigail (Howe) Howe; born in Marlboro, 6 June, 1798; died 28 Feb., 1863. Was a wheelwright and resided in Concord, Mass.

Children, 2 eldest born in Marlboro, others in Concord:
i Hepzibah Collins[7], b. 21 Oct., 1821; d. in Seaforth, Canada, 7 Aug., 1872; m. in Concord, 2 Nov., 1843, George Albert, son of Maj. Levi Stearns; b. in Lunenburg, Mass., 9 Sept., 1812; res. Quincy, Mass., and perhaps moved to Rouse's Point, N. Y. Ch. (Stearns), the two elder b. in Quincy:
1 *Georgiana Augusta*[8], b. 10 July, 1844.
2 *Elizabeth Lucy*, b. 15 July, 1846; d. Oct., 1848.
3 *Adelia Gertrude*, b. 26 Nov., 1848.
4 *Edward*; 5 *Ellen*; 6 *Winifred*; 7 *Ernest*.
630 ii William Eustis, b. 14 April, 1823.
iii George Howe, b. 5 Dec., 1824; res. Dorchester, Mass.; m. Melissa Wheelock of Newport, Vt. Ch.:
1 *Mary M.*[8], b. 11 June, 1856; d. 1860.
2 *Lillie*, b. 1861; d. 1862.

631   iv Alonzo Howe, b. 16 April, 1826.
     v John Edward, b. 9 March, 1828; m. Isabella Smith; res. Toronto, Canada. Ch.:
       1 *Frank*⁸, res. Toronto.
       2 *Mary*.
    vi Harrison Gray, b. 4 Nov., 1829; m. Josephine Garfield; res. Dorchester.
   vii Francis Eugene, b. 10 Oct., 1831; d. 11 Sept., 1833.
  viii Mary Ann, b. 3 May, 1834; m. Francis Bacon; res. Dover, Mass. Ch. (Bacon):
       1 *Ella*⁸; 2 *Lila*; 3 *Frank*.
    ix Lucy Jane, b. 3 July, 1836; d. Oct., 1873; res. Concord.

338   NATHANIEL PHILLIPS⁶, son of Henry⁵ and Anna (Phillips) Brigham; born in Barre, Mass., 1 Dec., 1785; died 5 Dec., 1866; married, April, 1810, Martha, daughter of Makepeace and Catherine (Smith) Gates; born in Barre, 3 Feb., 1784; died 14 Aug., 1869. Was a farmer and land surveyor.

Children, born in Barre:
632   i Martha Ann⁷, b. 22 Oct., 1811.
633   ıı William Harrison, b. 16 Dec., 1814.
634   ııı Orlando Sibley, b. 16 Dec., 1816.
    iv Nathaniel Nelson, b. 6 June, 1819; d. in Niagara Falls, Ont., 15 Sept., 1903; m. (1) 4 Nov., 1845, Sarah S. Hildreth, b. in New Braintree, Mass., 12 March, 1821; m. (2) Nov., 1880, Charlotte E. Wade of Palmerston, Ont.; res. Niagara Falls, Ont. Ch. (by first wife), b. in Barre:
      1 *Byron*⁸, b. 6 Sept., 1846; m. 23 April, 1877, E. P. Whittier of Kennebunk, Me.; res. s. p., in 1893, in Woburn, Mass.
      2 *Edward A.*, b. 8 Dec., 1854; m. 7 Feb., 1877, M. J. Wade; a gardener; has 3 daus.
      Ch. (by second wife):
      3 *Beatrice*, b. 21 Oct., 1883.
      4 *R. E.*, b. 21 Oct., 1887.
    v Nancy Phillips, b. 22 June, 1822; d. in So. Norwalk, Conn., 17 July, 1896; m. 5 Oct., 1843, Dexter Dennis, b. in Barre, 28 Jan., 1818; d. in So. Norwalk, 30 March, 1881. Ch. (Dennis), b. in Barre:
      1 *Lloyd Eugene*⁸, b. 16 Oct., 1844; m. (1) 16 Oct., 1865, Jane Sigourney Bassett; m. (2) 28 Nov., 1883, Augusta Mayhew Johnson; res. s. p., Worcester, Mass.
      2 *Agnes Eudora*, b. 4 March, 1852; m. 27 Jan., 1878, Abiathar Blanchard of Petersham, Mass.; s. p.
      3 *Frederick Walker*, b. 28 March, 1853; drowned 25 July, 1862.
      4 *Frederick Edgar*, b. 11 Jan., and d. 14 Jan., 1864.
    vi Louisa M., b. 11 June, 1825; m. in Sterling, 18 May, 1848, Sanford D. Smith, b. 2 July, 1823; res. Sterling, Ill. Ch. (Smith):
      1 *Clarence E.*⁸, b. 25 April, 1852; m. Nellie B. Brigham; res. Chicago. Ch.: Lura L.⁹, b. 3 Oct., 1877.
      2 *Harry N.*, b. 9 Sept., 1859; m. 1883, Maggie Bartow; res. Chicago. Ch.: i Harry⁹, b. 9 Dec., 1886; ii May, b. 30 May, 1889.

Thomas Brigham Rice, of Barre, Mass.   (339)

339 NANCY[6], daughter of Henry[5] and Anna (Phillips) Brigham; born in Barre, Mass., 4 March, 1789; died there, 26 Sept., 1873; married, 16 April, 1809, Francis, son of Thomas and Sarah (Nurse) Rice. Sarah Nurse was a direct descendant of Rebecca Nurse, who was hung in Salem, as a witch.

Children (Rice), born in Barre:

i Abigail[7], b. 5 Dec., 1810; d. 4 Sept., 1889; m. 18 April, 1832, Marshall D. Eaton, who d. 14 Sept., 1885; they adopted *Jennie*[8], dau. of her sister Juliana.

ii Francis D., b. 3 Jan., 1814; d. in Barre, April, 1885; m. 19 Nov., 1839, Harriet A. Tucker. Ch.:
1 *George E.*[8], res. Worcester.
2 *Mary A.*, res. Chicago.
3 *Alice*, and 4 *Hobart*, both d. y.
5 *Sybil L.*, m. Herbert Rogers of Barre.
6 *Justin F.*, m. Minnie Rogers.

iii Eliza Ann, b. 18 Jan., and d. 21 Feb., 1816.

iv Thomas Brigham, b. 30 Jan., 1817; m. 29 Oct., 1844, Maria Bacon, b. in Barre, 6 June, 1821; d. 9 March, 1855; was 30 years cashier of the B. & A. R. R.; retired and returned to Barre, where settled with daughter. Has great interest in friendless and orphaned children, and has had several in his home. He has always been a firm friend of the B. F. A.; is living, 1907, a genial and most interesting man, and a rare friend. Ch.:
1 *Lucy*[8], b. 22 Oct., 1845; res. in Barre; a quiet, but practical, philanthropist.

v Juliana M., b. 15 Oct., 1819; m. 12 Dec., 1843, Daniel H. Rice, who d. 8 Sept., 1857. Ch.:
1 *Edward*[8], b. 3 Sept., 1846; m. Christina L. Stover, b. 23 Dec., 1847; res. s. p., New Haven.
2 *Eliza*, m. Joseph R. Torrey of Worcester; has dau. Anne[9].
3 *Annie M.*
4 *Jennie*, adopted by Mrs. Eaton.

vi Henry E., b. 17 Jan., 1823; m. 1848, Elizabeth F. Rawson; a des. of Secy. Edward Rawson. Ch.:
1 *Olive*[8], m. Henry H. Brigham, 798.
2 *Frank H.*, b. 23 Feb., 1854; m. Lizzie J. Davis, b. 1 Jan., 1864. Ch.: i Florence H.[9], b. 16 Dec., 1881; ii Leslie F., b. 12 Dec., 1885; iii Harold, b. 18 March, 1896; iv Clair, b. 15 Sept., 1898; v Gerald, b. 21 Dec., 1903; res. Oakland, Cal.
3 *Fannie*, m. Seymour A., son of 632.
4 *Daniel H.*, of Barre.
5 *Arthur L.*, b. 14 May, 1870; m. 29 June, 1893, Annie E. Cook; res. Willamette, Ill. Ch.: i Kingsley L.[9], b. 24 Aug., 1898; ii Elizabeth B., b. 23 Jan., 1905.

vii Calista E., b. 22 Oct., 1827; d. May, 1891; m. Elam Shattuck of Worcester, who d. s. p., March, 1885.

340 HENRY[6], son of Henry[5] and Anna (Phillips) Brigham; born in Barre, Mass., 14 Nov., 1791; died in Rutland, Mass., 7 April, 1863; married, 6 May, 1818, Sally, daughter of Dea. Job Sibley; born 1794; died in Rutland, 19 Feb., 1864. Was a farmer

in Rutland; Capt. of the Militia and two terms Representative to the General Court.

Children, born in Rutland:
635 i Lawson Sibley[7], b. 15 Oct., 1820.
636 ii Monroe Bowman, b. 8 Sept., 1822.
    iii Mary A., b. 12 June, 1829; res. Coldbrook Springs, Mass.; m. 10 Jan., 1849, Daniel M. Parker, b. in Wolcott, Vt.; d. in C. S., 25 March, 1899; was a selectman, and res. Coldbrook Springs. Ch. (Parker):
        1 *Clarence Henry*[8], b. 31 Oct., 1849; m. 1872, Ida M. Bemis; has been St. Rep., selectman and postmaster. Ch.: Harry B.[9], a selectman.
        2 *Evander Leroy*, b. 28 Aug., 1851; m. 1880, Georgiana M. Hawkins. Ch.: i Maud E.[9]; ii Minnie L.
        3 *Floyd R.*, b. 30 Aug., 1853; m. 1875, Lizzie Cleveland. Ch.: i Virgil R.[9]; ii Mary A.
        4 *Daniel M.*, b. 8 July, 1855; m. Eldora E. Hawkins. Ch.: i Millicent A.[9]; ii Nellie M.
        5 *Maida Adele*, b. 5 April, 1857; m. 1877, Frank E. Stevens; s. p.

341 MARIA THERESA[6], daughter of Henry[5] and Anna (Phillips) Brigham; born in Barre, Mass., 20 Sept., 1800; died in Templeton, Mass., 8 March, 1861; married, 1 May, 1828, George Newton, who died in Templeton, 12 Oct., 1879. He was a farmer and resided in Templeton.

Children (Newton), born in Templeton:
    i Henry Phillips[7], b. 14 Nov., 1829; d. 25 Oct., 1886; m. 1854, Lucinda Severy; res. Boston. Ch.:
        1 *Olive M.*[8]; 2 *George Henry;* 2 ch., d. y.
    ii Peter Augustine, b. 10 May, 1831; m. Elizabeth Castle; res. Chicago. Ch.:
        1 *Henrietta*[8]; 2 *Agnes;* 3 *Leslie;* 4 *Charlotte;* 5 *Peter.*
    iii Samuel Dexter, b. 9 Jan., 1833; d. 9 July, 1886; 4 years in Civil War; res. Chicago.
    iv Edward Franklin, b. 28 Feb., 1835; res. Concord, Ill.
    v Ann Maria, b. 24 March, 1839; m. a physician.
    vi George William, b. 29 March, 1841; d. 23 Jan., 1889, in Chicago; in 57th Mass. Inf., Civil War.

342 JOSIAH FAY[6], son of Uriah[5] and Elizabeth (Fay) Brigham; born in Bakersfield, Vt., 11 Oct., 1801; died there, 28 Aug., 1878; married (1), 1828, Sally Warner, daughter of Foster Paige; born in Bakersfield, 5 Aug., 1808; died there, 11 March, 1829; married (2), 1831, Sylvina, daughter of Perley Hall, born in Berkshire, Vt., 6 Jan., 1812; died in Bakersfield, 20 Nov., 1844; married (3), 1847, Jane, daughter of John Fay; born in St. Armand, P. Q., 1820; died 30 Jan., 1899.

At the early age of 18, Fay took charge of the family estate because of the death of his father; became a man of wide reading;

was a good neighbor, husband, and father. Although of positive opinions and candid in the expression of them, he was highly esteemed in the community and exerted a large influence on public affairs. Although a Democrat in a Whig or Republican State, he was thrice elected to the Legislature, 1857, '69, and '76; was also frequently chosen selectman. In 1855, he was given the degree of Honorary A. M., by the University of Vermont. He took a great interest in the magnificent bequest left to the town by his brother, Peter Bent, and one of his last public acts was to attend the meeting which was to decide concerning the use of the fund and to vote for the school as now established.

Child (by first wife), born in Bakersfield:
    i Seneca Paige[7], b. 18 Feb., 1829; d. 10 March, 1831.
Children (by second wife), born in Bakersfield:
    ii Sarah Jane, b. 16 April, 1835; m. 27 April, 1866, William, son of William B. Kendall; b. in Rockingham, Vt., 8 April, 1823; d. in Newtonville, Mass., 7 Oct., 1893. Ch. (Kendall), b. in Boston;
        1 *Sylvina B.*[8], b. 6 July, 1870; was grad. Emerson Coll. of Oratory; m. 1 Jan., 1896, Charles H. Watson of Philadelphia. Ch. (Watson): Brigham Kendall[9], b. 1896.
        2 *J. Fay Brigham*, b. 29 July, 1871; educated Mass. Inst. Technology and Boston Univ. Law School.
        3 *Peter Bent Brigham*, b. 9 March, 1873; d. 21 March, 1873.
637 iii Albert Gallatin, b. 12 March, 1836.
    iv Roxana, b. 3 July, 1838; m. 20 April, 1861, Prof. Charles Bird, son of Richmond Hankinson, b. in Gravesend, Ont., 24 Nov., 1831; d. in Woodstock, Ont., 6 June, 1867. She was Lady Principal and teacher of French in "Canada Literary Institute," Woodstock; he was grad. from Univ. of Mich.; Prof. of Mathematics and Nat. Sciences in "Canada Literary Inst."; she is a teacher in Medford, Mass. Ch. (Hankinson):
        1 *Jennie B.*[8], b. 25 Dec.; d. 25 Feb., 1879.
        2 *Hattie B.*, b. in Woodstock, 17 Jan., 1865; res. Medford.
Children (by third wife), born in Bakersfield:
    v Frances Gertrude, b. 31 May, 1848; m. Robert Breck Brigham, 539; res. New York City.
    vi Col. Herbert Fay, b. 13 July, 1852; m. 17 Sept., 1894, Jennie M. C. Hill, a painter in oils; b. in W. Farnham, P. Q., 27 April, 1853; he attended the Univ. of Mich. Law School in 1874 and '75; admitted to the Franklin Co., Vt., bar; member of the Legislature of Vt., 1882 and '84; practices law in Bakersfield, where he res.
    vii Mary Fay, b. 24 June, 1856; m. 21 Feb., 1900, Arthur L. Weeks of St. Albans, Vt.
    viii Hattie F., b. 18 June, 1858; d. 6 Feb., 1864.

343   *PETER BENT[6], son of Uriah[5] and Elizabeth (Fay) Brigham; born in Bakersfield, Vt., 4 Feb., 1807, died, unmarried, Boston, Mass., 24 May, 1877.

* John Bent [1] (1596-1672), son of Robert Bent (1566-1631) came from Penton Grafton, Parish of Weygill, County of Hants, Eng., sailing from Southampton in

His father died leaving a widow and several small children dependent upon themselves for a livelihood. He came to Boston as a boy, making the first part of his journey on horseback, with saddlebags containing his food and scant apparel. His horse becoming useless, he made his way on foot and by working on a Middlesex canal boat. Starting in the fish and oyster business, selling at first from a wheelbarrow, he finally acquired a lease of Concert Hall, a well-known restaurant, corner of Court and Hanover Streets, which he conducted until about 1869, when the widening of Hanover Street required a portion of his building, and he retired from the restaurant business. His business always prospered, but his largest success was made in real estate, in which he invested shrewdly in his immediate vicinity. His judgment in matters of real estate, street widening, and general municipal improvement was often sought by the city officials. He was one of the early directors of the Fitchburg railroad and continued in office until his death. He never sought public office. He was a man of fine personal appearance, honest and straightforward in his dealings, and his habits and life were regular. Careful as to food, and a total abstainer from liquors and tobacco, his health was of the best. In manner he was cordial and of heart kindly. His innate sympathy was especially illustrated in his anti-slavery sentiments and the gentle kindness which he ever showed to the negro. Among his papers after his death were found two cancelled wills, dated before 1862, by which he gave the bulk of his estate for the emancipation of the slaves. He often lamented his want of a liberal education, and his will made generous provision for the improvement of the educational system of his native town, where Brigham Academy is named for him.* He died in his residence, still standing, on the northeast corner of Bulfinch and Allston Streets. He is buried in Magnolia Avenue, Mt. Auburn. The bulk of his estate, aggregating about $1,300,000, was given to found the Peter Bent Brigham Hospital. (See Appendix.)

the *Confidence*, of London, John Hobson master, in April, 1638. He became one of the founders of the town of Sudbury. He brought with him his wife, Martha, and five children. One son, Peter [2] (1629-1678) married Elizabeth ———, of Cambridge, about 1651, settled in Marlboro, for which town he was one of the petitioners, and died in England in May, 1678. His real estate at his death was valued at £431. His house was garrisoned, burned by the Indians and one of his sons was scalped during King Philip's War. His son Peter [3] married Abigail Barnes. Their son Peter [4] of Marlboro (1707-1798) served in the General Court and the first three Provincial Congresses. Peter Bent Brigham's mother was Elizabeth Fay, whose mother was Mary (Bent) Fay, wife of Josiah Fay of Southboro and daughter of Peter Bent [4] and sister of Abigail (Bent) Brigham, wife of Benajah Brigham. Robert Breck Brigham, nephew of Peter Bent Brigham, was fifth in descent from " the distinguished Peter Bent [4]."

* Mr. Brigham bequeathed $40,000 to his native town; $10,000 to be devoted forever to maintaining and beautifying the village cemetery, and $30,000 for educational purposes. The town voted " to use the income of the Brigham School

Peter Bent Brigham

344 BENJAMIN GOTT[6], son of Uriah[5], and Elizabeth (Fay) Brigham; born in Bakersfield, Vt., 10 June, 1808; died in Fairfax, Vt., 16 March, 1858; married in Fairfield, Vt., 25 Feb., 1835, Esther Potter, daughter of Thomas Northup, born in Fairfield, 17 June, 1809; died 25 Oct., 1879

He was many years treasurer and selectman of Fairfield, and represented the town in the Legislature. At the time of his death he was on the eve of receiving the appointment of U. S. Collector for the District of Vermont. He was a talented man with excellent powers as a debater. In his day he was one of the largest farmers in New England.

Children, the eldest born in Jericho, Vt., the others in Fairfield:
i Clarissa N.[7], b. 1 Feb., 1836; d. in Philadelphia; m. 4 May, 1859, Julian H. Dewey of Fairfax, Vt. Ch. (Dewey):
  1 *Gott*[8], who d.
  2 *Julian H.*, a physician in Philadelphia.
  3 *Archibald R.*, a lawyer in Philadelphia.
ii Uriah, b. 22 June, 1839; d. in Fairfield, 29 May, 1842.
iii Elizabeth F., b. 8 April, 1843; m. Ira Clark of Brandon, Vt., where she d. s. p.
iv Benjamin Gott, b. 17 April, 1847; d. 1 May, 1847.
v Henry Randolph, b. 31 July, 1848; d. in Boston, 24 Feb., 1884; m. 8 June, 1875, Ida E., dau. of Willard and Mandana (Gifford) Wight of Barnard, Vt.; b. there, 22 April, 1852. Mr. Brigham was admitted to the bar in Boston at the age of 21, and when he d. he was a member there of the firm of Proctor & Brigham, and had a large practice, especially in the Court of Insolvency. He was president of the Mercantile Co-operative Bank and associate justice of the District Court in Jamaica Plain, Mass., where he resided. He was an habitual student, had fertility of resources, and his knowledge of law and men, his nerve and firm will, made him equal to any emergency in his business, where he was respected for his integrity, conscientiousness and wisdom. In private life he maintained, in his home and in his friendships, the highest ideals, which were founded upon a deep religious faith. Ch., b. in Jamaica Plain: ,
  1 *Pauline Wight*[8], b. 4 Feb., 1877; drowned, accidentally, in Squam Lake, N. H., 6 Sept., 1905. She was grad, with high honors from Radcliffe Coll., Cambridge, 1898; she traveled and studied abroad for more than a year; a " flower-like " girl, with a brilliant mind and sincere character, her young life was full of promise of large achievement, because of her broad sympathies and indefatigable industry.

Fund for the maintenance of a high school to be called Brigham Academy." Mrs. Sarah B. Jacobs of Boston, sister of Peter Bent Brigham, Mrs. Roxana B. Hankinson of Bakersfield, and Mrs. S. Jane Kendall of Boston bought a large tract of land in the centre of the village, built and equipped a commodious brick structure and presented it to the town. Mrs. Jonathan Northrop of Sheldon, Vt., subsequently gave a public clock and bell. A bust of Mr. Brigham, by Millmore, stands in the building. Mrs. Jacobs died in 1891, leaving $100,000 to the Academy. The school was opened 26 Aug., 1879, and is one of the best in Vermont.

2 *Henry Randolph*, b. 6 April, 1880; grad. from Harvard Coll., 1901; after a year of travel abroad, he entered the Harvard Law School and grad. 1905; admitted to the bar in 1905, and practices law in Boston; res. unm., in Cambridge.

345 NANCY[6], daughter of Edward[5] and Beulah (Hawes) Brigham; born in Petersham, Mass., 10 May, 1796; died in Lancaster, Mass., 29 May, 1883; married, 10 Nov., 1819, Hon. Francis B., son of Francis Fay; born in Southboro, Mass., 12 June, 1793; died in Chelsea, Mass., 6 Oct., 1876. Mr. Fay removed from Southboro to Boston and thence to Chelsea about 1809, and became the first mayor of Chelsea when it was incorporated as a city.

Children (Fay):
  i Hon. Franklin Brigham[7], b. in Southboro, 24 Jan., 1821; d. in Chelsea, 20 March, 1904; m. (1) Rebecca, dau. of Judge William Bridges; m. (2) Mrs. Lucy P. Atwood. Mr. Fay was in the Legislature as Representative in 1857, and Senator in 1867. Became Mayor of Chelsea in 1861, and served also in '62 and '63· During the war, he spent nearly all the time at the front aiding sick and wounded soldiers, and was known as the " war mayor "; was a delegate to the Convention which renominated Lincoln, and a Mass. elector in 1868. In 1880 was appointed general agent and secretary for the S. P. C. C., having previously been connected with the S. P. C. A. It would be impossible in a few words to state the invaluable service that he gave to the work of this society, but it will not be forgotten for a long time to come. His public services were numerous and varied, and he always gave of his best whenever called upon. Ch.:
    1 *Harry F.*[8], res. Brookline.
    2 *Sibyl*, m. James W. Clark; res. N. Y. City.
  ii Norman Warren, b. 23 Feb., 1825; d. 23 April, 1826.
  iii Henry Gregg, b. 25 April, 1831; m. Clara Pearce; res. Chestnut Hill, Boston. Ch.:
    1 *Alice*[8]; 2 *George F.*, of Seattle, Wash.
  iv Eugene Francis, b. 10 March, 1840; m. Elizabeth Robbins of Walpole, Mass.; res. s. p., Boston.

346 ARTEMAS[6], son of Edward[5] and Beulah (Hawes) Brigham; born in Petersham, Mass., 22 Oct., 1799; died there, 22 June, 1894; married (1), 20 Dec., 1827, Sophronia, daughter of David Witt; born Hubbardston, Mass, 11 April, 1809; died in Petersham, 14 Jan., 1862; married (2), 10 June, 1863, Mrs. Mary A. Hammond, who died 27 April, 1881, æ. 76. Was a farmer and lived to a great age.

Children, born in Petersham:
  i *Norman C.*[7], b. 16 May, 1829; d. in Barre, 28 July, 1899; m. 31 March, 1852, Caroline Osgood, b. in Barre, 18 April, 1832. Ch., b. in Barre:
    1 *Fred A.*[8], b. 9 Jan., 1857; res. Spencer, Mass., where d. 16 May, 1897; m. 18 Jan., 1883, Minnie E., dau. of Hanson White; b. in Barre, 7 Jan., 1861. Ch.: i Edward H.[9], b. 15 May,

HENRY R. BRIGHAM, OF BOSTON (344)

1885; ii Daisy G., b. 4 Dec., 1886; d. y.; iii Carrie, b. 26 March, 1889.

2 *Nellie S.*, b. 7 April, 1862; m. 6 Oct., 1885, Frank Nye of Barre. Ch. (Nye): i Rosella C.⁹, b. 25 Sept., 1887; ii Minnie, b. 1891; d. 1891; iii Frank, b. 10 Jan., 1893; iv Frederic O., b. 17 Oct., 1897.

u Jane Sophronia, b. 17 Sept., 1835; d. in Barre, 26 March, 1867; m. 8 Feb., 1860, Henry M. Bassett, b. in Barre, 19 April, 1836. Ch. (Bassett), b. in Barre:

1. *Walter Artemas*⁸, b. 6 Aug., 1861; m. 20 March, 1884, Mary C. Peck, b. 12 May, 1863; res. on his grandfather Brigham's farm in Petersham. Ch.: i Henry E.⁹, b. 12 March, 1885; d. y.; ii Leslie Walter, b. 21 April, 1886; iii Ina Loretta, b. 5 Aug., 1888; d. y.

2 *Stella M.*, b. 30 April, and d. 4 Aug., 1863.

347   SARAH BRECK⁶, daughter of Edward⁵ and Beulah (Hawes) Brigham; born in Petersham, Mass., 22 May, 1808; died in Plymouth, N. H., 9 Nov., 1898; married, 20 May, 1833, Phillander, son of Stephen and Hannah (Briggs) Wood of Plymouth; born in Petersham, 11 April, 1809; died in Plymouth, 15 Sept., 1891.

Children (Wood), the 2 eldest born in Barre, Mass., the 4 youngest in Middlebury, Vt.:

i Stephen⁷, b. 8 Aug., 1834; d. 5 Sept., 1837.

ii Leander, b. 21 Dec., 1835; d. 16 May, 1870; m. 11 Feb., 1864, Cordelia Ryder, who d. 28 Feb., 1868; res. N. Y. Ch.:
  1 *Frank Fay*⁸, b. 29 July, 1866; d. 30 July, 1885.
  2 *Henry Hunt*, b. 29 Dec., 1867; d. 5 Feb., 1892.

iii Sarah D., b. in Salisbury, Vt., 27 May, 1837; d. 7 Dec., 1837.

iv Josephine A., b. in Salisbury, 6 Jan., 1839; res. unm., Laconia, N. H.; d. May, 1906.

v Edward D., b. 20 Sept., 1842; m. Mary P. Ostrom, b. 9 Oct., 1842; d. 30 Jan., 1894; res. Boston. Ch.:
  1 *Helen A.*⁸, b. 5 June, 1867; m. 24 June, 1904, Henry E. Urann.
  2 *Herbert B.*, b. 13 April, 1870; d. 5 Sept., 1882.

vi Perlin K., b. 16 May, 1844; m. 5 April, 1871, Julia A. Roberts of Charlestown, Mass., b. 21 July, 1849. Ch.:
  1 *Julia L.*⁸, b. 2 July, 1872; m. 18 June, 1892, Harry Fifield.
  2 *Sarah B.*, b. Sept., 1874; m. 18 June, 1900, Ernest C. Cheswell.
  3 *Alice M.*, b. 19 Aug., 1876; m. William Pelisser, 27 Nov., 1902.
  4 *Roxana D.*, b. 24 Feb., 1880; m. 31 Dec., 1900, Ralph E. Garvin.
  5 *George F.*, b. 7 July, 1882; unm.
  6 *Irving*, b. 9 Aug., 1885; unm.
  7 *Beulah H.*, b. 20 Dec., 1887; unm.
  All res. in Malden, Mass.

vii Maleska O., b. 28 Nov., 1846; res. Laconia.

viii Sarell H., b. 4 Nov., 1849; m. 26 Nov., 1874, John W. Clark, b. 13 Sept., 1848; res. Laconia. Ch. (Clark):
  1 *Josie A.*⁸, b. 25 Nov., 1875; unm.

348 EDWARD⁶, son of Edward⁵ and Beulah (Hawes) Brigham; born in Petersham, Mass., 1 Jan., 1814; died in Boston, 19 June, 1891; married, 28 March, 1839, Frances Tyler; born in Boston, 28 Oct., 1822; died 24 Jan., 1903. He was Supt. of the East Boston Ferries for 50 years, and resided in East Boston.

Children, born in E. Boston:

  i Edward Francis⁷, b. 27 July, 1839; m. 2 Nov., 1864, Josephine Crocker. Ch.:
    1 *Florence Tyler⁸*, b. 25 Aug., 1868; m. Charles P. Fernald.
    2 *Edna Josephine*, b. 4 March, 1884.
  ii Martin Tyler, b. 20 Oct., 1841; d. y.
  iii Frances Belinda, b. 20 Feb., 1843; d. 2 Aug., 1865.
  iv Martin, b. 20 Aug., 1845; d. 1848.
  v Harriet Amanda, b. 9 Sept., 1847; d. 1848.
  vi Tyler, b. 13 Dec., 1848; m. 1 June, 1882, Harriet A. Titcomb Fearing of Newburyport, Mass.; res. in Brookline, dealer in Ladies' Cloaks, in Boston.
  vii Elmina S. R., b. 9 March, 1852; m. 25 Dec., 1874, Corliss Wadleigh of Medford, Mass. Ch. (Wadleigh):
    1 *Mina Beulah⁸*, b. 19 March, 1875; m. 25 July, 1899, Wm. H. Brooks. Ch. (Brooks): Gertrude Wadleigh⁹, b. and d. 23 May, 1900.
    2 *Corliss*, b. 19 Aug., 1880.
  viii Charles Henry, b. 26 June, 1854; m. 3 Oct., 1878, Alice D. Poole; res. Wollaston, Mass.; manufacturer of ladies' waists in Boston. Ch.:
    1 *Edward T.⁸*, b. and d. 26 Jan., 1880.
    2 *Edward Tyler*, b. 29 Dec., 1880; a note salesman in Boston; res. Wollaston.
    3 *Clarence*, b. 31 Aug., 1883; d. 7 Dec., 1885.
  ix Harriet Nellie, b. 28 Nov., 1859; m. 3 Aug., 1883, Walter S. McLauthlin of Webster St., E. Boston. Ch. (McLauthlin):
    1 *Mina Brigham⁸*, b. and d. 1885.

349 TIMOTHY⁶, son of Phineas⁵ and Susanna (Howe) Brigham; born in Southboro, Mass., 8 Feb., 1786; died in Granville, Pa., 24 Aug., 1829; married (1) Patty Damon; married (2), 12 Oct., 1820, Abigail Mason, who died in Smithfield, Pa., 7 June, 1857. He was a farmer.

Children (by first wife):

638 i Ebenezer Damon⁷, b. in Granville, 15 Feb., 1808.
639 ii George, b. in Smithfield, 16 Oct., 1809.
    iii Mary Ann, m. Andrew Swain, and had several children.
640 iv Phineas, b. in Smithfield, 22 Jan., 1815.
    v Timothy.
    vi Joseph, m. ————. Ch.:
      1 *Julia⁸*, m. Charles Beach; d. s. p.
      2 *Clayton*, m. ————; had one son who res. N. Y. State.

Children (by second wife), born in Granville:

    vii Harriet, b. 4 Aug., 1821; d. in Burlington, Pa., April, 1859; m. Charles Taylor.
    viii Addison M., b. 24 Feb., 1823; d. in Leroy, Pa., Sept, 1883; m. Jane Carr; a farmer.

641 ix Henry C., b. 24 March, 1825.
      x Charles B., b. 6 Dec., 1826; d. in Smithfield, May, 1884; m.
        Lucilia Beach; he was a farmer.
642 xi Horace A., b. 29 May, 1828.

350 PHINEAS⁶, son of Phineas⁵ and Susanna (Howe) Brigham; born in Marlboro, Mass., 31 Dec., 1787; died in Madison, N. Y., 17 Sept., 1852; married 18 Feb., 1809, Susan Ames, born in Buckland, Mass., 11 March, 1792; died in Hamilton, N. Y., 4 April, 1876. He removed in 1810 to ,Eaton, N. Y., and also resided in Morrisville and Madison, N. Y.

Children, the eldest born in Southboro, the next 5 in Eaton, and the youngest in Madison:
643   i Lucy⁷, b. 18 Nov., 1810.
644   ii Lucius, b. 25 July, 1812.
      iii Mary, b. 12 Aug., 1814; d. 4 April, 1830.
645   iv Horace Ames, b. 14 Oct., 1817.
       v Emily, b. 16 Nov., 1819; m. Leonard Homes (see 643).
      vi George Howe (Rev.), b. 13 Aug., 1823; m. 1853, Eliza A. Perry;
         grad. from Hamilton Coll.; from Theological Seminary in 1853;
         was a clergyman in Central New York for 17 years; 23 years
         Dist. Secy. of the American Baptist Missionary Union; res. s. p.,
         Cortland, N. Y.
646 vii Edwin Pierson (Rev.), b. 11 Aug., 1828.

351 SOPHIA⁶, daughter of Phineas⁵ and Susanna (Howe) Brigham; born in Southboro, Mass., 5. May, 1792; died ————— ·
married Elijah Williams of Cazenovia, ,N. Y.

Child (Williams), born in Cazenovia:
     i (Rev.) Dwight⁷, b. 28 April, 1826; d. 13 June, 1898; m. 1855,
        Keziah E. Lane of New Hartford, N. Y.; licensed to preach, 1850,
        by the M. E. Church; held several charges on Litchfield Circuit,
        and others; his health was frail and he had to take vacations; an
        abolitionist and prohibitionist, he was N. Y. State Secy. for the
        party candidate in 1873; was Asst. Editor of the *Northern
        Christian Advocate,* and edited *The Watchword;* published 2
        volumes of verse, *The Beautiful City,* in 1876, and *Mother of
        the Wonderful,* in 1887; he was an idealist, and a writer of
        numerous booklets, hymns, songs, etc. He was interested in
        the B. F. A., and wrote and sent copies of poem " Brigham " for
        the Worcester Reunion, of which the following is the first stanza:.

> " Hail, sons of Brigham! Loyal stock!
>   A chapter in our story,
> Whose genesis is Plymouth Rock,
>   Its chivalry and glory;
> Hail, daughters of a sturdy band,
>   Who faced the sunset beauty,
> To build their altars long to stand,
>   Dear shrines of love and duty."

Ch. (Williams):
    1 *Susan B.*⁸; 2 *Prof. Dwight, Jr.,* of Cazenovia; 3 *Dau.* (Mrs.
    Vernon Bartow); 4 *Child,* d. y.

352   GEORGE HOWE[6], son of Phineas[5] and Susanna (Howe) Brigham; born in Southboro, Mass., 14 Dec., 1799; died in Chicago, 1882; married Sally Maria, daughter of Deacon Evarts of Auburn, N. Y.; born, 24 March, 1804; died 1880.   Resided in Auburn.

Children:
   i Caroline Matilda[7], b. 9 March, 1822; d. June, 1826.
   ii Charles Philip, b. 5 July, 1823; m. 3 Sept., 1850, Loraina Burdick, b. 29 Sept., 1827; d. 1899.   Ch.:
     1 *Alice*[8], b. 27 Dec., 1851.
     2 *Mary*, b. 17 June, 1855.
     3 *Clara*, b. 28 March, 1862; d. May, 1886.
   iii Mary Jane, b. 2 Jan., 1825; d. July, 1826.
   iv Mary Matilda, b. 9 Aug., 1826; living in 1905.
   v Caroline Matilda, b. 28 Dec., 1828; d. 4 July, 1829.
   vi George Fitch, b. 5 Oct., 1830; m. Maria Jones; res. 15 Lincoln Ave., Freeport, Ill.   Ch.:
     1 *William H.*[8], b. 24 Aug., 1857.
   vii James Rollins, b. 12 Oct., 1832; m. 31 Dec., 1861, Maria Parks, b. 17 April, 1844.   Ch.:
     1 *George H.*[8], b. 6 March, 1866; d. 21 Aug., 1893.
     2 *James R., Jr.*, b. 28 Nov., 1869.
     3 *Frederick W.*, b. 10 June, 1878.
   viii William Oscar, b. 17 Dec., 1833; m. 27 Nov., 1856, Ann Eliza, dau. of Seymour and Dorcas (Higgins) Scoville; b. 15 April, 1836; res. Toledo, O.   Ch.:
     1 *Frank Seymour*[8], b. 5 June, 1858.
     2 *William Oscar, Jr.*, b. in Auburn, N. Y., 14 June, 1864; m. 21 Oct., 1896, Ida May Herman, b. in Laselle, Mich., 4 Dec., 1867; res. Toledo.   Ch.: i Herman Corless[9], b. 25 Nov., 1897; ii Verne Elsworth, b. 22 Sept., 1902.
     3 *Alice Eliza*, b. 9 Feb., 1870.
   ix Dudley E., b. 12 Oct., 1838; d. 21 Nov., 1841.

353   SALMON[6], son of Phineas[5] and Susanna (Howe) Brigham; born in Eaton, N. Y., 15 July, 1805; died in Madison, N. Y., 24 Jan., 1890; married, 24 March, 1831, Mary Ann, daughter of Oliver Sumner; born in Eaton, 13 April, 1812; died in Madison, 29 June, 1887.   He lived in Eaton and Madison.

Children, the 6 elder born in Eaton, others in Madison:
   i Oliver Sumner[7], b. 16 Feb., 1832; d. in Madison, 24 June, 1866; m. 9 Sept., 1862, Virginia, dau. of Daniel Livermore; b. 15 Sept., 1839; d. 13 Feb., 1874.   Ch.:
     1 *Harry Blossom*[8], b. in Madison, 20 Dec., 1864; d. 19 March, 1869.
   ii Susan Howe, b. 3 March, 1834; d. 5 Aug., 1896; m. 25 June, 1855, Henry Martin Blossom of St. Louis, Mo.   Ch. (Blossom), b. in St. Louis:
     1 *Edmund Dwight*[8], b. 7 July, 1856.
     2 *Russell Nelson*, b. 22 June, 1859; d. 1 Feb., 1897.
     3 *May*, b. 28 Sept., 1861; m. 3 Nov., 1886, Thomas Chandler Kimber.
     4 *Susan Sumner*, b. 25 July, 1864.
     5 *Henry M., Jr.*, b. 10 May, 1866.

647 iii Orlando L., b. 19 Dec., 1835.
iv Dwight W., b. 10 June, 1838; d. 28 July, 1851.
v Caroline M., b. 30 Jan., 1840; d. 28 Jan., 1851.
vi Mary Wattles, b. 29 May, 1842; m. 20 Sept., 1865, Sanford Gillette Scarritt of St. Louis. Ch. (Scarritt):
    1 *Charlotte Mary*[8], b. 27 Oct., 1866; -m. 14 Nov., 1894, Charles Marie de Bremond. Ch. (De Bremond): i Mary Louise[9], b. 14 Dec., 1897; ii Edith Antoine, b. 21 March, 1900.
    2 *Edith Agnes*, b. 5 June, 1870; m. 22 Jan., 1895, Edmund Arthur Manny. Ch. (Manny): i Edmund Scarritt[9], b. 18 Sept., 1897; ii Mary Sanford, b. 29 March, 1904.
    3 *Daisy*, b. 9 April, 1872; d. 9 May, 1876.
vii Harriet Sophia, b. 21 July, 1844; m. 25 July, 1872, Marcus Dixon Dodd of St. Louis. Ch. (Dodd):
    1 *Agnes*[8], b. 8 May, 1873; m. 8 May, 1900, Thomas T. Richards. Ch. (Richards): Eleanor[9], b. 12 July, 1902.
    2 *Florence*, b. 2 Oct., 1874.
    3 *Grace*, b. 5 April, 1877.
    4 *Helen*, b. 16 Oct., 1878.
    5 *Ruth*, b. 3 Aug., 1880.
    6 *Samuel M.*, b. 28 Aug., 1882.
    7 *Marcus D.*, b. 28 Jan., 1888.
    8 *Randall*, b. 27 Dec., 1889.
viii Ellen Elizabeth, b. 9 May, 1846; m. 30 Sept., 1865, Daniel Livermore of Sangerfield, N. Y. Ch. (Livermore):
    1 *Katherine Ella*[8], b. 26 Sept., 1866.
    2 *Daniel Howard*, b. 28 Sept., 1868; m. Helen Hale. Ch.: Howard Jerome[9], b. 28 April, 1893.
    3 *Mary Virginia*, b. 16 Oct., 1873; m. Herbert Ray Burgess. Ch. (Burgess): i Daniel L.[9], b. 19 June, 1896; ii Jane, b. 13 Oct., 1898; iii Herbert R., b. 12 Aug., 1900; iv Katherine, b. 21 July, 1901.
    4 *Harry Brigham*, b. 19 Sept., 1875.
    5 *Agnes Sumner*, b. 15 March, 1879; m. Murray Moore Storke. Ch. (Storke): Elliot Gray[9], b. 7 Sept., 1900.
ix Arthur L., b. 2 Nov., 1849; m. 15 Jan., 1872; Minnie E., dau. of David Z. Brockett; b. 20 April, 1854; res. Madison. Ch.:
    1 *Hattie E.*[8], b. 20 March, 1873.
    2 *Faith Crosby*, b. 9 July, 1882.
x Agnes L., b. 2 Nov., 1849; m. 15 Dec., 1881, Jay W. Coolidge of Denver, Colo.
xi Delivan Dwight, b. 5 May, 1852; d. 23 March, 1857.

354 ASHBEL[6], son of Ashbel Samuel[5] and Persis (Brigham) Brigham; born in Marlboro, Mass., 1 July, 1800; died there 10 Oct., 1861; married Lydia H., daughter of Oliver Russell, born 23 Dec., 1795; died 1 April, 1888, in, or near Worcester, Mass.
Children, born in Marlboro:
    i Maria Elizabeth[7], b. 17 Oct., 1821; m. Aug., 1847, Edward Forbes Barnes, M. D., grandson of 170; b. 1809; d. 1878; was grad. Harvard Coll., 1838; res. Marlboro. Ch. (Barnes), b. in Marlboro:
        1 *Elizabeth Forbes*[8], b. 1848; d. 1869.
        (Josephine A., whom they adopted, was b. 1870; m. ————, and d. 1904.

ii Olive C., b. 29 Nov., 1823; m. 3 May, 1846, Charles L. Fay, son
of 408; b. in Marlboro, 29 Sept., 1822; d. 26 March, 1897, in
Marlboro. Ch. (Fay), b. in Marlboro:
   1 *Henrietta Adrian*[8], b. 5 April, 1847; m. Herbert Hudson. Ch.
   (Hudson): Lewis[9].
   2 *Mary Frances*, b. 23 July, 1852; m. Samuel P. Cannell of
   Everett, Mass.
   3 *Charlotte Sophia*, b. 23 June, and d. 2 Oct., 1854.
iii Nahum B., b. 21 Oct., 1825.
iv Mary J., b. 31 Dec., 1827; m. in Lancaster, 26 Sept., 1849, Charles
B. Russell of Marlboro.
v Ann Janette, b. 7 April, 1830; m. 1850, George W. Loud of
Randolph, Mass., b. 1828; d. 1875.
vi George Winslow, b. 9 Nov., 1832; d. in Boston, 5 Aug., 1898; m.
28 Dec., 1857, Joanna H. Claflin of Holliston, Mass.; res. Worcester. Ch.:
   1 *William F.*[8], b. 1 Dec., 1858; d. 15 March, 1878.
   2 *John C.*, b. 6 Aug., 1860 ; d. 9 Oct., 1861.
vii Charles L., b. 9 Nov., 1838; m. Martha Washington, probably
dau. of Jonathan Brigham, grandson of 83.

355   VARNUM[6], son of Ashbel Samuel[5] and Persis (Brigham)
Brigham; born in Marlboro, Mass., ,8 July, 1802; died in Westboro, 25 July, 1848; married June, 1824, Mary D., daughter of
John Bigelow of Charlton, Mass.; born there, 4 April, 1807; died
in Chicopee, Mass., 6 March, 1873. Resided in Worcester, where
he was the first merchant tailor.

Children:
   i Persis P.[7], b. 1 Aug., 1825; d. 4 Jan., 1851.
   ii Mary J., b. 14 June, 1827; d. 25 Sept., 1857.
   iii Calvin L., b. 8 Sept., 1828; d. 15 Oct., 1850.
   iv Sarah J., b. 23 Sept., 1830; d. s. p., 23 Jan., 1856; m. William
   Eager.
   v Varnum B., b. 21 Feb., 1833; m. Cate Harris. Ch.:
      1 *Varnum Charles*[8], res. Worcester.
   vi Emery P., b. 18 Jan., 1835; d. Jan., 1835.
   vii Mary L., b. 18 May, 1836; d. in Providence, R. I., s. p., 1872;
   m. (1) John H. Robinson, who d.; m. (2) James Chaffee. Ch.
   (Robinson):
      1 *Willie H.*[8], d. y.
   viii Frances Felicia, b. in Worcester, 3 Sept., 1838; d. 24 May, 1900;
   m. Nathaniel Fenner Hopkins, b. 4 Feb., 1838; res. Salem, Mass.
   Ch. (Hopkins):
      1 *Clarence B.*[8], b. 4 July, 1862; d. 5 July, 1865.
      2 *Martha Amelia*, b. 18 Feb., 1865; m. Charles H. Kaler. Ch.
      (Kaler): i Carrie F.[9]; ii Herbert H.
      3 *Maude Frances*, b. 30 March, 1867.
      4 *Florence Evelyn*, b. 1 Oct., 1868; res. Salem, Mass.
      5 *Stella*, b. 17 June, 1870.
   ix Martha A., b. 25 July, 1840; d. s. p., 1864; m. George Shattuck.
   x John A., b. 18 Sept., 1843; d. 2 Aug., 1854.

xi Abby H., b. 31 Dec., 1845; m. 1865, Horace M. Emerson, who d. 1881. Ch. (Emerson):
  1 *Mary D.*, b. 1866; m. Walter E. Dyer. Ch. (Dyer): i Abby*; ii Jennie.
  2 *Oliver M.*, b. 1869.

356 CHARLES[6], son of Ashbel Samuel[5] and Persis (Brigham) Brigham; born in Marlboro, Mass., 26 Sept., 1806; married Mary Jane Day; born 23 Feb., 1810. Probably resided in Philadelphia.
Children:
  i Harriet J.[7], b. 2 July, 1830.
  ii Eleanora, b. 2 Dec., 1831.
  iii Charles E., b. 12 Oct., 1833.
  iv George F., b. 28 Feb., 1835.
  v Mary E., b. 3 March, 1837; res. Philadelphia.
  vi Joseph D., b. 27 Jan., 1838.
  vii John D., b. 15 Sept., 1840.
  viii Ashbel S., b. 18 Sept., 1842.
  ix Thomas T., b. 3 March, 1847.
  x William L., b. 15 Jan., 1849.

357 MARY[6], daughter of Ashbel Samuel[5] and Persis (Brigham) Brigham; born in Marlboro, Mass., 21 March, 1815; died in Providence, R. I., 30 April, 1879; married, 7 May, 1834, Jonathan Jenks, born in Brookfield, Mass., 8 Jan., 1811; died in Providence, 8 Oct., 1885. He was a direct descendant of Roger Williams in the 7th generation; the emigrant Jenks was an inventor, and had the first patent in this country; he made the dies for coining the " Pine Tree " shilling, and built the first fire engine in America; came from Hammersmith, Eng.

They moved to Providence in 1839, where he was a merchant. She was a woman of sterling character, whose influence will be felt for many generations.
Children (Jenks):
  i Charles Brigham[7], b. in Springfield, Mass., 27 Jan., 1836; d. 19 April, 1903, in Providence, where a merchant; m. 9 Dec., 1863, Amelia Peabody of Newport, R. I., b. 25 Dec., 1843, b. in P.:
    1 *Arthur Peabody*[8], b. 14 Dec., 1865; d. 24 Nov., 1869.
    2 *Richard Peabody*, b. 28 May, 1870.
    3 *Vincent Wait*, b. 22 Oct., 1872; d. 4 Aug., 1873.
  ii Adelaide Persis, b. 20 Nov., 1839; m. 14 Dec., 1864, Edward A. Peabodie, wool merchant of Providence; b. 29 Sept., 1825; d. 26 Dec., 1892. Ch. (Peabodie):
    1 *Mary Blanche*[8], b. 19 Sept., 1866; d. 24 Sept., 1866.
  iii William Samuel, b. 23 Jan., 1842; m. 14 June, 1865, Martha I. Kingsley; b. Aug., 1840. Ch.:
    1 *Harry Kingsley*[8]; 2 *Frederick Augustus.*
  iv Abby Mallard, b. 25 June, 1844; m. 29 March, 1865, Eliphalet I. Armington, b. in Seekonk, Mass., 30 June, 1841; was in the Civil War nine months; res. Dorchester. Ch. (Armington):

1 *Edith Blanche*[8], b. 18 Dec., 1866; d. in P., R. I., 21 Aug.,
1903; m. 18 Apr., 1887, Ralph F. Ketchum, b. in St. John,
N. B., 12 April, 1866. Ch. (Ketchum): Eleanor Armington[9],
b. 5 March, 1888.
2 *Betsey Brigham*, b. in Everett, Mass., 15 April, 1877; m. 25
June, 1903, Herman K. Higgins.
v Caroline Harrington, b. 19 Nov., 1846; d. 1 Aug., 1900; m. 3
Nov., 1886, Rich. W. Pinney, b. in Springfield, Mass., Dec., 1846;
res. there.

358   ARTEMAS[6] son of Lovewell[5] and Betty (Rice) Brigham;
born in Marlboro, 27 April, 1796; died 25 Jan., 1839; married Mary
Ann, daughter of Aaron Arnold, who died 5 Sept., 1838, æ. 31.

Children, born in Marlboro:
   i William H.[7], b. 18 Aug., 1831; probably had ch.:
      1 *Alfred*[8], who m. Elizabeth Barnes, granddaughter of 395.
   ii Lydia A., b. 28 Dec., 1833; d. 1 Oct., 1834.
648 iii John Baker, b. 11 Aug., 1835.
   iv Mary S., b. 25 Feb., 1837; m. D. O. Frost of Saxonville, Mass.

359   CAPT. FRANCIS[6], son of Ivory[5] and Sally (Wilkins)
Brigham; born in Marlboro, Mass., 12 April, 1813; died in Hudson,
Mass., 7 Dec., 1880; married (1), 5 Jan., 1835, Sophia, daughter
of Francis Gleason; born 18 April, 1814; died 31 Aug., 1845; married (2) Emily N. Houghton, who died 6 Dec., 1855; married (3)
24 May, 1856, Persis E. Watkins, born 20 May, 1818; died 22
June, 1886.

He resided in Feltonville, now Hudson, where he founded the
firm of F. Brigham & Co., shoe manufacturers, erecting a very
complete factory on part of the fine waterpower which he owned.
In 1861, although there were 17·shoe shops in ₊the place, his was
the principal one and he employed 300 men.   They made large
quantities of shoes for soldiers in the Civil War.   To-day, the firm
of F. Brigham & Gregory Co., is the oldest shoe manufacturing
concern in the United States, with large facilities.   Was selectman
for Marlboro 1846-1847; Representative, 1850-1852.

Children (by first wife), born in Marlboro:
   i Francis D.[7], b. 27 Oct., 1835; d. 20 Sept., 1836.
649 ii Rufus H., b. 9 June, 1837.
   iii Wilbur F., b. 9 April, 1839; d. unm., 13 Nov., 1901. Educated
      at Monson Academy and learned his father's business in all its
      details; was in the Civil War 100 days, and prevented from
      further service by poor eyesight; an active worker in the tem-
      perance cause, and supporter of the Baptist church.   In 1865
      went into business with his father and became Vice-President of
      the F. Brigham & Gregory Shoe Co.
   iv Capt. William F., twin to Wilbur, enlisted 6 Aug., 1862, and
      d. in the hospital in Annapolis, Md., 6 Feb., 1865; was in the
      battles of Fredericksburg and Vicksburg; was a remarkable
      mathematician, with good powers of oratory, and known in his

youth as the "Eloquent Brigham," taking part in many debates
with older and riper men, and showing unusual ability.
650 v Waldo B., b. 23 June, 1841.
    vi Laura S., b. 14 Sept., 1843; m. Charles A. Wood of Hudson,
       and d.
Children (by second wife), born in Marlboro:
    vii Infant, b. Jan., 1853; d. y.
    viii Ida M., b. 6 April, 1855.

360 CHARLES[6], son of Ivory[5] and Sally (Wilkins) Brigham;
born in Marlboro, Mass., 11 Dec., 1815; died in Hudson, Mass., 2
Jan., 1899; married, 5 Oct., 1841, Sarah H. Barnard; born in
Harvard, Mass., 30 July, 1820; died 30 July, 1880.
    Mr. Brigham was one of the last survivors of the sixth genera-
ation of Brighams. He was a farmer and contractor. Was assessor
in Marlboro in 1849, and for many years overseer of the poor.
Was a great temperance laborer and an anti-slavery man; very
public spirited and one of the founders and leading men in the
Unitarian church.
Children, born in Feltonville:
    i Charles G.[7], b. 9 July, 1842; res. unm., in Hudson; in the Navy
       in 1862, in the South Atlantic, on the *Ino;* then in the Light
       Battery in Virginia.
    ii Warren S., b. 14 Jan., 1844; d. 19 Feb., 1904; res. Marlboro,
       and Randsburg, Cal.; m. Isabella S. Leighton of Marlboro, who
       d. 14 Nov., 1875. Ch.:
         1 *Lena Isabella*[8], b. 11 March, 1872; m. 24 Nov., 1892, Carl L.
           Hanson, b. in Sweden, 1863; res. Los Angeles, Cal. Ch.
           (Hanson): i Charles L.[9], b. 11 March, 1894; ii Irma I., b. 1
           April, 1897; iii Leighton J., b. 18 Sept., 1903.
         2 *Cora,* m. ———— Howe of No. Adams, Mass.
         3 *Ralph W.,* m.; has 1 ch.; res. Bakersfield, Cal.
         4 *Grace,* m.; res. Los Angeles.
         5 *Leslie,* res. unm., Los Angeles.
    iii Sarah L., b. 26 June, 1845; m. Everett Hussey of Hudson. Ch.
       (Hussey):
         1 *Harry E.*[8], grad. Tufts College; res. s. p., Pittsfield, Mass.
    iv Francis W., b. in Hudson; m. ————————; a farmer, res.
       Hudson. Ch.:
         1 *Clifford*[8], m.; 4 ch.
         2 *Irving,* m. s. p.
    v Harriet H., d. 30 Aug., 1860, æ. 10.
    vi Caleb B., res. s. p., Hudson.
    vii Horace, b. 12 June, 1857; d. 30 Dec., 1861.
    viii Infant, twin to Horace; d. y.

361 ARTEMAS WARD[6], son of Artemas[5] and Mary (Cornish)
Brigham; born in New Marlboro, Mass., 25 Dec., 1781; married,
5 Feb., 1814, Sophia Phelps of Chatham, N. Y. Resided in Westmoreland, Oneida Co., N. Y., but we are not informed as to his
later years and time of death.

Children, born in Westmoreland:

 i Origen S.⁷, b. 15 March, 1815; d. 24 Dec., 1850; m. Sept., 1842, Frances E. Waterman of Troy, N. Y. Ch.:

  1 *Adeline F.⁸,* b. 20 May, 1846, in Troy.

 ii Austin P., b. 18 Sept., 1819; d. 3 May, 1822, in Westmoreland.

651 iii Edwin W., b. 4 Feb., 1825.

362   BETSEY⁶, daughter of Artemas⁵ and Mary (Cornish) Brigham; born in New Marlboro, Mass.; died in Clinton, N. Y.; married, Harvey, son of Walter Pollard of Clinton.

Children (Pollard), born in Clinton:

 i H. Franklin⁷, b. 28 April, 1816; d. in Verona, N. Y., 22 Dec., 1862; was a dwarf.

 ii Mary Eleanor, b. 21 June, 1819; d. in Hartland, N. Y., 7 Jan., 1887; m. 29 Oct., 1845, Levi H., son of David Ingersoll of Clinton; moved to Middleport, N. Y. Ch. (Ingersoll), b. in Middleport:

  1 *Ella Mary⁸,* b. 21 April, 1849; d. 26 Sept., 1849.

  2 *Henry Brigham,* b. 6 Dec., 1852; res. Hartland; m. 25 Sept., 1875, ———.

 iii Martha Ann, b. 5 May, 1823; m. 22 July, 1846, Parsons S., son of Rev. Rufus Pratt; res. Dorset, Vt. Ch. (Pratt), the second and third b. in Winfield, N. Y.:

  1 *Anna Serena⁸,* b. in Niles, Mich., 20 Jan., 1848; d. unm., 25 Nov., 1865.

  2 *Carrie Guyon,* b. 24 Aug., 1849; m. Charles B. Gilbert of Dorset, Vt.; 6 ch.

  3 *Ada Martha,* b. 13 July, 1852; m. John Sherman of Dorset, Vt.; 4 ch.

  4 *Bertha Mary,* b. in Dorset, 8 Aug., 1858; d. 4 Feb., 1904.

 iv James Harvey, b. 3 July, 1832; m. (1) 31 March, 1856, Lorania Ely; m. (2) 4 Aug., 1882, Mrs. Mary A. La Due; was in Serroll's Eng. Corps, Civil War; res. Middleport, N. Y. Ch. (by first wife):

  1 *Floyd⁸,* b. 19 Dec., 1857.

  Ch. (by second wife):

  2 *Martha Eleanor,* b. 5 July, 1884.

363   REV. JOHN CLARK⁶, D. D., son of John⁵ and Phebe (Clark) Brigham; born in New Marlboro, Mass., 10 Feb., 1794; died in Brooklyn, N. Y., 10 Aug., 1862; married, 23 Aug., 1840, Maria E. Evertson; born in New York City, 5 Feb., 1811; died in Brooklyn, 10 Dec., 1864.

Dr. Brigham was graduated A. B. from Williams College in 1819; completed his course at Andover Theological Seminary in 1822. He spent four years in South America and Mexico at the suggestion of the A. B. F. M., studying religious conditions; as a result, Protestant chaplaincies were established in Rio Janeiro and other centers. Returning home in 1826, became Corresponding Secretary of the Am. Bible Society, being the first secretary appointed to give all his time to the work; held this position until 1862 with singular ability and success. Largely through his influence the present Bible House in New York was erected. He received the degree of D. D. from Andover, in 1832.

Children, born in Brooklyn:
    i John Cotton⁷, b. 18 Sept., 1841; d. Sept., 1842.
    ii Eliza Roosevelt, b. 27 Dec., 1842; d. unm., 13 Oct., 1890.
652 iii Walter Evertson, b. 14 March, 1845.
    iv Mary Douglass, b. 18 Sept., 1847; m. 21 Dec., 1869, John Henry Cooke, b. in Litchfield, Conn., 11 Nov., 1843; he engaged in business, and res. retired in Brooklyn. Ch. (Cooke), b. in Brooklyn:
        1 Adelaide⁸, b. 3 Oct., 1870; m. 14 March, 1900, John Sayres, b. in B., 6 Feb., 1875; res. Brooklyn. Ch. (Sayres), b. in B.: i Clinton⁹, b. 23 March, 1903; ii Philip Isham, b. 28 Sept., 1904.
        2 May Roosevelt, b. 11 Nov., 1882.
653 v Amariah Ward, b. 14 Oct., 1850.
    vi John Knox, b. 29 Jan., 1854; was grad. Univ. City of New York, 1873, A. B.; P. B. K., 4th honor, 3d fellow; studied architecture; was in business as designer and importer and contractor in N. Y. City until appointed Inspector in Bureau of Water Purveyors in 1890, and Clerk in Bureau of Water Register in 1894; res. unm., New York City; is now engaged in mercantile pursuits.
    vii Antoinette Gibson, b. 29 April, 1856; m. 30 Sept., 1886, James Burling Hopper, b. in Paterson, N. J., 19 Feb., 1851; d. in El Paso, Texas, 14 March, 1901. Ch. (Hopper), b. in Brooklyn:
        1 Louise Roosevelt⁸, b. 31 July, 1887.

364 HARRY⁶, son of John⁵ and Phebe (Clark) Brigham; born in New Marlboro, Mass., 19 June, 1796; died in Chatham, N. Y., 16 Oct., 1864; married, 18 Jan., 1827, Sarah, daughter of Alexander Bowman; born in Chatham, 1 Feb., 1808; died in Jersey City, 30 Nov., 1885.

Children, born in Chatham:
    i Phebe Ann⁷, b. 17 June, 1829; a teacher for forty years; principal of No. 1 School, Bergen, N. J.; d. unm., Stamford, N. Y., 27 May, 1903.
654 ii Lewis Alexander, b. 2 Jan., 1831.
655 iii John Calvin, b. 15 Aug., 1833.

365 DR. AMARIAH⁶, son of John⁵ and Phebe (Clark) Brigham; born in New Marlboro, Mass., 26 Dec., 1798; died 8 Sept., 1849, in Utica, N. Y.; married, 23 Jan., 1833, Susan Root of Greenfield, Mass.; born 23 Aug., 1811; died 12 Nov., 1896. He went with his father to Chatham, N. Y., in 1805.

After early hardships he began to practice medicine in Enfield, Mass., soon after reaching his majority, and then went to Greenfield and established himself in competition with practitioners of age and established reputation. He became eminent in his pro-

fession in Massachusetts and in Hartford, Conn., where he began
to practice in 1831 after a year abroad.   He regarded infant
schools and religious revivals as frequent inducers of insanity.
His little volume " *Influences of Mental Cultivation on Health* "
and his later works, " *Influences of Religion on the Health and
Physical Welfare of Mankind,*" were in advance of their time;
they are behind the present expression of thought which he contributed to form.   His last special work, " *An Inquiry concerning the
Diseases and Functions of the Brain, Spinal Cord and Nerves,*"
only indicates what was then known on the subject.   In 1840,
Dr. Brigham was appointed Superintendent of the Retreat for the
Insane in Hartford; from there he went to a similar institution in
Utica.   Endowed with rare judgment, unselfishness, courage and
an iron will, he gave himself fully to the service of mankind in
a much needed field, educating the public and the Legislature as
to the needs of the insane, and in 1844, with his own means, established the *Journal of Insanity,* the first periodical of that character in the world, and which is still published.   He was the
pioneer in all modern methods for caring for the insane.   Pritchard, at the head of one of the greatest English asylums, advised
an American to seek in the Utica asylum a degree of perfection
not then found in England.   Dr. Brigham was truly a great man
in his day and generation, but is more highly appreciated now than
he was in his own time.   " Brigham Hall " Hospital, Canandaigua,
is named in his honor.

> *Children, the 3 eldest born in Hartford, the 2 youngest in Utica:*
>   i Susan M.[7], b. 25 Oct., 1833; d. 19 Feb., 1881.
> ii John Spencer, b. 7 July, 1836; d. 16 Aug., 1848; his early
>   death hastened his father's decease.
> iii Helen, b. 1839.
> iv Louise, b. 17 Aug., 1843; d. 1901.
>   v Mary L. (posthumous), b. 1 Feb., 1850; d. 10 June, 1871.

366 ELIZA[6], daughter of John[5] and Phebe (Clark) Brigham;
born in New Marlboro, Mass., 27 Aug., 1801; died 24 June, 1870;
married 6 Feb., 1825, Robbins, son of Jabez and Mary (Robbins)
Burrell of Sheffield, O., born 20 Sept., 1799; died 24 Aug., 1877.
She was a woman of strong character.

> *Children (Burrell), born in Sheffield:*
>   i Solon[7], b. 26 Feb., 1826; d. 1828.
> ii Phebe A., b. 2 Oct., 1827; d. 2 Feb., 1851.
> iii Solon J., b. 7 Dec., 1829; d. 5 Oct., 1854.
> iv Lewis Brigham, b. 1 April, 1832; he served in the Navy, 1864-65;
>   res. Portland, Oregon; retired from business; has always been
>   a helper of others.
>   v Edward P., b. 21 Jan., 1835; d. Nov., 1891; a man of high

AMARIAH BRIGHAM, M.D. (365)

integrity; m. 19 Nov., 1862, Rosa Clifton, and res. Sheffield, O.
Ch
　　1 *Harry C.*[8], b. 15 Dec., 1863; m. Tempe Garfield; res. Sheffield;
　　5 ch.
　vi Howard A., b. 4 Jan., 1838; m. (1) 15 Oct., 1863, Harriet Ever-
　　son, who d. 5 June, 1876; m. (2) 20 Dec., 1877, Martha Jackson;
　　he stands high as an editor in Iowa, and has a unique style; grad.
　　from Oberlin Coll.
　vii Julia E., b. 15 Nov., 1840; m. 19 Dec., 1866, John Merton; res., a
　　widow, in Oberlin; she is " a copy of her mother." Ch. (Merton):
　　1 *Lewis B.*[8], b. 4 March, 1868.
viii Dwight R., b. 1 March, 1843; m. 20 March, 1890, Clara B. Kent;
　　res. s. p., Canandaigua, N. Y.; a grad. of Oberlin Coll., and has
　　a medical degree from the Univ. of Mich.; he was given charge
　　of " Brigham Hall " Hospital for the Insane in 1876, and has
　　since remained at the head of the institution which was named
　　for his uncle, Dr. Amariah Brigham.

367　RUFUS[6], son of John[5] and Lucy (Howe) Brigham; born
in Alstead, N. H., 29 June, 1791; died in Ackworth, N. H., 23
Aug., 1867; married 24 Feb., 1814, Elizabeth, daughter of Isaac
Duncan, born in Alstead, 22 Sept., 1794; died 27 April, 1858. He
was a farmer and resided in Ackworth, N. H.

Children, born in Ackworth:
　　i Harvey Duncan[7], b. 23 May, 1815; was at Middlebury Coll. in
　　1840 and '41; a merchant and teacher; d. s. p., at Pana, Ill.,
　　31 Oct., 1868; m. 4 Nov., 1845, Mary L. Ulrich, who d. 1872.
656　ii Elizabeth Ann, b. 18 March, 1819.
　iii Marinda, b. 3 March, 1824; d. 25 Oct., 1836.
657　iv Martha Lucina, b. 23 Jan., 1831.

368　POLLY[6], daughter of John[5] and Lucy (Howe) Brigham;
born in Alstead, N. H., 16 Sept., 1797; married 10 April, 1817,
Samuel McKeen; resided in Ackworth, N. H.

Children (McKeen), born in Ackworth:
　　i Polly[7], b. 29 March, 1818; m. (1) 28 April, 1841, Lewis Beck-
　　with, who d. 22 Jan., 1845; m. (2) 19 June, 1847, Henry C.
　　Stickney. Ch. (Beckwith):
　　　1' *Henry*[8], b. 10 Sept., 1842; d. 17 Sept., 1859.
　　　Ch. (Stickney):
　　　2 *Augustine W.*, b. 27 April, 1848.
　　　3 *Albert; 4 Mary; 5 Charles;* and 2 others.
　ii Samuel, b. 7 May, 1820; m. 2 Nov., 1840, Clarissa Spencer; res.
　　Ackworth. Ch.:
　　　1 *Martha Ellen*[8], m. George Wallace.
　iii John, b. 13 March, 1822; m. 22 Dec., 1842, Sarah A. Brown;
　　res. Ackworth and Russell City, Kan. Ch.:
　　　1 *John G.*[8]; 2 *Lyman A.; 3 Dean W.; 4 Annie.*
　iv Lydia, b. 4 Aug., 1824; d. 20 June, 1855; m. 2 Nov., 1844, Free-
　　land Hemphill; res. Ackworth. Ch. (Hemphill):
　　　1 *Kathleen M.*[8], b. 20 Oct., 1845; m. Watson G. Pettingill; had
　　　a family.

    2 *Eugene F.*, b. 13 Nov., 1847.
    3 *Ashton G.*, b. 17 Sept., 1849; res. Holyoke, Mass.
    4 *Julian A.*, b. 17 Aug., 1853; d. 25 April, 1854.
  v Martha E., b. 21 Feb., 1828; m. (1) 28 June, 1849, Charles Ward
    of Wayland, Mass.; m. (2) James Hubbard Way, 2 Dec., 1852;
    res. Lempster, N. H.   Ch. (Ward):
    1 *Etta³*, b. 21 April, 1850. Ch. (Way).
    2 *Emma*, b. Sept., 1853.
 vi Jonathan L., b. 21 Feb., 1835; m. 17 May, 1859, Jennette L.
    George; res. s. p., Ackworth.
vii Catherine S., b. 14 Aug., 1839; m. George F. Youngman.   Ch.
    (Youngman):
    1 *Etta³*, res. Lempster, N. H.

   369   CAPT. AARON⁶, son of Stephen⁵ and Louisa (Howe)
Brigham; born in Alstead, N. H., 20 Oct., 1797; died in Marlboro,
N. H., 16 Feb., 1876; married (1) 13 June, 1825, Susan K.,
daughter of Philip Proctor of Sullivan, N. H., born 11 Jan.,
1797; died in East Alstead, 29 Jan., 1865; married (2) 1 May,
1867, Mrs. Elvira W., widow of Calvin Stone; she died s. p., 5
Oct., 1884.   In early life a school-teacher, became a farmer and
resided on the homestead in Alstead, N. H.

Children, born in Alstead:
   i Evelina Fidelia⁷, b. 11 April, 1829; d. 23 Feb., 1901; m. 25
    Nov., 1852, John Warren Sawyer, b. 28 July, 1826; a farmer of
    Marlboro, N. H.   Ch. (Sawyer):
    1 *Lestina A.³*, b. 1855; m. (1) 1876, Charles E. Richardson; m.
    (2) 1896, George E. Holbrook, grandson of 370; res. s. p.,
    Amherst, N. H.
  ii Lestina Amanda, b. 17 May, 1832; d. in Butler, Ill., 22 Feb.,
    1872; m. 23 Oct., 1855, David Smith Ware, b. in Gilsum, N. H.,
    25 Oct., 1828; moved to Butler.   Ch. (Ware), 7 youngest b. in
    Butler:
    1 *John³*, b. in Hillsboro, N. H., 7 Jan., 1857; res. Waverly, Ill.
    2 *Arthur*, b. in Hillsboro, 18 Nov., 1858; m. 27 Oct., 1881, Mary
      Adaline Aten (or Aiken).   Ch., b. in Butler. i Frank⁹; ii
      Roy; iii Mabel; iv Wilma.
    3 *David*, b. 2 Aug., 1860; m. 17 Dec., 1890, Charlotte Cass
      Mack.
    4 *Theoda*, b. 4 June, 1863; d. 2 Sept., 1864.
    5 *Lyman Trumbull*, b. 15 Feb., 1865.
    6 *Beulah*, b. 8 Oct., 1866.
    7 *Emily*, b. 5 Dec., 1868; m. 20 Nov., 1890, Jesse Ware Osborn.
      Ch. (Osborn): i Wesley⁹; ii Grace.
    8 *Clarence Brigham*, b. 13 Feb., 1872; d. 1 Aug., 1872.
    9 *Clara Lestina*, b. 13 Feb., 1872; d. 26 July, 1872.
658 iii Willard Proctor, b. 25 Aug., 1835.
  iv Luceba Augusta, b. 25 Aug., 1836; m. 26 Sept., 1860, Justus
    Hurd Ware of Butler; she taught in Butler, and res. there
    after m.   Ch. (Ware):
    1 *Mary Flora³*, b. 29 Nov., 1862.
    2 *Carrie Susan*, b. 5 May, 1864; d. 1 Dec., 1866.

3 *George Vincent*, b. 25 Sept., 1867; m. 12 Dec., 1893, Mary
Grace Bryce.
4 *Amy Lillian*, b. 24 April, 1873; m. 10 Oct., 1900, James A.
Busby. Ch. (Busby): Leland W.⁹, b. 24 Nov., 1901.

370 LYDIA⁶, daughter of Stephen⁵ and Louisa (Howe) Brigham; born in Alstead, N. H., 26 Feb., 1800; died 28 Feb., 1870;
married 3 Nov., 1819, Stephen Holbrook, born 15 March, 1797;
died 24 April, 1854.

Children (Holbrook):
   i Francis W.⁷, b. 23 Dec., 1820, in E. Alstead; d. 14 Dec., 1886;
     m. Olivia C. Howland of Franconia, N. H.; res. Amherst, N. H.
     Ch.:
       1 *Charles R.*⁸, b. in E. A., 28 Oct., 1847; m. 15 May, 1872, Evelyn
         M. Atwood, who d. 25 Aug., 1872; m. (2) 30 April, 1878,
         Mary W. Howlett; res. Manchester, N. H.; 2 ch.
       2 *Louisa A.*, b. in Manchester, 11 May, 1849; d. 24 Sept., 1849.
       3 *Mary O.*, b. in M. 23 Aug., 1850; m. 29 Jan., 1874, George A.
         Buzzell; res. Pasadena, Cal.
       4 *Frank A.*, b. 30 Jan., 1853; res. Amherst; m. Maria E. Davis,
         b. 1852, of E. Jaffrey, N. H.; res. Amherst; 2 ch.
       5 *(Dea.) George E.*, b. in Amherst, 12 Nov., 1854; res. there; m.
         (1) 6 Aug., 1885, Cora B. Fisher of Amherst, who d. 5
         March, 1894; m. (2) 7 May, 1896, Mrs. Lestina A. Richardson,
         granddau. of 369; 2 ch.
       6 *Jennie*, b. in A., 28 Dec., 1860; m. 21 Dec., 1881, Ola Ander-
         son; res. Concord, N. H.; 4 ch.
   ii Abigail Louisa, b. 3 March, 1823; d. 1 Dec., 1877.
   iii Stephen Hubbard, b. in E. A., 10 July, 1824; d. in Amherst, 30
     June, 1858; m. 1 Oct., 1850, Lovisa M. Smith of Rutland, Vt.;
     res. with son, 1905, in Detroit, æ. 81. Ch ·
       1 *Albert W.*⁸, res. Detroit.
   iv Samuel B., b. 25 Sept., 1830; d. 14 Oct., 1845.
   v Ellen Maria, b. 23 Aug., 1842; d. 18 July, 1902; res. in Amherst.

371 DAVID⁶, son of Stephen⁵ and Louisa (Howe) Brigham;
born in Alstead, N. H., 25 March, 1802; died in Auburn, N. H.,
8 Feb., 1867; married (1) 10 April, 1827, Sophia, daughter of
Dea. William Mark of Gilsum, N. H.; who died 4 Jan., 1852, æ.
48; married (2) 13 Jan., 1853, Lydia Smith, daughter of Jonathan
Hall of Manchester, N. H., born in Auburn, Sept., 1819.

He moved to Gilsum from Alstead in 1819; was a deacon in the
church in Gilsum; treasurer ten years; also town clerk; was the
first secretary of the anti-slavery society there, and gave the material to build a church. He operated a cotton mill and was in the
clothier's trade; was also a music teacher at one time. He met
with reverses in business and voluntarily chose poverty to help his
creditors. Also resided in Manchester and Derry, N. H., and in
the former place was again appointed a deacon of the church.

Children (by first wife):
  i Elizabeth M.[7], b. in Gilsum, 19 Aug., 1829; d. 17 Sept., 1829.
  ii Mary Louisa, b. 11 July, 1832; d. 11(March, 1905; res. Manchester.
  iii Ellen Sophia, b. 14 July, 1834; d. 25 Sept., 1835.
  iv Eliza Ann, b. 30 June, 1840; d. 12 April, 1859.
Children (by second wife):
  v George Munroe, b. in Manchester, 23 April, 1854; d. in Boston.
  vi Hattie Sophia, b. 21 Oct., 1856; res. New Haven, Conn.
  vii Minnie Ann, b. in M., 24 Nov., 1860; d.
  viii Fred Holbrook, b. in Auburn, 4 March, 1864; res. New Haven.

372   ABRAM[6], son of Stephen[5] and Louisa (Howe) Brigham; born in Alstead, N. H., 1 April, 1807; died in Fitchburg, Mass., 12 March, 1872; married 28 March, 1831, Alma Moore, who died in Fitchburg, 20 Dec., 1888, æ. 85. Was a machinist and resided in Lowell. The male line is extinct.

Children:
  i Maria Louisa[7], b. 28 Nov., 1831(; m. 10 July, 1855, George W. Reed of Montreal, a prominent business man, who d. 20 April, 1897, s. p.; they adopted two daus.
  ii Caroline K., b. 15 May, 1835; m. Charles A. Brooks, M. D., of Clinton, Mass., who d. 3 June, 1889; she res. in Montreal, but removed to —————. Ch. (Brooks):
   1 *Alice Maria[8]; 2 Caroline Stevens;* both res. Boston.
  iii Stephen H., b. 4 June, 1839; d. y., unm.
  iv George H., b. 10 Oct., 1841; d. 17 Aug., 1843.
  v Ellen E., b. 20 Oct., 1844; m. 24 Dec., 1868, Isaac Osgood of Fitchburg; she res. Lowell. Ch. (Osgood):
   1 *Walter B.[8],* who res. New York City.
   2 and 3 d. y.

373   WILLIAM[6], son of Abner[5] and Elizabeth (Childs) Brigham; born in Princeton, Mass., 23 Nov., 1789; died 26 Aug., 1829; married 8 Feb., 1822, Alethea Bream of Virginia. Resided in Kanawha County, West Virginia.

Children:
659 i Mary Elizabeth[7], b. 29 Jan., 1823.
660 ii Lavinia Virginia, b. 22 April, 1825.
  iii Maria Louisa, b. 30 July, 1827; d. 11 July, 1828.
  iv William Alexander, b. 6 June, 1829; d. 17 Aug., 1856; m. 21 June, 1853, Margaretta Nixon, b. 10 Nov., 1830; d. 27 March, 1855. Ch.:
   1 *Alethea B.[8],* b. 18 April, 1854; d. 29 Feb., 1855.

374   LUCIUS[6], son of Abner[5] and Elizabeth (Childs) Brigham; born in Princeton, Mass., 2 Dec., 1797; died in Marietta, O., 16 Dec., 1876; married (1) Caroline P. Goodnow; married (2) Lucy Roper. Resided in Marietta, O.

Children, born in Marietta:
  i William[7], b. 19 Sept., 1833; d. 28 Jan., 1884; m. (1) Joanna

Ellis; m. (2) Marie Huntsinger; m. (3) Anna P. Hubbard; res. Minneapolis, Minn. Ch.:

1 *Carrie*[8], b.·in M., 14 Feb., 1860; d. unm., 10 Oct., 1886.

2 *Charles,* b. 31 Aug., 1863; d. 6 May, 1864.

ii Caroline E., b. 27 June, 1835; d. 29 March, 1883; m. William. L. Rankin of White Cottage, O. Ch. (Rankin):

1 *Edward K.*[8], b. 9 March, 1865; m. Martha Merriam; res. W. Zanesville, O. Ch.: Caroline[9].

iii Alonzo P., b. 2 March, 1837; m. Matilda Crouse; res. Burlington, Kan. Ch.:

1 *Newton Curtis*[8], b. 16 May, 1865; m. Ruth Shirres; res. St. Louis, Mo.

2 *Blanche B.,* b. 31 Aug., 1866; m. Robert O. Mills; res. Zanesville, O. Ch. (Mills): i Helen O.[9], b. 25 Dec., 1893; ii Mary, b. 3 Nov., 1895; iii Florence, b. and d. 1896; iv Donald, b. 28 March, 1902.

iv Edward G., b. 21 June, 1839; res. Marietta; m. Sarah E. Ells. Ch.:

1 *Frank M.*[8], b. 1868; d. 1878.

2 *Carrie E.,* b. 12 Oct., 1870; m. J. William McKinley of Washington, D. C. Ch. (McKinley): i Carrie E.[9]; ii Edward B.

3 *Edward G.,* b. 2 April, 1873; d. 1874.

4 *William H.,* b. 27 Dec., 1874; res. Marietta.

5 *Mary F.,* b. 19 Aug., 1877; m. Charles S. Smoot of Parkersburg, W. Va.

6 *Bessie E.,* b. 23 Dec., 1879.

7 *John E.,* b. 19 Sept., 1881.

v Samuel, b. 24 Sept., 1841; d. 9 Sept., 1842.

vi Julia L., b. 2 Oct., 1849; res. unm., Boston.

375 JOHN[6], son of Asa[5] and Elizabeth (Marean) Brigham;. born in Princeton, Mass., 24 Nov., 1791; died in Cobden, Ill., 2 Nov., 1870; married 19 Nov., 1816, Mary Moore, born 10 Oct., 1796, probably in Ackworth, N. H.; died in Decorah, Ia., 27 Feb., 1879.

He was less than 3 years of age when his father died and he was brought up by his uncle Stephen Brigham in Ackworth, from which place he married his wife; removed to Keesville, N. Y. in 1826, and later went west.

Children, probably all born in Keesville, N. Y.:

i William Marean[7], b. 19 Sept., 1817; m. 6 Oct., 1842, Mary E. Rich of Burlington, Vt., who d. 28 Oct., 1893; he is a prominent citizen of Milwaukee, Wis., where he res., and in 1905 is one of the two surviving charter members of the Board of Trade there. Ch.:

1 *Charles R.*[8], b. 1850; d. unm., 1880.

3 ch. d. in infancy.

ii Mary Grout, b. 9 Jan., 1819; d. 17 Jan., 1820.

iii Mary Caroline, b. 9 Feb., 1825; m. as his second wife, 24 Dec., 1857, Isaac G. Goodrich, b. in Lockport, N. Y., 1814; (by his first marriage, to Catherine Ayers, he had a son James); res. in Cobden, Ill., and removed to Albert Lea, Minn., where res.. s. p.

iv Lucy Elizabeth, b. 18 June, 1827; d. 26 Aug., 1849.
v Martha Augusta, b. 10 Sept., 1830; d. 13 April, 1835.
vi Justinian Holden, b. 12 Feb., 1832; d. 30 Jan., 1854.
vii Sara Eliza, b. 16 Aug., 1833; m. 30 July, 1857, Judge Ezekiel
Cutler, A. M., b. in Waterford, Vt., 26 April, 1827; d. in Decorah,
Ia.; he grad. from the Univ. of Vt., in 1853; was Lieut. Col. of
the 31st Ia. Vols. in the Civil War; she res. Decorah, in 1903.
Ch. (Cutler):
  1 *John Francis*[8], b. 29 April, 1862; res. Eureka, Ore.
  2 *Mary Brigham*, b. 12 March, 1866; grad. Carlton Coll., Northfield, Minn.; was a teacher of German in this school; m.
  17 June, 1905, Clarence Wedger.
  3 *Horace Eaton*, b. 22 May, 1873; grad. Wisconsin Univ., 1904,
  a teacher in the Philippine Islands.
viii Martha Moriah, b. 2 Jan., 1837; m. 25 Aug., 1859, William Hazelton, lawyer and banker of Albert Lea, Minn., where she res.
Ch. (Hazelton):
  1 *William B.*[8], b. 18 May, 1860; d. 11 June, 1875.
  2 *Edward C.*, b. 11 Dec., 1865; d. 1 Sept., 1867.
  3 *Frances Sophia*, b. 11 April, 1868; m. 5 Oct., 1893, L. G.
  Hewitt, M. D., and res. Northwood, Ia. Ch. (Hewitt): i
  Leland H.[9], b. 11 Oct., 1894; ii Martha E., b. 12 Oct., 1897;
  d. 16 July, 1898.

376 BETSEY[6], daughter of Asa[5] and Elizabeth (Marean)
Brigham; born in Princeton, Mass., 18 May, 1793; killed in a runa-
way accident, 7 Sept., 1828; married, 4 July, 1811, James, son of
James and Elizabeth (Davis) Browning of Hubbardston, Mass.,
(both of Scotland), born 30 Nov., 1788; died 12 Nov., 1837.
They lived in Hubbardston. (By a second marriage he had two
sons, George D., who was killed in the Civil War, and Josiah.)
Children (Browning), born in Hubbardston:
  i Asa B.[7], b. 18 Oct., 1812; d. 14 Oct., 1815.
  ii Clara Sherman, b. 7 July, 1813; d. 22 Jan., 1878, in Cambridge,
  Mass., where she res.; m. 29 April, 1835, Appleton Clark (whose
  emigrant ancestor was Hugh Clark of Watertown and Roxbury);
  b. in Hubbardston, 10 Aug., 1807; d. 12 March, 1904. Ch. (Clark),
  b. in Hubbardston:
    1 *Mary H.*[8], b. 14 Oct., 1839; m. 24 June, 1868, J. Gilman Waite;
    res. Medford, Mass.; s. p.
    2 *Abby M.*, b. 2 April, 1841; res. Cambridge.
    3 *Cecilia W.*, b. 29 Oct., 1843; res. Cambridge.
    4 *Susan R.*, b. 9 Feb., 1845; res. Cambridge.
    5 *Herbert A.*, b. 17 Aug., 1847; m. Ella A. Fletcher, 1 Dec.,
    1870; res. Haverhill; 6 ch.:
    6 *Sybil E.*, b. 30 Dec., 1849; m. Ephraim Emerton, Prof. of
    Ecclesiastical Hist. at Harvard Univ.; 1 ch.
    7 *Alice C.*, b. 14 Dec., 1856; d. 21 Dec., 1859.
  iii Elizabeth M., b. 1 June, 1815; d. 23 Nov., 1815.
  iv Sally Brigham, b. 6 March, 1817; d. 24 Aug., 1819.
  v James, b. 2 Feb., 1819; d. 26 April, 1819.
  vi James, b. 14 April, 1820; d. 23 May, 1898; m. 2 April, 1844, Ann

W. Whittemore, b. in Hubbardston, 12 Oct., 1821; d. 22 Jan.,
1898; was Corporal of the Color Guard in the 53d Mass. Regt.,
Co. H, in the Civil War. Ch.:
1 *Elizabeth A.*, b. 18 Dec., 1846; d. 21 July, 1881; m. 22 Jan.,
  1872, Eugene D. Shattuck; res. Newburgh, O.
2 *Sybil H.*, b. 9 March, 1857; m. 25 Nov., 1879, Silas A. Greenwood; res. Winchenden, Mass.; 1 ch.
vii John, b. 21 Feb., 1822; d. 13 June, 1859; m. 2 Dec., 1847, Abigail
    D. Greenwood, b. 12 June, 1823; d. 14 Jan., 1903. Ch.:
    1 *Henry H.*, b. 11 April, 1856; m. 8 Dec., 1880, Jennie A.
      Whitney; res. Worcester, Mass.; grad. of Worcester Poly-
      technic School.
viii Betsey Brigham, b. 10 May, 1824; d. in Medford, Mass., 5 May,
    1904; m. 22 June, 1867, James O. Curtis, b. 1 Nov., 1804; d.
    3 March, 1890; res. Medford, Mass., s. p., where he was an im-
    portant citizen and a well-known builder of many ships.
ix Sybil Marean, b. 7 April, 1826; m. 9 Sept., 1852, Henry J. Hunt,
   who d. 14 Oct., 1861; she res. in Medford.

377 AARON[7], son of David[6] and Sarah (Veeder) Brigham;
born in Denmark, N. Y., 21 Aug., 1809; married 30 June, 1834,
Maria, daughter of Dea. Marther Bosworth of Lowville, N. Y.;
born 13 April, 1813.

Aaron removed in 1833 from Lowville to Genesee County, Mich.,
and in 1836 to Hadley, Lapeer County, where he opened a farm
remote from neighbors, schools or churches; in time, the region
was peopled and he was successful in his enterprises.

Children, the eldest born in Genesee Co., Mich., the others in Hadley:
  i George W.[8], b. 29 Feb., 1836; m. 27 May, 1857, Lydia A. Pierson
    of Atlas, Mich., b. 31 Dec., 1836, in Norwich, Canada; he was
    the first male child born in Genesee Co. Ch.:
    1 *Mary Ella*, b. in Hadley, 21 May, 1859.
  ii David C., b. 6 June, 1838.
  iii Morris, b. 5 Feb., 1844; d. 29 July, 1845.
  iv Mary Jane, b. 2 July, 1846.
  v Horace Alfred, b. 20 Aug., 1851; d. 22 Jan., 1852.
  vi Stephen Henry, b. 10 July, 1853.

378 EDMUND SANFORD[6], son of Silas[5] and Rhoda (Morey)
Brigham; born in Brownington, Vt., 11 July, 1808; died in Brown-
ington, 25 Aug., 1862; married 14 June, 1840, Mary Buttrick,
daughter of Silas Wolcott, born 28 Jan., 1811; died 5 Jan., 1869.
Resided in Boston where he was for several years overseer at the
State House.

Children, born in Boston:
  i Charles Edmund[7], b. 13 May, 1841; m. 25 April, 1872, Alice Hut-
    ton, dau. of Richard Sims; b. in Salem, Mass., 5 April, 1843;
    he is a P. O. clerk in Boston, and res. Medford, Mass. Served in
    12th Mass. Vols. and U. S. N., Civil War. Ch., b. there:
    1 *Bertha Hamilton*[8], b. 8 Sept., 1874.

2 *Fred William,* b. 19 Dec., 1875.
3 *Florence Alice,* b. 22 April, 1881.
ii Elizabeth.
iii Frederick George, b. 10 Feb., 1846; d. in Memphis, Tenn., 15 Nov., 1867; was in the Civil War, Co. I, 45th Mass. Vols.
iv William James, b. 16 Feb., 1849; m. 20 Oct., 1886, Mary Elizabeth, dau. of Stephen H. De Be Voise; b. in Brooklyn, N. Y., 11 June, 1857; he is a planter, Hollywood, Miss. Ch., b. there:
    1 *Josephine Elizabeth*[8], b. 25 Aug., 1887.
    2 *Hattie Marsh,* b. 3 Dec., 1888.
    3 *Mary Frances,* b. 18 June, 1890.

379 EMILY[6], daughter of Silas[5] and Rhoda (Morey) Brigham; born in Brownington, Vt., 17 Dec., 1809; died in Newport, Vt., 30 April, 1893; married 3 July, 1833, Hon. Thomas Carlisle, son of Amherst and Anne (Carlisle) Stewart; born 26 Oct., 1804; died, 2 Sept., 1865.

Children (Stewart), born in Brownington:
i (Judge) Edward Amherst[7], b. 13 June, 1834; d. in Newport, 2 June, 1900; m. 1 Aug., 1860, Lucy Jane, dau. of Daniel and Lydia (Cook) Kelley of Derby; he was admitted to the bar in 1858; Asst. Clerk of the House of Representatives, Vt., 1859-61; Clerk, 1862-63; also elected Judge of the Probate Court for Orleans County; in 1872 he bought a half interest in the *Express and Standard* of Derby, and was editor for 9 years; from 1881 was in the insurance business and settled estates; was long a deacon and treasurer of the church. Ch.:

    1 *Emily Lydia*[8], b. 26 Aug., 1862; m. Axel W. Hallenborg.
    2 *Charles Edward,* b. 1 Jan., 1865; d. 28 July, 1880.
    3 *John Carlisle,* b. 6 Nov., 1868; d. 2 Feb., 1869.
    4 *Kate Maria,* b. 16 May, 1871; m. Jesse Holbrook.
ii John Brigham, b. 14 July, 1835; d. in Auburndale, Mass., 17 Oct., 1892; m. 12 April, 1864, Nancy A., dau. of Judge Isaac and Arabella (Cobb) Parker, of Coventry, Vt.; she was born there 20 Feb., 1839; res. Beebe Plain, P. Q. Ch.:
    1 *Cora Lydia*[8], b. 5 Feb., 1867; res. in Boston.
    2 *George Sawin,* b. 30 March, 1870; m. 31 March, 1897, Mary Alice Heckman; res. Newton Highlands, Mass.; is a genealogist; 4 ch.
    3 *Florence Mae,* b. 7 June, 1872; m. Harry Brown[10]. Stewart of Beebe Plain, P. Q.; he is a descendant of Eunice[5] Brigham Newton, dau. of 23.
    4 *Annie Carlisle,* b. 28 May, 1874; m. (1) Clinton W. Crandall of Woodland, Mass.; m. (2) Joseph Neal Day of Woolwich, Me.
    5 *Helen Louise,* b. 9 Nov., 1879; m. Dr. Nathaniel Niles Morse; res. Brooklyn, N. Y.
iii Persis Anne, b. 26 April, 1837; d. 13 June, 1880, in Sparta, Wis.; m. April, 1858, Capt. Martin Warner Davis of Coventry. Ch. (Davis):
    1 *Edward Warner*[8]; 2 *Frederick Everett;* 3 *Laura Brigham;* 4

CHARLES BRIGHAM, OF BOSTON   381)

LIEUTENANT J. G. CHARLE H. BRIGHAM LATE U.S.N.

*Jane Stewart; 5 Mabel Persis; 6 Carlisle Eleazer; 7 Persis
Stewart; 8 John Tyler.*
iv Thomas Tyler, b. 24 March, 1841; d. 2 Feb., 1901; m. 13 May,
    1891, Mrs. Alice (Wick) Powers.
v Martha Louise, b. 16 May, 1846; m. 12 July, 1870, Dwight C.
    Robbins. Ch. (Robbins):
    1 *Herbert Stewart*[8], b. 27 Oct., 1872.

380   JOHN MOREY[6], son of Silas[5] and Rhoda (Morey) Brigham; born in Brownington, Vt., 30 April, 1812; died ———;
married, 30 March, 1836, Maria Grow, born in Hyde Park, Vt.,
12 June 1811. Was a tanner and currier in Derby, Vt., and later
kept the " Brigham Hotel " in Derby Center.

Children, born in Brownington:
    i George Morey[7], b. 27 May, 1837; d. in Derby, where he res. a
       farmer, 10 Dec., 1879; m. 5 June, 1872, Julia Chandler, b. in
       Dorset, Vt., 10 Oct., 1852; she m. (2) Rev. Mr. Johnson of Iras-
       burg, Vt. Ch.:
       1 *John M.*[8], b. 10 Oct., 1874.
       2 *George Chandler*, b. 19 July, 1879.
    ii Silas H., b. 26 Dec., 1841; m. 14 Feb., 1868, Olive J. Merrick,
       b. in Compton, P. Q., 1 May, 1845; he is a hotelkeeper in
       Lisbon, N. H., and was county sheriff in 1892 and 1893. Ch.:
       1 *Harry S.*[8], b. 17 June, 1869; m. Florence R. Clough, b. 10
          Oct., 1869; res. Lisbon. Ch.: Fannie J.[9], b. 10 Aug., 1887.
       2 *George Merrick*, b. 31 March, 1875.
       3 *Fanny J.*, d. y.
       4 *Frank L.*, b. 23 Jan., 1879.

381   CHARLES[6], son of Silas[5] and Rhoda (Morey) Brigham;
born in Brownington, Vt., 26 Oct., 1814; died in Boston, 13 Jan.,
1900, æ. 85; married, 28 July, 1862, Mary Frances, daughter of
Samuel Adams and Lydia (Stoddard) Locke of Boston, born 15
Dec., 1828; died in Boston, 21 Jan., 1883.

He was a noted Boston Post-office employee, who entered the
service in 1837 and at the time of his retirement was the oldest
in the service in the United States; he was a faithful worker and
a most genial man.

Child, born in Boston:
    i Lieut. Charles Henry[7], b. 14 Nov., 1863; m. 29 April, 1898, Eliza-
       beth, dau. of Hugh and Elizabeth (Munroe) MacDonald; res.
       Jamaica Plain. He served in the Spanish War, on U. S. S.
       Prairie, as Senior Watch and Division Officer on blockade of Cuba
       and Porto Rico. Was in engagement resulting in destruction of
       Spanish S. S. *Alphonso XII.*, near Mariel, 5 July, 1898. He was
       commissioned Lieut., U. S. N., 23 April, 1898; resigned 28 Sept.,
       1898. Ch.: i Marion Ray, b. 5 Jan., 1902.

382   ALBERT SMITH[6], son of Silas[5] and Rhoda (Morey)
Brigham; born in Brownington, Vt., 19 Aug., 1816; died 4 Jan.,

1890; married, 11 Dec., 1847, Martha A., daughter of David G. and Mary Doe (Jenness) Merrill, born 10 March, 1823; died 5 Jan., 1883. He resided in Boston.

Children:
    i Emily Maria[7], b. 27 Feb., 1845; d. 12 Aug., 1850.
    ii Mary Upton, b. 13 Dec., 1846; m. 30 April, 1872, Charles Washington Bryant. Ch. (Bryant)
        1 *Bertha Williams*[8], b. 20 Nov., 1876.
        2 *Ethel Merrill*, b. 14 July, 1881.
    iii George Albert, b. 1 Jan., 1849; d. 12 Dec., 1849.
    iv Rhoda Martha, b. 23 Dec., 1850; d. 14 June, 1852.
    v Edmund Sanford, b. 5 Oct., 1853; m. 22 March, 1881, Martha J. Hunter; he is in the banking business; res. Dorchester, Mass. Ch.:
        1 *Grace Hunter*[8], b. 27 April, 1883; d. 31 March, 1884.
    vi Charlotte Stearns, b. 6 July, 1858; m. 3 July, 1876, Botsford Ralph Clarke. Ch. (Clarke):
        1 *Walter Ralph*[8], b. 23 June, 1877.

383 HON. ELBRIDGE G.[6], son of Aaron[5] and Charlotte (Read) Brigham; born 29 April, 1810; died ————; married (1) 10 March, 1840, Mary Mitchell, born 11 March, 1816; died 25 Jan., 1849; married (2) 4 Sept., 1850, Mattie E., daughter of Ziba Corbett of Palmyra, Mich., born 17 July, 1830. In 1832 he established himself in Monroe, Mich., as a manufacturer and dealer in furniture; held the offices of supervisor, alderman, city treasurer and mayor.

Children (by first wife), born in Monroe:
    i Mary L.[7], b. 13 Feb., 1841.
    ii Charlotte E., b. 23 Nov., 1842.
    iii Edwin, b. 1 Sept., 1846; d. 21 Oct., 1846.
    iv Emma, b. 15 March, 1848; d. 25 Jan., 1849.
Child (by second wife), born in Monroe:
    v Mattie B., b. 9 Dec., 1855.

384 MICAJAH R.[6], son of Aaron[5] and Charlotte (Read) Brigham; born in New Hampshire, 3 April, 1819; died 12 Feb., 1889; married, 10 Dec., 1845, Lucy Stowell, born in Monroe, Mich., 6 Dec., 1825; died 16 April, 1904. Resided in Monroe and Erie, Mich., and in Toledo, O.

Children, the eldest born in Monroe, others in Erie:
    i Estella[7], b. 15 Oct., 1846; m. 26 Sept., 1871, William R. Gifford, M. D., b. in Dundee, Mich., 6 May, 1843; res. Toledo, O. Ch. (Gifford), b. in Erie, Mich.:
        1 *Walter Fay*[8], b. 2 Jan., 1874.
        2 *Jessica M.*, b. 5 March, 1877.
        3 *Gertrude*, b. 13 Sept., 1881.
    ii Mary Jane, b. 7 Sept., 1849; m. 28 Dec., 1870, Frederick W. Himes, b. in Oswego, N. Y., 23 April, 1840; res. Toledo. Ch.

1 *Malcolm R.*[8], b. 16 Oct., 1871.
2 *Bessie B.*, d. y.
3 *Lottie E.*, b. 14 June, 1876.
4 *Robert A.*, b. 5 Jan., 1880.
5 *Frederick W.*, b. 29 July, 1881.
6 *Louis B.*, d. y.

iv Oshea Stowell, b. 17 Aug., 1852; m. 27 Oct., 1881, Caroline
A. Mulhollen, b. in Erie, 6 April, 1853; was grad. Ph. B., Univ. of
Mich., 1874; M. D., 1876; Ph. M., 1877; res. Toledo. Ch ·
    1 *Read Oshea*[8], b. in Toledo, 20 Dec., 1888.

v William Elbridge, b. 6 Oct., 1858; m. 17 Feb., 1882, Ida M.
Brown, b. in Woonsocket, R. I., 16 April, 1859; is in the Grain
Commission business; res. s. p., Toledo.

vi Charlotte Fay, b. 31 Dec., 1860; m. 1879, Halbert B. Warren of
Chicago, Ill.; res. Sandusky, O. Ch. (Warren):
    1 *Lucy M.*[8], b. 12 May, 1880.
    2 *Helen B.*, b. 12 Jan., 1882.
    3 *Clarence C.*, b. 1891.

vii Charles Reed, b. 4 April, 1863; m. 3 Nov., 1886, Helen K., dau.
of Benjamin and Martha (Keeney) Jones, b. 28 Aug., 1860; res.
Toledo. Ch.:
    1 *Norman R.*[8], b. 13 Sept., 1887.
    2 *Donald*, b. 5 June, 1890.

385 GEORGE[6], son of Capt. Daniel[5] and Thankful[6] (Brigham) Brigham, born in Marlboro, Mass., 19 Oct., 1784; died in
Groton, Mass., about 1868; married (1) 11 June, 1810, Betsey,
daughter of Stephen and Rebecca (Howe) Morse of Marlboro,
born 14 March, 1791; died 6 May, 1820; married (2) 20 Dec.,
1820, Margaret, daughter of William Shattuck of Groton, born 9
Sept., 1795; died 30 Aug., 1853. Was a harness-maker and resided
in Groton.

Children (by first wife), born in Groton:
661   i Betsey[7], b. 10 May, 1811.
662   ii George Dexter, b. 2 May, 1813.
663 iii Emeline, b. 18 April, 1815.
      iv Son, b. 11 Nov., 1817; d. 12 Nov., 1817.
Children (by second wife), born in Groton:
       v Margaret Ann, b. 6 Jan., 1822; m. 8 Dec., 1846, Rev. Joseph C.
Smith, b. 18 July, 1819, in Waltham, Mass.; d. 29 Dec., 1857;
was a missionary to the Sandwich Islands. Ch. (Smith)·
    1 *Robert Boynton*[8], b. 21 Oct., 1847.
    2 *William*, b. 17 Nov., 1851; d. 1 July, 1852.
    3 *Daughter*, b. 25 Sept., 1853.
664   vi Mary Loring, b. 2 Nov., 1823.
      vii William Boynton, b. 18 May, 1827; d. s. p., 1 April, 1856, at
Burlington, Vt.; m. 17 June, 1849, Pamelia Wentworth of Starks-
boro, Vt., b. 7 April, 1826; she m. (2) George W. Sipes of Galva,
Ill. Ch.:
    1 *Infant*[8], who d.
     viii Jane Laura, b. 22 Oct., 1829; res. unm., 1905, in Boston; was
a teacher.
665   ix Theodore, b. 29 June, 1833.
666   x Charles Sumner, b. 15 Sept., 1835.

386 CAPT. DANIEL⁶, son of Capt. Daniel⁵ and Thankful⁶ (Brigham) Brigham; born in Marlboro, Mass., 7 Aug., 1786; died ———; married, 27 May, 1810, Nancy, daughter of William and Elizabeth (Howe) Gates, born 19 Oct., 1790. He was living in Morse's day and inherited the tannery of his ancestor, Samuel, being the fifth Brigham owner in direct succession. Retired from business and occupied a part of the original estate of Samuel.

Children, born in Marlboro:
667   i Henry⁷, b. 4 Oct., 1811.
     ii Dexter G., b. 13 Sept., 1813; d. unm., in Pontiac, Mich., 1 March, 1852.
668 iii Dennison, b. 23 May, 1816.
     iv Daniel F., b. 11 May, 1822; m. Sarah Camfield of Cambridge, Mass.; res. in Marlboro. Ch.:
        1 *Kate O'Brien⁸*, b. 24 Aug., 1853.
        2 *William Dexter*, b. 9 Feb., 1856.
        3 *Nancy E.*, b. 2 Dec., 1858.

387 WILLIAM⁶, son of Capt. Daniel⁵ and Thankful⁶ (Brigham) Brigham; born in Marlboro, Mass., 3 Aug., 1793; died, 14 June, 1872; married, 13 April, 1816, Sophia Sawyer, born in Hudson, Mass., 19 June, 1797; died 7 Feb., 1884. Resided in Dracut, Mass.

Children:
     i Sophia A.⁷, b. 9 Oct., 1817, in Northboro, Mass.; d. 15 Nov., 1897; m. 28 Feb., 1843, Edward Taylor of Lowell and North Adams, Mass., who d. 16 Jan., 1887. Ch. (Taylor), the eldest b. in Lowell, the others in North Adams:
        1 *Edward Brigham⁸*, b. 7 Dec., 1843; m. Olive M. Goodwin. Ch.: Infant⁹, who d.
        2 *Helen S.*, b. 3 Dec., 1845; d. 1849.
        3 *Charlotte M.*, b. 9 Feb., 1847; d. 17 Oct., 1899; m. George T. Whitney. Ch. (Whitney): i Charlotte⁹; ii Adeline, who m. David N. Patterson, M. D.; iii George Brigham.
        4 *George H.*, b. 2 Oct., 1848; d. 6 April, 1887; m. E. Jane Neal. Ch.: i George⁹; ii Jennie; iii William.
        5 *Annie C.*, b. 19 Sept., 1850; res. unm., 1903, E. Greenwich, R. I.
        6 *William H.*, b. 14 Sept., 1852; m. Fannie G. Brown. Ch.: Annie E.⁹
    ii William F., b. 18 March, 1819; m. 22 June, 1843, Jane Pike, b. 1 Dec., 1822; res. Lowell, Mass.; a machinist; he has a descendant, Mrs. Henry Hartley of Brookline, Mass. Ch ·
        1 *Loella J.⁸*, b. 28 Jan., 1846.
   iii George, d. y.
    iv Charlotte M., b. in Dracut, 23 March, 1822; m. in Lowell, Mass., 4 July, 1847, George Timothy, son of Timothy Whitney; b. in Essex, Vt., 4 April, 1819; res. Lowell. Ch. (Whitney):
        1 *Lottie J.⁸*, b. 19 April, 1850; m. Frank E. Fitts; res. Somerville, Mass.
        2 *George B.*, b. 13 Feb., 1853; res. St. Paul, Minn.
        3 *Adilene S.*, b. 14 Jan., 1855; m. David N. Patterson, res. Lowell.

v George Alfred, b. in Lowell, 11 Jan., 1830; m. 25 Dec., 1863, Ellen
E. Sawyer. Ch.:
1 *Edward Sawyer*[8], b. 18 Sept., 1864.
2 *Helen Sophia*, b. 5 May, 1866; m. 9 Feb., 1893, Herbert C.
Chase.

388 WINSLOW[6], son of Capt. Daniel[5] and Thankful[6] (Brigham) Brigham; born in Marlboro, Mass., 29 May, 1795; killed by
a horse, 2 Nov., 1864; married, 27 July, 1817, Elizabeth Larkin,
who died 6 Dec., 1864. Resided in Marlboro.

Children, born in Marlboro:
  i Elizabeth G.[7], b. 20 June, 1817; m. 9 April, 1845, William Wallace
    Witherbee, son of 201; b. in M., 21 Feb., 1821; d. 11 June, 1888.
    Ch. (Witherbee), b. in Marlboro:
    1 *Ellen Howe*[8], b. 22 Feb., 1846; m. 1868, Edwin L. Knicker-
      bocker of Flint, Mich.
    2 *Frank Foristall*, b. 27 Sept., 1848; d. 9 Oct., 1851.
    3 *Elizabeth Winslow*, b. 21 Sept., 1850; res. Marlboro.
    4 *Frederick Wallace*, b. 15 Nov., 1852; m. 1875, J——— Ball;
      was a Ry. conductor, and killed, 17 Jan., 1890.
    5 *Mary Ide Brigham*, b. 8 Oct., 1856; res. Marlboro.
    6 *Sarah Dennis*, b. 30 Oct., 1858; res. Marlboro.
    7 *Anne Fisher*, b. 24 Sept., 1861; res. Marlboro.
    8 *Herbert Eugene*, b. 16 Jan., and d. 4 Feb., 1864.
 ii Anne Fisher, b. 16 Dec., 1821; d. 8 April, 1881; m. 15 May, 1845,
    Samuel Boyd, b. 3 June, 1815; d. 19 Sept., 1892; res. Marlboro.
    Ch. (Boyd). b. in Marlboro:
    1 *Delia Bucklin*[8], b. 1 Nov., 1846; m. 22 Oct., 1873, William
      Henry Aldrich of Newbury St., Boston. Ch. (Aldrich): i
      Roy S.[9], b. 19 Feb., 1879; ii Margery, who d. y.
    2 *Annie Frothingham*, b. 15 Oct., 1848; m. 1871, Hon. Samuel
      C. Darling of Somerville, Mass.
    3 *Florence Augusta*, b. 28 July, 1850; res. Marlboro.
    4 *Lydia Sophia*, b. 18 June, 1854; res. Marlboro.
    5 *Carrie Warren*, b. 25 May, 1855; d. 26 Feb., 1858.
    6 *Henry Irving*, b. 18 Dec., 1859; d. 24 March, 1860.
    7 *Fanny Brigham*, b. 2 Dec., 1862; d. 7 March, 1871.
669 iii Eugene Winslow, b. 21 Dec., 1833.

389 FREEMAN[6], son of Capt. Daniel[5] and Thankful[6] (Brigham) Brigham; born in Marlboro, Mass., 4 May., 1800; died 1894;
married, Harriet P. Gilson of Cambridge, Mass; resided there.

Children, born in Cambridge:
  i George W.[7], b. 19 July, 1827; d. in C., 13 April, 1872; m. Olivia
    E., dau. of Charles Carpenter of Derby, Vt. Ch.:
    1 *Frank Benjamin*[8], b. 23 Dec., 1853.
 ii Caroline C., m. 5 Dec., 1869, J. Henry, son of James H. White of
    Cambridge.
iii Lebina (or Lavina) S., b. 6 July, 1834.
 iv Harriet E., b. 13 May, 1836; m. Henry Blake, and moved West.
  v Webster.

390 CHARLOTTE⁶, daughter of Capt. Daniel⁵ and Thankful⁶ (Brigham) Brigham; born in Marlboro, Mass., 1 June, 1802; died there, 6 Sept., 1867; married, 19 May, 1825, Capt. Thaddeus, son of Jonah and Betty (Cranston) Howe of Marlboro, (and grandson of 117), born 12 May, 1799; died 6 Sept., 1872.

Children (Howe), born in Marlboro:

   i Harriet⁷, b. 1 Feb., 1826; d. 2 Jan., 1862, s. p.; m. Osborn Stearns.
   ii Emily B., b. 25 Feb., 1827; d. 12 Sept., 1848.
   iii Edwin, b. 6 Nov., 1828; d. 3 June, 1829.
   iv Pruman E., b. 9 Feb., 1830; d. 11 April, 1902; m. Mary McCracken. Ch.:
      1 *Mary L.*⁸, m. Charles E. Dorr, and has 3 ch.
      2 *Edwin L.;* 3 *Herbert H.,* d. y.; 4 *Alice M.*
   v Amariah, b. 29 Oct., 1831; d. 10 May, 1896; m. Ellen M. Stowe. Ch.:
      1 *Clarence E.*⁸*;* 2 *Lizzie M.*
   vi Laura A., b. 27 April, 1833; m. John Johnston.
   vii John, b. 14 Oct., 1834; m. Celesty Leavit.
   viii Heman S., b. 14 April, 1836; d. 19 Feb., 1841.
   ix Cranston, b. 19 Feb., 1839; d. 26 March, 1841.
   x Rufus, b. 27 May, 1841; d. 2 Sept., 1889.
   xi Cranston, b. 17 Sept., 1842.
   xii Charlotte E., b. 15 Jan., 1844; m. C. M. Twichel.
   xiii Amy S., b. 2 Feb., 1846; d. 21 March, 1865.

391 HARRIET⁶, daughter of Capt. Daniel⁵ and Thankful⁶ (Brigham) Brigham; born in Marlboro, Mass., 4 Dec., 1804; died there, March, 1889; married, 1 Jan., 1826, Jabez S. Witherbee, (son of 201), born in Southboro, Mass., 12 Sept., 1802; died 2 Dec., 1862. Resided in Marlboro where he was a Justice of the Peace and prominent citizen, and kept the " Williams Tavern."

Children (Witherbee), born in Marlboro:

   i George Witherbee⁷, b. 27 Dec., 1827; d. in San Francisco, 6 Jan., 1851, unm.
   ii Harriet Maria, b. 21 Feb., 1830; d. 19 March, 1859; m. 1856, Henry O. Russell.
   iii John Davis, b. 11 Feb., 1834; d. 10 June, 1836.
   iv Lorenzo F., b. 18 Dec., 1836; d. 8 Feb., 1837.
   v Charles Freeman, b. 29 April, 1840; d. in Marlboro, 16 Dec., 1883; enlisted in Marlboro Cornet Band with the 13th Mass. Vols., in 1861; m. Adelaide, dau. of Lambert Bigelow, b. 3 Aug., 1837. Ch.:
      1 *Ella Frances*⁸, b. 10 June, 1864; m. 13 Oct., 1889, Arthur William Furlong of Boston, b. 24 March, 1867; res. Somerville; 1 ch.
      2 *Hattie E.,* b. 16 July, 1867; d. 28 Feb., 1882.
   vi Francis Brigham, b. 25 Feb., 1842; d. 6 Feb., 1848.

392 LAURA ANN⁶, daughter of Capt. Daniel⁵ and Thankful⁶ (Brigham) Brigham; born in Marlboro, Mass., 17 March, 1807;

died in Shrewsbury, Mass., 13 Dec., 1882; married 31 March, 1828, Capt. Jesse Perry of .Sudbury, Mass., who moved to Shrewsbury, where he died, 10 April, 1807, æ. 81.

Children (Perry), born in Shrewsbury:

i Mary Elizabeth[7], b. 17 Dec., 1828; m. John S. Stevens of Marlboro, in 1846. Ch. (Stevens):
  1 *Eunice*[8].
  2 *Laura,* m. Charles Spearel of Marlboro.
  3 *Infant,* d. y.

ii Lucy Ann, b. 1 April, 1831; m. Samuel I. Howe of Shrewsbury, in 1859. Ch. (Howe):
  1 *Jennie*[8]; 2 *Frank P.;* 3 *Mary,* m. William H. Case.

iii Caroline Williams, b. 9 April, 1833; m. Stephen A. Reed of Shrewsbury, in 1851; he d. 18 Jan., 1904. Ch. (Reed):
  1 *Bessie*[8]; 2 *Annie;* both d. s. p.

iv George Harrison, b. 30 Aug., 1836; m. (1) Anna Batcheller of Northboro, in 1864; m. (2) Laurilla Moore. Ch.: 3 who d. y.

v Laura Brigham, b. 14 Dec., 1840; d. 1891; m. 1882, Samuel I. Howe of Shrewsbury.

vi Franklin Jesse, b. 28 June, 1843; enlisted Co. H, 25th Mass. Vols., and was killed, Cold Harbor, 3 June, 1864.

vii Ella Arbella, b. 14 Oct., 1845; m. 1869, Everett Walker of Shrewsbury. Ch. (Walker):
  1 *Frederic*[8]; 2 *Herbert;* 3 *Alice;* and 1 d. y.

393   COL. AARON[6], son of Capt. Aaron[5] and Betty (Barnes) Brigham, born in Marlboro, Mass., 20 March, 1798; died there, 1874; married, 9 Jan., 1821, Sally, daughter of Josiah and Hepzibeth (Collins) Fay of Marlboro and Southboro, born there, 30 July, 1801; died in Marlboro, 26 May, 1871. Was assessor in 1852.

Children, born in Marlboro:

i Maria E.[7], b. 27 May, 1821; m. (1) in M., 6 April, 1842, Perry G., son of Joseph Wood; b. in Upton, Mass.; d. in Marlboro, 29 June, 1856; m. (2) 27 Nov., 1858, Anthony Bull. Ch. (Wood):
  1 *Emily M.*[8], who d. y.
  2 *Clara E.,* b. 10 May, 1845.
  3 *Alice A.,* b. 3 April, 1848.

ii Abbie Howe, b. 23 June, 1823; m. 23 Nov., 1847, Isaac Conant of Dover, Ill. Ch. (Conant):
  1 *Herbert*[8]; 2 *Lelia;* 3 *Fremont.*

670 iii John Winslow, b. 4 Sept., 1825; m. Mary Putnam.

iv Sarah Hepsibah, b. 6 July, 1829; m. 22 June, 1853, Elisha Gore.

v Orissa Amber, b. 30 April, 1833; m. 21 July, 1881, John Kimball of South Braintree, Mass., who d. 21 Nov., 1883.

vi Aaron Augustus, b. 27 May, 1836; m. and res. Minn. Enlisted in Co. F, 8th Minn. Vols.; was killed in the battle of Murfreesboro, 7 Dec., 1864.

vii Caroline Augusta, b. 13 Aug., 1838; m. 8 June, 1859, Francis C. Curtis of Dudley, Mass.; res. Marlboro. Ch. (Curtis):
  1 *Chester Wellington*[8], b. 1862.
  2 *Harry Millis,* b. 1868.

3 *Mary Willis*, b. 1870.
viii Henry Harrison, b. 20 Aug., 1840; d. 19 Nov., 1885; m. 31
Oct., 1865, Charlotte E. Woodbury of Chicago, Ill.
ix Ellen Althea, b. 20 July, 1843; d. 22 Sept., 1881; m. April, 1865,
Frank H. Lowell of Bangor, Me. Ch. (Lowell):
1 *Herbert*[8]; 2 *Edward;* 3 *Grace;* 4 *Charles.*

394 JANE[6], daughter of Maj. Jedediah[5] and Lydia (Boyd)
Brigham, born in Marlboro, Mass., 23 April, 1798; died in Norwood, Mass., 26 Jan., 1866; married, 19 April, 1819, Lyman, son
of Gershom Bigelow, born in Marlboro, 25 April, 1795; died 13
March, 1842. He moved to Boxboro, Mass., where was merchant,
selectman, Representative, Postmaster, etc.

Children (Bigelow), born in Boxboro:
i Jane E.[7], b. 5 Feb., 1820; d. in Norwood, Mass., 13 Feb., 1888;
m. (1) James Brown; m. (2) Hon. Joseph Day; 1 ch., d. y.
ii Mary Louisa, b. 15 Dec., 1821; d. in Norwood, 29 March, 1888;
m. Josiah W. Talbot. Ch. (Talbot):
1 *Emma*[8], m. Stanford Mitchell of So. Boston.
2 *Mary*, m. Oscar Winship.
iii Augusta B., b. 10 Sept., 1823; d. 1 Sept., 1852; m. George B.
Talbot. Ch. (Talbot):
1 *Augusta*[8], m. M. W. Sanborn of Norwood.
iv Caroline, b. 29 Oct., 1825; d. s. p., 29 Jan., 1851; m. Cephas Hoar.
v Lyman Waldo, b. 7 March, 1828; d. 6 Dec., 1886; m. Catherine
Howard; a prominent merchant at Norwood. Ch.:
1 *Erwin*[8]; 2 *Edgar;* 3 *Waldo;* 4 *Alfred;* 5 *Lyman;* 6 *Caroline;* 7 *William A.;* 8 *Bernard;* 9 *Gertrude.*
vi Lydolf Willis, b. 16 Aug., 1836; d. 1856.

395 ASHLEY[6], son of Maj. Jedediah[5] and Lydia (Boyd)
Brigham; born in Marlboro, Mass., 9 Oct., 1804; died there, 14
May, 1881; married, 14 May, 1825, Mary B., daughter of Ephraim
Bigelow, born in Marlboro, 12 Aug., 1802; died there, 3 Aug.,
1857. Was a stone mason and resided in Marlboro.

Children, born in Marlboro:
i William Emerson[7], b. 19 Nov., 1826; d. unm., 12 Dec., 1847.
ii Lydia, b. 28 May, 1828; m. 6 April, 1853, Lewis H., son of
Benjamin W. Allen; b. in So. Vernon, Mass., 28 Nov., 1826; res.
Rockbottom, Mass. Ch. (Allen), b. in Rockbottom:
1 *Charles H.*[8], b. 27 Nov., 1865; res. Marlboro.
2 *Lewis H.*, b. 8 Aug., 1855; d. 24 Aug., 1855.
671 iii Humphrey, b. 5 Jan., 1830.
iv Marilla, b. 1 Sept., 1832; m. 9 Oct., 1850, Henry Franklin, son
of Henry Morse; b. in Marlboro, 27 Oct., 1826; res. and d.
there, 21 Sept., 1878; she res. Peterboro, N. H. Ch. (Morse),
b. in Marlboro:
1 *Charles E.*[8], b. 12 Jan., 1854; d. 20 March, 1854.
2 *Clara J.*, b. 4 July, 1856; m. 9 Dec., 1886, Forrest G. Field,
Jr., b. 20 Feb., 1856; res. Peterboro, N. H.
v Mariette, b. 22 July, 1834; d. 2 Feb., 1885; m. 28 June, 1854,

William Barnes, Jr., b. in Marlboro, 1828; res. there. Ch. (Barnes),
b. in Marlboro:

1 *George H.*, d. y.
2 *George H.*, b. 18 Jan., 1858; m. 1895, Nellie R., dau. of David
Heywood; res. Marlboro.
3 *Stella B.*, b. 29 Dec., 1864; m. 1891, Johnson P., son of Benjamin Shaw; b. in Nova Scotia, 1864; res. Marlboro.
4 *Elizabeth*, b. 25 Dec., 1868; m. 6 April, 1889, Alfred, probably
son of William H. Brigham, who was son of 358; b. in
Marlboro, 3 Aug., 1865; res. there. Ch. (Brigham): i Chester Albert, b. in Marlboro, 11 March, 1893; ii Lester Alfred,
b. 11 March, 1893.
5 *Marion*, b. 16 Oct., 1871; m. 1898, Edward Corbett of Southboro, Mass. Ch. (Corbett): i Myra P.; ii Mildred E.
vi Ashley, b. 19 April, 1837; m. 15 Nov., 1891, Martha E., dau.
of Cyrus and Cynthia (Bemis) Brigham, 688; res. s. p., a merchant in Marlboro.
vii Octavia, b. 17 Jan., 1842; res. unm., Marlboro.

396 JOEL⁶, son of Maj. Jedediah⁵ and Lydia (Boyd) Brigham; born in Marlboro, Mass., 16 Dec., 1808; died there, 26
July, 1892; married, 1 Jan., 1835, Lydia S., daughter of Capt.
Job Dickinson of Northfield, Mass.; born 18 April, 1811; died
14 March, 1854. He was a merchant in Marlboro, where resided;
the male line is extinct.

Children, born in Marlboro:
i Stella Morton⁷, b. 25 Jan., 1836; d. 22 July, 1854.
ii Flora Holton, b. 8 Sept., 1838; d. 25 Oct., 1865.
iii Julia Porter, b. 7 Aug., 1841; res. unm., in Marlboro.
iv Fanny Elnora, b. 6 March, 1846; m. 30 Jan., 1873, Oliver Hawes;
s. p.
v Henrietta Marsh, b. 1 Aug., 1848; at Mt. Holyoke College in
1868; res. unm., in Marlboro.

397 WILLIAM PITT⁶, son of Maj. Jedediah⁵ and Lydia
(Boyd) Brigham, born in Marlboro, Mass., 30 Aug., 1811; died
there, 10 Feb., 1884; married, 9 April, 1835, Lavinia, daughter of
Dr. John Baker, born in Marlboro, 30 Dec., 1815; died there Feb.,
1907. Was a merchant and resided in Marlboro, Boxboro and West
Acton, Mass.

Children, born in Marlboro:
672 i Harriette Augusta⁷, b. 29 Jan., 1836.
673 ii Henrietta Augusta, twin to Harriette.
674 iii Henry Augustine, b. 21 Aug., 1837.
iv Helen Adelaide, b. 19 Oct., 1839; m. Allan Dexter Howe. Ch.
(Howe), b. in Marlboro:
1 *Bertha M.*, b. 20 June, 1862.
2 *Alice Lavinia*, b. 2 Dec., 1866; m. William K. Winchester of
Brighton, Mass. Ch. (Winchester): i Fitch; ii Rosalind.
v William Frank, b. 4 April, 1842; d. in Washington, D. C., 18
July, 1864; was Corp. in Co. F, 13th Mass. Inf., and served 3
years in the Civil War.

vi Albert Quincy, b. 12 March, 1848; d. 24 Sept., 1849.
675 vii Alfred Adams, twin to Albert.
viii Emma Baker, b. 24 Oct., 1849; m. Herbert W. Brigham, son of 584.
ix Edwin Eugene, b. 15 Nov., 1855; m. 20 Dec., 1882, Hattie I. Johnson; an engineer and res. Marlboro.

398 JAMES MADISON[6], son of Artemas[5] and Lydia (Brigham) Brigham; born in Bridgton, Me., 14 March, 1805; died in Dorchester, Mass., 11 Dec., 1895; married in Boston, 15 Nov., 1832, Mary Frances, daughter of Daniel and Mary (Adams) Sawin (who lived in Milton, Mass.), born 9 Dec., 1812; died 25 July, 1893. He lived for a great many years in Bumstead Pl., Boston, opposite Park Street Church.

Children, born in Boston:
    i Mary Emma[7], b. 28 Oct., 1834; d. 1 April, 1859.
    ii James Henry, b. 17 Aug., 1840; d. 2 March, 1868.
676 iii William Dexter, b. 17 Oct., 1851.

399 SAMUEL[6], ·son of Fortunatus[5] and Martha (Barnes) Brigham; born in Northboro, Mass., 20 Sept., 1796; died ———; married Polly (Mary) Newton, born 7 May, 1798. Resided in Binghamton, N. Y.

Children, born in Binghamton:
    i Eunice Johnson[7], b. 6 Dec., 1826.
    ii Jane Electa, b. 17 Jan., 1829.
    iii Samuel Leander, b. 19 Aug., 1830.
    iv Mary Frances, b. 30 Nov., 1832.
    v William Edward, b. 14 March, 1835.
    vi Martin Gilson, b. 9 Feb., 1839.
    vii Lois Genevieve, b. 5 May, 1843.

400 MARTIN[6], son of Fortunatus[5] and Martha (Barnes) Brigham; born in Northboro, Mass., 25 Aug., 1799; died in Springfield, Mass., 1882; married (1) Mary Barnes, born 15 April, 1799; married (2) Eunice Gates, born 3 Oct., 1802. Resided in Palmer, Mass.

Children, born in Palmer:
    i Mary A.[7], b. 16 May, 1823.
    ii Harriet E., b. 4 Aug., 1824.
    iii Charles L., b. 27 Jan., 1827.
677 iv Lincoln Lafayette, b. 9 March, 1829.
    v William M., b. 12 April, 1832.
    vi Henry A., b. 18 Aug., 1835; was living in Springfield, in 1905.
    vii Lorenzo D., b. 10 Aug., 1837.

401 LINCOLN[6], son of Fortunatus[5] and Martha (Barnes) Brigham; born in Northboro, Mass., 13 May, 1803; died 16 May, 1883, in Marlboro, Mass.; married, 24 April, 1832, Susan A.

WILLIAM PITT BRIGHAM, OF MARLBORO (397)

Maynard, born in Shrewsbury, Mass., 3 April, 1811; died 15 May, 1885. Resided in Marlboro; the male line is extinct.

Children, born in Marlboro:
    i Sophia E.[7], b. 15 May, 1834; d. *ibid.*
    ii George A., b. 6 Oct., 1835; d. 20 Sept., 1886; m. 26 May, 1856, Nellie D., dau. of R. W. Flagg; b. in Sutton, Mass., 7 Dec., 1835; res. in Marlboro, where a hardware merchant. Ch., b. in Marlboro:
        1 *Leon E.*[8], b. 4 Dec., 1857; d. unm., 27 Feb., 1888; a jeweler.
    iii Ella Abba A.[7], b. 21 Jan., 1849; m. Albert E. Leighton.

402   EDWARD LEONARD[6], son of Fortunatus[5] and Martha (Barnes) Brigham; born in Marlboro, Mass., 8 Oct., 1806; died in Worcester, Mass., 13 Sept., 1898; married (1) 13 Sept., 1831, Eliza Brewer of New York, born 29 May, 1811; died in Worcester, 20 Feb., 1840; married (2) 25 April, 1844, Susan H. Sawyer of Berlin, Mass., born 13 Aug., 1818; died 31 Dec., 1872; married (3) 27 Jan., 1875, Annie J. (Tarlton) Sawyer, born 2 Aug., 1823; died 26 Dec., 1905; was a nurse in the Civil War, 4th N. H. Regt., and served until the end; was with Sherman on his " March to the Sea." Mr. Brigham resided in Worcester, where he learned the tailor trade, and was the first dealer in ready-made clothing. He was the senior Odd Fellow of Worcester.

Children (by first wife), born in Worcester:
    i Walter A. C.[7], b. 19 July, 1832; d. in New York, 6 Jan., 1878; m. 1864, Sarah H. E. Wood, who d. March, 1900.
    ii Lucian T., b. 29 June, 1835; d. 13 May, 1836.
    iii Eliza A., b. 31 Jan., 1837; m. 17 May, 1860, George E. Barrett, b. 14 Feb., 1834; res. Worcester. Ch. (Barrett):
        1 *Emma S.*[8], b. 10 July, 1868.
Children (by second wife), born in Worcester:
    iv Eleanor L., b. 9 April, 1847.
    v Edward L., b. 2 May, 1850; d. 31 March, 1906; m. 2 June, 1874, Teresa I. Davis, b. 14 May, 1845. Ch.:
        1 *Olive D.*[8], b. 15 Dec., 1875.

403   HON. and MAJOR ASA[6], son of Lewis[5] and Mary (Rice) Brigham, born in Marlboro, Mass., 31 Aug., 1788; died in Washington, Texas, 3 July, 1844; married (1) Jan., 1811, in Framingham, Mass., Elizabeth S. Babcock, who died in Brazoria County, Texas, in 1833; married (2) Ann ———, who married (2) ——— Walker of Austin, Texas.

In his youth he learned the tailor's trade. He settled in Framingham at the age of 21, where he bought a house and built a shop in 1809, which he sold in 1812, removing to Jaffrey, N. H., where he was tavern-keeper; was burned out 16 Dec., 1816, and, embarrassed financially, removed to Alexandria, La. In 1831 removed to Texas, and in the war between Texas and Mexico he served as commissary to the army; was one of the signers of the Declaration of Independence of Texas and early became Treasurer of the Republic. This office he held until his death, which occurred prior to the annexation of Texas to the United States.

Children (by first wife):

    i Adeliza Lewis[7], b. in ˙Framingham, 15 Dec., 1811; m. Edwin Richeson. Ch. (Richeson):

        1 *Sue Elizabeth*[8], m. 12 Nov., 1855, Hon. John Hancock of Austin, Tex. Ch. (Hancock): Edwin Brigham[9], b. 26 Oct., 1856.

    ii Samuel, b. 1814; res. Matagorda, Tex.

    iii Benjamin Rice, b. Jaffrey, N. H., 21 April, 1815; slain in battle of St. Jacinto, on his 21st birthday, 21 April, 1836.

404 OTIS[6], son of Jotham[5] and Lucy (Thompson) Brigham; born in Marlboro, Mass., 8 Oct., 1788; died there, 1833; married Lucy Stratton, who died Dec., 1830. Resided in Marlboro.

Children, born in Marlboro:

    i Mary Ann[7], b. 22 July, 1818; m. (1) George Emery, son of Sampson Bailey; b. in Sterling, Mass., 3 April, 1815; d. July, 1840; m. (2) George Gates of Stow, Mass.; res. Bolton, Mass. Ch. (Bailey):

        1 *Harriet M.*[8], m. John Dolan.

        Ch. (Gates):

        2 *Lyman B.;* 3 *Lucy S.*

    ii Lucy Jane, b. 30 June, 1819; d. May, 1880; m. Lyman Coolidge, who d. June, 1887; res. Bolton. Ch. (Coolidge):

        1 *Walter*[8], b. 28 May, 1844; d. 2 June, 1903; m. 3 June, 1869, Sarah A. Ryder of Bolton. Ch.: i Walter R.[9], b. 30 July, 1870; ii Sarah W., b. 6 Dec., 1873; iii Holden L., b. 19 Oct., 1876; iv Ruth P., b. 18 Jan., 1879; v John E., b. 13 Aug., 1882; vi Lucy J., b. 17 Dec., 1884; res. in Hudson, Mass.

    iii John H., b. 20 Aug., 1821; d. unm., 19 June, 1881; interred in Hudson.

    iv Harriet S., b. 14 Sept., 1823; was a teacher in Auburn, Kan.; res. 1905, Hudson.

    v George H., b. 19 Oct., 1825; m. Anna Lucas of Bolton; res. Hammoton, N. J. Ch.:

        1 *Le Grand S.*[8], b. 1850; res. Bolton.

        2 *Fanny*, b. 1852.

        3 *William*, b. 1854.

        4 *George*, b. 1859.

    vi Elizabeth A., b. 26 Oct., 1827; d. ————————; m. James S. Welsh, who d.; res. Hudson. Ch. (Welsh):

        1 *Fred O.*[8]; 2 *Annella E.;* 3 *Winifred*, who d.; 4 *Lucy D.;* Two d. y.

405 HENRY[6], son of Jotham[5] and Lucy (Thompson) Brigham; born in Marlboro, Mass., 3 May, 1790; died in Abington, Mass., 9 March, 1867; married (1) 7 May, 1812, Mary, daughter of Col. Aaron Hobart,* born in Abington, 3 Sept., 1787; died 27

* Whose wife was a widow of a brother of President Adams; Col. Hobart was the first manufacturer of brass cannon in America.

May, 1853; married (2) 31 May, 1854, Abigail S. Hersey. Was a clothier and resided in Abington.

Children (by first wife), born in Abington:
678   i Henry Hobart⁷, b. 22 Jan., 1813.
    ii Joseph W., b. 2 Oct., 1814; d. s. p., in New Orleans, La., 1886.
    iii Charles, b. and d. 1816.

406 JOHN⁶, son of Jotham⁵ and Lucy (Thompson) Brigham; born in Marlboro, Mass., 1 Aug., 1792; died in Abington, Mass., 19 Sept., 1831; married, 12 Nov., 1817, Ruth, daughter of Joseph Winslow born in Pembroke, Mass., 16 Dec., 1797; died in Bridgewater, Mass., 29 Oct., 1869; (she m. (2) Cotton Graves of Sunderland, Mass., and had 2 daus.). He was a machinist and resided in Abington.

Children, born in Abington:
    i John⁷, b. 31 Dec., 1818; res. unm., in 1870, in Bridgewater.
    ii Charles, b. 2 April, 1820; d. April, 1822.
    iii Charles Lee, b. 10 Sept., 1823; d. 26 Nov., 1837.
    iv Susan Baker, b. 26 Sept., 1825; m. 24 Dec., 1846, Henry Thomas, son of Howard and Lucia (Harding) Keith; b. 27 Oct., 1820; d. in Bridgewater, 19 May, 1853.

407 HASTINGS⁶, son of Jotham⁵ and Lucy (Thompson) Brigham; born in Marlboro, Mass., 4 Aug., 1794; died 15 July, 1865; married, 30 Jan., 1821, Nancy, daughter of Jonathan Spear of Hartland, Vt., born 17 Feb., 1796; died 23 Feb., 1843. Resided in Marlboro.

Children, born in Marlboro:
679   i Charles Hastings⁷, b. 1 June, 1822.
680   ii William Eustace, b. 10 Oct., 1823.
681   iii Nancy Sophia, b. 12 Sept., 1825.
    iv Abigail C., b. 26 Nov., 1827; m. Gamaliel Fisher; res. Marlboro.
682   v Henry O., b. 2 Sept., 1830.
    vi Andrew J., b. 4 Feb., 1832; m. Elizabeth Brown; res. Ossining, N. Y.
    vii Benjamin F., b. 7 Oct., 1834; d. 20 July, 1854.
    viii Lucy R., b. 26 Oct., 1836; m. John Brown; res. Marlboro. Ch. (Brown):
      1 *Emma*⁸.
    ix Mary F., b. 25 Dec., 1838; res. Ossining.
    x Elizabeth M., b. 15 Feb., 1843; res. Ossining.

408 SOPHIA⁶, daughter of Jotham⁵ and Lucy (Thompson) Brigham; born in Marlboro, Mass., 11 July, 1796; died in Sudbury, Mass., 22 May, 1878; married, 5 Dec., 1817, Mark, son of Josiah Fay, born in Southboro, Mass., 29 Jan., 1793; died in Marlboro, 20 June, 1876. Settled in Marlboro, where was Town Treasurer, Asst. Treasurer of Savings Bank and Pres't. of Fire Insurance Co.

Children (Fay), born in Marlboro:
  i Harriet Hastings[7], b. 11 June, 1818; d. unm., 2 April 1885.
  ii William Howe, b. 13 June, 1820; d. 1897; m. Sophia, dau. of Robert Fowler; a Ry. Official in Marlboro. Ch ·
    1 *Effie*[8], d. y.
    2 *Emma S.*, m. James Doak of Belfast, Me.
  iii Charles Lewis, b. 29 Sept., 1822; m. Olive C. Brigham, dau. of 354.
  iv Sidney Granville, b. 17 June, 1825; d. in Boston, 1882; m. Olive, dau. Daniel Hill; banker of Marlboro. Ch.:
    1 *Florence*[8], m. George A. Loring of Boston.
    2 *Mark;* 3 *Henry;* 4 *Everett.*
  v Eliza Jane, b. 24 Oct., 1827; m. Thomas Corey of Marlboro. Ch. (Corey):
    1 *Edwin*[8]*;* 2 *Eliza;* 3 *Blanche*, m. C. F. Holyoke, son of 673.
  vi Caroline Sophia, b. 21 Dec., 1829; m. Edmund Blake of Stoughton, Mass. Ch. (Blake):
    1 *Walter*[8]*;* 2 *Fanny;* 3 *Mary.*
  vii Charlotte Amanda, b. 10 Oct., 1832; m. George N. Cate of Marlboro; 1 ch., which d. y.

409 COL. CHARLES[6], son of Capt. Charles[5] and Susanna (Baylis) Brigham; born in Grafton, Mass., 22 May, 1799; died there, 22 Sept., 1871; married, 17 April, 1826, Anna E., daughter of Capt. Pierpont[6] and Anna (Warren) Brigham, (186), who died 15 June, 1895. He resided in Grafton on a tract of his ancestor's estate, farmed and settled estates, wrote wills, etc., and surveyed land; also acted officially in the town business. Male line is extinct.

Children, born in Grafton:
  i Josephine Maria[7], b. 1 Aug., 1827; d. 16 Nov., 1853.
  ii Ellen Augusta, b. 25 June, 1829; d. 4 Feb., 1832.
  iii Charles Pierpont, b. 10 July, 1831; d. 13 Feb., 1832.
  iv Sarah Prentice, b. 22 Jan., 1833; representative of the Lend a Hand Club in distributing reading matter through the South to the poor.
  v Anna Eliza, b. 6 March, 1835; d. 4 Feb., 1862; m. 1 June, 1859, Hon. Jonathan H., son of Liberty Wood; b. in Grafton, 10 Aug., 1822; a merchant in Grafton, and held many town offices; was Rep. in 1868, Senator in 1871; first Supt. of the Dummy Ry. Ch. (Wood):
    1 *Anna Eliza*[8], b. in Grafton, 21 Jan., 1861.
  vi Susan Baylis, b. 24 May, 1837; m. 1860, William F. Merrifield, son of 574; res. s. p., Brookline, Mass.
  vii Augusta Louisa, b. 7 Feb., 1841; a teacher in Boston.
  viii Mary Ellen, b. 31 Oct., 1844; a teacher.

410 HON. WILLIAM[6], son of Capt. Charles[5] and Susanna (Baylis) Brigham, born in Grafton, Mass., 26 Sept., 1806; died 9 July, 1869, from overwork; interred in Mt. Auburn; married, 11 June, 1840, Margaret Austin, daughter of Isaac and Mary (Austin) Brooks of Charlestown, Mass., born 6 July, 1817; died in Brookline, Mass., 1 Feb., 1886. She was descended from Thomas

Brooks, who emigrated from Suffolk County, England, to Watertown in 1630; also descended from the Tufts, Boutwell and Boylston families of Massachusetts.

Mr. Brigham graduated from Harvard Coll. A. B., 1829; read law with Hon. George Morey of Boston; admitted to Suffolk Bar in 1832, and subsequently to that of the U. S. Supreme Court on motion of Daniel Webster; settled in Boston as a lawyer and attained to eminence. He represented Boston in the General Court in the years 1834-'36, inclusive and in 1841 and 1849; in 1856 was a member of the Republican National Convention in Philadelphia, and was therefore, one of the founders of the Republican Party. He appeared as a reviewer in the *North American Review* and in the *Christian Examiner,* and made an address at the two hundredth centennial of Marlboro, 13 June, 1860; he compiled the Laws of Plymouth Colony; was a member of the Massachusetts Historical Society; delivered addresses before the Worcester County Agricultural Society and the Westboro Agricultural Society, 1855 and 1859, respectively; at the centennial celebration of his native town, in 1836, he gave the address of the day. He was six feet two inches in height, and well proportioned. His summer home was on the Grafton estate.

Children, born in Boston:
  i William Tufts[7], b. 24 May, 1841; grad. Harvard Coll., A. B., 1862; A. M., 1864; with Horace Mann, made a scientific exploration of the Hawaiian Islands in 1865, discovering many new plants; became professor in Vahu Coll.; resigned Oct., 1865, to make explorations in India and China. Was admitted to the bar in 1867, and practiced law in Boston; was instructor in Botany in Harvard Coll., 1868-69; 6 years on Boston School Board, and instituted systematic instruction in drawing; introduced Sargent method of Anthropometry now in use in colleges; removed to Honolulu, 1888, where in charge of Bishop Museum of Ethnology; is F. A. A. of A. & S., California Academy of Science, and Philadelphia Academy of Natural Science, etc.; has published, among other things, *Guatemala, the Land of the Quetzal, Volcanic Manifestations in New England, Hawaiian Feature Work,* etc.
683 ii Charles Brooks, b. 17 Jan., 1845.
  iii Edward Austin, b. 23 Feb., 1846; m. 5 April, 1876, Anne De Wolf Bartlett. Went to Lewiston, Me., in 1868, to learn cotton spinning, and after 3 years went to Europe and was appointed agent in the U. S. by Higgins & Co., mfrs. of Cotton Machinery, Manchester, Eng.; went to India, 1875, to build and fit up a large cotton mill; is now in business in Boston, residing in Grafton. Ch.:
    1 *Caroline W.*[8], b. 21 May, 1877.
  iv Mary Brooks, b. 26 Dec., 1851; m. 6 May, 1875, McPherson, son of Ben Henri Le Moyne, banker of Montreal, Can.; res. Brookline, Mass., and Isle Aux Graus, Can. Ch. (Le Moyne):
    1 *Charles*[8], b. 13 June, 1876; large sheep owner, Idaho.

2 *Margaret Brigham*, b. 1 Feb., 1880; m. 8 April, 1905, Stafford Wentworth of Cambridge, Mass.
3 *Edith B.*, b. 8 April, 1882.
4 *Henry*, b. 17 Jan., 1884; in Harvard Coll., class 1907; a noted athlete.
5 *Frances Moseley*, b. 8 Dec., 1891.
v Arthur Austin, b. 8 June, 1857; m. ————; res. Weston, Mass.

411 NICHOLAS[6] H., son of Capt. Charles[5] and Susanna (Baylis) Brigham; born in Grafton, Mass., 2 Oct., 1808; died there, s. p., 10 Nov., 1903; married in 1838, Sarah E., daughter of Hon. Samuel Wood of Grafton.

He was the oldest resident of Grafton at the time of his death. On his 94th birthday, it was said of him that " physically and mentally he is more alert, erect and vigorous than many men of seventy-five years. His face is scarcely wrinkled, being especially full. His voice is strong and his figure straight and tall. . . . His hearing and eyesight are especially excellent. He is fond of the open air and an inveterate walker in suitable weather."

He engaged in the boot and shoe business in Boston when he came of age, and later went to New Orleans where he was successful in the commission and shipping business, dealing with houses in the north. Soon after 1850 he went to New York and for 40 years thereafter conducted one of the large shipping concerns of that city. He retired 31 Dec., 1889, to Grafton to spend the rest of his days. He was the oldest person present at the B. F. A. reunion of 1902 in Boston. In 1904, at the meeting again held in Boston, Judge Forbes responded to the request for an obituary of Mr. Brigham.

412 HANNAH[6], daughter of Capt. Charles[5] and Susanna (Baylis) Brigham; born in Grafton, 11 March, 1813; died in Marlboro, Mass., 5 March, 1879; married, 21 Aug., 1849, (as his third wife) Rev. Stillman, son of Dea. Benjamin Pratt of Reading; born there, 24 April, 1804; died in Middleboro, Mass., 1 Sept., 1862.

He was especially adapted to pioneer work and founded the Congregational churches in Adams and Melrose, Mass.; also settled over churches in Orleans, Eastham and North Carver. As an editor he published the *Mothers' Assistant* and the *Middleboro Gazette*; also wrote and published the life of Gen. John C. Fremont, besides various religious works; was a graduate of Andover Theological Seminary, and a man of strong convictions.

Children (Pratt):
i Susan Kittredge[7], b. in Melrose, Mass., 31 Aug., 1850; m. 1878, Francis W. McIntire; res. s. p., in Attleboro, Mass.

ii Mary Bradford, b. in Carver, Mass., 20 Dec., 1851; m. 11 Sept.,
1873, Fred L., son of Ansel Morse of Marlboro and Attleboro,
Mass. Ch. (Morse), the 2 eldest b. at Marlboro:
  1 *Susie Brigham*[8], b. 14 March, 1876.
  2 *Helen Frances*, b. 11 Sept., 1877; d. 2 Jan., 1878.
  3 *Edward Ansel*, b. in Attleboro, 21 April, 1882.
iii Lucy B., b. 8 Feb., 1853; m. 28 April, 1885, Charles M. Robbins
of Attleboro. Ch. (Robbins):
  1 *Lawrence Brigham*[8], b. 27 April, 1886.
  2 *Chester M.*, b. 20 Oct., 1896.
iv Hannah M., b. 8 July, 1854; unm.
v Charles B., b. 21 Sept., 1855; d. 2 Dec., 1856.
vi Homer B., b. 7 Sept., 1856; d. 20 Nov., 1856.
vii Helen L., b. 22 March, 1858; d. 26 Dec., 1860.

413 SARAH[6], daughter of Capt. Charles[5] and Susanna (Bay-
lis) Brigham; born in Grafton, Mass., 7 May, 1815; died 26
March, 1871; married, 9 July, 1840, Rev. Charles Baker Kit-
tredge of Westboro and Munson, Mass., born in Mt. Vernon, N.
H., 4 July, 1806; died 25 Nov., 1884. She was a graduate of Mt.
Holyoke Seminary in the year 1838, and taught there one year.

*Children (Kittredge), the 3 eldest born in Westboro, the others in
Munson:*
  i Charles Brigham[7], b. 29 Sept., 1841; m. 1868, Katherine S., dau.
of Ephraim T. and Catherine (White) Forbes, and gr.-granddau.
of 175; res. Westboro, and Glyndon, Minn. Ch. (Kittredge):
    1 *Ellen L.*[8], m. William T. Lapp; res. Alaska.
    2 *Susie A.;* 3 *Alice F.;* 4 *Francis W.;* 5 *Frank A.;* 6 *Mar-
guerite E.;* 7 *Katie*, d. æ. 12; 8 *Charles*, d. æ. 20.
  ii Sarah Blackwell, b. 20 June, 1843; d. 5 Jan., 1844.
  iii Alvah Baylis, b. 3 Feb., 1845; d. 4 Oct., 1870; m. 3 Oct., 1870,
Alice W. Gordon of Boston.
  iv Harriet Dyer, b. 23 Jan., 1847.
  v Maria Abigail, b. 30 Jan., 1849; m. Jonathan E. Forbes of
Westboro, and Kansas City, Mo. Ch. (Forbes):
    1 *Lucy K.*[8]; 2 *Hattie A.*
  vi Ellen Louise, b. 16 Aug., 1851; d. 4 May, 1868.
  vii Sarah Amelia, b. 19 Feb., 1854; d. 12 April, 1870.
  viii Mary Clark, b. 25 Sept., 1856.

414 MARIA CAROLINE[6], daughter of Capt. Charles[5] and
Susanna (Baylis) Brigham, born in Grafton, Mass., 26 June, 1820;
died 28 Jan., 1891; married, (second wife), 9 May, 1847, William
Trowbridge Merrifield, whose first wife was Margaret Brigham,
(574). They resided in Worcester, Mass.

Children (Merrifield), born in Worcester:
  i Charles Brigham[7], b. 9 May, 1851; d. 17 May, 1851.
  ii Andrew Lucian, b. 3 Dec., 1852; d. 26 Aug., 1853.
  iii Maria Josephine, b. 9 July, 1854; d. 26 Sept., 1878.
  iv Harriette, b. 22 Oct., 1856; m. 5 Feb., 1884, Hon. William Trowbridge, son of Ephraim Trowbridge and Catherine (White)

Forbes, and gr.-grandson of 175; b. 24 May, 1850, in Westboro. Mrs. Forbes is the editor of the portion of the *Diary of the Rev. Ebenezer Parkman,* published by the Westboro Hist. Soc., and the author of *The Hundredth Town,* a sketch of Westboro. Judge Forbes grad. from Amherst Coll. in 1871; was instructor in Mathematics in Robert Coll., Constantinople 3 years; studied law, and in 1888 was appointed Judge of the Court of Probate and Insolvency for Worcester, having been standing Justice, 1st Dist. Court, Worcester. They res. in Westboro, where he practiced law and held many town offices; was representative to the Legislature in 1881-82, and senator, 1886-87. Removed to Worcester, where they now live. Ch. (Forbes):

1 *William Trowbridge*, b. 23 April, 1885.
2 *Allan White,* b. 20 June, 1886.
3 *Cornelia Brigham,* b. 14 July, 1888.
4 *Katherine Maria,* b. 23 Sept., 1889.
5 *Esther Louise,* b. 28 June, 1891.
6 *Malcolm Stuart,* b. 22 Nov., 1892; d. 4 Feb., 1893.

SEVENTH GENERATION

SEVENTH GENERATION

415   COL. BELA BREWSTER⁷, son of Moses⁶ and Wealthy (Johnson) Brigham; born in Hanover, N. H., 4 Feb., 1784; died 5 Dec., 1870, probably at Bath, N. Y.; married (1) 26 Dec., 1816, Hannah, daughter of Richard Davenport of Richfield, N. Y.; married (2) 30 Jan., 1823, Abby, daughter of Nathan Whitney, Conn., born 9 March, 1796.

Col. Brigham was a clerk in the store of P. S. Whitney of Boston for two years after his father's removal to Canada. In 1803 Bela joined his father, settled in London and became a loyal subject of England. He was on the side of the British in the War of 1812, and had command of a rifle company in the First Regt. of Oxford Militia and commanded the regiment during the Rebellion of 1837. He was often on duty during these years, acquiring for life a taste for a soldier's career. Morse found him, in his 76th year, living in Bath, N. Y., and relates that he had a retentive memory and a hand as steady as in youth. At 74 he amused himself with skating on his birthday, and in his 76th year he still went without a cane.

Children (by first wife):
    i Wealthy Clarinda⁸, b. 13 Oct., 1817; m. in 1841, Gideon Bullen, D. D.; d. in Chicago, 29 Jan., 1892.
    ii Eliza Ann, b. 9 July, 1819; d. 1 June, 1837.
    iii Twin boys, b. 5 May, 1821; d. unnamed.
Children (by second wife):
    iv Eugenia Maria, b. 26 April, 1824; d. in Washington, Ia., Aug., 1870; m. 12 Sept., 1848, S. Morris Seymour, C. E.; res. Bath, N. Y.
684   v Charles Brewster, b. 6 Aug., 1827.
    vi Adelaide Fidelia, b. 16 Nov., 1829; d. 26 July, 1832.
    vii Caroline Whitney, b. 10 Aug., 1831; d. 1 June, 1857, in Nebraska; m. Truman W. Woods, M. D., of Woodville, Neb., 10 Aug., 1853.
685 viii Henry Gustavus, b. 13 Sept., 1836.

416   PHINEAS⁷, son of Phineas⁶ and Lydia (Batherick) Brigham; born in Westboro, Mass., 28 March, 1782; died ———; married Lydia, daughter of Edmund Wilkins of Marlboro, Mass., where they resided.

Children, born in Marlboro:
    i Edward Elkins⁸, b. 4 Sept., 1805; d. unm., in Marlboro, æ. 37.
    ii Bela Brewster, b. 10 May, 1807; m. Harriet Frost.
686 iii Alden, b. 25 June, 1809.
    iv George, d. unm., æ. 33.

v Austin, b. 5 March, 1811; m. Elizabeth Hastings; res. Hudson, Mass. Ch., names of the 2 elder unknown:
3 *Willis F.*[9], b. in Hudson; m. 15 Dec., 1877, Lora Jeannette, dau. of Levi and Sarah (Crosby) Taylor; b. in Marlboro, 17 Oct., 1858; res. there. Ch., b. there: i Frederick Levi[10], b. 8 Aug., 1878; ii Everett F., b. 7 Feb., 1881; iii Ralph, b. 1882.
vi Lydia Ann, b. 28 Jan., 1815; m. (1) John Hastings; m. (2) Rufus Temple; res. Marlboro.
687 vii Sidney, b. 4 Aug., 1817.
688 viii Cyrus, b. 9 June, 1820.

417 WILLARD[7], son of Phineas[6] and Lydia (Batherick) Brigham; born in Westboro, Mass., 20 Sept., 1784; died in Sutton, Mass., 14 Oct., 1858; married, 21 Nov., 1811, Betsey, daughter of Aaron and Sarah (Kimball) Sherman; born in Westboro, 26 June, 1793; died in Worcester, Mass., July, 1880.

Children, born in Westboro:
i Leonard B.[8], b. 4 March, 1812; d. in Sutton, 22 Feb., 1894; m. (1) Harriet Alexander, b. in Holden, Mass., 16 Sept., 1829; m. (2) Charlotte Black, who d. in Holden, 31 Jan., 1886; was a farmer, town treasurer and tax collector. Ch.:
1 *Hollis B.*[9], b. in Holden, 6 Sept., 1836; d. unm., in Holden, 19 April, 1882.
689 ii Eliza J., b. 8 Oct., 1813.
iii Orison W., b. 3 Nov., 1816; d. in Northbridge, Mass., 8 April, 1882, s. p.; m. Laura, dau. Capt. Amos White of Northbridge; was a tool maker, and res. Northbridge.
iv Almira, b. 1 Jan., 1818; d. 17 Sept., 1852; m. (1) Elias Adams, who d.; m. (2) Lewis Holbrook. Ch. (Adams):
1 *Elias*[9], b. 15 Aug., 1841; res. Uxbridge, Mass.
Ch. (Holbrook):
2 *Adelaide M.*, b. 24 July, 1845.
690 v Eli A., b. 1 July, 1820.
vi Emmons B., b. 7 June, 1822; d. unm., 23 June, 1842, in Sutton.
vii Emily M., b. 26 Dec., 1824; m. 1859, Barnabas Hewitt of Northbridge; d. s. p., 4 Jan., 1891; res. So. Sutton.
691 viii Hannah L., b. 6 Feb., 1827.
ix Catherine M., b. 1 April, 1829; m. 19 Jan., 1853, Henry O., son of Hosea Sprague of E. Douglass, Mass.; b. 13 Nov., 1828; d. in Westfield, 9 Jan., 1896. Ch. (Sprague), b. in Westfield:
1 *Alvin L.*[9], b. 18 Sept., 1855; d. 21 Oct., 1892, in Gardner, Mass.; m. Fannie I. Shurtleff, b. in Blanford, Mass., 1857. Ch.: i Harry L.[10]; ii Charles E.; iii Florence.
2 *Clara L.*, b. 23 Aug., 1858; m. Charles S. Axtell of W. Springfield.
3 *Katie A.*, b. 20 June, 1866; m. James T. Case of Bristol, Conn. Ch. (Case): Catherine B.[10]
4 *Effie G.*, b. 18 July, 1868; m. Henry L. Sherwood of Westfield. Ch. (Sherwood): Alvin L.[10]; and 2 d. y.
x Phineas Forbes, b. 9 June, 1831; d. in Worcester, 1880; m. Lorenza Miller. Ch.:
1 *Melvina*[9], b. 26 Aug., 1855; d. in Worcester; m. ————.
2 *Lizzie*, b. Sept., 1861; m. (1) Omer Davis; m. (2) Frank

Jordan; res. Worcester. Ch. (Davis): Myrtou O.[10], b. Dec., 1882; m. Lila Hiatt.

xi Henry M., b. 29 Oct., 1833; m. 28 Nov., 1855, Hannah J. Sherman, b. in Sutton, 19 May, 1839; he moved to Sutton; has one of the best houses in the town, and is prosperous. Ch.:

    1 *Ella J.[9]*, b. in S., 16 June, 1859; m. 5 Nov., 1879, Henry W. Putnam of S.; s. p.

xii Sarah, b. 21 Sept., 1836; m. (1) 17 Jan., 1855, Loren Bolster of Worcester, who d. s. p.; m. (2) Fred Hawes, and res. Elk City, Neb. Ch. (Hawes):

    1 *Charles[9]*, who has ch.: George[10] and Buena.
    2 *Ada*, d. y.

418 LAMBERT[7], son of Phineas[6] and Lydia (Batherick) Brigham; born in Westboro, Mass., 7 June, 1794; died about 1833; married Sophia Buck, and resided in Sterling, Mass.

Children, born in Sterling:

  i Augustus[8], b. 26 May, 1820; m. 9 Nov., 1840, in Boston, Mary A. Allard. He res. in Worcester, was a carpenter, and was in the Civil War. Ch.:

    1 (*Dr.*) *Henry F.[9]*, b. at Wayland, 3 May, 1842; m. Lydia A. ————, who res. Geneva, O.; was in the Civil War.
    2 *Mary A.*, b. in Natick, 2 Oct., 1843.
    3 *Harriet*, b. in Framingham, 14 March, 1845.
    4 *James A.*, b. in Princeton, 26 Nov., 1846; m. Hannah ————; was a contractor and builder in Worcester, and was in the Civil War.
    5 *Owen W.*, b. in Sterling, 26 April, 1848; d. in Worcester; was in the Civil War.
    6 *Charles E.*, b. in Sterling, 26 Jan., 1850; d. 5 Sept., 1850.
    7 *Fanny A. W.*, b. 1 June, 1851, in Sterling.
    8 *Enoch A.*, b. 5 Sept., 1853; d. in Worcester.
    9 *Eler Emer J.*, b. 1 March, 1855, in Shrewsbury.
    10 *Rased A.*, b. 1 Sept., 1856; d. in Worcester.

  ii Aurelius, b. 3 Feb., 1830; m. 10 Sept., 1853, Olive Wilson; res. Boylston. Ch.:

    1 *Edward L.[9]*, b. 6 Dec., 1854.
    2 *John W.*, b. 4 Nov., 1855, in Boylston.

419 JOHN HAZELTINE[7], son of Capt. Ebenezer[6] and Judith (Hazeltine) Brigham; born in Townshend, Vt., 14 Aug., 1783; died in Townshend, 7 May, 1876; married in 1817, Orpha R. Hazelton, born in Townshend in 1801, died in 1841. He was a farmer and stockdealer, town officer and State Representative.

Children, born in Townshend:

  i to viii inclusive, d. young, unm.; names not given.

  ix Clarinda O.[8], b. 4 Jan., 1817; d. unm., May, 1872; a teacher.

  x Mary Ann, b. 13 July, 1819; d. in Wardsboro, Vt., June, 1888; m. in 1875, ———— Thresher, who d. 1876.

  xi (*Dr.*) John Wells, b. 19 Oct., 1823; m. 13 May, 1852, Lestina S. Gore, who d. at Union, Wis., 3 April, 1879; res. Union. Ch.:

    1 *Lock Wells[8]*, b. 15 May, 1853; d. in Union, Wis., 11 Jan., 1886; m. in 1876, Ada J. Elwood, b. in Union, in 1860; she

m. (2) ————, and res. in Evansville, Wis. Ch.: Bertha
Blanche[10], b. 11 April, 1879; res. unm., Madison, Wis.; grad.
B. L. Univ., Wis., 1900; post-grad. student, 1903.
xii Haley Forester, b. 12 Jan., 1827; m. (1) 1863, ———— Caney;
m. (2) 1870, Widow Wilder, *née* Smith; res. Wardsboro, Vt.;
a blacksmith.
xiii Bela Brewster, b. 3 March, 1831; m. in 1856, Mary E. Holbrook,
b. in Townshend, in 1836; a farmer, and has held town offices.
Ch., b. in Townshend:
1 and 2 d. y., unnamed.
3 *John H.*[9], b. 14 June, 1858; LL. B.; a lawyer, res. Duluth,
Minn.
4 *Bertha C.*, b. 2 Sept., 1870; grad. of Normal School.
5 *Blanche B.*, b. 7 Jan., 1872.

420 MOSES[7], son of Capt. Ebenezer[6] and Judith (Hazeltine)
Brigham; born in Townshend, Vt., in 1789, where he died in 1844;
married, 14 Nov., 1814, Sally Oaks, who died in Townshend, in
1862.

Children, all but the fourth born in Vermont:
i Mary Ann[8], b. 1815; d. 1818.
ii Judith, b. 1818.
iii Ebenezer, b. 1820; d. 1887.
iv Calvin Oaks, b. in Frankfort, N. Y., 30 Aug., 1822; m. 16 Feb.,
1851, Almira Smith of Roxbury, Vt., b. 20 Jan., 1825; d. in
Oakland, Cal., 21 July, 1893; is a merchant in Oakland. Ch.,
b. in San Francisco, Cal.:
1 *Frank Eugene*[9], b. 11 April, 1856; m. 16 Feb., 1886, Mary L.
Alexander, b. in Milwaukee, Wis., 29 April, 1864; a merchant in Oakland. Ch., b. in Oakland: i Beulah[10], b. 22 Jan.,
1887; ii Gladys, b. 25 Oct., 1888.
v Lyman H., b. 1825; d. 1891.
vi Emeline A., b. 1831; d. 1868.
vii Mary L., b. 1834.

421 JOSEPH CLARENDON[7], son of Joseph[6] and Sally
(Woods) Brigham; born in Marlboro, Mass., 20 Dec., 1800; died
in Northfield, Mass., 22 Jan., 1879; married, 15 June, 1828, Hannah Clapp, daughter of Gen. Thomas Lincoln; born in Taunton,
Mass., 1 March, 1807; died in Northfield, 4 Oct., 1855.

He was, early in life, a dry goods clerk in Boston; later in business for himself on Washington Street; in 1832 he moved to
Taunton, Mass., where he had a large store; moved to Clappville,
Mass., where became an extensive wool buyer; moved to Northfield,
in 1841, where he settled the important estate of John H. Dexter
of Boston. Was an occasional writer of prose and verse.

Children:
692 i Joseph Thomas[8], b. in Taunton, 1 Nov., 1829.
ii Augusta Hannah, b. in Northfield, 9 April, 1842; m. 1 May,
1881, Samuel G. Priest, M. D., of New York City, who d. s. p.,
27 Oct., 1893.

422 POLLY[7], daughter of Edmund[6] and Mary (Martyn) Brigham; born in Westboro, Mass., 6 Feb., 1780; died 25 April, 1875; married Sylvester, son of Heman Fay, born in Southboro, Mass., 2 Sept., 1781; resided in Southboro.

Children (Fay), born in Southboro:

i Charles Merrick[8], b. 12 Aug., 1804; m. 14 May, 1829, Sarah, dau. of Perry Whipple. Ch.:
  1 *Sarah[9]*; 2 *Olive,* m. William Brigham; 3 *Alice;* 4 *Walter;* 5 *Harriet.*

ii Maria, b. 8 June, 1806; m. Alexander Marsh. Ch. (Marsh):
  1 *Harriet[9];* 2 *Mary;* 3 *Henry;* 4 *Ann;* 5 *George.*

iii Jerome, b. 7 July, 1808; d. 1 March, 1868; when a young man saved up a few hundred dollars, suddenly left home, and was not heard from for years; in the seventies a lady, purporting to be the daughter of Fay Brigham of Philadelphia, applied to Peter Bent Brigham of Boston, for information concerning her father's family. After much trouble on the part of Mr. Brigham, by the aid of family pictures, it was discovered that Jerome Fay had changed his name in Philadelphia, married, and died there, under the name of Fay Brigham; he had 2 daughters.

iv Jane, b. 1 June, 1810; m. Martin, son of Dea. Brigham Fay; she d. Feb., 1888.

v Sylvester, b. 29 Feb., 1813; m. (1) 1837, Catherine Cook; m. (2) Abbie Parker. Ch., by 1st m.:
  1 *Mary[9];* 2 *William;* 3 *Frederick;* 4 *George;* 5 *Frank;* 6 *Catherine.*

vi Martha Ann, b. 21 May, 1816; m. 1835, Samuel S. Howe. Ch. (Howe):
  1 *Warren[9];* 2 *Annie,* who is a teacher.

vii Heman, b. 21 July, 1819; m. 1848, Adaline, dau. of Phineas Rice; res. Northboro; Ry. conductor B. & A. Ch.:
  1 *Ella[9].*

viii Edmund Brigham, b. 18 June, 1823; m. Eliza Trowbridge; res. Framingham Cen.; 2 ch.

423 JOHN[7], son of Edmund[6] and Mary (Martyn) Brigham; born in Westboro, Mass., 7 June, 1782; died in Whitingham, Vt., 21 Feb., 1863; married (1) 14 Nov., 1808, in Phillipston, Mass., Rebecca, daughter of Gamaliel and Sarah (Freeman) Smith; born in Truro, Mass., 2 Nov., 1783; died in Whitingham, 23 Feb., 1833; married (2) 4 Dec., 1833, Huldah, daughter of Minor Wheeler, born in Halifax, Vt., 24 Dec., 1804; died in Whitingham, 8 Oct., 1839; married (3) 22 April, 1841, Mrs. Rebecca (Rawson) Bardwell-Goss, born in Montague, Mass., 30 Sept., 1785; died in Whitingham, 5 July, 1844; married (4) 2 May, 1845, Betsey (Preston) Brigham, widow of his brother Lyscom, born in Whitingham, 11 July, 1800; died in Heath, 8 April, 1874.

He was six feet in his stockings and very muscular; his native ability was large, his energy enormous and he accomplished a great deal of business in his long life. When about 25 years old he bought land in southern Vermont, cleared it and built a house. Once, starting in the morning, he walked to Phillipston, 40 miles, and danced all night, apparently unwearied. He was the most prominent man in the section where he lived; he manufactured scythe snaths and annually carried thousands of dozens to market in Worcester County and eastern Massachusetts; he bought the surplus produce of the farmers and carried it with his own to Boston, a hundred miles with horse or ox teams, for years; he was the largest sheep raiser in southern Vermont. Although solicited, he never accepted public office, but was on several important committees and chairman of the building committee for the Universalist church; it was owing to his efforts that a society was formed in Whitingham. His geniality made his home a rallying point for all his kin.

Children (by first wife), born in Whitingham:
693   i Martyn Freeman[8], b. 19 Oct., 1809.
       ii Sally Smith, b. 29 Dec., 1811; d. 30 July, 1815.
694   iii Harriet, b. 2 Sept., 1814.
695   iv Sally Maria, b. 12 Aug., 1816.
696   v Rebecca Elvira, b. 23 March, 1820.
697   vi John Addison, b. 25 Jan., 1824.
       vii Francis Edmund, b. 1 Aug., 1826; d. s. p., in Orion, Ill., where
           he was a large farmer, 14 Feb., 1884; m. 16 Jan., 1855, Millicent
           A., dau. of Rufus Brown of Wilmington, Vt. Ch.:
           1 *John Rufus[9]*, b. 7 July, 1859; d. Sept., 1864.
           2 *Twins*, d. y.
Children (by second wife), born in Whitingham:
       viii Lewis, b. 17 Sept., 1834; d. 8 Oct., 1834.
698   ix Emeline Minerva, b. 16 March, 1836.
699   x Hosea Wheeler, b. 30 May, 1837.

424   LYSCOM[7], son of Edmund[6] and Mary (Martyn) Brigham; born in Templeton, Mass., 28 March, 1792; died in Whitingham, Vt., 19 Nov., 1844; married, 4 June, 1823, Betsey Preston, who married (2) John Brigham, of Whitingham; was a farmer in Whitingham.

Children, born in Heath:
       i Abigail[8], b. 5 March, 1824; m. 31 March, 1854, Elisha, son of
         Elisha Hagar; b. in Halifax, Vt., 2 Aug., 1819; d. 8 Dec., 1902;
         res. Dell, Mass. Ch. (Hagar), b. in Heath:
         1 *Frank Elisha[9]*, b. 17 July, 1855; m. 15 May, 1884, Julia P.
           Leonard, b. 31 July, 1858. Ch.: i Ernest R.[10], b. 13 June, 1885;
           ii Alice L., b. 9 Sept., 1886; iii Grace E., b. 13 Aug., 1889;
           res. in Auburn, R. I.
         2 *Clifford James*, b. 1 April, 1862; m. 15 April, 1884, Ella A.
           Purrington, b. 4 Feb., 1862. Ch.: i Infant[10], d. y.; ii May
           E., b. 13 June, 1892; d. 17 Oct., 1892; res. in Dell, Mass.
       ii Charles L., b. 2 Dec., 1825; d. 22 July, 1829.
       iii Samuel Dexter, b. 11 July, 1827; d. 8 Oct., 1838.

JOHN BRIGHAM, OF WHITINGHAM, VT. (423)

iv Mary, b. 25 Aug., 1830; d. unm., in North Heath, 15 June, 1887; a schoolteacher.
v Elizabeth A., b. 28 Oct., 1832; d. 27 Aug., 1838.
vi Lewis L., b. 12 May, 1835; d. in Colrain, Mass., 14 Jan., 1903; m. 15 Feb., 1859, Marcia A., dau. of Philander Shearer; b. in Colrain, 22 May, 1836; d. in C., 9 June, 1903. He was a farmer in Colrain. Ch.:
  1 *Alice A.*, b. in Halifax, 21 May, 1861; d. 8 Dec., 1863.
  2 *Frank Lewis*, b. in Cambridge, N. Y., 6 Oct., 1867; m. 26 Oct., 1892, Florence E. Miner, b. at Leyden, Mass., 14 Nov., 1876; res. Elm Grove, Mass. Ch., b. in Halifax: i Clarence H.[10], b. 17 Nov., 1894; ii Byron A., b. 24 May, 1898.

425 EDWARD[7], son of Edmund[6] and Mary (Martyn) Brigham; born in Templeton, Mass., 26 May, 1795; died in Whitingham, Vt., 10 April, 1880; married in April, 1824, Laura Cummings, born in Phillipston, Mass., 28 April, 1802; died in Whitingham, Sept., 1880.

Edward settled first in Heath, Mass.; removed to Whitingham in 1843. He first ran a saw-mill, then engaged in farming.

Children, born in Heath, except the youngest:
  i Mary[8], b. 23 Feb., 1825; d. 10 March, 1825.
  ii Augusta A., b. 7 July, 1827; d. 4 March, 1842.
700 iii Charles Edward, b. 4 June, 1833.
  iv Joseph L., b. 16 June, 1838; m. 2 July, 1861, Elmina C. Bunn, b. in Winchenden, Mass., May, 1841; res. in Fitchburg, Mass.
    1 *Eva E.*, b. 29 May, 1863; m. July, 1885, Frank M. Patch of Fitchburg, who d. Ch. (Patch): Leon F.[10], b. 16 Nov., 1890.
    2 *George E.*, b. 17 Nov., 1865; m. 28 July, 1887, Martha Shepard; res. Fitchburg. Ch.: Ruby E.[10], b. 4 Dec., 1890.
  v Henry, b. 5 Dec., 1844, in Whitingham; d. 27 July, 1863.

426 LEWIS[7], son of Edmund[6] and Mary (Martyn) Brigham; born in Templeton, Mass., 4 June, 1806; died there, 29 Aug., 1886; married (1) 27 May, 1834, Martha, daughter of Elisha Hagar of Halifax, Vt., and widow of Otis Holbrook; born 20 June, 1808; died 2 Jan., 1852; married (2) 7 Jan., 1856, Rebecca H. Whitney; born in Groton, Mass., 7 July, 1812; died 23 Dec., 1856; married (3) 13 Oct., 1857, Mrs. Clara W. Page; born in Woodstock, Vt., 23 Dec., 1815; died in Templeton, 14 Feb., 1891. Lewis inherited the farm in Templeton.

Children, born in Templeton:
  i Mary Martha[8], b. 7 March, 1835; d. 24 May, 1869; m. 27 Oct., 1853, Andrew J. Starkey, b. in Richmond, N. H., 4 March, 1831; d. 3 April, 1873. Ch. (Starkey):
    1 *James Lewis*, b. 27 July, 1854; d. 28 April, 1874.
    2 *Mary A.*, b. 27 May, 1859; d. 14 June, 1862.
    3 *Otis A.*, b. 23 June, 1861; res. W. Swanzey, N. H.
    4 *John W.*, b. 27 Jan., 1865; m. Oct., 1888, Anna Wood; res. W. Swanzey. Ch. (Starkey): i Chester A.[10]; ii Lena V.

5 *William H.*, b. 7 May, 1866; d. 10 Feb., 1888.
6 *Lydia G.*, b. 23 Jan., 1868; m. 21 Jan., 1891, John A. Joslin; res. Spofford, N. H. Ch. (Joslin): Ruth G.¹⁰, d. 10 Sept., 1905.

701   ii Edmund Monis, b. 21 Feb., 1837.
    iii Otis Holbrook, b. 14 Jan., 1839; d. in Boston, at the home of his cousin, John Addison Brigham, 16 Dec., 1861.
    iv James Lewis, b. 3 March, 1841; d. in Dakota, 26 May, 1891; m. (1) Delia A. Greenwood, who d. 5 June, 1875; m. (2) 10 Jan., 1878, Martha A. E., daughter of Benjamin Frye of Royalston, Mass.; b. 26 March, 1846; d. there, 20 Dec., 1892. Ch. (by second wife):
      1 *George Lewis*⁹, b. in Templeton, 6 Jan., 1879; res. in 1905, unm., in Boston.
      2 *Emma Winifred*, b. in Templeton, 14 Sept., 1881; res. Boston.
    v Susan Arnold, b. 9 April, 1843; d. *ibid.*

427   SAMUEL⁷, son of Samuel⁶ and Lydia (Ball) Brigham; born in West Waterford, Me., in 1788; died in Sweden, Me., 20 March, 1870, æ. 82; married (1) Hannah Stevens; married (2) Lovina Paterson, who died in March, 1863. The male line is extinct.

Children (by first wife), born in Sweden, Me.:
    1 Charlotte⁸, b. 4 Oct., 1812; d. in Sweden, 7 Oct., 1891; m. Benjamin Nevers of Sweden. Ch. (Nevers):
      1 *George*⁹, d. y.
      2 *Albion*, d. y.
      3 *Albion*, d. in 1900; 6 ch.
      4 *Charlotte C.*, m. Charles W. Bennett of Sweden; 2 sons and 2 daus.
    ii Lydia Ann, b. Aug., 1814; m. (1) Isaac Stevens of Marblehead, Mass., by whom she had 2 ch., 1 d. y.; m. (2) Asa Critchett of East Boston, Mass.; 2 sons.
    iii Martha, b. in 1816; d. March, 1864; m. J. H. Pate of Boston, Mass.; 1 son and 2 daus., all deceased.
    iv Lucretia, d. unm., in 1864.
    v Harriet O., d. unm., in Lowell, Mass., in 1901.
    vi Hannah, b. 25 Dec., 1825; m. Joseph Meader of Concord, N. H., and Boston, Mass.; 2 sons and 1 dau. About 1864, moved to California.
Child (by second wife), born in Sweden:
    vii Son, d. at birth.

428   LYSCOM⁷, son of Samuel⁶ and Lydia (Ball) Brigham; born (probably) in West Waterford, Me.,* 15 Nov., 1791; died in Hopkinton, Mass., 7 Sept., 1871; married, 8 Nov., 1814, Experience daughter of Dea. Dudley; born in Hopkinton, 27 Jan., 1791; died 29 Jan., 1862. He was a farmer.

Children, born in Hopkinton:
    i Pierpont⁸, b. 8 July, 1816; d. in Southboro, Mass., 12 March, 1876; m. ——————, 23 Aug., 1840.

* One record says Hopkinton, Mass., but all his brothers and sisters were born in Waterford.

ii Mary, b. 30 Aug., 1818; m. 18 Jan., 1852, ——————; res. Westboro.
iii Edmund, b. 14 Jan., 1821; m. 25 Nov., 1844, Abigail, dau. of Calvin Graves; res. in Marlboro. Ch.:
   1 *Abby Lucinda*⁹, b. in Fayville, Mass., 11 Oct., 1850; d. 1 Jan., 1874.
   2 *Emma Louise*, b. 25 Nov., 1856.
iv Betsey, b. 3 Nov., 1822; m. 3 Nov., 1846, ——————; she is a nurse, and res. Southboro, Mass.
v Lydia, b. 3 Aug., 1824; d. in Southboro, Mass., Sept., 1872.
vi Isannah, b. 7 Nov., 1825; was a hotelkeeper in Boston Highlands.
vii Lucy Ann, b. 9 Nov., 1827; d. in Hopkinton, 1860.
viii Samuel, b. 29 Dec., 1829; hotelkeeper, Medway, Mass.
ix Sarah, b. 28 Dec., 1832; d. in Hopkinton.
x Martha, b. 1 June, 1834; d. in Hopkinton.

429   DEA. GEORGE BALL⁷, son of Samuel⁶ and Lydia (Ball) Brigham; born in West Waterford, Me., 23 Jan., 1793; died 19 May, 1842; married (1) in 1815, Nelly, daughter of Robert Fay of Southboro, Mass.; born in Southboro, 2 April, 1789; died 18 Jan., 1840; married (2) 3 Sept., 1840, Anna, sister of his first wife, and widow of Seth Belknap of Westboro, Mass., by whom she had three children; born 20 Feb., 1793, died s. p., by second marriage. He resided in Westboro.

Children (by first wife), all born in Westboro, except the eldest:
702   i Harrison, b. in W. Waterford, in 1812.
703   ii George B., b. 5 Oct., 1818.
     iii Charles A., b. ——————; res. in California.
     iv Clarissa E., b. ——————; d. ——————; m. George Johnson; res. Framingham, Mass.
     v Samuel R., b. in 1828; d. in Westboro, 30 March, 1875; m. Ellen S. ——————; b. in 1831; d. in W., 25 Aug., 1875. Ch.:
        1 *Clare*⁹, m. —————— Emerson of Brockton, Mass.
        2 *Nellie*, m. —————— Archibald of Marlboro, Mass.
     vi Harriet D., m. Levi Smith; res. Westboro.

430   BRYANT⁷, son of Samuel⁶ and Lydia (Ball) Brigham; born in West Waterford, Me., 10 Feb., 1794; died, Westboro, Mass., 8 July, 1848; married (1) Betsey Dudley, who probably died in Maine; married (2) Mary Smith, who died in Westboro, 27 Dec., 1877, æ. 79 yrs., 2 mos., 6 days. He resided in Westboro.

Children (by second wife), born in Westboro:
     i Edmund Reed⁸, b. 19 March, 1826; m. (1) 15 April, 1852, Sarah Ball Williams, b. in Royalston, Mass., 6 June, 1828; d. 12 July, 1865; m. (2) 7 Oct., 1866, Mrs. Caroline Williams Fuller, b. in Warwick, Mass., 30 March, 1830. He res. in Worcester, and was living in 1906. Ch. (by second wife), b. in Worcester:
        1 *Sarah Jane*⁹, b. 11 July, 1868; m. 16 July, 1887, at Worcester, Archie Dwight Jennings; she res. Winchester, N. H. Ch. (Jennings): i Earle Brigham¹⁰, b. 13 March, 1890; ii Dwight Edmund, b. 23 Aug., 1892; iii Marguerite Ellis, b. 12 Feb., 1901.

2 *Melzar Williams,* b. 14 Aug., 1870; m. in Buffalo, N. Y., 22
Nov., 1893, Sarah Hanley. Ch.: i Mary Edna[10], b. March,
1895; d. Aug., 1895; ii Edmund Thomas, b. 23 June, 1896.

ii Mary Elizabeth, d. 2 Jan., 1841, æ. 9 yrs., 6 mos., 5 dys.

iii Susan Smith, d. 23 Aug., 1836, æ. 18 dys.

431 LEVI[7], son of Samuel[6] and Lydia (Ball) Brigham; born
in Waterford, Me., 27 May, 1796; died in Boston, 13 March,
1832; married, 5 Dec., 1821, Betsey Mixer; born in Southboro,
Mass., 3 Oct., 1796; died 3 Nov., 1831. He resided in Boston,
was a contractor.

Children, born in Boston:

 i Silas O.[8], b. 7 May, 1823; m. in San Francisco, 7 May, 1863,
 Adelaide Landgraf, b. in Nordhansen, Prussia, 16 June, 1824;
 went to California in 1849; res. New York City; office 16 So.
 Williams St. Ch., b. in San Francisco:
  1 *Charles H.[9]*, b. 6 March, 1864; m. 2 July, 1888, Hattie E.
  Hawley; res. Brooklyn, N. Y., s. p.

 ii Persis Elizabeth, b. 17 Dec., 1824; m. 7 Aug., 1851, William Harris
 Johonnot of Boston, receiving teller of the City Bank for 36
 years; res. Newton, Mass. Ch. (Johonnot), b. in Boston:
  1 *Elizabeth Brigham[9]*, b. 1 March, 1854; d. 16 July, 1855.
  2 *Charles Otis,* b. 4 Sept., 1856; d. 19 Dec., 1861.
  3 *John Oliver,* b. 21 July, 1858; m. 14 Nov., 1883, Sarah S.
  Kendall; with the N. Y. Edison Co.; educated at the Mass.
  Inst. of Technology. Ch.: Addie E.[10], b. in 1886.
  4 *Frank Brigham,* b. 26 Dec., 1859; res. 14 St. Andrews Pl.,
  Brooklyn, N. Y.
  5 *Charles Otis,* b. 4 Feb., 1865; m. 30 March, 1892, Elizabeth
  S. Oakes; res. 375 Putnam Ave., Brooklyn, N. Y. Frank
  and Charles Johonnot are partners in the manufacture of
  proprietary medicines. Ch.: Mildred P., b. in 1896.
  6 *Harris Edwards,* b. 25 March, 1868; electrician, Newton, Mass.

 iii Mary Jane, b. 18 Oct., 1826; d. 4 Feb., 1831.

 iv Levi S., b. 15 Feb., 1829; d. 10 March, 1832.

 v Charles H., b. 17 March, 1831; burned to death in Sacramento,
 Cal., 3 Nov., 1852.

432 LINCOLN[7], son of Samuel[6] and Lydia (Ball) Brigham;
born in West Waterford, Me., 22 Nov., 1801; died in Westboro,
Mass., 5 March, 1876; married, 20 March, 1831, Susanna Maria,
daughter of Nathan ——— and Frances (Brigham) Brigham;
born in Southboro, Mass., 5 April, 1807; died in Westboro, 6 Aug.,
1892, æ. 85. He resided in Westboro.

Child, born in Westboro:

 i Francis A.[8], b. 6 Nov., 1838; d.; m. 3 July, 1865, Juliana A., dau.
 of Warren Buck; b. in Southboro, 19 Dec., 1840; d. 12 Feb., 1876.
 Ch., b. in Westboro:
  1 *Walter Lincoln[9]*, b. 30 April, 1866.
  2 *Lillian Susan,* b. 21 Dec., 1867.
  3 *Sarah Frances,* b. 16 April, 1869.

SEVENTH GENERATION 349

4 *Irving Arthur*, b. 27 May, 1871; in the Spanish War, Co. C, 2d
Mass. Regt.
5 *Edward Frederick*, b. 23 May, 1874; m. 11 June, 1900, Caroline
L. Stevens. Ch.: i Elizabeth S.[10], b. 2 June, 1901; ii Laurence
S., b. 2 Aug., 1903.
6 *Juliana Angelina*, b. 6 Feb., 1876; d. y.

433 DEXTER[7], son of Samuel[6] and Lydia (Ball) Brigham;
born in Waterford, Me., 24 Sept., 1808; died in Westboro, Mass.,
in 1884; married, 16 Sept., 1834, Martha W., daughter of Capt.
Pierpont —— and Anna (Warren) Brigham, (186); born in
Westboro, 3 April, 1813; died in Westboro, 6 April, 1889.

He resided on Pierpont Brigham's homestead in the north-east
part of Westboro, probably the place where Capt. Edmund Brigham resided. The male line is extinct.

Children, born in Westboro:
i Marion Sophia[8], b. 26 March, 1835; d. 18 Feb., 1841.
ii Adaliza, b. 20 Oct., 1839; d. 7 Jan., 1877; m. 15 March, 1866,
Andrew Otis. Ch. (Otis):
1 *Francis[9]*, b. 1871; d. *ibid.*
2 *W. I.*, b. 25 Sept., 1875; m. in 1900, ——————.
3 *Fred*, b. 15 Jan., 1885.
iii Mary Elizabeth, b. 8 Aug., 1843; d. 7 April, 1869; m. 14 Nov.,
1865, William C. Penniman. Ch. (Penniman):
1 *Lizzie P.[9]*, b. 11 Dec., 1868; m. in 1897, Edgar H. Bates.
iv Dexter Pierpont, b. 14 Oct., 1845; res. in 1904, in Westboro;
m. (1) 14 Nov., 1867, Diana Tufts; m. (2) 5 Dec., 1894, Alice
J. Forbush. Ch. (by first wife):
1 *Jessie[9]*, b. 6 April, 1869; m. 28 July, 1897, William Sanford.
v Albert, b. 11 July, 1846; d. 8 July, 1887; m. 28 Jan., 1870, Kate
Pettigrew. Ch
1 *Nellie E.[9]*, b. 20 June, 1872; m. 25 Dec., 1897, Albert H.
Daniels.
vi Ella Sophia, b. 14 June, 1848; d. 27 Jan., 1870.
vii Lora, b. 26 March, 1851; d. 30 Aug., 1851.

434 CURTIS[7], son of Dea. Lyscom[6] and Martha (Fay) Brigham; born in Westboro, Mass., 21 May, 1793; died in Gun Plains,
Mich., 24 Feb., 1872; married in Boston, 14 Aug., 1817, Lydia,
daughter of John Woodbury; born in Salem, Mass., 5 April, 1789;
died in Gun Plains, Mich., 28 Nov., 1876.

He was a shoemaker and farmer. In 1812 he walked 90 miles to
Boston for work; then engaged on a coast vessel and was captured
in the War of 1812. He kept a shoeshop in Boston. In 1833, he
started for the West; drove to Brattleboro, Vt., thence took stage to
Troy, N. Y., canal to Buffalo; by lake to Detroit; then walked
125 miles to Gun (or Gull) Prairie, Mich.; then he returned for his
family and drove back the next year. He cleared a farm and saw
hard times. He began the first regular Sunday meetings in Al-

legan County, Mich., in 1835, and was licensed to preach. For 10 years he led meetings, Sunday-school and attended funerals, besides doing his farm-work. At the age of 75 he wrote an interesting life-sketch for his family from which this is taken.

Children, the eldest born in Boston, the second and third in Charlestown, and the others in Shutesbury, Mass.:
   i Lydia W.[8], b. 11 Jan., 1820; d. in Plainwell, Mich., 27 Aug., 1891; m. in Gun Plains, 17 Dec., 1845, William Y., son of John Gilkey; b. in Vt., 10 June, 1805; d. in Richland, Mich., 13 Jan., 1868. Ch. (Gilkey), all b. in Richland, except the eldest:
     1 *Curtis O.*[9], b. in Gun Plains, 3 Sept., 1848.
     2 *Martha*, b. 28 Feb., 1852.
     3 *Willard E.*, b. 24 March, 1854.
     4 *Mary O.*, b. 5 April, 1856.
     5 *John W.*, 1 Feb., 1859.
704 ii Curtis, b. 13 April, 1821.
   iii John W., b. 27 May, 1822; res. in Plainwell, Mich., a farmer and broker. He is also a Baptist deacon; s. p.
   iv Martha Fay, b. 19 Nov., 1823; m. ——— Monteith; res. Elkhart, Ind.
   v Elizabeth S., b. 4 Nov., 1825; unm.
705 vi Lyscom, b. 31 Jan., 1827.
   vii Mary, b. 29 March, 1828; d. in 1888; m. in 1855, ——— Woodhams; res. Plainwell, Mich.
   viii Stillman B., b. 13 Nov., 1829; res. in Plainwell, Mich.; son, a photographer, and one dau.
   ix Hannah, b. 12 April, 1831; m. 1855, ——— Metcalf; 5 daus.; res. California.
   x Ebenezer, b. 10 Dec., 1832; m. in 1855, Sarah S. Warrant, b. in 1836. Ch.:
     1 *Edward Morris*[9], b. in 1857; grad. from Michigan Univ.; South American explorer, and lecturer; commercial traveler; res. Battle Creek, Mich.

435 BENJAMIN FAY[7], son of Dea. Lyscom[6] and Patty (Fay) Brigham; born in Pelham, Mass., 25 Aug., 1800; died in Springfield, Mass., 16 March, 1884; married in 1823, Abigail, daughter of Shadrach Hoar; born in New Salem, Mass., 7 March, 1803; died in Springfield, 21 Oct., 1868.

He was a merchant, and in 1835 moved to Westboro, Mass., where he remained for 16 years; thence to Springfield. He also resided for a time at Shutesbury, Mass. The male line is extinct.

Children, born in Shutesbury:
   i Charles Austin[8], b. 10 June, 1824; d. 6 June, 1906; m. 11 Oct., 1846, Eliza Ann, dau. of Charles Hyde; res. Westboro, s. p.
706 ii Dexter Hammond, b. 17 June, 1826.
   iii Elizabeth Abigail, b. 16 Feb., 1833; m. in Springfield, 5 Nov., 1851, Benjamin Nourse, son of Joseph Davis; b. in Grafton, Mass., 4 Oct., 1826; d. in Dayton, O., 10 June, 1899, to which place they moved in 1858. Ch. (Davis), b. in Springfield:
     1 *Lizzie Amelia*[9], b. 15 Sept., 1852; m. at Dayton, O., 24 March,

1877, Samuel Thomas Evans, b. in Dayton, 31 Aug., 1849; d. 20 Nov., 1888. Ch. (Evans): i Florence D.[10]; ii Samuel T.; iii Walter Brigham; iv Maynard B.; v Winifred H.

436 DR. HUBBARD HAMMOND[7], son of Dea. Lyscom[6] and Betsey H. (Hoar) Brigham; born in Shutesbury, Mass., 31 Oct., 1819; married (1) 25 July, 1840, Deborah, daughter of Dea. Jacob Thomas of Shutesbury; born in New Salem, Mass., 9 March, 1817; died in Fitchburg, Mass., 7 June, 1850; married (2) 25 March, 1851, Mrs. Sarah C. Randall, daughter of Henry Read; (she had a daughter by her first marriage, Harriet, who goes under the name of " Brigham "); born in Brattleboro, Vt., 25 Oct., 1824.

Dr. Brigham resided and practiced in Fitchburg for many years. In 1906 he retired and removed to Dorchester, Mass. The male line is extinct.

Children (by first wife):
  i George[8], b. in Shutesbury, 11 Oct., 1841; killed by a fall on ship in the Indian Ocean, 12 Dec., 1862.
  ii Leonella, b. in Ware, Mass., 17 July, 1845; d. there, 1 Sept., 1845.
  iii Howard, b. in Fitchburg, 15 Feb., 1847; d. there, 14 Aug., 1849.
  iv Fred R., of Fitchburg, is an adopted son, and m. 2 Nov., 1896, Kate F. Killelea of No. Leominster, Mass.; has a son, Frederick Hubbard Brigham, b. 5 Sept., 1902; res. Dorchester.

437 EDMUND FAY[7], son of Eli[6] and Polly (Fay) Brigham; born in Bolton Mass., 28 Oct., 1813; married, 6 Jan., 1836, Hannah, daughter of Isaac Temple, who died 7 Jan., 1897, æ. 78. A manufacturer of baskets. In 1903 was living in West Boylston, Mass., where he had been selectman 10 years and overseer of the poor 15 years.

Children, born in West Boylston:
  i George T.[8], b. 7 July, 1836; m. 1863, Catherine Amanda Sawyer; he is J. P., and res. W. Boylston. Ch., b. there:
    1 *Minnie Frances*[9], b. April, 1864; d. 19 July, 1865.
    2 *Minnie Frances*, b. 16 Dec., 1865.
    3 *Nellie Eva*, b. 1 Nov., 1869; m. Charles Emory Gault of W. Boylston, 25 Dec., 1892; res. Bedford, Mass. Ch. (Gault): Charles E.[10], b. 25 Nov., 1893.
707 ii Elliott Fay, b. 13 Jan., 1839.
  iii Harriet A., b. 13 Aug., 1841; m. 12 Feb., 1865, Capt. George P. Lyon of Weymouth, Mass., who enlisted in 1861, private Co. H, 12th Mass. Infantry; became Capt. in 1863, Co. H, 35th Mass. Infantry; resigned because of ill-health, April, 1864; d. 1906. Was G. A. R. Post Commander; res. in Weymouth. Ch. (Lyon), b. in Weymouth:
    1 *Hattie Belle*[9], b. 23 Jan., 1866; d. 25 Aug., 1866.
    2 *Edith Blanche*, b. 7 March, 1869.

      3 *Frank Clemence*, b. 21 Sept., 1874; enlisted in 1898 in U. S. Signal Corps; promoted to Sergeant and served through the Spanish War in Cuba; re-enlisted and went to the Philippines 3 years as Sergt. in the Signal Corps; res. Boston.

  iv Ellen C., b. 1 Aug., 1844; m. 1 June, 1871, Arthur A. Eames of Worcester, Mass. Ch. (Eames), b. in Worcester:

      1 *Mabel Frances*[9], b. 26 April, 1872.

      2 *Arthur Benjamin*, b. 2 Nov., 1873; m. 19 June, 1901, Mabelle Albee; res. Worcester. Ch. (Eames): Alice F.[10], b. 19 Aug., 1902.

708   v Eli Howard, b. 5 Sept., 1847.

  vi Mary F., b. 31 July, 1850; m. 8 Sept., 1877, Charles H. Baldwin of Worcester. Ch. (Baldwin).

      1 *Henry Fay*[9], b. 17 Dec., 1879; grad. Worcester Polytechnic Inst.

  vii Edmund Davis, b. 16 July, 1853; m. Sept., 1875, Mary A. Cather; is a basket mfr.; res. W. Boylston. Ch., b. there:

      1 *Chester E.*[9], b. 11 June, 1876; m. 1897, Mary McQuillan. Ch.: Francis[10].

      2 *Francis*, b. 13 Aug., 1877; d. 15 June, 1895.

      3 *Bertha L.*, b. 8 Feb., 1879; d. 8 June, 1895.

      4 *Edmund D.*, b. 14 April, 1883; d. 4 Oct., 1884.

      5 *Hazel I.*, b. 15 July, 1893.

  viii Willie Porter, b. 14 Sept., 1859; m. 3 Dec., 1895, Ida R., dau. of Ezra Pierce of W. Boylston; is a basket manufacturer. Ch., b. in W. Boylston:

      1 *Charles Albert*[9], b. 3 Jan., 1902.

438 CATHERINE WARREN[7], daughter of Dexter[6] and Catherine (Warren) Brigham; born in Westboro, Mass., 11 Dec., 1816; died 19 March, 1849; married, 19 May, 1840, Daniel Mitchell, of Bridgewater, Mass., born 7 Feb., 1807; died 23 July, 1877, in Prescott, Arizona. He married (2) his first wife's sister, Angeline.

Mr. Mitchell was a civil engineer and surveyor, and an early contractor on the B. & A. R. R.; moved to Kansas in 1855, and resided in Ogden and Junction City, where was Recorder, Treasurer and Surveyor for the County; also County Commissioner, Mayor and Dept. Collector of Internal Revenue; moved to Arizona, in 1875, where was Dept. Territorial Surveyor. Mitchell County, Kan. was named for him.

Children (Mitchell), born in Bridgewater:

  i William Dexter[8], b. 31 July, 1841; he enlisted in the Civil War in 1861, and was killed 10 March, 1865; he was Capt. of Co. K, 5th Ky. Cav., on the "March to the Sea."

  ii Daniel Francis, b. 3 Jan., 1843; unm., in 1903; was in Quartermaster's Dept., in the Civil War; res. in Junction City, Kan., where he was Dept. Treas., Civil Engineer, etc.; moved to Prescott, Arizona, in 1876, where he is a R. E. and Ins. agent.

  iii Catherine Warren, b. 15 March, 1849; d. 28 Sept., 1849.

MARY A. BRIGHAM (441)
First President of Mt. Holyoke College

439 DEXTER, JR.[7], son of Dexter[6] and Catherine (Warren) Brigham; born in Westboro, Mass., 23 Jan., 1819; died 6 Oct., 1892; married (1) 16 Feb., 1842, Hannah Abigail, daughter of Rev. Elisha Rockwood; born in Westboro, 1 Feb., 1817; died 26 April, 1882; married (2) Mrs. Rosa ———. He was early connected with the Boston & Albany R. R. and later interested in the first express line between Boston and New York. He moved to San Francisco, Cal., and later to Australia. The male line is extinct.

Children, born in Westboro:
    i Susan Emily[8], b. 19 April, 1846; d. 27 Aug., 1846.
    ii Rockwood, b. 24 July, 1848; d. 7 Feb., 1874, s. p.
    iii Constance Dexter.

440 ANGELINE[7], daughter of Dexter[6] and Catherine (Warren) Brigham; born in Westboro, Mass., 27 Jan., 1824; died in Salt River, Indian Reservation, Maricopa, Arizona, 21 July, 1906; married, 3 Oct., 1850, Daniel Mitchell of Bridgewater, Mass., (widower of her sister Catherine). She studied at Mt. Holyoke College, in 1846, but did not graduate.

Children (Mitchell), born in Bridgewater:
    i Charles Warren[8], b. 16 Feb., 1852; d. 18 Aug., 1852.
    ii Angeline Brigham, b. 5 Oct., 1854; m. 20 April, 1881, George Edward Brown; res. s. p., Maricopa, Arizona, in Salt River Indian Reservation.

441 MARY ANN[7], daughter of Dexter[6] and Mary Ann (Gould) Brigham; was born in Westboro, Mass., 6 Dec., 1829; she was instantly killed in a railway accident near New Haven, Conn., 29 June, 1889.

When Miss Brigham died, she was the President-elect of Mt. Holyoke College, Mass. In her youth, fondness for study led her to the best school of her time for women, Mt. Holyoke Seminary, at whose head was the pioneer in women's education, Mary Lyon. Miss Brigham returned to the Seminary as a teacher during 1855- '58, then was assistant principal at Ingham University, Le Roy, N. Y., for 3 years. In 1863 she began to conduct a post-graduate course in connection with the Brooklyn (N. Y.) Heights Seminary, at that time the leading private school for girls. Here Miss Brigham found her real life-work, and she remained, first as teacher and then as Associate Principal, for 26 years. In 1889, Miss Brigham accepted the unanimous call of the Trustees to become President of Mt. Holyoke College. She had twice refused the presidency of Wellesley College, also positions of honorable responsibility at Smith and Vassar College. The school had just been granted a college charter; but Mt. Holyoke was not destined to open its doors to its first President.

Conservative yet liberal in her educational policy, she retained what was good in the older system while assimilating the best in the modern methods. Gifted with remarkable discrimination, well-balanced judgment, wide knowledge of human nature and unfailing tenderness and sympathy, she became to thousands of girls their ideal of womanly wisdom and of Christian character. The Alumnæ of the Brooklyn Heights Seminary have equipped a Memorial Hall as a permanent reminder of her work for young girls. Another fitting tribute is the "Mary Brigham Cottage" at Mt. Holyoke College, the gift of the Mt. Holyoke Alumnæ Association of New York and vicinity, of which Miss Brigham was, for years, President. It is a beautiful and permanent memorial to Mt. Holyoke's first president.

442 ACHSAH ELIZABETH[7], daughter of Dexter[6] and Mary Ann (Gould) Brigham; born in Westboro, Mass., 10 April, 1832; died 14 April, 1882; married, 1 May, 1860, Joseph Milton Myers, born in Ohio, 25 Jan., 1830; died 21 Oct., 1897. He was a hotel-keeper, at Beloit, Kas., and Seligman, Arizona; member of the Board of Supervisors, Commissioners, etc., and a rancher.

Children (Myers):
    i Joseph Milton[8], b. Oct., 1862; d. *ibid.*
    ii Charles Henry, b. 23 Jan., 1864; m. 17 Dec., 1889, Iva Leonore Seaver, b. 19 Aug., 1866; res. Mesa, Ariz. Ch.:
        1 *Arey E.[9]*, b. 1892.
        2 *Dau.*, b. 1899.
    iii Mary Emma, b. 24 Dec., 1866; m. 5 Oct., 1887, Theodore James Pomeroy; res. Guadalajara, Mexico. Ch. (Pomeroy):
        1 *Theodore H.[9]*, b. 1889.
        2 *Charles J.*, b. 1892.

443 CHARLES EDMUND[7], son of Dexter[6] and Mary Ann (Gould) Brigham; born in Westboro, Mass., 3 July, 1834; died in Boston, 23 Aug., 1896; married, 6 May, 1858, Elizabeth Catherine, daughter of Phineas Gay of Boston, born 29 June, 1829 ; died 18 March, 1901.

He prepared for college at Thetford Vt., Academy, and entered Dartmouth College, but gave up his course and became an iron and steel merchant, doing a very large and successful business in Boston, where he resided for many years.

Child, born in Boston:
    i Arthur Gay[8], b. 9 April, 1864; d. s. p., in Colorado Springs, Colo. (where he had gone for his health), Oct., 1905; m. Jessie, dau. of Dr. McDougal, a dentist of Jamaica Plain, Mass.

444 SARAH LOUISA[7], daughter of Dexter[6] and Mary Ann (Gould) Brigham; born in Westboro, Mass., 13 Jan., 1845; mar-

ried 1 Jan., 1868, Junius Welch Hill of Boston; born in Hingham, Mass., 18 Nov., 1840.

Prof. Hill was educated in the Boston Public Schools, a " Franklin Medal " scholar; graduated from the English High School, and from Leipsic (Germany) Conservatory of Music. He has been a teacher of piano and organ in Boston, for many years, and organist in several churches; was Prof. of Music in Wellesley College 13 years. Residence, Newton, Mass.

Children (Hill):
    i Frederic Warren[8], b. 7 March, 1869; m. 2 Aug., 1890, Grace Hall Williams, b. 2 Jan., 1870. Ch. (Hill):
        1 *Dexter Brigham*[9], b. 25 Dec., 1891.
        2 *Philip M.,* d. y.
    ii Mary Brigham, b. 19 Nov., 1870; res. Colorado Springs, Colo., in 1906.

445 BAKER[7], son of Lieut. William[6] and Sarah (Baker) Brigham; born in Southboro, Mass., 9 Jan., 1792; died 19 Dec., 1868; married in 1818, Fanny, daughter of Nathaniel Fay of Southboro, born 23 Dec., 1790; died 27 May, 1881.

Children:
    i S. Maria[8], b. in Southboro, 26 Feb., 1820; d. 20 April, 1886; m. 20 June, 1848, William H. Buck of Southboro, b. 26 Aug., 1818; d. 13 Nov., 1902. Ch. (Buck), b. in Southboro:
        1 *Frank H.*[9], b. 14 Nov., 1850; res. Southboro.
        2 *George W.,* b. 14 March, 1852; m. 3 Nov., 1879, Jennie Robertson of Boston, b. 1 Feb., 1852. Ch.: i George R.[10], b. 24 Jan., 1883; ii Howard H., b. 27 March, 1889.
        3 *Wallace B,.* b. 14 Feb., 1857; res. Southboro.
    ii William Baker, b. 16 Nov., 1829; d. 26 June, 1889; m. in 1858, Olive A., dau. of Charles Fay of Southboro; b. 3 Sept., 1833. Ch.:
        1 *Charles B.*[9], b. 21 Sept., 1861; res. in Boston.
        2 *Edward H.,* b. 20 April, 1874; d. July, 1876.

446 WILLIAM CHAMBERLAIN[7], son of Col. Ephraim[6] and Lucy (Rice) Brigham; born in Marlboro, Mass., 7 Aug., 1795; died in Wardsboro, Vt., 12 Aug., 1875; married (1) 4 Dec., 1817, Lydia B., daughter of Stephen Rice; born in West Medway, Mass., 12 April, 1796; died in Wardsboro, 22 April, 1862; married (2) in 186—, Rebecca Farnham of New Hampshire; who died s. p., in 1884. Was a Sergeant under his father, in the War of 1812; was a mechanic and wheelwright, and resided in Wardsboro, Vt., where he removed from West Medway.

Children (by first wife), the first 4 born in Medway, others in Wardsboro:
    i Sophia[8], b. 3 Oct., 1819; d. 30 Dec., 1836.
    ii Laura, b. 15 Jan., 1821; m. 20 Oct., 1846, Andrew Hawks, b. in Saugus, Mass., 27 Aug., 1822; res. Lynn, Mass. Ch. (Hawks):
        1 *George W.*[9], and 2 others, all d. young.

    iii Lydia, b. 23 July, 1824; m. in 1844, Ira Leonard, b. in Allentown,
        N. H., 14 Feb., 1806; res. Lowell, Mass. Ch. (Leonard):
        1 *Mary A.*, d. young.
        2 *Lillian*, d. young.
        3 *Caroline*, m. Ammi L. Corliss, and res. Lowell.
    iv Dana, d. in infancy.
    v Dana, b. 8 Aug., 1827; d. unm., in Wardsboro, 1869; a farmer.
709 vi Loraon, b. 16 Feb., 1829.
    vii Frances, b. 11 June, 1830; d. 18 Jan., 1840.
    viii Dexter Elbridge, b. 6 April, 1831; m. 1858, Edith S. Twitchell;
        res. a farmer in Wardsboro, s. p.
    ix Mary Eliza, b. 1 May, 1833; d. 9 April, 1855.
    x Ansel Merriam, b. 6 Sept., 1835; d. in Tacoma, Wash, 29 Jan.,
        1889, s. p.; m. in Starkville, Vt., 13 Sept., 1868, Martha J.
        Champion, b. there, 29 Nov., 1840; res. there.
    xi Charles Wesley, b. 2 July, 1837; m. (1) 29 Nov., 1866, E.
        Augusta, dau. of Otis Metcalf; b. in Ashburnham, Mass., 29
        May, 1844; d. in Lowell, Mass., 24 Jan., 1891; m. (2) 25 April,
        1894, Inez M., dau. of Nathan Currier; b. in No. Troy, Vt., 15
        July, 1848. Was grad. Dartmouth Coll., M. D., 1859; a musician,
        2d Brigade Band, 3d Div., 24th Army Corps, Civil War; res.
        Wardsboro and Lowell, where a tanner and currier. Ch., b. in
        Wardsboro:
        1 *George Dexter*, b. 23 May, 1870; d. 11 Aug., 1870.
        2 *Charles Edmund*, twin to George; music teacher.
    xii Francis Edmund, b. 10 March, 1839; m. 29 Jan., 1869, Ida M.,
        dau. of Horace Bissell; b. in Wardsboro, 1 Dec., 1849. In the
        Civil War, musician 2d Brigade Band, 3 Div., 24th Army Corps;
        is postmaster, selectman, overseer of the poor and town auditor
        in Wardsboro, where res. a tanner and currier. Ch., b. there:
        1 *Carlos Buddington*, b. 15 May, 1878.

    447 MATTHIAS[7], son of Col. Ephraim[6] and Lucy (Rice)
Brigham; born in Marlboro, Mass., 29 Nov., 1796; died at Cin
cinnati, O., about 1854; married in Cincinnati, 3 Oct., 1821,
Caroline Crossman.

    Children, born in Cincinnati:
    i Caroline[8], b. 14 April, 1823; unm.
    ii Matilda, d. y.
    iii John C., b. 5 Feb., 1826; unm., res. Washington, D. C., in 1893.
    iv Lucilia S., b. 11 March, 1832; m. in 1857, Thomas H. Looker;
        Purser, U. S. N.; later Paymaster Gen.; retired; b. in Cincinnati,
        in 1829. Ch. (Looker), all res. in Washington, D. C.:
        1 *Henry B.*, deceased; 2 *Herbert H.*, deceased; 3 *Edward F.;*
        4 *William C.;* 5 *Bertha H.;* 6 *Reginald B.*

    448 LUCY[7], daughter of Col. Ephraim[6] and Lucy (Rice)
Brigham; born in Marlboro, Mass., 11 March, 1798; died in Marlboro, 5 Feb., 1861; married (1) 1 Feb., 1816, Luther Howe of
Marlboro; born 24 Sept., 1792; died 1 April, 1826; married (2)
1851, Jonah Howe. Resided in Marlboro.

Children (Howe), by first marriage, born in Marlboro:
 i Ezra L.[8], b. 1 Aug., 1817; d. 4 Jan., 1891; m. July, 1838, Sarah
  C. Hammond. Ch.:
   1 *Lucy[9]*; 2 *Adelaide,* both d. y.
 ii Sophia, b. 28 May, 1820; d. 31 March, 1848; m. 26 Nov., 1846,
  Samuel Hammond. 1 son, d. y.
 iii Sophronia, b. 27 Dec., 1821; m. 3 Dec., 1844, Luther S. Wheeler.
  Ch. (Wheeler):
   1 *Hattie B.[9],* b. 4 Jan., 1847; m. George S. Russell. Ch. (Russell): i Clifton[10]; ii Bertha.
   2 *Frances A.,* b. 17 Aug., 1849; d. 1850.
   3 *Frank H.,* b. 23 Feb., 1851; m. Hattie J. Estabrook. Ch.
   (Wheeler): i LeRoy[10]; ii Lloyd.
   4 *Fred A.,* b. 19 Sept., 1855; m. Orah M. Trull.
 iv Archelaus, b. 21 April, 1823; m. Janette H. Brigham, 548.
 v Harriet, b. 2 Dec., 1824; d. 11 June, 1870; m. 1 Jan., 1845,
  Sewall H. Bowker. Ch. (Bowker):
   1 *Charles H.[9],* b. 22 Oct., 1848; m. Mary Grant. Ch. (Bowker):
   i Frank[10]; ii Mary; iii Charles; 2 d. y.
   2 *Frank S.,* d. y.

449 EPHRAIM[7], son of Col. Ephraim[6] and Lucy (Rice) Brigham; born in Marlboro, Mass., 21 Oct., 1799; died in Natick, Mass.
————; married, 25 Nov., 1821, (Morse also says "Dec. 6"),
Sophia, daughter of Archelaus Howe, of Marlboro; born 15 March
1799; lived and died in Natick.

Children, born in Natick, except the eldest:
 i Ephraim Harris[8], b. in Dedham, Mass., 26 Sept., 1822; d. 21 Aug.,
  1877; m. 2 Dec., 1842, Catherine Hastings of Millbury, who d.
  2 Jan., 1881. He res. at Natick, and was a commission merchant, town clerk and deputy sheriff. Ch., b. in Natick:
   1 *Emma A.[9],* d.
   2 *Edward Harris,* d.
   3 *Alice Fay,* b. 7 Oct., 1855; m. George H. Randall of Falmouth, Me., b. 17 April, 1851. Ch. (Randall): i Kathryn[10],
   b. in Wellington, Mass., 26 Dec., 1884; ii Marguerite, b. 28
   Oct., 1892.
 ii Thomas Hartwell, b. 12 March, 1825; res. unm., in California
  in 1858.
710 iii Alfred Milo, b. 21 Oct., 1828.
711' iv Laura Sophia, b. 26 Dec., 1830.
 v Matthias, b. 25 June, 1833; m. Nancy Helen, dau. of David
  Bacon of Natick; res. Natick. Ch ·
   1 *Harris[9].*
 vi Mary Hubbard, b. 1 June, 1838.

450 HARRIET[7], daughter of Col. Ephraim[6] and Lucy (Rice)
Brigham; born in Marlboro, Mass., 14 March, 1801; died in Berlin, Mass., 11 Jan., 1892, æ. 90; married (1) Nov., 1821, Major
Merrick, son of Roger and Elizabeth (Rice) Phelps; born in Marlboro, 13 Oct., 1798; died there, 21 Nov., 1829; he was a tailor;
she married (2) 31 Oct., 1844, Capt. Paul[7] Brigham, son of 213.

She resided in Marlboro during her first marriage and with her second husband in Berlin.

Children (Phelps), born in Marlboro:

 i Edmund W.[8], b. 13 Sept., 1822; d. in Milford, Mass., 18 July, 1875; m. 17 Sept., 1843, Hopestill C. Pond; res. in Milford; was 2 years in the Civil War. Ch.:
  1 *Ella[9];* 2 *Augusta.*

 ii Susan E., b. 12 April, 1824; m. 5 April, 1849, Lewis L. Carter, son of Lewis; b. in Berlin, 10 Nov., 1822. Ch. (Carter), b. in Berlin:
  1 *Sidney Brigham[9],* b. 23 Sept., 1852; res. Berlin; m. ————.
  2 *Lewis Paul,* b. 17 Jan., 1856; res. Worcester, Mass.; m. ————.
  3 *Cora Isabelle,* b. 17 June, 1860; m. 21 Feb., 1879, Calvin Hastings; res. Boylston, Mass.
  4 and 5 *Infants,* d. y.

 iii Henry Brigham, b. 15 Dec., 1825; m. 6 May, 1849, Adeline P. Andrews; res. Hyde Park, Mass.; was alderman; 3 years in Civil War. Ch.:
  1 *William H.[9];* 2 *Hattie;* 3 *Lizzie.*

 iv Harriet Augusta, b. 17 March, 1827; m. 9 Sept., 1846, James M. Simonds, who d. in 1879; res. Leicester, Mass. She d. in Worcester, Mass., 1865. Ch. (Simonds):
  1 *Ada[9];* 2 *Fred;* 3 and 4 d. y.

 v Stephen D., b. 3 Dec., 1828; d. in Brooklyn, O., 2 Oct., 1873; m. 25 June, 1850, Sarah C. Burr. Ch.:
  1 *Walter M.[9]*

451 COL. SIDNEY[7], son of Col. Ephraim[6] and Lucy (Rice) Brigham; born in Marlboro, Mass., 28 Dec., 1802; died 17 June, 1840, at Hamilton, Georgia; married, 30 Jan., 1825, Eliza Brigham, daughter of Capt. John and Mary (Brigham) Stevens, and grand-daughter of 162; born in Marlboro, 10 Sept., 1803; died in Francestown, N. H., 2 Nov., 1839, æ. 36.

He moved to Francestown, N. H., in 1828, where he was prominent in the Fire Department, and was a colonel in the Militia. He was a merchant tailor in Marlboro, Tewksbury, and Weare, N. H.

Children, the 2 elder born in Marlboro:
712 i Algernon S.[8], b. 13 March, 1826.
 ii Mary Elizabeth, b. 14 Dec., 1827; d. 13 Oct., 1890; m. 10 June, 1846, George C. Temple of Worcester, Mass., d. in Ashland, Mass., 11 May, 1883, æ. 63. Ch. (Temple):
  1 *Alice Shepard[9],* b. 30 Aug., 1850.
  2 *Marlie E.,* d. æ. 14 days.
  3 *Willis B.,* b. 1 May, 1854.
  4 *Carrie L.,* d. æ. 2 years.
  5 *Harvey W.,* d. in 1892, æ. 31.
713 iii Loriman Stevens, b. 30 Jan., 1832.

452 REV. ELIJAH[7], son of Col. Ephraim[6] and Lucy (Rice) Brigham; born in Marlboro, Mass., 17 Nov., 1804; died in Newtonville, Mass., 5 Jan., 1878; married, 5 June, 1827, Mary, daughter of Paul Locker of Wayland, Mass.; born 15 Feb., 1809; died in Newtonville, 5 March, 1895.

He was early a captain in the Militia in Marlboro; also a member of the firm of E. Brigham & Co., leading carriage manufacturers, in Worcester, Mass; became a minister and was licensed to preach in 1835, made a Deacon in 1840, and an Elder in 1845. He was the father of Methodism in Fitchburg and Worcester; retired in 1863, and lived in Newtonville.

Children, all but the 2 elder and the youngest born in Fitchburg:
714   i Elijah⁸, b. in Marlboro, 12 May, 1828.
    ii Dexter, b. in Marlboro, 28 Oct., 1829; went to sea in 1848, and became an officer in the merchant marine; was in California in 1849; wrecked on the Pacific Ocean; was in the U. S. Navy, stationed on the African coast to intercept the slave trade; in 1853 was an officer of the " Albany," which, in 1854, was lost at sea with all on board.
715 iii Mary Louisa, b. 20 Oct., 1831.
716 iv Anna Dorothy, b. 31 Aug., 1833.
717   v John Wesley, b. 11 March, 1835.
718 vi Maj. Charles Olin, b. 1 Dec., 1836.
  vii Adaline A., b. 21 April, 1838; d. in Boston, 14 March, 1859; m. 22 Dec., 1855, George Barnard, adopted son of Joseph Brown (a wealthy master builder of Boston whom he succeeded); b. in 1833. He m. (2) Abbie F. Brigham, sister of his first wife; m. (3) Hannah E. Dunbar (dau. of Gilbert), of Brewster, Mass., by whom he had one son. Ch. (by first wife) (Brown):
      1 *Joseph Brigham⁹*, b. 13 Feb., 1857; m. Emma F. Gates. Ch.: Ralph W.¹⁰
  viii Abby Frances, b. 12 Nov., 1841; d. in Boston, 7 Dec., 1861; m. 12 Nov., 1861, George Barnard Brown, widower of her sister Adaline.
    ix Emma Isabella, b. in Boston, 11 Nov., 1849; d. April, 1907; m. 20 Nov., 1873, William, son of Hon. Levi Spalding; b. in Stanstead, P. Q., 27 July, 1834; she was active in temperance work; he is a merchant in Derby Line, Vt.; have one adopted child, *Annie Katherine Spalding*, b. 28 Sept., 1883; taken by them in 1884.

453   PETER⁷, son of Col. Ephraim⁶ and Lucy (Rice) Brigham; born in Marlboro, Mass., 18 Sept., 1806; died ———; married, 17 Sept., 1832, Lydia, daughter of Abel Maynard of Marlboro. Resided in Cambridge.

Children, born in Cambridge:
    i Harriet Eliza⁸, b. 16 Aug., 1833; d. 13 Sept., 1837.
   ii Josiah Merrick, b. 2 Feb., 1836; m. 24 Feb., 1864, Betsey K., dau. of William Little of Antrim, N. H.; res. Westboro. Ch.:
      1 *Son⁹*, b. 5 Dec., 1864.
      2 *Harriet Elizabeth*, b. 25 Oct., 1866.
      3 *Walter Josiah*, b. 28 July, 1868.
  iii Peter Maynard, b. 24 Sept., 1838.
   iv Susan Harriet, b. 16 Sept., 1841.
    v William Maynard, b. 7 Oct., 1843; d. 27 June, 1849.

454 LYDIA[7], daughter of Col. Ephraim[6] and Lucy (Rice) Brigham; born in Marlboro, Mass., 2 Jan., 1809; died 22 Dec., 1893; married, 9 Sept., 1830, Matthias Walker, Jr., of Northboro, Mass.; born in Framington, Mass., 13 Feb., 1801; died in Northboro, 11 Sept., 1870. Was a farmer and resided in Northboro.

Children (Walker), born in Northboro:
i Charles S.[8], b. 2 July, 1831; d. s. p., in So. Carver, Mass., 11 July, 1865; m. Harriet Day.
ii James B., b. 17 Nov., 1832; d. in Westboro, Mass., 30 Jan., 1893; m. Mary A. Maynard. Ch.:
  1 *Sumner*[9]*;* 2 *Carrie.*
iii Emily Lucy, b. 12 Oct., 1834; m. Rev. George F., son of Capt. Jacob Warren; b. in Ashby, Mass., 1831; res. in later years in Brooklyn. Ch. (Warren):
  1 *Cora B.*[9]*;* 2 *Florence E.,* d. y.; 3 *George F., Jr.,* res. a lawyer, N. Y. City; 4 *Edith H.,* grad. Wellesley College; 5 *Harry W.,* a R. E. broker.
iv Ellen S., b. 12 April, 1838; m. Theodore T. Wemott; res. Kansas City, Mo. Ch. (Wemott)
  1 *Ada*[9]*;* 2 *Arthur,* alderman in Butler, Mo.; 3 *Herbert S.;* 4 *Mary A.;* 5 *Claudia L.;* 6 *Stella B.;* 7 *Hattie W.;* 8 *Bessie;* 9 *Maud I.*
v Hattie J., b. 1 Dec., 1840; m. 2 Oct., 1866, Leonard W., son of Leonard Brewer, a farmer of Berlin, Mass. Ch. (Brewer):
  1 *Nellie W.*[9]*,* m. George E. Keizer of Berlin. Ch. (Keizer): i Althea[10]; ii Verlie; iii and iv d. y.
  2 *Mabel H.,* m. Alfred E. Hapgood of Hudson, Mass.
  3 *Arthur L.,* m. Cora E. Wheeler; res. Berlin. Ch.: i Samuel[10]; ii Leon.
  4 *Frank W.;* 5 *Alfred D.;* 6 *Ruth E.*
vi Lydia M., b. 1 Oct., 1843; d. 16 March, 1854.
vii Mary E., b. 24 Nov., 1844; m. Guilford P. Heath; res. Northboro. Ch. (Heath):
  1 *Roie*[9]*;* 2 *Edith;* 3 *Annie;* 4 *Florence.*
viii Henry F., b. 2 Oct., 1846; m. Jessie K., dau. of Rev. Geo. Hill; res. Norwood, Mass. Ch.:
  1 *Lewis*[9]*;* 2 *Esther;* 3 *James;* 4 *Laura.*
ix Fred M., b. 27 Aug., 1853; res. Milford, Mass.; m. Mary E. Hancock. Ch.:
  1 *Willie F.*[9]*;* 2 *Alice;* 3 *Carrie;* 4 *Eva.*

455 JANE ELIZABETH[7], daughter of Col. Ehpraim[6] and Mary (Hubbard) Brigham; born 20 Dec., 1818; died in Chelsea, Mass., 5 Sept., 1903; married 5 Dec., 1838, Samuel Woodward, son of S. W. Kendall; born in Marlboro, 1 Oct., 1815; died in Newton, Mass., 1 Oct., 1894.

Children (Kendall), the 2 elder born in Framingham, Mass.; the 3 younger in Natick, and the others in Bolton, Mass.:
i Henry W.[8], b. 17 June, 1841; in wholesale dry goods business in Boston; res. W. Newton. Ch.:
  1 *Isadore*[9]*;* 2 *Mary.*

ii Samuel W., b. 25 Oct., 1842; d. in Newton, Mass., 7 Dec., 1888;
m. Minerva Howe of Weymouth, Mass. Ch.:
1 *Clifford H.*[9]; 2 *Kenneth H.*
iii Sarah W., b. 20 June, 1844; d. 5 Sept., 1847.
iv Eugene S., b. 4 Nov., 1845; d. 7 Sept., 1847.
v Jane E. B., b. 25 Aug., 1847; m. Edward P. Briggs of Chelsea,
Mass.
iv Charlotte, b. 19 June, 1849; d. 29 April, 1850.
vii Eugene W., b. 23 Sept., 1850; m. 1890, Flora M. Kendall; res.
New York City, a merchant. Ch.:
1 *Winifred I.*[9]; 2 *Charles H.*; 3 *Allie J.*; 4 *Hazel M.*; 5
Samuel W.
viii Charlotte R., b. 10 Dec., 1852; d. 6 June, 1856.
ix Ada M., b. 25 Nov., 1854; d. 12 Sept., 1855.
x Edward, b. 3 Aug., 1856; d. in Newton, Mass., 2 May, 1887; m.
Ida F., dau. of Wm. Howe. Ch.:
1 *Herbert B.*[9]; 2 *Fred K.*
xi George Bancroft, b. 29 July, 1858; d. 19 Sept., 1858.
xii Frederick Hobbs, b. 23 May, 1860; d. 4 Oct., 1862.

456 CHARLES F.[7], son of Col. Ephraim[6] and Mary (Hubbard) Brigham; born in Marlboro, Mass., 5 June, 1829; married,
1 Nov., 1854, Elizabeth M., daughter of William B. Morrison.

He resided for a time in Worcester, Mass., and was an engineer
in Boston; has been connected with business in Chicago for several
years. Resides in Boston (Allston).

Children:
i Lizzie M.[8], b. 25 July, 1855; res. Boston.
ii Ralph H., b. 27 May, 1867; m. 18 July, 1892, Lucy A. White
of Worcester; ¬res. in Worcester; was in Co. A, 2d Mass. Regt.,
in the Spanish War, and at El Caney and San Juan Hill. Ch.:
1 *Rollin W.*[9], b. in Worcester, 7 Aug., 1893.

457 LUCIUS L.[7], son of Col. Ephraim[6] and Mary (Hubbard)
Brigham; born in Marlboro, Mass., 1 Sept., 1832; died in Worcester, Mass., ————, 1904; married, 6 June, 1861, Abbie H.,
daughter of Elijah D. Hayes of Lawrence, Mass.

He was a dealer in flour, grain, etc., in Worcester, where he had
a fine residence; had been an alderman. He was local chairman of
the B. F. A., at the Reunion in Worcester in 1896.

Children, born in Worcester:
i Annie Hubbard[8], b. 3 Jan., 1863; m. 27 Oct., 1887, James H.
Wheeler, Jr.,, of W. Newton, Mass. Ch. (Wheeler):
1 *Donald B.*[9], b. 27 July, 1888.
2 *Lucius B.*, b. 8 March, 1890.
ii Clara Lawrence, b. 15 Oct., 1868; m. 1 June, 1892, Louis W.
Southgate; res. Worcester, Mass. Ch. (Southgate):
1 *Richard B.*[9], b. 5 May, 1893.
2 *Prescott W.*, b. 12 Nov., 1895.
iii Kate, b. 9 Dec., 1870; d. 24 Jan., 1873.
iv Harry Prescott, b. 19 Aug., 1877; m. July, 1905, Marion Tanner
of Springfield; he is a mfr. Ch.: *Harry Prescott, Jr.*, b. 1907.

458 ABIGAIL[7], daughter of Willard[6] and Abigail (Munroe) Brigham; born in Marlboro, Mass., 22 May, 1807; died in Belmont, Mass., 15 March, 1894; married, 12 Oct., 1836, Joseph, son of James Hill of Belmont, who died 25 May, 1860. Had been selectman in Belmont.

Children (Hill), born in Belmont:
    i and iv Infants[8], d. y.
    v Joseph Willard, b. 4 Aug., 1840; m. Louisa D. Wetherbee of
        Lunenburg, Mass.; who d. 30 Dec., 1895; a commission merchant
        in Boston; res. Belmont. Ch., b. Belmont:
        1 *Clarence Ordway*[9], b. 27 Oct., 1869; res. Belmont.
        2 *Willard Munroe,* b. 9 May, 1877.
        3 *Florence Abigail,* b. 5 Oct., 1879.
        4 *Alfred Cowden,* b. 23 Dec., 1881; res. Belmont.
    vi Harriet, res. unm., in Belmont.

459 SARAH FOYE[7], daughter of Willard[6] and Abigail (Munroe) Brigham; born in Marlboro, Mass., 5 May, 1809; died in Brighton, Mass., 6 May, 1885; married, 30 May, 1833, George Livermore of Brighton; born 21 Sept., 1798; died 17 Oct., 1867.

Before Brighton became a part of Boston, Mr. Livermore held various town offices, selectman, etc., and served in the Legislature 1833-35.

Children (Livermore), born in Brighton:
    i Sarah Fisher[8], b. 23 April, 1834; d. 22 Dec., 1895; m. 29 Jan.,
        1868, Henry Judson Murdock of Charlestown, Mass. Ch. (Murdock):
        1 *Carrie L.*[9], b. 26 April, 1869.
        2 *Belle B.,* b. 14 Dec., 1871.
    ii George Brigham, b. 11 May, 1836; m. 18 June, 1867, Bessie
        Duncklee, who d. 19 March, 1874. He res. in Brighton; was in
        Legislature 1880-81. Ch.:
        1 *Georgia D.*[9], b. 18 Sept., 1870; m. Herbert A. Wilson, 14 Oct.,
        1896.
        2 *Harry B.,* b. 26 Sept., 1873; unm., an art student in Florence,
        Italy.
    iii Henry Munroe, b. 5 Jan., 1841; d. in Boston, 4 Dec., 1891; m.
        30 July, 1868, Kate L. Willcut; res. Brighton. Ch.:
        1 *Gertrude W.*[9], b. 14 May, 1869; m. 23 Nov., 1893, Hiram A.
        Henderson. Ch. (Henderson): i Mildred L., b. 5 April, 1895;
        ii George A., b. 5 Sept., 1901.
        2 *George,* b. 13 June, 1870; d. unm., 4 Dec., 1901.

460 CAPT. WILLARD CHAMBERLAIN[7], son of Willard[6] and Abigail (Munroe) Brigham; born in Marlboro, Mass., 10 April, 1811; died 28 March, 1900; married (1), 18 Nov., 1841, Abigail N., daughter of Thomas and Abigail (Briggs) Gould of Winchester, N. H., who died 11 Feb., 1843; married (2), 6 July, 1843, Harriet A. Gould, sister of his first wife, who died 7 April, 1899.

He was captain of the Militia, and a farmer, in Rindge, N. H.; was many years on the school committee, also selectman.

Child (by first wife), born in Rindge:
    i Charles Gould[8], b. 7 Feb., 1843; res. Winchendon, Mass.; three years in the regular army.

Children (by second wife), born in Rindge:
    ii Abbie Ann, b. 4 May, 1844; res. in Newport, R. I.
    iii Henry Foye, b. 18 Feb., 1846; a farmer in Rindge.
    iv Elizabeth Maria, b. 13 Dec., 1847; d. unm., 19 Nov., 1897; she was a successful teacher for many years in Ashburnham, and elsewhere.
    v Ella Munroe, b. 6 May, 1850; res. unm., in Rindge.
    vi Jane Newton, b. 19 Dec., 1851; m. 18 Aug., 1880, Joseph, son of Joseph and Sarah (White) Ballard of Vernon, N. Y.; b. 16 Feb., 1852. She res. in Winchendon, Mass. Ch. (Ballard):
        1 *Albert Willard*[9], b. in Westminster, Mass., 12 Sept., 1881; res. Winchendon.
        2 *Elizabeth Forge*, b. in Rindge, N. H., 7 Aug., 1883; res. Winchendon.
        3 *Rutherford Carlton*, b. in Winchendon, 4 June, 1887.
        4 *Helen Brigham*, b. in Winchendon, 13 July, 1889.
    vii Lucretia Augusta, b. 30 Oct., 1854; m. 15 May, 1877, Isaac M. Gleason; res. Newport, R. I. Ch. (Gleason):
        1 *Daisy H.*[9]; 2 *Nellie M.*

461 SAMUEL[7], son of Ebenezer[6] and Betsey (Champney) Brigham; born in Southboro, Mass., 23 Oct., 1789; died 17 Aug., 1872; married, 5 Jan., 1816, Lydia, daughter of Joseph Ball of Concord, Mass. He resided on a part of the (Lieut.) Nathan Brigham homestead in Southboro.

Children, born in Southboro:
    i Betsey[8], b. 27 Nov., 1818; m. Warren Buck, and res. Southboro. Ch. (Buck)
        1 *Juliana A.*[9], m. Francis A. Brigham, son of 432.
        2 *Oscar B.; 3 Walter W.; 4 Delia L.; 5 Leona B.; 6 Leander,* twin to Leona, d. under a year; 7 *Arthur.*
    ii Susan Forbes, b. 16 Sept., 1821; d. unm., 8 Aug., 1843.
    iii Lydia Ann, b. 10 Nov., 1827; m. Nahum B. Outhank, an artist, res. Newton, Mass.

462 CURTIS[7], son of Ebenezer[6] and Elizabeth (Rice) Wilder Brigham; born in Southboro, Mass., 17 March, 1801; died 20 Sept., 1884; married, 5 April, 1829, Mary Ann, daughter of Capt. John and Mary (Brigham) Stevens; born in Marlboro, Mass., 24 Oct., 1805; died 9 April, 1885. Resided in Marlboro.

Children, born in Marlboro:
    i Ann Elizabeth[8], b. 29 Dec., 1829; d. 17 Feb., 1905; m. J. S. Woodworth of Worcester; res. there.
    ii Curtis Freeman, b. 17 Oct., 1831; m. 25 Dec., 1859, Sarah J. Howe, who d. 24 April, 1902; res. in 1903, Hudson, Mass. Ch., b. in Hudson:

1 *George Clifton*[9], b. 2 Nov., 1862; d. 19 July, 1864.
2 *Lilla Frances*, m. 1889, Rolla Lamson, and d. in Hudson, May, 1891.
3 *Frank C.*, res. Hudson.
iii Mary Jane, b. 16 Nov., 1833; d. unm., 27 July, 1884.
iv James Henry, b. 11 April, 1836; enlisted in 1861, Co. F, 13th Mass. Infantry; served through the war; m. Emma A. Fay, and d. s. p., 12 Aug., 1866.
v Adaline Stevens, b. 26 July, 1838; m. 26 May, 1861, Winslow D. Walker of Marlboro, who d. there, 2 Dec., 1904. Ch. (Walker), b. in Marlboro:
  1 *Charles Austin*[9], b. 2 July, 1862; d. 14 Aug., 1863.
  2 *Herbert Francis*, b. 29 April, 1866; m. 1891, Ora Morrison. Ch.: Prescott H.[10]
  3 *Caroline Louise*, b. 8 Sept., 1876; m. 1899, Harry C. Graham. Ch. (Graham): Warren J.[10]
vi Sidney Augustine, b. 28 Jan., 1841; d. in Hingham, Mass., 4 Feb., 1905; m. 7 Dec., 1865, Lois Ella Shaw. Enlisted in 1861, Co. F, 13th Mass. Regt.; captured 2d battle of Bull Run; paroled; discharged for disability, 1863. Res. in Marlboro, Quincy and Hingham, at different times, and established the Brigham Electric Co. in Boston, with his son. Ch., b. in Marlboro:
  1 *Melville Sidney*[9], b. 6 Sept., 1866; m. 4 Oct., 1893, Lina Wright; removed to Detroit, Mich. Ch.: Dexter[10], b. 26 Nov., 1894.
vii Francis Stevens, b. 9 March, 1843; m. Ellen A. Leland; 1 ch., d. y.
viii Abby Louisa, b. 23 Jan., 1846; m. 1873, Charles J. Macomber of Worcester. Ch. (Macomber)
  1 *Harry W.*[9], b. 10 March, 1880; m. 26 Jan., 1905, Nora Long of Sebring, O.

463 DANA[7], son of Ebenezer[6] and Elizabeth (Rice) Wilder Brigham; born in Southboro, Mass., Oct., 1802; died in Southboro, 9 Oct., 1881; married (1), Miranda Fessenden, who died 8 March, 1835; married (2) Susan (Flagg) Amsden, daughter of Elijah Flagg of Southboro; she died 29 June, 1882, æ. 80. He resided on a part of the (Lieut.) Nathan Brigham homestead in Southboro.

Child (by first wife), born in Southboro:
i Harriet M.[8], b. 15 Feb., 1834; m. Curtis Hyde; res. Southboro. Ch. (Hyde):
  1 *Lillian*[9], b. 29 June, 1865; m. 6 Nov., 1888, Norval Lamprey. Ch. (Lamprey): i Randolph[10], b. 15 April, 1891; ii Twins, Rachel and Clarence, b. 20 April, 1894.
Child (by second wife), b. in Southboro:
ii Dana E., b. 29 Dec., 1837; m. (1) 25 March, 1859, Sarah J. Dalrimple; m. (2) 8 March, 1887, Alice Weatherbee, b. 24 Oct., 1862. Ch. (by first wife), b. in Southboro:
  1 *Ida A.*[9], b. 11 Sept., 1860; m. 22 Feb., 1887, Levi P. Ball of Winchendon, Mass., who was b. 12 Sept., 1859.
  2 *Clifton*, b. 20 Sept., 1865.

464 DENNIS[7], son of Sylvester[6] and Patty (Nichols) Brigham; born in Southboro, Mass., 10 Dec., 1795; died in Brooklyn,

N. Y., 18 Jan., 1875; married (1), Sept., 1819, Roxorenna, daughter of Heman and Patty Fay of Southboro; she was born at the original seat of the New England Fays, in the north part of Southboro, 5 Feb., 1796; died 22 Aug., 1842; married (2), Sept., 1843, Harriet, daughter of Josiah Bigelow of Boston, who died Sept., 1901; resided in New York City.

Children (by first wife):
719   i Charles Henry[8] (Rev.), b. in Boston, 27 July, 1820.
     ii Caroline Elizabeth, b. 26 Oct., 1821; d. 6 Nov., 1889; m. 20 Sept., 1843, John Maxwell; res. Brooklyn, N. Y. Ch. (Maxwell):
       1 *Matilda Rogers*[9], b. 5 Aug., 1844; d. 11 Jan., 1869; m. J. C. Whiting.
       2 *Charles Edward*, b. 7 Oct., 1845; d. 8 June, 1888; m. Alice Perry.
       3 *John Rogers*, b. 20 Nov., 1846; m. Maria Washburn.
       4 *Henrietta Frances*, b. 24 Oct., 1848; m. Joseph H. Lester.
       5 *Henry William*, b. 7 Dec., 1850; d. 9 May, 1902; m. Celia G. Alexander, who d. in France, in 1888.
       6 *Eugene Lascelles*, b. 3 April, 1853; m. Ida Carlton, and d. Feb., 1895.
     iii Henrietta Frances, b. 24 Jan., 1824; m. 16 Jan., 1856, John Safford, Jr., who d. Jan., 1861; res. Orange, N. J. Ch. (Safford):
       1 *Caroline*[9], b. 28 Feb., 1857; d. unm., Nov., 1873.
       2 *Mary Doremus*, b. 17 June, 1861.
     iv Edward Marshall, b. 3 Sept., 1826; d. 11 Aug., 1838.
     v Anna Matilda, b. 6 Dec., 1829; d. 7 Feb., 1840.
720   vi Lucian Fay, b. in N. Y. City, 9 Aug., 1842.
Children (by second wife):
     vii Virginia, b. 20 July, 1844; d. 11 July, 1857.
     viii Harriet, b. 11 Nov., 1846; d. unm., June, 1884.
     ix Edward Dennis, b. 20 Nov., 1850; d. unm., Dec., 1873.
     x Albert Hillard, b. 12 Jan., 1858; d. unm., 1882.

465   WILLIAM ASHBEL[7], son of Sylvester[6] and Patty (Nichols) Brigham; born in Southboro, Mass., 24 Oct., 1798; died in Boston, 26 Feb., 1876; married, June, 1827, Lydia, daughter of John Johnson of Southboro; born there, 8, Sept., 1800; died in Boston, 17 June, 1862. He was a merchant in Boston where he resided.

Children:
     i Helen Ann[8], b. in Boston, 3 April, 1828; res. Roxbury.
     ii Katherine J., b. 20 Oct., 1830; d. 3 May, 1857.
     iii John Lowell, b. 6 June, 1832; m. Frances C., dau. of Luther Towne of Chelsea, Mass.; was in business in Boston. Before the war he belonged to the Boston Lancers and the Boston Light Guards. Enlisted in 1st Mass. Cavalry, 17 Dec., 1861; in 1862 was Regt. Commissary Sergt. and 1st Lieut. and Regt. Commissary of Subsistence; Capt. of Commissary of Subsistence. On staff of Gen. P. H. Sheridan in 1864. Mustered out 9 Oct., 1865, as Brevet Lt. Col. for long and continued distinguished services. Was comrade of Encampment John A. Andrew Post 15, G. A. R.

Was 32d deg. Mason and member of St. John's Lodge; member of the Ancient & Hon. Artillery Co. Ch.:

1 *Kate*[9], b. 19 Jan., 1858; m. Harry M. Howard, res. Brookline.
iv William Henry, b. 16 Feb., 1834; d. 7 Oct., 1864. He was an artist of promise in 1858, and painted the portrait of Rev. William Jenks, LL. D., for the Genealogical Society of N. E.; he painted scenes from Shakespeare, and was engaged on one from " King Lear " at the time of his death (Vide *N. E. Hist. Gen. Register,* vol. xviii, p. 89).
v Francis Stanton, b. 28 Dec., 1835.

466 LOWELL[7], son of Sylvester[6] and Patty (Nichols) Brigham; born in Southboro, Mass., 6 Dec., 1800; died in Southboro, 24 April, 1840; married (1) Sept., 1831, Ann, daughter of John Johnson; born in Southboro, 20 Aug., 1802; died 20 Sept., 1834; married (2) Harriet Williams. The male line is extinct.

Children (by second wife), born in Southboro:
i Harriet Ann[8], b. 2 Sept., 1837; d. 25 Sept., 1874; m. 1 Jan., 1861, Watson W. Bridge of Wilbraham, Mass. Ch. (Bridge):
    1 *Mattie A.*[9], b. 16 Dec., 1861; m. 1886, Burton E. Dibble of Westfield, Mass. Ch. (Dibble): i Wallace[10]; ii Ralph.
    2 *Watson;* 3 *Lowell;* both d. y.
ii Martha Elizabeth, b. 8 Sept., 1839; d 7 March, 1885; m. 15 Oct., 1862, John Avery of Boston. Ch. (Avery):
    1 *Harriet*[9], b. 29 Feb., 1864; m. 1888, Ellery Peabody of West Newton, Mass. Ch. (Peabody): i Margaret[10]; ii Ellery.

467 TROWBRIDGE[7], son of Sylvester[6] and Patty (Nichols) Brigham; born in Southboro, Mass., 27 Sept., 1802; died 16 March, 1875; married, 27 Nov., 1833, Sarah ,F., daughter of Joseph and Olive (Fairbanks) Morse; born 19 Jan., 1806; died 15 April, 1888. He resided in Southboro.

Children, born in Southboro:
    i Edgar Morse[8], b. 21 June, 1835; res. Nova Scotia.
721 ii Alfred Willard, b. 19 June, 1837.
    iii George Henry, b. 5 Feb., 1839; d. unm., 20 April, 1886.
    iv Mary Eliza, b. 4 July, 1840; d. unm., 5 Nov., 1862.
    v Ann Maria, b. 26 June, 1842; d. 31 Aug., 1848.
    vi Otis Lowell, b. 2 Jan., 1844; d. unm., 18 Nov., 1878.
    vii Adelia Augusta, b. 5 Dec., 1845; d. 26 Aug., 1848.
    viii Charles E., b. 1 Dec., 1847; d. 26 Aug., 1848.

468 ELIJAH SPARHAWK[7], son of Capt. Elijah[6] and Sophia (Houghton) Brigham; born in Southboro, Mass., 20 April, 1813; died in Boston, 11 July, 1863; married in Boston, 1 Jan., 1840, Sarah Jane, daughter of Luke and Sarah Wright (Brown) Rogers; born in Concord, Mass., 24 Jan., 1822. He resided in Boston.

Children, born in Boston:
722 i Edwin Howard[8], b. 27 Sept., 1840.
    ii Adeliza, b. 10 April, 1843; d. 26 Jan., 1845.

469 EMILY[7], daughter of Trowbridge[6] and Asenath (Eaton)
Brigham; born in St. Albans, Vt., 1 Jan., 1805; died ————;
married in St. Albans, 1 Jan., 1827, Orrin D. Snow. They resided
at Milton and Niles, Mich.

   Children (Snow), probably all born in Milton, except the 2 younger·
      i Alvira A.[8], b. 3 Oct., 182—; d. 17 June, 1840, at Niles.
     ii Susan L., b. 20 Jan., 1829; m. 20 May, 1844, James W. Granger
        of Pipestone, Mich. Ch. (Granger):
        1 Hartwell H.[9], b. 3 Sept., 1845.
        2 Delia E., b. 20 Aug., 1847.
        3 Emma A., b. 1 Nov., 1850.
        4 James W., b. 10 Aug., 1853; d. 11 Aug., 1857.
        5 Frank, b. 28 March, 1857.
    iii Delia D., b. 14 May, 1831; m. 18 Sept., 1851, John H. Young of
        Niles. Ch. (Young):
        1 Edwin D.[9], b. 13 Oct., 1852; d. 2 May, 1854.
        2 Alfred D., b. 25 Sept., 1854.
        3 Harry D., b. 19 Aug., 1856; d. 21 Sept., 1857.
        4 Walter D., b. 21 Nov., 1857.
     iv Lyman L., b. 28 March, 1833; d. 12 May, 1833.
      v Fanny R., b. 15 April, 1834; m. 28 March, 1858, Noah Michael
        of Berrien. Ch. (Michael):
        1 Genevia[9], b. 29 Dec., 1858.
     vi Trowbridge B., b. 19 June, 1836; m. 25 Dec., 1858, Melinda Marrs
        in Niles.
    vii Laphelia A., b. 10 Sept., 1838.
   viii Ellen E., b. 15 Nov., 1841.
     ix Lucinda E., b. 7 Oct., 1843.

470 STOWELL[7], son of Trowbridge[6] and Asenath (Eaton)
Brigham, born in St. Albans, Vt., 1 Aug., 1809; drowned in Canton,
N. Y., in 1874; married (1), in Potsdam, N. Y., 19 Oct., 1834,
Mary D. Dailey, who died at Madrid, N. Y., 26 April, 1849; mar-
ried (2), in Madrid, Feb., 1850, Elizabeth Bowen; married (3)
Mrs. Gamble, who died in California.

   Children (by first wife):
      i Harriet[8], m. D. G. Griswold of Canton, N. Y., who d.
     ii Samantha, m. Cyrus Abernathy of Waddington, N. Y.
    iii Helen, m. ———— Spaulding; res. Batavia, N. Y.
   Child (by second wife), b. in Madrid, N. Y.:
723 iv William Hartwell (christened " Myron Hartwell "), b. 4 Oct.,
        1853.

471 JOSEPH LINCOLN[7], son of Lincoln[6] and Lucy (Forbes)
Brigham; born 15 Nov., 1804, in Cambridge, Mass.; died in Rox-
bury, Mass., 8 Nov., 1889; married, 14 Nov., 1830, Sally Gay,
daughter of John and Mary (Scammell) Wheeler, formerly of
Medway, Mass. Her father was a highly esteemed merchant of
Cambridgeport of the firm of Wheeler, Gay and Griggs. She was

born 13 June, 1808.   Mr. Brigham was a merchant in Boston and resided in Roxbury.

Children, born in Roxbury:

 i Mary Wheeler⁸, b. 27 Nov., 1831; m. 25 May, 1854, Robert C. M. Bowles of Roxbury. Ch. (Bowles):
  1 *William Cushing⁹*, b. in Roxbury, 21 May, 1855; d. 3 April, 1858.
  2 *Joseph Brigham*, b. 11 Jan., 1858; m. 6 June, 1887, Sarah Newton Morse, b. in Chicago, 13 Dec., 1861. Ch.: i Mary¹⁰, b. 3 May, 1888; ii Albert Morse, b. 1 June, 1891; iii Robert Brigham, b. in Houston, Tex.
  3 *Frances Elizabeth*, b. 22 Feb., 1859.
  4 *Sallie*, b. 13 Jan., 1867.
 ii Daniel Webster, b. 20 June, 1833; d. 3 Sept., 1836.
 iii Charles Lincoln, b. 19 Dec., 1835; d. 14 Dec., 1836.
 iv Lucy Forbes, b. 25 Nov., 1839; res. unm., in Brookline, Mass.
 v Anna Scammell, b. 3 Aug., 1841; m. 10 June, 1864, George E. Foster of Roxbury, who d. 6 Sept., 1881. Ch. (Foster), b. in Roxbury:
  1 *Lucy Brigham⁹*, b. 24 March, 1865; m. 4 April, 1888, John Chandler. Ch. (Chandler): i Dorothy¹⁰, b. 16 June, 1889; ii John, Jr., b. 12 June, 1890.
  2 *George Blanchard*, b. 2 Aug., 1874; d. 27 Sept., 1875.
  3 *Helen Fowle*, b. 12 May, 1878.
724 vi Dana Bullard, b. 25 April, 1845.

472 ERASTUS FORBES⁷, son of Lincoln⁶ and Lucy (Forbes) Brigham; born in Cambridge, Mass., 26 Aug., 1807; died ————; married, 17 Oct., 1832, Sophia De Wolf, daughter of Andrew Le Pierre Homer of Cambridge, Mass. She died in St. Paul, Minn. He was a merchant in Boston, and resided in Woburn, Mass.

Children:

 i Emeline De Wolf⁸, b. 14 Feb., 1834, in Troy, N. Y.; d. unm., in Houghton, Mich., March, 1861.
 ii Sophia Homer, b. 18 Oct., 1835, in Troy; d. 28 Nov., 1848, in Cambridge.
 iii Le Grand Bliss, b. 31 Aug., 1838, in Brooklyn, N. Y.; m. in Brooklyn, and had one child; whereabouts unknown; supposed to have died.
725 iv Joseph Lincoln, b. 3 Dec., 1840.
 v Frances Homer, b. 3 April, 1847, in Brooklyn; d. 3 Feb., 1848, in Cambridge.
 vi Andrew Le Pierre Homer, b. 10 June, 1850, in Cambridge; d. s. p., in Hazleton, Mich.

473 LUCY FORBES⁷, daughter of Lincoln⁶ and Lucy (Forbes) Brigham; born in Cambridge, Mass., 9 Sept., 1818; died in Boston, ————; married, 19 Aug., 1839, John Parker Bullard, A. M.; born 30 Nov., 1809; died in Clinton, La.; he was a great temperance worker.

Children (Bullard):
    i John Lincoln⁸, b. in Jackson, La., 17 Aug., 1840; d. in Short
        Hills, N. J., 2 July, 1899; was grad. Harvard Coll., 1861; m. (1)
        10 June, 1863, Sarah W., dau. of Walter P. and Lydia (Gardner)
        Spooner of New Bedford, Mass., who d. 1 June, 1866; m. (2) 3
        Nov., 1868, Charlotte Green, dau. of Elisha and Alice (Hathaway)
        Haskill of New Bedford, who d. 20 Feb., 1898; was, at the time
        of the Civil War, chief clerk in the Boston office of the Commis-
        sioners of Subsistence; then Commissioner of Subsistence (rank
        of Capt.), Boston; then brev. Major; later in N. Y. City, with
        Osborne, Bullard & Co., jobbers of India goods; then in the
        firm of Bullard & 'Wheeler, cotton and bagging brokers. Ch.
        (by first wife):
        1 *John Thornton⁹*, b. in Boston, 31 March, 1864; was grad. A. B.
            Harvard College, 1884; M. D., 1887; m. 18 June, 1889, Emily
            Morgan Rotch; res. New Bedford; 5 ch.
        2 *Sarah Spooner*, b. in New Bedford, 20 May, 1866; m. 18 June,
            1895, Charles Henry Leonard, son of George Delano; res.
            New Bedford., s. p., 1903.
        Ch. (by second wife):
        3 *Lucy Forbes*, b. in Staten Island, N. Y., 17 Nov., 1877; m.
            16 March, 1898, Louis P. Bayard, Jr., who was grad. Princeton
            College, 1898; res. Short Hills, N. J.; 4 ch.
    ii Dana Brigham, b. 5 June, 1842; d. 26 Sept., 1844.

474 (CHIEF JUSTICE) LINCOLN FLAGG⁷, son of Lincoln⁶ and Lucy (Forbes) Brigham; born in Cambridge, Mass., 4
Oct., 1819; died in Salem, Mass., 27 Feb., 1895; married, 20 Oct.,
1847, Eliza Endicott, daughter of Thomas and Lydia (Perry)
Swain; born in New Bedford, Mass., 11 July, 1826.

In his youth Judge Brigham entered the counting-room of the
late Samuel Austin, Jr., in Boston, and remained two years. In
1837 he began to study for college under the direction of Rev. David
Peabody, his brother-in-law. He was graduated from Dartmouth
College in 1842, and received the degree of LL. B. from the Harvard Law School in 1844. He went to New Bedford, Mass., and
further equipped himself for the practice of his profession in the
office of John H. Clifford and Harrison G. O. Colby and was admitted to the bar in June, 1845. He then formed a law partnership with Mr. Clifford, in New Bedford, which was maintained
until that gentleman was elected Governor of Massachusetts. In
1853, Mr. Brigham was appointed district attorney for the southern
district of Bristol County, and when the office was made elective,
in 1856, he was chosen to the same position, which he held until
appointed to the bench of the Superior Court by Gov. Banks, in
1859. Although Judge Brigham was associated with remarkably
able jurists on that first Superior bench, he was the peer of any.
Ten years after his appointment, he became Chief Justice, a position which he held for 21 years with great honor to the Common-

wealth and to himself, holding the office longer than the chief justice of any other court of the Commonwealth, save Lemuel Shaw. He possessed a commanding presence, an expressive countenance and dignified manners, and was noted for his unfailing patience and good temper; his kindness to young attorneys was characteristic.

Hon. William T. Forbes of Worcester delivered an eloquent eulogy of Judge Brigham at the Boston Reunion of 1902 of the Brigham Family Association. Among other tributes to his memory, he paid the following:

" He is likely to remain for generations to come, as he is now, the most prominent Justice of the great trial courts of this State.

As a judge, he was sufficiently learned but not pedantic; self-poised, but not self-opinionated; firm, but not obstinate; always dignified, but never haughty."

It is stated that a place on the Supreme Bench was tendered Judge Brigham more than once, while he was on the Superior Bench, but he declined. He resigned in 1890, owing to failing health and increasing deafness.

In 1866 he moved to Salem, where he resided for the rest of his life. He had a summer home at Bar Harbor.

In 1883 he received the degree of LL. D. from Dartmouth College, and from Harvard University in 1886. He was a member of the Mass. Historical Society.

Children, born in New Bedford, Mass., except the youngest:
  i Thomas Swain⁸, b. 22 April, 1849; m. 4 Aug., 1873, Barbara Jean Bentz, b. in Baden Baden, Germany; was 3 years in a military school; 24 years on the plains with cattle, hunting, etc., in Colorado, New Mexico and Kansas; res. Colorado Springs, Colo.; a stockdealer. Ch.:
    1 *Sylvia Swain⁹*, b. 11 June, 1875.
    2 *Ruth Forbes*, b. 12 Jan., 1887.
  ii Lincoln Forbes, b. 26 July, 1855; m. May, 1895, Kate G. Coit; is C. S. D. Harvard Univ.; was engaged in the lumber business for a while in Wisconsin; res. Salem, Mass. Ch.:
    1 *Katherine⁹*, b. 20 Nov., 1896; d. y.
    2 *Lincoln Flagg*, b. Feb., 1902.
  iii Clifford, b. 22 Sept., 1857; m. 9 Oct., 1900, Amy H. Johnson; was grad. A. B., Harvard Univ., 1880; was grad. Harvard Law School; practices chiefly in U. S. courts; Prest. Salem Common Council, 1891, '92, and '93.
  iv Augustus Perry, b. in Boston, 5 March, 1861; m. (1) Oct., 1897, Maude Rich; m. (2) June, 1901, Marion Ely; for a time he practiced law in Salem; then went into business in Colorado Springs. Ch.:
    1 *Dorothy⁹*, b. Sept., 1898; d. y.

475 AARON⁷, son of Ephraim⁶ and Sarah Brigham; born in Grafton, Mass., 29 March, 1771; died in E. Burke, Vt., ———;

Lincoln Brigham

married Abigail Maynard, born in New London, Conn., 1768. Probably resided in St. Johnsbury and Charlston, Vt.

Children, the eldest born in Marlow, N. H., the fourth, fifth, sixth and seventh born in Waterford, Vt.:

  i Lucretia⁸, b. 1794.
726 ii Ezra, b. in Charleston, 13 Sept., 1796.
727 iii Abigail, b. 30 Dec., 1798.
  iv Lucy, b. 1801.
  v Aaron E., b. 1803; d. in W. Concord, Vt.; m. ———— Knight of W. Charleston; a farmer. Ch.:
    1 *Lucius⁹;* 2 *Julius;* 3 *Julia* (twins); 4 *Susan.*
  vi Rebecca, b. 1805; d. s. p.; m. ———— Owen of St. Johnsbury.
  vii Lot, b. 1808.
  viii Paul, b. St. Johnsbury, 1811; d. s. p., Tilton, N. H.; m. ————.
728 ix Thomas, b. Charleston, 1816.

476 THOMAS⁷, son of Ephraim⁶ and Sarah Brigham; born in Colebrook, N. H., 7 July, 1786; slain in battle on Chippewa Plains, Canada, 5 July, 1816, after three years' service in the War of 1812; married Mary W. Lacy; born in Piermont, N. H., 24 Aug., 1782; died at the home of her son Ephraim in Dover, N. H., 16 June, 1865.

He started from Colebrook, one day, for Plymouth, N. H., to get his wife's sister to nurse his wife through her approaching confinement. When he got to No. Haverhill, N. H., he met a recruiting officer and enlisted for 9 months in the War of 1812. He was told that he would not have to serve for several weeks. Late that night he received orders to march; hastily sending a messenger to Plymouth, he marched with his company, after sending word to his wife. When he was slain he was with a scouting party, who were all killed and buried in a trench on the Canadian side of the Niagara River. A few years ago a trench full of human bones was found on the bank of the river, and from some buttons found it was known that the remains were those of American soldiers. The Canadian government permitted the U. S. soldiers to come into Canada and give the remains a military burial. These may have been the bones of that scouting party.

Children:
729 i Azel Parkhurst⁸, b. in Enosburg, Vt., 7 April, 1809.
730 ii William Lacy, b. in Enosburg, 20 Dec., 1810.
  iii Ephraim Thomas, b. in Colebrook, 9 June, 1813; d. 26 Oct., 1895; m. (1) Sophronia A. Langley of New Market, N. H., b. Sept., 1815; d. 15 Oct., 1849; m. (2) 2 Aug., 1851, Rebecca C. Smith of Dover, N. H., b. 1 June, 1827; res. Wentworth Home, Dover. Ch. (by first wife):
    1 *Annie A.⁹,* b. 5 Nov., 1843; d. unm., 27 May, 1866.
    2 *Lavenia K.,* b. 13 Oct., 1847; d. unm., 7 Dec., 1867.

477 AARON[7], son of Ithamar[6] and Catherine (Barnes) Brigham; born in Marlboro, Mass., 29 Dec., 1785; died in Lexington, Mass., 3 Oct., 1863; married, 2 Aug., 1808, Comfort, daughter of William and Elizabeth (Jones) Valentine; born 10 March, 1783, Northboro, Mass.; died in Lexington, Mass., 19 Dec., 1863. He was a merchant on Long Wharf, Boston; moved to Lexington, Mass., 1853.

Children:

    i Catherine Jones[8], b. in Northboro, 9 June, 1809; d. unm., in Lexton, 29 Dec, 1863.
731 ii William, b. in Northampton, Mass., 1 Oct., 1812.
    iii Sophia, b. in Athol, Mass., 17 Jan., 1815; m. Wm. J. Valentine of London, Eng. (son of Col. S. L.); b. in Bangor, Me., 3 Aug., 1817; was in lumber trade in Boston; in 1852, in the commission business in London; in 1854 *ibid.* and banking in France; Pres. U. S. Commissioners at Paris Fair, 1855, and decorated by Napoleon III. with Legion of Honor; a banker in London, 1862; Fellow of the Royal Geographical Soc., 1873. Ch. (Valentine):
        1 *William Brigham[9]*, b. 1840; res. London.
        2 *Garafelia*, d. y.
        3 *Francena Sophia*, m. George F. Marlow, and res. London.

478 ELI[7], son of Ithamar[6] and Catherine (Barnes) Brigham; born in Marlboro, Mass., 18 July, 1794; died in Marlboro, 21 Oct., 1850; married 5 Sept., 1819, Lydia, daughter of Jedediah and Lydia (Felton) Howe; born Sept., 1800; died in Northboro, Mass., March, 1885. He was a farmer.

Children, born in Marlboro:

    i Sarah Ann[8], b. 3 Oct., 1820; d. in Northboro, 15 March, 1884; m. 1844, Alonzo, son of Capt. Jedediah and Betsey (Wilkins) Wood; b. in Marlboro, 17 Aug., 1817; res. Hudson, where was assessor in 1867; d. 16 Oct., 1873. Ch. (Wood), b. in Hudson:
        1 *Ann E.[9]*, b. 27 July, 1845; d. May, 1857.
        2 *Alonzo, Jr.*, b. 18 Jan., 1847.
        3 *Frank J.*, b. 23 Aug., 1851; m. Kittie A., dau. of Albion Howe of Marlboro.
        4 *Hiram H.*, res. Hudson.
    ii Jonas Edward, b. 17 Jan., 1823; d. in Marlboro, 22 Aug., 1898; m. 16 Dec., 1852, Sarah Davenport, b. 1829; d. in Marlboro, 1894; farmer, res. Marlboro. Ch., b. there:
        1 *Sarah Eliza[9]*, b. 10 Nov., 1853.
        2 *Edward A.*, b. 10 Aug., 1856.
        3 *Hattie E.*, b. 7 March, 1862.
    iii Silas Edwin, b. 20 Feb., 1825; m. Nov., 1858, Martha A., dau. Elisha Ellis, b. in Westboro. He settled on his great-uncle Silas Brigham's place in Southboro. Ch., b. there:
        1 *Silas O.[9]*, b. March, 1862; d. 8 Aug., 1875.
        2 *Charles E.*, b. 19 Sept., 1864.
        3 *Herbert E.*, b. 25 Feb., 1867.
    iv Caroline Sophia, b. 19 Oct., 1831; m. Francis Brown of Ipswich, Mass.; res. Northboro, in 1885.
    v George Webber, b. 20 June, 1833; a farmer in Northboro.

479   DEA. ABEL[7], son of Ithamar[6] and Catherine (Barnes) Brigham; born in Marlboro, Mass., 13 Feb., 1797; died Marlboro, 16 March, 1871; married (1), 13 May, 1821, Mary, daughter of Augustus Bigelow; born in Berlin, Mass., 19 Jan., 1799; died 23 May, 1843; married (2), 3 Jan., 1844, Sally, daughter of William and Lois (Bartlett) Felton; born 26 June, 1809; died 13 Feb., 1878, s. p.   She was very industrious and among the last to use a hand loom.   He was a farmer and resided on his father's homestead half a mile north of the Academy in Marlboro.

Children (by first wife), born in Marlboro:
732   i Levi Samuel[8], b. 4 Aug., 1825.
733   ii Catherine Elizabeth, b. 27 Feb., 1831.

480   DANIEL[7], son of Daniel[6] and Anna (Beaman) Brigham; born in Bridgton, Me., 4 June, 1794; died in Bridgton, 1862; married, 19 June, 1822, Sophronia, daughter of William and Sally (Kimball) Emerson of St. Stephens, New Brunswick; born 12 May, 1798.   He resided on the homestead in Bridgton.

Children, born in Bridgton:
  i William H.[8], b. 6 March, 1823; m. Sept., 1849, Lydia Stuart of Harrison, Me., b. Aug., 1826; d. in Bridgton, s. p., 1901; they res. in Naples, Me.
  ii Silas, b. 29 June, 1824; d. 5 Jan., 1850, in Cincinnati, O., unm.
734   iii Edward, b. 24 Jan., 1826.
  iv Sarah A., b. 8 June, 1828; d. in Bridgton, unm., 1863.
  v Ruth, b. 6 July, 1830; d. 15 July, 1855, unm.
  vi Otis, b. 24 Dec., 1832; m. Elizabeth Houghton, who d. s. p., 22 May, 1905; he resides in Ayer, Mass.
735   vii Seth E., b. 2 June, 1834.
  viii Roxana, b. 19 Dec., 1835; d. 9 May, 1836.
  ix Roxana, b. 7 May, 1836; m. Edwin Ingalls; res. s. p., Bridgton Highlands, Me.
  x Eliza, b. 28 April, 1838; d. 2 Dec., 1856.

481   AARON[7], son of Daniel[6] and Anna (Beaman) Brigham; born in Bridgton, Me., 11 March, 1796; died there, 7 June, 1872; married, 16 April, 1823, Asenath, daughter of Ebenezer Carsley; born in Bridgton, 9 June, 1802; died there, 10 Dec. 1878.

Children, born in Bridgton:
  i Ruth Anna[8], b. 8 March, 1824; m. 5 Sept., 1843, Joel Howe, son of Luke Fosgate of Berlin, Mass.; b. 16 March, 1818; d. 3 April, 1903; she res. in Berlin.   Ch. (Fosgate), b. in Berlin:
    1 *Francis O.*[9], b. 1 Nov., 1845; m. Emma Symms; res. Shrewsbury, Mass.; a farmer.   Ch.: Raymond[10].
    2 *Emily A.,* b. 28 June, 1847; m. Herbert A. Cook; res. Shrewsbury.   Ch. (Cook): i Lester[10]; ii Maurice; iii Elsie.
    3 *Frederick A.,* b. 17 June, 1852; m. Ella F. Swan; res. Berlin.   Ch.: i Ruth[10]; ii Jennie; iii Fred.

4 *Angelina B.*, b. 13 Oct., 1855; m. Henry Davis of Shrewsbury. Ch. (Davis): i Myron; ii Lucille; iii Forest.

5 *Alvah Dana*, b. 23 April, 1859; d. 20 Oct., 1896; m. 15 Nov., 1882, Nellie Clark; a farmer.

ii Elizabeth, b. 26 Sept., 1825; d. 14 April, 1903; m. 6 April, 1851, Addison A., son of Rufus Sawyer of Reading, Mass.; d. 4 March, 1893. Ch. (Sawyer), b. in Reading:

1 *Eugene N.*[9], b. 23 Feb., 1852; d. 4 Dec., 1902; res. Malden, Mass.; m. Hattie Parker. Ch.: Marion[10], and one d. y.

2 *Jennie M.*, b. 23 Aug., 1858; m. Geo. W. Wilkinson of Reading, Mass. Ch. (Wilkinson): i Emily[10]; ii Blanche.

3 *Euleyetta*, b. 16 Nov., 1859.

iii Alvina, b. 17 Sept., 1828; d. 16 Aug., 1833.

iv Otis, b. 1 July, 1830; d. 12 July, 1831.

v Angelina, b. 8 March, 1834; d. 5 May, 1855; m. 1 Jan., 1851, D. Augustus Russell of Reading, Mass. Ch. (Russell), b. in Reading:

1 *Edgar W.*[9], b. 31 Dec., 1851; d. 24 Sept., 1852.

2 *Chester O.*, b. 15 Aug., 1853; m. Mary Richtering. Ch.: i Edward M.[10]; ii Maud; iii W. Dale; iv May; v Daniel; he res. in Chicago.

vi Jane, b. 25 April, 1836; m. 10 March, 1861, Alvin, son of Jesse Gibbs of Pasadena, Cal. Ch. (Gibbs).

1 *Stella A.*[9], b. 14 Sept., 1865; m. 14 March, 1858, Orville G. Cummings of Pasadena. Ch. (Cummings): Lester F.[10], b. 1889; d. 1892.

2 *Lula A.*, b. 3 Oct., 1869; d. 1870.

vii Aaron, b. 2 July, 1839; m. 30 Dec., 1861, Mary P., dau. of William Morrison; res. No. Attleboro, Mass. Ch.:

1 *Edgar W.*[9], b. in Bridgton, 20 April, 1863; m. 29 May, 1883, Josephine Foshner. Ch.: Willie[10], b. 29 July, 1885.

2 *Fred B.*, b. 6 May, 1865.

3 *Harry E.*, b. 4 June, 1871; d. 3 Sept., 1871.

4 *Mabel J.*, b. 26 Sept., 1872.

viii Austin, b. 20 Feb., 1843; m. 29 Nov., 1870, Elizabeth, dau. of Henry Carter; res. Bridgton. Ch., b. there:

1 *Beulah L.*[9], b. 19 Dec., 1871; m. Nov., 1893, John Gore of Bridgton. Ch. (Gore): i Adaline M.[10]; ii Harry B.

2 *Harry A.*, b. 3 July, 1873.

ix Martha, b. 25 April, 1847; d. 23 Nov., 1849.

x Adelia L., b. 2 Nov., 1852; m. (1) 22 June, 1875, James E. Fellows, who d. 1899; m. (2) 1901, Edwin M. Varney of Windham, Me., where res. s. p.

482 HENRY[7], son of Daniel[6] and Anna (Beaman) Brigham; born in Bridgton, Me., 24 Sept., 1798; died 6 March, 1851; married, 6 Feb., 1826, Mary Estes of Bethel, Me.; resided in Waterford and North Bridgton, Me.

Children:

736 i Louisa[8], b. 30 June, 1830.

ii Charles H., b. 5 Sept., 1832; res. unm., in Waterford, Me.

iii Mary E., b. 4 July, 1834; res. unm., in Medfield, Mass.

iv Nancy, b. 25 Nov., 1837; m. 26 Oct., 1872, Fred Monks, a farmer of Bridgton, Me.

v Joel F., b. 25 Sept., 1842; m. 22 April, 1877, Emma Childs;
a farmer in Wabasha, Minn. Ch.:
   1 *Charles F.*[9], b. 24 Jan., 1886.
   2 *Joel E.*, b. 18 Feb., 1893.

483 LORING[7], son of Abner[6] and Dorothy (Wood) Brigham;
born Marlboro, Mass., 19 March, 1795; died Osceola Mills, Wis.,
10 Jan., 1878; married (1), May, 1817, Clarissa A., daughter of
Thaddeus Fay of Northboro, Mass.; who died Sept., 1829; married (2), 1866, ————. He resided in Morse's day in Ann Arbor,
Mich.

Children:
   i Arethusa Augusta[8], b. 14 May, 1818; m. 1838, Jonathan L.
    Patch, and res. Troy, N. Y.; she d. 13 May, 1851, leaving one ch.
    (Patch):
      1 *Clarissa Augusta*[9], who was adopted by Edward A. Brigham,
      son of 203, and her name was changed to " Brigham "; she
      res. Worcester, Mass.
737 ii Eliza Maria, b. 30 Oct., 1821.
   iii Charles Dexter, b. 12 Dec., 1823; d. 11 Feb., 1852; m. 24 March,
    1848, Martha R. Laurence (who m. [2] Judson Gleason, and had
    son Fred); she d. 29 June, 1894, æ. 64. Ch.:
      1 *Helen*[9], b. 29 March, 1851; m. 18 July, 1871, Charles A.
      Cleveland, and res. s. p., Worcester, Mass.
   iv Edward Henry, b. 1825; d. unm., 1847.
   v Clarissa M., b. and d. 1829.

484 ABNER[7], son of Abner[6] and Dorothy (Wood) Brigham;
born in Marlboro, Mass., 21 June, 1793; died 29 Nov., 1877; married, 1 Nov., 1837, Lucinda, daughter of John Maybee; born 9
Sept., 1811; died 1 March, 1885. He was a farmer and resided in
Yarmouth, Ontario.

Children:
   i William Austin[8], b. 30 Aug., 1840; m. (1) 22 April, 1873, Emma
    G. Clarke, b. in Hudson, O., 1839; m. (2) 7 April, 1885, Mrs.
    Amelia, widow of George H. Reed; is a lawyer and resides in
    Coweta, Indian Territory. Ch. (by first wife):
      1 *Ethel*[9], b. 1 Aug., 1878; m. 12 June, 1899, William Rack of
      Denver, Colo.
      2 *Olga*, b. 30 Nov., 1880; m. 11 Sept., 1900, James J. Moran of
      Kansas City, Mo.
   ii Charles, b. 12 Nov., 1847; is an agriculturist, and res. unm. in
    Stockton, Cal.

485 DR. ADOLPHUS[7], son of Abner[6] and Dorothy (Wood)
Brigham; born in Marlboro, Mass., 4 Dec., 1802; died in Shrewsbury, Mass., 30 April, 1859; married (1), 10 Nov., 1828, Eliza A.
Parker of Southboro, Mass., who died 21 March, 1831, æ. 27; married (2), 13 June, 1832, Rebecca W., daughter of Thomas Knowl-

ton, Jr., of Shrewsbury; born there, 9 Oct., 1810; died 11 June, 1894.

Dr. Brigham taught school during the winter seasons from 1821 to 1825 and studied the remainder of the year. In 1823 he " studied Latin and Greek under the instruction of Rev. Seth Alden," a clergyman of Marlboro. In May, 1824, he began the study of medicine with Dr. J. B. Kittredge of Framingham, with whom he remained two years. June 24, 1826, he removed to Shrewsbury to " attend to the study and practice of medicine," under Dr. Seth Knowlton, then a prominent physician of that town. He attended medical lectures at Harvard Medical School; was licensed as a physician and surgeon by the censors of the Second Medical District at Worcester, 20 June, 1827; began the practice of medicine and surgery in Shrewsbury, 18 Nov., 1827, and remained there until his death. For many years before his death he was called " The Doctor of Shrewsbury," and not only had the larger part of the practice in that town but much in several adjoining towns. He lived respected and honored, and died greatly lamented and mourned by those to whom he had ministered for a generation, and justly merited the name of " The Good Physician."

Children (by second wife), born in Shrewsbury:
738 i Frederick A.[8], b. 1 April, 1835.
739 ii Franklin Whiting, b. 13 Sept., 1841.
iii Arthur Knowlton, b. 12 Dec., 1850; d. 15 Feb., 1851.

486 DEA. PIERPONT[7], son of Dea. Paul[6] and Fanny (Brigham) Brigham; born in Marlboro, Mass., 2 Aug., 1785; died of cholera, in Buffalo, N. Y., 21 Sept., 1838; married, Dec., 1809, Lovisa Conger. He is believed to have lived in Buffalo.

Children:
i Lovisa Jane[8], b. 18 Jan., 1812; d. 25 April, 1837.
ii Fanny McD., b. 16 April, 1814; m. W. W. Mason; res. Buffalo, N. Y.
iii Harriet N., b. 23 Jan., 1817; m. Jacob Swartz; res. Buffalo.
iv Lorinda S., b. 5 June, 1819; m. ———— Emery; res. Aurora, N. Y.
v John Stratton, b. 9 June, 1821; m. Frances Burke; ch. four; res. Ravenna, O.
vi Sophia W., b. 14 Aug., 1823; d. 28 Jan., 1847.
vii Amanda W., b. 15 Oct., 1825; d. 4 Jan., 1844.
viii Lovina N. Ward, b. 13 May, 1827; d. 22 Jan., 1829.
ix Elizabeth, b. 29 Sept., 1830; d. 16 Feb., 1858; m. ———— Gunn.

487 WILLIAM D.[7], son of Dea. Paul[6] and Fanny (Brigham) Brigham; born in St. Albans, Vt., 14 Jan., 1806; died 17 July, 1875; married Lucy Doane; born 2 Feb., 1805; died 15 June, 1883. He resided in St. Albans.

Adolphus Brigham

Children, born in St. Albans:
    i Lummus[8], b. 11 Jan., 1833; d. 20 Oct., 1855.
    ii Edmund D., b. 7 Sept., 1834; res. in St. Albans; enlisted in
        Co. C, First Vt. Vols., in the Civil War.
740 iii Sidney S., b. 15 Feb., 1836.
741 iv Sanford J., b. 31 Jan., 1838.
    v Fanny L., b. 22 Dec., 1839; d. 5 Oct., 1882; m. 4 Nov., 1862,
        E. W. Jewett. Ch. (Jewett):
        1 *Jessie Brigham*[9], b. 6 Dec., 1865.
        2 *Mary F.*, b. 7 Oct., 1867; d. 2 Oct., 1869.
        3 *Nellie H.*, b. 8 Sept., 1869.
        5 *Walter C.*, b. 25 May, 1873.

488 BARNABAS[7], son of Samuel[6] and Asenath (Bailey) Brigham; born in Berlin, Mass., 13 March, 1791; died Sept., 1855; married Persis, daughter of Elihu and Phebe (Belcher?) Maynard, born Marlboro, Mass., 1 Nov., 1795. Resided in Marlboro on the Thomas[2] homestead and built the present house on the place, about 1825.
Children, born in Marlboro:
    i Benjamin[8], b. 17 March, 1818; d. 2 Sept., 1819.
    ii Benjamin Warren, b. 21 May, 1820; d. y.
    iii Phebe Maria, b. 22 March, 1822; d. in home of daughter in
        Roxbury, Mass., 4 Oct., 1902; m. Nicholas Wise, who d. Ch.
        (Wise):
        1 *Helen*[9], m. Alonzo G. Stockwell, who d. Feb., 1906.
    iv Benjamin Thomas, b. 31 May, 1823; d. about 1866; m. Harriet
        Webster. Warren Brigham, who owned Thomas[2] Brigham's old
        home, made him his heir. He was the last male Brigham owner
        of the place; was a merchant tailor in Boston, and his father
        carried on the farm. Ch.:
        1 *Alice*[9]; 2 *Warren*.
    v Lucy, b. 24 June, 1824; d. 4 March, 1899; m. Sidney Brown;
        res. Marlboro.
    vi Henry Quincy, b. 23 Oct., 1827; was a dentist in Boston.
    vii Austin Dana, b. 6 June, 1836; d. May, 1904, in soldier's home in
        Togus, Me.; was a soldier in the Civil War; res. in Boston.

489 THOMAS[7], son of Thomas[6] and Azubah (Babcock) Brigham; born in Berlin, Mass., 17 Oct., 1797; died in Northboro, Mass., 19 June, 1855; married 29 March, 1822, Ann Carter, of Berlin. He resided in Berlin until 1851, and then removed to Northboro.
Child, born in Berlin:
    i Eliza Ann[8], b. 24 Sept., 1824; d. in Northboro, 22 Nov., 1861;
        m. 29 May, 1849, Samuel I. Rice, b. in Northboro, 11 Sept., 1821;
        d. there, 6 Nov., 1903. Ch. (Rice), born in Northboro:
        1 *Thomas Chandler*[9], b. 1 Aug., 1850.
        2 *Samuel Wilson*, b. 27 March, 1856; d. in Westboro, Mass., 31
          Oct., 1890; m. 8 April, 1880, Jennie M. Moore. Ch. (Rice):
          i Anna Eliza[10], b. 21 Nov., 1880; m. Charles S. Knight; ii
          Carrie Louise, b. 24 Feb., 1882; iii Gertrude Alice, b. 8 July,
          1884; iv Edith Mabel, b. 1886; d. 1891; v Bessie Wilson, b.
          13 Dec., 1890.

490 JOEL[7], son of Gardner[6] and Sarah (Rice) Brigham; born in Northboro, Mass., 13 Dec., 1788; died 16 Oct., 1869; married, 19 Aug., 1808, Nancy, daughter of Fortunatus Brigham, 168; born in Marlboro, Mass., 29 June, 1791; died 10 June, 1850. Resided in Berlin, Mass. (Carterville), but returned to Northboro.

Children:
742   i Ira[8], b. in Berlin, 12 Jan., 1809.
    ii Lewis, b. 1 July, 1812; m. Almira (Hewes) Bemis; res. s. p., in Northboro.
    iii Phebe, b. 5 Aug., 1813; d. 13 March, 1885; m. Thomas B., son of Benjamin Warren; b. 5 Dec., 1816; d. 8 Jan., 1899. Ch. (Warren):
      1 *Martha A.*[9], b. 13 Jan., 1844; m. 31 July, 1890, William Lowe, who d. s. p., 5 May, 1904; she res. Northboro.
      2 *John F.*, b. 1845; m. Lydia A. Ball; 4 ch.; res. Northboro.
      3 *Edward H.*, b. 7 Oct., 1848; m. Mary Temple; 7 ch.; res. Northboro.
      4 *George A.*, b. 25 Nov., 1853; m. Myra Walker; 4 ch., 3 d.; res. Boylston, Mass.
743   iv Abraham, b. in Northboro, 23 Jan., 1816.
744   v John, b. in Northboro, 11 June, 1819.
745   vi Samuel, b. in Berlin, 5 April, 1822.
    vii Anne, b. 30 Dec., 1824; m. Seth Flagg, who d. 11 Nov., 1883; m. (2) 9 Aug., 1890, J. B. Manning; res. s. p., in Northboro.
    viii Martha, b. 12 Jan., 1828; d. 9 Jan., 1895; m. Levi Stratton; res. s. p., Northboro.
    ix Mary Ann, b. 26 Oct., 1830; m. Henry L. Stone; res. Westboro; 10 ch.
    x Henry J., b. 10 Sept., 1833; d. 20 July, 1889; m. Mary Blodgett; res. s. p., Northboro.

491 JOHN SWARROW[7], son of John[6] and Lois (Fisk) Brigham; born in Paxton, Mass., 24 May, 1803; married 21 Jan., 1828, Parmelia Brace.

Children:
    i Harriet[8], b. 29 Oct., 1828; m. George White; res. 9 Waverly Pl., Chicago. Ch. (White):
      1 *Fred*[9]; 2 *Caroline;* 3 *Emma.*
746   ii Charles H., b. near Rochester, N. Y., 30 June, 1830.
    iii Rhoda, b. 1832; d. 6 Dec., 1877; m. 24 Dec., 1855, Stephen G. Scott. Ch. (Scott):
      1 *George*[9]; 2 *Francis;* 3 *Flora;* 4 *John;* 5 *Josephine.*
    iv Jerome, b. 1834; d. 5 Nov., 1886; m. Mrs. Lovinda Oliver; no children.
    v John, b. 1836; m. Elizabeth Hall; res. Tipton Ford of Newton Co., Mo. Ch.:
      1 *Joseph*[9], d. 1891; 2 *Martha.*
    vi Artemas, b. 25 Aug., 1838; m. 24 Dec., 1868, Althea Cooley; no ch.
    vii George, b. 1841; d. unm., in Chicago, 12 Nov., 1888.

492 HENRY[7], son of Henry[6] and Susanna (Harrington) Brigham; born in Northboro, Mass., 30 Oct., 1798; died ————; married Lucy W., daughter of Benjamin Howe; she died 28 March, 1844, æ. 38. Resided in Northboro.

Children, born in Northboro:
   i Benjamin D.[8], b. 5 June, 1825; d. in So. Framingham, Mass., where he was a dealer in straw goods, in 1884; m. 1853, Hannah A. Rich, b. in Northboro, 15 June, 1831. In Co. M, 32d Mass. Infantry, Civil War. Ch., b. in So. Framingham:
      1 George W.[9], b. 1858; m. 1885, Helen Lake; res. Chicago, Ill. Ch.: i Walter I.[10]; ii Minnie; iii George W.
      2 Irving D., b. 9 Aug., 1864; m. 4 July, 1886, Lizzie Nichols, b. in England, 30 Nov., 1865; res. Framingham. Ch.: i Charles W.[10], b. 18 Sept., 1887; ii Frederick I., b. 28 Aug., 1889; iii Ralph T., b. 2 Sept., 1892.
   ii Seraph J., b. 2 June, 1829, and d.
   iii Thomas H., b. 25 Nov., 1831.
   iv George G., b. 10 June, 1836.
   v Susan M., b. 27 Oct., 1838.
   vi Artemas, b. 28 Jan., 1841.
   vii Charles H., b. 26 Jan., 1843, and d.

493 STEPHEN P.[7], son of Lovell[6] and Lucy (Phelps), Brigham; born in Northboro, Mass., 11 Oct., 1810; resided and died in Worcester, Mass., 13 June, 1846; married Sarah Allen, who died in Worcester.

Children, born in Worcester:
   i Jason Stephen[8], m. Ann Eliza Cashman of Milford, Mass.; res. there. Ch., b. in Milford:
      1 George[9]; 2 Henry; 3 Albert.
   ii Sarah, who d. about 1896.

494 WILLIAM RUSSELL[7], son of Lovell[6] and Lucy (Phelps) Brigham; born in Northboro, Mass., 27 Dec, 1812; died 20 Nov., 1858; married 5 April, 1837, Rebeckah Morse, daughter of Francis Flagg; born in Boylston, Mass., 23 Nov., 1819 died 2 Dec., 1896. He was a storekeeper in Worcester, Mass.

Children, born in Worcester:
   i Augustus E.[8], b. 14 July, 1838; d. 27 March, 1840.
   ii Henry E., b. 5 Aug., 1840; d. 6 Sept., 1841.
   iii Mary Augusta, b. 28 Aug., 1842; m. 17 Nov., 1868, Silas W. Goddard. Ch. (Goddard):
      1 Clifford W.[9], b. 7 Aug., 1875.
   iv Charles Augustus, b. 1844; d. 1846.
   v Charles Arthur, b. 30 April, 1850; m. (1) 12 June, 1878, M. Louise Mowry, who d. 1897; m. (2) 25 June, 1902, Evie M. Shippel of North Dana, Mass.; res. Worcester. Ch.:
      1 Walter E.[9], b. 31 May, 1880; d. y.
      2 George A., b. 12 March, 1884; d. 21 July, 1884.
      3 Rose I., b. 19 Sept., 1889.

    vi William Henry, b. 15 May, 1853; m. 8 May, 1879, Hattie Collins,
       dau. of Seneca Richardson; b. in Worcester, 18 Nov., 1856; res.
       Worcester. Ch.:
        1 *William Seneca*[9], b. 28 Nov., 1879; res. Worcester.
        2 *Bertha Emily,* b. 28 Oct., 1881; res. Worcester.
        3 *Katherine,* b. 16 April, 1891.
    vii Ellen, b. 29 June, 1855; d. *ibid.*
    viii Eleanor, twin to Ellen; d. *ibid.*
    ix Lily, b. 29 Oct., 1856.

495   LODASCA[7], daughter of John[6] and Sarah (Eaton) Brigham; born in Pomfret, N. Y., 13 Dec., 1807; died 14 Feb., 1885;
married 3 Aug., 1826, Aaron Mark, of Pomfret, N. Y. They resided near Silver Creek, N. Y.

    Children (Mark):
      i Reuben[8], b. 7 Aug., 1827; d. 1852.
      ii Calista, b. 19 June, 1829; d. 1861; m. William E. Powers. Ch.
        (Powers):
        1 *Frank E.*[9]
     iii Alfred, b. 16 Sept., 1831; m. Carrie Snyder; res., 1904, in
       Sheridan, N. Y.; had 2 daus.
     iv Aaron, b. 23 Aug., 1833; d. 1880; m. Almary Clark; 1 dau.
      v William C., b. 6 July, 1835; d. 1854.
     vi Martha M., b. 27 June, 1837; m. Reuben R. Hamlet of Sheridan,
       N. Y.; living in 1904; 1 son.
    vii Sarah L., b. 22 Dec., 1839; m. I. J. Ennis; living in 1904, Dunkirk,
       N. Y.; 1 son.

496   ORLANDO[7], son of John[6] and Sarah (Eaton) Brigham;
born in Dunkirk, N. Y., 5 Feb., 1813; died in Wasioja, Minn., 3
April, 1885; married (1) 8 April, 1838, Fanny Jane Safford, who
died 12 April, 1869; married (2) 9 Nov., 1870, Mrs. Betsey G.
Milliken.

He was in partnership with his uncle, Gen. Elijah Risley in
" Risley Seed Garden," Fredonia, N. Y. He resided for a time at
Pomfret, N. Y., where Brigham settlement and P. O. were named
for him. In 1859 he moved to Wasioja.

    Children (by first wife), born in Pomfret:
      i Charles Hanson[8], b. 27 May, 1839; d. unm., 5 Feb., 1861.
      ii Delia, b. 17 Oct., 1842; m. 1 Nov., 1870, Edward Doud of
       Rochester, Minn., and res. in Sheffield, Ala. Ch. (Doud), b. in
       Chattanooga, Tenn.:
        1 *Ralph Brigham*[9], b. 9 March, 1874.
        2 *Delia,* b. 14 April, 1875; m. 17 Oct., 1905, Rev. Lemuel J.
         Lewis.
        3 *Charles,* b. 9 Sept., 1876.
     iii Caroline, b. 29 July, 1846; m. 2 Oct., 1870, Charles W. Gibbons
       of W. Concord, Minn. Ch. (Gibbons):
        1 *Roy Brigham*[9], b. 16 Nov., 1872; d. 1 May, 1873.
        2 *Walter Fitz,* b. 31 Aug., 1875; m. 22 March, 1905, Bessie
         Hastings Wilde. Ch.: Laurene M.[10], b. 19 Jan., 1906.

Charles H. Brigham (746)   John S. Brigham (491)
Mrs. Ella Brigham Stevens   Edward D. Brigham (820)

3 *Fred Carl*, b. 17 Dec., 1877; d. 28 Feb., 1883.
4 *Margaret Ethel*, b. 27 April, 1883.
5 *Frank Eldon*, b. 4 Oct., 1884.
iv Fanny Jane, b. 10 Jan., 1850; res. unm., W. Concord, Minn.

497 NABBY[7], daughter of John[6] and Sarah (Eaton) Brigham; born 1818; died ————· married 7 April, 1839, Seth Griswold of Pomfret, N. Y.

Children (Griswold):
 i Walter E.[8], m. Isadore Frost; res. s. p., Kenmore, N. Y.
 ii Mary, (d.); m. Walter Cobb; 1 ch.; res. Buffalo.
 iii Adaline, m. Thomas Erwin; res. Cherry Creek, N. Y.; 1 son.
 iv Pamelia, m. James Scott; 1 son.
 v Fanny, (d.); m. Lowell Sheffield of Cherry Creek, N. Y.; 1 son.
 vi Emma, m. Edwin Bentley of Cherry Creek, N. Y.; 1 son.
 vii George, d. unm.
 viii Ella, m. Lynn Bentley; res. near Pittsburgh; 1 son and 2 daus.
 ix Benjamin, m. Nellie Emory of Cherry Creek, N. Y.; 1 dau.

498 NELSON[7], son of John[6] and Sarah (Eaton) Brigham; born in Dunkirk, N. Y., 11 June, 1822; died in Chicago, Ill., 9 Oct., 1893; married 25 May, 1852, in Pomfret, Charlotte E., daughter of Simeon A. and Nancy (Merrill) Stoddard; born in Arkwright, N. Y., 12 Aug., 1832.

He was a farmer and seedsman. He moved to Cropsey, Ill., and thence to Chatsworth, Ill., and finally resided at 7528 Normal Ave., Chicago.

Children, the second and third born in Cropsey:
 i Eldon Tappan[8], b. in Pomfret, N. Y., 6 Nov., 1853; m. 27 Dec., 1876, Maggie Emma, dau. of Henry Rayburn of Saybrook, Ill. Was grad. D. D. S., Northwestern Univ.; res. Sheldon and Watseka, Ill., and Albuquerque and Carlsbad, New Mexico, for health, Ch., b. in Saybrook:
  1 *Edith Eldora[9]*, b. 21 Oct., 1877; m. 21 June, 1899, Frank E. Lake of Dixon, Ill.; s. p., 1901.
  2 *Roy Emerson*, b. 18 Feb., 1882; d. 30 Dec., 1884.
 ii Helen Belle, b. 26 Aug., 1858; m. 15 Nov., 1877, Orman H. Brigham, D. D. S., of Chatsworth, Ill. Ch. (Brigham), b. in Cropsey:
  1 *Nina Ethel[9]*, b. 13 Sept., 1880.
  2 *Adella Bell*, b. 5 Dec., 1882.
  3 *Everett Eldon*, b. 20 May, 1889.
  4 *Virginia Ellingwood*, b. 10 Sept., 1895.
 iii Simeon Avery, b. 2 Nov., 1864; d. 31 Oct., 1865.
 iv Lottie Adella, b. in Chatsworth, 27 June, 1867; d. unm., 8 Nov., 1893.

499 FIDELIO WILLIAMS[7], son of James[6] and Fanny (Risley) Brigham; born in Fredonia, N. Y., 5 Dec., 1812; died in Tibaderville, La., 1 Jan., 1866; married (1) 2 Feb., 1833, Adaline

E. Smith; who died 1 March, 1855, in Nashville, Tenn.; interred in Fredonia; married (2) 30 Nov., 1858, Amelia V. Webb, who died in Cincinnati, O., 6 Sept. 1859, s. p.; married (3) about 1863, Harriet R., daughter of Barnabas Gilbert; born in Gary, N. Y., 9 Nov., 1820; died in Fruitvale, Cal., 19 Dec., 1904.

He lived in Youngsville, Pa., where he was a merchant, Postmaster and lumber dealer; he moved to California in 1851, where he was successful; returned and took extensive railroad contracts in Kentucky and was one of the proprietors of a very extensive coal mine on the Ohio River. The Civil War required him to abandon this business. Later he went to Louisiana and engaged in cotton raising with his brother Wesley and their sons.

> *Children (by first wife):*
> i Risley Hanson[8], b. 6 June, 1834; d. in Cheyenne, Wy., 20 Jan., 1870.
> ii Charles Edgar, b. 3 July, 1836; d. 12 Feb., 1839.
> iii Mary Ellen, b. 18 Dec., 1837; d. 7 Feb., 1839.
> iv William Fidelio, b. 16 Feb., 1840; living somewhere in Ohio in 1904.
> v Delia Harriet, b. 16 April, 1842; d. 27 Jan., 1846.
> vi Delia Adaline, b. 17 Oct., 1845; d. 22 Jan., 1904; m. (1) 1867, George Clark of Fredonia, who d. 1870; m. (2) 18 Feb., 1873, Noel B. Chamberlain of Niagara Falls, N. Y. Ch. (Chamberlain):
> 1 *Eleanor Risley*[9], b. 30 May, 1879; d. 14 July, 1881.
> vii Kate Adaline, b. 26 March, 1850; d. 7 April, 1853.

500 WESLEY HERVEY[7], son of James[6] and Fanny (Risley) Brigham; born in Fredonia, N. Y., 13 May, 1819; died at residence in Corry, Pa., 10 April, 1906; married in Youngsville, Pa., in 1842, Harriet N. Smith, born in Dunkirk, N. Y., 17 May, 1819; died Corry, Pa., 6 April, 1905.

In his early years he was in the mercantile line of business. In 1851 he went to California with his brother Fidelio and after engaging successfully in the water business in San Francisco, they both returned in 1853. Joined with his brother in carrying out extensive railroad contracts in Kentucky and Tennesee, and after the Civil War engaged in cotton raising in Louisiana. Later he was interested in farming.

> *Children, the 5 elder born in Youngsville, Pa., the others in Fredonia, N. Y.:*
> i James Risley[8], b. 3 June, 1843; m. 25 Nov., 1868, Alice Matteson, dau. of Sidney Stearns of Van Buren, N. Y.; b. 25 April, 1848; prominent citizen and hardware dealer in Corry, having filled numerous municipal offices. Ch., b. in Corry:
> 1 *Eugene Barney*[9], b. 15 Jan., 1871; m. 12 Nov., 1896, Glenn L. Pope. Ch.: Alice Louise[10], b. 14 Sept., 1900; a clerk in the Corry P. O.
> 2 *Walter Stearns*, b. 30 Nov., 1875; in business with his father.

ii Mary Adaline, b. 19 Feb., 1845; res. Corry.

iii Henry Clay, b. 21 March, 1847; d. 1 May, 1847.

767 iv Charles Fidelo, b. 18 April, 1848.

v Ella Sophia, b. 29 July, 1851; d. in Fredonia, 31 Oct., 1863.

vi George Wesley, b. 30 Aug., 1855; d. 25 May, 1879.

vii Frank Cushing, b. 14 Feb., 1857; m. 1 Jan., 1885, Elizabeth J. Kinny, b. in Ohio, 23 Feb., 1862; engaged in dairy farming and stock raising on a 300-acre farm in Corry. Ch., b. in C.:

1 *Ella Louise*[9], b. 1 Oct., 1886.

2 *Roscoe Fidelio*, b. 2 June, 1888.

3 *Alice Marie*, b. 16 Nov., 1897.

4 *Ruth Elizabeth*, b. 1 July, 1903.

viii Edward Levi, b. 18 Nov., 1862; d. s. p., 14 Feb., 1891; m. 1 Jan., 1884, Mrs. Edith O. Leach; was a highly respected merchant in Corry. Mrs. Brigham's dau., Ora Leach, took the name of " Brigham."

501 LEVI[7], son of James[6] and Fanny (Risley) Brigham; born in Fredonia, N. Y., 6 Jan., 1824; died in Parkersville, N. Y., 3 July, 1889; married 29 Oct., 1844, in Hartland, N. Y., Mary E., daughter of Anson Hutchinson; born in Pomfret, N. Y., 2 July, 1825; died 6 Aug., 1904, in Council Grove, Kas.

Mr. Brigham was Postmaster in Tidioute, Pa. With two brothers, in 1851, he went to California where they purchased the only well in San Francisco and made money. Returning east contracted to build a portion of the Louisville and Nashville Ry., and opened a coal mine in Paducah, Ky.; on account of the war he went to farming in Wisconsin and Illinois. In 1871 moved to Kansas and was agent of the M. K. & T. Ry. in Parkersville where was appointed Postmaster in 1873 and held the office 18 years. He contributed to papers and was a lecturer.

Children, the 3 elder born in Deerfield, Pa.:

i Helen Fanny[8], b. 3 Aug., 1846; m. 4 Jan., 1866, William Lewis, son of William J. Pierce; b. in Sacketts Harbor, N. Y., 13 March, 1843; in the Civil War 1 year, Co. G, 2d Wis. Cav.; res. s. p., Ironwood, Mich.

ii Hanson Hutchinson, b. 13 Aug., 1847; m. 7 Sept., 1868, Sarah K. Mabie; is superintendent of a large farm attached to a Presbyterian School for boys of white people of the mountains, in Asheville, N. C.; no ch.

iii Flora Ann, b. 2 May, 1850; m. 1 Oct., 1874, Adam Moser, Jr., Co. Atty. for Morris Co., Kansas, and Cashier of Farmers' and Drovers' Bank, Council Grove, Kan. Ch. (Moser):

1 *Maude Brigham*[9], b. 23 Feb., 1876.

2 *Helen Flora*, b. 4 Jan., 1878; d. 20 Nov., 1881.

3 *Levi Adam*, b. 1 Dec., 1879.

4 *Hanson Edgar*, b. 23 April, 1882.

iv Frederick Matteson, b. in Fredonia, 29 Nov., 1859; res. Kansas City, Mo., where in the Ry. Mail Service, P. O. Dept.; a member of the B. F. A., and has given efficient help to our genealogist in preparing family records.

    v Levi Hanaford, b. in Fredonia, 28 Feb., 1862; m. 6 June, 1893,
       Lalla Rookh Maloy; asst. cashier of Farmers' and Drovers' Bank,
       Council Grove, Kan. Ch.:
       1 *Rosalee Elizabeth⁰*, b. 6 Jan., 1895.
       2 *Marion Kathryn*, b. 27 Oct., 1897; d. 9 April, 1898.
       3 *Niva Hattie*, b. 9 March, 1900.
       4 *Mary Louise*, b. 28 Dec., 1904.
    vi Fidelio Wesley, b. Lyndon, Wjs., 16 April, 1865; grad. from the
       Dental Dept. of Washington Univ., St. Louis, Mo.; m. 22 Dec.,
       1897, Mabel H. Simpson of Knoxville, Tenn.; res. Edmond, Okla.
       Ch.:
       1 *Twins*, b. and d. 1899.

    502   REV. GEORGE FRENCH⁷, son of James⁶ and Fanny
(Risley) Brigham; born in Fredonia, N. Y., 18 Nov., 1827; married
13 June, 1853, Aurilla E., daughter of Edmund Douglass of South
Byron, N. Y.; died 7 Aug., 1904.

    In early life Mr. Brigham engaged in mercantile business, and
he owned his father's farm. In 1862, his business ruined by the
war, he removed to Chicago and entered the telegraph service. In
1866 he accepted the local agency of the C. & N. W. Ry., at
Sharon, Wis. This position he filled for 35 years, during which
time he prepared himself for holy orders in the Episcopal Church,
and became the founder of St. Mary's Mission in Sharon, of
which he is curate. He gave the address before the B. F. A. at
the first Marlboro meeting in 1894. He resides in Sharon.

Children, the 3 elder born in Dunkirk, N. Y.:
748   i Edmund Douglass⁸, b. 29 Dec., 1856.
     ii Fanny Risley, b. 30 June, 1858; d. in Byron, N. Y., May, 1860.
    iii Fanny Amelia, b. 10 June, 1860; m. 3 Sept., 1881, Luther S.
       Arnold. Ch. (Arnold):
       1 *Douglass Luther⁰*, b. 23 June, 1882; in State University, Madi-
       son, Wis., in 1905.
       2 *Willard Henry*, b. 14 Dec., 1884; in State University in
       Madison, in 1905.
       3 *Fanny*, b. 8 Feb., 1887; d. 1887.
       4 *Harold A.*, b. 3 March, 1888.

749   iv George French, b. in Fredonia, 12 Jan., 1863.
     v Susan Risley, b. in Chicago, 21 Feb., 1865; d. 21 July, 1865.
750   vi Henry Hanson, b. in Sharon, Wis., 31 Aug., 1868.

    503   MARY ANN⁷, daughter of Walter⁶ and Mary Child (Dix)
Brigham; born 18 Dec., 1814; died 4 Aug., 1842, and was interred
in Fredonia, N. Y.; married 4 Dec., 1835, Rev. Abel Brown, born
in Springfield, Mass., in 1810; died in 1844.

    She became the editor of the western *Golden Rule,* published at
Albany, 1841-'2, to promote moral reform.

Children (Brown):
     i Walter Brigham⁸, b. 18 March, 1858; m. in Franklin Grove,
       Hester Ann Hook; res. Spirit Lake, Ia., and Deerfield, Mo., s. p.

DR. LEVERETT E. GOODELL, OF WILBER, NEB. (504)

ii Charles Henry, b. 3 July, 1842, in Albany, N. Y.; d. 14 Oct., 1891; m. Emeline Wills. Ch. (Brown):
 1 *Charles W.*[9], b. 1871; m. Jessie Lee Forsythe.
 2 *Edith M.*, b. 1875; m. Daniel A. Thomas. Ch. (Thomas): Lorenzo B.[10]
 3 *Robert M.*, b. 1877; unm., in 1903; in 1901 was a student at Harvard College.

504 ELMINA[7], daughter of Lieut. Joel[6] and Polly Ann (Durkee) Brigham; born in Augusta, N. Y., 2 July, 1810; died Dec., 1843; married 21 March, 1833, Rev. Joel Goodell, from Dunkirk, N. Y. to Lodi, O.; he died in Taber, Ia.; he married again after her death.

Children (Goodell), born in Lodi, O.:
 i Leverett Edward[8], M. D., b. 20 Sept., 1834; m. 8 Dec., 1863, Harriet Jones of Pilot Grove, Ia., b. in Ia., 19 Sept., 1845. He moved to Ia. in 1855; was grad. M. D., in Keokuk, Ia., 1858; in 1864 went to Pilot Grove; thence to Wilbur, Neb., and owns ranches in Nebraska and Kansas, and raises cattle. Ch., b. in Pilot Grove:
  1 *Alice Eleanor*[9], b. 31 Dec., 1864; m. 4 Sept., 1884, Harry Miller from England; res. Omaha, Neb.
  2 *Jessie Willmina,* b. 3 Feb., 1867; m. 7 Dec., 1897, Prof. Henry Jennings from London, Eng., who is Supt. of Schools in Wilbur, Ia.
  3 *Charles Brigham,* b. 30 May, 1869; m. 4 March, 1895, Edith Turner; he is a banker in Crete, Neb.
  4 *Edith May,* b. 10 May, 1871; d. 7 June, 1872.
 ii Milton P., b. 27 June, 1837; went to northern Iowa, enlisted in 1862; wounded and taken prisoner, and d. in Andersonville Prison, 9 May, 1864.
 iii George W., b. 4 July, 1839; m. (1) 1863, Marietta Pence, who d. 22 April, 1872; m. (2) 1873, Elizabeth Osborne, who d. 1883; m. (3) 9 Dec., 1884, Lillie Hubbard; a farmer, res. Clear Lake, Ia. Ch. (by 1st wife):
  1 *Lydia E.*[9], b. 7 Jan., 1864.
  2 *Joel G.,* b. 24 Oct., 1868.
  3 *Richard H.,* b. 4 Feb., 1870.
  Ch. (by 3d wife):
  4 *Hettie V.,* b. 7 Nov., 1885.
 iv Lois E., b. 17 Jan., 1842; m. 1 Oct., 1861, William Totten of Throop, Kan. Ch. (Totten):
  1 *Mary P.*[9], b. 29 April, 186—; m. 9 April, 1883, John C. Brace of Narka, Kan.
  2 *Milton Goodell,* b. 8 Aug., 1865; m. 6 Oct., 1886, Lulu E. Tabo; res. Rockford, Kan.
  3 *Elmina R.,* b. 13 Sept., 1867; m. 18 Jan., 1889, Charles A. Lendahl of Haddam, Kan.
  4 *Hattie E.,* b. 6 June, 1871; res. unm., Norka, Kan.
  5 *Edith E.,* b. 25 Feb., 1873; m. May. 1891, Albert E. Dagne of Washington, Kan.
  6 *Alice W.,* b. 25 April, 1877; m. 6 June, 1900, William E. Campbell of Throop, Kan.

7 *Celia*, b. 24 July, 1879; d. 24 Aug., 1879.
8 *William Clarence*, b. 15 Dec., 1881.
9 *Carl A.*, b. 8 June, 1883.

505 DEXTER[7]. son of Lieut. Joel[6] and Polly Ann (Durkee) Brigham; born in Augusta, N. Y., 28 Oct., 1812; died in Lodi, O., 19 Aug., 1844; married 10 May, 1840, Deborah, daughter of Thomas Shaw; born in Plainfield, Mass.; she married (2) Abram Falconer and died at Wauseon, O., 27 June, 1893. He moved to Lodi, O. The male line is extinct.

Children, born in Lodi:
    i Haven E.[8], b. 10 April, 1841; d. 12 Aug., 1841.
    ii Emma F., b. 10 Oct., 1842; m. 6 March, 1868, Rev. Howard B. Taft of Fairfield, Mich., b. in Van Buren, N. Y., 1830; he was grad., Kalamazoo, 1859; M. A., 1862; Theological Sem., 1861; ordained, 1862; she was grad. Oberlin College, 1864; res. Weston, Mich. Ch. (Taft):
        1 (*Rev.*) *Edwin Brigham*[9], b. 2 July, 1872; was grad., Kalamazoo Coll., 1895; Rochester, N. Y., Theol. Sem., 1898; removed to Prescott, Arizona, where a preacher.
        2 *Mary Alice*, b. 7 Oct., 1878; was grad. 1902, Kalamazoo Coll., Mich.; ordained 1898, and preaches in Rochester, N. Y.
    iii Elmira, b. 15 Oct., 1844; res. unm., Wauseon, O.

506 WINFIELD SCOTT[7], son of Joel[6] and Polly Ann (Durkee) Brigham; born in Otsego, N. Y., 30 Dec., 1814; died 17 April 1906, in Bowling Green, O.; married (1) 22 Sept., 1836, Mary E., daughter of James White of Sheridan, N. Y., who died 8 Feb., 1863; married (2) Susanna Falconer, who died 31 March, 1893.

He resided in Lodi, Chatham and Wauseon, O. Was a tailor by trade and had a large shop in Lodi, O., also a farm. He spent his last days with his son Joel. He was a perfect specimen of a man physically, very muscular and well built, and more than 6 feet tall.

Children (by first wife), the elder born in Lodi, the fifth, sixth and seventh in Chatham, and the younger in Wauseon, O.:
    i Frances E.[8], b. 23 July, 1837; d. unm., while teaching school.
751 ii Joseph Henry, b. 12 Dec., 1838.
    iii Mary Ann, b. 20 Aug., 1840; d. 20 March, 1862, s. p.; m. in 1861, Charles Bond.
    iv Christine E., b. 24 July, 1845; d. unm., 7 Dec., 1898.
    v James O., d. y.
    vi Augusta A., b. 30 March, 1849; m. at Wauseon, 20 Jan., 1876, Squire, son of Silas and Harriet (Pomeroy) Johnson of Adrian, Mich., b. 27 July, 1844; he is an extensive celery gardener; res. Adrian. Ch. (Johnson), b. in Toledo, O.:
        1 *Emma C.*[9], b. 4 April, 1878; m. 17 Sept., 1902, Earl G. Keeney.
        2 *Merle*, b. 27 Dec., 1881; m. 15 June, 1904, Howard Swift.
        3 *Millicent M.*, b. 10 Feb., 1887.
        4 *Christine M.*, b. 16 Aug., 1890.

752 vii Joel S., b. 28 Oct., 1850.
  viii Fannie E., b. 1 April, 1856; m. 16 Dec., 1880, Dr. Carl Bock,
    b. 1852; res. Greenville, Mich. Ch. (Bock), b. in Canandaigua,
    N. Y.:
      1 *Gertrude E.*[9], b. 20 May, 1883; m. 11 March, 1906, Henry E.
        Bitzer; res. Chattanooga, Tenn.
      2 *Wyman C.*, b. 31 Oct., 1886; a student; res. Greenville.
  Children (by second wife):
    ix Gertrude, b. 2 April, 1869; d. 2 March, 1871.
    x Bertha E., b. 6 July, 1876; m. Burt A. Gurden, res. Toledo, O.

507 HON. JOEL[7], son of Joel[6] and Polly Ann (Durkee)
Brigham; born in Dunkirk, N. Y., 10 Jan., 1818, first white child
born in that place; married 29 Nov., 1838, Betsey, daughter of Elias
Lyon of Chatham Centre, O.; born in Goshen, Mass., 20 Feb.,
1820; died in Wauseon, O., 25 Nov., 1892, after 54 years of married life.

In 1834, Mr. Brigham moved to Lodi, O., with his parents.
He and his wife lived in a log cabin 12 x 16 feet, one story, with
one room, lighted by 2 two windows; the door was provided with
a wooden latch with " latch string " through the hole to lift it,
" always out." This cabin was built on 80 acres given him by his
father. In 1844, he received a sprain and sold out. He then moved
to Chatham Centre, O., where he built a store, which he sold in
1853. He moved to Lena, where he bought 240 acres with a sawmill. In 1859, Mr. Brigham moved to Wauseon, O., formed a partnership with Isaac Springer and opened a store; in 1865 he bought
a flouring mill and in 1871 erected a two-story brick warehouse
and went into mercantile business in this place. In 1887 he turned
it over to his youngest son. Has been a Justice of the Peace,
assessor, town treasurer 15 years, Postmaster, and Mayor for 2
terms, when he declined further nomination. During the Civil
War he was County Commissioner on Dist. Military Commission.
He was one of three to buy the West Cemetery, of which he was
the leading official for 25 years. At 84 he superintended a large
farm in the suburbs. He has had a successful life.

Children, the 4 elder born in Lodi, the 2 younger in Wauseon:
    i Elvira I.[8], b. 15 Nov., 1839; d. 26 July, 1840.
    ii Ann E., b. 13 May, 1841; d. 21 April, 1843.
753 iii Walter Scott, b. 6 Aug., 1843.
754 iv Haven T., b. 7 May, 1846.
    v Willard H., b. Chatham Centre, 30 Aug., 1849; d. 18 May, 1850.
    vi Mary Eva, b. in Chatham Centre, 14 Jan., 1852; d. 7 May, 1853.
    vii Harriet A., b. 28 Feb., 1854; m. 7 Oct., 1880, William H., son
      of William Sohn; b. in Tiffin, O., 29 June, 1851; interested in
      telephone plants in Ohio and Iowa; res. Wauseon. Ch. (Sohn):
        1 *Howard*[9], b. 21 March, 1886.
    viii Celia A., b. 18 Nov., 1857; m. 10 Oct., 1878, Dr. Charles E.,
      son of Dr. J. H. Bennett of Evansport, O.; grad. Detroit Med.

College, 1876; in practice 20 years Surgeon for L. S. & Mich.
So. Ry.; afterward in same capacity for Detroit & Lima Northern Ry.; res. Wauseon, O. Ch. (Bennett), b. in Wauseon:

   1 *Fred H.⁹*, b. 16 Nov., 1881; d. 8 Sept., 1895.

   2 *Walter,* b. 9 July, 1885.

   3 *Florence,* b. 22 June, 1896.

  ix Clarence E., b. 16 Oct., 1860; m. 15 Oct., 1885, Inez Scott; in
1887 bought out his father's store.

  x Mary Elmina, b. 2 Oct., 1862; d. 13 Feb., 1871.

508   JANE ELIZABETH⁷, daughter of Joel⁶ and Basmath
(Hamilton) Brigham; born in Brookfield, Mass., on the original
homestead, 11 July, 1819; died 12 July, 1892; married, about 1843,
Stillman Butterworth of Brookfield, born 20 March, 1817; died
Aug., 1882.

Children (Butterworth), born in Brookfield:

  i Henry L.⁸, b. ——————; d. Aug., 1884; m. Nettie ———.
   Ch.:

   1 *Arthur⁹;* 2 *Louis.*

  ii James Theodore, b. 6 June, 1847; d. in Brookfield, May, 1876;
m. Emma King of B., b. 10 Oct., 1850. Ch., b. in Brookfield:

   1 *Florence Maud⁹,* b. 4 Nov., 1874; a teacher in So. Framingham, Mass.

   2 *Theodora May,* b. June, 1876; m. Walter C. Butterworth.

  iii Frank Hamilton, b. 26 Nov., 1849; m. (1) Nov., 1871, Sarah A.,
dau. of Eli H. Cummings of So. Framingham; b. 2 Sept., 1853;
d. 13 Oct., 1890; m. (2) Emma (King) Butterworth, widow of his
bro. James; a clerk, res. So. F. Ch.:

   1 *Walter Cummings⁹,* b. in Quincy, Mass., 9 Aug., 1873; m. 1
June, 1898, Theodora M. Butterworth (dau. of J. Theodore).

   2 *Herbert Stillman,* b. 19 Sept., 1875; d. 11 June, 1899; res.
So. F.

   3 *Ada Frances,* b. 16 May, 1881; m. C. Frank Holbrook of
Sherborn, Mass.; 2 ch.

  iv Ada, b. ——————; m. Charles Vizard of Brookfield; d. there,
s. p.

509   SALEM TILLY⁷, son of Joel⁶ and Basmath (Hamilton)
Brigham; born in Brookfield, Mass., 17 Oct., 1824; died at his
residence in Woburn, Mass., 8 Oct., 1903; married 6 Oct., 1850,
Maria Davis of Woburn.

He was born in the old house built by his great-grandfather James⁴
Brigham in 1722; inherited by Capt. Tilly⁵ in 1780 and next by
Joel. The old house was burned a few years ago. Joseph Brigham now owns the place. Salem enlisted in Co. G 5th Mass. Vol.
from Woburn, 27 July, 1864, for one hundred days. He was
honorably discharged 16 Nov., 1864.

Children:

  i Helen M.⁸, b. in Malden, Mass., 14 May, 1853; m. 25 Oct., 1876,
L. Waldo Thompson; res. in Woburn.

  ii Edward Tilly, b. in Woburn, 21 Oct., 1868; m. 29 Oct., 1902,
Edith C. Buckman.

Hon. Joel Brigham, of Wauseon, O. (507)

510 BOSTWICK[7], son of James[6] and Marcia (Hastings) Brigham; born in Brookfield, Mass., 6 Aug., 1821; died in Richford, Vt., 3 Oct., 1888; married 28 Jan., 1852, Emeline M. Goodrich, who died in Richford, 21 May., 1888.

Children, born in Richford:
  i Henry G.[8], b. 15 Oct., 1853; d. 6 July, 1866.
  ii Marcia E., b. 18 March, 1859; m. 6 June, 1883, George E. Barber, b. 7 Feb., 1855. Ch. (Barber):
     1 Henry E.[9], b. 21 June, 1883.
     2 Rosa B., b. 17 Sept., 1887.
     3 Edwin A., b. 29 March, 1896; d. 1 April, 1896.
     4 Ruth, b. 17 Sept., 1897.
     5 Frank, b. 1 June, 1899.
  iii Emma J., b. 2 May, 1862; d. 6 July, 1887; m. 15 Sept., 1886, Chas. M. Dickerson. Ch. (Dickerson):
     1 Emma J., b. 4 July, 1887.
  iv Charles E., b. 2 Sept., 1869; m. 1 Jan., 1889, Mary E. Genung; res. Richford. Ch.:
     1 Hazel B.[9], b. 17 Nov., 1889.
     2 Pranza B., b. 24 July, 1893.
     3 Genevieve Z., b. 13 June, 1896.

511 JAMES EDWARD[7], son of James[6] and Marcia (Hastings) Brigham; born in Caroline, N. Y., 17 July, 1827; died in Berkshire, Vt., 16 Dec., 1874; married 29 Nov., 1855, Elizabeth Witter, who died in Berkshire, 7 Aug., 1873.

Children:
  i Asa Witter[8], b. in Newark, N. Y., 26 April, 1857; m. 30 April, 1887, Bertha T. Smith of Huron, So. Dakota; res. W. Brookfield, Mass. Ch.:
     1 Jessie L.[9], b. 8 May, 1888; 2 Maud M., b. 1889; d. 1890; 3 Frederick C., b. 18 Nov., 1893; 4 Viola, b. 5 June, 1898; 5 Phebe L., b. 8 Aug., 1899; 6 Geo. H., b. 9 Nov., 1903.
  ii Louisa C., b. 22 Sept., 1858; d. 1 Feb., 1901; m. Lewis A. Gribert of Brookfield, Mass.
  iii Lewis Hastings, b. 14 March, 1860; res. unm., Berkshire.
  iv George John, b. 21 Sept., 1864; m. Henrietta Cameron of Huron, So. Dakota; res. Alphena, So. Dakota. Ch.:
     1 Allen J.[9]

512 ALEXANDER[7] son of Silvanus[6] and Sarah (Rice) Brigham; born in Brookfield, Mass., 10 Nov., 1815; died there, 21 Feb., 1891; married Olive Walker.

Children, born in Brookfield:
  i Andrew A.[8], b. 3 May, 1841; m. M. E. F. Lakin; res. Brookfield. Ch., b. there:
     1 Jennie O.[9], b. 12 July, 1869; d. 2 Aug., 1900; m. H. C. Pond. Ch. (Pond): Edna L.[10], b. 4 Sept., 1892.
     2 Charles A., b. 7 Dec., 1870; d. 13 Jan., 1871.
     3 Fred L., b. 23 Feb., 1881.
     4 Norman O., b. 9 March, 1886.

513   SAMUEL[7], son of Samuel[6] and Polly (Wood) Brigham; born in Malone, N. Y., 8 May., 1817; died Bainbridge, O., 5 Feb., 1890; married Emily Ann Sweet, of Monroe County, N. Y.; born 28 March, 1820; died 10 January, 1879. He was a farmer, and moved to Bainbridge, Geauga County, O., in 1842. He was musical.

Children, born in Bainbridge:
755   i Benjamin Franklin[8], b. 26 Aug., 1840.
   ii Martha R., b. 12 Nov., 1843; m. 24 Dec., 1865, Ira Fish of Auburn, O. Ch. (Fish):
      1 *Mortimer Samuel*[9], b. 20 Sept., 1869; m. Margaret Mayhew. Ch.: Hazel[10], b. 4 Dec., 1893.
   iii Helen E., b. 23 Sept., 1845; d. s. p., 25 Nov., 1865; m. 14 Feb., 1865, Silvester Gilbert of Grand Travers, Mich.
   iv Emelus, b. 12 Dec., 1847; d. y.
   v Edith D., b. 14 June, 1849; m. Leander A. Ely of Bainbridge, O. Ch. (Ely):
      1 *Ernest A.*[9], b. 5 Dec., 1870; m. Alice Neal.
      2 *Dell A.*, b. 26 Dec., 1876; m. Lila Allhouse.
   vi Theron, b. 20 July, 1853; d. y.
   vii Emily Ann, b. 23 April, 1855; d. 12 June, 1898; m. Frank Russell of Athens, Mich.; she was a singer of note, and while singing in church the words of a chorus, " Goodbye, Goodbye," she fell forward and expired. Ch. (Russell)·
      1 *Hershel*[9], b. 4 July, 1883.
      2 *Avelda*, b. 26 June, 1887.
   viii Elmer Adelbert, b. 20 July, 1860; m. 20 Oct., 1890, Etta Dean. He is musical, and res. in Willson's Mills, O. Ch·
      1 *Keston*[9].

514   LUTHER[7], son of Nathaniel[6] and Sarah (Mason) Brigham; born in Shrewsbury, Mass., 10 Oct., 1800; died in Boylston, Mass., 7 Nov., 1887; married (1) in 1826, Parmelia Barrie of Salem, Mass., who died 1 March, 1843, æ. 39; married (2) in 1854, Hulda P. Conant, who died 28 July, 1886, æ. 77.

Children (by first wife):
756   i Sarah Elizabeth[8], b. 27 Sept., 1825.
   ii Martha Chamberlain, b. 18 Nov., 1828; in 1850 m. George Keyes of Worcester, and d. soon after.
   iii William Henry, d. y.
   iv William Henry, b. 29 Aug., 1832; m. 1876, Jennie M. Frary; res. s. p., Northampton.
   v Susan Emily, b. 15 Aug., 1834; d. 13 March, 1856.

515   CALVIN[7], son of Nathaniel[6] and Sarah (Mason) Brigham; born in Shrewsbury, Mass., 23 May, 1802; died 5 Aug., 1866; married 16 Nov., 1830, Susan S., daughter of Amma Wetherbee; born 3 Feb., 1811. He resided in Worcester, and kept a meat and provision market. Was one of the first councilmen when Worcester became a city.

LEMUEL HAWLEY BRIGHAM, (536)

Child, born in Worcester:
  i George Albert⁸, b. 15 Nov., 1847; m. 1 Nov., 1877, Susan Moore of
    Petersham, Mass.; res. in Worcester. Ch., b. there:
    1 *Fred Clarence⁹*, b. 15 Sept., 1880; 2 *Carrie Elizabeth*, b. 3 Dec.,
    1882; 3 *Arthur E.*, b. 20 Oct., 1887.

516 JOHN MASON⁷, son of Nathaniel⁶ and Sarah (Mason)
Brigham; born in Bolyston, Mass., 26 March, 1808; died 2 Jan.,
1892; married 31 Oct., 1844, Arminda, daughter of Josiah Stillman of Grafton, Mass., who died 5 Dec., 1894, æ. 77. He was
in the provision business in Worcester.

Children, b. in Worcester:
  i Sarah Mason⁸, b. 12 July, 1845; res. unm., in Worcester.
  ii John Stillman, b. 12 May, 1847; d. 20 Feb., 1897; m. 26 June,
    1879, Nellie E. Spurr. He res. in Worcester, and was of the
    firm of " Logan, Swift & Brigham." Ch. b. in Worcester:
    1 *Dwight Stillman⁹*, b. 24 Aug., 1886.

517 DEA. HENRY HARDING⁷, son of Nathaniel⁶ and Sarah
(Mason) Brigham; born in Bolyston, Mass., 21 June, 1814; resided and died at Boylston, 19 June, 1888; married 1 Aug., 1837,
Rebecca W., daughter of Benjamin Houghton; born 1814; died
11 Oct., 1876.

He was Justice of the Peace many years; Representative in
1848 for 2 years; deacon for 50 years; church treasurer and clerk
and superintendent of the Sunday-school; town clerk for 40 years;
also selectman and assessor.

Children, born in Boylston:
  i Henrietta Martyn⁸, b. 1 April, 1838; m. 8 Jan., 1861, John T.
    Andrews of Boylston. Ch. (Andrews), b. in Boylston:
    1 *Florence Helen⁹*, b. 13 Oct., 1861; m. 22 Nov., 1882, George
    H. Lane of Worcester. Ch. (Lane): i Bertha A.¹⁰, b. 17
    Oct., 1890; ii Penniman M., b. 17 Dec., 1895.
    2 *Mary Elizabeth*, b. 22 July, 1863; m. 25 Nov., 1891, Herbert
    H. French of Boylston. Ch. (French): Harold Brigham¹⁰,
    b. 7 Feb., 1894.
    3 *Amelia Rebecca*, b. 2 Oct., 1865; d. 12 Dec., 1865.
    4 *Calvin Henry*, b. 1 Jan., 1871; grad. of Worcester Polytechnic
    Institute, 1893; teacher of Physics in High School in Wor-
    cester; m. 27 Aug., 1896, Martha E. Reed.
  ii Penniman Mason, b. 2 June, 1840; m. 6 May, 1862, Mary Amelia
    Wall of Ashland, Mass.; res. in Boylston; a selectman. Ch ·
    1 *Fannie Josephine⁹*, b. 30 April, 1864; d. 29 Jan., 1865.
  iii Calvin Henry, b. 30 June, 1845; d. 20 July, 1865.

518 JEROME RIPLEY⁷, son of David⁶ and Elizabeth (Rip-
ley) Brigham; born in Fitchburg, Mass., 21 July, 1825; died in
Milwaukee, Wis., 31 Jan., 1897; married, 7 Oct., 1857, Mary
Noyes, daughter of Edward Ilsley of Portland, Me., who died 13
Aug., 1894.

He was graduated Amherst College, 1845; studied law; was appointed clerk of Superior Court, Wisconsin, upon the organization of the State government in 1848. In 1851, he resigned and practiced law in Milwaukee, and was city attorney 1881-'82; was in the Legislature 1887-'88; U. S. Appraiser of Merchandise at Milwaukee, 1871-77; on School Board; Board of Regents Union of Wisconsin; he was a writer for papers.

Children, born in Milwaukee:
  i Bessie[8], b. 14 July, 1858; m. 1881, Charles W. Badgley, merchant of Denver, Colo., where they res.; 3 boys and 1 girl.
  ii Charles Ilsley, b. 4 Feb., 1862; was grad., Univ. of Wisconsin, 1885; res. a farmer, in Blue Mounds, Wis.
  iii Mary Ripley, b. 25 Sept., 1864.
  iv Ellen Deering, b. 12 July, 1866; d. 31 Aug., 1871.
  v Louise, b. 26 Sept., 1868; d. 2 Oct., 1869.
  vi Mabel, b. 23 June, 1871; d. 27 Sept., 1902, at B. M.
  vii Katherine, b. 8 April, 1876; m. in Milwaukee, 29 Oct., 1902, Philip R. Fox. Ch. (Fox):
    1 *Anna*[9], b. in Madison, Wis., 13 Jan., 1904.

519 SILVESTER[7], son of Joseph[6] and Polly (Fullam) Brigham; born in Fitzwilliam, N. H., 17 June, 1807; died in Neodesha, Kas., Jan., 1872; married, in Cleveland, O., (1) 7 June, 1840, Lucy Gunn, who died 17 Aug., 1841; married, in Keene N. H., (2) 10 May, 1842, Mary W. Bingham.

He moved to Illinois in 1829 and walked from New Hampshire and back again; was in the Black Hawk War, and noted for courage and strength; a farmer and real estate dealer and platted the town of Dover, Ill.

Children (by first wife), born in Dover:
  i Joseph[8], b. 25 April, 1841; d. 17 July, 1841.
  ii Mary, twin to Joseph; d. 6 Sept., 1841.
Children (by second wife), the elder born in Dover, the 4 younger in Cordova, Ill:
757 iii Elijah, b. 14 March, 1843.
  iv Lucy, b. 26 Oct., 1844; m. (1) 13 Feb., 1868, Joseph Torpin, who d. in Fredonia, Kan., 1886, s. p.; m. (2) 21 April, 1887, Francis J. Moore of Fredonia.
758 v *George*, b. 9 Oct., 1846.
  vi Adoniram Judson, b. 29 Aug., 1850; d. in Dufur, Or., 28 Nov., 1903; m. 1 May, 1873, Louisa Snodgrass; mfr. of patent medicines; went to Wash. Ter., 1875; thence to Or., where a J. P.; an occasional preacher; res. Dufur. Ch.:
    1 *Waldo P.*[9], b. 9 Feb., 1874.
    2 *Grace May*, b. 5 May, 1889.
  vii Joseph Webb (Rev.), b. 11 Sept., 1852; m. 3 Aug., 1881, Lizzie Florence Gunn; res. s. p., Dorchester, Mass., where several years pastor of Baptist Church; was grad. Univ. of Kan. and Theol. Sem., Newton, Mass.

viii Mary E., b. 10 Oct., 1854; m. 4 Dec., 1875, Stephen A. Taylor; res. Denver, Colo. Ch. (Taylor):
    1 Cora E.⁹, b. 15 Oct., 1876; 2 Ethel F., b. 1 Dec., 1880; 3 Lillian I., b. 11 Nov., 1882; 4 Mabel E., b. 24 Sept., 1884; 5 Stephen C., b. 11 June, 1887; 6 Clarence E., b. 29 March, 1891; 7 Ruth B., b. 29 Jan., 1893.

ix Rufus, b. 20 Feb., 1856; d. 10 May, 1856.

x Charles S., b. 20 May, 1858; d. Kansas City, Mo., 11 Oct., 1903; m. in Neodosha, Kan., 13 March, 1881, Larue Woodard, b. in Lawrence, Kan., 9 Aug., 1858; at age of 18 he took up the home farm duties because of the death of father; res. a banker, Fredonia, Kan.; 2 terms dist. clerk of Wilson Co., Kan. Ch.:
    1 Grace⁹, b. 29 May, 1882; 2 Mary, b. 9 Jan., 1884; 3 Maud, b. 6 Nov., 1887; 4 Nellie, b. 22 Oct., 1893; d. 22 Dec., 1894.

xi Hattie E., b. 6 Nov., 1860; m. 25 Dec., 1883, Thomas Owen of Neodosha, Kan., b. 3 June, 1860; d. there, 1 Nov., 1887. Ch. (Owen):
    1 Bertha⁹, b. in Neodosha, 8 March, 1885.

520 JOSEPH H.⁷, son of Capt. Joseph⁶ and Polly (Fullam) Brigham; born in Fitzwilliam, N. H., 31 Jan., 1823; married (1) 29 Feb., 1848, Jane E., daughter of Aaron Mercer, born in Ohio, 22 Jan., 1830; died 21 June, 1871; married (2) 1 Jan., 1873, Carrie A., daughter of John Dunbar, born in Pennsylvania, 21 April, 1841. He resides a farmer in Dover, Ill.; has held county offices.

Children (by first wife), born in Dover:
i Elisha⁸, b. 12 Oct., 1849; d. 12 Sept., 1850.

ii Harriet, b. 29 June, 1851; d. 1 Aug., 1890; m. 29 June, 1875, Michael Hoover of Princeton, Ill.

iii Silvester, b. 10 Sept., 1853; grad. Princeton Univ., 1876; a grain buyer, res. Princeton, Ill.

iv Sarah E., b. 6 Nov., 1855; m. 22 Feb., 1883, William Kissick of Dover; res. Ohio, Ill. Ch. (Kissick):
    1 Joseph⁹, b. 8 Nov., 1885; 2 Edna, b. 19 Oct., 1888; d. 1 July, 1891; 3 Lottie, b. 12 Sept., 1890; 4 Pearl, b. 6 Oct., 1892; 5 Earl, twin to Pearl.

v Mary, b. 6 Sept., 1858; d. 6 Sept., 1890; m. 25 Dec., 1887, Galen Belden of Quincy, Kan.

vi Joseph, b. 16 Jan., 1861; a farmer in Dover.

vii Eliza, b. 11 Oct., 1864; m. 25 Dec., 1887, Joseph Bartley; res. Wellington, Kan.

viii John, b. 9 Nov., 1866; d. 18 Oct., 1890; a farmer in Dover.

Children (by second wife), born in Dover:
ix Curtis Dunbar, b. 15 June, 1874; m. in Princeton, Ill., 1 Jan., 1901, Edith W., dau. of Arthur, Jr., and Elizabeth (Hughes) Bryant (a great-niece of William Cullen Bryant); b. in Princeton, 1 Dec., 1878. He matriculated in Northwestern Univ., in 1894, but did not graduate; res. in Edna, Kan. Ch.:
    1 Arthur Bryant⁹, b. in Waterloo, Ia., 11 Feb., 1902.
    2 Charles Joseph, b. in Edna, 7 Dec., 1903.

x Charles, b. 12 Aug., 1877; res. Waterloo, Ia.

521 ELIJAH PARKMAN[7], son of Major Elijah[6] and Nancy (Fisher) Brigham; born in Westboro, Mass., 13 Jan., 1807; died 19 Nov., 1870; married 5 June, 1831, Mary Ann Williams of Charlestown, Mass.

Children, born in Westboro:
- i Charles Parkman[8], b. 20 Jan., 1832; d. in Nebraska, May, 1896; m. (1) 1855, Hannah Durant; m. (2) ——— Anderson; m. (3) 1884, Rhoda Larkin. Ch.:
    - 1 *Mary Louise*[9], b. 1856; d. 1857; 2 *William E.;* 3 *Mary Ann;* 4 *Nora Dell;* 5 *Susan;* 6 *Elijah Parkman.*
- ii Susan Walter, b. 29 June, 1836; d. 20 Oct., 1899; m. 12 March, 1857, Samuel D. Nye of Barre, Mass. Ch. (Nye), b. in Barre:
    - 1 *Walter Brigham*[9], b. 11 Feb., 1862.
    - 2 *Mary Eggleston*, b. 9 March, 1867; d. 21 May, 1869.
    - 3 *Henry Pearson*, b. 26 May, 1870.
    - 4 *Susie C.*, b. 28 Oct., 1876; d. 28 Aug., 1877.
    - 5 *Arthur Eggleston*, b. 7 Nov., 1878.
- iii Mary Angeline, b. 24 April, 1841; m. 1 Dec., 1864, Linus E. Pearson of Charlestown, Mass. Ch. (Pearson):
    - 1 *Barnard Bailey*[9], b. 2 July, 1867.
    - 2 *Ruth Nye*, b. 8 March, 1871.
    - 3 *Francis Everett*, b. 15 Oct., 1877.
- iv Caroline Emmons, b. 9 July, 1844; d. 24 Aug., 1871.
- v Charlotte Adelaide, b. 27 July, 1850; d. 24 July, 1851.

522 SUSAN AUGUSTA[7], daughter of Nathaniel[6] and Dolly (Ball) Brigham; born in Northboro, Mass., 5 Jan., 1813; died in Dorchester, Mass., 13 June, 1896; married, 25 Oct., 1837, Lewis, son of William and Lois (Munroe) Rice, and grand-son of 86; born in Northboro, 23 Nov., 1809; died in Boston, Mass., 16 March, 1877. He was proprietor of the American House in Boston from 1835-1877.

Children (Rice), born in Boston:
- i Lewis Frederick[8], b. 17 May, 1839; m. 25 Oct., 1867, Caroline Elizabeth, daughter of Charles Draper and Hannah Bullard (Fisher) Ellis; born in St. Louis, Mo., 8 Jan., 1842. He was grad. from Rensselaer Polytechnic Inst., C. E. Served during the Civil War from Jan., 1862-Oct., 1865 as Lieut., Capt., and Major of 31st Mass. Vols. Practiced as C. E. from 1859-1861 and from 1866-1871; also as Architect and C. E. from 1871 to present time. Since 1890, Asst. Engineer and Consulting Architect for the American Bell Telephone Co. in Boston; res. Brookline, Mass. Ch.:
    - 1 *Lewis*[9], b. in Dorchester, 15 Aug., 1868; d. unm., in Brookline, Mass., 2 April, 1899, of typhoid fever; he was a dealer in railway and electrical supplies, in Philadelphia.
    - 2 *Frederick Ellis*, b. 7 Sept., 1880, in Brookline; was grad. Harvard Coll. in 1903.
- ii Augusta Maria, b. 26 Dec., 1841; d. 18 Aug., 1869.
- iii Henry Brigham, b. 21 July, 1843; d. unm., in Norwood, Mass., 8 Sept., 1903. He was grad. from Walpole High School, 1857;

LUTHER AYERS BRIGHAM (537)

English High School, Boston, 1860; received Franklin Medal, 1860; took a year's course in Comparative Zoology, Lawrence Scientific School, Harvard Univ., 1860-61, under Prof. Louis Agassiz. Visited Europe in 1863. Was in partnership with father as proprietor of American House, Boston, 1868-74; sole proprietor, 1874-1881; Prest. and Gen. Manager of The American Postal Machines Co., 1888-1893; M. V. M., 1861-1899, retiring with rank of Major. He belonged to 10 of the leading Boston clubs. He was a 32d deg. Mason.

 iv Ella Frances, b. 3 April, 1849; d. 25 Aug., 1876, s. p.; m. 6 July, 1870, Winslow Herrick.

523 DOLLY ANN[7], daughter of Nathaniel[6] and Dolly (Ball) Brigham; born in Northboro, Mass., 28 Feb., 1814; died in Spencer, Mass., 2 June, 1898; married, 1 Feb., 1842, Lewis Bemis; born 6 Nov., 1797; died 8 Nov., 1856. They resided in Spencer.

Children (Bemis), born in Spencer:
 i Abbie Maria[8], b. 29 May, 1843; d. 20 Aug., 1843.
 ii Charles Brigham, b. 3 Aug., 1845; d. 8 Aug., 1846.
 iii Annie Hudson, b. 17 June, 1847; d. in Spencer, 31 Aug., 1899; m. 25 Jan., 1871, Charles A. Bemis, b. May, 1838. Ch. (Bemis):
  1 *Lewis Tyler[9]*, b. 26 June, 1874.
  2 *Mary Brigham*, b. 21 Aug., 1876; m. J. Bennett Porter.
  3 *Emma Augusta*, b. Sept., 1880.
 iv Emma Augusta, b. 13 June, 1852; d. 3 July, 1860.

524 ELIJAH WINSLOW[7], son of Nathaniel and Dolly (Ball) Brigham; born in Northboro, Mass., 18 July, 1816; died in Waltham, Mass., 22 July, 1900; married, 4 Dec., 1860, Ella R., daughter of William Lefferman; born in Baltimore, Md., 11 Dec., 1840. He resided in Waltham and was in the Insurance business in Boston.

Children, the eldest and youngest born in Northboro:
 i Florence Lefferman[8], b. 3 Sept., 1861; m. ————, George H., son of Edwin Bowker of Waltham. Ch. (Bowker):
  1 *Charlotte[9]*, b. 22 Aug., 1885.
  2 *Edwin*, b. 7 Nov., 1890.
 ii Frank Winslow, b. in New York, 26 June, 1863; in business in Boston; res. unm., in Waltham.
 iii Ella Maria, b. 10 Dec., 1864.

525 CATHERINE BALL[7], daughter of Nathaniel and Dolly (Ball) Brigham; born in Northboro, Mass., 8 Sept., 1818; married, 8 Oct., 1839, George Gill, son of Gill and Sabra (Wood) Valentine; born in Northboro, 12 Feb., 1815; died there, 24 Feb., 1869. He was a selectman, assessor and postmaster in Northboro.

Children (Valentine), born in Northboro:
 i George Lewis[8], b. 13 May, 1841; d. 7 Oct., 1848.
 ii Helen Maria, b. 7 May, 1846; d. s. p., 4 June, 1891; m. 25 March, 1873, Orrin M. Robinson of Westboro.

    iii Sarah Elizabeth, b. 4 Dec., 1850; m. 30 April, 1874, George E.
        Goodrich of Westboro, s. p.
    iv Harriet Dolly, b. 19 Oct., 1853; m. 25 June, 1890, Lewis F.
        Stratton of Northboro; s. p.

526   ANNA ALLEN[7], daughter of Michael[6] and Polly (Tyler)
Brigham; born in Brookfield, Mass., 9 Dec., 1797; married 21
Sept., 1819, John Gould, a farmer, born 17 Jan., 1789. Resided
Ware, Mass.

Children (Gould), born in Ware:
    i Maria[8], b. 25 May, 1820; d. 12 Nov., 1855.
    ii William Bowdoin, b. 12 Jan., 1822.
    iii David, b. 4 Feb., 1824; res. in Ware.
    iv Minerva, b. 13 March, 1826; (d.).
    v Minerva, b. 5 July, 1827.
    vi John Brigham, b. 12 June, 1829; res. Ware; living, 1905.
    vii Daniel, b. 19 June, 1831; res. Springfield; living, 1905.
    viii Mary Ann, b. 13 June, 1833; m. Erskine Pease of Indian Orchard,
        Mass. Ch. (Pease), b. in Indian Orchard:
        1 *Minerva Eliza*[9], b. 31 Jan., 1865; m. 18 April, 1888, Andrew
          J. Miller of Easthampton, Mass., b. 10 May, 1866.
        2 ——————, m. Frank M. Clark; res. Indian Orchard.
        3 *Erskine Kibbe*, b. 7 July, 1869; d. 27 May, 1902.
        4 *Rosa Bella*, b. 25 Nov., 1872; res. unm., in Indian Orchard.
    ix James H., b. 27 May, 1835.
    x Eliza, b. 8 March, 1838.
    xi Joseph B., b. 2 Sept., 1841.

527   LORING W[7]., son of Michael[6] and Polly (Tyler) Brigham; born in North Brookfield, Mass., 30 Oct., 1799; married 7
Oct., 1821, Maria H. Wiswell; born 17 Aug., 1799. He was a
farmer and mason and resided in Ware, Mass.

Children:
    i Elbridge[8], b. 12 March, 1824; m. Mary B. Joslyn; res. Spring-
        field, Mass. Ch.:
        1 *James J.*[9]; 2 *Frank L.*
    ii Mary M., b. 14 April, 1826; res. Ware.
    iii Caroline M., b. 2 March, 1828; d. 4 June, 1858; m. Robert B.
        Moores.
    iv Sarah Jane, b. 12 Aug., 1830; d. 11 Dec., 1832.
    v Abby B., b. 22 Dec., 1832; m. Charles L. Chapin, who res. a
        merchant, Warren, Mass.
    vi Emily J., b. 22 Feb., 1836; res. Warren.
    vii Theodora C., b. 17 Sept., 1838.
    ix Addie A., b. 6 Feb., 1841.

528   SAMUEL SUMNER[7], son of Eli[6] and Mary (Harrington) Brigham; born in Bakersfield, Vt., 30 Oct., 1803; died there,
13 Jan., 1883; married 2 April, 1835, Mary Powers; born 4 July,
1812; died 18 Dec., 1895. Resided in Bakersfield.

Children, born in Bakersfield:
759   i William Oakley[8], b. 16 May, 1836.
     ii Julia S., b. 27 April, 1839; m. Ahiva Beach of Keeseville, N. Y
       30 Sept., 1837; they both d. s. p., in Feb., 1886.
     iii Mary E., b. 24 April, 1844; m. 27 Aug., 1867, W. N. Phelps of
       So. Hero, Vt.; res. East Albany, Vt. Ch. (Phelps):
        1 *Harold Brigham*[9], b. 13 Aug., 1875.
        2 *George Hopkins,* b. 14 April, 1882.
        3 *Henry Wheeler,* b. 2 Dec., 1883.
     iv Laura E., b. 8 Oct., 1848; m. 29 Oct., 1874, H. E. Rustedt of
       Richford, Vt. Ch. (Rustedt):
        1 *Marian Brigham*[9], b. 4 June, 1877; grad. Univ. of Vt., 1898;
        Ph. B., B. K.
        2 *Mary Elizabeth,* b. 31 Oct., 1880; 2 years in Univ. of Vt.
        3 *Henry Frederick,* b. 31 Dec., 1885.

529   SOPHIA[7], daughter of Eli[6] and Mary (Harrington) Brigham; born in Bakersfield, Vt., 29 Sept., 1806; died 19 Nov., 1898 ·· married, 15 Jan., 1837; Niles Bushnell of Keesville, N. Y

Children (Bushnell), born in Keeseville:
     i Orpha Sophia[8], b. 25 Oct., 1837; d. 29 Sept., 1893; m. 25 July,
       1858, Richmond B. Marsh.
     ii Mary Amanda, b. 10 Nov., 1839; m. 15 Sept., 1868, Matthew A.
       Thomas; res. Keeseville. Ch. (Thomas):
        1 *Annie B.*[9], b. 1873.
     iii Salome, b. 4 Aug., 1842; m. 19 Nov., 1867, Henry M. Mould.
       Ch. (Mould):
        1 *Fred W.*[9], b. in K., 1868.
     iv Emeline, b. 1 July, 1845; res. Keeseville.

530   ELI WHITNEY[7], son of Eli[6] and Mary (Harrington) Brigham; born in Bakersfield, Vt., 22 Jan., 1810; died in Hebron, Ill., 10 Aug., 1885; married in Dundee, Ill., 20 Nov., 1842, Mary D. Collson, born in Cheshire, Mass., 16 July, 1810; died in Hebron, 28 March, 1891. He was a farmer; moved to Napersville, Ill., in 1833; thence to Hebron, Ill., in 1836, where was the first white settler.

Children, born in Hebron:
     i Charles Morris[8], b. 7 Aug., 1845; d. in Hebron, 22 July, 1894;
       m. 13 Oct., 1869, Fannie Campbell. Ch., b. in Hebron:
        1 *Bertha B.*[9], b. 7 Aug., 1870; m. (1) 19 Nov., 1890, Loring O.
        Weeks of Richmond, Ill.; m. (2) 1899, M. M. Stone of
        Richmond, Ill. Ch. (Weeks): i Grace E.[10]; ii Bernice, d. y.;
        ch. (Stone): iii Helen M.
        2 *Florence E.,* b. 22 Aug., 1872.
        3 *Grace C.,* b. 17 Sept., 1875; m. 27 April, 1898, Edgar F.
        Swan of Libertyville, Ill. Ch. (Swan): Morris Edgar[10], b.
        7 June, 1905.
        4 *Whitney E.,* b. 9 Feb., 1878; m. 20 Feb., 1901, Clara Libbey
        of Hebron. Ch.: i Shirley F.[10], b. 24 Dec., 1901; ii Joyce, b.
        10 Aug., 1903; iii Jean, b. 19 June, 1905.

ii Mary A., b. 1 Oct., 1847; res. unm., in Hebron.
iii Eliza S., b. 22 Jan., 1850; d. in Running Creek, Colo., 24 Oct.,
1874; m. 7 Nov., 1872, Jefferson A. Bailey of Alden, Ill. Ch.
(Bailey), b. near Denver, Colo.:
   1 *Charles W.*[9], b. 20 Oct., 1874; was grad. Med. Coll., Chicago,
   1900; m. 3 Nov., 1904, Josephine Ida Groesbeck, b. in Alden, Ill.,
   7 Nov., 1874; res. Hebron.

531   HUBBARD[7], son of Eli[6] and Mary (Harrington) Brig-
ham; born in Bakersfield, Vt., 28 June, 1815; died in Minneapolis,
Minn., 26 Dec., 1898; married 31 Jan., 1850, Mary B. Whiting.
He resided in Boston.

Children:
   i Mary A.[8], b. 7 June, 1851; m. 1 Oct., 1873, in Boston, Samuel
   Mortimer Rich of Minneapolis. Ch. (Rich), the elder b. in
   Boston, the 2 younger in Minneapolis: ·
      1 *Mortimer Brigham*[9], b. 11 July, 1874; m. 9 Nov., 1902, Halle
      Johnson of Minneapolis; he is a builder in M. Ch.: Dorothy
      M., b. 26 March, 1904.
      2 *John Hubbard,* b. 5 March, 1876; an artist, and res. Boston.
      3 *Henry L.,* d. y.
      4 *Kenneth Whitney,* b. 27 May, 1889.
      5 *Harold Hunter,* b. 21 June, 1890; d. Jan., 1891.
   ii Hubbard, b. 16 Aug., 1853; res. unm., in Cortez, Colo.

532   HOLLOWAY TAYLOR[7], son of Jonas[6] and Eunice (Billings) Brigham; born in Bakersfield, Vt., 4 Nov., 1807; moved to
St. Cloud, Minn., where died 9 Dec., 1894; married 8 June, 1839,
Eunice, daughter of Ira Fay, of Bakersfield; born 23 April, 1817;
resided in 1904 in St. Cloud with her son Dr. George Brigham.

Children, born in Bakersfield:
   i Ellen[8], b. 18 June, 1841; m. J. W. Wood; res. Hutchinson, Kan.
760   ii George Stannard, b. 16 June, 1845.
   iii Edward, b. 30 May, 1857.

533   ERASTUS OAKLEY[7], son of Jonas[6] and Eunice (Billings) Brigham, born in Bakersfield, Vt., 11 Nov., 1809; died in
Brigham, Quebec, 18 April, 1878; married Bridget O'Brien.
   He was a merchant and manufacturer. It was his enterprise
which founded the village of Brigham, Que., which was named for
him. He was one of the organizers of the Eastern Township
Bank and a director of the same. The Southeastern Railway was
also organized in part by Mr. Brigham, and was afterward acquired
by the Canadian Pacific Railway. He gave the right of way over
his property to the Southeastern Ry. and built the station and
freight house. He owned a large tannery and store in Brigham,
and built the Congregational church and parsonage, and gave them
together with the burial ground, to that society, and also provided

WALDO BRIGHAM, OF HYDE PARK, VT. (538)

for the maintenance of the property after his decease. He is interred in this cemetery with his wife. After the death of his widow, his residence was converted into a grammar school for boys. Mr. Brigham had a brilliant mind and unusual gifts.

Child:

i Byron Oakley[8], b. in St. Albans, Vt., 13 May, 1837; m. 23 March, 1864, Helen S. Bell, b. in Akron, O., 26 April, 1839. He is a business man in Toledo, O. Ch.:

1 *Zella Bell[9]*, b. in Clyde, O., 14 Dec., 1867; m. 10 May, 1890, Otto Sand, b. in Berlin, Prussia, 2 Dec., 1858. She is an accomplished violinist of unusual powers.

534 MOSES BARTLETT[7], son of Jonas[6] and Eunice (Billings) Brigham; born in Bakersfield, Vt., 18 Sept., 1823; died in Somerville, Mass., 14 March, 1900; married in 1850, Almira Elizabeth, daughter of James and Weltha (Piper) Fillebrown; born in Cavendish, Vt., 20 Dec., 1833; died in Somerville, 17 Jan., 1900. He was early in the produce business and for 40 years an agent of the National Life Insurance Co. of Vermont; resided in Boston, but moved to Somerville in 1868.

Child, born in Boston:

761 i William Erastus[8], b. 16 Feb., 1865.

535 JEWETT BOARDMAN[7], son of Jonas[6] and Eunice (Billings) Brigham; born in Bakersfield, Vt., 25 Aug., 1826; died 19 (or 22) Oct., 1890; married Julia R., daughter of Nathan and Alma (Fay) Fuller; born in Bakersfield, 1833; died 14 Jan., 1875. Resided in Boston and Ute, Ia.

Children, born in Boston, except the second b. Bakersfield:

i Frank Lawson[8], b. 14 Jan., 1853; res. unm., Ute, Ia.

ii Flora Adelia, b. 17 June, 1857; d. Jan., 1888; m. Jan., 1884, Cyrus M. Smith, M. D.; res. Ute, Ia. Ch. (Smith):

1 *Mabel A.[9]*, b. 19 May, 1885; d. July, 1887.

2 *Daisy*, b. 31 Dec., 1886.

iii Florence Mabel, b. 10 April, 1866; m. 22 Oct., 1891, William Thomas Wright, M. D.; grad. A. B., Kenyon College; M. D., Mich. Univ.; P. B. K.; B. T. P. Ch. (Wright):

1 *Winifred W.[9]*, b. 1 Sept., 1892; 2 *Alma L.*, b. 20 July, 1894; 3 *Alice E.*, b. 1 Oct., 1896.

536 LEMUEL HAWLEY[7], son of Dr. Luther[6] and Eunice (Hawley) Brigham; born in St. Albans, Vt., 17 Aug , 1816; died in Palmer, Mass., 6 May, 1896; married (1) 22 Sept., 1836, Lucinda Denison, daughter of Asa and Mary (French) Bamford, of Lowell, Mass., born 22 Sept., 1820; died 14 Dec., 1856; married (2) 30 June, 1870, Mrs. Maria J., daughter of Hezekiah Root and widow of W. L. Ray, born in Ludlow, Mass., 21 Oct., 1832; died 16 April, 1889.

Mr. Brigham was a manufacturer. He was connected with the Dwight Manufacturing Company of Chicopee, Mass., as superintendent for 32 years, and in 1868 went to Ludlow, where he was 19 years agent for the Ludlow Manufacturing Company. He retired from business in 1887, when he went to Springfield, Mass., and bought a residence, but in 1890 he went to Palmer to live with his daughter, Mrs. E. P. Ball. He was a 32d degree Mason, a member of the Springfield commandery, Knights Templar, and was a director in the Masonic Mutual Insurance company for many years. His affiliations were with the Universalist denomination and he was an ardent abolitionist. During his residence in Ludlow he made every interest of the place his own, and the history of the town, at that time, was largely a history of Mr. Brigham. Brigham Lodge of Ludlow is named for him. The male line is extinct.

Children (by first wife), the 4 elder born in Chicopee:
   i L. Mina⁸, b. 26 Sept., 1837; m. 7 Aug., 1860, John Shepard, son of Samuel Aitcheson, b. in Hartford, Conn., in 1836; d. in Brooklyn, N. Y., 12 Oct., 1872; was 1st Lieut. 27th Mass. Vols., Civil War; Provost Marshal in Washington, N. C., under Gen. Burnsides. Mrs. Aitcheson res. in Mechanicsville, N. Y. Ch. (Aitcheson):
     1 *Thomas Brigham⁹*, b. 1865; res. Schuylerville, N. Y.; m. 12 March, 1889, Bertha, dau. Stephen Jaquith of Hinsdale, N. H. Ch.: John S.¹⁰, b. 1890.
     2 *Grace Bamford*, b. 19 Feb., 1870; m. 2 July, 1891, Adelbert J. Harvey, b. 7 Jan., 1855; res. Mechanicsville, N. Y. Ch. (Harvey): i Lillian¹⁰; ii Hawley Brigham.
   ii Lemuel Warren, b. 18 Sept., 1839; d. s. p., 18 Sept., 1875; m. Ellen F. Dudley, who d. 1891; was an accountant in New York and Chicopee.
   iii Ellen Ione, b. 9 July, 1844; d. in 1895; m. 2 Dec., 1869, Charles Frederick, son of Ephraim Howard, b. in Chicopee, 17 Jan., 1840. Ch. (Howard):
     1 *Lucinda Carolyn⁹*, b. 20 April, 1870.
     2 *Lemuel Frederick*, b. 4 July, 1873.
   iv Ada Iretta, b. 3 Dec., 1846; m. 2 Dec., 1869, Edwin Pliny, son of William Ball, b. in Chicopee, 6 Jan., 1846. Ch. (Ball), b. in Chicopee:
     1 *Mina Linda⁹*, b. 14 Sept., 1870; 2 *Gertrude Ada*, b. 14 Sept., 1872; 3 *Edwin Brigham*, b. 22 Dec., 1876; 4 *Sarah Walker*, b. 18 July, 1883.
   v Mary Eva, b. 5 May, 1852; d. 26 Aug., 1852.
   vi Linda Hawley, b. 6 Oct., 1856; res. Mechanicsville, N. Y., Miss Brigham lectures on Art, and English and European literature.
Child (by second wife), born in Ludlow:
   vii Arthur, b. 1 July, 1872; d. 28 Aug., 1872.

537 LUTHER AYERS⁷, son of Dr. Luther⁶ and Betsey (Ayers) Brigham; born in Ware, Mass., 7 Oct., 1832; died in Colrain, Mass., (Elm Grove), 10 Aug., 1895; married (1) Josephine Chapin, born 5 Oct., 1837; died 3 Sept., 1862; married

(2) 28 Feb.. 1865, Helen Juliette, daughter of Jabez and Mary (Boardman) Temple, born in Whitingham, Vt., 6 Oct., 1843. She is a talented public speaker. In Spiritualist circles she is known as an "inspirational" speaker, improvising poems, on such occasions, on any given subject. She is also musical.

Mr. Brigham, in early life was a machinist in Chicopee but in 1854 he bought the estate at Elm Grove, Mass., where he afterward lived, and where he carried on farming. He was musical, the leader of the Brigade Band of Springfield, Mass. His instrument was the "Kent" bugle, later changed to the cornet, when they first came into use. He was a man of genial nature and generous disposition.

Child (by first wife), born in Chicopee.
  i Jose C., b. 14 July, 1862; d. 1 Oct.. 1862.
Child (by second wife), born in Elm Grove:
762 ii Clarence Lincoln, b. 6 April, 1866.

538 HON. WALDO[7], son of Asa[6] and Sally (Hardy) Brigham, born in Bakersfield, Vt., 10 June, 1829; died in Hyde Park, Vt., 2 April, 1900; married Nov., 1858, Lucia Ellen, daughter of Lucius H. and Diadamia (Smalley) Noyes, born in Hyde Park, 25 March, 1837.

Mr. Brigham was graduated A. M., University of Vermont in 1854; admitted to the Lamoille Co. bar in 1857; practiced five years in Bakersfield, then formed the law partnership of Brigham & Waterman, later Brigham & McFarland in Hyde Park, where he continued to reside and practice. He served in the Legislature of Vermont in 1867 and 1868 and was a leading spirit in securing the charter for the Lamoille Valley Div. of the Portland & Ogdensburg R. R. Was the first president of the Lamoille Valley R. R. continuing in this position for 10 years. Was prominent in the Democratic party in Vermont, and candidate for Lieut. Gov., U. S. Senator, etc. He was president of the Lamoille Central Academy for 25 years; vice-president of the Vermont Bar Assn.. and trustee of the University of Vermont from 1875-'81.

Children, born in Hyde Park:
    i Julia[2], b. 23 Aug., 1860; m. 22 Dec., 1881, Henry M., son of
      Moses McFarland, b. 5 Aug., 1852; lawyer in Hyde Park; was
      grad. Univ. of Vt., A.B., 1878; admitted to Lamoille County Bar,
      1881; was partner with father-in-law; vice-prest. Lamoille Co. Sav-
      ings Bank & Trust Co. and Lamoille Co Nat. Bank; secy Civil &
      Military Affairs of Vt., 1890-92; G M., I. O. O. F. of Vt..,
      1897-98. Ch. (McFarland), b. Hyde Park:
      1 Helen Marion[8], b. 27 Nov., 1885; 2 Grace Brigham, b. 24 Sept.,
        1888; 3 Brigham Wheeler, b. 3 April, 1891.
   ii Mary, b. 21 June, 1870; m. 28 Aug., 1895, James, eldest son of
      Matthew H. Buckham, Prest. Univ. of Vt. She was grad. Univ.

(2) 28 Feb., 1865, Helen Juliette, daughter of Jabez and Mary (Boardman) Temple, born in Whitingham, Vt., 6 Oct., 1843. She is a talented public speaker. In Spiritualist circles she is known as an "inspirational" speaker, improvising poems, on such occasions, on any given subject. She is also musical.

Mr. Brigham, in early life was a machinist in Chicopee but in 1854 he bought the estate at Elm Grove, Mass., where he afterward lived, and where he carried on farming. He was musical, the leader of the Brigade Band of Spingfield, Mass. His instrument was the "Kent" bugle, later changed to the cornet, when they first came into use. He was a man of genial nature and generous disposition.

Child (by first wife), born in Chicopee:
i Josie C.⁸, b. 14 July, 1862; d. 1 Oct., 1862.
Child (by second wife), born in Elm Grove:
762 ii Clarence Lincoln, b. 6 April, 1866.

538 HON. WALDO⁷, son of Asa⁶ and Sally (Hardy) Brigham, born in Bakersfield, Vt., 10 June, 1829; died in Hyde Park, Vt., 2 April, 1900; married Nov., 1858, Lucia Ellen, daughter of Lucius H. and Diadamia (Smalley) Noyes, born in Hyde Park, 25 March, 1837.

Mr. Brigham was graduated A. M., University of Vermont in 1854; admitted to the Lamoille Co. bar in 1857; practiced five years in Bakersfield, then formed the law partnership of Brigham & Waterman, later Brigham & McFarland in Hyde Park, where he continued to reside and practice. He served in the Legislature of Vermont in 1867 and 1868 and was a leading spirit in securing the charter for the Lamoille Valley Div. of the Portland & Ogdensburg R. R. Was the first president of the Lamoille Valley R. R. continuing in this position for 10 years. Was prominent in the Democratic party in Vermont, and candidate for Lieut. Gov., U. S. Senator, etc. He was president of the Lamoille Central Academy for 25 years; vice-president of the Vermont Bar Assn., and trustee of the University of Vermont from 1875-'81.

Children, born in Hyde Park:
i Julia⁸, b. 23 Aug., 1860; m. 22 Dec., 1881, Henry M., son of Moses McFarland, b. 5 Aug., 1852; lawyer in Hyde Park; was grad. Univ. of Vt., A.B., 1878; admitted to Lamoille County Bar, 1881; was partner with father-in-law; vice-prest. Lamoille Co. Savings Bank & Trust Co. and Lamoille Co. Nat. Bank; secy Civil & Military Affairs of Vt., 1890-92; G. M., I. O. O. F. of Vt., 1897-98. Ch. (McFarland), b. Hyde Park:
1 *Helen Marion*⁹, b. 27 Nov., 1885; 2 *Grace Brigham*, b. 24 Sept., 1888; 3 *Brigham Wheeler*, b. 5 April, 1891.
ii Mary, b. 21 June, 1870; m. 28 Aug., 1895, James, eldest son of Matthew H. Buckham, Prest. Univ. of Vt. She was grad. Univ.

of Vt., 1893; he is author of *Where Town and Country Meet*, and several volumes of verse; res. Melrose, Mass. Ch. (Buckham):

  1 *Barbara*[9], b. 18 Feb., 1898; d. 9 Sept., 1898.
  2 *Waldo Brigham*, b. 14 Jan., 1900.
 iii Blanche, b. 15 Aug., 1875; was grad. Univ. of Vt., 1897; was preceptress of Lamoille Academy, Hyde Park, and is (1906) preceptress of High School in Dallas, O.

539 *ROBERT BRECK[7], son of Cheney[6] and Elizabeth (Brigham) Brigham[6], born in Bakersfield, Vt., 1 Nov., 1826; died in Boston, s. p., 2 Jan., 1900; married 17 Nov., 1870, in Boston, Frances Gertrude Brigham[7], daughter of 342.

An ambitious student at the academy in Bakersfield, he went to Boston at the age of 16 to earn money to complete his studies, but, on a suggestion of his former schoolmaster, continued in the restaurant business, in the employ of his uncle, the noted Peter Bent Brigham, corner Court and Hanover Streets, remaining ten years. He then opened a restaurant of his own farther down on Court Street, which he conducted successfully until ill health compelled him to sell out and go to Florida. Returning in 1860, he bought the estate and established "Brigham's" restaurant at 642 Washington Street, Boston, tearing down old buildings and building "Brigham's Hotel" in the rear about 1882.

This historic spot in 1635 was apportioned for a house and garden to Garrett Bourne, who built in 1636 and set out a number of elm trees. One he transplanted in 1646 a little northwest of his house. The house was transformed into a tavern and in 1760 was the meeting place of the "Sons of Liberty." Here the first public act of resistance to British authority occurred, 14 Aug., 1765, when the effigy of Andrew Oliver, the stamp officer, was hung from the branches of the transplanted tree; the old elm thus becoming known as the Liberty Tree and the location as Liberty Hall. The tree was cut down by the Tories in August, 1775; at the close of the Revolution a liberty pole was erected on its stump. In 1823-'24 the four-story brick Lafayette Hotel, built and kept by Ralph Haskins, replaced the old tavern; and it was from what is now Brigham's hotel that a beautiful young girl, with a silk sash of red, white and blue draped across her shoulders, presented the Marquis de Lafayette with his first refreshment upon entering the

* Rev. Robert Breck, son of Captain John Breck of Dorchester, was born 7 Dec., 1682, Harvard 1700, was settled at Marlboro 25 Oct., 1704. He was of great natural powers and had remarkable skill in the learned languages (reading from the Hebrew Bible at family prayers). He m. 8 Sept., 1707, Elizabeth Wainwright of Haverhill. His dau. Sarah m. Dr. Benjamin Gott of Marlboro and her dau., Sarah Breck Gott, m. Lieut. Uriah Brigham, great-grandfather of Robert B. Brigham. Hannah Breck, another daughter, married Rev. Ebenezer Parkman of Westboro, and was an ancestor of the Drs. Parkman of Boston and of two Brigham lines.

Robert B. Brigham

new City of Boston, a glass of wine, in 1824. Soon after, the hotel was secured by Asa de Costa, who managed it for a long time. William F. Bacon was its proprietor in 1860, when he was succeeded by Mr. Brigham, who lived there uninterruptedly until his death, although he sold the business to Bush & Willey in 1891. Soon after his occupancy and against the remonstrance of many friends Mr. Brigham, as a matter of principle, abolished the open bar maintained by his predecessor and enforced the custom, which afterward became the law of the Commonwealth, of serving liquors only at tables with food.

Mr. Brigham was one of the first to appreciate the movement of business toward the " South End " of Boston and at his death owned real property to the value of $3,000,000, all within a mile of his hotel. His purchases included (12 June, 1883) the " Meeting House in Hollis Street " (Unitarian), which Mr. Brigham transformed in 1885 into the Hollis Street Theatre, the leading playhouse of Boston. The new Globe Theatre also forms part of the Brigham estate.

In business life he was shrewd, honorable and reserved, but he was naturally of a lively, cheerful disposition and he was charitable in many quiet ways. His innate generosity will reach its full fruition in the Robert B. Brigham Hospital for Incurables. (See Appendix.) He is buried in Bakersfield.

540 LEANDER D⁷., son of Edward⁶ Brigham, (mother's name unknown); born in Milton, Vt., 16 Oct., 1820; died Westford, Vt., March, 1859; married 29 Feb., 1844, Eliza Bates of Westford.

Children:
    i Edgar Parkis⁸, b. 1845; m. 1866, Hannah Chadwick; res. St. Johnsbury, Vt., where a farmer; has several ch.
    ii (Dr.) Charles Orson, b. 23 Dec., 1847; was grad. Univ. of Vt., 1886; res. Pittsford and Rutland, Vt.; went to Alaska gold fields, where d. Dec., 1898; m. 25 April, 1876, Sarah A. Bishop of Westford, who res., his widow, in Rutland, Vt. Ch.:
        1 *Lynn B.⁹*, b. in W., 15 Jan., 1877; in business in Rutland.
    iii Orilla Laura, twin to Charles; m. D. D. Hall of Pittsford, Vt. Ch. (Hall):
        1 *Lillie⁹;* 2 *Mary;* 3 *Louise;* 4 *Mabel.*
    iv Mary Eliza, b. Aug., 1850; m. Geo. D. Bates of Pittsford. Ch. (Bates):
        1 *Douglas⁹;* 2 *Katherine.*
    v Edward Leander, b. in Ottawa, Can., 8 Dec., 1852; m. 7 Dec., 1876, Sabina Elizabeth Thompson, b. 8 Dec., 1851, in Kane Co., Ill.; res. a farmer, in 1904, Lamont, Ia. Ch., b. in Lamont:
        1 *Guy A.⁹*, b. 25 March, 1879.
        2 *Grace M.,* b. 15 March, 1881.
        3 *Leon Edward,* b. 25 Feb., 1883.

4 *Roy Oscar*, b. 9 April, 1885.
5 *Robin Henry*, b. 16 June, 1887.
6 *George Leslie*, b. 4 June, 1889.
7 *Earl Eugene*, b. 24 June, 1892.
8 *Dorr Douglas*, b. 24 Sept., 1896.

541 ADDINGTON MUNROE[7], son of Barnabas and Mary (Fife) Brigham; born in Marlboro, Mass., on the old Samuel Brigham farm, 27 March, 1837; married 7 May, 1861, Mary, daughter of John and Selecta (Gould) Estabrook of Westminister, Mass.

He was educated in the schools of Marlboro. In 1864 he enlisted in Co. E. 5th Mass. Inf. and was stationed in Baltimore and vicinity during most of the service. Became a dairy farmer on the ancestral estate, which originally covered 175 acres. It has been occupied by Brighams ever since it was redeemed from the wilderness, having been owned by Samuel[3] who left it to his son George[4], who left it to Ashbael Samuel[5], who sold it to Dr. Daniel[5], who was followed by Barnabas[6], and who, in turn, was followed by Addington[7]. George, Ashbael Samuel and Addington, were all born there. Also, Ulysses[9], grand-son of Addington. It was a garrison house as stated on p. 109 of the *History of Marlboro*. It is in the south part of the town, three quarters of a mile from Marlboro Junction. Addington has served the town as Road Commissioner and the city of Marlboro as a member of the Common Council, of which he has also been president. He was a charter member of the Marlboro Grange and has held the leading offices in that and the District Grange. He is a member of the G. A. R. He has been Curator of the B. F. A., many years, and is a member of the Publication Committee of the *Brigham Family History*.

Children, born in Marlboro:
    i Abbie Alice[8], b. 1 Feb., 1862; m. 15 March, 1893, George Fred Nichols. They live on the homestead of Thomas[2], s. p.
763 ii William Munroe, b. 24 Jan., 1864.
    iii Ella Amelia, b. 14 Aug., 1866; m. 19 June, 1895, William Aubrey, son of Harding and Annie (Lockhart) Porter of Marlboro, b. 9 Jan., 1872. Ch. (Porter), b. in Marlboro:
        1 *George Lockhart*[9], b. 12 Aug., 1896.
        2 *Aubrey Brigham*, b. 30 Aug., 1897.
        3 *Harding Lawton*, b. 28 Dec., 1900.
    iv Cora Estabrook, b. 27 Oct., 1868; d. unm., 2 Oct., 1892.

542 CHARLES AMORY[7], son of Daniel[6] and Sarah (Barnard) Brigham; born in Northboro, Mass., 26 Sept., 1814; died in 1899, æ. 84; married Eliza A. Fairbanks, born in Milford, Mass., 5 Sept., 1815; died 4 March, 1900. He resided in Nashua, N. H., where he was Street Commissioner. They celebrated their Golden Wedding.

Children, born in Nashua:

i Corp. Charles L.⁸, b. 3 June, 1843; d. 22 Oct., 1864; enlisted 14 Aug., 1862, Co. F, 9th N. H. Vols.; wounded 30 July, 1864, in mine explosion before Petersburg, Va.; 28 buckshot were taken out of his body.

ii Corp. Edward H., b. 27 March, 1845; d. 22 Oct., 1880; enlisted 9 Dec., 1861, Co. M, 1st N. H. Vol. Cavalry; re-enlisted 1 Jan., 1864; wounded and captured 29 June, 1864, in Ream's Sta., Va.; released from Libby Prison, 30 June, 1865.

iii George H., b. 28 Nov., 1846; d. 30 July, 1848.

iv Frederick A., b. 21 Feb., 1848; d. 5 June, 1849.

764   v George H., b. 1 March, 1851.

vi Albert W., b. 2 Oct., 1853; m. Minnie Davis; res. a retired merchant in Weston, Mass. Ch.:
1 *John⁹;* 2 *Paul.*

vii Frank M., b. 28 Jan., 1856; d. 1860.

viii Ira S., b. 30 Dec., 1858; m. Anna Merrill; has been in Nashua City Council; a traveling salesman, and res. Dorchester, Mass.

543 LYDIA MARIA⁷, daughter of Abraham Monroe⁶ and Mindwell (Brigham) Brigham; born in Boston, Mass., 23 Nov., 1824; married 23 Sept., 1850, Rev. Solomon, son of William Fay They resided in Dayton, Ohio, for a number of years, and now live in Dorchester, Mass.

Children (Fay), born in Dayton:

i Henry Brigham⁸, b. 18 May, 1853.

ii Ella Maria, b. 18 Nov., 1857.

iii Louis Payson, b. 24 June, 1861.

544 GEORGE OTIS⁷, son of Otis⁶ and Abigail (Bates) Brigham; born in Westboro, Mass., 9 Nov., 1821; died 13 Feb., 1898; he never married.

He was Treasurer of the Westboro Savings Bank for 24 years; cashier of the National Bank in Westboro for 26 years; Town Treasurer 24 years; Representative to the General Court 1878 and 1879. He was the leader of business life in the town and interested in all public works. The " Geo. Brigham Steamer Co." of the Fire Department was named for him.

545 JOSHUA BATES⁷, son of Otis⁶ and Abigail (Bates) Brigham; born in Westboro, Mass., 28 Sept., 1828; died in Brookline, Mass., 18 April, 1891; married (1) 27 Feb., 1862, Sarah M., daughter of James Abbot Lovejoy of Billerica, Mass.; born 18 Sept., 1835; died Nov., 1866; married (2) 17 June, 1868, Helen M., daughter of Nathaniel and Marcia (Bowen) Burgess of Providence, R. I. She died in Brookline, 27 Feb., 1906. Mr. Brigham was a philosophical instrument maker.

Child (by first wife).
  i Abbot Otis⁸, b. 19 Nov., 1863; d. *ibid.*
Children (by second wife):
  ii Agnes Otis, b. 3 Jan., 1875; a teacher.
  iii Donald P., b. 4 Oct., 1877.

546   DAVID SEWALL⁷, son of Rev. David⁶ and Elizabeth (Durfee) Brigham; born in East Randolph, Mass., 17 March., 1823; died in Fall River, Mass., Oct., 1873; married (1) 4 Dec., 1845, Elizabeth Gardner, daughter of Samuel and Eunice (Hathaway) Chace of Fall River; born there, 28 June, 1825; died there, 3 Feb., 1853; married (2) 16 Feb., 1854, Mary Howland Wady, who died 5 Jan., 1864; married (3) 2 Feb., 1870, Elizabeth Williams.   He was a merchant in Fall River, Mass.

Children (by first wife), born in Fall River:
  i Charles A.⁸, b. 18 Sept., 1846; d. 3 Jan., 1847.
  ii Charles A., b. 12 June, 1848; d. 23 Feb., 1850.
  iii Martha Chace, b. 3 April, 1850; m. 10 May, 1870, Herbert Chase of Newton, Mass. Ch. (Chase):
    1 *Merrill B.⁹,* b. 22 Feb., 1872.
Children (by second wife):
  iv Elizabeth Gardner, b. 26 March, 1856; d. 9 Nov., 1902; m. C. F. H. White. Ch. (White):
    1 *Mary B.⁹,* b. 8 Jan., 1884; m. 31 Dec., 1903, Robert B. M. Knight of Fall River.
    2 *Sanford B.,* b. 4 May, 1888.
  v George Sewall, b. 10 July, 1858; m. 13 Oct., 1886, Mary E. Sheen; res. Fall River (Belmont St.).
  vi James Wady, b. 9 May, 1860; m. 27 Sept., 1887, Mary Elizabeth, daughter of James Kendall. Ch., b. in Fall River:
    1 *James Kendall⁹, b.* 4 April, 1889.
    2 *David Sewall,* b. 11 Sept., 1891.
  vii Kate Sawin, b. 5 April, 1862; d. 14 March, 1863.

547   CHARLES DURFEE⁷, son of Rev. David⁶ and Elizabeth (Durfee) Brigham; born in Fall River, Mass., 21 July, 1831; married 9 Nov., 1851, Josephine H., daughter of Thomas F. Gibbs. He resides in Brockton, Mass.

Children:
  i Annie Josephine⁸, b. 1 April, 1855; m. 8 June, 1882, Edgar W., son of Rufus Davis; res. Fairhaven, Mass. Ch. (Davis):
    1 *Alfred B.⁹,* b. 4 June, 1883; 2 *Edna W.,* b. 25 Feb., 1888; 3 *Lena J.,* b. 28 April, 1893.
  ii David Foster, b. 3 June, 1859; m. Carrie W., dau. of Martin Kingman; res. Brockton. Ch.:
    1 *Arthur Foster⁹,* b. in Brockton, 18 May, 1884.
  iii Mary Agnes, b. 8 Nov., 1861; m. 25 Dec., 1888, Oscar, son of Warren Heath of Brockton. Ch. (Heath):
    1 *Donald B.⁹,* b. 15 May, 1892.
  iv Charles Angier, b. 15 Feb., 1871.

ADDINGTON M. BRIGHAM, OF MARLBORO (541)

548   JANETTE HANNAH[7], daughter of Hon. Elmer[6] and
Betsey C. (Parker) Brigham; born in Westboro, Mass., 9 Jan.,
1827; married 6 April, 1848, Archelaus M., son of Luther and
Lucy (Brigham) Howe, (448), born in South Vernon, Vt., 21
April, 1823; died 26 Dec., 1905.

After engaging in the manufacture of sleighs in Westboro, Mr.
Howe established the business of manufacturing cutting dies, which
he transferred to Worcester, Mass. in 1860; continued in this business until 1897, when he retired.

Children (Howe), born in Westboro:
    i Arthur L.[8], b. 27 Nov., 1848; d. 13 Oct., 1849.
    ii Elmer Parker, b. 1 Nov., 1851; lawyer in Boston; was grad.
       Worcester Polytechnic Inst., in 1871; Yale Univ., 1876.

549   MERRICK PUTNAM[7], son of Hon. Elmer[6] and Betsey
C. (Parker) Brigham, born in Westboro, Mass., 9 March, 1829;
died in Boston, 10 Dec., 1875; married in Boston, 21 May, 1851,
Sarah E. Wellington, born 1 Dec., 1825, who resides in Attleboro,
Mass.

Children, the eldest and youngest born in Boston:
    i Edward M.[8], b. 5 April, 1852; m. 24 Nov., 1874, Elizabeth C.,
       dau. of Thomas Brightman; he is a marketman, and res. Attle-
       boro. Ch.:
         1 *Elsie W.*[9], b. 4 April, 1877; m. 1899, Robert H. Selfridge.
            Ch. (Selfridge): Dorothy W.[10]
         2 *Clara E.*, b. 31 March, 1879.
         3 *Fred M.*, b. 9 Jan., 1882.
         4 *Sarah L.*, b. 24 May, 1892.
    ii Sabra L., b. in Illinois, 3 Nov., 1855; m. 4 Nov., 1876, George
       F. Cole, who d. 22 Oct., 1885. Ch. (Cole):
         1 *Ralph H.*[9], b. 5 Feb., 1878; 2 *Edith L.*, b. 22 Aug., 1879.
    iii Walter M., b. in Westboro, 16 Dec., 1857; d. in Attleboro, 27
       Aug., 1882; m. 27 Feb., 1881, Julia, dau. of Darius Briggs; was
       a jeweler, and res. Attleboro. Ch.:
         1 *Charles Wellington*[9], b. 9 Nov., 1881; a die cutter in Attleboro.
    iv Alfred W., b. 4 Oct., 1859; m. 24 June, 1883, Etta L., dau. of
       James Peckham; res. Attleboro. Ch.:
         1 *Carl A.*[9], b. 5 May, 1884; 2 *Clarence J.*, b. 1 Sept., 1886.

550   CYRUS[7], son of Capt. Holloway[6] and Frances (Read)
Brigham; born in Northboro, Mass., 27 Dec., 1838; died in Boston,
11 July, 1899; married in Boston, 6 Dec., 1865, Margaret A.,
daughter of Capt. John and Ann (Scott) Evans, of St. John, New
Brunswick; born 5 Aug., 1847; she resides a widow in Brookline,
Mass.

Mr. Brigham was the head of the well-known firm of C. Brigham
& Co., of Boston, milk contractors, said to be the largest distribu-
tors of milk, butter and cheese in the U. S. He was a tenor singer

and one of the founders of the "Apollo Club" in Boston.   He resided in Roxbury, with summer home in Nantasket.

Child, born in Boston:
    i Robert Otis⁸, b. 19 June, 1871; m. Vesta Stewart of Springfield Centre, N. Y.; res. in Waban, Mass.   Ch.:
        1 *Margaret S.⁹*, b. 1899; 2 *Stewart Evans,* b. 1902.

551   HIRAM WRIGHT⁷, son of Sylvanus⁶ and Amy (Cox) Brigham; born in Florida, N. Y., 29 Dec., 1799; died in Freeport, Ill.; married Mary Zeriah Sutliff.   Resided in Damascus, Pa., and removed to Freeport in 1869.

Children, born in Damascus.
    i Joseph Brigham⁸.
    ii Mary Ann, b. 21 May, 1827; m. 1 Sept., 1855, George T. Piersol. Ch. (Piersol):
        1 *Luther W.⁹;* 2 *Ida O.*
    iii George.
    iv Amy S., b. 15 Oct., 1832; m. 25 Aug., 1874, William F. Preston, b. in Gallipolis, O., 19 June, 1819; was State Fish Warden for Ill.; res. retired, in Freeport.
    v Webster.
    vi Hiram Truman.
    vii Carrie.
    viii Hattie, b. 17 Sept., 1845; m. 6 April, 1871, Byron L. Pickard, b. in Elroy, Ill., 28 July, 1844; a farmer, and res. Elroy.   Ch. (Pickard):
        1 *Charles N.⁹*, b. 2 Feb., 1873; 2 *Bert E.,* b. 3 July, 1877; 3 *Mamie E.,* b. 20 Jan., 1879.
    ix Luther A., b. 3 Feb., 1850; m. 17 Sept., 1872, Laura Luella Williams; res. Freeport, Ill.   Ch.:
        1 *Lillian Irene⁹*, b. 28 July, 1873; d. 20 Nov., 1874.
        2 *Ada V.,* b. 10 Dec., 1876.
        3 *George Adelbert,* b. 27 Sept., 1879.
        4 *Hattie Jemima,* b. 22 May, 1881.
        5 *Margaret Lorena,* b. 20 Dec., 1891.

552   CYNTHIA M⁷., daughter of Sylvanus⁶ and Amy (Cox) Brigham; born 26 April, 1807; died 16 April, 1892; married 5 Sept., 1827, Philander, son of Elisha Fox; born in New York, 17 Feb., 1806; resided a carpenter, in Dryden, Mich., where he died 15 Sept., 1877.

Children (Fox), the eldest born in N. Y. State:
    i Theodore B.⁸, b. 11 Nov., 1828; m. Lydia R. Sadler; res. Dryden.
    ii William V., b. 24 Jan., 1830; m. Ann Skinner; 3 yrs. in the Civil War, 12th Wis. Battery; res. a merchant in Kearney, Neb.
    iii Sarah Ann, m. Edwin R. Clark of Shelton, Neb.
    iv Ashbel C., b. 19 Feb., 1833; m. (1) ———— Havens; m. (2) ———— Skinner; res. Dryden.
    v Alexander Ervin, m. Sarah Soles.
    vi Amy Ann, m. Simon Hoenshett of Dryden.   Ch. (Hoenshett)·
        1 *Albert⁹;* 2 *Elizabeth.*

vii Sylvanus B., b. 10 Sept., 1838; m. Matilda Barnum; 3 years in
Civil War, Corp. Co. H, 21st Ia. Vols.; res. a farmer, Akron, Ia.
Ch.:
    1 *Horace*[9], a dentist in Bessemer, Mich.; 2 *Charles;* 3 *Laura.*
viii Laura A., b. 13 Feb., 1841; m. (1) ————— Watson, who was
killed in the Civil War; m. (2) ————— Ellsworth, a J. P. in
Dryden.
ix Elisha G., m. Elizabeth Smith.
x Louisa A., d. æ. 3 years.

553 WILLIAM C[7]., son of Sylvanus[6] and Amy (Cox) Brigham; born in Florida, N. Y., 1 July, 1802; died in Lorraine, N. Y.,
June, 1879; married Polly, daughter of Thomas Cox.

Children, born in Lorraine:
    i William Henry[8], b. 2 Sept., 1820; killed in a mill, 20 April, 1866;
    owned a box factory in Lorraine.
    ii Jane Kate, b. 5 April, 1824; m. 1841, Joseph M. Pooler of
    Mannsville, N. Y. Ch. (Pooler), b. in Mannsville:
        1 *Alsom H.*[9], b. 1842; res. Lorraine; 2 *William J.,* b. 1846; 3
        Delancy E., b. 1849; 4 *Delbert J.,* b. 1851; d. 1854; 5 *Eddie
        J.,* b. 1856; d. 1859; 6 *Martha J.,* b. 1853; d. 1873; 7
        Zelotus H., b. 1858; 8 *Flora C. D.,* b. 1864; 9 *James O.,* b.
        1866; d. 1868.
    iii Julia Ann, b. 4 Feb., 1827.
765 iv Hiram N., b. 3 May, 1829.
766 v Philip V. R., b. 27 Aug., 1831.
    vi Martin V., b. 13 Aug., 1834; m. 30 Dec., 1860, Terissa Watertown,
    b. in Lorraine, 23 Feb., 1843; res. Lorraine, and is a carpenter;
    was J. P. for 8 years. Ch., b. in Lorraine:
        1 *Andrew J.*[9], b. 7 Nov., 1861; 2 *Lillian B.,* b. 25 July, 1865; 3
        Frank E., b. 11 Sept., 1867; 4 *Wallace E.,* b. 8 July, 1869;
        5 *William W.,* b. 22 April, 1871; 6 *Ernest N.,* b. 20 March,
        1876.
    vii Sylvanus, b. 12 March, 1836; m. Polly Moore. Ch.:
        1 *Emery*[9]; 2 *Edwin;* 3 *Charles;* 4 *William.*
    viii John M., b. 5 Nov., 1838; m. 2 June, 1861, Ellen R., dau. of
    Hermon Waterman. Ch., b. in Lorraine:
        1 *Rosella R.*[9], b. 28 Feb., 1865; m. 1884, —————.
        2 *Edith F.,* b. 23 July, 1871; m. 1893, William R. Taylor. Ch.
        (Taylor): i Iola M.[10], b. 4 Sept., 1896; ii Herman, d. y.; iii
        Edwin, b. 1900; iv Leon, b. 1902.
        3 *Musette A.,* b. 23 Dec., 1878; m. 30 Oct., 1895, James D. Miller.
        Ch. (Miller): i Carl J.[10], b. 1896; ii Myrtle I., b. 1898; iii
        Royal E., b. 1901; iv Ellen I., b. 1902.

554 PHILIP P[7]., son of Sylvanus[6] and Amy (Cox) Brigham;
born in Springfield, N. Y., 5 Sept., 1810; died 14 June, 1887;
married 6 Dec., 1832, Jane A. Miller. Was a farmer and resided
in Galilee, Pa.

Children, born in Galilee:
    i James L.[8], b. 13 Sept., 1833; m. 1 July, 1857, Statira V. Keesler;
    a farmer and lumberman in Damascus, Pa. Ch.:
        1 *Clara J.*[9], b. 3 Nov., 1860; d. in Damascus; a music teacher.

2 *Virgil O.*, b. 11 Sept., 1862; m. 12 Nov., 1888, Gertrude Monington; a lumberman; res. Damascus. Ch.: Jay L.[10], b. 25 Jan., 1891.

767   ii Aaron S., b. 10 Nov., 1834.

iii Mary F., b. 16 Feb., 1838; m. Julius J., son of John Keesler; b. in Damascus, 4 May, 1837; res. Tylerville, Pa. Ch. (Keesler):
1 *Melville M.*[9], b. Aug., 1859; d. 1871.
2 *Veruleigh A.*, b. 20 June, 1867.

iv Orrin W., b. 20 Feb., 1840; m. 31 May, 1866, Ruth E. Marks; a farmer, res. Galilee. Ch.:
1 *Philip C.*[9], b. 15 Oct., 1877.

v Virgil D., b. 11 Nov., 1842; enlisted in 1862, Co. I, 84th Pa. Vols.; taken prisoner at Petersburg, 1864; d. in prison, Salisbury, N. C.

vi Maletta J., b. 1 Aug., 1847; m. 26 Dec., 1866, James S. Beattie of Rockland, N. Y.; she was a teacher.

vii Sophie E., b. 7 April, 1850; d. in Lestershire, N. Y., 18 March, 1902; m. 18 March, 1884, John, son of Thomas Gregg of Lestershire.

555   ORRIN A[7]., son of Sylvanus[6] and Amy (Cox) Brigham; born in Boylston, N. Y., 4 May, 1820; died in Damascus, Pa., 13 Feb., 1890; married 1 Jan., 1842, Rachel E. Broadhead. He was a farmer and undertaker.

Children, born in Damascus:
i Orville S.[8], b. 26 Nov., 1842; d. in Damascus, 16 June, 1864; m. 24 Nov., 1861, Caroline, dau. of Charles Keesler; res. Damascus. Ch.:
1 *Jacob L.*[9], b. 13 April, 1863; m. 19 Sept., 1882, Lauretta T. Terry; res. Hancock, N. Y. Ch.: i Emma M.[10], b. 25 June, 1884; ii Clarence L., b. 9 Nov., 1886; iii Nora A., b. 22 Dec., 1888.

ii Jacob W., b. 17 Aug., 1844; d. 1 Aug., 1864, from bullet wound in the Civil War.

iii William Henry, b. 14 Feb., 1846; m. 2 Oct., 1867, Sarah A., dau. of Edward Rutledge; b. in Rutledgetown, Pa., 27 June, 1845; a farmer, and res. Damascus. Ch., b. there:
1 *Marvin N.*[9], b. 24 April, 1868; m. 19 Oct., 1892, Hattie L. Jackson, b. in Tylerville, Pa., 30 March, 1871. Ch.: Arthur Willard[10], b. 4 Nov., 1895.
2 *Floyd T.*, b. 17 Oct., 1872.
3 *Viva E.*, b. 18 Jan., 1875.

iv Mary C., b. 23 Dec., 1847; d. 11 Feb., 1883; m. 2 July, 1870, Peter K. Valentine. Ch. (Valentine), b. in Damascus:
1 *Alonzo H.*[9], b. 5 June, 1878; 2 *Corwin H.*, b. 18 Dec., 1880.

v Hiram Wright, b. 22 May, 1853; d. in Damascus, 7 Feb., 1893; m. 27 Sept., 1874, Hattie, dau. of Jacob Ross; b. in Callicoon, N. Y., 1 July, 1856; res. Damascus. Ch., b. there:
1 *Rose E.*[9], b. 9 Sept., 1875.
2 *Frank V.*, b. 12 Sept., 1877.
3 *Mary Elizabeth*, b. 7 Oct., 1879.
4 *Mamie C.*, b. 24 March, 1885; d. 13 Aug., 1886.
5 *Marguerite*, b. 2 Dec., 1892.

556 CALVIN[7], son of Asa[6] and Lavina (Bellows) Brigham; born in Milton, Vt., in 1805; married in 1830, Hannah Baker of Essex, Vt. He resided in Essex.

Children, born in Essex:
  i Leonard[8], res. Jericho, Vt.
  ii Hiram, b. May, 1837; d. —————; m. June, 1859, Aletha P. Wheeler. Ch.:
    1 *George S.*[9]
    2 *Willis S.,* res. Essex.
    3 *Eva,* d. —————; m. —————. Ch.: Mae[10].
    4 *Frank C.,* res. Essex Center.

557 DANIEL MORGAN[7], son of Rufus[6] and Lydia (Morgan) Brigham; born in Essex, Vt., 25 Sept., 1832; married 4 March, 1861, Lydia P. Card, born in Painesville, O., 4 Oct., 1840. He was a merchant in Milwaukee, Wis., but now resides in Cleveland, O.

Children, born in Wilwaukee:
  i Card[8], b. 17 March, 1862; d. 1864.
  ii Daniel Rufus, b. April, 1865; d. in Denver, Colo., 19 Feb., 1902; m. 1 Sept., 1896, Lillian B. Rice; she res. in Peoria, Ill. Ch., b. in Denver:
    1 *Daniel Morgan*[9], b. 8 May, 1899.
    2 *Caroline Rice,* b. 1 March, 1901.
  iii Ann C., b. April, 1869; m. 5 April, 1899, Charles S. Britton; res. Cleveland.

558 NELSON[7], son of Silas[6] and Polly (Harding) Brigham; born in Harpersfield, O., 21 Oct., 1821; married (1) Oct., 1843, Roxana, daughter of Nathan Jennings; married (2) 11 June, 1878, Mrs. Celia Edson, daughter of H. P. Castle. He resides in Star, Kas.; is a farmer, mechanic, Justice of the Peace and a member of the Kansas Legislature.

Children (by first wife), born in Geneva, O
  i Arthur Nelson[8], b. 28 Oct., 1852; m. 4 Nov., 1873, Nettie M. Riley; a farmer, res. Star, Kan. Ch.:
    1 *Ralph*[9], b. 22 Jan., 1875; d. 5 March, 1877; 2 *Ross Jay,* b. 22 Oct., 1878; 3 *Frank,* b. 13 Sept., 1881.
  ii Jay P., b. March, 1869; d. 3 Nov., 1875.

559 HIRAM[7], son of Silas[6] and Polly (Harding) Brigham; born in Harpersfield, O., 14 Feb., 1823; died 21 April, 1897; married, 1850, Louisa, daughter of Nathan Jennings. Resided in Painesville, O., a farmer and carpenter.

Children, born in Geneva, O.:
  i Louis Delos[8], b. 22 Dec., 1850; m. 1 Jan., 1874. Osceola, dau. of R. C. Fugit; b. 8 March, 1853; res. Emporia, Kan. Ch.:
    1 *Leo Jay*[9], b. 29 Jan., 1875; m. 1900, in Emporia, Carrie Simmons; res. Paola, Kan. Ch.: i Florence G., b. 16 April, 1901; ii Edna L., b. 23 Oct., 1902; iii Arian M., b. 29 Dec., 1904.

    2 *Ava Hiram,* b. 9 Dec., 1876.
    3 *Grace Louisa,* b. 8 July, 1881.
    4 *Ermie Belle,* b. 11 Aug., 1883; m. David Love of Emporia.
    5 *Mira N.,* b. 24 Jan., 1889.
    6 *Flossie V.,* b. 18 July, 1891.
    7 *Arthur D.,* b. 25 Jan., 1894.
  ii George Henry, b. 8 May, 1855; m. 20 Oct., 1881, Mabel, dau. of
    D. Henry Gaylord; b. in Geneva, 6 Feb., 1861; res. Painesville,
    O. Ch.:
    1 *Edith E.*[9], b. 23 March, 1883; d. 27 March, 1885.
    2 *Lois M.,* b. 17 Nov., 1885; m. 1903, Lloyd A. McIlvaine.
    3 *Leon D.,* b. 9 Aug., 1887.
    4 *Jay C.,* b. 20 March, 1889.
    5 *Ralph E.,* b. 14 March, 1891.
    6 *Ruth M.,* b. 23 May, 1895.
    7 *Philip E.,* b. 6 Nov., 1899.

    560 ALBERT CRAWFORD[7], son of Silas[6] and Polly (Hard-
ing) Brigham; born in Harpersfield, O., 13 Nov., 1828; married
4 Oct., 1855, Hannah R., daughter of Chauncey Sackett, born in
Windsor, O., 3 Oct., 1830; died in Trumbull, O., 18 March, 1889.
He is a farmer and teacher and was 10 years town clerk. Resides
in Trumbull, O.

  Children, born in Trumbull:
    i Frederic Erwin[8], b. 10 Oct., 1856; m. 17 Oct., 1889, Nettie Lenora,
    dau. of Irving Crandall; grad. Oberlin, 1878; a teacher and
    farmer; res. Trumbull. Ch.:
    1 *Mary Ida*[9], b. 17 Feb., 1892.
    2 *Clair Crandall,* b. 14 Nov., 1894.
    3 *Albert Henry,* b. 30 July, 1896.
    4 *Harold Lynn,* b. 9 June, 1898.
    5 *Robert Nelson,* b. 4 March, 1900.
    6 *Estella Marcia,* b. 14 Dec., 1902.
  ii Henry Albert, b. 12 Sept., 1861; d. 31 Aug., 1875.

    561 LIEUT. GEORGE WASHINGTON[7], son of Silas and
Polly (Harding) Brigham; born in Harpersfield, O., 22 Sept.,
1836; married (1) 3 May, 1860, Arabella, daughter of William
Marshall, who died in Oshkosh, Wis.; married (2) 16 July, 1887,
Mary Elizabeth, daughter of Oscar Lee. Was 1st Lieut. and
Quartermaster 103d O. Vol. Infantry, Civil War; a bookkeeper;
resided Croton, O., Oshkosh, and Longmont, Colo.

  *Children (by first wife), the 3 elder born in Croton, the youngest in
Oshkosh:*
    i Nellie Inez[8], b. 28 July, 1861; m. and res. Perry, Ia.
    ii Leonard Earle, b. 12 June, 1867; photographer, res. Ogden, Ia.
    iii Harry, b. 3 Dec., 1869.
    iv Edward, b. 28 Feb., 1875.

    562 HON. MAVOR[7], son of Dea. Sullivan[6] and Amanda
(Spalding) Brigham; born 16 May, 1806, in a small log house on
a farm in Westmoreland. Oneida Count New York. to which his

M. Brigham

father had recently moved from New Hampshire; died in Toledo, O., 8 Jan., 1897; married (1) 29 Sept., 1830, Clarissa, daughter of Oliver Bill, born in Booneville, N. Y., 5 June, 1801; died in Toledo, 9 March, 1842; married (2) 27 July, 1843, Malinda P daughter of Jacob M. Merrell, born in Westmoreland, 21 Jan., 1822.

The farm on which he was born, as also the two others on which the family afterward lived, was chiefly uncleared land. With little schooling but a brilliant mind, he so fitted himself that he taught school for several years with great success; learned the carpenter's trade and until 1835 was both carpenter and building contractor, teaching school winters; he taught himself to play the bass viol and flute, sang well and taught singing school. In 1835, with wife and child, he removed to the new settlement in Ohio, afterward the city of Toledo, and resided there permanently except for a short return to New York State. Here, for 20 years, he was a builder and, at one time, a railroad constructor, etc.; also bought land upon which he built houses for sale; was in the hardware business 1858-1868, when retired on account of ill-health but frequently acted as executor or assignee of estates, etc. He was Justice of the Peace 6 years, successively township clerk and treasurer, member of the City Council and in 1853, Mayor of Toledo; also Collector of canal tolls; member of the first board of police commissioners by appointment of the Governor and later of the Water Works Board; these positions of public trust came to him unsought. In 1832 he organized one of the first Anti-Slavery societies in the United States and was long its secretary; also he greatly assisted to form public opinion against slavery and to aid negroes who had secured their liberty. Always, in adult life, a devout Christian, he was 53 years deacon and clerk of the First Congregational Church of Toledo, holding both offices when he died. For many years was the choir-master of his church. With mental faculties unimpaired, he passed away in his 91st year respected and loved by all.

Children (by first wife), the 2 elder born in Vienna, N. Y.:
    i Harriet Eliza[8], b. 4 July, 1831; m. 28 May, 1851, William A., son of Elisha Beach; b. in E. Bloomfield, N. Y., 22 April, 1822; d. in Toledo, 13 Dec., 1892. He was manager of the Western Union Telegraph Co., in Toledo, from its origin. Ch. (Beach), b. in Toledo.
        1 *Helen L.*[9], b. 28 April, 1857; m. 23 Aug., 1892, Samuel W. Jones, who d. 12 July, 1904; res. in Toledo, where Mr. Jones was Mayor. Ch. (Jones), b. in Toledo: Mason[10], b. 3 Oct., 1897.
        2 *Anna C.*, b. 10 Nov., 1861; m. 27 Dec., 1888, Selah R. Mac-Laren, who d. 29 Jan., 1905; res. Toledo. Ch. (MacLaren): Harriet Christine[10], b. 15 Oct., 1889; d. 8 April, 1901.

ii Celina Emily, b. 19 March, 1833; d. 19 Dec., 1834.
iii Sylvania Emeline, b. in Toledo, 17 Sept., 1835; d. 9 Aug., 1838.
768 iv Charles Oliver, b. in Dundee, Mich., 9 Sept., 1838.
v Franklin Sullivan, b. in Toledo, 9 Feb., 1842; d. 29 June, 1842.
Children (by second wife), born in Toledo:
vi Stanley Faber, b. 12 Dec., 1844; m. 22 June, 1871, Emma Hague; a clerk in Toledo.
vii Helen Cornelia, b. 7 Aug., 1846; d. 28 March, 1853.
viii George Mavor, b. 1 Feb., 1849; m. 10 Jan., 1883, Kate E. McCormick; he is a telegraph operator in Toledo.
769 ix William Augustus, b. 21 Sept., 1853.
x Edward Rollin, b. 28 Jan., 1856; d. 6 April, 1861.
770 xi Frederick Merrell, b. 17 July, 1864.
xii Harry Chase, b. 12 Oct., 1870; a wholesale druggist, Toledo.

563 ORVILLE P⁷., son of Dea. John⁶ and Susan (Moore) Brigham; born in Ogden, N. Y., 10 Sept., 1818; died in Spencerport, N. Y., 22 Oct., 1885; married 27 Jan., Delia Barnard, who died 11 March, 1904. He was a farmer and town officer and resided in Spencerport.

Children, born in Spencerport:
i Charles H.⁸, b. 30 March, 1843; m. 25 Oct., 1870, Cora C. Clark. Ch
1 *Elizabeth C.⁹*, b. 30 Dec., 1875; m. Charles L. Mosher, in 1903.
2 *Clara*, b. 3 July, 1878; d. 1887.
ii Edward D., b. 16 June, 1845; m. 23 Feb., 1887, Marie A. Munn; he d. 20 June, 1896, in Palmyra, N. Y., where res.; hardware merchant. Ch.:
1 *Mildred C.⁹*, b. 24 May, 1888.
iii Frederick G., b. 18 Feb., 1849; unm., a traveling salesman from Batavia, N. Y.
iv John C., b. 9 Sept., 1853; m. 2 March, 1898, Mary L. Merz; res. Spencerport.
v Clara B., b. 15 Aug., 1856; m. 26 Feb., 1873, Adelbert W. Whittier; res. Spencerport.
vi Elbert W., b. 15 Jan., 1863; m. 30 June, 1895, Hattie M. Chadsey; a farmer in Sweden, N. Y. Ch ·
1 *William E.⁹*, b. 2 Sept., 1900.

564 JOHN D⁷., son of Dea. John⁶ and Susan (Moore) Brigham; born in Ogden, N. Y., 4 Dec., 1820; died 28 Oct., 1894; married 19 Feb., 1845, Sophia Malinda, daughter of Sylvanus and Malinda (Atchinson) Willey; born in Ogden, 31 Oct., 1824; died 24 Nov., 1899. He was a farmer in Ogden and held town offices.

Children, born in Ogden:
i Alvan W.⁸, b. 25 Nov., 1845; m. June, 1888, Mary E. Girkin; a traveling salesman; res. Rochester, N. Y.
ii Virginia Sophia, b. 7 April, 1852; m. 12 June, 1878, Allen B. Welch of Victor, N. Y. Ch. (Welch), b. in Victor:
1 *Faith Virginia⁹*, b. 27 Aug., 1879.
2 *Ruby Florence*, b. 23 April, 1881; m. 30 Dec., 1903, Lewis M.

iii Florence Adelia, b. 20 Feb., 1858; m. 19 Oct., 1880, **Christie J.**
Pierce of Ogden.
iv Ella May, b. 29 March, 1866; m. 19 Oct., 1887, Frank K. **Austin**
of Owasco, N. Y. Ch. (Austin):
1 *Florence⁹; 2 Blanche.*
v Cora Miranda, b. 2 June, 1867; m. 29 Dec., 1892, Charles A.
Decker of Owasco, N. Y. Ch. (Decker):
1 *Gladys⁹; 2 Delwin B.*

565 ALONZO⁷, son of Dea. John⁶ and Susan (Moore) Brigham; born in Ogden, N. Y., 16 Nov., 1822; died Oct., 1859; married
3 Jan., 1849, Mary F. Wyman, who died 1 Jan., 1886. Resided
in Lafayette, Ind.

Children, born in Ogden:
    i Mary Janette⁸, b. 11 Oct., 1849; d. 1 Jan., 1885; m. Charles
    Barton. Ch. (Barton):
        1 *Howard S.⁹,* b. Oct., 1869; d. 1882.
        2 *Lillis A.,* b. 11 March, 1871; m. Fred. Castle.
        3 *Charles A.,* b. 1 May, 1877.   '
        4 *Alice H.,* b. 22 Jan., 1880.
        5 *Evelyn F.,* b. 28 Feb., 1882.
    ii Frank A., b. 2 Sept., 1858; m. (1) 31 March, 1882, Bessie Smith,
    who d. 1892; m. (2) Laura Brash; res. Rochester, N. Y. **Ch.**
    (by 1st wife):
        1 *Harry⁹,* b. 30 Jan., 1893; 2 *Pearl.*
        Ch. (by 2d wife):
        3 *Laura.*

566 DEA. MILTON⁷, son of Dea. John⁶ and Susan (Moore)
Brigham; born in Ogden, N. Y., 18 June, 1825; died 20 Sept.,
1897; married 25 Oct., 1850, Mary A. Finch of Spencerport, N.
Y.; born 19 July, 1830; residing in Spencerport, in 1905. Was a
farmer and resided in Spencerport; held many town offices and was
overseer of the poor; was deacon for 30 years.

Children, the eldest born in Spencerport, others in Ogden, N. Y.:
    i Carrie Louise⁸, b. 3 July, 1855; m. 11 Jan., 1882, Willard **Brower**
    of Ogden, N. Y. Ch. (Brower):
        1 *Milton Willard⁹,* b. 11 Aug., 1885.
        2 *Chester Lewis,* b. 1 May, 1892.
        3 *Henry Somerset,* b. 24 May, 1893.
        4 *Roy Brigham,* b. 15 Aug., 1894.
771 ii Henry Martyn, b. 19 Nov., 1859.
    iii John Hazzard, b. 22 Sept., 1862; m. 19 June, 1895, Louise Bev-
    eridge Stevenson, b. in Edinboro, Scotland, 20 July, 1875; he is
    V. P. of the Rochester (N. Y.) Lamp Co., and Gen. Manager;
    res. N. Y. City. Ch.:
        1 *Dorothy Louise⁹,* b. and d. 1896.
    iv Minnie A., b. 20 Dec., 1864; m. 23 June, 187—, George Clement
    Card of Los Angeles, Cal.. Ch. (Card):
        1 *Don Brigham⁹,* b. in Minneapolis, 8 March, 1888.
        2 *Henry Harold,* b. 1890; d. 1893.
        3 *Louise Du Bois,* b. in Spencerport, 27 Sept., 1892.
        4 *Dorothy,* b. 1898.

567 CHARLES[7], son of Dea. John[6] and Susan (Moore) Brigham; born in Ogden, N. Y., 15 March, 1827; married 7 June, 1860, Hannah Bailey. Is a fruit-grower in Spencerport, N. Y · Justice of the Peace doing much out-of-court legal work; ex-postmaster.

Children, born in Spencerport:
  i William A.[8], b. 30 May, 1861; d. 21 April, 1900; a business man of West Superior, Wis.; ex-postmaster.
  ii Alletta B., b. 16 April, 1863.
  iii Hattie, b. 14 March, 1866.

568 LEWIS E.[7], son of Elijah[6] and Lydia (Richards) Brigham; born in Vernon Center, N. Y., 4 Dec., 1820; married, 1843, Sophia, daughter of Warren and Sophia (Catlin) Johnson of Clinton, N. Y., born 29 April, 1825. He died 22 Feb., 1907.

Children, all but the eldest born in Clinton:
  i Frank M.[8], b. in Utica, N. Y., 29 Dec., 1845; m. in Syracuse, N. Y., 8 Feb., 1872, Antoinette, dau. of Thomas and Silna (Corbin) Allen of Mechanicsville, N. Y.; b. 13 Sept., 1850; a salesman, res. Dorchester, Mass. Ch., b. in Utica:
    1 *Maud Allen*[9], b. 8 July, 1873; res. Quincy St., Dorchester.
  ii Perry, b. 25 March, 1847; m. Nov., 1875, Julia, dau. of Nathan and Mehitable (Russell) Jewett of Amherst, Me.; b. 12 July, 1857; res. s. p., a bookkeeper, in Los Angeles, Cal.
  iii Edward, b. 21 Nov., 1850; res. a farmer, in Clinton, N. Y.
  iv Walter Scott, b. 25 Feb., 1852; m. 26 March, 1890, Emma, dau. of Norman and Catherine (Smellie) Randall of New York City; b. 12 Oct., 1861; is a carpenter, in business for himself in N. Y. City, where res. Ch., b. in N. Y. City:
    1 *Walter Dudley*[9], b. 29 July, 1893.
    2 *Edna Randall*, b. 2 Sept., 1896.
  v Newton J., b. 4 May, 1853; d. 1 Jan., 1883; m. in Utica, 13 May, 1872, Mary Platt of Jersey City, N. J., b. 21 Jan., 1850. Ch., the two elder b. in Utica:
    1 *Perry N.*[9], b. 6 Feb., 1874; d. in Utica, 12 Aug., 1874.
    2 *Caroline M.*, b. 9 April, 1875; m. 5 June, 1895, Frank B., son of Robert Bishop of New Zealand; b. 5 March, 1872; res. San Francisco, Cal. Ch. (Bishop), b. in San Francisco:
      i Isabella[10], b. 5 April, 1896; ii Carrie, b. 13 Nov., 1898.
    3 *Isabella*, b. in Detroit, Mich., 15 July, 1877; d. in Cal., 24 Nov., 1894; m. 6 June, 1894, Augustus Haskins of Salt Lake City, b. 6 March, 1870; res. San Francisco.
  vi Caroline, b. 22 March, 1858; d. 2 Dec., 1901; m. in Boston, Nov., 1884, James T., son of Gaylord D. Brown of Madison, N. Y.; b. 22 Aug., 1857; res. s. p., Somerville, Mass.
  vii Robert O., b. 23 May, 1861; m. 23 Jan., 1890, Minnie, dau. of James and Rebecca (Nicholson) McDonald of Quincy, Ill.; b. 27 Sept., 1870; he is an inventor, and res. Centralia, Ill. Ch., b. in Denver, Colo.:
    1 *Mabel*[9], b. 20 Oct., 1890.
  viii Frederick, b. 26 Nov., 1868; d. 18 Oct., 1897; m. 1 Sept., 1891,

Martha, dau. of Thomas and Mary (Binnen) Harris of Danville,
Pa.; b. 11 June, 1873. Ch., b. in N. Y. City:
1 *Lewis*[9], b. 15 July, 1892.
2 *Leroy*, b. 29 April, 1895; d. 2 Sept., 1902.
ix Benjamin, b. 8 June, 1871; a farmer, Clinton, N. Y.

569 LYMAN FARWELL[7], son of Dea. David[6] and Catherine
(Romaine) Brigham; born in Hartwick, N. Y., 26 Sept., 1828; died
in Sedalia, Mo., 19 Nov., 1892 or 1896; married 4 July, 1850,
Maria, daughter of James Boroughs; born in Green, N. Y., 14
Feb., 1828. He was a builder, was Sergeant, Co. G, 15th N. Y.
Vol. Engineers, Civil War. Resided in Dryden, N. Y.

Children, born in Dryden:
    i Fred[8], b. 11 July, 1853; m. (1) 3 Dec., 1873, at Castle Creek,
    N. Y., Sarah J., dau. of M. E. Bullock; d. 25 July, 1874; m. (2)
    20 Jan., 1877, Ella, dau. of R. Shevalin; b. in Harford, N. Y.,
    11 July, 1856; is a farmer in Castle Creek. Ch.:
      1 *Jane*[9], b. in Castle Creek, July, 1874; d. y.
      2 *Mary*, b. in Harford, 24 Sept., 1882.
    ii Frank, b. 20 May, 1855; m. Dec., 1874, widow Julia Porter;
    res. a blacksmith, West Saticoy, Cal. Ch., b. in Chester, Pa.:
      1 *Frank*[9], b. 15 May, 1876.
    iii Mary Kate, b. 20 July, 1857; a teacher; res. unm., at Chenango
    Forks, N. Y.
    iv Mariah Elizabeth, b. 6 July, 1859; m. 1 Feb., 1882, Augustus,
    son of Otis Hall; b. 24 July, 1848; a farmer, res. Chenango
    Forks, N. Y.; has been town assessor. Ch. (Hall), b. in Che-
    nango Forks:
      1 *Lyman F.*[9], b. 16 June, 1883; 2 *Mary Jane*, b. 8 Aug., 1886;
      d. 19 Sept., 1886; 3 *Frank Brigham*, b. 6 July, 1887; 4
      Benjamin H., b. 12 Oct., 1888; 5 *Lucy M.*, b. 14 Feb., 1890;
      6 *Guy*, b. 2 Sept., 1891.

570 NEWTON JOSIAH[7], son of Dea. David[6] and Catherine
(Romaine) Brigham; born in Hartwick, N. Y., 17 Sept., 1834;
married 25 Dec., 1856, Mary, daughter of Philip Oliver, born in
Dryden, N. Y., 22 April, 1838; died in Iola, Kas., 3 Jan., 1892.
He is a farmer in Whitney's Point, N. Y.

Children, born in Dryden:
    i William[8], b. Jan., 1858; d. 19 April, 1858.
    ii Edwin Perry, b. 19 May, 1859; m. 6 Jan., 1886, Mary, dau. of
    Vencel Rowck, emigrated from Germany to Missouri; b. 11 Nov.,
    1859; res. a merchant, in Iola, but formerly in Dodge City, Kan.
    Ch., the elder b. in D. C., others in Iola:
      1 *Nettie A.*[9], b. 10 Oct., 1886; 2 *Newton J.*, b. 10 May, 1888; 3
      Arthur Perry, b. 10 Jan., 1890; 4 *May Adaline*, b. 2 Nov.,
      1891.
    iii Henrietta C., b. 29 Aug., 1861; m. 2 Dec., 1885, Alexander
    Stewart Ewart of Sedalia, Mo., b. in Pa., 10 Oct., 1856; res. Iola.
    iv Charles Arthur, b. 29 June, 1864; m. (1) 31 July, 1887, Pauline
    Harline, who d.; m. (2) 5 March, 1894, widow Mary Leet; res.
    Denver, Colo.

571   STEPHEN NATHANIEL BROOKS[7], son of Edmond[6] and Mary (Brooks) Brigham; born in West Boylston, Mass., 18 July, 1811; died 6 June, 1856; married 30 March, 1842, Betsey Bathia Lee; born 12 Nov., 1822; died 20 Aug., 1902.

Children:
  i Ellen Maria[8], b. 26 Jan., 1844; d. ——————; m. Charles H. Damon; 2 ch.
  ii Silas Brooks, b. 11 Aug., 1845; d. 21 Oct., 1848.
  iii Eunice Delpha, b. 2 July, 1848; d. 6 Sept., 1904; m. Charles F. J. Kitchener; 3 ch.
  iv Sarah Emma, b. 29 April, 1851; m. 24 Dec., 1879, Walter E. Blanchard; res. s. p., Lynn, Mass.
  v George Henry, b. 23 Jan., 1853; d. 13 Oct., 1857.
  vi Herbert Irving, b. 28 Feb., 1855; d. 11 Aug., 1856.

572   MOSES[7], son of Jabez[6] and Nancy (Kingsbury) Brigham; born 10 May, 1798; died 8 Feb., 1866; married (1) 3 Dec., 1818, Chloe, daughter of Nathan Pond of Walpole, Mass.; born 1 Feb., 1798; died 30 May, 1846; married (2) in 1847, Sarah T. Huse, of Newburyport, Mass. He resided in Chicopee, Mass.

Children, born in Worcester:
772   i Charles Augustus Goodrich[8], b. 3 Dec., 1823.
  ii Olivia Ann, b. 13 May, 1826; d. 1849.

573   HOSEA[7], son of Jabez[6] and Nancy (Kingsbury) Brigham; born in Worcester, Mass., 6 Dec., 1802; died 26 July, 1837; married 17 March, 1825, Mary, daughter Nathaniel Pond of Walpole, Mass.; born 24 Dec., 1805.

Child, born in Worcester:
  i Harriet Maria[8], b. 15 Oct., 1826; d. 1 Sept., 1850; m. ——— Bates. Ch., b. in Worcester (Bates):
    1 *Ella M.[9]*, b. 26 Aug., 1846; d. 13 Aug., 1879; m. in Enfield, Conn., May, 1876, ———.
    2 *Mary K.*, b. 13 July, 1850; m. 1 June, 1871, Henry H. Ellis of Springfield, Mass. Ch. (Ellis): i Henry B.[10]; ii Leon T.

574   MARGARET[7], daughter of Jabez[6] and Nancy (Kingsbury) Brigham; born ———, 1808; died 17 March, 1846; married 30 April, 1830, William Trowbridge, son of Alpheus and Mary (Trowbridge) Merrifield of Worcester, Mass.; born 10 April, 1807. He married for his second wife, Maria C. Brigham, 414. He resided in Worcester.

Children (Merrifield):
  i Ann Brigham[8], b. 6 Nov., 1831; d. 30 May, 1854.
  ii Caroline Amelia, b. 2 Jan., 1834; d. 11 June, 1858; m. 20 May, 1857, Rev. Edward W. French of Bergen, N. J.
  iii William Frederic, b. 30 Aug., 1837; m. Susan B. Brigham, dau. of 409; res. s. p., Brookline, Mass.
  iv Henry Kingsbury, b. 21 July, 1840.

575 LUCY A.[7], daughter of Stephen[6] and Lucy (White) Brigham; born in Boston, 8 Dec., 1811; died 9 Sept., 1896; married 20 Sept., 1832, Benjamin Houghton of Ashland, Mass. Resided in Ashland.

Children (Houghton), born in Ashland:
i Henry Winslow[8], b. 13 July, 1833; m. Josephine Howard; both deceased.
ii Elizabeth, b. 1 April, 1835; d. 18 Sept., 1838.
iii *George Francis*, b. 14 Oct., 1837; and d.
iv Elziabeth Brigham, b. 12 March, 1839; d. 23 Dec., 1874; m. Daniel Franklin Evans of Denmark, Me. Ch. (Evans):
1 *George F.*[9], b. 28 April, 1859; d. 3 Oct., 1894; m. and had 1 ch.
2 *Henry Winslow*, b. 3 Aug., 1863; m. Inez L. Ramsdell, 20 March, 1893; 3 ch.
3 *Grace Darling*, b. 6 Sept., 1867; d. 30 March, 1894; m. George Larrabee; 1 ch.
v Benjamin Wesley, b. 10 June, 1841; d. 12 June, 1897; m. 21 Oct., 1863, Mary V. Jones of Ashland. Ch.:
1 *Carrie H.*[9], b. 2 Nov., 1874; d. 18 Sept., 1875.
2 *Margaret C.*, b. 18 Aug., 1877.
vi Charles White, b. 9 Feb., 1843; d. in 1867.

576 LEVI HENRY[7], son of Levi[6] and Eunice (Monroe) Brigham; born in Boston, 27 Nov., 1811; died in New York City, 18 April, 1881; married 27 Feb., 1849, Zenobia, daughter of John and Ann (Hunt) West of Bristol, Eng.; born in Bristol, 29 Dec., 1827; died in Brooklyn, N. Y., 3 Jan., 1866. He was a merchant. The male line is extinct.

Children, all born in Brooklyn, except the fifth:
i Harriet[8], b. 11 Jan., 1850; d. 29 Oct., 1852.
ii Zenobia West, b. 1 Dec., 1853; was grad. Vassar College, 1876; was class poetess; d. unm., 10 Dec., 1900.
iii Emma Frances, b. 11 April, 1855; d. in Brooklyn, N. Y., 25 Feb., 1881; m. 24 April, 1878, Eugene Winslow Durkee of Brooklyn; she was grad. Vassar College, 1877; was a successful sculptor; one work, a bust of Prof. Maria Mitchell, the astronomer, was cast in bronze, and given to her class; is now in Vassar College. Ch. (Durkee).
1 *Emma West*[9], b. in Brooklyn, 17 Feb., 1879; res. New York, and E. Patchogue, L. I.
2 *Helen Winslow*, b. in B., 26 Nov., 1880; res. N. Y., and E. P., L. I.
iv Henry, b. 27 Nov., 1857; d. 16 March, 1859.
v Ada Anne, b. in Orange, N. J., 5 July, 1860; res. unm., Brooklyn, N. Y., and Bennington, Vt.
vi Caroline W., b. 26 Dec., 1865; d. 28 Feb., 1866 (?).

577 JOSEPH DARWIN[7], son of Joseph[6] and Hannah (Hardy) Brigham; born in Westboro, Mass., 19 July, 1807; died in Princeton, Mass., 15 Jan., 1869; married 20 Dec., 1832, Ann,

daughter of Isaac Thompson; born in Princeton, 2 Dec., 1810. He was a carpenter and resided in Princeton.

Children, born in Princeton:

    i Henry[8], b. 15 Oct., 1833; d. s. p., 29 Dec., 1890; m. 2 June, 1869, Emma Donnell. He was a Ry. man, and res. Cambridge, Mass.; his widow res. Bath, Me.

    ii Elizabeth, b. 31 March, 1835; d. 16 Sept., 1835.

    iii Edward, b. 18 Aug., 1836; d. 15 Dec., 1836.

    iv Walter, b. 8 Dec., 1838; d. 1 Feb., 1839.

    v Harriet A., b. 31 July, 1840; d. 19 May, 1877; m. 4 Jan., 1865, Charles J. Cheney, who d. 6 Dec., 1872; a Ry. man, res. Cambridge, Mass. Ch. (Cheney):

        1 *Grace A.*[9], b. 25 Jan., 1866; m. 1888, Walter Newbert of Worcester. Ch.: Helen F.[10]

    vi Franklin D., b. 29 Dec., 1843; m. 6 Jan., 1870, Helen A. Bates, who d.; m. (2) Frances, dau. of Philander Harlow of Hyde Park, Mass.; res. provision dealer, in Hyde Park, s. p.

    vii Maria J., b. 2 May, 1847; res. Hyde Park.

578   WILLIAM BELKNAP[7], son of Joseph and Hannah (Hardy) Brigham; born in Westboro, Mass., 26 April, 1809; died in Springfield, Mass., 14 May., 1892; married 4 Dec., 1835, Susan Richardson, daughter of Samuel Willard; born in Sterling, Mass., 24 Dec., 1815; died 22 July, 1892. He was a machinist and settled in Worcester, Mass. about 1836, thence to Springfield, in 1844.

Children, all born in Worcester, except the youngest:

    i George William[8], b. 25 June, 1838; d. in N. Y. City, 25 Sept., 1892; m. (1) 1864, Josephine Pickens, who d. 1872; m. (2) Mary Lafond of New York, who survived him with 6 ch. Ch. (by first wife), b. in N. Y. City:

        1 *William E.*[9], b. 2 Feb., 1865; d. 28 Oct., 1873.

        2 *George F.*, b. March, 1868; d. Sept., 1870.

        3 *Charles*, b. May, 1872; d. June, 1872.

    ii Laura Susan, b. 6 Aug., 1841; m. 24 May, 1866, Louis J. Jenner of Springfield, Mass.

    iii Sarah Jane, b. 25 May, 1847; d. unm., 4 Oct., 1871.

    iv Charlotte E., b. 26 April, 1851; she adopted, 1894, *Frederic Orrin* (b. *Flood*, in Boston, 14 Feb., 1882; changed name by Act of Court to) Brigham.

    v Nellie Estey, b. in Springfield, 26 June, 1855; d. 7 May, 1863.

579   CHARLES CORRIDEN, son of Joseph and Hannah (Hardy) Brigham; born in Westboro, Mass., 1 Dec., 1812; died in Blackstone, Mass., 3 July, 1853; married, in Marlboro, Mass., 29 Aug., 1840, Sabra Butler, daughter of Lebbeus and Mary (Eager) Cook, born in Marlboro, 26 Dec., 1819; died in Worcester, Mass., 2 March, 1905, at the advanced age of 85 years. (The Cook line has been traced back to Walter Cook who was at Weymouth, Mass., in 1643, and has been printed in comprehensive form in the Newport *Mercury* during 1901). Mr. Brigham was a

LEWIS RICE AND H̱ s WIFE, SUSAN AUGUSTA BRIGHAM (522)

manufacturer of reeds, harnesses and other mill supplies. He was interred in Worcester and 25 years later the body was removed to Riverside Cemetery, Providence, R. I.

Children, the second and third born in Worcester, and the fourth and fifth in Woonsocket, R. I.:

    i Laurietta Ella⁸, b. 28 June, 1841, in Grafton, Mass.; d. in Waterbury Cen., Vt., in 1896; m. in Marlboro, 12 Nov., 1864, Benjamin Corliss Hutchins, b. in Whitefield, N. H., 18 May, 1835. Ch. (Hutchins):

        1 *Ernest Eaton⁹*, b. in Marlboro, 28 Aug., 1865.
        2 *Ila M.*, b. 11 June, 1868, in Westfield, Vt.
        3 *Maranda Jane*, b. 22 March, 1871, in Richford, Vt.
        4 *Clytie*, b. 23 Feb., 1879, in Waterbury.

    ii Charles Elwin, b. 26 Nov., 1844; d. 29 July, 1845.

    iii Charles Adalbert, b. 10 March, 1846; m. (1) 16 Feb., 1870, Alida Clarinelle, dau. of Lorenzo and Celia J. Wilmarth; b. in Victor, N. Y., 29 Jan., 1851; d. in Providence, R. I., 11 July, 1876; m. (2) 25 Dec., 1877, Mary Abbie, dau. of Abel Getchell of Waterville, Me., b. 28 Feb., 1853. He is a carpenter and block-maker, res. Norwood, R. I. Ch. (by first wife), b. in Providence:

        1 *Jennie Ballard⁹*, b. 16 May, 1871; m. 23 June, 1897, Frank Edwin, son of Jeremiah W. and Felicia H. Andrews; b. in Woodstock, Conn.

        2 *Florence Clay*, b. 1 July, 1873; m. 16 Dec., 1896, Walter Sage, son of Edwin G. and Margaret Baker; b. in Providence, 10 July, 1874. Ch. (Baker): Dorothy Deane¹⁰, b. in Providence, 15 April, 1898.

773 iv John Olin, b. 15 July, 1848.

    v Ethelyn Estella, b. 10 Oct., 1849; m. 14 Feb., 1871, William Richards, son of Samuel G. and Rhoda A. Howe; b. in Westboro, in 1850. Ch. (Howe), b. in Norwich, Conn.:

        1 *Joseph Olin⁹*, b. 16 Jan., 1875; m. 12 Jan., 1902, Anna Elizabeth Lawlor.
        2 *Winifred Eva*, b. 31 Dec., 1876.
        3 *William Brigham*, b. 23 Sept., 1887.

    vi Angenette Cook, b. in Blackstone, 1 June, 1853; m. 18 Oct., 1877, John Thompson, son of George C. and Mary M. Wheeler; b. in Berlin, Mass. Ch., the 2 elder b. in Worcester:

        1 *Daisy May⁹*, b. 31 March, 1880; d. 10 May, 1880.
        2 *Lois Mable*, b. 14 Feb., 1882; m. 10 June, 1902, Dwight Alberty. Ch. (Alberty): Richard Dwight¹⁰, b. 23 Aug., 1903.
        3 *George Brigham*, b. in Marlboro, 1 Feb., 1888; d. 1 Jan., 1889.

580 OWEN BENJAMIN⁷, son of Benjamin⁶ and Lucy (Hardy) Brigham; born in Westboro, Mass., 27 May, 1812; died in Cambridge, Mass., 19 Jan., 1872; married 30 Nov., 1836, Mary Duncan, daughter of Wales Paine, born in Westboro, 22 March, 1815. Resided in Worcester and other places and later in Cambridge.

Children, the 2 elder born in Worcester:

    i Caroline Augusta⁸, b. 9 March, 1839; d. in Lyndonville, Vt., 23 Dec., 1873; m. 10 May, 1866, Ira Wilmarth, son of J. T. G.

Cunningham of Lyndonville; b. there, 22 Feb., 1843. Ch. (Cunningham):

1 *Marion Brigham*[9], b. in Lyndonville, 25 Dec., 1870.

ii Henry Wales, b. 5 July, 1840; 3 yrs. in Civil War; res. unm., Cambridge.

iii Frederick Abbe, b. in Roxbury, Mass., 25 Aug., 1845; m. 19 July, 1875, Adelaide Maria, dau. of John Clark; b. in Waltham, Mass., 26 June, 1853; res. Cambridge. Ch.:

    1 *Caroline Adelaide*[9], b. 10 April, 1876.

    2 *George Frederick*, b. 9 Jan., 1879; d. 29 Dec., 1881.

    3 *Eva Jane*, b. 28 July, 1883.

    4 *Owen Benjamin*, b. 11 March, 1885.

    5 *Frederick Abbe*, b. 24 Dec., 1887.

iv Edwin Wetherbee, b. in Dorchester, Mass., 10 April, 1848; m. 5 June, 1878, Elizabeth Ann, dau. of William F. McIntosh; b. in Montville, N. S., 15 April, 1859; res. Dorchester. Ch.:

    1 *William Ira*[9], b. 3 May, 1886.

v Walter Owen, b. 18 July, 1854; m. 3 Jan., 1890, Mrs. Caroline M. (Burrill), widow of E. J. Adams of St. Johnsbury, Vt.; res. Lyndonville, Vt.

581 MARY M.[7], daughter of Willard[6] and Betsey (Russell) Brigham; born in Marlboro, Mass., 1 Oct., 1804, (perhaps, 1809); died 1883; married Ebenezer Brown, born in Marlboro, 1 Oct., 1802; died in South Boston, 1873.

Children (Brown), order uncertain in some cases.

i Mary Matilda[8], b. 1824, in Ashland, Mass.; m. Samuel Pillsbury; d. s. p., in Boston.

ii George Dana, b. in Marlboro, 15 May, 1830; m. 4 May, 1851, in Ashland, Josephine Merchants, b. 15 Oct., 1835, in Montague, Mass. Ch.:

    1 (*Dr.*) *Eugene Merchants*[9], b. Saugus Centre, Mass., 19 Aug., 1860; m. in N. Y., 14 Aug., 1891, *Georgiana* Armstrong, b. 30 March, 1863, in Boston; res. there. Ch.: Harold Eugene[10], b. 21 Oct., 1896.

iii Frank Brigham, b. in Ashland.

iv Emmons Augustine, b. in Ashland.

v Sarah Abbot, b. in Marlboro.

vi Samuel Ebenezer, b. in Marlboro; d. in Chicago; m. Sarah Moulton, who d. in So. Boston.

582 *REV. LEVI[7], son of Willard[6] and Betsey (Russell) Brigham; born in Marlboro, Mass., 14 Oct., 1806; died in Marlboro, 26 Dec., 1885; married 6 July, 1838, Mary, daughter of Dea. Dexter Fay; born in Berlin, Mass., 21 Oct., 1804.

He was graduated from Williams College 1833; Andover Theological Seminary, 1836; was ordained pastor of the Evangelical Church in Dunstable, N. H., 15 March, 1837; dismissed in 1850, at his own request; was elected Trustee of Pepperell Academy, 1841; pastor in Troy, N. H., 8 years and supplied in Winchendon; resided in Saugus, Mass., in later years.

* Vide Hist. *Dunstable and Fay Family.*

Children, born in Dunstable:
  i Eliza Catherine[8], b. 11 Feb., 1839; m. 10 Oct., 1861, Rev. Geo.
    A. Beckwith; res. s. p., Saratoga, N. Y.
  ii Mary Louisa, b. 25 June, 1840; d. 23 May, 1851.
  iii Edward Dexter, b. 4 Oct., 1841; d. 1 May, 1859; a student in
    Williams College at time of death and stood second in class; the
    first in rank d. about the same time, and the class put up a
    monument to them.
  iv Abby Ann, b. 13 Oct., 1844; m. 20 Aug., 1872, Dr. Carl G.
    Metcalf of Marlboro, Mass., b. in E. Unity, N. H., 21 April,
    1846; grad. of Albany Med. Coll., 1869; practiced in Troy, N. H.,
    Middletown and Marlboro, Mass., where he d. s. p., 1 Nov., 1884.

583 GEORGE[7], son of Willard[6] and Betsey (Russell) Brigham, born in Marlboro, Mass., 12 Oct., 1808; died April, 1889;
married, 1 May, 1832, Mary Ann, daughter of Thomas Hapgood
of Marlboro, born 20 July, 1813; died 24 Nov., 1878. Resided on
the homestead of his grandfather in Marlboro.

Children, all but the eldest born in Marlboro:
  i Frances Augusta[8], b. in Northboro, Mass., 27 March, 1833; d.
    in Westboro, 29 Jan., 1895; m. 1 July, 1849, John A., son of
    Ephraim Goddard; b. in Berlin, Mass., 11 July, 1827; was in
    the Mexican War and Regular Army, 1844-46, and 4th Mass.
    Heavy Art. in Civil War; res. Westboro, and d. there, 3 March,
    1905. Ch. (Goddard):
      1 *John Edward[9]*, b. 7 June, 1855; res. unm., Fitchburg.
      2 *Ada Frances,* b. 29 Jan., 1859; fine vocal teacher and church
        singer.
      3 *George Emerson,* b. 22 Oct., 1862; lost in wreck of *City
        of Columbus* off Gay Head, Mass., 18 Jan., 1884.
  ii Mary Eliza, b. 9 Dec., 1834; m. 1853, Francis L. Barnard of
    Marlboro. Ch. (Barnard):
      1 *Mary Frances[9]*, b. 19 Dec., 1853; m. George G. Douglas,
        b. in Malone, N. Y.; res. Wollaston, Mass. Ch. (Douglas):
        i Stella[10]; ii Grace, both d. y.; iii Carrie B., b. 1877; m.
        Edwin Stone; res. Winchendon, Mass.; iv George R.
      2 *Martha,* b. 30 April, 1855; m. 1891, Edward Webb, b. in
        Dorchester, Mass., 30 Nov., 1854; res. there, s. p.
  iii Caleb B., b. 14 Sept., 1836; m. 1879, Augusta Frye of Bolton,
    Mass.; res. s. p., Hudson, Mass.
  iv Willard Ebenezer, b. 9 April, 1839; d. 6 Nov., 1899; m. 25
    April, 1861, Abby Randall, b. Aug., 1841; a railway man, and res.
    Marlboro. Ch.:
      1 *Fred[9]*, d. y.
      2 *Alice Elvira,* b. Dec., 1866; m. Charles De Moyer. Ch. (De
        Moyer): i Fred[10]; ii Perry.
      3 *Oliver Francis,* m. Ella ————. Ch.: Willard D.[10], m. 1902,
        Kate Richie.
      4 *Willard Dana,* b. July, 1879; m. ————.
  v George W., b. 9 April, 1841; d. 23 June, 1843.
  vi Ellen S., b. 24 Dec., 1842; res. unm., Everett, Mass.
  vii Harriet Newell, b. in Hudson, 17 Aug., 1844; m. 2 June, 1864,
    Hiram W. Chase, b. in Holden, Mass., 21 July, 1840; d. ————;
    res. Hudson. Ch. (Chase):

1 *Mabelle N.*, b. 14 Nov., 1865; was grad. Smith Coll., 1888; a teacher in Everett.

2 *Aimee Florence*, b. 26 Nov., 1870; m. 16 July, 1891, Charles F. Reed. Ch. (Reed): Marion G.[10], b. 5 Oct., 1892; res. Brooklyn, N. Y.

3 Er*nest Leonard*, b. 23 Jan., 1879.

584   REV. WILLARD[7], son of Willard[6] and Betsey (Russell) Brigham; born in Marlboro, Mass., 4 May, 1813; died in Winchendon, Mass., 1 March, 1874; married (1) 4 May, 1843, Maria, daughter of Nathaniel and Zerviah (Maynard) Davenport; born in Boylston, Mass., 14 March, 1815; died 3 Sept., 1857; married (2) 23 Oct., 1860, Laura Cleveland, born in Medfield, Mass., 7 Feb., 1826; died 15 Jan., 1887.

Was graduated from Williams College, 1836; Andover Theological Seminary, 1839; was pastor in Wardsboro, Vt., 12 years; also in Bernardston, Ashfield, Wendell, South Wellfleet and Winchendon, Mass,; was member of school committee in Wardsboro and Wendell, where he held the office of Town Clerk.

Children (by first wife), born in Wardsboro:
i Helen F.[8], b. 27 Dec., 1844; attended the famous Sanderson Academy in Ashfield, where fitted for Mt. Holyoke Sem., which she attended in 1865; taught school chiefly in Boston, and retired after 35 years; res. in Cambridge, Mass., with a summer home at Brant Rock, Mass. Has been a loyal supporter of the B. F. A., and the History of the Brigham Family.
ii Albert J., b. 14 Aug., 1846; d. in Denver, Colo., 22 Sept., 1888; he was a journalist, and unm.; had a remarkable memory, and keen mind; a noted wit; his untimely death cut short a life which early gave promise of a brilliant future.
iii Herbert Willard, b. 10 Nov., 1848; m. 20 July, 1875, Emma B., dau. of William Pitt Brigham 397; b. in Marlboro, 24 Oct., 1849; foreman in shoe factory, Marlboro. Ch.:
  1 *Maud Lavinia*[9], b. 8 Dec., 1880.
  2 *Oscar Willard*, b. 28 June, and d. 30 July, 1887.
iv Mary M., b. 20 July, 1854; taught school in Greenfield, Montague, Winchendon, and Cambridge, Mass., where res. and teaches; has been Asst. Secretary Brigham Family Assn. for several years, and she and her sister are among its most faithful supporters.

585   AARON[7], son of Willard[6] and Betsey (Russell) Brigham; born in Marlboro, Mass., 7 April, 1817; married (1) Salinda, daughter of Daniel Stratton of Bolton, Mass.; born in Harvard, Mass., Nov., 1812; died 10 Aug., 1857; married (2) 20 March, 1857, Mrs. Sarah (Messenger) Houghton, who died; married (3) 14 Sept., 1887, Mrs. Betsey Holmes, who died; a farmer, and resided in Holliston, Ashland, and later in Milford, Mass.

Children (by first wife), the 3 younger born in Holliston:
i Delia Augusta[8], b. in Oneida, N. Y., 17 Sept., 1838; d. in Holliston, 25 Nov., 1896; m. 15 March, 1865, Asa, son of Ellery

Allen of Holliston; b. in Franklin, Mass., 25 Dec., 1825; d. 1
Jan., 1885. Ch. (Allen), b. in Holliston:
1 *Arthur Leon*[9], b. 21 Jan., 1866; m. 28 Oct., 1896, Annie Sinness;
  res. Pittsburg, Pa.
2 *Charles Vernon*, b. 7 July, 1869; m. 1894, Abigail ————;
  res. Mexico City. Ch.: i Howard Brigham[10]; ii Helen Louise.
3 *Carlton Brigham*, b. 3 Aug., 1880; res. unm., in Pittsburg.
ii Daniel Stratton, b. in Ashland, 17 April, 1841; d. about 1898;
  was a piano dealer in Boston, and res there, unm.
iii Martha Amelia, b. 12 Aug., 1845; d. in Holliston, s. p., 1893;
  m. Charles Batchelder; they adopted a son, *C.* Fred.
iv Alma Salinda, b. 2 Jan., 1849; res. unm., a teacher in Los Angeles,
  Cal.
v Alfred Aaron,᾽ b. 23 Dec., 1850; m. 24 April, 1873, Lizzie Decker,
  b. Sept., 1848; res. Worcester, Mass. Ch.:
1 *Alfred Russell*[9], b. 1 June, 1874; res. unm., Worcester.
2 *Charles Vernon*, b. 28 March, and d. 2 May, 1877.
3 *Ralph Willard*, b. 24 Oct., 1879; res. unm., Worcester.

586 ELIZABETH[7], daughter of Willard[6] and Betsey (Russell) Brigham; born in Marlboro, Mass., 1 Dec., 1821; married in
Vienna, N. Y., Jonathan Randall, born in Stow, Mass., 1817; died
6 Aug., 1853.

Children (Randall), all born in Feltonville, Mass., except the eldest:
i Lester V.[8], b. in Vienna, 19 Nov., 1842; m. 1873, Ella S. Hunt.
  Ch. the 3 younger b. in Hudson, Mass.:
1 *Maud B.*[9], b. in Auburn, Me., Nov., 1877.
2 *Chester B.*, b. Nov., 1883.
3 *Christine V.*, b. 21 Jan., 1886.
4 *Bernice E.*, b. May, 1888.
ii Herbert N., b. 21 Aug., 1846; d. 5 Sept., 1901, in Soldiers' Home,
  Chelsea, Mass.; m. Annie Rogers of Boston. Ch., b. in Wollaston,
  Mass.:
1᾽ *Florence M.*[9], b. 1 Sept., 1878.
2 *E. Grace*, b. 14 Dec., 1879.
iii Charles C., b. 1 Oct., 1848; m. Henrietta O. Brown, in 1869; res.
  Corona, Cal. Ch., b. in Hudson:
1 *Clarence L.*[9], b. 3 June, 1870.
iv Emma E., b. 24 Aug., 1851; m. 19 Dec., 1877, Frederick W.
  Trowbridge.

587 MARTHA CHAMBERLAIN[7], daughter of Caleb Jr.[6] and
Martha (Brigham) Brigham; born in Marlboro, Mass., 2 Oct.,
1803; died 20 Jan., 1883; married in Marlboro, 6 April, 1825,
Matthias, son of Capt. Eli and Lucy (Brigham) Rice, (167), born
in Marlboro, 10 July, 1802; went to Machias, Me., where he died,
8 June, 1841.

Child (Rice), born in Worcester, Mass.:
i Elvira Brigham[8], b. 23 July, 1827; m. Lewis G., son of Daniel
  and Rebecca (Burr) Tuttle of Fitchburg; b. 13 Feb., 1821; d.
  5 March, 1883. Ch. (Tuttle), b. in Fitchburg:
1 *George Lewis*[9], b. 17 Sept., 1847; d. 23 Sept., 1851.

2 *Frederick Gould*, b. 14 Oct., 1853; d. 22 Oct., 1903; m. 25 Oct., 1877, Clara A. Cole of E. Somerville, Mass.; 3 ch.

3 *Ella Frances*, b. 2 July, 1856; d. 23 Feb., 1859.

4 *Francis Dana*, b. 14 Sept., 1861; m. 3 Nov., 1885, Amy L., dau. of Jos. T. Goodwin of Fitchburg; b. in E. Boston, 12 Feb., 1859; 2 ch.

588   TILESTON[7], son of Caleb Jr.[6] and Martha (Brigham) Brigham; born in Marlboro, Mass., 25 Aug., 1822; died 28 March, 1896; married in Marlboro, 16 April, 1845, Maria Lovina, daughter of Otis and Lovina (Rice) Russell, born in Marlboro 31 Dec., 1825; died 13 Nov., 1887.

He was a shoe-maker and farmer; a member of the United Brethren Lodge F. & A. M. and a charter member of the Marl boro Lodge I. O. O. F.

Children, born in Marlboro:
i Frank Austin[8], b. 11 May, 1849; d. 22 May, 1858.
ii Alfred Winslow, b. 27 Feb., 1851; m. 7 May, 1874, Clara L., dau. of Joseph Proctor of Marlboro; b. 15 Dec., 1841; res. Marlboro. Ch.:
   1 *Alice Augusta*[9], b. 6 April, 1883; d. 15 Aug., 1883.
   2 *Annie Howe*, b. 8 Oct., 1884.
iii Otis Tileston, b. 26 March, 1856; m. 1 June, 1881, in Dubuque, Ia., Nellie R., dau. of J. F. Conant of Dubuque; b. 29 Nov., 1860; d. 28 Jan., 1900; res. Bancroft, Ia. Ch.:
   1 *Gertrude M.*[9], b. in Brainerd, Minn., 28 Jan., 1883; m. 12 Nov., 1903, Wilfred T. Johnson of Bancroft, Ia., b. 6 Aug., 1879.
   2 *Frank O. J.*, b. in Tower, Minn., 19 March, 1885.
774 iv Caleb Lewis, b. 12 March, 1858.
v Benjie Ellsworth, b. 9 Sept., 1861; m. Leonetta F. Scruton; res. s. p., in Marlboro.
vi Mabel Jeanette, b. 22 Dec., 1866; res. Pleasant Lake, Mass.

589   MARY LANCASTER[7], daughter of Benajah[6] and Sarah (Lancaster) Brigham; born in Boston, 28 Dec., 1808; died in Boston, 1 April, 1882; married (1) 14 Oct., 1831, Rev. Charles G. Safford, D. D., (son of Dudley); born in Exeter, N. H., 17 Nov., 1804; died 1846; married (2) 1849, Charles H. Estabrook of Fitchburg, Mass. Dr. Safford was a graduate of Dartmouth College and Andover Theological Seminary.

Children (Safford):
i Charles Benjamin Brigham[8], b. 28 Aug., 1833, in Gilmanton, N. H.; d. in Malta, Ill., 4 Oct., 1868; m. 25 Sept., 1860, Clara, dau. of Oliver Safford; b. 6 Jan., 1845. Ch.
   1 *Charles G.*[9], b. in Malta, Ill., 26 Feb., 1862; d. 14 June, 1904.
   2 *(Rev.) George Brigham*, Ph. D., b. in So. Grove, Ill., 8 Aug., 1866; m. 11 Aug., 1892, Luetta David; res. s. p., pastor 52d Ave. Presbyterian Church, Chicago, Ill.
   3 *Clara Eliza*, b. 21 Sept., 1868; d. 29 Jan., 1869.

ii Edward Payson, b. in Gilmanton, N. H., 14 March, 1837; m.
20 Dec., 1866, Sarah F., dau. of Henry Safford; b. 11 June,
1844; a farmer, Sycamore, Ill. Ch., all but the eldest b. in
Mayfield, Ill.:
1 *Mary E.*⁹, b. in So: Grove, Ill., 20 Oct., 1868; res. Mayfield.
2 *Infant.*
3 *Henry S.,* b. 29 July, 1872; res. Roswell, N. M.
4 *Charles H. E.,* b. 4 Oct., 1874, in Mayfield.
5 *Edward Brigham,* b. 14 June, 1880; m. 11 May, 1905, Edna
May Hammond; res. Albuquerque, N. M.
6 *Sarah Lancaster,* b. March, 1882; res. Sycamore.
Child *(Estabrook)*:
iii Mary E., b. 1851; d. 1853.

590 GEORGE⁷, son of Benajah⁶ and Sarah (Lancaster) Brigham, born in Boston, Mass., 20 Sept., 1815; died in Bloomington,
Ill., 12 May, 1878; married 5 Feb., 1837, Lydia, daughter of
Joab Shinn, born in Cincinnati, O., 20 Aug., 1819. She is still
living and has 33 living grand-children and 32 great-grand-
children. He was a farmer and resided in Bloomington.

Children, born in Bloomington:
775 i Joab⁸, b. 23 Nov., 1837.
ii Mary, b. 2 Feb., 1839; m. 25 Dec., 1866, Milton Weed of Union
Springs, N. Y., b. 30 July, 1842; res. Cooksville, Ill. Ch. (Weed):
1 *Charles Seth⁹,* b. 30 June, 1871; m. 20 July, 1892, Ettie Mc-
Cullom of Cooksville, b. 15 Feb., 1872; res. Cooksville. Ch.:
i Seth George¹⁰, b. 15 May, 1893; ii Frank Milton, b. 31 July,
1894; iii Charles Ray, b. 20 June, 1898; iv Fannie L., b. 12
Feb., 1900; v Willis, b. 17 Feb., 1905.
776 iii Benajah, b. 3 Nov., 1840.
iv Elizabeth, b. 20 Dec., 1843; m. 25 Dec., 1879, James, son of
Arnett Poindexter; b. 10 Sept., 1843; res. Bloomington. Ch.
(Poindexter):
1 *Jamesina Pearl⁹,* b. 31 Aug., 1883; m. 28 Dec., 1904, John
R. O'Neal of Bloomington.
777 v Fletcher, b. 13 Jan., 1845.
778 vi John, b. 16 April, 1847.
vii Nancy, b. 26 April, 1849; m. 23 Feb., 1876, A. T., son of Robert
T. Freeman of Monmouth, Ill., b. 29 Dec., 1849; res. Bloomington.
Ch. (Freeman), b. in Bloomington:
1 C. *Litney⁹,* b. 27 March, 1877; m. 3 April, 1899, Emma Yoder,
b. 5 Feb., 1876. Ch. Gladys¹⁰, b. 20 March, 1902.
2 *George Brigham,* b. 4 April, 1879; d. 17 Aug., 1879.
3 *Asa,* b. 16 Oct., 1882; m. 27 Oct., 1906, Muriel Van Scott.
4 *Theodore,* b. 7 April, 1884; m. 1 July, 1905, Lita Martin, b.
26 Nov., 1887. Ch.: Dartha B.¹⁰, b. 17 Oct., 1906.
5 *Ruth,* b. 11 June, 1886.
viii Charlotte, b. 1 Dec., 1851; d. 28 Aug., 1852.
ix Asa, b. 30 May, 1853; m. 7 Sept., 1887, Sophia, dau. of J. H.
Hoffman, b. 12 Feb., 1865; res. Bloomington. Ch., the 2 elder
b. in Ellsworth, Ill.:
1 *Lawrence⁹,* b. 2 Dec., 1890; d. 6 Jan., 1891.
2 *Leonard,* b. 30 Jan., 1892; d. 15 Dec., 1892.

3 *Asa*, b. in Bloomington, 8 Feb., 1894.

4 *Thomas*, b. in Sibley, Ill., 9 Sept., 1899.

x Eliza, b. 12 Aug., 1856; d. 27 Dec., 1856.

xi Annie, b. 17 Aug., 1861; d. 24 Jan., 1897; m. 15 Dec., 1887, L. F. Robuck of Dayton, O., b. 14 Oct., 1861; res. Bloomington. Ch. (Robuck):
    1 *Frank A.*⁹, b. 7 March, 1891; 2 *Stella*, b. 25 June, 1892; 3 *James L.*, b. 2 April, 1894; 4 *Elmer Brigham*, b. 7 Sept., 1895; 5 *Asa*, b. 19 Jan., 1897; d. 1897.

591 JOHN W.⁷, son of Ephraim⁶ and Hannah (Twitchell) Brigham; born in Westboro, Mass., 16 May, 1821; died in Boston, April, 1890; married (1) 22 March, 1845, Anna Dana Blake of Watertown, Mass., who died April, 1888; married (2) 10 June, 1889, Merial L. Wilder of Malden, Mass. He was an extensive shoe manufacturer in Worcester; resided in Boston, after 1836.

Children (by first wife), born in Boston:
i John William⁸, b. 16 April, 1850; m. 1 June, 1882, Frances E. Bowen of Newton Center, Mass.; was partner with his father 23 years; then public accountant in Boston; res. Newton. Ch.:
    1 *Florence*⁹, b. 7 Feb., 1886.
    2 *Sylvia B.*, b. 28 Nov., 1897.
ii Frederick Dana, b. 10 July, 1858; d. 10 Feb., 1876.
iii Arthur F., b. 27 Aug., 1859; d. Jan., 1886.
Child (by second wife), born in Boston:
iv Harold W., b. Aug., 1890.

592 WILLIAM AUGUSTUS⁷, son of Peter W.⁶ and Lydia (Valentine) Brigham; born in Boston, Mass., on Hollis Street, 29 August, 1808; died in Newton, Mass., 12 Oct., 1878; married (1) 15 April, 1830, Maria, daughter of Matthew and Millicent (Dickerman) Gray of Westboro, Mass.; born in Worcester, Mass., 20 Oct., 1808; died 21 May, 1847; married (2) 3 May, 1848, Hannah Smith, daughter of Daniel C. and Nancy (Smith) Chapman of Belchertown, Mass.; born there, 10 Sept., 1819; died in Boston, 7 Aug., 1899.

He was a man of enormous energy, for years was with Sampson, Davenport & Co., publishers of Boston and other directories; was noted for accomplishing more work than other men; a statistician of note, and occupied many places of responsibility. He was in charge of the City Agricultural Grounds at Worcester from 1855 till about 1861.

Children (by first wife), the 3 elder born in Westboro, the 3 younger in Worcester:
i Ann Maria⁸, b. 12 Aug., 1831; d. in Elmira, N. Y., 1902; m. 26 April, 1854, George R. Bowman; res. Elmira. Ch. (Bowman), b. in Almond, N. Y.:
    1 *Louis Wellington*⁹, b. 13 April, 1860; m. 24 Oct., 1888, Lillie M. Buckhont, b. 25 Jan., 1869. Ch.: i Beatrix W.¹⁰, b. 30 July, 1890.

PHINEAS BRIGHAM, OF CANTON, PA. (640)

2 *Charles Augustus,* b. 2 April, 1862; m. 29 Dec., 1886, Cora
    Hagadorn, b. in Elmira, 16 Oct., 1865.
ii Augustus Appleton, b. 31 July, 1833; d. s. p., in Worcester, 23
    Jan., 1868; m. 1 May, 1860, Martha E. Jones of Stafford Springs,
    Conn.
iii Sarah Waldo, b. 14 Feb., 1837; m. (1) 12 Sept., 1861, Stephen
    Fairfield Logee of Pascoag, R. I., b. 6 Aug., 1841; d. s. p., in
    Elmira, 6 March, 1868; m. (2) 24 Aug., 1871, Edward B. Boden,
    b. 17 March, 1841; res. s. p., Melrose Highlands, Mass.
iv Susan Baker Davis, b. in Northboro, Mass., 25 July, 1839; m.
    9 June, 1864, Stephen J. Waite of Worcester, b. in Worcester, 11
    Sept., 1841. Ch. (Waite), b. in W.:
        1 *William Jennison*⁹, b. 7 June, 1869.
v Elizabeth Valentine, b. 9 Sept., 1841; d. 13 Aug., 1849.
vi Mary Chapman, b. 30 Aug., 1844.
vii Amelia Gray Perry, b. 15 March, 1847; m. 25 Dec., 1871, James
    O. Egerton, b. in Boston, 8 Oct., 1848. Ch. (Egerton), b. in So.
    Boston:
        1 *Charles Ozro*⁹, b. 14 March, 1880.
Children (by second wife), born in Worcester:
viii Hannah Augusta, b. 22 Feb., 1849; d. 29 Aug., 1849.
779 ix William Valentine, b. 17 May, 1850.
780 x Louis Kossuth, b. 30 Jan., 1852.
    xi Oliver Smith Chapman, b. 13 March, 1856; d. 22 Jan., 1876.
    xii Georgiana Nancy, b. 2 March, 1858; res. Boston.
    xiii Sylvia Augusta, b. 9 Jan., 1860; d. 1 Feb., 1860.

593 FRANKLIN⁷, son of Jabez⁶ and Sophia (Hunt) Brigham;
born in Lancaster, Mass., 19 July, 1805; died in Boston, Mass.,
27 Sept., 1883; married 18 March, 1830, Ann Whitman, daughter
of John Taylor of Lancaster; born there, 3 March, 1808; died
in Boston, 14 Aug., 1882. He had the military titles of Lieut.,
Capt., and Major. During his later years was Supt. of The
Clinton Mfg. Co. of New Jersey.

Children, born in Lancaster, except the 2 youngest.
i Sarah Ann⁸, b. 7 Jan., 1831; m. Feb., 1847, Mial, son of David
    Cushman; b. in Duxbury, Mass., 19 June, 1819; d. in Winchester,
    Mass., 27 Nov., 1884. Filled many town offices. Ch. (Cushman):
        1 *Frank Brigham*⁹, b. 1 Jan., 1859, in Methuen, Mass.; d. 1871.
ii Almira Low, b. 27 April, 1832; m. 17 Oct., 1852, James Miller,
    son of John Morehead; b. in Marshfield, Mass., 21 Aug., 1818;
    res. N. Y. City; was a "49r" in California. Ch. (Morehead):
        1 *Annie Taylor*⁹, an artist, N. Y. City.
iii Francis Low, b. 22 July, 1833; accidentally killed, in So. Orange,
    N. J., 15 Dec., 1859; C. E., Knight Templar, and Knight of
    Pythias.
iv Harriet Augusta, b. 2 Sept., 1835; d. s. p., in Boston, 26 Feb.,
    1897; m. 20 Dec., 1854, Daniel P. M. Cummings, b. in N. H.,
    25 Aug., 1831; d. in Boston, 7 Oct., 1860; a piano manufacturer.
v Abbie Elizabeth, b. 13 Aug.. 1878, Edwin Rice, b. in Brookfield,
    Mass, 11 April, 1814; d. ————; was retired; owner of
    extensive estate; director Quincy Mining Co. Ch. (Rice), b.
    in Boston:
        1 *Edwin Brigham*⁹, b. 5 Dec., 1879.

781 vi Daniel Taylor, b. 30 May, 1840.
   vii Arthur Charles, b. in Somerville, Mass., 25 Dec., 1846; m. in
       Denver, Col., 14 March, 1883, Eliza Medora, dau. of Capt. William
       Tarkington; b. in Indiana, 19 Nov., 1850; agent for National
       Tube Works Co., and res. s. p., Pittsburg, Pa.; Knight Templar.
  viii Ella Josephine, b. in Cambridge, Mass.; res. Boston.

594   ABIGAIL[7], daughter of Jabez[6] and Sophia (Hunt) Brigham; born in Grafton, Mass., 24 Oct., 1807; died in Worcester,
Mass., 1901; married 12 May, 1830, Ezra K. Pratt of Grafton.

Children (Pratt), born in Grafton:
   i Hon. Francis B.[8], b. 19 April, 1831; went to California early;
     was then a planter in Madison Co., Miss., till 1871; lawyer in
     Canton, Miss., where res.; J. P., Prest. Co. Board of Supervisors;
     Dist. Atty. 14th Dist., Miss.; St. Senator, 1875.
  ii Jerome G., b. 1 Jan., 1834.
 iii Adelia M., b. 27 April, 1836.
  iv Henry H., b. 12 Aug., 1840.
   v George D., b. 16 Aug., 1842.

595   PHEBE[7], daughter of Jabez[6] and Sophia (Hunt) Brig-
ham; born in Boston, 2 Aug., 1810; married William Holden of
Grafton, Mass. She was living in 1904 with daughter, Mrs. J. L.
Bacon, in Roxbury, Mass.

*Children (Holden), the 4 elder born in Grafton, the others in Tem-
pleton, Mass.:*
   i George W.[8], b. 25 Jan., 1835; m. Mary Whitney. Ch.:
     1 *Mary L.[9]*, m. George Bemis.
  ii James A., b. 15 May, 1837; d. Oct., 1837.
 iii Jane A., twin to James; d. Oct., 1837.
  iv Jane A., b. 29 Sept., 1838; m. Joel Bacon of Roxbury, where
     they res. Ch. (Bacon):
     1 *Nellie[9]*, d. y.; 2 *Lillian.*
   v Rozelia V., b. 17 Feb., 1843; d. 14 April, 1888; m. Albert T.
     Milliken of Boston. Ch. (Milliken)·
     1 *Lyman[9].*
  vi Electa A., b. 25 June, 1848; d. 22 April, 1891; m. James K. P.
     Wood. Ch. (Wood):
     1 *Ida[9]*; 2 *Edward*; 3 *Herbert*; 4 *Ethel.*
 vii Harrison A., b. 22 March, 1853; m. Rosella Gault.

596   SARAH ELIZABETH[7], daughter of Jabez[6] and Sophia
(Hunt) Brigham; born in Grafton, Mass., 9 Sept., 1822; married
6 June, 1849, James Allen of Putnam, Conn.; born 26 Dec., 1815;
died 23 April, 1883. He was a farmer. She resides with her son
in Boston.

Children (Allen), born in Putnam:
   i Charles Edgar[8], b. 7 Oct., 1857; m. 1 Jan., 1890; Mary Elizabeth
     Willcox of Sheffield, Mass.; was grad. LL. B. from Boston Uni-
     versity, 1887; is a practicing lawyer in Boston. Ch.:
     1 *Raymond W.[9]*; 2 *Ralph C.*; 3 *Robert B.*, d. y.
  ii Mary Louise, b. 11 June, 1863; res. in Boston.

597 ELISHA WARREN[7], son of Leonard Warren[6] and Polly (Wilcox) Brigham; born in Roxbury, Vt., 15 Nov., 1814; died 13 Oct., 1848; married 9 April, 1840, Elizabeth L., daughter of Joseph Faunce; born in Enfield, N. H., June, 1814; died 10 Oct., 1900. He was a farmer and resided in Brookfield and Northfield, Vt.

Children, the second and third born in Brookfield, Vt.:

782   i Leonard Warren[8], b. in Elmore, Vt., 25 May, 1841.
      ii Ellen Manora, b. 25 June, 1843; m. 14 Feb., 1863, James O. Bemies, b. 11 March, 1808, at Littleton, N. H.; res. Springfield, Mass. Ch. (Bemies), the two elder b. in Northfield:
          1 William H.[9], b. 7 June, 1864; m. March, 1889, Emma Sanders.
          2 Charles O., b. 19 March, 1867; m. 14 Aug., 1891, Lena Stracke. Ch.: Carl[10], b. in Beaver Falls, Pa., 24 July, 1893.
          3 J. F., b. in Springfield, 9 Jan., 1873.
      iii Mary Elizabeth, b. 26 March, 1846; m. 1 Jan., 1870, James N. Glover, who d. s. p., 10 Dec., 1902.
      iv Elisha Newell, b. Northfield, 4 Aug., 1848; m. 14 June, 1880, —————. Ch.:
          1 Joseph Walter[9], b. 26 Feb., 1882; m. 30 Aug., 1899, —————.
          2 Nelson Elisha, b. 9 March, 1884.

598 DR. GERSHOM NELSON[7], son of Elisha[6] and So— phronia (Ryder) Brigham; born in Fayston, Vt., 3 March, 1820; died in Chicago, Ill., 21 June, 1886; married (1) in Fayston, 23 Aug., 1846, Laura Elvira, daughter of Merrill and Zelinda (Whitcomb) Tyler; born in Fayston, 25 Oct., 1823; died in Montpelier, Vt., 11 March, 1873; married (2) 12 Feb., 1875, Agnes Ruth, daughter of Ephraim Walker; born in Springfield, Vt., 26 Oct., 1845; died in Rogers Park, Ill., 18 April, 1894; she was early a Preceptress of Vt. M. E. Female Seminary in Montpelier, and in other schools.

Dr. Brigham had large ambitions from boyhood. Prevented from entering college, he studied medicine, with Dr. D. C. Joslyn of Waitsfield, Vt.; was graduated from the Vt. Medical College at Woodstock, in 1845. Later in life he became a practitioner of the Homeopathic School. Was one of the founders of the Vt. State Homeopathic Society of which he was President. He published medical works, one on " Phthisis " and one on " Catarrh "; also a volume of poems entitled " The Harvest Moon and Other Poems "; was also a frequent contributor to Medical Journals and the secular press. He practiced medicine in Vermont for 30 years and in 1875 removed to Grand Rapids, Mich., where he built up a large practice and resided until death.

Children (by first wife):
      i Julia Estelle[8], b. 29 July, 1847; d. ibid.
      ii Julia Lena, b. 10 Nov., 1848; res. Lowell, Mass.
783 iii Homer Colby, b. in Waitsfield, 10 July, 1851.

    iv Ida Leonore, b. 16 Nov., 1854; d. 13 Aug., 1856.
784 v Willard Irving Tyler, b. in Montpelier, 31 May, 1859.
Children (by second wife), all but the youngest born in Grand Rapids, Mich.:
    vi Miriam Allyn, b. 15 Nov., 1875; m. Harry Rindge of Grand
       Rapids.
   vii Ruth Rayder, b. 20 Dec., 1876; m. Dr. Frank D. Harter of Grand
       Rapids.
  viii Gershom Walker, b. 1 Sept., 1883; d. *ibid.*
    ix Beulah Evangeline, b. 5 Aug., 1885.
     x Breta Manning, b. in Rogers Park, Ill., 5 March, 1887.

599 ELISHA ALDIS[7], son of Elisha[6] and Sophronia (Ryder) Brigham; born in Fayston, Vt., 22 Dec., 1821; died in Chippewa, Mich., June, 1899; married 20 June, 1849, Celia, daughter of Hon. Eber H. Baxter, born in Moretown, Vt., 16 March, 1826; died in Chippewa, 17 Jan., 1897.

He was Justice of the Peace and town clerk; prominent in the M. E. church where was a class leader; an occasional writer of prose and verse; Mrs. Brigham often contributed to the papers, and her brother has collected 200 of her poems.

   Children, born in Fayston:
    i Ziba Whittier[8], b. 8 May, 1850; m. 27 May, 1877, Mattie J., dau.
      of Perry Clark; b. 1 Oct., 1850; res. Chippewa. Ch., b. there:
       1 *Edwin Perry[9]*, b. 10 Oct., 1880.
       2 *Emily Blanche*, b. 10 July, 1882.
       3 *Herbert Guy*, b. 13 Sept., 1883.
       4 *Clarence Elisha*, b. 22 June, 1885.
       5 *Albert Glen*, b. 11 July, 1887.
       6 *Irma Celia*, b. 7 Jan., 1890.
   ii Elisha Kossuth, b. 23 Dec., 1851; m. 25 Dec., 1876, Maria C.
      Green, b. in Pa., 10 Dec., 1857; res. Chippewa, and thence to
      Bayfield, Wis. Ch., first 5 b. in Chippewa, last 3 in Bayfield:
       1 *Ernest Jerrold[9]*, b. 6 Aug., 1877.
       2 *Elisha Earl*, b. 19 Aug., 1879.
       3 *Celia May*, b. 18 May, 1883; d. 8 Sept., 1887.
       4 *Aldis Leonidas*, b. 25 Aug., 1884.
       5 *Son*, b. and d. 1886.
       6 *Nelson*, b. 11 Oct., 1887.
       7 *Hazel Laura*, b. 1 March, 1890.
       8 *Lloyd*, b. 18 Sept., 1891.
  iii Edwin Baxter (Dr.), b. 1 Oct., 1857; m. 27 Sept., 1885, Nina
      F., dau. of H. C. Denison; b. in Cascade, Vt., Feb., 1864; res.
      and practiced in Hartwick, and Rose Lake, Mich., and Indianapolis,
      Ind. Ch., the 2 youngest b. in Rose Lake:
       1 *Fred M.[9]*, b. in Hartwick, 15 Aug., 1886.
       2 *Helen*, b. 21 Sept., 1889.
       3 *Marshall H.*, b. 3 July, 1891.
   iv Rosina, b. 4 April, 1859; d. 5 June, 1878, unm.

600 EUSEBIA MIRANDA[7], daughter of Elisha[6] and Sophronia (Ryder) Brigham; born in Fayston, Vt., 23 Oct., 1826;

married 1 Jan., 1844, John Chaffee of Fayston, who died in Dayton, Mich., Sept., 1886.

Children (Chaffee):
 i Ewin or Edwin Elisha⁸, b. in Chelmsford, Mass., 26 May, 1846; m.
  Oct., 1885, Mary E. Perry; res. Maysville, Mich. Ch.:
   1 *Edwin⁹*, b. in M., 1889; *2 Ada*, b. 1893; *3 Altha*, d. y.
 ii Oscar Herbert, b. in Fayston, 13 Sept., 1848; m. (1) 1872, Annie
  Grigor; m. (2) 26 May, 1886, Emma M. Chaffee; res. Maysville. Ch. (by 1st wife):
   1 *Geo. A.⁹;* 2 *Charles A.*, twins, b. 1873, d. 1875.
   3 *Arthur*, b. 1874; d. 1875.
   4 *Mary M.*, b. Feb., 1876.
   Ch. (by second wife):
   5 *Cara A.*, b. 10 Feb., 1891.
 iii John Julius, b. in Fayston, 15 Aug., 1850; res. unm., Dayton,
  Mich.
 iv Arthur Ernest, b. in Ogdensburg, N. Y., 21 July, 1852; d. 14
  April, 1884; m. 1883, Emma M. Worth.
 v Alice Florence, b. in Ogdensburg, 5 Feb., 1855; m. William
  H. Ormsbee, Oct., 1876. Ch. (Ormsbee):
   1 *John C.⁹*, b. 1877; 2 *Mabel L.*, b. 1879; 3 *Florence L.*, b.
   1881; 4 *Jessie E.*, b. 1883; 5 *Alice*, b. 1886.
 vi Mary Frances, b. 17 Oct., 1857, in Flint, Mich.; d. 17 Oct., 1888;
  m. June, 1886, Avery Worth; res. Watertown, Mich.
 vii Henry Lincoln, b. in Flint, 21 Dec., 1864; m. April, 1887, Ida A.
  Worth; res. Dayton, Mich. Ch.:
   1 *Mary⁹*, d. y.

601 REV. LEANDER HOWE⁷, son of Elisha⁶ and Sophronia (Ryder) Brigham; born in Fayston, Vt., 17 April, 1828; married 14 Nov., 1850, Loraine A., daughter of Amasa Russ. They reside in Warren, Vt.

In early life he was a farmer on the old homestead. At the age of 45 he began preaching, his work being largely that of a missionary in central and northern Vermont. He was President, for 10 years, of a State undenominational Christian Union Association. The male line is extinct.

Children, born in Fayston, except the second and youngest:
 i Mary L.⁸, b. 20 July, 1851; m. 10 Feb., 1869, Orlando S. Davis;
  res. in Montpelier, Vt., and for a time in Randolph, Vt. Ch.
  (Davis):
   1 *George M.⁹*, b. in Fayston, 16 Aug., 1870; m. in M., Aug.,
   1892, Lilla White; designer and engraver of granite. Ch.:
   Harold W.¹⁰, b. in Montpelier, 13 May, 1893.
   2 *Clairon A.*, b. in Randolph, 6 Feb., 1872; unm.; res. Montpelier.
   3 *Viola M.*, b. in Fayston, 6 April, 1873; m. 10 March, 1889, W.
   R. Granfield. Ch. (Granfield): i Raymond E.¹⁰; ii Daphene
   L.
   4 *Hermon O.*, b. in Randolph, 28 Sept., 1877; m. 2 July, 1901,
   Evelyn Emerson Staples; b. 30 Sept., 1882; electrician. Ch.:
   Alfred Hermon¹⁰, b. in Montpelier, 23 Feb., 1904.
   5 *Florence E.*, b. in Fayston, 17 Nov., 1886.

    ii Sarah F., b. in Waitsfield, Vt., 26 Feb., 1853; m. in Fayston, 10 Feb., 1869, Edgar A. Davis of No. Fayston. Ch. (Davis), b. in Fayston:

        1 *Merton E.⁹*, b. 7 July, 1870; m. 1 May, 1896, Minnie C. Morse of Duxbury: Ch.: i Frank Brigham[10], b. in F., 31 May, 1900; ii Laura S., b. 21 June, 1904.

        2 *Gertrude M.,* b. 17 Jan., 1872; m. 30 April, 1889, Charles Granfield of Fayston. Ch. (Grandfield): i Estella G.[10]; ii Ralph E.

        3 *Ina L.,* b. 22 Sept., 1885; m. 13 Aug., 1902, Walter Lester Johnson of Waterbury, Vt. Ch. (Johnson): Ray Edgar[10], b. 20 Sept., 1903.

    iii Sophronia A., b. in Fayston, 24 Jan., 1857; m. 1 Jan., 1873, George H. Camp of Randolph, Vt. Ch. (Camp), b. in Randolph:

        1 *Winifred E.⁹*, b. 2 Oct., 1873; m. 12 Feb., 1898, George Greenslit of Warren, Vt. Ch. (Greenslit), b. Warren: i Ruth I.[10]; ii Evelyn Loraine, b. 15 Aug., 1901; iii Ivan Leander, b. 24 April, 1903; iv Ila May, b. 6 June, 1904.

    iv Charles L., b. 1 Dec., 1859; d. 8 Dec., 1859.

    v Hattie M., b. in Waitsfield, 22 Sept., 1864; m. 31 Dec., 1881, William A. Collins of Lowell, Mass. Ch. (Collins):

        1 *Grace C.,* b. 6 April, 1882 (adopted).

602 REV. ALBERT⁷, son of Elisha⁶ and Sophronia (Ryder) Brigham; born in Fayston, Vt., 17 Oct., 1832; married, 12 Nov., 1853, Almira M. Durkee of Fayston, Vt. He is a farmer, but also preaches; is a Second Adventist; moved from Fayston to Grant, Mich.

Children, born in Fayston:

    i Daughter⁸, d. y.

    ii Albert Erwin, b. 24 Feb., 1855; m. 4 July, 1874, Almeda Harper of Grant, Mich.; a farmer and dealer in pine lands, and res. Grant. Ch., b. in Grant:

        1 *Dora Almeda⁹*, b. 17 Sept., 1875; m. 21 July, 1899, Joseph T. Bell; res. Manistee, Mich.

        2 *Harvey Pierson,* b. 5 Oct., 1877.

        3 *Clarence,* b. 28 Jan., 1880.

        4 *Ralph,* b. 2 Jan., 1882.

        5 *Gordon,* b. 19 April, 1884.

        6 *Ellsworth,* b. 8 March, 1889.

    iii Glen Alcott, b. 15 Jan., 1862; m. 6 June, 1889, Kate Coates of Grant, Mich.; a farmer and dealer in pine lands. Ch., b. in Grant:

        1 *Ethan Kinley⁹*, b. 15 April, 1896.

        2 *Gerald Hobart,* b. 29 July, 1897.

603 SARAH⁷, daughter of Elisha⁶ and Sophronia (Ryder) Brigham; born in Fayston, Vt., 17 Oct., 1836; died in Lebanon, N. H., 15 April, 1898; married 12 April, 1855, Martin Mansfield, born in Fayston, 24 May, 1834; died in Lebanon, 20 March, 1903. She was an occasional contributor to periodicals, in prose and verse, and wrote the "Roxbury" chapter in the *Vermont Gazetteer.* They resided in Lebanon.

Children (Mansfield), born in Fayston:
    i *Kate M.*[8], b. 6 Dec., 1856; m. 12 Sept., 1874, Alverton Waterman; res. Burlington, Vt. Ch. (Waterman):
        1 *Dr. Vance W.*[9], b. 9 April, 1876.
        2 *Rex A.*, b. 1884; d. 1888.
    ii Bessie I., b. 15 Sept., 1858; m. (1) 27 Nov., 1872, George A. Marsh; m. (2) 1890, Willard H. Crozier. Ch. (Marsh):
        1 *Nina*[9], b. in Roxbury, Vt., 9 Nov., 1874; d. in Lebanon, 7 Jan., 1899.
    iii William R., b. 3 Oct., 1860; m. (1) Alice Bowers of Montpelier, Vt.; 1 ch., d. y.; moved to Mexico, where m. (2); has dau.; Ry. Supt. in San Luis Potosi. •

604 LAURA ARTEMESIA[7], daughter of Elisha[6] and Sophronia (Ryder) Brigham; born in Fayston, Vt., 27 Feb., 1840; married 22 Nov., 1855, George O. Boyce of Fayston. He is a farmer who resided on the old Boyce homestead and then moved to Montpelier, Vt. She is an occasional writer of prose and verse and has written poems and hymns for the Brigham Family Association meetings.

Children (Boyce), born in Fayston:
    i Leonore[8], b. and d. Sept., 1856.
    ii Ida Lucinda, b. 22 Nov., 1857; m. —————.
    iii Alice Minerva, b. 2 Sept., 1859; d. unm., 9 April, 1803.
    iv Ada Leonore, b. 5 Sept., 1861; killed in Kirksville, Mo., by cyclone, 27 April, 1899; m. 8 Aug., 1884, Dr. Herman K. Sherburne. Ch. (Sherburne):
        1 *Theodore*[9], d. y.
    v Lucy Lillian, b. 6 Feb., 1865; m. April, 1892, Frank A. Hayden; res. Montpelier. Ch. (Hayden):
        1 *Philip Sherburne*[9], b. 7 Feb., 1897.
    vi Clayton Brigham, b. 27 Aug., 1876; unm., in 1901; res. Montpelier.

605 WILLIAM BAXTER[7], son of Alvin Lucas[6] and Flora H. (Baxter) Brigham; born 17 Nov., 1826; married 1 May, 1860, Sarah B., daughter of Washington Wardner; born 30 Dec., 1840. He is a farmer and resides in Roxbury, Vt.

Children:
    i George W.[8], b. 7 June, 1862; Ry. sta. agt., and telegrapher; res. Matlock, Ia.
    ii Effie F., b. 27 Dec., 1863; m. 3 May, 1893, Elmer E. Chase. Ch. (Chase):
        1 *Hazel Irene*[9], d. young.
    iii Lovette E., b. 30 Aug., 1868; d. 13 Jan., 1885.
    iv Eunette A., b. 30 Aug., 1868; d. 12 March, 1884.
    v Flora A., b. 26 Aug., 1870; a teacher.
    vi Ozro Don, b. 3 Nov., 1874; d. 10 Nov., 1874.
    vii Blanche L., b. 25 June, 1878; was a teacher, Lowell, Mass.; m. William A. Ellis, A. M., Northfield, Vt., Librarian Norwich University.

606 SARAH[7], daughter of Alexander[6] and Sarah (Whitten) Brigham; born in Buckland, Mass., 11 Sept., 1796; died 19 Jan., 1867; married 1819, Elisha Wright; born in Williamstown, Mass., 1784; died 6 March, 1852.

Children (Wright):
    i Lucy B.[8], b. 23 Feb., 1820; m. Norman Matteson; res. Plainfield, N. Y. Ch. (Matteson):
        1 *Delia*[9]; 2 *Elisha*; 3 *Mary.*
        4 *Guy*, m. Clara Chapman; res. Des Moines, Ia. Ch.: i Grace Ivon[10]; ii Gertrude; iii William; iv Agnes.
        5 *Eliza;* 6 *Etta;* 7 *O. J.;* 8 *Theodore.*
    ii Rachel, b. 15 Sept., 1821.
    iii George, b. 15 July, 1823.
    iv Martin W., b. 23 March, 1825.
    v Josiah, b. Jan., 1827.
    vi Sarah, b. May, 1828; d. 2 July, 1830.
    vii Levantia, b. 23 Feb., 1830.
    viii Leticia, b. 1833.
    ix Elizabeth, b. 31 March, 1836.
    x Menzo Deforest, b. 13 March, 1839; d. 22 Jan., 1861.
    xi Fanny, b. 1847.

607 GEORGE[7], son of Alexander[6] and Sarah (Whitten) Brigham; born in Richfield, N. Y., 6 March, 1808; died in Clayton, N. Y., 7 Nov., 1897; married Almena, daughter of Abner Smith of Perch River, N. Y.; born 26 Aug., 1813; died 1868. He kept the first hotel in Limerick, N. Y., and was a pioneer of the town.

Children:
785   i Theodore S.[8], b. 25 March, 1833.
    ii William Jasper, b. April, 1839; d. Sept., 1859.

608 LEWIS[7], son of Don Ferdinand[6] and Lois (Palmer) Brigham; born in Coventry, Conn., 22 March, 1809; died in Mansfield, Conn., 17 Jan., 1873; married (1) 19 Feb., 1833, Louisa Tilden, who died 20 June, 1849; married (2) 12 Jan., 1851, Lucy Starkweather, who died 26 Jan., 1883.

Children (by first wife), born in Mansfield:
    i Walter Tilden[8], b. 26 July, 1834; d. 23 April, 1861; m. (1) 13 April, 1858, Caroline Bethia, dau. of Austin Pearl of Willington, Conn.; m. (2) ——— Warren, and res. E. Brookfield, Mass.; was a Ry. man and merchant, Mansfield Depot. Ch.:
        1 *Ann Elizabeth*[9], b. 4 April, 1859; m. Walter Linley, 1886; res. Spencer, Mass.
786   ii Don Ferdinand, b. 5 Jan., 1839.
    iii Lewis Henry, d. y.
Children (by second wife), born in Mansfield:
    iv Lewis Starkweather, b. 27 July, 1852; m. 9 Nov., 1885, Hattie Childs Spafford; res. Sturgis, So. D. Ch.:
        1 *Lucy S.*[9], b. 16 Dec., 1888; 2 *Alice F.*, b. 15 Feb., 1892; 3 *Pauline.*

Elijah Winslow[7] Brigham   (524)

v Dr. Lucy Louise, b. 27 April, 1854; d. unm., Hartford, Conn., 1901; she was a practicing Homeopathic physician.
vi Nathan, b. 26 Feb., 1856; m. 9 July, 1889, Lena Huntington, b. in Eagleville, Conn., 11 Nov., 1867; he is a lumberman, and res. Whitewood, So. Dakota. Ch ·
  1 *Lillian*[9], b. 4 March, 1890; 2 *Ruth S.,* b. 26 July, 1893; 3 *Ralph H.,* b. 11 Sept., 1894; 4 *Howard N.,* b. 19 Sept., 1896; 5 *Lewis H.,* b. 30 Oct., 1902.
vii Ida Celestia, b. 13 Jan,, 1858; d. s. p., 7 Aug., 1903; m. Frederick E. Miller of Brooklyn, Conn.
viii Lillian Estelle, b. 12 Aug., 1860; d. unm., 2 April, 1886.
ix Dr. Walter Irving, b. 17 Feb., 1863; m. 25 June, 1890, Clara B. Taylor; a dentist, So. Framingham, Mass. Ch.:
  1 *Ferdinand*[9], b. 23 April, 1891.
  2 *Philip Taylor,* b. 1892; d. 1893.

609 ROYAL[7], son of Royal[6] and Hannah (Tracy) ,Brigham; born in Coventry, Conn., 17 July, 1805; died in Randolph, Vt., 22 Sept., 1878; married 5 Dec., 1832, Eliza West, born 1803, died 1866.

  i Charles West[8],, b. 20 Sept., 1833; at the age of 19 went to Brazil, S. A., to oversee a large plantation, and d. in Bahia, 15 June, 1854.
  ii Hannah Tracy, b. in Strafford, Vt., 21 Sept., 1836; d. in W. Randolph, Vt., 7 Dec., 1899; m. 1861, Norman Nichols, b. in 1832. Ch. (Nichols):
    1 *Janette E.*[9], b. 1862; d. 1890; m. David Dyer.
    2 *Charles H.,* b. 1864; m. 1889, Isa Dyer; res. N. Y. City. Ch.: i Lucy[10]; ii Norman; iii Charles H.
    3 *Martha A.,* b. 1867; m. 1891, Edward H. Nichols of Braintree, Vt. Ch. (Nichols): i Royce[10]; ii Ralph; iii Ray.
    4 *Anna M.,* b. 1869; d. 1875.
    5 *Ruth M.,* b. 1871; m. 1894, Frank C. Angell, M. D., of Randolph. Ch. (Angell): i Cyril[10]; ii Wilmer.
    6 *Hannah L.,* b. and d. 1873.
  iii William Henry, b. 31 Oct., 1843; d. 28 Oct., 1862, in U. S. Hospital.

610 POLLY[7], daughter of Dr. Thomas[6] and Polly (Dana) Brigham; born in Norwich, Vt., 21 July, 1794; died ——; married, 11 Jan., 1815, Willard Hutchinson of Norwich, born in Braintree, Vt., 22 Aug., 1792; died in Windsor, Vt., Jan., 1845.

Children (Hutchinson):
  i James Dana[8], b. 18 April, 1817; d. in Boston (Roxbury), ——; m. 11 Aug., 1852, Louise, dau. of Otis French of Pawtucket, R. I.; a merchant in Boston; res. Roxbury. Ch.:
    1 *Fannie B.*[9], b. 22 May, 1853; d. in girlhood of consumption.
    2 *Henry Dana,* b. 6 March, 1855.
    3 *Alice,* m. William M. Seavey, who d.
  ii Thomas B., b. 16 June, 1821; d. y.
  iii Henry A., b. 16 March, 1826; d. y.

iv Mary M., b. 1 May, 1829; m. Charles E. Blaisdell of Norwich.
   Ch. (Blaisdell):
   1 *Charles Willard*, b. 29 Dec., 1848.
   2 *Emma L.*, b. 22 Aug., 1852.
v Martha A., b. 22 Feb., 183—; d. y.

611   LUCIA[7], daughter of Dr. Thomas S.[6] and Polly (Dana) Brigham; born in Norwich, Vt., 8 March, 1796; married, 17 Feb., 1819, John Warner, son of Alexander ,L. Leslie, born 18 Aug., 1791, in Londonderry, N. H.; a descendant of the Scotch who settled there. Mr. Leslie became a lumber dealer and later engaged in farming.

Children (Leslie):
   i Charles Brigham[8], b. in Wells River, Vt., 5 Nov., 1819; m. 15 Jan., 1845, Harriet Heaton, dau. of Smith Skinner; b. in Thetford, Vt., 9 May, 1822; Judge of Probate for several years; res. Wells River. Ch., b. in Wells River:
      1 *Julius Hayden*[9], b. 7 Nov., 1845; 2 *Elizabeth Butler*, b. 7 Sept., 1847; 3 *Charles Edward*, b. 3 July, 1854.
   ii Elizabeth B., b. 19 Oct., 1822; m. 31 Aug., 1843, Julius Hayden of St. Louis; she d. s. p., 5 March, 1845, in Memphis, Tenn.
   iii Lucia Ann, b. 17 April, 1835; res. (in 1903) unm., in Wells River.

612   JAMES DANA[7], son of Dr. Thomas S.[6] and Polly (Dana) Brigham; born 10 Oct., 1806; died 2 March, 1900; married Oct., 1850, Maria R. Grant of Bath, Me.

Children:
   i Carlton Baxter[8].
   ii Franklin Pierce, m. Laura E. Hamilton of Breckenridge, Mo. Ch.:
      1 *Fred H.*[9]; 2 *Curtis D.*; 3 *Harry H.*
   iii Frederick Howard.
   iv Laura Etta, m. Edward T. Hodgsdon of Phippsburg, Me. Ch. (Hodgsdon):
      1 *Viola M.*[9]
   v Ellen Augusta, m. Frank E. Williams; res. Brooklyn, N. Y. Ch. (Williams):
      1 *Edith A.*[9]

613   PAUL WOOSTER[7], son of Paul Wooster[6] and Mary (Ayers) Brigham; born in Sharon, Vt., 2 Nov., 1802; died in Norwich, Vt., 4 Nov., 1898; married 3 April, 1826, Louisa M. Slack; born 20 Sept., 1806; died 17 Jan., 1894.

Children, born in Norwich:
   i Louisa Ann[8], b. 11 July, 1827; m. Jan., 1845, Stillman C. Armstrong of Norwich, b. Aug., 1820. Ch. (Armstrong), b. in Norwich:
      1 *Charles A.*[9], b. Sept., 1847; m. 1872, Arabell Grub; res. Minn.
      2 *Byron D.*, b. April, 1849; m. 1883, Nellie Church; res. Worcester, Mass.

3 *Clara E.,* b. Feb., 1852; m. 1872, W. M. Swan of Tunbridge, Vt.

4 *Frank B.,* b. June, 1856; m. 1885, Nellie Huntington; res. Lebanon, N. H.

5 *Andy A.,* b. Feb., 1858; m. 1886, Lou Nye; res. San Jose, Cal.

6 *Willie E.,* b. June, 1863; m. 1884, Addie Blair.

7 *Nellie A.,* b. June, 1863; m. 1885, John Hull; res. Lebanon, N. H.

787   ii George C., b. 1 Jan., 1831.

iii Mary A., b. 23 May, 1830; d. unm., 23 March, 1885.

iv Elizabeth, b. 27 March, 1834; d. 3 Oct., 1851.

v Ellen C., b. 3 June, 1838; d. 19 March, 1856.

788   vi James M., b. 11 May, 1843.

vii Alma J., b. 27 Feb., 1846; m. George Brown; res. Tunbridge, Vt.

614   WILLIAM⁷, son of Paul W.⁶ and Mary (Ayers) Brigham; born in Norwich, Vt., 20 March, 1808; died ,there, 18 April, 1888; married 26 Sept., 1832, Ann F., daughter of John and Lydia (Lord) Proctor; born in Norwich, 7 June, 1812; died there, 31 March, 1887. He resided on the Governor Paul Brigham homestead at Norwich.

Children, born in Norwich:
    i Charlotte E.⁸, b. 10 Aug., 1833; d. unm., 30 June, 1859.
    ii Ellen A., b. 6 Oct., 1835; d. unm., 2 April 1857.
    iii John P., b. 5 Jan., 1838; d. 11 Jan., 1840.
    iv Francis A., b. 12 March, 1840; d. 16 Oct., 1856.
    v Louisa A., b. 18 Feb., 1843; res. unm., 1903, on the old Gov. Brigham homestead.
789   vi Andrew William, b. 31 Jan., 1847.
    vii Albert Carlton, b. 23 Sept., 1849; m. (1) 23 Sept., 1872, Alice M., dau. of William Maxham; b. in Worcester, 5 Oct., 1850; d. 4 Jan., 1889; m. (2) 11 May, 1897, Mrs. Jennie F. Camp, dau. of Rowell Bryant; b. Hanover, N. H., 2 May, 1848; res. on the old Gov. Brigham estate, a farmer. Ch., b. in Norwich:
    1 *Mary A.⁹,* b. 13 March, 1875; res. Norwich.

615   JAMES A.⁷, son of Paul Wooster⁶ and Mary (Ayers) Brigham; born in Norwich, Vt., 24 June, 1816; died in Manchester, N. H., where he resided, 31 Jan., 1901; married April, 1841, Mary Wheeler who died 6 Dec., 1878

Child, born in Manchester:
    i Emily A.⁸, b. 29 May, 1842; m. 5 Sept., 1867, Jasper P. George, and res. Manchester. Ch. (George):
    1 *Milton Brigham⁹,* b. 7 Aug., 1874; m. Emma L. Furney. Ch.: i Walter B.¹⁰; ii Jasper.

616   CHARLES FREDERICK⁷, son of Charles⁶ and Betsey (Royce) Brigham; born in Woodstock, Vt , 13 Nov., 1825; died in White River Junction, Vt., 30 Dec., 1903; married (1) 23 June, 1856, Caroline A. Havens; who died 3 June, 1862; married (2)

15 June, 1868, Mary Antoinette Dow, who died 15 April, 1897.
Was a bookkeeper and resided in Tampa, Fla.

Child (by first wife):
  i Charles Norman[8], b. 30 Dec., 1858; m. 4 Feb., 1885, Eva B. Gibson;
    he is a merchant and bookkeeper; res. Tampa, Fla. Ch.:
      1 *Anna C.[9]*, b. 3 July, 1886; d. 23 Aug., 1886; 2 *Norman H.,*
        b. 25 Dec., 1888; 3 *William Ernest*, b. 23 Jan., 1892; 4
        Frederick H., b. 23 Jan., 1895.
Children (by second wife):
  ii Carrie Augusta, b. 28 June, 1869.
  iii Herbert Dow, b. 30 April, 1871; res. unm., in South Woodstock,
    Vt.
  iv Frederick Newton, b. 14 Nov., 1873; unm.

617 CAPT. GEORGE NEEDHAM[7], son of Daniel R.[6] and
Eliza (Needham) Brigham; born in South Coventry, Conn., 2
May., 1831; died in Rockville, Conn., 25 March, 1896; married
(1) 25 Oct., 1854, Sarah P., daughter of Henry Bodge; born in
Lebanon, Conn., 27 Aug., 1831; died 22 Oct., 1878; married (2)
27 Nov., 1879, Mary E. Bodge (sister of first wife); born 20
Feb., 1834. He learned the trade of the weaver. Was two years
in California, during the gold excitement; enlisted 20 Aug., 1862,
as Sergeant of Co. D, 14th Conn. Vol. Infantry, and became
Capt. Co. B same Regt.; discharged because of ill health 8 Dec.,
1864; wounded at Gettysburg, Morton's Ford and Reams Station.
Was Postmaster in Rockville 1866-86; tax collector and member
of the School Board; prominent in the Congregational Church.

Children (by first wife), born in Rockville:
  i Charles Henry[8], b. 22 Oct., 1855; d. unm., in New Haven, Conn.,
    25 June, 1893.
  ii Frank Markham, b. 20 Feb., 1858; res. Rockville, where a lead-
    ing clothier; m. 16 Nov., 1887, Minnie C., dau. of Isaac Sill.
    Ch.:
      1 *Persis E.[9]*, d.
      2 *Christine Sill,* b. 26 Dec., 1889.
      3 *Marion Francis,* b. 19 March, 1891.
      4 *Teressa Marjorie,* b. 4 Sept., 1894.
      5 *George Newton,* b. 13 Feb., 1896.
      6 *Lucille Markham,* b. 18 June, 1897.
      7 *Frances Minnie,* b. in Ellington, Conn., 18 Feb., 1904.
  iii Martyn E., b. 21 May, 1870; d. 23 May, 1870.
  iv Mary E., b. 21 May, 1870; d. 14 June, 1870.

618 ABEL[7], son of Joel[6] and Elizabeth (Brown) Brigham;
born in Sudbury, Mass., 11 Jan., 1814; died in Troy, Wis., 14
Feb., 1884; married Emeline Hibbard, born in North Hadley,
Mass., 23 Aug., 1824; died in Troy, 2 June, 1902. A farmer and
moved to Troy.

Children, the first 5 born in N. Hadley:
    i Maria⁸, b. and d. 1841.
790 ii Truman E., b. 3 March, 1842.
~   iii Emma Salina, b. 14 April, 1844; d. 1885; m. James Hooper; res. Troy.
    iv Emerson Abel, b. Nov., 1847; m. Rose Meecham of Troy; res. Darien, Wis.
    v Susan Emeline, b. 1849; m. Emory Atkins; res. Troy.
    vi Clara Levina, m. Charles Finch; res. Lincoln, Neb.
    vii Allen C., b. in Troy, 1861; m. —————; res. Troy.
    viii Frank M., b. in Troy, 1868; m. at North Adams, Mass., Hattie Buck; res. Lincoln, Neb.

619 CHARLES WILLIAM⁷, son of Danforth Phipps⁶ and Hannah (Walcott) Brigham; born in Lowell, Mass., 12 Aug., 1834; married 22 June, 1870, Annie Maria, daughter of Ransom E. Cady; born 16 June, 1850. Three years in the Civil War, in the 7th Mass. Artillery, and Richardson's Infantry; has been for many years in the Fire Marshall's Office, State House, Boston; resides in Lowell.

Children, born in Lowell:
    i Albert Danforth⁸, b. 13 Dec., 1870.
    ii Edward William, b. 9 Jan., 1873.
    iii Charles Richardson, b. 29 April, 1885.

620 WILLIAM⁷, son of John⁶ and Mary (Leveritt) Brigham; born in Georgia, 19 July, 1819; died in Girard, Ga., 2 June, 1893; married 10 April, 1844, Caroline M. T. White of Georgia, who died 24 Feb., 1883. He succeeded to the ownership of his father's plantation in Girard, where he resided.

Children, born in Girard:
791 i John Christopher⁸, b. 16 June, 1846.
792 ii William Henry, b. 23 July, 1848.
793 iii Thaddeus Rudolf, b. 25 Aug., 1849.
    iv Mary Ann Elizabeth, b. 12 April, 1851; m. 30 June, 1873, Matthew M. Daniel of Ga. Ch. (Daniel):
      1 *William Morgan⁹,* b. 21 May, 1874.
      2 *Nina Thayer,* b. 13 Feb., 1876.
      3 *James Cochrane,* b. 17 Feb., 1878.
      4 *Charles,* b. 17 May, 1880.
      5 *Ethel,* b. 17 March, 1882.
    v Sarah Martha Jane, b. 10 Nov., 1853; m. April, 1886, Howard S. Royal of Ga. Ch. (Royal):
      1 *Irene⁹,* b. 16 July, 1887.
      2 *William B.,* b. 2 Oct., 1889; d. July, 1890.
      3 *Howard Seaborn,* b. 2 Oct., 1891.
      4 *Warren B.,* b. 27 Dec., 1895.
    vi Erasmus Horatio, b. 17 April, 1854; d. 14 May, 1864.
794 vii Clarence Russell, b. 6 Sept., 1856.
    viii Infant, b. 7 Sept., 1858; d. 2 Nov., 1858.
795 ix Charles, b. 3 Oct., 1860.

796 x Walter Breckenbridge, b. 25 June, 1863.
  xi Caroline, b. 3 Jan., 1865; d. 20 May, 1875.
  xii Harry White, b. 21 Dec., 1871; m. 5 April, 1896, Bessie Lee
    Cochrane. Ch.:
      1 *Caryl Bessie*[9], b. 7 Feb., 1897.

621 ELIZABETH ANN EUNICE[7], daughter of John[6] and
Mary (Leveritt) Brigham; born in Girard, Ga., 15 Jan., 1824;
died in Watertown, Mass., 20 March, 1857; married 6 May, 1846,
Artemas B. Rogers, a merchant in Watertown, born in Newton,
Mass., 19 April, 1817; died in Watertown, 17 July, 1901.

Children (Rogers), born in Watertown:
  i Frank[8], b. 3 April, 1847; d. 14 Nov., 1873.
  ii George Leveritt, b. 24 April, 1849; d. 15 Dec., 1875.
  iii Frederick W., b. 15 Sept., 1851; m. 18 Aug., 1874, Ella L. Frost;
    res. Waltham, Mass. Ch.:
      1 *Artemas Bixby*[9], b. 8 Feb., 1876.
  iv John Brigham, b. 25 April, 1854; res. unm., in Watertown.
  v Lucy Maria, b. 17 April, 1856; m. 24 Aug., 1885, Albert C.
    Wright, b. 13 Aug., 1857; d. in Waltham, 19 June, 1888; she
    res. Watertown.

622 JOHN[7], son of John[6] and Mary (Leveritt) Brigham;
born in Burke County, Ga., 13 Feb., 1827; died in Watertown,
Mass., 20 Dec., 1871; married 5 Jan., 1852, Mary Elizabeth,
daughter of Capt. William C. Tainter of Boston; born 3 Jan.,
1830. Was in business as a lumber merchant in Watertown, with
his father.

Children, born in Watertown:
  i Cora E.[8], b. 7 Oct., 1852; d. 12 Oct., 1860.
  ii Nellie Maria, b. 11 Oct., 1857; d. 27 Sept., 1858.
  iii Harry Webster, b. 12 Jan., 1869; m. 12 March, 1894, Ella May
    Leavitt, b. in Newtonville, Mass., 21 March, 1869; res. Water-
    town.

623 WILLIAM THEODORE[7], son of William[6] and Adeline
(Cole) Brigham; born in Watertown, Mass., 12 Sept., 1835; married 2 Feb., 1864, Marion Billings Cole of Baltimore, Md.

He went to Baltimore in the employ of his uncle, a prominent
hat manufacturer; later succeeded to the business and upon its incorporation became President of the Brigham-Hopkins Company;
retired in 1899 and resides in Shelter Island, Suffolk County,
N. Y.

Children, born in Baltimore:
  i Charles Pliny[8], b. 3 Feb., 1867; m. 11 July, 1900, Mary Lapham
    Walker of Glens Falls, N. Y.; was grad. A. B., Johns Hopkins
    Univ., 1888; Ph. D., 1891; is secy. and treas. of the Greenport
    Basin & Construction Co., Greenport, L. I.; res. s. p., Shelter
    Island.

ii Walter Cole, b. 11 Jan., 1870; at Johns Hopkins Univ., 1888-91; an artist, res. unm., Shelter Island.

iii Theodore William, b. 5 Jan., 1876; studied naval architecture at Institute of Technology, Boston; is a naval architect, in the employ of the Greenport B. & C. Co.; res. unm., Shelter Island.

624 CHARLES[7], son of William[6] and Mary (Crafts) Brigham; born in Watertown, Mass., 21 June, 1841; married 13 Dec., 1892, Rebecca S., daughter of George V. Jordan of Saco, Me.

He entered the office of an architect in Boston, to study his chosen profession. The war coming on, he served nine months in Co. K, 5th Regt. Mass. Vol. Infantry, at New Berne, North Carolina. Returned to Boston, finished his architectural course, and formed a partnership under the firm name of "Sturgis & Brigham." After the death of the senior partner, the firm became "Brigham & Spofford." Many Boston buildings and numerous buildings in other parts of New England and the United States have been built after their designs. After a competition between the leading architects of the United States Mr. Brigham was awarded the work of building the large extension to the Massachusetts State House on Beacon Hill, Boston, which work occupied a decade, from 1890 to 1900. He resides in Watertown, a highly respected and honored citizen; has filled the office of selectman many times, and served on the school board. He has no children.

625 ABEL[7], son of Samuel[6] and Alethina (Howe) Brigham; born in Boylston, Mass., 26 Oct., 1815; died there, 6 May, 1893; married, 21 June, 1843, Charity Brewer, born in Boylston, 10 Aug., 1819; died 21 May, 1886. Was a farmer of Boylston and his house still stands.

Children, born in Boylston:

i Walter A.[8], b. 29 Feb., 1844; m. 13 Oct., 1869, Julia A., dau. of Robert Andrews, b. in Boylston, 7 May, 1847; res. Worcester, Mass., where a fruit grower. Enlisted in 1861 in Co. D, 25th Mass. Vol. Inf. and served 3 years, and was in 24 engagements. Ch.:

1 *Frederick W.*[9], b. 23 Dec., 1870; m. Vanna King. Ch.: i Dorothy[10]; ii Hazel; iii Walter.

2 *Lucy J.*, b. 1872; d. 1874.

3 *Robert A.*, b. 1879; d. 1903.

4 *Flora G.*, b. 4 Sept., 1875; m. J. A. Carter; res. Winthrop, Mass. Ch. (Carter): Kenneth Cranston[10]

5 *Ralph H.*, b. 6 April, 1886.

ii Josephine C., b. 7 Sept., 1847; d. 1853.

iii Leland N., b. 4 Nov., 1850; m. 17 June, 1874, Jennie Bradley of Dickerson, N. Y.; res. Clinton, Mass., where shipping agent of Clinton Wire Cloth Co. Ch.:

1 *Lilian Mae*[9], b. 20 Oct., 1879.

    iv Orrison W., b. 11 Feb., 1854; d. s. p., 12 Aug., 1903; m. Mary
Eliza Robshaw. He was a merchant of Worcester.

    v Carrie J., b. 25 March, 1857; m. 18 May, 1876, William A. Taylor
of Clinton. Ch. (Taylor):

        1 *Mabel F.*[9], b. 1 July, 1877.

        2 *Clara N.*, b. 2 Aug., 1879; m. 30 Sept., 1903, Clifton W.
Cheney. Ch. (Cheney), Barton Taylor[10], b. 1 April, 1905.

        3 *Herbert D.*, b. 6 Sept., 1881.

        4 *Leland B.*, b. 4 Nov., 1884.

        5 *Mildred J.*, b. 25 Sept., 1890.

  626 DOLLY[7], daughter of Samuel[6] and Alethina (Howe) Brigham; born 30 Oct., 1817; died 21 May, 1882; married, 5 Oct.,
1842, James F. Maynard, of the old firm of Maynard, Skinner &
Co., Wholesale Grocers, State Street, Boston.

Children (Maynard):

    i Ellen[8], b. 27 Aug., 1843; m. 27 June, 1869, William H., son of Dr.
Hartshorn. Ch. (Hartshorn):

        1 *Edward H.*[9], b. 17 July, 1870; a physician.

        2 *Harry,* b. 1 Nov., 1874.

    ii Calvin, b. 5 Nov., 1845; m. (1) Laura Hunt; m. (2) Mary
Stickney of Williamstown, Mass. He is a farmer in So. Lancaster, Mass. Ch. (by first wife):

        1 *Charles A.*[9], b. 27 Aug., 1867.

        2 *Nellie F.*, b. 15 March, 1870.

        Ch. (by second wife):

        3 *Nahum A.*, b. 3 Nov., 1880.

        4 *James Forrest,* b. 6 Jan., 1888.

        5 *Stanley,* b. 14 Oct., 1890.

        6 *Raymond,* b. 6 April, 1898.

  627 SAMUEL DAVIS[7], son of Samuel[6] and Alethina (Howe)
Brigham; born 22 March, 1821; died about 1893; married Sarah
Read of Machias, Me., where he settled for a time; returned to
Clinton and went west; was the seventh Samuel in regular succes-
sion.

Children:

    i Frances[8], d.; ii Samuel, eighth in regular succession, d.; iii
Caroline, d.; iv Josephine, d.; v Austin.

    vi Faustina, b. in Clinton, Mass., 20 Sept., 1859; m. 28 April, 1880,
Alexander Robertson; res. Clinton. Ch. (Robertson):

        1 *Tina*[9], b. 7 July, 1881; m. 10 April, 1902, John Holden of
Gardner, Mass.; 2 *James,* b. 3 Nov., 1882; 3 *Alix,* b. 12
Feb., 1883; 4 *Lina,* b. 6 Sept., 1886; 5 *William,* d. y.; 6
Caroline, b. 16 Dec., 1894; 7 *Grace,* b. 7 July, 1898.

    vii and viii Infants, d. y.

  628 LEVI EDWIN[7], son of Samuel[6] and Alethina (Howe)
Brigham; born in Lancaster, Mass., 17 Jan., 1825; died in Clinton,
Mass., 26 Oct., 1895; married 30 March, 1850, Ann Janette Barnes

of Berlin, Mass. Resided in Jaffrey, N. H. from about 1863 to 1873.

Children:
    i Edmund L.[8], b. 18 Sept., 1851; m. 18 Sept., 1880, Julia Paupau, who d. 30 Oct., 1887.
    ii Webster D., b. 1 Jan., 1853; d. 14 March, 1853.
    iii Daniel W., b. 7 July, 1854; m. 22 Sept., 1904, Mrs. Caroline Stebbins.
    iv Ella J., b. 28 Oct., 1856; m. at Clinton, 24 Oct., 1888, Albert S. Stuart of Stowe, Mass., b. 5 April, 1849. Ch. (Stuart), the 3 younger b. in Sterling, Mass., where she resides:
        1 *Leon E.*[9], b. in Clinton, 9 April, 1890; 2 *Harold A.*, b. 16 Dec., 1893; 3 *Walter L.*, b. 22 Sept., 1896; 4 *Amos E.*, b. 30 June, 1898.
    v Isadore, b. 14 July, 1858; d. 21 June, 1882; m. 5 Jan., 1881, Fred. Bagster; res. Clinton. Ch. (Bagster):
        1 *Nellie*[9], b. 26 Oct., 1881.
    vi Dolly A., b. 13 July, 1860; m. 3 Oct., 1883, at Clinton, William J. Melvin, a compositor, for many years with the Boston *Daily Globe;* b. in Scotland. Ch. (Melvin):
        1 *Robert Levi*[9], b. in Boston, 22 Dec., 1889.
        2 *William Prescott,* b. in Greenwood, Mass., 4 Nov., 1902.
    vii Lizzie J., b. 25 April, 1863; m. 5 Dec., 1883, Dean S. Moulton of Charleston, Vt., b. 1859. Ch. (Moulton), all but the eldest b. in Clinton:
        1 *Vera L.*[9], b. in W. Burke, Vt., 20 May, 1886; m. 23 Nov., 1904, Newell W. Wilson; res. Derby, Vt.
        2 *Ralph,* b. 22 April, 1888; d. Aug., 1888.
        3 *Ray,* b. 22 April, 1888; d. Sept., 1888.
        4 *Elsie,* b. 11 July, 1890.
        5 *Martha,* b. 2 Jan., 1893.
        6 *Ruth,* b. 9 Jan., 1897.
        7 *Ada,* b. 15 May, 1899; d. 18 Oct., 1901.
        8 *Lizzie,* b. 15 May, 1899.
        9 *Harry E.,* b. 27 Sept., 1902.
    viii C. Herbert, b. 30 May, 1867; d. 14 June, 1868.

629 JOHN D.[7], son of Samuel[6] and Alethina (Howe) Brigham; born in Machias, Me., 5 Aug., 1834; died in Clinton, Mass., 27 Feb., 1900; married Oct., 1863, Betsey J. Cutting of Vermont, who died in Clinton, suddenly, in the street, of heart disease, 22 Feb., 1897. He was in the Civil War and was taken prisoner; after his release he settled in Clinton.

Child, born in Clinton:
    i Mabel A.[8], b. 25 July, 1864; res. Clinton, unm.

630 WILLIAM EUSTIS[7], son of John Gott[6] and Lucy (Howe) Brigham; born in Marlboro, Mass., 14 April, 1823; died in Jamaica Plain, Mass., 8 May, 1896; married 10 May, 1855, Eliza Ann, daughter of Jeremiah G. and Nancy C. (Parker) Shattuck of Pepperell, Mass.; born there 12 Dec., 1830.

He was Superintendent and Manager of the Jamaica Pond Ice Co. until consolidation with the Boston Ice Co., and a member of that firm until death. He was treasurer of the Forest Council of the Royal Arcanum and a 32d degree Mason. He was highly esteemed in business and private life.

Children:

i George Edward[8], b. in Pepperell, 17 Feb., 1856; m. 28 Oct., 1885, Ada, dau. of Alexander and Susannah (May) Dickson of Jamaica Plain; he is treasurer of Simpson Bros. Corporation, Boston; res. Jamaica Plain. Ch:·

   1 *Margherita*[9], b. 23 April, 1887.

ii Will Ellsworth, b. 11 Aug., 1864. Is in business with the Boston Ice Co.

631 ALONZO HOWE[7], son of John Gott[8] and Lucy (Howe) Brigham; born in Concord, Mass., 16 April, 1826; died there, 5 Jan., 1892; married 4 Jan., 1863, in Neponset, Mass., Mary, daughter of Armory M. Parmenter of Marlboro, Mass., born 17 June, 1836. Was a farmer and resided in Concord.

Children, born in Corcord:

i Frank A.[8], b. 15 Dec., 1863; d. 5 Aug., 1866.

ii Lucie Howe, b. 3 June, 1865; m. 3 April, 1888, Frank, son of Edwin Wheeler of Concord; b. 3 April, 1855. Ch. (Wheeler), b. in Concord:

   1 *Hilda*[9], b. 15 July, 1889; 2 *Esther Howe*, b. 26 July, 1891; 3 *Priscilla*, b. 8 March, 1894; 4 *Elizabeth Rice*, b. 26 March, 1899; 5 *Irene*, b. 18 April, 1901; 6 *Frances Brigham*, b. 5 Dec., 1904.

iii John Burt, b. 18 Dec., 1866; m. 7 Aug., 1904, Flora Stuart of E. Boston, b. 20 May, 1884; res. s. p., Boston; been ten years in the Militia.

iv Harry Winthrop, b. 22 Dec., 1868; a farmer, res. Concord; member of the Militia.

v Amy Belle, b. 11 Jan., 1871; d. 25 Dec., 1871.

vi Alice May, b. 14 Sept., 1877; m. 25 March, 1897, Harry Sidney, son of George P., son of Josiah Walcott; b. in Concord, 27 May, 1871. Ch. (Walcott), b. in Concord:

   1 *George Brigham*[9], b. 11 April, 1898; 2 *Roger Nelson*, b. 4 Oct., 1899; 3 *Mary Elizabeth*, b. 19 May, 1901; 4 *Malcolm Lester*, b. 31 Dec., 1903.

632 MARTHA ANN[7], daughter of Nathaniel Phillips[6] and Martha (Gates) Brigham; born in Barre, Mass., 22 Oct., 1811; married 22 Oct., 1835, Horatio H. Wheelock.

Children (Wheelock), born in Barre:

i Frances E.[8], b. 1 Dec., 1836; d. s. p., 5 Oct., 1863; m. 1858, Lyman W. Adams.

ii George Nelson, b. 2 May, 1838; killed at Gettysburg; was in Co. G, 15th Mass. Vol. Infantry; unm.

iii Nancy M., b. 24 Jan., 1840; m. 1859, Elliot Howe, a farmer, res. Barre. Ch. (Howe):

   1 *Martha*[9]; 2 *Nelson*; 3 *Henry*.

HON. LEWIS ALEXANDER BRIGHAM (654)

iv Harriet A., b. 8 April, 1842; m. James E. Holden; res. Barre.
Ch. (Holden), b. in Barre:
1 *Dr. George Walter[9]*, b. 17 Sept., 1866; m. 1896, Elsie L.
Greene of Boston; was grad. M. D., Univ. of Vt., 1895; ex-
Prof. of Clinic. Med. U. Denver Med. Coll.; Supt. and Med.
Director Agnes Memorial Sanatorium, Denver, Col.
v Olivia M., b. 9 May, 1843; m. 1872, George N. Harwood; res.
Barre, where he is selectman and overseer of the poor. Ch.
(Harwood):
1 *Ethel[9]*.
vi Everett B., b. 26 March, 1846; m. 1881, Alice Leland; a broker,
and res. Willamette, Ill. Ch.:
1 *Harold[9]; 2 Alice; 3 Mabel; 4 Earl*.
vii Seymour A., b. 20 April, 1848; m. 26 March, 1872, Fannie, dau.
of Henry E. Rice; a Com. Merchant, res. Willamette, Ill. Ch.:
1 *Bertha C.[9]*, b. in Barre, 9 Jan., 1873; 2 *Seymour E.*, b. 15
July, 1879, in Chicago; 3 *Bessie E.*, b. 30 Dec., 1882, in Chicago; 4 *Grace*, b. 30 March, 1885, in Willamette; 5 *Raymond*,
b. 25 June, 1887, in Willamette.
viii Edward C., b. 10 May, 1850; a marble dealer, res. Hiawatha,
Kan.

633 WILLIAM HARRISON[7], son of Nathaniel Phillips[6] **and**
Martha (Gates) Brigham; born in Barre, Mass., 16 Dec., 1814;
died there, ———; married (1) 14 Nov., 1838, Hannah Nash
of Warnick, born 1818; died 7 July, 1879; married (2) 1 Sept.,
1884, Lydia F. Hodge of E. Jaffrey, N. H., born 24 Nov., 1829;
died s. p.

Children (by first wife), born in Barre:
i Clarissa M.[8], b. 12 July, 1841; m. 22 Oct., 1867, Albert Rice of
Barre; b. there, 4 Oct., 1840; res. there. Ch. (Rice), b. in Barre:
1 *Franklin Harrison[9]*, b. 27 April, 1873.
2 *Frederick Dexter*, b. 13 June, 1875; d. y.
797 ii Henry H., b. 8 Dec., 1846.
iii Martha Eva, b. 22 May, 1852; m. 11 May, 1875, John S. Roper,
b. 11 Dec., 1851; d. in Barre, 31 Oct., 1887. Ch. (Roper), b. in
Barre:
1 *H. Louise[9]*, b. 10 May, 1879; 2 *Alice E.*, b. 27 Jan., 1882; 3
Grace E., b. 19 April, 1884; 4 *Charles H.*, b. 1 June, 1887.

634 ORLANDO SIBLEY[7], son of Nathaniel Phillips[6] **and**
Martha (Gates) Brigham; born in Barre, Mass., 16 Dec., 1816;
died in Springfield, Mass., 11 Feb., 1901; married 31 Dec., 1840,
Lucy A, daughter of William and Rebecca (Allen) Rice, born in
Hubbardston, Mass., 23 Oct., 1818; died in Springfield, July, 1895;
Resided in Hubbardston and Springfield. The male line is ex-
tinct.

Children, born in Springfield:
i Louisa A.[8], b. 12 June, 1842; m. 3 May, 1864, Edward Bigelow
of Rutland, Mass. Ch. (Bigelow):
1 *Robert Edward[9]*, b. 18 July, 1868; m. Amelia S. Gulick; res.
Worcester. Ch.: Lenox E.[10]

    ii Lucy Agnes, b. 4 Sept., 1843; d. 1887; m. George W. Stowe.
    Ch. (Stowe):
      1' *Gertrude L.*[9], b. 1869; m. Wm. H. Sanford; res. Worcester.
      Ch. (Sanford): Agnes B.[10]
      2 George, b. 1871; m. Nellie M. James.
  iii Stella J., b. 7 Aug., 1845; m. William G. Pond of Springfield,
    Mass. Ch. (Pond):
      1 *Lucy A.*[9], b. 28 Sept., 1876.
   iv Ella S., b. 25 Dec., 1848; d. 1899; m. Leroy W. Brown of
    Springfield. Ch. (Brown):
      1 *Ernest L.*[9], d. y.
    v Carrie Maria, b. 1 March, 1855; m. 6 June, 1877, Frank P. Frost
    of Springfield. Ch. (Frost):
      1 *Douglas B.*[9], d. y.

635 LAWSON SIBLEY[7], son of Henry[6] and Sally (Sibley)
Brigham; born in Rutland, Mass., 15 Oct., 1820; died there, 28
March, 1898; married 7 Nov., 1844, Martha Jane, daughter of
Capt. Asa Bigelow,* born in West Boylston, Mass., 3 April, 1826.

Children, born in Rutland:
    i Eliza Jane[8], b. 7 Sept., 1846; m. 30 Nov., 1869, Freeland S., son
    of Andrew Gleason of Hubbardston, Mass. Ch. (Gleason), b.
    in Hubbardston:
      1 *Mabel Frances*[9], b. 3 June, 1871; m. 1899, Harry H. Roper
      of E. Hubbardston. Ch. (Roper): i Sarah E.[10]; ii Howard
      G.; iii Harold B.
      2 Alice Estelle, b. 7 Feb., 1873.
    ii Edna Augusta, b. 15 Dec., 1848; d. 2 Sept., 1850.
  iii Frances Ann, b. 12 Aug., 1852; m. 4 Jan., 1881, Charles M.,
    son of John Hartwell of Barre, Mass. Ch. (Hartwell), b. in
    Barre:
      1 *Hattie Lilian*[9], b. 23 April, 1884; *2 Edith Myrtle*, b. 1 Aug.,
      1886.
798   iv Herbert Elliot, b. 10 Jan., 1857.
    v Henry Lester, b. 19 May, 1859; d. 22 Aug., 1861.
   vi Hattie Olivia, b. 27 Jan., 1864; m. 28 June, 1893, Allen Sherman,
    son of Lyman Woodward of Hubbardston, Mass. Ch. (Wood-
    ward), b. in Hubbardston:
      1 *Gladys Sherman*[9], b. 13 Dec., 1897; *2 Everett Brigham*, b.
      26 Jan., 1899; *3 Marion Ella*, b. 20 Aug., 1900.

636 MONROE BOWMAN[7], son of Henry[6] and Sally (Sibley) Brigham; born in Rutland, Mass., 8 Sept., 1822; died in
Danvers, Mass., 2 May, 1874; married 15 Aug., 1845, Eliza Smith,
born 25 Aug., 1825, in Chester, Vt. Was a market-gardener
of Danvers, Mass., and deacon in the First Baptist Church.

Children, born in Danvers:
    i Henry Artemas[8], b. 17 Aug., 1847; d. 19 Feb., 1849.
    ii Henrietta L., b. 1 Jan., 1852; d. 24 Feb., 1871.
  iii Harriet E., b. 1 Nov., 1856; m. 1 Nov., 1877, Dr. I. H. Bascom,
    b. in Hinsdale, N. H., 1846; res. in Hinsdale. Ch. (Bascom),
    b. in Hinsdale:

* Vide *Bigelow Genealogy.*

1 *Harold Irving*[9], b. 12 Oct., 1886; d. 4 Jan., 1887.
2 *Harold Earle*, b. 6 Dec., 1887; d. 14 Feb., 1888.
iv George Monroe, b. 15 Nov., 1860; m. 10 April, 1890, Lydia A.
Balster, b. 21 May, 1863, in Peabody, Mass.; a market gardener,
and res. s. p., Danvers, Mass.
v Walter Seymour, b. 11 Oct., 1862; d. 5 Aug., 1873.

637   ALBERT GALLATIN[7], son of Josiah Fay[6] and Sylvina
(Hall) Brigham; born in Bakersfield, Vt., 12 March, 1836; married (1) 16 April, 1856, Marietta, daughter of ¡Josiah Houghton;
married (2) 26 Oct., 1869, Celina S., daughter of George Larrabee
of Berkshire, Vt.; born 18 May, 1846.   Resides in Bakersfield,
where a farmer, selectman, etc.; in 1853 moved to Boston, for
two years, where he was in business.

Children (by first wife), born in Bakersfield:
    i Charles William[8], b. 25 Sept., 1860; m. 1 Nov., 1893, Mary
       Darrow, b. in E. Plymouth, O., 1863; a farmer in St. Albans, Vt.
   ii Fred Hamilton, b. 1 Dec., 1862; m. 23 Sept., 1890, Minnie Chaffee
       of Berkshire, b. 1869; a farmer, res. Waterbury, Vt.   Ch.:
       1 *Mary Chaffee*[9], b. in Berkshire, 19 July, 1892.
       2 *Frank A.*, b. 10 Nov., 1901.
Children (by second wife), born in Bakersfield:
  iii George Fay, b. 25 July, 1874; farmer, and res. Bakersfield.
   iv Cynthia Jennie, b. 22 April, 1876; was a teacher; was grad. Brigham Academy, Bakersfield; m. 4 Oct., 1900, Harvey A. Churchill
       of Bakersfield.   Ch. (Churchill):
       1 *Winston*[9], b. 1901.

638   EBENEZER DAMON[7], son of Timothy[6] and Patty
(Damon) Brigham; born in Granville, Pa., 15 Feb., 1808; died
————; married Mary Aldrich, born 4 June, 1816.

Children, born in E. Smithfield:
     i Harriet Amanda[8], b. 12 March, 1836.
799 ii Alasco De Lancey, b. 9 March, 1838.
   iii Dwight William, b. 6 Sept., 1842; d. s. p., in Florida, in 1901;
       m. Abbie Carpenter.
    iv Mary Rosaile, b. 2 Aug., 1848; m. 16 Aug., 1869, John A. Murray,
       b. in Geneva, N. Y., 12 April, 1847; res. Detroit, Mich.   Ch.
       (Murray):
       1 *John Alexander*[9], b. 2 March, 1871; d. 14 March, 1873.
       2 *Herbert De Lancey*, b. 21 April, 1876; m. 1 Sept., 1904, Clara
          Aline Harshaw.
     v Frank Clifford, b. 2 June, 1851; m. Lucy Taggart; res. s. p.,
       in the West.

639   GEORGE[7], son of Timothy[6] and Patty (Damon) Brigham; born in Smithfield, Pa., 16 Oct., 1809; died in Villa Ridge,
Ill., 20 Sept., 1872; married 5 May, 1831, Amy Stockwell of
Granville, Pa., born 20 Feb., 1810.   Resided in Granville.

Children, born in Granville:
800   i Reader Smith⁸, b. 16 June, 1832.
     ii Urania, b. 9 May, 1834; m. 18 Aug., 1854, Lathan Andrews.
    iii Wallace, b. 8 Oct., 1837; d. 2 May, 1864; m. 15 April, 1860, Matilda Thompson.
    iv Helen, b. 7 April, 1840; m. (1) 11 Jan., 1862, Hiram Shriver; m. (2) 5 April, 1869, Rush Robinson.
     v Mary A., b. 10 Nov., 1843; d. 9 Sept., 1880; m. 7 April, 1866, Joseph Kendall.
    vi Eaton (twin to Mary), m. 14 March, 1869, Fanny Ferguson; was a drummer in the 31st O. Infantry; res. in Danville, Ill.
   vii Lucina, b. 10 April, 1846; m. 6 Sept., 1870, Henry Goe of Villa Ridge, Ill.
  viii Luman P. (twin to Lucina), d. 3 March, 1846.
    ix Luman P., b. 8 Dec., 1848; d.
     x Julia A., b. 15 May, 1850.
    xi Juliette (twin to Julia), d. 5 Oct., 1850.

640   PHINEAS⁷, son of Timothy⁶ and Patty (Damon) Brigham; born in Smithfield, Pa., 22 Jan., 1815; died in Canton, Pa., 20 May, 1889; married (1) 10 Oct., 1838, Eliza, daughter of Ezekiel Johnson, born 10 Feb., 1822; (divorced soon after the war and married (2) 1877, P. C. Stone of Round Grove, Ill., whom she survives, residing with her son in Des Moines, Ia.); married (2) Jan., 1872, Myra, daughter of)David Andrews, born Leroy Township, Bradford Co., Pa., 15 April, 1836; died in Philadelphia, 8 July, 1902.

His parents dying early, when a mere child he was placed in the family of William Baldwin, proprietor of " Old Fountain Inn " near Wellsburg, Pa., where he lived for several years. He ran away after a severe flogging, returned, and at last set out for the home of his uncle Salmon Brigham in Madison County, N. Y., working for his food and lodging on the way. He intended to prepare for the Methodist ministry, but after a brief experience as an exhorter, he abandoned the idea. He became state agent of an insurance company and later a retail shoe merchant in Elmira and Watkins, N. Y. After his second marriage he lived at Canton, Pa., where he is interred. He enlisted in the Civil War in Co. B of the 153d N. Y. Infantry and served three years, the last months of his term in the Veteran Reserve Corps.

Children (by first wife), born in Cherry Valley, N. Y ·
801   i Mary Louise⁸, b. 11 Nov., 1839.
    ii William, b. 1 June, 1841; d. 2 Jan., 1842.
802 iii Johnson, b. 11 March, 1846.
    iv William Loomis, b. 14 Feb., 1851; d. Jan., 1853.
Children (by second wife), born in Canton, Pa.:
     v Elizabeth, b. 28 May, 1873; res. Philadelphia.
    vi Anna, b. 10 April, 1875; m. in Philadelphia, 20 April, 1904, George B. Somerville, b. in Dumferline, Scotland, 24 March, 1875;

was grad. Dickinson Law School, Carlisle, Pa., 1897; member of the Philadelphia bar, with res. there; she taught the violin and mandolin before marriage.

641 HENRY C[7]., son of Timothy[6] and Abigail (Mason) Brigham; born in Granville, Pa., 24 March, 1825; died in Smithfield, Pa., 31 Jan., 1892; married 6 Jan., 1848, Sally Kingsley, born in Smithfield, 1 April, 1828; died 26 Nov., 1892. Was a farmer of Smithfield.

Children, born in Smithfield:
   i Marian[8], b. 12 Oct., 1848; d. 2 May, 1850.
   ii Howard T., b. 26 July, 1851; m. 11 Oct., 1871, Lauretta Phelps; a farmer, and res. No. Dakota.
   iii Almeron S., b. 28 Dec., 1852; m. 20 Aug., 1879, Eva M. Snyder; a farmer, and res. Smithfield.
   iv Evangeline, b. 4 March, 1855; d. 3 Feb., 1874.
   v Emma J., b. 19 May, 1858; m. L. A. Courttenden of No. Dakota.

642 HORACE A.[7], son of Timothy[6] and Abigail (Mason) Brigham; born in Granville, Pa., 29 May, 1828; died 14 Feb., 1900; married 1 May, 1853, Sarah C. Young, born in Middletown, Conn., 15 Oct., 1834. Was a farmer of East Smithfield, Pa.

Children, born in E. Smithfield:
803   i Clarence Elmer[8], b. 24 July, 1854.
   ii Helen Augusta, b. 19 April, 1856; d. in E. Smithfield, 15 Nov., 1895; m. 24 Oct., 1877, Orpheus Bird Sumner of E. Smithfield, b. 8 April, 1846. Ch. (Sumner), b. in E. Smithfield:
     1 *Louise*[9], b. 6 Aug., 1878; m. 27 Oct., 1903, E. K. Drake. Ch. (Drake): Charles Sumner[10], b. 4 Nov., 1904.
     2 *Jesse*, b. 29 Aug., 1882.
     3 *Burt*, b. 24 July, 1886.
     4 *Fred*, b. 21 Feb., 1892.
   iii Harriet Louisa, b. 29 April, 1859; m. 17 Feb., 1886, Calvin Van Kirk Woodworth, b. in Cohocton, N. Y., 1 Jan., 1856; res. Minco, Ind. Territory. Ch. (Woodworth):
     1 *Marvin Brigham*[9], b. 25 Dec., 1889; 2 *Ernest Fenwick*, b. Aug., 1895; 3 *William Alexander*, b. Aug., 1898.
   iv Horace J., b. 23 April, 1861; d. 21 April, 1864.
   v Ida May, b. 16 May, 1865; m. 15 May, 1890, Ernest Wood, b. 26 July, 1865; d. 20 June, 1892, in Elmira, N. Y.; she lives in East Smithfield, s. p.
   vi Fred Russell, b. 10 Nov., 1868; m. 5 Sept., 1890, Lena Chapel, b. 5 Nov., 1872; a R. R. man, and res. St. Louis, Mo. Ch.:
     1 *Helen Francis*[9], b. 17 April, 1892; 2 *Anna*, b. 3 Jan., 1894.

643 LUCY[7], daughter of Phineas[6] and Susan (Ames) Brigham; born in Southboro, Mass., 18 Nov., 1810; died in Madison, N. Y., 20 May, 1855; married 2 April, 1829, Leonard Homes, a farmer of Madison. He married (2) Aug., 1856, Emily, (sister of his first wife) who was born in Eaton, N. Y., 16 Nov., 1819;

died 18 Dec., 1904; she resided a widow in Syracuse, N. Y., for some years.

Children (Homes), by first wife, born in Madison:

    i Mary[8], m. Rev. E. P. Bond, Baptist clergyman and army chaplain; editor and teacher. Ch. (Bond)

        1 *Infant*[9], d.; 2 *Ella*, missionary to Assam, Asia; 3 *Alfred*, was grad. from Brown Univ., became a teacher, and d. in Mt. Pleasant (?), Pa.

    ii Chester, was a farmer, and d. in Detroit, Mich. Ch.:

        1 *Elvin*[9], res. Detroit.

    iii Sarah Ann, m. Asa Hartshorn, a farmer of Lebanon, N. Y. Ch.:

        1 *Son*[9], d. æ. about 20.

    iv Eliza Ann, m. Rev. Hardin Wheat, a grad. of Colgate Univ.; she d. in Palmyra, N. Y. Ch. (Wheat):

        1 *Leonard H.*[9], photographer, Newark, N. J.

        2 *Lena*, m. George Eveland, editor and postmaster, Franklin, N. Y.

        3 *Mary E.*, teacher; m. Prof. Elmer G. Frail of Erie, Pa.

        4 *Carrie*, d. æ. 16.

        5 *Helen*, m. Prof. M. Multer of Perry, N. Y.

    v Fidelia, d. in North East, Pa.; m. Rev. Marcus C. Mason, Baptist missionary, Assam, Asia. Ch. (Mason):

        1 (*Rev.*) *Walter*[9], was grad. Colgate Univ. and Rochester Theol. Seminary; missionary with father in Assam.

    vi Ella, m. Rev. E. G. Phillips, a graduate of Colgate Univ., and missionary, Tura, Assam, Asia.

Child (Homes), by second wife:

    vii Arthur L., m. Amy Homes; machinist, res. Syracuse, N. Y. Ch

        1 *Horace L.*[9], student at Syracuse Univ.; 2 *Newell*, architect; 3 *Harold*; 4 *Ella*; 5 *Dau.*

    644   LUCIUS[7], son of Phineas[6] and Susan (Ames) Brigham; born in Eaton, N. Y., 25 July, 1812; died in Syracuse, N. Y., 30 June, 1881; married, 1 Feb., 1840, Prudence Merchant, born in Fenner, N. Y., 25 Aug., 1817; died 13 Aug., 1889. Was proprietor of a restaurant and hotel in Syracuse. The male line is extinct, but the children of a daughter have assumed the name of " Brigham."

Children:

    i Emma L.[8], b. in Fenner, 22 Sept., 1841; m. Tyler Mason of Indianapolis, Ind., who d.; res. in Syracuse.

    ii Alice A., b. in Syracuse, 20 Oct., 1844; m. Frank Roraback, from whom divorced; has assumed her maiden name of " Brigham," as her children have also done; res. in Syracuse. Ch., b. in Syracuse:

        1 *Frederick Lucius*[9], b. 7 Jan., 1865; m. ——————; res. Syracuse. Ch.: i Lucius W.[10], b. 9 Feb., 1893; ii Donald F., b. 29 Aug., 1894; iii Howard B., b. 24 June, 1896; iv George K., b. 6 Jan., 1898.

        2 *Emma*, b. 20 Oct., 1867.

645 HORACE AMES[7], son of Phineas[6] and Susan (Ames) Brigham; born in Eaton, N. Y., 14 Oct., 1817; died, 16 March, 1904; married 1 May, 1845, Julia Perry of Wyoming, N. Y., born 31 Jan., 1819; died 30 July, 1870. Was a farmer of Perry, N. Y.

Children, born in Perry:
    i Ellen A.[8], b. 12 April, 1846; d. 17 Sept., 1875, unm.
    ii Mary, b. 17 Aug., 1849; m. George H. Bemus; she is an artist. Ch. (Bemus):
        1 *Albert*[9]; 2 *Walter*, twins, b. 1878; 3 *George*, b. 1883.
804 iii Albert Perry, b. 12 June, 1855.

646 REV. EDWIN PIERSON[7], son of Phineas[6] and Susan (Ames) Brigham; born in Morrisville, N. Y., 11 Aug., 1828; married (1) Mary Hopkins; married (2) Calista Hazen; married (3) 1 Sept., 1870, Mrs. Hannah (Halloway) McDermott, born 17 Jan., 1837; died 9 Feb., 1875; married (4) Mrs. Lucina (Armstrong) Buck.

He was graduated from Hamilton College A. B. 1856; Theological Seminary 1857; has had many charges in New York State and is now preaching in Conklin Center, N. Y.; been in active service in ministry for 46 years in 1903.

Children (by third wife):
    i Edwin[8], b. in LeRoy, N. Y., 31 Aug., 1872; he is an invalid.
    ii Mary Hannah, b. 9 Feb., 1875; m. 20 Oct., 1897, Clarence V. June, photographer of Addison, N. Y.; she was graduated from Vassar College, A. B., 1897; res. Addison. Ch. (June):
        1 *Lawrence B.*[9]

647 ORLANDO L.[7], son of Salmon[6] and Mary Ann (Sumner) Brigham; born in Eaton, N. Y., 19 Dec., 1835; married (1) 8 Sept., 1862, Abigail Elizabeth, daughter of Sidney Putnam of Madison, N. Y., born 26 Aug., 1836; died 7 Feb., 1868; married (2) 12 Jan., 1870, Sarah Rebecca Cole, who died 15 July, 1899. Resides in Madison.

Children (by first wife), born in St. Louis, Mo.:
    i Elizabeth Gardner[8], b. 22 Nov., 1863; res. Madison.
    ii Arthur Putnam, b. 18 Oct., 1865; m. 24 Feb., 1898, in St. Louis, Sidney, dau. of Lucien M. Chipley of St. Louis; res. there. Ch.:
        1 *Lucien Morris*[9], b. 13 Feb., 1899.
        2 *Arthur Putnam*, b. 10 July, 1902.

648 JOHN BAKER[7], son of Artemas[6] and Mary (Arnold) Brigham; born in Marlboro, Mass., 11 Aug., 1835; married 6 May, 1860, Ann Mary, daughter of Amos Gleason Jr., born in Groton, Mass., 16 May, 1841. He enlisted in 1862, in Co. D, 35th Mass.

Vols.; served 3 years, and came back with broken health; resided for a time in Wayland and Weston and West Newton, Mass., and now resides in Greendale, Worcester, Mass.

Children, the 3 elder born in Wayland, 7 youngest in West Newton:
 i Minnie Elizabeth⁸, b. 25 March, 1861; d. 1 April, 1861.
 ii Emma F. S., b. 23 May, 1862.
 iii Arthur L., b. 5 March, 1866; m. 1890, Nellie G. Brown; res. Melrose, Mass.
 iv Oscar Everett, b. in Weston, 27 March, 1867; m. 1895, Lizzie Corliss; employed by Laconia Car Co., Laconia, N. H., where res. Ch.:
   1 *Gertrude E.⁹*, b. 9 Dec., 1896; 2 *Allen E.,* b. 18 Nov., 1898; 3 *Lilian E.,* b. 1 Aug., 1900.
 v Minnie F., b. in Weston, 22 March, 1868; d. 15 April, 1887.
 vi Eugene C., b. 23 May, 1871.
 vii Alden B., b. 30 Jan., 1873; farmer, and res. Worcester.
 viii Ada G., b. 7 June, 1875; m. 1902, Henry Jackson; res. Chelsea, Mass.
 ix Charles L., b. 9 Feb., 1878; res. Worcester.
 x Walter E., b. 22 Nov., 1880; d. 22 March, 1888.
 xi Lizzie M., b. 7 Oct., 1882; res. Boston; m. 1901, John Sargent.
 xii Frank W., b. 13 Feb., 1887.

649 RUFUS H.⁷, son of Capt. Francis⁶ and Sophia (Gleason) Brigham; born in Hudson, Mass., 9 June, 1837; died there, 2 March, 1899; married 7 Nov., 1860, Basha A., daughter of Moses Mossman, born in Searsport, Me., 14 July, 1844. She resides with her son, Gen. Brigham, in Hudson.

He was the senior member of the firm of F. Brigham & Co. at the time of his death, having succeeded, with his brothers, to his father's business of shoe manufacturer in Hudson; was a conservative and honorable business man. A member of the Doric Lodge A. F. & A. M.; the Houghton R. A. Chapter, Trinity Commandery and Allepo Temple M. N. S. Was interested in the Fire Department and a member of the Massachusetts State Firemen's Association. Was Chief of Hudson's Fire Dept. and for many years foreman of the famous Eureka Engine Co.

Child, born in Hudson:
805 i William H.⁸, b. 1 Feb., 1863.

650 WALDO B.⁷, son of Capt. Francis⁶ and Sophia (Gleason) Brigham; born in Hudson, Mass., 23 June, 1841; married Ruth A. Pedrick, born in Marblehead, Mass. Mr. Brigham succeeded with his brothers to his father's shoe manufacturing business, but has been retired for some years. He is a resident of Cambridge, Mass., in the coal business.

Children:
 i Frank Ellsworth⁸, b. in Hudson, 31 July, 1861; m. 31 July, 1884, Eva Miranda Whitney, b. in Ludlow, Vt., 16 May, 1866.

Ch., b. in Hudson:
1 *Persis Eva*[8], b. 11 April, 1885.
2 *Alice Ruth,* b. 28 Jan., 1887.
3 *Mabel Florence,* b. 11 July, 1888.
4 *Cora Miranda,* b. 29 April, 1890.
5 *Rachel Whitney,* b. 31 Oct., 1898; d. 9 April, 1899.
ii Florence, b. April, 1864; d. 17 June, 1866.
iii Alice, twin to Florence, d. 28 May, 1868.
iv Julia S., b. April, 1868; d. 9 Aug., 1870.
v Waldo D., b. Dec., 1869; d. 31 Aug., 1871.
vi Wilbur B., b. April, 1872; d. 9 March, 1877.
vii Maud, b. April, 1875; d. 20 Oct., 1876.
viii William P., b. Dec., 1876; d. 23 Aug., 1877.
ix Annie.
x Evelyn R., m. William R. Pedrick, Jr., of Hudson; res. Hudson.
Ch. (Pedrick):
1 *Laurena M.*[9], b. 24 Feb., 1903.

651 EDWIN W.[7], son of Artemas Ward[6] and Sophia (Phelps) Brigham, born in Westmoreland, N. Y., 4 Feb., 1825; died there, 1884; married 14 Dec., 1845, Louisa Hulbert of Yates County, N. Y.

Children, born in Westmoreland:
    i Fannie S.[8], b. 10 Nov., 1846; m. 13 Oct., 1869, Park M. Bardin of West Winfield, N. Y. Ch. (Bardin):
        1 *Edith L.*[9], b. 2 May, 1871; m. Clayton E. Clark of West Winfield. Ch. (Clark): i Valeria[10]; ii Hazel B.
        2 *Earl C.,* b. 13 April, 1873; m. Rena M. Button of West Winfield. Ch.: Dorothy[10].
        3 *Ward N.,* b. 15 March, 1875; m. Blanche E. Lamb of Utica, N. Y.
    ii Ellen L., b. 13 Nov., 1850; m. 3 Sept., 1883, Irwin C. Ruth of Westmoreland. Ch. (Ruth):
        1 *Irma M.*[9], b. 25 Oct., 1884; 2 *Edwin Brigham,* b. 26 Jan., 1886; 3 *Vincent E.,* b. 27 July, 1887; 4 *Irwin H.,* b. 11 June, 1889; 5 *William H.,* b. 13 Nov., 1892.
    iii Origen S., b. 8 Nov., 1853; m. 26 Jan., 1876, Clara E. Stone of Utica, N. Y., b. 1855. Ch.:
        1 *Ward E.*[9], b. 10 Feb., 1878; 2 *Laura L.,* b. 5 Sept., 1880; 3 *Clarence A.,* b. 5 Sept., 1880.
    iv Carrie H., b. 18 April, 1860; m. 13 Oct., 1886, Henry D. Stebbins of W. Winfield. Ch. (Stebbins):
        1 *Reba E.*[9], b. 15 July, 1887; 2 *Millie E.,* b. 7 Aug., 1888.

652 WALTER EVERTSON[7], son of Rev. John Clark[6] and Maria E. (Evertson) Brigham; born in New York City, 14 March, 1845; married, near Evansville, Ind., 15 May., 1877, Frances Bryant Armistead, born in Henderson, Ky., 11 Sept., 1855. He is an illustrator and engraver and resides in Evanston, Ill.; received an academic education.

Children:
    i Elizabeth[8], b. in Evansville, Ind., 30 Nov., 1878.
    ii Eloise, b. in Des Plaines, Ill., 3 Sept., 1883; m. 25 July, 1895, in So. Evanston, Ill. (where they res.), Carl Forster.

653 AMARIAH WARD[7], son of Rev. John Clark[6] and Maria E. (Evertson) Brigham; born in Brooklyn, N. Y., 14 Oct., 1850; married there, 9 Oct., 1873, Emma Jocelyn Wilde, born 9 Sept., 1851, in Brooklyn; died in East Orange, N. J., 24 Nov., 1904. He is a manufacturer, doing business in New York City and resides in East Orange, N. J.; received an academic education.

Children:
   i Lowell Irving[8], b. in Rutherford, N. J., 14 June, 1875; church organist, and res. with father.
   ii Florence, b. in Brooklyn, 6 Dec., 1880.

654 HON. LEWIS ALEXANDER[7], son of Harry[6] and Sarah (Bowman) Brigham; born in Chatham, N. Y., 2 Jan., 1831; died in Bergen, (Jersey City) N. J., 19 Feb., 1885; married 6 Nov., 1855, Elizabeth Ann, daughter of Jacob Van Winkle, born in Bergen, 4 Oct., 1835; died in Jersey City, 20 Sept., 1881. He was graduated A. B. from Hamilton College 1849; taught school in Albany and Monticello, N. Y.; had a private school in Bergen while studying law; lawyer in New York City, Member of Congress from New Jersey in 1878-1880.

Children, born in Bergen:
   i Louis Francis[8], b. 29 Aug., 1857; d. April, 1892; m. 26 May, 1881, Lavina Frost; civil engineer and surveyor. Ch.:
     1 *Jennie Louise*[9], b. 29 Aug., 1882.
   ii Charles Frederick, b. 16 Aug., 1859; d. 30 Oct., 1862.
   iii Harry Van Winkle, b. 9 Aug., 1861; res. unm., Jersey City; with " Hudson Co. Gas Co."
   iv Bertie, b. 12 March, 1864; d. 6 May, 1864.
   v Margaret S., b. 3 Sept., 1865; unm. 1903.
   vi Arthur, b. 19 Jan., 1868; m. 30 Oct., 1890, Ella Woodhull Brown; connected with " The Provident Institution for Savings " in Jersey City, where res. Ch.:
     1 *Arthur*[9], b. 12 June, 1892; 2 *Lula Brown*, b. 25 Jan., 1898.
   vii William Clarence, b. 8 May, 1872; m. 30 Oct., 1893, Anna Chapin; connected with the Inspection Dept. of U. S. " Rural Free Delivery "; res. Trenton, N. J. Ch.:
     1 *William C., Jr.*[9], b. 1 Aug., 1895; 2 *Harold Frederick*, b. 25 May, 1897; 3 *Lewis Maitland*, b. 24 Oct., 1900.

655 JOHN CALVIN[7], son of Harry[6] and Sarah (Bowman) Brigham; born in Chatham, N. Y., 15 Aug., 1833; died in New York City, 21 Jan., 1869; married 15 Jan., 1856, Anna E. Titus of Brooklyn, N. Y. He enlisted on the 8th of June, 1861 in the 9th N. Y. Vols., and was honorably discharged 16 July, 1862; resided in New York City. The male line is extinct.

Children, born in New York City:
   i Catherine A.[8], b. 24 Oct., 1856; d. in Newburgh, N. Y., 14 July, 1903; m. 1879, Francis F. Clark. Ch. (Clark):
     1 *Frank Brigham*[9], d. y.

ii Phœbe Elizabeth, b. 8 Jan., 1859; m. 1887, Rev. William E. Scofield of the M. E. Church) of Greenwich, Conn.; she taught 12 years in the public schools of Brooklyn. Ch. (Scofield):
  1 *Alice Brigham*[9], b. 20 Feb., 1890.
  2 *Gertrude E.*, b. 3 Aug., 1894.
iii Anna R., b. 22 Dec., 1861; d. ————; m. 1884, Benj. W. Martin of Brooklyn, N. Y. Ch. (Martin):
  1 *Edna G.*[9], b. 1884; 2 *Harold W.*, b. 1891; 3 *Herbert S.*, b. 1897.

656 ELIZABETH ANN[7], daughter of Rufus[6] and Elizabeth (Duncan) Brigham; born in Ackworth, N. H., 18 March, 1819; died there, 10 Dec., 1865; married, 11 Sept., 1849, Daniel A. Ryder, born 24 July, 1821; died in Ackworth, 8 Dec., 1868; he married (2) Mrs. Harriet Dunham and had a daughter who died young. Was a farmer of Ackworth.

Children (Ryder), born in Ackworth:
  i Herbert Daniel[8], b. 12 Nov., 1850; m. 30 Nov., 1881, Margaret E. Ball, b. 3 July, 1861, in Springfield, Vt.; was grad. Dartmouth Coll., 1876; A. D. Phi.; Principal of High Schools in Springfield and in Bellows Falls, Vt., 1876-1887; studied law and practiced in Bellows Falls, where res.; has held many town offices; is County Examiner of Schools. Ch., b. in Bellows Falls:
    1 *Jessie Elizabeth*[9], b. 18 Feb., 1884.
    2 *Margaret Sarah*, b. 26 April, 1885.
    3 *Helen Winifred*, b. 27 June, 1887.
    4 *Charlotte Divoll*, b. 4 Sept., 1889.
    5 *Katherine Foster*, b. 26 July, 1895.
    6 *Daniel Franklin*, b. 9 Jan., 1900.
    7 *Mary Scott*, b. 18 June, 1904.
  ii Elizabeth, b. 7 Aug., 1852; m. 6 April, 1880, James E. White of Springfield, Vt.; he is a farmer, and owns 600 acres; has been St. Representative; does a large probate business, and has held various town offices. Ch. (White):
    1 *Ralph Herbert*[9], b. 1 Jan., 1884; d. 1 Sept., 1895.
  iii Clarence Delmere, b. 9 Feb., 1855; d. in Abingdon, Ill., 19 Sept., 1878.
  iv Helen Maria, b. 17 Feb., 1857; m. Osman S. Ellison of Springfield, Vt., who d. May, 1888; she res. Worcester, Mass. Ch. (Ellison):
    1 *Edith Helen*[9], b. 30 May, 1878; m. William E. Putnam; res. Birmingham, Ala.

657 MARTHA LUCINA[7], daughter of Rufus[6] and Elizabeth (Duncan) Brigham; born in Ackworth, N. H., 23 Jan., 1831; married 8 June, 1854, David C. Anderson of Windham, N. H., born 26 June, 1826. He is a farmer.

Children (Anderson), born in Ackworth:
  i Mary Estelle[8], b. 9 Nov., 1855; m. James F. Dickey, a merchant of Holyoke, Mass. Ch. (Dickey):
    1 *Christine E.*[9], b. 1887.
  ii Walter Harvey, b. 7 Nov., 1857; d. 13 May, 1859.

iii Emma Elizabeth, b. 19 Sept., 1859; m. Herbert N. Harding, a
merchant of Little Falls, Minn. Ch. (Harding).
1 *Bertha A.⁹;* 2 *Glen S.;* 3 *Ruth A.*
iv George Weston, b. 1 Sept., 1861; m. Minnie E. Mitchell of
Boston, where he res.; was grad. Williams Coll., 1886; is a brilliant
lawyer in Boston, where he was six years on the school board.
Ch.:
1 *Clara M.⁹;* 2 *Robert D.*
v Alice Lucinda, b. 29 Jan., 1864; unm.; res. Windham.

658 WILLARD PROCTOR⁷, son of Capt. Aaron⁶ and Susan
(Proctor) Brigham; born in Alstead, N. H., 25 Aug., 1835; married 5 Feb., 1865, Mary J., daughter of Lucius and Cynthia
(Clay) Taft of Keene, N. H., born in Putney, Vt., 14 March,
1842; died 6 Jan., 1895. Was a farmer of Marlboro, N. H.,
thence to Surrey, N. H., and now resides with his son.

Children, born in Marlboro, N. H.:
i Albert W.⁸, b. 17 June, 1869; m. 19 Oct., 1892, Clara M. Stone
of Bellows Falls, Vt., b. in Keene, N. H., 20 Nov., 1872; in
1905 res. Walpole, N. H.; fireman on the Fitchburg Ry. Ch.:
1 *Mary Louise⁹,* b. 17 Sept., 1898.
2 *Albert Stone,* b. 13 April, 1902.
ii Belle E., b. 31 March, 1874; m. 8 May, 1901, Selwyn I. Carter,
b. 20 Oct., 1869; res. Laurel, N. H. Ch. (Carter):
1 *James Brigham⁹.*

659 MARY ELIZABETH⁷, daughter of William⁶ and Alethea
(Bream) Brigham; born 29 Jan., 1823, in Virginia; married 5 Sept.,
1841, Rev. Stuart Robinson, D. D. In 1903 she resided a widow
in Louisville, Ky.

Children (Robinson):
i Martha Porter⁸, b. 2 Sept., 1846; d. 2 Dec., 1891; m. Bennet H.
Young. Ch. (Young):
1 *Mary P.⁹,* b. 7 April, 1867; m. 12 Oct., 1892, Burt McVay
Allison, b. 7 Oct., 1864; d. 25 Jan., 1905; she res. s. p.,
a widow, in Cincinnati, O.
2 *Stuart Robinson,* b. Aug., 1868; d. 26 Nov., 1901; m. Elizabeth Wymond; s. p.
3 *Lawrence Andrew,* b. 23 May, 1870; m. 11 Jan., 1894, Mabel
Wheeler, b. 2 Sept., 1872; res. Chicago. Ch.: i Henry
Wheeler¹⁰, b. 2 Dec., 1894; ii Alice, b. 23 May, 1898; iii
Lawrence Robinson, b. 8 Feb., 1903.
4 *Josephine,* b. 10 July, 1873; d. 4 June, 1892.
ii Lawrence Carr, b. 15 March, 1845; d. 2 Oct., 1869; m. Amelia
Owsley. Ch.:
1 *Lalla R.⁹,* m. Embry L. Swearingen; res. Louisville, Ky. Ch.
(Swearingen): i Amelia¹⁰; ii Lalla; iii George.
iii Elizabeth, b. 7 Feb., 1855; m. John G. Cecil. Ch. (Cecil):
1 *Mary⁹;* 2 *Stuart;* 3 *Martha;* 4 *Russell;* and 2 who d. y.

660 LAVINIA VIRGINIA PATRICK⁷, daughter of William⁶
and Alethea (Bream) Brigham; born in West Virginia, 22 April,

1825; died in Denver, Colo., 30 Sept., 1894; married 17 June, 1845, William Chauncey Brooks of Charleston, West Va., Frankfort and Louisville, Ky.

Children (Brooks), the 8 younger born in Louisville:
    i Walter Boone[8], b. in Charleston, 1 May, 1846; m. Money Blatterman; res. Charleston. Ch.:
        1 *George B.[9]; 2 Eleanor; 3 Walter.*
    ii Alethea[8], b. in Frankfort, 20 Oct., 1848; m. 1873, Charles H. Small of Charleston, b. 1842; res. in Denver. Ch. (Small), b. in Charleston:
        1 *Lavinia Alethea Brigham Brooks[9],* b. 14 Aug., 1876; a teacher in Denver.
        2 *Charles H.,* b. 28 Oct., 1879; d. 13 Sept., 1904.
    m Lavinia, d. in infancy.
    iv Fanny Oden, b. 26 Feb., 1854; m. Benjamin L. James; res. s. p., Denver; author of several books.
    v Mary, d. in infancy.
    vi William Brigham, b. 1 Jan., 1858; unm., res. Chichuachua, Mex.
    vii Chauncey, d. in infancy.
    viii Nona Lovell, b. 22 March, 1861; unm., res. Denver; an ordained minister.
    ix Frederick, d. y.
    x Henry Frederick, b. 12 April, 1866; m. Louise McNamara; res. s. p., Denver.
    xi Hallie, d. in infancy.

661 BETSEY M.[7], daughter of George[6] and Betsey (Morse) Brigham; born in Groton, Mass., 10 May, 1811; died 21 Feb., 1836; married 12 April, 1834, Jonathan Preston of Boston.

Children (Preston), born in Boston:
    i George Brigham[8], b. 15 Feb., 1836; m. (1) 28 April, 1859, Annie E. Merrill, who d. 17 Oct., 1867; m. (2) 24 July, 1871, Mary F. (Bowen) Merrill (sister of first wife); res. Medford, Mass. Ch. (by first wife):
        1 *Edith[9],* b. 20 Sept., 1860.
        2 *John M.,* b. 9 Feb., 1863; m. 1889, Carrie Barker; 3 ch.
        3 *Jonathan,* b. 29 May, 1865; m. 1891, Mary L. Waggott; s. p., 1903.
        4 *Fannie,* b. 10 Sept., 1867; unm., 1903.
        Ch. (by second wife):
        5 *Ethel,* b. 16 March, 1874.
        6 *George B.,* b. 30 July, 1876.
        7 *Charles W.,* b. 16 Dec., 1881.

662 GEORGE DEXTER[7], son of George[6] and Betsey (Morse) Brigham; born in Groton, Mass., 2 May, 1813; died there, Dec., 1892; married 23 April, 1837, Mary Jane, daughter of Isaac and Nancy (Edgell) Brigham, of Groton, who died in 1895; was town clerk and J. P. in Groton many years.

Children, born in Groton:
    i Betsey[8].
    ii Emily, b. 12 Oct., 1840.

   iii Emily Jane, res. Washington, D. C.
   iv Ellen M., m. Col. Daniel Needham of Groton.
   v George E., res. Boston.
   vi Dexter.
   vii Ida.
   viii William K., res. Meriden, Conn.

663 EMELINE[7], daughter of George[6] and Betsey (Morse) Brigham; born in Groton, Mass., 18 April, 1815; died 7 Aug., 1903; married, 29 Nov., 1838, Johnson Carter, son of Josiah and Ruth (Kilburn) Burrage of Leominster, Mass., born there, 20 Jan., 1816; died 6 April, 1881. Was a merchant of Boston of the old firm of J. M. Beebe & Co., in which business he acquired a fortune.

Children (Burrage):
   i Frances Morse[8], b. 18 Dec., 1839; m. Benjamin J. Lang of 8 Brimmer St., Boston, who is at the head of the musical profession in Boston; he is an organist, composer, director, etc. Ch. (Lang):
      1 *Margaret Rosamond[9];* 2 *Malcolm.*
   ii Edward Carter, b. 13 June, 1841; m. Julia L. Severance; is with the Boston Safe Deposit and Trust Co. Ch.:
      1 *Severance[9]*, Prof. of Sanitary Science in Purdue Univ., Lafayette, Ind., and an author.
      2 *Caroline;* 3 *Emeline;* 4 *Bessie,* d. y.
   iii Herbert Emery, b. 14 Dec., 1845; m. Ruby M. Childs; res. Boston. Ch.:
      1 *Francis[9]*, with Boston Safe Deposit & Trust Co.
      2 *Harry,* Prest. Eliot National Bank, Boston.
      3 *Alice;* 4 *Eleanor.*
   iv Helen, b. 10 July, 1847; m. John W. Carter. Ch. (Carter):
      1 *Lucy[9];* 2 *Richard;* 3 *Margaret;* 4 *Philip.*
   v Emma, b. 8 Dec., 1850.
   vi Marion, b. 18 Jan., 1853; m. 12 Jan., 1887, Charles T.[8] Morse, son of 664.

664 MARY LORING[7], daughter of George[6] and Betsey (Morse) Brigham; born in Groton, Mass., 2 Nov., 1823; died 28 Feb., 1856; married 20 Dec., 1843, Gardner Morse, a prominent citizen of New Haven, Conn.

Children (Morse):
   i Elliot Howe[8], b. 31 July, 1846; m. 15 April, 1879, Grace Adele Bowns. Ch.:
      1 *John M.[9],* b. 22 Feb., 1881; 2 *Gardner W.,* b. 30 Nov., 1883; 3 *Dorothea H.,* b. 1 Sept., 1887.
   ii Mary Adelaide, b. 5 June, 1848.
   iii Joseph Bulkeley, b. 3 Oct., 1850; m. (1) 14 Sept., 1875, Annie Basset, who d. 19 April, 1881; m. (2) 18 May, 1898, Bessie May Jones. Ch. (by first wife):
      1 *Stephen[9],* b. 20 July, 1879; d. 27 July, 1886.
      2 *Julia A.,* b. 26 March, 1881.

Ch. (by second wife):
3 *Joseph B.*, b. 26 April, 1899.
iv Charles Theodore, b. 4 April, 1853; m. 12 Jan., 1887, Marion
Burrage, dau. of 663.
v Reginald Brigham, b. 9 Aug., 1854; d. 5 March, 1855.

665 THEODORE[7], son of George[6] and Betsey (Morse) Brigham; born in Groton, Mass., 29 June, 1833; killed by a cyclone,
27 April, 1899; married, 2 Jan., 1868, Sarah F. Terry of Kingston, N. Y.

He enlisted in the United States Navy in 1857 and went to the
Mediterranean; enlisted in the Civil War in the 6th Mass. Vols.
and was in the Baltimore Riot. After the war was a merchant
at Napanock, N. Y. and in 1872 removed to Kirksville, Mo.,
where was city alderman, and County Treasurer. He resided
finally in Kansas City, Mo.; was a very religious man.

Children:
    i Stella F.[8], b. 15 Oct., 1868; d. 27 Sept., 1888.
    ii Harriet E., b. 12 Aug., 1872; d. 1 Aug., 1873.
    iii Edwin Terry, b. 12 Feb., 1874; m. Bessie Sheets of Paris, Ill.;
    Asst. Supt. of Helping Hand Inst., Kansas City, Mo. Ch.:
    1 *Ralph[9]*; 2 *Lawrence.*
    iv Herbert D., b. 4 Oct., 1876; m. Maud G. Wing.
    v Theodore V., b. 17 April, 1881; at Denver Univ.
    vi Mabel J., b. 10 Jan., 1883; d. 20 Jan., 1898.

666 CHARLES SUMNER[7], son of George[6] and Betsey
(Morse) Brigham; born in Groton, Mass., 15 Sept., 1835; mar-
ried, 17 Aug., 1859, Caroline Eliza Seymour, born in Salem, N.
Y., 2 Jan., 1840. Is a business man of Napanock, N. Y.

Children, born in Napanock:
    i Florence Margaret[8], b. 12 Sept., 1860.
    ii Ralph Sumner, b. 25 March, 1862; m. 1 Feb., 1888, Ellen Cush-
    ing Ransom of Tonawanda, N. Y.; is a designer in Topeka,
    Kan. Ch.:
    1 *Helen Ransom[9]*, b. 28 May, 1890.
    iii Jennie Seymour, b. 23 May, 1866; m. 12 June, 1888, Ellis L.
    Martling; res. Atchison, Kan. Ch. (Martling):
    1 *Merrifield G.[9]*, b. 11 Oct., 1890.
    iv Ernest Shattuck, b. 1 June, 1868; theater manager; res. Atch-
    ison.
    v Archibald Rutherford, b. 17 Dec., 1869; theater manager; res.
    Fremont, Neb.

667 HENRY[7], son of Capt. Daniel[6] and Nancy (Gates) Brigham; born in Marlboro, Mass., 4 Oct., 1811; died in Savannah,
Ga., 8 Jan., 1883; married (1) 6 Nov., 1843, Mary H. Bemis,
who died 15 Sept., 1849; married (2) 22 Sept., 1851, Mary Catherine O'Brien, who died 4 June, 1887. Resided in Savannah.

Child (by first wife):
  i Sarah Warren⁸, b. 2 Sept., 1845; d. 17 May, 1903.
Children (by second wife):
  ii Henry Hartstene, b. 16 July, 1855; m. 22 Oct., 1879, Minnie
    Louise Day; res. E. Orange, N. J. Ch.:
      1 *Henry Day⁹*, b. 2 June, 1881; 2 *Mary Lester*, b. 4 March, 1886.
  iii Mary Harcourt, b. 17 Jan., 1858; d. Aug., 1866.
  iv Nancy Gates, b. 28 July, 1860.
  v James Harcourt, b. 28 June, 1862; d. Jan., 1866.
  vi William Sinclair, b. 1 May, 1864; d. 23 May, 1906; m. 26
    April, 1894, Heda Forster Schultz; res. Murray Hill, N. J.
    Ch.:
      1 *Gertrude Louise⁹*, b. 29 Jan., 1895.
      2 *Helen Sinclair*, b. 10 Nov., 1898.
  vii Clayton Harcourt, b. 17 Jan., 1866; d. 28 July, 1897.
  viii Kate O'Brien, b. 15 Sept., 1869.
  ix Harcourt, b. 29 Aug., 1873.

668 DENNISON⁷, son of Capt. Daniel⁶ and Nancy (Gates)
Brigham; born in Marlboro, Mass., 23 May, 1816; died there,
26 April, 1874; married 3 May, 1844, Sarah, daughter of Jonathan and Sarah (Clark) Weeks, born in Marlboro, 19 Dec., 1819;
died in Malden, Mass., 23 June, 1883. Resided on the tannery site
of Samuel in Marlboro.

Children, born in Marlboro:
  i George Henry⁸, b. 26 Feb., 1846; m. 11 Feb., 1868, Sarah E.
    Rockwood; res. Marlboro.
  ii Charles Dennison, b. 25 Jan., 1848; m. 16 May, 1870, Ellen
    Christian; res. Marlboro.
  iii Sarah Elizabeth, b. 25 Nov., 1849; d. 13 Jan., 1874.
  iv Mary Bemis, b. 8 Sept., 1851; d. 13 Aug., 1877, s. p.; m. 20
    Dec., 1871, James V. Schermerhorn.
  v Kate Hartwell, b. 16 June, 1853; d. 21 July, 1867.
  vi Nellie Gates, b. 13 Feb., 1857; m. 13 March, 1879, James V.
    Schermerhorn, widower of her sister Mary; res. Malden, Mass.
    Ch. (Schermerhorn):
      1 *Mary Gates⁹*; 2 *Lyman Gibbs*.
  vii Charlotte Warren, b. 2 Feb., 1859; m. 6 Oct., 1881, Arthur A.
    Brigham, son of 670.

669 EUGENE WINSLOW⁷, son of Winslow⁶ and Elizabeth
(Larkin) Brigham; born in Marlboro, Mass., 21 Dec., 1833; mar-
ried 29 Nov., 1855, Caroline Frances, daughter of Elijah Stearns.
He is a merchant in Marlboro and Manchester, N. H.

Children:
  i Edward Winslow⁸, b. 25 Jan., 1857; d. 19 Sept., 1858.
  ii Eugene Carroll, b. 16 Dec., 1860; m. 12 Sept., 1892, Fannie
    Bell, dau. of Holmes Pettee, b. in Manchester, 9 July, 1861; d.
    23 Aug., 1901; a commercial traveler, and res. Manchester.
  iii Martha Alice, b. 24 April, 1865; m. 28 Feb., 1901, Charles G.
    Ranno; res. Manchester.

iv Ella Frances, b. 18 May, 1867; m. 26 June, 1889, Nathaniel Doane,
Jr., a merchant of Manchester. Ch. (Doane):
1 *Allen N.*, d. y.; 2 *Ray Winslow*, b. 11 Sept., 1892; 3 *Nathaniel*, b. 20 June, 1894.

670 JOHN WINSLOW[7], son of Col. Aaron[6] and Sally (Fay)
Brigham; born in Marlboro, Mass., 4 Sept., 1825; died 9 Oct.,
1901; married 4 July, 1852, Mary Rebecca, daughter of Samuel
Putnam of Worcester, Mass.; born 25 Sept., 1828; died 9 March,
1885. Was a farmer and ice dealer of Marlboro.

Children, born in Marlboro:
  i Arthur Amber[8], b. 6 Oct., 1856; m. 6 Oct., 1881, Charlotte W.*
Brigham, dau. of 668; b. in Marlboro, 2 Feb., 1859; he was graduated Massachusetts Agricultural College, 1878; Professor of
Agriculture in Imperial Agric. Coll. Sapporo, Japan, 1888-1893;
studied in George Augustus Univ., Göttingen, Ger., 1894. Ch.,
the eldest b. in Marlboro:
1 *Reuben*[9], b. 13 Dec., 1887; 2 *Ruth*, b. 12 Sept., 1892.
 ii John Putnam, b. 4 Aug., 1859; d. 27 Sept., 1859.
iii Walter Irving, b. 10 Oct., 1863; d. 30 Sept., 1864.
 iv Lottie Maria, b. 25 Jan., 1865; m. 16 Sept., 1891, Edward N.
Stratton, b. 18 Aug., 1866; grad. Mass. Agricul. Coll.; a farmer
of Marlboro. Ch. (Stratton):
1 *Edward Winslow*[9], b. 16 Dec., 1900.
  v Anna Rebecca, b. 9 May, 1867; d. 5 May, 1886.

671 HUMPHREY[7], son of Ashley[6] and Mary (Bigelow)
Brigham; born in Marlboro, Mass., 5 Jan., 1830; died Dec., 1902;
married 1 Jan., 1863, Ellen, daughter of Benjamin F. Gleason.
Was a shoe manufacturer in Hudson, Mass.

Children, the eldest born in Rockbottom, Mass.:
  i Frank L.[8], b. 2 April, 1864; d. 22 March, 1894.
 ii Whitney Gleason, b. 3 July, 1868; m. 21 June, 1894, Gertrude L.,
dau. of John Peters, b. in Hudson, 26 Dec., 1868; was grad. Dartmouth Coll., B. S., 1892; is a C. E. in Hudson, Mass. Ch.:
1 *Dorothy A.*[9], b. 14 Feb., 1897; 2 *Alfred G.*, b. 9 Dec., 1900.
iii Louisa F., b. 25 Jan., 1872; m. 25 Jan., 1894, John Melvin Lewis,
b. in Maine, 11 Dec., 1870; res. Hudson. Ch. (Lewis):
1 *Franklin Brigham*[9], b. 2 Oct., 1894.

672 HARRIETTE AUGUSTA[7], daughter of William Pitt[6]
and Lavinia (Baker) Brigham; born in Marlboro, Mass., 29 Jan.,
1836; married 1 Jan., 1857, Hon. S. Herbert, son of Samuel Howe,
born in Marlboro, 21 Dec., 1835.

He is a shoe manufacturer in Marlboro; has been selectman,
Representative to the General Court, member of the Governor's
Council, and was the first mayor of the city of Marlboro.

Children (Howe), born in Marlboro:
  i Alice Baker[8], b. 19 Dec., 1857; d. 19 Oct., 1858.
 ii Louis Porter, b. 29 May, 1858; m. 1 Jan., 1887, India Howe
Arnold; Supt. of a shoe manufactory; is a Knight Templar.

iii Charlotte Adelaide, b. 9 May, 1861; m. Oscar H. Stevens, a
dentist; res. Marlboro.   Ch. (Stevens):
1 *Herbert H.*; 2 *Oscar L.;* 3 *Louis W.*
iv Annie Brigham, b. 15 June, 1871; d. 7 Sept., 1887.

673   HENRIETTA AUGUSTA[7], daughter of William Pitt[6]
and Lavinia (Baker) Brigham; born in Marlboro, Mass., 29 Jan.,
1836; married 30 Nov., 1854, Freeman, son of William Holyoke,
born in Marlboro, 18 Aug., 1818; died there, 24 April, 1876. He
was a carpenter and a market-man, and they resided in Marlboro.

Children (Holyoke), born in Marlboro:
i Charles Freeman[8], b. 27 Dec., 1855; m. Blanche E., dau. of
Thomas Corey, and gr.-dau. of 408; is Treas. of Marlboro Savings Bank. Ch
1 *Thomas C.*; 2 *Charles F.*
ii Frank Henry, b. 6 Jan., 1857; d. 15 April, 1865.
iii Adaline Lavinia, b. 25 June, 1862; m. 31 March, 1885, Walter
P., son of John A. Frye; b. 7 Feb., 1863; he is a shoe mfr. in
Marlboro; a Knights Templar. Ch. (Frye):
1 *John F.*, b. 6 April, 1886; 2 *Robert P.*, b. 18 Aug., 1887; 3
Russell Brigham, b. 6 June, 1889.

674   HENRY AUGUSTINE[7], son of William Pitt[6] and Lavinia (Baker) Brigham; born in Marlboro, Mass., 21 Aug., 1837;
married Mary Plank.   Is an engineer and mining expert, and resides in California.

Children:
i Emma Louise[8], b. in Nevada City, Cal., 22 Sept., 1862; m. Walter
S. Bigelow of Oakland, Cal., b. 19 Nov., 1859   Ch. (Bigelow), b.
in Oakland:
1 *Ethel Lavinia*, b. 16 Jan., 1885; 2 *Ruth.*
ii Charles Francis, b. in Sweetland, Cal., 24 March, 1864; m. **Ida**
B. Campbell; is Supt. of a shoe factory in Marlboro. Ch., b.
in Marlboro:
1 *Eleanor M.*, b. 7 May, 1887; 2 *Henry,* b. 2 Sept., 1888; 3
Carl, b. 4 May, 1890; 4 *Robert,* b. 1 Dec., 1894.
iii Edward Bigelow, b. in No. San Juan, Cal., 26 Nov., 1870; m.
1895, ——————; res. Baker City, Ore.
iv William P., b. in No. Columbia, Cal., 7 March, 1875.

675   ALFRED ADAMS[7], son of William Pitt[6] and Lavinia
(Baker) Brigham; born in Marlboro, Mass., 12 March, 1848;
married, Eliza D. Marsh.   Is a foreman in a shoe factory **in**
Marlboro, where he resides.

Children, born in Marlboro:
i Frank LeRoy[8], b. 21 Nov., 1869; m. Nellie A. Stephenson. Ch.:
1 *Dorothy L.*, b. 17 Feb., 1891.
2 *Kenneth Stephenson,* b. 30 April, 1896.
ii Gertrude A., b. 16 Sept., 1872; m. 1 June, 1896, Reuben Leonard;
res. Sutton, Mass.

William Dexter Brigham, of Boston (676)

676 WILLIAM DEXTER[7], son of James Madison[6] and Mary F. (Sawin) Brigham; born in Boston, Mass., 17 Oct., 1851; married in Dorchester, Mass., 7 Oct., 1885, Lizzie, daughter of Francis and Rebecca C. (Greene) Fuller of Boston; born 17 Oct., 1856.

Mr. Brigham was born in Bumstead Pl., Boston, but has lived in Dorchester for the last 40 years; has been connected with the Dennison Mfg. Company for 37 years, and has been a member of the firm since its incorporation, in 1878. Is deeply interested in religious work; for the last 27 years has been clerk of the old historic Second Church in Dorchester; is a member of the Boston Congregational Club and an ardent Republican.

Children, born in Dorchester:
  i Ernest Fuller[8], b. 11 Oct., 1886; d. 24 Aug., 1887.
  ii Arthur Dexter, b. 16 Dec., 1890.
  iii William Winthrop, b. 9 May, 1893.
  iv Stanley Fuller, b. 8 Jan., 1895.

677 LINCOLN LAFAYETTE[7], son of Martin[6] and Mary (Barnes)* Brigham; born in Marlboro, Mass., 9 March, 1829; died 1899, æ. 69 years and 10 mos.; married 1851, Emily C. Perham, born 1833.

Children:
  i Samuel[8], b. 17 Aug., 1854; m. 13 June, 1884, Anna E. Holcomb, b. 18 Feb., 1866; a salesman; res. Hartford, Conn. Ch.:
    1 *Alfred H.[9]*, b. 19 April, 1885.
    2 *George H. O.*, b. 26 March, 1887.
    3 *May R.*, b. 26 May, 1889; d. 30 Sept., 1889.
    4 *Nettie May*, b. 1 Feb., 1893.
    5 *Clarence D.*, b. 3 July, 1898; d. Feb., 1899.
    6 *Addie L.*, b. 19 Feb., 1902.
    7 *Robert E.*, and 8 *Ada*, twins, d. y.
  ii Walter E., b. in Amherst, Mass., 1856; m. Harriet ———— b. 14 Oct., 1863; res. W. Hartford. Ch.:
    1 *Lucy[9]*, b. 2 Feb., 1884; 2 *Myrtle Edna*, b. 18 Nov., 1892.
  iii Ernest A. E., res. Albany Ave., Hartford.
  iv Emma L., m. Charles Morgan of Brooklyn, N. Y.

678 COL. HENRY HOBART[7], son of Henry[6] and Mary (Hobart) Brigham; born in Abington, Mass., 22 Jan., 1813; died in Whitman, Mass., 16 June, 1879; married (1) 16 Oct., 1834, Mary Ripley, daughter of John and Joan (Phillips) Corthell, born in Abington, 19 Dec., 1816; died in Whitman, 14 July, 1847; married (2) 12 April, 1854, Drusilla B., daughter of Daniel Keen, born in Maine, 17 June, 1824.

Mr. Brigham was Lieut.-Col. of the 3d Regt. 1st Brigade, 5th Div. Mass. Militia, from 1836-1839; was early a prominent anti-

* Or Eunice Gates.

slavery man, and for a long time Secretary of Plymouth Co. Anti-Slavery Society; in 1855 became a manufacturer of tacks and nails and built up a large business; retired after 30 years.

Children (by first wife), born in Whitman:
806   i Andrew Corthell[8], b. 5 May, 1837.
       ii Joseph Henry Hobart, b. 22 June, 1844; d. s. p., 17 Jan., 1866; m. Eliza Ann Cood.

679   CHARLES HASTINGS[7], son of Hastings[6] and Nancy (Spear) Brigham; born in Marlboro, Mass., 1 June, 1822; died there, 16 Jan., 1877; married (1) Nov., 1849, Jane B., daughter of William Felton, born in Marlboro, 25 Feb., 1822; died there, 10 Oct., 1869; married (2) 1 June, 1870, Mrs. Kessie, daughter of John Wood and widow of Joseph P. Johnson; born 17 Oct., 1838. By her first marriage she had a son and daughter. Mr. Brigham was a shoemaker, and took out several patents in the leather business.

Children (by first wife), b. in Marlboro:
       i Charles H.[8], b. 3 Aug., 1852; m. June, 1879, Hattie A. Blodgess; res. Leominster, Mass.
       ii Eugene O., b. 25 July, 1855; m. April, 1878, Annie F., dau. of Dea. John F. Cotting of Marlboro; is Asst. Depot-master and tax collector in Marlboro. Ch.:
          1 *Charles H.[9]*, b. in Marlboro, 9 Feb., 1880.
       iii Morrill F., b. 5 April, 1857; committed suicide, 16 April, 1895; m. Jan., 1883, Mary E. Grant; one child.
Children (by second wife), born in Marlboro:
       iv Elbert I., b. 12 July, 1871.
       v Ruth M., b. 28 March, 1874.

680   WILLIAM EUSTACE[7], son of Hastings[6] and Nancy (Spear) Brigham; born in Marlboro, Mass., 10 Oct., 1823; died 6 Sept., 1894; married Lydia Russell Tobey of Sandwich, Mass., born 17 Oct., 1834.

Children, born in Marlboro:
       i Mary E.[8], b. 23 June, 1855; m. Mark Wesley Fay; a banker in St. Paul, Minn., where they res., s. p.
       ii Martha T., b. 5 Feb., 1858; m. C. F. Whitney.
       iii Eustace Hastings, b. 11 March, 1860; m. 8 April, 1885, Carrie M. Whitney in Marlboro, b. 20 Sept., 1861, in Marlboro; res. Winthrop, Mass. Ch., b. in Marlboro:
          1 *Alice Whitney[9]*, b. 3 Aug., 1886.
          2 *Nancy Sophia*, b. 31 July, 1892.
       iv Nancy Sophia, b. 29 Sept., 1862; m. 6 Sept., 1892, Herbert E. Murdock. Ch. (Murdock):
          1 *Russell B.[9]*, b. 7 Sept., 1893; 2 *Phyllis*, b. 15 Nov., 1895; 3 *Marjorie*, b. 3 Aug., 1897.
       v Anna E., b. 28 Feb., 1868; m. Charles H. Buckley of Delhi, N. Y.; res. St. Paul, Minn. Ch. (Buckley):
          1 *Fay[9]*, b. 13 April, 1890; 2 *Lydia*, b. 22 May, 1903.

681 NANCY SOPHIA[7], daughter of Hastings[6] and Nancy (Spear) Brigham; born in Marlboro, Mass., 12 Sept., 1825; died 31 March, 1891; married, 25 June, 1850, Thomas Emerson, son of Thomas Hapgood, born in Marlboro, 11 May, 1824.

Mr. Hapgood established the firm of Hapgood & Phelps, one of the first shoe factories in Marlboro; in 1862 removed to Providence, R. I. to employ convicts in shoemaking; thence, in 4 years to Sing Sing, N. Y. for the same business, where he was also an alderman for 6 years, when he declined further service. He was chairman of the Board of Education, etc.

Children (Hapgood), the 4 eldest born in Marlboro:
   i Alice Sophia[8], b. 29 April, 1851; m. George Washington Kiff of Sing Sing. Ch. (Kiff):
      1 *Howard H.[9]*, was grad. Wesleyan Univ.; 2 *Dorothy.*
   ii Frank Emerson, b. 29 April, 1856; d. 8 July, 1858.
   iii Fred Hastings, b. 12 March, 1859; d. 30 March, 1859.
   iv Ben Andrew, b. 12 June, 1860; m. Emma E. Layley of New York City.
   v Annie Yerington, b. in Providence, 22 July, 1863; m. Hiram R. Reynolds; res. Williamsport, Pa. Ch. (Reynolds):
      1 *Katherine[9]*.
   vi Edward Thomas, b. in Providence, 8 Dec., 1866; m. Elizabeth M. Smith.
   vii William Henry, b. in Sing Sing, 29 Dec., 1870; was grad. Cornell Univ.; res. Sing Sing.

682 MAJ. HENRY O.[7], son of Hastings[6] and Nancy (Spear) Brigham; born in Marlboro, Mass., 2 Sept., 1830; died in Detroit, Mich., 22 Jan., 1868; married 30 May., 1852, Mahala Jane, daughter of Lucas Bigelow, born in Marlboro, 4 Aug., 1833; died there, 11 May, 1886.

Major Brigham was educated at Norwich, Vt., Military Academy. He was a drummer boy in the Mexican War at 16 years of age; then became 1st Lieut.; then government clerk at Washington; in 1861, a paymaster in volunteer service; at the head of the Pay Dept. of the Gulf from 1863 to 1865; then in Regular Service, stationed at Detroit.

Child, born in Marlboro:
   i Hattie Josephine[8], b. 21 Aug., 1860; m. 13 Jan., 1887, Edward C. Hawkes of Newton Center, Mass., where resides. Ch. (Hawkes):
      1 *Frances B.[9]*; 2 *Jennie E.*; 3 *Marjorie A.*

683 DR. CHARLES BROOKS[7], son of William[6] and Margaret Austin (Brooks) Brigham; born in Boston, Mass., 17 Jan., 1845; died in San Francisco, Cal., 24 Aug., 1903; married 26 April, 1879, Alice W. Batcock of San Francisco.

Dr. Brigham was graduated from Harvard College A. B., 1866;

A. M., 1872; Nov., 1866, matriculated at the Harvard Medical School; April, 1869 was House Surgeon of the Boston City Hospital; M. D. Harvard, 1870; studied in Europe. Aug., 1870, was Surgeon-in-Chief " Ambulance Internationale Francaise de l'Ecole Forestiene de Nancy " and through 7 months of the Franco-Prussian War. President Thiers decorated him with " Legion of Honor " and the Emperor of Germany with the " Iron Cross," for his distinguished services. Also presented with cross of " International Society " and diploma for exceptional services. He published numerous surgical cases in France and England. In 1872 he removed to San Francisco, where he was surgeon to the French Hospital.

Children, the 2 youngest born in San Francisco:
  i Alice⁸, b. in Paris, France, 1880.
  ii William B.
  iii Katherine.

EIGHTH GENERATION

EIGHTH GENERATION

684 CHARLES BREWSTER[8], son of Col. Bela Brewster[7] and Abby (Whitney) Brigham; born in Delaware, Ont., 10 Aug., 1827; died in Chicago, Ill., 25 Dec., 1899; married 11 Nov., 1860, Sarah Ann, daughter of Job Galloway; born in Penn., 20 April, 1831.

He was an early settler of Chicago, where he dealt in real estate. He was a photographer by trade, and also musical. Was President of the Union Dispatch Co. before the fire of 1871.

Children, born in Chicago:
  i Gustavus Brewster[9], b. 30 May, 1863; m. Catherine, dau. of Dr. William Holton of Mt. Vernon, Ind. He was the leading baritone in the Hess Opera Co. in 1883; was with the Lillian Russell Opera Co. in 1884; author and librettist of the comic opera *Marcella,* and three other musical comedies which have had professional presentation; also *Kafoozalaam,* which was recently given in Chicago; another comic opera will be produced in the spring of 1907, *The Unkissed Son,* dealing with Dowie and Zion City. He occupies the position of superintendent of Agencies and Branch Stores with the Strohber Piano Co. in Chicago. Ch.:
    1 *Charles David[10],* b. 24 Aug., 1897; d. 3 March, 1899.
  ii Charles Frank, b. 11 May, 1867; m. 15 Sept., 1895, Annie E., dau. of Watson D. Crocker, Prest. and founder of Crocker Chair Co. of Sheboygan, Wis.; res. Superior, Wis., where he is secy. and treas. of Webster Mfg. Co. of Superior. Ch.:
    1 *Marion[10],* b. 9 Jan., 1897.
    2 *Jean,* b. 17 March, 1898.
    3 *Watson Crocker,* b. 30 Sept., 1901.
  iii Samuel Fred, b. 27 Jan., 1873; m. Ada, dau. of Frank G. Springer. He is of the firm of Brigham & Emrich in Chicago. Ch.:
    1 *Florence[10],* b. 23 Dec., 1897.
    2 *Frank Brewster,* b. 15 March, 1901.

685 CAPT. HENRY GUSTAVUS[8], son of Col. Bela Brewster[7] and Abby (Whitney) Brigham; born in Delaware, Ontario, 13 Sept., 1836; married, 13 Sept., 1871, Fanny M., daughter of Theodore Hazlett; born in Zanesville, O., 7 Nov., 1849. Was Capt. in the 107th N. Y. Vol. Regt., in the Civil War. A business man in Florida.

Children, born in Chicago:
  i Robert Seymour[9], b. 5 Sept., 1874; res. Des Moines, Ia.; m.
  ii Harry, b. 12 June, 1882.

686 ALDEN[8], son of Phineas[7] and Lydia (Wilkins) Brigham;

born in Marlboro, Mass., 25 June, 1809; died ————; married
Asenath Hastings.

Child, born in Marlboro:
  i Thomas B.⁹, b. 4 June, 1840; d. 20 March, 1901; m. 28 Nov.,
    1867, Madeline, dau. of Martin Kirwan; b. 19 April, 1848. Ch.,
    b. Marlboro:
      1 *Charles Alden*¹⁰, b. 1 Oct., 1868; res. unm., Whitman, Mass.
      2 *Clifton John*, b. 6 Sept., 1870; m. 14 May, 1896, Mary Bour-
        gious, b. 1875; he res. in Marlboro. Ch.: i Clifton William¹¹,
        b. 17 Feb., 1898; ii Herbert Joseph, b. 4 Nov., 1898; iii
        Ethel, b. 11 Dec., 1900; iv Evelyn, b. 19 Jan., 1903.
      3 *Madeline Gertrude*, b. 13 Dec., 1874; is m. and res. Marlboro.
      4 *Gerald Nelson*, b. 25 Nov., 1877; res. Marlboro, unm.
      5 *Mary Elizabeth*, b. 16 July, 1881; m. and res. Marlboro.
      6 *Annie Veronica*, b. 1 Aug., 1883; res. Marlboro.
      7 *Effie Amelia*, b. 20 July, 1886; res. Marlboro.
      8 *Thomas Benton*, b. 1 Aug., 1888; res. Marlboro, unm.
      9 *Asenath Hazel*, b. 27 April, 1895.

687 SIDNEY⁸, son of Phineas⁷ and Lydia (Wilkins) Brigham; born in Marlboro, Mass., 4 Aug., 1817; died in Richwood,
Minn., 30 April, 1878; married 8 June, 1839, Fanny N., daughter
of Richard Hemmingway; born 8 July, 1818; died in Spokane,
Wash., 24 Jan., 1892. Moved to Richwood in 1872, where he was
town treasurer and supt. of a shoe factory; was a temperance worker
and sung in the church choir. The male line is extinct.

Children, the elder born in Stow, Mass.; the 3 younger in Marlboro:
  i Lucy Sophia⁹, b. 2 July, 1840; d. 2 June, 1844.
  ii Sidney Eugene, b. 4 June, 1842; d. 23 Sept., 1844.
  m Clara Jane, b. 19 March, 1844; res. unm., Spokane.
  iv Amelia Rebecca, b. 10 Jan., 1846; m. 1 Jan., 1875, John H.
    Sutherland; s. p.
  v Mary Lucy, b. 9 Nov., 1848; d. 29 May, 1854.
  vi Richard Eugene, b. 17 Jan., 1851; d. 13 Sept., 1854.
  vii Hattie Marion, b. 2 Dec., 1853; m. 19 Dec., 1875, William A.,
    son of William Norcross; moved from Richwood to Spokane.
    Ch. (Norcross), b. in Minn.:
      1 *Mildred Carlton*¹⁰, b. 2 Oct., 1876; m. 1898, Leon H. Graham
        of Spokane; she is a literary worker.
      2 *Marion Brigham*, b. 11 Oct., 1880; d. 9 Feb., 1893.
  viii Nellie Frances, b. 27 Nov., 1855; m. 1876, Charles H., son of
    J. A. Potter of Detroit, Mich.; moved to Spokane. Ch. (Potter):
      1 *Sidney Brigham*¹⁰, b. in Minn., 10 Nov., 1882.
      2 *Millie Sutherland*, b. in Wash., 29 March, 1885.
      3 *Fred Dart*, b. 24 Sept., 1886; d. 18 Aug., 1887.
  ix Angie Sophia, b. 11 Nov., 1859; m. 1887, Curtis H. Dart of
    Spokane.

688 CYRUS⁸, son of Phineas⁷ and Lydia (Wilkins) Brigham;
born in Marlboro, Mass., 9 June, 1820; died there, 22 Dec., 1895;
married 17 Dec., 1840, Cynthia M., daughter of Lewis Bemis; born

Martyn Freeman Brigham, of Boston (693)

in Billerica, Mass., 5 Oct., 1824; died in Marlboro, 19 Jan., 1892. Resided in Marlboro.

Children, born in Marlboro:

    i Sarah Paulina⁹, b. 21 Feb., 1841; m. 3 April, 1884, George Balcom; res. Marlboro.

    ii Cynthia E., b. 13 Jan., 1843; m. 15 Sept., 1865, Albert H., son of Asa D. Perry; b. in Natick, Mass., 19 May, 1840; res. in Marlboro. Ch. (Perry):
       1 *Lillian Brigham*¹⁰, b. 28 Feb., 1874.

    iii Lydia F., b. 3 Oct., 1844; m. Jan., 1867, Timothy C., son of Eben Ordway of Marlboro. Ch. (Ordway), b. in Marlboro:
       1 *Frank Irvin*¹⁰, b. 17 June, 1869.
       2 *Cyrus*, b. 11 March, 1883.
       3 *Maud Frances*, b. 26 Aug., 1886.

    iv Martha Edwina, b. 19 Jan., 1847; m. Ashley Brigham, son of 395.

    v Mary Deborah, b. 1 Jan., 1849; m. 22 Feb., 1875, Samuel Alexander; res. Philadelphia.

    vi Cyrus Waldo, b. 17 Dec., 1850; m. Ellen N. Winch, b. in Framingham, Mass., 15 Oct., 1849; res. Marlboro. Ch.:
       1 *Archie Waldo*¹⁰, b. 29 March, and d. 27 Sept., 1870.
       2 *Cyrus Harrison*, b. 7 Jan., 1880.
       3 *Lester Eugene*, b. 29 Sept., 1881.
       4 *George William*, b. 10 June, 1885; d. 16 May, 1889.

    vii William Henry, b. 11 Dec., 1852; m. Margaret Cosgrove; a musician; res. s. p., Marlboro.

    viii Sidney Eugene, b. 28 March, 1855; m. 24 Dec., 1885, Nettie, dau. of Charles I. Forbush; is a musician and formerly the leader of the " Brigham Band "; res. Marlboro. Ch.:
       1 *Cynthia Mary*¹⁰, b. 25 Jan., 1887.
       2 *Sydney Eugene*, b. 16 July, 1889.

    ix Caroline E., b. 28 April, 1857; unm.

    x George Albert, b. 11 June, 1859; m. 17 March, 1885, Kate Lavalle; a musician; s. p.

    xi Harrison Ellsworth, b. 18 May, 1861; m. 1 Jan., 1882, Annie E., dau. of Willard Pond. Proprietor of " Harry E. Brigham Band "; res. Marlboro, s. p.

    xii Irvin, b. 19 April, 1864; d. 1 Aug., 1866.

    xiii Edith, b. 23 March, 1867; and d. 24 March, 1867.

689 **ELIZA J.**⁸, daughter of Willard⁷ and Betsey (Sherman) Brigham; born in Westboro, Mass., 8 Oct., 1813; died in W. Boylston, Mass., 28 Aug., 1894; married 4 March, 1839, Lyman, son of Abijah and Betsey (Burden) Putnam of Sutton, Mass.; born there, 28 Jan., 1813; died in Uxbridge, Mass., 24 May, 1902. A farmer and lived in Sutton.

Children (Putnam), born in Sutton:

    i Sarah J.⁹., b. 4 Jan. 1840; d. in Warwick, R. I., April, 1900; m. 1860, Van Buren Dorr. Ch. (Dorr):
       1 *Henry L.*¹⁰, res. Warwick, R. I.
       2 *George E.*, m. Emma Morrell; res. Warwick; 3 ch.

3 *Frederick F.*, m. Ellen Graves; res. Sutton; 3 ch.
4 *Amy J.*, m. Eben Crowell; res. Warwick; 6 ch.
5 *Julia A.*, m. William Sprague; res. Warwick; 1 ch.
6 *Minnie I.*, m. Charles Austin; res. Warwick; 1 ch.
ii Julia M., b. 31 Dec., 1846; m. Dec. 1867, William R. Foskett; res. a widow, in Uxbridge. Ch. (Foskett):
    1 *Albert L.*[10], b. 4 May, 1871; res. Uxbridge.
iii Laura A., b. 12 April, 1848; m. 21 April, 1870, Stephen C. Hall; res. a widow, in Greendale, Worcester, Mass. Ch. (Hall):
    1 *Walter A.*[10], b. 10 Aug., 1871; res. Worcester.
    2 *Arthur C.*, b. 4 Sept., 1873; res. W. Boyleston; m. 9 March, 1898, Lena Hurtle; 2 ch.
    3 *Robert T.*, b. 23 Aug., 1875; res. Worcester.
    4 *Charles C.*, b. 4 July, 1878; res. Worcester.
    5 *Lucius S.*, b. 8 April, 1880; res. Worcester.
    6 *Frank E.*, b. 27 Feb., 1889; res. Worcester.
iv Orison L., b. 17 Dec., 1850; d. 19 Sept., 1869.
v Emma A., b. 27 Nov., 1859; m. 20 June, 1883, Horace Porter Whipple; res. Whitinsville, Mass. Ch. (Whipple):
    1 *Amos Earle*[10], b. in W., 9 Nov., 1889.

690 ELI A.[8], son of Willard[7] and Betsey (Sherman) Brigham; born in Westboro, Mass., 1 July, 1820; died in Russell, Mass., 20 Feb., 1892; married (1) 28 Nov., 1844, Satira B., daughter of Stiles Stearns; born in Northbridge, Mass., 28 Feb., 1821; died in Blandford, Mass., 16 March, 1859; married (2) 17 Oct., 1860, Isabella, daughter of Patrick Gillespie; born in Camohy, Ireland, 6 Nov., 1836. He was a tanner and currier, and resided in Montague, Worcester, Blandford, and Russell, Mass.

Children (by first wife), the 3 younger born in Blandford:
  i Pliny Stearns[9], b. in Montague, Mass., 15 Oct., 1845; d. in Chicago, Ill., 12 Jan., 1881; m. 2 Dec., 1875, Sarah Elizabeth, dau. of Simeon Mayo; b. in Worcester, Mass., 21 Oct., 1853; res. Chicago, where a paying-teller in a bank. Ch., b. in Chicago:
    1 *Frank Pliny*[10], b. 24 March, 1877; m. 17 Sept., 1900, Fanny G. Paschal; res. E. St. Louis. Ch.: i Marjorie E.[11], b. 18 June, 1901; ii Frances E., b. 1903; d. *ibid.*
  ii Serviland Theodore, b. in Worcester, 28 Feb., 1847; d. 13 July, 1847.
  iii Edwin Eli, b. 6 Sept., 1850; d. in Springfield, Mass., 2 Nov., 1904, where interred; m. 16 July, 1876, Lizzie, dau. of William Foye; b. in Lockport, N. Y., 16 Feb., 1852; res. Chicago, Russell and E. Longmeadow, Mass.; a bookkeeper. Ch., the 2 elder b. in Chicago, 2 younger in E. Longmeadow:
    1 *Eli Edwin*[10], b. 18 April, 1877; m. 28 May, 1900, Ella C. Collins; res. Springfield.
    2 *Maud Mabel*, b. 18 Aug., 1881; m. 26 April, 1905, Frank T. Tate; res. Springfield.
    3 *Fred Willard*, b. in Russell, Mass., 27 Oct., 1883.
    4 *Franklin*, b. 24 Dec., 1885; d. 1885.
    5 *Grace Estella*, b. 12 Nov., 1887.
    6 *Viola Jessie*, b. 30 April, 1892.

iv Emma Satira, b. 12 June, 1853; m. 25 Dec., 1873, Sylvanus W., son of Ansel E. Brooks; res. Westfield, Mass. Ch. (Brooks), b. in Chicago:

1 *Cora Bell[9]*, b. 2 Sept., 1874; m. 1894, William Burlingame; res. Westfield. Ch. (Burlingame): Emma[11].

2 *Judson Oliver*, b. 30 Sept., 1876; m. Blanche H. Harding; res. Westfield.

3 *Frank Pliny*, b. 25 Oct., 1882; m. Jennie E. Williams.

4 *George Henry*, b. 29 Sept., 1887.

5 *Elsie Irene*, b. 15 Feb., 1891.

v Agnes Louise, b. 29 June, 1857; d. 19 Sept., 1857.

Children (by second wife), born in Russell, Mass.:

vi Henry Oscar, b. 31 July, 1861; m. Millie B., dau. of William Holmes; b. in Russell, 30 June, 1864; res. a mfr., in Westfield.

vii Mary Isabella, b. 1 Nov., 1863; m. George Murphy; res. Westfield.

viii Kate Elmira, b. 2 June, 1867; m. Homer B. Fletcher, b. Hamlin, Pa., 8 Feb., 1871; res. in Chicopee Falls, Mass. Ch. (Fletcher):

1 *Henry B.[10]*

ix Florence Gertrude, b. 20 Feb., 1870; d. 9 July, 1870.

x Cora Adelaide, b. 6 Oct., 1872; d. 14 June, 1893.

xi Nellie Ethel, b. 28 Sept., 1875; m. Everett Bogardus; res. in Chicopee Falls.

691 HANNAH L.[8], daughter of Willard[7] and Betsey (Sherman) Brigham; born in Westboro, Mass., 6 Feb., 1827; married 10 April, 1848, Joseph R. Danforth of Hardwick, Mass.; born 1819; died in Worcester, Mass., 4 Sept., 1880. She resides a widow in Morgan Park, Ill.

Children (Danforth):

i Susan W.[9], b. in Montague, Mass., 14 April, 1850; m. 20 Oct., 1873, Frank N. Wilder, Bank Cashier of Worcester, Mass.; b. 8 Aug., 1850. Ch. (Wilder).

1 *Ralph E.[10]*, b. 23 Feb., 1875; m. Charlotte White of Tracy, Ill., 20 Sept., 1900; a cartoonist on the Chicago *Record-Herald;* 1 ch.

2 *E. Josephine*, b. 4 Nov., 1879.

3 *Roland D.*, b. 23 May, 1888.

ii Ella J., b. in Worcester, Mass., 19 May, 1853; d. 3 Nov., 1856.

iii George L., b. in Ft. Wayne, Ind., 19 Nov., 1855; m. Catherine De Kay of Toledo, O.; res. Toledo. Ch.:

1 *Frederick E.[10]*, b. 3 Nov., 1883.

692 JOSEPH THOMAS[8], son of Joseph Clarendon[7] and Hannah C. (Lincoln) Brigham; born in Taunton, Mass., 1 Nov., 1829; died in Northfield, Mass., 12 Feb., 1904; married 17 Nov., 1854, Sarah Emily, daughter of Willard Stratton.

Children, born in Northfield:

i Infant[9], b. 6 Sept., 1857; d. 14 Sept., 1857.

ii Herbert Lincoln, b. 20 March, 1860; d. 1905; m. 31 Jan., 1900, Harriet M. Moody of Fitchburg, Mass.

iii Clara Elizabeth, b. 27 March, 1863; d. 23 July, 1894; m. 3

Aug., 1887, Edward E. Gallup of North Adams, Mass. Ch. (Gallup):

1 *Ruth Brigham*[10], b. 9 June, 1891.

iv Walter Joseph, b. 16 May, 1866; res. unm., in Northfield.

v Anna Augusta, b. 4 Feb., 1869; d. 21 Aug., 1894.

vi Alfred Clarendon, b. 28 Oct., 1872; d. 23 Jan., 1880.

vii Albert Sherman, b. 10 May, 1875; m. 10 May, 1899, Cora B. Lee; res. Dorchester, Mass. Ch.:

1 *Sherman L.*[10], b. 16 Nov., 1903.

viii Paul Printess, b. 26 March, 1884; in business in Boston.

693 * MARTYN FREEMAN[8], son of John[7] and Rebecca (Smith) Brigham; born in Whitingham, Vt., 19 Oct., 1809; died in Boston (Dorchester), 17 Oct., 1897; married 12 Jan., 1836, Elizabeth Maria, daughter of Gamaliel and Elizabeth (Kendall) Smith of Phillipston, Mass.; born there, 22 April, 1810; died in Boston (Roxbury), 8 May, 1876.

He established the first tannery in Wilmington, Vt.; removed to Cambridge, Mass. about 1844, thence to Boston where he was in business in partnership with his brother, John Addison (under the firm name of M. F. & J. A. Brigham), and also for himself, over 25 years. He lived longer than any of his Brigham ancestors save one, Lieut. Nathan[4], who reached the age of 91. He was a man of sterling character with a wonderfully sweet spirit, and was greatly beloved. Was a member of the Roxbury M. E. church for over 40 years, and one of the official board nearly all of that time.

Children, the 2 elder born in Wilmington, Vt., the youngest in Boston:

i Francis Henry[9], b. 19 July, 1837; d. s. p., in Boston (Dorchester), after years of invalidism, which were borne with courage and patience, 23 May, 1904; m. 8 July, 1862, Harriet A., dau. of Adna Buxton; b. in Salem, Mass., 2 Nov., 1835; d. in Boston (Dorchester), 4 Sept., 1870.

807 ii Ellen Maria, b. 3 Oct., 1841.

iii Emma Elizabeth, b. 12 Jan., 1852; res. in Boston. Was secretry of the B. F. A. during the reconstruction period, 1896-1900; treasurer, 1900-02, and 1904 to present time. A member of the Publication Committee of the *History of the Brigham Family,* she was appointed by that Committee to compile the manuscript left by the late Willard I. Tyler Brigham, and in collaboration with William E. Brigham of Somerville, Mass., one of the Committee, has edited this book. She is now (1907), compiling the Tyler Family manuscript left by Mr. Brigham at the time of his decease.

694 HARRIET[8], daughter of John[7] and Rebecca (Smith) Brigham; born in Whitingham, Vt., 2 Sept., 1814; died there, 29 Jan., 1872; married 4 Jan., 1840, Luke Wolcott, son of Thomas

* He was descended from Constant Freeman the emigrant and ancestor of the Freeman family in America, and from Richard Martyn of Portsmouth, N. H., an early settler.

Emma E. Brigham (693)
Editor of "The History of the Brigham Family"

Farnsworth; born in Halifax, Vt., 1 Oct., 1808; died in Hyde Park, Mass., 12 Aug., 1890.

Children (Farnsworth), born in Whitingham:

i Charles Luke⁹, b. 24 Nov., 1840; m. 15 Jan., 1868, Nellie D., dau. of John and Ruth (Woodbridge) Clifford; b. in No. Edgecomb, Me., 19 July, 1838; in business in Hyde Park; for 35 years a director in the B. F. A. Ch., all but the eldest b. in Hyde Park:

　1 *Harrie Clifford*¹⁰, b. in Boston, 9 Nov., 1868; m. 12 June, 1894, Florence Gordon Page of Hyde Park. Ch. i Augustus Page¹¹, b. 15 March, 1895; ii Charles Wolcott, b. 8 May, 1899.

　2 *Edith May*, b. 16 March, 1873.

　3 *Nettie Maud*, b. 4 Oct., 1874; m. 29 Sept., 1896, Frederick Whitney of Charlestown, Mass. Ch. (Nason): Edith Farnsworth¹¹, b. 14 Feb., 1898.

　4 *Alice Brigham*, b. 12 Feb., 1882; res. Hyde Park.

ii Sophia Harriet, b. 25 Aug., 1843; m. Charles E. Chase, son of 695.

iii Eliza Rebecca, b. 25 July, 1845; m. 19 Oct., 1880, Trueworthy Heywood; res. s. p., Boston.

iv John Addison, b. 13 Jan., 1851; m. 21 Dec., 1881, Hannah Elizabeth, dau. of Thomas J. Jordan; b. in Rural, Ill., 3 June, 1857; res. Hyde Park. Ch.:

　1 *Nellie May*¹⁰, b. in Western, Ill., 9 May, 1886.

　2 *Mildred Arlene*, b. in Hyde Park, 18 April, 1892.

　3 *Myron Addison*, b. in Hyde Park, 18 April, 1892; d. 19 April, 1895.

v Laura E., b. 9 May, 1856; m. 12 May, 1875, Cyrus W. Boyd of Whitingham, who d. Nov., 1900. Ch. (Boyd):

　1 *Clinton*¹⁰, d.

　2 *Ethel Jane*, b. 21 March, 1885.

　3 *Alice May*, b. 29 Dec., 1890.

vi Ellen Maria, b. 16 May, 1859; m. 5 June, 1889, Fred W., son of Woodbridge Clifford of No. Edgecomb, Me.; b. 21 Sept., 1856. Ch. (Clifford), b. in No. E.:

　1 *Ruth W.*¹⁰, b. 29 June, 1890.

　2 *Esther F.*, b. 16 April, 1893.

　3 *Woodbridge K.*, b. 27 Dec., 1895.

　4 *Rebecca E.*, b. 12 Feb., 1900.

695 SALLY MARIA⁸, daughter of John⁷ and Rebecca (Smith) Brigham; born in Whitingham, Vt., 12 Aug., 1816; died in Orion, Ill., 16 Feb., 1897; married 11 Sept , 1835, Merrick, son of Benjamin Chase; born in Douglas, Mass., 13 Dec., 1811; died in Orion, 3 Jan., 1887. He was Deputy Co. sheriff; moved from Vt. to N. Y. State, and thence to Orion.

Children (Chase), the 4 elder born in Whittingham, the 3 younger in Somerset, Mass.:

i Sylvester S.⁹, 3 Sept., 1836; m. (1) 1859, Maria B., dau. of Benj. Seaver of Boston; d. 1863; m. (2) Sophia Eddy; res. Chittenden, Vt. Ch. (by first wife), adopted by mother's family, and name changed to " Seaver " :

1 (*Judge*) *Henry E.*[10], b. in Boston, 1860; d. in Canton, N. Y., 23 May, 1898; m.; 1 ch.; was grad. Harvard Univ., 1881; admitted N. Y. bar, 1885; had high reputation as a speaker. Ch. (by second wife) (Chase):

    2 *Hattie*, m. ———— Smith.

ii Elvira Rebecca, b. 10 Feb., 1839; m. 3 April, 1856, Dr. Daniel A. Chase, b. 13 Jan., 1830, in Athens, Vt.; was grad. Cincinnati Eclectic Med. Inst.; surgeon U. S. Navy, in Civil War; traveled extensively; a remarkable botanist and natural doctor; d. in Cambridge, N. Y., 7 April, 1899. Ch. (Chase):

    1 *Maria P.*[10], b. 13 Aug., 1858; m. 22 Nov., 1876, Albert Holland; res. s. p., Chelsea, Mass.

    2 *Estelle*, b. 11 May, 1860; m. 12 Aug., 1880, Dr. Harry Blackfan; res. Cambridge, N. Y. Ch. (Blackfan): i Hallie M.[11]; ii Kenneth D.; iii Harry C.

    3 *Mary Elizabeth*, b. 3 April, 1862; d. in Davenport, Ia., 1880.

iii John Brigham, b. 6 May, 1841; m. Ann Hay. Ch.:

    1 *Elwin*[10]; 2 *Clinton*; 3 *Hattie*; 4 *Francis*; 5 *Charles*; 6 *Herbert*; 7 *George*; 8 *Fred.*

iv Charles Emerson, b. 13 Jan., 1844; m. 26 Feb., 1874, Harriet Sophia Farnsworth, dau. of 694; a farmer and stock-raiser on a large scale in Orion, Ill.; prominent in his township. Ch., b. in Orion:

    1 *Arthur Francis*[10], b. 1 March, 1879; was grad. 1901, Knox Coll., Galesburg, Ill.; joined father in extensive farm operations; res. Orion; m. 20 Aug., 1902, Etta Love of Orion.

v Sarah Maria, b. 12 Oct., 1847; d. in Oakland, Neb., 30 Aug., 1900; m. 19 Feb., 1879, at Orion, Valentine Neumann, b. 15 April, 1841; a banker in Oakland, and one of the leading men of the community. Ch. (Neumann), the elder b. in Lynn, Ill., the youngest in Oakland:

    1 *Ernest Valentine*[10], b. 9 Dec., 1879; m. 11 June, 1902, Nellye M. Lenton of Pender, Neb.; res. Pender.

    2 *Clyde Chase*, b. 18 May, 1881; res. Oakland.

    3 *Cornelia Barnes*, b. 6 Jan., 1884; m. 30 May, 1905, Joseph Harker of Mitchell, S. D.; res. there.

vi Addison Martyn, b. 30 Oct., 1856; m. 5 Oct., 1892, Bertha Calloway of Orion, b. 17 Dec., 1869; res. a farmer and stock-raiser, in O. Ch., b. in O.:

    1 *Myron Forrest*[10], b. 29 Aug., 1894.

    2 *Harold Addison*, b. 10 Sept., 1896.

696   REBECCA ELVIRA[8], daughter of John[7] and Rebecca (Smith) Brigham; born in Whitingham, Vt., 23 March, 1820; died in Jamaica Plain, Mass., 14 April, 1893; married (1) 15 March, 1843, Joseph Goodnow, Jr., of Whitingham; born there, 20 May, 1815; died there, 14 Sept., 1847; married (2) 11 Sept., 1858, Nathaniel Y., son of Gardner and Sarah (Smith) Lord of Athol, Mass., born there, 22 Sept., 1819; died there, s. p., April, 1876.

Child (Goodnow), born in Whitingham:

i Joseph Wilson[9], b. 28 Dec., 1843; m. 22 April, 1869, Helen M. Colman; a successful business man; retired, res. in Jamaica Plain. Ch.:

1 *Albert Wilson*[10], b. 29 April, 1871; m. Henrietta F. Barton.
Ch.: Anna Hortense[11], b. 16 Sept., 1894; res. in Jamaica Plain.
2 *Marion Colman*, b. 8 Sept., 1876; was grad. Radcliffe Coll., 1900;
m. 14 June, 1904, Deen L., son of ex-Lieut. Gov. Robinson of
Mich.; res. Houghton, Mich.

697 JOHN ADDISON[8], son of John[7] and Rebecca (Smith)
Brigham; born in Whitingham, Vt., 25 Jan., 1824; died in South
Braintree, Mass., 12 Dec., 1902; married (1) 15 March, 1855,
Emily Corinthia, daughter of Jeremiah Parmelee; born in Wilming-
ton, Vt., 19 Jan., 1826; died in Boston, 8 Feb., 1865; married (2)
7 June, 1866, Lydia Y., daughter of Paul R. Kendall; born in
Phillipston, Mass., 1 May, 1829; died in Boston, two weeks after
her marriage from a carriage accident, 23 June, 1866; married (3)
Mrs. Mary Luvia E. Harvey, born in Burke, Vt., 4 Oct., 1839, who
survives him.

He was a business man in Boston about 35 years, retiring in 1884
to a farm in So. Braintree. Was an Odd Fellow, a Knight Templar
and a Knight of Malta, and belonged to the Roxbury Horse Guards.
A member of the Roxbury Universalist church. Was administrator
of his father's estate.

Children (by first wife), born in Boston:
  i Carrie Emily[9], b. 31 May, 1856; m. 19 Jan., 1881, Charles S.
    Chase, b. in Whitingham, 13 May, 1855; an official court reporter,
    lawyer, and State Senator, 1906-07; res. Whitingham. Ch. (Chase),
    b. in Whitingham:
      1 *Robert Martyn*[10], b. 22 Feb., 1883; m. 22 April, 1904, Kate
        J. Benjamin of Colrain, Mass., b. 21 July, 1882; res. Whit-
        ingham.
      2 *Harrie Brigham*, b. 9 Aug., 1889; student at Phillips Exeter
        Academy.
      3 *Paul Addison*, b. 13 Nov., 1895.
  ii Gilbert Addison, b. 22 July, 1858; d. 20 Nov., 1858.
  iii Addie Rebecca, b. 2 Jan., 1860; d. 17 Aug., 1882.
  iv Alice Corinthia, b. 9 Dec., 1861; d. 17 May, 1878.
  v John Martyn, b. 25 July, 1864; d. 9 April, 1881.
Child (by third wife):
  vi Ethel May, b. 18 April, 1878; m. 21 July, 1901, Nelson Everson
    Hayden, Jr., of So. Braintree, b. 25 Dec., 1874; res. So. Brain-
    tree.

698 EMELINE MINERVA[8], daughter of John[7] and Huldah
(Wheeler) Brigham; born in Whitingham, Vt., 16 March., 1836;
married (1) 20 Oct., 1857, Stephen H. Nelson; born in Wardsboro,
Vt., 22 Oct., 1825; died 10 Dec., 1864, from the effect of treatment
in Libby Prison; married (2) 29 Oct., 1879, Edwin Legate, a farmer
of Halifax, Vt., born in Charlemont, Mass., 29 Aug., 1817.

Children (Nelson):
  i Charles H.[9], b. in Wardsboro, Vt., 12 July, 1858; m. (1) 9 May,
    1888, Della Roberts; m. (2) 30 March, 1904, Emma M. Benton,
    b. 27 June, 1850; res. Greenfield, Mass.

    ii George H., b. in Whitingham, 10 March, 1861; m. 21 Feb., 1893,
       Gertrude F., dau. of Joseph Martin, b. in Leyden, Mass., 27 July,
       1874; res. Winchester, N. H. Ch.:
        1 *Herbert R.*[10], b. 18 July, 1894.
        2 *Evelyn D.*, b. 5 June, 1902.
    iii Herbert S., b. in Newfane, Vt., 11 Nov., 1863; res. Cal.
Child (*Legate*).
    iv Blanche, b. in Halifax, Vt., 20 March, 1881; m. Lewis Worden
       Sumner, b. 16 July, 1877. Ch. (Sumner), b. in Halifax:
        1 *Mary E.*[10], b. 18 May, 1902.

699   HON. HOSEA WHEELER[8], son of John[7] and Huldah
(Wheeler) Brigham; born in Whitingham, Vt., 30 May, 1837; mar-
ried, 14 Sept., 1858, Florilla R., daughter of Joseph Farnham; born
Whitingham, 4 June, 1841.

His ambition was to study law, and in 1872 he was admitted to
the Windham County, Vt., bar, and later to the Supreme and United
States circuit and district courts. Postmaster in Sadawga, Vt.,
1872-78. In 1881, removed to Winchester, N. H., and is a member
of the Keene, N. H., bar; was a member of the N. H. constitutional
convention in 1889 and in 1904; State Representative, 1893-'94;
chairman Board of Education for 15 years, and town clerk in Winchester for 12 years; county commissioner for Cheshire Co. at pres
ent time and Justice of the Peace and Chancellor. Enjoys the confidence of all with whom he has contact, and is widely known over
the State. Prominent in Masonry, and a member of the Royal Arch
Council and a Knight Templar.

    Children, the eldest and youngest born in Whitingham:
      i Eva Corsella[9], b. 14 Aug., 1861; m. 22 March, 1881, Edelbert J.
        Temple, b. in Wilmington, Vt., 3 June, 1856; a lawyer in Hinsdale,
        N. H. Ch. (Temple):
        1 *Charles H.*[10], b. in Winchester, 19 Feb., 1882; was grad. Tufts
          College, 1905; student Theological School, and pastor Uni-
          versalist Church, Medford Hillside, Mass., in 1906-07.
        2 *Mabel E.*, b. in Hinsdale, 9 Nov., 1883.
        3 *Madelon M.*, b. in Hinsdale, 7 Aug., 1890.
      ii Ulric Ulysses, b. in So. Braintree, Mass., 15 Aug., 1865; m. 29
        June, 1889, Ada R., dau. of Lyman Dalrymple; b. in Whitingham,
        2 Dec., 1867; a pharmacist; res. Whitingham. Ch., b. Hinsdale:
        1 *Christine A.*[10], b. 5 Oct., 1890.
        2 *Fortice U.*, b. 17 March, 1894.
        3 *Flora J.*, b. 4 Jan., 1896.
      iii Maude Flora, b. 22 March, 1879; was grad. Smith College, 1903.

700   CHARLES EDWARD[8], son of Edward[7] and Laura (Cummings) Brigham; born in Heath, Mass., 4 June, 1833; married 27
Aug., 1855, Sarah A. Lake; born in Halifax, Vt., 4 Feb., 1837; died
3 Jan., 1892. Resided in Whitingham, Vt., and later in Fitchburg,

Hosea W. Brigham, of Winchester, N. H. (699)

Mass.; moved to Longwood, Fla., and now resides there winters, returning summers to No. Attleboro, Mass.

Children, the 2 elder born in Whitingham:
    i Mervin⁹, b. 4 July, 1856; d. 20 Dec., 1858.
    ii Murray Edward, b. 18 Dec., 1862; m. 1 Jan., 1888, in Kansas City, Mo., Hatty, dau. of Bethnel Roberts; an accountant; res. s. p., Maywood, Ill.
    iii Arthur Henry, b. in Ashburnham, Mass., 13 April, 1867; m. 24 Dec., 1896, Eva G., dau. of Dr. Francis Prince; b. in Bessemer, Alabama, 11 Oct., 1870; a photographer, res. No. Attleboro. Ch.:
        1 *Sarah Marguerite*¹⁰, b. 17 Feb., 1900.
        2 *Edward F.*, b. 9 Nov., 1901.

701 *EDMUND MONIS⁸, son of Lewis⁷ and Martha (Hagar) Brigham; born in Templeton, Mass., 21 Feb., 1837; married 11 Jan., 1863, Mary Elizabeth, daughter of Francis and Adeline (Stearns) Dodge; born in Newcastle, Me., 29 Oct., 1843. Mr. Brigham came to Boston in early life and entered the employ of his cousins, M. F. & J. A. Brigham; continued with the latter until he retired, and has since remained in active business in the city.

Children, born in Boston:
    i Martha Adeline⁹, b. 4 Sept., 1864; m. 29 Oct., 1889, Walter G., son of James S. and Amelia (Corey) Crowther; b. in Concord, N. H., 3 Feb., 1866; res. Dorchester, Mass. Ch. (Crowther), b. in Boston:
        1 *Ralph Frank*¹⁰, b. 2 Feb., 1892; 2 *Frederick Stewart*, b. 21 March, 1894; 3 *Roland Lewis*, b. 21 March, 1898; 4 *Merton Warren*, b. 7 May, 1900.
    ii Abbie Swallow, b. 28 June, 1867; m. 22 July, 1890, Arthur F., son of Isaac Richardson; b. in Orland, Me., 8 March, 1868. Ch. (Richardson):
        1 *Albert B.*¹⁰, b. 22 Aug., 1899; 2 *Hazel E.*, b. July, 1902.
    iii Otis Albert, b. 5 June, 1869; m. 31 Aug., 1899, Elsie May, dau. of Frank Thayer of Medford, Mass.; b. 24 Feb., 1880; he is clerk in Boston P. O.; res. Dorchester. Ch.:
        1 *Marion M.*¹⁰, b. 22 March, 1901; 2 *Mildred*, b. 25 May, 1904.
    iv Frank Edgar, b. 30 May, 1872; m. 26 Aug., 1896, Lulu Agnes, dau. of Horace W. Littlefield; b. in Prospect, Me., 13 April, 1876; he is a bookkeeper in Boston; res. Dorchester. Ch., b. in Boston:
        1 *Raymond L.*¹⁰, b. 20 June, 1897; 2 *Ruth E.*, b. 28 Sept., 1901.

702 HARRISON FAY⁸, son of Dea. George Ball⁷ and Nelly (Fay) Brigham; born in Waterford, Me., 10 June, 1817; died in Westboro, Mass., 18 Sept., 1877; married in 1838 or '39, Susan

---

* The name of Monis came into the Brigham family because of a friendship, formed in Harvard College, between the Rev. John Martyn (ancestor of Edmund ⁶ Brigham's descendants), and Rabbi Judah Monis, the young Hebrew Instructor of 1722, who retired from the college to live with Mr. Martyn, in Northboro, in his old age. Mr. Monis married a sister of Rev. Mr. Martyn's wife, became a Christian, and is buried in the Martyn lot in Northboro. Gifts of communion silver from him are in the possession of the old church in Northboro.

Neat; born 19 June, 1822; died in Lynn, Mass., 9 Dec., 1906. She resided in Westboro.

Children, the 4 elder born in Boston, the youngest in Westboro:

i Charles R.⁹, b. 1839; d. 15 Dec., 1886; m. 18 Aug., 1862, Mary E. Kirkup; was in the 13th Mass. Regt. Band, Civil War; moved to Wampum, Wis., where overseer in the State Prison. Ch.:
  1 *Charles Augustus*¹⁰, res. Pa.; m. ——— ———, and has 1 ch.

ii Samuel Neat, b. 15 Nov., 1843; d. in Westboro, 28 Jan., 1872; m. 31 Oct., 1865, Nellie A. Budd, who d. 1875, æ. 32; a midshipman in the Navy, with a res. in Westboro. Ch.:
  1 *Walter H.*¹⁰, b. 1869; d. in Westboro, 1887.

iii Harrison Fay, b. 10 Sept., 1847; d. 10 Feb., 1896; m. 15 June, 1871, Mary Jennie Sullivan; res. Brockton, Mass. Ch.: 1 boy and a girl, adopted by persons unknown.

iv George Cushing, b. 1849; d. in Brockton, 1889; Corporal in the Civil War; m. (1) Etta ———; m. (2) ———.
  Ch. (by first wife):
  1 *Georgie Etta*¹⁰, b. in Worcester, Mass.; m. ——— Shaw; res. Pomfret, Conn.; ch.: 3 boys and 1 girl.
  Ch. (by second wife):
  2 *Infant*, d. y.

v Susan Torrey, b. 23 March, 1854; d. 27 May, 1891; m. 23 March, 1874, Andrew Noble, son of Thomas Hewitt; b. 23 June, 1852; res. Westboro. Ch. (Hewitt), b. in Westboro, except the sixth:
  1 *Mabel Olive*¹⁰, b. 4 Feb., 1875; m. George K. Sarness of Lynn, b. in Harpoot, Turkey, 1870. Ch. (Sarness): Hortense Brigham¹¹, b. in Haverhill, Mass., 15 June, 1900; res. Lynn, Mass.
  2 *Bertha Adelaide*, b. 28 Jan., 1877; m. James R. Lowe, b. 18 March, 1845. Ch. (Lowe): Mary Elizabeth¹¹, b. in Leominster, Mass., 8 June, 1901; res. L.
  3 *Arthur Noble*, b. 24 July, 1878; res. Westboro.
  4 *Mary Etta*, b. 12 Nov., 1879; res. Worcester, Mass.
  5 *Flora Abbie*, b. 10 Sept., 1881; res. Westboro.
  6 *Harvey Leroy*, b. in Templeton, Mass., 12 Oct., 1888; res. Lynn.
  7 *Irvin Gay Brigham*, b. 23 Dec., 1889.

703 GEORGE BALL⁸, son of Dea. George Ball⁷ and Nelly (Fay) Brigham; born in Westboro, Mass., 5 Oct., 1818; died there, 27 Jan., 1891; married (1) 10 April, 1844, Caroline Jones, daughter of John and Sally (Bickford) Leland, of Sherburne, Mass.; born 10 Oct., 1818; died 7 Feb., 1858; married (2) Mary Phipps, daughter of Michael and Susan (Phipps) Homer of Hopkinton, Mass., born 25 Feb., 1838.

For 50 years the leading boot and shoe manufacturer of Westboro, he employed two or three hundred people. In 1843, he entered the grocery and produce business in Boston; 1849-'57 was supt. of Newton's Shoe Factory, also in the lumber business; 1858, manufacturer of shoes, later taking in his sons John and Horace under the firm name of George B. Brigham & Sons. Held town offices and was Representative, 1887; was chosen one of the Committee for publishing the town history; very active in the Baptist Church.

Children (by first wife), the 2 elder born in Sherburne, the others in Westboro:

    i Ella Lucile⁹, b. 18 Jan., 1845; d. 22 Nov., 1858.

    ii Atherton Fontenelle, b. 16 Oct., 1846; d. 4 Sept., 1852.

    iii Carrie Georgiana, b. 14 Dec., 1853; m. 29 June, 1886, H. O. Barr, and res. Westboro. Ch. (Barr):

        1 *Ella C.*¹⁰

    iv John Leland, b. 11 Sept., 1855; m. 25 Dec., 1884, Aldusta Harding; boot and shoe mfr., and bank president; res. Westboro, s. p.

808   v George Bickford, b. 8 Oct., 1856.

    vi Bertram Fay, b. 7 Feb., 1858; m. 22 Dec., 1884, Nellie M. Brewster; was grad. Andover Academy, 1878; R. E. agent; res. Brockton, Mass. Ch.:

        1 *Herbert B.*¹⁰, b. 9 Feb., 1887.

Children (by second wife), born in Westboro:

809 vii Frank Fontanelle, b. 15 Oct., 1859.

    viii Horace Eugene, b. 27 Aug., 1862; m. 20 Oct., 1885, Sarah Crocker; boot and shoe mfr.; was grad. Brown Univ., 1885; res. s. p., Westboro.

    ix Lillie Josephine, b. 26 Sept., 1864; unm.

    x Marion Homer, b. 27 Aug., 1867; m. 24 Dec., 1891, William M., son of Lucius R. and Martha (Matthews) Bates; b. 15 Sept., 1867; res. Westboro. Ch. (Bates):

        1 *Lucius Ray*¹⁰, b. 21 Oct., 1894; 2 *George Brigham*, b. 3 Dec., 1897; 3 *Marion*, b. 22 Sept., 1900.

    xi Ernest Phipps, b. 14 July, 1871; a dentist in Westboro.

704 DEA. CURTIS, JR.⁸, son of Dea. Curtis⁷ and Lydia (Woodbury) Brigham; born in Charlestown, Mass., 13 April, 1821; died in Lenville, Idaho, 8 Jan., 1888; married in Sylvan, Mich., 8 Nov., 1849, Esther, daughter of Moses Metcalf; born in Ohio, 15 May, 1830; died in Washington Co., Cal., 11 Jan., 1875.

He moved from Shutesbury Mass., to Plainville, Mich., in 1834; moved to California in 1854, via the Isthmus; tried mining then farming in Alameda Co.; in 1880 became an Idaho pioneer in Latah Co., where he took up a homestead of 160 acres and was a deacon in the Baptist Church.

Children, the 3 younger born in Washington, Cal.:

    i Alfred Curtis⁹, b. in Orangeville, Mich., 19 May, 1851; m. 18 Oct., 1887, Mrs. May M. Sigler; a farmer; went to Placer Co., Cal., 1856; moved to Genesee, Latah Co., Idaho, 1878, where has a homestead and is a fruitgrower. Ch., all d. y.:

810 ii Ervin Frank, b. in Sylvan, Mich., 16 April, 1853.

    iii Hon. John Warren, b. in Niles, Cal., 22 March, 1857; m. 31 Dec., 1893, Nellie Wilson. He went to Lenville, Idaho, 1876, where res. s. p.; has 320 acres of orchard and farm land. Is a member of the Legislature of Idaho, and was member of Textile Committee (Senate), and introduced the bill locating the State University in Moscow; member of the Constitutional Convention of 1889; member of the 1st State Senate, 1890; 5th and 7th Legislatures, and President *pro tem* of the Senate of the 7th Legislature; acting Lieut. Gov., 1904.

iv Ella Caroline, b. 7 Sept., 1859; m. 7 April, 1885, Rev. James Berreman, a farmer and preacher for the United Brethren; res. Philomath, Ore. Ch. (Berreman):

1 *George*[10], b. in Cameron, Idaho, 7 May, 1886; 2 *Hattie;* 3 *Dora;* 4 *James W.;* 5 *Frank B.;* 6 *Joel;* 7 *Daughter.*

v Eddie, b. 29 April, 1866; m. 24 July, 1887, Belle Sigler; a fruit grower, res. Genesee, Idaho. Ch.:

1 *Lienella*[10]*;* 2 *Edna;* 3 *Bessie.*

vi Burnice B., b. 12 Nov., 1871; m. 13 Nov., 1892, Minnie Sigler; inherited his father's homestead, Lenville, Idaho, where a farmer. Ch.:

1 *Caddie E.*[10]*,* b. 24 March, 1894.

2 *Boyd L.,* b. 22 July, 1897.

705 LYSCOM[8], son of Dea. Curtis[7] and Lydia (Woodbury) Brigham; born in Shutesbury, Mass., 31 Jan., 1827; married (1) 29 Jan., 1852, Mary, daughter of Theron Norton of Cooper, Mich., who died 6 Nov., 1869; married (2) 26 Jan., 1870, Calista, daughter of Erastus Cressy of Prairieville, Mich.

He studied at Olivet College, Mich.; resided in Orangeville, Mich., thence to Decatur, Ill., where a prominent citizen and the largest mint distiller in the state; has a 520 acre farm. He patented a marsh shoe for horses to work in the swamp.

Children (by first wife), born in Decatur:

i Curtis L.[9], b. 3 April, 1855; m. Kate Lindsey; res. Plainwell, Mich. Ch.:

1 *Olive*[10].

ii Lydia M., b. 12 Sept., 1860; res. unm., with father.

811 iii Dexter E., b. 14 May, 1862.

iv Charles W., b. 29 June, 1867; m. Lucy Cady; res. Decatur, Mich., where a grower and distiller of mint. Ch.:

1 *Geneva R.*[10]

Children (by second wife), born in Decatur:

v Arthur E., b. 28 Nov., 1871; m. Mabel Culverhouse; res. Decatur. Ch.:

1 *Thomas A.*[10]

vi John F., b. 29 Nov., 1877; m. Allie Willson; mint grower, Decatur.

vii Frank M., b. 11 Feb., 1880; unm.

viii Alfred C., b. 29 Jan., 1883.

ix Leslie A., b. 31 Aug., 1886.

706 DEXTER HAMMOND[8], son of Benjamin Fay[7] and Abigail (Hoar) Brigham; born in Shutesbury, Mass., 17 June, 1826; died in Springfield, Mass., 14 Dec., 1898; married 6 Nov., 1849, Lomira Cheever Forbush; born in Westboro, Mass., 17 Jan., 1829. Resides in Springfield, Mass.

Mr. Brigham moved early to Westboro where, at 18, he was in

DEXTER H. BRIGHAM, OF SPRINGFIELD, MASS. (706)

the firm of Fay, Brigham & Co.; at 23 he moved to Springfield, and opened a gentleman's clothing store; made uniforms during the Civil War; in 1860 was the pioneer in the paper collar industry; from 1888 he dealt exclusively in ladies' wardrobes. He had 80 people on his pay-roll. He was a gentleman of the old school, courteous and refined. He took a great interest in the movement to publish a history of the Brigham family and his untimely death was a great loss to the Association, with which he had closely allied himself. He traveled abroad and at the first meeting of the Association in Marlboro, in 1894, he presented to each person at the banquet, a beautifully prepared copy of a picture of the old church in Brigham, Cumberland Co., Eng., with a delightful note of explanation.

Children, born in Springfield:
  i Emma Cheever[9], b. 26 May, 1852; d. in Springfield, 15 June, 1898; m. 15 Oct., 1873, Frank May, son of D. Leverett Bugbee; b. in Hartford, Conn., 9 Aug., 1849; d. in Springfield, 25 March, 1892. He was a clothier in Springfield. Ch. (Bugbee), b. in Springfield:
    1 *Ernest Dexter*[10], b. 10 July, 1874; m. 27 Oct., 1897, Maud M. Blaisdell.
    2 *Harold Sprague*, b. 26 Aug., 1877; d. 29 July, 1878.
    3 *Florence May*, b. 21 May, 1879; m. 22 May, 1901, Irving Sprague Russell.
    4 *Harwood Chapin*, b. 4 May, 1881; d. 8 Feb., 1889.
    5 *Frank May*, b. 20 Aug., 1883; d. 19 Jan., 1889.
  ii Ella Eliza, b. 4 Dec., 1856; m. 14 Jan., 1880, Willard Morgan, son of Joseph P. White of Springfield. Ch. (White), b. in Springfield:
    1 *Howard Morgan*[10], b. 20 May, 1881.
    2 *Edith Muriel*, b. 16 March, 1890.

707 ELLIOTT FAY[8], son of Edmund Fay[7] and Hannah F. (Temple) Brigham; born in West Boylston, Mass., 13 Jan., 1839; married 1 May, 1859, Jane E., daughter of Benjamin Wadsworth of W. Boylston. He enlisted as a private in the 4th Mass. Cavalry; became 1st Lieut., and served until Nov., 1865. Is supt. in a boot and shoe factory.

Children, born in West Brookfield:
  i Clifford H.[9], b. 8 Nov., 1859.
  ii Elliott Wadsworth, b. 18 Aug., 1861; m. (1) 1890, Minnie M. Wheeler, who d. s. p.; m. (2) her sister, Carrie Wheeler. Ch.:
    1 *Lester H.*[10], b. 6 March, 1895.
    2 *Dorothy W.*, b. 2 March, 1897.
  iii Harry L., b. 30 Sept., 1863; m. 16 Oct., 1886, Hattie L. Peck of No. Brookfield, Mass.; res. Bridgeport, Conn. Ch.:
    1 *Francis*[10]; 2 *Minnie May*.
  iv Jennie T., b. 1 Feb., 1867.
  v Edmund Fay, b. 15 March, 1872; m. 1895, Eva Burr of Worcester, Mass.; res. Boston. Ch.:
    1 *Wesley Joseph*[10], b. 3 April, 1898.

708 ELI HOWARD[8], son of Edmund Fay[7] and Hannah F. (Temple) Brigham; born in West Boylston, Mass., 5 Sept., 1847; married 6 April, 1876, Augusta, daughter of Dea. William Richardson of Sterling, Mass., Mr. Brigham is a basket manufacturer and resides in Medford, Mass. Mrs. Brigham is a newspaper correspondent.

Children:
    i Gertrude Rebecca[9], b. 1 Nov., 1876; was grad. Normal Art School, Boston; supervisor of drawing in the public schools for several years; res. Boston.
    ii Howard Richardson, b. 27 Feb., 1878; res. Brooklyn, N. Y.
    iii Frances Augusta, b. 14 Jan., 1880; res. Westboro, Mass.
    iv Florence Margery, b. 28 Aug., 1881; res. Sterling.
    v William Burpee, b. 29 Jan., 1883; res. Boston.
    vi Helen Blanche, b. 27 March, 1884; res. Boston.
    vii Hattie Idelle, b. 26 July, 1886.

709 LORAON[8], daughter of William Chamberlain[7] and Lydia B. (Rice) Brigham; born in Wardsboro, Vt., 16 Feb., 1829; married 14 March, 1847, Rev. Silas G., son of Silas Kellogg; born in Oswegatchie, N. Y., 24 March, 1823; died in Hudson, N. H., 21 Dec., 1891. He resided in Wardsboro, Vt., Norwich, New Ipswich, Claremont, N. H., and Croydon, N. Y.

Children (Kellogg), born in Wardsboro:
    i (Rev.) George Newell[9], b. 2 July, 1848; was grad. Tilton Sem., N. H.; m. 1873, Alice J. Anthony; res. Morrisville, Vt. Ch.:
        1 Maud[10]; 2 Charles; 3 Nellie.
    ii (Hon.) William Channing, b. 11 July, 1850; m. Emma J. Lewis; was grad. Middlebury Coll.; a lawyer and Judge in Yonkers, N. Y.; has office in N. Y. City. Ch.:
        1 Lewis[10]; 2 Ruth.
    iii Charles Prescott F., b. 24 Oct., 1856; m. Nellie B. Burnham; was grad. from Tilton Sem.; wholesale merchant; res. Dorchester, Mass. Ch.:
        1 Grace[10]; 2 Priscilla.
    iv (Rev.) Frederick Brigham, b. 9 July, 1866; was grad. Boston Univ., and Union Theol. Sem., N. Y.
    v Florence Sophia, b. 27 Aug., 1877 (adopted).

710 ALFRED MILO[8], son of Ephraim[7] and Sophia (Howe) Brigham; born in Natick, Mass., 21 Oct., 1828; killed by a shell, before Petersburg, Va., 15 June, 1864; married Caroline, daughter of Sewell Damon; born in Wayland, Mass., 12 April, 1828; died in Auburn, Mass., 5 June, 1892. Mr. Brigham was a shoe manufacturer of Natick, and held town offices; Postmaster, 16 years; Adjutant 4th Regt., Colored Troops; also served in Co. I, 39th Mass. Vols.

Children, born in Natick:
812   i Walter Damon[9], b. 4 Sept., 1853.
813   ii Nathaniel Maynard, b. 8 March, 1856.

iii Helen Sophia, b. 28 Dec., 1858; m. 1 Aug., 1877, Irving E. Glidden; res. Natick. Ch. (Glidden):
  1 *Helen Hall*[10], b. 31 Aug., 1878; m. 19 Nov., 1902, William Howland Bassett of Bridgewater, Mass.

711 LAURA SOPHIA[8], daughter of Ephraim[7] and Sophia (Howe) Brigham; born in Natick, Mass., 26 Dec., 1830; died in Winstead, Conn., 26 June, 1905; married 16 Oct., 1853; Gilbert Park, son of Park Fay; born in So. Framingham, Mass., 6 March, 1826; died in Chelsea, Mass., 9 May, 1893.

Children (Fay), all but the eldest born in Natick:
  i Martha Fuller[9], b. in Boston, 15 Sept., 1854; m. July, 1885, John Eastman Clark; res. s. p., Winsted, Conn.
  ii Brigham Park, b. 31 Jan., 1855; m. Ida M. Hemenway of Wayland, Mass.; res. Everett, Mass. Ch.:
    1 *Park S.*[10]; 2 *Lloyd W.*, d.; 3 *Olive M.;* 4 *Carl G.*
  iii (Dr.) Irving Wetherbee, b. 30 Nov., 1861; m. Aug., 1897, Elizabeth Schoefel; res. Brooklyn, N. Y. Ch.:
    1 *Ernestine*[10], b. Aug., 1898.
  iv Janet Williams, b. 24 Nov., 1866; m. Sept., 1888, Clarence E. Cozzens; res. Indianapolis, Ind., s. p.
  v Alfred Chase, b. 21 April, 1868; m. Henrietta Martin; res. Bridgewater, Mass. Ch.:
    1 *Eliot Gilbert*[10], b. 20 Jan., 1902.
  vi Harrison Gilbert, b. 10 May, 1869; m. 31 March, 1900, Ella C. Colt; res. Nashua, N. H.; Principal of High School. Ch.:
    1 *Henry C.*[10], b. 26 Jan., 1901.
    2 *Priscilla Brigham*, b. 22 Feb., 1902.

712 ALGERNON SIDNEY[8], son of Col. Sidney[7] and Eliza B. (Stevens) Brigham; born in Marlboro, Mass., 13 March, 1826; married 1 May, 1849, Matilda M. Hayden, born 25 July, 1828; died 10 Jan., 1899. He is a shoe manufacturer and resides in Marlboro.

Children, born in Marlboro:
  i Ida Matilda[9], b. 15 Aug., 1850; d. 23 Aug., 1854.
814 ii Ernest Algernon, b. 29 July, 1852.
  iii Percival Hayden, b. 16 Nov., 1855; m. Laura G. Hicks of New York, 13 April, 1886; mining engineer; went to So. Africa, where d. of yellow fever, 28 Dec., 1887.
  iv Clarence Hale, b. 23 Aug., 1857; m. (1) 18 Sept., 1879, Cora Maria Curtis of Marlboro, who d. 3 June, 1886; m. (2) 11 Nov., 1889, Annie Louise Forbush of Marlboro, where res. Ch. (by first wife), b. in Marlboro:
    1 *Cora Elsie*[10], b. 30 May, 1886.
      Ch. (by second wife), b. in Marlboro:
    2 *Harold Lewis*, b. Feb., 1893.
    3 *Algernon Raymond*, b. 31 Aug., 1895.
  v Laurie Stanton, b. 30 Nov., 1861; m. 23 Aug., 1888, Mary A. Talcott of Dorchester, Mass.; res. s. p., Columbus, Ga., a druggist.
  vi Elsie Hudson, b. 14 April, 1867; res. Marlboro.

vii Shirley Keeler, b. 29 May, 1870; m. 14 Sept., 1892, Susie Elvira
    Clough of So. Londonderry, Vt.; res. in St. Johnsbury, Vt. Ch.,
    b. in So. Londonderry:
    1 *Dorothy Matilda*[10], b. 5 Nov., 1894.
    2 *Eda Sarette*, b. 11 Feb, 1900.

713 LORIMAN STEVENS[8], son of Col. Sidney[7] and Eliza B.
(Stevens) Brigham; born in Francestown, N. H., 30 Jan., 1832;
died in Marlboro, Mass., 18 Dec., 1903; married (1) 25 Nov., 1855;
Caroline, daughter of Lyman Howe; born in Westboro, Mass., 13
June, 1837; died in Marlboro, 28 Oct., 1865; married (2) 22 Nov.,
1869, Emma Sophia, daughter of Franklin Field of Northfield
Farms, Mass., died 20 Jan., 1871, æ. 26; married (3) 9 Jan., 1873,
Mary Snow, daughter of John Percival, a noted pharmacist of Bos-
ton; born in Cohasset, Mass., 20 June, 1847.   She was a well-
known singer in her youth.

He went to Marlboro after the death of his parents, and lived
with his uncle Winslow Stevens; he learned the jewelry and watch-
repairing business and in 1857 purchased a jewelry store in Marlboro; when he died he was the oldest merchant in the city, senior
member of the firm of Brigham and Eager, and had a handsome
fortune.   For many years was President of the People's National
Bank of Marlboro; trustee, vice-president, and later, president
of the Marlboro Savings Bank, and member of the Board of Invest-
ment for 31 years.   He was a very successful organist and choir
director.   His cheerful and kind disposition and love of fun rendered
his home life very happy.   Though tendered him, he always refused
town offices.   He crossed the continent several times.   He belonged
to the Trinity commandery of Knights Templar of Hudson, and the
United Brethren Lodge, A. F. and A. M., and Houghton Royal
Arch chapter of Marlboro.

Children (by third wife), born in Marlboro:
    i Loriman Percival[9], b. 24 Oct., 1878; m. 21 Oct., 1903, Ethel
      Annie, dau. of Charles H. and Anna G. (Barnes) Stone; b. in
      Northboro, 19 Oct., 1877; was grad. Amherst Coll., 1900; in jewelry
      business in Hudson, Mass. Ch.:
      1 *Loriman Stone*[10], b. 7 Feb., 1906.
    ii Lilla May, b. 7 Feb., 1881; m. 7 June, 1905, Russell B. Tower
      of Cohasset, Mass.
    iii Drusilla Percival, b. 14 Sept., 1883.

714 ELIJAH[8], son of Rev. Elijah[7] and Mary (Locker) Brigham; born in Marlboro, Mass., 12 May, 1828; died in Worcester,
Mass., 2 March, 1889; married (1) 3 Oct., 1850, Fanny Augusta,
daughter of John Norcross; born in Shrewsbury, Mass., 19 Jan.,
1832; died in Sutton, Mass., 17 Jan., 1878; married (2) 29 Oct.,
1884, Hassie Melissa, daughter of Richard Ware; born in Buckland,
Mass., 14 April, 1839.

Loriman S. Brigham.

At 17 he went around Cape Horn, on a 3 years' cruise. Was Sergt. Co. H, 10th Mass. Infantry, Civil War; disabled and honorably discharged; re-enlisted Co. C 1st Mass. Cavalry March, 1864, and served through the war. Resided in Wayland, Mass., and then moved to Sutton.

Children (by first wife), born in Wayland:
    i Anna Augusta⁹, b. 3 Jan., 1852; d. 26 March, 1852.
    ii Anna Frances, b. 15 July, 1853; m. 14 June, 1873, John A., son of Enoch Hammond of Douglass, Mass., from whom divorced; res. unm., s. p., Spencer, Mass.

715 MARY LOUISA⁸, daughter of Rev. Elijah⁷ and Mary (Locker) Brigham; born in Fitchburg, Mass., 20 Oct., 1831; died in Milford, Mass., 26 Jan., 1879; married (1) 18 Feb., 1849, George Taft, son of John Daniels of Holliston, Mass.; born 14 March, 1822; died 24 Oct., 1874. He was a boot manufacturer, selectman, assessor, and a prominent 32d degree Mason. She married (2) 21 June, 1876, Stephen Mathewson of Milford, Mass. (first wife Harriet W. Day of Attleboro); born in Rhode Island, 26 July, 1820 and died —————

Children (Daniels), b. in Holliston:
    i Emma Genevieve⁹, b. 6 Dec., 1849; m. 1870, Albert P. Pond; a prominent hotel man who d. in Chicago, 1892.
    ii Mary Louise, b. 16 Dec., 1851; d. 15 Oct., 1887; m. Edwin M. Battles, who was in the Civil War; he res. Boston. Ch. (Battles):
        1 *George E.*¹⁰, res. Philadelphia, Pa.
    iii George Dexter, b. Aug., 1860; d. Jan., 1863.

716 ANNA DOROTHY⁸, daughter of Rev. Elijah⁷ and Mary (Locker) Brigham; born in Fitchburg, Mass., 31 Aug., 1833; died in Mt. Vernon, Ia., 26 June, 1863; married 22 Aug., 1855, Rev. Denison Gage, Jr., of Lynn; born in Malden, Mass., 1829; died in Mt. Vernon, 25 July, 1862. Mrs. Gage taught languages in Amenia Seminary, N. Y., and drawing and painting in Cornell College, Mt. Vernon. Mr. Gage was graduated from Wesleyan College in 1855; was Principal of Stanstead Academy, P. Q.; Principal Amenia (N. Y.) Seminary; Prof. Latin, Cornell College.

Children (Gage):
    i Anna Frances⁹, b. 17 Feb., 1857; m. William H. Sylvester, who was grad. from Harvard Univ., 1879. Ch. (Sylvester)·
        1 *Harold*¹⁰, d. y.
    ii Minnie Adaline, b. 3 May, 1859; m. Rev. Edgar E. Davidson of Newtonville, Mass. Ch. (Davidson):
        1 *Helen W.*¹⁰, b. 1887.

717 DR. JOHN WESLEY⁸, son of Rev. Elijah⁷ and Mary (Locker) Brigham; born in Fitchburg, Mass., 11 March, 1835;

died in Sutton, Mass., 14 Sept., 1898; married 14 Sept., 1856, Betsey Ann, daughter of Capt. Alonzo Jelleff (a pioneer of Fon Du Lac, Wis.) and widow of John A. Delancey of Ripon, Wis.; she was born in Columbia, Pa., 11 Dec., 1828. Dr. Brigham was educated in Wilbraham Academy and practiced medicine in Massachusetts, Wisconsin, and Iowa; later resided in Sutton where he held town offices.

Children, the second and third born in Green Lake, Wis.:

 i Dea. Dexter Alonzo[9], b. in Rushford, Wis., 30 July, 1857; m. 2 March, 1881, Jennie Abbie, dau. of John S. Burnap; b. in Sutton, 4 Dec., 1857; res. Sutton, where selectman, etc.; a farmer and mechanic. Ch.:
   1 *Mary Ethel*[10], b. 13 May, 1884.
   2 *Alice Minerva,* b. 8 Sept., 1887.
   3 *Minnie Ann,* b. 6 Sept., 1889.
   4 *Mabel Louise,* b. 3 May, 1891.

 ii Alphonso Gilderoy, b. 5 April, 1860; m. 16 April, 1884, Sarah Elizabeth, dau. of John S. Burnap; b. in Sutton, 1 Jan., 1865; res. Fisherville, Mass.; with bro. Sidney; did business as contractor and builder until 1893. Ch., b. in Sutton:
   1 *Ralph Bertram*[10], b. 2 Sept., 1886.
   2 *Bertha Gertrude,* b. 30 Dec., 1891.

 iii Sidney D., b. 26 Aug., 1862; m. 6 Jan., 1885, Fannie Ellen, dau. of Pierre Chabotte; b. in Grafton, Mass., 16 April, 1867; res. Whitinsville, Mass.; head of firm S. D. Brigham & Bros. until 1893, when dissolved. Ch.:
   1 *Wallace Grover*[10], b. 1887; d. 1888.
   2 *Carl Sidney,* b. 3 Dec., 1889; d. 15 May, 1895.

 iv Curtis Mortimer Jelleff, b. in Whitewater, Wis., 14 Aug., 1868; m. Lillian W. Ferry, b. in Northboro, Mass., 17 Oct., 1868; a contractor and builder; res. Fisherville.

718 MAJOR CHARLES OLIN[8], son of Rev. Elijah[7] and Mary (Locker) Brigham; born in Fitchburg, Mass., 1 Dec., 1836; died, s. p., in Derby Line, Vt., 24 June, 1890; married Clara A. Spalding; born in Province of Quebec, 4 April, 1842.

Major Brigham had a fine war record. He was in Wesleyan College, Middletown, Conn., when he enlisted, in 1861, in Co. G, 4th Conn. Infantry; was in the Army of the Potomac until his discharge in 1865; was 1st Sergt., 2d and 1st Lieut., Capt., and finally breveted Major for bravery before Petersburg, Va. He resided in Derby Line, Vt., where was a prominent lawyer.

719 REV. CHARLES HENRY[8], son of Dennis[7] and Roxorenna (Fay) Brigham; born in Boston, Mass., 27 July, 1820; died in Brooklyn, N. Y., 19 Feb., 1879.

He was graduated, Harvard College, A. B., 1839, receiving the Bowdoin prize of $40; was graduated Cambridge Divinity School, 1843, in which year he received the degree of A. M. from Harvard College. Ordained in Taunton, Mass., 1844, he remained there many years. Later was Prof. of Biblical Archaeology and Ecclesiastical History in Meadville (Pa.) Theological Seminary. In 1865 he organized the United Society at Ann Arbor, Mich., and remained there until obliged from ill health to retire. He traveled extensively through the East and Europe, and wrote tirelessly for periodicals, and published many sermons and lectures. Was Secy. Board of Trustees Bristol Academy 15 years. He was corresponding secretary of the Old Colony Historical Society for 5 years, and was on the Executive Committee of the American Unitarian Association for 2 years. Before his fortieth year he had accomplished more than many men in a lifetime.

720 LUCIEN FAY[8], son of Dennis[7] and Roxorenna (Fay) Brigham; born in New York City, 9 Aug., 1842; married (1) 7 Dec., 1870, Louise, daughter of G. W. Alexander, who died in Pottsville, Pa., 26 June, 1890; married (2) 18 Oct., 1892, Laura Sherbrooke, daughter of Dr. John T. Carpenter of Pottsville, where he resides.

Children (by first wife), the 2 elder born in Brooklyn, N. Y., the third and fourth in Plainfield, N. J.:
  i Alexander Fay[9], b. 21 Feb., 1872; m. in Capetown, So. Africa, 2 Sept., 1902, Helen A. Pruner; is a mining engineer; res. Kimberly, So. Africa. Ch., b. there:
    1 *Fay*[10], b. 5 Aug., 1903.
    2 *Patricia*, b. 12 Sept., 1904.
  ii Lucien Maxwell, b. 6 June, 1874; a business manager in New York City, where he res.
  iii Charles Henry, b. 15 March, 1877; res. New York City.
  iv John Gardner, b. 9 Nov., 1880; d. 9 April, 1902, unm.
  v Celia Louise Caroline, b. in Pottsville, 21 June, 1890.
Children (by second wife), born in Pottsville:
  vi Edward Carpenter, b. 22 Aug., 1893.
  vii Adelaide Hill, b. 9 July, 1895.
  viii Robert Hill, b. 23 Nov., 1896.
  ix Laurence Fay, b. 4 Oct., 1903.

721 CAPT. ALFRED WILLARD[8], son of Trowbridge[7] and Sarah F. (Morse) Brigham; born in Southboro, Mass., 19 June, 1837; married 30 May, 1876, Annie H., daughter of Col. Ruel Hough of Boston; she was educated in the Ursuline Convent, Columbus, O.

Capt. Brigham enlisted on the eve of the firing on Fort Sumter, as Corp. Co. B, 13th Mass. Vols; was wounded at Antietam and discharged; re-enlisted as 1st Lieut. Co. C, 3d Mass Heavy Artillery, 1863; A. A. Q. M. 3d Brigade Hardin's Div., 22d A. C. from April to Oct., 1864; Capt. Co. C, 3d Mass. Art., Oct., 1864; Judge Advocate Gen., Court Martial in Fort Stevens, D. C., June and July, 1865; commanded Fort Mahan, D. C., fall to spring, 1864-'65;

mustered out, Oct., 1865; retired, disabled by wounds. Resides in Boston.

Children, born in Boston:
> i Mary Worcester[9], b. 25 April, 1879; m. 20 April, 1904, Burt W., son of Samuel Emmes; res. Brookline, Mass. Ch. (Emmes):
> 1 *Arthur Bertram*[10], b. in Brookline, 15 Aug., 1905.
> ii Helen Adelia, b. 23 Nov., 1882.

722 DR. EDWIN HOWARD[8], son of Elijah Sparhawk[7] and Sarah J. (Rogers) Brigham; born in Boston, 27 Sept., 1840; married in Watertown, Mass., Jane Spring, daughter of Moses and Mehitable (Nye) Peirce; born in Medford, Mass., 5 Sept., 1845.

During the Civil War he was in the 13th Mass., Vols., Co. A, from 20 July, 1861 to 24 Feb., 1864, when he became Hospital Steward, U. S. A. He was graduated from Harvard Medical College in 1868; in 1875 became Asst. and Resident Librarian of the Boston Medical Library, and is head of the Nurses Directory for Medical Library; in 1884, became Librarian of the Mass. Medical Society.

Children, born in Boston:
> i Percy[9], b. 14 July, 1874; d. in Boston, 2 June, 1875.
> ii Ethel, b. 23 June, 1878; m. 15 Oct., 1901, Albert Thompson, son of Andrew F. and Florence (Thompson) Leatherbee; b. in Boston, 20 Dec., 1876; res. Allston, Mass.
> iii Edwin Howard, b. 9 Dec., 1883; d. 25 Dec., 1883.
> iv Ralph Peirce, b. 10 June, 1888; student in Mass. Inst. Technology.

723 WILLIAM HARTWELL[8], son of Stowell[7] and Elizabeth (Bowen) Brigham; born in Madrid, N. Y., 4 Oct., 1853; married (1) in Watertown, N. Y., 1875, Margaret Hickey, who died 19 Aug., 1881; married (2) in Troy, N. Y., 1884, Mary F. Wallace, who died s. p., 8 Dec., 1904.

He resides in Washington, D. C., where he is in the Government Printing Office; is President of the Royal Arcanum Hospital Bed Fund Association.

Children (by first wife):
> i George J.[9], b. 21 April, 1876; m. 17 Sept., 1899, Mary J. Mety of Long Island City, N. Y.; b. 1 April, 1877. He is in the R. E. and Ins. business; res. Blissville, L. I. City. Ch.:
> 1 *Gertrude M.*[10], b. 25 Aug., 1900.
> 2 *John W.*, b. 10 June, 1902.
> 3 *Helen*, b. Sept., 1903.
> ii John, on the death of his mother lived with his maternal uncle in Watertown, N. Y., and has assumed the family name of his mother, "Hickey"; m. Angelina Cooper of Perth Ontario, Canada. He res. New York City. Ch. (Hickey):
> 1 *Elizabeth M.*[10], b. Aug., 1905.

SETH E. BRIGHAM, OF FITCHBURG (735)

724 DANA BULLARD[8], son of Joseph Lincoln[7] and Sally Gay (Wheeler) Brigham; born in Brooklyn, N. Y., 25 April, 1845; married 10 April, 1872, Frances, daughter of Edward Slade, a dry goods commission merchant of Baltimore, Md.; born 1 March, 1853. Mr. Brigham is a commission merchant in New York City.

Children, the 3 elder and the youngest born in New York City:
  i Joseph Lincoln[9], b. 15 Jan., 1873; d. 20 Aug., 1873
  ii Dana Bullard, Jr., b. 16 Feb., 1874; a business manager; res. Flushing, L. I.
  iii Ellen Slade, b. 1 Dec., 1875.
  iv Edward Slade, b. in Flushing, N. Y., 22 Nov., 1877; d. 6 Aug., 1878.
  v Sally, b. in Petersham, Mass., 20 Aug., 1880; res. Flushing.
  vi Francis Gorham, b. 27 Sept., 1882; in 1905 a student in Colgate University.

725 JOSEPH LINCOLN[8], son of Erastus Forbes[7] and Sophia De Wolf (Homer) Brigham; born in Brooklyn, N. Y., 3 Dec., 1840; married in Houghton, Mich., Feb., 1868, Elizabeth, daughter of Joseph Schnitzer of St. Paul, Minn.; born 17 Nov., 1847; died 10 April, 1893. Mr. Brigham claims a residence in St. Paul, Minn., but he is engaged in business in New York City.

Children, born in St. Paul:
  i Emeline Marie DeWolf[9], b. 5 Dec., 1870; m. 26 Sept., 1899, Henry M., son of Niven Agnew; res. St. Paul. Ch. (Agnew):
    1 Elizabeth J.[10], b. 8 Feb., 1901.
    2 Janet M., b. 1 Nov., 1903.
    3 Nell Brigham, b. 2 May, 1905.
  ii Lincoln Flagg, b. 21 March, 1878; unm., 1905.

726 CAPT. EZRA[8], son of Aaron[7] and Abigail (Maynard) Brigham; born in Charleston, Vt., 13 Sept., 1796; died there 20 March, 1883; married 26 Aug., 1821, Mary Pierce of St. Johnsbury, Vt., who died 21 March 1888, æ. 83. He resided in Charleston, Vt., and was a carpenter. He was also Capt. in the militia.

Children:
  i Levi P.[9], b. 12 April, 1822; d. in St. Johnsbury, 7 July, 1854; m. 1844, Ann Sylvester of St. J. Ch.:
    1 Emma[10], m. Carlton Woodbury, and d. 8 Feb., 1882, in St. Johnsbury.
    2 Ella M., m. Charles Perrigo of St. Johnsbury. Ch. (Perrigo):
      i Lilla[11]; ii Robert; iii Harry.
  ii Lucy, b. 14 April, 1824; d. 1 May, 1842.
  iii Lewis W. b. 12 Feb., 1827; d. 28 Feb., 1873; m. Ellen Garvin of Boston, Mass. Ch.:
    1 Ezra G.[10], b. 1871; res. Irondale, O.
  iv Lucius T., b. 6 June, 1829; d. 27 March, 1830.
  v Lucian L., b. 20 Jan., 1831; d. in Dudley, Mass., 8 Dec., 1888; m. 1874, Nellie M., dau. of Richard and Mary (Ashworth)

Hargreaves of England; b. 4 Aug., 1842; she res. Peru, N. Y., before marriage. Ch.:

1 *Nellie A.*[10], b. 5 July, 1876; m. 17 Oct., 1904, Fred E., son of LaFayette W. and Lucia (Brigham) Stevens of Island Pond, Vt., where they res.

2 *Nettie L.*, b. 20 Oct., 1881; m. 30 Oct., 1900, Ralph W. Nichols of Saundersville, Mass. Ch. (Nichols): Corydon R.[11], b. 18 Feb., 1904.

vi Loren M., b. 6 Sept., 1842; d. on field of battle at Gettysburg, 3 July, 1863; he was in Co. F, 1st Vt. Cavalry.

vii Lucia A., b. 2 Sept., 1845; m. 1872, Lafayette W. Stevens, b. 14 Aug., 1850; res. Island Pond. Ch. (Stevens).

1 *Fred E.*[10], b. 3 Sept., 1872; m. Nellie A., dau. of Lucian L. Brigham.

727 ABIGAIL M.[8], daughter of Aaron[7] and Abigail (Maynard) Brigham; born 30 Dec., 1798; died 28 Oct., 1876; married 27 Nov., 1845, Leonard Gilson of East Burke, Vt.; born 8 May, 1795; died 24 Oct., 1869.

Children (Gilson), probably born in E. Burke:

i Lucinda[9], b. 24 Oct., 1821; m. 27 Nov., 1845, John Graves.

ii David, b. 30 April, 1824; d. 21 Dec., 1897; m. 21 Oct., 1850, Fanny Phippen.

iii Clara, b. 16 June, 1826; m. 14 Feb., 1851, Hollis Shorey.

iv Daniel B., b. 18 July, 1828; m. 22 Aug., 1858, Harriet E. Hill; res. E. Burke, Vt. Ch., b. there:

1 *Fred O.*[10], b. 7 June, 1859; d. 7 Oct., 1863.

2 *Alvah D.*, b. 28 March, 1863; m. 20 Jan., 1885, Mary E. Brown.

3 *George A.*, b. 21 Aug., 1867; m. 7 June, 1899, Lettie B. Stearns.

4 *Eda M.*, b. 13 Aug., 1872; d. 29 Sept., 1883.

v Lemon, b. 21 Oct., 1830; m. Emily Kimball, 2 May, 1858; d. 11 Aug., 1863.

vi Abigail M., b. 18 Jan., 1834; d. 13 Sept., 1867.

vii Mary, b. 24 April, 1836; d. 27 July, 1852.

728 THOMAS[8], son of Aaron[7] and Abigail (Maynard) Brigham; born in Charleston, Vt., 1816; died in Lawrence, Mass., 1873; married (1) in St. Johnsbury, Vt., 1843, Abigail Pierce, who died in 1861; married (2) 1866, Phoebe Watson. Was a marble cutter in St. Johnsbury; thence moved to Lawrence.

Children, born in St. Johnsbury:

i Charles W.[9], b. 2 Oct., 1845; m. 1870, Abbie Harvey of Burke, Vt.; res. Pelham, N. H. Ch., b. in Concord, Vt ·

1 *Sidney L.*[10], b. 1875.

ii Helen, b. 1851; m. 1872, in St. Johnsbury, Almon N. Bryant, who d. in Lawrence, 1896; she res. there, a widow. Ch. (Bryant), b. in St. Johnsbury:

1 *Mary L.*[10], b. 1873; res. Lawrence.

2 *Seth P.*, b. 1875; res. Lawrence.

iii Sidney H., b. 10 March, 1853; d. in Lawrence, 23 Nov., 1903; m. 1875, Sarah A., dau. of Eben Woodbury of Andover and

Lawrence, Mass.; b. in Andover, 1856; res. in Lawrence. He was connected with the Lawrence Post Office over 25 years. Was postmaster 1898-1902. Ch.:

1 *Helen*[10], b. in Lawrence, 1886; d. 1904.

729 REV. AZEL PARKHURST[8], son of Thomas[7] and Mary W. (Lacy) Brigham; born in Enosburg, Vt., 7 April, 1809; died in Plymouth (or Lebanon), N. H., 28 Sept., 1843; married 7 April, 1834, Amanda Adams of Henniker, N. H. They resided in Henniker. Mrs. Brigham resided in Lebanon, N. H., in 1905.

Children, born in Henniker:

    i Carrie Augusta[9], b. 6 Oct., 1835; m. 1 Jan., 1857, George W. C. Dudley of Hanover, N. H.; res. Lebanon. Ch. (Dudley):

        1 *Sarah Amanda*[10], m. Eugene C. Chase of Lebanon. Ch. (Chase):
            i Helen[11]; ii Lyle; iii Eula; iv Lawrence.

        2 *Emma Gertrude*, m. William H. Jones of Nashua, N. H. Ch. (Jones): i Rae[11]; ii Leon; iii Forest.

    ii Emma Amanda, b. 7 May, 1843; res. 1903, unm., Lebanon.

730 WILLIAM LACY[8], son of Thomas[7] and Mary W. (Lacy) Brigham; born in Enosburg, Vt., 30 Dec., 1810; died in 1893; married, in Bath, N. H., 24 Nov., 1831, Achsah, daughter of Enoch and Ann (Bedel) Blake (who were also married in Bath, 25 Nov., 1799).

Children, born in Exeter, N. H., except the eldest:

    i Azel P.[9], b. in Littleton, N. H., 7 Sept., 1832; res. Milford, N. H.; is m. and has a family. See No. 816.

    ii Atlanta Ann, b. 27 May, 1837; d. at Exeter, 3 Sept., 1838.

    iii Ephraim Thomas, b. 31 March, 1839; d. in Key West, Fla., 16 Feb., 1894. See No. 816.

815   iv William Henry Brewster, b. 13 Aug., 1841.

816   v George Albert Draper, b. 29 Oct., 1843.

    vi Annie A., b. 28 March, 1847; d. in Tewksbury, Mass., 15 April, 1903; m. (1) Jan., 1866, Daniel W. Dudley of Exeter; m. (2) 10 May, 1877, John G. Atherton of Exeter. Ch. (Dudley):

        1 *Leola A.*[10], b. 16 Dec., 1866; m. 28 June, 1884, Charles A. Parker of Exeter. Ch. (Parker): i Dora I.[11], b. in Exeter, 13 July, 1887; ii Walter A., b. in S. Newmarket, N. H., 10 May, 1889.

        2 *George A.*, b. 28 Feb., 1868; m. 26 June, 1895, Grace B. Waldron of Portsmouth, N. H. Ch., b. in Exeter: i Ralph A.[11], b. 21 March, 1896; ii Gertrude M., b. 7 May, 1897.

817   vii Orange Scott, b. 15 Jan., 1852.

731 WILLIAM[8], son of Aaron[7] and Comfort (Valentine) Brigham; born in Northampton, Mass., 1 Oct., 1812; died in Westboro, Mass., 12 Aug., 1853; married (1) Jane C. Munroe of Boston, who died 16 May, 1838; married (2) in Concord, Mass., 14 June, 1839, Lucy Ann Merriam of Concord, who died 21 Jan., 1872.

Children (by second wife), all but the eldest born in So. Boston:

i William Cleveland⁹, b. in Boston, 2 Sept., 1840; d. 4 Dec., 1894; m. 2 Oct., 1867, Marcia W., dau. of Samuel and Anna (Marshbank) Sheppard; b. 24 Oct., 1844; d. 2 May, 1877; res. Concord, Mass. Ch., the 3d and 4th b. in Boston:

1 *Waldo¹⁰*, b. in Salem, 16 June, 1869; d. 18 Nov., 1893.

2 *Emma S.*, b. in Cambridgeport, 27 June, 1871; d. 22 Oct., 1871.

3 *Lucy M.*, b. 23 April, 1873; res. Boston.

4 *Louise A.*, b. 10 Jan., 1875; res. N. Y.

5 *Anna E.*, b. in Medford, Mass., 9 Feb., 1876; m. 29 Jan., 1902, Edward M. Fisher; res. N. Y.

ii Jane Munroe, b. 30 Aug., 1842; m. William Le Brun, 3 June, 1866, in Hanover, Germany; he d. in York, Me., Aug., 1883.

iii Charles P., b. 23 May, 1844; d. 28 July, 1846.

iv Alice, b. 11 Aug., 1847; d. Jan., 1893; m. George S. Parsons, in Framingham, Mass., 31 Dec., 1868; he also d. Ch. (Parsons):

1 *Lucy Brigham¹⁰; 2 Joseph L.; 3 Alice Munroe; 4 Ethel.*

732 LEVI SAMUEL⁸, son of Dea. Abel⁷ and Mary (Bigelow) Brigham; born in Marlboro, Mass., 4 Aug., 1825; died in Ayer, Mass., 1 April, 1892; married (1) 7 Sept., 1845, Sophronia, daughter of Luke and Anna (Gleason) Rice of Marlboro; born 1 April, 1828; died 16 May, 1848; married (2) 22 Jan., 1850, Elizabeth Davenport, born 11 Feb., 1826; died 10 Nov., 1891. Resided in Ashby and Ayer, Mass.

Children (by first wife), born in Ashby:

i Abel Rice⁹, b. 21| Nov., 1846; d. in Milford, Mass., 18 May, 1906; m. 7 Oct., 1874, Addie, dau. of George Tabor of Rockville, R. I.; b. 7 Sept., 1844; he was in Co. B, 6th Mass. Infantry, Civil War, and member Post 22, G. A. R., Milford; a pattern maker; res. Milford. Ch., b. in Woonsocket, R. I.:

1 *Della Adelaide¹⁰*, b. 1 Aug., 1877; m. 26 Sept., 1900, Francis Ballou Follet.

2 *Everett Linwood*, b. 24 Feb., 1880; res. Indianapolis, Ind.

Children (by second wife), born Ashby:

ii Edwin Davenport, b. 13 Nov., 1850; m. 23 Aug., 1876, Elis Wanstrom of Sweden; res. in Ashburnham, Mass., a coal and ice dealer. Ch.:

1 *Charles Edwin¹⁰*, b. in Seekonk, Mass., 12 June, 1878; d. unm., 8 April, 1902.

2 *Fred W.*, b. in Ashburnham, 7 July, 1882; is a photographer.

iii Orison Orlando, b. 1 Aug., 1852; d. s. p., March, 1901, in Gardner, Mass.; m. 1887, Edwina A. Chapman.

iv Mary Alice, b. 12 June, 1854; d. 7 Aug., 1855.

v Lizzie Jane, b. 15 June, 1856; d. 8 Sept., 1856.

vi Lyra Sophronia, b. 5 Dec., 1857; d. 22 Jan., 1902, in Gardner; m. W. E., son of Samuel Knight of Harrisville, N. H.; res. Gardner. Ch. (Knight):

1 *Howard L.¹⁰; 2 Flora M.; 3 Harry O.; 4 Lizzie.*

vii Lucien Elmer, b. 29 Dec., 1861; res. unm., a farmer in Gardner.

viii Bertis Bigelow, b. 17 June, 1870; m. 24 June, 1891, Mary E.,

Lewis Frederick Rice and Hs Wife, Caroline Elizabeth Ells   522

dau. of Samuel R. Sprague of Malone, N. Y.; b. 21 March, 1871; res. a carpenter, Westboro. Ch., b. in Barre Plains, Mass.:
1 *Clara Estella*[10], b. 17 April, 1895.

733 CATHERINE ELIZABETH[8], daughter of Deacon Abel[7] and Mary (Bigelow) Brigham; born in Marlboro, Mass., 27 Feb., 1831; married 5 April, 1849, Alden Phelps; born 13 Dec., 1823; died 20 July, 1890. Resided Fitchburg, Mass.

Children (Phelps):
  i Samuel Dennis[9], b. in Marlboro, 8 Dec., 1849; d. there, 19 Oct., 1853.
  ii Mary Bigelow, b. in Sterling, Mass., 9 Nov., 1851; m. 30 March, 1875, Edward M. Palmer, b. 2 Oct., 1854. Ch. (Palmer):
    1 *Hattie E.*[10], b. 8 March, 1876; m. 4 March, 1899, Chas. W. Rumrill; 1 ch.
    2 *Almira E.*, b. 5 June, 1878; m. Herbert F. Rumrill.
    3 *Adelaide C.*, b. 1 July, 1880; m. 6 Feb., 1901, Willis Whitten.
    4 *Edna M.*, b. 1 Jan., 1882.
    5 *Frank H.*, b. 22 Oct., 1884.
    6 *Kathie L.*, b. 2 Feb., 1886.
    7 *Rufus A.*, b. July, 1888; d. Jan., 1890.
    8 *Irene L.*, b. 29 Oct., 1890.
    9 *Cecil E.*, b. 16 Dec., 1893; d. 17 Dec., 1896.
  iii Austin A., b. 22 July, 1854; unm.
  iv Lizzie Rebecca, b. 20 Jan., 1857; d. 4 Feb., 1905; m. 17 Feb., 1882, Stuart J. Park, b. 10 May, 1854; d. 13 Oct., 1900. Ch. (Park):
    1 *Arthur Stuart*[10], b. 4 July, 1883.
    2 *Ray Silas*, b. and d. 1887.

734 EDWARD[8], son of Daniel[7] and Sophronia (Emerson) Brigham; born in No. Bridgton, Me., 24 Jan., 1826; died in Westboro, Mass., 14 June, 1868; married 9 June, 1859, Ellen, daughter of Nathan and Eliza (Stevens) Whitney; born in Bolton, Mass., 11 Dec., 1838; died in Worcester, Mass., 3 June, 1887.

Child, born in Westboro:
  i Merrill Draper[9], b. 26 Jan., 1866; m. 9 Oct., 1889, Alice Gray Brown of Newburyport, Mass., b. 27 Nov., 1863; in business in Worcester, Mass., where he res. Ch.:
    1 *Lawrence Whitney*[10], b. 17 Oct., 1890; 2 *Ruth Montague*, b. 24 May, 1892; 3 *Harold Kingsbury*, b. 1 Feb., 1894; 4 *Ellenore A.;* 5 *Margaret;* 6 *Alden I.*

735 SETH E.[8], son of Daniel[7] and Sophronia (Emerson) Brigham; born in Bridgton, Me., 2 June, 1834; married 12 Jan., 1859, Louisa M., daughter of George and Sophronia (Houghton) Fitch of Lancaster, Mass.; born 5 Dec., 1832; died in Fitchburg, Mass., after a lingering illness and great suffering, 22 Nov., 1902. He is a blacksmith and resides in Fitchburg.

Children, born in Fitchburg:
    i Helen Sophronia⁹, b. 22 Oct., 1859; res. unm., Boston, a book-keeper, holding a very responsible position.
    ii Everett Edward, b. 23 June, 1861; d. in Fitchburg, unm., 12 Dec., 1884.
    iii William Emerson, b. 18 July, 1864; res. unm., Fitchburg; with the Fitchburg Ry.
    iv Melville Webb, b. 25 Feb., 1873; d. in California, unm., 16 Feb., 1899.

736 LOUISA⁸, daughter of Henry⁷ and Mary (Estes) Brigham; born in Waterford, Me., 30 June, 1830; died in Minnesota, 7 Jan., 1892; married May, 1849, Albert Valentine Hamlin of Waterford; born 16 June, 1821; died 17 Oct., 1864, drowned in White River, Arkansas, while going south to join his regiment. They removed to Wabasha Co., Minn., from No. Bridgton or Waterford.

Children (Hamlin):
    i Florence L.⁹, b. in N. B., 10 Aug., 1850; m. 22 Dec., 1867, Hiram P., son of Minot Boyd; b. 19 Oct., 1841; res. Plainview, Minn. Ch. (Boyd):
        1 *Hattie E.*¹⁰, b. 21 June, 1870.
        2 *Carrie G.*, b. 10 Dec., 1872; m. 26 June, 1895, Arthur Hale Davis; 4 ch.
        3 *Olive B.*, b. 17 April, 1879; m. 8 March, 1900, William Drury; 2 ch.
        4 *Walton H.*, b. 16 Jan., 1886.
    ii Isabella M., b. in Smithfield, Minn., 31 July, 1858; d. 25 Feb., 1891.
    iii Charles Lincoln, b. 27 June, 1864; m. 25 Dec., 1896, Isabelle Woods; res. Plainview. Ch.:
        1 *Eva*¹⁰, b. 27 Sept., 1897.

737 ELIZA MARIA⁸, daughter of Loring⁷ and Clarissa A. (Fay) Brigham; born in Northboro, Mass., 30 Oct., 1821; married 15 April, 1840, Benjamin, son of Aaron Hastings; born in Boylston, Mass., 27 May, 1817; died 28 April, 1892. They resided in Grafton, Shrewsbury, Northboro, and Boylston, Mass. She resides now in Boylston Centre.

Children (Hastings), the 4 younger born in Boylston:
    i Charles Henry⁹, b. Grafton, 17 Jan., 1841; m. (1) 1868, Ellen O. Ball; m. (2) Mary I. Cooley. Ch.:
        1 *Ellen*¹⁰; 2 *Edward.*
    ii John Edward, b. in Shrewsbury, Mass., 14 Dec., 1842; d. in Boylston, 25 Nov., 1860.
    iii Clarissa Augusta, b. in Northboro, 26 Aug., 1845; unm.
    iv Benjamin Eugene, b. in Boylston, 25 Jan., 1848; m. 1877, Carrie L. Frye. Ch.:
        1 *Charles*¹⁰; 2 *Carrie*; 3 *Benjamin*; 4 *William*; 5 *Frank.*
    v Miriam Maria, b. in Northboro, 2 July, 1850; d. in Lewiston, Me.; m. Daniel Lynch.

vi Nancy Sophia, b. 6 March, 1853; m. 1872, Charles F. Hale. Ch.
    (Hale):
    1 *Ralph*[10]*;* 2 *Charles;* 3 *George;* 4 *Marion.*
vii Walter, b. 20 Sept., 1856; m. 1889, Emma Harland. Ch.:
    1 *Leslie*[10].
viii George, b. 29 May, 1860.
ix Ida Janette, b. 5 June, 1865; d. 1880.

738 FREDERICK A.[8], son of Dr. Adolphus[7] and Rebecca W.
(Knowlton) Brigham; born in Shrewsbury, Mass., 1 April, 1835;
married 16 Oct., 1860, Mary A. H., daughter of Stephen Flagg;
born in Boylston, Mass., 16 Oct., 1842; died 5 Sept., 1894.

Mr. Brigham is a real estate dealer in Topeka, Kansas.

Children:
    i Arthur Alden[9], b. 26 May, 1862; d. 12 Sept., 1863.
    ii Alice Rebecca, b. 10 Jan., 1865; m. 13 Sept., 1890, Prof. Horace
       E., son of Horace L. Horton; a grad. of Harvard University;
       a chemist; res. Waukegan, Ill. Ch. (Horton):
       1 *James E.*[10], b. 2 July, 1891.
       2 *Alice C.,* b. 22 Sept., 1892; d. 1 Oct., 1893.
       3 *Margaret W.,* b. 13 Dec., 1895.
       4 *Horace B.,* b. 9 Jan., 1899.
    iii Edward Franklin, b. 16 Oct., 1866; a singer (basso profundo) of
        wide reputation; in 1902 he gave a recital before the B. F. A., and
        again in 1904. Res. New York City.

739 DR. FRANKLIN WHITING[8], son of Dr. Adolphus[7] and
Rebecca W. (Knowlton) Brigham; born in Shrewsbury, Mass., 13
Sept., 1841; died in Shrewsbury, 28 Feb., 1899; married 14 Sept.,
1869, Alice R., daughter of Joseph Bates of Providence, R. I.;
born 10 Feb., 1850; died 3 Feb., 1872.

Dr. Brigham was graduated from Harvard Medical School in
1865, and after serving two years as Acting Asst. Surgeon, U. S. N.
(1863-1865), settled in his native town, where he continued to reside, one of its most beloved and useful citizens. His father had
been known as " The Doctor of Shrewsbury," which applied with
equal force to the son. Not only Shrewsbury, but all surrounding
towns looked to him for health when ill. Probably no physician
in central Massachusetts was so often sought in consultation; none
have been more universally mourned. He was long conspicuous in
the Massachusetts Medical Society and repeatedly at the head of
the Worcester District Medical Society, always having been a close
student. Without political aspirations, his opinions were sought,
irrespective of party lines, upon all local improvements; chiefly to
his influence the town owed its public library; to all the needy, he
was a generous friend. His home, with its beautiful old-fashioned
furnishings, was charming, and none who ever visited there will forget it or the cordial greeting of the master of the house.

He was one of the officers of the Brigham Family Association from its inception and was always present at the meetings until 1898, and none gave it a heartier " God-speed."

He was an occasional poet and essayist. The following verses, written by him, were sung at the funeral of his mother, and were rendered by the quartet of his choice, at his own obsequies:

> "Father of all, to Thee returns my soul,
> Worn with the travail of the earthly strife;
> Henceforth, Thy mansions blest shall be my goal,
> And the glad leisure of celestial life.

> "Friends of my heart, I will not say adieu,
> For you shall follow me, ere many days;
> Impatient I shall there be waiting you,
> Where funeral dirges change to songs of praise."

Child, born in Shrewsbury:
    i Estella^9, b. 29 March, 1871; d. 12 Sept., 1871.

740   REV. SIDNEY S.^{8}, son of William D.^{7} and Lucy (Doane) Brigham; born in St. Albans, Vt., 15 Feb., 1836; married 27 May, 1861, Anna Beals. He is a retired minister of the M. E. Church, and resides in Underhill, Vt. He enlisted as a private, Co. H, 3d Vt. Vols., and was mustered out Capt., July, 1864, having been in 27 battles and skirmishes.

Children:
    i William Sidney^9, b. in Swanton, Vt., 6 Dec., 1863; m. 8 June, 1892, Lulu V. Crowell; res. a merchant in Westfield, Mass. Ch.:
       1 *Wesley C.*^{10}, b. 12 Dec., 1894.
    ii Fannie Ainsley, b. 24 Dec., 1871; m. 30 Oct., 1895, R. C. Ballard, a farmer of Fairfax, Vt. Ch. (Ballard):
       1 *George Kenneth*^{10}, b. 31 Oct., 1898.
    iii Winona L., b. 10 July, 1877; m. 16 Dec., 1901, R. W. Taft of Burlington, Vt. Ch. (Taft):
       1 *Robert Brigham*^{10}, b. 4 Oct., 1902.

741   SANFORD J.^{8}, son of William D.^{7} and Lucy (Doane) Brigham; born in St. Albans, Vt., 31 Jan., 1838; married 4 Nov., 1862, Sarah J. Bronson, who died 20 March, 1901. He is a farmer and resides in St. Albans.

Children, born in St. Albans:
    i Henry S.^{9}, b. 20 July, 1864; m. Dec., 1892, Carrie A. Holyoke; res. St. Albans. Ch.:
       1 *Marion S.*^{10}, b. 24 Aug., 1893; 2 *Anice S.*, d. y.; 3 *Dorothy*, b. 30 Aug., 1899; 4 *John H.*, b. Jan., 1901.
    ii Lummus, b. 28 Nov., 1865; d. while a student at Dartmouth Coll., 13 March, 1891.
    iii Elbert S., b. 19 Oct., 1887; was grad. B. S., Middlebury Coll., 1903.

Franklin W. Brigham

ENGRAVED FOR THE BRIGHAM FAMILY HISTORY

742 IRA[8], son of Joel[7] and Nancy (Brigham) Brigham; born in Berlin, Mass., 12 Jan., 1809; died 11 Feb., 1892; married Betsey, daughter of Luther Carter; born 20 March, 1814; died 12 April, 1856. They resided in Berlin but died in Northboro.

Children, born in Berlin:
- i George L.[9], b. 5 Dec., 1835; d. y.
- ii Louisa E., b. 3 March, 1838; d.
- iii George Henry, b. 5 Dec., 1841; m. 5 Aug., 1863, Elizabeth Hastings; res. Northboro. Ch., b. in Northboro:
  - 1 *George E.*[10], b. 9 Oct., 1864; m. Lillian Hastings, Boston.
  - 2 *Bessie E.*, b. 31 May, 1868; m. 11 Sept., 1889, Frank A. Hadley. Ch. (Hadley): i Mildred W.[11], b. 29 Aug., 1892; ii Walter C., b. 6 Feb., 1894; res. Greendale (Worcester), Mass.
  - 3 *Grace V.*, b. 5 Dec., 1872; m. 1 Feb., 1893, Maitland D. Bailey.

743 ABRAHAM[8], son of Joel[7] and Nancy (Brigham) Brigham; born in Northboro, Mass., 23 Jan., 1816; died in Chicago, Ill., 23 Nov., 1857; married 2 Dec., 1840, Hannah A. Stone of Westboro, Mass.; born 15 Sept., 1822; died in Berlin, 26 Dec., 1857. He resided for a time at Berlin (Carterville) from 1852, where he manufactured shoes under the firm name of "Brigham & Stone." The male line is extinct.

Children, born in Northboro.
- i George A.[9], b. 8 Sept., 1841; d. from fright, 26 Jan., 1856.
- ii Marion S., b. 25 Nov., 1843; married 1 July, 1860, Charles B. Rathbun of Berlin. Ch. (Rathbun), b. in Berlin:
  - 1 *Alice M.*[10], b. 3 Oct., 1867; m. 3 Oct., 1893, Dr. Frank L. Harvey of Leominster, Mass.; res. Milford, Mass.; he has a private hospital.
- iii Annie Louisa, b. 22 March, 1845; m. 18 April, 1861, Benjamin F. Seymour; res. Ohio.
- iv Henrietta D., b. 7 June, 1848; m. 28 May, 1867, Edward S. Bryant from Hyde Park, Vt., to Berlin, Mass.; removed to Sullivan, N. H., 1885, where he d. 23 Aug., 1889; he was in the Civil War. After his death she returned to Berlin. Ch. (Bryant), b. in Berlin:
  - 1 *Edith L.*[10], b. 19 May, 1869; 2 *Eva E.*, b. 19 May, 1869; m. Lester, son of Rufus Wheeler; res. Sullivan, N. H.; 3 *George E.*, b. 15 March, 1873; 4 *Lillian E.*, b. 26 Aug., 1877; 5 *Carroll W.*, b. 28 May, 1884.

744 JOHN[8], son of Joel[7] and Nancy (Brigham) Brigham; born in Northboro, Mass., 1818; died there 1 June, 1893; married 22 April, 1842, Mary S., daughter of Edward Bemis; born in Westboro, Mass., 5 Jan., 1820; died 19 Sept., 1892. He was a farmer and resided in Northboro.

Children:
- 818   i Charles L.[9], b. in Berlin, 22 April, 1844.
- 819   ii Walter Augustus, b. in Boylston, 22 May, 1846.
-      iii Ellen M., b. 3 March, 1850; m. March, 1870, Alvin Wheeler of Marlboro; d. s. p., 3 Dec., 1872.

iv Delia F., b. 16 Sept., 1858; m. in Baltimore, Md., 3 Dec., 1884, Edwin S., son of T. F. Corey; b. 31 Dec., 1861, in Brighton, Mass.; she was grad. State Normal School; res. Northboro. Ch. (Corey), b. in Northboro:
    1 *Florence E.*[10], b. 1 Oct., 1885; 2 *Marjorie M.*, b. 30 July, 1889; 3 *Dorothy Brigham*, b. 6 Nov., 1899.
v George A., b. 17 Nov., 1859; m. 29 June, 1880, Sarah A., dau. of Rev. Edward A. Goddard; b. 9 Sept., 1858; a farmer in Northboro. Ch.:
    1 *Ellen Marion*[10], b. in Boylston, 27 Aug., 1883; res. in Northboro; 2 *Robert Goddard*, b. in Northboro, 18 April, 1892.
vi Florence A., b. 3 Oct., 1862; m. 21 Feb., 1884, William J., son of Cyrus Potter; res. Northboro. Ch. (Potter):
    1 *Raymond B.*[10], and 2 *Norman B.*, twins b. 5 July 1886.

745 SAMUEL[8], son of Joel[7] and Nancy (Brigham) Brigham; born in Berlin, Mass., 5 April., 1822; died 9·Oct., 1878; married 3 Nov., 1857, Mrs. Sarah E. Bemis, daughter of Asa P. and Hannah (Pierce) Miller; born in Westboro, Mass., 25 Jan., 1826. Mr. Brigham was a teacher of the violin in early life, and later became a farmer. Resided in Northboro, Mass.

    i Emma L.[9], b. in Berlin, 27 Sept., 1860; m. 27 June, 1876, Clarence W., son of Daniel Rowland of Boston; b. 18 Feb., 1853; was grad. Amherst Agricultural College; d. 10 June, 1886. Ch. (Rowland):
        1 *Caroline*[10], b. 3 Sept., 1879; m. 21 June, 1906, Robert, son of Robert MacKenzie of Auchinines-Dalbeattie, Scotland, and of Barre, Vt.; she is a soloist and church singer in Boston.
        2 *Ethel*, b. 9 Dec., 1883; was grad. from Boston Normal School, 1904.
    ii Lilla E., b. in Northboro, 13 Aug., 1866; m. 7 Oct., 1885, Herbert A. Smith of Bridgewater, Mass.; s. p.

746 CHARLES H.[8], son of John Swarrow[7] and Parmelia (Brace) Brigham; born near Rochester, N. Y., 30 June, 1830; married (1) Phalla House, who died 22 April, 1873; married (2) Lelia P. Wheeler, in 1876. He has resided in Somnauk, Ill., Hamilton, Mich., and Page Co., Ia.

Children (by first wife):
    i Charles W.[9], b. 27 Sept., 1858; m. 31 Dec., 1880, Elizabeth Cain; res. St. Joseph, Mo. Ch.:
        1 *Oscar Leroy*[10], b. 27 Nov., 1881; m. Charlotte ———. Ch.: Oscar Denton[11], b. 1 Dec., 1901.
        2 *Robert*, b. 22 Oct., 1883; 3 *Kenneth*, b. 7 Oct., 1887; 4 *Charles*, b. 7 Jan., 1889.
    ii Frank, b. 8 June, 1860; m. 15 Feb., 1881, Nellie L., dau. of A. E. Ames of Somnauk, Ill.; b. 17 April, 1863; res. in Fostoria, Ia. Ch., the 2 younger b. in Mason City, Ia.:
        1 *Wesley Duane*[10], b. in Wedron, Ill., 21 Jan., 1882; d. 16 Oct., 1890.
        2 *Alice May*, b. in Sandwich, Ill., 21 April, 1884; m. 4 Jan., 1905, Archibald Cutler of Langdon, Ia., b. 11 Dec., 1882.

3 *Henry Arthur*, b. in Primghar, Ia., 24 Dec., 1887; 4 *Leslie Harold*, b. 29 Dec., 1895; 5 *Harriet Dorris*, b. 11 Oct., 1897.

820 iii Edward D., b. 22 Feb., 1863.
iv Ellen M., b. 29 July, 1865; d. s. p., 1 Dec., 1903; m. 29 June, 1899, Ezra H. Stevens.
v Nelson J., b. 6 Dec., 1870; d. 6 Sept., 1886.
vi Oscar Duane, b. 23 Nov., 1873; m. Rachel Mackie; res. Chicago, Ill. Ch.:
1 *Mildred M.*[10], b. 6 Aug., 1896; 2 *Marjorie M.; 3 Arthur Brigham.*
vii Mae, b. 7 March, 1879; m. 6 Jan., 1899, William W. Shannon. Ch. (Shannon):
1 *Lloyd*[10], b. 3 Aug., 1900; 2 *Earl*, b. 29 Sept., 1902; 3 *Infant*, b. 18 Feb. 1905.
viii Grace, b. 6 April, 1880.
ix Harry, b. 12 May, 1881.
x Elroy C., b. 21 Feb., 1884; d. 12 Sept., 1904.
xi Flora, b. 1 Oct., 1887.

747 CHARLES FIDELIO[8], son of Wesley Hervey[7] and Harriet N. (Smith) Brigham; born in Youngsville, Pa., 18 April, 1848; married (1) 1869, Mary Keller, born 9 June, 1851; died 23 Dec., 1884; married (2) 7 Feb., 1887, Margaret Jack, born 29 April, 1851; died in New York City, 4 March, 1899; married (3) 14 Sept., 1905, Electa Groger, born 3 April, 1847. He has been employed on the Pa. Ry. for more than 30 years, and has won meritorious distinction. He resides in Oil City, Pa.

Children (by first wife):
i Harry Risley[9], b. in Alexandria, Va., 5 Nov., 1869; m. 24 July, 1889, Cora Blakeley, b. in Corry, Pa., 7 June, 1870; Ry. Engineer. Ch., b. in Oil City:
1 *Edward L.*[10], b. 10 May, 1891; d. 5 Oct., 1891.
2 *Florence E.*, b. 9 Oct., 1892.
ii Harriet Louisa, b. 27 May, 1877; d. 15 Nov., 1877.
iii Harriet Louisa, b. in Oil City, 12 Nov., 1878; m. 12 Sept., 1905, Oliver M., son of Rev. O. C. Sherman of Plum, Pa.
Children (by second wife), b. in Oil City:
iv Charles Fidelio, b. 27 April, 1888.
v Samuel Jack, b. Feb., 1890.
vi Richard Douglass, b. 5 May, 1892.

748 EDMUND DOUGLASS[8], son of Rev. George French[7] and Aurilla E. (Douglass) Brigham; born in Dunkirk, N. Y., 29 Dec., 1856; married, 12 Aug., 1879, in Republic, Mich., Edith, daughter of Prof. John Northmore (a well-known educator in Northern Michigan).

He is General Freight Agent for the Chicago and North-Western Railway and largely interested in successful gold mining properties in Sonora, Mexico, and California. Resides in Glencoe, a suburb of Chicago.

Children, the 2 younger born in Chicago:
822 i George Samuel⁹, b. in Ishpeming, Mich., 27 May, 1880.
ii Edmund Douglass, Jr., b. in Fond du Lac, Wis., 13 June, 1884; a student in Colorado School of Mines, Golden, Col.
iii John Northmore, b. 1ˑ Sept., 1887; a student in Yale University.
iv Fanny, b. 29 Sept., 1890.

749 GEORGE FRENCH, JR.⁸, son of Rev. George French⁷ and Aurilla E. (Douglass) Brigham; born in Fredonia, N. Y., 12 Jan., 1863; married in Kansas City, Mo., 14 Jan., 1891, Nellie Carrie, daughter of James Watkins.

He is General Agent for the Freight and Passenger Department of the C. & N. W. Ry., St. Louis., Mo., and resides there.

Children, the 2 younger born in St. Louis:
i James Watkins⁹, b. in Kansas City, 20 Oct., 1891.
ii Aurilla Douglass, b. 10 May, 1895.
iii Godfrey Macdonald, b. 15 Dec., 1897.

750 HENRY HANSON⁸, son of Rev. George French⁷ and Aurilla E. (Douglass) Brigham; born in Sharon, Wis., 31 Aug., 1868; married in Burlington, Wis., 27 Nov., 1894, Ethelyn Belle, only daughter of Adams J. Hanna.

He is General Traffic Manager for the Booth Company of Chicago, Ill., and of the Booth Line of Lake Superior Steamers. Resides in Glencoe, Ill.

Children, born in Chicago:
i Frances Elizabeth⁹, b. 22 Jan., 1896; d. 9 Oct., 1896.
ii Erwin Risley, b. 9 April, 1897.
iii Edith, b. 10 Jan., 1902; d. 12 Feb., 1902.
iv Edith Margaret, b. 21 Jan., 1903.

751 COL. JOSEPH HENRY⁸, son of Winfield Scott⁷ and Mary E. (White) Brigham; born in Lodi, Ohio, 12 Dec., 1838; died in Delta, O., at the home of his son Roy, 30 June, 1904; married 1 Dec., 1863, in Wauseon, O., Edna Allman, who died 20 Nov., 1903.

He enlisted as a private in Co. F, 12th O. Infantry, in 1861, for three months, and re-enlisted in Co. A, 69th O. Infantry, of which he became Captain; was promoted to be Lieut.-Col. of the regiment and later was brevetted Colonel, but not mustered out as such because there were too few men left in the regiment. He commanded a brigade on Sherman's March to the Sea. In 1873 he joined the order of Patrons of Husbandry; was Master of the State Grange for 10 years; Master of National Grange in 1888 and for 9 years; 3 terms sheriff of Fulton Co., O.; State Senator 1 term; trustee of State University; member of Board of Control of Ohio Experiment Station; member of Board of Managers of Ohio State Peni-

COLONEL JOSEPH H. BRIGHAM, OF DELTA, O. (751)

tentiary, 6 years, appointed by Gov. McKinley; member of Ohio State Board of Agriculture of which president 1 term; appointed U. S. Asst. Secretary of Agriculture by Pres't. McKinley, 22 March, 1897, by whom appointed Chairman Board of Management of Trans-Miss. and International Exposition at Omaha; also of the Pan American Exposition at Buffalo and of the Louisiana Purchase Exposition, St. Louis. He was 6 ft. 6 in. in height, and weighed 250 pounds. He was noted as being the tallest man in official life in Washington, D. C. He resided in Delta, O., when not in Washington.

Children:
    i Kate[9], b. 14 Nov., 1865; m. 18 March, 1887, William Leist. Ch. (Leist):
      1 *Henry*[10],
    ii Georgie, d. y.
    iii Bessie M., b. 12 Jan., 1873; m. Sept., 1893, Prof. R. H. Dunbar, Prin. of School, Delta, O. Ch. (Dunbar):
      1 *Fred D.*[10]; 2 *Marguerite.*
    iv Roy S., b. 2 July, 1874; m. April, 1896, Carrie E. Mason; he is a farmer. Ch.:
      1 *Helen*[10].
    v Harry H., b. 26 April, 1876; m. Mabel Coffin; res. Portland, Ore.
    vi Mary M., b. 12 Aug., 1879; m. S. S. Cline; res. Washington, D. C.
    vii Josephine, b. 22 Nov., 1882; res. with sister, Mrs. Cline, in Washington.

752   JOEL SEBASTIAN[8], son of Winfield Scott[7] and Mary E. (White) Brigham; born in Chatham, O., 28 Oct., 1850; married (1) 1875, Everna E. Overman of Pleasant Hill, Neb.; married (2) 27 Sept., 1880, Carrie A. Kellogg. He resided in Welles Point, Texas, and Toledo, O.; is an extensive gardener in Bowling Green, O.

Child (by first wife):
    i Erle W.[9], res. Lincoln, Neb.
Children (by second wife), the 2 elder born in Welles Point, the younger in Texas:
    ii Joel Winfield, b. 22 Jan., 1883.
    iii Stella May, b. 1 Dec., 1885.
    iv Helen M., b. 10 July, 1887.
    v Haven A., b. 13 July, 1893.

753   WALTER SCOTT[8], son of Joel[7] and Betsey (Lyon) Brigham; born in Lodi, O., 6 Aug., 1843; died in Wauseon, O., of apoplexy, 1 Jan., 1906; married (1) April, 1864, Julia, daughter of Warren Williams of Huron Co., O., who died 18 Jan., 1865; married (2) 13 Dec., 1866, Ellen, daughter Harvey Buchanan of Norwalk, O.

He enlisted 27 May, 1862, at the age of 18, as private; Co. I, 87th O. Vols. Inf., and was honorably discharged 3 Oct., 1862, a paroled prisoner, having been captured in Harper's Ferry. He was 14 years Ry. P. O. clerk, between Detroit and Cincinnati; Pres't. McKinley, in 1897, appointed him Postmaster in Wauseon, where he resided. It was through his influence that the first Rural Free Delivery was established in Fulton Co. He was highly esteemed in the community.

Children (by second wife), born in Wauseon:
  i Etta B.⁹, b. 7 Feb., 1869; was grad. 1888, N. W. Coll Inst.; m. 8 July, 1891, Bert W. Crissey; res. Oak Park, Ill. Ch. (Crissey), b. in Wauseon:
      1 *Lucel*¹⁰, b. 7 Nov., 1893; 2 *Mildred,* b. 4 Sept., 1895; 3 *Joel Brigham,* b. 8 Oct., 1898.
  ii Richard J., b. 2 Dec., 1870; d. 18 Jan., 1871.
  iii Ralph W., b. 11 Jan., 1874; expert electrician; m. Fanny Parsons; res. Wauseon. Ch.:
      1 *Walter Pearson*¹⁰, b. 29 July, 1904; 2 *Joel Harvey,* b. 8 July, 1906.

754 HAVEN T.⁸, son of Joel⁷ and Betsey (Lyon) Brigham; born in Lodi, O., 7 May, 1846; married 28 Sept., 1876, in Madison, N. Y., Elizabeth Harriet, daughter of John S. and Julia (Coe) Lucas; born in Madison, 3 Oct., 1852. At 16 he enlisted as a private in the Civil War, and served for six months; was honorably discharged. Early in life he was a partner in a book and stationery store; afterward became interested in telephone plants in Ohio and Iowa. Resides in Wauseon, O.

Children, born in Wauseon:
  i Laurence⁹, b. 7 Jan., 1880.
  ii Helen, b. 6 April, 1883.

755 BENJAMIN FRANKLIN⁸, son of Samuel⁷ and Emily Ann (Sweet) Brigham; born in Bainbridge, N. Y., 26 Aug., 1840; married (1) 22 Feb., 1866, Elizabeth J., daughter of Syrenus Luce; born in Orange, O., 1845; died in Chardon, O., 30 July, 1887; married (2) 17 June, 1891, Lynda B., daughter of H. J. Cleaves; born in Orwell, O., 15 July, 1860. He is a farmer and resides in Chardon.

Children (by first wife), born in Chardon:
  i Byron Franklin⁹, b. 9 Aug., 1867; m. 20 Dec., 1891, Lucy Harold; res. Windsor, O. Ch.:
      1 *Zelda J.*¹⁰, b. 29 April, 1893; 2 *Walter,* b. 5 Nov., 1894.
  ii Rudolph Clayton, b. 28 Dec., 1869; d. 4 May, 1886.
  iii Samuel Adrian, b. 3 July, 1877; m. 13 Feb., 1897, May D. Griffin; res. Chardon. Ch.:
      1 *Jesse Franklin*¹⁰, b. 5 Aug., 1902; 2 *Mildred,* b. 9 June, 1904.
  iv Benjamin Forest, b. 5 Dec., 1880.

756 SARAH ELIZABETH⁸, daughter of Luther⁷ and Parmelia (Barrie) Brigham; born 27 Sept., 1825; died in Northampton,

Mass., 25 July, 1886; married 16 June, 1847, Sylvester J. Bosworth of Northampton; born in 1818; died 14 Oct., 1886.

Children (Bosworth), born in Northampton:
    i Mary Ella⁹, b. 11 April, 1848; res. Florence, Mass.
    ii Helen Josephine, b. 19 Dec., 1849; d. 16 July, 1860.
    iii Jennie Lind, b. 20 Oct., 1852; d. 25 Sept., 1865.
    iv Herbert Sylvester, b. 22 July, 1854; d. 30 April, 1898, s. p.; m. June, 1886, Kate Eager; res. in Florence, Mass.
    v Luther Henry, b. 22 Aug., 1857; m. 5 Sept., 1882, Lillie C. King; res. Florence. Ch.:
        1 *Robert A.*¹⁰, b. 26 May, 1883; 2 *Nettie A.*, b. and d. 1886; 3 *Arthur K.*, b. 28 May, 1887.
    vi Emily Parmelia, b. 31 Oct., 1859; res. Florence, Mass.
    vii Jessie Fremont, b. 1 Feb., 1863; m. 13 Nov., 1886, Louis H. Bailey of Florence. Ch. (Bailey):
        1 *Henry S.*¹⁰, b. 1 Nov., 1887; 2 *Frederick L.*, b. 31 May, 1889; 3 *Irving*, b. 8 May, 1894; 4 *Helen L.*, b. 22 Jan., 1904.
    viii Anna Josephine, b. 12 April, 1866.

757 ELIJAH⁸, son of Silvester⁷ and Mary W. (Bingham) Brigham; born in Dover, Ill., 14 March, 1843; married 5 March, 1874, Julia P. Huntley. He was in the 134th Ill. Regt., Civil War; educated University of Chicago; in Real Estate and Fire Ins. business, Trinidad, Colo., where he resides.

Children, born in Trinidad:
    i Frank Elijah⁹, b. 27 Nov., 1877; d. 10 Jan., 1880.
    ii Eva Maud, b. 11 Oct., 1882.
    iii Dora M., b. 30 May, 1884.
    iv Leslie Elijah, b. 17 June, 1889.

758 GEORGE⁸, son of Silvester⁷ and Mary W. (Bingham) Brigham; born in Dover, Ill., 9 Oct., 1846; married 26 Feb., 1874, Mrs. Martha E. (Canover), widow of William Lawrence. He is a farmer and resides in Elk Falls, Kans.

Children, born in Elk Falls:
    i Hattie E.⁹, b. 8 Feb., 1875; d. 26 March, 1889.
    ii Clara C., b. 28 Dec., 1876; d. 3 April, 1877.
    iii Addie M., b. and d. 1878.
    iv Sylvester William, b. 24 Sept., 1879.
    v Charles M., b. 31 Dec., 1881.
    vi Clarence F., b. 16 Aug., 1884.
    vii Ray S., b. 11 Sept., 1886; d. 6 Feb., 1894.
    viii Arthur E., b. 24 April, 1889.
    ix Mary E., b. 25 Dec., 1891.

759 HON. WILLIAM OAKLEY⁸, son of Samuel Sumner⁷ and Mary (Powers) Brigham; born in Bakersfield, Vt., 16 May, 1836; married (1) 17 February, 1864, Nella M., daughter of John Perkins; born in Bakersfield, 6 March, 1844; died 10 Dec., 1893; married (2) 22 Oct., 1895, Rilla (Field) Worthing; born 26 Aug., 1846.

He was educated at Bakersfield Academy; from 1858-60 was in Illinois. Enlisted Sept., 1862, Co. G, 13th Vt. Vols.; was in the battle of Gettysburg; honorably discharged in 1863. Is a farmer and resides on his father's homestead in Bakersfield; he has held many town offices, selectman, etc.; 14 years overseer of the poor; Commander of the G. A. R. of Bakersfield; was in the Legislature in 1882.

Children (by first wife), born in Bakersfield:
821   i Clarence Sumner[9], b. 5 Feb., 1867.
    ii Clara S., b. 5 Feb., 1867; m. 23 Sept., 1896, Myron C. Boutwell; res. Shrewsbury, Mass. She was grad. from the Boston Art School; taught several years in Brigham Academy, Bakersfield. Ch. (Boutwell):
      1 *Doris Nella*[10], b. 21 May, 1898; 2 *Charles M.*, b. 16 April, 1902.
    iii John P., b. 18 July, 1872; matriculated Univ. Vt., but did not take a degree; was grad. Boston Dental Coll.; m. 29 Dec., 1896, Mabel A. Powers; practices dentistry in Winchendon, Mass. Ch.:
      1 *Muriel Adele*[10], b. 21 March, 1898.

760   DR. GEORGE STANNARD[8], son of Holloway Taylor[7] and Eunice (Fay) Brigham; born in Bakersfield, Vt., 16 June, 1845; married 22 June, 1875, Mrs. Benjamin Farrar (Emily Cook Burr); born in Fairfield, Vt., 6 May, 1840. He is a physician with a large practice in St. Cloud, Minn.; was graduated M. D., McGill Coll., Montreal, 1869, and M. D., Univ. Vt., 1870.

Children, the 2 younger born in St. Cloud:
    i Charles Fay[9], b. in Lancaster, Mass., 29 April, 1876; was grad. M. D., Univ. Minn., 1901; in practice with father in St. Cloud; m. 11 Nov., 1903, Frances A. Harmer of Minneapolis, Minn.
    ii Florence Louise, b. 11 March, 1878.
    iii Frank Taylor, b. 18 April, 1880; M. D., Univ. Minn., 1905.

761   WILLIAM ERASTUS[8], son of Moses[7] and Elmira E. (Fillebrown) Brigham; born in Boston, 16 Feb., 1865; married (1) 6 Sept., 1888, Lettie Jane, daughter of Francis Mitchell; born in Hartland, Me., 19 Nov., 1863; died in Somerville, Mass., 3 Aug., 1891; married (2) 21 Jan., 1899, Carrie Emerson, daughter of Jacob Everett Brown; born in Rye, N. H., 18 March, 1872.

He was graduated from the Somerville High School, 1884; 7 years on editorial staff of the Boston *Globe;* 2 years managing editor Lynn *Daily Press;* 3 years manager Somerville *Citizen;* in 1898 attached to and later legislative and political writer Boston *Transcript;* since 1902 private secretary to Eugene N. Foss; is of musical tastes and education. He was President of the Brigham Family Association during the reconstruction period, 1896-1900; one of the Publication Committee, and associate editor of the History of the

WILLIAM E. BRIGHAM (761)
President of the Brigham Family Association, 1896-1900

Brigham Family; resided in Somerville since 1868. Was the chief instrument in preparing the present accurate history of the resideuces of the Puritan Thomas in America, which has never before been published.

Children (by first wife), born in Somerville:
    i Editha⁹, b. 3 Dec., 1889; d. 14 July, 1893.
    ii Son, b. and d. 3 Aug., 1891.

762 CLARENCE LINCOLN⁸, son of Luther Ayres⁷ and Helen Juliette (Temple) Brigham; born in Colrain, Mass., 6 April, 1866; married 26 Jan., 1887, Lizzie P., daughter of William P. March; born in Stuttgart, Germany, 17 April, 1866. He resides in Elm Grove, Mass., on the family place; is a musician and music dealer, also a band-master; has been in charge of music in the public schools of Colrain, Buckland, Shelburn, Leyden and Leverett for several years.

Children:
    i Warren Luther⁹, b. in Brattleboro, Vt., 2 Dec., 1887; he is a professional violoncellist; he and his father gave their services at the meeting in 1904, of the B. F. A.
    ii Arthur Temple, b. 12 Jan., 1890.
    iii Rose Marie, b. 26 Dec., 1894.

763 WILLIAM MUNROE⁸, son of Addington Munroe⁷ and Mary (Estabrook) Brigham; born in Marlboro, Mass., 23 January, 1864; married 21 June, 1889, Florence Rhoda, daughter of John and Catherine (Constable) Eyers; born in Northampton, Eng., in 1866.

He was graduated from Boston University, College of Liberal Arts, A. B., in 1887; LL. B., in 1889; admitted to Middlesex Co. bar in 1889; practiced law in Marlboro; appointed Associate Justice of Marlboro Police Court; served as Representative from 21st Middlesex Dist. (which includes the city of Marlboro and the towns of Sudbury and Wayland), 1899-1907, inclusive. Was on Recess Committee for Revising Pub. Statutes; on Committee to receive Pres't. McKinley in 1899; chairman of Committee on Cities 6 years.

Children, the first and third born in Marlboro:
    i Ulysses Addington⁹, b. 31 Aug., 1890.
    ii Alfred Estabrook, b. in Belchertown, Mass., 3 Aug., 1892.
    iii William Munroe, Jr., b. 12 Dec., 1894.

764 GEORGE H.⁸, son of Charles Amory⁷ and Eliza A. (Fairbanks) Brigham; born in Nashua, N. H., 1 March, 1851; married Sarah M. Peaseley; born 15 Sept., 1857.

He resides in Nashua where he has been Councilman, Alderman, State Representative, Street Commissioner, etc. In the '70s he carried the U. S. Mail across Nebraska; carried dispatches in the Sioux War; is a member of the Nashua Board of Trade; member of the Legislature of New Hampshire in 1907 and in previous years.

Children, born in Nashua:
    i Sadie P.^{9}, b. 3 June, 1879.
    ii Charles E., b. 29 Aug., 1882.
    iii Jessie P., b. 14 March, 1887.
    iv Rosalie, b. 31 July, 1895.
    v Mary E., b. 8 Jan., 1898.
    vi Kathryn, b. 16 May, 1900.

765   HIRAM N.^{8}, son of William C.^{7} and Polly (Cox) Brigham; born in Lorraine, N. Y., 3 May, 1829; married 12 Oct., 1854, Amanda, daughter of Warren Horr; born in LeRoy, N. Y., 1 Jan., 1835. Resides in Pilot Knob, Wis.

Children, the first 7 born in Lorraine:
    i Wellington C.^{9}, b. 12 Nov., 1855; m. 1881, ————; a farmer, res. Pilot Knob.
    ii Annie, b. 15 June, 1857; d. 18 Oct., 1875.
    iii Ella J., b. 24 Jan., 1859; m. 1886, Byron T. Plugh; res. Rhinelander, Wis., where town treasurer; 3 yrs. in 12th Wisconsin Hvy. Arty. in Civil War. Ch. (Plugh):
        1 *Nellie D.*^{10}, b. 6 March, 1882.
    iv Etta, b. 5 Feb., 1861; m. 1885, ———— Dimmock; res. Sackett Harbor, N. Y.
    v Orin, b. 6 March, 1863; res. Havre, Mont.
    vi Byron, b. Aug., 1865; res. Westfield, Wis., where he has a dairy farm.
    vii Henry, b. 15 June, 1868; a farmer, res. Pilot Knob.
    viii Minnie, b. Pilot Knob, 15 Sept., 1872; m. ———— Farnsworth.
    ix Viola, b. 16 July, 1875; d. 2 Jan., 1876.

766   PHILIP VAN RENSSELAER^8, son of William C.^{7} and Polly (Cox) Brigham; born in Lorraine, N. Y., 27 Aug., 1831; married, Mrs. Helen Cordelia, daughter of Clark Remington and widow of Lester Lawrence; born in Lorraine, 1830; died 1889. He resides with his daughter in Lake Forest, Ill. The male line is extinct.

Children, born in Lorraine:
822   i Brayton A. R.^{9}, b. 1 Jan., 1862.
    ii Nettie May Dora, b. 3 Dec., 1872; m. (1) 17 Sept., 1892, John D. Furlong; m. (2) John Hart; res. s. p., Lake Forest, Ill.

767   AARON S.^{8}, son of Philip P.^{7} and Jane A. (Miller) Brigham; born in Galilee, Pa., 10 Nov., 1834; married 10 Feb., 1858, Clarissa, daughter of Charles Keesler.

Children, born in Galilee:
    i Melitta V.^{9}, b. 29 May, 1862; m. 21 June, 1880, Jeremiah Canfield, a farmer, b. 21 June, 1856; res. Galilee. Ch. (Canfield):
        1 *Forest L.*^{10}, b. 15 March, 1881; 2 *Bertha E.*, b. 22 July, 1883; 3 *William J.*, b. 26 Feb., 1885; 4 *Frank A.*, b. 15 Oct., 1888.

Very truly
C. O. Brigham

ii Charles P., b. 22 May, 1869; m. 3 March, 1887, Jane Blackwell;
res. Tobyhanna, Pa. Ch.:
   1 *Howard L.*[10], b. 20 April, 1889; 2 *Lulu M.;* 3 *Ernest James,*
   b. 30 May, 1895.
iii Rockwell L., b. 25 Oct., 1871; m. 7 June, 1888, Lucy Henderson;
res. Galilee.
iv Flora Musetta, b. 19 Sept., 1877; m. 16 July, 1895, Rev. Albert
C. Brackenberry, from England to the U. S.; res. Galilee.
v Cora May, b. 28 May, 1880.

768 CHARLES OLIVER[8], son of Hon. Mavor[7] and Clarissa
(Bill) Brigham; born in Dundee, Mich., 9 Sept., 1838; died in
Toledo, O., of apoplexy, 2 May, 1906; married (1) 11 October,
1860, Sarah M., daughter of Hosmer and Sarah A. (Goodman)
Graham; born 10 Sept., 1840; died in Toledo, 9 Feb., 1870; mar-
ried (2) 23 Nov., 1871, Mary L., daughter of Perez Porter and
Clarissa (Goodman) Peck; born 21 Dec., 1834; died in Toledo, 25
March, 1903.

Mr. Brigham received the best education obtainable in a pioneer
country; at 15 entered the telegraph service with the Erie and
Mich. Telegraph Co., and upon the reorganization of the Western
Union Co., entered the Toledo office, where he continued as Manager
for 45 years, or until Oct., 1900. For 20 years he was correspondent of the Western Associated Press for Northwestern Ohio;
for several years superintendent of the Toledo electrical system;
was for 18 years trustee of Central Congregational Church. He
gave time, thought, and money to charitable work in Toledo. A
man of the highest integrity, he had a keen sense of honor in social
and business life. His tastes were broad and refined. His favorite
study was ornithology. He was a brilliant, magnetic public speaker,
and his fine carriage and expressive face gave additional power to
his eloquence. He was deeply interested in the Sons of the American Revolution. Pres. of Anthony Wayne Chapter, he presided at
a banquet given by himself to this chapter in Toledo, the night
before his death, making one of his grandest addresses. Was the
first President of the Brigham Family Association, elected in 1893,
and serving until 1896; again elected in 1900 and continuing until
his death; presided at meetings of 1893, '94, '95, '96, 1902, '04,
always speaking eloquently. He was a cordial and generous supporter of the History of the Brigham Family, and without his
active leadership and strong co-operation the History might not
now be written. It is impossible to estimate fully the service which
he has so freely given as President and as Chairman of the Publication Committee. Those who have been associated with him know
how large is the debt the family owes him. No finer character ever
bore the Brigham name.

Child, born in Toledo:
    i Charles Graham⁹, b. 24 Dec., 1869; m. 1? Dec., 1894, Minnie
    Aldora, dau. of Adam Cully, b. 28 April 1874; res. Toledo.
    Ch
        1 *Harriet Elizabeth¹⁰*, b. 9 Dec., 1896.

769 WILLIAM AUGUSTUS⁸, son of Hon. Mavor⁷ and Malinda
P. (Merrell) Brigham; born in Toledo, O., 21 Sept., 1853; married
22 Sept., 1875, Cora Frances, daughter of Denison and Hetty (Cole)
Steele. Mr. Brigham is Asst. Manager of the Woolson Spice Co.,
and resides in Toledo.

Children, born in Toledo:
    i Cora Steele⁹, b. 3 Oct., 1876.
    ii Bessie Louise, b. 26 Aug., 1882.

770 FREDERICK MERRELL⁸, son of Hon. Mavor⁷ and Malinda P. (Merrell) Brigham; born in Toledo, O., 17 July, 1864;
married in Ripon, Wis., 8 Sept., 1893, Alice Ballou, daughter of
Gustavus F. and Anna (Ballou) Horner; born in Ripon, 19 Sept.,
1866. Mr. Brigham is a lawyer in Toledo.

Child, born in Toledo:
    i Robert⁹, b. 26 Aug., 1899.

771 HENRY MARTYN⁸, son of Dea. Milton⁷ and Mary A.
(Finch) Brigham; born in Ogden, N. Y., 19 Nov., 1859; married
in Huntington, L. I., 17 Aug., 1887, Marie Antoinette Whiting of
Spencerport, N. Y.; born 2 June, 1857.
    Mr. Brigham was graduated from Rochester Univ., A. B., 1883.
Studied law in New York City and admitted to the bar in 1885;
practices in New York City, and resides in Brooklyn. Has devoted
his attention largely to patent and corporation law and has acted
as counsel for the National Lead Company and other large corpora-
tions; director Northern National Bank of New York; member of
the Crescent Athletic Club, St. Maurice Club, and Clove Valley
Rod and Gun Club.

Child, born in Brooklyn:
    i Henry Whiting⁹, b. 19 Dec., 1890.

772 REV. CHARLES AUGUSTUS GOODRICH⁸, son of
Moses⁷ and Chloe (Pond) Brigham; born in Worcester, Mass., 3
Dec., 1823; resided and died in Enfield, Conn., 12 Oct., 1897; mar-
ried in 1853, Eleanor M., daughter of John Smith, of Middletown,
Conn. He was graduated from Wesleyan University in 1847, and
later from the Bangor Theological Seminary.

Children, born in Enfield:
    i Nellie, d. y.
    ii Charles S.⁹, b. 1 May, 1854; m. 11 Jan., 1876, Hattie J. Ranney,

b. in Conway, Mass., 3 Feb., 1854; Ry. conductor, res. Hartford,
Conn. Ch.:
  1 *H. Eleanor*[10], b. 6 Oct., 1876.
  2 *Edna L.*, b. 6 Feb., 1882; d. 3 Jan., 1883.
iii William M., b. 15 Jan., 1857; m. 16 Sept., 1878, Josephine A.
Deming, b. 13 May, 1858, in Middletown; res. Hartford. Ch.:
  1 *William C.*[10], b. 20 Sept., 1879; 2 *Lillian H.*, b. 3 July, 1884; 3
  Charles, b. 18 Nov., 1889; d. *ibid.*

773 JOHN OLIN[8], son of Charles Corriden[7] and Sabra Butler
(Cook) Brigham; born in Woonsocket, R. I., 15 July, 1848; married,
14 October, 1874, Alice, daughter of Peleg and Keturah (Gavitt)
Saunders, of Westerly, R. I.; born 6 July, 1854.

In early life Mr. Brigham removed to Carolina, R. I., and
at the age of 18 came to Providence, R. I., and accepted a position
with his uncle, John Kendrick, manufacturer of harnesses. In 1873
he entered the wholesale grocery business and in 1885 with Joseph
H. Babcock established the firm of Babcock & Brigham. This firm
was dissolved in 1890 and Mr. Brigham went into the real estate
business in which he has continued to the present time.

Children, born in Providence, R. I.:
  i Herbert Olin[9], b. 15 Dec., 1875; entered Brown Univ. in 1895, but
    did not grad., owing to ill health. In 1899 became second asst.
    librarian in Brown Univ. Library, and in 1903 was appointed
    State Librarian of Rhode Island, which position he now holds.
    He is Secy. of the R. I. Library Assn. and a member of the Am.
    Library Assn. and of the Am. Hist. Assn.
  ii Clarence Saunders, b. 5 Aug., 1877; entered Brown Univ. in 1895,
    graduating in 1899; a member of the Phi Beta Kappa Soc. After
    a short service in Brown Univ. Library, he was appointed libra-
    rian of the R. I. Hist. Society in Jan., 1900, which position he
    still retains. Is a member of the Am. Antiquarian Soc., Am.
    Bibliographical Soc., Am. Hist. Assn., Am. Library Assn., and
    the R. I. Library Assn., and numerous local clubs. Is Archivist
    of Brown Univ., and an editor of *Brown Alumni Monthly.*
    His contributions to historical literature include the following:
    Memorial of Amos Perry, 1900; Records of Town of Ports-
    mouth, 1901; Hist. of R. I., 1902; Bibliog. of R. I. Hist., 1902;
    The Harris Papers, 1903; Roger Williams and Butler's Fourth
    Paper, 1903; 17th Cent. Place-Names of Providence. 1903; Re-
    port on the R. I. Archives, 1904, and is a contributor to historical
    and genealogical magazines.

774 CALEB LEWIS[8], son of Tileston[7] and Mary L. (Russell)
Brigham; born in Marlboro, Mass., 12 March, 1858; married in
Hudson, Mass., 24 Sept., 1885, Anna Eliza, daughter of Charles
H. and Ada J. (Bragdon) Robinson of Marlboro; born 7 Jan., 1865.

Mr. Brigham is the fourth of the name of Caleb. Was graduated
from the N. E. Conservatory of Music in Boston, 1876, and studied
piano and organ in the Boston University College of Music.

Entered the Hudson National Bank as clerk and was appointed cashier, which position he now holds. Has been an organist for many years and is leader of the church orchestra in the Unitarian church of Hudson, where he resides. A member of the Doric Lodge F. & A. M., Rawson Council, R. A., and of the Corinthian Chapter Eastern Star.

Children, born in Hudson:
    i Ada Maria², b. 12 Oct., 1887; ii Eva Belle, b. 20 Nov., 1888; iii Laura Grace, b. 27 Sept., 1891; iv Marion Robinson, b. 14 July, 1896; v Everett Russell, b. 9 Aug., 1898; vi Doris Ruth, b. 11 June, 1900.

775 REV. JOAB⁸, son of George⁷ and Lydia (Shinn) Brigham; born in Bloomington, Ill., 23 Nov., 1837; married (1) 10 Oct., 1866, Narcissa Quinn; married (2) 10 Sept., 1872, Mrs. Mildred, daughter of John McDonald and widow of William·D. Doolittle. A minister of the Christian Church and resides in Padua, Ill.

Children (by second wife):
    i George McDonald⁹, b. 20 Sept., 1873; d. June, 1876; ii Hattie M., b. 24 June, 1875; iii P. Whitmer, b. 20 Sept., 1878; iv Elwood, b. 15 Nov., 1881; d. 15 May, 1892; v Emma J., b. 20 Nov., 1884.

776 BENAJAH⁸, son of George⁷ and Lydia (Shinn) Brigham; born in Bloomington, Ill., 3 Nov., 1840; married 25 Aug., 1868, Elizabeth, daughter of Jacob Sherer of Griggsville, Ill. Five years in the Civil War, Co. C, 33d Ill. Vols.; wounded at Vicksburg. Resides, a farmer, in Fletcher, Ill.

Children:
    i Edna M.⁹, b. 5 Feb., 1871; m. 15 April, 1890, Marion Parr of Cooksville, Ill. Ch. (Parr):
        1 *Leland W.*¹⁰, b. 2 Nov., 1892; 2 *Arthur E.*, b. 5 Feb., 1895; 3 *Edith L.*, b. 28 July, 1901.
    ii William B., b. 11 Aug., 1874.
    iii Alice G., b. 2 Nov., 1876; m. William C. Pickering, 19 April, 1894. Ch. (Pickering):
        1 *Ethel G.*¹⁰, b. 19 April, 1895; 2 *Elizabeth E.*, b. 28 Aug., 1897; 3 *Edna M.*, b. 31 Jan., 1900; 4 *Wilbur L.*, b. 29 Sept., 1903.
    iv Carrie H., b. 5 Oct., 1878; m. John W. Stipp, 23 Jan., 1901. Ch. (Stipp):
        1 *Muriel E.*¹⁰, b. 13 Dec., 1901; 2 *Stanley*, b. 22 Aug., 1903; 3 *Eveline*, b. 10 June, 1905.
    v Myra P., and vi Mary B., twins b. 22 Sept., 1882.

777 FLETCHER⁸, son of George⁷ and Lydia (Shinn) Brigham; born in Bloomington, Ill., 13 Jan., 1845; married 19 Dec., 1872, Charlotte C., daughter of John Pray of Le Roy, Ill.; was in

the Civil War, Co. C, 33d Ill. Vols.; wounded in a railway wreck; a farmer and resides in Bloomington.

Children, born in Bloomington:

 i Dora May[9], b. 5 Oct., 1873; m. (1) 16 Aug., 1893, John Woolums of Ohio; m. (2) 30 Aug., 1899, H. Nelson Harne of Maryland. Ch. (Woolums):
  1 *Lydia Esther*[10], b. 16 June, 1894. Ch. (Harne): 2 *Dora Mabel,* b. 15 Oct., 1901; 3 *Fletcher Brigham,* b. 28 July, 1905.
 ii George W., b. 15 Jan., 1875; m. 20 Sept., 1899, Annie Pretzlaff of Sibley, Ill. Ch.:
  1 *Ruth Elizabeth*[10], b. 9 Aug., 1901; 2 *Rachel Esther,* b. 8 Aug., 1903.
 iii Rachel E., b. 10 Oct., 1876; m. 19 Feb., 1896, William H. Foster. Ch. (Foster):
  1 *William Lawrence*[10], b. 29 April, 1900; 2 *Charlotte,* b. 3 Dec., 1902.
 iv Nora Mabel, b. 19 Oct., 1879.
 v Mary Esther, b. 22 Oct., 1881; m. 18 Feb., 1903, Fred Eastman, Jr., of Ill. Ch. (Eastman):
  1 *Edith Barbara*[10], b. 27 Jan., 1904; 2 *Fred Fletcher,* b. 19 Oct., 1905.
 vi Annie, b. 29 Jan., 1885.
 vii Charlotte F., b. 28 June, 1888.

778 JOHN[8], son of George[7] and Lydia (Shinn) Brigham; born in Bloomington, Ill., 16 April, 1847; married 2 March, 1871, Louisa, daughter of L. Fossett of Blue Mound, Ill. A farmer, and resided in McLean Co., Ill., until 1892, when he removed to Tomora, Neb.

Children:

 i John R.[9], b. in LeRoy, April, 1874, and d. 1874.
 ii Gertrude, b. 20 Aug., 1876.
 iii Annie, b. 4 Jan., 1878; m. 16 Feb., 1898, F. C. Vawter, Jr., of Butler Co., Neb. Ch. (Vawter):
  1 *Walter F.*[10], b. 22 Dec., 1898; 2 *J. Wayne,* b. 15 Nov., 1901.
 iv Bertram E., b. 12 Dec., 1880; m. 5 Feb., 1902, Pearl, dau. of John Wimberly; b. in Ulysses, Neb., 26 Dec., 1880. Ch.:
  1 *Nadeen*[10], b. 3 Dec., 1903.
 v Byron D., b. 6 Feb., 1882.
 vi Walter L., b. 13 Oct., 1885.

779 WILLIAM VALENTINE[8], son of William Augustus[7] and Hannah S. (Chapman) Brigham; born in Worcester, Mass., 17 May, 1850; married, 1868, Lillion Lillie of Willimantic, Conn.; born there, 14 May, 1846; died in Newton Highlands, Mass., 17 March, 1892. A stock broker in Boston, where he resides.

Children:

 i Louis Stanhope[9], b. in Stanhope, N. J., 30 Aug., 1869; m. 8 Aug., 1900, Edith May, dau. of Pliny Nickerson of Newton Highlands; b. in Boston, 14 Feb., 1873; is principal man in the Brigham Gelatine Co. in Newton Highlands. Ch.:
  1 *Stanhope*[10], b. 18 Oct., 1903.

  ii Charles Lillie, b. in Brooklyn, N. Y., 1 Jan., 1871; d. 2 Jan., 1871.
 iii Oliver Henry Harrington, b. in Willimantic, 8 Oct., 1871.
  iv Charles Edwin, b. in Carmel, N. Y., 26 July, 1873; m. ————,
       res. Lowell, Mass.
   v George Ernest, b. in Springvale (now Islington), N. Y., 13 May,
       1875.
  vi Lillie Chapman, b. in So. Boston, 23 March, 1877; d. 24 April,
       1877.
 vii Lotta May, b. 1 May, 1880; d. 4 Feb., 1881.
viii Ruth Chapman, b. in Newton Highlands, 15 Dec., 1881; m.
       Leslie Briggs; res. Lowell.
  ix Lillian Estella, b. 5 Feb., 1884.
   x Harold Augustus, b. 22 Sept., 1887.

780   LOUIS KOSSUTH[8], son of William Augustus[7] and Hannah S. (Chapman) Brigham; born in Worcester, Mass., 30 Jan.,
1852; married 5 Jan., 1876, Abbie Ware, daughter of John and
Ellen (Cunningham) Richardson; born in Newton, Mass., 23 Sept.,
1853. A business man in Boston.

Children, born in Newton:
  i Edmond Francis[9], b. 13 April, 1878; res. Boston.
 ii Harriet Ellen, b. 18 March, 1881.

781   DR. DANIEL TAYLOR[8], son of Franklin[7] and Ann Whitman (Taylor) Brigham; born in Lancaster, Mass., 30 May, 1840;
married 22 Aug., 1867, Ellen Jane, daughter of James G. Brown;
born in Hingham, Mass. Has been, for many years, a dentist in
Boston with a large practice; resides in Dorchester, Mass.

Children, born in Boston:
  i Percy Herbert[9], b. 14 June, 1871; a dentist in Boston.
 ii Arthur Winsor, b. 14 July, 1883.

782   REV. LEONARD WARREN[8], son of Elisha Warren[7] and
Elizabeth L. (Faunce) Brigham; born in Elmore, Vt., 25 May,
1841; married 5 April, 1862, Henrietta M. Hubbard.
   Educated in Vermont; prepared for the ministry with clergymen
in active service; licensed to preach about 1865; ordained in 1868;
became a Universalist and settled in La Crosse, Wis., in 1874; held
the position of superintendent of churches in Illinois for 7 years.
For 18 years was director in an Insurance organization in Illinois,
and also general supervisor for several years. Re-entered the
ministry in 1905, which he left on account of throat trouble. A
prominent I. O. O. F., he was grand patriarch in Vermont and grand-
master in Wisconsin, 1882-83. Resides in Chicago.

Children:
  i (Rev.) Leonard Ward[9], b. 21 May, 1865, in Dover, Vt.; m. 15 May,
       1888, Emma Ballou; res. 1904, Brooklyn, N. Y. Ch.:
       1 *Warren Ballou*[10], b. in Munda, Ill., 17 May, 1889.
       2 *Eva Marie*, b. in Rochester, Minn., 3 July, 1901.

ii Bret Hugh, b. in Rutland, Vt., 6 May, 1871; m. 20 July, 1892,
Mildred Woods; a lawyer; res. Milwaukee, Wis. Ch:
1 *Grace E.*[10], b. in Chicago, 8 Jan., 1894.
2 *Cecilia H.*, b. Simi, Cal., 31 May, 1897.
iii Frederick Guy, b. 8 June, 1874; d. 1 Oct., 1874.
iv Paul Laflin, b. 20 June, 1882; m. 8 Oct., 1904, Eleanor Hunt;
a business man. Ch.:
1 *Donald Hunt*[10], b. 4 Oct., 1905.

783 DR. HOMER COLBY[8], son of Dr. Gershom Nelson[7] and
Laura E. (Tyler) Brigham; born in Waitsfield, Vt., 10 July, 1851;
married (1) Nellie Atherton of Waterbury, Vt.; married (2) Harriet, daughter of Hon. Whitman Ferrin of Montpelier, Vt.

Was graduated from the New York Homeopathic College in 1872,
and has practiced in Montpelier, Vt., Grand Rapids, Mich., and New
York City; has been President of the Vt. Homeopathic Society, and
Vice-President of the Mich. State Homeopathic Society; also U. S.
Pension Examiner; resides in Montpelier and New York City.

Children (by first wife), born in Montpelier:
i Roy[9], d. æ. about 1 year.
ii Conrad, d. æ. about 1 year.
Child (by second wife), born in Montpelier:
iii Laura, d. æ. about 1 year.

784 WILLARD IRVING TYLER[8], son of Dr. Gershom
Nelson[7] and Laura E. (Tyler) Brigham; born in Montpelier, Vt.,
31 May, 1859; died s. p. in Auburn, Cal., 26 Sept., 1904; married 22
March, 1893, M. Hazel Morse; born in Concord, Vt., who married
after his death, her cousin, Edwin E. Nelson, and resides in Texas.

Willard was a natural leader in the local grammar school, and
class orator of Grand Rapids, Mich., High School, 1878. He
taught a year, then entered the University of Michigan, Class of
'83; elected Freshman Historian, principal contributor to the
Sophomore " Oracle," corresponding secretary Alpha Delta Phi;
for his excellence in Greek and Natural History was advised by
the professor of each to adopt that branch of teaching for his life
work. Leaving college through ill health, he studied law in Grand
Rapids, also a year with the leading practitioner of Petosky, Mich.,
where, for services rendered the Pottowatomie Indians, he was
adopted by the tribe under the name of " Kenoshaus " (pickerel,
big-mouth—hence orator).

Long a student of Shakespeare and excelling as a reader and
amateur actor, he now accepted a flattering offer from Thomas
Keene, the tragedian. The next 5 years were spent in touring the
United States with such eminent players as Booth, Barrett, Sheridan, Haworth, Marie Prescott, and under " the Frohmans." He be-

came a B. P. O. E. and a recognized "leading heavy," with bright prospects; but finding the life too exacting for his nervous type, he returned to practice at Grand Rapids, incidentally writing the chapter, "Bench and Bar," for Baxter's History of Grand Rapids. In 1890 he removed to Minneapolis, where he continued in the law, and was a chief assistant in the preparation of Judge Atwater's excellent history of that city. He removed to Chicago in 1893 and continued there until 1901, when ill health sent him to Phoenix, Ariz. During this period he was attorney for the State Board of Dental Examiners and interested also in important cases, one being a division suit among minors of the real estate of his deceased father, valued at $100,000. He went to Auburn in Sept., 1904.

Genealogically, he traced back, among others, to Richard Warren of the *Mayflower* and to those early governors of Massachusetts, Thomas Dudley and Simon Bradstreet; the latter the first public man who dared brave the savage furies of the Salem Witchcraft in 1692 and his wife, Anne, the first American woman of letters, whose old mansion is still standing at Andover, Mass. Through his mother he was descended from John[2] Brigham, thus having 2 lines of descent from Thomas[1] Brigham. Always an eager student of history and genealogy, Willard turned naturally to literary work along these lines when failing health compelled him to abandon the law. Since 1893 he continued uninterruptedly the historianship of the Brigham Family Association, then organized (see Appendix) and published an official report of seven reunions filled with historical matter involving years of labor and invaluable to the family. In 1901 he was formally engaged to write the History of the Brigham Family, and it was literally upon his dying bed that his final work upon the present volume was done. How generously and enthusiastically he gave of his time and strength to the family without recompense, how uncomplainingly he later bore the indifference and discouragements incident to some phases of his work, how bravely he battled for life that he might finish his noble, his almost self-imposed task—all this can never be sufficiently known to his kinsmen. His editors marvel at his erudition and his industry. He spent the summer of 1900 in Great Britain and France in researches. In fact, he contracted the disease from which he died while searching the archives in the damp stone buildings of London. He founded the Tyler Family Association (his mother's family), of 5 of whose reunions he published complete reports; and was engaged at the time of his death in tracing all the families of that name in this country. Mr. Brigham was a member of the New England Historic Genealogical Society, Southern History Association, Society of Colonial Wars, Sons of the Revolution, British Record Society; also corresponding member of the New Hampshire and

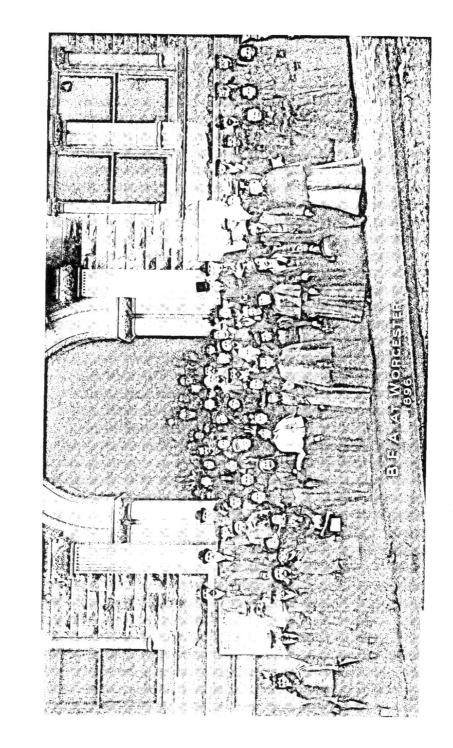
B.F.A. AT WORCESTER
896

Maine Historical Societies. With all these his rank as a genealogist was established. He is buried in Montpelier.

785 THEODORE SMITH[8], son of George[7] and Almena (Smith) Brigham; born in Clayton, N. Y., 25 March, 1833; married 3 July, 1859, Olivia Delight Porter; born 7 Nov., 1840. A farmer and resides in Clayton.

Children, born in Clayton:
    i Laura Almena[9], b. 17 April, 1863; d. 28 March, 1872.
   ii William Jasper, b. 7 Dec., 1864.
  iii Rosa Belle, b. 24 Jan., 1871.
   iv George Asa, b. 30 March, 1874; m. Florence R. Graves, b. 30 Jan., 1875. Ch.:
        1 *Jasper Irvin*[10], b. 2 April, 1898; 2 *Ronald Graves*, b. 21 Sept., 1899; 3 *George Asa*, b. 12 Oct., 1900; 4 *Theodore William*, b. 5 Feb., 1902.
    v Maud Louisa, b. 26 Nov., 1876; d. 10 Oct., 1887.

786 DON FERDINAND[8], son of Lewis[7] and Louisa (Tilden) Brigham; born in Mansfield, Conn., 15 Jan., 1839; died 27 Feb., 1888; married 26 Nov., 1863, Harriet Maria Storrs; resided in Hartford, Conn.

Children:
    i Herbert Storrs[9], d. y.
   ii Ernest Ward, b. 13 Feb., 1869; m. Edith Bennett. Ch.:
        1 *Ferdinand B.*[10]; 2 *Robert B.*
  iii Clement Hugh, b. 20 June, 1873; m. Lilian Talcott. Ch.:
        1 *Storrs Talcott*[10].
   iv Alice, b. 9 Aug., 1876; was grad. Wesleyan Univ., 1900; a teacher.
    v Clara, b. 8 Oct., 1878; m. Arthur P. Bennett; he attended Amherst Coll., 1859-61; res. Oxford, N. J. Ch. (Bennett):
        1 *David B.*[10]

787 GEORGE CARLETON[8], son of Paul Wooster[7] and Louisa M. (Slack) Brigham; born in Norwich, Vt., 1 Jan., 1831; died there, 18 Sept., 1900; married 28 Feb., 1858, Wealthy C., daughter of Joseph Rogers; born in Norwich, 1 Jan., 1832. Was a farmer and resided in E. Randolph, Vt.

Children, born in Norwich:
    i George Edward[9], b. 13 Oct., 1858; m. 28 Dec., 1880, Phena F. Burroughs; res. E. Randolph. Ch.:
        1 *Phelina May*[10], b. 30 Aug., 1885; 2 *Frank George*, b. 27 Oct., 1887; 3 *Paul Andrew*, b. 3 March, 1896; 4 *Lillian M. Sprague*, b. 15 June, 1898.
   ii Nellie Elizabeth, b. 10 June, 1865; m. 28 Dec., 1886, George Arthur Robinson of E. Randolph. Ch. (Robinson):
        1 *Nellie Ethel*[10], b. 20 May, 1888; 2 *Jennie Welthea*, b. 6 June, 1894; 3 *Ina May*, b. 30 Sept., 1898.
  iii Jennie May, b. 13 Sept., 1872; m. 3 Jan., 1893, Gilbert Morrill Blaisdell of E. Randolph. Ch. (Blaisdell):
        1 *Ernest Gilbert*[10], b. 9 Oct., 1893; 2 *Infant*, b. and d. 1896.

788   JAMES M.[8], son of Paul Wooster[7] and Louisa M. (Slack) Brigham; born in Norwich, Vt., 11 May, 1843; married 25 Dec., 1872, Harriet, daughter of L. S. Partridge; born in Norwich, 5 May, 1854. A farmer and resides in Norwich.

Children, born in Norwich:

i James B.[9], b. 6 June, 1873; m. 18 Nov., 1896, Mattie B. Hutchinson; res. New London, Conn., where manager for Swift & Co. (packers).
ii Paul W., b. 26 Sept., 1874; d. 4 April, 1881.
iii Laughton E., b. 25 March, 1878; res. Fitchburg, where manager for Swift & Co.; removed to Burlington, Vt.
iv Elizabeth Ellen, b. 13 May, 1880; res. Medford, Mass.
v Charles R., b. 4 July, 1883; buyer for Swift & Co.; res. Manchester, N. H.
vi Frederick Lewis, b. 28 Aug., 1885.
vii Nina Ethel, b. 26 Sept., 1887.
viii Minnie Maud, b. 9 Oct., 1889.
ix Bessie Edith, b. 4 Oct., 1891.
x Lillian Margaret, b. 2 Feb., 1892.
xi Vivian Rosetta, b. 21 Oct., 1895.

789   ANDREW WILLIAM[8], son of William[7] and Ann T. (Proctor) Brigham; born in Norwich, Vt., 31 Jan., 1847; married 4 Feb., 1868, Abbie S., daughter of Edson Johnson; born in Strafford, Vt., 29 Nov., 1848. Resides (1903) on the Governor Brigham homestead in Norwich.

Children, born in Norwich:

i Annie A.[9], b. 3 Feb., 1869; m. 31 Dec., 1896, Arthur L. Douglass of Norwich; s. p.
ii Grace L., b. 5 March, 1872; m. 21 Aug., 1895, Grant C. Thornton, who d. 15 May, 1898; res. Lawrence, Mass. Ch. (Thornton):
  1 Gladys[10], b. 6 Feb., 1896.
iii William E., b. 12 June, 1875; m. 7 Jan., 1903, Myra Parrizo; a teacher and res. Lawrence.
iv Paul A., b. 9 Feb., 1883; res. unm., in Norwich.

790   TRUMAN ELBRIDGE[8], son of Abel[7] and Emeline (Hibbard) Brigham; born in North Hadley, Mass., 3 March, 1842; married 10 May, 1866, Harriet Newell Hibbard; born in North Hadley, 2 June, 1845. He resides in Amherst, Mass.

Children, born in No. Adams, Mass..

i Laura Belle[9], b. 23 Feb., 1867; d. 8 Feb., 1875.
ii Clarence Truman, b. 4 Dec., 1869; m. 4 Oct., 1892, Estelle Wetmore; res. No. Adams. Ch.:
  1 Willard Clarence[10], b. 2 Nov., 1893; 2 Ruth Estelle, b. 8 Aug., 1895; 3 Carolyn, b. 14 May, 1898; 4 Proctor K., b. 5 Jan., 1902.
iii Allen Eugene, b. 27 Aug., 1872; m. 8 Oct., 1895, Helen Beatty; res. No. Adams. Ch.:
  1 Leonard Allen[10], b. 22 Feb., 1898.
  2 Ralph Armond, b. 20 Feb., 1900; d. 8 April, 1901.

iv Harriet Emeline, b. 19 Feb., 1875; m. 19 Dec., 1900, Ransom P. Nichols; res. San Juan, P. R. Ch. (Nichols):
1 Doris Adelaide[10], b. in Amherst, Mass., 16 Oct., 1901.
2 Ransom Brigham, b. in San Juan, P. R., 8 Dec., 1902.
v Ethel Clara, b. 1 Aug., 1879; d. N. A., 29 July, 1881.
vi Arthur Abel, b. 7 April, 1882; d. 1907.
vii Ralph Hibbard, b. 10 Oct., 1883.

791 DR. JOHN CHRISTOPHER[8], son of William[7] and Caroline (White) Brigham; born in Girard, Ga., 16 June, 1846; married 17 Oct., 1872, Julia D. Odom. He is a physician in Girard.

Children, born in Girard:
i William Randall[9], b. 17 Jan., 1874.
ii Annie Beulah, b. 2 Oct., 1875; d. 6 Feb., 1900; m. 11 Dec., 1895, George F. Brinson.
iii John Christopher, b. 5 Aug., 1877; d. 22 June, 1885.
iv Arthur Julian, b. 19 May, 1879; m. 28 Oct., 1902, Josie Parnell; res. a farmer, in Girard.
v Jennie Freeland, b. 28 March, 1885.
vi Savannah, b. 7 April, 1887.
vii Ernest Talmadge, b. 11 July, 1889.
viii Julia Pauline, b. 9 March, 1893.

792 WILLIAM HENRY[8], son of William[7] and Caroline (White) Brigham; born in Girard, Ga., 23 July, 1848; married (1) 8 Feb., 1877, Mary E. Cochran; married (2) 7 April, 1881, Jennie F. Rutherford of Augusta, Ga.

Child (by first wife), born in Girard:
i James Cochran[9], b. 31 Oct., 1877; d. 3 May, 1878.
Children (by second wife), born in Girard:
ii Charles Stanley, b. 26 June, 1882; d. 25 Dec., 1887.
iii William Henry, b. 13 June, 1883; d. 10 Oct., 1887.
iv Constantia Louise, b. 27 Oct., 1884.
v Eugenia B., b. 13 Nov., 1887.
vi Grace, b. 20 Jan., 1891.
vii Jennie Rutherford, b. 18 Aug., 1892.

793 THADDEUS RUDOLF[8], son of William[7] and Caroline (White) Brigham; born in Girard, Ga., 25 Aug., 1849; died 1 May, 1898; married, 25 Jan., 1894, Mary Burton Powell of Georgia.

Children:
i Thaddeus Powell[9], b. 11 Jan., 1895.
ii Gladys, b. 23 March, 1896.
iii Aramintha, b. 9 Nov., 1897.

794 CLARENCE RUSSELL[8], son of William[7] and Caroline (White) Brigham; born in Girard, Ga., 6 Sept., 1856; married 19 Dec., 1878, Georgia V. Odom.

Children:
    i Carrie Maud[9], b. 1 Feb., 1880.
    ii Infant, b. 12 Sept., 1882; d. y.
    iii Clarence Evans, b. 13 Sept., 1884; d. 1 March, 1887.
    iv Horace, b. 17 Feb., 1886.
    v Clifford, b. 24 Feb., 1889.
    vi Essie, b. 30 Oct., 1890.
    vii Harold, b. 17 Oct., 1892.
    viii Hazel, b. 18 Nov., 1894.
    ix Russell, b. 2 Nov., 1897; d. 24 April, 1899.
    x Infant, b. 25 April, 1900; d. y.

795   CHARLES[8], son of William[7] and Caroline (White) Brigham; born in Girard, Ga., 3 Oct., 1860; married (1) 6 May, 1886, Julia Rowland, who died 26 June, 1890; married (2) 15 Dec., 1891, Ada Mariah Lewis, who died 10 May, 1896.

Child (by first wife):
    i Alma[9], b. 15 July, 1889; d. Sept., 1889.
Children (by second wife):
    ii Ada Ruth, b. Dec., 14, 1892.
    iii William Lewis, b. 19 June, 1893.
    iv Sarah Caroline, b. 20 Nov., 1895; d. 20 June, 1903.

796   WALTER BRECKENBRIDGE[8], son of William[7] and Caroline (White) Brigham; born in Girard, Ḡa., 25 June, 1863; married, 29 July, 1884, Lillie Ann Tabb of Georgia. He is a wholesale grocer in Augusta, Ga.

Children:
    i Walter Breckenbridge[9], b. 26 May, 1885; m. 1 June, 1905, Susie Wood of Aiken, Ga.
    ii Eugene Foster, b. 4 Oct., 1886.
    iii Tulia Loween, b. 28 Dec., 1888.
    iv Lillie May, b. 29 July, 1890; d. 9 Aug., 1892.
    v and vi Twins, b. 15 May, 1892; and d.
    vii Mary Freeland, b. 12 July, 1893; d. 6 Sept., 1896.
    viii Lillian, b. 26 Nov., 1895.
    ix John Christopher, b. 31 Dec., 1897.
    x Dorothea, b. 13 Oct., 1899.
    xi William Roscoe, b. 9 Feb., 1902.

797   HERBERT ELLIOT[8], son of Lawson Sibley[7] and Martha J. (Bigelow) Brigham; born in Rutland, Mass., 10 Jan., 1857; married 30 Nov., 1876, Olive Augusta, daughter of Homer M. and Olive (Houghton) Adams of Hubbardston, Mass.; born 27 July, 1852. Is a farmer and resides in Hubbardston.

Children:
    i Stella Hattie[9], b. in Hubbardston, 14 Oct., 1877; m. 29 May, 1904, Anson E. Nutting.
    ii Edith Augusta, b. in Oakham, Mass., 3 Sept., 1879; m. 14 Oct., 1897, Herbert A., son of Aaron Ware of Barre, Mass.

ALASCO DE LANCEY BRIGHAM   799

MRS. ROSE BRIGHAM COXFORD

iii Jennie Henrietta, b. 21 Jan., 1881.
iv Bertie Lawson, b. 21 June, 1884; d. 6 Oct., 1884.
v Herbert Elliot, b. 17 Oct., 1891.

798 HENRY HARRISON⁸, son of William Harrison⁷ and Hannah (Nash) Brigham; born in Barre, Mass., 8 Dec., 1846; died there, 24 March, 1891; married 22 Oct., 1867, Olive, daughter of Henry E. and grand-daughter of Francis and Nancy (Brigham) Rice (339), born in Barre, 5 Jan., 1851. He was a farmer and resided in Barre where his widow now lives.

Children, the eldest born in Hubbardston, Mass.:
   i Francis Henry⁹, Rev., b. 3 Nov., 1873; m. 6 May, 1899, Alice
      Shock of Sedalia, Mo., b. 1 March, 1872.
      He was grad. from Lawrence Univ., Wisconsin, in 1904; was a
      very noted football player and athlete; is 6 feet, 2¾ inches in height,
      and weighs 200 pounds. Was in charge of the gymnasium work
      and out-door athletics at Lawrence Univ. before graduation.
      Represented Mass. at the athletic event in connection with the
      31st International Convention Y. M. C. A. of No. America, in
      1895, at which he was the winner. In the mile run he "beat
      the field so badly he seemed to be running alone." He was or-
      dained an elder in the M. E. Church in 1903. He has been preach-
      ing 10 years. Ch.:
      1 *Dorothy¹⁰*, b. in Green Bay, Wis., 21 May, 1900.
      2 *Jean*, b. in Appleton, Wis., 14 Sept., 1901.
      3 *Ruth*, b. in Kankanna, Wis., 8 April, 1904.
   ii Myron Pinkerton, b. 13 Aug., 1883; drowned in a lake in
      Waupaca, Wis., 9 July, 1906. He was a student at Lawrence
      Univ., and had completed the sophomore year; he excelled in
      athletics, oratory, languages and mathematics. Was in charge
      of an M. E. Church in Detroit Harbor, Wis., in the summer of
      1905, and in the spring of 1906 received a call to the Congre-
      gational Church in Chilton, Wis., where he preached the day before
      his death. His young life, so suddenly cut short, was full of
      promise in his chosen profession, and his loss is irreparable to a
      large circle.
   iii Henrietta Harrison, b. 21 June, 1891; res. Barre.

799 ALASCO DE LANCEY⁸, son of Ebenezer Damon⁷ and Mary (Aldrich) Brigham; born in E. Smithfield, Pa., 9 March, 1838; died in New York City, 10 Nov., 1881; married 4 April, 1870, Ella Eudora, daughter of William H. Grey; born in Geneva, N. Y., 9 Nov., 1849. He was editor of the "Weekly Underwriter," in New York City, where he resided. Was vestryman in St. Ignatius Church, W. 40th street.

Children, born in New York City:
   i Rose Ella⁹, b. 28 April, 1871; m. 26 April, 1893, William F., son
      of William H. Coxford of New York City; b. in 1848; he is a
      manufacturer of firearms, and they res. s. p., in New York City.
      Mrs. Coxford has taken a great interest in the B. F. A., and with
      her mother has attended most of the meetings.
   ii Grey Mills, b. 8 Nov., 1873; d. 17 May, 1881.

800 DR. READER SMITH[8], son of George[7] and Amy (Stockwell) Brigham; born in Granville, Pa., 16 June, 1832; died in New Albany, Ind., 11 March, 1890; married, 10 April, 1860, Mary, daughter of John Goe; born in Ohio, 5 Oct., 1835. She resides a widow in New Albany. Dr. Brigham was one year in the U. S. N. as surgeon; practiced in Weston, Mo., Cairo, Ill., and Indianapolis, Ind.

Children:

    i Frank Payne[9], b. 28 June, 1861; a druggist in Louisville, Ky.
    ii Birdie, b. 8 May, 1866; d. 18 April, 1870.
    iii Fred Lincoln, b. 22 Aug., 1871; a druggist in New Albany.
    iv Pearl, b. 30 July, 1873.
    v John Goe, b. 4 Sept., 1875.
    vi Lieut. Claúde Ernest, b. 14 April, 1878; was grad. West Point Military Academy, 1901; thence to the Philippines, 31st Co., Coast Art.

801 MARY LOUISE[8], daughter of Phineas[7] and Eliza (Johnson) Brigham; born in Cherry Valley, N. Y., 11 Nov., 1839; married 6 March, 1856, Norris M. Compton; born in Sullivanville, N. Y., 26 April, 1836. They reside in Horseheads, N. Y., and he is Deputy U. S. Marshal, West District, N. Y.; is a veteran of the Civil War.

Children (Compton):

    i Ida Brigham[9], b. 31 July, 1857, in Sullivanville; m. in Alpine, N. Y., 3 July, 1873, James Robert Fitzgerald, b. 1850; res. Sugar Grove, Ill. Ch. (Fitzgerald), the 4 youngest b. in Oswego, Ill.:
        1 *Clifford Compton*[10], b. in Sullivanville, 23 Oct., 1876; res. Sugar Grove.
        2 *Mary Belle,* b. in W. Almond, N. Y., 4 Sept., 1881; res. Morgan Park, Ill.
        3 *Anna Maude,* b. 19 Jan., 1885.
        4 *James Robert,* b. 8 Nov., 1892; d. 25 Aug., 1893.
        5 *Wilbur Norris,* b. 17 Dec., 1896.
        6 *Harold Leon,* b. 17 Dec., 1898.
    ii Hon. William R., b. 8 April, 1860; m. (1) Alice Forshea; m. (2) 27 April, 1899, Helen R., dau. Samuel M. Tubbs, b. 8 Dec., 1877; he is U. S. Marshal, West Dist. N. Y., and real estate dealer; res. Horseheads. Ch. (by first wife):
        1 *Amy*[10], b. in Elmira, N. Y., 23 March, 1882; d. Aug., 1882.
        2 *Isabelle,* b. in E., 11 Jan., 1884.
        3 *Leon,* b. in Sullivanville, 25 Sept., 1886; res. Wichita, Kan.
        4 *Fasset Brigham,* b. 8 June, 1889.
        Ch. (by second wife):
        5 *William R.,* b. in Horseheads, 9 July, 1902.
    iii Johnson Brigham, b. 9 June, 1863; d. 4 March, 1886.
    iv Mary Edith, b. 1 April, 1875; m. 10 Oct., 1900, Lewis Henry Lent, b. in Tompkins Cove, N. Y., 27 July, 1871; res. New York City. Ch. (Lent):
        1 *Worthington Compton*[10], b. 14 Nov., 1902.
    v Lena May, b. 12 March, 1879; m. 1 Feb., 1898, Rev. John Ford Leffler, of Shelbyville, Ind., b. 28 Sept., 1867; he is a member

Falls, N. Y., in 1905. Ch. (Leffler):
1 *Compton Alba*[10], b. 26 May, 1900.

802   HON. JOHNSON[8], son of Phineas[7] and Eliza (Johnson)
Brigham; born in Cherry Valley, N. Y., 11 March, 1846; married
(1) 1 Sept., 1875, Antoinette Gano, in Watkins, N. Y.; married
(2) 20 Dec., 1892, Lucy H., daughter of William W. Walker;
born in Cedar Rapids, Ia., 17 Jan., 1860; Mrs. Brigham studied at
Wellesley College.

In 1869, Mr. Brigham studied at Cornell University, where he
was an organizer of A. D. Chapter and its first president; at
Hamilton College in 1871.   Became a journalist and was editor
and proprietor of the Cedar Rapids *Republican* and founder
and managing editor of the *Midland Monthly*.   Was Collector of
the Port of Brockport, N. Y., and one term U. S. Consul at Aix la
Chapelle, Germany, under Pres't. Harrison.   In 1898 became State
Librarian of Iowa, with a residence in Des Moines, Ia., which position he now holds.   Was Pres't. of the Iowa Library Com., 1890
04; Pres't. Iowa State Library Association, 1902-03; and Chair
man Iowa Fifth Congressional Committee and Pres't. of the Iowa
State Republican League, 1892, etc., etc.   Contributes both prose
and poetry to the leading magazines of the country, and has published a novel, " An Old Man's Idyll," under a nom de plume.   Mr.
Brigham is now, 1907, editing the papers of the late Senator Harlan,
of Iowa, at the request of his daughter, Mrs. Robert T. Lincoln,
preparatory to writing the Senator's biography for the State Historical Society.

He is an occasional speaker before colleges and institutions and
on public occasions; has contributed poems for the B. F. A. meetings; in 1895 delivered the address at the banquet of the Association in Boston, and in 1904 delivered the address at the meeting
in St. Louis.   He has traveled extensively in America and Europe,
and has resided at Elmira, Watkins, Brockport, and Hornellsville,
N. Y., and Cedar Rapids and Des Moines, Ia.   He has taken a
deep interest in the family history.   As first Vice-President of the
Association he became, by the death of President C. O. Brigham,
President of the Association and Chairman of the Publication Committee.   The following verses were written for the B. F. A. in 1900:

THOMAS BRIGHAM, THE PURITAN
I

No " doubting Thomas " was our family's founder;
In faith he rode the wide Atlantic's waves.
On yonder rock-ribbed shore he lived, expounder
Of simple creed that Service only Saves.*

* A free translation of our Brigham Family Association motto, " In Cruce Salus."

II

His name shall stand with us for strenuous living,
    For honest thinking, and for righteous laws;
For humble doing and for noble giving
    Of self for conscience or for freedom's cause.

III

Soul calls to soul, by kinship's ties united;
    From out the past we hear a hale godspeed;
Soul answers soul, by trials unaffrighted,—
    We, too, would serve, or bravely do the deed.

IV

Our course should mark the way of progress plainly,
    And bid the true and daring walk therein;
Against it must detraction war but vainly,—
    Who strives for progress can but grandly win.

Child (by first wife):
    i Anna Gano⁹, b. 17 Jan., 1877; m. Charles P. Hartley, asst. in Physiology and Plant Breeding, Dept. of Agriculture, Washington, D. C.

Children (by second wife):
    ii Ida Wilkinson, b. 22 Aug., 1895.
    iii Mary Walker, b. 27 Jan., 1898.

803   CLARENCE E.⁸, son of Horace A.⁷ and Sarah (Young) Brigham; born 24 July, 1854, in Smithfield, Pa.; married 19 Jan., 1876, Ophelia M. Bourne; born in Burlington, Pa., 2 Aug., 1854. Is a farmer of Athens, Pa.

Children, born in Athens:
    i Russell Elmer⁹, b. 9 Dec., 1877; unm. 1905; res. a jeweler, Oneonta, N. Y.
    ii Alice May, b. 10 Jan., 1879; m. 21 March, 1904, Albert F. A. Schlotzhauer of Canajoharie, N. Y.; res. Briarclif, Manor, N. Y.; he is manager of Dairy Dept. of Briarclif Manor. Ch. (Schlotzhauer):
        1 *Grace Louise*¹⁰, b. 13 Feb., 1905.
    iii Arthur Bourne, b. 13 Aug., 1880; m. 21 Jan., 1904, Charlotte Williams; res. Athens. Ch.:
        1 *Ernest Lee*¹⁰, b. 21 March, 1905.
    iv Clarence Ray, b. 25 Aug., 1885; d. 19 Dec., 1891.
    v Sarah Effie, b. 16 Oct., 1887; d. 22 Dec., 1891.
    vi Horace D., b. 30 Oct., 1888.
    vii Agnes Ora, b. 9 June, 1892.

HON. JOHNSON BRIGHAM, OF DES MOINES, IA. (802)
President of the Brigham Family Association, 1906

804 REV. PROF. ALBERT PERRY[8], son of Horace Ames[7] and Julia (Perry) Brigham; born in Perry, N. Y., 12 June, 1855; married in Amsterdam, N. Y., 27 June, 1882, Flora Winegar of Amsterdam, born 1 July, 1861.

Prof. Brigham was graduated from Colgate (then Madison) University, A. B., 1879; from Hamilton Theological Seminary 1882, and received degree of A. M. Was ordained to the ministry in 1882; was pastor of the Baptist Church in Stillwater, N. Y., 1882-1885; pastor Tabernacle Baptist Church, Utica, N. Y., 1885-1891; graduate student of Harvard University, 1891-1892, receiving degree of A. M.; Prof. of Geology in Colgate University, 1892 to present time; Instructor in Geology, summer sessions, Harvard Univ., 1891, 1894, 1895, 1900; Prof. of Geology, Colorado Summer School, 1893; Prof. of Geology and Geography, Cornell Univ., summer sessions 1901-02-03-04; has been Chairman of the Committee of Physical Geography, National Educational Association; Associate Editor Bulletin American Geographical Society; Pres't. N. Y. State Science Teachers' Assn.; secretary and treasurer Association of American Geographers; Follow of the Geological Soc. of America and of American Association for the Advancement of Science; member of the Association of American Geographers and of the National Geographic Society. Has contributed many papers to leading journals of a scientific and educational character, and is a contributor to the New International Encyclopædia. He has published *" Text-book of Geology "*; *" Introduction to Physical Geography "*; *" Geographic Influences in American History "*; *" Student's Laboratory Manual of Physical Geography."*

Children:
i Charles Winegar[9], b. in Stillwater, N. Y., 22 Oct., 1883; d. 2 Jan., 1899.
ii Elizabeth, b. in Hamilton, N. Y., 3 Aug., 1895.

805 GEN. and HON. WILLIAM H.[8], son of Rufus H.[7] and Basha (Mossman) Brigham; born in Hudson, Mass., 1 Feb., 1863; married in Hudson, 25 Nov., 1884, Cora Belle, daughter of Benjamin Dearborn; born in Stowe, Mass., 1 March, 1863.

Gen. Brigham is the Pres't. of the F. Brigham and Gregory Co., of Hudson and Boston, the oldest shoe manufactory in the U. S. He is a director in various banks and of the N. E. Shoe & Leather Assn. Was a member of the Mass. House of Representatives in 1892-93, serving on the committee of Military Affairs and Banking. Was a member of the Mass. Senate in 1897-98 in the sixth Middlesex Dist. and served on the committees for rules, towns, education, railroads and military affairs. Was a member of the Board of Selectmen of Hudson 1890-96, inclusive. Has been connected with the Mass. Militia for many years, as follows:

First Lieut. of Co. M, 5th Infantry, 1887; Major and Asst. Inspector of Rifle Practice on staff of the first Brigade; was Lieut. Col. and Inspector Gen. Staff of Gov. Crane, 1900; Brig. Gen. and Inspector General staff of Gov. Crane, 1901-03; Brig. Gen. and Inspector Gen., staff of Gov. Bates, 1903 and 1904; staff of Gov. Guild, 1906.

He resides in Hudson.

Children, born in Hudson:
  i Mildred Ellen⁹, b. 29 April, 1888.
  ii William Mossman, b. 5 July, 1896.

806 HON. ANDREW CORTHELL⁸, son of Col. Henry Hobart⁷ and Mary Ripley (Corthell) Brigham, born in Whitman, Mass., 5 May, 1837; died there, 4 Feb., 1907; married, 23 Oct., 1857, Helena Sophia, daughter of Martin L. and Maria P. (Bearse) Peterson; born 13 Nov., 1840.

He was superintendent of a tack factory in Whitman, his father having been a manufacturer of tacks. Was in the Civil War, 4th Mass. Infantry. Was a member of the Mass. Legislature, and was on the board of selectmen for the town of Whitman for 7 years; always resided in Whitman, where he was greatly respected.

Children, born in Whitman:
  i Albert Henry⁹, b. 25 Feb., 1860; m. 25 Feb., 1882, Hannah Jane Stevens, b. April, 1859; a tack maker and inventor; res. s. p., Whitman.
  ii Mary Hobart, b. 4 Jan., 1873; m. 4 Jan., 1894, Harry, son of George H. Stanley, b. in Manchester, Eng., 19 April 1870; res. Whitman. Ch. (Stanley):
    1 *Henry Brigham*¹⁰, b. 4 March, 1896.
    2 *Donald Hobart*, b. 14 Feb., 1901.
  iii Herbert Andrew, b. 8 Nov., 1876; d. 8 July, 1903.
  iv Stella, b. 16 June, 1881; d. 14 July, 1884.

NINTH GENERATION

NINTH GENERATION

807 ELLEN MARIA[9], daughter of Martyn Freeman[8] and Elizabeth M. (Smith) Brigham; born in Wilmington, Vt., 3 Oct., 1841; married in Boston, 27 May, 1867, Thomas D., son of William and Mary (Watson) Cook of Scotland; born in East Boston, 1 July, 1840; died in Dorchester, Mass., 26 Jan., 1906; a business man in Boston about 40 years; she resides in Dorchester.

Children (Cook), born in Boston:
    i Walter Freeman[10], b. 20 July, 1868; m. 13 Aug., 1900, Minnie Louise, dau. of John A. Crotty of Boston; was grad. from the Institute of Technology, Boston, 1890; carries on the business and is administrator of the estate of his late father. Ch.:
        1 *Frank Brigham*[11], b. in Dorchester, 1 July, 1901.
    ii Frank William, b. 20 July, 1870; d. 14 Jan., 1876.
    iii Ernest Brigham, b. 31 Jan., 1875; d. 21 Sept., 1875.
    iv Marion Brigham, b. 9 Nov., 1877; m. 10 Sept., 1900, Benjamin Simpson, son of Thomas Frost of Boston; b. 21 June, 1873; of the firm of T. D. Cook & Co., Boston. Ch. (Frost):
        1 *Katherine*[11], b. in Dorchester, 1 Jan., 1902.
    v Emma Eleanor, b. 26 May, 1879; d. 4 Jan., 1880.
    vi Ellen Maria, b. 20 Aug., 1881; d. 13 Jan., 1882.

808 GEORGE BICKFORD[9], son of George Ball[8] and Caroline J. (Leland) Brigham; born in Westboro, Mass., 8 Oct., 1856; married 30 Oct., 1884, Lottie B. Mathewson of Millbury, Mass. Was graduated from Brown University, A. M., 1881. Is a boot and shoe manufacturer in Ayer, Mass.

Children:
    i George B.[10], b. 1889.
    ii Flora B., b. 1886.
    iii Roger W., b. 1897.

809 DR. FRANK FONTANELLE[9], son of George Ball[8] and Mary Phipps (Homer) Brigham; born in Westboro, Mass., 15 Oct., 1859; died in Lynn, Mass., 10 March, 1903; married 26 April, 1888, Ida McDonald.

Dr. Brigham was graduated from Brown University in 1882, Harvard University, M. D., 1885; was house surgeon of Lynn Hospital 1885-86; member board of health of Lynn, 1887-91; School Board 1894-98. He was a practicing physician in Lynn until his untimely death, and prominently identified with the philanthropic and Christian movements of the city.

Children, born in Lynn:
    i Ruth McD.[10], b. 1889; ii Frank D., b. 1889.

810   ERVIN FRANK[9], son of Dea. Curtis[8] and Esther (Metcalf) Brigham; born in Sylvan, Mich., 17 April, 1853; died in Lenville, Idaho, 3 June, 1893; married in Moscow, Idaho, 5 Oct., 1880, Emma, daughter of William Overacker of Iowa; born 22 July, 1859; she resides a widow in Kipling, Wash. Was a fruit-grower in Idaho. Justice of the Peace and Sunday School superintendent. He was 6 ft 1½ in. in height.

Children, all but the eldest born in Lenville:
  i William Curtis[10], b. in Moscow, 4 Sept., 1881; educated Univ. of Idaho; a teacher and medical student; in 1905 went to Des Moines, Ia., and thence to Los Angeles, Cal., to study Osteopathy.
  ii Frank Howard, b. 17 May, 1883; d. 17 July, 1894.
  iii Harrison Benton, b. 11 Nov., 1888.
  iv Fleda Adaline, b. 18 Dec., 1891.
  v Ella Gladys, b. 20 Oct., and d. 14 Nov., 1893.

811   DEXTER E.[9], son of Lyscom[8] and Mary (Norton) Brigham; born in Decatur, Mich., 14 May, 1862; married 27 Jan., 1892, Clara W., daughter of William and Olive (Wait) Lindsey; born in Prairieville Township, Mich., 9 Sept., 1861.   He resides in Decatur, Mich., where he is a grower and distiller of essential oils; is a member of the Village Council.

Children, born in Decatur:
  i Margaret Wait[10], b. 15 Aug., 1893.
  ii Doris Mary, b. 15 June, 1895.
  iii Lyscom Dexter, b. 2 Oct., 1901.

812   WALTER DAMON[9], son of Alfred Milo[8] and Caroline (Damon) Brigham; born in Natick, Mass., 4 Sept., 1853; married in Manchester, N. H., 17 July, 1879, Carrie B., daughter of Charles Brigham; born E. Kingston, N. H., 2 Sept., 1860.   He resided in Willimantic, Conn., for many years, where he was superintendent in the factory of the Willimantic Linen Co.; was also Postmaster and alderman.   Removed to Plymouth, Mass.

Children, all but the eldest born in Willimantic:
  i Abbie Wood[10], b. in Lowell, Mass., 22 Oct., 1881.
  ii Helen Idora, b. 21 Sept., 1884.
  iii Barbara Louisa, b. 26 Nov., 1884.
  iv Paul Goodrich, b. 25 Sept., 1894.

813   NATHANIEL MAYNARD[9], son of Alfred Milo[8] and Caroline (Damon) Brigham; born in Saxonville, Mass., 8 March, 1856; married 18 June, 1894, Mrs. Luella Cobb Young of Salt Lake City, Utah.

He is a graduate of Harvard University in the famous class of 1880 (Roosevelt); a member of the 'Varsity crews of 1877, '78, '79,

Mr. and Mrs. Dexter E. Brigham   (811)

'80, and celebrated as the tenor soloist of the Harvard Glee Club. His beautiful voice made him famous all over the country. Resided in Utah for 9 years, and for 4 years (1893-97) was United States Marshal for the territory and warden of the Territorial Penitentiary. For the last 5 years he has been on the illustrated lecture platform. Resides in Chicago.

Children:
i Nathalie Frances[10], b. 10 Jan., 1896.
ii Virginia Howe, b. 22 Nov., 1898.

814 ERNEST ALGERNON[9], son of Algernon S.[8] and Matilda M. (Hayden) Brigham; born in Marlboro, Mass., 29 July, 1852; married 2 Oct., 1870, Adeline Frances, daughter of Otis and Frances (Pond) Cole; born in Ashland, Mass., 22 Feb., 1853. Resides in Los Angeles, Cal.

Children, born in St. Louis, Mo.:
i Archie Valentine[10], b. 26 April, 1871; m. in Hot Springs, Ark., 11 Nov., 1896, Elaine Bryant McCarter; is the Gen. Baggage Agt. in St. Louis for the Mo. Pacific Ry. Co., and res. there. Ch.:
1 *David Ralston*[11], b. 26 Oct., 1897; d. 29 Jan., 1899. '
2 *Elizabeth Townsend,* b. 3 Aug., 1900.
3 *Natalie Adeline,* b. 24 Sept., 1905.
ii Ethel Percy, b. 5 Nov., 1873; res. Chicago.
iii Amy Frances, b. 26 Feb., 1876; res. St. Louis.

815 WILLIAM H. BREWSTER[9], son of William Lacy[8] and Achsah (Blake) Brigham; born in Exeter, N. H., 13 Aug., 1841; married Aug., 1871, Mary E. Spead, born in New Market, N. H., 3 May, 1847. See No. 816. In 1863-4 was on the U. S. S. Ohio. He resides in Wakefield, Mass.

Children:
i Annie Gertrude[10], b. 3 May, 1877; d. 27 May, 1879.
ii Harry, b. 13 Jan., 1881; res. Summersworth (Great Falls), N. H.

816 GEORGE ALBERT DRAPER[9], son of William Lacy[8] and Achsah (Blake) Brigham; born in Exeter, N. H., 29 Oct., 1843; married (1) April, 1868, Ida R. Albee, who died; married (2) Mrs. Mary E. Carver. Mr. Brigham and his 3 elder brothers enlisted as musicians in the Civil War, 27 April, 1861, in the 11th Mass. regiment. After the first Bull Run battle their regiment was formed into Hooker's Brigade. Saw service on lower Potomac at Budd's Ferry, Md., and then were in the Peninsula campaign under McClellan. They officiated at the Siege of Yorktown, battles of Williamsburg, Seven Pines, Savage Station, Glendale, Malvern Hill, and lay at Harrison's Landing when discharged 8 Aug., 1862, under

a general order doing away with regimental bands. They came home and all re-enlisted; Azel P. in the N. Y. Cavalry, and William H. B. in the 15th N. H. George then spent 2 years on U. S. S. Ohio, and then joined the army in front of Petersburg, 1 Oct., 1864, attached at headquarters of Gen. Mott's Div. of (the 2d) Hancock's Corps. Was at Appomattox at Lee's surrender. Discharged 8 June, 1865. He does business in Charlestown, Mass., where he has long resided.

Children (by first wife):
    i Ida Florence[10], b. in Somerville, Mass., 13 Sept., 1869; a violinist of repute.
    ii Ethel May, b. 13 Sept., 1871; d. Feb., 1872.

817 ORANGE SCOTT[9], son of William Lacy[8] and Achsah (Blake) Brigham; born in Exeter, N. H., 15 Jan., 1852; married, 1884, Ida Bell Glover; born in Exeter, 14 March, 1866. Resides in Exeter.

Children, the first and third born in Boston:
    i Carl Eugene[10], b. 29 Jan., 1885.
    ii Florence Leola, b. in Exeter, 10 March, 1886.
    iii Anna Atalanta, b. 24 Dec., 1888.
    iv Abby Elizabeth, b. in Exeter, 16 Nov., 1891.

818 CHARLES LEWIS[9], son of John[8] and Mary S. (Bemis) Brigham; born in Berlin, Mass., 22 April, 1844; married 1 Sept., 1868, Laura A., daughter of Nathaniel Hastings; born in Clinton, Mass., 16 June, 1850. A farmer in Northboro, Mass.

Children, born in Northboro:
    i Charles Montford[10], b. 26 July, 1873; married at W. Somerville, Mass., 15 Sept., 1897, Helen E., dau. of Rev. Edward A. Goddard of Northboro; b. in Huntington, Mass., 15 Jan., 1872; res. s. p., in Northboro.
    i Walter O., b. 14 Sept., 1877; m. 22 Dec., 1897, Alice L., dau. of James Bowes; b. in Northboro, 22 Jan., 1878; res. Northboro. Ch.:
        1 *Charles Clayton*[11], b. 16 Aug., 1898.
        2 *Harold Montford*, b. 6 April, 1900.
        3 *Ernest Lynden*, b. 9 April, 1902.

819 WALTER AUGUSTUS[9], son of John[8] and Mary S. (Bemis) Brigham; born in Boylston, Mass., 22 May, 1846; died 23 Aug., 1903; married 29 March, 1868, Jennie M., daughter of Alexander Smith; born 22 Jan., 1878. For 6 years he was superintendent of the Northboro Town Farm; for several years in the milk and ice business in Boston.

Child, born in Boylston:
    i Herbert Augustus[10], b. 6 April, 1869; m. in Westboro, Alice C., dau. of John Gilman; b. 5 Aug., 1866; res. Boylston Cen.,

NATHANIEL MAYNARD BRIGHAM, OF GLEN ELLYN, ILL. (813)

P. O., Northboro. Ch., the eldest and 2 younger b. in Medford, Mass.:

1 *Charlotte E.*[11], b. 26 Sept., 1888.
2 *Walter Gilman*, b. in Boylston Cen., 25 Jan., 1890.
3 *Hazel A.*, b. in Boylston Cen., 13 Aug., 1892; d. 10 Oct., 1892.
4 *Herbert L.*, b. 21 July, 1894.
5 *Marion E.*, b. 19 June, 1896.

820 HON. EDWARD D.[9], son of Charles H.[8] and Phalla (House) Brigham; born in Somnauk, Ill., 22 Feb., 1863; married (1) 5 July, 1887, Mary, daughter of Michael Corcoran; born in Boscobel, Wis., 1867; died 17 Dec., 1889; married (2) 8 Dec., 1892, Clara L., daughter of Charles A. McCoy of Seattle, Wash.; born in Monteith, Ia., 8 Dec., 1873.

Mr. Brigham is the Labor Commissioner for the State of Iowa, appointed to his second term in 1905. He began at the age of fifteen in the railway service and worked up to conductor; was employed from 1890 to 1902 by the Chicago Great Western Railway Co. In 1902 left active service to become Commissioner of the Bureau of Labor Statistics. Resides in Des Moines, Ia.

Child (by first wife):
i Jay Edward D.[10], b. Mason City, Ia., 7 April, 1888; d. 12 Dec., 1899.
Children (by second wife):
ii Leon Herbert, b. in Des Moines, 8 Feb., 1896.
iii Lyle Duane, b. in St. Joseph, Mo., 5 Oct., 1899.

821 DR. CLARENCE SUMNER[9], son of William Oakley[8] and Nella M. (Perkins) Brigham; born in Bakersfield, Vt., 5 Feb., 1867; married (1) 20 Sept., 1893, Anna H. Tracy of Hamburg, N. Y., who died 27 Feb., 1898; married (2) 7 Nov., 1901, Mrs. Jennie B. Kinney of Los Angeles, Cal. Was graduated A. B. Univ. of Vt., 1889; M. D., same 1891; post-graduate N. Y. Polytechnic School, 1896; practiced in Jamaica, Vt., and in 1903 resided in Leominster, Mass.

Children (by first wife):
i Paul Tracy[10], b. 17 Sept., 1896.
ii Helen Pearl, b. 28 Oct., 1897.

822 GEORGE SAMUEL[9], son of Edmund Douglass[8] and Edith (Northmore) Brigham, born in Ishpeming, Mich., 27 May, 1880; married in New Haven, Conn., 1902, Christine, only daughter of Mrs. Anne Hempstead. He is a Yale graduate, 1901, and took up Engineering and Maintenance of Way on the C. & N. W. Ry. upon leaving College. He is now General Manager of the Blue Ridge Copper Co., at Stanleyton, Va., where he resides.

Children, born in Mankato, Minn, 1:
i Edmund Hempstead[10], b. 1905.

823   DR. BRAYTON ALVARO REMINGTON[9], son of Philip
V [8] and Helen C. (Remington) Brigham; born in Lorraine, N. Y.,
1 Jan., 1862; died in Lake Forest, Ill., Oct., 1901; married 15 Feb.,
1887, Mrs. Amanda, daughter of J. T. McManus and widow of J.
B. Blackwood, from whom he was divorced in 1893.

Dr. Brigham was the founder of the Brigham Family Association
1893.   He was connected with the Battle Creek Sanitarium 2 years.
Was graduated from the College of Physicians and Surgeons,
Chicago, Ill., and was a lecturer at the Harvard Medical College in
Chicago.   His specialty was Gynecology; was considered a good
operator; had several medical works planned but none published.
Began a history of the Brigham Family, which was unfinished at
his death; the results are embodied in this volume.

Children, born in Chicago:
    i Mabel Olive[10], b. 24 March, 1888.
    ii Henry Cox, b. 1889; d. ibid.

Dr. B. A. R. Brigham, of Chicago (823)
First Secretary of the Brigham Family Association, 1893-1896

APPENDIX

APPENDIX A.

"BRIGHAM FARME ON YE ROCKS."

In 1648 there was laid out by the town of Cambridge to Thomas[1] Brigham " 72 acres on ye Rocks on Charlestown line." In view of the important error of Mr. Morse in locating upon this plot the homestead in which Thomas died in 1653, the place has borne a distinction in Brigham family history which is unwarranted by its actual position as a Brigham possession. Morse, mistaking the well-known ledges of Clarendon Hill for " ye Cambridge Rocks," declares that the last habitation of Thomas was in Somerville. Having done this, he easily draws a graphic picture of the Brigham Farm as it might have appeared in the last days of its owner; and he even goes so far as to offer the baseless conjecture that Thomas was buried in Medford.

The " Cambridge Rocks " were, as Morse says, a well-known ancient landmark, but they were not where Morse places them. They begin in Cambridge on the Watertown line, at a point which is now the corner of Pleasant Street and Concord Avenue, Belmont. They skirt the western boundary of Pleasant Street to the corner of Massachusetts Avenue, Arlington, where the public library now stands. This site was originally the corner of the old Watertown road. Thence they cross Massachusetts Avenue and, following the line of the present Water Street, extend to Fowle's Mill Pond and thence northwesterly along the mill pond and brook, and northerly across the brook to the Charlestown line. (This brook, Sucker Brook, was originally Alewive Meadow Brook, and should not be confounded with the present Alewive Brook, flowing out of Fresh Pond, originally the Menotomy [a] River.) " The Rocks " continued along the Charlestown line to a point near the present Lexington and Arlington line. The territory to the west—Lexington since 1713—was originally known as Cambridge Farms.

It was colloquial to refer to the grants in this immediate vicinity as the " small farms "; hence the item in the inventory of the property of Thomas[1] Brigham, " a small farme at Charlestown line, £10." The ancient use of the term " farm " did not imply that the land was under cultivation.

It will thus be seen that all the present Arlington Heights, also the well-known Turkey Hill (which is *half an inch* lower), was included in what was anciently known as the Cambridge Rocks.

Of the 72-acre grant to Thomas[1] Brigham, it may be said, in modern terms, that it is now in a northwest part of Arlington. While originally bounded on the north by Charlestown line, a change in the line at the incorporation of Winchester (originally Woburn) in 1850 left a triangular piece in the northwest corner lying in Winchester. Turkey Hill is near the center of the grant. Forest Street runs across the property, about a mile from Massachusetts Avenue, where one leaves the electric car.

The 48-acre grant of Nicholas Wyeth, which adjoined that of Thomas[1] Brigham on the northwest, later passed into possession of Henry Dunster, first president of Harvard College, and was held by his descendants many years. In a bill of sale of the Dunster piece given by John Steadman, county treasurer, to Thomas Danforth, in 1674, the lot is described as bounded " n. (n.e.) by Woburn line . e. (s.e.) by a small farm layed out to Thomas Brigham." The Brigham grant also adjoined, on the Charlestown line, a 300-acre farm of Increase Nowell and also the 480 acres of " Squa Sachem," which the Colony reserved to her when settlement was made with the Indians for the territory comprising Charlestown and Cambridge. The familiar Indian monument on the Peter C. Brooks place in West Medford was erected by Mr. Brooks in memory of the son of Squa Sachem, Sagamore John.

Thomas[1] Brigham died 8 Dec., 1653, leaving this 72-acre grant, with all his other property, to his widow and five children. In 1656 the General Court gave the overseers of his will the right to sell all his real estate. It would appear that this " Brigham Farm," as many ancient deeds refer to it, was bought for £16 by Hon. Thomas Danforth, an executor of the will, although no deed of the property is recorded. In 1695 the farm on the Rocks figures in the suit brought by the children of Thomas Brigham to recover, apparently, all the property which the overseers of their father's will had sold. In the formal ceremony of claiming the " Brigham Farm," as quaintly attested by the witnesses in the chapter on " Thomas Brigham the Emigrant," it will be noted that the " ffarme " is described as " upon the Rocks within the bounds of Cambridge."

Settlement was reached apparently in 1703, when on 26 Feb., Thomas[2], Samuel[2] and John[2] Brigham quitclaimed " that tract or p[r]eell of land commonly called or known by y[e] name of Brighams farme: Scituate, lying and being on y[e] Rocks neer Oburn line within the Township of Cambridge . . . containing by Estimation Seventy Two acres be the same more or less . . . ," to Francis Foxcroft, Esq., Samuel Sparhawk and Daniel Champney, joint executors of the will of Hon. Thomas Danforth. This deed was given " in consideration of the Sum of Sixteen Pounds pd to yᵉ Children of Thomas Brigham late of Cambridge Dece'd by Thomas Danforth Esq. and Thomas Fox called Overseers of yᵉ Estate of sᵈ Thomas Brigham Dece'd: and Thirty pounds in money to us in hand etc." From this document, and others affecting the other properties, it might be inferred that the suits grew out of the dissatisfaction of the children of Thomas, now of age, with the disposition of their property while they were yet minors.

In 1706 the property was bought by Thomas[3] Prentice for £68. It was then bounded " N.E. by Charlestown line, N.W. by Nathaniel Patten Senor and John Carter of Ohuru, W. by Walter[3] Russell E. and S. E. by the land of Jason Russell." Thomas[3] Prentice was a brickmaker and resided on what is now the west side of Garden Street opposite the Botanical Garden. He died 7 Dec., 1709; and the inventory shows: " 72 acres, Brigham's Farm, £68." In the distribution of his property the Brigham Farm went to his son, Rev. Thomas[4] Prentice (b. 1702, H. C. 1726, d. 1782), who made his first sale, of nine acres, in 1724, as if to aid him through Harvard, to Andrew Mallet, who built the Old Powder House in Somerville. A second purchaser, of twenty acres, was Deacon John Bradish, a celebrated real estate trader of his day. He always styled himself, even in his deeds, " glazier of Harvard College," and he held this unique position for forty years. By 1753 Rev. Thomas Prentice had disposed of more than 70 acres of the original grant for £443. Much of the property remained within the Prentice family.

In 1773 John[5] Hutchinson, whose descendants at the present time own all but about ten acres of the original grant, made his first purchase from the Brigham tract, paying Henry Prentice, an uncle of the Rev. Thomas, £50, 13s. 4d. for 9½ acres " on * Turkey Hill " —the first mention of this name in the deeds. John Hutchinson owned and occupied the Nowell-Broughton-Gardner farm of about 70 acres adjoining on the Charlestown side of the line, and at his death in 1783 had acquired also some 40 acres of the Brigham place. In 1817 his son Thomas[6], to whom the farm later descended, bought 22½ acres more, 20 of which were " Brigham land," of Daniel Reed of Charlestown, making all but about eight acres, on the southwest side, of the original grant. At the death of Thomas[6] in 1863, the property was divided among his six children, and most of it is still held by their heirs. No building ever has been erected on the land originally owned by Thomas Brigham. It is now partly tilled. The Hutchinson homestead, on the original Charlestown side on the old Nowell farm and replacing the buildings erected in

* In olden times this was a favorite sighting point for vessels making Boston Harbor, as it was heavily wooded and Arlington Heights was not.

1743-45 and burned a few years ago, stands on the corner of Ridge Street and Hutchinson Road (Fruit Street), Winchester. It is occupied by Mrs. Mary A., widow of Thomas[7] O. Hutchinson, a daughter, Miss Mary A., and a son, Thomas[8] M. Hutchinson, the well-known antiquarian, to whose generosity and exhaustive researches, covering many years, the writer is indebted for many of these authenticated facts relative to the " Brigham Farme on Ye Rocks."

APPENDIX B

BRIGHAMS IN THE EARLY WARS

In every stage of the nation's progress whenever it has become necessary to resort to arms, the Brigham family has loyally responded to every call for volunteers. The colonial and revolutionary periods brought to the front a remarkable quota of Brighams, and the roll of honor is a heritage which their descendants may justly transmit with pride to coming generations. The civil war, the greatest conflict of modern times, found earnest defenders of the Union among the Brighams, and the intelligent bravery displayed by them on various battlefields would furnish an interesting chapter of history. We have not attempted to give a complete list of the Brighams in this war, but where known the records have been entered under individuals.

In the Black Hawk war, which was one of the incidents of the early settlement of the western section of the United States, Sylvester Brigham (519), who was a pioneer from Massachusetts, did his part in opening to civilization that vast region, which has since furnished many of the largest and most prosperous States to the Union.

About the same period Asa (403) and Benjamin (403-iii) served in the war with Mexico under Major Morse; and Henry O. (682), who entered the service as a drummer boy, earned by merit the ranks of lieutenant and major—a great distinction in view of the fact that regular troops of the United States preponderated in that contest and junior officers from that branch were usually selected for promotion.

In the war with England, 1812-15, the Brigham family sent the following named representatives:

Dexter B. (189), pri.; Pierpont (186), capt.; Elijah (198) capt.?; Jonas (208-iv), officer?; John (278), pri.; Josiah (251), (Morse, p. 43); Bela (415), capt. (Morse, p. 54); Uriah (147-iii) (Morse, p. 76); Pliny (153-iii); Joel (227), lieut.; Silas (274);

William C. (446), sergt.; Ephraim (192), col.; Ebenezer (179), capt.; Curtis (434), captured as a civilian; Thomas (476), killed Chippewa Plains, Canada, after three years' service; Orleans (307); Asa (403), Maj. Morse; Benjamin (403-v); Henry (682) drummer boy, lieutenant and major.

It is difficult to present satisfactorily a story of the revolutionary heroes, as the records of that period are incomplete and probably inaccurate. Every known source of information, however, has been sought in securing the list and every means of verification has been tried. It is interesting to note that the "minute men" of 1775 had a remarkable percentage of Brighams, who not only marched to Lexington and Concord but also to other points which were threatened by English troops.

BRIGHAMS IN THE REVOLUTION.

Aaron, Marlboro (163), pri., Capt. Edward Langley's Co., Col. Cogswell's Regt.; served three months in fortifications around Boston; later six months in Continental Army.

Abel, Sudbury (51-i), pri., Capt. Andrew Haskell's Co., Col. Thomas Marshall's Regt.; served from 23 June, 1776, to 1 Dec., 1776, 5 mos., 9 days; also in Capt. Moses Barnes' Co., Lieut.-Col. Pierce's Regt., from 29 May, 1779, to 1 July, 1779 in Rhode Island; served in Continental Army for 6 mos.; in Capt. Ashael Wheeler's Co., Col. Read's Regt., 41 days' service with Northern Army, in 1776; in Capt. Edward Langley's Co., Col. Cogswell's Regt., 3 mos. service in 1778, to guard and fortify posts around Boston.

Abijah, Sudbury (51), sergt., and reported with the "minute men" at Cambridge by the way of Concord 19 April, 1775; 2nd lieut. 7th Sudbury Co., Capt. Ashael Wheeler, of Col. Ezekiel Howe's Regt.; commissioned 5 July, 1776; also served as 2nd lieut. in Capt. Amasa Cranston's Co., Col. Denny's Regt.; enlisted 30 Oct., 1779, discharged 23 Nov., 1779.

Abner Croyden (residence not given) (79-i), corp. in Capt. Luke Drury's Co., Col., Jonathan Ward's Regt., enlisted for service in Quebec under Col. Arnold; was sergt. in 1779 under Col. Chase.

Abraham (residence given as Bolton), (62), joined Capt. Barnes' Co., Col. Timothy Bigelow's Regt., in Continental Army; enlisted for 3 years in 1777 and promoted to sergt.

Amariah, Sutton (12 under 77), pri. in Northern Department of Continental Army and did duty in Rhode Island for eight months.

Antipas, Westboro (106), marched to Cambridge on 19 April, 1775, and marched to Hadley to reinforce the Northern Army; in the army in 1775, 1777, 1778 and 1779.

Antipas, Marlboro (64), corp. in Capt. Daniel Barnes' Co.; marched on alarm of 19 April, 1775; also served for 13 weeks, 6 days as sergt. with Capt. Barnes; promoted from corp. to sergt. 9 June, 1775.

Artemas, Northboro (85), pri., Capt. Sam Wood's Co. of " minute men " in Gen. Ward's Regt., which marched on alarm of 19 April, 1775; later was sergt. in Lieut. Seth Rice's Co., of Col. Job Cushing's Regt.; saw service with the Northern Army in Berkshire County.

Artemas, New Marlboro (153), pri. in 1775, and marched on alarm at Lexington 19 April, 1775; promoted to corp. and saw service in New York State; served in several other organizations and discharged 16 Oct., 1780.

Asa, Westboro (40-vii), pri., Capt. Reuben Sibley's Co., Col. Josiah Whitney's Regt.; on duty in Rhode Island.

Barnabas, Westboro (105), pri., Capt. Edward Brigham's Co. of " minute men " in Gen. Ward's Regt., which marched to Cambridge on 19 April, 1775; in Capt. Todd's Co., Col. Crafts' Regt. of Artillery; in fortifications around Boston from 1 Feb. to 8 May, 1776.

Benjamin, Westboro, pri., Capt. Seth Morse's Co., Major-Gen. Ward's Regt., marched to Cambridge on alarm 19 April, 1775.

Benjamin, Upton, Col. Thomas Marshall's 10th Regt. of Continental Army; also served with Capt. Caleb Brooks in Col. Dike's Regt.

Daniel, Marlboro (209), pri., Capt. William Morse's Co., of Col. Jonathan Read's Regt., which marched to reinforce General Gates; later served six months in Continental Army in western part of Massachusetts; in Capt. Barnes' Co., Col. Cyprian Howe's Regt. from 24 May, 1779, to 1 July, 1779.

Daniel, Jr., Marlboro, pri., Capt. William Morse's Co., Col. Jonathan Read's Regt.; marched to reinforce General Gates; may have been the Daniel who served at age of fifteen as waiter in Capt. John Gleason's Co., Col. Josiah Whitney's Regt.

Daniel, Westboro (107), surgeon's mate, Col. John Rand's Worcester County Regt., served 3 mos., 12 days, and was at West Point when Major Andre was captured.

David, Shrewsbury (97), Capt. Ross Wyman's (Artillery) Co., of Col. John Wood's Regt., which marched to Cambridge on 19 April, 1775; also in Capt. John Maynard's Co., Col. Job Cushing; marched to Hadley 21 Aug., 1777, by order of Col. Denny on alarm from Bennington.

Ebenezer, Northboro(?), pri., Capt. Joseph Warren's Co., Lieut. Col. Wheelock's Regt.; also saw service of several months in

Rhode Island and marched to the western part of Massachusetts when Bennington, Vt., was threatened; his enlistments covered from 1777 to 1779 inclusive.

Edmund, Westboro (73), capt. of Company of "minute men," Major-Gen. Ward's Regt., which marched to Lexington 19 April, 1775; also Capt. in Col. Job Cushing's Regt., which marched to re-inforce Northern Army by order of General Stark and General Lincoln; remained in service until February, 1779, when resigned on account of injuries received by kick from a horse.

Edmund, Westboro, son of Capt. Edmund (181), pri., Capt. James Myrick's Co., Col. Nathan Sparhawk's Regt.; was in fortifi-cations around Boston for 2 months and 3 days.

Edward, Westboro (104), pri., Capt. Moses Bullard's Co., Col. Ebenezer Thayer's Suffolk County Regt.; responded to the alarm from Lexington; promoted to corp. and sergt., and served $4\frac{3}{4}$ mos. in New York and 8 mos. at Dorchester.

Edward, pri. (probably of Westboro, same as 104), Capt. Moses Bullard's Co., Col. Ebenezer Thayer's Suffolk County Regt.; did duty in Rhode Island for 3 mos.; as member of another organiza-tion marched on 40 days' expedition by order of His Excellency John Hancock.

Elijah, Southboro (76), lieut., Capt. Josiah Fay's Co., of "min-ute men" which marched to Cambridge, 19 April, 1775.

Elisha, Brookfield (93), pri., Capt. Asa Danforth's Co., Col. Converse's Regt.; served in the army of Gen. Gates and was at Battle of Saratoga.

Gardner, Northboro (215), pri., Capt. Nathaniel Wright's Co., Col. Denny's Regt.; served 3 mos., 20 days at West Point.

George, Marlboro (54), pri., Capt. Gates' Co.; did duty around Boston; also served in Company of Capt. Homes, Col. Jonathan Read's Regt.; was member of committee from Middlesex County to raise men for New York and Canada.

George, Jr., Marlboro (54-ii), pri., Capt. William Brigham's Co., Col. Jonathan Ward's Regt.; marched on alarm of 19 April, 1775, to Cambridge.

Gershom, Marlboro (125), marched to Cambridge in Capt. William Brigham's Co.

Gershom, Marlboro (120), was on the alarm list and did duty with Capt. Benjamin Monroe.

Henry, Marlboro (146?), sergt., Capt. William Brigham's Co., which went to Cambridge on 19 April, 1775; also sergt. in Capt. Silas Gates' Co., Col. Ward's Regt.

Hosea, Bolton, pri., Capt. James Mirick's Co., Col. Whitney's Regt.; went to reinforce Gen. Gates at Saratoga.

Isaac, Grafton (206), pri., Capt. Luke Drury's Co., Gen. Ward's Regt.; marched to Cambridge 19 April, 1775; also at the alarm at Bennington; later reinforced Continental Army; was promoted to corp. and sergt.

Ithamar, Marlboro (81), lieut., Capt. William Brigham's Co., Gen. Ward's Regt., which marched to Cambridge; also Capt. William Morse's Co., Col. Read's Regt.; went to reinforce Gen. Gates.

Ithamar, Marlboro (208), pri., Capt. William Morse's Co., Col. Jonathan Read's Regt., in 1777; pri., Capt. Joshua Leland's Co. of Guards in 1779, under Major Nathaniel Heath; manned forts around Boston by order of Governor Hancock.

James, credited to the 3rd Precinct of Brookfield as having served for 8 mos. in 1778.

Joel, Sudbury (135), pri., Capt. Aaron Haynes' Co.; marched to Cambridge 19 April, 1775; served in Continental Army and promoted to sergt.; was in the army nearly 7 years and attached to several organizations.

Joel, Jr., Marlboro, served in Capt. Barnes' Co., Col. Howe's Regt. for 9 mos.; afterwards made commissary.

John, Sudbury (141), pri., served 3 mos. at Claverack, and was also stationed at White Plains, N. Y.; his term of service was between 1776 and 1779.

John, pri., Col. John Rand's Worcester County Regt.; did duty at Princeton, N. J.

John, pri., Capt. Daniel Bowker's Co., Col. Webb's Regt.; went to reinforce the Continental Army.

John, Templeton, pri., Capt. Joel Fletcher's Co. of "minute men" and probably responded on alarm 19 April, 1775.

John, Bolton and Princeton (155), corp., James Mirick's Co., from 2 to 18 Oct., 1777; corp. in Capt. Homes' Co. from 1 April, 1778 to 4 July, 1778.

John, pri., Capt. Timothy Brigham's Co., 27 July, 1777, to 29 Aug., 1777; at Bennington.

John, pri., Capt. Ephraim Lyons' Co., from 24 June, 1778, to 13 July, 1778, at Rhode Island; also in Capt. Manasseh Sawyer's Co. from 30 July, 1778, to 13 Sept., 1778.

John, pri., Capt. Ephraim Stearns' Co., from 11 July, 1780, to 11 Oct., 1780.

John Gott, Marlboro (145), Capt. Morse's Co., Col. How's Regt.; marched to reinforce the Continental Army.

Jonas, Sudbury (136), pri., Capt. Jonathan Rice's Co., Col. Samuel Willard's Regt.; served 4 months in Continental Army.

Jonas, Westboro (352), probably capt.; saw 7 mos.' service at Dorchester and 3 mos. at New York.

Jonas, Brookfield (103), sergt., Capt. Jonathan Barnes' Co. of "minute men," Col. Jonathan Warner's Regt., which marched on alarm of 19 April, 1775; then 2nd lieut., Capt. Daniel Gilbert's (Ninth) Co., Col. James Converse's (Fourth Worcester County) Regt.; promoted to 1st lieut. and marched to relief of Gen. Gates. His term of service began April, 1775 and ended 9 Sept., 1779.

Jonathan, Brimfield, sergt., Capt. John Ferguson's Co., Col. Timothy Danielson's Regt.; did duty around Roxbury.

Jonathan (94) served to the credit of 3rd Precinct of Brookfield; 30 June, 1778, list dated.

Jonathan, Marlboro (probably 89), pri., Capt. Daniel Barnes' Co.; marched to Cambridge on alarm 19 April, 1775; also guarded stores in Boston and later marched to reinforce Gen. Gates.

Joseph, Jr., Marlboro (119), sergt. Capt. William Brigham's Co., Col. Ward's Regt., which marched to Cambridge 19 April, 1775; saw service in Rhode Island as 2nd lieut.

Josiah, Grafton, pri., Lieut. Seth Rice's Co., Col. Job Cushing's Regt.; went on 21 Aug., 1777, on alarm to reinforce Northern Army, but on arriving at Hadley found services not wanted; served 3 mos. in other parts of the army.

Levi (38), lieut.-col. of Col. John Goulding's (6th Worcester County) Regt., raised in Southboro, Westboro, Shrewsbury, Northboro and Grafton.

Lewis, Marlboro (169), pri., Capt. William Brigham's Co.; responded at Cambridge on alarm of 19 April, 1775.

Lovewell, Marlboro (151), pri., marched to Cambridge 19 April, 1775; also served in Northern Army in Rhode Island and in the Continental Army.

Ober, Northboro, pri., Capt. Thomas Fisk's Co., Col. Nathan Tyler's Regt.; saw service in Rhode Island.

Origen, New Marlboro (57-iii), surgeon's mate, enlisted for 3 years, Capt. Simeon Smith's Co., Col. Seth Werner's Regt.; saw service in Continental Army.

Paul, Marlboro (82), 2nd lieut., Capt. Daniel Barnes' Co.; marched to Cambridge 19 April, 1775; rose to rank of capt. and was in Army of Northwest.

Paul, Marlboro (211), served under Capt. Thomas Pritchard in Continental Army.

Phineas, Marlboro (149), on 2nd July, 1776, engaged to march to New York and remain in service until 1 Dec., 1776, unless sooner discharged; on 26 June, 1777, found in Capt. John Gleason's Co.,

Col. Josiah Whitney's Regt.; 27th Sept., 1777, enlisted in Capt. Joseph Warren's Co., Lieut.-Col. Wheelock's Regt.; discharged 23 Oct., 1777; probably enlisted 17 Oct., 1778, as pri. in Capt. Joseph Cole's Co., Col. John Jacobs' Regt., enlistment expired 1 Jan., 1779; next served until 1 July, 1779, in Col. Cyprian Howe's Regt. at Tiverton, R. I.; completed term of service in Capt. Moses Barnes' Co.

Phineas, pri., Capt. Jonathan Houghton's Co., Col. Smith's Regt.; year not given.

Phineas, Westboro (177), pri., Capt. Edmund Brigham's Co. of "minute men," Maj.-Gen. Ward's Regt.; marched to Cambridge 19 April, 1775; made sergt. and was stationed at North Kingston, R. I., for 6 mos. and 12 days.

Phineas, Marlboro (149), pri., Capt. Joseph Cole's Co., Col. John Jacobs' Regt.; did duty in Rhode Island; promoted to sergeant.

Roger, (82), pri., Capt. Seth Newton's Co., Col. Elijah Stearns' Regt.; saw service for 3 mos. and 2 days in Roxbury; was a corp. in Capt. Isaac Harrington's Co., Col. Samuel Denny's Regt.; joined Continental Army at Claverack.

Samuel, Sudbury (48v), pri., Capt. John Nixon's Co. of "minute men," Col. Abijah Pierce's Regt.; marched to Cambridge 19 April, 1775.

Samuel, Marlboro, pri., Capt. Caleb Brooks' Co., Col. Dike's Regt.; 3 mos. guarding stores in Boston; also under Capt. William Morse; Col. Jonathan Read's Regt.; marched to reinforce Gen. Gates.

Samuel, Shrewsbury, pri. in Capt. Job Cushing's Co. of "minute men," marched to Cambridge 19 April, 1775.

Samuel, Westboro, also given Grafton, fifer; later served in Capt. Josiah Fay's Co., Col. Jonathan Ward's Regt. at Dorchester; also member of Capt. Edward Brigham's Co. and served in the West.

Samuel, was in Capt. Samuel Monroe's Co., Col. Sprout's Regt.; in Rhode Island in 1778; muster roll dated at Stow.

Samuel, lieut., was detached from militia and sent to reinforce Continental Army in June, 1779; commissioned 30 June, 1780.

Seth, Westboro, marched to Cambridge and later was on duty in New York.

Stephen (probably 118), pri., Capt. John Maynard's Co., Col. Job Cushing's Regt.; went to Bennington, Vt., Aug., 1777.

Tilly (92), on list of men who served to credit of 3rd Precinct of Brookfield, dated 30 June, 1778, term of service 13¼ mos.

Timothy, Northboro, 1st lieut., Capt. Samuel Wood's "minute men"; marched to Cambridge 19 April, 1775; did duty at Dorchester; and reinforced the Northern Army when Bennington was threatened by attack; promoted to capt. in 1775.

Uriah, Jr. (147), pri., Capt. Silas Gates' Co., Col. Ward's Regt.; did duty at Dorchester and in the army of Gen. Gates.

William, Marlboro (74), capt., Col. Jonathan Ward's Regt.; marched to Cambridge on alarm from Lexington.

Winslow, pri., Capt. Seth Morse's Co., Major-Gen. Ward's Regt.; marched to Cambridge on alarm 19 April, 1775.

Winslow, on 2 July, 1776, agreed to march to New York and continue in service until 1 Dec., 1776. Nothing in the records conflicts with the belief that both these men may have been the Winslow who follows:

Winslow, Northboro (101), pri., Capt. Silas Gates' Co., Col. Ward's Regt.; was in service in Rhode Island 6 mos. and 12 days; also a member of Capt. Timothy Brigham's Co., Col. Cushing's Regt.; Capt. Ebenezer Belknap's Co.; and Capt. Nathan Fisher's Co. of Col. Wade's Regt.; service in North Kingston, R. I., from 23 June, 1778, to 1 Jan, 1779; also on muster roll Jan.—Nov., 1778.

The New Hampshire contingent was:
Don C. (132), Capt. Moulton's Co., 1781; pensioner 1832-1840.

Elnathan (45), Rudd's Co.; took part in battles of Newport and Long Island, 1778; with Capt. Waterman at New London, 1781.

Paul (128), 2nd lieut., Oct., 1776; capt. 7th Co., 12th Conn. Regt. Dec., 1776; in Col. Chandler's Regt., Feb., 1777; in 8th Regt., "Conn. Line," raised for entire war; camped at Peekskill, spring of 1777; at Germantown and Fort Miflin; wintered 1777-78 at Valley Forge and at White Plains; resigned 22 April, 1781.

Stephen (432), ensign 8th Co., 5th Regt., 1779.

Alpheus (110), Smith's Co., Hale's Regt., 1776.

Asa (40), Cheshire Co., 1776; Mellin's Co., Hale's Regt., at Ticonderoga, 1777; also served in Major Nichols' Regt.

Asaph (110-i), Philip Thomas' Co., 1781.

Abner (79-i), sergt., Chase's Regt.; reinforced Ticonderoga, 1777.

Asa (40-vii), Lewis' Co., Moor's Regt.; at Saratoga, 1777.

Isaac (206), Chase's Regt.; at Ticonderoga, 1777.

Jonathan (273), Chase's Regt.; at Ticonderoga, 1777.

Leonard (112), Parker's Co.; at Ticonderoga, 1776.

Samuel (144), Chase's Regt.; at Saratoga, 1777.

Stephen (113), Whitcomb's Co., 1775.

The list from Connecticut was:
Daniel C., Coventry, Capt. Wm. Moulton's Co., 1781.
Don C., Hartford.

Elnathan, Capt. Rudd's Co., Tyler's Brigade; took part in attempt to dislodge British from Newport; was in battle of Long Island.

Nathan B., Capt. Waterman's Co.; on duty at New London.

Paul B., Coventry; commissioned capt. 1 Jan., 1777, in 8th Regt., "Conn. Line"; took part in defense of Fort Mifflin; was in battle of Monmouth; wintered at Valley Forge and White Plains; commended by Connecticut Assembly for bravery.

Stephen B., Mansfield; 26 Sept., 1777, rendered distinguished service by transporting supplies to Boston much needed by army.

BRIGHAMS IN THE FRENCH AND INDIAN WARS.

(From Massachusetts Archives.)

Aaron (77), Grafton, on Train Band, 25 March, 1757 (Capt. Warren).

Abijah, Sudbury (85), pri. on Crown Point Expedition, 1755-6, 13 weeks, Capt. Samuel Dakin.

Abijah, Sudbury (28), 1758, Capt. Henry Spring, Col. Abraham Williams; served 22 days.

Artemas, Westboro (85), pri. in Train Band, 1757, Capt. Bezaleal Eager.

Asa (40), Shrewsbury, ensign on Train Band, 28 March, 1757; Capt. Artemas Ward.

Asa, Marlboro (63), corp., 26 April, 1757; Capt. (Col.) Abraham Williams' Co.

Antipas, Marlboro (64), 26 April, 1757; Capt. (Col.) Abraham Williams' Co.

Benjamin, Marlboro (44), sergt., 26 April, 1757; Capt. (Col.) Abraham Williams' Co.

Charles, Grafton (21), 25 March, 1757; Capt. Sam Warren (prob. 1725); "Centinel" 3 weeks, 1 day in Capt. Nathan Brigham's troop of horse.

Daniel, Grafton (21-ii), 25 March, 1757, Capt. Sam Warren; 1759, pri., Whipple's Co., Ward's Regt.; 18⅔ days at Pontosook (Pittsfield) to recruit forces.

Ebenezer, Southboro (75), pri., 1759, Capt. Maynard's Co., Col. Williams' Regt., 8 mos., 15 days.

Edmund, Southboro (19-iii), under Capt. Timothy Brigham.

Elisha, Grafton (80), 25 March, 1757, on Train Band, Capt. Warren.

George, Marlboro (54), 26 April, 1757; Col. Abe Williams.

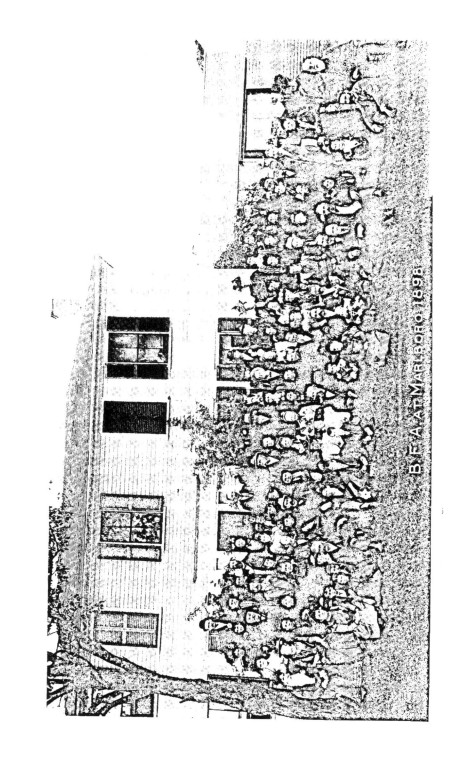

B.F.A. AT MARLBORO. 1898

Gershom, Westboro (43), 1 April, 1757; Capt. Fay's Train Band.

Ithamar, Marlboro (81), corp., 1757, 1st Marlboro Co., Col. Williams; ensign, Capt. Jesse Rice's Marlboro Co.

James (35), corp., 9 Aug., 1757; marched to Kinderhook, 17 days.

Jesse, Westboro (33), ensign, Train Band, 1757, 2nd Co., Capt. Bezaleal Eager, capt., 2nd Westboro Co., Col. Ward, 1762.

John (14-iv), on alarm list and in Sudbury Co., Capt. Josiah Richardson, 1757.

John, Shrewsbury (36), 1757, on alarm list, Capt. Artemas Ward; in Oct. and Nov., 1759, returned from army as invalid; went into service again (æ. 19) Col. Abe Williams' Regt., invasion of Canada; pri., 1760, Capt. Maynard's Co., to westward, 8 mos., 21 davs; " Centinel," Capt. Josiah Brown's troop of horse.

John, Jr., Shrewsbury (95), 1757, Capt. Ward, Train Band.

Jonas, Westboro (39), lieut., Train Band, Capt. Benjamin Fay, 1757; lieut. (acting capt.), 1758, Capt. Fay, Col. Williams, 14 days; on relief Fort William Henry

Jonathan, Jr. (32), 1757, in Col. Abe Williams' (1st Mr'l.) Co.

Joseph (42), (1725 prob.) " Centinel " under Capt. Nathan Brigham, 3 weeks, 1 day.

Levi, Shrewsbury (38), cornet, 1757, Third Regular Troop Horse, Capt. Benjamin Eager.

Nathan (71), on alarm list under Capt. Timothy Brigham; lieut., 1759; Capt. Taplin, Col. Bagley, 8 mos., 25 days; lieut., 1760, 8 mos., 21 days, Capt. Stephen Maynard; capt., 1761, 28 weeks, 2 days; capt., 1763, 43 weeks, 3 days.

Nathan, Jr. (22), (prob. 1725) " Centinel," Capt. Nathan Brigham, 3 weeks, 1 day.

Noah (83), Marlboro, 1st Co., under Col. Abe Williams; 1759, Lieut. Rice, Col. Williams, 14 days on relief of Fort William Henry.

Paul, Marlboro (82), 1757, 1st Co., Col. Abe Williams.

Samuel (52), surgeon, 1755, 14 weeks, 1 day on Crown Point Expedition, Col. Josiah Brown.

Samuel, Sudbury (48), Capt. Josiah Richardson's 2nd Sudbury Co.; 1759 (æ. 42), Col. Elisha Jones, invasion of Canada.

Silas (37), pri., Train Band, 1757, Shrewsbury 1st Co., Capt. Ward.

Stephen (59), 1757, 2nd Marlboro Co., Capt. J. Weeks, Train Band.

Thomas (23), (prob. 1722), " Centinel," Col. Buckminster, 1 week, 4 days, with detachment of Shrewsbury men under Sergt. Nahum Ward, Westboro and Shrewsbury scout.

Timothy, Westboro (84), Train Band, Capt. Bezaleal Eager,

1757; 1758, 46 days, Capt. Maynard, Col. Williams; 1759, Capt. Maynard, 7 mos., 20 days, for reduction of Canada.

Timothy, Southboro (20), capt. and colonel in 1757.

Uriah (53), lieut., 1762, 3rd Marlboro Co., Capt. Thomas How, Jr., Col. Ward.

William (74), Southboro Co., Train Band, Col. Timothy Brigham, 1757; Grafton, 1757, Train Band, Capt. Sam Ward.

Winslow (60), pri., 1756, Rutland (? or pos. Mr'l.), Capt. Samuel How, 15 weeks, 1 day; in Col. Willard's Regt., Crown Point; 1757, pri., 2nd Marlboro Co., Capt. J. Weeks, Train Band.

APPENDIX C.

AMERICAN BRIGHAM PLACES.

BRIGHAM CITY, a hamlet in Apache Co., Arizona, whose P. O. is Winslow.

BRIGHAM, a hamlet in Greenwood Co., Kansas, whose P. O. is Flint Ridge.

BRIGHAMVILLE, a hamlet in Red River Co., Louisiana, whose P. O. is East Point.

BRIGHAM HILL and BRIGHAM SCHOOL, Grafton, Worcester Co., Mass.

BRIGHAM, a hamlet in Allegany Co., N. Y., P. O. Spring Mills.

BRIGHAM, a hamlet in Chautauqua Co., N. Y., P. O. Fredonia.

BRIGHAM, a hamlet in Clinton Co., N. Y., P. O. Black Brook.

BRIGHAM, a hamlet in Franklin Co., N. Y., P. O. Saranac Lake.

BRIGHAM, a post village in Brome Co., Quebec, on the Canadian Pacific Ry., having saw mills, a tannery and sash factory, population, in 1895, 275.

BRIGHAM JUNCTION (near the above), a station on the Canadian Pacific Ry.

BRIGHAM CITY, post town, capital of Boxelder Co., Utah, at west foot Wahsatch Mts., on Southern Pacific, Utah Northern Branch U. P., and Cent. Pac., Rys., (2½ miles from "Brigham Station") 56 miles north of Salt Lake City; has a church, seminary, public library, flour mill, woolen factory and a bank; engaged in fruit-growing and agriculture; waterworks owned and operated by the municipality. Population, in 1900, 2859.

BRIGHAM HILL, a delightful viewpoint near Burlington, Vt.

BRIGHAM PRAIRIE, a hamlet in Dunn Co., Wisconsin, P. O. Menomonie.

APPENDIX D.

BRIGHAM YOUNG NOT A BRIGHAM.

Because of Brigham Young's Christian name, the author of this work often has been called upon to explain a seeming consanguinity. Fortunately, the truth is not far to seek. Brigham Young was a son of John Young, once of Hopkinton, Mass., who married Abigail Howe, daughter of Phineas Howe of Hopkinton. Said Abigail had a sister Susanna Howe, who married Phineas Brigham of Southboro, Mass., and Eaton, N. Y. Susanna and her race were such estimable people that Brigham Young was honored by being christened after his Brigham aunt. This (*Deo laudamus!*) is the utmost opprobrium the Brigham family has to bear in the matter of " The Prophet."

APPENDIX E.

TWO BRIGHAM HOSPITALS.

It is a matter of profound pride with the Brigham Family that the name of Brigham is to be perpetuated by two of the noblest charities the spirit of beneficence could devise; that the two men of the Brigham name who won the greatest success, from the material point of view, should have sought to outrival each other in generous provision for the helpless and suffering of posterity.

The careers of Peter Bent Brigham and his nephew, Robert Breck Brigham, were singularly alike in many respects. Both men came from the country without means and laid the basis of their fortunes in the restaurant business. Both owed their greatest financial success to their foresight in the purchase and development of real estate. Both confined their investments to property within a short distance of their places of business. Both were men of the highest integrity and correct personal habits, kindly, unassuming and little influenced by ambitions outside their own sphere of activity. Neither sought public life, yet both were keenly interested in the issues of the day and contributed materially to the upbuilding of the community in which their business lives were passed. Alike in life and effort, in death each made identically the same disposition of his property for the benefit of humanity.

Peter Bent Brigham died at his home in Boston 24 May, 1877, leaving a will which was duly admitted to probate 17 Oct., 1877. According to the inventory of his estate, filed in 1877, the real estate was valued at $690,000, and the personal estate at $659,-075.74, as follows:

Real Estate:

Land and bldgs. 79 to 89 Causeway st. and 178 to 210 Portland st.	$75,000.00
Land and bldgs. 166 to 176 Portland st.	65,000.00
Land and bldgs. 36 to 46 Canal st. and 36 to 46 Friend st. (Mortgaged for $100,000)	130,000.00
Land and bldgs. 217 to 229 Friend st.	30,000.00
Land and bldgs. 61 to 63 Blackstone st.	21,000.00
Land and bldgs. 11 Charlestown st.	25,000.00
Land and bldgs. 5 to 10 Tremont Row	185,000.00
Land and bldgs. 90 and 92 Court st.	85,000.00
Land and bldgs. 223 and 225 Washington st.	70,000.00
4 shares in Chardon St. Club stable at $750	3,000.00
Tomb in Mt. Auburn Cemetery	1,000.00
	$690,000.00

Personal Estate:

$50,000 U. S. 5.20 bonds 1865	*$52,000.00
$21,000 U. S. 5.20 bonds 1867	*22,260.00
$29,000 U. S. 5.20 bonds 1868	*31,030.00
$5,000 currency 6s (U. S.), $120	6,000.00
1000 Lancaster R. R. bonds, $40	40,000.00
312 sh. Fitchburg R. R., $106	33,072.00
1000 sh. Lancaster R. R., shs., $10	10,000.00
183 shs. Nashua, Acton & Bos. R. R., $1	183.00
5 sh. Framingham & Lowell, $1	5.00
64 sh. Boston Gaslight Co., $800	51,200.00
15 sh. Union Nat'l Bk., $136	2,040.00
7 sh. State Nat'l Bank, $107	749.00
Note of Fitchburg R. R.	100,000.00
Note of Fitchburg R. R.	100,000.00
Note of Fitchburg R. R.	88,000.00
Note of Fitchburg R. R.	14,000.00
Mtg. note Henry Farnum et ux	20,000.00
Mtg. note Harvey D. Parker	30,000.00
Mtg. note John F. Wells	30,000.00
Note of Devlin	200.00
Horses, carriages, etc.	1,500.00
Watch and chain in possession of Mrs. Jacobs	40.00
Gold watch and chain	100.00
Cash	26,696.74
Total	$659,075.74

There were debts of about $150,000, personal bequests of $55,500, personal annuities of $14,600; and provision also was made for the distribution of $138,000 among the children of the annuitants, if living, at the death of the latter. The sum of $40,000 was be-

* Pledged to secure notes of P. B. Brigham for $100,000.

queathed to the Town of Bakersfield, Vt.; the income of $10,000 to be expended for the care of the graves of the parents, brothers and sisters of the testator and of the burying ground generally, and the remaining $30,000 to be invested as a permanent fund, "which shall be called the Brigham School Fund and the income thereof shall be expended for educational purposes, either in the district schools or for a school of higher grade, as the said town shall from time to time determine."

The supremely important provision of the will was as follows: "At the expiration of said term of twenty-five years from time of my decease, my said Executors shall dispose of said rest and residue of my property and estate, and of all the interest and accumulations which shall have accrued thereon, for the purpose of founding a hospital, in said Boston, to be called the Brigham Hospital, for the care of sick persons, in indigent circumstances, residing in the said County of Suffolk, in the following manner, that is to say; they shall procure the formation of a corporation to be called the 'Brigham Hospital,' with suitable provisions as to officers, their powers and duties for control, direction, conduct and administration of the corporation and the care and management of the funds in its charge; and upon the legal formation and organization of said corporation, my said Executors shall transfer to it all the property and estate provided for it as aforesaid, to be by it used and employed for the purposes above declared, and I give, devise, and bequeath said rest and residue of my property and estate accordingly."

The Executors were given full power as to sale, lease and management of the real estate, to change and alter investments, and to treat stock dividends, in their discretion, as belonging either to the principal or income of the estate.

The will was witnessed by J. P. Healy, C. F. Kittredge, and Fisher Ames. Robert Codman and Joseph Healy of Boston were appointed Executors of the will; and it was expressly directed by the testator that no bond should be required of either of them.

Mr. Healy died soon after the testator, and the property remained in the sole control of Mr. Codman until his death in January, 1901. In all the annals of trusteeship, there is no more splendid example of faithful and able administration of a trust than was exhibited by Robert Codman in his management of the property of Peter B. Brigham. It was not Mr. Codman's nature to speculate, and it is said of him that in the various and important trusteeships with which he was honored, he never lost a dollar. With property representing $1,349, 075.74 committed to his care in 1877, Mr. Codman's Twenty-second Annual Report, made just before his death, showed a book value of $2,846,718.47, or representing an actual value considerably in excess of this figure.

Upon the death of Robert Codman, his son, Edmund D. Codman, and Laurence H. H. Johnson were duly appointed trustees under the will, 25 January, 1901. On 8 May, 1902, they procured the formation of a corporation called the " Peter Bent Brigham Hospital." On 22 May, 1902, the General Court, by Chapter 418 of the Acts of 1902, authorized the Hospital to hold, " for the purposes for which it was incorporated, real and personal estate, to an amount not exceeding $5,000,000 in value, including the amount that it is already authorized by law to hold " ($1,500,000).

On 24 May, 1902, exactly twenty-five years after the death of the testator, the Peter B. Brigham Hospital took over the real and personal estate, amounting to $4,323,168 appraised value. On 24 May, 1906, this immense property had appreciated more than $700,-000, and had a book value of $5,045,255.54.

The Peter Bent Brigham Hospital is composed (1907), as originally, of the following named: Alexander Cochrane, president; Edmund D. Codman, treasurer; Laurence H. H. Johnson, secretary; Eben S. Draper, Augustus Hemenway, Walter Hunnewell, Henry S. Howe, and William Ropes Trask.

Except for litigation upon certain technical points, the outcome of which is not feared by the Trustees, the Peter Bent Brigham Hospital already would be an established institution. The corporation has made an agreement to purchase of Harvard College, upon advantageous terms, a site adjoining the new Harvard Medical School on the Back Bay Fens. The corporation has made a friendly arrangement with the Harvard authorities which, it is expected, will be mutually beneficial to the Hospital and the Harvard Medical School. In view of some misunderstandings created by this action, it may be said that the Peter B. Brigham Hospital will remain wholly independent of the Harvard authorities in point of purpose and administration. The terms of the alliance between the Peter B. Brigham Hospital and Harvard College are sufficiently illustrated by the following extract from a letter of the Trustees to the authorities of Harvard:

" So far as the charitable purposes of this trust shall in our opinion permit, we hereby declare our desire to promote the objects of your Medical School by seeking advice from its Faculty, and by giving careful consideration to its nomination in making appointments to our Medical Staff, and by permitting access for students to the Hospital. Except for the purchase of the land, subject to the defeat, as above stated, of all claims of the Brigham heirs, we do not enter into any agreement or contract in any sense, but we are ready if you so desire to spread this letter upon our records."

Robert Breck Brigham died 2 Jan., 1900, leaving a will wherein he appointed Charles O. L. Dillaway, Halsey J. Boardman and Sylvester G. Willey as Trustees. Mr. Boardman and Mr. Willey have since died and their places were filled by William E. L. Dillaway and Hiram M. Burton who, with Charles O. L. Dillaway, constitute the present (1907) Trustees under the will. Charles O. L. Dillaway acts as surviving Executor, the others having died. The Trustees are to be succeeded, after ten years, by the New England Trust Company as Trustee.

Mr. Brigham left an estate valued at about $3,000,000. This was represented by about $750,000 of personal and about $2,250,-000 real estate, the latter including, besides Brigham's Hotel, the Hollis Street Theatre and much of the remainder of the property on Hollis Street, Burroughs Place and Hollis Place; the building occupied for years by Cobb, Aldrich & Co., corner of Washington and Kneeland Streets; the building formerly occupied by Cobb, Bates & Yerxa, corner Washington and Beach Streets, now the site of the Globe and a smaller theatre; a large block on Eliot Street, and a block on Beach Street; parcels corner Shawmut Avenue and Dover Street and elsewhere.

The will provided for small bequests to individuals ranging from $100 to $1000, amounting to about $15,000; two personal life annuities of $200 each and one of $300; a gift of $2000 to the Boston Emergency Hospital and an annuity (in perpetuity) of $1000, payable every year, to each of the following named charitable institutions: Massachusetts Charitable Eye and Ear Infirmary, Associated Charities of Boston, Boston Dispensary, Boston Provident Association, Channing Home, Children's Hospital, Children's Mission to the Children of the Destitute, City Missionary Society, Home for Aged Men, Home for Aged Women, Massachusetts Infant Asylum, New England Home for Little Wanderers, Home for Aged Couples, Boston Children's Aid Society, Boston Home for Incurables, Perkins Institution and Massachusetts School for the Blind, New England Hospital for Women and Children, Massachusetts Society for the Prevention of Cruelty to Children, Boston Lying-in Hospital, Home for Aged Colored Women, Burnap Home for Aged Women, all of Boston; and the Warner Home of St. Albans, Vt.

In line with the tender solicitude of the testator for the helpless, whether by reason of extreme youth, old age, or other infirmity, the will provided also that the balance of the *net income* from the estate should be paid to the " Robert B. Brigham Hospital for Incurables "; said corporation to be organized " for the purpose of maintaining an institution for the care and support and medical and surgical treatment of those citizens of Boston who are without necessary means of support and are incapable of obtaining a comfortable livelihood, by reason of chronic or incurable disease or permanent physical disabilities."

All the net income of the estate over and above the annuities— these amounting to $22,000—is to be invested by the Trustees and held by them for accumulation until the accrued income, with interest thereon, is of an amount which is large enough, in the opinion of the Directors of the Hospital, for the purchase of land in the city of Boston and the erection and thorough equipment of a building or buildings of size and capacity adequate for the purposes of said Hospital. On the erection of the Hospital, the Trustees are to convey the same, together with the land, to the Robert B. Brigham Hospital for Incurables, and thereafter the Trustees under the will are to pay all the rest, residue and remainder of the net income from the estate as the same shall be collected to the Robert B. Brigham Hospital for Incurables forever.

In accordance with the direction of the will that " said Trustees shall select not less than seven citizens of Boston, well known and of high character and reputation, who shall associate themselves together and form a corporation under the provision of Chapter 115 of the Public Statutes of Massachusetts, or under a special act of the Legislature, if deemed advisable," the Robert B. Brigham Hospital for Incurables was organized 11 Feb., 1903, with the following named persons as incorporators: John Shepard, Charles J. Lincoln, Francis H. Manning, Andrew J. Bailey, Michael J. Anagnos, Hiram M. Burton, Ubert K. Pettingill, Eugene N. Foss and Charles F. Whittemore. The following named are directors of the Hospital: Andrew J. Bailey, Miss Elizabeth F. Brigham, Eugene N. Foss, William S. Crosby, Francis H. Manning, Ubert K. Pettingill, Wallace L. Pierce, John Shepard, C. F. Whittemore. The foregoing, with the following named, compose the present (1906) membership of the Corporation: John Quincy Adams, Hiram M. Burton, James S. Conant, Ernest W. Cushing, M. D., Charles O. L. Dillaway, Wm. E. L. Dillaway, Robert B. Dixon, M. D., William J. Fegan, Charles H. Olmstead, John F. Souther.

In 1902 the Trustees under the will purchased about ten acres of land on the top of Parker Hill, Roxbury District, as a site for the Hospital. The site is about 230 feet above sea level and is one of the highest and most commanding locations in the city of Boston, within whose limits, according to a provision of the will, the buildings must be erected.

Under the terms of the will, the total net income after the construction of the buildings must be applied to the maintenance of the Hospital; thus precluding, inferentially if not absolutely, additions, whether of land or buildings, to the original Hospital estate. The Trustees under the will are restrained also, except on order of the Court, from acquiring or disposing of real estate except for the Hospital purposes specified. The estate is now free of litigation, but for the reasons stated, and others, the Directors of the Hospital are awaiting a sufficient accumulation of the fund before beginning construction. The Trustees under the will have accummulated a large surplus for Hospital purposes, and expect to begin construction within a very few years. It is provided in the will that on the completion of the Hospital a tablet of stone or bronze bearing the inscription " Erected by Robert B. and Elizabeth F. Brigham " shall be set in an appropriate place in the building or in one of the buildings if there be more than one.

APPENDIX F.

BRIGHAM FAMILY ASSOCIATION.

* The Brigham Family Association owes its origin to the late Dr. Brayton A. R. Brigham of Chicago, upon whose call Brighams resident in Chicago met in his office 15 Aug., 1893, to consider " the question of holding a reunion of the Brigham Family in Chicago during the Columbian Exposition." Besides Dr. Brigham, Rev. Leonard W., and Messrs. Edward D. and Gus. B. Brigham attended, and took action which led to a gathering of 107 persons, representing the Brigham name, held in the Illinois State Building of the Exposition 18 Oct., 1893.

The Brigham Family Association was then organized with these officers: President, Charles O. Brigham of Toledo, O.; vice-presidents, Captain H. G. Brigham of Chicago, O. A. Brigham of Lowell, Mass., Hon. Johnson Brigham of Des Moines, Iowa, Thomas Brigham Rice of Barre, Mass., James R. Brigham of Corry, Pa.; secretary, B. A. R. Brigham, M. D., of Chicago; treasurer, E. D. Brigham of Chicago; historian, Willard I. Tyler Brigham of Chicago; librarian, Emma E. Brigham of Boston; orator, Rev. George F. Brigham of Sharon, Wis.; and a board of trustees consisting of these and Charles W. Brigham of Lowell, Mass., Gus. B. Brigham of Chicago, H. C. Brigham, M. D., of Grand Rapids, Mich., Colonel J. H. Brigham of Delta, O., and Jerome R. Brigham of Milwaukee. The features of the meeting were a description, by Hon. Johnson Brigham, of a visit to the town of Brigham, Cockermouth, England; an address, " The Lineage of Brigham," treating of the English origin and heraldry of

* This sketch is an abstract of an article by William E. Brigham (President B. F. A., 1896-1900), published in the " Official Report of the First Six Meetings of the American Brigham Family Association," in 1900.

the Brigham Family, by the Historian, W. I. T. Brigham; an address by Rev. George F. Brigham of Sharon, Wis.; an exhibition of relics, deeds and other heirlooms; and the singing of a quartet, " Brigham," the words and music by the venerable Mavor Brigham, father of the first President of the Association. A Constitution was adopted (superseded in 1898); and a full coat of arms exhibited, as follows: Ar. a fleur de lis within an orle of martlets sable; crest, a boar's head bendways couped sa; motto, *In cruce salus.* From the address of the Historian it was learned that " Dr. B. A. R. Brigham has in his possession a letter elicited from an English-American Brigham, who can trace his descent through very many generations, who speaks of this motto as being won in Palestine in the time of the Crusades for acts of bravery on the part of an ancestor." * The valuable pamphlet descriptive of this meeting is now out of print.

The second meeting was held at Marlboro, Mass., 12 Sept., 1894, with Loriman S. Brigham as Local Chairman. It was voted to adopt the coat of arms, crest and the motto, " In Cruce Salus," as the emblem of the Association. Mayor William M. Davenport welcomed the Association at the dinner in City Hall.

All Odd Fellows Building was utilized for the reunion held in Boston, 5 Oct., 1895, William E. Brigham of Somerville, Mass., Local Chairman. Not less than 500 persons attended the banquet in the afternoon and the ball in the evening. Thanks to Miss Emma E. Brigham, the first, and Addington M. Brigham, the present Librarian-Curator, the general display of antiquities at Marlboro in 1894 and the portrait show in Boston in 1895 constituted two of the most noteworthy exhibitions of the kind ever given under the auspices of a family association in this country. Among these family treasures were the carved oak box in which Mercy Hurd, wife of Thomas Brigham the Emigrant, brought her caps from England; the original deed, in parchment, by Benjamin Rice to Thomas^2 Brigham, of the Thomas Brigham farm in Marlboro; a silver salt cup which belonged to a daughter of Mary Chilton, the first woman to land on Plymouth Rock in 1620—it having been held in the Brigham Family for generations; the chair in which Thomas^2 Brigham died; and scores of other priceless articles. Of the portrait show, one writer has said: " The opportunity to trace the Brigham characteristics in those old portraits was improved with eagerness; and it was clearly shown that two or three types have come down to the present day with great persistence. The peculiar droop of the eyelids, noticed in many of the visitors, was seen also in a large number of the portraits." The Committee on

* For reasons stated in an early chapter of this volume, the Brigham Family Association never has claimed for the family a title to arms.

Family Badge made a report, showing a pin of design picked out from a Brigham coat-of-arms, already described, which was formally adopted.

The Worcester reunion of 14 Oct., 1896, Lucius L. Brigham, Local Chairman, was held in the Y. M. C. A. building and Salisbury Hall. It was noteworthy as being the last held under strictly local auspices and at the personal expense of local residents; and for an important change in administrative policy. President Charles O. Brigham, an ideal official, voluntarily retired, and William E. Brigham of Somerville was elected president and Miss Emma E. Brigham of Boston secretary.

The new administration entered upon its duties with a well-defined policy, prominent in which was the purpose to raise the B. F. A. to an independent financial position, thus relieving individuals of the heavy expense incident to the reunions; and to insist that the Association fulfil its original mission of undertaking the preparation and publication of a History of the Brigham Family. It was with great satisfaction, therefore, that the Treasurer was able to report to the fifth meeting, held in Marlboro, 14 Sept., 1898, that all bills had been paid by the Association, and nearly $100 remained in the treasury. A simplified Constitution, providing for biennial, instead of annual, reunions was adopted; the President outlined plans looking to the ultimate publication of a History of the Brigham Family, and urged also the preservation, in pamphlet form, of the admirable historical papers prepared by the Historian, W. I. T. Brigham, for every meeting of the Association.* At this meeting, as at Worcester in 1896, a successful group picture of the Association was taken.

Charles O. Brigham reassumed the presidency and Willard I. Tyler Brigham was elected Secretary-Historian of the Association at the sixth meeting held in the American House, Boston, 10 Oct., 1900. At the dinner, the Historian exhibited photographs and gave an interesting account of his recent visit to historic Brigham places in England.† Upon the menu was a poetic illumination of the family motto, " In Cruce Salus," by Hon. Johnson Brigham.

The seventh reunion, held in the American House, 10 Sept., 1902, marked an epoch in the history of the Association and the great work it had undertaken. In 1900 President William E. Brigham had said: " The past of the Brigham Family Association has been such that we review it with inexpressible pride. Our greatest successes, however, must be of the future. For a year or two after its

* These papers were gathered in a pamphlet in 1900, and form the basis of the historical chapters of this volume.

† The Historian was aided materially in extending his British researches by the special contributions of members of the Brigham Family Association.

organization, the B. F. A. held hopefully to its original plan of making itself the means of the publication of a " Lineage of Brigham," which should complete the honorable work so well begun by Rev. Abner Morse, A. M., in 1859; but an unexpected change of circumstances rendered the immediate consummation of this project impracticable, and the officers, abandoning with regret the earlier proposition, concentrated their efforts upon a development of the social features of the organization; depending upon time and strength gained from social contact to indicate the way toward a fresh start. This policy has proved its own wisdom. . . . The Brigham Family Association, as such, is in a position to authorize the preparation of a ' Lineage of Brigham,' under its own auspices."

Confidence had been restored; and at this meeting in 1902 it was reported that a sufficient guaranty fund had been raised to secure the preparation of a History of the Brigham Family. The details of the plan were worked out by President C. O. Brigham. A Committee on Publication was appointed and Willard I. Tyler Brigham, secretary-historian of the B. F. A. and a trained genealogist, was engaged to prepare the book. His own painstaking researches had continued, modestly and without reward, since 1893; and no better choice could have been made. The valuable genealogical documents collected by the late Dr. B. A. R. Brigham were purchased by the B. F. A., thus materially shortening the task of the Genealogist.

At the eighth meeting of the B. F. A., held in the American House, 14 Sept., 1904, none of the social features which had made all the reunions so successful were lacking.* At the seventh and eighth reunions, papers were read as follows, in addition to the regular contributions of the Historian: " Hon. Lincoln F. Brigham, Jurist and Scholar," by Hon. William T. Forbes of Worcester; " Dr. Amariah Brigham, a Distinguished Specialist," by Dr. D. R. Burrell of Canandaigua, N. Y.; " Nicholas Brigham," by Hon. William T. Forbes. Secretary Willard I. T. Brigham had planned a " Brigham Day " at the St. Louis Exposition, which was held, but without his presence, Hon. Johnson Brigham making an address; and at the time of the Boston reunion he lay upon his death bed, writing to the last. He died within a few days; his work unfinished, but so far advanced that it was practicable for others to attempt its completion. How well this duty has been performed by Miss Emma E. Brigham of Boston and her associates,

---

* It is deeply regretted that there is not space to treat herein of the social features of the B. F. A. reunions and to give due credit to the many talented Brighams and others who made them so delightful. These were described in the published report of 1900.

B. F. A. AT BOSTON 1904

the present volume attests. C. O. Brigham, the first and last president of the Association, here greeted his kinsmen for the last time, for he died in May, 1906. He is succeeded by Hon. Johnson Brigham of Des Moines, State Librarian of Iowa. At this writing, the ninth meeting of the Association is called to take place at Marlboro, Mass., June 6, 1907, when it is expected that "The History of the Brigham Family" will be ready for distribution.

In closing this imperfect sketch of a noble organization, its difficult task and its measurable achievement, can more fitting words be used than those of the beloved President C. O. Brigham in his magnificent and what proved to be farewell address to the Brigham Family Association in 1904:

"No one, I think, can look back over the history of our Association without discovering the fact that since its organization in Chicago at the time of the World's Fair in 1893, up to the present hour, we have easily enjoyed a position at the head of the family associations of America; and I cannot doubt that even if many of the older ones, myself included, are to be swept aside in the all-devouring process of time, there will be raised up to this association another generation who will take up the work where we are compelled to lay it down. Our lips shall teach this to our sons, and they again to theirs, that generations yet unborn may teach their sons, and so shall we hand down this work to succeeding generations; adding to its interest and value as times goes on."

So mote it be!

EUNICE[5], daughter of Lieut. Nathan (See 22-ii) and Dina (Rice) Brigham, b. in Marlboro 4 Oct., 1721; m. 8 Sept., 1742, Hezekiah Newton, son of Isaac and Sarah Newton of Marlboro, b. 28 July, 1719, Marlboro, d. 4 Feb., 1786, in Paxton, Mass.

Children, (Newton) the 3 eldest born in Southboro, the 4th in Leicester, the others in Rutland:

i Persis Newton, b. 14 June, 1743; m. 16 April, 1766, in Rutland, Mass., Daniel Estabrook, Jr., who d. in Rutland 11 Sept., 1816, in his 75th year. She d. 25 Dec., 1828, in Rutland.

ii Silas, b. 10 Dec., 1744.

iii Catherine, b. 10 Jan., 1746-7, prob. d. young.

iv Mehitable, b. 22 Feb., 1748-9.

v Catherine, b. 16 May, 1751.

vi Ruth, b. 25 April, 1753; m. 1772, John Stewart, (afterward General) and removed to Brattleboro, Vt. He d. in 1812 and she survived him 8 mos.

vii Hezekiah, b. 25 June, 1755; m. 8 Oct., 1783 in Rutland, Lucy Cogswell of Paxton. He d. in Rutland 6 Jan., 1848. He was a Revolutionary pensioner.

viii Eunice, b. 17 March, 1758

ix Nathan Brigham, b. 28 March, 1760; m. Mary Stewart of Paxton, (sister of Gen. John Stewart, above) and settled in Royalston, Mass. He d. in Royalston 18 Dec., 1843, æ. 84 and she d. 15 Dec., 1842.

x Elizabeth, b. 4 Feb., 1763; m. Samuel Richardson, Jr., of Leicester, int. pub., 15 March, 1781. He d. in Leicester, 11 Oct., 1838 æ. 84, and she d. 5 Jan. 1840.

xi Edmund, Capt., b. 9 June, 1765.

OWNER'S LINEAGE

FIRST GENERATION

Name. . . . .

Number. . . . .   Pages. . . . .

SECOND GENERATION

Name. . . . .

Number. . . . .   Pages. . . . .

THIRD GENERATION

Name. . . . .

Number. . . . .   Pages. . . . .

FOURTH GENERATION

Name. . . . .

Number. . . . .   Pages. . . . .

FIFTH GENERATION

Name. . . . .

Number. . . . .   Pages. . . . .

SIXTH GENERATION

Name...

Number.............   Pages..............

SEVENTH GENERATION

Name...

Number.............   Pages........ ......

EIGHTH GENERATION

Name...

Number.............   Pages..............

NINTH GENERATION

Name...

Number.............   Pages..............

TENTH GENERATION

Name...

Number.............   Pages..............

ELEVENTH GENERATION

Name...

Number.............   Pages..............

TWELFTH GENERATION

Name...

Number..............   Pages..............

INDEX

INDEX

This index refers only to the genealogical section, and to numbers, not pages. The letter *u* preceding a number indicates that mention of the person is to be found *under* or in connection with the record carrying that number. The letters *f u* signify reference to a *footnote under* the number.

604 INDEX

INDEX 617